DATE DUE

FEB 12	OCT 0 1 1999		
JAN 02			
JAN 23			
APR 1 5 1997			
MAY 2 2 2001			

HIGHSMITH #45115

A History of Russian Architecture, the most comprehensive study of this subject to date, surveys the development of Russian architecture, from the masonry churches of tenth-century Kievan Rus to the prefabricated built environments of the present.

Subject to cultural and stylistic influences from both east and west, Russian architecture nonetheless developed its own distinctive approaches to building, as demonstrated in the four parts of this study: early medieval Rus up to the Mongol invasion in the midtwelfth century; the revival of architecture in Novgorod and Muscovy from the fourteenth to seventeenth centuries; the cultural revolution in architecture during the reigns of Peter the Great and his successors in the eighteenth and early nineteenth centuries; and the advent of modern architecture, ranging from the colorful eclecticism of the nineteenth century to the rigorous experiments in avant-garde design of the early twentieth century, which were followed by a return to monumental eclecticism in the Soviet period. Analyzing stylistic developments within their historical contexts, this volume serves as a rich cultural history that will be invaluable to scholars and general readers alike.

Lavishly illustrated, *A History of Russian Architecture* includes line drawings, plans and elevations, and a full complement of photographs taken by the author.

A History of Russian Architecture

A History of Russian Architecture

Text and photographs by

WILLIAM CRAFT BRUMFIELD

CAMBRIDGE
UNIVERSITY PRESS

Published by the Press Syndicate of the University of Cambridge
The Pitt Building, Trumpington Street, Cambridge CB2 1RP
40 West 20th Street, New York, NY 10011-4211, USA
10 Stamford Road, Oakleigh, Melbourne 3166, Australia

First published 1993
Reprinted 1993

Printed in the United States of America

Library of Congress Cataloging-in-Publication Data
Brumfield, William Craft, 1944-
A history of Russian architecture / text and photographs by
William Craft Brumfield.
p.   cm.
Includes bibliographical references and index.
ISBN 0-521-40333-2
1. Architecture – Russia (Federation) – Themes, motives.   I. Title.
NA1181.B72   1993
720′.947–dc20   92-29554
                                                                                        CIP

A catalog record for this book is available from the British Library

ISBN 0-521-40333-2 hardback

FRONTISPIECE: Church of the Savior on the Stores, Rostov Kremlin.
1675. Photograph by William Brumfield

Contents

Acknowledgments

This volume represents the cumulative experience of some two decades of study and photography of Russian architecture. During that time, various institutions and individuals have assisted in the evolution of my work. In this country, my research has been greatly advanced by the resources of the Library of Congress, and by the Kennan Institute for Advanced Russian Studies at the Woodrow Wilson International Center for Scholars, part of the Smithsonian Institution. I am much indebted to the staff of the Photographic Archives at the National Gallery of Art. The archives' acquisition of several thousand of my negatives of Russian architectural monuments has facilitated the printing of many of the black-and-white photographs in this book. I would also like to thank friends and colleagues such as Priscilla Roosevelt, Declan Murphy, and Ruth Mathewson for their hospitality during the many essential trips to major research libraries.

My gratitude to Russian colleagues is beyond measure, not only for their efforts on my behalf, but also for the information shared from their own research. I am deeply appreciative of the unfailing generosity over many years of Aleksei Komech, at the Institute of Art History in Moscow. In Petersburg, my greatest debt is to Iurii Denisov, the most knowledgeable historian of that city's architecture. Numerous other Russian scholars have made my visits in that country both pleasant and productive, and I would like to mention a few as representative of the many: Evgeniia Kirichenko, Dmitrii Shvidkovskii, Vladimir Kirillov, Grigorii Kaganov, Elena Stolbova, and Vladimir Lisovskii.

To study Russian buildings *in situ* and compile detailed photographic documentation are not easy tasks – because of the distances involved, many bureaucratic obstacles, and the lack of adequate photographic supplies. My efforts to cope with these conditions have been assisted by Russian friends and by travel opportunities arranged through institutions such as the International Research and Exchanges Board, the Cooper-Hewitt Museum in New York, and Tulane University.

In producing this volume, and in particular its color plates, Cambridge University Press has been supported by generous grants from the J. J. Medveckis Foundation and from The Howard Gilman Foundation. I am grateful to both of them. The Regents of the University of California have granted permission to use portions of my book *The Origins of Modernism in Russian Architecture* (University of California Press, 1991) in Chapters 13 and 14 of the present volume.

Finally, it is my pleasant duty to express gratitude to Beatrice Rehl, Fine Arts Editor at Cambridge University Press, who combines consummate editorial skills with an appreciation of Russian culture that is informed, sensitive, and shrewd. Without her support, I suspect that this history of Russian architecture would not exist.

W. C. B.

Author's Note

In transliterating from Russian, I have used the Library of Congress system, modified by the omission of the soft sign (') in the body of the text. In the spelling of names, I have usually transliterated directly from the Russian, although in the case of certain saints, I have used the Greek form (e.g., "Sergius," instead of the Russianized "Sergii"). In the nomenclature of churches and icons dedicated to Mary, the literal translation of the Russian term *Bogomater* (*Bogoroditsa*) is "Mother of God"; but in some instances, the accepted western term "Virgin" reads more easily, and I have used it. Russian architectural terms are illustrated in Appendix II. It must be emphasized that there are considerable differences of opinion in the dating of a number of Russian architectural monuments, and my goal has been to assign dates on the basis of the most recent or in my opinion the most reliable research.

One of the priorities in western studies of Russian architecture must be adequate photographic documentation. My photographs for this book were taken on numerous trips, beginning with the summer of 1970 and extending to August 1991. Many of the photographs – especially the color plates – were taken with a medium-format camera. The rigors of extensive travel without special privileges in Russia, however, often restricted my equipment to two 35-mm cameras with an assortment of lenses – not an ideal situation, yet one redeemed by the versatility of certain 35-mm films available in the west. The captions for the black-and-white photographs are followed by the appropriate reference number to my collection in the Photographic Archives of the National Gallery of Art.

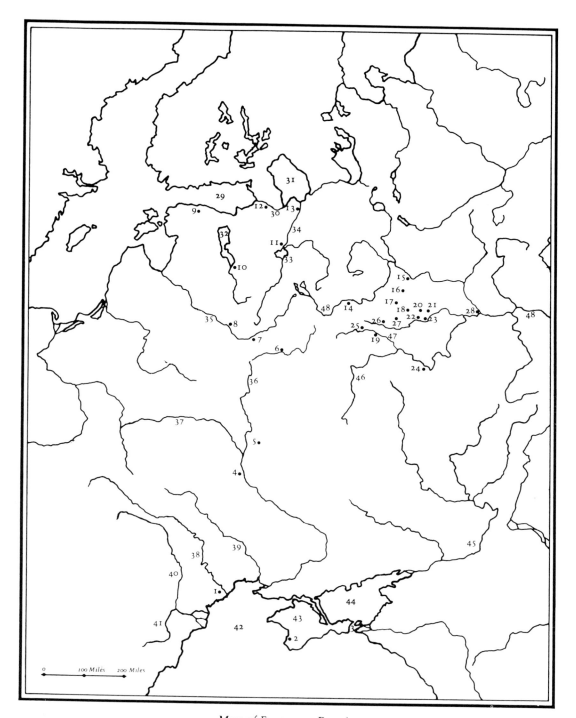

Map of European Russia

1. Belgorod	11. Novgorod	21. Kideksha	31. Lake Ladoga	41. Danube River
2. Kherson	12. Petersburg (Leningrad)	22. Vladimir	32. Lake Chud	42. Black Sea
3. Tmutarakan	13. Ladoga	23. Bogolyubovo	33. Lake Ilmen	43. Crimea
4. Kiev	14. Tver	24. Ryazan	34. Volkhov River	44. Sea of Azov
5. Chernigov	15. Yaroslavl	25. Zvenigorod	35. West Dvina River	45. Don River
6. Smolensk	16. Rostov	26. Zagorsk	36. Dnieper River	46. Oka River
7. Vitebsk	17. Pereslavl-Zalessky	27. Alexandrov	37. Pripyat River	47. Moscow River
8. Polotsk	18. Yurev-Polsky	28. Nizhny-Novgorod	38. Dniester River	48. Volga River
9. Revel (Tallin)	19. Moscow	29. Gulf of Finland	39. South Bug River	
10. Pskov	20. Suzdal	30. Neva River	40. Prut River	

Introduction

In his article "On the Architecture of the Present Time" (1834), the Russian writer Nikolai Gogol presented what he considered a "strange idea": "I thought it would not be bad to have in a city a street that would serve as an architectural chronicle. It ought to begin with ponderous, gloomy gates, from which the viewer would emerge to see on both sides the sublime, magnificent buildings of the primordial savage taste common to all peoples. Then a gradual change through a series of views: the high transformation to a colossal Egyptian [style], suffused with simplicity; then to that beauty, the Greek; then to the sensuous Alexandrine and Byzantine, with its squat domes; then to the Roman, with arches in several rows. . . ." The literal high point would be Gothic architecture, the "crown of art," and the promenade would end with some undefined new style. "This street would become in a sense a history of the development of taste, and anyone too lazy to leaf through weighty tomes would only have to stroll along it in order to find out everything."[1]

There is not in this fantasy one mention of medieval Russian architecture, in any of its manifestations; and the article's oblique references to Russian neoclassical architecture are not flattering. Gogol praises the cathedrals of Milan and Cologne as well as the Islamic architecture of India; yet the "everything" that Gogol's cultured but indolent Russian might inspect includes nothing from eleventh-century Kiev or Novgorod, nothing from twelfth-century Vladimir or sixteenth-century Moscow. This omission by Gogol, a gifted amateur critic of architecture, reflects an indifference by most of the educated elite toward a native Russian architectural heritage. Indeed, very little was known of this heritage until the rise of romantic nationalism and an interest in the distinctive history of peoples stimulated the beginnings of a sustained scholarly approach to Russian architecture at institutions such as the Academy of Arts in St. Petersburg.[2]

Even then, Russian architecture was for many decades interpreted as a receptacle for foreign influences: Mongol, Lombard, Venetian, Syrio-Byzantine, Indian – not to mention the imposing of western styles (brilliantly assimilated in Russia) by Peter and his successors. The process, as interpreted by early nineteenth-century historians, was not one of borrowing and interchange, but of imposition – of Russia as a pliable amorphous material on which more highly developed cultures placed their stamp. There were no "Lives" of Russian artists and architects, no Renaissance, no sense of continuity. Yet the decline of neoclassicism in Russia in the midnineteenth century was accompanied by an interest among Russian architects and writers in exotic architectural styles from abroad. This meant above all the glorification of Gothic architecture, an attitude typical of the Romantic period everywhere. In Russia it inspired not only pseudo-Gothic caprices, but also stimulated a desire to exalt Russian medieval architecture. Alexander Benois, writing of Russian architects on tours of Europe during the nineteenth century, noted: "They believed in the theory that the medieval architecture of Italy had much in common with old Russian architecture, and therefore set for themselves the task of resurrecting this native architecture on their return to Russia."[3]

Yet these two forms of medieval building differed

so fundamentally as to make impossible any comparison between the European sense of architectural development and that of Russia. Even the term "medieval" can mislead when applied to Russian art and architecture, although it is widely used by Russian scholars to refer to a protean grouping of styles and periods before the eighteenth century. For Russians, there was no "idea of scholasticism" in the complexity of great Gothic cathedrals; and there are no Russia documents similar to those of Villard de Honnecourt, the thirteenth-century French architect whose notebooks provide an insight into the architectural mind of medieval Europe.[4]

Indeed, for the nineteenth-century Russian, "Old Russian" architecture would most likely mean a rather modest, if highly decorated, church built only a century and a half earlier, during the long reign of Peter the Great's father. Furthermore, the scholarly grounding of Russian architecture in the Byzantine tradition was tenuous, owing both to the lack of research and to the diversity of Russian styles (hence the references to Syrian, Mongol, and Lombard influences). As Elena Borisova has remarked in her study of nineteenth-century Russian architecture: "The hypnotic effect of the word 'Byzantine' replaced all attempts to comprehend the relations between Byzantine and pre-Petrine architecture and cut off any possibility of such attempts."[5] In the nineteenth century, the concept of Byzantine was equated with the neo-Byzantine, a style appropriated for official ecclesiastical architecture during the reign of Nicholas I. As Russian architecture became an object of study, it surrendered some innate sense of identity – neoclassical or medieval – to technology and the various ideological positions of historicism.

What, then, was Russian architecture before the advent of self-conscious historicism? Above all it began, and in many ways continued to be, a signifier of the central relation between Church and state. The major cathedrals and monastery churches were commissioned, or endowed, by princes who had disavowed paganism for the culture and regalia of Byzantium and the Orthodox Church. To the best of our knowledge, architecture, like other aspects of that culture, was imported in a radical fashion; yet Russian masons and carpenters, guided by Byzantine masters, assimilated and modified the eastern Mediterranean heritage, with its emphasis on both plasticity of form and tectonic clarity. The centralized plan of the Orthodox church encouraged the development of a vertical point at the main cupola (located over the central

crossing), whose architectural form merged with religious symbolism as an expression of the relation between man and the deity on high. In larger churches, the flanking, lesser domes created a pyramidal effect, but in any event, little detracted from the priority created by the main cylinder, or drum, and its dome. The Orthodox rejection of statuary and the general lack of adequate quarries and stone carvers – with the enigmatic exception of the twelfth-century Vladimir churches – ensured the primacy of the unadorned, molded structure of thin brick and layers of mortar in early medieval churches among the eastern Slavs. (The design of log churches before the sixteenth century is a matter for speculation, but here, too, it is reasonable to assume an emphasis on centrality and height.)

Whatever their size, churches built in stone and brick stood in sharp constrast to their environment of wooden dwellings and walls clustered around the base of the larger churches. In the most visible way, the church stood for light – reflected from the exterior walls and flooding the interior through the windows of the drums and the lights of innumerable candles. It has been noted that the opposition between the light of the church and the darkness of the surrounding dwellings (not only those inhabited by the poor) reinforced the image of ecclesiastical power and glory. Indeed, there is evidence to suggest that this symbolic resonance was cultivated by both secular and ecclesiastical authorities as a means of instilling sentiments of awe and reverence in the population.[6]

To a certain extent, parallels can be noted in the development of western Gothic cathedrals. Yet among the eastern Slavs (in medieval Rus and subsequently Russia), secular rulers played a greater and more direct role in supporting church construction – a role reflecting the close relation between the Church and princely authority that had been inherited from Byzantium. Thus, it can be argued that just as the link between Church and ruler in the east differed from the separate status and spiritual influence of the Papacy over princes in the west, so the impetus for church architecture in Russia differed profoundly from the corporate effort and scholastic spirit that produced the large medieval churches of western Europe.

In addition, the harsh climate and great distances of the eastern plains and forests mitigated in many and complex ways against the formation of civil, secular institutions that laid architectural claims of their own in the west: universities, banking houses, palaces and mansions, hospitals. There were princely palaces in Rus during the early medieval period, and some were apparently built of stone; yet none has survived and the available documentary references give little evidence of splendor. Despite the lacunae in our knowledge of secular medieval architecture in Russia, it must be supposed that throughout the medieval period, masonry churches formed the overwhelming majority of architectural monuments – from the opus mixtum walls of Novgorod cathedrals to the limestone temples of Vladimir and Suzdal. It is their design that illustrates most brilliantly the technical and aesthetic capabilities of medieval Russian culture.

Indeed, during the two centuries following the devastating Mongol invasion (1237–41), the Church in a physical sense remained the most visible symbol of a unifying force over the vast area of what would become Russia. Yet with the attainment of ever greater power by Muscovy's grand princes during the late fifteenth and early sixteenth centuries, the design of churches acquired other, more explicitly secular connotations. During this period, the need to express new concepts of political destiny and national identity led to a second wave of foreign builders, educated in the ideals of the Italian quattrocento. Their influence, on both design and construction technology, was incalculable and capable of the most varied interpretation. The rebuilding of the Kremlin cathedrals and the concurrent abrogation of Mongol authority signaled Moscow's legitimacy as heir to the culture of the pre-Mongol Vladimir principality, just as the design of the Dormition Cathedral symbolized the reunion of the architectural heritage of Vladimir with construction principles imported by Italian architects and engineers.

The remarkable, creative extent of this grafting of different cultural stocks is embodied in the Cathedral of the Intercession on the Moat, popularly known as St. Basil's. Built by Ivan the Terrible in commemoration of his conquest of the khanate of Kazan, the cathedral displays numerous elements in both plan and detail that can be traced to the geometrical rigor of fifteenth-century Italian architectural thought, yet without the cultural ambience that nurtured the ideas of Antonio Filarete and his contemporaries in Europe. It is at this formative point in the rise of a national state that concepts and motifs from western culture begin to appear in Russian architecture as part of a process of highly selective and indiosyncratic adaptation.

If the architecture of the pre-Mongol church, with its inscribed-cross plan, had reflected an attempt to assimilate the culture and spiritual ideals of Byzantine Orthodoxy, the development of new architectural forms – derived from fortress walls and cathedrals built with Italian guidance – celebrated the rise of the Muscovite state and its ruthless autocrats. The emphasis on verticality, which can be detected to a limited extent in pre-Mongol churches with their pyramids of cupolas, now achieves an innovative and more rigorous interpretation in tower churches that signified the special relation between the heavenly hosts and the Muscovite prince, whose power was absolute. Although this period in Russian culture was replete with accomplishments, a concern with humanistic individualism was not among them.

The practice of incorporating foreign elements in Russian architecture at sporadic intervals and for specific, pragmatic purposes represents an admission that in architecture, as in other areas, Russia could not thrive without the west; yet it viewed western culture with a suspicion merging into xenophobia. The architecture of Muscovy, represented above all by the sixteenth-century votive churches commissioned by the grand princes (or tsars), is a striking manifestation of this expression of identity and separateness – not merely as a cultural statement, but as a form of political defense against alien and agressive powers. Russian architecture in the late medieval period thus signals, to a degree unknown elsewhere in Europe, the survival of the nation and its ruling dynasty.

In creating dramatic new forms to express this dominant idea – particularly in the tower votive churches – the sixteenth and seventeenth centuries also witnessed the proliferation of architectural ornament in brick, stucco, and ceramic. The festive appearance of churches brightly decorated with polychrome ornament and gilded onion domes (which may have originated as late as the sixteenth century) represents for many the essence of the Russian style in architecture and design; but ornamentalism is only one part of the national genius in architecture. Since the fifteenth century, if not earlier, Russian architecture has manifested an alternation between extremes of monolithic, tectonic clarity and ornamental saturation. And although this opposition originates in church design, by the eighteenth and nineteenth centuries, it appears in secular architecture as well. In a context of social instability and invasion during the late medieval period, ornamentalism represented an affirmation and celebration of the nation's resilience.

The architecture of national survival maintained its central importance in subsequent periods of Russian history, even as the Church lost its predominant role as the symbol of that survival. The great monastery ensembles of the seventeenth century illustrate Orthodoxy's attempt to reassert its primacy as the bearer of the national spirit, despite the inexorable expansion of secular authority at the expense of the Church. Not until the reign of Peter the Great, however, did architecture reflect the new secular order in an imported style (primarily northern baroque) that reflected Peter's fascination with European industry and technical knowledge. And although Peter shared certain artistic interests and political assumptions with his contemporaries among absolute monarchs, his cultural revolution – so evident in the formal vocabulary of architecture – was again impelled by an intensely pragmatic desire to create and maintain Russia's viability among the great European powers. This impulse occurred despite (or perhaps because of) Russia's lack of the cultural traditions and ideals that had nurtured the baroque and had provided a brilliant facade for what most impressed Peter: political and military power. Even Rastrelli's magnificent late baroque palaces for the Empress Elizabeth – obvious symbols of an absolutist state – had their specific, pragmatic political purpose as indices of the status, wealth, and power of the Russian Empire during a series of pan-European wars.

To be sure, during the reign of Catherine the Great, in the latter half of the eighteenth century, a coherent architecture for the institutions of civil society and individuals appeared in the forms of neoclassicism, which were related to other manifestations of Enlightenment culture (again, such as it existed in Russia). Nonetheless, the overwhelming supremacy of the interests of the autocratic state remained evident in such early nineteenth-century architectural masterpieces as the Admiralty (by Andreian Zakharov) and the Headquarters of the General Staff (by Carlo Rossi) – with their hypertrophied dimensions, triumphal columns, chariots, and other regalia in celebration of the military might and victories of the imperial state at the point of its highest, and final, glory. Even in a style so clearly derived from the west, Russian architects – and architects at work in Russia – created with a geometric rigor and on a scale unique to that country.

The decline of neoclassicism in the 1830s brought with it a loss of tectonic unity, as the interests of the state moved toward engineering projects such as railroads. Having yielded its pragmatic role as a symbol of state power and national survival, architecture also lost its cohesive sense of style and aesthetics. At the same time, the renewed growth of civil society in the wake of the Great Reforms of the 1860s made it evident that however eclectic contemporary architecture, it now functioned in service to individuals and insti-

tutions necessary for a modern urban society based on commerce and individual enterprise in the broadest sense. The tsarist regime viewed these developments with deep suspicion and supported its own forms of historicist "national" architecture, particularly in church construction. Yet the driving force behind imperial architecture had long since vanished in favor of individual experiments in modernism – both functional and aesthetic – that culminate in the work of Fedor Shekhtel at the beginning of the twentieth century.

Despite a hobbled economy and an anachronistic political system, the integration of Russia into "bourgeois" Europe at the turn of the century seemed plausible. Yet the lack of stylistic unity in architecture and the flamboyant ornamentalism of the Russian "style moderne" were widely interpreted as a sign of social disarray, of the loss of a proper standard for social and cultural values. During the decade before the First World War, the attempt to revive neoclassicism as a reaffirmation of the past glories of the empire only further demonstrated the pervasive influence of commerce in determining architectural style.[7] As private capital created a new urban environment, market forces and entrepreneurs exerted on architecture a formative influence that could not be denied by nostalgia or Parnassian aestheticism. For those who benefited from this transformation, the architecture of national survival had been replaced by one of individual preservation.

But not for long. The expropriation of private property and the development of radical theories for cooperative and communal housing after the Bolshevik Revolution replaced capitalist individualism with the socialist ideal of an egalitarian, industrial society. Yet the emphasis of Soviet architecture in the 1920s was also on the individual, whose social and cultural identity was to be transformed by an international modern style that reached from Moscow to Dessau and beyond. For the first time in its history, Russian architecture, closely related to the avant-garde in the visual arts, assumed a position at the center of European developments in design and theory. The unprecedented influence of Russian architects during this period is, of course, closely related to political events of international significance and to the belief, widespread among western intellectuals (including Le Corbusier and Frank Lloyd Wright), that the Soviet Union stood at the crest of a new social era. But though few have recognized it, the avant-garde in Russian architecture, like that in painting, is connected in significant ways with some of the oldest principles in medieval Russian design – in particular the unadorned, volumetric shapes of early medieval churches.

The collapse of an idealistic, internationalist view of the architectural environment – due to political factors and a devastating gap between theory and praxis – was accompanied by obligatory criticism against the monotony of the modern functionalism in Soviet Russia. It is hardly coincidental that the appearance of historicist styles such as totalitarian pseudo-classicism took place during the 1930s with the implementation of the five-year plans, essential to Stalin's concept of "socialism in one country." The perceived – and manipulated – threat of capitalist, imperialist encirclement led once again to xenophobia and repression; and once again architecture became a symbol of authority, hierarchy, and national survival. The culmination of Stalinist grandomania occurred after the war with the construction of "tall buildings," considered by western visitors to be another Russian idiosyncrasy, but whose model ultimately derived from early twentieth-century Manhattan skyscrapers. As in the sixteenth century, foreign technology and formal elements were adapted in Russia to a profoundly different cultural and ideological context. Indeed, one can interpret the unremitting mediocrity of the prefabricated, industrialized buildings from the post-Stalinist era as a signal of the decline of a virulent ideology and its cultural pretentions.

This pattern of intense engagement with, followed by isolation from, the varieties of western architecture created a tradition that cannot be easily defined, one that seems rarely essential to western civilization as defined by the academic syllabus and by cultural critics. Yet it is precisely this rhythm that not only makes of Russian architecture a remarkable record of the heroic – yet often tragic and destructive – history of a great people, but also provides illuminating perspectives on western cultural and aesthetic values, seen through the distorting glass of Russian buildings. In recording their story, this volume also serves as a commemoration, both of the Russian architectural tradition and of those whose generosity inspired my understanding of it.

Joseph-Volokolamsk Monastery. Cathedral of the Dormition. 1688–96. Walls and tower, second half of seventeenth century. Northeast view. (MR 20–18)

PART I

Early Medieval Architecture

CHAPTER 1

Kiev and Chernigov

And gaze upon thy city, radiant in its splendour, upon churches flourishing, upon Christianity increasing, gaze upon thy city, illuminated with holy icons, brilliant, surrounded with fragrant darkness, filled with hosannas and divine song.

– Ilarion, "Oration to Prince Vladimir"

Little remains of the Kiev that Metropolitan Ilarion praised in his encomium to Vladimir (at some point between 1037 and 1050). Centuries of war and devastation, culminating in the unique barbarism of twentieth-century totalitarianism, have effaced most of the city's early monuments; and those extant ensembles that suggest the city's glorious past – such as the churches of the Near and Distant Caves at the great Monastery of the Caves (see Plate 1) – are often the product of seventeenth- and eighteenth-century baroque architecture in Ukraine. Yet an observer of the eleventh century might indeed have marveled at the flourishing of the grand prince's city, whose towers, palaces, and churches had risen within a brief period, beginning in the latter part of the tenth century. For monumental architecture began among the eastern Slavs with the coalescence of a Kievan state dominating the Dnieper River trade route (from the "Varangians to the Greeks," from the Baltic to the Black Sea), and with the acceptance of Orthodox Christianity after Vladimir's baptism in 988.

There has been much dispute over the circumstances by which this occurred – and, in particular, over the role assigned to Norse adventurers in the formation of a cohesive political unit. One of the earliest medieval sources, *The Primary Chronicle*, states that in 860–2, the inhabitants of Novgorod, on the upper reaches of the trade network, summoned a Varangian, or Viking, leader named Riurik and his two brothers to "come and rule over them."[1] The reasons for this summons are unclear, the historicity of Riurik is uncertain, and the validity of the source, written some two centuries later, is unsubstantiated. None-

theless, Riurik is considered the founder of Russia's first dynasty, the Riurikovich line, which lasted until 1598.

Kiev came into prominence in 882, according to the chronicles, when Prince Oleg of Novgorod undertook a successful campaign against the settlement, found its central location on the trade route favorable, and in effect established the capital of an emerging Slavic state, to be known as Kievan Rus. We know of Kiev's earliest princes, Oleg and Igor, from both Russian and Byzantine sources, for the Slavs frequently made raids against the Byzantine Empire, for spoils and to gain a more advantageous trading position. Hard pressed by the Arabs to the south and the Bulgarians to the northwest, Byzantium concluded a number of agreements with the Russians, but cultural contacts remained minimal – at least until Princess Olga, widow of Igor, journeyed to Byzantium with her retinue in 957. Olga is celebrated in Russian legend for the calculated and horrific revenge she exacted on the murderers of her husband; but she was also the first Kievan ruler to accept Christianity (for which she was later canonized by the Orthodox Church).

Nonetheless, relations with the eastern rite remained undefined. The patriarch in Constantinople resisted any assertion of autonomy on the part of a Kievan Church, and a pagan revival during the reign of Olga's son Sviatoslav (964–72) threatened what limited gains had been made by the Church. After Sviatoslav's death (following a campaign against Byzantium in 972), tension between his three sons erupted into warfare, resolved in 978 in favor of Prince Vladimir of Novgorod and his Viking auxiliaries. For the first 10 years of his reign (c. 980–1015), Vladimir continued the policies of his predecessors in waging war with the nomadic tribes to the east, in defining a boundary with Poland, and in strengthening the authority of Kiev over its neighboring cities. The question of ties with Byzantium, and the concomitant struggle between paganism and Christianity, remained unsettled until 988, when Vladimir carried out one of the most decisive acts in the history of the eastern Slavs – the establishment of Orthodox Christianity as the official religion of Kiev.

Vladimir's motives for accepting Christianity were no doubt pragmatic. In the early years of his reign, he had continued the attempt of his father, Sviatoslav, to reaffirm the worship of pagan deities, and apparently gathered them into some sort of pantheon – indicative of his desire to create a cohesive religious structure. Paganism could not, however, provide the cultural and ideological base that Vladimir needed for his increasingly complicated state. Familiar with Judaism, Islam, and Christianity (both Roman and eastern), the grand prince decided in favor of eastern Christianity – a logical choice in view of Kiev's commercial and political ties with Byzantium, and the large number of people within his realm who had converted to Christianity. Medieval accounts also note the favorable impression made on Russian envoys to Constantinople by the Orthodox ritual and by Byzantium's magnificent achievements in the arts.

The final political maneuvering in 987 centered on negotiations for Vladimir's marriage to Anne, sister of the Byzantine emperor Basil II, in return for the official acceptance of Orthodox Christianity in Kiev and for Russian assistance in suppressing a revolt against Basil in Asia Minor. Despite the complicated situation in the empire and the disdain of many in Byzantium for the barbarians of Rus, Basil and Vladimir succeeded in fulfilling the terms of the agreement: Vladimir accepted Christianity and was baptized, presumably at the beginning of 988; the baptism of the Kievans in the Dnieper River occurred in the spring of 988; and shortly thereafter Anne arrived in Kiev. From this course of events, it can be inferred that Vladimir's acceptance of Christianity had diplomatic ramifications of considerable importance for both Kiev and Byzantium: While Basil consolidated his position on the Byzantine throne and converted a troublesome neighbor into an ally, Vladimir married a Porphyrogenite and acquired the cultural and social luster of the Byzantine court and Church.[2]

The first Kievan clerics were Greeks (many from Kherson on the Black Sea), and the Kievan metropolitan was chosen in Constantinople. Yet the rituals and Church literature were translated into Slavonic in order to facilitate propagation of the new religion, which encountered resistance that lingered for several decades in parts of Kievan Rus, particularly in the north. This melding of the Slavic and the Byzantine applied as well to the development of church architecture: wooden churches, which could be rapidly assembled by a people thoroughly skilled in the use of the ax, must in some cases have achieved great complexity. But the more substantial architectural presence that would signal Kiev's political and cultural status could come only in the form of stone and brick, of mosaics and frescoes produced by Greek and Balkan masters.[3] The basic principles of architectural design derived from Byzantium, and particularly from the flourishing of the inscribed-cross church of the middle Byzantine period (ninth through the twelfth centuries). Yet the builders of Kievan Rus soon developed their own modifications of the basic plan, and local craftsmen quickly learned the necessary skills for masonry construction and its decoration.[4]

Only the most fragmentary evidence remains of Kiev's first major monument – the Church of the Tithe (Desiatinnaia), built between 898 and 996 by Prince Vladimir, who dedicated it to the Virgin Mary and supported it with a tenth of his revenues. Destroyed by a fire in 1017 and reconstructed in 1039, the church was looted in 1177 and 1203 by neighboring princes, and finally destroyed in 1240 during the siege of Kiev by the Mongol armies of Khan Batu. There are different versions as to the cause of the structure's collapse: As one of the last bastions of the Kievans, it came under the assault of Mongol battering rams, and may have been further weakened by the survivors' attempt to tunnel out. Nonetheless, part of the eastern walls remained standing until the nineteenth century, when, in 1825, church authorities decided to erect a new church on the site. Rejecting the idea of incorporating the old walls into the new, they leveled what stood down to the foundations and commissioned the distinguished neoclassical architect Vasilii Stasov to construct an ungainly "neo-Byzantine" church; it was razed in 1935 and the site covered with pavement.

From twentieth-century excavations, however, we have a plausible, if incomplete, notion of the original church's plan; and although there is no way of determining with any accuracy the church's appearance, fragments of mosaics, frescoes, and marble ornaments give some sense of its decoration.[5] The walls were probably composed of alternating layers of stone and flat brick (plinthos) in a mortar of lime and crushed brick. What is left of the foundations suggests a prototype for the plan of medieval Russian masonry churches – the "inscribed-cross," or cross-domed, design (Figure 1), which evolved in Byzantium in the eighth century (cf. the Koimesis in Nicaea).[6] Composed of three, and in rare cases five, aisles laid along

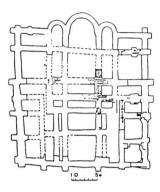

Figure 1. Church of the Tithe. Kiev. 989–96. Plan reconstructed by Mikhail Karger.

an east–west axis, the design is characterized by a widening of the central aisle, whose width is reflected in a north–south, or transept, aisle – thus delineating a cross within a quadrilateral. The space at which the arms of the cross intersect is marked by four piers that support the central cupola, elevated on a cylinder, or drum. With the addition of aisles in the west, a narthex could be formed; but the core of the plan consisted of the inscribed cross and the central cupola, whose interior contained a representation of Christ as Pantocrator. The eastern wall was marked by at least one apse and frequently by three (containing the prothesis and diaconicon). For all its apparent simplicity, the inscribed-cross plan not only suited the complicated movment of the Orthodox service, but also achieved a metaphor of centrality; for each church, whose walls depicted the work of God on earth and in heaven, could symbolize to its congregation the center of the universe, observed by an image of the Savior at its highest, central point.

Kiev in Glory: The Reign of Iaroslav the Wise

With the establishment of the Orthodox Church in Russia, Vladimir had created an enduring cultural and religious bond with the eastern empire, despite his successors' extensive contacts with the west – in particular, Scandinavia. Indeed, the west in the tenth and eleventh centuries was backward when measured against Byzantium and fragmented in comparison with the great territory of the eastern Slavs. Yet the rapid expansion of Kievan Rus contained the seeds of its own fragmentation, which began even before the death of Vladimir, in 1015. That year his son Iaroslav, prince of Novgorod, refused to render tribute to Kiev, and upon Vladimir's death, during preparations for a campaign against the recalcitrant, the Kievan throne became a prize in a struggle among the old prince's many sons. Sviatopolk – "damned Sviatopolk," as he is known in the chronicles – managed to kill three of his brothers, two of whom, Boris and Gleb, accepted death at the hands of Sviatopolk's minions rather than enter the fray. For their piety and refusal to meet violence with violence, they were canonized in 1015 as the first Russian martyrs.

In 1016, the main struggle emerged between Iaroslav and Sviatopolk, and it continued until 1019, when Iaroslav defeated Sviatopolk and his nomadic allies, the Turkic Pechenegs, near the walls of Kiev. On the site of this battle, Iaroslav was to raise his Cathedral of St. Sophia, inspired by the Hagia Sophia in Constantinople. But for some eighteen years, Iaroslav contended with further challenges to his power – the most serious coming from his brother Mstislav, prince of Chernigov and another patron of architecture. During this feudal strife, Iaroslav remained for the most part in Novgorod and little was built in Kiev: a small wooden church with five cupolas that served as a mausoleum for Sts. Boris and Gleb, and possibly (there are no remains) a wooden church dedicated to St. Sophia.[7]

With the consolidation of power after the death of Mstislav in 1036, Iaroslav – who as a young prince had refused to give tribute to Kiev – continued the work in that city begun by his father, whose original plan was now considerably expanded, with a new wall and three large gates, including the "Golden Gate," fragments of which still survive. But the great and lasting achievement of Iaroslav's reign is the cathedral dedicated to St. Sophia (or the Divine Wisdom), which dominated his city as the Church of the Tithe had dominated Vladimir's.[8] The cathedral was a monument not only to the ascendancy of Iaroslav, now called "the Wise" (owing to his judicial wisdom), but also to the increasing prestige of the Orthodox Church in Kievan Rus, whose metropolitanate, created in 1037, was to be seated at St. Sophia's for the next two centuries.

Although the exterior of the cathedral has been modified by reconstruction in the seventeenth and

Figure 2. Cathedral of St. Sophia. Kiev. 1037(?)–50s(?), with seventeenth- and eighteenth-century accretions. East view, with stucco stripped from portions of the apses to reveal the opus mixtum (stone and flat brick) construction. (KI 1–3; this and subsequent numbers refer to the catalog of the author's photographs.)

12

Figure 3. Cathedral of St. Sophia. Kiev. Drawing by A. Westerfeld, a German mercenary in the army of Prince Radziwill. Made during the Polish occupation of Kiev (1651), the view shows the cathedral after its restoration by Peter Mohila, in the 1630s–40s. The exterior of St. Sophia still retained an eleventh-century silhouette; its cur-rent baroque panoply dates from the turn of the eighteenth century, in a restoration supported by Mazepa (the Ukrainian hetman) and by Peter the Great. Courtesy of Shchusev State Historical Architectural Museum, Moscow.

eighteenth centuries (it had fallen into ruin after the Mongol invasion in 1240), excavations in the 1930s and the study of possible variant designs have furnished what is considered a definitive version of the original composition. In its basic parts, the plan of Kiev's St. Sophia conforms to the cross-domed model as developed in the middle Byzantine period; but its complexity and scale exceeded that of the Desiatinnaia Church – and of most subsequent Russian Orthodox churches. Of its five aisles, each of which culminates in an apse, the central aisle is twice the width of those flanking – a proportion that also characterized the transept along the building's north–south axis. The main cupola, focal point of the exterior, is elevated on a high drum over the central crossing and surrounded by twelve cupolas, arranged in descending order, to create a pyramidal silhouette (Figures 2 and 3).

The origins of this plenitude of domes are obscure: Although early wooden churches may have had com-plex roof designs, no clear derivation has been established, nor can it be proven that there was any numerological significance to the arrangement.[9] Whatever their provenance, the cupolas – or, more precisely, their drums – serve both a practical and an aesthetic purpose as the primary source of natural light for the cathedral's interior. The thick walls, enclosed by two exterior arcaded galleries, allow almost no light from the outside, and what little enters from the windows under the vaulting is obscured by choir galleries along the northern and southern walls.[10]

On entering the cathedral one sees – or is plunged into – a dimly lit space, which yields to a brilliant display of color under the central domes. The light that illuminates the area before the altar reveals not only piers and walls covered with eleventh-century frescoes (well preserved, in view of the cathedral's frequent despoilation), but also the only extensive mosaics to have survived in Kievan architecture.[11] Much of the central apse is obscured by an icon-

13

ostasis dating to the eighteenth century. From the medallion of the Pantocrator in the center of the main cupola, 100 feet above the floor, to the great Virgin orant within the central apse – blue robe on a gold background – the mosaics of St. Sophia display what for Byzantium would be a provincial style; but the Greek masters who executed both the mosaics and the frescoes succeeded in transmitting the Byzantine fusion of religious art and architectural space (Figures 4 and 5).

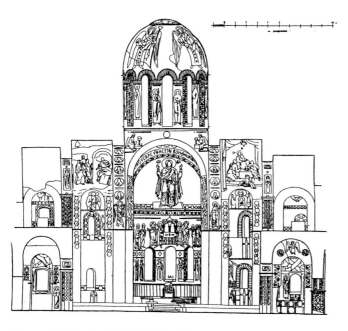

Figure 4. Cathedral of St. Sophia. Kiev. Transverse section by Iu. Nelgovskii and L. Voronets, with a schematic drawing of the mosaics and frescoes of the central dome and the altar.

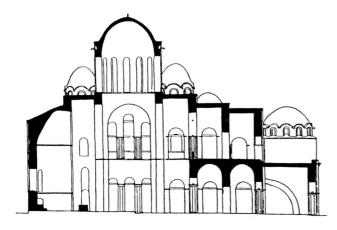

Figure 5. Cathedral of St. Sophia. Kiev. Longitudinal section, plan. From the reconstruction by Kresalskii, Volkov, and Aseev.

In contrast to the monumental art of its interior, the exterior of the St. Sophia Cathedral demonstrates an austerity characteristic of Byzantine church architecture during the tenth and eleventh centuries (cf. the Bodrum Camii and the Fenari Isa Camii North Church, both early tenth-century Constantinople). The walls, constructed in *opus mixtum* (alternating courses of stone and flat brick – or *plinthos* – in a mortar of lime and crushed brick), had decoration consisting of niches, pilasters, and various ornamental patterns in brick – most frequently, the meander. Although parts of the facade were probably decorated with frescoes, and carved marble capitals provided a more elaborate form of architectural ornament, little distracted the eye from the structural mass of the church, rising in pyramidal form to the central cupola. The pink masonry walls were later covered with white stucco, but even their original, more colorful appearance was restrained in comparison with the interior. This contrast between an austere facade and a profusely decorated interior continued to predominate in the Russian church until the sixteenth century – the monolithic austerity separating the church from its surrounding structures, usually of wood, and the profusion conveying the worshipers to the inner world of the Church and its saints.

◇ ◇ ◇

During the construction of St. Sophia, other major centers of medieval Rus had also initiated the building of large churches, although none as complex as the Kievan cathedral. Iaroslav's rival Mstislav had as early as 1034 or 1035 commissioned a cathedral dedicated to the Transfiguration of the Savior in Chernigov (some 120 kilometers to the north of Kiev).[12] The chronicler notes that by the time of Mstislav's sudden death (while hunting), in 1036, the cathedral walls had attained a height that could be "reached by a man sitting on a horse." There is no further word on its construction, which must have been interrupted and then completed during the reign of Iaroslav, or that of his son Sviatoslav, who ruled in Chernigov from 1054 until he became Grand Prince in Kiev in 1073.[13] The plan of the cathedral is similar to that of Vladimir's Desiatinnaia Church – cross-domed, three-aisled, and with a narthex – yet the sharp delineation of its central aisle, separated from the transept by a two-story arcade formed by arched columns, creates a perception of linear development unusual for Orthodox churches in this area and reminiscent of the basilica (Figure 6). Although badly damaged in the aftermath of the Mongol invasion of 1240, the fragments of the mosaics, frescoes, and carved marble

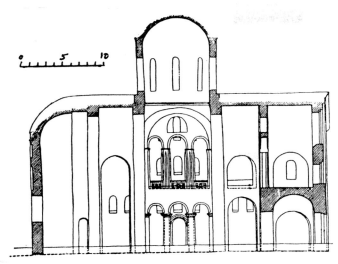

Figure 6. Cathedral of the Transfiguration of the Savior. Chernigov. 1031–50s(?). Section.

that decorated the interior characterize a style still largely dependent on Greek masters and their materials.

On the exterior, the cross-domed plan of the church is reflected in the delineation of the facade into bays that correspond to the interior structure and vaulting. The central, major bay of each facade represents an extension of the arms of the inscribed cross, and each contains the traditional three windows beneath its curved gable, or *zakomara* (Figure 7). The west front has at its north corner a tower with stairs leading to the choir gallery over the narthex (Figure 8). (During a reconstruction in the 1790s, a companion tower was added to the south corner and conical steeples were placed over both.) The walls, about 1.5 meters thick, are of opus mixtum, marked on the exterior with brick niches and decorated with brick patterns such as the meander, which were covered in later centuries by stucco. Rising above the structure are five drums with cupolas. Although less elaborate than the great conglomeration of cupolas at St. Sophia in Kiev, the domes of the Cathedral of the Transfiguration nonetheless achieve that pyramidal, vertical emphasis that would become a distinctive feature of the medieval Russian church (see Plate 2).

The Monastery Churches

After the death of Iaroslav the Wise, in 1054, an uncertain principle of succession, combined with the distribution of lands among his five sons, once again threatened the fragile unity of the Kievan state. A period of cooperation among the three elder brothers, controlling most of the territory, collapsed under the pressure of feudal infighting, attacks by the nomadic Polovtsi (a Turkic group occupying the southeastern steppes), and popular discontent, which in 1068 led to rioting in Kiev. The struggle that developed at this point between Kiev's prince, Iziaslav, and his brothers continued for another generation without resolution: No prince wished the demise of Kievan Rus, and yet none could be compelled to surrender autonomy to the nominal capital.

The Church was unsuccessful in its attempt to mediate among the various parties (it condemned Iziaslav for his Roman Catholic, Polonophile tendencies, and condemned his brothers for usurping the place of the eldest); but it benefited from the largess of the various claimants to the Kievan throne, who tendered land and valuables to the city's churches and its growing number of monasteries. Of these institutions, the first, the richest, and for several centuries the primary Orthodox monastery in medieval Rus was the Kiev-Percherskii ("Cave") Lavra, or monastery, founded in the middle of the eleventh century as a retreat near Kiev. It is significant that the Lavra was the only Kievan monastery not founded by a prince, but by the monastic brotherhood led by the venerable Feodosii. By virtue of its cohesiveness, the monastery quickly assumed a leading role in the affairs of the Church, as well as in the development of a literary tradition in Kiev. From the eleventh through the thirteenth centuries, its monks compiled the chronicles that provide most of the written information we have about Kievan Rus.[14]

As the monastery's holdings and wealth increased, its first small wooden church was replaced by the Cathedral of the Dormition, begun in 1073 (with a major donation from Iaroslav's son Sviatoslav), completed around 1077, but not consecrated until 1089. (Considerable time was allowed for the masonry walls of Kiev's large churches to settle and thoroughly dry during construction and before the interior was decorated.) Although the cathedral was damaged by an earthquake in 1230, sacked by the Mongols in 1240, and rebuilt in the fifteenth century, much of its original core survived until an explosion destroyed it during the occupation of Kiev in 1941. The remnants – a chapel in the southeast corner, portions of the eastern walls, the foundations, and massive fragments of opus mixtum – have been preserved (Figure 9).

In contrast to the major churches constructed during the reigns of Vladimir and Iaroslav – with their complex array of aisles and exterior galleries, and tiers of cupolas surrounding a central dome – the mon-

15

Figure 7. Cathedral of the Transfiguration of the Savior. Chernigov. West facade. An enclosed baroque porch obscures the original portal, but the removal of stucco reveals decorative brick patterns of the opus mixtum walls, not originally stuccoed. (CH 1–3)

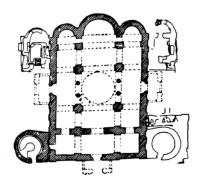

Figure 8. Cathedral of the Transfiguration of the Savior. Chernigov. Plan by I. Morgilevskii.

astery Cathedral of the Dormition represents both a simplification of plan and a pronounced development of the vertical, which created a greater visibility above the monastery walls.[15] Although by no means small, the structure contained only three aisles in addition to a narthex (Figure 10). There were no flanking galleries and initially only one cupola (with twelve windows), and as a result, there was no distraction on either the exterior or the interior to hinder a perception of the building's considerable height.

Within a few years of the cathedral's completion, a much smaller church with baptistry, dedicated to John the Baptist, was constructed adjacent to the

16

Figure 9. Cathedral of the Dormition, Monastery of the Caves. Kiev. 1073–8. East view. In ruins after the Mongol sack of Kiev in 1240, the cathedral was restored in 1470, renovated by Peter Mohila in the 1640s and by Mazepa during the 1690s, at which time it was given a baroque exterior. During the occupation of Kiev in 1941, an explosion destroyed all but portions of the east structure and a baroque chapel at the southeast corner. (KI 3–6)

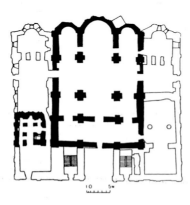

Figure 10. Cathedral of the Dormition, Monastery of the Caves. Kiev. Reconstructed plan by Morgilevskii.

north corner of the west facade. Alterations in the fifteenth, seventeenth, and eighteenth centuries obscured the original appearance of the Cathedral of the Dormition, but its structural principle can be observed in other churches built during the next century, such as the Cathedral of St. George at the Iurev Monastery in Novgorod (1119–30; see Figures 29 and 31). The interior had not only frescoes, but also mosaics, on both the walls and the floor, and there is no reason to doubt the statement of the monastery chronicles that the Dormition Cathedral was designed and built by masters from Constantinople. This was still the common practice for Kievan churches, whose scale posed special problems in the technology of construction and decoration – such as the preparation of smal-

17

tos for mosaics. Nonetheless, one can assume not only local participation in the process of building and decoration (the chronicle mentions the work of the monk Alimpii in painting the frescoes), but also in the development of a style of church architecture distinctive to Kievan Rus.[16]

Shortly before the construction of the Cathedral of the Dormition, another of Iaroslav's sons, Vsevolod, established the Vydubetskii Monastery near his estate to the south of Kiev, and in 1070 provided for the construction of a church dedicated to the Archangel Michael. Much smaller than the Dormition Cathedral, the church at Vydubetskii Monastery was consecrated only in 1088, after delayed construction of a narthex and tower on the west front (Figure 11). The structure's picturesque location on a bluff above the west bank of the Dnieper River proved to be an unending source of trouble, for a few decades after its completion, the east foundation began to give way. The construction of a major retaining wall by the Kievan architect Peter Miloneg in 1199 only postponed the catastrophe, and at some later date, the entire eastern part of the church collapsed into the Dnieper. Only since 1945 has archaeological research provided the information for a hypothetical reconstruction (Figure 12) of this, one of the few remaining Kievan monuments from the late eleventh century.[17] Despite its relatively small size and the mishaps connected with its construction, the Cathedral of the Archangel Michael incorporated a number of unusual refinements in design. Its cupola was shifted one bay to the west, thus presenting a more imposing appearance to the west entrance. The walls, originally unstuccoed, display the texture of opus mixtum, but with a more highly profiled articulation of facade details such as decorative niches and windows.

The most impressive of the new monastery churches was dedicated to the Archangel Michael and built between 1108 and 1113 at the Monastery of St. Dmitrii, established in the middle of the preceding century by Iziaslav. The monasteries founded by the rival sons of Iaroslav continued to be maintained by their own descendents as a sort of patrimony. Thus, in 1085, Iziaslav's son Iaropolk commissioned the first stone church (long since destroyed) at the Monastery of St. Dmitrii; and another of his sons, Sviatopolk, commissioned the much larger Church of the Archangel Michael, which was comparable to the Cathedral of the Dormition at the Monastery of the Caves in its elaborate decoration. Indeed, the church was referred to in the chronicles as "the Golden-Domed," and the monastery itself eventually adopted the name of the church.

Figure 11. Cathedral of the Archangel Michael, Vydubetskii Monastery. Kiev. 1070–88. West facade. (KI 6–1)

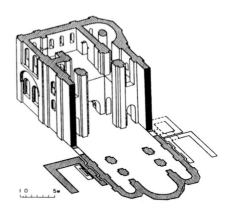

Figure 12. Cathedral of the Archangel Michael, Vydubetskii Monastery. Kiev. Reconstruction by M. Karger. The collapsed eastern portion is outlined at the foundation level.

Like the Dormition Cathedral, the Church of the Archangel Michael contained mosaics (placed in the apse, as in the Cathedral of St. Sophia), as well as the less technically demanding frescoes for the main part of the interior.[18] In addition, the structure incorporated features that were to enter the mainstream of medieval Russian art – most notably the placement of arched gables, or *zakomary*, along a horizontal line at the culmination of the walls.[19] Regrettably, this landmark in the evolution from the art and architecture of Byzantium to an indigenous style in medieval Rus did not survive the extensive destruction of Kiev's religious monuments in the 1930s, and only a few of its mosaics were hastily salvaged during the church's demolition in 1934–5.

With the death in 1113 of Iziaslav's son Sviatopolk, who was buried in the recently completed Church of the Archangel Michael, the line of Iziaslav came to an end as a power in Kievan politics. The new grand prince, Vladimir Monomakh, was the son of Vsevolod and grandson of Iaroslav the Wise. Yet he ruled in Kiev not by hereditary right, but only after having been summoned by the Church in the wake of rioting and looting precipitated by economic crisis and the death of the unpopular Sviatopolk. Vladimir's own domains were in Rostov-Suzdalia – far to the east of Kiev – and much of his architectural patronage was expended there. Kiev's Cathedral of the Dormition is assumed to have served as the prototype for his cathedrals in Rostov and Suzdal – of which only the foundations remain.[20]

Nonetheless, Vladimir proved to be one of the most vigorous leaders of medieval Rus. During his reign, from 1113 to 1125, he not only succeeded in containing the centrifugal tendencies of the Kievan principalities and in repulsing the Polovtsy, the latest of Kiev's nomadic raiders from the steppes, but he also wrote a document entitled the *Testament*, a remarkable account of his reign and the incessant struggle with Kiev's external enemies. It is one of the few major secular documents of medieval Russian literature, and the only one to provide such a detailed insight into the life of a Kievan prince. From one of Vladimir Monomakh's eight sons, Iurii Dolgorukii, there ensued the princely line that would rule Russia until the extinction of the Riurikovich dynasty at the end of the sixteenth century.

At some point in his reign (the precise dates of construction are not known), Vladimir Monomakh commissioned one of the most distinctive of Kiev's churches, the Savior at Berestovo, which served as the family chapel and burial crypt of the Monomakhs. Although smaller in size than the major monastery churches, the Church of the Savior was notable for its height and the imposing dimensions of the arched entrance into the main part of the church. In addition, it contained a complex narthex with a baptistry and chapel in the north section and a stair tower (to the large choir gallery) in the south (Figure 13). In previous churches such as the Dormition and Michael the Golden Domed, the baptistry was placed adjacent to but beyond the main structure. Its inclusion within the Church of the Savior would account for the size and complexity of the narthex, which is wider than the body of the church.[21]

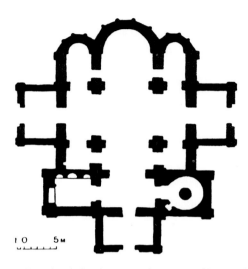

Figure 13. Church of the Savior at Berestovo. Kiev. 1113(?)–25. Reconstructed plan by M. Karger. The narthex (the only surviving part of the original structure) included a baptistry in the north bay and a gallery staircase in the southwest corner.

The narthex is in fact the only part of the Church of the Savior to have survived the despoilation and neglect that followed the Mongol invasion. As one of Kiev's ruined monuments rebuilt in 1640–2 by the distinguished scholar and metropolitan of Kiev, Peter Mohila, the remaining walls were preserved, albeit beneath an overlay of Ukrainian baroque decoration. A restoration by Peter Pokryshkin in 1909–13 revealed not only the good condition of the west front, but also the brickwork, which represents a transitional stage from the earlier opus mixtum to walls entirely of brick, with decorative patterns such as the meander and the inserted cross (Figure 14).[22]

After Vladimir Monomakh's death in 1125, two of his sons succeeded to some degree in maintaining the cohesion that he had imposed on the Kievan state; but by the middle of the twelfth century, the internecine strife inherent in the division of the patrimony among the grand prince's sons once again threatened the unity of Kiev. Andrei Bogoliubskii, whose extraordinary patronage of architecture in the Vladimir-Suzdal area is examined in Chapter 3, refused to re-

Figure 14. Church of the Savior at Berestovo. Kiev. Southwest view. The extant twelfth-century walls provide the first example in Kiev of solid brick construction in a technique known as submerged row: Alternating courses of flat brick are recessed with a pink mortar of lime and crushed brick. The decorative patterns (a meander frieze, crosses, recessed niches) are typical of middle-Byzantine architecture. (KI 5–9)

turn to Kiev upon his accession to power in 1157 (following the death of his father Iurii Dolgorukii). Indeed, in 1169, his son sacked the city. Nonetheless, the construction of monastery churches in Kiev continued, on a less extensive scale.[23]

Of these churches, the most significant, and the best preserved, is the Church of St. Cyril at the monastery of the same name. Situated to the north of the city and founded by Prince Vsevolod Olgovich of Chernigov shortly after his forces wrested power from the Monomakhs in 1140, the monastery functioned as a personal holding of yet another of the princely clans contending for power in Kiev. The dates of the monastery church are not certain, but apparently it was completed several years after Vsevolod's death in 1146. One interpretation of the chronicles suggests that Vsevolod's widow, Maria, was responsible for the completion of the Church of St. Cyril,[24] after

which it served as the burial crypt for the Olgovich line – including, in 1194, Vsevolod's son Sviatoslav, one of the main princes in the most famous of medieval Russian epic poems, the *Tale of the Host of Igor*. Although not severely damaged in 1240, the abandoned church gradually fell into ruin until its reconstruction in the style of the Ukrainian baroque at the end of the seventeenth century. It was reconstructed again in the middle of the eighteenth century by Ivan Grigorovich-Barskii, who designed the pediment over the west front (see Plate 3).

In its original form, the Church of St. Cyril had one large drum and cupola over the central crossing (the other four now on the church were added at the end of the seventeenth century). The plan included the features common to large Kievan churches: a tripartite apsidal structure, a choir gallery in the west, and a narthex, with a baptistry in the south corner and a burial chamber in the north (Figure 15). Access to the choir gallery was provided not through a tower incorporated into the narthex, but by a set of narrow stairs placed within the north wall – a common device in less elaborate churches. The walls were entirely of brick, and were among the earliest to have been covered in a type of stucco: lime with fragments of crushed brick of a pinkish hue.

The twelfth-century frescoes on the interior had subsequently been covered under layers of plaster, and in 1880, an attempt was made to uncover and restore a number of scenes, including in the narthex a depiction of the Last Judgment (an innovation for

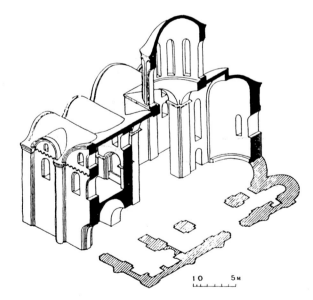

Figure 15. Church of St. Cyril, Monastery of St. Cyril. Kiev. Reconstruction of midtwelfth-century form by Iu. Aseev.

the late twelfth century). The main dome contained a representation of Christ Pantocrator, the north and south walls contained compositions on the Nativity of Christ and the Dormition of Mary, and the apse displayed the canonical representations of Mary Mother of God and the Eucharist. The south section of the apse also contained extensive scenes from the life of St. Cyril of Alexandria. Unfortunately, the restoration of the 1880s included extensive overpainting of fragmented or missing areas with oil paints, which themselves did considerable damage to surviving parts of the original frescoes. Recent restorations have attempted to recover and maintain as much as possible of the original work, and have in the process rediscovered the remarkable vitality of composition and color in the frescoes.[25]

Chernigov in the Twelfth Century

Although St. Cyril's is a rare example of midtwelfth-century church architecture extant in Kiev, its structural form is related to two surviving twelfth-century churches in Chernigov. As Chernigov's princes continued to be major rivals for power in Kievan Rus throughout the century, the city itself witnessed the construction of a number of major projects, including a cathedral dedicated to the martyred princes, Sts. Boris and Gleb. Situated near the Cathedral of the Transfiguration of the Savior and adjacent to the prince's residence (not extant), the Cathedral of Sts. Boris and Gleb was undoubtedly commissioned by the prince of Chernigov. The commonly accepted patron is Prince David Sviatoslavich, who died in 1123 and is mentioned in medieval sources as having been buried in the Cathedral of Sts. Boris and Gleb, which he built. However, there is no specific mention of the construction of this church (tentatively dated between 1115 and 1123), and the discovery of the foundations of an earlier structure beneath the present cathedral has given rise to the hypothesis that the church associated with Prince David was completely rebuilt in a style characteristic of the latter half of the twelfth century.[26]

After the Second World War, the Cathedral of Sts. Boris and Gleb was restored to what is thought to have been its original appearance (see Plate 4), although certain aspects of the restoration – in particular the roof line – must necessarily remain conjectural. The elegantly simple exterior, which resembles the original form of the Church of St. Cyril in Kiev, is divided along the east–west axis into four bays, culminating in a semicircular *zakomary*. Among the few decorations to have been preserved are limestone basket capitals – probably of Byzantine provenance – displaying various fanciful animals in a web of rinceaux. The capitals now visible on the attached columns of the exterior (Figure 16) are rough copies of the originals, on exhibit within the church. The presence of carved capitals, decorative arcade friezes, and profiled portals suggests western influence in the twelfth-century architecture of Kievan Rus – possibly a reflection of early dynastic ties between Kiev and the west.[27]

The cathedral plan included the usual three apses, six piers that define the arms of the inscribed cross, and a choir gallery in the west. The north and west facades originally had attached galleries on the exterior, and a small chapel was attached to the southeast corner shortly after the construction of the main structure (Figure 17). This proliferation of attached chapels was quite typical throughout medieval Russian architecture, including churches in Novgorod, Vladimir-Suzdal, and Muscovy. In some cases, the chapels are still visible; in others, they have been incorporated into subsequent enlargements of the church or removed altogether in later restorations. The walls were of solid brickwork (no fieldstone), covered with a thin layer of stucco and scored to resemble ashlar stonework – a detail ignored in the reconstruction.

A similar structure – and similarly related to St. Cyril's in Kiev – is the Cathedral of the Dormition at Eletskii Monastery, one of two monasteries founded

Figure 16. Cathedral of Sts. Boris and Gleb. Chernigov. Midtwelfth century(?). Northwest view. (CH 1–10)

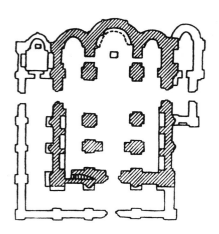

Figure 17. Cathedral of Sts. Boris and Gleb. Chernigov. Plan.

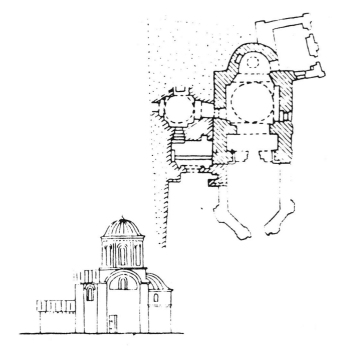

Figure 18. Church of Elijah, Trinity-Elijah Monastery. Chernigov. Early twelfth century, with seventeenth-century additions. Section and plan of original structure by P. Iurchenko.

in Chernigov in the latter half of the eleventh century by Sviatoslav, son of Iaroslav the Wise. The cathedral has been provisionally dated to the middle of the eleventh century, although there is no precise documentary evidence and earlier datings have been proposed.[28] The basic structure has been well preserved – with the usual overlay of late seventeenth-century baroque decoration – and corresponds on most essential points to the Cathedral of Sts. Boris and Gleb: a cross-inscribed plan with three apses, a choir gallery, and walls lightly coated on the exterior with stucco scored to resemble stonework. The Dormition Cathedral is slightly larger than the Cathedral of Sts. Boris and Gleb and has a clearly defined narthex that connects with an exterior gallery along the south facade.

A much smaller monument, which has been dated no more precisely than the twelfth century, is the monastery Church of Elijah at the Trinity-Elijah (Il-inskii) Monastery, another foundation of Sviatoslav Iaroslavich (in 1069) at the site of a cave retreat inhabited the preceding year by Antonii of the Caves. Antonii, one of the most revered eremites of medieval Rus, had founded the Kiev Cave Monastery in 1051, and his brief presence in Chernigov was sufficient to institute a similar monastery on the outskirts of Chernigov. The Church of Elijah, located on the slope of a hill and connecting with a subterranean complex of caves and chapels, was substantially reconstructed at the end of the sixteenth century, and again in 1649. Nonetheless, its basic structure is clearly defined: a narthex in the west, a single apse in the east, and braced walls – without free-standing piers – to support a single dome (Figure 18).[29] This simple and logical plan would serve as a prototype for the de-velopment of other small masonry churches in Kievan Rus.[30]

Architecture at the Turn of the Thirteenth Century

As the last of the churches commissioned by Svia-toslav were coming to completion, a number of innovative church structures were being created elsewhere under the patronage of Sviatoslav's rival, Riurik Rostislavich of Smolensk. In fact, the apparent inability of Kiev's princely factions to create a stable political situation had been temporarily resolved in 1181 with a division of power between Sviatoslav Vse-volodovich (of the Chernigov Olgovich dynasty), who became grand prince in Kiev, and Riurik (of the Smolensk Rostislavich dynasty), who assumed the title of grand prince of Rus. In this unequal division, Riurik and his brothers became major patrons of the arts and builders of churches in Smolensk, Polotsk, Ovruch, and eventually Kiev itself.

The Church of St. Basil in Ovruch is perhaps the most significant of Riurik's churches to have survived – although the term "survived" must be qualified here, for the structure had become little more than a shell of ruined walls by the beginning of this century.

In 1907–9, it was reconstructed by the architect Aleksei Shchusev, who during the decade before the First World War was the most accomplished designer of churches in Russia. Although the reconstruction was carried out with the advice and supervision of the archeologist P. Pokryshkin, and although Shchusev's proposal had the approval of the Archeological Commission, it is now recognized that Shchusev's design of the upper walls and the roof is based on no authority other than his own supreme talent as a modern interpreter of medieval architecture (Figure 19).[31]

Subsequent research indicates that the church was originally built between 1190 and 1192, and that its drum and cupola were steeply pitched above an ascending pyramid of corbelled arches – in fact, a form similar to that of St. Paraskeva-Piatnitsa in Chernigov (see Plate 5). A series of these compact, vertically accented brick churches was built around the turn of the thirteenth century, and like the Ovruch church, they all had four piers and no narthex. St. Basil's in Ovruch was distinctive, however, in having two tow-

Figure 19. Church of St. Basil. Ovruch. 1190–2. Reconstruction by Aleksei Shchusev, 1907–9. Photograph from *Ezhegodnik Moskovskogo arkhitekturnogo obshchestva* (Annual of the Moscow Architectural Society), 1912–13.

ers attached to the west front, and it also displayed the unusual device of placing large polished stones within the exterior facing of the brick walls. The roof was composed of sheets of lead – the usual material for those masonry churches in Kievan Rus that were not roofed in wooden shingles (a common practice in Novgorod). However, because the church was known as the "Golden-Domed," it is possible that its cupola was covered with gilded copper.[32]

After the death of Sviatoslav Vsevolodovich in 1194, Riurik asserted his claim to be the one ruler of both Kiev and Rus – a claim inevitably to be disputed by rival princes. Indeed, the greater political power resided in the Vladimir-Suzdal area, where Prince Vsevolod III, son of Iurii Dolgorukii, ruled over a large area of Rus from 1176 to 1212 and oversaw the building of some of the greatest Russian cathedrals of the medieval period (see Chapter 3). Nonetheless, fighting resumed over the throne in Kiev in 1203, when the city was again sacked. During the brief interval before the renewal of the struggle, the chronicles note that in 1197, Riurik commissioned another church dedicated to the Byzantine theologian St. Basil the Great (Riurik's baptismal name was Basil). There has been no concensus as to the precise archeological identification of this church, but its general form is assumed to have resembled that of St. Basil's in Ovruch.[33]

One monument of the period has, after many vicissitudes, survived and been restored to a form that seems so strikingly innovative in the context of earlier Kievan architecture. The Church of St. Paraskeva Piatnitsa in Chernigov can only be roughly dated to the turn of the thirteenth century, and it was substantially reconstructed at the end of the seventeenth century. In the aftermath of severe bomb damage in 1943, much of the original structure was revealed (only the east and north parts were relatively intact); and after extensive preparatory work, a reconstruction of the church was begun in 1959 and completed four years later.[34]

Patterned brickwork decorates the central part of the facades (Figure 20), but the overwhelming aesthetic impression is created by the shaping of the structure. The church is modest in its dimensions (16 by 12 meters; approximately 24 meters in height) and in its plan: a small cuboid space, with four interior piers supporting a single drum and cupola (Figure 21). The soaring height of the drum and cupola is created by three corbelled arches, whose massed contours provide a visual transition from the upper part of the walls to the cupola. The recessed portals, outlined with arched brickwork, the blind arcade along

Figure 20. Church of St. Paraskeva-Piatnitsa. Chernigov. Early thirteenth century. West facade. (CH 2–8)

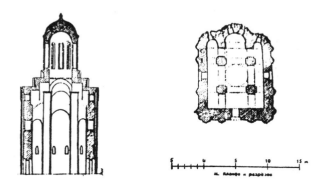

Figure 21. Church of St. Paraskeva-Piatnitsa. Chernigov. Section and plan (after Baranovskii).

the upper part of the apse, the attached profiled columns (all elements suggestive of late Romanesque architecture), and the detailing of the cornice reinforce a perception of the structure as an aesthetic whole (see Plate 5). Although not of uniform size, the width of the bricks exceeds that of the mortar seams (a de-

velopment of the twelfth century, which saw a decline in the use of the earlier plinthos), thus giving a consistent and clear definition of the structural material. The construction technique of the walls – whose stability was demonstrated beyond all measure in subsequent centuries – called for an interior and exterior surface of bricks, with an infill of brick rubble and lime mortar. At every five to seven rows, cross rows of brick linked the two facades. The piers and vaulting were of solid brick.[35]

The vertical thrust achieved in the structure of the Church of St. Paraskeva is curiously similar to that of the great votive Church of the Ascension at Kolomenskoe, near Moscow (1532; see Chapter 6). The similarity is manifest in the way by which structural features, particularly the vaulting arches, reveal an aesthetic as well as architectonic purpose, and in the use of brick to emphasize the texture and plasticity of the walls. There is no evidence to suggest influence or continuity between these two monuments, so distant from each other in every respect; and yet there is a broader affinity that speaks of medieval Russian architecture's remarkable expression of the vertical.

Kiev in Desolation

By the time of the construction of St. Paraskeva in Chernigov, Kievan Rus no longer existed in any effective, cohesive sense. With the death of Vladimir Monomakh in 1125, the struggle for the Kievan throne among princes whose power base lay elsewhere undermined the concept of the city as the center of a unified state. In addition to a flawed political system that encouraged disunity by the lack of a clear principle of dynastic succession, there were undoutedly collateral developments in the economic and social structure that undermined the unity of the vast (too vast) territory of medieval Rus.[36] Shifting trade routes in the twelfth century brought new prosperity to Novgorod, busy at trade with the west and colonization in the far north. In political terms, the principality of Vladimir-Suzdal supplanted Kiev's dominance in central Russia. Monomakh's successor in Suzdalia, Iurii Dolgorukii, strove for the throne in Kiev and finally gained it shortly before his death in 1157; but his son Andrei had no desire to rule there. The city was raided in 1169, and devastated again in 1203 – a year before the sack of Constantinople by the Crusaders, an event that dealt another blow to the status of Kiev. This decline should not imply that all productive cultural and economic activity had ceased: In some respects, the population and the monastic foundations could

24

exist apart from the princely feuds and even flourish. Yet in absolute terms, Kiev at the beginning of the thirteenth century was unable to exercise control over Russia's warring principalities, all of which, with the exception of Novgorod, fell before the destructive fury of the Mongol invasion of 1237–40.

Desolate, depopulated (a contemporary account notes that barely 200 people survived in the city after the Mongol conquest), Kiev would gradually regain a semblance of order, but the circumstances that had once allowed it to rule from Poland to the Volga were not to be recreated. As Muscovy expanded in the east, Kiev came under the domination first of Lithuania, and then of Poland (after the Union of Lublin, in 1569), both Roman Catholic. Only in the seventeenth century, after prolonged and vicious warfare between Poland and Cossacks from the Dnieper region, did Kiev and much of the Ukraine unite with Russia (in 1654). During this period, many of its ruined churches were repaired or rebuilt, under the energetic direction of Metropolitan Peter Mohila – who fostered an intellectual renaissance in the city and provided Moscow with a conduit for western culture. Major architectural projects included the restoration of the Cathedral of St. Sophia and the rebuilding of the Monastery of the Caves. Indeed, in their zeal to create a new Kiev, patrons rebuilt eleventh- and twelfth-century churches in a seventeenth-century style that properly belongs to the development of a separate, Ukrainian culture among the Slavs of the Dnieper River basin.[37]

In surveying the cultural significance of early Kievan architecture, one notes the virtually complete dominance of the church in masonry construction. If wooden churches (none extant) are added to the number – and in some cities of Kievan Rus, they would have outnumbered stone churches – then it becames clear that the princely families and a large part of the population had accepted and supported the Orthodox Church within a remarkably short period. Yet the Church, which had canonized Boris and Gleb for their martyrdom in the face of political violence, had not been effective in halting that same violence.

The Orthodox Church and its monastic institutions served as mediator and, in the short term, beneficiary of the princely disputes. The proliferation of church construction and regional stylistic peculiarities are evidence of a competition for the Church's favor, as well as a statement of the prestige, wealth, and political power of the donor and his clan. Although the fragmentation of Kievan Rus has often been given as a reason for the conquest of the area by the Mongols, it seems unlikely that a more cohesive political system – by the standards of the time – could have resisted that force. Despite the ensuing devastation of churches and of written documents, enough remains to testify to the rise of a vital new culture within the orbit of Byzantium.

For 200 years, Kiev had served as a point for the assimilation and development of the Byzantine architectural legacy, with cathedrals of astonishing scale and complexity that testified to the entry of Rus into the cultural heritage of the Mediterranean. At the same time, the spread of smaller parish and monastery churches demonstrated the propagation of Orthodoxy and its art among the population of a vast area. Although subsequent events would isolate Russia from the classical world, the architectural principles established in Kiev – a combination of classical tectonics and plasticity of design – would evolve over the centuries in striking ways, in some periods, emphasizing the logic of the classical system, and in others, exploring a free-form approach to structure and decoration. Indeed, by the twelfth century, other cities, to the north and east of Kiev, were to expand this legacy in ways unknown to the first capital.

CHAPTER 2

Novgorod and Pskov: Eleventh to Thirteenth Centuries

That same year [1156] the overseas merchants built the Church of Paraskeva Piatnitsa on the market place.

– Novgorod First Chronicle

The city of Novgorod is, by a fortunate set of circumstances, the great repository of medieval Russian art, with more than fifty churches and monasteries extending from the eleventh through the seventeenth centuries. The recipient of Byzantine architectural forms via Kiev, the city rapidly developed an indigenous architectural style in churches commissioned by its princes during the eleventh and twelfth centuries, as well as in the "commercial" and neighborhood churches of the fourteenth and fifteenth centuries. Even with the surrender of its independence to Moscow in the late 1400s, Novgorod sustained a vital creative tradition in its adaptation of a new, "Muscovite" style – a tradition that ceased only in the 1700s, as the city lost its strategic importance and sank into an almost total stagnation.

Medieval chronicles first mention Novgorod in connection with events between 860 and 862, when the local Slavs summoned the Varangian Riurik to assume control of their disordered affairs.[1] After the Riurikovich dynasty transferred its power to Kiev at the end of the ninth century, Novgorod continued to exercise control over a vast area of northern Rus. In 989, following the official acceptance of Christianity in the domains of Grand Prince Vladimir, Novgorod was visited by Vladimir's ecclesiastical emissary, Bishop Joachim of Kherson. In his energetic imposition of Christianity on Novgorod, the bishop overturned pagan idols into the Volkhov River and commissioned the first stone church (dedicated to Sts. Joachim and Anna; it is not extant), as well as a wooden Church of St. Sophia, with thirteen "tops," or domes.

The political history of Novgorod was far from calm, for the city not only frequently challenged its leaders, including Riurik, but also participated in the princely feuds that wracked the Kievan state. Nevertheless, Novgorod prospered during the eleventh and twelfth centuries as part of the Dnieper trade route from the Baltic to the Black Sea, and in its prosperity, the city had the means to create a citadel and an imposing architectural ensemble of churches.[2] The Volkhov River, which separated the city into the Trading, or Commercial, Side and the Sophia Side (after the Cathedral of St. Sophia, in the Novgorod citadel), provided an essential link for trade and exploration within a network of waterways that led in every direction. The extent of its commercial activity produced a relatively large group of literate citizens, independent of Kiev and of its princely representative in Novgorod (usually the brother or son of the grand prince in Kiev).

At the beginning of the twelfth century, the assembly of citizens, or *veche*, assumed the responsibility of electing a *posadnik* to direct the city's business. Novgorod's status as a republic was finally established in 1136, when Prince Vsevolod was told by the citizens: "We do not want you. Go wherever you wish." Henceforth, the Novgorod prince was retained as a military leader with strictly limited privileges, while effective power lay with a merchant oligarchy and the archbishop. Novgorodians spoke of owing allegiance only to their city, "Lord Novgorod the Great."

During the twelfth century, this city of 30,000 inhabitants, with a trading network extending from the Baltic to the Urals, was among the most advanced in eastern Europe: the streets were paved with wooden blocks, literacy was widespread, commercial transactions were recorded on birchbark, and an extensive water system was developed. In their chronicles, the monasteries compiled a comprehensive, if laconic, account of the city's history, with frequent references to the building and alteration of churches; and from these sources, as well as from archaeological research, we know more about the life and art of Novgorod than of any other medieval Russian city.[3]

The achievement of Novgorod's medieval architecture is based primarily on a resourceful adaptation of Byzantine and Kievan prototypes to local conditions, as illustrated in the choice of building materials. The builders who worked in Novgorod did not have a source of high-quality surface stone, such as the white limestone used in twelfth-century churches of the Vladimir area (see Chapter 3), nor was brickmaking as extensively developed as in Kiev. Instead, they devised a method of placing blocks of rough-hewn gray limestone of various sizes within a cement composed of crushed brick and lime, which imparted to the facade a pink hue similar to that of early Kievan churches, though coarser in texture. The use of brick was limited in most cases to ornamentation on the facade, the detailing of window and door arches, and the pilaster strips dividing the exterior bays.[4] Stucco was originally applied only in the interior, which was then covered with frescoes painted by local and foreign masters (from Greece and the Balkans). As in Kiev, all too few of these remarkable paintings have survived. Many were destroyed in the Second World War, others by overpainting in earlier centuries. It is only through prewar photographs that we have some idea of the stunning contrast between the lavish interior and the stark exterior of churches such as the Savior on the Nereditsa River.[5]

Architecture of the Eleventh Century in Novgorod

The oldest surviving and the most imposing monument in the city is the Cathedral of St. Sophia (see Plate 6), built between 1045 and 1050 and located in Novgorod's *detinets*, or citadel, on the west bank of the Volkhov River. The cathedral was commissioned by the prince of Novgorod, Vladimir Iaroslavich, as well as by his father, Iaroslav the Wise, and by Archbishop Luke of Novgorod.[6] It is fitting that Iaroslav, whose own Sophia Cathedral in Kiev was entering its final construction phase at this time, should have played a role in the creation of the Novgorod St. Sophia. Novgorod had been the base of Iaroslav's power, not only during the reign of his father, Grand

Prince Vladimir, but also until the death of his rival Mstislav of Chernigov. With the building of large masonry cathedrals dedicated to the Divine Wisdom in both Kiev and Novgorod, Iaroslav rendered homage to one of the most sacred mysteries of the Orthodox Church, and established a link between the two major cities of his realm and "Tsargrad," or Constantinople.

In addition, Iaroslav's participation would have been essential from a very immediate and practical point of view. Masonry construction was virtually unknown in Novgorod before the middle of the eleventh century (the city's earlier church dedicated to St. Sophia had been built of oak), and a cathedral of such size and complexity could only have been constructed under the supervision of imported master builders, presumably from Kiev and ultimately Byzantium. It is thought that some of the brick (for the lower part of the central apse) was also imported from Kiev.[7] The basic material for the construction of the walls and the piers, however, was obtained in Novgorod and was rougher than that used in Kiev: fieldstone and some undressed blocks of limestone set in a mortar of crushed brick and lime. Plinthos applied in the recessed row technique was used for the interior arches and vaulting, but appeared in the main walls only for detailing and occasional stabilizing rows, as well as for the apsidal structure and the drums of the subsidiary cupolas. On the exterior, therefore, the walls of St. Sophia in Novgorod would have presented a highly textured appearance, even with the spreading of mortar to reduce the unevenness of the surface. (The earliest reference to the application of whitewash to the walls appears in the Novgorod chronicle under the year 1151.[8])

The plans of the Novgorod and Kiev cathedrals show clear similarities: five aisles for the main structure (but only three apses in Novgorod), with enclosed galleries – eventually reaching a height of two stories – attached to the north, west, and south facades (Figure 22). Although originally intended to be only one story, the attached galleries evolved during the building of the Novgorod cathedral into an integral part of the structure on both levels. The north and south galleries each contain chapels on the ground level, and the west gallery includes a round stair tower that leads to the upper levels of all the galleries, including the choir gallery inside the main structure.[9] Despite its structural complexity, the Novgorod Sophia is smaller than its Kievan counterpart, both in its central structure and in the size of the attached galleries, which in Kiev comprise the equivalent of two additional aisles on each side (see Figure 5).

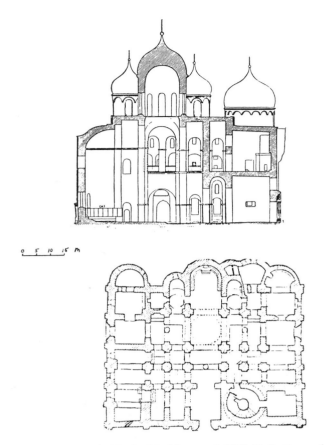

Figure 22. Cathedral of St. Sophia. Novgorod. 1045–52. Section and plan by N. Travin and R. Katsnelson.

Yet the two cathedrals are of approximately the same height, and therein lies an explanation for the much sharper sense of vertical development in the Novgorod cathedral. Indeed, the proportional relation of height to the area of the central structure in the Novgorod cathedral is one and a half times greater than that of Kiev. The emphasis on height is maintained in the interior, where the piers of the main aisles soar directly to the barrel vaults without the visual impediment of lowered arches of the type frequently suspended between the piers of St. Sophia in Kiev (Figure 23). The choir gallery is 10 meters above the main floor (in contrast to 8 meters in Kiev), and the central apse reaches the height of the east wall.

Most of the original painting of the interior has long since vanished under centuries of renovations. Although there is some evidence of decorative mosaics in the apse and floor, the Novgorod cathedral lacked the elaborate mosaics characteristic of major churches in Kiev before the middle of the twelfth century.

Nonetheless, the Novgorod chronicles, in their cryptic way, indicate that the interior was painted with frescoes over a period of several decades. According to the Novgorod Third chronicle, soon after the completion of construction, "icon painters from Tsargrad" painted Christ with his hand raised in blessing (probably an image of the Pantocrator in the central dome) and other representations of the Savior. Fragments of the eleventh-century work, including full-length paintings of Emperor Constantine and Elena, have been uncovered, as well as early twelfth-century frescoes.[10] The exterior facade above the west portal also displays frescoes (poorly preserved and relatively late work), but the most distinctive element is the portal itself, with its magnificent bronze Sigtuna Doors (Figure 24), produced in Magdeburg in the 1050s, and taken as loot from the Varangian fortress of Sigtuna by Novgorod raiders in 1117.

The culminating point in the structure of the Novgorod Cathedral of St. Sophia is the massing of cupolas. Although their original form would probably have had a lower pitch than do the helmet-shaped domes now in place, the design is without doubt one of the most visually impressive moments in medieval Russian architecture (Figure 25). The structure itself provides an admirable base, with its almost total lack of surface decoration and only the simplest of architectural details – the profiled entrance arch of each facade and the massive lesenes, or pilaster strips, that mark the bays of the exterior gallery walls. The attached galleries, although wide, are visually integrated into the higher walls of the central structure. The arched gables, or *zakomary*, of the galleries echo the more sharply etched roof line of the main structure, with its arched and pointed *zakomary* that conform to the interior vaulting contours.

The drum and dome over the central crossing predominate in both height and diameter, but the four subsidiary domes are so closely placed in relation to the central dome as to appear part of one perfectly devised whole. (The "inner" walls of the flanking drums rest on the same line of transverse vaulting arches as do the east and west arcs of the main drum, thus conveying the impression of an enclosed pentacupolar structure.) The central group is balanced by a sixth cupola, lower than the rest, but considerably larger in circumference, over the stair tower in the west gallery. It is precisely on the west front that the horizontal space occupied by the structure and its exterior galleries is most evident and most likely to overcome the vertical development of the cathedral (Figure 26). Yet the west cupola reasserts the vertical principle without detracting from the unity of the cen-

Figure 23. Cathedral of St. Sophia. Novgorod. Interior. East view
of central dome and crossing. (N 13–35)

Figure 24. Cathedral of St. Sophia. Novgorod. West facade, Sigtuna Doors. Produced in Magdeburg in the 1050s and modified upon their installation at St. Sophia. The panels depict saints, bishops, a centaur, and biblical scenes. (N 2–7a)

tral group. The Cathedral of St. Sophia in Novgorod lacks the pyramidal ascent created by the thirteen cupolas of its counterpart in Kiev, and its form may have been determined to no small degree by a series of practical considerations that materialized as the construction progressed.[11] Nonetheless, the consummate skill of the cathedral's builders (either from Kiev or Byzantium) not only incorporated local requirements and materials into a functional design with a clear vertical development, but also calculated the height and mass of the cupolar structure to achieve a visual effect unmatched in early medieval Russian architecture.

Early Twelfth-Century Churches

Although no subsequent church in Novgorod rivals the Cathedral of St. Sophia in the grandeur of its conception and execution, the twelfth century saw a continuation of major projects initiated by the city's princes. As their hold on political power, and the citadel itself, loosened, Novgorod's princes maintained a show of architectural force by constructing large masonry churches elsewhere in the city. Some of these structures have been destroyed and most have been modified; but four of them, built between 1113 and 1130, provide evidence of a style characteristic of the princely church: the Cathedral of St. Nicholas in Iaroslav Court (1113), the Church of the Nativity of the Virgin at Antoniev Monastery (1117–19), the Cathedral of St. George at Iurev Monastery (1119), and the Church of John the Baptist in Petriatin Court (1127–30). Each is a simplification of the multiaisled plan at St. Sophia and indirectly reflects the influence of Kiev's Cathedral of the Dormition: the number of aisles has been reduced to three; the inscribed-cross plan has been retained, with an additional bay, or narthex, on the west end; and the east – or altar – end is completed by a triple apse, usually rising the full height of the sanctuary wall. The lead roof typically followed the contours of the interior vaulting – a feature obliterated by later, hipped roofs. In each case, the interior division into bays is reflected on the exterior by pilasters that divide the austere facade into arched segments.

The earliest of these, the Church of the Annunciation in Gorodishche (a settlement at the southeastern edge of the city), was founded around 1103 by Mstislav, son of the Kievan grand prince Vladimir Monomakh.[12] The church was destroyed and rebuilt in 1342, but remnants of the original foundation are sufficient to place the structure within the class defined before.[13] Much more remains of the Church of St. Nicholas in Iaroslav Court, also commissioned by Mstislav and built within the *dvorishche*, or Court – the new residence of the Novgorod prince. Located across the Volkhov River from the *detinets*, the church was highly unusual in its original pentacupolar design (since destroyed), whose purpose was undoubtedly to rival the form of St. Sophia in a citadel the prince no longer possessed.[14] In other respects, the church followed the typical plan, including a contoured roof with sheets of lead nailed directly over the barrel vaulting (Figure 27). The walls were of alternating rows of brick and limestone slabs in a mortar of crushed brick, and were covered with a light layer of stucco.

A variation on the princely church appeared in the Church of the Nativity of the Virgin at Antoniev Monastery (1117–19). Although commissioned by the founder of the monastery, Antonii Rimlianin ("the Roman," a convert to Orthodoxy from the west), the

Figure 25. Cathedral of St. Sophia. Novgorod. South facade. (N 1–10)

Figure 26. Cathedral of St. Sophia. Novgorod. Northwest view. (N 1–6)

Figure 27. Cathedral of St. Nicholas in Iaroslav Court. Novgorod. 1113–36. South facade. Reconstruction by Grigorii Shtender.

Figure 28. Church of the Nativity of the Virgin, Antoniev Monastery. Novgorod. 1117–19. Southeast view. (N–1)

church could not have been constructed without the assistance of the Novgorod prince, both for political reasons and because the prince still held a monopoly on the materials and the builders necessary for masonry construction.[15] The Church of the Nativity displays the expected elements of Novgorod church architecture during this period, but it also contains a number of innovative features (Figure 28). The two west piers under the central crossing are octagonal (as opposed to the cruciform piers almost universally used in medieval Russian church architecture), which creates a sense of space in the center of what is a relatively narrow structure. The choir gallery above the narthex is reached by a stair tower attached to the northwest corner of the building (similar to the earlier Church of the Annunciation), but its shape is round, rather than the usual square extension housing a round stairwell. This unexpected form, in conjunction with a simplification of exterior details, heightens a sense of the plasticity of the structure, whose walls were more crudely molded than those of the early twelfth-century princely churches.[16]

Of the latter, the culminating and most imposing example is the Cathedral of St. George, commissioned in 1119 at the Iurev (St. George) Monastery by Prince Vsevolod, son of Mstislav. According to the chronicles, the builder was a certain Master Peter, one of the few medieval Russian architects (in addition to Peter Miloneg) whose name has been recorded.[17] In comparison with the Antoniev Monastery church, the Cathedral of St. George adheres more faithfully to the accepted architectural elements of large Russian churches of its time. On the exterior, the vertical de-

velopment, created by massive pilaster strips that divide the facade into bays, is counterposed to the horizontality of alternating rows of windows and niches (see Plate 7). On the interior, the cruciform piers define the cross-inscribed space, with narthex and attached stair tower on the northwest corner. In an era that emphasized the vertical structure, the walls of St. George's reach a height of 20 meters, with a cross-centered design whose piers soar to the barrel vaults with no visual impediment (see Plate 8).

Master Peter applied these familiar elements on a scale and with a fluency that suggest an intention to comment on the very art of building a princely church. To have had his name recorded in the chronicles, he must have been a compelling personality; and in this, his one attested church, he did not work on a modest scale: in its central space, the Cathedral of St. George is larger even than St. Sophia.[18] As noted, the plan of the cathedral is rectangular (with an additional bay, or narthex, on the west end), but from the southwest, the structure appears to be a massive cube – an impression produced by the construction of the stair tower in the form of an additional bay on the west facade (Figure 29). Only from the northeast does one see the tower, leading to the choir gallery, as a rec-

Figure 29. Cathedral of St. George, Iurev Monastery. Near Novgorod. 1119–30. Southwest view. (N–2)

in a dogtooth brick pattern that had appeared in the Novgorod Sophia Cathedral. All three domes have scalloped niches. In contrast to the austere monumentality of the facades, the interior was covered with frescoes and contained icons from the prince's workshop – including some of the rarest examples of twelfth-century icon painting.[19]

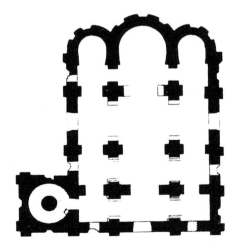

Figure 30. Cathedral of St. George, Iurev Monastery. Near Novgorod. Northeast view. (N 8–7)

tangular projection from the main structure (Figure 30). With the northwest bay matching the narthex extension on the south facade, Master Peter imposed an overall symmetry within which the second, larger, bay of each facade corresponds to the arms of the inscribed cross (Figure 31).

The asymmetrical facade of the St. George Cathedral contains a massive blind arcade and rows of windows seeming to foreshadow the horizontal sweep of Petersburg's palaces. The restrained detailing of the exterior centers on major structural elements: the narrow windows and double-recessed niches complement the rhythm of the facade arches, whose extrados repeat the indentation of the windows and portal. The walls originally culminated in *zakomary* that followed the contours of the vaulting and provided a visual transition to the three cupolas: the largest over the crossing, the middle over the stair tower, and the smallest situated at the southwest corner. The present domes, in the "helmet" shape, probably replaced smaller domes prevalent in Rus during the eleventh and twelfth centuries. In a final decorative touch, the two drums supporting the larger cupolas repeat the arched-window motif of the facade, and the largest and smallest drums are crowned with arcading edged

Figure 31. Cathedral of St. George, Iurev Monastery. Near Novgorod. Plan.

33

Figure 32. Church of John the Baptist in Petriatin Court. Novgorod. 1127–30; rebuilt in 1453. Southeast view. (N 3–9)

Late Twelfth-Century Architecture in Novgorod and Pskov

The instability of the position of Novgorod's princes during the twelfth century led to a decrease both in the number and the size of churches they commissioned (Figure 32).[20] Some 60 years elapsed between the construction of the final princely church in the commercial district – the Church of the Dormition in the Trading Side, built in 1135 by Vsevolod – and the last of Novgorod's churches to be built by a prince –

the Transfiguration of the Savior on the Nereditsa River (1198; see what follows). In the interval, princes throughout Rus were involved in the incessant struggle for the Kievan throne. This does not imply that Rus was beset by ruin, but with certain exceptions (primarily in the area of Vladimir-Suzdal), there was a decrease in the number of masonry construction projects initiated by princes. Indeed, the churches endowed during this period often reflected some aspect of the political struggle, as is exemplified by the design of the Cathedral of the Transfiguration of the

Savior at Mirozhskii Monastery in Pskov.

Pskov was one of the few cities in the domain of "Lord Novgorod" that could claim an indigenous artistic style of considerable vitality. Located some 120 miles to the southwest of Novgorod, at the confluence of the Pskov and Velikaia rivers, the city was founded probably at some point in the tenth century as a trading settlement, prospering as part of the Kiev–Novgorod network. Pskov's social and cultural institutions developed parallel to those of Novgorod, with a *veche*, or citizens' assembly, that on occasion challenged the authority of Novgorod. Pskov never rivaled Novgorod as a commercial center, yet the self-reliant spirit of its citizens – who declared independence from Novgorod in 1348 – was soon told in the turbulent history of their city.

It was to Pskov that Prince Vsevolod retreated after his expulsion from Novgorod in 1136, and it is possible that he was supported in his bid to regain Novgorod by Archbishop Nifont, who, like Vsevolod, was an energetic supporter of church construction. In any event, Vsevolod died in 1137 or 1138, but there is evidence that before his death, he endowed, with the support of Nifont, a church dedicated to the Transfiguration of the Savior.[21] From the time of Mstislav of Chernigov through the thirteenth century, dedications to the Transfiguration of the Savior appear to have been used exclusively for churches built by a prince; yet it has been argued that another group of princes participated in the foundation of the Savior Mirozhskii Monastery in Pskov in the late 1140s.[22] Whether Vsevolod or Nifont's subsequent ally Iurii Dolgorukii was a leading contributor to the building of the cathedral and monastery on the banks of the Mirozh River, it appears that the structure and its frescoes were completed by the time of Nifont's death in 1156.

It also appears that the unusual design of the structure had an ideological meaning; Nifont was a Grecophile, a believer in the authority of Byzantium over the Russian Church, and his cathedral in Pskov is comparable to Byzantine prototypes in Asia Minor (perhaps by way of Kherson) – a simple cruciform plan, with low corner bays and one large cupola situated on a combination of east piers and the indented corners of the west wall (Figure 33).[23] This design, with its exposed central bays, proved impractical in a much colder, northern climate and the corner bays of the west facade were soon built to the height of the main structure (Figure 34). The interior the cathedral was painted with frescoes, which have, miraculously, survived largely intact (Figure 35). Their style has been related to the still vital tradition of

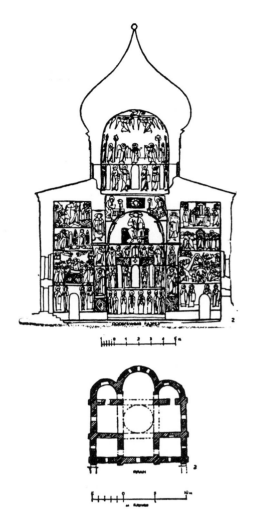

Figure 33. Cathedral of the Transfiguration of the Savior, Mirozhskii Monastery. Pskov. 1140s–50s. Plan and section by G. Alferova; reconstruction by Iu. Spegalskii.

Byzantine wall painting in Rus at a time when Greek painters were still active in the area, yet the pictoral themes are chosen and interpreted in a manner that suggests the work of local masters.[24]

Some four decades after the completion of the Cathedral of the Transfiguration of the Savior in Pskov, Prince Iaroslav Vladimirovich commissioned the last of the churches to be endowed by a prince in medieval Novgorod. Also dedicated to the Transfiguration of the Savior, the church was located on the Nereditsa River (a small tributary of the Volkhov) near the Gorodishche district, the site of a residence compound for the Novgorod prince and his retinue. Constructed within three and a half months in 1198, the Nereditsa church represents a considerable dimunition in comparison with earlier princely churches, and it prefi-

Figure 34. Cathedral of the Transfiguration of the Savior, Mirozhskii Monastery. Pskov. Northwest view. (PK–1)

gures the simplified cube form that would become the dominant pattern in Russian parish church architecture for the next three centuries. In 1903–4, the church was carefully studied and restored by Peter Pokryshkin (shortly thereafter to be involved with Shchusev's rebuilding of the Church of St. Basil at Ovruch); and although Pokryshin's restoration of what he assumed to be the original form of the cornice and roof was not without controversy, his documentation proved invaluable for a rebuilding of the church after much of it was destroyed by artillery fire during the fighting around Novgorod in the fall of 1941.[25]

The restored roofline, defined by *zakomary*, conforms to the construction techniques applied in earlier large twelfth-century churches, and the three apses have been retained, although the flanking apses are diminished. The number of bays along the length of the church was reduced from 4 to 3, thus creating a compact form dominated by a single cupola (Figure 36). With the exception of an arcade band, edged in the dogtooth pattern, on the cupola drum, the exterior is devoid of ornamentation.[26] The walls are of alternating rows of brick and red shellstone (*rakushechnik*), whose rough, irregular lines endow the church with a peculiar sculpted texture, emphasized by the partial covering of the surface with a reddish stucco (see Plate 9). It appears that wood was used extensively in the structural work: the walls contained oak tie beams (at certain places, they seem to have extended to the piers); the portals were topped by a simple wooden lintel, with a brick relieving arch above (Figure 37); and the original roof was apparently of wooden shingles – a technique commonly adopted for smaller masonry churches in Novgorod.

Originally part of a small monastery endowed by the Novgorod princes, the Church of the Savior fell into neglect with the eventual disappearance of princely authority in Novgorod by the beginning of

Figure 35. Cathedral of the Transfiguration of the Savior, Mirozhskii
Monastery. Pskov. Central crossing. (LG 101–5)

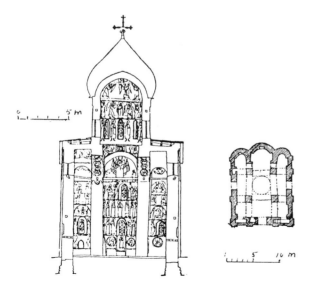

Figure 36. Church of the Transfiguration of the Savior on the Nereditsa. Novgorod. 1198. Plan and section by P. Pokryshkin.

the fourteenth century. After 1764, the church was
open only once a year for the Feast of the Transfiguration of the Savior, and thus its frescoes, painted
in the summer of 1199, escaped the extensive repainting that damaged so many works of art in more active
churches. Before the war, the Church of the Transfiguration of the Savior on the Nereditsa contained
one of the very few extensively preserved sets of frescoes among medieval Russian churches; only a small
portion survived to be restored with the reconstructed
church.[27]

Urban Churches at the Turn of the Thirteenth Century

With the decline of the Novgorod prince, both as
political leader and as patron of architecture, the primary role in the building of churches (which remained
virtually the only significant masonry structures) was

37

Figure 37. Church of the Transfiguration of the Savior on the Nereditsa. Novgorod. South facade. (N–7)

assumed by the monastic clergy, by merchant families or corporations, and by neighborhood associations of artisans and tradespeople. The transition in sponsorship did not occur abruptly, nor was it signaled by a radically innovative architectural design; but the smaller scale of construction projects offered greater flexibility in contracting locally for builders and artisans. Only a very few of the late-twelfth-century churches built by these groups of patrons have survived. Although all are four-piered structures with a choir gallery and no narthex, each is distinctive in design and suggests the considerable variety of church architecture at this time.

The Church of the Annunciation at Miachino, commissioned by Archbishop Elijah and built in 1179 at the monastery of the same name, now stands in a much altered form. In the seventeenth century, the vaulting and the large drum with cupola collapsed, to be replaced with a much smaller drum. The rest of the structure, however, is basically sound, with walls composed of rough limestone, brick of irregular sizes, and fieldstone, reinforced by wooden beams. The stairs to the choir gallery were placed within the west

wall. Despite damage to the structure over the centuries, the interior still contains large fragments of the original frescoes (particularly in the apsidal structure) painted in 1189 (see Plate 10).[28]

Located near the Annunciation Church is the Church of Sts. Peter and Paul (1185–92; Figure 38), which was built for the monastery of the same name on Sinichia Hill. It is interesting to note that the labor for the church, if not the design, was provided by a group of residents from a particular street in Novgorod. Although much modified by later brick reinforcement, the original walls were probably the thinnest of any known architectural monument in medieval Novgorod, due to the unusual composition of the walls: opus mixtum for the lower level yielding to brick applied in the recessed row technique for the upper walls.[29] There are no preserved medieval frescoes on the interior.

The most notable church of the period was built in 1207 on the Trading Side by an association of foreign trade merchants and dedicated to St. Paraskeva Piatnitsa, considered the patron of the marketplace. It was not the first church in her honor and on this site: In 1156, the same corporation had built a wooden church to St. Paraskeva, which was replaced by yet another in 1191. The masonry structure erected at the beginning of the thirteenth century was substantially altered in the fourteenth and sixteenth centuries, but an investigation of the considerable remnants of the original walls and vaulting arches has provided the plan for a partial reconstruction.[30]

The Church of St. Paraskeva represents an elaboration of the simple cuboid plan developed during the latter part of the twelfth century, with four piers, a single cupola, and three apses. The plan is still cross-

Figure 38. Church of Sts. Peter and Paul on Sinichia Hill. Novgorod. 1185–92. Southeast view. (N 18–28)

Figure 39. Church of St. Paraskeva Piatnitsa on the Marketplace. Novgorod. 1207, with extensive modifications in the fourteenth and sixteenth centuries. Partially reconstructed in the 1960s. (N 3–1a)

inscribed, but the arms of the cross are now marked in the north, south, and west by three large covered porches (Figure 39), divided into two stories, the upper of which functions as a gallery. The three galleries are reached by a stairway beginning in the wall of the north porch and concluding on the upper level of the west porch. The galleries are connected on the upper level by a passageway within the main walls (approximately 1.5 meters thick). This ingenious plan enabled the builders to dispense with the choir gallery, thus achieving an openness of space that is amplified by the round columns – instead of cruciform piers – supporting the central drum and dome. The eastern wall consists of a rectangular projection, containing the two side chapels, and a greatly extended central apse (Figure 40). The derivation of this plan –

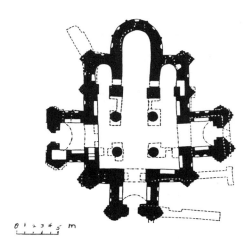

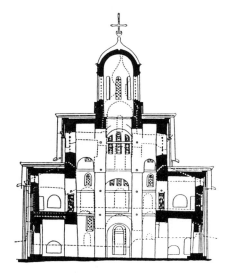

Figure 40. Church of St. Paraskeva Piatnitsa. Novgorod. Plan and section by G. Shtender.

unique in Novgorod – has been traced to Smolensk, whence came the architect who designed the Church of St. Paraskeva.[31]

Smolensk, benefitting from the patronage of the Rostislavich princes, had a flourishing architectural school of its own during the latter part of the twelfth century. Although relatively compact in plan, its brick churches were structurally complex, with the use of corbelled arches under the central dome to achieve a vertical emphasis comparable to that of the Paraskeva church at Chernigov. They frequently had enclosed porches (some with their own chapels on the east end) extending from the portals of the north, west, and south facades. Profiled attached columns marked the division of bays. All of these features appear to have been present in the Church of the Archangel Michael, built at some point between 1180 and 1190 by the prince of Smolensk, David Rostislavich, as well as in the cathedral built at the turn of the thirteenth century for the Trinity Monastery on the Klokva River.[32] The Church of the Archangel Michael had a trefoil roofline, which appears to have been a feature of other Smolensk churches of the period, such as the Church of St. Basil at the Smiadino Monastery (1191), also commissioned by David.

Although the mixed construction of its walls differed from the solid brickwork of the Smolensk churches, the unusual design of the Novgorod Church of St. Paraskeva shows a clear resemblance to the forms characteristic of Smolensk architecture: the general plan, the enclosed porches, the attached profiled columns, and the trefoil roofline, which would become a distinctive part of Novgorod church architecture in the fourteenth century (see Chapter 4). For these reasons, it is now generally assumed that the Novgorod church was designed by an architect from Smolensk – possibly the architect of the Klokva church. Furthermore, on the basis of an analysis of the extant walls, Grigorii Shtender has concluded that the Novgorod church was begun by masons from Smolensk, who left the project to local builders after the first building season.[33]

In terms of its influence on the architecture of Novgorod, the most notable feature of the Church of St. Paraskeva is the shape of the roof and its effect on the appearance of the facade: Instead of a series of low arches placed on the same level, the facade assumes a trefoil shape with a large central arch, corresponding to the barrel vaulting over the arms of the cross (Figure 41). The central arch leads downward to halved arches, which are placed over the quadrant vaults at the corners of the church. The roof itself probably consisted of wooden shingles (a distinctive

Figure 41. Church of St. Paraskeva Piatnitsa. Novgorod. Reconstruction by G. Shtender.

Figure 42. Church of the Nativity of the Virgin at Peryn. Near Novgorod. Early thirteenth century. Southeast view. (N–9)

Novgorod trait), which endowed the contours with a textured pattern.

Indeed, the trefoil roof reappeared in the design of a small church for the monastery of the Nativity of the Virgin at Peryn, to the south of the city (Figure 42). Although the date of construction has not been established, archaeological evidence suggests the first half of the thirteenth century.[34] The profiled cornice of the trefoil gable emphasizes the plasticity and height of this compact structure of stuccoed brick and rough limestone blocks. So small was the church – 7.8 meters wide and 9.8 meters long, including the apse – that the existence of a choir gallery is doubtful (there are no stairs within the structure or its walls). Despite its height and small size, prefiguring the development of the tower church in Russia, the interior still contained four piers under the dome (Figure 43).

There were few other churches constructed in Novgorod during the thirteenth century, which was a period of general unrest in the city. The chronicles make frequent reference to fire, flood, and famine, as well as to feuds among the townspeople, with the city's right bank, or Trading Side, pitted against the St. Sophia side. The brawls often culminated on the wooden Volkhov bridge, where the object was to beat and throw into the river as many opponents as possible. During the more violent scrimmages, each side would destroy its part of the bridge. Occasionally, the crowd's wrath was directed against an unpopular archbishop or prince, as, for example, in 1225, when the people drove Archbishop Arsenii from town, "beating him almost unto death."

But Novgorod soon faced a far more serious crisis.

In 1238, the Mongols, having begun their conquest of Kievan Rus, advanced to within 60 miles of Novgorod. Although at this point they turned back because of terrain unsuited to cavalry operations, the following years brought invasions by the Swedes,

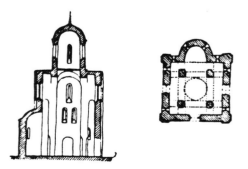

Figure 43. Church of the Nativity of the Virgin at Peryn. Near Novgorod. Section and plan by R. Katsnelson.

41

from the north, and the Teutonic Knights, from the west – both intent on colonizing the area. In a series of decisive campaigns directed by Prince Alexander Nevskii ("of the Neva"), Novgorod and its allies checked both invasions (the Swedes in 1240 near the Neva River, the Teutonic Knights in 1242 at Lake Pepius, in the "Battle on the Ice"), for which victories Alexander became a symbol of Russian military valor. In 1259, however, a delegation of Mongols, with their wives and retainers, entered the city to take a census for taxation, with the threat of a punitive expedition if their demands were not met; when the enraged mob threatened to kill them, Alexander counseled submission (one of the reasons given for his elevation to sainthood by the Russian Orthodox Church).[35] Although later to be sacked and subjugated by Moscow's grand princes, Novgorod was spared the devastation that covered so much of Russia, and thus became a center of cultural and artistic revival during the fourteenth century that formed a connection to the past and, moreover, stimulated the creation of new forms.

CHAPTER 3

Vladimir and Suzdal Before the Mongol Invasion

And in that year [1160] the Church of the Holy Mother of God was completed in Vladimir by the devout and beloved of God Prince Andrei; and he decorated it with wondrously many icons, and precious stones without number, and holy vessels, and covered it with gold, for by his faith and devotion to the Holy Mother, God brought him masters from all lands. . . .

– Laurentian Chronicle, on the Cathedral of the Dormition

While Novgorod and Pskov pursued their commercial interests and the authority of Kiev eroded under the impact of princely feuds, a third center of power arose in Russia, to the northeast, in the upper reaches of the Volga River and its tributaries. Settled as early as the first century by Finno-Ugric tribes, these lands were colonized during the tenth century by Slavs from the west, drawn to the rich forests and tillable land. During the eleventh century, Kievan princes extended their authority over the northeast (in 1024, Iaroslav the Wise suppressed a rebellion incited by pagan priests in the Suzdal area), and strengthened settlements such as Rostov and Suzdal, which formed a major principality.[1] Kiev's control proved tenuous, however. In 1071, one of Rostov's first bishops, Leontii, was killed in yet another pagan uprising, and the area underwent the constant threat of raids by Volga Bulgars. At the turn of the eleventh century, the town of Suzdal was fortified and acquired its own prince.

Suzdal was soon overshadowed by the fortress of Vladimir, established in 1108 a few miles south of Suzdal, on the Kliazma River. Its founder, Vladimir Monomakh, grandson of Iaroslav the Wise and grand prince in Kiev from 1113, was the last of Kiev's great rulers (see Chapter 1). Monomakh is recorded in the chronicles as having built in Vladimir, at some point between 1108 and 1117, a church dedicated to the Savior (the Transfiguration).[2] Its site has not been discovered, but the foundation of his earlier church dedicated to the Nativity (or perhaps the Dormition) of the Mother of God has been analyzed at the site of the extant Suzdal Cathedral of the Nativity (see what

follows). Both of these churches would most likely have been built of brick.

Monomakh's death in 1125 led to competition for succession to the throne at Kiev among his numerous sons, including the heir to Suzdalia, Iurii Dolgorukii. Iurii finally gained Kiev shortly before his death, in 1157, but during the protracted struggle, he built much in Vladimir, center of his principality, and established a number of settlements in Suzdalia – among them a small fortified post called Moscow, after the river on which it was located. Information from the chronicles indicates that his major building activity occurred in the 1150s, as though he had despaired of ever gaining Kiev and wished to create an architectural legacy in Suzdalia toward the end of his life.

Although the white limestone Church of St. George (c. 1157) and palace built by Iurii Dolgorukii in Vladimir are not extant,[3] two of his churches – at Kideksha and Pereslavl-Zalesskii – provide early examples of an architectural style that would soon lead to an extraordinary series of monuments. The Church of Sts. Boris and Gleb at Kideksha, near Suzdal, has been severely altered since its construction in 1152, particularly by renovations in the 1660s and in 1780 (Figure 44).[4] Nonetheless, the walls of the central and western bays of the structure are well preserved and illustrate the basic construction technique that would apply to churches in the Vladimir–Suzdal area over the next eight decades. The walls are faced with limestone ashlar on both interior and exterior, between which is a rubble core. An arcade frieze decorates the facades

Figure 44. Church of Sts. Boris and Gleb at Kideksha. Near Suzdal. 1152. South facade. The earliest extant church in the Vladimir–Suzdal region. A rebuilding in the seventeenth century destroyed the original vaults, roofline, drum, and cupola. Limestone blocks from the original walls are visible at the base of the seventeenth-century enclosed porch. (KD–5)

from the palace to the choir gallery of the main cathedral was not uncommon in medieval Rus.) Structural evidence suggests that the original roofing

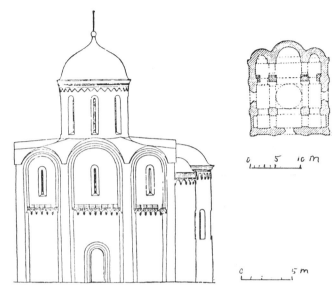

Figure 45. Church of Sts. Boris and Gleb at Kideksha. Near Suzdal. South elevation reconstructed by I. Ern; plan by Iu. Savitskii.

at midpoint, above which the surface of the bay is recessed within a profiled arch that culminates in *zakomary*. The present roof obscures the original gable line, which followed the vaulting of the interior, but it has been relatively easy to reconstruct the initial form of the church, with its cuboid cross-inscribed plan (Figure 45). The small choir gallery was apparently reached by a wooden staircase, yet the uncertainty of its relation to the structure reveals a problem typical of twelfth-century limestone churches.

The Cathedral of the Transfiguration of the Savior at Pereslavl-Zalesskii (1152–7) has retained most of its original structure (Figure 46).[5] Although it lacks the harmony of proportions that characterizes later churches built by Iurii Dolgorukii's sons, the plan is finely calculated (particularly in the main vaulting arches) and demonstrates the facility with which limestone ashlar was used as the basic structural material. No other area of Rus produced cut stonework of such precision for structural purposes, and the reasons for its sudden appearance in Suzdalia are still unresolved.

As at Kideksha, the upper bays of the walls are recessed, but the facades are devoid of decoration, except for an ornamental frieze on the apse and drum. Access to the choir gallery presumably occurred through an opening in a bay of the north facade, linked by a wooden passageway to the princely residence—also of wood. (Construction of a passage

material consisted of wooden shingles.[6] The Cathedral of the Transfiguration provides the basic design for all but one of Suzdalia's major twelfth-century churches: a cross-domed plan, with a triple apse and four piers supporting a single cupola (Figure 47). Within a year of its completion, Iurii's son Andrei Bogoliubskii had commissioned the Cathedral of the Dormition, the first of the great churches in Vladimir.

Andrei Bogoliubskii: the Flourishing of Stone Architecture

Prince Andrei has entered Russian history as a controversial figure, feared by those who supported the power of Kiev and Novgorod, but venerated in Vladimir, the city he considered his own. Throughout his reign, he ruthlessly and with great tenacity pursued a policy of aggrandizement at the expense of both Kiev and Novgorod. His intention was not to rule from a capital in the south, but to transfer power to Vladimir; in this he was largely successful. In 1169, Kiev was sacked by his son Mstislav – some 70 years before its devastation by the Mongols. Kiev continued to exist as the religious, and perhaps cultural center of Rus, but its military and political strength had col-

Figure 46. Cathedral of the Transfiguration of the Savior. Pereslavl-Zalesskii. 1152–7. Northwest view. Originally, the structure had exterior galleries leading to the choir level through the upper tier of the northwest bay (visible on left), and its cupola was much lower in shape. (PZ 3–6)

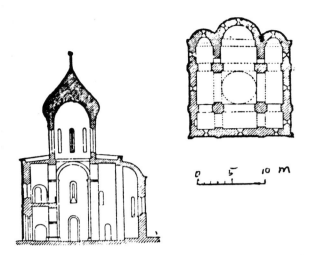

Figure 47. Cathedral of the Transfiguration of the Savior. Pereslavl-Zalesskii. Section and plan by A. Chiniakov.

lapsed. During the same period, Andrei's forces marched on Novgorod, and although his army was repulsed – in a battle commemorated in Novgorod's chronicle and icons – Andrei succeeded in blocking the city's grain supply from the south, so that Novgorod, like Kiev, was forced to accept his candidate for resident prince.[7]

It seems to be axiomatic in the history of Russian architecture that the expansion or establishment of political power is inevitably accompanied by intensive building activity on the part of a ruler who wishes to impress with his structures, particularly churches. One is tempted to add that in Russia, the more bloodthirsty and driven the prince, or tsar, or emperor, the greater is his architectural legacy (Andrei, Ivan the Great, Ivan the Terrible, Peter the Great). Exceptions come to mind, but it is beyond question that Andrei Bogoliubskii, despoiler of Kiev, is one of the great patrons of Russian architecture. Even though only a fraction of what he built has survived, that is more than sufficient to support the claim.

His first church, the Cathedral of the Dormition in Vladimir (1158–60), conformed to the elongated, six-pier plan typical of large churches in Kiev and Novgorod during the same period, and it displayed, on a limited scale in comparison to later Suzdalian churches, high-relief carvings on its facade of limestone ashlar.[8] Among the distinctive features of the structure were a large drum and cupola, with twelve windows and twenty-four columns with carved capitals. The ingenuity required to raise such a structure far exceeded that needed for Iurii Dolgorukii's churches during the preceding decade. If the source

of their design remains unclear, the enigma is all the greater in the case of the Dormition Cathedral. The Laurentian chronicle mentions the bringing of masters from "all lands," and there are later references to *Nemtsi*, or "Germans" – a term broadly used. In fact, it has been proposed, on slim evidence, that the artisans were sent to Bogoliubskii by Frederick Barbarossa.[9] Nonetheless, if certain features of the Vladimir churches – such as the portals and decorative stonework – suggest a western medieval, particularly German Romanesque, presence, the basic plan remains firmly in the tradition of Byzantine church architecture as adapted in early medieval Rus.

The appearance of the Dormition Cathedral – located in the center of Vladimir's citadel, on a high bluff above the Kliazma River – would surely have been spectacular. Gilded copper sheets covered the cupola as well as the walls of the drum; the columns of the arcade frieze at the facade midlevel were gilded; and the surface between the columns contained frescoes – presumably, a row of saints.[10] As with the temples of ancient Greece, the large twelfth-century churches of the Vladimir area so impress the viewer with the monumentality of the stonework that it is difficult to comprehend that their facades often displayed vivid polychromatic decoration, evident on the limestone facades of the late fifteenth-century Cathedral of the Dormition in the Moscow Kremlin (see Plate 25). Most of the decorative work, however, was effaced at the end of the century, when the church that Andrei built became the nucleus of a much larger structure (see what follows).

The second of Andrei's major projects in Vladimir also dates from the beginning of his reign, and involved not only a church, but also a dominant point in his new fortifications for the city. Like much else in Andrei's architectural patronage, the Golden Gates of Vladimir (1158–64) were based on a larger structure (of the same name) in Kiev, which in turn based its major fortress gates on the model of Constantinople. The original form – substantially modified in a 1795 rebuilding – consisted of parallel walls with pilasters that supported six vaulting arches.[11] Above the gates themselves and the various guard posts, the platform supported the Church of the Deposition of the Robe. The construction of a church over a main gate was a feature of the walls of Constantinople, with obvious connotations of divine protection for the city's defenses. Kiev adopted the same practice, not only for the central fortress gates, but also at the Monastery of the Caves, whose example inspired the construction of gate churches at the entrance to major Russian monasteries over the next six centuries.

46

The Palace Ensemble at Bogoliubovo

The greatest part of Andrei Bogoliubskii's architectural legacy occurred not in Vladimir itself, but in Bogoliubovo, a special settlement built between 1158 and 1165 and located some 10 kilometers to the east of Vladimir. The center of Bogoliubovo consisted of a walled compound with the princely residence and limestone cathedral dedicated to the Nativity of the Virgin (Figure 48), as well as one – or perhaps two – additional churches.[12] The cathedral was a cuboid structure similar in form to those built by Iurii Dolgorukii, but more elaborately decorated with carved masks, an arcade frieze at the midpoint of the facades, and carved capitals for the columns (not the usual cruciform piers) at the central crossing (Figure 49). The choir gallery was reached through a passageway leading directly to the palace, situated to the north, although it would appear that there was a second entrance from a free-standing tower at the southwest corner.[13]

Figure 49. Cathedral of the Nativity of the Virgin. Bogoliubovo. Reconstruction by N. Voronin.

Figure 48. Cathedral of the Nativity of the Virgin and passage to Andrei Bogoliubskii's palace. Bogoliubovo (near Vladimir). 1158–65. Reconstruction by N. Voronin.

The lavish decoration of the Cathedral of the Nativity was an object of wonder commented upon in the sparse chronicle entries: "[Bogoliubskii] adorned it with a luster that could not be looked upon, for all the church was of gold. . . . He adorned it with precious icons, with gold and valuable stones, with a priceless pearl of great size, with various ornaments of jasper, and many precious things with carved patterns."[14] The repeated references to gold (sheets of gilded copper) remind of the decoration of the Dormition Cathedral in Vladimir and suggest the forthright nature of the grand prince's taste for extravagant architectural display.

There is no reliable evidence as to the appearance of the palace, apart from the fact that it was built of stone, as were the other buildings of the compound – a notable exception to the preference for wood in the building of dwellings – even on a grand scale – in medieval Russia. The surviving stairtower and passageway that linked the palace and church provide another glimpse of what appear to be borrowings from western medieval architecture, particularly in the arcade band and the columns of the north arch (Figure 50). It was on this site, in the summer of 1174, that Andrei met his death, at the hands of drunken conspirators (probably from his own retinue) exasperated by his strong temper and autocratic rule. Having stabbed the prince and left him for dead, the assassins heard groans from the staircase in the passageway, where they finally delivered the coup de grace and then proceeded to ransack the palace.[15] Many of the local inhabitants, indifferent to princely feuds and their ruler's fate, took part in the pillage. Two days later, a Kievan recovered the corpse and placed in on the porch of Cathedral of the Nativity of the Virgin; not until 6 days after the murder did a delegation from Vladimir retrieve the body for burial in the city.

The Bogoliubovo compound was converted into a monastery in the thirteenth century, and in 1702, Andrei Bogoliubskii was canonized. Although much damaged in the Mongol devastation of Suzdalia in 1238, many of the ancillary structures remained until

Figure 50. Stair tower. Bogoliubovo. Northwest view. (BG 1–9)

the latter part of the eighteenth century, when "improvements" were made to the monastery grounds. Andrei's elevation to sainthood undoubtedly hastened the destruction of his Bogoliubovo. As for the Cathedral of the Nativity, an inept attempt to enlarge the windows at the turn of the eighteenth century upset the delicate structural balance and led to the collapse of the church in 1723. Fragments of the limestone carvings were placed on the walls of the church that now stands on the site.

Yet the vigorous building campaign that Andrei Bogoliubskii initiated has not been entirely effaced or rebuilt over the centuries. Indeed, the one church from his reign that has survived in something like its original form, the Church of the Intercession on the River Nerl, is arguably the most perfect thing created by medieval Russian architecture. Located a short distance from the palace at Bogoliubovo, the church honors the holy festival of the Intercession of the Virgin, derived from a Byzantine miracle, but elevated to a major religious holiday by Andrei (over the opposition of Kievan and Byzantine religious authorities).[16] Built within one construction season in 1165 or 1166,

the church follows the cross-inscribed design, with four piers, a single dome, and a tripartite facade culminating in *zakomary* (Figure 51). Yet subtle modifications in design and articulation create a sense of proportional harmony unsurpassed in medieval Russian architecture.

This mastery over material and form is expressed most clearly in the unknown architect's understanding of the vertical principle in the design of the Russian cruciform church. The architect was aided by the choice of site – and a very unlikely one, on low, marshy ground near the confluence of the Kliazma and Nerl rivers. (The Kliazma has since shifted course, leaving a small oxbow lake on two sides of the church.) On this unpromising location, exposed to spring floods as high as 4 meters, the builders fashioned an artificial hill, paved with stone, that not only protected the church from high water and provided a buttress for the deep foundation walls (5 meters), but also served as the first stage of the visual ascent (Figure 52). In its original form, the structure appears to have been buttressed by a 1-story gallery on the north, west, and south facades (Figure 53).[17] In addition, the gallery provided access to the choir gallery through an entryway still visible on the upper level of the south facade (west bay).

From its well-engineered and durable foundation, the structure rises in two tiers: a lower story of thick walls, culminating in an arcade band; and the upper-facade panels, deeply recessed within the three bays of each wall. The vertical thrust, defined by the proportions of the building, is reinforced by the receding surface of the walls, and by a slight calculated lean inward, which creates a foreshortened effect. The per-

Figure 51. Church of the Intercession of the Virgin on the Nerl. Near Bogoliubovo. 1165. Longitudinal section by B. Dedushenko; plan by N. Kucherova.

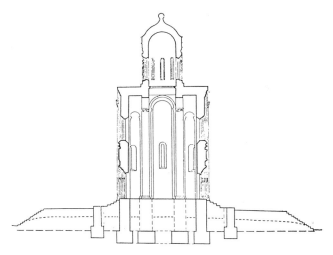

Figure 52. Church of the Intercession of the Virgin on the Nerl. Near Bogoliubovo. Section, with diagram by N. Voronin of the artificial hill and foundation.

spective arches of the portals define a focal point at the base of the structure (Figure 54), and continuity between the two levels is maintained by pilasters, accentuated by attached columns ascending from

Figure 54. Church of the Intercession of the Virgin on the Nerl. Near Bogoliubovo. West portal. (BG–2)

Figure 53. Church of the Intercession of the Virgin on the Nerl. Near Bogoliubovo. Reconstruction by N. Voronin of the original form, with exterior gallery.

plinth to *zakomary*. This rhythm, established by the arched bays, is repeated in the arcade strip and in the narrow stepped windows of the upper tier. The ascent is completed by the drum, whose eight recessed windows echo those of the walls and whose placement seems in perfect balance with the rest of the structure. Although the onion dome is a nineteenth-century distortion and the current roofline obscures the base of the cupola as well as the relation between the *zakomary* and the drum, the builders' original design is still clearly in view (see Plate 11).[18]

The vertical lines of the Church of the Intercession are determined by an unusual proportional system among the facade bays. A simple method of expressing the proportions is provided by the number of arches, in the blind arcade, contained within each bay: on the north and south facades, the numbers (counting from the east) are three, six, and five; on the west facade, four, six, and four. Each of the three facades (north, south, and west) contains fourteen arches of equal width and each central bay – the extension of the axes of the church – contains six arches.

The complexity of the arrangement arises from the spacing of the side bays along the north and south facades. The need to extend the west end of the church in order to accommodate the congregation was usually accomplished by adding another bay (as in the Cathedral of St. George at Iurev Monastery in Novgorod), or simply by lengthening the west bay. By contrast, the Church of the Intercession obtains the additional space in the west by shifting the central crossing slightly to the east – as indicated by the number of arches in the east and west bays (three to five).[19] On the east end of the church, the apses (Figure 55) rise to the archivolt of the *zakomary* and display the same sense of proportion that characterizes the central structure.

The elegance of the design brings to a culmination the architectural principles first stated in the simpler churches from the reign of Iurii Dolgorukii, with their two-tiered structure, sharply molded facades, and splayed window niches. Its sculptural decoration may also have had precedents in Suzdalia, but the Church of the Intercession is the earliest surviving monument to display an iconographic message in stone.[20] The white limestone quarried in the area provided a durable material suitable for carving, yet apart form the arcade frieze at Pereslavl-Zalesskii, the sculptural possibilities of stone had not been exploited before the building of the Cathedral of the Dormition in Vladimir, which contained a few carved figures and columns. The rapid development of this form of exterior ornamentation at Andrei's Bogoliubovo churches (the Nativity and the Intercession, both completed by 1165) and the appearance of perspective portals suggest the participation of foreign masters familiar with the Romanesque style in central Europe.[21]

The variety of carvings can be divided into two general categories – both of which are highly unusual in medieval Rus: the stylized foliated patterns on the archivolts of the portals and on the capitals of the engaged columns, and the bestial and human figures on the facades. The dominant element in the latter group is a high-relief carving of King David, placed in each of the central *zakomary*. Enthroned, with the right hand raised in blessing and the left holding the Psalter, David is flanked by two birds and two lions, signifying both submission and protection.[22] The prominence allotted David suggests various interpretations: as God's anointed, the king of Judah, he rep-

resents the warrior-leader who defeated his enemies and united the various factions within his kingdom – deeds Andrei would have compared to his own frequent campaigns to consolidate power within Rus and to defeat such external enemies as the Volga Bulgars. Built to commemorate a victory over the Bulgars, the church testifies to the power of divine intercession invoked in the Psalms.

More precisely, however, the name of the church honors the intercession of the Virgin, whose protection is extended to the people of Vladimir and their just, God-fearing ruler. No representation of Mary appears on the Church of the Intercession, but the

Figure 55. Church of the Intercession of the Virgin on the Nerl. Near Bogoliubovo. Apse. (BG 1–4)

concept of feminine protection is expressed in the twenty high-relief masks of braided maidens, placed sightly below the *zakomary*. Striking in their stylized primitive form, the masks suggest not only the exaltation of the feminine in Orthodox religious art, but also the indigenous celebration of fertility and the reverence for the Russian earth as a female being.[23]

Although much of the carving was obscured by the construction of the exterior gallery, a variety of forms proliferated on the consoles supporting the columns of the arcade band – female masks, lion faces, leopards, pig snouts, griffins, and other chimeras.[24] These figures were undoubtedly drawn from the *Physiologus*, a work that had considerable impact on architectural sculpture and manuscript art throughout medieval Europe, and – more to the point – one of the secular texts imported to Rus from Byzantium.[25] The appeal of the *Physiologus* derived from its blending of popular tales of nature with an allegorical, Christian interpretation of the beasts (often fantastic) depicted therein. Thus, the carvings on the surface of the church had a symbolic significance comprehensible to the prince and at least a part of his retinue.

But however extensive the symbolic system, the dominant figure was that of David, both in terms of its position at the center of the main *zakomary* and as the iconic image of the ruler. Although written sources refer to Andrei as a "second Solomon" (similar comparisons had been made of Iaroslav the Wise), it is probable that Andrei intended himself to be compared to King David, a strong ruler and victorious warrior.[26] In endeavoring to unite the Russian lands around a new center of power in the northeast, Andrei had clearly been aware of the symbolic uses of architecture. He intended his churches to rival those of Kiev and is reported in a Kievan chronicle to have said of the Bogoliubovo Church of the Nativity: "I wish to build just such a church as that one with the golden doors [in Kiev], that it may be a remembrance to my land."[27]

At the same time, Andrei Bogoliubskii's work represents a disavowal of much in Kievan culture and architecture. Having left Kiev in 1155 and having rejected his father's political goal of ruling from Kiev, Andrei looked elsewhere for the means to create a new princely architecture. It seems likely that he found in central Europe a source of builders familiar with precise stonework and trained in a culture that encouraged the use of statuary in church decoration – in contrast to the Byzantine tradition, accepted elsewhere in Rus, which rejected such uses. To be sure, the interior of the Church of the Intercession was in the usual Russian manner covered with frescoes (not extant after 1877). But Andrei had also achieved the means of conveying to all who passed his churches – and not just to those who entered – the images of a stone poem in praise of his power and the glory of what he had created.

Architecture and Ornament in the Reign of Vsevolod III

The period following Andrei Bogoliubskii's assassination in 1174 was marked by the usual struggle among contenders for power over Suzdalia. By 1177, the issue had been resolved in favor of Vsevolod Iurevich, half-brother of Andrei, who in 1162 had driven Vsevolod's mother, Elena, and her sons into exile in Constantinople. Vsevolod's return to Vladimir ensured not only the continuation of the Monomakh princely line as the dominant power in the eastern lands of Rus, but also a renewal of the creative spirit of Greek art in medieval Russian architecture. The Cathedral of St. Dmitrii, with its frescoes and elaborate carving (see what follows), provides ample testimony to the influence of Greek culture during the reign of Vsevolod.

Furthermore, Vsevolod would come to understand, no less than Andrei, the uses of architecture in projecting the authority of the prince. He ruled at a time of able and ambitious rival princes, including Sviatoslav Vsevolodovich of Chernigov (and grand prince in Kiev); Riurik Rostislavich, grand prince of western Rus; and his brother, David Rostislavich of Smolensk. As has been noted in the preceding chapters, these princes actively supported the construction of large masonry churches, and one can assume that they did so not only as an expression of religious devotion and support for the Orthodox Church, but also as a statement of the power and wealth that they commanded.

Not until 1185, however, did Vsevolod III – known as "Great Nest" for the number of his male progeny – turn his attention to a major building campaign. The immediate cause was a fire that destroyed much of Vladimir and severely damaged the Dormition Cathedral. Vsevolod's builders ingeniously retained the walls of the earlier structure, weakened by fire, as the core of the cathedral, and added another aisle on each side (Figure 56). The bays of the now interior walls were widened to create piers (bolstered by pylons), and the choir gallery was extended over cross vaults to the west aisle. On the east, the apsidal structure was completely rebuilt, with a substantial increase in depth.[28] On the other facades, the new walls were raised 2 stories, but not to the full height of the original structure. The relation between the old and the new was thus clearly defined in the structure, and the additional aisles served as a form of gallery. Indeed, it could be said that the rebuilding of the Dormition Cathedral achieved the consummate in-

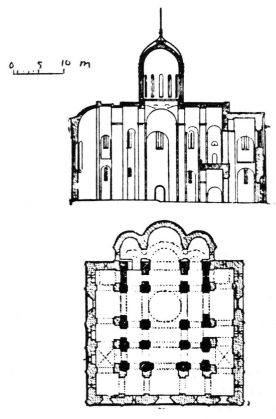

Figure 56. Cathedral of the Dormition. Vladimir. 1158–60; enlarged in 1185–9. Longitudinal section and plan by N. Karabutov.

tegration of attached gallery and central structure that had so often challenged medieval Russian architects.

The exterior walls are marked at midlevel by an arcade frieze but relatively little carved ornament (Figure 57). Nonetheless, the extant console blocks from Vsevolod's time demonstrate the preservation of the technique, if not the scale, of carving introduced 20 years earlier by Andrei Bogoliubskii's Romanesque masters.[29] In a broader sense, the walls themselves possess a sculpted quality, with the recessed upper bays delineated by attached columns, and the festive row of *zakomary* outlined in decorative metalwork. The most spectacular change in the design of the new cathedral consisted of four additional cupolas, placed over bays to the north and south of the corners of Andrei's original structure (see Plate 12). Again, Vsevolod's builders demonstrated remarkable assurance in integrating the two structural layers. As before, the walls of the drums were sheathed in gilded copper; and although the basic roofing material was sheet lead, there is evidence that the large central cupola was also covered with gilded copper.

The rebuilding of the Cathedral of the Dormition

produced one of the largest masonry structures in medieval Rus.[30] As the center of religious authority in the large domains of Suzdalia, the cathedral also represented a monument to Vsevolod's power (none of his rivals in Rus built so large a church) and to the cultural renaissance that it fostered. The Dormition Cathedral was followed in 1192–6 by a stone church with one dome and four piers for the Monastery of the Nativity of the Virgin in Vladimir. Although not as large as the Dormition Cathedral, it apparently possessed the same monumental form, with little ornamental carving apart from the perspective portals.[31] Long in ruins by the middle of the nineteenth century, the church was razed and a copy of what was presumed to be the original form was rebuilt on the site by N. A. Artleben – only to be destroyed in the 1930s.

In view of the austerity of sculpted ornament on Vsevolod's earlier churches (compared with those of Andrei Bogoliubskii), the profusion of stone sculpture for his palace church, dedicated to St. Demetrius of Salonika, must be attributed to its role as a statement of princely authority. Built between 1193 and 1197, the church is similar in plan to the cuboid structure of the Bogoliubovo churches, with an arcade frieze separating two tiers, the upper of which is covered in carved limestone (Figure 58; see Plate 13).[32] Although Vsevolod's sculptors undoubtedly drew on motifs and techniques developed three decades earlier at Bogoliubovo, there is no clear source for the extraordinary iconographic exercise of the facades of the Cathedral of St. Dmitrii. The western medieval elements introduced in Bogoliubskii's churches are still in evidence, but some have argued in favor of borrowings from Balkan churches or from the carved tufa facades of Armenian churches.[33]

No reliable evidence exists for any one theory of derivation, and in view of the transience of motifs and craftsmen – from Byzantium, the Balkans, central Europe, and, possibly, the Caucasus – it is likely that Vsevolod's artisans adapted and brilliantly combined elements from several sources. As Meyer Schapiro has noted, Romanesque art is distinguished by its eclectic use of elements from widely diverse sources: "There is in western art from the seventh to the thirteenth centuries an immense receptivity matched in few cultures before that time or even later; early Christian, Byzantine, Sassanian, Coptic, Syrian, Roman, Moslem, Celtic, and pagan Germanic forms were borrowed then, often without regard to their context and meaning."[34] The late twelfth-century Suzdalian churches exhibit the same receptivity and pose the same challenges in determining provenance and derivation.

Figure 57. Cathedral of the Dormition. Vladimir. Southwest view.
(VL 10–3)

Apart from the issue of provenance, there is the iconographic question posed by the carvings, whose order has been partially preserved despite reconstruction and renovation over a period of eight centuries – the most extensive being a "restoration" begun in 1832. Like the Church of the Intercession on the Nerl, St. Dmitrii was originally constructed with an exterior gallery that gave access to the choir gallery within.[35] The removal of this attached structure (much dilapidated) in the 1830s enhanced the perception of the exterior carving, but also introduced a rearrangment of some of the carved blocks of the facade. Nonetheless, the extant original carvings on the exterior display a system of religious, secular, and ornamental motifs that comprise a message in stone. Furthermore, it is likely that a number of the reconstructed elements would have conformed to the iconographic function of the original carvings they replaced.

Although certain of the plant and animal carvings are associated with motifs widespread in Indo-European folklore – and, more directly, with the *Phy-*

siologus – their function seems primarily decorative, the repetition of highly stylized elements in an ordered setting.[36] In addition, the chimeras and masks – particularly evident in the console blocks of the apse arcade (Figure 59 and 60) – no doubt play the thaumaturgic role allotted to them elsewhere in medieval architecture, including the Church of the Intercession on the Nerl. The human figures, however, have in many cases been identified, and it is possible to read the facades as a text on the prince whose authority is sanctioned by God, by the Orthodox Church and its saints, and by legendary rulers of antiquity. Furthermore, the military component, so essential to the maintenance of princely power, is emphasized not only in references to Alexander the Great and King David, but also to the "warrior saints," or Roman officers martyred for their faith and canonized by the Orthodox Church. This would not appear to be a setting congenial to the cult of Sts. Boris and Gleb, yet they figure prominently in the arcade frieze of the north facade (right bay).

53

As at the Church of the Intercession, the central *zakomara* is dominated by King David, so inscribed on the west facade (Figures 61 and 62). The significance of David has already been noted in the discussion of the Church of the Intercession on the Nerl, but he is joined here (on the left bay of the west facade) by the figure of Solomon, law-giver, poet, and builder of the Temple.[37] Surrounding David are creatures of the sky and the earth, among them eagles, doves, peacocks, lions, panthers, pheasants, hares, as well as fantastic creatures such as griffins, centaurs, and the basilisk. As representations of the wise and strong ruler, David and Solomon are complemented by mythological and historical figures such as Hercules and Alexander the Great, the latter known through the Alexander Romance, a legendary version of his deeds that circulated in Byzantium and medieval Europe.[38]

Indeed, the emphasis on great rulers seems to overshadow the image of Christ, whose baptism on the left *zakomara* of the south facade is balanced by the apotheosis of Alexander the Great on the right bay (Figures 63, 64, and 65). In symbolic terms, however, all of the previous rulers and mythological figures would have been interpreted as part of an elaborate system of commentary on the glory and majesty of Christ (references to classical mythology as well as to the Old Testament were justified as a prefiguration of Christ's mission). The final link in the uppermost row of images occurs on the north facade, of which the left *zakomara* displays a donor group containing Vsevolod and his five sons, one of whom he holds on his knee (Figure 66).[39] From Alexander, David, Solomon, and Christ, the sense of authority bequeathed to Vsevolod and to his sons is emphatically proclaimed.

Below the row of *zakomary* are further depictions of religious and secular figures, each category of which contains emblems of physical and martial prowess, as wrestlers and hunters are joined by galloping warrior-saints such as Theodore Stratilates and George of Cappadocia. Of the several half-figure portraits of ascetic saints and churchmen, only a few can be dated to the twelfth century (Figure 67); the rest are replacements sensitive to the style and identification of the originals. Much the same can be said of the arcade frieze: It is possible that only sixteen of the seventy carvings are original work, yet the overall iconographic system has been maintained.[40] The figures of the divinity, of Mary, and of the evangelists on the west (main) facade are seated, thus indicating their regal position in the cosmic hierarchy. The south facade contains statues of Russian princes, including Alexander Nevskii – proof that later sculptors used

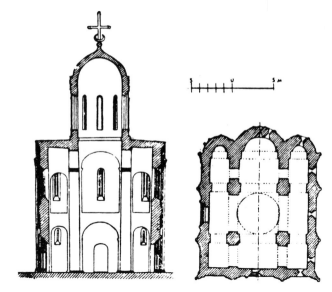

Figure 58. Cathedral of St. Dmitrii. Vladimir. 1193–7. Transverse section and plan by A. Rukhliadev.

the cathedral as a pantheon for the portrayal of medieval Russian saints and leaders.

Regardless of the changes introduced by the carving of new statuary, the renovations succeeded in maintaining the visual integrity of the structure, with its rich texture of limestone reliefs set within sharply defined bays. The recessed portals are framed by carved archivolts (Figure 68), which provide a focal point to the central bays and complement the rounded forms of the *zakomary*. A restoration of the roofline now illuminates not only the relation between the *zakomary* and the interior vaulting, but also the gilded cupola and drum (Figure 69), whose attached columns frame windows and strapwork containing fanciful beasts and half-figures.[41] The cross is of iron, with gilded copper ornamental work and a copper dove at its crown.

On the interior (Figure 70) carved details such as the crouching lions on impost blocks are preserved, but most of the frescoes have been destroyed. However, the central and south vaults beneath the choir gallery still display a remarkable set of frescoes, probably painted around 1195, on the theme of the Last Judgment. The predominant scholarly opinion now assigns the major part of this work to a master from Constantinople, with frescoes by Russian assistants in the south vault.[42] Although discussion of the paintings lies beyond the scope of this study, the quality of the composition and execution form a part of the artistic culture reflected throughout the building of St. Dmitrii. As Viktor Lazarev has noted, Vsevolod's

Figure 59. Cathedral of St. Dmitrii. Vladimir. Northeast view. (VL 1–1)

Figure 60. Cathedral of St. Dmitrii. Vladimir. Central apse, console blocks. On the left, nineteenth-century mask; on the right, twelfth-century figure of bird. (VL 7–27)

Figure 61. Cathedral of St. Dmitrii. Vladimir. Southwest view. (VL 3–8)

mother was a Byzantine princess, Vsevolod himself spent 7 years of his youth in Constantinople, and his brother Mikhail established in Vladimir a school with Greek clerics and a library with extensive holdings of Greek manuscripts.[43] Although the library is long destroyed, its manuscripts suggest a source for the iconographic motifs of Vsevolod's own psalm in white stone.

Early Thirteenth-Century Churches in Suzdalia: The Culmination of Ornamentalism

Following the construction of the Cathedral of St. Dmitrii, Vsevolod commissioned the Dormition Cathedral of the Kniaginin Convent in Vladimir (1200, substantially rebuilt at the beginning of the sixteenth century)[44]; but although he continued to rule effec-

tively throughout much of Rus until his death in 1212, he added little to his architectural legacy after the completion of St. Dmitrii. His sons, however, continued the building of churches in their respective fiefdoms within the Vladimir-Suzdal principality. The most active builder among them was Konstantin, Vsevolod's eldest son, who had ruled in Rostov since 1207. In 1213, he commissioned the rebuilding of Andrei Bogoliuskii's Dormition Cathedral in Rostov, and in 1215 and 1216, he undertook two major projects in Iaroslavl: the Cathedral of the Dormition, begun in 1215 and consecrated in 1219; and the Transfiguration of the Savior at the Spasskii (Savior) Monastery, built between 1216 and 1224. Both of the Iaroslavl churches were of brick, with carved limestone details.[45]

None of Konstantin's churches is extant and only a slightly better fate occurred with the architectural work of his brother Iurii, with whom he struggled for control of the northeast. For political reasons having to do with the need to maintain the central authority of Vladimir – as opposed to that of Rostov – Vsevolod had appointed not Konstantin, but the next son, Iurii, to be his successor as grand prince in Vladimir-Suzdal. Rivalry between the two increased with Konstantin's establishment in 1214 of an independent episcopate in Rostov, and in 1216, the two factions clashed in a battle on the river Lipitsa. Although Iurii was supported by three of his brother-princes, the victory went to Konstantin (reinforced by Novgorod), who assumed power in Vladimir. Iurii endured peaceful exile in Suzdal.

After Konstantin's death in 1219, Iurii returned to the capital, Vladimir, but his long association with Suzdal led him to rebuild its Cathedral of the Nativity of the Virgin. An earlier church on the site, constructed around 1102 by Vladimir Monomakh, had undergone a number of major repairs (including one in 1194 of which the Laurentian chronicle notes that

Figure 63. Cathedral of St. Dmitrii. Vladimir. South facade, upper tier of left bay. Relief, under the arch, of the baptism of Christ; presumed to be early nineteenth century. (VL–7)

Figure 62. Cathedral of St. Dmitrii. Vladimir. West facade, upper tier of central bay. In the *zakomara*, King David surrounded by angels and chimeras. (VL 3–1a)

the work was done not by "Germans," but by craftsmen from Vladimir); and in 1222–5, the structure was rebuilt in stone – primarily a light tufa, with limestone for the details. Rubble from the plinthos walls of the Monomakh church was used for the core infill.[46] In 1445, the upper part of the cathedral collapsed. When rebuilt in 1528–30, the remaining stone walls were lowered to the level of the arcade frieze, and the upper structure and five drums were rebuilt of new brick in the style of large Muscovite churches (see Plates 14 and 15). Thus, the form of the thirteenth-century cathedral must remain in part conjectural.[47]

The Nativity Cathedral in Suzdal shows substantive differences with earlier limestone churches in the area, in both plan and detail. The main bay of each facade contains an enclosed extension with portal, thus giving the plan a cruciform aspect (Figure 71).

Figure 64. Cathedral of St. Dmitrii. Vladimir. South facade, upper
tier of central bay; with King David and warrior saints. (VL 1–9)

58

The arcade band, which in earlier churches functioned as a support for the drip cornice at midlevel, is here recessed into the wall surface, thus assuming a decorative role. The surface iconography is limited to female masks (indicative of the dedication of the cathedral) placed on the pilaster strips (Figure 72), with heraldic lions at the corners and on certain of the capitals of the attached columns framing the portals (Figure 73). This emphasis on the ornamental, as opposed to iconographic, function in the carved

Figure 65. Cathedral of St. Dmitrii. Vladimir. South facade, upper tier of right bay; with a relief, under the arch, of Alexander the Great ascending to heaven. (VL–4)

Figure 67. Cathedral of St. Dmitrii. Vladimir. North facade, central bay. Half-figure carvings of saints. (VL 7–20)

Figure 66. Cathedral of St. Dmitrii. Vladimir. North facade, left bay. The patron, Prince Vsevolod, with five of his sons. (VL 7–17)

stonework is particularly evident in the elaborate strap motifs that cover the shafts of the attached columns of both the arcade band and the portals, and the leaf detail of the capitals. The primary iconographic setting of the cathedral was transferred from the structural surface to the "Golden Doors" of the west portal, tentatively dated 1233, and to a later pair

59

Figure 68. Cathedral of St. Dmitrii. Vladimir. West facade, portal. (VL 4–11)

the church collapsed in the 1460s (a distressingly frequent event among Russian churches during the fifteenth century), Ivan III, grand prince of Moscow, commanded the architect Vasilii Ermolin to rebuild the structure as part of a campaign to restore the luster of the ancient centers of the Monomachus princes in Suzdalia, now absorbed into Muscovy (see Chapter 5).

In 1471, Ermolin completed his task – successfully, to judge by the sound state of the structure, but with scant concern for the original appearance. Perhaps there was little choice, because the original design, which seems to have daringly elevated the large drum and cupola above the main walls (Figure 74), may have been unstable.[49] (In this case, Suzdalian builders approached the experiments in Chernigov, Smolensk, and Novgorod to impart a vertical thrust to the upper structure.) Furthermore, the patterned carving that covered the facades could hardly have been recreated in the absence of a concern for scholarly accuracy in such matters. It is fortunate that many of the carved blocks were restored to the new walls in whatever

Figure 69. Cathedral of St. Dmitrii. Vladimir. Drum and cupola, viewed from the west. (VL 3–1)

in the south portal (c. 1248). The scenes portrayed in the panels of both sets of doors were executed by applying gold foil to copper plate; and although the combination of biblical scenes, Byzantine theologians and saints venerated in Rus, and heraldic beasts can yield ingenious religious and political interpretations,[48] the setting of the doors and the artistic medium create a miniaturization of the iconographic message.

The full measure of the tendency toward ornamentalism was revealed in the limestone cathedral constructed in Iurev-Polskoi by Sviatoslav Vsevolodovich. Founded by Iurii Dolgorukii in the middle of the twelfth century, the town had been included in the Vladimir principality; but with the distribution of lands among Vsevolod's sons in 1212, it became the seat of a small principality under Sviatoslav. In 1230, he commissioned a rebuilding of Dolgorukii's Church of St. George (1152), and by 1234, the new cathedral was completed. When the upper part of

Figure 70. Cathedral of St. Dmitrii. Vladimir. Interior, central crossing. (VL 6–2)

fashion, yet a number were used for the vaulting, or for other hidden structural purposes. Much of the extant surface, therefore, resembles carved chaos, with the exception of the relatively intact north wall.[50]

Although considerably smaller than the Nativity Cathedral in Suzdal, the Cathedral of St. George is similar in its three extensions for the portals of the north, west, and south facades. As at Suzdal, the west extension is considerably larger: two stories, with an upper level replacing the usual choir gallery within the main structure. (At Suzdal, the west extension contained stairs that led to a large choir gallery.) Because it lacked a choir gallery, the interior of this four-piered church was unusually spacious and well illuminated by two tiers of unobstructed windows. The interior walls would have had the usual complement of frescoes, but the more striking iconographic display remained on the exterior. It is thought that the Cathedral of St. George was built to celebrate a major victory of Sviatoslav's forces over the Volga Bulgars

in 1220, and, consequently the biblical scenes, saints, and church fathers that appear in relief carving signify the divine protection extended to the prince and his people. Not only are there carved blocks with separate motifs, but also at least three large stone icons (including the Transfiguration) composed of several blocks.[51] In addition, the surface was covered with a low-relief vegetal pattern carved when the blocks were already in place. The dense ornament covered all of the lower structure, including the attached col-

Figure 71. Cathedral of the Nativity of the Virgin. Suzdal. 1222–5; upper tier rebuilt of brick in 1528. South facade. (SD 1–2)

umns, so that architectural detail – clearly delineated at the St. Dmitrii cathedral – is subsumed within a monolithic carved block.

The exuberance expressed in the form and decoration of the Cathedral of St. George at Iurev-Polskoi is an indication of the relative wealth of the grand principality of Vladimir in thirteenth-century Rus. Despite the setback dealt to Iurii Vsevolodovich and his quest for unification at the battle of Lipitsa, the principality continued to expand and colonize in the east. After his brother Sviatoslav's victory over the Volga

Figure 72. Cathedral of the Nativity of the Virgin. Suzdal. South facade, detail. (SD 1–12)

Bulgars in 1220, Iurii founded Nizhnii Novgorod at the confluence of the Oka and Volga rivers and built two limestone churches in the new town: the Transfiguration of the Savior (1225) and Archangel Michael (1227).[52] The fragmentation of Rus did not, under normal circumstances, mean a loss of vitality in the major principalities. Circumstances, however, were rapidly changing.

The Mongol Conquest

"[1224] The same year, for our sins, unknown tribes came whom no one exactly knows, who they are, nor whence they came, nor what their faith is; but they call them Tatars. . . ."[53] Thus, the Novgorod chronicle described the first appearance of the Tatars in Russia.

Other chronicles were to give more precise information – the "Tatars" were in fact part of the Mongol hordes of Genghis Khan – but all accounts contain the same interpretation, drawn from the lamentations of the Old Testament prophets: that an unprecedented calamity had overtaken Russia as a punishment for its sins. (The same explanation was given by Kievan chroniclers for the sack of that city by Andrei Bogoliubskii.) After a crushing defeat of Russian forces on the river Kalka (in the southern steppes,

near the Sea of Azov) in 1223, the Mongols returned to the eastern steppes, where they were to reorganize following the death of Genghis Khan (1227), and launch another attack to the northeast. Let by Batu, a grandson of Genghis Khan, a Mongol army of some 150,000 troops struck the disorganized Russian principalities, first at the southern principality of Riazan in 1237, and then at Vladimir in the winter of 1237–8. The invasion eventually carried them to Kiev (1240) and Galicia, then Poland and Hungary (1241); and at each stage, the sequence of events was essentially the same: the capture of a town by cunning or superior force, its destruction, and the massacre of its inhabitants.

According to the detailed account in the Galician-Volhynian chronicle, the catastrophe at Vladimir began with the defeat of Russian forces and the death of Grand Prince Iurii, killed while raising another force. When the Mongols approached the city and attempted by threats to gain the city without a siege, Bishop Mitrofan assumed leadership (Iurii's young son Vsevolod was thoroughly demoralized) and exorted the citizens to fight:

The people of the city hearkened to [his] words and began to fight with greater strength. The Tatars battered the town with their wall-battering instruments; they released arrows without number. Prince Vsevolod saw that the battle waxed yet more fierce, took fright because of his youth, and went forth from the town with his small group, carrying with him many gifts and hoping to receive his life. Batu, like a wild beast, did not spare his youth, but ordered that he be slaughtered before him, and he slew all the town. When the bishop, with the princess and her children, fled to the church [the Cathedral of the Dormition], the godless one commanded it to be set on fire. Thus they surrendered their souls to God.[54]

With the death of Grand Khan Ugedei, Batu with-

Figure 73. Cathedral of the Nativity of the Virgin. Suzdal. Detail, south portal. (SD 1–4)

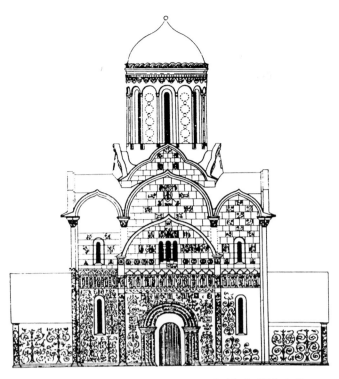

Figure 74. Cathedral of St. George. Iurev-Polskoi. 1230–4. Reconstruction of west facade by G. Vagner.

drew from Europe to the lower part of the Volga, where he established his leadership of that part of the Mongol empire known as the Golden Horde. From their capital of Old Sarai, Batu and his successors exacted tribute from Russia, conferred the title of Grand Prince on Russian leaders whom they favored, and made periodic raids to maintain their dominance. Russian princes were frequently required to accompany Mongol punitive expeditions against rebellious Russian cities; the ambitious princes of Moscow were adept in exploiting this role to their own advantage.

The "Tatar Yoke," which was not formally abrogated until 1480, led to a general cultural decline that was particularly noticeable in architecture, for both technical and economic reasons. Brilliant as they were

in military organization, the Mongols had little to offer the more highly developed Russian culture, from which they remained detached by both religion and secular custom. (Alexander Pushkin remarked: "The Tatars were not like the Moors. Having conquered Russia, they gave her neither algebra nor Aristotle."[55]) As the process of assimilation increased during the fifteenth century, the direction was invariably toward the acceptance by the Mongols of the Russian Orthodox faith and other cultural traditions.

In the period following the Mongol invasion, a modicum of organized existence returned to the devastated towns of Suzdalia, even though the principality was exposed to frequent raids. In 1252, the title of Grand Prince of Vladimir was bestowed by the Mongols on Alexander Nevskii – prince of Novgorod and grandson of Vsevolod III – whose policy of accommodation provided a fragile stability to the area. However, the predominance of Vladimir in Russian affairs had passed. In 1328, Moscow's Grand Prince Ivan I (Kalita, or "Moneybags") persuaded the metropolitan of the Russian Church to transfer his residence from Vladimir to Moscow; and by the end of his reign, Vladimir had been incorporated into the Moscow principality. Throughout two centuries of harsh Mongol rule, the Church provided the most important link with the culture of early medieval Rus, and during the fourteenth and fifteenth centuries, it continued to play a leading role in the resurgence of the Russian culture, from Novgorod to Moscow.

The limestone monuments of Suzdalia would also provide a model for the halting recovery of masonry architecture in Muscovy during the same period; but the genius of the early limestone churches eluded later generations of builders, and Muscovite architecture developed in directions little related to carved stone. Indeed, the architecture of the Vladimir-Suzdal principalities before the Mongol conquest represents an anomaly in the general development of Russian architecture, which throughout its history emphasized the plasticity of brick (and wood), and only occasionally resorted to the more precise discipline of stonework.

CHAPTER 4

The Revival of Architecture in Novgorod and Pskov

In the summer of 6886 [1378] was painted the Church of the Divine Transfiguration of Our Savior Jesus Christ, at the behest of the noble and God-fearing boiar Vasilii Danilovich and with the residents of Elijah Street. And the Greek master Theophanes painted [the frescoes]. . . .

– Novgorod Third Chronicle

As political and military relations with the Mongols achieved a modicum of stability in the first half of the fourteenth century, there were modest attempts to revive the techniques of masonry construction in Russia – now defined by Novgorod and its lands in the north, and by the area of central Russia formerly ruled from Vladimir but increasingly under the dominance of Moscow during the fourteenth century. Novgorod, relatively secure behind its forest barrier and well situated to explore commercial relations to the west through the Baltic Sea, was the first to benefit from this revival on a significant scale. Its new prosperity was reflected above all in the number of churches commissioned by the city's merchants, or by the citizens of a particular district.

Because their use was limited primarily to parish and donor, these churches were of compact design, even though in rare cases their dimensions (in particular, their height) were considerable. The four piers under the central dome organized the interior space, and the west corner bays were occasionally enclosed as donor chapels. Brick and fieldstone continued to be the major building materials, together with extensive use of wood for roofing and structural supports, and the walls were in most cases stuccoed and whitewashed – as had become common by the twelfth century. In comparison with earlier churches, however, the facades of fourteenth-century monuments show a marked increase in the use of extended brick ornamental figures. Such exuberant ornamentalism is usually associated with the creation of new wealth, and the link between the two is evident in the facade decoration of major Novgorod donor churches during

the fourteenth and early fifteenth centuries. (Pskov, by contrast, developed elaborate, multiplanar roof structures over whitewashed walls.) However profuse the ornament, Novgorod architecture maintained its characteristic molded, free-form plasticity, as dictated by the soft brick and rough stone of its walls.

Novgorod Churches of the Fourteenth Century

The harbinger of Novgorod's revival in architecture is the Church of St. Nicholas at Lipno (1292; to the southeast of Novgorod), one of the first masonry churches to be built in the area after the Mongol invasion. Despite its modest size (10 by 10 meters), the cuboid structure with four piers, one dome, and one apse established a prototype for more spacious fourteenth-century churches (Figure 75). In turn, there are certain features of St. Nicholas – in particular, the trefoil roofline and the compact, molded form of the structure – that suggest borrowings from the Church of the Nativity of the Virgin at Peryn, built at the beginning of the thirteenth century (see Chapter 2). The walls of the Lipno church were primarily of rough stone (flagstone, shellstone, and some sandstone), with details in brick of a larger, firmer type than the plinthos used in earlier churches. Although the structure was severely damaged in World War II, enough remained to allow a reconstruction to what is considered to have been its original, trefoil form.[1]

Only fragments remain of Novgorod's masonry churches from the first half of the fourteenth century,

Figure 75. Church of St. Nicholas at Lipno. Near Novgorod. 1292. Plan and transverse section; reconstruction of west facade by P. Maksimov.

although archeological evidence suggests that the basic forms varied between those with a trefoil facade and those with a horizontal row of *zakomary*.[2] The earliest fourteenth-century church extant in something close to its original form is the Church of the Savior at Kovalevo, built on the outskirts of Novgorod in 1345 and now reconstructed after its virtual destruction in the World War II. Its central structure resembles that of the Nereditsa church (see Chapter 2), but the enclosed extensions from the north, west, and south facades form a plan similar to that of the Paraskeva-Piatnitsa church, which was in fact undergoing reconstruction in 1345 after being severely damaged in the great fire of 1340.

The Kovalevo church was commissioned by the Novgorod boyar Ontsyfor Zhabin, and at least one of the extensions, on the south facade, served as a burial chamber for the donor and his family (Figure 76). Lazarev suggests that the interior frescoes, commissioned by the boyar Afanasii Stepanovich and painted in 1380, are related to Serbian painting.[3] Although the question of Serbian authorship remains unresolved, the major Russian principalities did, in fact, experience an influx of artists and churchmen from the territory of the south Slavs in the fourteenth and

fifteenth centuries, as the Turks extended their control over the Balkans. It is likely that Novgorod, as well as Moscow, benefited from their presence. Perhaps a greater complement of frescoes, also tentatively dated to 1380, was contained in the neighboring Church of the Dormition on Volotovo Field (1352; not extant), which followed the trefoil design developed at the Peryn and Lipno churches.[4]

The most notable of Novgorod's fourteenth-century monuments are the Church of St. Theodore Stratilates on the Brook (1360–1) and the Church of the Transfiguration of the Savior on Elijah Street (1374). Unlike the earlier trefoil churches at Peryn, Lipno, and Volotovo, whose compact, molded form dispensed with an exterior segmentation of the facade, the churches of St. Theodore and the Transfiguration revealed a more rational articulation in the use of pilaster strips to emphasize the dimensions of the structure. Both churches display intersecting gabled roofs along the axes of the vaulting, but the restored roof of St. Theodore Stratilates is closer to its original design, whose contours are defined by the trefoil facade (Figure 77). As was frequently the case, the church roofs were modified during the sixteenth century to an eight-slope form, which facilitated the application of sheet metal; it was also believed that a single plane would shed snow and ice more easily than a contoured design, although apparently this is not so.[5] In fact, the original roofing material for churches of this period must have been wooden shingles. No traces of roofing tiles have been discovered, and lead would have been used only to repair the roofs of large cathedrals from the eleventh and twelfth centuries.[6]

The Church of St. Theodore was commissioned by Semion Andreevich, the *posadnik,* or mayor, of Novgorod, whose generosity made this one of the larger fourteenth-century churches. Its trefoil facade is extended to the west in order to reconcile the basic cuboid plan with the need to provide space for the congregation (Figure 78). The extension is clearly indicated in the articulation of the north and south facades: The central bay contains a trefoil crown and the east bays culminate in a halved trefoil, whereas those on the west display the outlines of a halved pentafoil. The north and south facades each have a recessed portal with a profiled arch. The two rows of ogival windows are placed in a one-to-one arrangement across the facade, and the upper part of the central bay contains an elaborate cross beneath a single window niche. An extension from the west facade, perhaps used as a chapel, was replaced in the seventeenth century, and its dimensions are unclear.[7]

The curvilinear form of the St. Theodore church is

65

Figure 76. Church of the Transfiguration of the Savior at Kovalevo. Novgorod. 1345. Southwest view. The burial chamber of the donor, Ontsyfor Zhabin, with its tripartite roof, extends from the south facade. The gash along the facade indicates the level of the ruins after the Second World War. (N 7–1)

repeated on the apse, divided by a series of attached columns that in turn are linked by two series of arches above each of the rows of windows. The lower series is outlined in a sawtooth pattern (reappearing on the cornice and drum) and spans the entire distance between the columns, and the upper group contains a secondary series of short columns framing paired windows and thus creating an arcade within an arcade. It is possible that the blind arcading on the apse is related to western, perhaps German, sources, although a similar pattern appeared on the twelfth-century Vladimir churches. The rhythm of curve and arch is repeated on the drum, whose narrow windows are capped by eyebrow arches and a scalloped-wave cornice beneath the dome.

On the interior, a high wall separated not only the northwest and southwest bays of the choir gallery from the main space (a device used in midfourteenth-century churches to create additional chapels), but also the center bay, which was converted into a chapel. The frescoes, which were whitewashed in the 1870s (a period when much extant medieval art was destroyed), were first restored in 1910, and at one time, they were thought to have been painted by the greatest artist to work in Russia in the late fourteenth century: Theophanes the Greek, who arrived in Novgorod in the late 1370s. Subsequent restoration of the frescoes has revealed substantial differences in detail when compared with the work of Theophanes; and it has been suggested that the paintings, for which

Figure 77. Church of St. Theodore Stratilates on the Brook, Novgorod. 1360–1. Southeast view. (N 4–8)

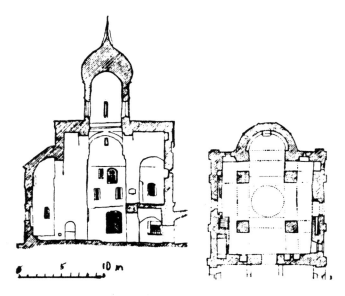

Figure 78. Church of St. Theodore Stratilates. Novgorod. Longitudinal section and plan by L. Shuliak.

there is no documentary evidence, were done in the late 1370s by a Novgorod artist who was intimately familiar with the style of the Greek master.[8]

The most significant monument of the Novgorod revival, both for its structure and its frescoes, is the Church of the Transfiguration of the Savior on Elijah (Ilin) Street, built in 1374 by the residents of the major street through the Slavno district of the Trading Side. The new structure replaced a wooden church that had housed the miraculous icon of the Virgin of the Sign, the palladium of Novgorod.[9] The importance of this church – second only to St. Sophia in the fourteenth and fifteenth centuries – may account for the festive decorative patterns on its exterior (see Plate 16). The motifs are essentially those used at St. Theodore, but their application reveals a more complex attempt to emphasize the building's vertical lines.

This is particularly noticeable in the distribution of the windows on the north and south facades, where the simple rows at St. Theodore are replaced by larger groupings in the central bay (Figure 79). From the deeply recessed portal, with a brick archivolt, the main bay rises to a group of three narrow windows separated by blind niches. The central, larger, window provides the focal point, and the entire group is capped with a pentafoil arch, thereby creating a pattern that echoes the division of the facade as a whole. Above this ensemble is an elaborate melange of windows and niches – circular and rectangular – surmounted by a trefoil arch leading to the final burst of detail: a patriarchal cross (in relief), a single window, and a decorative brick band, all culminating in the final trefoil arch. In recapitulation, the drum displays eyebrow arches over the windows, a band of scalloped indentations, a band of hollow brickwork, and a wave cornice. It is probable that when first built, the walls of brick and rough stone were left unstuccoed, which would have created a richly textured surface of reddish-brown hue, as in the restored Church of Sts. Peter and Paul in Kozhevniki (see Plate 19).

The plan of the Church of the Transfiguration of the Savior differs little from that of the slightly smaller St. Theodore – the same four-pillared arrangement with the bias to the west, reflected on the exterior panels (Figure 80).[10] On the interior, the northwest and southwest bays were enclosed as corner chapels, dedicated to the Trinity and to Sts. Kozma and Demian, respectively. The north chapel was reached by a stairway within the thickness of the west wall – a common device in medieval Russian brick churches. The central bay in the west is spanned by a wooden passageway leading to the entrance of the south chapel.

Figure 79. Church of the Transfiguration of the Savior on Elijah Street. Novgorod. 1374. South facade. (N 4–3)

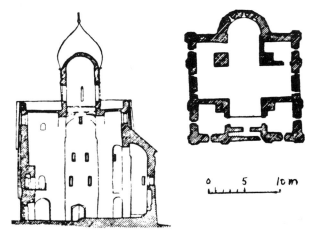

Figure 80. Church of the Transfiguration of the Savior on Elijah Street. Novgorod. Longitudinal section and plan by L. Shuliak.

The absence of a choir gallery for the favored elite in this, as in several other Novgorod churches of similar plan, suggests a certain "democratization" appropriate to the Novgorod social order. Yet the Church of the Transfiguration on Elijah Street was no austere meeting house. In 1378, the boyar Vasilii Danilovich commissioned frescoes for the church from Theophanes the Greek, an experienced artist from Constantinople who had recently arrived in Novgorod as part of a wave of artists and intellectuals fleeing the beleaguered Byzantine and Balkan states.[11] Theophanes – or Feofan Grek, as he was known to the Russians – painted icons as well as frescoes, and the Church of the Transfiguration is his only documented church interior in Novgorod. Although only fragments have survived, they are sufficient to establish his reputation as one of the greatest painters of medieval Russia.

These remarkably free and vigorous paintings lie beyond the limits of the present study, yet it must be noted that the two major extant portions – the Pan-

tocrator, surrounded by archangels, in the central dome, and the Old Testament Trinity and the Byzantine stylites in the northwest Trinity chapel – demonstrate Theophanes' understanding of the relation between monumental painting and architectural space.[12] The relation between the dynamism of Theophanes' style, with its slashing highlights on a reddish-brown, amphoralike ground, and the spiritual and social upheavals of the late fourteenth century has been much discussed in recent scholarship. Some see in the freedom of his style a reflection of the various heretical movements that attacked the power, and the wealth, of the church in Novgorod (e.g., the Strigolniki).[13] More profoundly, the references to spiritual, monastic purity and to eschatology (linked with the Second Coming) that appear throughout the frescoes have been related to the influence of Hesychasm, a mystical movement that emphasized intense spiritual contemplation as a means to perceiving the Divine light. Although Lazarev proposes that Theophanes and others left Byzantium because of the grip of dogmatic Hesychast influence in the final century of Paleologan rule, there is a general agreement that Hesychast spirituality, as a response to a time of profound uncertainty and social upheaval (appropriate to Russia as well as to Byzantium in the latter part of the fourteenth century) could not but effect the work of this supremely intelligent artist.[14]

The colorful, earthy vitality of the four-piered, trefoil-roofed structure in Novgorod is remarkably evident in the Church of Sts. Peter and Paul in Slavno (1367), the same district as the Transfiguration on Elijah Street.[15] With the removal of the stucco from the original walls, the texture and hue of fieldstone characteristic of the exterior of late fourteenth-century churches are now on view (see Plate 17). Other noteworthy examples include the Church of the Nativity of the Virgin at Mikhalitsa (1379; rebuilt in the seventeenth century and only partially restored), with portions of the south wall stripped to reveal inset limestone crosses.[16] Indeed, many Novgorod churches, including the Transfiguration on Elijah Street, display inset crosses, which were usually transferred from the graves of clerics buried adjacent to the church.

Still more modest in design is the Nativity of Christ at the Cemetery (1381–2), which contains poorly preserved fragments of an excellent set of frescoes (artist unknown), thus demonstrating the broad extent of artistic culture in Novgorod during the second half of the fourteenth century.[17] In these smaller churches, whose walls were not sufficiently thick to contain a stairway, the choir gallery was reached either by means of a corner staircase of stone (as in the Nativity of the Virgin at Mikhalitsa) or by steep wooden stairs (as in the Nativity at the Cemetery). Despite their restricted dimensions, the facades of a few of the Novgorod churches of this type were exuberantly decorated, such as the Church of St. John the Divine at Radokovitsi, on the Vitka (1383–4; see Plate 18).[18]

Novgorod Architecture in the Fifteenth Century

At the beginning of the fifteenth century, the traditional church plan that had developed over the preceding half century still retained its vigor. Indeed, the Church of Sts. Peter and Paul in Kozhevniki (1406) displays a number of stylistic refinements in comparison with the Church of the Transfiguration on Elijah Street, which it closely resembles. The decorative patterns are focused on the middle bay – particularly on the west and south facades – rather than distributed over the entire surface. The appearance of new ornamental motifs in brick, such as rosettes and a continuous band of eyebrow arches on the main drum, provides a textural contrast to the main surface of the walls, constructed of a deep-red, rough shellstone that was originally unstuccoed (see Plate 19). Brick is also used for the pilaster strips, which delineate the facade, and for the arcaded attached columns on the apse (Figure 81).

Every feature of the exterior of the Church of Sts. Peter and Paul, whether minor or of major structural significance such as the recessed portals, emphasizes the unity of form and plasticity of material character-

istic of Novgorodian architecture during the height of its revival in the late fourteenth and early fifteenth centuries. As was often the case, this church underwent substantial modifications in the sixteenth century, including the replacement of the roof and the creation of a second story by building a wooden floor on the level of the choir gallery.[19] After substantial damage in the Second World War, a meticulous restoration by Grigorii Shtender and L. M. Shuliak stripped the remaining stucco from the facades and recreated the trefoil cornice with its wooden shingled roof.

In comparison with Sts. Peter and Paul in Kozhevniki, other churches of the period – such as the Church of St. Vlasii, built the following year (1407) on Volosov Street – seem archaic in their treatment of the cuboid form (Figure 82). The church also illustrates the residual influence in the far north of pre-Christian beliefs in its dedication to St. Vlasii, whose popular role as protector of cattle was assumed from the pagan god Volos. The final extant Novgorod church that originally conformed to the cuboid, trefoil design is the Church of St. John the Compassionate

Figure 81. Church of Sts. Peter and Paul in Kozhevniki. Novgorod. 1406. Southeast view. (N 15–18)

Figure 82. Church of St. Vlasii. Novgorod. 1407. Northeast view. (N 12–36)

at Lake Miachino (1421–2). Although it was substantially modified in the seventeenth century, the church in its present form retains a number of recognizable structural and decorative features from an earlier period. Of particular interest are excavations that reveal the presence of a relatively large enclosed space attached to the north facade.[20] Its function could have been that of chapel or burial chamber, but it is unusual in having been the first known structure in Novgorod (indeed, in Russia) with one central column supporting the ceiling vaults.

The final stage of Novgorod's history as an independent political and cultural center is dominated by the figure of Evfimii (Euthymius), archbishop of Novgorod from 1429 to 1458. As the tenacious princes of Muscovy realized their campaign of aggrandizement through military, political, and religious means, Novgorod remained preoccupied with maintaining its European trade. The city's refusal to participate in the first major offensive of the Russians against the Mongols (in 1380, with Russian forces under the command of Prince Dmitrii of Moscow) signified its increasing isolation from the center of power in Russia. In resisting Moscow's domination in the fifteenth century,

Novgorod's oligarchy even considered allying itself with its Roman Catholic neighbors – Lithuania, in particular.

Archbishop Evfimii, however, chose architecture as a means of reaffirming Novgorod's glorious past in the face of an uncertain future. It was he who initiated the rebuilding in an earlier medieval style of a number of dilapidated churches, such as John the Baptist in Petriatin Court (see Figure 32) and the Church of the Dormition on the Trading Side. In addition, he commissioned eighteen new churches, of which only two are extant, including the Church of the Twelve Apostles by the Gully (1454–5), a simplified design with almost no exterior decoration.[21] The increased use of brick throughout these structures exemplifies a trend that would have considerable ramifications not only in the architecture of Novgorod, but also that of Moscow.

The greatest of Evfimii's architectural endeavors arose within the Novgorod citadel as a product of his determination to create an ensemble that would reflect both his own power and that of a revitalized Novgorod. The major components in this ensemble are the archbishop's reception chambers (the "Faceted Chambers," or *Granovitaia palata*, built in 1433 as part of the archbishop's palace) and the great free-standing bell tower that bears Evfimii's name (1443). Both structures were largely of brick, whose production and use were expanded in Novgorod during this period.[22] The increased adaptability of brick stimulated new architectural forms that are particularly evident in the large reception hall of the Faceted Chambers, with ribbed star vaults radiating from a single column in the center of the structure (Figure 83). Although the plan of the hall would appear to resemble the north extension of the Church of St. John the Compassionate, the design is more clearly related to refectory structures in central Europe; and indeed, the Novgorod chronicles note that Evfimii hired as construction masters "Germans from across the Sea."[23] The hall, incidentally, remains in excellent condition. Much less is known of the original appearance of the Evfimii bell tower, which served as an observation point within the archbishop's compound. The tower collapsed in 1671 and was rebuilt in the Muscovite style 2 years later (Figure 84).

After the death of archbishop Evfimii in 1458, the rebuilding of churches continued on a reduced scale. The 1464 version of the Church of the Convincing of the Apostle Thomas (also known as the Church of the Resurrection at Miachino) followed to a remarkable degree a style appropriate to the original form of the church, built in 1195–6 and completely dismantled in the fifteenth century. The rough stone walls with brick detailing provide an excellent example of traditional Novgorodian construction methods, yet the ornamental brick bands on the upper facade are typical of the fifteenth century (Figure 85). The builders' recreation of a horizontal row of *zakomary* reminds that the original church dated from the same period as the Transfiguration on the Nereditsa (see Plate 9).

A less archaic reconstruction occurred at the Church of St. Dmitrii (Figure 86), located near St. Theodore Stratilates. Originally constructed in 1381–3, the church was rebuilt in 1463 with modifications typical of the period, such as the insertion of a wooden floor to create a 2-storied structure. In a reflection of Novgorod's pragmatic business sense, the lower floor served as storage for valuable goods belonging to the neighborhood merchants or craftsmen. The new variant repeated the trefoil facade of its predecessor, but with a more elaborate use of decorative brick patterns (*begunets* and *porebrik*) at the top of the center bay.[24] The conservative design of this and other churches of the period reflects an entrophy in Nov-

Figure 84. Evfimii bell tower. Novgorod citadel. 1443; rebuilt in 1673. (N 1–6)

gorod's culture as the city's future seemed increasingly threatened by Moscow.

Novgorod After the Triumph of Moscow

Novgorod's position between two centers of power – Catholic Europe and Orthodox Muscovy – ultimately proved untenable, and as Muscovy rose, Novgorod was compelled to submit. As early as 1386, Dmitrii Donskoi laid siege to the city, which paid a large sum to him and accepted his nominal authority. In 1456 (2 years before the death of Evfimii), Grand Prince Vasilii II imposed by force a treaty that reduced the rights and territory of Novgorod. Subsequent resistance on the part of the city's governing elite was ineffectual and lacked support not only among the common citizens, but also among segments of the Church, fearing Catholic influence in an alliance with Lithuania. Indeed, resistance provided Ivan III with convenient cause for a campaign against Novgorod, in which he won a complete victory over the city's divided forces in 1471. The last futile attempts to se-

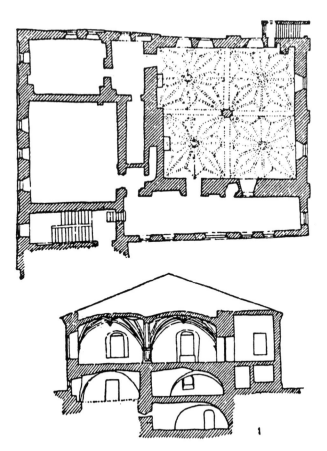

Figure 83. Chambers of the Archbishop's Court (*Granovitaia palata*). Novgorod citadel. 1433. Plan.

71

Figure 85. Church of the Verification of the Apostle Thomas (Resurrection at Miachino). Novgorod. 1195–6; rebuilt in 1464. East view. (N 5–7)

cure help from Lithuania led to Ivan III's occupation of Novgorod without a battle in 1478, and to the complete subordination of the city to Moscow.

As would be expected, the conquest affected construction in Novgorod, but in often paradoxical ways. Many of the city's assets were transferred to Moscow, and the Iaroslav Court, or commercial center, renamed the Sovereign's Court (Gosudarev dvor), came under the control of the Muscovite grand prince. At the same time, Ivan the III, seeing in Novgorod a valuable strategic outpost in the northwest of his expanding realm, initiated in 1484 one of the city's major construction projects: a brick fortification wall to replace the earthen and log ramparts of the detinets (Figure 87). Completed in 1490, the wall displays advances in Moscow's military engineering that were still more apparent in the rebuilding, with Italian guidance, of the Moscow Kremlin during the same period (see Chapter 5).

By the beginning of the sixteenth century, it became evident that Novgorod would retain much of its cultural and commercial vitality under the suzerainty of Moscow. As in the past, the building of new churches reflected the return to a stable, relatively prosperous climate; yet the patrons were now in many cases merchants from Moscow who had been resettled in Novgorod by Ivan as a means of ensuring control over the city's valuable trading network.[25] (Concomitantly, a large number of Novgorod merchants were resettled to Moscow or various Muscovite outposts.) Thus, one of the first major churches of the new era – the Church of Women Bearing Myrrh (1508–11) – was commissioned by the Muscovite merchant Ivan Syrkov for reasons that, in the Novgorod tradition, had much to do with commerce. The modest sanctuary, with two small chapels on a fourth floor at the west end, was situated over not one but two levels used as a storehouse for valuable goods (Figure 88). Otherwise the design of the structure showed little deviation from its predecessors in Novgorod. Even the distinctive appearance of its roof, with pitched gables and plank covering, is known to have occurred in other area churches of the period (Figure 89).[26]

A more complex example of the continuation of the Novgorod ecclesiomercantile architectural tradition is the Church of St. Prokopii, built by Dmitrii Syrkov in 1529 and situated next to his father's Church of the Women Bearing Myrrh. As in most such churches,

Figure 86. Church of St. Dmitrii. Novgorod. 1381–3; rebuilt in 1463. Southeast view. (N–15)

Figure 87. Novgorod Detinets (citadel). Brick walls constructed in 1484–90, with towers dating from the thirteenth to the seventeenth centuries. Kokui Tower (right background) constructed in 1691. (N 11–24)

wooden staircases, here originally attached to the north, west, and south facades, allowed access to a church situated above a warehouse with its separate entrance.[27]

Figure 88. Church of the Women Bearing Myrrh. Novgorod. 1508–11. Reconstruction by T. Gladenko of the original form. The lower levels were used for storage of valuable goods.

The foregoing evidence of continuity with earlier architecture in Novgorod should not imply that the construction of masonry churches continued without influence from Moscow. This influence was particularly evident in large monastery churches in the area surrounding Novgorod, most notably the Cathedral of the Transfiguration commissioned by Basil III in 1515 at the Khutyn Monastery.[28] Among its notable Muscovite features are the use of a triple apsidal structure, and the return to a pentacupolar design that had long been abandoned in Novgorod architecture, only to reappear in a number of sixteenth-century churches such as Sts. Boris and Gleb in Plotniki, built in 1536 by a group of merchants from Moscow and Novgorod (Figure 90). It has been argued that a major factor in the greater complexity of Novgorod church architecture in the 1530s was the strongly pro-Muscovite sentiments of archbishop Makarii (Macarius), who served in Novgorod from 1526 until his elevation to Metropolitan of all Russia in 1542.[29]

The development of more elaborate forms reached its apogee throughout Russia in the seventeenth century (see Chapter 6); but even in less imposing Novgorod churches, the new style brought forth a greater

Figure 89. Church of the Women Bearing Myrrh. Novgorod. East view. (N 3–7)

Figure 90. Church of Sts. Boris and Gleb in Plotniki. Novgorod. 1536. Southwest view. (N–18)

ornamentalism that paralleled that of Muscovy during the same period. The best extant examples are the Church of the Trinity at the Holy Ghost Monastery (1557; Figure 91) and the ensemble created in the middle of the sixteenth century by the rebuilding of two adjacent churches: the Archangel Michael and the Annunciation on the Trading Side (Figure 92).[30] The characteristic use of wooden structural elements and decorative details in masonry churches (roofing shingles, attached galleries, porches, stairs) was particularly extensive during this period. Yet, the architectural revival in Novgorod could not be sustained. In 1570, Ivan the Terrible's paranoid dementia led him to seize the city, slaughter a great number of its inhabitants, and ravage what was still one of Muscovy's leading commercial centers – all on groundless suspicions of sedition. Thereafter, Novgorod went into a steady decline that was only partially reversed in the latter part of the seventeenth century.

The Architecture of Pskov During the Fifteenth Century

Pskov, like its more prosperous neighbor and rival Novgorod, experienced a return to major construction activity in the fourteenth century. Although the city was located in the northern area not invaded by the Mongols, the preceding century had been unusually turbulent with incursions by the Lithuanians and Teutonic Knights and incessant feuding with its nominal overlord Novgorod (in 1348, Pskov formally rejected the authority of Novgorod). Pskov was, however, fortunate in having an exceptionally able military leader, Dovmont – a Lithuanian exile who arrived in Pskov in 1266, expelled the local prince, and successfully defended the city's interests until his death in 1299.[31] Adjacent to the Pskov citadel (or *krom*), Dovmont built a stone wall around an area that became known as Dovmont Town and contained at least four of the earliest stone churches (none extant) to be built by local masons in Pskov.[32]

During the fourteenth century, construction activity expanded considerably, both within the walled city and outlying regions. Although Pskov was one of the few medieval Russian cities to develop a style of secular masonry architecture, here, as elsewhere, the major resources were allotted to the construction of churches. The culminating point in the early architectural development of the city occurred with the rebuilding in 1365–7 of the Trinity Cathedral, located in the citadel. Although the cathedral was razed in 1682 and subsequently rebuilt, preserved sketches seem to indicate that it used corbeled arches to achieve a strong vertical effect in the manner of Smolensk and Chernigov.[33]

Most of Pskov's churches, however, were of modest dimensions and often designed, as in Novgorod,

Figure 91. Church of the Trinity at the Holy Ghost Monastery. 1557. Novgorod. Southwest view. (N 5–4)

with a lower level or basement used for storage by merchants and guild associations. The patrons included monasteries, guilds, and neighborhood districts (the so-called *kontsy*) around which the city was organized. The approach to church building in Pskov was eminently practical, with the use of hired labor under strict contractual obligations for the project. The basic material was a local flagstone, with plinthos brick, and to protect the relatively soft surface, the walls were covered with a thin layer of stucco that revealed the underlying texture.[34]

Of twenty-two churches dating from the first half of the fifteenth century, only one is still standing: the Church of St. Basil the Great on the Hillock (1413). Built on the site of a fourteenth-century church of the same name, St. Basil's underwent extensive modification in the seventeenth century; but its basic design illustrates the model for church architecture in Pskov during the next two centuries (Figure 93). The simple four-piered plan, augmented by surrounding galleries, chapels, and a bell gable over the west facade, is dominated by a single cupola and drum, raised over the vaulting by a system of corbeled arches (the builders of Pskov's churches were unusually inventive in the use of the corbeled arch). The primary decoration – on the cupola drum and the apses – consists of ornamental bands fashioned from blocks of limestone (Figure 94). Archaeological evidence suggests that the original roof followed the vaulting contours as outlined by zakomary.[35]

Very few of the some forty churches built in Pskov during the fifteenth century are extant, but they provide evidence of certain new developments, such as the proliferation of chapels and galleries around

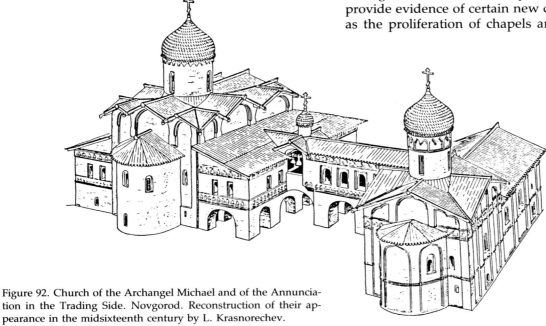

Figure 92. Church of the Archangel Michael and of the Annunciation in the Trading Side. Novgorod. Reconstruction of their appearance in the midsixteenth century by L. Krasnorechev.

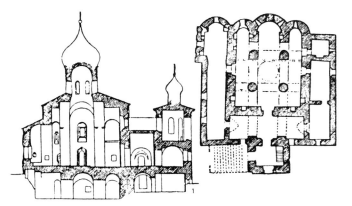

Figure 93. Church of St. Basil the Great on the Hillock. Pskov. 1413, with modifications in the seventeenth and nineteenth centuries. Longitudinal section and plan by K. Firsov.

Figure 94. Church of St. Basil on the Hillock. Pskov. South facade. (P–2)

the main cuboid structure. Perhaps the most striking change – one peculiar to Pskov – was a new roof design, introduced as wood planks became the preferred roofing material. This led to a multiplanar covering divided into segments whose level corresponded to the vaulting (the corner segments, e.g., were lower than the central gable).[36] Novgorod, by contrast, evolved a trefoil facade and roofline for a similar structure. Ultimately, the complex sixteen-slope roofs proved impractical and they yielded toward the end to the century to simpler forms, whereas those that remained were rebuilt. One such example of the transition is the Church of Sts. Kozma and Demian by the Bridge, designed with a sixteen-slope roof in 1462 and rebuilt in 1507 with a eight-slope roof after an explosion of gunpowder stored

in one of its chapels damaged much of the structure (Figures 95 and 96).[37]

Among the remaining fifteenth-century churches, St. George on the Slope (1494) has been considerably altered by later rebuildings, yet its basic structure remains as an excellent example of parish church design in Pskov in the late fifteenth and sixteenth centuries (see Plate 20). Considerably larger and more complex is the Church of the Epiphany across the Pskov River (1496), now devoid of the east chapels that comple-

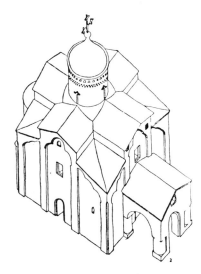

Figure 95. Church of Sts. Kozma and Demian by the Bridge. Pskov. Reconstruction of form in 1462 by Iu. Spegalskii.

Figure 96. Church of Sts. Kozma and Demian by the Bridge. Pskov. Northwest view. (P–5)

Figure 97. Church of the Epiphany across the Pskov. Pskov. 1496.
Southwest view. (P–6)

mented this symmetrically planned structure (Figure 97).[38] The symmetry is, however, resolutely broken at the west facade by a great belfry, whose open gables and massive pillars make it one of the most impressive examples of this distinctive Pskovian form. A free-standing belfry of similar porportions was also built for the Church of the Dormition at the Ferry (1521). The culminating development of the Pskov belfry, however, is to be found some 15 kilometers beyond the city, at the Pskov Monastery of the Caves, where the sixteenth- and seventeenth-century *zvonnitsa* has been preserved in working order and still rings forth majestically (see Plate 21).[39]

The more typical integration of belfry and church in Pskov is exemplified by the Church of St. Nicholas on the Dry Spot, originally constructed in 1371 and rebuilt in 1535–7. At the time of its completion, it was the city's second largest church, after the Trinity Cathedral – a fact now obscured by the accretion of soil to a height of almost 2 meters above the original

ground level. A partial restoration of the structure has returned the belfry to its original position above the north facade, where it is particularly effective in mediating the transition from the miniature northeast chapel to the great wood-shingled onion dome above the central structure (Figure 98).[40] A similar design applied to the early sixteenth-century Church of St. Anastasia of the Smiths, subsequently modified (Figure 99).

The simplest but in a sense the most remarkable demonstration of tectonic creativity in Pskov parish architecture is the Church of the Nativity and the Intercession of the Virgin, tentatively dated to the sixteenth century (see Plate 22). The design consists of two churches attached along a common central wall and symmetrical in articulation. The pitch of the roof and the bell gable, and the articulation of the entire structure – virtually without ornament – conveys a sense of harmony that transcends cultural traditions and historicist concepts of architectural style. But in

Figure 98. Church of St. Nicholas on the Dry Spot. Pskov. 1371; rebuilt 1535–7. Northeast view. (P–3)

a more specific, historical context, this ability of Pskov's builders to integrate attached structures into a unified ensemble proved one of the most important of their contributions to the development of sixteenth-century architecture in Moscow.

Indeed, from the late fourteenth through the middle of the sixteenth century, artists and architects from both Novgorod and Pskov contributed greatly to the development of new artistic forms during the rise of a centralized Russian state dominated by Moscow. Just as the departure of Theophanes the Greek for Moscow in the 1390s signaled the beginning of the great era of Muscovite icon painting, so the increasing presence of Pskov's highly trained masons in Muscovy reflected an architectural era that would combine Russian and foreign elements in an unprecedented manner.

Although at the beginning of the sixteenth century, Pskov, like Novgorod, had surrendered its ancient freedoms to Moscow, the smaller, more remote city

was spared the punitive expeditions inflicted upon Novgorod. Pskov's acceptance of Muscovite rule, in 1510, opened a new period in its history – one firmly linked to the fortunes of Moscow itself. In 1511, Philotheus, a monk from Pskov's Eleazar Monastery, proclaimed Moscow the "Third Rome" in an epistle to Grand Prince Vasilii III: "Two Romes have fallen [Rome and Constantinople], a third [Moscow] stands, a fourth there shall not be."[41] However varied its interpretations, Philotheus's statement suggests that important segments of the clergy of Novgorod and Pskov may well have favored Moscow's authority as a means of preserving the Orthodox faith and combatting heretical tendencies, be they local or imported through these two centers of democracy and foreign trade in Russia. Henceforth, Pskov was to serve as a defensive outpost on Muscovy's western march.

Figure 99. Church of St. Anastasia of the Smiths. Pskov. Sixteenth century. Northeast view. (P–4)

Joseph-Volokolamsk Monastery. Cathedral of the Dormition. Interior completed in 1696. East view, with iconostasis. (MR 20–34)

PART II

The Muscovite Period

CHAPTER 5

Moscow: Architectural Beginnings

And that church was exceedingly wondrous in its majesty and height, illumination and resonance and extent, such as had not before been in Rus, except for the Vladimir church; and having stepped back a little, anyone would see it as if [it were of] one stone. . . .

– Moscow Chronicle, on the Dormition Cathedral in the Kremlin, 1479

"Come to me, brother, in Moscow." Iurii Dolgorukii's laconic invitation to his ally Prince Sviatoslav of Chernigov in 1147 is the earliest historical reference to a small outpost on the banks of the Moscow River, a part of the Vladimir-Suzdal principality. 1147 is now officially taken as the year of the city's founding; but, as the invitation implies, some form of settlement existed before then – probably a collection of log structures, among which would have been a compound sufficiently large to accommodate a "hearty feast" celebrating their alliance.[1] However modest the town's appearance at the time, its position at a strategic juncture of trade routes and political boundaries was recognized by Iurii Dolgorukii, who in the course of his princely wars shifted the center of power in pre-Mongol Russia from Kiev to his domains in Suzdalia.

In 1156, on high ground at the confluence of the Neglinnaia and Moscow rivers, Iurii built a wooden fortification placed on an earthen rampart that protected a cluster of workshops and trading rows. Over the following eight centuries very little has changed in this general arrangement: The Kremlin today occupies the site of Iurii's original fortification and the city's largest department store (formerly the Upper Trading Rows) stands slightly to the north of the oldest trading center. The infrequent references to Moscow in the early chronicles note that the town was burned in 1176 during a raid by a neighboring prince, was fought over by the sons of Vsevolod III (of Vladimir) in the 1210s, and was overrun in January 1238 by the Mongol armies of Batu on their way to Vladimir.

Despite the devastation, the town quickly rebuilt and, indeed, grew with the influx of refugees from other, more exposed territories. For the century following the Mongol invasion, Moscow – afforded some protection from Tatar raids by a barrier of forests and rivers – gradually increased its territory by a policy of collaboration with the Horde and the skillful acquisition of neighboring real estate through marriage, purchase, and inheritance. The rise was by no means steady, and submission to Mongol overlordship was an absolute precondition to local autonomy; Prince Daniil Aleksandrovich (1261–1303), who inherited the city from his father Alexander Nevskii, ruled in Moscow from 1283 until 1303 with the *iarlyk*, or Mongol seal of authority. During the reign of Daniil, the city made its first clear gains in the move toward primacy in central Russia.[2]

After the death of Daniil, there occurred a prolonged fractious interlude in which Russian princes, aided by hired Tatar forces, fought over precedence and control of the central Russian heartland.[3] It soon became apparent that the main contenders would be the cities of Moscow and Tver (to the northwest of Moscow), and the ensuing diplomatic maneuvering involved not only the Golden Horde, which wished to maintain a rough parity among the competing forces, but also the hierarchy of the Russian Orthodox Church, whose metropolitanate had moved from Kiev to Vladimir in 1300. Moscow's success in this struggle derived from several sources, but one of the most significant was the presence of a singularly cunning and unscrupulous leader, Ivan I (son of Daniil), who assumed power in Moscow in 1325.

Ivan quickly grasped the strategy of using an alien

military force for internal political purposes – and quickly applied it. In 1327, he participated in the Mongol suppression of an uprising provoked by Mongol "representatives" in Tver; for his services, he was invested with the *iarlyk* and title of grand prince by Khan Uzbek in 1331, and given the authority to collect taxes for the Horde.[4] This position (providing his nickname, Kalita: "Moneybags") worked considerably to the advantage of Moscow, where Ivan continued to reside rather than in Vladimir, the traditional seat of the Russian grand prince. Of equal importance to the prestige of the young city-state was the favor of the church, liberally bestowed upon Moscow by Metropolitan Peter, who in 1325 made the city his unoffical residence.

This move, carefully cultivated by Ivan, was fraught with significance not only for the political and religious status of Moscow (the two could hardly be separated), but also for its architectural development; for in 1326, Ivan, with the participation of Peter, lay the foundation for what may have been the first stone church in the Moscow Kremlin, the Cathedral of the Dormition.[5] Later that year Peter was buried in the cathedral walls in a tomb that he had himself prepared, thus endowing the site with added religious significance when Peter as canonized in 1339. The cathedral's dedication to the Feast of the Dormition also served as a symbol of the continuity between Vladimir, the political center of pre-Mongol Russia, and its inheritor, Moscow. Little is known of the appearance of this or the other early limestone churches in the Kremlin, although in their plan, they can be compared with the Cathedral of St. George in Iurev-Polskoi (see Figure 74).[6] They undoubtedly represented an attempt, however modest, to revive the tradition of Vladimir architecture, yet it would be some time before Moscow possessed the resources or the motive to raise a monument comparable to the Vladimir cathedrals.

The union of interests between Moscow and the Orthodox Church continued under Peter's successors, Feognost and Aleksei, who perceived in Moscow a bulwark against possible alliances of Russian princes with western, Catholic powers, and whose grand princes had successfully maintained favor – and a measure of stability – in their relations with the Mongols.[7] The results of Kalita's realpolitik came to bear during the reign of his grandson Dmitrii Donskoi ("of the Don"), who ruled as grand prince of Moscow between 1359 and 1389, and who led the combined forces of several Russian principalities to major victories over the fragmenting Horde in 1378 and 1380 (at Kulikovo Pole, near the Don River). Dmitrii also continued the work of his predecessors in expanding Moscow's political dominance (Tver submitted to Muscovite power in 1375) and in strengthening the city's defenses. In 1367, the Kremlin walls, of oak logs on an earthen rampart, were replaced with limestone and extended to roughly their present length (2 kilometers), and a number of fortress-monasteries were established to protect the city's southern and northern approaches.[8]

The increasingly militant Orthodox Church, which had long counseled acceptance of the authority of the khan in Sarai, played a major role in rallying Russian forces around the banner of Moscow in a crusade against the Horde. Shortly before the battle at Kulikovo Pole, Dmitrii was exhorted by Sergius of Radonezh, abbot of the Holy Trinity Monastery (see what follows) and the most repected leader of the Russian Church, to "concern himself with the flock entrusted to him by God and to go against the infidels."[9] Dmitrii's victory was not, however, decisive in any immediate sense. In 1382, another Mongol army, led by Tokhtamysh, besieged Moscow in Dmitrii's absence, took the Kremlin by ruse, burned and looted the city, and left with a great number of captives. Although Tokhtamysh was later routed by a rival Mongol horde led by Tamerlane (who ravaged the Golden Horde's capital, Old Sarai, on the Volga), Moscow continued to pay tribute to the Horde for several decades, and its lands continued to suffer devastating raids. Even without these incursions, Moscow was built almost entirely of wood and therefore prey to fires that periodically destroyed large parts of the city.

Early Fifteenth-Century Stone Churches

By the end of the fourteenth century, the first stone churches in the Kremlin formed a modest ensemble that would later be entirely rebuilt. For what is probably the earliest surviving example of the revival of masonry architecture in the Moscow area, one must go to the small village of Kamenskoe, some 80 kilometers to the west of Moscow. Dedicated to St. Nicholas and presumed to date from the latter half of the fourteenth century, this small limestone church was located on the lands of Prince Iurii of Zvenigorod, who commissioned other churches in a similar but more refined design. The Kamenskoe church has been only partially restored (Figure 100), but the cornice may have originally have culminated in decorative point *zakomary*. On the interior, the piers were not free-standing but attached to the interior corners – a feature of Balkan architecture that again raises the

Plate 1. Ensemble of the Near and Distant Caves, Monastery of the Caves, Kiev. Left foreground: Church of the Elevation of the Cross, 1700. Background: Church of the Nativity of the Virgin, 1696; the bell tower of the Distant Caves, 1754–61, architect: Ivan Grigorovich-Barskii.

Plate 2. Cathedral of the Transfiguration of the Savior. Chernigov. C. 1034–50s. Southeast view, apsidal structure.

Plate 3. Church of St. Cyril, Monastery of St. Cyril. Kiev. Midtwelfth century, with seventeenth- and eighteenth-century alterations. West facade.

Plate 4. Cathedral of Sts. Boris and Gleb. Chernigov. Midtwelfth century(?). Southeast view.

Plate 5. Church of St. Paraskeva-Piatnitsa. Chernigov. Late twelfth–early thirteenth century. Southeast view.

Plate 6. Cathedral of St. Sophia. Novgorod. 1045–52. East facade.

Plate 7. Cathedral of St. George, Iurev Monastery. Novgorod. 1119–30. South facade.

Plate 8. Cathedral of St. George, Iurev Monastery. Interior, central drum and crossing, with nineteenth-century paintings.

Plate 9. Church of the Transfiguration of the Savior on the Nereditsa. Near Novgorod. 1198. East facade.

Plate 10. Church of the Annunciation at Miachino. Novgorod. 1179. Frescoes in north apse.

Plate 11. Church of the Intercession on the Nerl. Near Bogoliubovo. 1165. Southwest view.

Plate 12. Cathedral of the Dormition. Vladimir. 1158–60; enlarged in 1185–9. Northeast view.

Plate 13. Cathedral of St. Dmitrii. Vladimir. 1193–7. West facade.

Plate 14. Cathedral of the Nativity of the Virgin. Suzdal. 1222–5; upper tier rebuilt (in brick) in 1528. Northwest view, with seventeenth-century bell tower and archbishop's palace (on right).

Plate 15. Cathedral of the Nativity of the Virgin. Suzdal. East view.

Plate 16. Church of the Transfiguration of the Savior on Elijah Street. Novgorod. 1374.

Figure 100. Church of St. Nicholas. Kamenskoe. Late fourteenth century. Northeast view. (MR 1–10)

The founding of what was subsequently known as the Savvino-Storozhevskii Monastery (after its location on Storozhi, or "Lookout," Hill) was complemented by Iurii's efforts to develop the center of his town. At some point around the turn of the fifteenth century, he commissioned two stone cathedrals: the Dormition, which served as the court church within the city's fortress, and the Nativity of the Virgin, located in the monastery.[12] Both churches follow the plan of their predecessors at Vladimir and Bogoliubovo, with a central cube containing four piers, which support a single drum and cupola, and with three apses extending from the sanctuary's eastern wall. Each facade is divided into three parts by attached columns, and as in the Vladimir churches, the portals are framed by perspective arches. These similarities are more readily perceived in the unobstructed central form of the Dormition Cathedral (Figures 101 and 102).

Yet, in comparison with the limestone churches of pre-Mongol Vladimir, Iurii's cathedrals display a simplified notion of design, in which the complex relation of structure and ornament characteristic of Vladimir is replaced by a few insistently repeated decorative

persistent question of Serbian influence in Russian architecture during the century before the collapse of Byzantium.[10] Despite the extreme simplicity of the design, the surviving perspective portals and the plinth molding refer to the traditions of stonework in the Vladimir area.

More impressive, however, are the cathedrals of Zvenigorod, some 60 kilometers to the west of Moscow. Although its early history is obscure, the town probably existed as an outpost of one of the western principalities (Chernigov, most likely) during the twelfth century.[11] By the fourteenth century, written records place Zvenigorod within the domains of Moscow's princes, and in 1389, Dmitrii Donskoi bequeathed the town to his fifteen-year-old son Iurii. As had his father, Iurii maintained close relations with the Holy Trinity Monastery, founded by Sergius and soon the preeminent religious center of Muscovy. By the end of the fourteenth century, Iurii had amassed the resources to endow a monastery of his own in Zvenigorod, under the spiritual direction of the monk Savva, who had served as prior of the Trinity Monastery for 6 years after the death of Sergius in 1392.

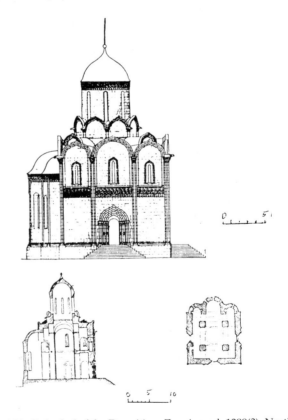

Figure 101. Cathedral of the Dormition. Zvenigorod. 1399(?). North elevation, longitudinal section, and plan by B. Ognev.

85

Figure 102. Cathedral of the Dormition. Zvenigorod. Northeast view. (ZV 1–17)

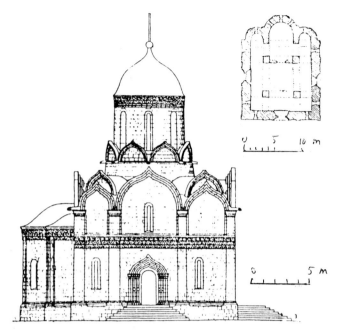

Figure 103. Cathedral of the Nativity of the Virgin, Savva-Storozhevskii Monastery. Zvenigorod. 1405(?). North elevation and plan by V. Kaulbars.

motifs, such as the profusion of ogival arches between the cornice and the cupola drum of the Nativity Cathedral (see Plate 23). The Cathedral of the Dormition, whose pointed arches were removed in a rebuilding of the roof, bears a greater resemblance to the churches of Andrei Bogoliubskii, with its emphasis on verticality (enhanced by a slight tapering of the walls), than does the Nativity Cathedral, which has a lower silhouette (Figure 103).

But though the debt to Vladimir-Suzdal is obvious – and to be expected – the differences in Zvenigorod are several and in some cases prefigure a distinctly Muscovite ornamental style that emerged in the sixteenth and seventeenth centuries. The rounded arches and *zakomary* of Vladimir have been replaced by pointed forms. The exterior division of the walls no longer corresponds to the interior arrangement of pier and vault.[13] And on the facades, the ornamental frieze that in Vladimir had served to demarcate the thicker, lower part of the wall from its upper panels now assumes an inverted form unrelated to the struc-

ture of the wall: The highest of the three strips composing the band overhangs the other two in what is assumed to be a means of protecting the intricate limestone carving from moisture erosion. (In the Vladimir churches, this purpose was served by the blind arcading of the facade frieze.) The greatest difference is the nature of the motifs composing the strips; instead of the profusion of mythological and biblical subjects – displayed with instructive as well as decorative intent on the facades of the Vladimir churches – the ornamental strips at Zvenigorod consist of a foliate pattern repeated without variation for the length of the band.[14]

Although the destruction of Muscovy's earliest churches makes it impossible to trace the evolution of a Muscovite style derived from Vladimir, the cathedrals at Zvenigorod provide evidence of a departure from the close integration of structure and decoration, a greater freedom in the relation between interior and exterior design, and a heavier reliance on ornamental effects – such as *kokoshniki* (pointed arched gables) – with no structural purpose. The tendency to ornamentalism was to assume many forms in the development of Muscovite architecture, some trivial and others indicative of a highly imaginative, if idiosyncratic, genius. The full expression of this tendency would occur only in the sixteenth century, when brick had replaced stone as the primary building material.

Yet for most of the fifteenth century, the Zvenigorod cathedrals provided a pattern for Muscovy's stone churches, such as the Trinity Cathedral at the Holy Trinity Monastery (*lavra*), to the northeast of Moscow.[15] The cathedral was jointly endowed in 1422 by Prince Iurii of Zvenigorod and Grand Prince Vasilii I to provide an imposing monument to Sergius of Radonezh (1319?–92), founder of the monastery and one of the inspiring forces in the development of Russian monastic communities. A log chapel had been built over the grave of Sergius almost immediately after his death, and in 1412, a larger log church was consecrated on the site after the burning of the monastery during a large-scale Tatar raid in 1408. In 1422, the year of Sergius's canonization, the latter church was replaced by the one now in existence. The rebuilding of the monastery after 1408 and the expeditious manner in which the community constructed and to build the stone cathedral were in both cases due to the tireless efforts of Abbot Nikon, a devoted disciple of Sergius.[16]

In comparison with the Zvenigorod churches, the Trinity Cathedral is retrogressive: its decoration is more austere (a repetition of the carved ornamental strips along the upper facade and drum), and the relation between the interior and the design of the facade is awkward. The substantial shift of the main crossing and cupola toward the east coexists with the rigidly symmetrical division of the side facades with pilasters (Figure 104), and thus violates the usual emphasis on centrality – or an illusion of centrality – characteristic of the structure of the single-cupola Russian church.[17] The off-center portal of the north facade further reveals the disjuncture between interior and exterior. Only from the east and west perspectives is the structural balance evident, emphasized by the buttressing inward lean of the walls and the cupola drum (Figure 105). Curiously, this balance and the resulting focus on verticality make it seem that the structure is considerably longer than its width. Despite the peculiarities of its design, the Trinity Cathedral at the time of its construction would have presented a striking contrast to the log construction of the monastery complex and its surrounding low wall.

The site, and the saint that it commemorated, also served as an inspiration for one of the greatest Russian painters, Andrei Rublev, who in his youth had been a monk at the Lavra. Although the precise date is unknown, Rublev had already painted what is now regarded as medieval Russia's most famous icon, the

Old Testament Trinity, for the church dedicated to Sergius. Around 1425–6, Rublev and Daniil Chornyi returned to the monastery from Moscow at the urging of Abbot Nikon to paint the cathedral frescoes, which were completed shortly before Nikon's death in 1427 and remained in the church for two centuries. Poorly preserved – a condition no doubt hastened by the prolonged seige of the monastery by the Poles at the beginning of the seventeenth century – the frescoes were replaced in 1635.[18]

In 1427, Rublev and Chornyi, with various assistants, also painted the cathedral iconostasis, into which Rublev's earlier Trinity icon was placed.[19] Although the development of the high icon screen had already begun in Russia by the end of the fourteenth century (with the powerful stimulus of the icons of Theophanes the Greek), the Trinity Cathedral iconostasis appears to have been the first example that extended, without interruption, across the entire width of the main structure and concealed the east piers as well as the apsidal structure from the center of the church.[20] Indeed, the shift of the cupola and drum to the east in the Trinity Cathedral may have been an experiment in illuminating the iconostasis. Consequently, at this formative stage in Muscovite architecture, the evolution of the iconostasis intro-

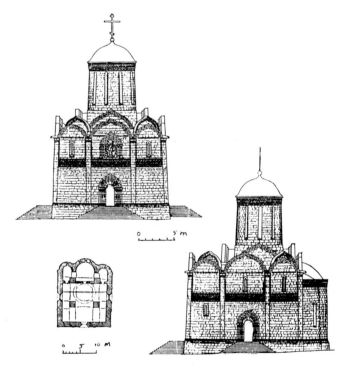

Figure 104. Cathedral of the Trinity, Trinity-Sergius Monastery. Zagorsk. 1422. West and south elevations and plan by V. Baldin.

Figure 105. Cathedral of the Trinity, Trinity-Sergius Monastery. Zagorsk. East view, with Nikon Chapel (1548). (Z 4–2)

cated in the center of monastery ensembles. The ascent of pointed *zakomary* and decorative *kokoshniki,* culminating in a high drum and cupola over the center of the structure, creates a vertical thrust that is reinforced by a lowering of the corner vaults. It has been suggested that this design, with an octagon of *kokoshniki* serving as a visual transition from the central cube to the drum, is a prototype for Moscow's tower churches of the sixteenth century.[21] Although other sources could be proposed, there is little doubt that the Savior Cathedral prefigures much in later Moscow architecture – and in a much more specific manner than do the Zvenigorod churches.

But though the cathedral at Andronikov Monastery represents a new variation on the tradition of Vladimir's limestone churches, it, like the early monuments at Zvenigorod and Trinity Monastery, represents a limited attempt to reaffirm an earlier and

duced a new visual, if not structural, principle to the design of the interior of the Russian church, and brought with it fundamental changes in the perception of interior space.

Centrality and symmetry are emphatically reaffirmed, however, at the Cathedral of the Transfiguration of the Savior, located within the Savior-Andronikov Monastery (named for its first prior, Andronik, another of the disciples of St. Sergius). The church is considered the earliest preserved monument in the city, although the date of its construction is unattested. At some point between 1410 and 1427 – or perhaps earlier – the church was apparently endowed by the Ermolins, among the first in a distinguished line of Muscovite merchant-patrons of architecture. The structure is by far the most ornamental to be found in Muscovy at that time (Figure 106); and it displays the strong vertical development common since the eleventh century to churches lo-

Figure 106. Cathedral of the Transfiguration of the Savior, Savior-Andronikov Monastery. Moscow. 1410–1427(?). Southeast view. (M 109–2)

more distinguished style. None achieves the subtlety of design and construction demonstrated at Vladimir and Bogoliubovo. In their ornamentalism, the closest affinity is with the Cathedral of St. George in Iurev-Polskoi. Indeed, in the history of medieval Russian culture, these churches are of less importance for their design than for the fact that Andrei Rublev participated in the decoration (frescoes and icons) of at least three of them. Indeed, some redactions of the vita of St. Sergius note that Andrei Rublev participated in the building, as well as the fresco painting, of the Transfiguration Cathedral at Andronikov Monastery.[22]

The construction of small cross-inscribed churches with a single cupola continued in Moscow during the late fifteenth and early sixteenth centuries, at a time when the resources and technical abilities to create larger structures had greatly expanded. Apart from their traditional plan, the churches of this later group share certain innovative features. Athough they were built on a limestone base and had carved stone details such as recessed portal arches, their walls were of brick. The production and use of brick as a major structural element apparently had begun in the Moscow area after the middle of the fifteenth century, possibly for the reconstruction of one of the Kremlin towers.[23] Yet the broader possibilities of material – far more versatile than limestone – were introduced to Moscow not only by the Italians who rebuilt the Kremlin and transformed Russian architecture in the fifteenth and sixteenth centuries, but also by Russian masters, presumably from Novgorod. Furthermore, it is known that in 1474, builders from Pskov were brought by Ivan III to Moscow, where they skillfully adapted their practice of building in stone slabs to the design of brick churches that conform to the basic plan described before. Contemporary accounts also note that the masters from Pskov had worked among the "Germans" – most likely in the Baltic area – and thus were particularly well-qualified specialists.[24]

Of particular note in this group is the Church of the Holy Spirit, built in 1476 on a site directly to the east of the Trinity Cathedral at the Trinity-Sergius Monastery. The unusual distinction of this cuboid, cross-inscribed structure is its polygonal belfry, placed above the central crossing and beneath the cupola drum (Figure 107). This design has no clear prototype, and yet the squat, massive columns that form the belfry are clearly derived from the bell gables of Pskov, which in other respects are formed in an entirely different manner. It should be noted that the belfry also served as a watchtower (essential in those uncertain times), and was apparently reached by a passageway from an adjacent wooden structure (there is no evidence of a staircase within the church or against its exterior).[25] Pragmatism aside, the design of the structure provides striking evidence of the Muscovite emphasis on centrality that would lead to far more ambitious tower churches in the next century.

The innovative design of the church also included the use of ceramic tiles, glazed and unglazed, to create a decorative frieze along the upper part of the facades and the drum. Ornamental strips in stone and brick had long appeared in the churches of Suzdalia and Novgorod as well as Pskov, but the polychromatic tiles – whose leaf pattern derives from the limestone decorative strip on the Trinity Cathedral (see Figure 105) – provide a new example of the Muscovite fondness for boldly stated architectural ornament. At the same time, the whitewashed brick facade and the precision of the ornamental ceramic work seem deliberate echoes of the pre-Mongol era of Suzdalian limestone churches.[26]

The subsequent work of the Pskov builders in Moscow includes two churches within the Kremlin itself. The first of these, the Deposition of the Robe (dedicated to the holiday commemorating the taking of the Virgin's robe from Palestine to Constantinople in the fifth century), was built in 1484–5 for Metropolitan Gerontii.[27] Its decoration resembles that of the Church of the Holy Spirit, particularly in the ornamental terracotta band on the brick facade, yet the proportions and the scale are altogether more modest than those of the prototype (Figure 108). The influence of the Pskovian tradition is more evident in the decorative brickwork on the drum, and in the design of the three apses, low and richly ornamented with attached columns and a decorative frieze. In structural terms, however, the Church of the Deposition is possibly a simplified variant of the cathedral at the Savior-Andronikov Monastery.[28]

In contrast to the simplicty of the Deposition Church, the Annunciation Cathedral (1484–9) has been so extensively modified that the late fifteenth-century work seems hidden within later chapels and a proliferation of cupolas (see Plate 24). As the court church of Moscow's grand prince, the earliest structure, a small cross-inscribed limestone church, was erected in the latter part of the fourteenth century, perhaps in the 1360s. Here again, a modest church proved a milestone in Russian art history: In 1405, Theophanes the Greek, Andrei Rublev, and Prokhor of Gorodets painted frescoes as well as icons for an iconostasis that is considered the earliest known example of a tall icon screen.[29] The extant, restored icons are now considered national treasures; the frescoes

Figure 107. Church of the Holy Spirit, Trinity-Sergius Monastery. Zagorsk. 1476. West facade. (Y 5–30)

Figure 108. Church of the Deposition of the Robe, Kremlin. 1484–5. Southeast view. (M 107–13)

were, of course, destroyed when the dilapidated church was razed for rebuilding in 1484.

The Pskov builders used the old limestone foundation, strengthened and enlarged in 1416, as the basis for their brick church, which in its orginal appearance closely resembled the Church of the Holy Spirit – without the belfry.[30] A blind arcade of attached columns on the three apses and the side facades suggests the link with ancient Vladimir, but otherwise the building represented a melding of Pskovian and Muscovite decorative and structural motifs. Because the eastern (apsidal) part of the cathedral faced the evolving central space of the Kremlin – Cathedral Square – the builders added two cupolas, over the northeast and southeast corner bays. Seriously damaged in the great Moscow fire of 1547, the building was remodeled in the 1560–70s, at which time four chapels were added at the corners above the gallery that surrounded the main structure (Figure 109). An additional two cupolas were placed over the west bays, and all nine cupolas, as well as the roof, were covered with gilded copper (Figure 110).

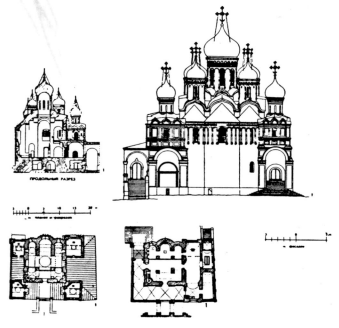

Figure 109. Cathedral of the Annunciation, Moscow Kremlin. 1484–9. Plan by V. Suslov.

Figure 110. Cathedral of the Annunciation, Moscow Kremlin. Northeast view. (M 150–21)

Although overshadowed by far larger structures, the forms developed by the Pskov builders proved viable and adaptable well into the sixteenth century. The small limestone Church of St. Trifon in Naprudnyi, built in the 1490s on one of the estates of Ivan III, is of particular interest for its use of the Pskovian technique of vault design without the use of interior piers (Figure 111), in which the drum is supported on a combination of groin and domical vaults (*kreshchatyi svod*). On the exterior, the debt to Pskov is clearly stated in the small gabled belfry spanning the southwest corner (Figure 112). Of similar design and size is the Church of the Conception of St. Anne on the Corner, probably built in the 1530s and located in Kitai-gorod, the old trading district.[31] The walls are of limestone to the level of the vaulting arches, demarcated by a decorative strip (*begunets*) in the Pskov style (Figure 113). Small brick is used for the upper part of the structure, including the trefoil gables, which provide an effective transition for the elevated drum beneath the main cupola. As at St. Trifon, there are no interior piers.

A more complex variation on the same theme is the Cathedral of the Nativity of the Virgin at the Nativity

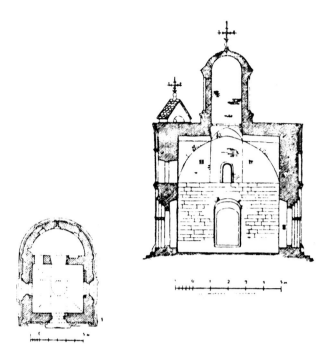

Figure 111. Church of St. Trifon in Naprudnyi. Moscow. 1490s. Section and plan by L. David.

Figure 112. Church of St. Trifon in Naprudnyi. Moscow. South facade. (M 7–12)

(Rozhdestvenskii) Convent. Probably built between 1500–5, the church has been much disfigured by subsequent additions (particularly in the nineteenth century), and has been only partially restored.[32] Although built of brick, not limestone, its extant core bears a close resemblance to the Andronikov monastery cathedral. In both cases, lowered corner vaults provide a visual base for a pyramidal ascent of kokoshniki leading to the elevated drum and cupola (Figure 114). The vertical thrust of the structure is clearly defined on the interior, where corbeled arches join the four piers whose spring arches support the drum (Figure 115). The Nativity Cathedral provides yet another example of the inexorable structural logic with which church design in Moscow was moving toward a new, and unprecedented, expression of verticality in architecture. Its culmination, however, did not come from the modest, superbly constructed churches surveyed before, but from an entirely different source.

Rebuilding the Kremlin: The Cathedral of the Dormition

The arrival of the first Italian architects in Moscow in 1475 profoundly changed the building techniques that had been laboriously accumulated in Muscovy over the past century. Although Russian architecture remained far from integration into the rapidly progressing art of building during the Renaissance, the architects of the quattrocento nonetheless endowed Moscow with the tools by which to pursue its own idiosyncratic destiny – as it had every intention of doing. Indeed, it can be said that from 1475 until the end of the sixteenth century, architecture became the primary mode of expression for Muscovite culture.

To comprehend this radical shift, one must return to the political events surrounding the rise of Muscovy. The process of consolidating the central Russian lands around Moscow, aided by the disintegration of the Golden Horde, continued fitfully during the reign of Vasilii I (1389–1425), although Moscow's tenuous hold on power was tested by severe Tatar raids in 1408 and 1410. This modest recovery, reflected in the early fifteenth-century stone churches described before, was interrupted at the end of the 1420s by a protracted struggle between the followers of Vasilii's son, Vasilii II – who was 10 years old at the beginning of his reign (1425–62) – and Prince Iurii of Zvenigorod, whose power base was in the rich lands of Galich to the north of Iaroslavl. As the second son of Dmitrii Donskoi, Iurii had assumed according to traditional

Figure 113. Church of the Conception of St. Anne, Kitai-gorod. Moscow. 1530s(?). In the background, Hotel Rossiia. 1964–8. Architect: Dmitrii Chechulin et al. (M 132–24)

Kievan rules of succession that the title of grand prince belonged to him. After Iurii's death, in 1434, his sons, Dmitrii Shemiaka and Vasilii Kosoi, continued the debilitating, chaotic feud, in the course of which both Vasilii II and Vasilii Kosoi were blinded. By 1450, however, Moscow and the principle of direct male succession to its throne emerged triumphant.

At the same time, momentous events in the Orthodox Church had both immediate and far-reaching consequences for Moscow. The Byzantine Church, in a final desperate move to relieve the pressure of the Turks on Constantinople, agreed to reunite with the Roman Catholic Church (the Union of Florence, 1439) on terms that reflected doctrinal concessions and an acceptance of the authority of the Pope. The recently appointed metropolitan of Russia, Isidore, enthusiastically supported the union, but a number of the accompanying Russian delegates in Florence did not,

and they ultimately succeeded not only in rejecting the union, but also in expelling Isidore from Russia. With this repudiation of the authority of the Patriarch in Constantinople, the Russian Church had in effect become autocephalous. The break was made formal in 1448 when a convocation of Russian bishops elected Archishop Jonah of Riazan to the post of metropolitan. The fall of Constantinople in 1453 no doubt increased the sense of isolation of Russian Orthodoxy, yet it would also reinforce the mission of the church – and of Muscovy – as defender of the Orthodox faith.

As the metropolitan of the Russian Church and Grand Prince Vasilii II asserted their respective powers at the midpoint of the century, major construction projects became feasible for the first time in almost 25 years.[33] Although the buildings of this period, particularly in the Kremlin, have since been reconstructed or replaced, the impetus provided by projects

93

Figure 114. Cathedral of the Nativity of the Virgin, Nativity Convent. Moscow. 1500–5(?). (M 58–23a)

fourteenth-century version of the Dormition Cathedral in the Kremlin (see the foregoing).

By the beginning of the reign of Ivan III in 1462, that Dormition Cathedral was already at the point of collapse, with some of its vaults supported only by large wooden beams.[35] In view of the close connection of the cathedral with the ruler of Moscow, it is worth noting that the original impetus for rebuilding the cathedral apparently came from Metropolitan Philip, the successor to Jonah. It was Philip who commissioned the rebuilding in 1471, who began the cutting of the limestone from the Miachkov quarry near Moscow, and who hired the architects Ivan Krivtsov and Myshkin. The enormous scale of the project, which was to be modeled on but larger than the Dormition Cathedral in Vladimir, required unusual financial measures such as special levies and large donations from Moscow's merchants. There is no documentary

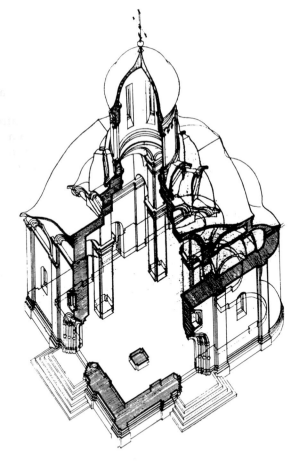

Figure 115. Cathedral of the Nativity of the Virgin, Nativity Convent. Moscow. Axonometric reconstruction. Courtesy of Shchusev Museum, Moscow.

such as the Kremlin residence and church of Metropolitan Jonah not only created symbols of authority, secular and ecclesiastical, in Moscow, but also prepared the way for much larger structures during the reign of Ivan III (1462–1505). The attention also devoted by Ivan III to the preservation of the ancient monuments of Suzdalia is a further statement of cultural continuity as well as a preparation to resurrect the glories of a heroic age. Of particular interest is the restoration in 1471 of the Cathedral of St. George in Iurev-Polskoi, which had collapsed for unknown reasons in the middle of the century. Although by no means a complete restoration in the modern sense, the project was executed with considerable skill under the supervision of the wealthy Moscow merchant and contractor Vasilii Ermolin.[34] And the cathedral itself, relatively modest in size but richly decorated, was viewed as an important model in the rebuilding of Muscovite architecture – including, most notably, the

evidence of a contribution from Ivan – perhaps an oblique reference to a quarrel between the grand prince and the metropolitan.[36]

On April 30, 1472, Metropolitan Philip, in the presence of Ivan III, lay the cornerstone of the new cathedral, which encompassed the old structure, soon to be razed after the graves of Moscow's princes and metropolitans were removed to their burial sites in the new walls. In the spring of 1473, Philip, who by all accounts was obsessed with the building projects he had initiated, suffered a fatal stroke; but work on the cathedral continued unabated under his successor, Metropolitan Gerontii. By May 1474, the walls and the vaulting were completed and construction of the large central drum had begun, when, on the night of May 20 or 21, the vaults collapsed, and with them much of the rest of the structure. Many reasons have been given for the disaster: the poor quality of the mortar; the unsuitability of the local stone for extensive vaulting over such an extensive space; the placement of a staircase (to the choir gallery) within the north wall, thus weakening a large structure that was already unsound in its use of the old technique of rubble core infill for limestone walls. In addition to flawed structural calculations, there had been a perceptible, and very unusual, earthquake the day before.[37]

Ivan III promptly intervened and assumed control of the project, whose completion had now become a matter of state – and of Ivan's own credibility as a ruler. To assess the cause of the collapse, he summoned the group of master builders from Pskov, who praised the stonework, but found the mortar too thin, refused to assume further responsibility, and undertook other, more modest projects that have been discussed before. In June of the same year, Ivan dispatched his envoy Semion Tolbuzin to Italy on a mission that included the hiring of an architect-engineer capable of building on a large scale.

Tolbuzin was not the first Russian envoy to appear in Italy during Ivan's reign. After the death of his first wife, the grand prince in 1472 married Sophia (Zoe) Paleologue, niece of the last Byzantine emperor, Constantine XI. After the fall of Constantinople, Zoe had been taken to Rome, where she became the ward of the Pope. Her entourage included Vissarion of Nicea, a Byzantine churchman and scholar who had supported the Union and subsequently was elevated to Cardinal. Vissarion's successful role in arranging the marriage, stimulated no doubt by a desire to create an alliance against the Turks, had an effect on Russian cultural politics that might be compared with Prince Vladimir's marriage into the Purple some five centuries earlier.[38] Although Vissarion died in 1472, 3 years before Tolbuzin's arrival, his extensive contacts among the artistic elite of northern Italy would have provided a network known to Zoe and invaluable to Tolbuzin.

The details of Tolbuzin's embassy are at best sketchy, and his own account of his meeting with the Bolognese architect Aristotele Fioravanti are fanciful to the point of improbability.[39] Yet he succeeded in recruiting not only the architect, but also his son and an assistant. By this time, Fioravanti (1420–85?) had already established a long, if not always rewarding, career as engineer, architect, and artist. He had worked extensively in northern Italy, and in 1458 had entered the service of Francesco Sforza in Milan, where he met Antonio Averlino Filarete, chief architect to the Sforzas and author of one of the most famous architectural treatises of the Renaissance.[40] Fioravanti collaborated with Filarete in the building of Milan's Ospedale Maggiore, but his major extant work is the arcaded Palazzo del Podestà in Bologna.

When Fioravanti arrived in Moscow at the end of March 1475 (some 2 months before the beginning of the building season), he immediately directed the razing of the remaining walls of the Dormition Cathedral (Muscovites were startled to see what had taken 3 years to build dismantled, with the Italian's technological ingenuity, in a week), and in June, he began the construction of a new foundation. Placed on oak piles, the foundation walls were the deepest (more than 4 meters) yet seen in Russia for such a structure, ensuring a reliable base for the limestone walls, which were unusually thin by Russian standards and were constructed of solid bond masonry instead of rubble infill.[41] He also established a brickworks (near Andronikov Monastery), whose large, well-fired bricks were stronger than those previously produced in Moscow, and he corrected the deficiency in mortar that had been noted by the Pskov masters. The thickness of the cement provided the firm bonding that had been known in Vladimir and Novgorod but had been lost – along with much else in the art of building – during the period following the Mongol invasion.

Having initiated the construction of the cathedral and entrusted its supervision to his son Andreas, he traveled to Vladimir to inspect what was, in a broad sense, to be the model for the Dormition Cathedral. Both the Vladimir and Moscow cathedrals are pentacupolar (see Plate 25), with zakomary to effect the transition from facade to roof; both have an arcade band at the midlevel of the facade, delineated to reflect the interior division of bays; and both use perspective arches to frame the portals.

Fioravanti's plan, however, contained a number of significant deviations from the traditional cross-inscribed design characteristic of Russia's masonry churches. In part, the differences derive from construction techniques that mitigated the stress on key points of the building (it should be remembered that the Dormition Cathedral in Vladimir contained a structure within a structure). The lightness of Fioravanti's cathedral was made possible by the use of brick, instead of stone, for the vaulting as well as the drums, and by the insertion of iron tie rods within the masonry and across the vaulting. For Russian builders, these were innovations. On the exterior, the walls were buttressed by large pilasters, dividing the facade into equal vertical segments whose proportions were determined by the a variation on the golden section.[42]

Indeed, Fioravanti transmitted the contemporary Italian interest in rationalism by applying the concept of structural harmony as determined by the rules of geometry to a degree unknown in Russia on such a large scale. He in effect abandoned the cross-inscribed plan, which had dictated a widening of the central axes to delineate the figure of the cross. The Cathedral of the Dormition is composed of twelve quadrilateral bays (Figure 116), equal in size and cross – rather than barrel-vaulted – a design that increased the span of the brick vaults, whose light weight enabled a corresponding reduction in the size of the six piers (four of them round, but with two square piers at the altar to provide support for the iconostasis). Despite the equal size of the bays, Fioravanti achieved the characteristic Russian pentacupolar silhouette, with its

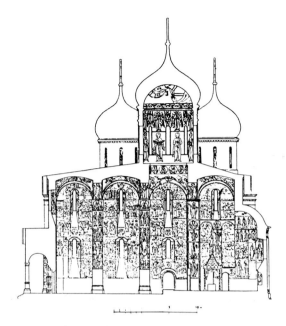

Figure 117. Cathedral of the Dormition, Moscow Kremlin. Section by F. Rikhter.

dominant central drum and cupola, by extending the main drum over, rather than within, the central bay – a resolution that has been compared to Filarete's centralized design for a chapel at the Ospedale Maggiore (c. 1455).[43]

The sense of spaciousness created by Fioravanti's design and technical innovations was enhanced by the decision to eliminate a significant and traditional element in the design of Russian masonry churches: the choir gallery.[44] Thus, the entire interior, from the iconostasis to the west facade, was washed in a natural light that illuminated the vibrant colors of the frescoes and icons. Work on the painting of the interior began almost immediately after the structure's completion in 1479, and by 1515, the entire space was covered with frescoes (Figure 117). In addition, an iconostasis of three rows was painted in 1481 by the reknowned artist Dionisii and his assistants, who may also have been involved in the painting of the original frescoes.[45]

The unity of the sculpted form – as if cut from one stone, according to a Russian chronicler – is especially evident in the south facade (Figure 118), and in the design of the eastern wall, whose five apses extend slightly from the central block of the church and are screened by massive pylons at either corner. Furthermore, they are unified by large attached columns and the plinth molding that compress the apsidal contours into an imposing east facade confronting the

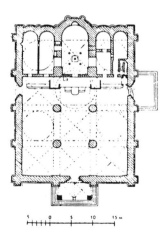

Figure 116. Cathedral of the Dormition, Moscow Kremlin. 1475–9. Plan by F. Rikhter.

Figure 118. Cathedral of the Dormition, Moscow Kremlin. South facade. (M 108–31)

Figure 119. Cathedral of the Dormition, Moscow Kremlin. East facade. (M 107–10)

main entrance to the Kremlin's cathedral space (Figure 119). On the north and south facades, the portals are framed by iconic wall paintings, including the portrayal of saints within the blind arcade – a technique similar to that applied on the surface of Andrei Bogoliubskii's Dormition Cathedral. The culmination, in every sense, of Fioravanti's design is the ensemble of five gilded cupolas over the central and east bays. It is thought that the original domes were of plates of "German" iron, prepared in Novgorod and polished to a high gloss. After the great fire of 1547, the domes were reconstructed and covered with gilded copper sheets, which to this day provide a particularly rich hue to the gold surface.[46]

Conceived as a grand and solemn space for the crowning of Russian rulers and the investiture of metropolitans (later patriarchs) of the Russian Orthodox Church, Fioravanti's Cathedral of the Dormition represents the felicitous meeting of two cultures: the Russian, with its Byzantine heritage, and the western European, as expressed in the architectural ideas of the Italian Renaissance. Indeed, the cathedral can be seen as the culminating monument of the Vladimir tradition, the last of the great limestone churches.

Although limestone continued to be used in a few smaller churches such as St. Trifon, its use would be limited henceforth primarily to the structural base (as at the Annunciation Cathedral) and to decorative details. The new forms of brick were easier to obtain and more adaptable than limestone, and by the end of the fifteenth century, brick had become the primary building material of major construction projects – of which none was more major than the rebuilding of the Kremlin walls.

A New Fortress

The Kremlin walls, so potent a symbol of Russian power and inscrutability, undoubtedly owe much of their appearance to the native imagination – specifically, the tower spires added in the seventeenth century by local architects. Yet their main structure, indeed the towers themselves, is very much the product of Italian fortification engineering of the quattrocento, already long outdated in Italy by the time of their construction in Moscow. Nonetheless, the walls proved adequate against Moscow's traditional enemies from the steppes, whose cavalry was capable of inflicting great damage on unwalled settlements, but had little or no heavy siege equipment.

By the 1460s, the condition of Dmitrii Donskoi's limestone Kremlin walls had reached a dangerously vulnerable state of disrepair. As noted before, Russian contractors had been commissioned to rebuild sections of the wall,[47] but the need for a fundamental reconstruction would have led, once again, to Italy, whose fortification engineers were the most advanced in Europe. Between 1485 and 1516, the old fortress was replaced with brick walls and towers extending 2,235 meters and ranging in thickness from 3.5 to 6.5 meters (the brick was particularly well-fired and heavy – up to 8 kilograms). The height of the walls varied from 8 to 19 meters, with the distinctive Italianate "swallowtail" crenellation that is particularly reminiscent of the castle and Ponte Scaligeri in Verona (late fourteenth century). The highest sections of the wall faced Red Square, which had no natural defensive barrier such as the Moscow and the Neglinnaia rivers on the other two sides of the Kremlin triangle. In 1508, however, a moat was dug along the Red Square wall.[48]

Of the twenty towers, the most elaborate were placed on the corners or at the main entrances to the citadel. Among the most imposing is the Frolov (later Savior, or Spasskii) Tower (see Figure 120), built in 1464–6 by Vasilii Ermolin and rebuilt in 1491 by Pietro Antonio Solari, who arrived in Moscow from Milan

in 1490. The elaborate decorative crown with its pseudo-Gothic motifs was added in 1624–5 by Bazhen Ogurtsov and the Englishman Christopher Halloway.[49] At the southeast corner of the walls, the magnificent round Beklemishev Tower (1487–8, with an octagonal spire from 1680; Figure 120) was constructed by Marco Friazin, who frequently worked with Solari. This and similar Kremlin towers have led to comparisons between the Moscow citadel and the fortress at Milan.[50] Anchoring the southwest corner is the Vodozvodnaia (Water; also called Sviblovo) Tower, built in 1488 by one of the first Italian engineers to arrive in Moscow, Anton Friazin (friazin being a generic term for "Franks"). The name of the tower derives from a machine installed by Halloway to lift water drawn from the river to the Kremlin gardens; its spire was added in 1672–86.[51] The walls connecting the several towers were rebuilt concurrently, with immediate attention given to the seriously damaged areas of Dmitrii Donskoi's fortress.

Although he built no cathedrals, Pietro Antonio Solari played a major role in the renovation of the Kremlin, not only with his four entrance towers – the Borovitskii, the Constantine and Helen, the Frolov, and the Nikolskii (all 1490–3) – as well as the forbidding corner Arsenal Tower and the Kremlin wall facing Red Square, but also for his role in the completion of the "Rusticated Chambers" (Granovitaia palata), so named for the diamond-pointed rustication of its limestone main facade (Figure 121). Used for banquets and state receptions within the Kremlin palace complex, the hall was begun in 1487 by Marco Friazin, who designed the 3-storied structure with a great hall whose vaulting was supported by a central pier. A similar plan had been used for the archbishop's palace in Novgorod (see the foregoing), but the distinctive feature of the Kremlin structure was its Italianate decoration, thought to have been the work of Solari, who assumed control of the project in 1490.[52]

Solari was an accomplished sculptor as well as architect, whose work in northern Italy demonstrated a regional propensity for liberally applied ornament. His talents were reflected not only in the main (east) facade of the building, marked at each end by narrow attached columns with a spiral incision and capitals, but also in a lavish entrance porch on the south facade (not extant). The original unstuccoed brick side walls were painted a dark red, which provided a dramatic contrast to the limestone front. Much of the ornamental detail, however, was modified or effaced during a rebuilding of the Chambers by Osip Startsev in 1682. The original pairs of narrow windows in a late-Gothic style were replaced by the present wider

Figure 120. Beklemishev Tower, Moscow Kremlin. 1487–8. Architect: Marco Friazin. Spire added in 1680. In the background, Frolov (later Savior, or Spasskii) Tower. 1491. Architect: Pietro Antonio Solari. Superstructure added in 1624 by Bazhen Ogurtsov. (M 2–2)

Figure 121. Rusticated Chambers (*Granovitaia palata*), Moscow Kremlin. 1487–91. Architects: Marco Friazin and Pietro Antonio Solari. Northeast view. (M 4–4)

frames, with elaborate carved columns and entablature; and the steep roof was replaced with one much lower.[53] The diamond rustication had an enduring appeal in Russian architecture during the sixteenth and seventeenth centuries, but it was rarely applied in stone: Local architects preferred to paint the facets on brick walls as gaudy trompe l'oeil.

It is of interest to compare the *Granovitaia palata*, even in its modified form, with one of the few other surviving "palace" structures of the fifteenth century in Russia: the Chambers of the Appanage Princes in Uglich, located some 220 kilometers to the northeast of Moscow on the Volga River. Although Uglich was no rival to Moscow, its location in one of the most vital areas of medieval Russian culture (Moscow–Rostov–Iaroslavl) and a favorable trading position on the Volga provided its energetic local prince Andrei the Big with the means to build a brick residence in the 1480s (Figure 122).[54] Time and various restorations have obscured many of the original features of the building (part of a larger palace complex), yet much of the basic structure is intact, including the three levels of windows in this towerlike design. A number of the facade details appears to derive from Novgorod decorative work – such as the "eyebrow" arches over the window and the decorative brick bands. Other details, such as the terra-cotta relief ornaments along the upper structure, resemble the decoration of the Church of the Holy Spirit at the Trinity–St. Sergius Monastery (see Figure 107), built by architects from Pskov just a few years earlier, in 1476. Entirely lacking, however, is any trace of contemporary Italian

Figure 122. Chambers of the Appanage Princes. Uglich. 1480s; partially reconstructed in 1890–2. (Ug 3–29)

design – perhaps a reflection of the smoldering feud between Andrei and his older brother Ivan III.

The Cathedral of the Archangel Michael

The final stage in Ivan the Great's reconstruction of the Kremlin began in 1505 (the year of his death), with the commissioning of the Cathedral of the Archangel Michael on the southern flank of Cathedral Square, to replace the earlier church of that name from the time of Ivan Kalita (1333). Its architect, identified in Russian chronicles as Aleviz Novyi (Aleviz "the New," to distinguish him from the "Elder" Aleviz, who built the northwest Kremlin walls), had arrived in Moscow in 1504, after completing a palace for the Crimean khan Mengli-Girei at Bakhchisarai.[55] It is known that Aleviz was first recruited during the ambassadorial mission of Dmitrii Ralev to Venice and other northern Italian cities in 1500, and there are clear similarities between the architecture of late fifteenth-

101

century monuments in the Venetian area and the work of Aleviz in Moscow; yet his identity has only recently been established (tentatively) as Alvise Lamberti da Montagnana, a student of Mauro Codussi in Venice.[56]

By the beginning of 1505, Aleviz was at work on the cathedral that was to serve as the final resting place for Russia's grand princes and tsars until the time of Peter the Great, 200 years later. On first view, the Archangel Cathedral displays the most extravagantly Italianate features of the Kremlin's Italian period (Figure 123).[57] The decorative detail and the articulation of the facade of the Archangel Cathedral are particularly close to that of Venetian monuments during the late quattrocento (cf. the entablature and gables of the Scuola di San Marco in Venice). In addition, the four intricately carved and painted limestone portals – three of which are on the west facade (Figure 124) – expand upon the elaborate entrance to the Rusticated Chambers, which would have been visible from the cathedral's west facade. (The main portal is surrounded on the exterior by frescoes on the theme of the acceptance of Christianity in Russia.)

In its structure, however, the Archangel Cathedral represents a return to the traditional Russian cross-inscribed plan in which the arms of the cross are delineated by their greater width and by the massive square piers (Figure 125). In comparison with the spacious modification of that plan in Fioravanti's Dormition Cathedral, Aleviz appears to have implemented an archaic design, although on a grand scale. And yet the structural core of the Archangel Cathedral resembles in significant ways the design of Venetian monuments, which are also ultimately related to Byzantine architecture, such as the Cathedral of St. Mark, one of the purest examples of cross-in-square planning. And the similarities are still more evident in comparison with smaller Venetian churches.[58]

These motifs from the quattrocento would have been more clearly visible at the beginning of the sixteenth century, when the Archangel Cathedral had an open, arcaded gallery along all but the east facade (a feature redolent of northern Italian architecture, as well as that of twelfth-century architecture in Vladimir).[59] Since then, the cathedral has undergone significant modifications, including the rebuilding of the roof, whose original form, in red and black tile, rested directly over the contours of the structure's barrel vaults. The present sheet-metal roof, overhanging the zakomary, obscures the limestone pyramidal ornaments that originally crowned the arches and gives an obtrusive, weighty effect to the roofline. Nonetheless, the carved limestone scallops – a Venetian

motif that firmly entered the repertoire of Moscow's architects – remains intact and accentuates the cathedral's brick walls, which are divided into two tiers by a system of arches, pilasters, and cornices. The lower tier, in the form of a blind arcade rising from a clearly defined limestone base, is separated from the upper tier by a cornice resting on a series of classical capitals. The entablature of the upper tier in turn isolates the scallop-form zakomary, creating the effect of a large square structure with a lavishly decorated roof. The contrast between the brick structure and the limestone decoration was intensified by the application of red paint directly over the brick walls – a feature lost in the eighteenth century when the walls were stuccoed.[60]

The segmentation of the facades of the Archangel Cathedral has been criticized as an interruption of the vertical unity of the bays, a destruction of the monolithic quality inherent in the relation between the vaulting and the design of the facades in earlier Russian churches – including Fioravanti's Dormition Cathedral. (A similar criticism has been made in regard to early fifteenth-century Muscovite churches, which had introduced rudimentary elements of the order system on the facade with no direct correlation to the interior division of bays.) The sense of fragmentation is intensified by the large number of bays: five, of unequal size, on the north and south facades (the fifth, containing the choir gallery, includes a third floor with a special gallery for the use of the grand princess and her suite).

The Archangel Cathedral should not, however, be judged by the formal systems of its predecessors. Alevis's bold use of classical elements on the facades created a new interpretation of the sculpted form, whose plasticity and exuberance complement, rather than follow, the work of Fioravanti and Solari. Furthermore, the introduction of clear references to the classical order system – however isolated from the context provided by the Italian Renaissance – prefigures the development in Russian architecture of a layered plasticity, a hierarchical combination of elements that suggests parallels with the classical tectonic system without directly imitating it.

Indeed, there was no possibility of transferring the classical system in any fundamental way to Muscovy. Russia's legacy from the classical world had been filtered through Byzantium, which provided in the cross-domed church an infinitely adaptable plan, but one narrowly focused on religious architecture. The reinterpretation of Greco–Roman architecture during the Renaissance could only be selectively applied in Muscovy, which had yet to form the secular institu-

Figure 123. Cathedral of the Archangel Michael, Moscow Kremlin.
Northeast view. (M 108–35)

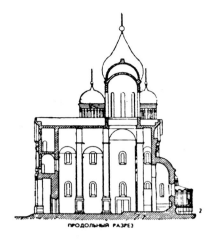

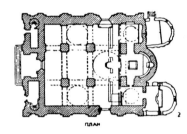

Figure 124. Cathedral of the Archangel Michael, Moscow Kremlin. 1505–8. Architect: Aleviz Novyi. West facade. (M 107–27)

Figure 125. Cathedral of the Archangel Michael, Moscow Kremlin. Plan and section by A. Vlasiuk.

tions that would require an architectural idiom expressive of the ideal of public life – what John Summerson, characterizing the revival of classical forms in the Renaissance, calls "the grammar of antiquity as a universal discipline."[61] It is possible to use terms such as "renaissance" and "orders" in referring to developments that occurred in Russian culture and architecture at the beginning of the fifteenth century; yet despite the need to recognize cultural processes that place the formation of a Russian state within the broader frame of Europe, the idiosyncratic ways of Russian history frustrate attempts to define the connections precisely – or even convincingly.[62]

Despite its importance as a symbol of cultural evolution in Muscovy, the Italianate design so skilfully articulated by Aleviz on the facade of the Archangel Cathedral did not have immediate, substantive ramifications in the development of Russian Church architecture.[63] The system that it embodied would reappear only at the end of the seventeenth century. Yet a number of isolated elements were readily

accepted, perhaps in dim acknowledgment of its expression of a new sense of state power. If the Annunciation Cathedral served as the court church, the Archangel Michael represented the full majesty of Moscow's rulers, who were buried within it. Consequently, many of its motifs were repeated in other major churches, such as the Cathedral of the Ascension Convent, which had been founded in the Kremlin in 1386 by Eudoxia, wife of Dmitrii Donskoi. The original cathedral, begun in 1407, became the burial site of the Moscow grand princesses and it was rebuilt on a larger scale in 1519, presumably by Aleviz. No visual evidence of its form exists, but a third rebuilding of the structure around 1588 quoted liberally from the Archangel Cathedral, which was, in a sense, its counterpart (each was used as a place of burial for the ruling family).[64] Indeed, the decorative system of the Archangel Cathedral acquired a special political resonance during the era of Boris Godunov at the end of the sixteenth century (see Chapter 6).

The final, and culminating, monument in the re-

104

Figure 126. Bell tower of Ivan the Great, Moscow Kremlin. 1505–8, with third and higher tiers and cupola added in 1600. Architect: Bon Friazin and others. Southwest view. On the left: the Belfry and Church of the Nativity of Christ, and the Filaret Annex, both destroyed in 1812 and rebuilt by Giovanni Gilardi to designs by Ivan Egotov and Luigi Rusca. (M 107–24)

building of the Kremlin is the Bell Tower of Ivan the Great, begun, like the Archangel Cathedral, in 1505 and completed in 1508. Virtually nothing is known of its architect, Bon Friazin, who had no other recorded structure in Moscow. Yet he was clearly a brilliant engineer, for not only did his bell tower – of 60 meters in two tiers – withstand the fires and other disasters that periodically devastated much of the Kremlin, but it also survived intact a French explosive charge in 1812 strong enough to level two large adjacent structures. The tower, whose height was increased by an additional 21 meters during the reign of Boris Godunov, rests on solid brick walls that are 5 meters thick at the base and 2.5 meters on the second tier (Figure 126). In addition, the walls of the first tier are reinforced by iron beams set within the masonry.[65] Bon Friazin also understood the virtues of simplicity. The facades of the octagonal structure are recessed in the center, with an arcade strip at the top of the panels and a modest ornamental brick cornice, with dentilation, above each tier. The rest is a matter of perfect proportion, based on the golden section and outlined by the vertical corner strips.

With the construction of the bell tower by Bon Friazin, the Kremlin had achieved a core, defended by massive walls, that would evolve over the following centuries but would not substantially change (see Plate 26). The remarkable speed with which this major architectural ensemble was created – some five decades – is a tribute to the resources and the shrewd intelligence brought to bear on the project by Ivan the Great, as well as to the adventuresome spirit of the Lombard and Venetian architects who embarked on such an uncertain venture. Whether this adaptation of the forms of the quattrocento reflected a deeper understanding of, or curiosity about, the Italian culture that had so transformed Muscovy's provincial architecture is a question with no clear answer. It is known that among the frescoes painted in the north and south galleries of the Annunciation Cathedral during the first half of the sixteenth century were representations of classical philosophers and writers such as Plutarch, Thucydides, Aristotle, Homer, and Virgil.[66] Certainly, the interest in Italian culture continued in Moscow during the sixteenth century.

There were two important factors, however, that worked against an extended Russian acceptance of Renaissance thought. The first was the profound suspicion on the part of the Russian Orthodox Church toward a culture so closely related to Roman Catholicism (the increased secularization of western society notwithstanding – or precisely for that reason). The second concerns the evolving nature of autocratic power in Russia. Although Ivan the Great was the first Muscovite grand prince to use the title "tsar," the term would not come into official use for Moscow's ruler until the reign of Ivan's grandson, Ivan IV (the Terrible). Nonetheless, even by the end of the fifteenth century, the inexorable rise of Muscovy – for all of its catastrophic reverses – involved a concept of despotism inherent in the term "tsar" and derived from the legacy of the Mongol khans rather than from contemporary concepts of the secular nation-state in the west.[67] The ramifications of the establishment of autocratic power in Russia go beyond architectural history; yet Russian architecture in the sixteenth century would adapt western stylistic elements and construction techniques to give unprecedented – and unwestern – expression to the concepts of centrality and hierarchy.

CHAPTER 6

The Ascent of Architecture in Muscovy

When they rise in the morning, they goe commonly in the sight of some steeple, that hath a crosse on the toppe: and so bowing themselves towardes the crosse, signe themselves withal on their foreheads and brests.

– Giles Fletcher on Moscow, 1591

With the completion of the central Kremlin ensemble during the reign of Vasilii (Basil) III (1505–33), Russian architecture had achieved a transformation from provincialism to monuments of technical and aesthetic distinction. The genius of the Italian architect-engineers who recreated the Kremlin consisted not merely in their adaptation of northern Italian decorative motifs and construction techniques to local needs, but also in their acceptance of the legacy of pre-Mongol Russian architecture. The resulting fusion allowed sixteenth-century Russian architects to assimilate western innovations without rejecting their native tradition. And if the use of Italianate motifs often seems improvised and awkward, it must be remembered that the intention of Russian builders was not to accept an entire architectural system from the west, but to reaffirm in brick and stone the centrality of the Russian Orthodox Church and the will of divine providence as extended to the ruler of Muscovy.

At a time when western architecture had increasing numbers of secular patrons, a revived Russian architecture was thoroughly beholden to the Orthodox hierarchy and to an autocrat (often at odds with the Church hierarchy) who believed in his special relation to the deity and in his unlimited power over his subjects. Combined with an abundance of timber and the Russian preference for living in wooden houses, masonry architecture in Russia thus continued to be almost entirely a matter of churches and fortresses – each of which served to defend Muscovy from alien (often western) incursions. However skillfully builders in Russia applied the lessons of the quattrocento, their work became more, not less, distinct from that in the west.

Church construction in sixteenth-century Muscovy was by no means an unbroken procession of major monuments. Numerous churches commissioned by the grand princes were quite modest in design (cf. the Church of St. Trifon; Figure 111), as were most parish and monastery churches. As noted in the preceding chapter, architects from Pskov and their followers were active in constructing small cuboid churches, whose design represented an amalgam of early fifteenth-century Muscovite architecture with the building traditions of Pskov. Some of these churches, such as the cathedral at the Nativity Convent (see Figure 115), involved a complex integration of structure and decoration.

By the second decade of the sixteenth century, builders of cross-inscribed churches (with four piers and one cupola) began to incorporate elements from the two major Kremlin cathedrals – particularly, the Archangel Michael. An early example of this process is the Cathedral of the Intercession of the Mother of God at the Intercession (Pokrovskii) Convent in Suzdal (see Plate 27). Commissioned by Vasilii III and built in 1510–14, the cuboid brick structure displayed features of early Muscovite churches, such as the pointed *kokoshniki* in an octagonal arrangement at the base of the drum and the ornamental brick and terracotta motif beneath the main cupola (Figure 127); yet it also has blind arcading on the facade and a level row of zakomary – devices common in early Suzdalian architecture and revived through Moscow's Dormition Cathedral.[1]

The Intercession Cathedral has three cupolas – two over chapels within the eastern corner bays, in the manner of the Kremlin Annunciation Cathedral – and

107

Figure 127. Cathedral of the Intercession, Intercession Convent. Suzdal. 1510–14. Southwest view. (SD 3–4)

dal. The Aleksandrov cathedral has only one large drum and cupola and has been much altered by later additions, yet its still visible core structure has *zakomary* whose profiled archivolts spring from capitals at the top of pilasters. Much of the building's finish is of limestone, including a decorative strip along the facade (now hidden by the attached gallery), the pilasters and capitals, and the interior walls. Indeed, the considerable height of the structure derives from the elevation of its brick-surfaced walls upon a limestone base, a feature of major sixteenth-century churches such as the Archangel Michael.[3] Although remote from the elaborate facades of the Archangel Michael Cathedral, the articulation of the Intercession Cathedral is no less indebted to Italian influence.[4]

By 1525, the looming dynastic crisis compelled Vasilii with the support of the Church, to anull his marriage to Solomoniia Saburova, who entered the same Suzdal Intercession Convent where churches had arisen a decade before in supplication for the birth of a son. Vasilii's second marriage, to Elena Glinskaia,

an exterior gallery. Its polygonal bell tower, connected to the main gallery, originally had a second-floor chapel. Although the upper level was rebuilt in the seventeenth century, it may have been one of the earliest examples in Muscovy of a brick tower church with a conical roof.[2] The convent gate church, dedicated to the Annunciation and built around 1516 (Figure 128), has three cupolas and a main drum similar in design to the convent's cathedral. The proportions of the structure, with its arcaded gallery on the upper level and recessed entrance arches, show a masterful handling of form that could be the work of Kremlin masons, especially because all of these structures were commissioned as votive churches by Vasilii III and his first wife, Solomoniia Saburova, in supplication for the birth of an heir.

Early in his reign, Vasilii established a new compound on a favored site for hunting and pilgrimage to the north of Moscow. Called Aleksandrova Sloboda, the walled compound with its lodges and ancillary buildings centered around the Cathedral of the Intercession (Figure 129), built in 1513 to a design resembling that of the Intercession Cathedral in Suz-

Figure 128. Gate Church of the Annunciation, Intercession Convent. Suzdal. C. 1516. Southwest view. (SD 3–3)

did not initially produce the desired issue, and the royal couple resumed the practice of pilgrimage to monasteries. The Trinity-Danilov Monastery in Pereslavl-Zalesskii was particularly revered by Vasilii and as an offering of gratitude for the birth of Ivan IV, he commissioned the superb Trinity Cathedral, built between 1530 and 1532.[5] Despite the modification of the roofline, which originally followed the contour of the zakomary, the basic form of the cathedral (Figure 130) is intact and represents one of the most carefully pro-

Figure 129. Cathedral of the Intercession. Aleksandrova Sloboda. 1513. Northwest view. (A 1–1)

portioned examples of the early sixteenth-century cuboid structure. During the seventeenth century, the cathedral was enhanced by a large "tent" bell tower (1689) and an ensemble of frescoes (see Plate 28) painted in 1662–8 by two masters from Kostroma, Gurii Nikitin and Sila Savin, who were also involved in the repainting of the frescoes at the Archangel Michael Cathedral in Moscow.[6]

The viability of the cuboid design for large brick churches is demonstrated by its use in Pereslavl-

Zalesskii almost three decades later for the votive church of St. Theodore Stratilates at the Fedorovskii (Theodore) Monastery. Commissioned by Ivan IV apparently as a votive offering in celebration of the birth of his son Fedor in 1557, the structure has a lower silhouette than the Trinity Cathedral and has been even more severely disfigured by the addition of chapels and by modifications to the roofline. The most noticeable difference between the designs of the two churches is the appearance of the five cupolas at the Cathedral of St. Theodore, which anticipates the decorative use of the pentacupolar form in relatively small churches during the seventeenth century.[7] In the sixteenth century, however, the revival of the pentacupolar design appeared primarily in large monastery churches that had an additional bay, or narthex, at the west end.

Monastic Cathedrals: Symbols of State Power

In the Dormition and Archangel Michael Cathedrals of the Moscow Kremlin, Fioravanti and Aleviz Novyi had reintroduced the ensembles of five cupolas, largely neglected since the twelfth century in Suzdalia, over an elongated variant of the cross-inscribed structure. This distinctive arrangement of drums and cupolas subsequently became an obligatory feature of imposing cathedrals built in the style – if not the plan – of the Kremlin Dormition Cathedral. One of the earliest examples is the Cathedral of the Dormition in Rostov (Figure 131), built perhaps as early as the late fifteenth century on the site of two earlier limestone

Figure 130. Cathedral of the Trinity, Trinity-Danilov Monastery. Pereslavl-Zalesskii. 1530–2. Northwest view. On the left: bell tower, 1689; and Church of All Saints, 1687. (PZ 3–10)

Figure 131. Cathedral of the Dormition. Rostov. Late fifteenth or early sixteenth century. Southwest view. (RO 3–28)

versions of the cathedral dating from the twelfth and thirteenth centuries.[8] The design of the new cathedral thus incorporated elements of the pre-Mongol Suzdalian style – in some cases quite literally, because decorative fragments of the thirteenth-century cathedral were placed into the brick walls of the new cathedral.

Whatever the new Rostov Dormition Cathedral derived from its antecedent structures, it was more directly influenced by the design of the Moscow Dormition Cathedral, which in turn derived much of its exterior detail from the twelfth-century Vladimir Dormition Cathedral. Thus, the blind arcade outlined beneath the windows of the second tier of the Rostov cathedral is a Suzdalian motif reinterpreted in the manner of the fifteenth century. With no structural purpose, the arcading displays decorative elaborations (on the column shafts and the pointed arches) characteristic of the ornamentalism of early fifteenth-century Muscovite churches. Indeed, it has been suggested that the sheaflike motif of the capitals in the limestone arcading not only follows the pattern of the Annunciation and Deposition churches in the Moscow Kremlin, but equally derives from carved wooden decoration.[9] The main effect of Moscow's great cathedrals is visible, however, in the five cupolas over bays delineated by the six interior piers.

Whether it occurred in the reign of Ivan III or of

Vasilii III, the rebuilding of the Rostov Cathedral was unquestionably an event of much significance – a demonstration of Moscow's dominant political position as well as its determination to maintain and enhance the ancient centers of Russian religious culture. During the same period, however, the dedication of new churches moved toward symbolic commentary on major events occurring within the reign of the grand prince. For example, the Cathedral of the Icon of the Smolensk Mother of God at Moscow's Novodevichii (Newmaiden) Convent was founded by Vasilii III in 1524 to commemorate the incorporation of the strategic city of Smolensk within the Russian state in 1514 (it had been under the control of Lithuania for the preceding century).[10]

Although simpler in articulation, the Smolensk Cathedral (1524–5; Figure 132) is no less imposing than the Rostov Dormition by virtue of the height of its four longitudinal bays. In contrast to the Kremlin Dormition Cathedral and a number of its successors, the main zakomara of each facade of the Smolensk Cathedral is distinguished by greater height and width

Figure 132. Cathedral of the Smolensk Mother of God, Novodevichii Convent. Moscow. 1524–5. South facade. (M 127–5)

– thus signifying the arms of the inscribed cross. The verticality is further developed by elevating the church above a ground floor, or *podklet*. As in other churches of simliar design – such as the Transfiguration Cathedral in Iaroslavl – the podklet served as a burial chamber for wealthy nobles or members of the princely family. The cathedral culminates in massed domes, whose peaks support gilded crosses of a height commensurate with the proportions of the drums and cupolas (Figure 133).

The implicit dedication of this impressive form to a political event – and, more specifically, a military victory – confirms a tendency toward merging secular and religious symbolism in sixteenth-century Muscovy. To an extent, this impulse was present as a motive underlying the reconstruction of the Kremlin; yet the Kremlin churches, like the rebuilt cathedrals of Rostov and Suzdal, had existed well before the expansion of the Muscovite state, whose ascent to power was reflected in the rebuilding of ancient cathedrals, but not explicitly commemorated by their very dedication and existence. Whatever the original dedication, the proliferation of major churches in imitation of the Moscow Dormition Cathedral not only symbolized Mucovy's gathering of the Russian lands, but also in a tangible sense recreated the sanctum of Moscow at strategic points throughout its expanding territory.

The symbolic importance of Fioravanti's Dormition Cathedral as a prototype for major cathedrals in Muscovy, and the direct involvement of Moscow's ruler in their creation are illustrated in two of the last of these structures, one of which was built in the most revered of Muscovite monasteries and given the same dedication as the Kremlin cathedral. The Cathedral of the Dormition at the Trinity-Sergius Monastery (Figure 134) was commissioned by Tsar Ivan IV (the Terrible), who in 1559 personally attended the religious service initiating the project. A disastrous fire that leveled much of the monastery in 1564 impeded construction, as did the tsar's mistrustful attitude toward the monastery hierarchy during the latter part of his reign. The church was not completed and consecrated until 1585, after Ivan's death.

Despite the century that separates them, the Dormition Cathedral at the Trinity-Sergius Monastery remains the most faithful recreation of its Kremlin prototype on both interior and exterior. Although larger than the Kremlin Dormition (29.2 meters by 42.3, as opposed to 27 meters by 39.75), it reproduces such distinctive structural details as a five-part apse merged within the pylons of the east facade, a large arcade band at midlevel, a uniform height for the

Figure 133. Cathedral of the Smolensk Mother of God, Novodevichii Convent. Moscow. East facade. (M 71–11)

zakomary, an equal division of the bays, and a large central drum and dome.[11] (The domes were originally similar in shape to those of the Moscow cathedral, but were later replaced with onion domes.) There are also obvious differences, such as cruciform piers rather than round columns that had enhanced the perception of interior space in the Moscow Dormition Cathedral, and the use of brick as the basic structural material. Yet the general similarity exists on the exterior as well as the interior, although the frescoes (extant) were not painted until 1684 – a reflection of the troubled century following the completion of the cathedral. Once commissioned, however, the frescoes were completed in the remarkably short period of 3 months by a group of thirty-five painters headed by the Iaroslavl master Dmitrii Grigorev.[12]

The symbolic uses of the Kremlin Dormition Cathedral culminated in the building of the main cathedral of Vologda, a trading and administrative center in the north of Russia during the sixteenth and sev-

enteenth centuries. (Vologda was the primary distribution point for the increasingly profitable trade with England, and subsequently Holland, via Arkhangelsk and the Dvina River.) Ivan IV devoted much attention to Vologda in the late 1560s, when he formed his personal state (oprichnina) within Muscovy. Although legends that Ivan intended to make the city his new capital have little basis in fact, it is possible that he wished to establish a fortified refuge from the chaos that he himself had created. Construction of a large masonry citadel began in 1565 under the tsar's supervision, but only a portion of the walls and towers (not extant) was completed.

An essential part of the enhancement of Vologda was the building of a cathedral (1568–70) for the bishopric that was transferred to the city in 1571. Modeled on Fioranvanti's Dormition Cathedral, the cathedral was also to have been dedicated to the Feast of the

Figure 134. Cathedral of the Dormition, Trinity-Sergius Monastery. Zagorsk. 1559–85. Northwest view. (Z 7–21)

112

Dormition. Church politics however, led, to its unusual dedication to the Divine Sophia – a reflection of Vologda's rivalry with Novgorod, whose religious as well as secular power had been steadily reduced by Moscow's rulers. For a brief period in the latter part of the sixteenth century, Vologda – formerly subordinate to Novgorod – was a direct beneficiary of this policy.[13] Having appropriated the name of Novgorod's great cathedral, the architects at Vologda effected a graceful, simplified interpretation of the Moscow Dormition, with pilaster strips leading to a horizontal row of four zakomary, above which are five domes. Of the major Dormition offspring, the Vologda cathedral bears the closest resemblance to the cathedral at the Novodevichii Convent. The interior of St. Sophia – with a vivid "Last Judgment" on the west wall – was painted in 1686–8 by a group of some thirty artists from Iaroslavl led by the same Dmitrii Grigorev (or Plekhanov) who supervised the painting of the Dormition Cathedral at the Trinity-Sergius Monastery.

Fortress Walls and Towers

The massive brick walls of the new Muscovite churches – and the military impulse behind the dedication of churches such as the Smolensk Cathedral at Novodevichii Convent – remind that the reign of Vasilii III was a period of intensive effort to fortify the approaches to Moscow, with major fortresses constructed at Nizhnii Novgorod (1500–11), Tula (1507–20), Kolomna (1525–31), Zaraisk (1528–31), and Kashira (1531).[14] These citadels served as anchors for the *Zasechnaia cherta*, a defensive line established and expanded in the sixteenth and seventeenth centuries to guard Muscovy's southern borderlands.[15] The walls and towers of the Trinity-Sergius Monastery were also strengthened in this period – to good effect when the monastery endured a prolonged siege by Polish forces at the beginning of the seventeenth century (see Chapter 7).

Typically built of brick on a base of limestone blocks, these citadels followed the general design of the Moscow Kremlin, and testify to the facility of Vasilii's Russian builders to assimilate imported construction techniques (there is no documentary evidence of Italian participation in the foregoing projects). Like the Moscow Kremlin, the fortresses were obsolete by European standards, but under Russian conditions, they provided urgently needed protection. The building of a new citadel at Kolomna, one of Moscow's major southern gateways, attained priority following

the sack of the town during a devastating attack on Moscow by the Crimean khan Mohammed Girei in 1521. Completed in 1531, the Kolomna Kremlin had seventeen towers and walls as thick as 4.5 meters (Figure 135).[16] The citadel at Tula was one of the earliest examples of a Russian masonry fortress designed according to a geometric (rectangular) shape. Similar in shape, although more complex in design, was the fortress at Ivangorod, built and enlarged in 1492–1507 to confront the Livonian Order at Narva, on Muscovy's northwestern border. In Pskov, another strategic western fortress, expansion of the city's extensive network of stone walls increased during the reign of Basil and continued into the 1570s.[17]

The most advanced example of fortification architecture in Russia appeared in Moscow itself, with the construction between 1535–8 of a brick wall some 2.5 kilometers in length encompassing the city's commercial district, the "Kitai-gorod," extending from the

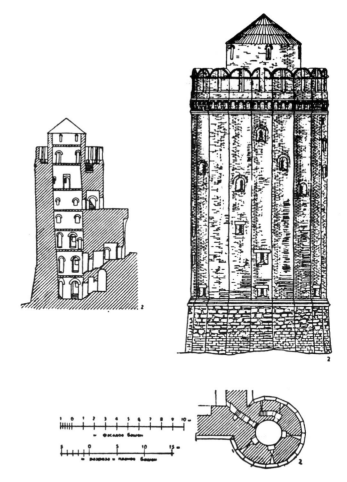

Figure 135. Marinkina Tower, Kolomna Kremlin. 1525–31. Elevation by L. Pavlov.

113

eastern side of the Kremlin and Red Square.[18] In contrast to the imposing brick fortifications of the Kremlin, the relatively low silhouette of the Kitai Gorod wall took into account recent developments in siege warfare and the use of artillery, which in Europe had made the high walls of the late medieval and early Renaissance fortresses obsolete. Although Moscow did not face the likelihood of an intensive artillery bombardment, the dimensions of the wall – as much as 6 meters thick with a typical height of 6.5 meters – and the various defensive configurations of its fourteen low towers provided a new level of security.[19]

The architect of the Kitai-gorod wall, Petrok Malyi (or Petr Friazin), was a part of the third – and final – wave of Italian architects to work in Muscovy. The little biographical information available seems to indicate that Petrok Malyi arrived in Moscow in 1528, rather than 1522, as presumed in earlier scholarship; yet his earliest documented project, the Church of the Resurrection in the Moscow Kremlin, dates from 1532.[20] In view of Muscovy's rapid assimilation of such valued foreign talent, it is unlikely that Petrok – who was sent to Russia on the recommendation of Pope Clement VII (nephew of Lorenzo de Medici and patron of numerous Renaissance artists) and was one of only three Italian architects identified as *arkhitekton* in the Russian chronicles – would have spent 4 years in inactivity or on trivial projects. The nature of Petrok's early work in Muscovy remains the subject of speculation. It is possible that precisely in the years 1529–32 – shortly after his arrival and before his documented work in the center of Moscow – Petrok created the engineering and architectural marvel that would initiate the great era of sixteenth-century Muscovite votive architecture.

The Church of the Ascension at Kolomenskoe

The peculiar Muscovite centralized church in the form of a tower has a complex and obscure provenance in Russian architecture. Compact structures with corbeled arches for a single drum and cupola had appeared no later than the beginning of the thirteenth century, as exemplified by the Church of St. Paraskeva in Chernigov (see Figure 20). In fifteenth-century Muscovy, the variations on the single-cupola design with vertical emphasis include the Church of the Transfiguration at the Savior-Andronikov Monastery and the brick Church of the Holy Spirit at the Trinity-St. Sergius Monastery. In the early sixteenth century, the cathedral at the Nativity Convent in Moscow (see

Figure 114) demonstrated the transition from a cuboid form to an octagon with ascending kokoshniki. Indeed, it has been argued that the cross-inscribed church as it developed in Muscovy contains in its core the essence of the tower church.[21]

Recent research suggests a more obvious prototype in the Church of the Metropolitan Peter (part of the Upper Petrovskii Monastery), now considered to have been built in 1514–15 by Aleviz Novyi.[22] Its unusual plan begins with an octafoil first level, with the bays at the points of the compass larger than those on the diagonal (Figure 136). The upper tier is octagonal and may have had narrow windows, resembling the lancet form, in each of the eight bays. The brick structure culminated in a short arcade frieze, above which is a cornice and a helmet roof of eight facets covered in dark tile, Aleviz's preferred roofing material. On the interior, the lobes of the octafoil provided additional space and buttressed the structure – sound enough to allow a considerable widening of the windows at the turn of the eighteenth century (Figure 137). Despite its small scale, the church prefigures the development of votive churches as well as the return to smaller, ornamented tower churches at the end of the seventeenth century.

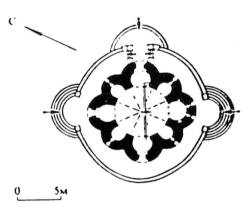

Figure 136. Church of the Metropolitan Peter, Upper Petrovskii Monastery. Moscow. 1514–15. Architect: Aleviz Novyi(?). Plan.

Other extant structures that might serve as antecedents for the tower form in sixteenth-century Russian church architecture are rare and involve chapels placed in bell towers. The lower two tiers of one such structure, built around 1515 and attached to the cathedral of the Intercession Convent in Suzdal, still exist (see Figure 127); but the upper part was rebuilt in the seventeenth century, thus effacing the original resolution of the top. At the Savior-Evfimii Monas-

Figure 137. Church of the Metropolitan Peter, Upper Petrovskii Monastery. Moscow. Northwest view. (M 37–8)

Nothing from this period, however, quite prepares for the first of Muscovy's great tower churches, the Ascension at Kolomenskoe (Figure 139), commissioned by Vasilii III in 1529 as a votive offering for the birth of an heir, Ivan IV. Not only is it of unprecedented height – both in absolute terms and in relation to the size of the floor plan – it also culminates in an elongated brick conical roof (the *shatior,* or "tent" roof) rather than the cupolar form traditional in Russian churches (see Plate 29). The impression of the Church of the Ascension was intensified by its site on a steep bank above the Moscow River with a view of the princely domains. Its location in the middle of a compound of wooden structures, including a large palace of haphazard form (burned in 1571 and twice rebuilt), created an ensemble whose silhouette was undoubtedly richer than it is today, when the sur-

Figure 138. Bell tower and Church of John the Baptist, Savior-Evfimii Monastery. Suzdal. C. 1515. Northeast view. (SD 6–33)

tery, also in Suzdal, there exists a tower chapel in three tiers dedicated to John the Baptist and presumably dating from the early part of the sixteenth century. The structure was subsequently modified with the construction and enlargement of an adjoining belfry in 1599 and again in 1691 (Figure 138).[23] The most imposing of the early sixteenth-century bell towers was, of course, that of Ivan the Great (see Figure 126), which originally contained a small church, dedicated to John Climacus, on the first tier. In all of these examples, there is no reliable means of determining the initial appearance of the roof.

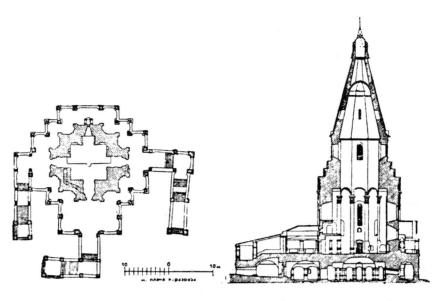

Figure 139. Church of the Ascension at Kolomenskoe. Moscow.
Plan and section by I. Rylskii and B. Zasypkin.

viving masonry monuments are viewed in a splendid isolation.[24]

The distinctive form of the Church of the Ascension, and in particular its "tent" roof over an octagonal tower on an attenuated cruciform base, has led to frequent comparisons with the design of Russian wooden tower churches (see Appendix I). Additional support for the uniquely Russian derivation of the form occurred with the discovery and publication in 1941 of a chronicle reference to the design of the Church of the Ascension with a top "in the manner of wood" (*vverkh na dereviannoe delo*).[25] Yet the notion of a prototype in wood cannot be easily accepted. Not only is there no evidence of wooden tent churches antedating the Church of the Ascension, but the chronicles also refer to the unprecedented nature of the form, whose conical tower sharply deviates from accepted Orthodox practice. A. I. Nekrasov, who rejected the theory of wooden origins as a late nineteenth-century nationalist maneuver unworthy of serious attention, argued that the Ascension church represented a late development of Romanesque towers with pyramidal roofs.[26] It has also been suggested that the tent roof, introduced specifically for a votive church, might be related to the form of the ciborium, which had been used in Russia to mark sites of special significance (e.g., over a holy well) and the baldachin, placed within the church to protect the throne of the metropolitan or grand prince.[27] In this view, the chronicle reference to a wooden form might derive

from a comparison with the common, and documented, practice of placing pyramidal wooden roofs over fortress towers in medieval Russia.

Yet the imaginative leap implied in so bold a design at Kolomenskoe eludes a final explanation. To be sure the technical problems of balancing so much vertical weight had been successfully addressed by Bon Friazin in the Bell Tower of Ivan the Great, yet the plan of the bell tower is simpler than that of the Ascension church, with its cruciform plan and unusual roof. Thus, it has been argued, with considerable evidence, that another Italian master – most likely Petrok Malyi – guided the resolution of this complex challenge.[28] Petrok was not only an experienced engineer, but also the consummate *arkhitekton*, as the walls of Kitaigorod demonstrated. Unfortunately, nothing remains of his Church of the Resurrection in the Kremlin, begun the year following the completion of the church at Kolomenskoe. Yet the limited visual evidence of its form indicates that it, too, was a towering structure, equal in height to the adjoining Bell Tower of Ivan the Great (before the additions of 1599–1600) and considerably larger in ground plan.[29]

The Church of the Ascension embodies the skills required by a fortification engineer as well as a designer of large eccleciastical structures. Its walls, which rest on massive brick cross vaults reinforced with iron tie rods, vary in thickness between 2.5 and 3 meters (considerably more than needed for the weight of the *shatior*, or "tent"), and they are further

116

supported by the buttressing effect of the cruciform configuration. The raised terrace (originally without a roof) girding the lower part of the church is reached by three staircases, each with a perpendicular turn that would have increased the visual drama of ritual processions. The main block of the tower, edged with massive pilasters, leads upward to three tiers of pointed *kokoshniki* whose design is echoed in the cornice of the octagon (Figure 140). From this point, the "tent" ascends in a pyramidal shape of eight facets delineated by limestone ribs. The rise is accentuated by a rhomboid pattern, also in limestone, that narrows toward the culmination of each facet (Figure 141; see Plate 29).[30] The tower concludes with an octagonal lantern, a cupola, and, at the height of 58 meters, a cross.

The hand of Petrok (or some other Italian master) can also be seen in the detailing of the exterior facades of the Church of the Ascension, which include details of the order system as interpreted in the Renaissance. Such elements had appeared in the Archangel Michael Cathedral, with its pilasters, capitals, and rudimentary form of entablature. The Ascension church has no entablature, but it has an abundance of other elements that point to a fluent knowledge of decorative forms from the Renaissance and, interestingly, from the Gothic: pilasters with ornate capitals that brace the corners of the octagonal bays and support the water spouts; similar capitals as consoles for the *kokoshniki* at the top of the octagon's bays; window surrounds with pilasters and capitals; and in the bays of the lower structure, steeply pitched pediments that point to the massed *kokoshniki*, but also frame narrow windows, each with its own ogival pediment. These pediments rest on slender attached columns (of particular interest as a late Gothic detail), each with a capital and volutes.[31]

Many of the same details appear on the church interior, which emphasizes the vertical to even more dramatic effect. The basic plan is a square with a side dimension of 8.5 meters – a limited space that does

Figure 140. Church of the Ascension at Kolomenskoe. Moscow. Detail of octagonal tower. (M 13–25)

Figure 141. Church of the Ascension at Kolomenskoe. Moscow. Axonometric projection by V. Podkliuchnikov.

eastern wall that served as an apse, yet the church had no apsidal structure. In its place on the exterior terrace was a setting, perhaps similar to a baldachin, for the throne of the grand prince, who could survey his domains across the Moscow River. Thus, the essentially secular nature of this unique structure was confirmed in the place most sacred in traditional Orthodox architecture.[32] Yet the clergy recognized the signal importance of a votive structure built by Vasilii III, anointed defender of the faith; and the Metropolitan Daniel himself – a loyal supporter of the grand prince, who had in effect appointed Daniel to the metropolitanate – participated in the three-day ceremony consecrating the church.

Paradoxically, the Orthodox Church had so linked its policies and pronouncements to the fortunes of the Muscovite state that it willingly accepted such a rad-

Figure 142. Church of the Ascension at Kolomenskoe. Moscow. Interior. (M 54)

not permit free-standing piers. The piers are, however, recast as pilasters attached at the intersections of the shallow arms of the cross and the main structure, thus dividing each wall into three segments with a framed recessed bay in the center (see Figure 141). The capitals of these shafts serve as a spring point for arches that effect the transition from the square to the octagon and, ultimately, to the tent roof that billows upward in a perfectly defined union of structure and space (Figure 142). Although the tower interior was perhaps decorated with abstract ornamental forms, the unadorned whitewashed walls are now marked only by light from the narrow windows of the octagon and tent.

The interior of the Church of the Ascension originally had an iconostasis as well as a niche in the thick

ical departure, motivated by purposes of secular power, from the traditional – one might say canonical – forms of church design. Not until the middle of the seventeenth century would the Russian Orthodox hierarchy attempt to contain the spread of the *shatior*, in both wood and masonry. As an expression of the Muscovite ruler's special relation to the deity, the form of the Ascension at Kolomenskoe can be compared to a votive candle, a fortress tower, a beacon – all serving as metaphors of the authority of the grand prince, the endurance of the princely dynasty, and the centrality of Moscow in the formation of the Russian state.[33]

The Church of John the Baptist at Diakovo

Within two decades of the completion of the Church of the Ascension, Vasilii III's heir, Ivan IV (1529–84), had commissioned another votive church related to the fortunes of the dynasty. The date of construction is unclear, but it presumably occurred between Ivan's coronation, in 1547, and the birth of his son Ivan in 1554.[34] Situated at Diakovo, a village attached to the grand prince's estate of Kolomenskoe and separated from it by a wide ravine, the Church of the Decapitation of John the Baptist rivals the Church of the Ascension in its strikingly innovative form (see Plate 30). As with the church at Kolomenskoe, the visual effect of the Diakovo church is enhanced by its location on a bluff overlooking the Moscow River. Although it lacks the vertical *point* provided by the "tent" at Kolomenskoe, the Church of John the Baptist can be classified as another variant of the tower church – the "pillar," or *stolp* – with a massively articulated drum beneath the central dome. The debate about the possible wooden derivation of the shatior is here irrelevant, thus permitting a more productive analysis of the origins and ramifications of this complex form.

The central structure of the Diakovo church is an octagonal column, each of whose bays is defined not by pilasters – as at Kolomenskoe – but by doubly recessed panels, reminiscent of the side facades of the Archangel Michael Cathedral by Aleviz. Above the cornice, a tier of kokoshniki yields to pediments in a transition to the great drum, composed of a series of semicylinders placed on a high octagonal base. Despite the unusual appearance of these forms, they reduce the weight of the drum without decreasing its strength.[35] A circle of panels above the cylinders isolates the cupola from the variety of forms beneath it. The relation of rounded and octagonal volumes, of circular and pointed surfaces, creates a dynamic that is reinforced by the four ancillary chapels (*pridely*), also octagonal and with a design similar to that of the main tower.

From a structural perspective, this symmetrical arrangement of small churches around the central mass – all resting on the same base (Figure 143) – is the most innovative feature of the Church of John the Baptist, and poses a greater enigma than the "tent" tower at Kolomenskoe. Following the example of his father, Vasilii III, Ivan and his clerics dedicated the separate altars as an affirmation of the personal relation between the tsar – as he was now formally called – and the deity. The central church, from which the entire structure derives its name, commemorates a solemn event from the Gospels – an event whose day of observance on the church calendar also served as the name day of Ivan (and a premonition of the violent nature of his later reign). Two of the four secondary tower churches were dedicated to the Church holidays of the Conception of St. Anne and

Figure 143. Church of the Decapitation of John the Baptist at Diakovo. Moscow. 1547–54(?). Section and plan by F. Rikhter.

119

the Conception of John the Baptist, thus signifying the primary votive purpose of supplication for an heir to the throne. This assumed a particular urgency after Ivan's first son, Dmitrii, born in 1552, died the following year. The other two tower churches were dedicated to Church fathers – to the Twelve Apostles and to the Moscow Metropolitans Peter, Aleksei, and Jonah – whose benevolent protection strengthened the role of the tsar as God's chosen ruler. On the gallery above the main entrance to the church (west facade), an additional, much smaller chapel was dedicated to Saints Constantine and Helen. As the first Christian emperor and his mother, their place in the symbolic pattern of the church is evident, with the additional memorial to Ivan's mother, also named Elena.[36]

Identifying the meaning of the dedications of these ancillary chapels does not, however, account for the unprecedented form of the Diakovo church. Most large, and many not so large, Russian churches had attached chapels with their own dedications. In rare examples, they were placed in a symmetrical arrangement to the main structure, but in any case, they were not elements of a single comprehensive architectural plan. At Diakovo, to the contrary, the subsidiary chapels were part of a highly integrated design that reproduced the central form at the four corners of a square base, and they linked the five components with a surrounding gallery. The complexity was increased by the presence of a large semicircular apse attached to the main tower, but also linked to the two flanking east chapels (Figure 144). The interiors of the towers, whose minimal decoration is not extant, are each articulated with a clarity that integrates tectonic detail and aesthetic form – as in the corbeled levels of brick effecting the transition from the lower to upper structure (Figure 145). Whatever the possible prototypes for the tower form itself, the precision and complexity of the plan of the Diakovo church have their origins elsewhere, most likely in the Italian Renaissance.

The concept of direct Italian participation in the design of the church would be easier to conceive were the date of construction still accepted as 1529. That is not the case, however, and two decades later, the presence of Italian architect-engineers in Muscovy is a matter of the past (Petrok is among the final "generation," active in the 1520s and 1530s).[37] Furthermore, the structure shows no sign of Italian work in details such as pediments, capitals, and attached columns that regularly appeared on major sixteenth-century Italian churches in Moscow.[38] Yet the general concept of a centralized design with integrated sat-

ellite structures could well have been conveyed to local masters by their Italian counterparts, who would have had ample knowledge of early Renaissance experiments in complex designs for centralized churches.

In this regard, the most obvious source – one with remarkable similarities to the Diakovo church – can be found in the work of Antonio Averlino Filarete (c. 1400–69), architectural theoretician and builder whose manuscript *Trattato d'architettura* was widely circulated in Italy. In it, he set forth his concept of an ideal planned community, called Sforzinda in honor of his Sforza patrons in Milan, that was arranged in strict symmetry around an octagonal town square. The treatise contained sketches for a number of idealized structures, including centralized church designs also organized around an octagonal core.[39] The octagon had the virtue of clearly organizing numerous ramifications, be they streets or ancillary structures, into a symmetrical whole – as displayed, for example, in the church designed for Sforzinda. Although the four corner towers are higher than the central structure and have an air of fantasy about them, the conceptual similarity with Diakovo is readily apparent (Figure 146).

Filarete's designs in the *Trattato* were often absurdly impractical in their abstract geometrical complexity. Impractical, that is, for Italy, but not in Muscovy, where the limitations on masonry construction created an emphasis on symbolic, rather than functional, structures. Relying on wood for most building purposes – urban as well as rural – and without the economic or cultural institutions requiring more durable and costly edifices, Muscovy placed its resources in brick, stone, and lime into the construction of fortress walls and churches, reflective not only of the defense of the interdependent interests of state and church, but also, in the sixteenth century, of a new militancy that would be most forcefully expressed in the colorful towers of the greatest of Moscow's votive churches, on Red Square.

If, therefore, the tsar wished to commission a votive church representing hierarchy, centrality, and the multitude of bishops and heavenly hosts interceding for the ruler, it is possible that the appropriate Italian model was at hand. Among Moscow's Italian architects, Fioravanti had worked for the Sforzas in Milan, as had Pietro Antonio Solari, builder of the *Granovitaia palata* in the Kremlin (see Chapter 5). Solari, in fact, participated in the construction of Milan's Ospedale Maggiore, designed by Filarete on a commission from Francesco Sforza in 1451. In addition, Filarete designed for the hospital a church (unbuilt), square in

Figure 144. Church of the Decapitation of John the Baptist at Diakovo. Moscow. East view. (M 10–13).

plan and consisting of a central dome with four high-domed chapels in the corners. Thus, Fioravanti and Solari could have possessed direct knowledge of Filarete's architectural concepts, either from the treatise or from collaboration in his work in Milan. No doubt there were other Italians in Moscow, including perhaps Petrok Malyi, who were also acquainted with the ideas of Filarete, if only by virtue of their outlandish fantasy.

In these circumstances, it would have been a relatively simple – indeed expected – gesture to repro-duce sketches of such intriguing temples for a receptive Muscovite audience. Whether a more detailed plan was transmitted is unknown, although in the Quattrocento, the use of geometrically accurate architectural plans, developed by Filippo Brunelleschi, became accepted practice among Italian architects – and perhaps among certain of their Russian contemporaries.[40] Just who these contemporaries were in the case of the Diakovo church is more than usually difficult to determine due to the lack of historical sources. Barring direct Italian participation at this late

Figure 145. Church of the Decapitation of John the Baptist at Diakovo. Moscow. Interior. (M 55)

level of the central structure without hindering a perception of its form. The pitched decorative gables on all of the towers have an air of fantasy about them, and the entire edifice projects a very unchurchly appearance. (Despite its size, it has no stairs for ceremonial purposes and is the most private of the tsar's votive churches.) Yet the flat domes remind of pre-Mongol churches forms directly influenced by Byzantium, and the system of corner chapels can be seen as a variant of the pentacupolar design. These rich possibilities were soon to be exploited in the most renowned of Russia's architectural monuments, the Cathedral of the Intercession on the Moat, popularly known as the Temple of Vasilii the Blessed.

Cathedral of the Intercession on the Moat

The fame of the building that has come to epitomize the color – and, for some, the barbarism – of Muscovite imagination rests on more than its extravagant exterior. The notorious character of Ivan IV (the Terrible) – who commissioned the Cathedral of the Intercession in 1555 as a commemoration of his taking of Kazan in 1552 – and the savagery of the latter part of his reign have fostered the notion of a structure devoid of restraint or reason (see Plate 31). Yet the architects of record, Barma and Postnik Iakovlev (the latter from Pskov), created a coherent, logical plan that represents a development of the Diakovo church, both in structural terms and in the signification of its components.[42] Like the churches at Kolomenskoe and Diakovo, the Intercession Cathedral is located on high ground above the left bank of the Moscow River and thus provides a visual dominant over a very large space – even in the middle of a crowded urban area, whose wooden structures were lower than the cathedral towers. The visibility of the structure was enhanced by its location on a large square called the *Pozhar* ("fire," as in an area swept by fire) and known by the middle of the seventeenth century as Red (or "beautiful") Square. The church thus served as a visual and symbolic link between the Kremlin, center of political power, and the *Posad*, the densely settled mercantile area in Kitai-gorod, where Ivan enjoyed considerable popularity.[43]

The Intercession Cathedral's ensemble of towers and domes echoes the urban ambiance of sixteenth-century Kitai-gorod, with its many churches.[44] It consists of a central tower surrounded on a common base by eight free-standing churches, each with its own entrance (Figure 147). This proliferation of forms – increased by seventeenth-century additions – is dominated by the "tent" of the central tower, and by the

date, it is reasonable to assume that the architect was from Pskov – not only because of the long tradition of Pskov collectives at work in the Moscow area (see Chapter 5) and their highly regarded skill as brick masons, but also from certain features suggestive of the Pskov style, such as the open belfry on the west facade. Furthermore, there is documentary evidence concerning masons from Pskov in service to Ivan IV as fortification engineers and as architects within Moscow itself, most notably of the Cathedral of the Intercession (St. Basil's).[41]

Although John the Baptist at Diakovo is overshadowed by its spectacular predecessor at Kolomenskoe and its successor on Red Square, it represents the essence of masonry construction in sixteenth-century Muscovy – massive, fortresslike, and skillfully modeled both in its individual components and in the union of its separate forms, creating a texture of light and shadow. The corner chapels reach the cornice

Figure 146. Church of the Decapitation of John the Baptist at Diakovo. Moscow. Southwest view. (M 186–29)

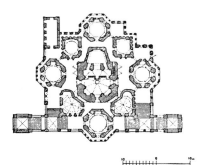

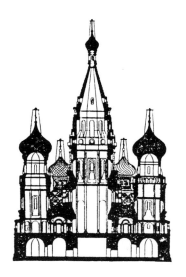

Figure 147. Cathedral of the Intercession on the Moat (Temple of Basil the Blessed). Moscow. Transverse section; plan at terrace level by F. Rikhter.

center of the plan, but is shifted westward to accommodate its apsidal structure (see Figure 147). The Cathedral of the Intercession thus has a dual center: the tower itself and that of the structure as a whole, whose north–south axis runs from the center of the south tower to its counterpart on the north.[47] There is a greater distance between the main tower and its eastern satellites than between those on the west, which appear foreshortened and compressed, with a concomitant increase in the density of their mass and color (Figure 149; see Plate 31).

The origins of the Cathedral of the Intercession are as complex as its form. Soon after his storm of the city of Kazan on October 1–2, 1552, Ivan commanded that a church dedicated to the Holy Trinity be erected on the square outside the Kremlin at the Frolov Gate.[48]

Figure 148. Cathedral of the Intercession on the Moat. Moscow. West elevation by F. Rikhter.

alternation of height in the eight surrounding churches: small on the diagonal and large at the compass points.[45] The octagonal motif at the base of the plan is repeated in the drum and tent roof of the central tower, as well as in the four octagonal churches on the compass points. The remaining, smaller churches (partially obscured by the seventeenth-century enclosure of the cathedral terrace) are cuboid, with a cupola and round drum raised on three tiers of *kokoshniki*.[46] When viewed from the west side (Figure 148; see Plate 31), the cathedral and its flanking stairways to the entrance project a regulated, imposing design appropriate to the ceremonial functions that culminated on this side, facing one of the main entrances to the Kremlin (the Frolov – later Savior – Tower).

When viewed from the river to the south or from Red Square to the north, however, the cathedral presents a multiaxial silhouette inherent in the nature of the design: the central tower is not in the geometric

In view of the national significance of his victory, Ivan perhaps wished to place the church-monument closer to the populous Kitai-gorod area. And, indeed, the brick Church of the Trinity, completed in 1553 and located on a moat in front of the Kremlin, immediately became a popular shrine with seven attached wooden chapels.[49] There is no reliable evidence as to the ap-

Figure 149. Cathedral of the Intercession on the Moat. Moscow. South view. (M 146–16)

pearance of this ensemble, and no reason to assume that its proliferation of chapels had a particular architectural plan that served as a prototype for the subsequent masterpiece. The accrual of chapels around a shrine was a frequent practice.

But Ivan intented to rebuild the church on a scale consonant with the importance of his defeat of Kazan, which not only eliminated an ancient and troublesome relic of Mongol power, but also opened a vast area for colonization and trade. And with the conquest in 1554–6 of the khanate of Astrakhan, at the mouth of the Volga on the Caspian Sea, one of the most important Eurasian trading arteries came into Muscovy. In addition, and more significant from the religious point of view, the conquest of the eastern Islamic khanates signaled a triumph for Russian Orthodoxy at a time when the church still faced challenges to its wealth, its institutions, and to its most sacred doctrines from various heretical movements such as the persistent antitrinitarian groups (hence, the symbolic dedication of the original church to the Trinity).[50]

A new monument was, therefore, to express the triumph of Orthodoxy and of Muscovy, a dual purpose evident in the sponsoring of the Intercession Cathedral by both the Metropolitan Macarius and the tsar. Manuscript accounts indicate that the Trinity Church was to be joined by a church dedicated to the Intercession and seven chapels, with the Intercession as the central church, but the Trinity rivaling it in importance. Concerning the total number, at least one seventeenth-century source indicates that the Metropolitan Macarius initially stipulated eight churches (the number at the original shrine), but that the architects advocated a ninth to achieve a symmetrical arrangement of the ensemble.[51]

The cathedral design clearly derives in part from the preceding votive churches: the central tent tower from Kolomenskoe and the subsidiary towers from Diakovo. There is no convincing evidence of an indigenous prototype in wood,[52] although the practice of grouping wooden chapels around a shrine can be considered a conceptual antecedent. In western church architecture, there are many octagonal designs, from medieval baptisteries to Brunelleschi's St. Maria degli Angeli (1434; construction halted at the ground floor in 1437), with a plan consisting of a central octagon whose bays opened onto eight surrounding chapels. In addition, Leonardo da Vinci created a number of sketches for octacupolar churches. Indeed, the ground plan of Bramante's design for the Basilica of St. Peter in Rome bears an abstract resemblance to the plan of the Cathedral of the Intercession.[53] Yet, with the exception of St. Peter's, the foregoing projects – like Filarete's ideal churches – were not realized, and they exemplify only an innate logic peculiar to certain geometric designs, not an octagonal system of separate churches. Although this geometric logic may have been transmitted to Moscow by Italian architects, there is no basis to assume their participation in the making of the exuberant forms of the Intercession Cathedral.

Whatever the borrowed motifs in its design (and a number are of Italian origin), the ultimate form is a resolute proclamation of the unique and separate identity of Muscovy at a time of militant expansion. Nor was the territorial growth solely to the east and south: Initially, successful campaigns in Livonia to the west gave rise not only to visions of taking the ancient lands of Kievan Rus, but even to a "reverse" crusade bringing Orthodoxy even into the lands of the Germans.[54] In the 1560s, such megalomania soon faced the reality of a vital Polish state; but in 1555, with the exaltation of the eastern victories still present, the force of the messianic idea suffused the complex design of the cathedral with a combination of violence and religious mysticism. Ivan the Terrible's victories were not simply the repulse of an enemy or an episode in interminable border warfare, but a defining event in the identity of a nation, endowed with a sense of inexorable destiny.

To celebrate these ideas, each of the components of the Intercession Cathedral was endowed with multiple iconographic and symbolic meanings. The main axis begins on its eastern end with what has been construed as the original church, dedicated to the Trinity (Figure 150). Although the Intercession tower contains an apse, the Trinity Church can be seen as the holy of holies for the ensemble in general, not only because of its eastern position but also by virtue of its dedication to the trinitarian mystery, which forms the basis of the numerological system of the cathedral. Each axis, each diagonal, each side has three towers, whose structure from the terrace level is divided into three parts: the main level (octagon or cube), tiers of kokoshniki (semicircular or ogival), and the culminating octagon, above which is the cupola (see Figure 148).

The steeply pitched triangular pediments of the Trinity Church form a contrast to the billowy onion-dome turban, placed there – as were the other onion domes – in a restoration of the cathedral in 1586 following its damage during the catastrophic Moscow fire in 1583. Because of the absence of sixteenth-century illustrations of the monument, the original form of the cupolas, apparently of monochromatic tin over iron sheets, can only be surmised – most likely helmet-shaped or low domes similar to those at Diakovo.[55] The machicolation beneath the dome of the Trinity Church appears to a greater or lesser degree in each of the four major satellite churches.

At the center of the main axis is the tower dedicated to the Intercession of the Virgin, one of the most revered of Russian church holidays (see Chapter 3). Apart from its significance as a celebration of the divine protection extended to Russia, the day of its observance, October 1, coincided with the start of the final storming of Kazan. By virtue of this dual significance, the Intercession tower is the largest component of the cathedral, and until the completion of

Figure 150. Cathedral of the Intercession on the Moat. Moscow. East view with Church of the Trinity (main cupola) in center foreground; Chapel of Basil the Blessed (1588), lower right; and Church of Sts. Cyprian and Ustinia, upper right. (M 147–9)

the Bell Tower of Ivan the Great in 1600, it was the highest structure in Moscow: some 61 meters (comparable to its prototype at Kolomenskoe). Indeed, from a structural perspective, the Intercession owes much to the octagonal design of the great Kremlin bell tower – thus illustrating the peculiar and immensely productive fusion of Italian Renaissance and Muscovite design in this most Russian of structures. The base of the tent, an eight-pointed star arising from massed tiers of *kokoshniki*, originally served as a platform for eight small drums and cupolas, reproducing on the central tower the larger configuration of the cathedral.[56] The exterior decoration of the tent combined gilded and twisted metallic strips along the ribs of the *shatior* with glazed terra-cotta ornaments (see Plate 31).

During the 1950s, an exploration of the interior surface of the central tower uncovered at the base of the

tent an original inscription noting the dedication of the Intercession Church on June 29, 1561 (the feast day of the Apostles Peter and Paul), in honor of the Holy Trinity and in the presence of the tsar, the tsareviches Ivan and Fedor, and Metropolitan Macarius. (The surrounding, lesser churches had been consecrated in 1560.) The restoration of the interior also revealed a restrained decorative pattern, presumably resembling the interiors of the votive churches at Kolomenskoe and Diakovo.[57] The main part of the interior was painted brick red, with white seams limned to resemble the mortar – a technique known as *pod kirpich*, or in imitation of brick. This practice, applied also to the exterior brick walls of the cathedral, was imported from Italy, and it appears that a number of the Kremlin structures of the early sixteenth century, such as the Rusticated Chambers, were originally painted in the same manner.[58] Not only did the paint protect the walls from moisture seepage, but the brick pattern also enhanced the color of the surface. Although at least half of the adjoining churches later acquired frescoes, the return to the original brick pattern in some of the interiors has revealed its appropriateness to the narrow, confined space. The interiors of the chapels culminated in a pinwheel spiral on the vaulting beneath the cupola – as in the side chapels of the Diakovo church (see Figure 145). The interior of the larger Intercession tower (46 meters in height from the floor) had more elaborate ornamentation, including on the interior facets of the tent a painted imitation of the rhomboid pattern used on the exterior at Kolomenskoe.[59]

If the Trinity Church represents the sanctum or the apse of the entire ensemble, and the Intercession Church the central temple, then the primary entrance to the ensemble is the west church, dedicated to the Entry of Christ into Jerusalem (see Plate 31). While completing the main axis in homage to Palm Sunday, the west church also symbolizes the triumphal entry of Ivan the Terrible into Kazan. The association of the two events – Kazan and Jerusalem – led as early as 1557 to the institution of an annual ritual in which the tsar, led on a horse caparisoned as a donkey, simulated the Palm Sunday procession.[60] The ritual at first was circumscribed by the Kremlin cathedrals (the Dormition Cathedral contained an altar dedicated to the Entry into Jerusalem); but, evidently, by 1559, the procession had been reoriented beyond the Kremlin to the Trinity Church, under construction as the enlarged Intercession Cathedral. The inference is that the new shrine – and not the Kremlin and its cathedrals – represented the sacred city, Zion, Jerusalem.[61] Indeed, the Intercession Cathedral was often called simply "Jerusalem," a designation recorded in the seventeenth century by western visitors to Moscow such as Adam Olearius (Figure 151).[62]

The enormous resonance of Jerusalem in the formulation of a Muscovite ideology appears not only in the architecture of Ivan the Terrible's reign, but for a century thereafter. Yet the agglomeration of tent towers in the Cathedral of the Intercession represents more than an image of the heavenly city; it is an identification of the messianic idea with Moscow itself. All that Moscow strove for in asserting its national identity against hostile states in the east, south, and west – the gathering together of component parts, the enclosure of those parts within a single base, the imitation of fortress architecture (even to the use of machicolation), the sense of hierarchy and centralization – all are represented in the form of the cathedral, even as it mediates between the Kremlin and the secular, popular world of the *posad* and of Kitaigorod.

With the establishment of the primary religious and symbolic concepts in the main axis, from east to west, the other six churches assumed a symbolic program referring to the Kazan campaign, memorialized by four churches – in addition to the more general memorial of the Intercession Church. The northwest chapel is dedicated to Bishop Gregory of Armenia, on whose feast day (September 30) occurred two major events preceding the storm of Kazan: the defeat of a sortie of enemy troops on the Field of Arsk, and the spectacular explosion of the Arsk Tower, one of the main bastions of the city. The north church (see Fig. 150; see Plate 32), dedicated to Sts. Cyprian and Ustinia (October 2), commemorates the completion of the conquest after the storming of the city the preceding day. The northeast chapel, dedicated to three Byzantine patriarchs (Alexander, John, and Paul), represents the victory on August 30 over the Tatar cavalry led by Prince Epancha, thus eliminating a major threat to the siege of Kazan. This battle appears to be commemorated again in the southeast chapel, dedicated to St. Alexander of Svir, whose day also occurs on August 30.

The remaining two churches – both on the south flank (see Figure 149) – refer to the tsar's family in continuation of a practice established in earlier votive churches such as at Diakovo. The dedication of the southwest chapel (see Plate 33) to St. Varlaam of the Khutynskii Monastery near Novgorod commemorates the tsar's father, Vasilii III, who shortly before his death assumed the traditional role of monk and adopted the name Varlaam.[63] The south church is dedicated to the icon of St. Nicholas of Velikoretsk

Figure 151. Cathedral of the Intercession on the Moat. Moscow. East view, midseventeenth century (after Olearius).

(after the River Velikaia in the area of Pskov), a venerated image brought to Moscow for reconsecration. The role of Pskov's monks in formulating the mission of Muscovite autocracy was noted at the end of the preceding chapter, and it is not unexpected that the shrine should pay homage to a saint in the Pskovian monastic tradition. To this one must also add the inestimable contribution of Pskov's builders to the development masonry construction in Muscovy during the fifteenth and sixteenth centuries, culminating in the Intercession Cathedral.[64]

When all of the original churches are accounted for, one is still left with the popular "dedication" of the Intercession Cathedral to Vasilii the Blessed (1469–1552), a Muscovite *iurodivyi* – or "fool in Christ" – revered by the tsar himself as well as by the common people for his saintliness, his gift of prophecy, and his courage. By coincidence Vasilii died in the year of the taking of Kazan, and a wooden shrine in his honor was erected to the east of the original Trinity Church.[65] The shrine was maintained during the building of the Intercession Cathedral, and in 1588, it was replaced with the small brick Chapel (*pridel*) of Vasilii the Blessed, attached to the northeast corner of the cathedral (see Figure 150). Despite the modest size of the church in relation to the surrounding towers, the cult of Vasilii grew to such proportions as to usurp in common usage all of the cathedral's previous designations, official or unofficial. Even its apparently unpretentious structure – a single drum and cupola over a domical vault without interior piers – established a form of structure typical of a series of churches in the "Godunov style" at the end of the century.[66]

Indeed, Boris Godunov may well have been responsible for the creation, after the fire of 1583, of the cathedral's distinctive onion domes (*lukovitsa*), which are among the earliest authenticated examples of that form in Russian masonry architecture. It has been suggested that their bulbous shape derives from a late fifteenth-century reliquary that reproduced the cupola of a medieval canopy over the Holy Sepulcher, and thus represents another manifestation of the Jerusalem theme that enthralled Godunov (see what follows).[67] Would the onion dome – sanctified by the notion of recreating Zion in Moscow – have spread so rapidly at the end of the sixteenth century, replacing innumerable cupolas on earlier churches and setting a pattern for subsequent architecture? Like other theories on the origins of the Russian onion dome (from eastern sources such as India, or as a gradual development of northern prototypes, perhaps of wood), this one remains a matter of conjecture.

The ensuing evolution of the Intercession Cathedral culminated in the seventeenth century with the enclosure of the terrace, the building of another church adjoining Vasilii the Blessed on the east side, and numerous additions to the ground floor, including thirteen chapels removed from their original location along the Red Square moat. These shrines "on the blood" had been built on the site of various public executions during the time of Ivan the terrible; most of them were dismantled in the renovation of the cathedral during the 1780s. Around 1680, the large free-standing bell tower at the southeast corner of the cathedral (see Figure 149) was reconstructed in a seventeenth-century ornamental style, with polychromatic decoration and a tent roof of ceramic tile. Much

of the painted ornamentation on the exterior walls, particularly of the new gallery, was also added in the latter part of the century.[68] As the major cathedral in one of the most populous sections of Moscow, the Intercession, or Trinity, Cathedral – or the Temple of Vasilii the Blessed, or simply Jerusalem – stood like a massive outcropping swept by waves of rebuilding in each successive era, retaining some of the modifications, but never losing the form that celebrated Muscovy's accession to an empire in the East.

Late Sixteenth-Century Architecture

The form of the tower churches would provide some of the most distinctive examples of Russian architecture over the century following the building of the Intercession Cathedral; yet the traditional pentacupolar design retained its viability, even in the construction of votive churches during the decade after the conquest of Kazan and Astrakhan. The Cathedral of the Dormition at the Trinity-St. Sergius Monastery (see Figure 134), begun in 1559, can be considered as one such example, even though it was not consecrated until 1585. In Kazan itself, the establishment of an archiepiscopate in 1555 led to the construction in 1556–62 of a pentacupolar cathedral on the site of what had been the main mosque within the citadel.[69]

Indeed, the Kremlin Annunciation Cathedral, considered the court church of the grand prince, was itself the object of votive expansion in 1564–6 with the construction of four chapels built above the covered gallery along the north and south facades of the structure (see Figures 109 and 110). It has been proposed that Ivan added the chapels in fulfillment of a vow after the taking of Polotsk in 1563 during the opening stages of the Livonian War.[70] The chapel dedications included the Entry into Jerusalem, whose symbolic significance has been discussed before; the Convocation of the Mother of God; and the Archangel Michael, protector of the ruler – appropriate both symbolically and stylistically, in view of the chapels' miniature replication of the Italianate features on the facade of the adjacent Archangel Michael Cathedral.

The early 1560s were not, however, auspicious for Ivan, particularly after the death of his first wife, Anastasia, in 1560. Despite initial successes, Ivan's western campaign in Livonia met with a vigorous Polish response led by King Stephen Báthory, and by the middle of the decade the strain had begun to place intolerable burdens on the state system and on the tsar himself. From that point, Muscovite architecture entered a period of stagnation linked to the social collapse and dementia that suffused the final two de-

129

cades of Ivan's reign. Although an element of rationality existed in foreign policy and in the administrative chanceries, the implacable suspicion and hostility of the tsar toward the ever larger groups of those he considered his enemies – including many of the boyars and certain segments of the clergy – led him in 1565 to divide Muscovy into two parts, one of which he claimed as his own "estate" (the *oprichnina*). The rest of the country was given a separate administration (the *zemshchina*), which fell prey to the depredations of Ivan's personal army.[71] The widening circle of arrests and executions combined with plague and famine to depopulate large parts of the country. The greatest victim was Novgorod, which was sacked at the beginning of 1570 and hundreds of its residents executed under false suspicion of treasonous relations with Moscow's enemy Poland. Reverses in the Livonian War to the west and ineffectual resistance to a large-scale raid on Moscow in 1571 by the Crimean Tatars increased the burden on the state, although subsequent raids by the Tatars were soundly repulsed after the liquidation of the *oprichnina* in 1572.

The center of architectural patronage during the *oprichnina* was Ivan the Terrible's walled compound at Aleksandrova Sloboda, an estate much favored by his father, Vasilii III, at the beginning of the sixteenth century (see Figure 129). It was here that Ivan established his separate court in January 1565, and for almost 10 years, the compound served as the center of the Muscovite state. A number of foreigners – emissaries and mercenaries – produced accounts of life at Aleksandrova Sloboda that stretch the limits of credulity. The tsar instituted a pseudo-monastic regime, with his personal guard, the *oprichniki,* as monks; religious services and prayers alternated with the torture and execution. In the words of one recent history of Aleksandrova Sloboda: "Hypocrisy, having become a tradition with the majority of Moscow princes, and later tsars, acquires in the character of Ivan the Terrible a hypertrophied resonance, an apotheosis."[72]

After savage punitive campaigns against Tver in 1569 and Novgorod in 1570, Ivan commissioned for the "redemption of his sins" two churches at Aleksandrova Sloboda, both of which were placed over large vaulted cellars designed to store the treasure from his despoilation of Novgorod and other Russian towns.[73] The refectory Church of the Trinity (1570–1; subsequently renamed the Church of the Intercession) displays a tent tower on a truncated octagon over the place of worship; its refectory was enlarged and a bell tower added on the west in the 1660s (Figure 152). Ivan's palace was attached to this structure, which serves as another example of the evolution to-

Figure 152. Refectory Church of the Trinity. Aleksandrova Sloboda. 1570–1. North elevation (with seventeenth-century additions) by N. Sibiriakov.

ward the "refectory church" of the seventeenth century, with the *shatior* yielding to a pentacupolar roof. The neighboring Church of the Dormition originally had one cupola when built in the early 1570s, but received its pentacupolar form, as well as an array of chambers and a refectory, in the 1660s.[74] Both churches show extensive use of limestone, in addition to brick, for wall construction – a feature peculiar to late sixteenth-century Muscovite architecture.

The most distinctive structure created at Aleksandrova Sloboda in the 1570s, and the one most closely related to the votive tower, is the bell tower and church, dedicated to the Crucifixion at the end of the seventeenth century (Figure 153). The original octagonal bell tower, which forms the nucleus of the later structure, was probably commissioned by Vasilii III concurrently with the Intercession Cathedral (1515). In the mid-1570s, apparently after the abolition of the *oprichnina*, the tower was encased within the massive pylons of a 2-story polygonal arcade, supporting three tiers of *kokoshniki*, an open octagon, and a tent roof with cupola soaring to a height of 56 meters.[75] With this monument, Ivan not only provided Aleksandrova Sloboda with the vertical dominant characteristic of the great Russian monastic ensembles, but also commemorated his own apocalyptic rule from this compound. The formal debt to the central tower of the Intercession Cathedral in Moscow is clear, but its innovation (apart from the unprecented scale and shape of the arcade) lay in the adaptation of the *shatior* to the bell tower – a device that would spread through-

Figure 153. Bell tower and Church of the Crucifixion. Aleksandrova Sloboda. 1570s. Northwest view. (Z 3–11)

The opposite chronological adjustment has been applied to the refectory Church of the Dormition at the Savior-Evfimii Monastery in Suzdal (Figure 155). Formerly dated to 1525, the church now appears to have been constructed no earlier than the last quarter of the century.[77] Its tent tower is similar to, and perhaps influenced by, the tower of Moscow's Cathedral of the Intercession on the Moat. Also in favor of the later date is the lack of clearly delineated refectory churches until the latter part of the century. This Russian monastic institution, which flourished in the seventeenth century, seems to have begun as an austere refectory structure with no differentiated altar space attached – as illustrated by the refectory Church of the Conception of St. Anne (1551) at the Intercession Convent in Suzdal (Figure 156).

The Savior-Evfimii refectory, however, has a clearly defined church structure with a tent tower above rows of *kokoshniki*, as well as an apse and attached chapel on the southeast. Although the Church of the Dormition overshadows the modest structure of the refectory proper, later combinations of refectory and church will reveal a closer integration of form. It

Figure 154. Bell tower and Church of St. George, Kolomenskoe. Moscow. 1534(?). Southeast view. (M 9–3)

out Russian church architecture after the tent was abandoned for use over the church proper.

Certain tower churches attributed to the closing decades of Ivan's reign remain imprecisely dated. It has been suggested recently that the tower Church of St. George at Kolomenskoe (Figure 154), formerly dated to the latter part of the sixteenth century, was in fact built in 1534 as a votive church upon the birth the preceding year of Iurii (George), brother of Ivan IV.[76] The round tower displays some of the Italianate features present in early sixteenth-century architecture, but its plan and decorative features such as kokoshniki suggest that its builders applied foreign motifs in a superficial manner, particularly when compared to the coherence of the design of the Church of the Metropolitan Peter, attributed to Petrok (see Figure 136).

Figure 155. Refectory Church of the Dormition, Savior-Evfimii Monastery. Suzdal. Late sixteenth century. Southeast view. (SD 4–10)

should be noted in passing that the Savior-Evfimii monastery contains one genuine anachronism: the Cathedral of the Transfiguration of the Savior (1582–94; see Plate 34), built in the style of monastery cathedrals of the middle of the century, which were themselves an imitation of Fioravanti's Dormition Cathedral. Its blind arcading represents both fifteenth-century Muscovite and thirteenth-century Suzdalian motifs.

The vitality of the tent form in late sixteenth-century architecture is nowhere more forcefully stated than in the Church of the Transfiguration at the village of Ostrov, another country estate of the grand princes, and later tsars, on the southern outskirts of Moscow.[78] In the absence of documentation, much in the construction history of this striking form (Figure 157) remains unclear. Indeed, it is possible that the *shatior* was completed by a different architect considerably later than the lower part of the structure – perhaps as late as the first half of the seventeenth century (the church was dedicated in the presence of Tsar Aleksei Mikhailovich in 1646).[79] The central part of the lower church is a massive limestone cruciform structure, reminiscent of the Ascension at Kolomenskoe, yet substantially different in the configuration of its east, apsidal end. Whereas the Kolomenskoe church had

Figure 156. Refectory Church of the Conception of St. Anne, Intercession Convent. Suzdal. 1551. South facade. (V 10–33)

132

no exterior apse, the church at Ostrov reveals a pronounced extension of the eastern end, which produces on the interior a less coherent delineation of space. On the exterior, the decorative masses of *kokoshniki* on both the corner chapels and, in two tiers, on the central tower represent a mannered interpretation of a form that had achieved its greatest expression in the middle of the sixteenth century.

The commemorative uses of the tent tower were often effectively exploited on a considerably smaller scale, as in the Church of the Metropolitan Peter in Pereslavl-Zalesskii (Figure 158), built in 1585 to honor the early fourteenth-century metropolitan of the Orthodox Church who provided significant support to the Muscovite principality at an early stage of its development (see Chapter 5).[80] The Church of the Metropolitan Peter shares certain formal features with its prototype, the much larger Ascension Church at Ko-

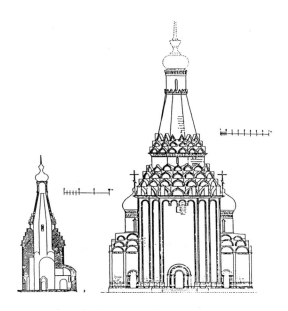

Figure 157. Church of the Transfiguration at Ostrov. Near Moscow. Late sixteenth century. West elevation, longitudinal section by A. Khachaturian.

lomenskoe: The lower part of its cruciform structure was buttressed by an open terrace (subsequently enclosed) over arcaded vaults. The upper part of the brick structure is reinforced with wooden beams instead of the iron tie rods of the larger Moscow votive churches. Despite the resemblances between early and late sixteenth-century tent churches, the intervening half century led to a greater emphasis on the ornamental – such as *kokoshniki* – and a clearly defined separation between the tent and the main structure,

as opposed to the monolithic ascent of the Kolomenskoe church.[81]

Although churches remained the primary form of monumental architecture in Moscovy, the troubled circumstances and incessant warfare of the latter part of Ivan's reign ensured that fortress architecture would continue to place major demands on Muscovy's resources, as it had in the reign of Vasilii III. The mobile defense required by the open spaces of the southern border gave rise to log fortified towers ingeniously constructed and capable of rapid assembly. Indeed, the Muscovite campaign against Kazan had been facilitated by the design of precut log structures that were transported and rapidly assembled, such as the fort of Sviiazhsk some 30 kilometers to the north of Kazan in 1551.[82] For more substantial fortifications on the country's northern and western marches, however, brick and stone continued to be widely used, particularly in the construction of fortified monasteries such as St. Nikita in Pereslavl-Zalesskii, whose brick walls were built in the 1560s and show much the same principles of fortification introduced by Petrok Malyi in the design of the Kitai-gorod walls.

Although they lacked the monumentality of the brick fortresses of the time of Vasilii III, those dating from the reign of Ivan proved durable and on occasion withstood a major siege, such as that mounted in 1581 by Polish King Stephen Báthory against Pskov, whose stone walls had been extended in 1516 by an Italian engineer and renovated in the middle of the century. The south wall and towers were subjected to concentrated fire in 1581; and despite the fact that the great Intercession Tower (Figure 159) was eventually taken by the Poles, a secondary wooden wall enabled the defenders to repulse the attack and repair the breach. The reconstructed tower illustrates the preference for a lower, broader silhouette (against artillery fire) similar to that used by Petrok Malyi in Moscow.[83]

The most ingenious Russian fortress design of the Livonian War was built in 1553–65 at the Pskov Cave Monastery, in a ravine some 40 kilometers to the southwest of Pskov. Its stone walls, which follow the rugged terrain, were guarded by nine towers, including the immense Tower of the Upper Grates (Figure 160) through which the stream Kamenets at the bottom of the ravine flowed into the monastery. Its six levels of firepoints covered all four directions, and the high pyramidal wooden roof culminated in a watchtower. In 1581, the Cave Monastery successfully repulsed a detachment of Báthory's troops, and over the next two centuries, its ensemble of churches and the Great Belfry (see Plate 21) were expanded in a colorful, archaic ornamental style.[84]

Figure 158. Church of the Metropolitan Peter. Pereslavl-Zalesskii. 1585. Northwest view. (PZ 2–10a)

Figure 159. Intercession Tower, Pskov citadel. Sixteenth century. (P 12)

Figure 160. Tower of the Upper Grates, Pskov Monastery of the Caves. 1565. (P 11)

Architecture in the Reign of Boris Godunov

The end of the sixteenth century witnessed a brief architectural revival under the patronage of Boris Godunov, who became tsar in 1598 and ruled until 1605. Although not of the ruling dynasty, Godunov had risen to power as one of the most able administrators of Ivan's *oprichnina*. After the death of Ivan, he strengthened his power both through ruthless infighting and through the marriage of his sister Irina to the pious but weak Tsar Fedor, the third son of Ivan the Terrible and the last Riurikovich tsar (of the Daniilovich line). During the reign of Fedor, between 1584 and 1598, Godunov served as an unofficial regent under whose guidance Muscovy began to repair the damage inflicted during the latter years of Ivan. In addition to consolidating its hold on Siberia and in the steppe regions to the south, Muscovy achieved a truce with its western foes – particularly Poland – and expanded trade and diplomatic contacts with England. In terms of political and ecclesiastical prestige, the most important event was the approval in 1589 of Moscow as the seat of a patriarchate in the Orthodox Church. In the strenuous negotiations with the

patriarch of Constantinople, Godunov had supported the metropolitan of Moscow, Job, who became the first Russian patriarch.[85]

Godunov's influence and wealth were reflected in an active building program that began in the late 1580s and created a "Godunov style" of church – a single-cupola structure, often with no interior piers, and a pyramidal bank of *kokoshniki* above the main cornice. The technique of modified domical vaulting that distinguishes the interior of the Godunov churches first appeared in the Chapel of Basil the Blessed on the east end of the Cathedral of the Intercession (1588;

see Figure 150), but the earliest example of the style in its developed form occurred no later than 1593 with the completion at Donskoi Monastery of the Cathedral of the Don Mother of God.[86]

Donskoi Monastery, located at the southern approaches to Moscow, was the last of the major monastic strongpoints constructed to defend the medieval city. In 1591, an army of the Crimean khan Kazy-Girei made a full-scale raid on Moscow; and at a site between the Kaluga and Tula roads leading to the south of the city, Boris Godunov deployed a movable wooden fortress (a tactic refined during the time of Ivan the Terrible) to protect his forward artillery. Godunov subsequently achieved a decisive victory over the invading forces – the last Tatar raid ever to reach the outskirts of Moscow. After the rout, Godunov donated much of the considerable wealth conferred upon him for his military leadership to the foundation of a monastery at the location of his wooden fort.[87] The monastery cathedral was dedicated to the much revered Icon of the Don Mother of God, associated with the first major Russian victory over the Tatars, on Snipe Field near the Don River in 1380. Godunov's choice was thus an extension of the Russian iconographic celebration of divine protection in the incessant war against the southern infidels.[88]

The Donskoi monastery cathedral, while not on the scale and in the dramatic form of votive churches built during the reigns of Vasilii III and Ivan the Terrible, nonetheless follows a pattern of celebratory architecture, with its pyramid of *kokoshniki* etched in white on a background of painted stucco over brick (see Plate 35). The vertical development of the cathedral has long been obscured by two attached chapels flanking the apse (dedicated to St. Nicholas the Miracle Worker and St. Theodore Stratilates), a refectory, and bell tower – all added in the 1670s. But from the east side, the central form is relatively unobstructed and reveals the proportional relation between the structure and the three-tiered transition to the drum, supported on the interior by corbelled arches within the domical vault (Figure 161).[89] The transition of *kokoshniki* on the exterior resembles that of the Crucifixion Church at Aleksandrova Sloboda, yet the rejection of the *shatior* in favor of a single cupola established a new style whose precedents extended back to the fourteenth-century parish architecture of Novgorod.

The precise dates of the subsequent Godunov churches remain open to question. His personal estates at Khoroshevo, Besedy, and Viaziomy provided the settings for three churches, of which the closest to the Donskoi cathedral is the limestone and brick Church of the Trinity at Khoroshevo (Figures 162 and

Figure 161. Small Cathedral of the Don Mother of God, Donskoi Monastery. Moscow. 1593, with chapels and bell tower added in the 1670s. Longitudinal section and plan by N. Sobolev.

163; tentatively dated to 1598), whose vaulting system and the semicircular *kokoshniki* beneath the single cupola of the central structure adhere to the pattern described before.[90] Unlike the initial form of the Donskoi cathedral, however, the Trinity Church was designed with a monolithic apsidal structure of limestone that included the apses of two flanking chapels as a part of the original plan. The resulting apse, in both detail and general form, is related to the apsidal

Figure 162. Church of the Trinity at Khoroshevo. Moscow. C. 1597. Southeast view. (M 10)

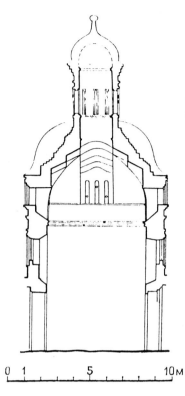

Figure 163. Church of the Trinity at Khoroshevo. Moscow. Plan, section.

to rely upon the Archangel Cathedral not only for its refined facade segmentation, but also its association with the ruling house of Muscovy.[92] If the Trinity Church represents the perfected combination of the single-domed, ornamental form at the Donskoi monastery with an Italianate resolution of the cornice, these motifs are transformed at another, larger Church of the Trinity, built in the late 1590s on the Godunov estate of Viaziomy.[93] Elevated on a high limestone base, the Viaziomy Church of the Trinity (Figure 164; renamed the Transfiguration of the Savior at the end of the seventeenth century) retains the semicircular niches of the smaller churches, but places them within a more traditional and monumental pentacupolar design whose facade is articulated in the manner of Aleviz. In addition to the precise delineation of the facade bays by pilasters and the double

structure of the much larger Dormition Cathedral by Fioravanti (see Figure 119).

Yet the articulation of the facades of the Trinity Church at Khoroshevo also suggests a deliberate, perhaps politically motivated, return to that most influential of Muscovite cathedral designs, the Archangel Michael by Aleviz. The symbolic significance of the cathedral as the burial shrine of Moscow's rulers, as well as its influence on the design of the neighboring Ascension Convent cathedral (the burial site for the wives of Muscovite rulers) have been noted in the preceding chapter. In 1587–8, the Aleviz cathedral again served as a model for a rebuilding of the Ascension Cathedral, supported in this instance by Irina and Boris Godunov. It has been argued that the project, launched at a time when Godunov was engaged in a crucial struggle to prevent a rival court faction led by the Shuiskii clan from arranging a divorce between his sister and Tsar Fedor, is a most obvious example of the use of architectural style in the service of political power – particularly within a situation that required the support of the church hierarchy.[91]

It is plausible, therefore, that after Godunov's victory over his rivals by 1589, his architects continued

Figure 164. Church of the Trinity (from the late seventeenth century, Church of the Transfiguration of the Savior). Viaziomy. Near Moscow. C. 1598. Northwest view. (ZV 1–1)

136

segmentation of the cornice, the Viaziomy architect paid homage to the Italian master in the use of profiled arches at the upper level of each bay, thus emphasizing the verticality of the structure (Aleviz had placed the arcade motif on the first tier of the Archangel Michael Church).[94]

Indeed, the Viaziomy church uses the visual language not only of the Archangel Michael Cathedral, but also of Fioravanti's Dormition Cathedral: the walls are of limestone up to the cornice level, with brick for the vaulting and cupola drums; and the original roof, covered with oak shingles, followed the contours of the semicircular zakomary.[95] The apsidal structure of five ashlar limestone bays resembles the limestone monolith at the east end of the Dormition Cathedral in the Kremlin. Like the Trinity Church at Khoroshevo, which also derived its apsidal design from the Dormition Cathedral, the incorporation of flanking chapels on either side of the central structure (with the usual three bays) permitted the expansion of the east facade to a width of five apses. Although the chapels' height is much less than that of the main structure, the disparity is mediated by a pyramid of *kokoshniki* leading to a small cupola over each attached chapel. The greater width at the east end of the church is integrated into the main structure by a raised terrace attached to the central cube on the south, west, and north facades (Figure 165).

The architect of the Viaziomy church thus combined with consummate skill the decorative pyramidal clusters of *kokoshniki* with elements from the Kremlin cathedrals and from the tower votive churches with elevated terraces. The Trinity Church was further enhanced by the unique design of its free-standing brick belfry, built at the same time and situated to the northeast of the church (Figure 166). Like the Trinity Church itself, the belfry rises from an elevated terrace, with two levels of triple arches culminating in *kokoshniki* and tent gables. In design, it is related to the bell gables of the Pskov region, but interpreted with a precision of detail characteristic of the best examples of late sixteenth-century Muscovite architecture.[96]

If the Trinity at Viaziomy is the most accomplished church of Godunov's reign, the most impressive was the tower Church of Sts. Boris and Gleb, built at the turn of the seventeenth century and located at the walled compound of Borisov Gorodok, a Godunov estate near Mozhaisk to the southeast of Moscow. In some respects, Borisov Gorodok, which was demolished at the beginning of the nineteenth century, seems to have been Godunov's answer to Ivan the Terrible's compound at Aleksandrova Sloboda – with

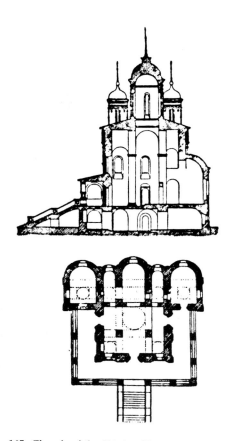

Figure 165. Church of the Trinity. Viaziomy. Longitudinal section and plan by V. Suslov.

which Godunov was well familiar. But the elongated form of the *shatior* of the Church of Sts. Boris and Gleb (Figure 167) suggests above all the votive church at Kolomenskoe, and with good dynastic reason. The dedication of the church to St. Boris and the very name of the settlement (lit., "Boris town") signaled a clear intent to celebrate the founding of a new dynasty with the accession of Boris to the throne after the death of Fedor in 1598. (Fedor left no male heir, thus ending the legitimate succession of the Moscow Daniilovich line of the Riurikovich dynasty; and Irina Godunova entered the Novodevichii Convent after his death.) Other tower forms during the Godunov era include the Church of the Nativity of Christ constructed in the late 1590s on his estate at Besedy to the south of Moscow.[97] And it is possible that the church at Ostrov (see Figure 157) was also largely built during the same period. Like the Ascension at Kolomenskoe, the churches at Besedy and Ostrov were placed to overlook the Moscow River and thereby proclaim the power of the Muscovite ruler along its serpentine path through this Ile de Russe.[98]

137

Figure 166. Church of the Trinity. Viaziomy. Bell tower. (ZV 1–2)

Figure 167. Church of Sts. Boris and Gleb at Borisov Gorodok (not extant). Northwest view. Reconstruction by P. Rappoport.

The sixteenth century in Muscovy thus concludes with a return to the secular, dynastic message of the votive church that had appeared in the reign of Vasilii III. Yet the stylistic evolution over the preceding seven decades (the Boris and Gleb Church was consecrated in 1603) had its effect, for the lower structure of the church at Borisov Gorodok bore a striking resemblance to the Viaziomy monument, with a raised arcaded terrace and similar segmentation of the facade. The three tiers of *kokoshniki* above the cornice represent the Godunov style, in contrast to the traditional pentacupolar Viaziomy church; but the compound at Borisov Gorodok also had a free-standing bell tower apparently similar in configuration to the one at Viaziomy.[99]

The similarities between these and other churches of the Godunov era have led to speculation on the identity of their architects, on whom there is no recorded information. It has been suggested, for example, that most of the churches are the work of the extraordinarily gifted engineer Fedor Kon, the builder of enormous fortification works initiated by Godunov

in Smolensk and in Moscow (see what follows).[100] A different hypothesis suggests that an architect other than Kon built the major Godunov churches, whose stylistic similarities could only have come from one master.[101] And yet another view maintains that Kon, master of fortifications, could have built the walled ensemble and the church at Borisov Gorodok, but makes no reference to the other churches.[102]

Whatever the degree of Kon's involvement in the construction of the Godunov churches, his place in the history of Russian architecture is ensured by the massive fortress at Smolensk. Built between 1595 and 1602 as part of Godunov's foreign policy vis-à-vis Poland, the fortress had thirty-eight towers (Figure 168) along a perimeter wall 6.5 kilometers in length – among the largest Russian construction projects before the reign of Peter the Great. And like the herculean ventures of Peter, it required the mobilization of resources and forced labor from a large area of Muscovy, including monastery and private brickyards enlisted in state service. (As during the intensive early stages of the building of Petersburg, masonry construction not connected with state service was prohibited on pain of death.[103])

The production of the 100 million bricks needed for the Smolensk walls and the great quantity of limestone blocks used for their base – in addition to lime, iron, and other components – could only have occurred with the standardization of building materials (particularly, brick sizes) and the organization of production and the labor force under the centralized administrative system expanded under Godunov's able guidance. One of the main components of that system was the Office of Masonry Work (*Kamennyi prikaz*), created in 1584 and used by Godunov to encourage masonry construction for personal as well as state projects. In Moscow, plagued by fires from unregulated wooden construction, civilian access to materials needed for masonry building was eased, long-term loans were arranged, and builders were encouraged to adhere to more regular street lines.[104]

The benefits of the new organization of construction were soon visible in Moscow itself with the construction in 1584–93 of the massive brick wall of Tsar Gorod or Belyi Gorod (*gorod* originally meaning walled enclosure or citadel) to protect the rapidly expanding trading districts beyond the Kremlin and Kitai-gorod. The walls were coated with whitewash, which gave them their name (*belyi*, or white) and en-

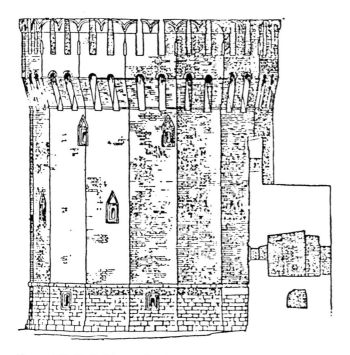

Figure 168. Eagle Tower, Smolensk citadel. 1595–1602. Architect: Fedor Kon. Elevation by P. Pokryshkin.

dowed the city with a more imposing appearance. In addition, the memory of Crimean Tatar raids – the last occurring in 1591 – stimulated the construction of a still larger circumference composed of an earthern rampart with log walls (Figure 169). The rapidity with which they were built, within the one season of 1591, gave rise to the name Skorodom ("rapid building").[105]

The architectural center of Muscovy remained, however, the Kremlin, for it was here that Godunov devised his most ambitious plans for the remaking of the very image of Moscow in a reconstruction of the Kremlin cathedral ensemble as a "Holy of Holies" (*Sviataia sviatykh*). The idea for a vast temple on the square adjacent to the Bell Tower of Ivan the Great and overshadowing the existing cathedrals appears to have arisen from Godunov's grandiose vision of Moscow as the new Jerusalem, and from the increased authority of the Russian Church after the establishment of the patriarchate in Moscow in 1589.[106] Only fragmentary information is available on the form of Godunov's intended project; but it is now accepted that the model – in a general if not precise sense – was to be drawn from the Anastasis (Church of the Resurrection) in Jerusalem, with particular emphasis on its rotunda over the Holy Sepulcher.[107] Although preparations for construction began in 1598, the project met with opposition at the beginning of the seventeenth century, and events following Godunov's death in 1605 rendered the plans irrelevant. (The revival of the architectural vision of New Jerusalem would return to Muscovy in the middle of the seventeenth century; see Chapter 7.)

Nonetheless, one component apparently intended for the Holy of Holies in the Kremlin materialized when, in 1599–1600, the Bell Tower of Ivan the Great was extended by the two additional tiers that brought it to its present height of 81 meters (see Figure 126). This project also had its dynastic significance, stated clearly in an inscription composed of three bands of gold letters on a dark blue background beneath the gold cupola. The statement proclaimed that the addition was done "by command of his great majesty the tsar and grand prince Boris Fedorovich ruler of all Rus . . . and his son the tsarevich prince Fedor Borisovich." Boris made every effort to inculcate the values of a powerful and intelligent ruler in his son, whose inclusion in the inscription on the highest structure in Moscow signaled the arrival of a new dynasty.

Godunov's vision ultimately collapsed under a succession of natural catastrophes (exacerbated by the weakness of the country after the reign of Ivan the Terrible) over which this energetic and intelligent

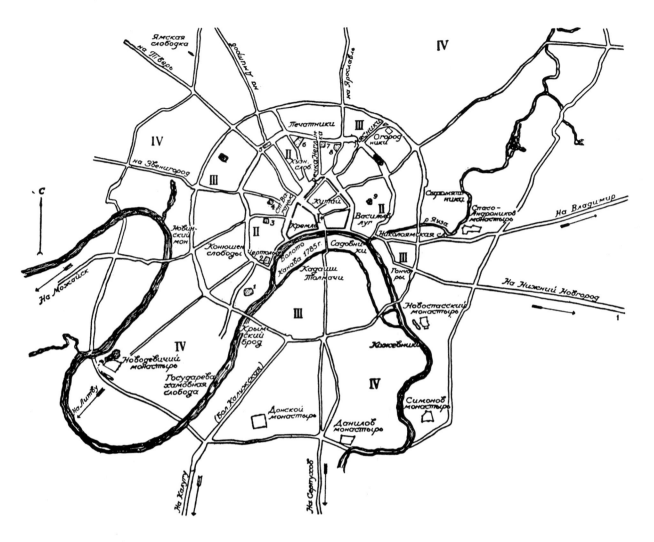

Figure 169. Plan of sixteenth-century Moscow, with circumference walls and major monasteries.

ruler had no control. Furthermore, his power – and, more important, that of his heir – was undermined by the considerable political maneuvering involved in his accession to the throne. The weakness inherent in his tenuous claims to the crown was further exposed in the aftermath of the death in 1591 of Ivan the Terrible's sole remaining son, the nine-year-old Dmitrii, prince of Uglich. Although the offspring of an uncanonical marriage and thus ineligible for the throne, Dmitrii's death (apparently self-inflicted in an epilectic seizure) gave rise to persistent rumors of Godunov's complicity and, after his death, to a series of pretenders to the throne. From the time of his death in 1605 until the end of the 1610s, Russia was wracked by foreign invasion (primarily Poles and Swedes), and brigandage known as the Time of Troubles.[108] In 1611, the walled city of Smolensk fell after a prolonged siege to the Poles, who were to control it for the next half century. In the following year, however, a levée en masse originating in Nizhnii Novgorod produced a national army that liberated Moscow in the fall of 1612 and made possible the accession of the Romanov dynasty in 1613. Despite the general social collapse and the cessation of building, the arduous task of national recovery led to a revival of the forms of late sixteenth-century church architecture in a transition between the last phase of the medieval period and the beginnings of the modern age.

CHAPTER 7

The Seventeenth Century: From Ornamentalism to the New Age

With the establishment of the Romanov dynasty in 1613 and during the recovery of Russia after the "Time of Troubles," the drama of national resistance inspired new churches that repeated the commemorative and celebratory forms of sixteenth-century architecture, both in the tower church and in the ornamentalism typical of the Godunov era. Although Godunov's success at court intrigue had resulted in the banishment of the Romanov clan (the family of Ivan the Terrible's first wife, Anastasia), and although their accession to power after the Time of Troubles ensured that his name would long be consigned to obloquy, the churches endowed by Godunov – ornamental, compact in design, and often without interior piers – served as prototypes for parish churches in Moscow throughout the seventeenth century.

The commemorative uses of the Godunov style are particularly evident in the brick Church of the Intercession at Rubtsovo (Figure 170), commissioned by Tsar Mikhail Romanov in 1619 to mark the repulse of the last Polish-led attack on Moscow on October 1, the Feast Day of the Intercession.[1] The significance of the Intercession has been noted with regard to the cathedral on Red Square; yet the design at Rubtsovo derives not from the tower votive churches, but from the cathedral at Donskoi Monastery, where one of the decisive checks to the Polish attack was delivered – and from whose site the Crimean Tatars had been driven back in 1591. Thus, the adaptation of the Donskoi design for a monastery church at the opposite (northeast) end of the city can be seen as a parallel expression of gratitude for a successful military operation. The Rubtsovo church is an agglomeration of

several of the Godunov churches, with its two attached chapels and a raised terrace, but the pyramid of *kokoshniki* under the single cupola reminds most obviously of the Donskoi Monastery cathedral.

The decorative possibilities of the cuboid structure with tiers of *kokoshniki* were exemplified in the votive Cathedral of the Icon of the Kazan Mother of God, built in the 1620s near the north end of Red Square and demolished in the early Soviet period. Its donor, Prince Dmitrii Pozharskii, was the military leader of the Russian national liberation effort in 1612, and the Kazan Cathedral memorialized that movement, with the additional connotation of Ivan the Terrible's victory over Kazan.[2] Indeed, the Kazan icon joined the Don Mother of God as symbols of the divine protection of Russia in her struggle with foreign enemies – inevitably seen as infidels. Although the Kazan Cathedral was not consecrated until 1637, the combinations of its five tiers of *kokoshniki* may well have influenced the decorative patterns of other churches in the Kitai-gorod district, such as the Trinity in Nikitniki (see Figure 181).

The movement of liberation was honored in the more dramatic tower form of the Church of the Intercession at Medvedkovo, originally built in wood around 1620 on Pozharskii's recently enlarged estate north of Moscow. It commemorated not only the events of the 1610s, but, by implication, Pozharskii's contribution to the Russian recovery. Just as Godunov had benefitted from the victory over the Tatars in 1591, so Pozharskii – of minor Suzdalian noblility – received the rank of boyar and many grants of land, which he not only revived as productive estates, but

141

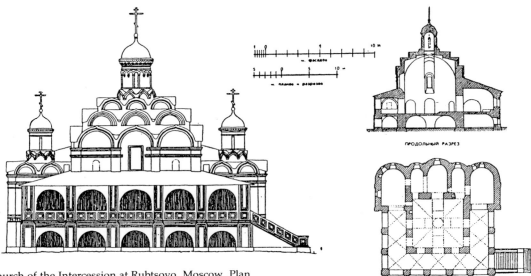

Figure 170. Church of the Intercession at Rubtsovo. Moscow. Plan and longitudinal section by V. Suslov.

frequently graced with churches.[3] The Medvedkovo estate, located near the road to the Trinity-St. Sergius Monastery, had been used by Pozharskii as a final camp before his liberation of Moscow in 1612, and therefore gained particular resonance as a historical site. Estate records show that the wooden church had a tent roof.

Because of the still considerable demands for his military skills in the 1620s, Pozharskii was rarely at Medvedkovo in the 1620s, and the rebuilding of the tower in brick apparently did not occur until 1634. In that year, the truce of Deulino was replaced with the peace treaty of Polianovo in which the Polish king renounced his claims to the Muscovite throne, a diplomatic victory that may have stimulated the rebuilding of the church in more durable materials.[4] Its form is related to late sixteenth-century churches with a *shatior* above rows of kokoshniki, which in turn rest on the octagon and cube of the main structure (Figure 171). The four cupolas flanking the base of the octagon and the attached chapels (Figure 172; later obscured by an enclosed gallery) suggest a reference to its namesake on Red Square.[5]

The adaptability of the *shatior* to commemorative purposes ensured its reproduction throughout Russia in new church architecture. Beyond Moscow, church memorials appeared in considerable numbers during the 1620s–50s in the Nizhnii Novgorod area, and reconstructed elevations of several of the Nizhnii Novgorod churches from this period – both wood and masonry – reveal a preponderance of the tent tower

form.[6] Nizhnii Novgorod, in addition to Moscow, was among the first cities to experience an intensive resumption of construction, in part because of the city's stategic location on the Volga, but also by virtue of large donations for the construction of churches and for the expansion of local monasteries. Nizhnii Novgorod's leading role in the campaign for national redemption had made it, like the Trinity-St. Sergius Monastery, the beneficiary of gifts not only from the court, but also from private donors.

The elaborate forms of the early seventeenth-century brick tower churches are epitomized at the refectory Church of the Dormition (1628) at the Monastery of St. Aleksii in Uglich.[7] Known in contemporary accounts as the *Divnaia* (Wondrous), the church has three tent spires (Figures 173 and 174), placed over the central cube and the two flanking chapels on the east end in a symbolic reference to the Trinity. Although there is no specific votive dedication, the fact that the church was part of rebuilding the monastery after its opposition to and sack by the Poles is sufficient to characterize it as yet another memorial to national deliverance, particularly because the towers – unlike those at Kolomenskoe and related tent churches – admit almost no light to the cramped and unprepossessing interior.[8] Attached to the church on the west is a large refectory that provides ballast to the structure with its simple rectangular form.

A more rigorous development of the ribbed tent tower is the Church of Sts. Zosima and Savvatii at the Trinity-St. Sergius Monastery (1635–7; Figure 175).

142

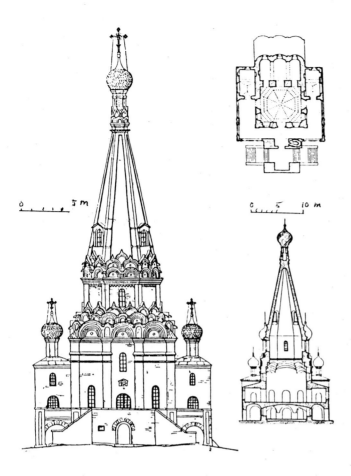

Figure 171. Church of the Intercession at Medvedkovo. Moscow. 1634–5. Reconstructed west elevation by V. Kozlov, plan, and transverse section.

After the Time of Troubles, the entire monastery became the object of lavish gifts that supported its expansion and the repair of the damage inflicted on existing structures during the monastery's resistance to a Polish siege between September 1608 and January 1610. There are special commemorative elements in the dedication, the form, and the location of the Church of Sts. Zosima and Savvatii, which honors two monks, Zosima and Savvatii, who in the first half of the fifteenth century were among the founders of the Monastery of the Transfiguration on the Solovetsk Islands in the White Sea. Both monasteries, which anchored Russia's major artery to the north and thence to Europe, were connected by a long tradition of monastic cooperation: the Solovetsk monastery was established as a direct result of the monastic revival inspired by St. Sergius, and it contributed a number of talented administrators to the Trinity Monastery, including Avraamii Palitsyn, who compiled a daily

written account of the Polish siege of the Trinity-St. Sergius Monastery in 1608–10. Moreover, the martial exploits of the Trinity-St. Sergius Monastery during the Time of Troubles were complemented in the far north with the repulse of a Swedish force by the Transfiguration Monastery.[9] Thus, the dedication of the tower church to the brotherly Transfiguration Monastery subsumes both a monastic and a military alliance.

In addition, the location of the Church of Sts. Zosima and Savvatii, rising from a space created in the middle of the second story of the monastery infirmary, signifies the charitable role of the monks in accepting and treating great numbers of wounded from Moscow after the Polish suppression of an uprising in the city in March 1611. (So complex was the political maneuvering during the Time of Troubles that even the lifting of the monastery siege in 1610 did not resolve the larger questions of dynastic succession and the Polish occupation of Moscow.) Indeed, Prince Pozharskii initially recuperated here

Figure 172. Church of the Intercession at Medvedkovo. Moscow. Northwest view. (M 17–6a)

143

Figure 173. Church of the Dormition, Monastery of St. Aleksii. Uglich. 1628. (UG 3–8)

from serious wounds before moving to his estate to await the call to lead a national liberation army.[10] The *shatior* of the church, towering over the northwest wall (in the direction of Solovetsk), served as a memorial not only to the wounded and dying from all of the campaigns, but also to those who defended the monastery itself – represented in depictions of cannons and soldiers on a number of the green ceramic tiles that decorate the tent.[11] The commemorative purpose of the design is all the more evident in the isolation of the tent from the rest of the structure by a vaulted ceiling at the base of the *zakomary*, which permitted the year-round use of the heated church.

Even the church hierarchy adopted the *shatior*, as exemplified by the Church of the Trinity at Troitsko-Golenishchevo (1644–6; Figure 176), located to the south of Moscow at a summer residence of the Moscow metropolitanate. The structure – whose design is attributed to A. Konstantinov, builder of the Kremlin Terem Palace – has flanking chapels (each with a small *shatior*) and a surrounding gallery.[12] The most florid use of the tent tower appears in central Moscow at the Church of the Nativity of the Virgin in Putinki (1649–52; Figure 177), with three over the main church (none of which opens into the structure), and three more of various sizes over: a miniature second church dedicated to the Burning Bush, the bell tower, and the entrance porch. The structure was built at the

144

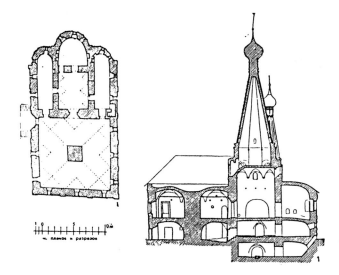

Figure 174. Church of the Dormition, Monastery of St. Aleksii. Uglich. Plan and section by P. Baranovskii.

Figure 175. Church of Sts. Zosima and Savvatii, Trinity–St. Sergius Monastery. Zagorsk. 1635–7. Southeast view. (Z 5–2)

command of Tsar Aleksei Mikhailovich to replace a wooden church, burned in 1648, that also had three tent towers.[13] Despite the likely origins of the *shatior* in masonry construction, the use of the form in wood had an influence on the increasingly decorative use of the tent in brick churches. The wooden prototype may also explain the picturesque silhouette of the entire "micro ensemble," as well as the asymmetrical arrangment of space within the plan (Figure 178), which ultimately included a low vestibule and yet another chapel.

The decorative *shatior* appeared in many small churches, such as the Church of the Holy Spirit (1642), with two towers, in the Riazan Kremlin.[14] The Nativity in Putinki, however, was the last Moscow church to display tent towers over the main structure. Perhaps its exuberant asymmetry demonstrated for the ecclesiastical hierarchy the conversion of church structures into decorative displays little related to Christian dogma. The secular impulse behind the construction of tent churches had been evident from the very beginning; and by the middle of the seventeenth century, the Russian patriarchate would make a vigorous attempt to reassert its authority by purifying religious expression of uncanonical elements. Under these circumstances, use of the *shatior* was discouraged; yet the fondness for the tent reappeared in the design of attached bell towers, as urban prosperity continued to support ornamental architecture.

The shifting usage of the tent tower is illuminated by the Church of Elijah the Prophet in Iaroslavl – a stunning example of ornamentation Russian architecture (Figure 179). Since the time of Ivan the Terrible, Iaroslavl's strategic position on the trade route from the White Sea to Siberia and the east had attracted colonies of Russian and foreign merchants (English, Dutch, German), whose commerce greatly increased the resources available for the construction and decoration of local churches.[15] The donors of the Elijah Church, the Skripin brothers, possessed great wealth gained from the Siberian fur trade, and they had access both to the tsar and to the patriarch.[16] In 1647, they endowed in the central part of Iaroslavl a pentacupolar brick church on an elevated base that also supported an enclosed gallery (Figure 180). The roofline of the main structure originally followed the contours of the zakomary, which are still visible despite a simplification of the roof design in the eighteenth century.

Thirty years after its completion in 1650, the widow

Figure 176. Church of the Trinity in Troitsko-Golenishchevo. Moscow. 1644–6. Southwest view. (M 23–10)

Figure 177. Church of the Nativity of the Virgin in Putinki. Moscow. 1649–52. Southwest view. (M 11)

of one of the Skripin brothers commissioned the painting of the interior of the main church by the distinguished artists Gurii Nikitin and Sila Savin. This splendid complement of frescoes is among the best-preserved in Russia and is illustrative of the growing secular influence in Russian religious art during the late seventeenth-century.[17] In a further expression of "merchant taste," the exterior of the church was painted with colorful ornament similar to that added in the same period of Moscow's Cathedral of the Intercession on the Moat.

Like many churches of its period, the Elijah Church had chapels flanking the apse on the east, of which the north chapel represents a small self-contained church with a pyramid of *kokoshniki* beneath its cupola. The balanced asymmetry of the ensemble is most clearly stated by the two towers attached to the west of the structure: the bell tower at the northwest corner and the separate Chapel of the Deposition of the Robe, placed at a greater remove from the southwest corner of the church, to which it is connected by an extension of the raised gallery. Above this chapel, whose plan is of modest dimensions, rises

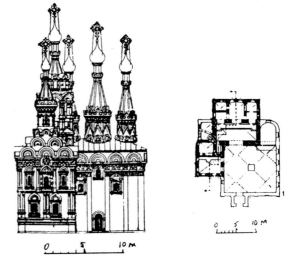

Figure 178. Church of the Nativity of the Virgin in Putinki. Moscow. Reconstructed west elevation.

what is perhaps the last great tent tower to be placed over a church. Indeed, the *shatior* is not a part of the main church, as though its presence were increasingly

146

Figure 179. Church of the Prophet Elijah. Iaroslavl. 1647–50. (RO 4–27)

remote from the accepted structure of the Orthodox Church.

New Forms of Ornamentalism

The ornamental component of the Elijah Church was already well developed in Russian architecture by the middle of the seventeenth century, and is indicative of a new national confidence after the Time of Troubles. The economic basis of ornamentalism is demonstrated at the Church of the Trinity in Nikitniki (Figure 181), situated on a small street in Moscow's Kitai-gorod, endowed by the merchant Grigorii Nikitnikov, whose vast wealth made him an occasional banker to the tsars.[18] After its completion in 1634, the original pentacupolar structure, consisting of the central cube and a vestibule, acquired over the next two decades two chapels (at the northeast and southeast) and an enclosed gallery leading to a bell tower with tent roof on the northwest corner (Figure 182). This is the earliest example of the placement of a bell tower within the church ensemble – a practice that would become general in parish architecture in the seven-

teenth century. At the corner of the bell tower, the gallery turns at a right angle and descends by a covered staircase to a porch at the southwest corner,

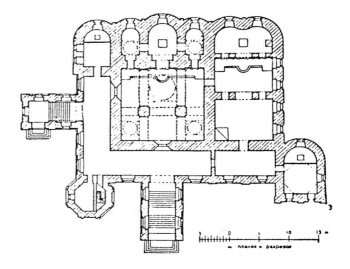

Figure 180. Church of the Prophet Elijah. Iaroslavl. Plan.

147

Figure 181. Church of the Trinity in Nikitniki. Moscow. 1628–51.
West view. (M 18–12)

Plate 17. Church of Sts. Peter and Paul in Slavno. Novgorod. 1367. East facade.

Plate 18. Church of St. John the Divine at Radokovitsy, on the Vitka. Novgorod. 1383–4. Southeast view.

Plate 19. Church of Sts. Peter and Paul in Kozhevniki. Novgorod. 1406. West facade.

Plate 20. Church of St. George on the Slope. Pskov. 1494. Northeast view.

Plate 21. Pskov Monastery of the Caves, belfry. Near Pskov. Sixteenth and seventeenth centuries.

Plate 22. Church of the Nativity and the Intercession of the Virgin. Pskov. Sixteenth century.

Plate 23. Cathedral of the Nativity of the Virgin, Savva-Storozhevskii Monastery. Zvenigorod. 1405(?). South facade, with Savva Chapel (midseventeenth century).

Plate 24. Cathedral of the Annunciation. Moscow Kremlin. 1484–9. Southeast view.

Plate 25. Cathedral of the Dormition. Moscow Kremlin. 1475–9. Architect: Aristotele Fioravanti. Southeast view.

Plate 27. Intercession Convent. Suzdal. Sixteenth–eighteenth centuries. Northeast view.

Plate 26. The Kremlin, Moscow. Southeast view. From left to right:
Cathedral of the Archangel Michael;
second tower (1480s; 1680s); Cathedral of the Dormition;
bell tower of Ivan the Great, with adjoining structures.

Plate 28. Cathedral of the Trinity, Trinity-Danilov Monastery. Pereslavl-Zalesskii. 1530–2. Central dome and pendentives. Frescoes by Gurii Nikitin and Sila Savin, 1662–8.

Plate 29. Church of the Ascension at Kolomenskoe. Moscow. 1529–32. West facade. Photograph taken in 1972.

Plate 30. Church of the Decapitation of John the Baptist at Diakovo. Moscow. 1547–54(?). South view.

Plate 31. Cathedral of the Intercession on the Moat (Temple of Basil the Blessed). Moscow. 1555–61. West view.

Plate 32. Cathedral of the Intercession on the Moat. Moscow. North view (from Red Square).

Figure 182. Church of the Trinity in Nikitniki. Moscow. West elevation by V. Suslov.

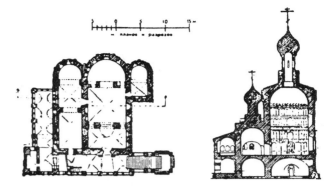

Figure 183. Church of the Trinity in Nikitniki. Moscow. Plan and transverse section by V. Suslov.

capped by *kokoshniki* and a pyramidal roof. The ornate south Chapel of Nikita (St. Nicetas) the Warrior, whose form echoes the main church, served as the family burial chapel.[19]

This array of forms has led some to suggest a resemblance to the agglomeration of wooden structures in the Russian countryside, as well as to estate churches such as the Transfiguration at Ostrov[20]; and yet the building's design is determined by and adapted to the constraints of an urban setting. When viewed from the southwest corner, the ascent from entrance to sanctuary impresses not only with the harmony of its shapes, with the balancing of various projecting chapels and galleries, but also with the clarity, the logic of its design, which effects the transition from the street, or southern, side to the main east–west axis of the Orthodox church (Figure 183).

The saturated ornamentation of the Church of the Trinity, like its structure, evolved over several years, during which Nikitnikov was able to draw on the services of the tsar's own artisans, who were then engaged in the completion of the Kremlin's Terem Palace (Figure 184).[21] The decorative elements of the latter, built in 1635–6 under the supervision of Antip Konstantinov, Bazhen Ogurtsov, Trefil Sharutin, and Larion Ushakov, show a clear similarity to the exterior details of the Trinity Church (particularly, the window surrounds) and indicate a further intrusion of secular culture into the design of the Russian Orthodox church. The facades of this monument provide an inventory of ornamental devices applied in Muscovite architecture during the seventeenth century: carved limestone *nalichniki* in Romanesque or Moorish patterns (Figure 185), limestone window pediments, deeply recessed decorative squares (*shirinki*), *kokoshniki* sculpted with perspective arches, limestone pendants (*girki*) within the entrance arches, attached columns, pilasters, arcading of the cupola drums, arches of every conceivable sort – all subsumed in a color pattern of red with white trim (see Plate 36). This by no means exhausts the array, whose application must in some cases be judged capricious. Despite the fact that Russian masters had assimilated certain details of western architectural orders (e.g., the capital), their context was ignored in favor of a decorative approach that might place a ''classical'' window pediment on the same facade as a series of ogival arches.

The interior of the central cube of the Trinity Church contained no piers, and the primary sources of natural light were the windows on the south facade and the main drum. The four flanking drums were ''blind,'' closed by the single domical vault supporting the roof. The interior surface was covered with frescoes, painted between 1652 and 1658 in a style whose lavish detail is both secular and more naturalistic (western) in comparison with earlier Russian frescoes.[22] It is assumed that the artists were among those involved in the repainting of the major Kremlin cathedrals in the middle of the seventeenth century, and particularly the Archangel Michael Cathedral.[23] Prominent among them were Osip Vladimirov and the young Simon Ushakov (1626–86), who would become the most distinguished icon painter of the seventeenth century.

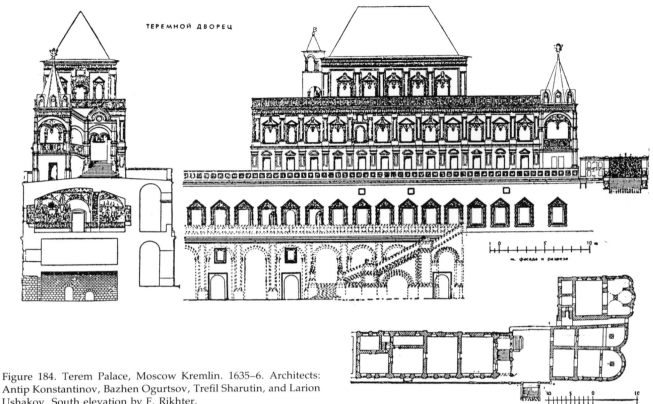

ТЕРЕМНОЙ ДВОРЕЦ

Figure 184. Terem Palace, Moscow Kremlin. 1635–6. Architects: Antip Konstantinov, Bazhen Ogurtsov, Trefil Sharutin, and Larion Ushakov. South elevation by F. Rikhter.

The collision between Muscovite ornamentalism – which appears as early as the decorative strips on the Zvenigorod cathedrals – and decorative borrowings from the west was to be resolved in favor of the latter during the eighteenth century. Before that time, however, Moscow's architects and artisans had ample resources to fashion the ornament displayed at the Church of the Trinity in Nikitniki. The long and relatively peaceful reign of Tsar Aleksei Mikhailovich (1645–76) stimulated a proliferation of brick churches, in both city and country parishes, that were decorated in bright polychrome. Yet despite the decorative effusion, the design of such churches achieved an unusual degree of stability in a plan known as the "ship," consisting of a cuboid main structure with a low spacious apse and, extending along the same axis from the west facade, a low vestibule (*trapeza*) and a bell tower culminating in the tent form.[24] The tower provided a counterpoint to what might be considered the "sails" of the ship: its five cupolas, usually gilded or decorated with bright metallic stars (see Figure 190).

Although the beginnings of the return to a pentacupolar form can be detected in the Intercession Church at Medvedkovo, with four cupolas around a central tent tower, the Trinity Church at Nikitniki was the first to combine the unobstructed cuboid space of the small Godunov churches (no interior piers and a simplified vaulting structure) with five decorative cupolas and an attached bell tower. It should be emphasized that this transfer of the tent from the central structure to the bell tower antedates the church's rejection, in the midseventeenth century, of the *shatior* over the church proper. The transition seems rather to have been motivated by a structural logic that placed less weight on the vaulting and allowed an expansion of the central space, whose walls were reinforced with oak beams and iron tie rods (Figure 186).[25] In formal terms, the revival of a system of five cupolas – on a smaller, ornamental scale – enhanced the decorative possibilities of the main church while retaining the tent tower on an ancillary structure.

In the urban environment, these churches provided focus to neighborhoods still composed of wooden structures and often organized around settlements of craft guilds.[26] Hence, the origins of the extended names of many Moscow churches, such as the Church of the Dormition *v Goncharakh* – or "in the Potters'

150

district'' (Figure 187; built in 1654, with a bell tower added in the mideighteenth century). Despite its miniature size, the Dormition Church is perhaps the earliest known example of the use of a sloped roof above a horizontal cornice with decorative *kokoshniki*.[27] The greater simplicity of this design led throughout Russia to the extensive rebuilding of rooflines by filling in the original contours of the upper walls as defined by curved gables (*zakomary*). The church is also remarkable for its bands of ornate polychromatic ceramic tile along the upper walls of the vestibule, and for the ceramic icons on the drum of the chapel of St. Tikhon, which was attached to the south side of the church in 1702.[28]

The application of the tripartite plan (main church, vestibule, bell tower) was by no means restricted to neighborhood churches. Much the same pattern was adopted for the brick Church of the Kazan Mother of God (1649–53; see Plate 37) adjoining the tsar's residence at Kolomenskoe. The construction of a masonry church connected to a residence, usually of wood, had been adopted by Russian princes from the earliest days of Christianity in Russia, but in the seventeenth century, the practice became widespread among powerful and wealthy citizens as well. The Church of the Trinity in Nikitniki, for example, originally adjoined the Nikitnikov residence (razed in 1657). In 1656, the prominent Moscow official Averkii Kirillov replaced a wooden Church of St. Nicholas on his urban estate fronting the Moscow River with a brick church dedicated to the Trinity – but persistently known as the Church of St. Nicholas on Bersenevka. Completed the following year, the church was attached to a rare example of seventeenth-century brick domestic architecture in Moscow (Figure 188). That structure was subsequently much rebuilt, as were ancillary parts of the church, but the central part has been well restored, particularly the roof (Figure 189).[29]

The durability of the ''ship'' form of church persisted even into the eighteenth century, despite the dramatic changes in church design over the same period. Not only did it provide an easily assimilated model that could be reproduced in the country as well as in a confined urban setting, but it also allowed for inexhaustible variations in detail. One of the ''purest'' examples of the form is the Church of St. Nicholas in Khamovniki (1679–82; Figure 190), built for the wealthy settlement of weavers (*khamovniki*) located in this southwest district of Moscow.[30] The prosperity of the guild is evident in the decoration of the church, whose main structure retains the complex layering of *kokoshniki*. The attached columns and consoles sup-

Figure 185. Church of the Trinity in Nikitniki. Moscow. South facade. Window detail. (M 18–10)

porting the *zakomary*, as well as the decorative window surrounds, are all outlined in bright polychrome on a background of whitewashed brick. The same use

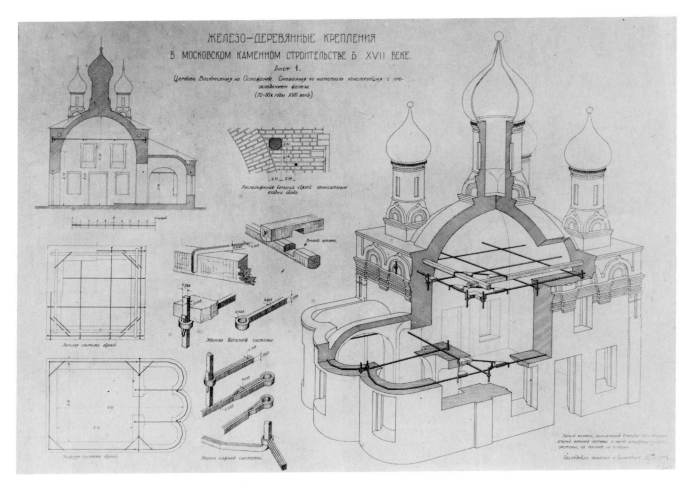

Figure 186. Church of the Resurrection in Ostozhenka (not extant). Moscow. 1670s. Sketch of structural system. Courtesy of Shchusev State Museum of Architecture.

of color extends to the magnificent bell tower – one of the tallest attached to a church in Moscow – whose height allowed both a greater distribution of sound and a surface for ornament such as the dormer windows on the tent tower. Similar features reappear in the rebuilding during the 1680s of the bell tower placed to the southeast of the Cathedral of the Intercession on the Moat.

A different approach to ornament and surface texture appeared at the same period in the Church of the Trinity on the Cherkasskii family estate of Ostankino to the north of Moscow (1678–83). The builder, identified as the serf master Pavel Potekhin, exploited the decorative contrast of molded brick and limestone detail, which is particularly striking in the window surrounds and the structural detail on the east facade (Figure 191).[31] The Ostankino church is notable both for its size (large for an estate church) and for the contemporaneity of its ornamental style. Other estate

churches adhered to designs of a half century earlier, such as the Church of the Archangel Michael at Arkhangelskoe (1667; Figure 192) whose decorative *kokoshniki* remind of the Godunov period. The effect of this anachronism is increased by the peculiar interior, with two piers supporting the west vaulting of the main structure and a domical vault for the eastern part. The small size and idiosyncratic design of the Archangel Church may have been due to the estate's frequent change of ownership: the donor of the church was Ia. N. Odoevskii, who owned the estate from the 1660s to 1681, after which it passed into the control of Mikhail Cherkasskii.[32]

The largest of the estate churches, however, were those built for the tsar, such as the Church of the Annunciation at Taininskoe (see Plate 38), built in 1675–7 on an estate belonging to Tsar Fedor Alekseevich. The brief reign of Fedor, between 1676 and 1682, witnessed a continuation of the church styles

152

Figure 187. Church of the Dormition in Gonchary. Moscow. 1654, with mideighteenth-century bell tower. Northeast view. (M 173–33)

decorative nature. The Church of the Archangel Michael at Troparevo (a village belonging to the Novodevichii Convent) conforms perfectly to the pattern in its basic elements, yet is distinguished by its horseshoe *zakomary* and the doubled polygonal drums whose receding forms increase the impression of height and suggest the mannerisms of an incipient baroque style. Indeed, its date of construction (1693) places it within a period designated as the "Moscow baroque" (see what follows), and the interrupted pediments of its window surrounds exhibit the ornament that distinguishes this style: more ordered in its design and decoration when compared with the preceding church architecture, yet still remote from the western system of orders.

A key monument in this decorative system is the Church of the Resurrection in Kadashi (1687–95; Figure 194), situated in view of the Kremlin across the Moscow River, and the center of the district of weavers attached to the tsar's court.[34] The appearance of

Figure 188. Church of St. Nicholas on Bersenevka. Moscow. 1656–7. Southeast view. (M 126–36a)

established under Aleksei Mikhailovich, yet the Taininskoe church deviates from the "ship" form. It would appear that the pious Fedor constructed the church, located near the road from Moscow to the Trinity-St. Sergius Monastery, as a pilgrimage halt, and certain features of the design – particularly on the west – reflect the demands of ritual procession. The vestibule is enclosed within a gallery, supported by massive decorated pillars, that leads at either corner of the west front to descending steps (Figure 193). The point of their meeting, in the center of the west facade, is marked by a large open barrel gable.[33] The verticality of this superbly engineered royal church (without interior piers) is emphasized by 2 stories of large windows framed in decorative strips, which lead upward to tiers of *kokoshniki* supporting the narrow drums and five cupolas.

Through the final decade of the century, the "ship" form proved capable of new variations, usually of a

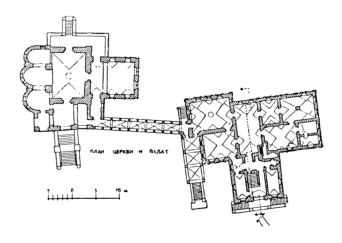

Figure 189. Church of St. Nicholas on Bersenevka. Moscow. Reconstructed plan by D. Razov, with attached Chambers of Averkii Kirillov.

the Resurrection Church has been distorted by nineteenth-century additions, and its view is partially obstructed by a cannery; yet in its scale and the harmony of its proportions, the church still dominates the surrounding area, as it did almost three centuries ago when Moscow's neighborhoods were defined by such structures. The design, attributed to Sergei Turchaninov,[35] adheres to the traditional ship form (Figure 195), although the bell tower was not added until 1695. Its form resembles the spires placed on the Kremlin towers in the latter part of the seventeenth century, and there is also an affinity with the campaniles of the seventeenth-century baroque in central and western Europe (Amsterdam, for example).

The most distinctive feature of the Kadashi church is its intricate limestone ornament, whose carving was supported by the wealth of the court weavers.[36] In addition to this carved lacework, which also appears

Figure 190. Church of St. Nicholas in Khamovniki. Moscow. 1679–82. South facade. (M–19)

154

Figure 191. Church of the Trinity at Ostankino. Moscow. 1678–83.
Architect: Pavel Potekhin. East facade. (M 41–8)

Figure 192. Church of the Archangel Michael at Arkhangelskoe. Near Moscow. 1667. West facade. (M 13)

in the more innovative structures of the "Moscow baroque" tower churches, the limestone ornament replaces the *kokoshniki* as a transition from the main cube to the five drums and cupolas: three symmetrical tiers of carved limestone composed of scroll pediments, scallops, and other elements. The original structural design enhanced the lapidary display with an open terrace and balustrade (Figure 196), placed above a ground floor arcade. Access to the terrace was provided by three flights of steps, leading to the north, west, and south portals. This design, which was substantially modified with the building of the bell tower and further defaced in the nineteenth century, proved influential in the development of grand ornamental stairways for the exterior of the "Naryshkin" tower churches.

Iaroslavl Church Architecture: Second Half of the Seventeenth Century

For all the variety of Moscow's brick parish churches during the final decades of the seventeenth century, the apogee of the traditional forms of church architecture occurred in Iaroslavl, with its proliferation of richly decorated churches erected and maintained by a combination of wealthy merchants, city districts, and trade associations. Not since the late fourteenth and early fifteenth centuries in Novgorod had there been such a concentrated expression of neighborhood cohesiveness, wealth, and pride as in the Iaroslavl churches of the seventeenth century, when forty-four

masonry churches – most of considerable size – were erected within thirty-five parishes in the Iaroslavl area.[37] The most impressive single monument of this era is the Church of the Prophet Elijah (see Figure 179), which also served as a prototype for the subsequent development of the district church in Iaroslav, typically with an attached gallery on three sides and an array of secondary structures. Indeed, from a structural point of view, the core design of the Iaroslavl churches appears "archaic" in comparison with the flexibility allowed by the ship form that evolved elsewhere in Muscovy during the second half of the seventeenth century.

If the Elijah Church can be seen as a transitional monument and a prototype for the Iaroslavl school of church building, its successors quickly developed a system of integrating the attached structures into a symmetrically balanced design. This process is first, and in some ways, most impressively demonstrated in the church ensemble at Korovniki, a suburban district near the confluence of the small Kotorosl River with the Volga. The area takes its name from the Russian word *korova* (cow) and was used as pasturage, but its inhabitants also engaged in ceramic crafts, brickmaking, and pottery, all of which play a major role in the structure and decoration of the this ensemble of two churches, with a large free-standing bell tower situated between them on the west (Figure 197).[38]

The main structure of the Korovniki ensemble is the Church of St. John Chrysostom, commissioned by the merchants Ivan and Fedor Nezhdanov, who are buried in its south gallery. Constructed in 1649–54, the church was remodeled with more elaborate decoration in the 1680s and thus represents an amalgam of two periods. Its central plan remained untouched, however, and it epitomizes the return to an earlier, "classical" form of church structure with four interior piers (Figure 198). Yet the plan deviates from tradition in one significant respect: Both the east and west piers are shifted away from the center, thus creating an extended rectangle under the central drum and considerably extending the length of the church.[39] This extension of a four-piered structure would in turn give rise to changes in the tectonic system, particularly in the construction of the cornice and roof. Innovative systems of reinforced vaulting obviated the structural purpose of the zakomary and led to an increasingly decorative resolution of the cornice beneath a sloped roof.

The Chrysostom Church is flanked by galleries whose east ends lead to attached chapels with tent towers; their apses merge into a general five-part ap-

Figure 193. Church of the Annunciation at Taininskoe. Near Moscow. 1675–7. West facade. (M 16)

sidal structure (Figure 199). Many large Iaroslavl district churches integrated their attached chapels within the main structure by means of this design, which in its basic points had appeared in the plan of the Godunov church at Viaziomy (see Figure 165). Yet its appearance in Iaroslavl is altogether different, not only because of the texture of the unstuccoed brick work, but also the proliferation of shapes around the great pentacupolar mass – the height of the drums and cupolas exceeds that of the main structure (see Figure 198). Each point of entry to the gallery has a semidetached porch (added in the 1680s) with a sloped roof, and when seen from the west or east, they initiate the pyramidal crescendo that overwhelms the cuboid central structure.

In the balance of its parts, the Chrysostom Church is simpler than its predecessor, the Church of Elijah, but its ornamentalism is of a different order. Whereas the exterior decoration of the Elijah Church consists of patterns painted on stucco, the Korovniki monument is a prototypical example of the intricate use of polychrome ceramic ornament that symbolized wealth and artistry in church decoration throughout

Muscovy during the latter half of the seventeenth century. In Iaroslav, however, it served the additional purpose of visually enriching the conservative limits of the four-piered structural design. Iaroslavl builders countered the possibility of monotony with a soaring cupolar superstructure and with polychrome ornament at key structural points. Of particular note in the Chrysostom Church is the window surround of the central apse (Figure 199), whose great size enables it to be seen from the Volga – the best vantage point for the church as a whole.

Indeed, the primary way of reaching the Korovniki churches at that time was from the river to the east, and the successive builders of the ensemble exerted considerable effort to endow the east side with a festive appearance. Although the second, paired church of the Korovniki ensemble is more modest in structure and in decoration than the Chrysostom Church, it provides a balance to the main structure, particularly from the east. Dedicated to the Icon of the Vladimir Mother of God and built in 1669, the church was intended for winter services and thus had a separate vaulted ceiling between the first and second stories

Figure 194. Church of the Resurrection in Kadashi. Moscow. 1687– 95. South view. (M 123–30)

Figure 195. Church of the Resurrection in Kadashi. Moscow. Longitudinal section by G. Alferova. Courtesy of Shchusev State Museum of Architecture.

Figure 196. Church of the Resurrection in Kadashi. Moscow. East elevation by G. Alferova. Courtesy of Shchusev State Museum of Architecture, Moscow.

158

Figure 197. Church of St. John Chrysostom (left) and Church of the Vladimir Mother of God (right) and bell tower at Korovniki. Iaroslavl. Second half of seventeenth century. Northwest view. (Y 2–36)

in order to preserve heat (see Figure 197). The entire upper story of the central cube, as well as its drums and cupolas, was closed from view in the interior and east facade essentially served only as a visual complement to the Chrysostom Church.[40] On the west, the church was extended with a 1-story vestibule, an awkward arrangement, but not visible from the river. This three-dimensional trompe l'oeil is an extension of the use of large structural elements such as the *shatior* for purely external effect (cf. the Church of Sts. Zosima and Savvatii), and demonstrates a sensitivity to the larger architectural environment.

The culminating point of the ensemble at Korovniki occurred in the 1680s with the construction of the bell tower, 37 meters in height (see Figure 197). The existence of such a structure in a semirural setting is unusual (bell towers of this size were usually built within monasteries), but it was not the only freestanding campanile in Iaroslavl. The final element of

the ensemble at Korovniki consists of a decorative Holy Gate and wall constructed at the end of the seventeenth century between the eastern corners of the two churches and fronting on the Volga. The position of the Holy Gate gave formal acknowledgment to the dominant role of the river in the livelihood and geography of the district inhabitants.

Other districts up the Kotorosl River from Korovniki engaged in church building – perhaps in rivalry to the city of Iaroslavl proper on the other side of the Kotorosl. The Church of John the Baptist at Tolchkovo is comparable in scale to St. John Chrysostom, and may lay claim to surpass it as a single monument. The church was constructed between 1671 and 1687 with funds provided largely by Rodion and Leontii Eremin, whose wealth derived from leather-working enterprises located in the district. Its basic plan followed that of the Chrysostom Church, with an enclosed gallery flanking three sides of the rectangular

159

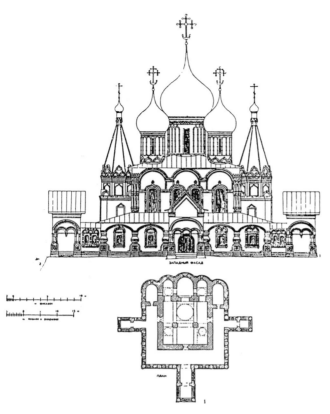

Figure 198. Church of St. John Chrysostom at Korovniki. Iaroslavl. Plan and west elevation by A. Pavlinov.

supports the sloped roof, although they are of little structural importance.

Greater ingenuity is shown in the design of the east chapels, whose cornice is elevated to the height of the main structure. This creates not only a uniform roof level, but also gives the east facade a monumental unity unequalled in seventeenth-century church architecture. The culminating points of this resolution are the two miniature groupings of five cupolas on elongated drums over each chapel.[42] The brilliance of this device is equalled by its ostentation, relying for its effect on the external expansion of structure with no interior gain: the chapels are only 1 story in height. Not that they lacked for magnificence: The intricate carving of their iconostases was complemented by frescoes on the interior of both the gallery and the church.[43] Painted under the supervision of the Iaroslavl master Dmitrii Grigorev Plekhanov between 1694 and 1700, the frescoes extend the brightly colored portrayal of a local, secular environment for biblical motifs that had appeared in the Church of the Trinity in Nikitniki, endowed by another merchant of Iaro-

pentacupolar structure and two symmetrical chapels at each eastern corner. Entrance porches with steeply pitched roofs are located at the center of the north, west, and south galleries. As noted earlier, this design is inherently conservative and lacking in flexibility, and the builders of the Tolchkovo church tried assiduously to introduce variations within the plan, both in the ornamentation of the facade and in the articulation of the attached chapels.

The spacing of clusters of attached columns as a decorative means of segmenting the facades had been introduced at the Resurrection Cathedral (1670–8) of the neighboring town of Tutaev, but at Tolchkovo, their symmetrical placement within a melange of minor decorative elements represents the triumph of saturated ornament over the clarity of individual elements (Figure 200).[41] The elaborate forms of the brick were complemented by bright polychrome tiles encrusting the facade. Indeed, the decorative relief work of the upper tiers can be distinguished only with difficulty from the colorful trompe l'oeil rustication on the apsidal structure. Above the projecting entablature of the cornice is a row of zakomary that visually

Figure 199. Church of St. John Chrysostom at Korovniki. Iaroslavl. Northeast view. (Y 2–32)

160

Figure 200. Church of John the Baptist at Tolchkovo. Iaroslavl.
1671–87. Southeast view.

slavl origins. Although fanciful western (medieval) architectural motifs frequently dominate the background of these wall paintings, the figures themselves and the details of the biblical scenes indicate an unambiguous approval of and sense of sufficiency with the prosperous commercial milieu of Iaroslavl.

The Church of John the Baptist had its ancillary structures, including a separate winter church (not extant) and an entrance framed by a Holy Gate. The dominant feature of the ensemble is the campanile (Figure 201), built at the turn of the eighteenth century in the florid style known as "Moscow baroque." Forty-five meters in height, the bell tower is decorated with limestone elements, including balusters and pinnacles that emphasize the ascent of its receding octagons (an amalgam of Russian and Dutch design). In both height and wealth of measured architectural detail, the one structure comparable to the Tolchkovo tower is the bell tower at Novodevichii Convent (see Plate 41).

By the time the Church of John the Baptist was completed in 1687, the decorative saturation that it epitomizes had reached an impasse. Although ingenious in detail and monumental in concept, the encrustation of the structure admitted no possibility of further development, and subsequent Iaroslavl churches show a simplification. Much of the wealth of the Tolchkovo district derived from the processing of fine leather, and in the year of the completion of John the Baptist, a group in the same district initiated the construction of another large church, dedicated to St. Theodore Stratilates. Indeed, the building of the church was the subject of a detailed written account that emphasized the collective labor of local inhabitants who chose the model from an existing church in Iaroslavl, determined the dimensions so that it would rival the prototype in size, laid the foundation, and only then summoned master builders.[44] The upper part of the church is austerely decorated by a form of entablature whose base consists of several strips of

161

Figure 201. Church of John the Baptist at Tolchkovo. Iaroslavl. Bell tower. Late seventeenth century. (Y 3–8)

molded brick. Above the projection of this profiled band are the recessed semicircular forms of zakomary that provide a decorative rhythm, and serve as relieving arches for the soaring pentacupolar structure. On the interior, the high walls provided the space for seven tiers of frescoes painted in 1715 by Fedor Ignatev and Fedor Fedorov.[45]

Within the central districts of Iaroslavl, churches generally displayed a more compact design, and financial vicissitudes often influenced form, as at the Church of the Nativity of Christ, begun by the merchant brothers Akindin and Gurii Nazarev as a four-piered cuboid structure with five cupolas and an attached gallery (Figure 202).[46] Neither of the brothers gained great wealth, and it was completed in 1644 by the sons of Gurii Nazarev. The Chapel of St. Nicholas the Miraculous, built at the northeast corner of the church, was subsequently balanced at the southeast by the donor Chapel of St. Akindin. Both were complemented by the masterful addition of a southwest

corner chapel, dedicated to the Icon of the Kazan Mother of God and raised to the upper level of the main gallery. The cupola of the chapel retains its tile surface and gives an indication of the original impression produced by the five cupolas (not extant) of the main structure, covered with contoured tiles in bright colors. This early example of the Iaroslavl fondness for ceramic ornamentation culminates in a glazed inscription along the upper walls of the Church of the Nativity – unusual not only for the reproduction in tile of ornate letters, but also for the acknowledgment in the inscription to the secular donors.[47]

The final element of the Church of the Nativity is its gate bell tower and chapel, built after a large fire in Iaroslavl in 1658 and capped with a richly decorated *shatior*.[48] The tower was originally connected to the northwest corner of the main church by an extension of the second-story gallery. The painting of the major complement of frescoes on the interior occurred in 1683–4, long after the completion of the building. An overextension of resources in Siberia led to the financial collapse of two of the three sons of Gurii Nazarev in 1667, but the youngest brother remained solvent and the painting of the church was supported by his sons. Although not among the most accomplished of Iaroslavl frescoes, their bright palette and the admixture of secular elements reflect the role of the Nazarev-Gurev donors into the making of their church.[49]

Less complex examples of Iaroslavl neighborhood churches include the Archangel Michael, built in 1658 just beyond the southeast wall of the central Monastery of the Transfiguration of the Savior. In 1682, the church was rebuilt in a more imposing style, but still maintained the compact arrangement of an enclosed gallery surrounding the pentacupolar church, with a bell tower attached to the northwest corner. The portal is the most refined structural detail of the church, but the cupola design is crowded by the width of the drums, and the decoration is relatively modest.

This cannot be said of the last major architectural work in seventeenth-century Iaroslavl, the Church of the Epiphany, donated by the merchant Aleksei Zubchaninov near the west wall of the Savior Monastery in 1684–93. Although similar in plan to the Archangel Church, the vertical emphasis of the Epiphany Church and the concentrated use of ceramic decoration on a background of brick walls painted dark red make of this monument a summation of the Iaroslavl school (Figure 203). From the 1-story gallery around the base of the church and the bell tower, the vertical ascent is marked with elongated window shafts framed in pilasters, which are decorated with a string of polychrome tiles set diagonally. The tops of the window shafts end in a slight ogival point that is repeated in the three tiers of *kokoshniki* above the cornice.

The horizontal lines of the church are defined with polychrome ceramic tiles that reach their apogee in the profiled entablature at the top of the walls.[50] The tiles are of two sorts: a glazed element used for architectural details such as the architrave; and square tiles in five patterns, repeated in five different colors.[51] The Epiphany Church thus combines the Iaroslavl arrangement of structural components (bell tower, gallery, chapels, and church) with Moscow ornamentalism: a pyramid of *kokoshniki* over a cube with no interior piers, and bright ceramic ornament on the exterior.

The precise brickwork and the buttressing effect of the exterior gallery at the Epiphany Church permitted an unusually large space to be devoted to windows that illuminate the interior, with its eight levels of frescoes painted in 1692–3 and devoted primarily to

Figure 203. Church of the Epiphany. Iaroslavl. 1684–93. West view. (RO 4–34)

Figure 202. Church of the Nativity of Christ. Iaroslavl. 1644; expanded after 1658. West view, with Kazan Chapel (right). (Y 4–13)

scenes from the life of Christ, with particular emphasis on his teachings and ministry. The lack of interior piers further enhances the perception of the wall paintings, which contain decorative motifs that repeat certain of the ceramic designs of the exterior. The curved planes of the domical vault are ingeniously adapted to complex compositions such as the Dormition, the Resurrection, and the Ascension.[52]

During the extraordinary renascence of Iaroslavl architecture, supported by a flourishing local economy, many other provincial cities also found the means – both secular and ecclesiastical – to erect or rebuild masonry churches and monasteries on an unprecedented scale. Most followed variations on the "ship" pattern adopted in Moscow, but others, such as the Church of the Resurrection in the Grove in Kostroma, show a similarity to the Iaroslavl churches, with a gallery flanking three sides of the central structure and attached chapels on the east. Kostroma and Ia-

163

roslavl are in the same general region on the Volga River; and although the precise date of its construction is unknown, the Resurrection Church was completed by 1652, contemporary with the rise of Iaroslavl architecture.[53] A large area of the exterior wall was covered with brightly painted trompe l'oeil rustication, traces of which remain on the east facade. The west facade is preceded by entrance gates (Figure 204) with towers and arched portals, the smaller of which leads into the churchyard, and the larger opens onto a stairway leading to the gallery and main entrance to the church. In addition to decorative brick work, the portals display carved limestone medallions with various beasts from Slavic mythology, including the bird Sirin.

The Resurrection Church in Kostroma is exceptionally rich in its design, yet throughout central Russia, seventeenth-century parish churches commonly display an inventive use of decorative motifs together with a sure sense of structural proportion. Riazan and Kaluga to the south of Moscow, and Vologda, Velikii Ustiug, and Murom to the north and east created a distinctive architectural environment focused on the construction of parish churches that to this day provide provincial Russia with its best examples of the art of building.[54]

Architecture as Incarnation of the Sacred Environment

Although the long reign of Aleksei Mikhailovich, sole son of Mikhail Romanov, fostered the stability and prosperity that underlay the wave of new church construction, the same period was marked both by religious dissent and by grave social and economic unrest that ignited widespread peasant and cossack uprisings. A new code of Russian laws in 1648–9, confirming and strengthening the existence of serfdom, and attempts during the middle of the century to correct certain errors in sacred texts and liturgical practices led to the alienation and greater oppression of a large segment of the Russian population, particularly in rural areas.

At the center of these events stood Patriarch Nikon (1605–81), a cleric of peasant origins, who began as a member of the married clergy, but took the monastic vows after the early deaths of his children. It is telling that Nikon spent his first years as monk (1635–43) at the northern fortress Monastery of the Transfiguration on Solovetsk Island, whose heroic traditions had recently been tested during the Time of Troubles and whose austere, monumental architecture embodied the ideal of the remote and sacred community.[55] By force of will and intelligence, Nikon rose rapidly in the church hierarchy; and after appointment in 1646 as archimandrite (abbot) of the Novospasskii Monastery in Moscow (see Figure 223), he came to the attention of the tsar as a member of a select group of churchmen known as the Zealots of Piety. In 1648, he became metropolitan of Novgorod, where his attempts to modify the Cathedral of St. Sophia met with the determined resistance of the local populace. Nikon had gained access to the governing elite in Muscovy and was well aware of the role recently played in the country's resistance and recovery by church leaders such as the Patriarchs Hermogen, who had died in Polish captivity, and Philaret, who had guided his son Mikhail Romanov in the tenuous early years of his reign.

At the same time, the inexorable logic of the formation and maintenance of a secular state could only lessen the political power of the patriarch. When Nikon acceded to the patriarchate in 1652, he brought both energy to the process of reform within the Church and intolerance of any form of opposition. He intended to reassert the preeminence of the Church in Muscovy and to defend its economic privileges, which had been curtailed by the legal code of 1649. Furthermore, his reinvigorated Orthodox Church was to withstand encroachments both from the Catholic west and, even more insidious, from the Protestant north – a policy that swayed the tsar to peace with Poland and an unsuccessful war with Sweden.

Nikon's insistence on the power of his office and the autonomy of the Church led him into conflict with the tsar, who for all his piety and generous donations to the Church recognized the threat to secular power posed by the patriarch's claim to senior authority in Muscovy. In 1658, the public rift between the two led to the inevitable triumph of civil authority and the eventual removal of Nikon from the patriarchate.[56] This did not, however, resolve the issue of Church reforms, nor did Nikon go quietly from the scene. The Church council of 1666–7 irrevocably banished him from any participation in the governing of the Orthodox Church (he was defrocked and exiled); yet the council also approved the changes promulgated by Nikon, who was consequently seen by many "Old Believers" as an agent of the Antichrist.

After the resolutions of the council, all hope vanished for a peaceful settlement of what became a social and political, as well as theological, struggle. The state, acting as the defender of a Church whose prerogatives it increasingly usurped, in effect declared

Figure 204. Church of the Resurrection in the Grove. Kostroma. 1652(?). Kostroma. West view and main gates. (KO 2–28)

war on a large portion (perhaps as many as 20 percent) of a population that refused to surrender the ritual ways of the Old Faith. In turn, their resistance, known as the Schism, or *raskol*, seems to have developed into a form of protest against the new forces of secularization and the increase of the exploitative power of the state.[57] The theocratic principle underlying the authority of the tsar yielded as a rationale for power to the process of secularization that accompanied Muscovy's evolution into a modern bureaucratic state. The reign of Aleksei Mikhailovich thus represents both the apogee of medieval religiosity in Muscovy and its decline.

Within this historical context, the architecture of the official Orthodox Church during the late seventeenth century reflects an ever greater ornamentalism expressive of material wealth, both of the church and its donors, within an increasingly secular society.[58] At the same time, architecture had become irrelevant for those such as the Old Believers, who retreated to

worship in modest log structures (a distant reflection of the sixteenth-century movement of the "nonpossessors," advocating the rejection of Church and monastic wealth). Paradoxically, the decline in the power and prestige of the Orthodox Church was accompanied by a last flourish in the construction of grand architectural ensembles reflecting the power and resources of individual churchmen and their vision of an ideal built environment, tangible evidence of a still greater heavenly kingdom.

Foremost among them was Patriarch Nikon himself, an indefatigable builder who intended to use architecture as a reflection of his concept of a reformed and pure orthodox faith. As metropolitan of Novgorod, he had noted the beauty of the area of Valdai, some 130 kilometers to the southeast of the city; and in 1653, after his appointment to the patriarchate, he founded at Valdai a monastery dedicated to the Iversk Mother of God. Its main Cathedral of the Dormition was modeled after the Resurrection Church in Jerusalem and contained a wonder-working icon of the Mother of God, brought from one of the spiritual centers of the Orthodox Church, the complex of monasteries on Mount Athos.[59] Indeed, Athos had provided many of the documents used in Nikon's attempt to purge Russian Church texts of accumulated errors. Thus, in the dedication of his monastery as well as the form of its central church, Nikon commemorated two of the most sacred sites of Orthodoxy.

In a similar gesture, he constructed adjacent to the Patriarchal Palace in the Moscow Kremlin a church dedicated to the Apostle Philip, in implicit homage to the Metropolitan Philip, who had achieved martyrdom for his opposition to the terror of Ivan IV.[60] The design and detailing of this large brick church, built in 1652–6 and rededicated in 1681 to the Twelve Apostles (Figure 205), were derived from the twelfth-century limestone churches of Vladimir, which had previously inspired Moscow's rulers as the epitome of Russian Orthodox architecture. Nikon intended that his church serve as a model for symbolically correct forms. Thus, the pentacupolar design with low domes was particularly significant, as was the absence of all references to the onion dome and to the *shatior*, or tent tower, which had gained such popularity in Russian votive and parish churches. By 1655, it would appear that Nikon and his hierarchs considered the tent form inappropriate for the Orthodox Church, although it was permitted for bell towers.[61] The evident intent was to return the Church to the purity of its pre-Mongol forms, and to curtail the diversity of essentially secular, commemorative interpretations of the *shatior*.[62]

The fact that Nikon himself reverted to the conical form at the greatest of his structures reflects the arrogance and lack of consistency that infuriated the opponents of his liturgical reforms. In 1657, Nikon had conceived of recreating the Anastasis, or Church of the Resurrection in Jerusalem, at a picturesque site on the Istra River, to the west of Moscow. The cathedral was to be surrounded by the buildings of the Monastery of the Resurrection, and the entire community was to be known as New Jerusalem.[63] Nikon received support in this visionary plan from Tsar Aleksei, who made generous donations to each of the three monasteries founded by Nikon; and by 1658, construction was well underway, supervised by the patriarch himself. To complicate matters, Nikon, like later obsessed autocratic builders in Russia, often undid what had just been done and revised the design. Indeed, in order to obtain building material for his New Jerusalem, he began the demolition of one of the most distinctive structures from the reign of Ivan the Terrible – the Cathedral of Sts. Boris and Gleb in

Staritsa (1560–1; razed in 1804), with an elaborate plan and a *shatior* tower.[64] This act of vandalism should not, however, be seen as a rejection of the tent form: Not only did Resurrection Cathedral have a conical dome, but the Mount Eleon Chapel at New Jerusalem (1657) – also drawn from a prototype in the Holy Land – had the purest of tent towers over its low octagonal form.[65]

To guide his builders, Nikon had available various sources of information on the Jerusalem monument, of which the most important seems to have been the published description, with illustrations and plans, of the holy monuments in Jerusalem by Bernadino Amico.[66] The similarities in design are close enough to warrant such an assumption, despite the anomaly of a colossal monument possibly based on western architectural drawings appearing in remote Russia (cf. the hypothetical connection between Filarete's *Trattato* and the design of Ivan the Terrible's votive churches). The form of the Resurrection Cathedral at New Jerusalem, with massive rotunda and conical dome (see Plate 39), is at once unprecedented and yet firmly within the Russian tradition of visionary structures – such as the Cathedral of the Intercession on the Moat, which was also referred to as "Jerusalem" and which had a vertical point with an array of subsidiary towers. As in its Jerusalem prototype, the Resurrection Cathedral contained several components, including the church proper, a bell tower, and attached chapels with cupolas, all situated to the east of the rotunda (Figure 206).

Nikon's reasons for creating a replica of the Jerusalem shrine involved the desire to transplant the sacred shrine of Christendom to Orthodox soil, free from the control of infidels; and to inspire the faithful by the contemplation of ideal forms in service to the central tenets of Christian dogma – above all the resurrection.[67] At the same time, his concept, which involved construction on a scale far larger than the usual seventeenth-century Russian standard, represented a continuation of the idea of Moscovy as locus of the heavenly city (Zion), first implemented during the reign of Ivan the Terrible and subsequently undertaken, unsuccessfully, by Boris Godunov in his design for the Holy of Holies in the Kremlin (also intended as a replica of the Anastasis).

But whereas the Cathedral of the Intercession was popularly "rededicated" to Vasilii the Blessed, both Godunov's project and Nikon's were closely associated with the person of their creators (cf. the Godunov inscription at the top of the addition to the bell tower of Ivan the Great), and aroused opposition for the overweaning ambition of their scale.[68] Nikon's in-

Figure 205. Church of the Twelve Apostles. Moscow Kremlin. 1652–6. Architect: Antip Konstantinov. South view. (M 4–1)

volvement in the project intensified after his abandonment of the patriarchal throne in 1658, when he retreated to the New Jerusalem compound – a gesture reminiscent of Ivan the Terrible's retreat to Aleksandrova Sloboda, but with different results. Following the church council of 1667, Nikon was cast out of the New Jerusalem paradise, within which he had an isolated monastic residence, and sent into exile at the St. Cyril-Belozersk Monastery in the north. In 1681, after his release from exile, he died in Iaroslavl on the return journey to Moscow.

Although work was halted at New Jerusalem after the expulsion of Nikon, the project was resumed in 1679 at the command of Tsar Fedor. After the completion of the cathedral in 1684, surrounding wooden structures in the monastery were rebuilt of brick in the ornamental "Moscow baroque" style. The cathedral itself had a significant influence in the development of some of the most distinctive features of that style, including the revival of centralized tower churches and certain forms of exterior ornamentation of western provenance.[69] Despite its impressive engineering, the rotunda and brick roof collapsed in 1723 as the result of a failure of the westernmost wall. In 1756–61, the rotunda walls were repaired and the conical roof rebuilt in wood by Karl Blank, with projecting baroque window surrounds (see Plate 39). During the same period, Bartolomeo Francesco Rastrelli redid the interior in a florid late baroque style (Figure 207), which stood until the end of 1941, when the cathedral was severely damaged during the battle of Moscow.[70]

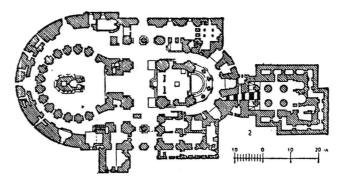

Figure 206. Cathedral of the Resurrection, New Jerusalem (Resurrection) Monastery on the Istra. Near Moscow. 1658–85. Architects: Patriarch Nikon and Sergei Turchaninov. Rebuilt in mideighteenth century by Bartolomeo Francesco Rastrelli and Karl Blank. Plan and east elevation.

Figure 207. Cathedral of the Resurrection, New Jerusalem Monastery. Near Moscow. Longitudinal section.

The Court of the Rostov Metropolitan

For all of the vicissitudes of New Jerusalem, the idea of a comprehensive, enclosed ensemble representing in material terms the realm of the spiritual continued to exert impressive force on the imagination of Church hierarchs who controlled sufficient resources to implement their will. None succeeded more visibly than Nikon's protégé, the Metropolitan Jonah of Rostov (c. 1607–90). The son of a country priest, Jonah Sysoevich rose through the monastic structure in Rostov, and in 1652 was appointed by the newly elected Patriarch Nikon to the metropolitanate in Rostov. Although devoted to his mentor, Jonah was appointed caretaker of the patriarchal throne after the departure of Nikon in 1658. The divided loyalties of Jonah's position brought him to the disfavor of the tsar during Nikon's attempt to reassert his authority in the 1660s.

Nonetheless, Jonah regained the sovereign's trust and proceeded from his position in Rostov to marshall the resources for the building of what was in fact an ideal city, whose scale may have served as an example to Peter the Great in the creation of his "window on the west," despite the fact that the spirit and the derivation of the metropolitan's creation were altogether different from those of secular Petersburg.[71] Although Jonah had at his command only 16,000 serfs as well as the best craftsmen of his large and prosperous eparchy, he seems to have used his limited means more rationally than would Peter; for within 20 years – between 1670 and 1690 – Jonah's masons erected not only several large churches and buildings for the metropolitan's court and residence (often referred to as the Rostov Kremlin), but also magnificent walls with towers and gate churches (Figure 208), situated on the north shore of Lake Nero.[72] The adjacent Dormition Cathedral (see Figure 131) provided a monumental example for the metropolitan's compound, to which it is linked visually by the great belfry. Apparently built between 1682 and 1687, the

Figure 208. Rostov Kremlin (Court of the Metropolitan of Rostov). West view, belfry. (R 3–32)

Figure 209. North wall and Gate Church of the Resurrection. Rostov Kremlin. 1670. North facade. (R 2–17)

belfry is composed of two adjoining structures, of which the taller (and later) contains the greatest of the bells – the 36-ton "Sysoi," named after Jonah's father. The larger segment of the belfry, with three bays, contains the twelve bells.[73]

From the belfry, the northern entrance to the Kremlin is flanked by two towers with bulbous domes, between which is the north facade of the gate Church of the Resurrection (1670; Figure 209). Its pointed gables beneath cupolas remind of wooden architectural forms, as does the attached raised gallery along the south and west facades of the church. The facades are divided into three bays by pilaster strips, with a multitude of arched forms for the various portals on the ground floor and in the gallery arcade above. The interior is without piers, and is entirely covered in frescoes whose color palette and composition match the best Iaroslavl work.[74]

Within the walls, the compound is occupied by

buildings associated with the metropolitanate, including the Red Chambers or palace (*palata*), used as the metropolitan's residence (Figure 210). Built in the southwest corner of the walls in 1672–80, the chambers form an L-shaped 2-storied structure with a sloped roof; the main level is reached by a covered porch and steps, with tent towers over the successive landings. The interior space contains a large hall supported by a central pillar, a design introduced in Novgorod in the fifteenth century. Attached to the palace by passageways is the Church of the Savior on the Stores (see Frontispiece), built in 1675 above a provisions cellar, which served as the metropolitan's chapel for devotional purposes, and for the performance of sacred music.[75] The interior of the church was decorated with the richest of wall paintings in the entire compound.[76] Beyond the palace on the west wall is the ensemble's second major gate church, dedicated to St. John the Theologian and flanked by large

Figure 210. Red Chambers. Rostov Kremlin. 1672–80. North facade.
(R 2–8)

towers (1683; Figures 211 and 212). It is elaborately
decorated, with a frieze of ogival arches in imitation
of the adjacent Dormition Cathedral.[77] The apsidal
structure on this, as on all of the Kremlin churches
built by Jonah, is a low projection of three bays roofed
in the manner of wooden construction.

After the death of Jonah in 1690, his work was
continued by the Metropolitan Josephat, who over
the next decade built a number of ancillary structures,
as well as the Church of the Icon of the Mother of
God Hodegetria (Figure 213), covered on the exterior
with the trompe l'oeil diamond rustication imported
to Muscovy by the Italians in the early sixteenth century. The surge of ornamentalism at the end of the
seventeenth century brought a revival of the technique throughout Muscovy, from Kostroma to Zagorsk. With the death of Josephat in 1701, little else
was built in the Rostov Kremlin and nothing of architectural distinction. The ensemble had been conceived as a total environment, and was incapable of
further development without destruction to the fabric
of the original design. In that sense, it serves as an
illuminating reprise to medieval Russian culture.

There were other visions of community, secular but
also reliant on the enterprise and authority of churchmen. The development of Siberia offered possibilities
for the creation of new settlements, such as the city
of Tobolsk, with its three adjacent citadels – the St.
Sophia Court (*dvor*), the trading district, and the
Kremlin, all overlooking the Irtysh River.[78] After damage from repeated fires, the rebuilding of central parts
of the city and its fortifications was initiated in the
1680s by Metropolitan Paul of Siberia, with the support of Moscow's Siberian Office (*prikaz*).[79] In the
1690s, the strategic importance of the city spurred
Tsar Peter I to expend greater resources on this enterprise, whose implementation was entrusted to a
local surveyor, Semion Remezov, brought to Moscow
in 1698 to improve his limited knowledge of city planning and architectural design through the reading of
an "Italian" (*friazhskii*) construction manual. Remezov's plan of 1699 for a new kremlin was approved,
and the installation of a new governor (M. V. Gagarin)
in 1711 gave impetus to the venture, as did the work
of Swedish prisoners-of-war who brought needed
skills to a number of Siberian projects. But despite

169

Figure 211. Gate Church of St. John the Theologian. 1683. Rostov Kremlin. West elevation.

energetic beginnings, Remezov's vision of the regulated building of houses and a comprehensive city plan were not realized for lack of resources.[80]

During the late seventeenth century, other cities also gained new fortress walls and towers – often more for symbolic effect than for military value. Kazan in particular benefited from a reconstruction of its kremlin walls after a fire in 1672.[81] Its dominant landmark is the Siuiumbeki Tower (Figure 214), named after a Tatar princess of the time of Ivan the Terrible. Many legends have associated the princess with the tower (or some earlier variant), but the existing structure was built in the latter part of the seventeenth century as a watchtower, most likely by a master builder from Moscow.[82] It was during this period (1660s–80s) that the towers of the Moscow Kremlin gained their tiered superstructures, often with spires; and the Borovitskii Tower (built on the southwest wall of the Kremlin in 1490 by Pietro Antonio Solari, with receding superstructure added in 1666–80s) seems in particular to have served as a model for the Kazan structure. The engineering of so tall a structure (58 meters in height) depended on brick of high quality and on a base whose thickness is comparable to that of the Bell Tower of Ivan the Great.

170

The Flourishing of Monastic Architecture

Although the wealth of monasteries (in both land and labor, city and country) was restricted by the Legal Code of 1649, their economic, political, and cultural influence remained considerable during the latter half of the seventeenth century. Many still received major patronage from members of the tsar's family, as well as from wealthy nobles and merchants. Some initiated expansion whose scale reminds of the work undertaken by Jonah, particularly the great walled citadel and twelve towers of the Savior-St. Evfimii Monastery in Suzdal (Figure 215), which was built in 1664, shortly before the beginning of the Metropolitan's Court in Rostov.

Indeed, the St. Evfimii monastery, which possessed over 10,000 serfs, may have imitated the Moscow Kremlin in yet another attempt by the Church to reassert its political authority. As the burial place of Prince

Figure 212. Gate Church of St. John the Theologian. Rostov Kremlin. East view. (R 3–8)

Figure 213. Church of the Mother of God Hodegetria (left), Dormition Cathedral (center), and Church of the Resurrection. Rostov Kremlin. South view. (R 1–37)

Dmitrii Pozharskii (1642), the monastery had the character of a secular shrine and was much used for purposes of state at the turn of the eighteenth century.[83] The main tower, square in plan and 22 meters in height, provided an imposing entrance not only in its size, but also with decorative friezes, including a row of "gothic" ogival window surrounds. Other Suzdal monasteries also benefited from the largess of the tsarist family. The superb Church of the Ascension at the Monastery of St. Alexander Nevskii (Figure 216), built in 1695 with funds provided by Natalia Naryshkina (second wife of Tsar Aleksei and the mother of Peter I), displays the decorative elements of late seventeenth-century architecture in an accomplished design that speaks of Muscovite work.

Certain monasteries maintained their role as centers of learning, even as secular academies were beginning to enter Russia by way of the Ukraine. Notable among such centers was the Trinity-Ipatevskii (Hypation) Monastery in Kostroma, which possessed one of the most important collections of Old Russian chronicles. In the turbulent year 1613, the monastery also served as the refuge for the young Mikhail Romanov and his mother at the time of his election to the throne, and the monastery benefited from the generosity of the tsarist family over the next three centuries.[84] When in 1649 the monastery Cathedral of the Trinity, originally built in 1590, collapsed from an explosion of powder kegs in its cellar (not an uncommon occurrence in Muscovite towns, where masonry churches were often the only secure storage areas), Tsar Aleksei promptly provided for its reconstruction. Its monumental design (Figure 217) combines the early sixteenth-century Iaroslavl Cathedral of the Transfiguration with the plan of Iaroslavl district churches a century later.

The most powerful of Muscovy's monasteries remained the Trinity-St. Sergius, whose heroic role in the repulse of the Polish–Lithuanian forces gained it not only vast respect, but also increasing donations

Figure 214. Siuiumbeki Tower. Kazan Kremlin. Latter half of seventeenth century. (KZ 2–14)

acquired new buildings of palatial ambience. The most striking is the refectory Church of St. Sergius (1686–92), donated by Tsars Peter and Ivan V, and built in a style whose wealth of facade detail epitomizes late Muscovite ornamentalism (Figure 218). The Russian institution of a refectory (or monastic dining hall and kitchen) with attached stone church had first appeared in the Kremlin Chudov Monastery at the end of the fifteenth century.[86] Thereafter, the arrangement spread to several major monasteries and convents, including the Trinity-St. Sergius, whose earlier refectory dated from the 1560s, with a church added in 1621.[87] The late seventeenth-century refectory Church of St. Sergius, 85 meters in length (including the exterior terrace), contained a refectory 34 meters long without a central column, and a 2-story church with domical vault (Figure 219). The interior is decorated with wall paintings and gilded ornament. The exterior has window surrounds with molded columns, first introduced in 1682 with the widening of the windows of the Faceted Chamber in the Moscow Kremlin (see Figure 121). The exterior walls are covered with polychrome diamond rustication – also derived from the Faceted Chamber.[88]

Similarly decorative is the monastery's main (east) gate church, dedicated to John the Baptist, which was orginally erected in 1513 and rebuilt in 1692–9 with funds provided by the Stroganovs (Figure 220). In style, it belongs to a group of such churches constructed during the same period as wealthy Muscovite monasteries (such as the Novodevichii Convent; see Figure 229). Typically, these brightly painted churches use the shell motif above the cornice, and apply elements of the order system decoratively, with no tectonic purpose; yet they serve admirably to focus attention at the point of entry into the sacred precincts.

The ornamental exuberance, symbolic of paradise, affected even the fortress towers, which had been massively reinforced during the middle of the seventeenth century. By the end of the century, some of the towers received purely decorative superstructures of brick and limestone – such as the Utochii Tower at the northeast corner (Figure 221), so named for the carved figure of a duck at its spire.[89] The tiered design of this folly, built between 1672 and 1686 and equal in height to the base tower structure, has led to the suggestion of Dutch influence – not unlike that of the bell tower of the Church of John the Baptist at Tolchkovo in Iaroslavl (see Figure 201).

Within Moscow itself, what has survived of late seventeenth-century monastery architecture gives proof of its considerable variety, beginning with the

throughout the seventeenth century. The last two decades of the century presented an unparalleled display of magnificence, due in part to its role in two crucial events in the ascendancy of Peter I. In 1682, Peter, his half-brother and cotsar Ivan V, and the latter's sister Sophia (who was serving as regent) fled to the monastery to escape a rebellion of the Muscovy's professional soldiers, the *streltsy*. And in 1689, Peter once again took refuge in the monastery to elude the machinations of Sophia and her advisors who wished to seize power from the young tsar after the death of Ivan V. Peter's complete triumph, and its brutal repercussions, began from the very walls of the Trinity-St. Sergius Monastery.[85]

During the 1680s and 1690s, the monastery thus

Figure 215. Savior–St. Evfimii Monastery. Suzdal. Walls and square
main entrance tower (right) built c. 1664. (SZ 3–2)

Figure 216. Church of the Ascension and bell tower, St. Alexander
Nevskii Monastery. Suzdal. 1695. (SZ 3–7)

Figure 217. Cathedral of the Trinity, Trinity–Ipatevskii Monastery. Kostroma. 1590; rebuilt 1650–2. Southeast view. (KO 1–23)

Cathedral of the Icon of the Sign (Znamenie) at the Znamenskii Monastery in Kitai-gorod. Located within the compound of the Boiars Romanov (whose "Chambers" were restored in 1857–9 by the court architect Friedrich Richter), the monastery was generously endowed by the mother of Mikhail Romanov upon its founding in 1631.[90] Yet the cathedral, built in 1679–84 by masons from Kostroma, is not lavishly decorated; it adheres to a monumental archaic style that reminds both of Novgorod architecture and, in its gable and roof structure, of wooden architecture (Figure 222).[91] In contrast, the Cathedral of the Transfiguration of the Savior (1645–51) at the New Savior (Novospasskii) Monastery reproduces the pentacupolar design of large sixteenth-century monastery catherals (Figure 223). Long patronized by the rulers of Muscovy, the monastery was looted during the Time of Troubles, but rebuilt with support from Tsars Mikhail and Aleksei, and it continued to enjoy the favor of the Romanov family as well as the Sheremetevs, a number of who are buried on its precincts.[92]

The pentacupolar form was capable of ornamental variations, such as the extensive use of decorative ceramic tiles on the exterior of the Cathedral of the Intercession at Izmailovo (1671–9; Figure 224), a village belonging to the Romanovs and subsequently converted to a crown estate on the northeast edge of Moscow. In 1663, it became a model estate, supported by Tsar Aleksei as a means of encouraging the development of horticulture in Russia.[93] Surrounded by a canal and dominated by the large domes of the cathedral, the central part of Izmailovo is comparable to the ideal architectural ensembles described before, with the ambience of a wealthy monastery. Yet its purpose was both secular and prosaic, at the service of the tsar, who built a palace there (not extant) and in 1682 erected the main gates (Figure 225), whose design with tent tower resembles the main gateway, with chiming clock, to the royal estate at Kolomenskoe (1672–3). Similar gateways were also built at monasteries during this period, as is colorfully illustrated at the entrance to the Convent of the Deposition of the Robe of the Mother of God at Suzdal. Built in 1688 by Andrei Shmakov and comrades, the design has the typical two arches of different size, with two tent towers on low octagons (see Plate 40). At Izmailovo, a second entrance point was guarded by a brick tower (the *Mostovaia bashnia;* 1679), whose terraced form is composed of an octagon over a cube – usually reserved for church architecture – with decorative detail outlined in white (Figure 226). Although lower than the spire of the Main Gates, the pyramidal roof of the tower posesses a similarly festive appearance. Unfortunately, the most innovative building at Izmailovo, the multitiered Church of Josaphat, is not extant.

Elaborate fortress architecture is exemplified in the far northern St. Cyril–Belozersk Monastery (Figure 227), and in Moscow's Simonov Monastery, on the southeast approach to the city. Founded in 1370, the ensemble was rebuilt in the midseventeenth century as the last of the great monastery fortresses. Much of it was destroyed in the 1930s with the expansion of the ZIL Autoworks, but the Dulo, or "Muzzle," Tower remains as one of the most impressive examples of late Muscovite fortress architecture. Built in the 1640s, the tower is composed of a round base ribbed with pilaster strips and decorated with limestone blocks in a checkered pattern. The superstructure recedes to a two-tiered watchtower over a conical roof that prefigures the design of the Resurrection Cathedral at New Jerusalem.

As at the Trinity-St. Sergius Monastery, lavish ornamentation was reserved for the monastery refectory, rebuilt in 1677–85 by Parfen Petrov (Potapov ?)

Figure 218. Refectory Church of St. Sergius. Trinity–St. Sergius Monastery. 1686–92. Northeast view. (Z 6–3)

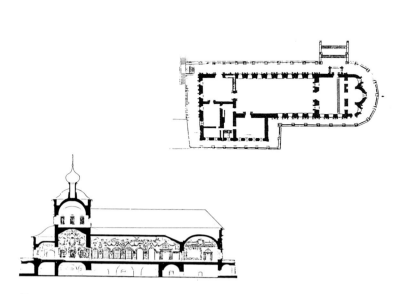

Figure 219. Refectory Church of St. Sergius. Trinity–St. Sergius Monastery. Section by V. Baldin.

Figure 220. Gate Church of John the Baptist. Trinity–St. Sergius Monastery. 1692–9. West facade. (Z 2–7)

Figure 221. Utochii Tower. Trinity–St. Sergius Monastery. Midseventeenth century; 1676–82. Southeast view. (Z 6–15)

and Osip Startsev. Although designed in the usual rectangular form of monastery refectories, with painted diamond restication, the west facade culminates in a stepped gable, with volutes, that has been compared with both Polish and Dutch architecture of the period (Figure 228).[94] The attached columns also adhere more closely to the classical order system, in comparison with the usual ornamental columns of the "Moscow baroque." This rare surviving evidence of the increasingly knowledgeable assimilation of western decorative forms in Muscovite architecture has been disfigured by subsequent conversion to industrial use, but contemporary drawings suggest that there were other Moscow structures with similar stepped gables.

Of all Moscow's monastic institutions, none prospered more openly than the Novodevichii (New Virgin) Convent, whose early sixteenth-century Smolensk Cathedral (see Figure 132) served as a prototype

– along with the Kremlin cathedrals – for major monastery churches. At the end of the sixteenth century, the convent received donations from Irina Godunov and her brother Tsar Boris to rebuild its walls, which had also played a role in the repulse of Crimean Khan Kazy Girei in 1591.[95] The elaborate crowns of the towers were added in the late seventeenth century.

The major building campaign at the convent was supported by the Tsarevna Sophia during the years of her regency (1682–9). She was assisted in this endeavor by her main advisor Prince Vasilii Golitsyn, an architectural innovator much interested in western forms.[96] The palatial, secular orientation of the style is reflected in the refectory Church of the Dormition (1685–1687)[97]; and the Church of the Transfiguration,

Figure 222. Cathedral of the Icon of the Sign, Znamenskii Monastery. Moscow. 1679–84. East facade. (M 18–6)

Figure 223. Novospasskii Monastery. Moscow. Walls: 1640s; Cathedral of the Transfiguration of the Savior, 1645–51. Southeast view. (M 126–0)

Figure 224. Cathedral of the Intercession at Izmailovo. Moscow. 1671–9. West facade, with nineteenth-century structures attached on either side. (M 129–0)

over the north gates (1687–9; Figure 229), whose gilded five domes and crosses crown a cornice of scallop shell *zakomary*, and the facade displays "Moscow baroque" window surrounds. The south gate Church of the Intercession (1683–8; Figure 230) is more modest in detail, but has the unusual design of three towers of ascending octagons with gilded cupolas. Both of the gate churches have terraces over the gates, the base of the church proper, thus creating a platform for the jeweled structure above.[98]

The culminating element of the Convent's expansion was the great bell tower, finished in 1690 (see Plate 41). One of the tallest in Russia at that time (72 meters, as compared with 81 meters for the Bell Tower of Ivan the Great), the tower of receding octagons displays great technical ingenuity as well as the decorative exuberance of the Moscow baroque. Its balustrades and pinnacles at the base of each octagon remind of the Tolchkovo bell tower in Iaroslavl, yet the finely calculated proportions of the Novodevichii tower are more spacious, and the onion dome provides a dramatic, luminescent concluding accent. By the time the bell tower was completed, the power of the convent's benefactress Sophia had been broken by Peter in the unsuccessful coup attempt of 1689, after which Sophia was confined to house arrest at Novodevichii.

Figure 225. Main Gates *(Paradnye vorota)* at Izmailovo. Moscow. 1682. East view. (M 129–9)

Following the suppression of that uprising, Peter commissioned the refectory Church of St. Sergius (Figure 231) at the Upper Petrovskii Monastery in memory of his refuge at the Trinity-St. Sergius Monastery during the uprising of *streltsy* in 1689. Completed in 1694, the church is related to the decorative style of the Novodevichii convent. In 1694, work was also completed on the monastery bell tower, placed above the gate Church of the Intercession (Figure 232). The open arcading of the two-tiered octagon over the gate church is a daring exercise in structural design that functions admirably to disseminate the bell tones.[99]

The innovations evident in monastery architecture were largely decorative in character, emblematic of the wealth donated to monasteries, but not intended to change the basic features of church design based on a pentacupolar cuboid structure. As seen at the Izmailovo Intercession Cathedral, however, even very conservative church forms could serve as a base for a startling display of intricate polychrome deco-

ration in the form of ceramic tiles. This tendency is illustrated at its extreme by two uniquely related seventeenth-century ensembles, of which the more conservative is the Monastery of St. Nicholas at Viazhishche (see Plate 42), 12 kilometers to the northwest of Novgorod.[100]

Between 1674 and 1695, the Orthodox Church in Novgorod was guided by Metropolitan Kornilii, a pious churchman little inclined toward elaborate displays of church wealth, despite his Muscovite origins. The monastic complex at Viazhishche, however, was ruled between 1683 and 1697 by the energetic archimandrite Bogolep Sablin, who had every intention of creating an environment reflective of his own power and that of his monastery.[101] The contrast between the two personalities suggests an explanation for the conservative, if imposing, design adopted for the rebuilding of the monastery Cathedral of St. Nicholas (1681–5; see Plate 43). The four-piered structure has the traditional pentacupolar culmination, with a concession to Novgorod tradition in the multigabled roof line (cf. the Church of the Trinity at the Holy Spirit Monastery in Novgorod; Figure 91). The most

Figure 226. Entrance tower *(Mostovaia bashnia)* at Ismailovo. Moscow. 1679. Southeast view. (M 129–17)

complex part of its form is the ascending entrance gallery, culminating in a single zakomara gable and flanked by two towers with pyramidal roofs – a design that can be compared with that of the royal church at Taininskoe (see Plate 38).

By 1694, work had begun on a new refectory and church adjacent to the cathedral. The accepted practice for refectory churches in the seventeenth century called for greater ornamentation, perhaps in acknowledgment of their secular ambiance as centers of monastic conviviality. The sparse information available suggests that the St. Nicholas Monastery under archimandrite Bogolep was a lavish institution, and nothing in the appearance of the refectory Church of St. John the Theologian belies that assumption (see Plate 44). Its imposing length culminates in the west with a bell tower (the last element to be completed, in 1704) and in the east with a 2-story structure containing churches dedicated to St. John the Theologian (below), and to the Ascension (above). The long facade is marked with two strips of ornamental tiles on a green base, depicting primarily floral patterns, but also containing mythological beasts (unicorn, two-headed eagle) and iconographic motifs. The church and bell tower have additional strips decorating their greater height, and the church has elaborate ceramic window surrounds rivaled only by the Iaroslavl churches at Tolchkovo and Korovniki.

Figure 227. Northeast tower, St. Cyril-Belozersk Monastery. 1660s.

Figure 228. Refectory, Simonov Monastery. Moscow. 1677–85. West facade (much disfigured by factory works). (M 39–7a)

those churchmen like Bogolep, who made no apologies for a display of the wealth and power of the Church.[103] To this end, he supported the ongoing process of rebuilding his legation, the Krutitskoe Podvore, located in the eastern part of the city within sight of the Novospasskii Monastery.

The reconstruction had begun before his time with the Church of the Dormition (1667–85), typical of the period with domical vault and a decorative penta-cupolar top. From the church, an elevated, arcaded gallery led to the residence and refectory, the entrance to which led through a brick gateway – the Teremok, or tower – whose upper facade was covered in polychrome tile of the most intricate design, including ceramic columns (Figure 233; see Plate 45). The bays of the gateway are additionally delineated and decorated with carved limestone columns. The architect of this display (which, facing north, rarely receives

The provenance of the extraordinary tile work at Viazhishche remains unclear, although Moscow and Iaroslavl are possible sources, because both produced such tiles for sale in other cities. It is also known that Nikon imported Belorussian potters, who refined the polychrome faience technique at the ceramic workshop for his monastery at Valdai (in the Novgorod region), but the patriarch subsequently transferred them to work on the Resurrection Cathedral at New Jerusalem.[102] However, if Abbot Bogolep initiated the refectory decoration, it is likely that he had the support of Evfimii, who succeeded Kornilii as metropolitan of Novgorod from 1695 to 1696, and who during his preceding tenure as Metropolitan of Saratov and the Don region had commissioned the most remarkable single display of ceramic ornamentation in Russian architecture.

It must be noted that the metropolitans of the various eparchies of the Russian Orthodox Church typically had a legation (*podvore*), or residence, in Moscow. Indeed, some of them spent most of their tenure in the capital in order to remain close to the centers of administrative power. The Sarskii and Podonskii (Saratov and Don) Eparchy had traditionally been one of the most important, because its area brought it into contact with the Mongol khanates. Metropolitan Evfimii, who occupied this significant post between 1688 and 1695 (after holding other major ecclesiastical appointments in Moscow), belonged to

Figure 229. Gate Church of the Transfiguration, Novodevichii Convent. Moscow. 1687–9. East view. (M 73–12)

Figure 230. Chambers of Tsarevna Mariia Alekseevna and Gate Church of the Intercession, Novodevichii Convent. Moscow. 1683–8. Northeast view. (M 127–4)

direct light) was Osip Startsev, with the assistance of L. Kovalev, and the decorative work – ceramic and limestone – came from the workshop of Osip Startsev and his son Ivan.[104] The Krutitskii gateway, begun in 1693, was completed the following year, just before Evfimii's departure for Novgorod, where he in some unspecified way probably assisted in the implementation of Abbot Bogolep's refectory church.

The one Moscow monastery that can claim a genuinely innovative structure from the late seventeenth century is Donskoi Monastery, whose Small (malyi) Cathedral had defined the decorative Godunov style at the turn of the century. The reasons for the monastery's increase in prestige were related to its commemoration of the victory over Khan Kazy Girei; for with the Russian effort to deal decisively with the threat of its southern frontier from the Crimean Tatars and their Turkish sponsors during the 1670s, Donskoi Monastery moved from a symbolic function in the struggle against the infidel to the status of an active participant, blessing and encouraging campaigns to the south. In this respect, the monastic hierarchy developed particularly close relations with Vasilii Golitsyn, the most influential proponent of an aggressive – and ultimately disastrous – southern policy during the regency of Sophia.[105]

With the monastery's new wealth and patronage, the small cathedral no longer sufficed (fortunately, it was preserved), and in 1684, the regent Sophia commissioned the building of a new cathedral (the "Bolshoi," or large) also dedicated to the Icon of the Don Mother of God. Its form is unlike that of other large monastery cathedrals: the four subsidiary cupolas, for example, are placed at the points of the compass rather than on the diagonal (Figure 234). The major changes, however, are in the structure itself and the plan, which approaches a cruciform shape (Figure 235). The central bays of each facade project substantially, and the corner bays of the main "cube" are lowered in height to 1 story, thus increasing the depth

181

Figure 231. Refectory Church of St. Sergius of Radonezh, Upper Petrovskii Monastery. Moscow. 1690–4. Southwest view. (M 20)

the renewal of Russian culture at the end of the century, and it is therefore probable that the Kievan area provided general concepts of new architectural forms, as Belorussian craftsmen had influenced the development of architectural ornament.[107]

The cathedral walls were completed by 1687, but after the unsuccessful outcome of Golitsyn's Crimean campaigns in 1687 and 1689 (which led to factionalism within the army and the collapse of Sophia's regency

of the arms of the cross. Access to the main level is achieved through a raised gallery surrounding the structure. The centralized characteristics of the design are maintained on the interior, with four columns supporting the drum above the central crossing.

Throughout its history, Russian religious architecture has devised centralized forms with a strong vertical emphasis that would accommodate liturgical needs as well as symbolize important secular events (cf. the sixteenth-century votive tower churches). The late seventeenth century witnessed a new stage in this process, within which the catheral at Donskoi Monastery is a seminal monument. It has been suggested that the impulse behind the new centralized church designs came from the recently incorporated western lands, particularly Ukraine, which by the middle of the seventeenth century had developed a cruciform church plan typically composed of four tower bays grouped around a central bay with the main drum.[106] Golitsyn maintained close ties with Kievan scholars and clergy who served as a catalyst in

Figure 232. Bell tower, Upper Petrovskii Monastery. Moscow. Completed in 1694. Southwest view. (M 37–9a)

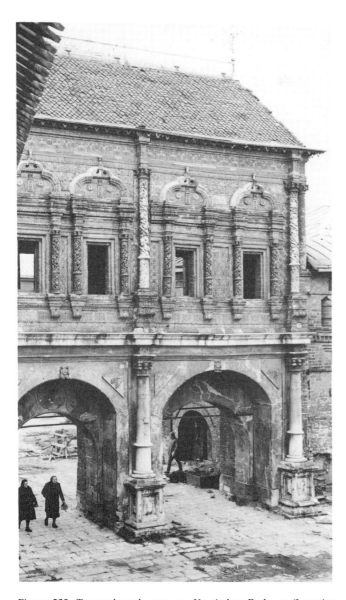

Figure 233. Teremok and gateway, Krutitskoe Podvore (Legation of the Metropolitan of Saratov and the Don region). Moscow. 1693–4. North facade. (M 40–7)

Figure 234. Great (Bolshoi) Cathedral of the Don Mother of God, Donskoi Monastery. Moscow. 1684–98. Southeast view. (M 128–33)

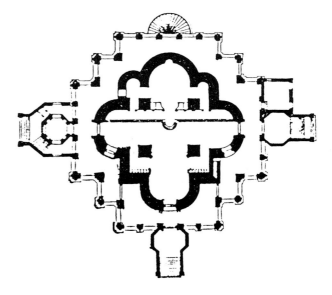

Figure 235. Great Cathedral of the Don Mother of God, Donskoi Monastery. Moscow. Plan.

after an attempt to overthrow the young tsar Peter), further building was halted. Peter, however, would continue the campaigns against the Turks and Tatars; and after his rapprochement with the monastery, work on the cathedral was resumed in 1692 and finally completed in 1698.[108] The elaborately carved, gilded seven-tiered iconostasis, which defines the great height of the interior, was begun in 1695 by Karp Zolatarev and completed in 1699. By that time, the innovations of the new Donskoi cathedral had been been superceded by more rigorous expressions of the tower church.

The "Naryshkin Baroque" and the Revival of Tower Churches

The transformation in Russian society and culture at the end of the seventeenth century – and the premonition of more radical changes to come – led to new church forms sponsored by some of Russia's most powerful and wealthy families, perhaps as an expression of changing cultural identity. The ensuing style is often designated the "Naryshkin baroque," after the boiar family (related to Peter I) that built such churches on its estates. Indeed, the term "Naryshkin baroque" is often used interchangeably with "Moscow baroque," which in the examples illustrated before (the Kadashi church, the Simonov Monastery refectory, the Krutitskii Teremok) was largely a decorative style with little structural impact.[109] In this sense, there are questions as to the validity of the term, which suggests misleading comparisons with the contemporary baroque of central Europe, without the structural – or ideological – complexities of the latter.[110]

Nonetheless, both terms have endured, and there is a certain convenience in designating as "Naryshkin style" a series of estate tower churches erected by a small group of grandees oriented toward western culture (notably, the Naryshkins and Sheremetevs associated with Peter I), rather than by the craft guilds, merchants, and churchmen responsible for the more traditional decorated forms of Moscow baroque architecture. For the Naryshkin style, the balance and symmetry of the carved limestone cornices, window surrounds, and attached columns, as well as an increasing understanding of the classical system of orders, suggests a new sophistication of taste on the part of both patron and builder. This was no longer the *horror vacui* that led to the exuberant application of ornament highlighted by bright colors. The new form of ornamentation consisted of sculpted details (usually of limestone), frequently borrowed from western handbooks[111] and placed on the facade in a more coherent fashion than had been the case with churches such as the Trinity in Nikitniki and the Trinity at Ostankino.

At the same time, the distinctive tiered (*iarusnyi*) estate church – composed of octagonal levels above a central cube and first appearing in masonry construction at the beginning of the 1680s – represents a reassertion of the Russian fondness for a vertical silhouette, temporarily in abeyance with the rejection of the tent tower, or *shatior,* over the church structure. Like its tower precessors, the tiered church was often

considered to have derived from a wooden prototype, and perhaps with more historical justification, because examples of wooden tiered churches dating from as early as the midseventeenth century have survived (see Appendix I). But here as well, the formal similarity of the pyramidal shape is overshadowed by the greater complexity of the brick-tiered church.[112]

For not only does the "Naryshkin" church reinterpret the centralized tower structure, it also integrates the bell tower by placing it in an octagonal tier above the main part of the church, thus permitting a symmetry in which the apse is balanced by a vestibule of identical configuration on the west end.[113] Furthermore, a number of the Naryshkin designs have projections added to all four sides of the central cube, thus creating a tetrafoil pattern reminiscent of the Church of the Metropolitan Peter at the Upper Petrovskii Monastery (now dated to the early sixteenth century; see Figure 136). The resulting compact form did not allow for a large sanctuary – unnecessary in an estate church – and the thick walls that supported the weight of the tower and contained the steps to the bell octagon placed further constraints on the size of the interior.

Among the two dozen or so late seventeenth-century tower churches known to have been built to the tiered design, the first examples – dating from the early 1680s and no longer extant – were awkward structures with little ornamentation.[114] Fortunately, there is considerable documentary evidence on the Church of the Indian Prince Josaphat (*Ioasaf Tsarevich indiiskii,* razed in the late 1930s), begun at Izmailovo in 1678 and rebuilt in 1687–8. Despite its retention of some features of the "ship" design, such as the attached (rather than superimposed) bell tower, the church as rebuilt in 1688 was the first to display a clearly defined tiered structure, with symmetrical domed projections on east and west (Figure 236).[115] Shortly thereafter, the same basic design reappeared in the Church of Sts. Boris and Gleb at Ziuzino (1688–1704; see Plate 46), an estate acquired from the crown by Prince B. I. Prozorovskii in 1687.[116] Although still awkward in the proportion if its ascending octagons, in its integration of decorative detail and structure, the Ziuzino church is a major step in the evolution of the tiered church form.

A further stage of development is the tiered Church of the Smolensk Mother of God (Figure 237), built in 1691 on the estate of Safarino – or Sofrino – belonging to the boiar F. P. Saltykov. The church is picturesquely located on a hill (near the road to Zagorsk), and Saltykov stipulated that it be attached to his masonry house (not extant).[117] This unusual arrangement al-

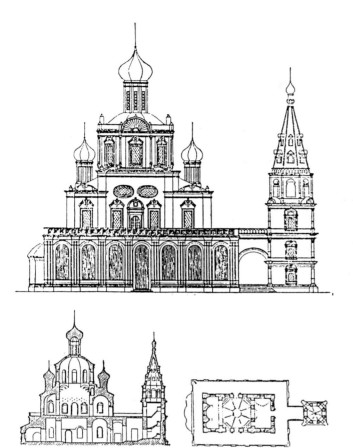

Figure 236. Church of Josaphat at Izmailovo. Moscow. 1687–8. Architect: T. Makarov. Reconstructed north elevation and longitudinal section by A. Chiniakov.

lowed both church and mansion to preside over the surrounding village and fields. Although the form of four receding octagons over the main cube is imposing, the proportions and the transition from one to the next are still clumsily modulated, due perhaps to the thickness of the walls, which contained a narrow stairway to the belfry. The architect also reverted to the asymmetry of the ship design for the apsidal structure, and applied the ornamental detail with simple abandon. Of greater refinement is the Church of the Icon of the Sign (late 1680s) built by the boiar Lev Naryshkin, uncle of Peter I, at his estate compound in the center of Moscow.[118] Yet it, too, has features of the traditional ship design, such as an apse with two attached chapels on the east, and a vestibule on the west.

The first indisputable masterpiece of the Naryshkin style is the Church of the Intercession at Fili, built in

1690–3 by Lev Naryshkin. Its plan is both decorative and tightly organized: a cube with four projecting lobes, of which the east and west are elongated. All projections but the east have a staircase with balustrade descending from the gallery that encircles the structure (see Plate 47). The festive, ceremonial function of this design of steps, in two landings with a right-angle turn, had been explored at the Ascension Church at Kolomenskoe, and is here perfected with the decorative panoply of the Naryshkin style.

In comparison with certain later examples of the tiered church, the exterior ornament at Fili is restrained: most notably cornice crests ("combs") and attached columns without ornamental carving on the shafts. The distinctive quality of church, emphasized by the application of decorative detail, is the impeccable handling of proportion and structural development, from the raised gallery – which reinforces the plasticity of the projecting lobes, each with its own gilded cupola – to the culminating cupola above the central tower and belfry (Figures 238 and 239). Despite the stylistic distance that separates the Fili church from contemporary European architecture, its un-

Figure 237. Church of the Smolensk Mother of God at Safarino. Near Moscow. 1691. South view. (MR 8–1a)

Figure 238. Church of the Intercession at Fili. Moscow. 1690–3. South view. (M 85–6a)

above four lobes, which are themselves above the main gate.

Before completing the gate church, Bukhvostov had undertaken a much larger project in the city of Riazan, whose Metropolitan Avraamii undertook a rebuilding of the city's main cathedral, dedicated to the Dormition. Work had begun in 1684, but the completed walls collapsed in 1692; and Bukhvostov, who assumed control of the project from his hapless predecessor, was also to have much trouble with the foundations and the roof vaulting for the immense

Figure 239. Church of the Intercession at Fili. Moscow. Axonometric projection. Courtesy of Shchusev State Museum of Architecture.

known architect possessed an unerring sense of an ordered tectonic system relating all parts to a harmonious whole.[119] The sumptuously outfitted but small interior, with carved iconostasis, is essentially a cylinder, linked at the base of the main cupola with iron tie rods.

There is one architect of the Naryshkin style whose career is known in unusual detail – largely derived from the depositions in a series of lawsuits brought against him by irate patrons. Iakov Bukhvostov, born around 1630, was a serf on an estate belonging to Mikhail Tatishchev near the town of Dmitrov (in the Moscow region).[120] Although the details are unknown, his enlightened owner seems to have noted his talent as a builder and allowed him to resettle as a free laborer in Moscow, where he is first mentioned in 1681 as a bidder for two construction projects. His name reappears in 1690, in connection with the major upgrading of the walls of the monastery at New Jerusalem. Included in Bukhvostov's work was the gate Church of the Entry into Jerusalem, completed in 1694 and recently restored to an approximation of its original form – four octagonal tiers over a cube that rises

structure (Figure 240).[121] The interior plan contains four massive columns for the central and west bays, and two extended piers at the east bay and iconostasis (Figure 241). Over 40 meters in height, with five large drums and cupolas as well as extensive window space, the structure is balanced on Bukhvostov's system of cellar vaults, which also provide a terrace platform for the cathedral.

Like its predecessor by Fioravanti, the Riazan Dormition Cathedral resembles a great 3-story hall. Its roofline was designed as a horizontal dentilated cornice, and the tall windows were framed with carved limestone columns and pediments (the some 5,000 blocks comprising the limestone details were standardized, thus enabling the architect to complete the structure by 1699, a relatively short period in view of the complexity of the project and Bukhvostov's ongoing work elsewhere).[122] The window surrounds and the paired brick columns (painted white) that vertically segment the brick facades provide a secular, palatial ambience to one of the largest churches of the seventeenth century – larger, in fact, than Moscow's Dormition Cathedral.

Concurrently with the work at Riazan, Bukhvostov had contracted for another project, which, although smaller than his cathedral, was structurally more complex. Commissioned in 1694 by the choleric Peter Sheremetev the Younger for his estate at Ubory (to the west of Moscow), the Church of the Transfiguration of the Savior was hampered by the late delivery of construction materials and by the interference of Sheremetev, who, like the metropolitan of Riazan, brought criminal suit against Bukhvostov when the church was not finished by the time stipulated by the contract (July 1696). After winning his case in court, Sheremetev found it politic to make peace with the architect, and the basic structure was finished the following year – just before the death of Sheremetev, who never saw the interior of his church.

With its articulated four-lobed plan (Figure 242), the Ubory church is one of the most interesting structures in the "Naryshkin style," yet the structure shows a disjunction of parts that appears to have been due to Sheremetev, who insisted that the octagonal tower rise from an elevation of the central cube, rather than directly above the intersection of the four lobes. As a result, the harmony of proportions in relation to the size of the ground plan is lost, particularly when compared with the simpler plan at Fili. Spatially, however, the Ubory church is the most accomplished of the period, with the volume of the attached lobes flowing into the cylindrical core of the tower (Figure 243). On the exterior, the terrace – lower and wider

Figure 240. Cathedral of the Dormition. Riazan. 1693–1702. Architect: Iakov Bukhvostov. Southwest view. (RZ 3–35)

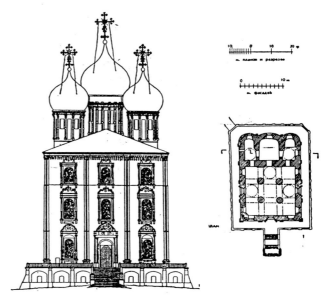

Figure 241. Cathedral of the Dormition. Riazan. Plan and section.

187

Figure 242. Church of the Transfiguration of the Savior at Ubory. Near Moscow. 1694–7. Architect: Iakov Bukhvostov. Plan and west elevation by V. Podkliuchnikov. Courtesy of Shchusev State Museum of Architecture.

Figure 243. Church of the Transfiguration of the Savior at Ubory. Section by V. Podkliuchnikov. Courtesy of Shchusev State Museum of Architecture.

than at Fili – amply frames the lobes, whose trefoil contours are marked by unusual "rustic" hewn limestone columns.

Of the many great estates that surrounded Moscow in the seventeenth century, most have been absorbed into the city's gargantuan housing developments, with only a name to mark their existence. There remain, however, tenuous oases that seem little touched by the twentieth century. One such village is Troitse-Lykovo, located on the far bank of the Moscow River in the northwest part of the city. Owned by the boiar Boris Lykov from 1627 to 1644, the estate temporarily reverted to the tsar's holdings; but in 1690, it was added to the demesnes of Lev Naryshkin, who at the end of the century built there a stunningly beautiful church dedicated to the Trinity – also attributed to Bukhvostov.[123]

The Church of the Trinity at Troitse-Lykovo is not large – none of the estate churches was, apart from those belonging to the tsar. It impresses, rather, by the proportions of the central tower, which rises from a cube to an octagon, to yet another octagon (with bells), to an octagonal drum, culminating in the golden cupola and cross (see Plate 48).[124] The tower is flanked on the east and west by two projections – the apse and the vestibule – which ascend in octagonal tiers to a cupola and cross (Figure 244). Although symmetrical in plan, the church presents two very

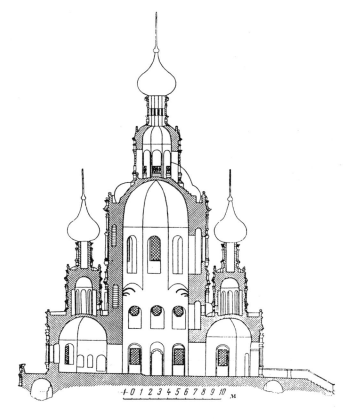

Figure 244. Church of the Trinity at Troitse-Lykovo. Moscow. 1698–1703. Architect: Iakov Bukhvostov(?). Section and plan.

different facades: from the north and south, a pyramid with flanking projections (Figure 245), and from the east and west, a straight vertical profile. The brick facades, with decorative portals and lucarnes, are outlined by elaborately carved limestone columns and cornices.

The interior (undergoing a laborious restoration after a postwar fire that destroyed most of the wood carving) was consummately theatrical, with red walls and black detail as a background for a gilded wood iconostasis ascending to a full relief, life-size crucifix (Figure 246) – an unusual, not to say unorthodox, feature that speaks of Polish influence. To observe the service, the Naryshkins had loges, with carved decoration and a balustrade, projecting from the upper tier, which was reached by a narrow stairway within the brick walls. The space of this gallery was so constricted as to make it virtually impossible to genuflect. The ostentatiously festive, secular quality of the Naryshkin style, so thoroughly represented here, created in essence a merging of exterior and interior. The motifs of the carved iconostasis frame were transferred to the facades, where they served to frame the structure as an expression of wealth and innovative taste.[125]

The saturation point of the Naryshkin style was reached in the Church of the Icon of the Sign on the estate of Dubrovitsy (near Podolsk, to the west of Moscow). Commissioned in 1690 by Boris Golitsyn, tutor of Peter I, the basic structure was completed in 1697, yet the church was consecrated only in 1704, in the presence of Metropolitan Stefan Iavorskii and Tsar Peter. The identity of its builders and the sculptors of its profuse statuary (Figure 247) has been the subject of much speculation, yet all hypotheses have so far proved untenable.[126] Whatever the resolution to that question, the church spans the most productive years of the tiered style, and is a catalog of its experiments in structure and in the decorative arts – both interior and exterior.

In the symmetrical plan of the Dubrovitsy church (Figure 248), the tower rises directly from the four lobes of the first tier – apparently what Bukhvostov had intended at Ubory. Thus it is, along with the church at Fili, one of the early examples of the centralized plan. But other than a certain structural logic, the provenance of the design is unresolved. It would appear that by far the earliest example in Muscovite architecture is the Church of the Metropolitan Peter at the Upper Petrovskii Monastery; and in view of the close connection of the Naryshkin family with that institution (see the foregoing), it is possible that the Naryshkin architect used it as a conceptual model for

Figure 245. Church of the Trinity at Troitse-Lykovo. Moscow. North facade. (M 27–11)

his far grander elaboration of the tiered church at Fili.

At the same time, however, a church with a similar lobed design, if more modest in scale, was begun on yet another Golitsyn estate – Perovo, at the northeast fringe of the city. It, too, was dedicated to the regal Icon of the Mother of God of the Sign, and consisted of eight lobes: four major, at the points of the compass, and four minor at the interstices. On the exterior, the semicircular bays are separated by attached columns in the corinthian order, which is maintained on the octagon of the second tier (Figure 249). This design has an indisputable logic, evident not only in the plan of the Metropolitan Peter Church, but even in the outline of the plan of St. Basil's. The buttressing strength of this configuration allowed not only a large area given to windows (now filled in), but also created on the interior an elaborate play of volumes (Figure 250) that would not have been unfamiliar to Carolingian architects.

Whether or not the monuments at Perovo and Dubrovitsy were conceived at the same source, the Gol-

189

Figure 246. Church of the Trinity at Troitse-Lykovo. Moscow. Iconostasis, upper tier, with sculpted crucifix. (M 29–1)

and the cathedral at Iurev-Polskoi; yet its ambience is largely western, in the statuary and the decidedly unorthodox crown above the tower (see Figure 247). It is symbolic that Peter I – in the early stages of a desperate war with Sweden – should have attended the dedication of this church, built by a tutor who had played his role in the opening to the west. For the church at Dubrovitsy represents at once an extreme variant of Muscovite ornamentalism and the quickening pace of westernization that would turn Russian architecture from Byzantium to Rome.

But while Peter traveled to western Europe in the late 1690s and gained the experience that enabled him to determine the appearance of his new capital, Moscow church architecture continued to discover new variants of the centralized design, such as the Church of St. Anne (1698–1704) at the Streshnev estate of Uzkoe, reminiscent of Ukrainian baroque churches with four projections attached to a central space (Figure 251). Yet the greatest of all late seventeenth-century churches, the Dormition on Pokrovka Street

itsyn churches are the most thorough expression of the centered tower design in late seventeenth-century architecture.[127] The unique quality of the Dubrovitsy church, however, lies in the texture of the structure. Not only are the walls of limestone (with the first use in Russia of smooth or chamfered rustication), but the structure and its flowing terrace serve as pedestals for an unprecedented proliferation of statuary in a culture that had from its beginnings rejected sculpture as idolatrous.[128] Peter I would import classical statues – nude or seminude – from Italy as a signal of his cultural revolution (see Chapter 8). The statuary at Dubrovitsy is still religious and fully clad, but it is assumed that the craftsmen – particularly for the interior stucco work – were Italian–Swiss.[129]

The church itself became a work of sculpture at Dubrovitsy. The plasticity of the curvilinear stone walls, accented by the broad steps leading to each projection, creates a sculpted effect reinforced by the carved details and statues that cover the church above the cornice. In the sheer luxuriance of its stonework, the church can be compared only to such pre-Mongol monuments as the Church of St. Dmitrii in Vladimir

Figure 247. Church of the Icon of the Sign at Dubrovitsy. Near Moscow. 1690–7; 1704. Southwest view. (MR 2–7)

190

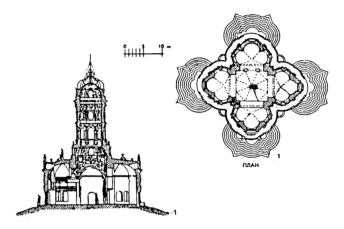

Figure 248. Church of the Icon of the Sign at Dubrovitsy. Near Moscow. Section and plan.

Figure 250. Church of the Icon of the Sign at Perovo. Section. Courtesy of Shchusev State Museum of Architecture.

Figure 249. Church of the Icon of the Sign at Perovo. Moscow. 1690–1704. South view. (M 30–1)

(1696–1699; Figure 252), was built not on an estate, but in the densely settled eastern part of the city with funds provided by the wealthy merchant I. M. Sverchkov, who built the church on a lot adjoining his house. The church, demolished as one of the most wanton acts of cultural destruction in the 1930s, united both the centralized and elongated church designs within the confines of an urban street.[130]

The genius of the Dormition Church (Figure 253) lies in its combination of the most productive elements of the Moscow baroque styles with new, western idioms. Among its innovative aspects was the use of the order system, with paired columns on consoles at the corners of the structure and smaller attached

Figure 251. Church of St. Anne at Uzkoe. Moscow. 1698–1704. Southeast view. (M 30)

Under Stroganov's aegis, N. Diletskii published the first theoretical guide to musical composition in Russia (the *Musical Grammar*), and the Stroganov church choirs were famed for the intricacy of their singing. This may have influenced the similarly intricate decor of the Stroganov cathedral at the Monastery of the Presentation of the Virgin in the Temple (1689–93).[131] Its 3-story cuboid form with three bays (Figure 254) resembles Bukhvostov's larger Dormition Cathedral in Riazan, but the window surrounds and cornice are effulgent, and the arcaded gallery has no equal in

Figure 252. Church of the Dormition on Pokrovka. Moscow. 1696–9; with eighteenth-century bell tower. Drawing by Giacomo Quarenghi. Courtesy of Shchusev State Museum of Architecture, Moscow.

columns framing the windows. The decorative limestone carving, fragments of which have been preserved, was the most refined in Moscow, both in detail and in delineating the facade. The rounded gables of the upper tier, beneath the central cupola, show a familiarity with the northern European baroque.

The changes in late seventeenth-century church architecture did not go unnoticed in the provinces, where the wealth of the Stroganovs created palatial churches of limestone and brick whose ornamental exuberance exceeded even that of contemporary Moscow churches. In the unlikely, far northern settlement of Solvychegodsk (from the word for salt and the Vychegda River), which was the center of their monopoly on salt production for central Russia, the Stroganovs built an entrepreneurial community with a number of large churches. At the end of the seventeenth century, the cultural leader of the family was Grigorii Stroganov, a personal associate of Peter I.

Figure 253. Church of the Dormition on Pokrovka. Plan and elevation.

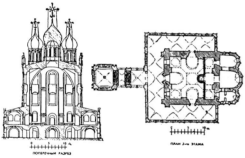

Figure 254. Cathedral of the Presentation of the Virgin in the Temple, Presentation Monastery, Solvychegodsk. 1689–93. South elevation, section, and plan.

Muscovite architecture (it also serves to buttress the structure, which has no interior piers).

The Stroganov style was defined by its decorative extravagance rather than by structural innovation, as illustrated by the Church of the Nativity in Nizhnii Novgorod, built in 1697–1703, but not dedicated until 1715 – a delay caused by the expense of decoration as well as waning Stroganov interest in the city after their loss of the salt monopoly to the state in 1705.[132] The church, located adjacent to the Stroganov compound on a steep incline above the Volga River, has a large bell tower located up the hill and at a right angle to the west entrance (Figure 255). Thus, despite its conservative design (a cuboid structure with no interior piers), the church can be appreciated from an unusual variety of perspectives. The exterior stone work with its cornucopia of plant motifs resembles Muscovite interior wood carving; yet the facades also

display an awareness of the Corinthian order, not only in the capitals of the attached columns, but also in the entablature that encircles the church and bell tower.

Although the Stroganovs were to become proponents of the latest in European architecture in Petersburg, the "Stroganov style" continued to remain vital in provincial architecture, exemplified in the Cathedral of Sts. Peter and Paul in Kazan (1722–6). Built with funds provided by the merchant Mikhliaev to commemorate the fiftieth birthday of Peter I, who had awarded him a monopoly in cloth manufacturing, the church is a design typical of four decades earlier, with octagons over the main cube and an extended refectory (Figure 256).[133] The Stroganov style appears in the separate bell tower, as well as in the painted and carved exterior of the church, which seems improbably to reflect Italian–Swiss origins.

Transitions in Moscow Architecture During the Petrine Era

The incursion of new western elements into the design of Orthodox churches is a defining characteristic of Russian architecture during the latter part of the seventeenth century. At the same time, however, large masonry structures for secular purposes were primarily "chambers," whose owners began to apply "baroque" decorative mannerisms to structures built as unpretentious living quarters and as storehouses for goods. The most monumental of the unadorned original buildings can be found in Pskov, with its well-developed merchant traditions. Although much modified, the largest known example of the combination of living and storage quarters is the Pogankin Chambers, built around the 1530s (Figure 257).[134] The walls originally supported a log superstructure (the living quarters); yet even in its reduced form, the building gives an excellent idea not only of the solid masonry techniques of Pskov, but also the unstable conditions that called forth such private citadels for the city's merchants.

In Moscow, the best surviving example of masonry architecture for mercantile purposes is the Old English Court, first built in the early sixteenth century for the merchant Ivan Bobrishchev (the lower walls, of limestone, remain). Ivan the Terrible subsequently made the building available to English merchants after the negotiation of an Anglo–Russian trade agreement in 1556.[135] The building was frequently modified; and after the expulsion of the English merchants in 1649, it passed through a succession of owners.

Figure 255. Church of the Nativity and bell tower. Nizhni Novgorod. 1697–1703; 1715. East elevation.

The Old English Court has now been restored to its appearance at the first half of the seventeenth century (Figure 258), when it contained offices and storage rooms for the company. Its form is largely functional, and yet the use of decorative recessed panels, or *shirinki*, and the central bay and steps exemplify the decorative asymmetry of the medieval Russian buildings. There were several such brick structures built in Kitaigorod during the seventeenth century, particularly after the issuance of an edict in 1681 forbidding wooden construction in the central parts of the city, including Belyi Gorod (White City). Yet Moscow's buildings, with the exception of churches, remained primarily of logs and resistant to attempts to regulate construction.[136] After another devasting fire in Kitaigorod and Belyi-gorod in 1699, the same decree was again promulgated in 1701.

By the end of the century, with the increasing security of Muscovy's borders and the expansion of Moscow's own fortifications beyond the "White City," the possibility of constructing residences that expressed the wealth of the owner and bore some resemblance to "architecture" produced such palaces as the Chambers of the boiar Volkov, built at the end of the seventeenth century (Figure 259).[137] Although still constricted in design and access, the proto-

baroque window surrounds on a red-brick background, and the picturesque asymmetry of the steep roofs reveal again the juncture of two cultural epochs (it should be noted that the chambers were restored in 1892 by Nikolai Sultanov, one of the leading proponents of the "Russian Revival" style, which greatly valued the decorative plasticity of late seventeenth-century architecture).

The juncture of two cultures is resolved differently in the Chambers of Averkii Kirillov, adjacent to the Church of St. Nicholas on Bersenevka. Initially built at the beginning of the sixteenth century, the house was reconstructed in 1657 (together with the church) with the usual asymmetrical cluster of roofs and levels (see Figure 188). The exterior was decorated with recessed panels that framed inset tiles (blue decorative motifs on a white ground). At the beginning of the eighteenth century, the son of Averkii Kirillov undertook to redesign the central part of the central part

Figure 256. Cathedral of Sts. Peter and Paul, with bell tower. Kazan. 1722–6. Southeast view. (KZ 1–28)

194

Figure 257. Pogankin Chambers. Pskov. C. 1530. (PS 1–35)

of the house by adding another floor and another wing on the south side of the house to balance the earlier design.[138] The center of the mansion was extended forward in a 2-story structure culminating in an arched pediment braced by volutes (Figure 260). The rigor and balance of this facade, edged with quoins, are entirely of the new Petrine era, as is the strict order of decorative details. Yet most of the interior remained in its original configuration.

The coming of the new secular order, incarnate in Petersburg, was preceded in Moscow with the construction of such buildings as the Sukharev Tower, erected in 1692–5 at the northern gates of the city as a watchtower and barracks for L. P. Sukharev's regiment of *streltsy*. Above its several portals and a balustraded terrace rose the regimental quarters and an octagonal tower. By the end of the century, the rebellious *streltsy* were disbanded and replaced by Pe-

ter's new guards regiments, and the building was converted in 1701 to use as a mathematics and navigation school, presumably with an observatory. At this point, it gained another floor, with a row of paired windows, as well as an extension of the tower under the supervision of Mikhail Choglokov (Figure 261).[139] Its carved limestone window surrounds and attached columns are similar to those of such churches as the Dormition on Pokrovka Street. The use of the order system, however, is still fragmented and decorative. A more compact design was adopted for the Main Pharmacy on Red Square (1699; not extant); yet it followed a similar method of stacking horizontal elements – unregulated by the order system – with an octagonal tower above.

During this transitional period, the traditional forms of the parish church were reinterpreted in monuments such as the Church of the Deposition of the Robe on Don Street (1701; see Plate 49), whose extended baroque domes on narrow drums resemble the late seventeenth-century Iaroslavl style, and whose scallop motif and window surrounds continue the festivity of the Novodevichii gate churches. The "ship" form (church, vestibule, bell tower) underwent certain modifications,[140] exemplified in churches such as Sts. Peter and Paul on Basman Street (1705–17), and Church of St. John the Warrior (1709–17; see Plate 50). Instead of the usual cuboid structure for the church proper, the builders (possibly Ivan Zarudnyi for the latter) created a cruciform structure with large semicircular gables over each arm of the cross. The next tier consisted of a broad octagon with a receding octagonal superstructure.

The "palatial" elements introduced in the Church

Figure 258. Old English Court. Moscow. Early sixteenth and seventeenth centuries. (M 132–32)

Figure 259. Chambers of the Boiar Volkov. Moscow. C. 1690s. (M 118–24)

Figure 260. Chambers of Averkii Kirillov. Moscow. 1657; beginning of the eighteenth century. (M 67–12)

Figure 261. Sukharev Tower. Moscow. Elevation and section by V. Skoldinov.

of the Dormition on Pokrovka Street are reinterpreted at St. John the Warrior, notably above the arms of the cross in the windows whose volutes and pediments remind of the mansion of Averkii Kirillov. The detailing on the exterior shows a rigor characteristic of the new baroque forms of Petrine architecture, and the balustrade above the main octagon at the Church of St. John creates a platform overlooking one of the most picturesque locations of Zamoskvoreche. Despite the ascending octagons, St. John the Warrior differs from the Naryshkin estate church, because the needs of a parish church required the greater space that led to the widening of the lower octagon, thus altering the silhouette.[141]

The ultimate statement of the vertical in Moscow church architecture was also the first to proclaim the new order of Petrine architecture. The Church of the Archangel Gabriel, built in 1701–7 on the city estate of Alexander Menshikov (hence, its common name, the "Menshikov Tower"), is rectangular in plan, with a semicircular gable at the center of each facade (Fig-

ures 262 and 263). The triumphal nature of the church is expressed in its stucco festoons and cherubim, as well as its use of a major Corinthian order for pilasters and fluted columns that frame the center bay and portal. The main entrance on the west front (see Plate 51) is massively framed by pylons, volutes, columns, and a stucco relief of the Ascension of Christ. (A similar style was used for the Gate Church of the Tikhvin Mother of God at Donskoi Monastery: see Plate 52.)

The initial form of the church, with a wooden, metal-sheathed spire of 81 meters, consisted of three octagonal tiers above the rectangular base, thus showing a continuity with the Naryshkin baroque. The main octagon originally supported statues of archangels (similar to the use of statuary at Dubrovitsy). The general design has been attributed to Ivan Zarudnyi, but it is known that the project also included for varying periods of time Italian architects and sculptors.[142] The brickwork for so demanding a structure was implemented by a team of masons from Iaroslavl and Kostroma, both centers of brick production and craftsmanship.[143]

Just as the Menshikov Tower embodies the superimposition of two cultural epochs, the palace that Peter I commissioned for one of his most valued foreign assistants François Lefort – on the banks of the Iauza

196

Figure 262. Church of the Archangel Gabriel (Menshikov Tower). Moscow. 1701–7. Architect: Ivan Zarudnyi(?). South facade. (M 118–1)

River in the eastern, "German" district of the city – reflects the rapidity with which old aesthetic principles were replaced. The Lefortovo Palace was first built in 1697–9 by Dmitrii Aksamitov in a symmetrical form with early baroque window surrounds, but it nonetheless retained the steeply pitched Muscovite roofs over each of the building's five parts (Figure 264). After Lefort's death in 1699, the palace was given to Menshikov, who had it greatly enlarged and rebuilt in 1707–8 by Giovanni Mario Fontana. Although hardly luxurious, the palace was capacious: a large quadrangle incorporating the original structure into the east facade and extending with a single enfilade of rooms on the other three sides (Figure 265).[144] Its horizontal profile and the severe, correct detailing of its main gateway, with Corinthian pilasters, have nothing of Moscow's architectural traditions in them.

Although the effective reign of Peter dates from

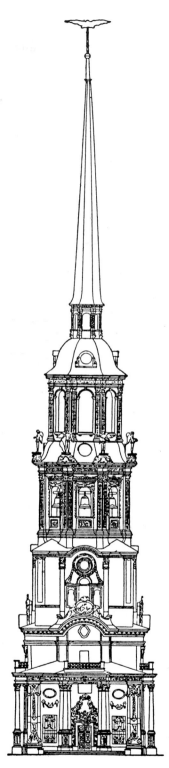

Figure 263. Church of the Archangel Gabriel (Menshikov Tower). Moscow. Plan and reconstructed elevation by E. Kunitskaia.

197

Figure 264. Palace at Lefortovo. Moscow. 1697–9. Architect: Dmitrii Aksamitov. Reconstructed elevation by R. Podolskii.

1689, Petrine architecture in any meaningful sense begins with the founding of Petersburg in 1703. At that point, the western architectural models introduced as emblems of Peter's new secular order were unambiguously stated, and their impact would be felt throughout the empire. With this radical shift, Moscow suffered accordingly. Nowhere is this more evident than in the Kremlin, whose one Petrine building

is, tellingly, the Arsenal, intended both as an arms storehouse and a military museum. Construction, begun in 1702 under the supervision of Mihail Choglokov and Mikhail Remezov, was interrupted in 1707 by the war and not resumed until 1711. Around 1713, the gilded tile roof collapsed and with it the upper vaulting of the structure, which lay in disrepair until its completion in the mid-1730s, when it received the baroque south entrance.[145] The building seems to have suffered from every subsequent cataclysm in Moscow's turbulent history. Yet its walls, with their embrasure windows, remind of both the austerity and the heroism of the Petrine era. They also suggest that in comparison with the last flourishing of Muscovite ornamentalism, the monuments of Petrine Moscow represent a lowering of expectations, an impoverishment of the spirit of the city. Such is to be expected in view of the concentration of resources for the prosecution of Peter's wars and, above all, for the construction of Petersburg.

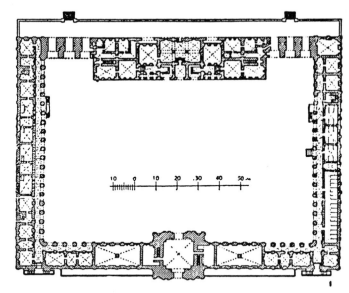

Figure 265. Palace at Lefortovo. Moscow. 1707–8. Architect: Giovanni Mario Fontana. Elevation and plan by R. Podolskii.

PART III

The Turn to Western Forms

CHAPTER 8

The Foundations of the Baroque in Saint Petersburg

> An aerial ship and touch-me-not mast, serving as a straightedge for the successors
> of Peter, its lesson is that beauty is no demigod's caprice: it is the simple carpenter's
> ferocious rule-of-eye.
>
> – Osip Mandelstam, "The Admiralty"

Historians have long debated the significance of Peter I's accomplishments. Although certain of his projects and reforms were ephemeral, it is beyond question that Peter the Great oversaw the transformation of the Muscovite state into a major European power. This transformation, occurring in the face of considerable opposition from many levels of society, was realized through massive forced-labor enterprises, as well as a series of wars demanding as much as 90 percent of the state budget and occupying 28 of the 31 years of Peter's effective reign (from 1694, following his mother's regency, to his death, in 1725). For this sacrifice exacted from an unwilling populace, Peter established an empire with acquisitions ranging from the Baltic to the Caspian seas; he introduced fundamental social, economic, religious, administrative, and educational reforms; he created a modern army and navy, which roundly defeated Sweden, one of Russia's oldest and most troublesome enemies; and he laid the foundations of Europe's newest capital.[1]

Peter was not, however, present at the founding of Saint Petersburg (May 16, O.S., 1703), nor did he at first intend to "hack a window through to Europe." In the third year of a conflict with Sweden that would last until 1721 and finally establish Russia's power in northern Europe, his concerns at this time were intensely practical: to create a fortified point on the Neva estuary, the key to Russia's position on the Gulf of Finland. The Great Northern War had begun inauspiciously for Peter, but the 18-year-old Swedish king, Charles XII, lulled by his early success over the Russians at the battle of Narva, turned his attention to Peter's ally, Augustus II of Poland. During this res-

pite, Peter rebuilt the Russian army and went on the supervise, with the assistance of his aide Alexander Menshikov, the methodical conquest of Swedish garrisons along the northeastern Baltic.

Peter was particularly interested in the area around Lake Ladoga and the Neva River (Figure 266) – contested by the Swedes and Russians since the thirteenth century. By May 1703, after a series of sharply contested local victories, Russian forces could sail unhindered from Ladoga down the Neva to the Gulf of Finland; but to control access to this tenuous acquisition, Peter needed a fortress at the mouth of the Neva. A reconnaissance of the estuary indicated a small, well-protected island (Hare's Island, as it was called by the local Finns) as the site of his fortification. Some 20,000 men were conscripted to surround the island with earthen walls and bastions under conditions that defy description.[2] The tsar himself lived in a small log house whose walls were painted and lined to resemble brick (Figure 267). The number of fatalities mounted rapidly, yet work proceeded at a brisk pace, and by November, the fortress of Sankt Piter Burkh – "Saint Peter's Burg" – was essentially completed. It was named in honor of the Russian Orthodox feast day of Saints Peter and Paul (June 29) but rendered in Dutch, the language of a culture much admired by Peter. However limited the tsar's immediate intentions, the name of the city expressed a far-reaching, ambitious sense of his own greater mission to redirect Russia toward the ways of the west.

After the completion of the fortress, the first structures were placed haphazardly on the surrounding islands, but as early as 1704, Peter initiated plans for

201

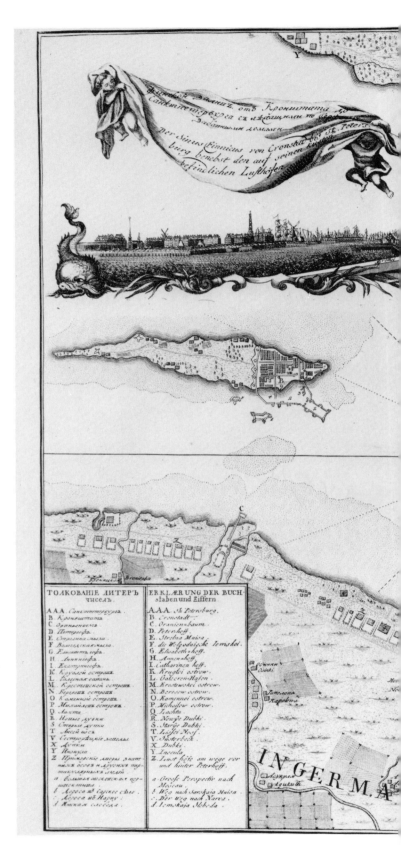

Figure 266. The Neva estuary. Engraving by Grimel. 1737. The fortress island of Kronstadt (left) protected access to the city of St. Petersburg at the mouth of the Neva River (right). On the southern shore of the Gulf of Finland, Peter and Alexander Menshikov built their country palaces – at Strelna (E), Peterhof (D), and Oranienbaum (C). By permission of the Houghton Library, Harvard University.

ЗНАТНѢЙШІЯ МѢСТА
ВЪ КРОНШТАТѢ.

1. Кронштатъ.
2. Военная Гавань.
3. Пороховые Анбары.
4. Купецкая Гавань.
5. Цитаделя.
6. Императорской Дворецъ.
7. Карабельной артиллерiской домъ.
8. Шлюпочной анбаръ.
9. Казармы для морскихъ солдатъ.
10. Морской спиталь.
11. Казармы для сухопутной солдатъ.
12. Карабельной каналъ.
13. Карабельные доки.

VORNEHMSTE PLÆTZE
in und um Cronstadt.

1. Cronoschlofs.
2. Kriegs-hafen.
3. Pulver Magazin.
4. Kauffardey hafen.
5. Die Citadelle.
6. Der Kayserliche Pallast.
7. Das Schiffs Artillerie haufs.
8. Schaluppen Anbar.
9. Caserne für das Schiffsvolck.
10. See Hospital.
11. Caserne für die Feld-Regimenter.
12. Schiffs Canal.
13. Schiffs Docken.

C A R E L I E N

КАРЕЛЬСКАЯ СТОРОНА

ИНГЕРМАНЛАНДІЯ

203

Figure 267. House of Peter the Great. Petersburg. 1703. (P 55–31)

a shipbuilding and commercial center that would provide much of the activity for a functioning city – and a new capital.[3] That year, the government instituted an annual conscription of 40,000 peasants for the construction of the city in shifts of 2 or 3 months (from April to October); and although only 30,000 to 34,000 peasants were actually summoned, and far fewer appeared owing to administrative inefficiencies, significant progress was made in draining marshes, driving piles, and building such basic institutions as the Admiralty and its shipyards.[4] In addition to peasant conscripts, criminals, and Swedish prisoners of war employed in heavy construction, Peter brought craftsmen, tradesmen, and members of the nobility to populate his new city. The lower classes settled in neighborhoods according to their crafts or trade, and the noblemen were expected to build houses of a certain type and size, determined by their wealth (as measured by the number of serfs they possessed).

Working conditions remained abysmal, even by Russian standards. Conscripted peasants, who rightly viewed work in Petersburg as little better than hard labor in Siberia, frequently deserted their convoys in large numbers; for not only were they subjected to the rigors of building a city on a swamp, they were also taken from their land at the height of the planting and harvesting seasons, to be sent – in some cases hundreds of miles – to an incomprehensible undertaking. Government measures for dealing with evasion or flight were predictably harsh. Workers were often marched to Petersburg in chains, families of escapees were liable to imprisonment, and many of those captured in flight were knouted or executed. Gradually, a measure of pragmatism was introduced into these draconian recruitment policies, and by the

end of the decades, hired labor had largely replaced the conscription system, which was not only wasteful of manpower, but also inefficient.

Designing Petersburg

In the first 10 years of its existence, there was little to distinguish Petersburg from a frontier outpost. Although its Department of Construction had been established in 1706, the town's buildings, almost entirely wooden or clay-walled (Figure 268), were distributed with little concern for geometric precision. Peter was still preoccupied with his Swedish war, and even though the final assault on Petersburg was repulsed in 1708, the city was not secure until the decisive Russian victory over Charles at Poltava, in July 1709. In 1710, the capture of Vyborg, on the coast of the Gulf of Finland to the north of Petersburg, provided additional insurance, and in the same year, the tsar – now "Imperator" – established a monastery in honor of Alexander Nevskii, who had defeated the Swedes in this area almost five centuries earlier. With the transfer of the saint's relics from Vladimir, Peter had given his city the status of a major religious center, however secular his intentions. In 1712, the imperial court was moved from Moscow to Petersburg, even though many important administrative departments continued to function in the former capital.

Construction of the city at this point accelerated under the supervision of Peter, or of his delegate Alexander Menshikov. No detail was too small for the ruler's attention, from the design of model houses to the decree ordering citizens to boil the moss used in insulating wooden structures (supposedly to prevent

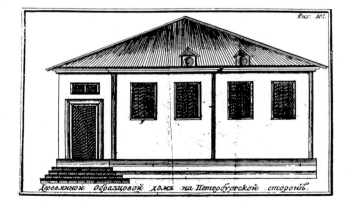

Figure 268. Early eighteenth-century house. Petersburg. Although the Russian caption states "wooden model house," the structure is probably the *mazanka*, or clay, type. Engraving from the first history of the architecture of Petersburg, written by Andrei Bogdanov in 1750. Widener Library, Harvard University.

cockroach infestation). In 1706, he established an Office (*Kantselariia*) of City Affairs, endowed with police powers to regulate construction according to rigidly defined standards.[5] Peter's ideal was the well-ordered, solidly built city of the type he had seen in Holland – or England – during his tour of Europe (1697–9), with steeples and spires for visual emphasis, a rationally planned network of streets, and ensembles of buildings surfaced in durable and monumental stone.

So eager was Peter to achieve urban monumentality that he ordered the early wooden buildings, including the first version of the Cathedral of Saints Peter and Paul begun in 1703 in the fortress (Figure 269), painted to resemble stone and brick. In 1714, he forbade masonry construction throughout the rest of his empire, in order to ensure a supply of qualified workers and materials for Petersburg. Stone for foundations and streets was obtained by a "stone duty," levied from 1714 to 1776: three stones of not less than 5 pounds each were exacted from wagons entering the city, and ten to thirty stones were paid by ships entering the port. Indeed, every form of building material – glass, lead, construction stone, bricks, roofing tile, cement, lumber (everything but dirt) – was imported or in some cases produced by workshops and mills hastily erected on site.[6] Despite this effort, spurred by a series of ukases from Peter and his assistant Menshikov, resources proved inadequate, and after 1714, only certain areas of the city were reserved for masonry construction. For lack of materials, even this decree was honored in the breach, and by 1723, masonry construction was actually forbidden throughout most of the city, with the exception of the Neva embankments and a few streets on Vasilevskii Island, the city's putative center and the site of one of Peter's grand schemes.[7]

Peter possessed an indefatigable and pragmatic interest in the arts, as well as a talent for visualizing project designs – be it for a ship or for a fortress. It is not improbable, therefore, that the essential elements in the early design of Petersburg were his own, liberally cribbed from his travels and observations in western Europe.[8] Nonetheless, to implement his vision, he relied on the skill of professional architects who worked closely with the Office of City Affairs. In this respect, the central figure was the Italian–Swiss architect Domenico Trezzini who designed model houses to be reproduced in various parts of the city according to financial means and social class of the residents.[9] By 1716, Trezzini had collated the development plans of specific districts into a general view of the city in accordance with Peter's views. These

Figure 269. Fortress of Sankt Piter Burkh. 1703. Engraving from the history of Petersburg by Bogdanov, who describes this earliest version of the fortress cathedral of Sts. Peter and Paul as "wooden, in the shape of a cross, with three spires from which pennants were flown on Sundays and holidays." Widener Library, Harvard University.

views were by no means immutable, and the plan of the city underwent a number of modifications during the tsar's lifetime, as various cherished projects yielded to topographical and social reality.

Among them, the plan for Vasilevskii Island, the dominant geographical feature of the delta, experienced the greatest modifications.[10] Peter's ideal for the island as a new Amsterdam, covered with a network of canals and a precise grid of streets with mansions, administrative buildings, and large public parks (Figure 270), was hindered by its inaccessibility during the formation and melting of river ice in the fall and spring. Although Peter's wealthier subjects

Figure 270. Plan of St. Petersburg, c. 1720, by Jean Covens. The jumble of buildings on the Admiralty and Petersburg sides of the Neva (south and north, respectively) stands in contrast to the ordered grid of streets and canals initially designed for Vasilevskii Island. Widener Library, Harvard University.

PLAN
de la Ville & du Fort de
St. PETERSBOURG,
Nouvelle Capitale & Residence des
EMPEREURS DE RUSSIE:
Bâtie par l'Empereur PIERRE I. sur quelques Isles du
GOLFE de FINLANDE, a l'embouchure de la
Riviere de NEVA.

A AMSTERDAM.
Chez JEAN COVENS et CORNEILLE MORTIER
Geographes.

ISLE BERESOW

ISLE St. PETERSBURG

Jardin des Simples, &
Cimetiere des
Allexandi.

Ourvage à Couronne.

FORT DE St. PETERSBURG

Magazin
Hôpital.

Grande
Brasserie.

NEVA RIVIERE

PARTIE DE FINLANDE

L'ISLE DE L'AMIRAUTÉ

Marais

Marais

Marais

Marais

FORT
de la
NEVA
Demoli.

INGRIE.

207

were ordered to build houses on this island, the location proved so impractical that many left their houses unfinished and continued to live on the left bank of the Neva, in defiance of decrees between 1719 and 1725. Contemporary accounts of Vasilevskii Island convey the impression of an abandoned project, imposing from a distance, but on close inspection, rotting and uninhabited.[11]

A still more radical vision for Vasilevskii Island was submitted by Jean-Baptiste Alexandre Le Blond, a student of the great landscape architect André LeNôtre. In June 1716, Peter interviewed Le Blond in France and subsequently hired him as "General-architect" of the new city, along with an entourage of skilled craftsmen.[12] Le Blond offered a highly critical assessment of the new, often unfinished buildings in a city that seemed to have no comprehensive plan, but his proposal for the redesign of Petersburg would have involved a massive expenditure in money and labor to create a fortified wall in the shape of an ellipse, encompassing four islands (including Vasilevskii) in the Neva delta and containing a system of parks and squares arranged in rectangular and diagonal configurations (Figure 271). No serious attempt was made to implement the plan, which was quietly rejected by Peter in a note to Menshikov.[13]

Although Peter's hopes for a thriving city on Vasilevskii Island were not realized until decades after his death, the island's streets – or "lines," whose horizontal vistas were laid out with a straightedge – conform to the pattern reproduced in Trezzini's early plans. And on the left (south) bank of the Neva, the magnificent arrangement of three major "prospects" radiating from the Admiralty that would define the later development of Petersburg probably originated with Peter's concept of a grand avenue leading into the city.[14] But apart from these specific features, reaffirmed with the adoption of a master plan in the late 1730s, Peter's greatest legacy to the form of his city consisted in the very notion of a comprehensive urban design, within which Petersburg's architects created the palaces, churches, parks, and squares that compose the most remarkable eighteenth-century ensemble in Europe.

Very little remains from the first decades of construction in Petersburg, but surviving sketches and plans provide a sense of the early architectural forms, shaped by a variety of European styles. As in the time of Ivan III and Vasilii III, Russia had capable and skilled builders, but their isolation from developments in European construction technology and engineering required the importation of technical specialists.

208

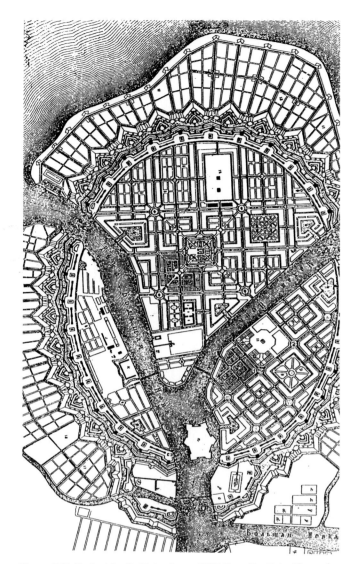

Figure 271. Project for St. Petersburg. 1717. Jean-Baptiste Alexandre Le Blond. From I. N. Bozherianov, *Nevskii Prospekt*. Widener Library, Harvard University.

The early Petrine architects were of widely differing origins – Italian, Dutch, German, French – whose work for the courts of Europe included Denmark and Sweden. The guiding presence remained Peter himself, who was fascinated by architectural details and not uncommonly changed his mind about the proposed appearance of a building as soon as its foundation was laid. In Igor Grabar's description: "Quite often one architect would begin a certain building, another would continue it, a third finish it, and at the very end a fourth would again redo it."[15] However generously Peter paid certain of his foreign architects (Le Blond, for example, received the princely sum of 5,000 rubles per annum), both the physical and administrative conditions under which they worked strained their endurance to the limit, and the rate of attrition from death or early departure was extremely high. (In sad example, Le Blond died of smallpox in March 1719.) Nonetheless, the architects Peter hired from abroad not only created a coherent baroque style, but also trained a new generation of Russian architects.[16]

Dominico Trezzini and the Rebuilding of the Peter–Paul Fortress.

It would appear that even before the victory at Poltava, Peter had intended the fortress at the center of his city to serve not only – or primarily – a military function, but also as a tangible symbol of his union of state and religious institutions within a new political order in Russia. In the heroic attempt to implement this reformation in the very architecture of Petersburg and its fortress, he was capably served by Dominico Trezzini, one of the most talented and long-lived of the Petrine architects. Born in 1670 in the village of Astano, near Lugano (the region that had produced Carlo Maderna and Francesco Borromini), Trezzini received his education locally, and by 1699 was employed in Denmark as a fortification engineer. In this capacity, he was hired by the Russian envoy to the court of Frederick IV in the spring of 1703 and arrived in Moscow, via Arkhangelsk, with a group of craftsmen in August 1703.[17] By February 1704, Trezzini had been summoned to Petersburg to supervise the construction of the Kronshlot bastion guarding the western approach to the city from the Gulf of Finland. Although unorthodox from the perspective of military engineering, this octagonal log and earth structure that rose from the shallows off the southern tip of Kotlin Island (later the site of the Kronshtadt naval base) played a major role in the repulse of sizeable Swedish attacks in the summers of 1704 and 1705.[18]

Having demonstrated his skills as an engineer, Trezzini was entrusted with the rebuilding of the fortifications of Narva, heavily damaged during the successful Russian storm of the city in August 1704. Trezzini remained in Narva almost a year, but with the death of the supervisory engineer of the Peter–Paul Fortress (the Saxon Johann Kirchenstein), Peter elevated Trezzini to the position as architect of the country's main citadel. Although the earthen fortress was complete, Peter already intended to replace it with masonry walls. In May 1706, the tsar assisted with the laying of the foundation stone of the Menshikov Bastion, and for the rest of Trezzini's life (until

1734), the design and building of the Peter–Paul fortress, with its six bastions, would remain one of his primary duties.[19] In contrast to the Muscovite importation of dated Italian fortification methods two centuries earlier, Peter was thoroughly acquainted with the latest advances in defensive works, and could expertly assess the needs of the fortress, whose design conformed to the standards of western military engineering.[20]

Yet the Peter–Paul Fortress was never tested in battle, and its design was also calculated for symbolic, political effect (Figure 272). The major sections of the fortress – and most visibly, the six bastions – were named either for a leading participant in Peter's reign, such as Menshikov, or for a member of the imperial house, not excluding Peter himself.[21] Nowhere are the secular nature of the Petrine era and its rejection of the symbolism of the Muscovite past more clearly stated. The Cathedral of the Intercession on Red Square had also symbolized a new vision of Russia's destiny and its successful claim to territory – in this case to the Volga and beyond; yet the dynastic and military allusions in the naming of the various parts of that structure were couched within the terms of the Orthodox Church calendar and its feast days (see Chapter 6). Despite the growing power of the secular state, the sixteenth-century tsars and their Romanov successors would not openly challenge the premise that their power rested on divine protection and intercession.

For Peter I, however, secularism was the essence of social order, and in his great fortress, even the religious allusions (Peter was well acquainted with the Bible) are subsumed within an aesthetic and symbolic context that is turned toward the west – and away from Muscovite Orthodoxy. There can be no clearer example than the triumphal Peter Gates (Figure 273), constructed in wood by Trezzini in 1708 and subsequently rebuilt in masonry in 1715–17 with classical detailing in the manner of the seventeenth-century baroque (cf. Christopher Wren's 1672 design for the entrance to Temple Bar, London). The edifice was originally surmounted by a wooden statue of the Saint Peter, below which was a bas relief, carved in wood by Conradt Ossner, entitled "The Casting down of Simon Magus by the Apostle Peter."[22] There can be no doubt that the references to Saint Peter were linked allegorically to the tsar (and in the case of the bas relief, to his victory over Charles XII), as was the dedication of the cathedral within the fortress. Whereas Ivan the Terrible's Cathedral of the Intercession symbolized at its main entrance the Entry of Christ into Jerusalem, the statue of Peter over the

Figure 272. Peter–Paul Fortress, with Cathedral of Sts. Peter and Paul. Petersburg. Southeast view. (P 33–4)

entrance to the Petersburg fortress held the keys to heaven and hell itself. It is precisely the attainment and possession of power that underlies all the major allegorical systems of the Petrine period – be they Christian or classical (as in the statues of Bellona, goddess of war, and Minerva in niches on either side of the Peter Gates). The key as a symbol of power and of enclosure (imprisonment) is additionally significant because Aleksei Petrovich, heir to the throne and an opponent of his father's policies, died here in June 1718 after an interrogation in which his father presumably participated.

Within the fortress, Trezzini's design of the Cathedral of Saints Peter and Paul represents a radical departure from traditional Russian church architecture, based on the cross-domed or centralized plan. To replace the original wooden church, Trezzini created a greatly elongated basilical structure, whose modest baroque dome, on the eastern end, is subordinate to the tower and spire placed over the west entrance

(see Plate 53; Figure 274). Indeed, the tower was the main focus of Peter's interest, and had priority over the rest of the structure, which was not completed until 1732. Rapid construction of the tower not only created a platform from which Peter could, in his obsessive way, survey construction progress over the entire area, but it also provided a frame for the carillon, with chiming clock, that he had commissioned in Holland.[23] By 1717, Trezzini had completed the basic structure of the tower (the spire was assembled in 1720), and in 1720, the carillon was installed. Once again, the tsar had bestowed upon his city an artifact that both paralleled and challenged the landmarks of Moscow – in this case, the clock and chimes over the Savior Gate at the entrance to the Kremlin. By 1723, the spire, gilded and surmounted with an angel holding a cross, reached a height of 112 meters, which exceeded the bell tower of Ivan the Great by 32 meters.

The spire, like the body of the cathedral, resembles

Figure 273. Peter Gates, Peter–Paul Fortress. Petersburg. 1715–17. Architect: Domenico Trezzini. (P 57–22)

of Russian artists.[24] The centerpiece of the interior, however, is the gilded iconostasis beneath the dome in the eastern end of the church (see Plate 54). Its design, by Ivan Zarudnyi, bears a closer resemblance to the triumphal arches erected to celebrate events of state – particularly Peter's victories – than to the elaborate icon screens of the late seventeenth century. Yet the craftsmanship of the latter was readily adaptable to the demands of the baroque style, of which this iconostasis is a most accomplished example. The frame, with allegorical figures, trumpeting angels, cherubim, twisted columns, and broken pediments surrounding a central icon of, appropriately, the Ascension, was carved between 1722 and 1726 by master craftsmen in Moscow, and assembled in the cathedral in 1727. It is now assumed that the icons were painted on site by the Moscow painter Andrei Merkurevich Pospelov and his assistants; but whatever the precise

the seventeenth-century baroque architecture of northern Europe, with its combination of large volutes bracing the lower tiers of the tower and elements of classical entablature in the segmentation of the ascending levels (Figure 275). The large windows that mark the length of the church are in articulation and design unprecedented in Russian church architecture, and provide ample illumination for the banners and other imperial regalia that mark the interior. It is not clear whether this great hall was originally intended to serve as a burial place for the Romanov tsars, but with the death of Peter the Great (whose funeral was held in a temporary wooden church erected within the walls of the uncompleted cathedral), this function was assumed from the Archangel Cathedral in the Kremlin. Indeed, the Peter–Paul tower and steeple can be seen as a counterpart to the bell tower of Ivan the Great – and to the Church of the Ascension at Kolomenskoe – as an expression of the majesty of the sovereign.

The interior of the cathedral, divided by faux marbre piers with gilded Corinthian capitals into three aisles, is decorated with pastel trompe l'oeil architectural detail that seems to extend the space of the vaulting. The upper parts of the walls display panneaux on religious themes, which, although done in the western manner, were painted by a collective

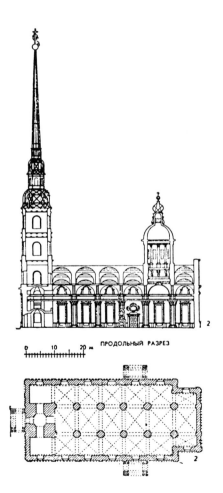

Figure 274. Cathedral of Sts. Peter and Paul. Petersburg. 1712–32. Architect: Domenico Trezzini. Plan and longitudinal section by A. Shelkovnikov (1826).

Figure 275. Cathedral of Sts. Peter and Paul. Petersburg. Northwest view. (P 57–35)

details of its assembly, the style of the painting is entirely western.[25]

Trezzini, Zarudnyi, and the other craftsmen and artists performed brilliantly in providing Peter with an unequivocal statement of his determination to turn the course of Russian identity. The many secular monuments of early baroque Petersburg display that intention clearly enough, but the rejection of Muscovite, Orthodox architectural culture was all the more emphatic when occurring in the first cathedral of the new capital. Indeed, the cathedral lacked one of the fundamental elements of the traditional church structure – the apse (the altar was placed within three rectangular segments at the east end). The east wall, directly

visible on entering the fortress, is instead another variation on the triumphal arch.

Peter was by no means heterodox, and the fact that the Cathedral of Saints Peter and Paul resembled a large western church was less significant than its lack of resemblance to traditional Orthodox architecture. The culture of the new style in church architecture and painting reflected the talents of a new, articulate generation of churchmen, such as Feofan Prokopovich, who firmly supported the ideology of Petrine society and adopted ornamental baroque devices in their own writings.[26] Some of the more elaborate ornamentation of the cathedral was lost after a lightning strike and fire in 1756, although a prompt response by the garrison preserved the iconostasis and much of the interior work. The rather dour rebuilding of the roof, cupola, and spire by Bartolomeo Rastrelli and Savva Chevakinskii, known for their lavish baroque churches (see Chapter 9), preserved the essential features of the original structure.[27]

Early Monuments of Church and State

Concurrently with the construction of the Cathedral of Saints Peter and Paul, Trezzini was at work on the design of the monastery dedicated to the Holy Trinity and to Saint Alexander Nevskii, established by Peter in 1710 and redesignated the Alexander Nevskii Lavra in 1797. Although major work on the monastery continued until the end of the eighteenth century – with substantial modifications to the architect's conception – Trezzini's plan of 1715 established patterns that would characterize much of Petersburg's religious architecture as a reaction against the traditional Russian forms. In contrast to earlier Russian monasteries created by the informal accrual of structures over a period of centuries, Trezzini envisioned a highly organized, symmetrical complex, whose school, churches, and administrative buildings were joined in a single structure, dominated by the monastery cathedral (Figure 276).

The plan of the Alexander Nevskii Monastery exemplified Peter's notion of a comprehensive architectural design, and the style was resolutely secular: the stuccoed walls, painted in red and white and delineated by pilasters and panels, closely resemble early Petrine palaces and administrative buildings such as the Twelve Colleges (see what follows). Indeed, Zubov's 1716 engraving of the original Trezzini design for the monastery's Trinity Cathedral shows not only a duplication of the tower and spire of Saints Peter and Paul, but an elaborate baroque entrance through

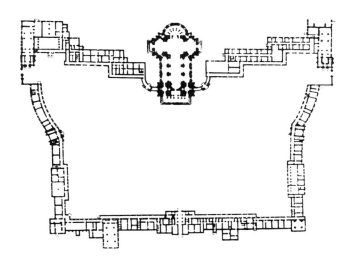

Figure 276. Alexander Nevskii Monastery. Petersburg. 1715. Plan according to design by Domenico Trezzini, with Ivan Starov's Trinity Cathedral (1776–90).

the east – traditionally apsidal – facade.[28] Trezzini's many competing duties removed him from active supervision of the monastery's construction, and his designs were implemented by Theodor Schwertfeger, who completed the dual Church of the Annunciation and of Saint Alexander Nevskii (see Plate 55), consecrated in August 1724.[29] In addition, Schwertfeger redesigned the Trinity Cathedral in his own effusive Bavarian baroque style and energetically began its construction. The vicissitudes of court politics interfered with the project in the 1730s, however, and the unfinished building was eventually dismantled in 1755 because of structural flaws (a wooden model remains).[30] Its splendid replacement will be discussed in Chapter 10.

The last of Trezzini's extant major projects, the Building of the Twelve Colleges (Figure 277 and 278), contained the offices of the ten state ministries ("colleges"), as well as the Senate (the highest judicial body) and the Holy Synod – all administrative units devised by Peter, with the advice of Gottfried Leibniz,

Figure 277. The Building of the Twelve Colleges, Vasilevskii Island. Petersburg. 1722–41. Architects: Domenico Trezzini, Theodor Schwertfeger, and Giuseppe Trezzini. Engraving by E. Vnukov from a drawing by Mikhail Makhaev. Courtesy of the Library of Congress.

Figure 278. Building of the Twelve Colleges, Vasilevskii Island. Petersburg. (p 20–7a)

in an attempt to base the Russian bureaucracy on modern principles of organization.[31] Emblematic of the rationalist ideology of Peter's reforms, the building, 383 meters in length, also exemplifies the era's experimentation with construction methods – organized in theory, but chaotic in practice. According to Peter's instructions of 1723, the various departments were to be joined in a single row, and each was to have its own uniform roof, with interior rooms arranged to the needs of each department (Figure 279). The concept of individual buildings linked by one plan was known to Trezzini from his stay in Copenhagen, whose Exchange, built in 1619–24 by Lourens and Hans van Steenwinkel, displays a similar arrangement.[32] As the structure cleared the foundation, however, Peter reopened the competition for the facade design; and while Trezzini's general concept was retained, much of the detail of the upper two floors is now attributed to Schwertfeger. Intended to give both flexibility and uniform construction tasks to each of the departments, the system created confusion in the delivery of materials and the coordination of schedules, thus greatly delaying work. After Trez-

zini's death in 1734, the project continued until its completion in 1741 under the direction of his son-in-law Giuseppe Trezzini, who constructed a gallery along the length of the "back," or west, facade.[33]

The site sketch for the Building of the Twelve Colleges also included a plan for a large church as dominant feature of the Point (*strelka*) of Vasilevskii Island. A number of competition entries was submitted by Petersburg architects, but the tsar also solicited a design from the Swedish architect Nicodemus Tessin the younger, whose proposal was virtually a copy of the cathedral that he had designed for Stockholm in 1708 in a florid Italian baroque style.[34] Although Vasilevskii Island cathedral was not built, the Tessin design (dated 1724) offers further evidence of the importance of Sweden and Denmark – in addition to Holland – as intermediaries in translating the baroque style into a northern European architectural idiom.[35] Both the elder and the younger Tessin had studied in France and Italy (as well as England and Holland), and in creating a high baroque style in Sweden, they pursued a course that would be repeated by eighteenth-century architects in Russia: adapting the rhet-

214

Figure 279. Building of the Twelve Colleges, Vasilevskii Island. Petersburg. Plan by A. Shelkovnikov.

oric of baroque ornamentation to structures, both public and private, situated in a harsher and damper climate than that of southern or western Europe. By way of comparison, Tessin's Baroque Royal Palace in Stockholm, begun in 1697 but not completed until the 1750s due to the economic havoc wrought by Charles XII's military adventures, was much influenced by the work of Claude Perrault and Gianlorenzo Bernini. Similar stylistic elements appear during the late 1710s in the palaces built by Giovanni Fontana and Gottfried Schädel for Alexander Menshikov (see what follows).

Throughout the early eighteenth century, the Russian baroque is distinguished by the striking effect created by the polychromatic, white-trimmed, stuccoed brick facades, enhanced by the delicate ambience of the northern light. This quality is demonstrated in another major Petrine project for Vasilevskii Island: the Kunstkammer, or Chamber of Curiosities, the first of Petersburg's academic institutions devoted to the diffusion of scientific knowledge. Peter was well aware of the role of modern scientific thought in the development of a secular state, and in February 1718, he issued a decree on the collection of various "rarities" to be displayed at the Kunstkammer for the edification of the populace and the promotion of scientific research. By the end of the year, the rapidly expanding collection was transferred from the Summer Palace to the former residence of Admiral Alexander Kikin (see Figure 286), which although enlarged on either wing, proved inadequate for both the public collection and the research quarters, and was also located at a considerable distance from the center of the city.[36]

The new Kunstkammer building was to be situated on the Neva embankment within the tip of Vasilevskii Island (near the future Twelve Colleges). Plans for the structure were submitted by the Swiss–German architect Georg-Johann Mattarnovy, who had arrived in Petersburg in 1714 on the recommendation of the renowned Prussian architect Andreas Schlüter, himself hired by Peter the previous year as chief architect of the city. (Neither withstood the rigors of Petersburg: Schlüter died several months after his arrival, and Mattarnovy died in 1719 – the year of Le Blond's death.) Although begun in 1718, the Kunstkammer

was not completed until 1734, by which time a succession of architects, including Gaetano Chiaveri and Mikhail Zemtsov, had modified Mattarnovy's original design, with its florid baroque pediments and statuary flanking the central tower (Figure 280).[37] Nonetheless, the basic outlines remain (Figure 281) and are marked by the extensive use of white trim on a pastel stuccoed facade – a device common to the work of Trezzini and Schwertfeger.

The symbolic significance of the Kunstkammer as a center of learning is expressed in the central tower, culminating in a polygonal lantern and globe representing Peter's interest in science and its applications for a new age of exploration in Russia. The tower design has been compared with that of Schlüter's Münzthurm in Berlin, and it is not improbable that Mattarnovy, Schlüter's protègè, would have had access to the master's sketches in Petersburg.[38] On the interior (Figure 282), the tower housed a circular anatomy theater and an observatory – the first in Russia. On either side of the tower extended the library and museum collection, which were in turn flanked by wings containing office space. The viability of this logical design is attested by the continuing function of the building as an ethnographic institute, with library and much of the original collection acquired by Peter. Within the context of Vasilevskii Island, the Kunstkammer tower not only provides a vertical dominant within the succession of classical facades along the island's embankment (see Plate 56), but also mediates between the spires of the Peter–Paul Cathedral and, on the south bank of the Neva, the Admiralty.

Palace Architecture

In addition to large projects for the military, the Church, and the civil administration, Peter initiated a transformation in the nature and style of palatial architecture, whose only precedent in Muscovy had been the unprepossessing *palaty*. Here again, Dominico Trezzini was centrally involved. In 1710, he began two residences for the tsar himself on the left bank of the Neva: a winter and a summer palace, both of stuccoed brick. The Winter Palace (not extant) was

215

Фасадъ Императорской Библиотеки и кунсткамеры на постокъ.

Aufriß von der Kayserlichen Bibliothec, und Kunstkammer, gegen Morgen

Façade de la Bibliotheque & des Sales des rarétés, vers l'orient.

Orthographia externa ædium, quibus Bibliotheca, et Gazophylacium rerum naturalium et artificiosarum continentur, Ortum versus.

Figure 280. Kunstkammer, Vasilevskii Island. Petersburg. 1718–34. Architect: Georg Johann Mattarnovy. Engraving by Grigorii Ka- chalov, 1741. By permission of the Houghton Library, Harvard University.

completed in 1711 and expanded at least twice in the following decade. During the same period, Peter commissioned a second palace, begun in 1716 by Mattarnovy. Although Mattarnovy's death in 1719 interrupted work on this and other projects, Trezzini in 1724 completed the second Winter Palace to Mattarnovy's plans (Figure 283), which resembled Le Blond's model design of a house "for notables" (*dlia imenitykh*).[39] The center of the palace is distinguished by three arched window shafts separated by attached columns (rather than the more common pilasters), and resembles Le Blond's passageway of three arches in the center of the country palace at Strelna (see what follows). A profusely decorated baroque cornice completes the theatrical display over the main entrance (the shadow detail in the engraving indicates that the elaborate cornice with entablature stood clear of the structure and its mansard roof, rather like a stage set).

The one extant example of Trezzini's work as a builder of palaces is the Summer Palace of Peter the Great, located within a corner of the Summer Garden at the confluence of the Fontanka and the Neva.[40] The small structure (Figure 284) was completed by 1712,

and decorated over the next 2 years. The plaster panels on the exterior are attributed to Schlüter, and portray scenes from classical mythology as an allegorical representation of the success of Russian arms – particularly the Petrine fleet. The palace, defined by an elegant simplicity in window detail and proportion in relation to the size of the building, is one of the most aesthetically harmonious of imperial residences in eighteenth-century Petersburg. Yet its modest size, which was outgrown even in Peter's time, caused it to be discarded by his successors in favor of much larger summer palaces – eventually destroyed, while Trezzini's gem remains in almost its original condition. The interior decoration followed Peter's fondness for Dutch tastes, but also contained at least one room built to a design by Le Blond in 1717–20, as well as seven ceiling paintings on allegorical themes.[41]

Early palace architecture could, however, achieve a grand scale, as in the case of the residence of Alexander Menshikov on Vasilevskii Island (Figure 285). Located on the Neva, with a garden extending into the center of the island, the masonry palace was begun in 1710 to a design by Giovanni Mario Fontana

216

and completed in the early 1720s – with attached wings converting much of the garden into a courtyard – by Gottfried Johann Schädel.[42] Menshikov and his family were summarily evicted from the palace following his downfall in 1727, during the reign of Peter II, and in 1732, the residence was converted to use as a military institute. Its steeply pitched mansard roof with flanking towers was removed, as was a row of allegorical statues over the entrance. A recent restoration has uncovered much of the original decorative work on the interior, including the lavish use of Dutch tiles, carved paneling, extensive stucco ornament, and several ceiling paintings.[43] The pilaster capitals on the second level of the main facade are among the early examples of the use of the composite order in Russia, and indicate an interest in reproducing elements of the order system in the new architecture.[44] Menshikov's Vasilevskii Island residence was not his only palace: On the Island of Kotlin, Menshikov commissioned the expansive "Italian Palace," built by Johann Friedrich Braunstein in 1720–3. An early engraving shows the extensive use of pilasters, a rus-

ticated ground floor, and statuary above the cornice at the center of the building. Again, the design suggests similarities with the work of Tessin the younger in Stockholm.[45]

Within Petersburg itself, most of the Petrine palaces were subsequently razed or incorporated into larger structures, but one of the best examples, on a small scale, of early palace architecture is the so-called Kikin *palaty*, or "chambers" (Figure 286). Constructed in 1714, the residence was one of several built for Admiral Alexander Kikin, an early favorite of the tsar, but condemned to death in 1718 for his implicit participation in the abortive flight abroad of Peter's son Aleksei. In the early 1720s, the wings of the palace were enlarged by an additional story to accommodate the Kunstkammer Museum. Although there is no certainty as to the architect of the Kikin residence, its style shows a similarity with Le Blond's design for the main palace at Peterhof, also begun in 1714.[46] The use of white trim – particularly the pilaster strips – delineates the proportions of the stuccoed facade and the large window frames, whose expanse of glass

Figure 281. Kunstkammer, Vasilevskii Island. Petersburg. (P 90–1)

Профиль Библиотеки и Кунсткамеры на пос-током. — *Durchschnitt von der Kayserlichen Bibliothec, und Kunstkammer, gegen Morgen.* — *Coupe de la Bibliotheque & des Sales des raretés, vers l'Orient.* — *Orthographia interna Bibliothecæ, & Gazophylacii rer. nat. et artificias. Ortum versus.*

Figure 282. Kunstkammer, Vasilevskii Island. Petersburg. Interior. The Academy of Sciences Library (right) and the Kunstkammer collection (left) flank the central tower, which housed an anatomy theater and an observatory. Engraving by Grigorii Kachalov, 1741. By permission of the Houghton Library, Harvard University.

provides a telling contrast to pre-Petrine dwellings, which seem to have been designed to exclude a view of the exterior world.

The Country Palaces

In addition to urban palaces, Peter the Great encouraged the construction of country residences on the south shore of the Gulf of Finland (see Figure 266) and in the forests to the southwest of the city. The most extensive of these projects, Peterhof, began on a small cape opposite Kronshtadt with the construction of a wooden house for Peter in 1710–11. In 1714, Peter commissioned two mansonry palaces: "Mon plaisir," on a slight bluff directly above the shore; and the main palace, situated on higher ground some 500 meters to the south. The work was supervised by one of Schlüter's main assistants, Johann Friedrich Braunstein, who within 2 years created the central structure of each palace, as well as the outlines of the Upper and Lower Parks, and a large grotto in front of the main palace.[47] In 1716, Le Blond assumed direction of the project, widened the canal leading from the gulf to the grotto, devised an extensive hydraulic plan for the parks, and supervised the interior decoration of the palaces, which assumed an opulent appearance.

Le Blond's work on the main palace at Peterhof, which he partially rebuilt and expanded from Braunstein's original structure, illustrates his approach to palace architecture, developed from principles set forth by the French master Jules Hardouin-Mansart (grandnephew of François Mansart), who served as Royal Architect to Louis XIV and supervised work at Versailles during the last quarter of the seventeenth century.[48] Symmetry was the supreme principle and began with the three-storied central structure, marked by a pediment and Corinthian pilasters, still clearly visible in Rastrelli's rebuilding of the palace (Figure 287). This area contained a vestibule, extending from the south to the north facade of the palace, and a grand stairway leading to enfilades of state rooms. In Le Blond's larger designs, more intimate quarters could be arranged as an "apartment," or cluster of rooms, around a large space.

Le Blond's greatest rooms at Peterhof were the Italian Salon and Peter's Oak Study, neither of which he lived to see completed. A fire in 1721 led to their restoration by Niccola Michetti, who retained the

218

paneling of light oak carved under the direction of Nicolas Pineau (a detail borrowed, perhaps, from Le Grand Trianon). The ceiling paintings included works by Pillement and Bartolomeo Tarsia, whose design for the main, Italian Salon was approved by Peter, but painted the year after his death. In 1721, Michetti expanded Le Blond's plan with the addition of galleries and end pavilions extending from either side of the central structure.[49] By 1725, the essential elements of the main palace were in place and ready for their vast expansion by Bartolomeo Francesco Rastrelli.

In contrast to the main palace, the Petrine form of "Mon plaisir" has been remarkably well preserved despite extensive war damage (Figure 288). Intimate in scale, the building was, as its name suggests, a pleasure retreat for the tsar, with a mansard roof over the central area that contains a large state room flanked by small rooms – including a Chinese Study decorated in chinoiserie lacquer work. On either side of the center block extend arcaded galleries (begun in 1717) consisting of an enfilade of semienclosed chambers and a small end pavilion, or "Lusthaus." In deference to the elements in this exposed location, the glazed arcade of the galleries faces south, and the north, gulf side is protected by a brick wall with niches and smaller arched French windows. (Mon Plaisir is one of the few examples in eighteenth-century Petersburg architecture to use brick without stucco on the exterior.) On the interior, Le Blond interpreted Peter's fondness for the Dutch style with superb craftsmanship – including plaster statuary designed by Carlo Rastrelli, carved oak paneling, and ceiling paintings on allegorical themes executed in 1718–22 by Phillipe Pillement, who also participated in the interior design of the Summer Palace and the Menshikov Palace in Petersburg.[50]

With the death of Le Blond in 1719, the role of supervising architect at Peterhof was assumed by Michetti, who continued work on the main palace and devoted particular attention to the development of the Upper and Lower Parks in the French style initiated by Le Blond. Braunstein, however, remained the actual designer of a number of buildings, including Mon Plaisir, where in 1721 Peter himself commanded that the gallery walls be faced in oak, with panels designed to accommodate his growing collec-

Figure 283. Second Winter Palace. Petersburg. 1716–24. Architects: Georg Johann Mattarnovy, Domenico Trezzini. Engraving by E. Vinogradov from a drawing by M. Makhaev. Courtesy of the Library of Congress.

219

Figure 284. Summer Palace of Peter the Great. Petersburg. 1711–14. Architects: Domenico Trezzini, with plaster panels attributed to Andreas Schlüter. (P 31–1)

Figure 285. Menshikov Palace. Petersburg. 1710–20s. Architects: Giovanni Mario Fontana and Gottfried Johann Schädel. (P 8–12)

Figure 286. Kikin Chambers. Petersburg. 1714. (P–5)

tion of seventeenth-century Dutch and Flemish paintings – considered the first art gallery in Russia. Braunstein's other work at Peterhof includes the small Marly Palace (1720–3; Figure 289), marked by rusticated pilaster strips and a finely calculated relation between the design of the windows and the proportions of the two floors.

Like every significant palace of the Petrine period, the design of Marly took into account the distribution of water as an element for the enhancement of architecture. Although this aquatic emphasis, particularly in Petersburg, might be characterized as making a virtue of necessity, it also reflects an essential goal of Peter's policies – access to and management of water, through his Baltic outlet, and by a system of canals initiated to provide a more efficient transportation network within the country. In addition to facilitating these specific political and economic goals, hydraulic engineering created at Peterhof one of the most complex ensembles of fountains, cascades, and decorative ponds in Europe, thus proclaiming the resources and might of Russia's transformed autocracy.[51]

In one sense, these elaborate hydraulic installations, like the Peterhof parks in general, are an imitation of Versailles and Marly. Yet there are also at Peterhof symbolic references to Peter's triumph not only over his enemies, but also over the natural elements. Beyond the great cascade at the main palace, the gilded statue of Samson (see Plate 57; designed by Carlo Rastrelli and first cast in 1735) forces open the jaws of the lion in an allegory of Peter's victory over Charles at Poltava, on the day dedicated in the Church calendar to Samson. Like Ivan IV, who combined the fall of Kazan and the Feast of the Intercession for his church-monument on Red Square, Peter skilfully exploited religious symbolism for political purposes. Yet apart from this specific allegory, the very force of the water channeled through the stat-

Figure 287. Main palace, Peterhof. 1714–52. Architects: Jean Baptiste Alexandre Le Blond, Johann Friedrich Braunstein, Niccola Michetti, and Bartolomeo Rastrelli. North facade, with canal to Gulf of Finland. (P 76–10)

uary is symbolic of Peter the Great's reshaping of the elements – not simply in this aquatechnic display (which required the excavation of a 24-kilometer canal), but in the very building of his city.

Water is no less evident in the design of the Hermitage pavilion, surrounded by a small moat and situated at the edge of the Gulf of Finland (Figure 290). Built by Braunstein in 1721–4, the Hermitage was intended entirely for leisure, with broad French windows opening onto views of the park and the gulf from the second floor. Even Mon Plaisir included an office and study for the conduct of business, but at the Hermitage, the entire upper floor served as a dining or reception hall.[52] Like the Summer Palace in Petersburg, Mon Plaisir, Marly, and the Hermitage were unsuited in both design and setting for the major expansion required by the displays of imperial pomp in the mideighteenth century. They remain untouched relics of the Petrine era, and as such reveal the rapid transference of western architecture and the

decorative arts to Russia, as well as the facility with which Russian craftsmen assimilated the highly specialized skills necessary to build on a level comparable to the major centers of culture elsewhere in Europe.

There were a number of other palaces built during the reign of Peter in the area of Peterhof and beyond. As a country residence for his second wife, Catherine, the tsar chose a wooded, hilly area inland at a site called Saari Mois ("elevated land") by the local Finnic inhabitants and eventually transformed into the Russian *tsarskoe selo*, or "Tsar's village" (now called Pushkin in honor of the poet, who attended the Tsarskoe Selo Lycée in 1811–17). In 1717–23, Braunstein built a small two-storied residence for Catherine, although it is not clear whether the design was originally his. Indeed, little is known of Catherine's palace, which was so thoroughly rebuilt by Rastrelli during the reign of Elizabeth.[53]

Far more from the Petrine period has been preserved at Oranienbaum, the large palace commis-

Figure 288. Mon Plaisir, Peterhof. 1714–22. Architects: Jean Baptiste Alexandre Le Blond and Johann Friedrich Braunstein. South facade. (P 90–9)

Figure 289. Marly (palace and park), Peterhof. 1720–3. Architect: Johann Friedrich Braunstein. (P 75–34)

222

Figure 290. Hermitage, Peterhof. 1721–4. Architect: Johann Friedrich Braunstein. The brackets under the main balcony are encased within protective winter covers. (P 74–20)

sioned by Alexander Menshikov and begun in 1710 by Giovanni Fontana, who had also done the initial work on Menshikov's palace in Petersburg. With Fontana's departure from Russia in 1713, supervision of Menshikov's projects was assumed by Gottfried Schädel, a colleague of Schlüter, who may well have been the source of the north German baroque influence in the design of the central palace structure.[54] The scale of the Oranienbaum palace seems exaggerated in the mideighteenth century depiction by Mikhail Makhaev (Figure 291), who generally provided a faithful representation of the imperial palaces.[55] The sweeping double terrace beneath the arcaded gallery conveys an impression of monumentality that was belied by the relatively compact structure of the palace itself. Nonetheless, Menshikov had again rivaled the tsar in the scale of his residence, elevated to a superb view of the gulf. After Menshikov's exile in 1727, the ownership of the estate eventually passed to various members of the imperial family, including the ill-fated Peter III, for whom Empress Elizabeth commissioned Rastrelli to redesign much of the interior. The second flourishing of Oranienbaum, however, occurred under the direction of Antonio Rinaldi during the reign of Catherine II (see Chapter 10).

Other notable Petrine country residences, now in various states of disrepair, include Strelna, which, as the closest of the imperial palaces to Petersburg, originally served the tsar as a resting place for more distant points along the gulf. Miraculously, his original wooden residence (c. 1710) at Strelna has been preserved, and with its modest classical detailing in wood, it might be taken for any number of nineteenth-century manor houses in Russia.[56] The main palace is on a far grander scale, and although much rebuilt,

it provides the purest example of the arrangement of interior space along enfilades as propagated by Le Blond, who worked on the structure in 1716–19. After Le Blond's death, palace construction was supervised by Michetti, who introduced a number of design modifications (Figure 292). Upon Michetti's departure from Russia in 1723, the project was given to his most talented Russian apprentice, Mikhail Zemtsov. With the growth of Peterhof, Peter had less use for Strelna, which became the property of his daughter, the future Empress Elizabeth, and was finally completed in the 1750s under the direction of Rastrelli. Despite the scale of its formal gardens and of the main palace itself, Strelna did not receive the focused attention devoted to the other imperial estates. Its notable architectural details – such as the triple-arched open passageway at the center of the main floor – are subsumed within an ungainly hybrid of a structure.[57]

The Petrine country palaces, like their European models, contain the variety of influences that had formed the baroque style, modified throughout Europe to meet local conditions and the individual tastes of the autocrat. Peter was intensely concerned with the development of the estates, and often defined the general plan of the parks as well as the specifics of the architectural design of his country palaces, which, like the architecture of Petersburg, combined elements of the Dutch, French, and Prussian baroque. In contrast to the country residences of Moscow's rulers, which were typically rambling wooden structures grouped around a masonry church (the most notable example being Kolomenskoe), the main palaces commissioned by Peter – and Menshikov – were brick structures organized on principles of symmetry, proportion, and logic in the distribution of the parts, from central structure to end pavilions. Even country life was to be regulated in accordance with European court rituals under the new regime.

Transition from Petrine Architecture

During the final years of Peter's life, most of the major structures in his capital were still under construction – apart from the various palaces of the tsar-emperor and his grandees, almost all of which were subsequently rebuilt. The bell tower of the Peter–Paul Cathedral had received its finishing touches, but the body of the church was still far from complete. Parts of the Holy Trinity–Alexander Nevskii Monastery were in place, but the new building of the Twelve Colleges was mired in disorganization, and the Kunstkammer fared little better. The Admiralty had been finished as a sprawling timber-frame complex

Figure 291. Main palace, Oranienbaum. 1711–25. Architects: Giovanni Mario Fontana and Gottfried Schädel. Engraving by F. Vnukov and N. Chelnakov from a drawing by Makhaev. Courtesy of the Shchusev State Museum of Architecture, Moscow.

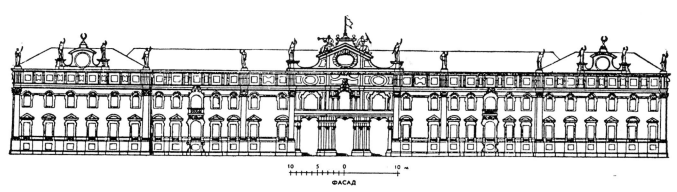

ФАСАД

Figure 292. Main palace, Strelna. 1716–50s. Architects: Jean Baptiste Alexandre Le Blond, Niccola Michetti, Mikhail Zemtsov, and Bartolomeo Francesco Rastrelli. Elevation and plan of central structure.

along the Neva, but by 1721, preliminary work for the construction of a masonry building was already underway.

The deaths of both Le Blond and Mattarnovy in 1719 temporarily disrupted projects in the city as well as at the imperial estates; but Michetti, who had worked in Rome under the tutelage of Carlo Fontana, quickly assumed direction of civil architecture with Peter's full confidence. In addition to his direct involvement in the development of palaces and parks at Peterhof and Strelna, Michetti also projected the Catherinental palace, commissioned by Peter near Revel (now Tallinn) for his wife Catherine. Although its exterior ornament is modest by baroque standards, the large interior state rooms reveal the full measure of Michetti's Roman exuberance, particularly in the White Hall with its ceiling painting and extensive plaster decoration – including fully modeled statuary.[58]

In these diverse responsibilities, Michetti had the assistance of one of the first Russian architects to master the new western architectural forms. Around 1709, Mikhail Zemtsov moved from Moscow to Petersburg, where he began studies in Italian and became a student-assistant to Trezzini.[59] His native talent and abilities as a draftsman – developed during his early apprenticeship at the Printing Works of the Kremlin Armory – brought advancement and notice within what was still a guild of foreigners. With the promotion of Michetti to "architect-general" in 1720, Zemtsov was given a leading role in the supervision of such projects as the Catherinental Palace, where he designed parts of the interior, as well as the park. Sent to Stockholm in 1722 at Peter's command to further his training and to hire Swedish craftsmen in specialities designated by the tsar, Zemtsov returned to Petersburg in 1723. In the same year, Michetti, having decided not to renew his contract, departed for Italy, thus leaving Zemstov in effective control of major projects such as the parks at Peterhof and the Summer Garden, where he not only oversaw the expansive design for the park itself, but also the Grotto pavilion and, in 1727, a large banqueting hall (neither extant).[60] By that time, however, political events had altered the course of construction in Petersburg.

At the end of Peter the Great's reign, in 1725, Petersburg had acquired an economic and administrative base for further development as a major city. Yet its position as the Russian capital remained a source of discontent among those who resented the westernization embodied by the new city. The brief reign (1725–7) of Peter's second wife, Catherine I, saw a continuation of many building projects; but Catherine had little of Peter's energy, and Menshikov remained the primary force behind the city's development. On the succession in 1727 of the 11-year-old Peter II (Peter's grandson by his first marriage), power was assumed by a Supreme Council dominated by the Dolgorukii family, which promptly exiled Menshikov

on the grounds of corruption (a readily verifiable charge). By 1728, reaction against Peter's reforms had gained momentum. The court returned to Moscow, Petersburg faced the exodus of a large part of its population, the army and fleet were neglected, and the country's strained financial position was exacerbated by the widespread refusal of an impoverished peasantry to pay taxes.

When in 1730 Peter II died of smallpox, the Romanov male line was temporarily exhausted. The eventual choice as empress of Anne, niece of Peter the Great (daughter of Ivan V) and widow of the duke of Courland, promised further limitation of imperial power by the Supreme Council and its allies among the hereditary nobility. Having accepted restrictions on her authority, Anne promptly nullified them upon her accession to the throne.[61] With the support of the guards regiments and large segments of the gentry in service to the state (both the creations of Petrine policies), Anne reestablished autocratic power, and announced her intention of returning to Petersburg

Figure 293. Admiralty. Petersburg. 1732–8 Engraving by G. Kachalov from a drawing by M. Makhaev. Courtesy of the Library of Congress.

226

and to the absolutist principles that the city represented as capital of the Petrine state. Although its buildings, streets, and canals had fallen into decrepitude, much had been restored through the efforts of the indomitable Trezzini (now 61) and Zemtsov as the imperial court resettled in Petersburg in 1732.

The revival of construction after the return of the court did not reach previous levels, but the dates of completion of a number of major projects, such as the Cathedral of Sts. Peter and Paul (consecrated in 1733) and the Kunstkammer (finished by Zemtsov in 1734), are evidence of a new continuity in the development of the city. Notable changes were also under way, such as the rebuilding of the central block of the Admiralty, begun in 1732 by Ivan Korobov. To a greater degree than Zemtsov, Korobov was a product of Peter the Great's support for the education abroad of Russian architects. Having studied in Holland between 1718 and 1727, Korobov obtained the position of architect for the college (ministry) of the Admiralty in 1728, only to find little work other than the construction of two wooden churches in the Petersburg area during the reign of Peter II.[62] Thus, the Admiralty project proved a turning point in his career as well as in the design of Petersburg.

The basic outlines of the Petrine Admiralty re-mained unchanged: a long facade with perpendicular wings on either side extending to the Neva and flanking the shipyard. The entire complex was fortified with ramparts and a moat (Figure 293). Peter had understood the need to distinguish the Admiralty architecturally, not only as a symbol of Russia as a major maritime power, but also by virtue of its central location on the south bank of the Neva – on what was then called Admiralty Island, but was in effect a part of the mainland. To that end, Peter had in 1711 commanded the building of a timber-frame tower, with clock and spire, over the central, brick portion of the main facade.[63] As the city expanded to the south and east of the Admiralty, the importance of the spire as a focal point for development became obvious, and Korobov exploited this position to create one of the most successful and enduring features of the Petersburg cityscape. For all of the references to the northern European baroque, the Admiralty spire, then as now, was situated to dominate a unique and vast system of intersecting spaces, from the Neva River to the prospekts and squares beyond. Korobov, following Peter's inspiration, had established the true line that would define the harmony of Petersburg's urban plan for the next century.

CHAPTER 9

The Late Baroque in Russia: The Age of Rastrelli

> When I entered and saw all the splendor and magnificence of our palace, there
> came upon me such a pleasurable rapture, that I was beside myself in delight.

> – Andrei Bolotov on the Winter Palace in the 1760s

Despite the idiosyncratic behavior of Empress Anne and the deadly intrigues of her court, Petersburg and its supporting bureaucratic and military institutions increased steadily during the 1730s, as the Russian Empire initiated campaigns against the troublesome Crimean Tatars and the Turks to the south, and became involved in the intricate maneuvering of European politics – most notably during the War of the Polish Succession. The spirit of exploration encouraged by Peter the Great culminated during Anne's reign in the expeditions of Vitus Bering, a Danish captain in Russian service who moved beyond Kamchatka and the Bering Strait to the shores of Alaska. In order to administer the expanding empire, Petersburg required not only the completion of monumental state projects begun in the Petrine era, but also the development of a functioning urban environment – houses, shops, parish churches – for its some 70,000 inhabitants.[1] This humbler aspect of Petersburg architecture, created at such cost to those who lived there, has long since disappeared, either from rebuilding or from the frequent scourge of Russian cities, fire.[2]

Two churches of the period, however, have survived and exemplify the extent to which the design of the Russian church, even on a modest level, had been altered by the importation of western mannerisms by architects such as Trezzini. The style of each is baroque, with steeples on the west end and elements of the classical order system on both exterior and interior. Mikhail Zemtsov's Church of Saints Simeon and Anna (1731–4) reflects the influence of Trezzini, not only in use of classical entablature, but also

in the design of the portico on the south facade (Figure 294). In comparison with the Zemtsov church, with its effective use of rusticated quoins to frame the south facade, the Church of St. Panteleimon (1735–9), attributed to Ivan Korobov, shows a more capricious – or perhaps rustic – use of baroque motifs. This is particularly evident in the detailing of the apse, whose crown is said to resemble the grenadier's helmet (Figure 295) – not inappropriate for a church built to commemorate the major Russian naval victory in 1714 over the Swedes at Cape Gangut (Finnish Hankö).[3]

Yet the presence of the apse at the Church of St. Panteleimon also signals the reintegration of traditional Russian forms in the design of Petersburg parish architecture. Furthermore, although both the Zemtsov and Korobov churches could be classified as basilican in plan, the presence of a large dome over the east bay of each suggests a resemblance to the "ship" form characteristic of seventeenth-century Russian church architecture. This adaptation of European baroque elements to centralized structures accommodating the Orthodox liturgy would attain more impressive solutions over the next two decades in the work of Rastrelli and Chevakinskii.

The rarity of the Zemtsov and Korobov churches reminds that despite Peter's energetic measures to counter the destructive effects of fire, the city remained prey to periodic fires that on occasion reached catastrophic proportions. In the summer of 1736, an entire district of Admiralty Island (the most densely populated area of the city) burned. As Zemtsov and other architects planned a revival of the area, an even more devastating fire the following summer de-

Figure 294. Church of Sts. Simeon and Anna. Petersburg. 1731–4. Architect: Mikhail Zemtsov. South facade. (P 66–20)

stroyed much of the remaining Admiralty district.[4] In order to organize the massive rebuilding and reordering of the central city, a new central planning agency was formed: the Commission for the Construction of St. Petersburg. Although the commission was headed by Count Buchard Christophe Münnich, commander of the army under the Empress Anne, its guiding, creative force was the architect Peter Eropkin, who had been sent by Peter the Great to Rome, where he studied with the architect Sebastiano Cipriani. Upon returning to Russia in 1723, he worked first in Moscow and then moved to Petersburg in 1726. Like many of his contemporaries, Eropkin participated in the work at the imperial estates of Peterhof and Strelna, but his interests and abilities were directed more toward the theory of architecture and urban design rather than the actual practice of building.

These qualities were amply proven in his work for the commission, which involved the first detailed topographical survey of the city with indications of existing, rather than planned, structures (Moscow was

also mapped with unprecedented accuracy in 1739).[5] The specific recommendations of the commission, which concluded its work in 1742, provided the most important single direction for the development of Petersburg in the eighteenth century. Many of its proposals for the rebuilding of the destroyed parts of the Admiralty district were promptly implemented under the direction of Zemtsov.[6] Eropkin emphasized the rational development of major thoroughfares and the building of architectural monuments that would dominate the city space at effective visual points.

Eropkin also initiated another, closely related undertaking in the form of a treatise that served as a compendium of architectural principles and as a guide to the practical organization of architecture – "public and private" – in Petersburg. Entitled *The Duties of the Architectural Office*, the treatise was not published until the twentieth century,[7] and it represents a collaborative effort that included Mikhail Zemtsov (who completed the document at the end of 1740) and Ivan Korobov. Each was an experienced pedagogue: Zemtsov had been accepting students since 1724,[8] and Korobov only slightly later. Indeed, Korobov's workshop provided training for three of the most success-

Figure 295. Church of St. Panteleimon. Petersburg. 1735–9. Architect: Ivan Korobov. Southeast view. (P 10)

ful native Russian architects during the late baroque period: Alexander Kokorinov, Savva Chevakinskii, and Dmitrii Ukhtomskii. In this sense, Eropkin's collaborators were well equipped to guide this early attempt to provide a formal structure to the practice of architecture in Russia.

Although the level and intent of the several sections of *Duties* vary considerably, Eropkin's introduction to the treatise, and certain of its sections, reflects his erudition in classical architectural theory as well as his specific interests in Palladio, whom he began to translate, in detail and from the original text, in the late 1730s.[9] Unfortunately, Eropkin did not live to bring these projects to fruition. In 1740, he was implicated in a plot by his powerful sponsor Artemii Volynskii to overthrow Anne and her German advisors in favor of the future Empress Elizabeth. The ensuing repression, associated with Anne's favorite Count Ernst Johann Bühren (or Biron, as he was known in Russia), has been seen as a logical culmination of an increasingly unpopular reign, one of whose most tragic victims was Eropkin. He was publicly executed near the Peter–Paul Fortress in June 1740.[10] Zemtsov was able to provide a measure of continuity in the realization of projects suggested by Eropkin; but not until the latter part of Elizabeth's reign did the capital assume the imperial aspect projected by Eropkin and his colleagues. Ironically, the spectacular success of the capital's development was largely due to the efforts of an architect who had been generously supported by Biron.

Rastrelli: Architectural Beginnings

Bartolomeo Francesco Rastrelli was able, by a twist of fate and his own supreme talent as an architect, to survive not only the Walpurgisnacht of the reign of Anne, whom he served so effectively, but also to advance rapidly to a commanding position during the reign of Elizabeth, whose taste for lavish decorative effects meshed perfectly with Rastrelli's approach to architecture. Born in 1700, Rastrelli spent his youth in France, where his father, the Florentine sculptor and architect Count Carlo Bartolomeo Rastrelli (the title was bestowed by the Pope), served at the court of Louis XIV.[11] Upon the death of Sun King in 1715, Peter the Great and his agents recruited French architects and artisans – newly without court appointments – for service in Russia, and among them was the elder Rastrelli. In 1715, he left Paris with his son and arrived early the following year in Petersburg,

where he began work on various projects at Strelna and Peterhof.

Because of an immediate and mutual antipathy between Le Blond and Carlo Rastrelli, the latter's career in Russia came to a halt in the summer of 1716; but the timely commission of a magnificent bronze bust of Menshikov as well as Le Blond's reputation for arrogance gained Rastrelli a valuable ally in the person of the prince, who soon reinstated him in the good graces of the tsar. As noted in the preceding chapter, Carlo Rastrelli's work for Peter consisted primarily of statuary, both free-standing and interior plaster decorative work – as in the main hall of Mon Plaisir. His son's first recorded project was the large wooden model for the palace and park at Strelna that he built with the guidance of his father in 1717.[12] In 1721–7, he constructed a mansion (not extant) in rather uncertain imitation of the baroque style for the Moldavian prince Dmitrii Kantemir – father of the noted Russian satirical poet Antiokh Kantemir.[13] In addition, he was involved in other projects – some unrealized, none extant – for the grandees of Petersburg.

There is no firm evidence that the young Rastrelli returned to Europe in the mid–1720s to supplement his education and hone his skills, although some biographers have suggested that his father sent him there for that purpose.[14] Whatever the facts of his apprenticeship, by the beginning of Anne's reign, Rastrelli had not only acquired the skills to maneuver among the shoals of court intrigue, but had also begun to show evidence of his remarkable abilities as an architect. In February 1730, both Rastrellis had moved to Moscow, temporarily again the capital; and later that year, either the father or the son – it is not entirely clear which – had been appointed court architect.[15] During this period, they were commissioned to construct two large wooden palaces (neither extant) for the empress in Moscow: the Winter Annenhof ("Anne's Palace," in the preferred language of this Germanophile), a wooden structure of some 130 rooms near the new building of the Kremlin Arsenal; and in the Lefortovo district, the larger Summer Annenhof, a palace of 220 rooms and an extensive park with formal gardens.

The Winter Annenhof, built during the second half of 1730, is one of the earliest examples of Rastrelli's mature work in the baroque style, although the configuration of the one-story structure appears to have been constrained by the adjacent Kremlin buildings. The interior decoration was apparently lavish, with a ceiling painting by Louis Caravaque in the Great Hall. In 1736, the palace, which had served only briefly as the imperial residence, was dismantled and moved to Lefortovo. The Summer Annenhof, a more elaborate structure, was completed in 1731 – also a remarkably short time and testimony to Rastrelli's ability to mobilize and direct a large labor force that included over 6,000 carpenters, masons, sculptors, and other craftsmen. Their efforts were evident from the project sketches of the decorative work on the interior and baroque window surrounds on the exterior. Although the court returned to Petersburg soon after the completion of the Summer Annenhof, the project had served as ideal preparation for Rastrelli's imperial work, with its gargantuan expansion of scale and expenditure during the next three decades.[16]

Rastrelli in the 1730s: Moscow, Petersburg, Courland

Even as work proceeded on the Moscow palaces, the empress, with her return to Petersburg in mind, had commissioned of Rastrelli a wooden Summer Palace on the Neva, constructed in 1731.[17] Other buildings, including a manege, soon followed on the open space along the Neva just beyond the Admiralty. The most prominent among them was the Third Winter Palace, located at the site of the former palace of Admiral Fedor Apraksin. The Apraksin Palace – there were several variants, including one designed by Le Blond – was basically the work of Domenico Trezzini, and it was he who at the end of 1731 began the conversion of the structure to meet the demands of Empress Anne. Almost immediately, the seemingly unrestrained growth of the imperial appetite for palaces dictated a more expansive project, which was entrusted to Bartolomeo Francesco Rastrelli, possibly assisted by the elder Rastrelli.

When completed in 1735, the three-story Winter Palace was the most imposing residence the city had seen, and the most richly appointed. Contemporary drawings by Mikhail Makhaev (Figure 296) convey a rather ungainly appearance, with an asymmetrical design on the main (Neva) facade consisting of the remodeled Apraksin Palace and the adjoining, much larger structure by Rastrelli, which extended an additional 60 meters along the Neva in the direction of the Admiralty.[18] Perpendicular to the Neva facade of his palace, Rastrelli constructed a large wing with an imposing, symmetrical facade on each side. The bulging mansard roofs that had characterized most of the Petrine palaces here seem outmoded, and Rastrelli was soon to discard them.

The interior of the Third Winter Palace, however, represents an unprecedented achievement for Rastrelli, both in terms of structural scale and in his application of the decorative arts. In Rastrelli's own description: "In this building there was a great hall, a gallery and theater, and also a grand staircase, a large chapel – all richly decorated with sculpture and painting, as were all of the state apartments. The number of rooms which were constructed in this large palace exceeded 200."[19] It should be noted that work on the interior continued until the closing of the palace for the construction of a still larger building in the reign of Elizabeth (see what follows). Among the most spectacular rooms in this later phase of the palace's history was the Amber Study, designed by Schlüter in 1709 for the Prussian king Friedrich-Wilhelm I, who presented it to Peter the Great in 1716. According to one reliable account, nothing was done with the amber panels until 1743, when Rastrelli placed them with twenty-six pilasters of mirrored glass in one of the rooms of the Winter Palace.[20] The luminous hue of the amber was perfectly suited to the baroque taste, but it is Rastrelli's use of glass that defined the interior as his own. From its early development by the French in the seventeenth century, mirrored glass had become an essential component in the decoration – and visual expansion – of interiors. Le Blond was familiar with its uses, but the full exploitation of this material, often in conjunction with transparent glass in French windows, would be a distinctive feature of Rastrelli's imperial palaces.

While the Winter Palace was under construction, Rastrelli began the design of what would become a series of residences for Anne's premier courtier, Count Ernst Johann Biron (Bühren), designated the Duke of Courland (now Latvia) in 1737. The palaces at Ruhental (1736–40) and Mitau (1738–40) fall outside the boundaries of this history, but they are, nonetheless, significant in the development of Rastrelli's mastery.[21] Although the decoration of the interiors of these palaces ceased with Biron's exile to Siberia in 1740, the structural work was completed and displays a plasticity and the balance of decorative detail that characterizes Rastrelli's mature work. If the palace at Ruhental was merely an imposing residence for a wealthy courtier, the Mitau palace, begun after Biron's selection as ruler of Courland, was already on an imperial scale comparable to the palace at Strelna.[22] Yet both Mitau and Ruhental reflect the early Petersburg baroque, particularly in the extensive use of pilasters to segment the main facade and the bold rectangular window surrounds that reinforce the ver-

Figure 296. View up the Neva River, c. 1753. On the right, the Third Winter Palace. 1732–5. Architect: Bartolomeo Francesco Rastrelli. Engraving by E. Vinogradov from a drawing by M. Makhaev. Courtesy of the Shchusev State Museum of Architecture, Moscow.

ticality of the pilasters. The young Rastrelli had no lack of examples of this grid of white stucco trim, not only in the work of Trezzini and Schwertfeger, but also in Michetti's design of the palace at Strelna. Rastrelli's later work, by contrast, would develop a horizontal background for rococo decoration and attached columns.

Rastrelli in Petersburg: The 1740s

With the death of Empress Anne in the fall of 1740 and the subsequent collapse of Biron's power, Rastrelli returned to Petersburg from Courland. Despite his cordial working relations with the duke, Rastrelli had remained detached from court politics, and emerged unharmed from the struggle among contending regency factions during the brief reign of Ivan VI and the subsequent seizure of power (in November 1741) by Elizabeth, daughter of Peter the Great by his second marriage. Nonetheless, Rastrelli's association with Biron impeded his access to court commissions during the first years of Elizabeth's reign. His appointment as Chief Architect (Ober Architektor) to the Court, officially approved in 1738, was called into question with severance of pay in 1742. After the death of Zemtsov in 1743, however, Rastrelli remained the only experienced architect capable of building on a scale required by the ritual of the new court. And Elizabeth, whose frank pursuit of pleasure had gained her much support among the Russian nobility and the guards regiments, fully intended to lift the residual gloom of Anne's ponderous, Teutonophile reign by spending with unprecedented largesse – both for herself and for favorites such as the Razumovskiis and the Vorontsovs. In these auspicious circumstances, Rastrelli petitioned for a reconfirmation of his rank and official position in 1744.[23]

Although Rastrelli was not officially reinstated to the position of Chief Architect until 1748, he was allowed to complete the building of a new palace (the Third, begun in 1741) in the Summer Garden. Rastrelli's Summer Palace was among his most effusive rococo creations, a pleasure palace built of wood and set within an elaborate park (incorporating Peter the Great's Summer Garden) at the intersection of two major canals, the Fontanka and the Moika (Figure 297). In Rastrelli's words: "The [Summer Palace] had more than 160 apartments, including a church, a grand hall, and galleries. All were decorated with mirrors and rich sculpture, just as the garden was decorated with splendid fountains and a Hermitage ... surrounded with rich trelliage and with decorations all gilded."[24] Despite the modest size of the palace – only 160 "apartments," contained primarily on a single story above the ground floor – its integration of structure and decoration, as well as the resolution of the roof line, show a break with Petrine architecture, with its northern European basis, and the beginnings of what might be called Elizabethan baroque, redolent of Italy and France.

The Third Summer Palace was razed in 1797 to make way for Paul's forbidding Mikhailovskii Castle (in each case, architectural taste providing insight into the ruler's character), but mideighteenth-century colored prints of the building, together with written evidence, give some idea of Rastrelli's pastel flourish. The walls, culminating in a balustrade with statuary, were light pink, trimmed in white, and rose from a gray–green rusticated round floor (the color of Petersburg facades often changed with the frequent repaintings required by the harsh climate).[25] Although pilasters segmented certain portions of the structure, the wider spacing of the windows on the main facade permitted a clearer perception of the wall surface and, most especially, its color as a background for rococo

Figure 297. Summer Palace. Petersburg. 1741–3. Architect: Bartolomeo Francesco Rastrelli. Engraving by A. Grekov from a drawing by M. Makhaev. Courtesy of the Library of Congress.

decorative elements. Boris Vipper has argued that the polychromaticism of Rastrelli's work – with colors ranging from pale pistachio and azure to orange – is analogous to the Russian fondness for brilliant color applied to the facades of brick churches, as is his profuse application of gold leaf and of ornamental detail derived from plant motifs.[26] Whatever the obvious features that Rastrelli's buildings share with other European monuments of the late baroque, it is evident that he had a broader view on the uses of color in architecture than did his European contemporaries – a fact unequivocally stated later in the century by western travelers who saw Rastrelli's palaces and commented upon the experience.

Concurrently with work on the Summer Palace, Rastrelli was involved in the completion of another imperial residence, the Anichkov Palace, situated at the intersection of Nevskii Prospekt with the Fontanka Canal. The palace was begun in 1741 to a design by Zemtsov; and although little had been built by the time of his death in 1743, a comparison of his project drawings with the Makhaev view of the structure as completed in the 1750s (Figure 298) shows that the building was essentially Zemtsov's.[27] Rastrelli's claim to have finished the Anichkov Palace must, therefore, refer to the interior work and to his design of gilded cupolar structures for the corner wings (comparable to his end pavilions at Peterhof). Elizabeth gave the palace to her courtier Aleksei Razumovskii, and Catherine the Great subsequently donated it to Grigorii Potemkin, at which time Ivan Starov introduced a number of modifications in the neoclassical style.

Due to the frequency with which it has been rebuilt, the Anichkov Palace retains virtually none of its original baroque ornament. Only through the engraving does one have a sense of its original appearance and its importance as an extension of imperial architecture to the boundary of the Fontanka, at a time when the Nevskii Prospekt was still a rather modest affair. The aquatic motif, so evident in Rastrelli's design of the Summer Palace, was developed here (perhaps by Zemtsov) in the form of a square basin situated in the main courtyard and accessible to canal boats from the Fontanka. The undesirability in the Petersburg cli-

234

Figure 298. Anichkov Palace. Petersburg. 1741–50s. Architects: Mikhail Zemtsov and Bartolomeo Francesco Rastrelli. Engraving by Ia. Vasilev from a drawing by M. Makhaev. Courtesy of the Library of Congress.

mate of bringing the water to the very walls of the palace was soon evident, and the basin was filled in; yet its original presence suggests the strength of the impulse to create a Venetian ambience in so unlikely a setting.

Rastrelli at Peterhof and Tsarskoe Selo

Rastrelli's accession to rococo magnificence began in 1745 with his commission to rebuild the main palace at Peterhof, where the basic structural work was completed in 1752, although the decoration continued until 1755 – and the remodeling began almost immediately thereafter. His design adhered to the spirit of Le Blond's early baroque, particularly the central structure (Figure 299), which followed the original form on the exterior and also preserved certain rooms associated with Peter the Great. The Petrine style is also evident in the mansard roof of both the central part and the end pavilions, which were considerably expanded by Rastrelli. The use of pilas-

ters and rusticated quoins – virtually the only ornamental features of the stuccoed facade – is restrained in comparison with the decoration of Rastrelli's later works.

The late baroque, however, is fully evident in the designs for the two end pavilions: the court church and the Imperial Insignia pavilion, so named for the two-headed eagle, in three dimensions, placed above the cupola. The cupolas in their turn rest above a pyramidal projection whose four edges are outlined with gilded festoons. These forms are distantly reminiscent of the bulbous wooden roofs of the great palace at Kolomenskoe, which Rastrelli probably saw on one of his many trips to Moscow; but it is the court church – whose inspiration has been attributed to sources as diverse as Savva Chevakinskii and the empress herself – that suggests most convincingly the baroque reinterpretation of traditional Russian forms. The link was all the clearer in the original pentacupolar design of the church, whose corner cupolas (see Figure 299; they have not been restored) represent one of the earliest examples of the return of that form

Figure 299. Main palace, Peterhof. 1745–55. Architect: Bartolomeo Francesco Rastrelli. Engraving from a drawing by M. Makhaev, 1761. North facade. Courtesy of the Shchusev State Museum of Architecture.

in post-Petrine architecture. The gilded cupolas of both pavilions not only provide a dramatic definition of the extent of the structure, but also complement the brilliant yellow of the facade, highlighted by white trim. As is so often the case with the architecture of Petersburg, the colors are enhanced by the continual variations in sunlight, the tone of the northern sky, and cloud patterns off the Gulf of Finland that match the most extravagant baroque fancy.

The plan of the palace reflected the informality of what was considered primarily a summer residence on the gulf. The main entrance and stairway are situated to the side of the palace, in the west wing (extending into the Upper Park) and lead directly to the grand state rooms: the Ballroom, the Chesme Hall (remodeled during the reign of Catherine II), and the

Great Throne Hall (Figure 300) – perpendicular to the west wing and extending for almost a quarter of the main facade. In the center is a cluster of salons or "apartments" that lead to two parallel enfilades connecting a series of dining rooms, studies, and other state rooms. Beyond this core structure, one-story galleries led to the palace church beyond the east wing, and the Imperial Insignia pavilion to the west. Although by no means modest in scale, the constellation of rooms in the Peterhof palace is imposing in arrangement than the grand enfilade at Tsarskoe Selo.[28]

The creation of the luxuriant interior at Peterhof demanded not only a large workforce of craftsmen, but also the subsequent collaboration of the architect Vallin de la Mothe in the 1760s.[29] In the 1770s, Georg Veldten redid much of the interior to suit Catherine's

tastes, but a number of the major rooms, such as the Great Hall retained much of Rastrelli's work. In addition to the characteristic use of plaster ornament, gilded rococo details, and mirrors – still preserved in the Ladies-in-Waiting, or Audience, Hall – the interior also contained ceiling paintings on allegorical themes, most notably by Bartolomeo Tarsia in the Portrait Hall and the Ballroom, and a series of painted oval portraits by Giuseppe Valeriani in the Ballroom.[30] (After their almost total destruction during World War II, many of the rooms have been reconstructed with most, if not all, of their interior decoration.)

If in the simplicity of its form, the main palace at Peterhof represents Rastrelli's homage to an earlier manifestation of the Russian baroque, his succeeding palaces express the spirit of Elizabeth's reign: extrav-

agant in design and execution, yet ordered by the rhythmic insistence of massed columns and baroque statuary. At Tsarskoe Selo, the major rebuilding of the earlier palace by Braunstein coincided with the beginning of the reign of Elizabeth, who had spend much of the 1730s there. Zemtsov, who with his assistant Ivan Blank built the Church of the Icon of the Sign at Tsarskoe Selo in the mid–1730s, began to enlarge the palace in 1741. After his death in 1743, the project was entrusted to the young Andrei Kvasov, who completed structural work on the end wings, linked to the central building by a wooden gallery in the form of a colonnade. In 1745, Kvasov also began work on the Circumference, a single-story enclosure that contained service quarters and framed the main entrance to the palace – which in Rastrelli's plan was

Figure 300. Main palace, Peterhof. Interior. (P 115–36)

Architect to the court was in charge of all palace construction, took over direct control of work at Tsarskoe Selo with the purpose of creating a palace on a scale befitting a major European power (the commemorative medal struck by Rastrelli on the rebuilding of the palace proclaimed "for the Glory of Russia").

To this end, Rastrelli demolished much of Chevakinskii's completed work (particularly the galleries) and added a third story to the main structure, which was extended the full length of the palace. The initial elegant design appropriate to a country palace, with galleries and an orangery, became a display of imperial wealth on an unprecented scale. With thousands of laborers and 400 masons from Iaroslavl, whose brick churches had been the glory of seventeenth-century Russia, Rastrelli oversaw the building and rebuilding of the palace in a process that Catherine the Great called "Penelope's labor. On the next day they destroyed what had been built today. This building was six times razed to the foundation and rebuilt before it reached its present condition."[31] Even allowing for a measure of sardonic hyperbole, the frequent revision and expansion of the palace's plans seems to have been devoid of any constraints usually imposed on architects by the realities of construction – most notably, expense.

As Rastrelli himself described it:

At Sarskoe selo I built a large masonry palace in three floors. . . . This extensive structure contains, in addition to the main apartment, a large gallery with several large reception rooms, a large main staircase, decorated with colonnades and statues, with rich plaster and painted decorations . . . all richly gilded. In addition there is a large room, faced with magnificent work in amber, executed in the city of Berlin and given by the King of Prussia to Peter the Great. . . . The facade of this large palace is decorated with magnificent architecture, all in capitals, columns, pilasters, window pediments, statues, vases, and in general everything gilded up to the balustrade.[32]

"Large," "magnificent," "rich," "gilded" – Rastrelli's apparent hyperbole is in fact a sober portrayal of the opulence that is the palace at Tsarskoe Selo (see Plate 58).

The removal during Catherine's reign of the gilt from much of the exterior impedes an impression of the effect this enormous mass must have produced in Elizabeth's time: gilded atlantes supporting white columns against a turquoise background, surmounted by a golden balustrade – decorated with golden vases and statuary – and culminating in the silver hue of a sheet-iron roof. In the second half of the eighteenth century, such ostentation was viewed

soon to tower above them (Figure 301). In 1745, Savva Chevakinskii, Korobov's brilliant assistant, assumed control of work at Tsarskoe Selo, completed the Circumference, redid the galleries in brick, built a court church on the east wing, balanced by an orangery on the west, and began the reconstruction of the central, masonry structure.

Chevakinskii's version of the Catherine Palace, completed in 1751, retained the basic plan stated by Zemtsov and Kvasov, and characteristic of other imperial estate palaces such as Peterhof: two wings and a central structure connected by galleries. Yet even as the building was completed, it became clear that this design could not accommodate the demands of an empress who saw court ritual as an expression of the majesty of state and who intended to make her beloved Catherine Palace (named, it will be remembered, after her mother) the main imperial residence outside of Petersburg. In 1752, Rastrelli, who as Chief

as the epitome of bad taste, by both Russians – notably Catherine herself – and European visitors. An English traveler, William Coxe, noted: "This palace, which was built by Elizabeth, is a brick edifice stuccoed white; is of disproportionate length, and in a most heavy style of architecture. The capitals of the outside pillars, many other exterior ornaments, and the series of wooden statues which support the cornice and adorn the roof are all gilded and exhibit a most tawdry appearance."[33] Another called it "the Completest triumph of a barbarous taste I have seen in these northern kingdoms."[34]

The palace is indeed of disproportionate length (over 325 meters), and the facade is perhaps best appreciated in fragments, as seen through clearings in the park or from the main palace gates. From this perspective, the palace, with or without gilt, reveals Rastrelli's genius for color and form. Above the rusticated ground floor, with its arcade of French windows separated by atlantes, the building is marked by white attached columns that give the azure facade a depth unknown in his earlier palaces. Despite the symmetry of the facade, its culminating point is not the central structure, but rather the pentacupolar church that anchors the east wing of the palace (Figure 302). The baroque articulation of the gilded cupolas shows an clear resemblance to his design for the Church of St. Andrew in Kiev (1748–62; see Plate 60), yet it also anticipates Rastrelli's sublime union of baroque and Russian Orthodox church architecture at the Smolnyi Convent.

The resolution of the Catherine Palace in favor of its end point (a corresponding domed pavilion on the west end was later modified during the reign of Catherine II) is in accord with the horizontal essence of the structure. This principle was reaffirmed in Rastrelli's plan for the interior (Figure 303), whose main entrance was from the west wing. From that point, two parallel enfilades extended the length of the palace without the interruption of a central cluster of rooms. The later central vestibule and grand stairway, built for Catherine II by Charles Cameron in 1780 and remodeled in 1860 by Ippolit Monighetti, established a midpoint that allows one to proceed to either half of the enfilade; yet the sense of one integral space in the original plan is undiminished.

The dimensions of this axial arrangement are almost beyond comprehension; yet they reflect the horizontal perspectives (*prospekt*) of Petersburg itself, as well as the imperial scale of construction in eighteenth-century Russia. At Tsarskoe Selo, Rastrelli's fondness for placing the main stairway to the side of the structure enabled the design of a series of ante-chambers leading to the Great Hall, 48 meters in length, whose arcades of French windows are interspersed with mirrors and rococo gilt decoration (Figure 304).[35] The combination of natural light and mirrored reflection enlarges the boundaries of the room, for the enormous allegorical ceiling painting (of Russia partaking the bounties of civilization, executed in 1753 by Valeriani) would otherwise weigh heavily on the space. It must be emphasized that the palace interior at Tsarskoe Selo, like that at Peterhof, is a scrupulous reconstruction, itself a heroic task that began almost immediately after World War II, and continues to this day.

In commenting on Rastrelli's rebuilding of Tsarskoe Selo, Boris Vipper has noted that his interiors deny the caprice of the French rocaille, and they also lack "the mystical fog and emotional exaltation" of the German–Austrian baroque.[36] Vipper's interpretation of the tectonic character of the Catherine Palace – pilasters segmenting the walls, with rectilinear and symmetrical ornament – has been supported by the later view that Rastrelli, in contrast to the French rococo, applied the order system to his interiors, and transferred the effusive mannerisms of the rococo to the exterior, thus converting a decorative style into a monumental expression of architecture.[37]

As work continued on the Catherine Palace, Rastrelli was further involved in the creation of the parks and pavilions that played an indispensable role in the ambience of European country palaces. Although the design of the parks lies beyond the subject of this study, the pavilions, by virtue of their compact size and refined decoration, represent some of the most accomplished Russian work in the rococo manner. The largest of these, the Hermitage (Figure 305), was originally designed by Zemtsov in 1743, and the structural work was completed by Chevakinskii and Kvasov in 1746. In 1748, Rastrelli was commissioned to redesign the exterior as well as the interior of the Hermitage. From 1749 to 1753, sculptors, plasterers, and master carpenters labored on the pavilion, which culminated in the ceiling paintings of Valeriani and assistants.

Again, the most appropriate description is by Rastrelli himself: "All the facades were decorated on the outside with statuary between the columns and above the cornice, where there are pedestals for statues and vases; and at the top of the cupolas is a group of figures, all gilded, as are the window surrounds, the pediments, and the balustrade. This splendid building is equipped with a large moat [not extant] and drawbridge, decorated with a magnificent balustrade with pedestals on which are placed statues six feet in

Figure 301. Catherine Palace. Tsarskoe Selo. Architects: Johann Braunstein, Mikhail Zemtsov, Andrei Kvasov, and Savva Chevakinskii. Final version by Bartolomeo Francesco Rastrelli. Courtyard facade, with Circumference (foreground). Engraving from a drawing by M. Makhaev, 1761. Courtesy of the Shchusev State Museum of Architecture, Moscow.

height and completely gilded."[38] It should be added that the central dome was crowned with a sculptural representation of the Abduction of Persephone.

These frequent references to sculpture (none of which has survived at the Hermitage) remind not only of its exceptional importance in Rastrelli's work, but also of a fundamental aspect of the Petrine cultural revolution, which had within a brief period introduced on a large scale the art of fully modeled, classical (and unclothed) statuary. Peter's own collection of Italian marble statues was displayed in the Summer Garden, but the park at Tsarskoe Selo also has a number of statues, imported during the Petrine period, that had formerly graced the grounds of the Menshikov estates.[39] Indeed, Rastrelli placed fully sculpted presentations of angels and cherubim within his church at Tsarskoe Selo.

The plan of the Hermitage consists of a central cube from which extend diagonally four "pods," or satellite rooms, also square in plan. This complex surface configuration is enhanced by Rastrelli's use of paired columns, supporting their own richly carved pediments, at every corner. (A similar device appears in the design of the St. Andrew Church in Kiev; see Plate 60.) The interior displayed the characteristic Rastrelli combination of mirrors and French windows, framed by elaborate gilt work.[40] The Hermitage was situated within a grove on the palace grounds, and the expansive view of the foliage through large, richly decorated window frames epitomized the juxtaposition of brilliant artifice with the natural setting in baroque country palaces.

The one pavilion at Tsarskoe Selo that was originally Rastrelli's design is the Grotto (Figure 306), begun in 1749, but completed on the interior only in the late 1770s to a design by Antonio Rinaldi. Located on

240

the edge of the Large Pond, the Grotto ultimately served as a sculpture gallery for Catherine. On the exterior, playful images of aquatic creatures are superimposed on a textured facade, with rusticated columns. The plan is composed of three rooms of equal size, on a single axis and molded with seashells and porous tufa. The formal garden shapes the perception of the pavilion as one approaches, unfolding its inventive stucco work.

Mon Bijou, the third of the major baroque pavilions at Tsarskoe Selo, was completely rebuilt in the pseudo-Gothic style – and renamed the Arsenal – by Adam Menelaws during the first decade of Nicholas I's reign, and thus we have only limited visual or documentary evidence (Figure 307) of its glory as one of the greatest monuments of the Russian baroque.[41] Mon Bijou was designed by Savva Chevakinskii in 1747 as a hunting lodge situated in the middle of the

Tsarskoe Selo game preserve (now occupied by the Alexander Park). As at the Hermitage, Rastrelli took the project to its completion, in 1754, but introduced far fewer changes into the original design, which consisted of a central, two-story octagon with 4 one-story rooms extended on intersecting diagonals. Rastrelli raised the octagonal dome and added a small cupola with a statue of trumpeting fame at the top. Other statues were placed along balustrades on the promenade extending from the second story, on the baroque exterior stairway, and around the pavilion at the edge of the moat that surrounded it. All of the statues were, of course, gilded. In terms of the complex rhythm of spatial forms and the highly refined decorative conceits – displayed within an intricate and clipped formal park – Mon Bijou was the quintessential late baroque monument in Russia. Yet the virtues of its miniature and compact design were to be su-

241

Figure 302. Catherine Palace. Tsarskoe Selo. Park facade, with palace church on far right. (TS 5–37)

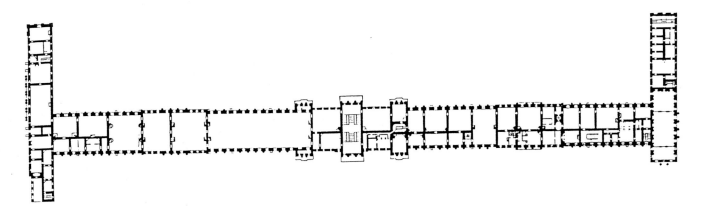

Figure 303. Catherine Palace. Tsarskoe Selo. Plan.

Figure 304. Catherine Palace. Tsarskoe Selo. Great Hall. (TS 1–21)

perceded during the final years of Elizabeth's reign by construction on the more typical Russian scale.

Rastrelli in Petersburg: The Winter Palace

Concurrently with his work on the imperial estates near Petersburg,[42] Rastrelli was engaged in the design of a series of palaces in the city itself that represent the final stage in his interpretation of the baroque. The first of these was begun in 1749 for Count Mikhail Vorontsov, one of the leaders of the coup that brought Elizabeth to power. Not unexpectedly, Vorontsov was rewarded with high positions in government (notably Vice-Chancellor and, from 1758, Chancellor) that gave him both influence and the means to procure great wealth, much of which he expended on his palatial residence. In this enterprise, he no doubt had the support of Elizabeth, who released her distinguished court architect to work on the project.[43] Nonetheless, financial difficulties impeded progress on the palace, which was completed only in 1758 with the conse-

cration of the domestic church and a housewarming ceremony attended by the empress.

Like the nearby Anichkov Palace, occupied by Aleksei Razumovskii, the Vorontsov mansion was located on the Fontanka, but its main facade was turned away from the canal and toward the newly fashionable Sadovyi (Garden) Street. The site plan (Figure 308) included a large courtyard before the main structure, with wings projecting on either side toward the street, separated from the ensemble by a cast-iron fence designed by Rastrelli. On the Fontanka side, a formal park with fountains extended to the canal. Although lacking the brilliant bichromatic contrasts characteristic of Rastrelli's work, the facade is richly textured with paired columns supporting an interrupted entablature and cornices (Figure 308). With the accession of Catherine the Great in 1762, a number of Elizabethan favorites, such as Vorontsov, were removed from – or asked to be relieved of – the onerous duties of high office. Unable to maintain their city palaces, they typically relinquished them to new grandees or, eventually, to the state treasury. Whatever the circumstances, most were remodeled to a significant degree on both the exterior and particularly the interior, as was the case with the Vorontsov Palace, which in 1810 was given to the imperial institution of the Corps des Pages.[44]

Fortunately, Rastrelli's greatest palace for a private individual survived relatively intact, as did the fortunes of the Stroganovs who commissioned it and remained there until 1917. Not only did the Stroganov clan possess fabulous wealth, dating to the fifteenth century and greatly expanded in the sixteenth and seventeenth centuries with the exploitation of salt mines and foundaries in the Urals, but they were also related by marriage to the empress – as was Vorontsov. Here, again, Elizabeth made available Rastrelli's services; but Baron Sergei Stroganov, unlike Vorontsov, had ample means to pay for the construction of his palace, which was completed in slightly over two years, from 1752 to 1754. Although small in comparison with the imperial palaces, the Stroganov residence (Figure 309) displays a command of the relation between structure and decoration, particularly in the articulation of the window surrounds. They are a marvel of ingenuity on both the Nevskii Prospekt and Moika Canal facades, as well as on the interior courtyard (Figure 310). Due to a considerable rise in the street level along the Nevskii facade, the proportions of the structure seem flatter than in the original design, yet the palace retains the dynamic quality admirably suited to the Stroganov motto: "Life in Energy."

In plan, the Stroganov Palace is constructed on the perimeter of its lot (Figure 311), bounded by Nevskii Prospekt and the Moika (the building code for the prospekt required construction flush with the street line). In addition, Stroganov himself stipulated that the Moika facade – often viewed as the "side" – should be as imposing as that facing the prospekt.[45] Indeed, Rastrelli surpassed the latter by creating a complex yet balanced grouping of attached columns, cornice, and pediment on the piano nobile overlooking the canal. Because of the unusual perimeter design, however, the design of the interior courtyard also assumed a special importance. Upon entering from Nevskii Prospekt through the large wooden gates – decorated with Rastrelli's signature, the baroque lion masks – one is in the midst of a protected space, which, although not as grand as either of the street facades, contains some of his most elaborate stucco decorative work (see Figure 310).[46]

In the early 1790s, much of the palace interior was destroyed by fire. Although the Stroganovs were fortunate to have the rooms redesigned by one of the greatest Russian architects, their own freed serf Andrei Voronikhin, most of the baroque interior work was lost. Therefore, we must draw upon Rastrelli's own words to summon an impression of the original design for a "three-story palace belonging to Baron Stroganov":

> The number of apartments consists of fifty rooms, including a great hall, decorated with stucco work by very skilled Italian masters. In addition there is a gallery decorated with mirrors and gilded sculpture, with ceilings in some of the apartments painted by Italian artists. The grand staircase is richly decorated with plaster work, and gilded iron railings. . . . The two main facades are decorated with splendid architecture in the Italian manner.[47]

The frequent references to Italian work and the Italian manner suggest that the northern European baroque, which had manifold connections to Italian architecture, had been supplanted in Russia by a direct perception of Italy as an inexhaustible source of architectural style and as an ultimate authority in the definition of proper architecture. Architects in eighteenth-century Russia – regardless of their national origin – developed a distinctive, inimitable interpretation of Italian prototypes in all of their variety. Indeed, by the time Rastrelli wrote the previous passage, the Italian style had already acquired a new connotation, oriented toward classical architecture and antipathetic to his use of the baroque. It would seem that incipient elements of the neoclassical style are already present in the design of Rastrelli's grandest work – a presence that may explain both the tension inherent in the structure and its ultimate success.

Figure 305. Hermitage. Tsarskoe Selo. 1743–53. Architects: Mikhail Zemtsov, Savva Chevakinskii, and Bartolomeo Francesco Rastrelli. (TS 4–28)

Figure 306. Grotto. Tsarskoe Selo. 1749. Architect: Bartolomeo Francesco Rastrelli. (TS 5–33)

Figure 307. Mon Bijou. Tsarskoe Selo. 1747–54. Architects: Savva Chevakinskii and Bartolomeo Francesco Rastrelli. Engraving from a drawing by M. Makhaev, 1761. Courtesy of the Shchusev State Museum of Architecture, Moscow.

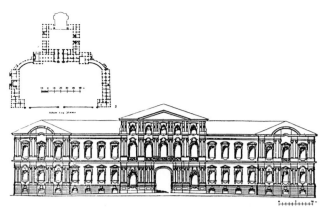

Figure 308. Vorontsov Palace. Petersburg. 1749–58. Architect: Bartolomeo Francesco Rastrelli. Plan and elevation by A. Shelkovnikov.

In approaching the horizontal mass of the Winter Palace, the last of Rastrelli's imperial residences, it must first be remembered that the architect operated under constraints similar to those imposed at Peterhof and Tsarskoe Selo: to incorporate a very large existing structure (in this case Rastrelli's own, Third, Winter Palace) into the design of a still larger work, staggering in both size and cost. Indeed, it is a telling comment on the state of Elizabeth's finances that the 859,555 rubles originally allotted for construction of the Winter Palace were to be drawn, in a scheme devised by her courtier Peter Shuvalov, from the revenues of state-licensed pothouses – frequented, no doubt, by Rastrelli's army of laborers, most of whom earned a monthly wage of 1 ruble. Despite the huge sums designated for the Winter Palace, cost overruns were chronic, and work was occasionally halted for lack of materials and money at a time when Russia's

Figure 309. Stroganov Palace. Petersburg. 1752–4. Architect: Bartolomeo Francesco Rastrelli. (P 79–31)

Figure 310. Stroganov Palace. Petersburg. Courtyard facade, window surround. (P 11)

resources were strained to the limit by involvement in the Seven Years' War (1756–63). Ultimately, the project cost some 2.5 million rubles, drawn from the alcohol and salt taxes placed on an already burdened population. Yet for all of Elizabeth's apparent caprices and the problems inherent in a project whose complexities strained the limits of rationality, Rastrelli's genius succeeded in creating not only one of the last major Baroque buildings in Europe, but also – in light of subsequent events – one of the central monuments in the history of the modern world.

Preliminary discussions for the creation of a new, fourth, Winter Palace began in the early 1750s, and by 1753, Rastrelli had submitted the final variant of his plan for the building.[48] As construction proceeded during 1754, Rastrelli concluded that the new palace would involve not simply an expansion of the old, but would have to be built over its foundations, thus necessitating the razing of the previous structure – a

246

step the empress was initially reluctant to take. (In removing Elizabeth from her palace, the architect had also to design and build a temporary wooden residence, a large one-story structure located on Nevskii Prospekt and completed by the fall of 1755.[49])

Rastrelli had no hope of meeting Elizabeth's unrealistic expectations for constructing the Winter Palace within 2 years, yet he exerted his considerable experience and talent in directing the vast project, organized to a degree unprecedented even in Petersburg. Although construction continued year round, despite the severe winters, and although the empress – who viewed completion of the palace as a matter of state prestige during the Seven Years War – continued to issue orders for its completion and requests for supplemental appropriations, Elizabeth did not live to see the completion of her greatest commission. She died in the temporary palace on December 25, 1761. The main state rooms and imperial apartments were ready soon the following year for Tsar Peter III and his wife Catherine. For his services, Rastrelli was granted the rank of major general, and presented with one of the tsar's own decorations (from Holstein) – but no financial reward. Peter is reported to have said that he himself needed the money.[50]

The plan of the Winter Palace resembles, albeit on a far greater scale, the perimeter concept of the Stroganov Palace, with a quadrilateral interior courtyard decorated in a manner similar to the outer walls (Figure 312). Yet the intimate scale of the Stroganov Palace is entirely lacking. The exterior facades of the new imperial palace – three of which are turned toward great public spaces – can only be compared to those of the Catherine Palace at Tsarskoe Selo. On the river facade, the palace presents from a distance an uninterrupted horizontal sweep of over 200 meters (Figure 313), whereas the Palace Square facade (Figure 314) is marked in the center by the three arches of the main courtyard entrance, immortalized by Sergei Eisenstein as well as numerous lesser artists who portrayed the largely fictive "storming of the Winter Palace." The facade overlooking the Admiralty is the one area of the structure that contains substantial elements of the previous palace walls; and the decorative detailing of its central part of the facade, flanked by two wings, reflects the earlier mannerisms of Rastrelli's style.

Although a strict symmetry reigns in the articulation of the facades, each has its own formulation in the design of pediments and the spacing of attached columns, whose distribution provides an insistent rhythm to the horizontal expanse.[51] The 250 columns segment some 700 windows (not including those of

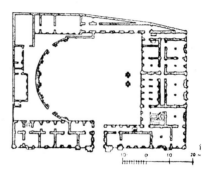

Figure 311. Stroganov Palace. Petersburg. Plan.

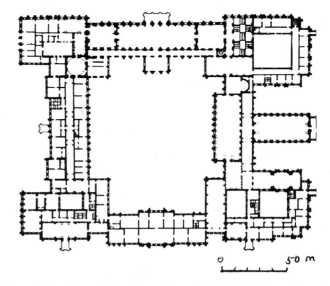

Figure 312. Winter Palace. Petersburg. 1754–64. Architect: Bartolomeo Francesco Rastrelli. Plan.

the interior court), whose surrounds are decorated in twenty different patterns reflecting the array of ornamental motifs – including lion masks and other grotesque figures – accumulated by Rastrelli over a period of three decades. The three main floors of the Winter Palace are situated over a basement level, whose semicircular window surrounds establish an arcade effect that is followed in the tiers of windows above. The horizontal dimensions of the palace are emphasized by a string course separating the two upper floors from the first, and by the complex profile of the cornice, above which is a balustrade supporting 176 large ornamental vases and allegorical statues.

Changes have inevitably occurred in the structure and decoration of the Winter Palace. Above the balustrade, the stone statuary, corroded by Petersburg's harsh weather, was replaced in the 1890s by copper figures; and the sandy color originally intended for the stucco facade has vanished over the years under

Figure 313. Winter Palace. Petersburg. Neva facade, with the Small Hermitage, the Old Hermitage, and the Hermitage Theater in the distance. (P 15–2, 3)

a series of paints ranging from dull red (applied in the late nineteenth century) to the present green (see Plate 59), which is lighter than that used for the Stroganov Palace.[52]

The interior of the Winter Palace, with its more than 700 rooms, has undergone far greater modifications. Rastrelli's original designs used decorative devices similar to those of his earlier palaces: gilded plasters and wooden ornamentation, elaborate pilasters to segment the walls of large spaces such as the Throne Room, and intricate parquetry for the floors.[53] Yet little of Rastrelli's rococo interior decoration has survived. Work on so elaborate a space was to continue for several decades, as rooms were changed and refitted to suit the tastes of Catherine the Great and her successors. And in 1837 the palace interior was destroyed by a fire that burned unchecked for over 2 days. During the reconstruction, most of the rooms were decorated in eclectic styles of the midnineteenth century or restored to the neoclassical style used by Rastrelli's successors in decorating the Winter Palace, such as Giacomo Quarenghi.[54] Only the main, or Jordan, staircase and the corridor leading to it (the Ras-

trelli Gallery; Figure 315) were restored by Vasilii Stasov in the manner of Rastrelli's original design.

For all of its modifications, the final version of the Winter Palace remains the great expression of imperial Russian architecture and of the autocratic state that willed its construction. Authority is connoted by the very scale of the building, whose horizontal lines are segmented by the repetition of column and statuary.[55] From the classical perspective, the ornament and much of the statuary seem superfluous on a structure whose mass is antithetical to the complexities of the baroque.[56] Nonetheless, the Winter Palace is admirably situated to display at greatest advantage qualities that might otherwise seem ponderous. The south facade, with the main entrance, opens onto a vast square, contained and completed by the genius of another imperial architect, Carlo Rossi (see Chapter 11); and on the north, the palace fronts the Neva, whose broad expanse – whether of ice or water – provides a setting commensurate with architecture of the grand design.[57] Whatever its faults, the Winter Palace represents the quintessence of Saint Petersburg's monumental style, an assimilation of western

principles applied in a manner and on a scale uniquely Russian.

Late Baroque Church Architecture

For all the grandeur of Rastrelli's palaces, the spirit of the late baroque in Russia is most fully expressed in the design of churches, particularly those by Rastrelli and Savva Chevakinskii. Although the confluence of secular and sacred architecture characteristic of the design of Petrine churches continued in certain ways – particularly in the decorative mannerisms applied to the churches – there was during the reign of Elizabeth a noticeable movement away from western basilical models and a return to traditional forms such as the centralized, pentacupolar plan. It would be unwise to exaggerate the specific nationalist component of this revival, yet there is little doubt that Elizabeth benefited politically from a perception of her support of traditional Russian ways, after the preponderance of German advisers and manners during the reign of Anne. Church architecture again became

a demonstrative expression of the connection between autocrat and subjects.

One of the earliest examples of this final stage of Russian baroque church architecture appears not in Russia proper, but in Kiev, which in the eighteenth century served as the spiritual capital of the Ukraine, or "Little Russia." The Ukraine had developed its own forms of church architecture during the seventeenth century, many of which churches are related to forms of the baroque in central Europe. Yet Rastrelli's design for the Church of St. Andrew is entirely an imported design, similar to the court church at Peterhof. The idea for the church occurred during Elizabeth's grand tour in 1744 of the native land of her lover (and perhaps morganatic husband) Aleksei Razumovskii. Enchanted by what she saw of Kiev, Elizabeth commissioned the building of a church overlooking the Dnieper River near a site associated with the legendary visit of the Apostle Andrew to Rus.

The initial project, submitted in 1745 by Schädel (who had resettled in Kiev after his work in Petersburg) was rejected, and Elizabeth assigned the project to Rastrelli, who had undertaken a series of major

Figure 314. Winter Palace. Petersburg. Palace Square facade. (P 77–6)

projects for her and could not afford to remain in Kiev to oversee construction. His approved plan was therefore entrusted in 1748 to one of the most talented of the new Moscow architects, Ivan Michurin, who coped valiantly with problems such as the water-soaked slope of the hill and finished the basic structure in 1753 (the decoration was not completed until 1767).[58] Michurin excavated much of the site and in effect created a three-story pedastal (used to house the clergy) from which rose Rastrelli's magnificently sculpted baroque church (see Plate 60). Indeed, the body of the church itself seems primarily a setting for the great central dome, which reminds of the sixteenth-century Muscovite tower churches, yet also of the pavilions designed at Tsarskoe Selo by Chevakinskii and Rastrelli.

The four flanking cupolas of this unusual variant of the pentacupolar design are placed not on drums above the vaulting of the church, but on clusters of free-standing Corinthian columns that in turn rest on pylons wedged within the corners of the cruciform structure (Figure 316). The pylons, which buttress the walls and in effect support the large dome, are decorated with paired Corinthian columns placed on high pedestals. The order of the columns is reproduced at the same height by the capitals of the pilasters on the facade of the church. In a recent restoration, all of the cast-iron capitals and certain other decorative elements have been gilded – as Rastrelli apparently stipulated.[59]

Rastrelli's daring, if somewhat impractical, plan for St. Andrews reflected the aesthetic of the baroque pavilion, and was constructed on a similar scale. The more remarkable accomplishment was his translation of this aesthetic to a much larger frame, without losing the sense of a cohesive, sculpted form illuminated by exuberant decoration. This culmination of his work occurred with the design of the Cathedral of the Resurrection at the Resurrection Newmaiden Convent – commonly known as the Smolnyi (from the Russian for "tar") because of its location near the site where tar had been stored for Peter's navy. This questionable

Figure 315. Winter Palace. Petersburg. Rastrelli Gallery. (L 81–37)

Monastery. The large square perimeter of the convent contained enclosed galleries linking the living and administrative quarters, as well as churches placed at the four corners. The center of the compound was, of course, occupied by the cathedral, which the empress specified to be built along the lines of the Cathedral of the Dormition in the Moscow Kremlin: a cross-domed plan with five cupolas. The reign of Elizabeth thus marks the resurgence of the traditional Russian Orthodox plan, however modified by western influence.[60] In addition, the entrance to the convent was to support a colossal bell tower, between 140 and 170 meters in height (depending on the variant design), constructed in a manner of ascending tiers derived from the bell tower of Ivan the Great (also in the Kremlin), but at least twice its height.

Construction proceeded slowly: After Elizabeth's approval in 1749 of the plan submitted by Rastrelli, 7 years (1750–6) were required for the completion of a detailed model – itself an example of the Russian genius for woodworking – but by 1760, the exterior of the cathedral had assumed its final shape. Because of technical difficulties, construction delays, and the enormous cost, the Smolnyi Convent was never completed as Rastrelli, or Elizabeth, had intended. In particular, work on the bell tower, which might have proved one of the most extraordinary of eighteenth-

association did not deter Elizabeth, who wished to found not only a convent, but also an institute suitably removed from the city for the education of young noblewomen. Indeed, there may have been a personal motive for the empress, who combined pleasure with piety, and wished to retire to a convent with a luxurient ambience that Rastrelli so thoroughly understood. There is a happy irony in Elizabeth's support of the project, because the threat of exile to a convent precipitated the coup that brought her to power in 1742. Furthermore, her establishment of this institution, whose magnificence was widely publicized, provided a highly visible means of demonstrating her support for the Russian Church.

Work on the foundations for the cathedral and the conventual buildings began in 1748, as shifts of soldiers (as many as 2,000) dug trenches and drove some 50,000 four- and twelve-meter piles into the marshy soil along the Neva. At this preliminary stage, Rastrelli submitted variants of a plan (Figure 317) that resembled Trezzini's design for the Alexander Nevskii

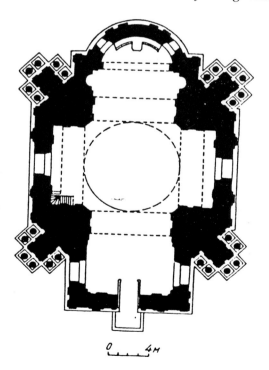

Figure 316. Church of St. Andrew. Kiev. 1748–67. Architects: Bartolomeo Francesco Rastrelli and Ivan Michurin. Plan.

251

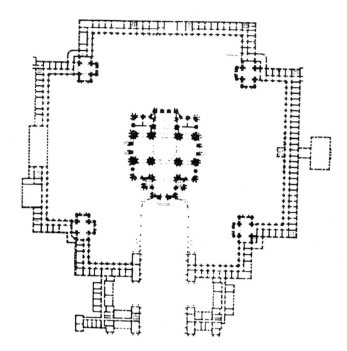

Figure 317. Resurrection (Smolnyi) Convent. Petersburg. 1748–64. Architect: Bartolomeo Francesco Rastrelli. Plan.

whose elongated single domes appear from a distance to be extensions of the main structure.

When viewed from the front, the corners of the successive planes that comprise the west facade – marked by pilasters and clusters of columns – advance toward the entrance portal and provide a suitably imposing base for the great dome, which rises to a height of almost 100 meters. The side facades present a more even, unified plane, with only a portal to mark the center of the luxuriant plaster decoration of the facade. As usual for the design of baroque churches in Petersburg, the apse is not given a major structural role, and is only slightly visible as a rectangular projection on the east facade. Also characteristic of baroque architecture in Russia is the use of color – in this case, white on a pastel-blue stucco facade – to delineate the building's structural and decorative elements. As a final touch, the crosses that soar above the five cupolas are mounted on golded orbs, whose

century engineering achievements, was halted with the onset of the Seven Years War (the empress's own palace was threatened by the cost of that war). After Elizabeth's death at the end of 1761, the bell tower was eliminated from the plan. The convent was completed only in 1764 under the direction of Georg Friedrich Veldten, and the cathedral interior was not decorated until the 1830s in a neoclassical style by Vasilii Stasov that bears little relation to Rastrelli's intention (Figure 318).

Rastrelli's design of the cathedral exterior, however, reveals the ingenuity with which he fused eastern and western elements. The four subsidiary cupolas, placed on double-tiered towers, are grouped around a central dome supporting the fifth cupola, in a pattern derived from the Russian pentacupolar church; yet their placement and design, as well as the form of the ribbed dome, are reminiscent of Borromini and the seventeenth-century Roman baroque (Figure 319). Nonetheless, the tightly integrated, monolithic mass of the central and subsidiary domes is related to two of the greatest of medieval Russian monuments – the Kremlin Dormition Cathedral and the Novgorod St. Sophia. (In his model of the structure, Rastrelli had placed the flanking cupolas at a visible distance from the central dome.) The vertical thrust of the cathedral is echoed by four corner chapels (Figure 320),

Figure 318. Cathedral of the Resurrection, Smolnyi Convent. 1748–64. Petersburg. Section by Rastrelli, showing the original rococo design for the interior. Reproduced in *Zodchii Rastrelli,* by Iu. M. Denisov and A. N. Petrov.

252

Figure 319. Cathedral of the Resurrection, Smolnyi Convent. Petersburg. West facade. (P 58–32)

Figure 320. Cathedral of the Resurrection, Smolnyi Convent. Petersburg. Northeast corner church. Southwest view. (P 58–78)

surface, in the proper light, glows with a celestial radiance (see Plate 61).

The one baroque church in Petersburg to rival Rastrelli's design at Smolnyi is the Cathedral of St. Nicholas, built in 1753–62 by Savva Chevakinskii, whose previous accomplishments had included extensive work on the imperial estates. Neither this nor his other works would be sufficient to proclaim him the first native Russian architect of genius in the eighteenth century. Nor would they materially distinguish him from Zemtsov, Korobov (Chevakinskii's mentor), and a few others who contributed to the rapid assimilation of western architecture, but cannot be considered among the best architects at work in Russia during the first half of the century. Chevakinskii can, on the basis of the St. Nicholas Cathedral.

The location of this azure structure, with white trim and golden domes (see Plate 62), is one of the most picturesque in Petersburg, near the intersection of the Catherine and Kriukov canals. The design of the cathedral combines a rigorous and finely calculated symmetry with an assured handling of profuse baroque decoration. Its plan can be classified as cruci-

form, with a single bay inserted within each corner of the cross (Figure 321). Although there are variations in the ornamental work on the separate facades – particularly the east, or apsidal facade – the north, south, and west are strongly centered by the triple Corinthian columns that frame the portal. These columns lead to a semicircular pediment with elaborate stucco decorative work that seems to exhaust the possibilities of cherubic faces. Indeed, the entablature of the main structure approaches that of the classical system of orders, broken by the gleeful bursts of cherubim on the capitals and by botanical ornament instead of triglyphs. Chevakinskii's design emphasizes the horizontal, in contrast to the verticality of the cathedral at Smolnyi. Its superbly proportioned central dome does not dominate the four widely spaced subsidiary domes, which gain spatial autonomy at the corners of the structure (they rest on the four "inserted" bays within the arms of the cruciform plan).

On the interior, the portals give access to a ground-level "winter" church, above which is the main church, brilliantly lit and of spacious proportions (Figure 321). It is reached by stairways in the two west corner bays,

253

Figure 321. Cathedral of St. Nicholas. Petersburg. Plan and section.

each of which is illuminated by its cupola drum. Chevakinskii calculated the relation between structure, function, and decoration as skilfully as any medieval Russian master; and he had the fortune, denied Rastrelli at Smolnyi, to implement his own design for the interior, whose centerpiece is a wooden iconostasis, intricately carved and decorated with baroque and classical elements.[61]

Chevakinskii's combination of tradition and innovation are perhaps most effectively stated in the cathedral's splendid bell tower (see Plate 63; Figure 322). Since the seventeenth century, bell towers were usually attached to the west structure of Russian churches, yet the traditional separate bell tower was still viable. Chevakinskii placed a free-standing tower on a direct axis with the west entrance of his cathedral, but at a distance of some 30 meters. Poised over the Kriukov Canal, the tower not only provides the vertical dominant that is muted in the structure itself, but also marks the west facade and the main entrance (the major street to the cathedral leads to its north facade). The St. Nicholas Cathedral and its bell tower comprise one of the most sublime monuments of the Russian baroque, yet they contain incipient elements of the coming neoclassical age, which will create its own masterpieces of church architecture in Petersburg.

Chevakinskii also designed palaces for such luminaries as P. B. Sheremetev, son of Peter the Great's fieldmarshal Boris Sheremetev. In a typical Petersburg pattern, a wooden house built by the elder in the 1710s, was replaced in the late 1730s by a brick mansion, which was in turn completely rebuilt by Chevakinskii in 1750–5 in the manner of Rastrelli's early work.[62] More elegant, and closer in style to the Stroganov Palace, was the palace that he built in 1753–5 for Ivan Shuvalov, one of the most cultured of Elizabeth's advisors.[63] (Both of these residences under-

went several modifications in the late eighteenth and nineteenth centuries.)

The Late Baroque in Moscow

Although in the middle of the eighteenth century, Petersburg continued to receive the greater share of building resources, both in terms of talent and money, Moscow had begun to reclaim its position as a major center of architecture. The wooden palaces built by Rastrelli for the Empress Anne proved short-lived (the Summer Annenhof was dismantled beginning in 1744 and his winter palace burned in 1753), yet they had signaled the presence of a mature baroque style in the ancient capital. The 1739 Moscow city plan (Figure 323), completed by Ivan Michurin, provided the first accurate topographical survey of the city; and in 1742, the imperial government issued an ukase concerning the regulation of construction in Moscow, which, like Petersburg, had suffered a devastating fire in 1737. In addition, Ivan Blank, one of the most accomplished local architects, was appointed to the newly created position as supervisory architect in Moscow. The ar-

Figure 322. Cathedral of St. Nicholas. Petersburg. Bell tower. (P 14–1)

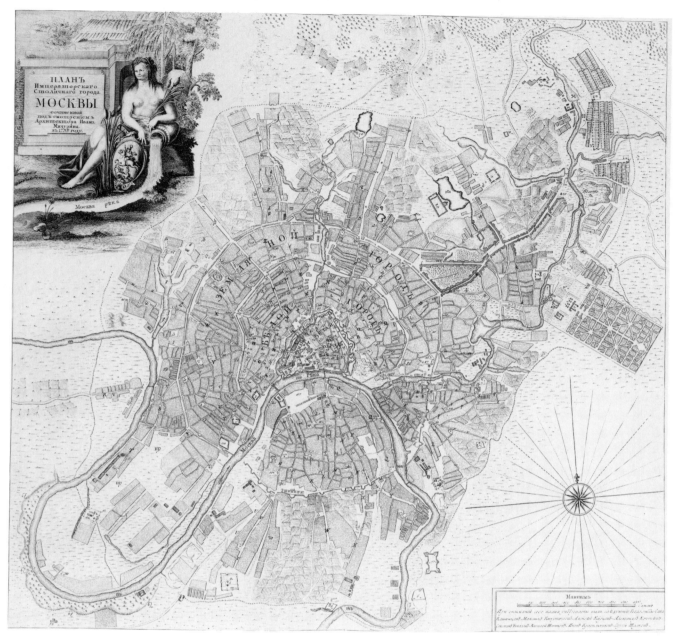

Figure 323. Plan of Moscow, 1739. Compiled by Ivan Michurin. By permission of the Houghton Library, Harvard University.

rival of Ivan Korobov from Petersburg in 1741 further enlarged the possibilities for developing a local architectural school. Indeed, the workshops of Michurin and Korobov (both of whom had studied in Holland) served as Moscow's closest equivalent to formal training for builders, and it was they who produced the greatest architect of the late baroque in Moscow – Dmitrii Ukhtomskii (1719–74).

With the death of Blank in 1745 and the ill health of Korobov, Ukhtomskii was appointed supervisory architect, and over the next two decades labored heroically to bring the city into a semblance of order. No project was too prosaic, and for that reason, much of his work has either disappeared or remained unnoticed: government buildings (some in the Kremlin), commercial structures (including a number near his Kuznetskii Bridge and in Kitai-gorod), stables, "eateries," fire stations, as well as widened streets and renovated city walls, monasteries, and churches.[64] Among the more elevated of his projects was the Red Gates (Figure 324), built on Miasnitskii Street in 1753–

Figure 324. The Red Gates (not extant). Moscow. 1753–7. Architect: Dimtrii Ukhtomskii. Photograph c. 1900.

7 as a triumphal point of entry for Elizabeth during a state visit to Moscow. The baroque statuary and ornament of this structure – extant until the 1930s – did not detract from its heroic design and scale (26 meters to the top of the trumpeting angel).[65] Ukhtomskii is also thought to have built one church in Moscow, the baroque Church of St. Nikita the Martyr (1751–2) on Basman Street (Figure 325).

His greatest achievement, however, lay in the design of bell towers, and most particularly the main tower at the Trinity–St. Sergius Monastery. This structure, 88 meters in height, organizes its surrounding architectural space (see Plate 64) even more thoroughly than does the Kremlin bell tower of Ivan the Great. The original version, by Ivan Shumacher, stipulated only three tiers. Work began in 1741 under the supervision of Michurin, whose departure for Kiev in 1747 (to implement Rastrelli's design for the St. Andrew church) enabled Ukhtomskii to assume control of the project. Although continuing to build to the stipulated height, he reinforced the large two-story base of the tower in order to support a substantial increase in height that he deemed necessary. During the visit of Elizabeth to the monastery in 1753, Ukhtomskii submitted his plan for an additional two tiers and gained the imperial assent. The structure was completed in 1758, but the installation and decoration of the tower continued until 1770.[66]

Ukhtomskii's decision to increase the height was entirely appropriate, both in terms of the structure itself and its relation to the rich environment of buildings dating from the three centuries. The strength of the tower is visually expressed with the use in the lower two tiers of paired columns that mediate between the massive pilasters of the base and the single attached columns that frame the uppermost tiers (Figure 326). The contrast between the shadowed openings for the bells and the brilliance of the white stucco trim and gilded baroque cupola offers an instructive comparison with the much simpler resolution of the Kremlin bell tower. Each establishes a clear tectonic hierarchy that can be related to the system of architectural orders without reproducing it.[67]

The ability of the Moscow architectural tradition to successfully assimilate the baroque style suggests hidden affinities established in the parallel evolution of architecture in Muscovy and the west since the Renaissance. The convergence of the two cultures is most clearly revealed in projects such as the restoration of the Resurrection Cathedral at the New Jerusalem Monastery (see Chapter 7). After the collapse of the large roof over the Nikon rotunda in 1723, various plans for its reconstruction were submitted

Figure 325. Church of St. Nikita the Martyr. Moscow. 1751–2. Architect: Dmitrii Ukhtomskii. (M 121–5)

by Moscow architects such as Michurin and Aleksei Evlashev; but the project ultimately fell to Rastrelli, who devised a magnificent wooden conical roof with three tiers of dormer windows, framed in white surrounds, that flood the elaborately carved and painted interior of the dome with light (see Plate 39).[68] This bold fusion of classical, baroque, and Muscovite – evident above all in the general resemblance to the Russian "tent" roof, but also containing references to the coffered ceiling of the Pantheon – suggests, in a manner very different from the Smolnyi cathedral, the genius of Rastrelli in extracting and recombining the distinctive elements of such diverse architectural traditions.

The actual implementation of Rastrelli's design was entrusted to Karl Ivanovich Blank, who by the time of its completion in 1760 had established a flourishing career of his own that spanned the transition between the baroque and the neoclassical. Blank's work at the suburban estate of Kuskovo will be noted in the following chapter; but his design for the Church of the Savior at the Vorontsov estate of Voronovo (south of

Figure 326. Bell tower of the Trinity St. Sergius Monastery. Zagorsk. 1741–58. Architect: Dmitrii Ukhtomskii. South view. (Y 5–28)

Figure 327. Church of the Savior at Voronovo. 1760s. Architect: Karl Blank. Northwest view. (MR 4–38)

Figure 328. Church of St. Clement. Moscow. 1762–70 (?). Architect:
Pietro Antonio Trezzini. Southwest view. (M 34)

258

Figure 329. Apraksin mansion. Moscow. Mideighteenth century. (M 89–9)

Moscow) deserves inclusion here as a late manifestation of baroque church architecture. Constructed probably in the 1760s, the church (Figure 327) displays typical features of the baroque style, with an emphasis on plasticity – particularly in the rounded corner bays – as well as elaborate stucco decorative work and window surrounds. (Blank, like Chevakinskii, made prolific use of cherabim.) The large drum and dome, with no flanking cupolas, suggest a baroque variant of the traditional Russian tower church. In the free use of the classical orders and the design of the facade pediments, however, Blank acknowledges the neoclassical era even in this deliberate and finely proportioned anachronism.[69] The classical is still more clearly stated in the bell tower, located almost 50 meters from the church and probably constructed at a slightly later date.

Within Moscow itself, the last great monument of baroque religious architecture is the Church of St. Clement (Figure 328), built in 1762–70(?) and attrib-

uted to the Petersburg architect Pietro Antonio Trezzini, although there is no documentary proof of his authorship. Trezzini was involved in the continuation of work at the Alexander Nevskii Monastery; but his most significant Petersburg church was the Transfiguration of the Savior (founded by the elite Preobrazhinskii Guards Regiment), begun in 1743 to a design by Zemtsov. After Zemtsov's death that same year, Trezzini assumed control of the project, which was completed only in 1754. The church, destroyed by fire in 1825 and rebuilt by Vasilii Stasov (see Figure 494), is considered the earliest example of the pentacupolar revival in Petersburg.[70]

In continuing this revival, the Moscow Church of St. Clement displays a compact, monolithic form similar to the Smolnyi cathedral (to which it is also comparable in size); yet the corner cupolas are placed at a greater distance from the large central dome, whose drum is of the same height as those on the diagonal. Although the vertical development is emphatically stated – particularly in the movement from the paired attached columns to the ribs of the central dome – the equality of height among the drums creates the effect of a bipartite structure: a clearly defined base, rising from the rusticated ground floor to the cornice, upon which rest the rotundas of the five drums and cupolas. The St. Clement Church provides another example of the revival of the pentacupolar plan, but its design is distinct from its predecessors by Rastrelli and Chevakinskii, and reveals the inexhaustible variety of a form ultimately derived from Byzantium.

As for domestic architecture in Moscow, the flurry of palace construction at the beginning of the eighteenth century and during the reign of Anne could not alter the city's enduring status as an overgrown village composed primarily of wooden houses or of brick *palaty* built in the pre-Petrine manner. One of the few exceptions was the mansion built for M. F. Apraksin at the Pokrovskii Gates in the northern part of the city. After its purchase by the Trubetskois in the early 1770s, the house was expanded on the wings, but retained the central structure, with its curved baroque facade and stucco decoration (Figure 329). The Apraksin house is in fact the surviving part of an ensemble of masonry houses on Pokrovka Street. Although the row originated in an attempt to regulate construction as prescribed in the Michurin plan for rebuilding Moscow, the individual houses were separated from their neighbors by relatively spacious plots – in contrast to the denser construction along the streets of central Petersburg. (Indeed, the different approaches to the placement of houses would continue to distinguish Moscow from Petersburg until the Soviet period.) Not until the liberation of the Russian gentry from obligatory state service, however, did the wealth of central Russia show itself in a series of remarkable neoclassical mansions.

CHAPTER 10

Neoclassicism in Petersburg: The Age of Catherine the Great

Its exterior does not shine with carving, gilt, and other lavish ornament; an ancient, refined taste is its virtue, simple but majestic.

– Gavriil Derzhavin on the palace of Prince Potemkin in 1790

In the work of Rastrelli and Chevakinskii, the late baroque gave rise to some of the most distinctive monuments in the history of Russian architecture. Yet it was the neoclassical era that ultimately created the ambience of imperial Petersburg and that fashioned of Moscow an appropriate setting for the Russian nobility at the apogee of its power. The formation of the neoclassical has its obvious precedents in western Europe, particularly France and England, and within Russia, it evolved from, as much as rejected, baroque architecture. Although the transition between the two styles produced intermediate forms combining the old and the new, there are, nonetheless, boundaries that clearly mark the displacement of the baroque by the neoclassical. The accession of Catherine II to the throne in 1762 (after the usual murderous intrigue, leading to the death of her husband Peter III) is the most obvious of these boundaries, in both a political and an aesthetic sense. For Catherine, who possessed an abiding interest in architecture, the extravagant tastes of Elizabeth reflected a lack of order and rationality in her conduct of state affairs as well as in the design of her palaces.

But even before the Catherinian era, the turn from baroque extravagance was evident in the design of practical structures in a developing urban environment for which the elaborate, festive statuary and decoration of palaces and churches seemed obviously inappropriate.[1] The most obvious example was the fate of the Gostinnyi Dvor (Merchants' Yard) project, for the rebuilding of the city's main trading complex on Nevskii Prospekt. Initially designed by Rastrelli in 1752 to replace a similar structure destroyed in the 1736 fire, the Gostinnyi Dvor was begun only in 1758 under the severe constraints imposed by the demands of Elizabeth's other mammoth construction projects. Rastrelli's perimeter design for a two-storied trapezoid, arcaded on both the exterior and interior, included extensive stucco decoration and statuary above the cornice.[2] Work on the complex was halted, however, at the end of 1760 and the design was submitted for review.

At this point, the project was revised by Jean-Baptiste Vallin de la Mothe (1729–1800), who arrived in Petersburg in 1759 and was to exert a profound effect on the development of neoclassicism in Russian architecture. Vallin de la Mothe preserved the basic features of Rastrelli's monumental plan, but stripped the design of its statuary in favor of a simple detailing of the structure, whose long arcades and massive porticos were, paradoxically, all the more impressively revealed (Figure 330). The classical element appeared most explicitly in the use of Doric columns to frame the entrances. Even with these simplifications, the structure, whose cost was borne by the merchants who used it, was not completed until 1785.[3]

Following the death of Elizabeth, Rastrelli's career suffered a further and irreversible decline. He had received the Order of St. Anne from Peter III and promotion to Major General at the beginning of 1762, but after the death of the emperor in July of that year, Ivan Betskoi replaced Rastrelli as director of imperial construction and granted him leave to go to Italy with his family for an extended vacation. Although Rastrelli returned the following year, he had in effect been given a polite dismissal, which was formalized with

Figure 330. Gostinnyi Dvor. Petersburg. 1758–85. Architect: Jean-Baptiste Vallin de la Mothe. Side facade. (P 15–8)

the grant of a generous pension. Upon leaving Petersburg in 1764, Rastrelli interrupted his journey to Italy with a prolonged stay in Courland, where Biron, returned from exile in Siberia for two decades, commissioned Rastrelli to expand the work that he had done almost three decades earlier at Mitau and Ruhental – a remarkable exercise in stylistic anachronism.[4]

The French Presence in Early Russian Neoclassicism: Vallin de la Mothe

In 1779, the seventeenth year of her reign (1762–95), Catherine the Great described her passion for architecture in a letter to her advisor on cultural matters, the philosophe Friedrich Melchior Grimm:

Our storm of construction now rages more than ever before, and it is unlikely that an earthquake could destroy as many buildings as we are erecting. Construction is a sort of devilry, devouring a pile of money, and the more you build, the more you want to build. It's simply a disease, something like a drinking fit – or, perhaps, just a habit.[5]

It would indeed seem that no other Russian ruler, with the exception of Peter the Great, was more addicted to the pursuit of architecture as a manifestation of progress and of imperial glory. Not only did Catherine initiate a multitude of projects in both Petersburg and Moscow – projects that led to the reconstruction of large areas within those cities – but she also founded a planning commission whose mandate was to impose order on provincial cities throughout the empire. The neoclassical architecture and planning of these administrative centers were to reflect the rationalism of the Enlightenment, even though the autocratic basis of government remained essentially unchanged. Although her accomplishments fell short of the ambitious goals, many Russian provincial cities still bear the imprint of her desire for architectural order.

It was Petersburg, however, that bore the brunt of the "storm," as Catherine presided over the extraordinary enterprise that defines the first phase of neoclassicism in Russia. The architects of this period are as cosmopolitan as those of previous reigns: Jean-Baptiste Michel Vallin de la Mothe, from France; Antonio Rinaldi and Giacomo Quarenghi, from Italy; Georg Friedrich Veldten, from Germany; Charles Cameron, a Scot; and an impressive array of native Russians, educated in Europe, or in the European manner. The designs of Vasilii Bazhenov (in Moscow as well as Petersburg) and Ivan Starov are of particular interest as examples of the assimilation of the western idiom by Russian architects.

The origins of neoclassicism in the eighteenth century are several: the Italian Renaissance and classical elements in seventeenth-century French architecture, as well as Palladianism in England all provided interpretations of what was seen as the essence of classical architecture – particularly as expressed in the writings and work of Palladio. (As noted, Russian interest in Palladio, Vignola, Vitruvius, and other codifiers of the classical order system dates from the beginning of the eighteenth century, but no sustained interpretation of their work occurred during the Petrine period.) Above all other nations, however, France provided for Russia the model for the application of classical architectural principles, as defined by the "Roman" imperial style of Louis XIV and by later variants derived from the more severe statement of Hellenism.[6]

The rapidity with which Russia accepted neoclassicism reflects the influence of the intellectual and artistic movement that occurred in France during the middle of the eighteenth century. Russia did not make any theoretical contribution to this development, merely appropriating it; but the reasons for its success are similar to those elsewhere in Europe: Neoclassicism was welcomed as a rejection of the "disorder" of the late baroque, and a reaffirmation of the principles of reason expressed in the philosophy and the architecture of antiquity. As one critic has described the movement in France: "This revulsion against the Rococo and all the values it was felt to express, or at any rate to imply and condone, amounted in certain cases to an instinctive nausea; but in general the new moralizing fervour which began to penetrate the arts around the midcentury was rational and stoic in tone. . . ."[7]

Much the same could be said of Russia, or, more precisely, of Catherine, who experienced "instinctive nausea" for the baroque extravagance of Elizabeth's style, and who took pride in the role of enlightened autocrat – a role assiduously cultivated by her correspondence with such French philosophes as Diderot, Voltaire, and d'Alembert, in addition to Grimm. The style of Catherine's neoclassicism varies considerably, depending on the function of the structure and the architect's interpretation of classical principles; but the general intent is clear: a new restraint – especially in the decoration of the exterior – and an adherence to elements of the classical system of orders.

Although the transformation of the Gostinnyi dvor project provides evidence of the impact of the change, the more significant project as a statement of neoclassical principles is the building of the Imperial Academy of Arts in Petersburg. Like Moscow University (founded in 1755), the Academy was established through the efforts of Mikhail Lomonosov with the support of Ivan Shuvalov, whose proposal was approved by the Senate in 1758. At that time, the Academy was affiliated with Moscow University, from which it drew most of its students for study in Petersburg (the academy was originally housed in Shuvalov's palace). With the accession of Catherine, Shuvalov was relieved of his duties, and his efforts on behalf of the academy were dismissed as the enterprise of a dilettante. In 1764, the academy, under the direction of Ivan Betskoi, received a new charter, and construction of a building on the Neva embankment of Vasilevskii Island began a year later.[8]

The predominant French influence in the design – and the curriculum – of the Academy of Arts derives not only from Vallin de la Mothe, trained in France and Italy and invited to Russia to teach at the Academy in 1759, but also from Alexander Kokorinov (1726–72), who had studied with Korobov and Ukhtomskii in Moscow. After moving in 1754 to Petersburg, where he was engaged in completion of the

interior at the palace of Ivan Shuvalov, Kokorinov was appointed the first professor of architecture at the academy in 1758. Both Shuvalov and Kokorinov were devotees of French culture, and the academy's early library holdings reveal an orientation toward the precursors and theoretical treatises of French classicism such as Nicholas-François Blondel's *Cours d'architecture* (1675), a similar treatise by D'Aviler (1691), and the four volumes of Jacques-François Blondel's *L'Architecture française* (1752–6).[9]

The Francophile sympathies of Shuvalov and his successor Betskoi were reinforced by such figures of state as Dmitrii Golitsyn, Russian ambassador to France from 1761 and a major intermediary between French and Russian culture. Not only did Golitsyn continue the practice of earlier Russian emissaries (Antiokh Kantemir and Mikhail Bestuzhev-Riumin) in providing sustenance and shelter to Russian architects sent to study abroad, but he also introduced them to such figures of the Enlightenment as Denis Diderot, in addition to arranging their placement with French architects such as Charles de Wailly and Jean-Jacques Sufflot.[10] Thus, two of the most imposing names in Russian architecture – Vasilii Bazhenov and Ivan Starov – had an advantageous entry during the 1760s into the rich cultural life of Paris.

In addition, Golitsyn was himself a devoted connoisseur of the arts, whose writings provide an insight into the assimilation of the aesthetic and cultural values of neoclassicism. Of special interest is his essay "On the Usefulness and Glory of the Arts," composed in 1766 and sent to the Academy of Arts, where it was translated into Russian and circulated within the academy. Golitsyn's views were indebted to those of Diderot (considered the founder of art criticism in France by virtue of his commentary on the *salons* at the Louvre), and espoused the usefulness of the arts – above all, architecture – for the formation of the noble character, as well as for the development of the traditions inherited from the classics, the source of all true greatness in the arts. The fundamental principle of magnificence in architecture was linked not to the rich decoration, but to simplicity, as illustrated by the ancient Greeks and Romans.[11]

When compared with the work of Rastrelli, whose Winter Palace had only recently been completed, Kokorinov and Vallin de la Mothe's design for the Academy of Arts is the essence of simplicity. Without elaborate statuary or plaster ornamentation, the main facade of the three-story building is marked by tetrastyle Tuscan porticos on either end and, in the center, a projecting pediment with two supporting columns on each side of a large window on the main

Figure 331. Academy of Arts. Petersburg. 1765–89. Architects: Jean-Baptiste Vallin de la Mothe and Ivan Kokorinov. (P 14–11a)

level (Figure 331). This five-part division of a neoclassical facade, with an advanced central pediment, had been established by Le Vau, Perrault, and Le Brun on the east front of the Louvre. Unlike the French prototype, however, the Academy of Arts uses the more modest pilasters, rather than a colonnade, to define the middle sections. Furthermore, the walls are not of natural stone, but of stuccoed brick, rusticated on the ground floor.

Despite the application of stucco, the building lacks the typical Petersburg bichromatic scheme of pastel facade and white trim – no doubt in deliberate contrast to the baroque, but also to create a closer approximation to stone facing. In fact, the street facades remained unstuccoed for the rest of the eighteenth century. Cost overruns and inflation caused by the Russo–Turkish War led to inordinate delays in construction of the building, whose official "completion" in 1789 referred only to the shell of the building, much of which remained unfurnished until 1810. Nonetheless, the academy continued to function in the completed parts of the enormous structure (125 × 140 meters), rivaled in size only by the Winter Palace.[12] The plan included a series of self-enclosed, autonomous units organized around four rectangular court-

yards, which are themselves attached to a great circular courtyard in the center of the structure (Figure 332). Not only are the facades regulated by a strict symmetry, but the plan itself represents an elaborate exercise in geometrical form.

In retrospect, it would seem that the Academy of Arts marks a clear division between the baroque and the neoclassical. Its cornice displays one of the earliest Russian uses of a proper entablature, above which is a simple attic with no ornamentation – both features

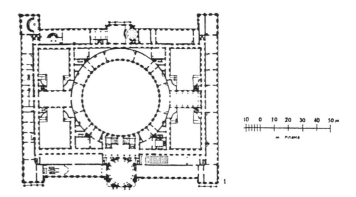

Figure 332. Academy of Arts. Petersburg. Plan.

264

signaling the advance of neoclassicism. Nonetheless, certain baroque features remained, such as the curved projection for the central pediment. And the maddeningly slow pace of the academy's construction could hardly have advanced the cause of neoclassicism, even though the large wooden model of the structure played a role in the propagation of the style within the academy itself. Indeed, the old style remained a forceful presence in the work of Vallin de la Mothe, as is evident in his Roman Catholic Church of St. Catherine (1762–83) on Nevskii Prospekt, where baroque elements such as oval windows, curved pediments, and statuary were combined with Corinthian columns and pilasters in a symmetrical arrangement (Figure 333). To be sure, the presence of the baroque at the Church of St. Catherine was motivated to no small degree by the cultural symbolism of Catholicism.

Vallin de la Mothe's other works – such as the Small Hermitage (1764–75; see Figure 313), designed to house Catherine the Great's art collection – demonstrate a clearer vision of neoclassicism: simplicity in the use of columns, which are frequently detached but not clustered; modest window decoration; and a cornice articulated with classical elements (triglyph, dentils, guttae). The Doric and Ionic were the most commonly used orders. In addition to a greater simplicity in design, the new austerity continued to be noticeable in a muting of the vivid colors that had characterized Petersburg architecture from its beginnings. Nonetheless, baroque forms, especially in the design of windows, continued to appear during this transitional period, as exemplified by the magnificent palace on the Moika for Elizabeth's favorite Kirill Razumovskii, begun in 1762 by Kokorinov and completed in 1766 by Vallin de la Mothe. At the center of the main facade, a hexastyle Corinthian portico frames an ascending series of arcaded windows, medallions, oculi, and festoons.[13] A more restrained, neoclassical design was implemented in Vallin de la

Figure 333. Church of St. Catherine. Petersburg. 1762–83. Architect: Jean-Baptiste Vallin de la Mothe. South facade, Nevskii Prospekt. (P 19)

Mothe's rebuilding in the 1760s of the former Peter Shuvalov mansion, also on the Moika, for the Iusupovs.[14]

The most monumental, and arguably the strongest, of Vallin de la Mothe's designs is the arch for New Holland, a complex of canals, basins, and wooden warehouses originally built by Ivan Korobov in 1732–40 for use as a storage area by the navy.[15] In 1765, Savva Chevakinskii began to rebuild the warehouses in brick (their function remained the same: to store lumber for the navy), but the design for the exterior facades and the major gateway to the complex was entrusted to Vallin de la Mothe. The unstuccoed brick facades (those that were completed before the project was halted in the 1780s) are detailed without decoration as a three-story monolithic arcade containing windows – a simple but noble resolution that, like the design of Gostinnyi dvor, demonstrated the viability of the neoclassical style in the design of large utilitarian buildings.

The magnificent arch, large enough for a boat to enter through the canal leading to a turning basin, is framed by paired Tuscan columns of gray granite supporting the projecting entablature (Figure 334). Within the brick facade behind each pair of columns is an arched niche, above which is a medallion. They are separated by a stone cornice that leads to the capital of a smaller Tuscan column on each side of the entrance arch. Thus, the major and minor orders are integrally linked. The entryway, with its highly pitched arch, is a marvel in the use of a void to define the harmony of structural proportions. Above and on either side of the arch is an abstracted festoon, also of stone; and the central part culminates in a continuation of the Doric entablature. Although less agressively archaic than C. A. Ehrensvärd's design some two decades later (c. 1785) of a dockyard gateway for Karlskrona, the New Holland Arch is one of the great exercises in European neoclassicism and anticipates the triumph of neoclassical geometry in Adrian Zakharov's design for the Admiralty (see Chapter 12).

Vallin de la Mothe, together with Kokorinov, had introduced to Russian architecture the new vocabulary of imperial classicism in what might be called the era of the column. Not that the uses of the column were unknown to Rastrelli, but the decoration of his palaces submerged the column within an array of statuary and plaster ornament. Vallin de la Mothe and subsequent architects of Catherine's reign – Velten, Rinaldi, Bazhenov, Quarenghi, Starov – exploited the column and pilaster as a means of segmenting an extensive facade, yet the articulation of their work is carefully measured in comparison with Rastrelli's ex-

uberance. For Vallin de la Mothe, the restraint derived from the late baroque exemplified in the French *hôtel* of the first part of the eighteenth century. For his distinguished successor, Antonio Rinaldi, a comparable model would be the Italian palazzo as interpreted by Luigi Vanvitelli.

Georg Friedrich Velten

Before Rinaldi, however, the possibilities of neoclassical architecture were expanded during the early part of Catherine's reign by Georg Friedrich Velten (1730–1801), who played a major role in the transformation of the Petersburg cityscape. Although born, raised, and schooled in Petersburg, Velten (or Veldten) continued his education in Tübingen after the death of his father, who had occupied a responsible position in the Academy of Sciences.[16] Velten's artistic training thus included a familiarity with the eighteenth-century masterpieces of Württemberg, including the palace at Stuttgart in whose construction he participated. In 1749, Velten returned to Petersburg for advanced training at the Academy of Sciences and Arts – as the combined institution was known from 1747 until the creation of a separate Academy of Arts in 1757. In 1754, Velten was accepted as an apprentice to Rastrelli, and after the latter's dismissal, continued his work on parts of the Winter Palace interior.

With Rastrelli's departure, Velten rivaled Vallin de la Mothe as one of the most active architects in Petersburg. His first major work involved the design of the South Pavilion of the Small Hermitage (1760s), located on Million Street (adjacent to Palace Square) and connected by a roof garden to the Hermitage that Vallin de la Mothe had created on the Neva embankment. As in the work of the French architect, the baroque presence lingers in this stage of neoclassicism, and the influence of Rastrelli is evident in the window surrounds and plaster ornament of the walls (Figure 335). In the following decades, the Small Hermitage, like the other parts of the palace complex, had almost all of its interior replaced; and in 1840, a fourth floor was added to the South Pavilion of the Hermitage by Vasilii Stasov.

During this period of sustained palace construction, the need to replace the wooden embankments along the Neva, with their unprepossessing appearance, became increasingly obvious. The initiative for this project, which had such significant ramifications for the architectural setting of Petersburg, came from one of the most important institutions for the direction of eighteenth-century Russian urban design: the Com-

Figure 334. New Holland Arch. Petersburg. 1765–80s. Architect: Jean-Baptiste Vallin de la Mothe. (P 18–3)

mission for the Stone [masonry] Construction of St. Petersburg and Moscow, established at the beginning of Catherine's reign in December 1762 as an agency of the Senate and directed by Ivan Betskoi. When the activity of the commission ceased with the death of Catherine in 1796, it had designed – if not implemented – over 300 new plans for the majority of Russia's cities.[17] In regard to Petersburg, the commission followed the general plan developed by Eropkin and Zemtsov, with an emphasis on the comprehensive planning of the urban space that surrounded new architectural ensembles such as the Winter Palace.

In the building of granite embankments along the south bank of the Neva, Velten was given the major responsibility for organizing the work, including parapets, sidewalks, iron street lamps, and a newly rein-

forced and paved street along the embankment.[18] The primary material was rough-hewn red Finnish granite, which combined durability and a rich texture. Particularly effective is the design of the oval descents to the water level and the gracefully arched bridges (Figure 336) over the three canals between the Winter Palace and the Summer Garden. Work on the embankment continued into the 1780s, by which time similar projects were underway on other waterways in the city. An integral part of the Palace Quay development was the design in 1770 of an ornamental fence along the embankment side of the Summer Garden. In this project, completed with the assistance of Peter Egorov and others in 1784, the stonework of the thirty-six monolithic granite columns, surmounted with decorative urns, was complemented by the pat-

Figure 335. Small Hermitage, South Pavilion. Petersburg. 1760s. Architect: Georg Friedrich Velten. Fourth floor added by Vasilii Stasov in 1840. (P 17–11a)

terned iron work of thirty-two sections of iron staves and three gates. Only the two smaller gates survive.[19] Velten was also involved in regulating the appearance of Palace Square and adjoining construction – an enterprise that was not completed until Carlo Rossi's design of the General Staff Building in the 1820s (see Chapter 12).

Velten also collaborated with the sculptor Etienne Falconet in the creation of Petersburg's – indeed, Russia's – greatest monumental statue. The monument to Peter the Great, popularly known as the "Bronze Horseman" (Figure 337), is the culminating work of European baroque sculpture. Within Russia itself, the statue possesses a mythic significance as a symbol of the country's modern history and culture. Yet the monument was created in an atmosphere of continual tension and hostility between Falconet, who had been recommended to Catherine by Diderot, and Ivan Betskoi.[20] In the event, Falconet, who had arrived in Petersburg in 1766, left Russia in 1778, 4 years before the statue was installed and unveiled in August 1782. Velten's contribution lay not only in the design of the embankment on this portion of the Neva (adjacent to and down river from the Admiralty), but also in the engineering and design work necessary to transport

as well as to install the sculpted granite monolith ("Thunder Rock") on which the statue rests.

During the 1770s, Velten was engaged in the remodeling of certain major rooms – including the Throne Hall – of the main palace at Peterhof, and he was also commissioned to build a palace to the south of the city in honor of the Russian naval victory over the Turks at Chesme Bay in the Aegean (June 1770).[21] With the conclusion of the Russo–Turkish war in 1774, Velten began work on the palace, triangular in plan and decorated to resemble a medieval castle, although without an interior courtyard (in its place was the main hall of the palace). The pseudo-Gothic style of the exterior not only symbolized the exoticism of Turkish architecture, but also reflected the Anglomania that affected Catherine and had a significant impact on the design of her palaces as well as the parks surrounding them.[22] The Chesme Palace, completed in 1777, was intended not as a major imperial residence, but as a transit (*putevoi*) palace to be used as a resting place during the annual shift of the court from Petersburg to the suburban palace at Tsarskoe Selo. In this respect, it is similar to the flamboyant pseudo-Gothic transit palace designed by Matvei Kazakov on the northern fringes of Moscow (see Chapter 11).

The conversion of the Chesme Palace into a veterans' hospital in the 1830s altered its original castellated appearance, although the main flanking towers and many of the large lancet windows remained intact. Much closer to its original form is the adjoining Church of John the Baptist, built between 1777 and 1780 in a style similar to that of Strawberry Hill Gothic (Figure 338). The finials, spires, and lancet windows are placed upon a structure whose quatrefoil design is reminiscent of certain estate churches in the "Moscow baroque" style of the late seventeenth century (e.g., the Church of the Transfiguration of Ubory). Indeed, it could be argued that the experimentation with unusual church forms during Catherine's reign reflects the intensified secularization of society, particularly the upper nobility at the turn of the eighteenth century (see Chapter 7). The decorative panoply of the miniature Chesme church suggests a resemblance to the pseudo-Gothic pavilions that proliferated in estate parks during the reign of Catherine – and subsequently.[23]

Velten was, in fact, engaged in the construction of such pavilions at Tsarskoe Selo, including most notably the "Ruin," an architectural conceit in the form of a massive ruined Doric column capped by fragments of a pseudo-Gothic pavilion (Figure 339).[24] Designed in 1771 and completed 2 years later, the Ruin exemplifies the tendency toward allegorical structures expressive of the grandeur and decay of past cultures, and can be compared with a still more radically gargantuan form built in France the same year: the fluted Column House at Désert de Retz, designed by the eccentric nobleman François Racine de Monville.[25]

Catherine considered herself the ruler of a new power among the comity of civilized nations, and the attraction of recreating ancient architecture (and its ruins) lay not only in its stimulus to the contemplation of history, but also its suggestion of Russia's inheritance of the mantle of greatness from ancient civilizations. In specific reference to the Ruin, an inscription above the large arch within the partially destroyed wall near the column-tower commemorates the humbling of the Turkish empire during the Russo–Turkish War of 1768–74. (As at the Chesme complex, the exoticism of the pseudo-Gothic suggests the colorful and "barbaric" culture of the Ottoman empire.) Thus, Velten's "Ruin" served as an initial stage in the creation of an elaborate system of architectural messages, proclaiming the expansion of the Russian empire, within the parks at Tsarskoe Selo.[26]

Beyond the ruined wall of the Ottomans and within the main Catherine Park, the pavilions adopted the architectural styles of classical antiquity, the Middle Ages, and even ancient Egypt, as was typical of this period of pluralistic taste throughout Europe. The 1770s saw a revival of interest in Chinoiserie, exemplied by the Chinese, or "Squeaky," Pavilion (from the noise of its weather vane), built by Velten in 1778–86 and picturesquely situated between two ponds in the Catherine Park (Figure 340). Similar exercises in both Chinoiserie and the pseudo-Gothic were implemented by Vasilii and Ilia Neëlov, father and son who in the latter part of the eighteenth century supervised much of the development of the Catherine Park (Figure 341).[27] In 1772–4, Vasilii Neëlov constructed the Great Caprice – an artificial stone hill, surmounted by a Chinese pavilion and containing a passage for one of the main roads to the palace. At the same period, an entire Chinese "village" arose in the adjoining Alexander Park, apparently under the direction of Vasilii Neëlov with the participation of Antonio Rinaldi and, later, Charles Cameron.[28] It would be proper to assume that the fascination with things Chinese

Figure 336. Neva Embankment (Palace Quay), Upper Swan Bridge. Petersburg. 1770s. Architect: Georg Friedrich Velten(?). (P 17–3)

Figure 337. Bronze Horseman (Monument to Peter the Great). Senate Square, Petersburg. 1766–82. Sculptor: Etienne Falconet. Architect: Georg Friedrich Velten. (P 60–8)

reflected a renewed interest in trade and political expansion in the direction of China, yet the creation of such artificial environments also signaled an ability to transform reality, a confrontation of nature and artifice characteristic of imperial estate design since the time of Peter I.

During the late 1770s, Velten and Ilia Neëlov also collaborated in the expansion of the main palace with two parallel wings extending at each end of the building into the courtyard. The south wing, subsequently known as the Zubovskii, was designed by Velten and entailed the destruction of Rastrelli's grand stairway, later to be replaced by a new one designed by Cameron in the center of the palace. The north wing is the work of Neëlov and extends from the palace

church. Neëlov's design imitated some of the baroque elements of the original structure, but Velten adopted a neoclassical style for the Zubovskii wing. It should be noted that a decade later, in 1788–92, Ilia Neëlov, constructed a large wing parallel to his church wing and connected to it by an overhead passageway on three arches. The rustication of the two ground floors and the clear delineation of the horizontal lines of the building created a harmonious addition to the palace ensemble, despite the great differences in style.[29] Originally intended as living quarters for the grand duchesses, the building was converted in 1811 to accommodate the newly established Lycee at Tsarskoe Selo, among whose first students was the poet Alexander Pushkin.

In 1764, Velten received a commission to construct adjacent to the Smolnyi Convent an institute for the education of girls of nonnoble background (later known as the Aleksandrovskii Institute, with students for the most part from prosperous merchant families). In some respects, the building reminds of the Petrine baroque, with a rusticated ground floor and recessed panels beneath the windows. Yet the lack of a bichromatic segmentation of the facade and the more detailed use of the order system reveal an interpretation of neoclassicism similar to the Academy of Arts. Despite the restraint of the exterior detail, the plan of the three-storied institute is complex: The main part consists of a rectangle enclosing three courtyards, to which is attached a semicircular structure flanking the central entrance. Ironically, the expense of this austerely imposing structure – whose construction required a much longer time than expected (from 1765 to 1775) – precluded the completion of the rococo interior of the Cathedral of the Resurrection at the Smolnyi Convent, which had been entrusted to Velten after Rastrelli's departure.[30]

Still more restrained is Velten's design for an extension of Catherine's "Hermitage" at the Winter Palace. Subsequently known as the Large, or Old, Hermitage (see Figure 313), the building was constructed in two stages: the first fronting the Neva (1771–6), and a further extension to the Winter Canal. The entire project was completed only in 1787.[31] Its simplicity offers a measure of visual relief within the richly detailed of palaces along the Neva embankment. Indeed, it epitomizes much of Velten's work: functional, solid, unobtrusive, and essential to the developing fabric of Petersburg.

Antonio Rinaldi

By the time of Rastrelli's departure from imperial service, another Italian architect had begun the next phase of palatial magnificence in Petersburg and its suburbs. Little is known of the biography of Antonio Rinaldi (1710?–94) before his arrival in Petersburg in 1754.[32] He was a student of Luigi Vanvitelli, and presumably assisted the latter in the construction of the

Figure 338. Church of John the Baptist, Chesme Palace. Near Petersburg. 1777–80. Architect: Georg Friedrich Velten. (P 21)

Figure 339. "Ruin" Pavilion. Tsarskoe Selo. 1771–3. Architect: Georg Friedrich Velten. (TS 5–20)

271

Figure 340. Chinese ("Squeaky") Pavilion. Tsarkoe Selo. 1778–86. Architect: Georg Friedrich Velten. (TS 5–22)

Royal Palace at Caserta, begun in 1751. Certainly, the influence of that Neapolitan masterpiece – the last of the great baroque palaces of Italy – appears in Rinaldi's Russian work. Although he extended the idiom of neoclassicism in Russian architecture, it should be noted that the roots of his style remained in the late baroque era, epitomized by the work of Vanvitelli and of Filippo Juvarra, architect to the royal court of Savoy, whose early eighteenth-century palazza in Turin prefigure Rinaldi's palaces in their combination of luxuriant decoration and austere monumentality.

Rinaldi's first major contribution occurred at Oranienbaum, where in 1756–61, he created the modest palace ensemble of Peterstadt for the heir to the throne, subsequently (and briefly) Emperor Peter III. The more grandiose stage of construction at Oranienbaum began with the reign of Catherine, who in 1762 commissioned the "Personal Dacha," an ensemble that included a palace and the Sledding Hill Pavilion. Although small by imperial standards, both are masterpieces that belong as much to the rococo as to the neoclassical. The one-story residence (1762–8; expanded in the 1840s by Andrei Shtakenshneider) was subsequently named the Chinese Palace for the wealth of its interior Chinoiserie, but the supreme

achievement is its rococo decoration.[33] The roster of masters who participated in the design of its interior comprises a catalogue of the decorative arts in mid-eighteenth century Petersburg: ceiling paintings by Giovanni Battista Tiepolo (the greatest master of the Venetian school of decorative painting) and other Venetian artists; wall and ceiling paintings in tempera by Stefano Torelli (from Bologna); marble bas-reliefs by Marie-Anne Collot (Falconet's assistant in the sculpting of the Bronze Horseman); and elaborate parquet designs by Rinaldi himself. The foregoing list includes only a small portion of the artists and decorators – primarily Italian and French – as well as Russian craftsmen involved in the interior work.

Equally suffused with the rococo spirit was the Sledding Hill pavilion (1762–74), for ice sledding in the winter and roller coasting – over a half-kilometer track – in warmer weather.[34] The highly centralized structure, with three wings extending from the core rotunda (capped by a bell-shaped cupola; Figure 342), is reminiscent of the pavilions by Rastrelli and Chevakinskii at Tsarskoe Selo, with elaborately terraced stairs and the use of pastel blue with white trim for the exterior. Despite the baroque elements, the imprint of neoclassicism is evident in the colonnade above the terrace and in the interpretation of the order system on the facade. Although the building of the Sledding Hill was completed by 1769, five more years were required for its interior, which displayed Chinoiserie and rococo elements similar to the Chinese Palace.[35] As in the palace, the pavilion demonstrates the tenacity with which Rinaldi balanced the baroque and the neoclassical styles in this transitional era.

Rinaldi created an altogether more severe and monumental ensemble for Catherine at Gatchina, the southernmost of the major country estates near Petersburg. During the reign of Peter the Great, the village had belonged to the tsar's beloved sister Natalia Alekseevna, after whose death in 1717, the estate changed hands frequently. In 1765, Catherine the Great presented it to her favorite Grigorii Orlov, who soon thereafter commissioned Rinaldi to create a grandiose palace and park. The palace, begun in 1766 but not completed until 1781, was designed as a three-story main block with one-story, square service wings – designated Kitchen and Stables – attached to either side of the main structure by curved colonnades. In a departure from the usual practice, Rinaldi surfaced the building in a type of limestone (one of the reasons for its austere, monumental appearance) found along the banks of the nearby Pudost River. The flanking towers of the main palace and its restrained architectural detail, consisting largely of pilasters separating

Figure 341. Upper Bath Pavilion. Tsarskoe Selo. 1777–9. Architect: Ilia Neëlov. (TS 4–23)

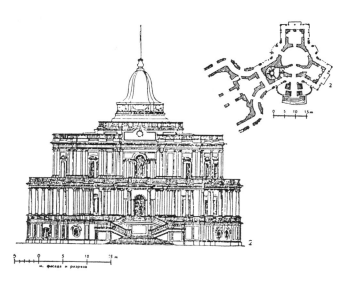

Figure 342. Sledding Hill Pavilion. Oranienbaum. 1762–74. Architect: Antonio Rinaldi. Elevation and plan.

the windows, endow the structure with the appearance of a castle (Figure 343).

Following the death of Orlov in 1783, the estate was presented by Catherine to her son and heir to the throne, Paul, who had the flanking wings greatly expanded under the direction of Vincenzo Brenna, with the participation of Adrian Zakharov. Nonetheless, the central style of the palace was established by Rinaldi, and it reveals a marked turn to the neoclassical, despite rococo traces in the plaster work of the interior and in the superb parquetry designs by Rinaldi for a number of the rooms.[36] Rinaldi also contributed to the development of the Gatchina park with an obelisk celebrating the victory of the Russian fleet at Chesme. The exact date of the obelisk is unknown, but it is assumed to have been commissioned by Orlov no later than the mid–1770s in honor of his brother Aleksei Orlov, general commander of the Russian forces at Chesme.[37]

Figure 343. Main palace. Gatchina. 1766–81. Architect: Antonio Rinaldi; expansion of wings in the 1780s by Vincenzo Brenna. Photograph taken in 1972, before restoration. (P 85–8)

The culmination of Rinaldi's work as designer of palaces occurred in Petersburg itself with the construction of another palace for Grigorii Orlov. The architect's sensitivity to the shades of natural stone, so evident in the Orlov Gates at Tsarskoe Selo, achieved the grand scale in the building known appropriately as the Marble Palace. Begun in 1768, the interior of the palace was not completed until 1785, by which time Catherine the Great had repurchased it – together with the Gatchina estate – from the surviving Orlov brothers.[38] The long period of construction was due not only to the elaborate interior work, but also to the unusual, and somewhat impractical, material of the exterior walls. Only during the latter half of the eighteenth century had sources of marble suitable for construction been discovered in the Urals, as well as in Karelia; yet the great distances and primitive transportation limited its use to the rare patron with endless resources and patience.

Rinaldi's Italian background seems to have predisposed him to the use of natural stone, and he superbly exploited the material in the Orlov (Marble) Palace, which, like the Winter Palace, is visually divided into two levels culminating in a cornice and attic (Figure 344). The ground floor, of rough-grained red Finnish granite, forms a sharp contrast to the subtle coloration of the two upper floors, with gray granite walls and architectural details in several varieties of marble: polished pink Karelian marble for the two-story Corinthian pilasters that provide both vertical and horizontal definition to the upper level; capitals and festoons (between the second and third floors) of white Urals marble; veined bluish gray marble from the Urals for panels beneath the festoons; Karelian marble for the attic frieze, above which are ornamental urns of Reval dolomite (from quarries near Reval, or Tallinn).[39]

The facades of the Marble Palace are designed with a rigorous symmetry, yet the trapezoidal plan of the structure (Figure 345) necessitates a different configuration for each. The rectilinear mass of three facades is broken on the fourth by a recessed courtyard containing the main entrance, marked by attached white marble columns. Even Orlov could not command the resources necessary for an interior comparable to the imperial palaces, yet the use of natural stone for the main stairway (in the style of the Italian Renaissance) and the elaborate stucco work remind of Orlov's imperial backing. Much of the palace was redecorated in 1844–51 by Alexander Briullov, who nonetheless preserved Rinaldi's design in a number of central spaces.[40]

Rinaldi, who had provided such a splendid example of a new style of Italian architecture in Petersburg, departed Russia in obscurity in the early 1790s (the date of his death remains tentative, like much else in his biography). Yet the Marble Palace stands as the most imposing residence built in Petersburg in

Figure 344. Marble Palace. Petersburg. 1768–85. Architect: Antonio Rinaldi. East facade. (P 17–10)

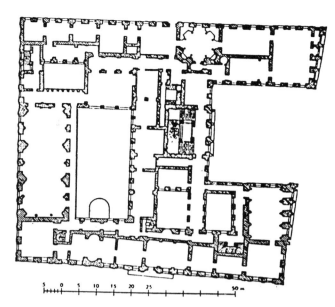

Figure 345. Marble Palace. Petersburg. Plan.

the late eighteenth century, and in its stern luxuriance, it epitomizes the final stage of Petersburg's transition from the baroque to the neoclassical.

Ivan Starov

The most influential architect of this transition, Ivan Starov (1745–1808), graduated with distinction in 1762 from the Academy of Arts, where he studied with Kokorinov and Vallin de la Mothe. He subsequently spent 4 years in Paris in the studio of Charles de Wailly, and in 1766–8, traveled extensively in Italy.[41] After his return to Petersburg, he accepted a teaching position at the Academy, and in the early 1770s, designed a number of country mansions in the environs of Petersburg and Moscow – most notably the neoclassical palaces commissioned by Catherine at Bobriki and Bogoroditsk (near Tula; Figure 346).[42] In 1772, Starov became a member of the influential Commission for the Masonry Construction of St. Petersburg and Moscow, under whose aegis he devised new plans for a number of Russian cities, including Voronezh and Pskov.[43]

Starov's first major project in Petersburg itself was the Cathedral of the Trinity at the Alexander Nevskii Monastery, a project that had become emeshed in a series of rejected proposals for its reconstruction after the razing of Schwertfeger's uncompleted structure (see Chapter 8).[44] Catherine, who inspected and ap-

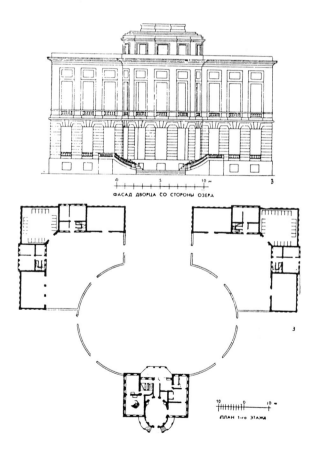

Figure 346. Bogoroditsk Palace. Near Tula. 1771. Architect: Ivan Starov. Elevation, plan.

proved Starov's project in 1776, was impressed by its monumental classicism, interpreted within a Roman basilical design (Figure 347). The great ribbed dome, on a rotunda with attached Corinthian columns over the main crossing, provides an instructive contrast to the complex baroque dome of Rastrelli's Smolnyi cathedral, which soars above the center of a cross-inscribed structure (see Figure 319). The greater amplitude and lower profile of the dome of the Trinity Cathedral suggests the work of Soufflot – particularly Ste. Geneviève (the Panthéon; 1755–1792), whose design would likely have been seen by Starov during his stay in Paris. To be sure Soufflot also adopted a centralized, cruciform plan – as had so many architects of the high baroque, Rastrelli included.

Thus, in retaining a basilical design, Starov simply followed the original plan for the monastery developed by Trezzini and elaborated by Schwertfeger (Starov created a new, much firmer foundation on the outlines of his predecessor's ill-fated building). Yet no stylistic contrast could be greater – or more tactfully stated – than that between the early baroque designs by Trezzini and Schwertfeger, and Starov's neoclassical temple, whose modest crossing, shifted to the east wall, poses little interruption to the rectangular plan (Figure 348). For the west front, facing the spacious monastery yard, Starov created a hexastyle Tuscan Doric portico that frames the main entrance and is in turn framed by two square bell towers outlined with Corinthian pilasters (Figure 349). This balance of elements provides a clearly articulated surface for which Fedot Shubin, one of the leading Russian sculptors, created panels with biblical themes: the Appearance of God to Moses in the Burning Bush and the Deliverance to Moses of the Ten Commandments (both on the west front); the Appearance of the Trinity to Abraham and the Return of the Prodigal Son (over the south and north entrances); Solomon's Sacrifice at the Consecration of the Temple and the Entry of Our Lord into Jerusalem (over the main portal on the west front).

The appearance of these panels – executed in the late 1780s after the completion of the structure in 1786 – is a landmark in the iconography of Russian neoclassicism. Not since Trezzini's design of the Summer Palace, with allegorical panels by Schlüter on the theme of Russia's naval power, had Petersburg architecture served directly to present an iconic message of belief and ideology. The decoration of baroque facades had mitigated against sculpted reliefs, and only in the latter part of Catherine's reign did classical statuary provide architecture with an iconographic system to replace the lost iconography of medieval religious art. Allegories of social virtues and national triumph henceforth would be drawn from ancient history or mythology, but the classical idiom also proved transferable to the Old and New Testaments. Both the building and decoration of the Trinity Cathedral marked the arrival of neoclassicism as a statement of civic grandeur in architecture.

Starov's next exercise in the Tuscan order proved in its way to be no less influential: the Tauride Palace (1783–9), commissioned by Catherine the Great for another of her favorites, Grigorii Potemkin, Prince of the Tauris. The palace is a model of neoclassical simplicity, and was widely imitated in the design of estate houses. Indeed, its setting in what was a relatively undeveloped part of Petersburg, near the Smolnyi Convent, endowed the palace with the air of a country mansion, surrounded by a park designed by the English master William Gould.[45] The front of the palace (Figure 350) is defined by a hexastyle Tuscan portico and a rotunda with a low dome; the lack of ornamentation is most striking in the facade, whose only decoration is a frieze of metopes and triglyphs. The courtyard is flanked by wings (Figure 351), each of which has a Doric portico of four columns. The back, or park, facade of the wings displays the Ionic order. Starov's minimal use of architectural decoration on the exterior contrasted to the richness of the interior, but in each case, an elegant neoclassical restraint dominates.

The interior of the Tauride Palace has not survived in its original form. The Emperor Paul, in a gesture of rage against the memory of Catherine and her supporters, converted the building into a stable for the Horse Guards, thus destroying much of the decoration. Despite a sensitive reconstruction by Luigi Rusca in 1802–4, Starov's design was in some ways substantially altered; and in 1819, the prominent Italian decorator Giovanni Battista Scotti repainted much of the interior wall and ceiling decor in the style of late Empire neoclassicism.[46]

Charles Cameron

Among the varieties of neoclassicism during the reign of Catherine the Great, the most productive was Palladianism, introduced to Russia by Charles Cameron and Giacomo Quarenghi. Cameron (1743–1812), an enigmatic Scotsman who was perhaps recommended to the Empress by Denis Diderot, had abandoned work in the employ of his father, a London building contractor of modest means, and spent several years in Rome, where he studied the classical monuments as well as the work of Palladio. A volume based on

Plate 33. Cathedral of the Intercession on the Moat. Moscow. Southwest view. Chapel of St. Varlaam Khutynskii.

Plate 34. Cathedral of the Transfiguration of the Savior, Savior-Evfimii Monastery. Suzdal. 1582–94. South facade, with seventeenth-century frescoes.

Plate 35. Small Cathedral of the Don Mother of God, Donskoi Monastery. Moscow. 1593. Southwest view.

Plate 36. Church of the Trinity in Nikitniki. Moscow. 1628–51. South facade, with Chapel of St. Nikita the Warrior.

Plate 37. Church of the Kazan Mother of God at Kolomenskoe. Moscow. 1649–53. Southeast view.

Plate 38. Church of the Annunciation at Taininskoe. Near Moscow. 1675–7. Southeast view.

Plate 39. Cathedral of the Resurrection, New Jerusalem. Near Moscow. 1657–84; mideighteenth century. Southwest view.

Plate 40. Gateway, Convent of the Deposition of the Robe. Suzdal. 1688. West view.

Plate 41. Bell tower, Novodevichii Convent. Moscow. 1690. Southwest view.

Plate 42. Monastery of St. Nicholas at Viazhishchi. Near Novgorod. West view.

Plate 43. Cathedral of St. Nicholas at Viazhishchi. Near Novgorod. 1681–5. West view.

Plate 44. Refectory Church of St. John the Theologian at Viazhishchi. 1694–1704. Southeast view.

Plate 45. Krutitskii Teremok. Moscow. 1693–4. Architect: Osip Startsev. North facade.

Plate 46. Church of Sts. Boris and Gleb at Ziuzino. Moscow. 1688–1704. Northwest view.

Plate 47. Church of the Intercession at Fili. Moscow. 1690–3. Northwest view.

Plate 48. Church of the Trinity at Troitse-Lykovo. Moscow. 1698–1703. Architect: Iakov Bukhvostov(?). West view.

Figure 347. Cathedral of the Trinity, Alexander Nevskii Monastery. Petersburg. Southwest view. (P 68–34)

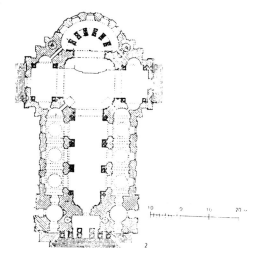

Figure 348. Cathedral of the Trinity, Alexander Nevskii Monastery. Petersburg. Plan.

Figure 349. Cathedral of the Trinity, Alexander Nevskii Monastery. Petersburg. 1776–90. Architect: Ivan Starov. West elevation by A. Shelkovnikov.

Figure 350. Tauride Palace. Petersburg. 1783–9. Architect: Ivan Starov. (P 22)

his studies, *The Baths of the Romans Explained and Illustrated, with the Restorations of Palladio Corrected and Improved* (published in London in 1772), established his critical reputation and served as an introduction to the style that he would apply for his Russian patrons in both architecture and interior design. In his introduction to Catherine, Cameron apparently played on the empress's sympathy for a deposed royal line by claiming affiliation with the Jacobites, but there is no evidence that he was associated with the cause in Rome.[47]

Cameron arrived in Petersburg apparently in 1779 and worked in Russia over the next two decades. His first task for Catherine consisted of redecorating a number of rooms in the palace at Tsarskoe Selo, her main summer residence. The empress was pleased with the results and wrote to Grimm in 1781: "I have an architect here named Kameron, born a Jacobite, brought up in Rome. He is known for his book on the ancient Roman baths; the man has a fertile brain, and a great admiration for [Charles-Louis] Clérisseau, so the latter's drawings will help Kameron to decorate my new apartments here, and these apartments will be superlatively good. So far only two rooms have been finished, and people rush to see them...."[48]

In the event, Cameron created three suites of rooms (or "Apartments"): two for Catherine's use, on the side of the palace adjoining the Zubovskii Wing; and another for Grand Duke Paul and his wife, Maria Fedorovna, on the opposite, or church, side of the palace. The luxury of Catherine's suites was epitomized by the Lyon Salon, with walls of lapis lazuli and damask silk from Lyons, and parquetry inlaid with mother-of-pearl. For the Empress's bedroom, the walls were of milk-colored glass, with thin glass col-

umns (a motif borrowed from Roman wall paintings) in deep lilac and Wedgwood medallions designed by the firm's preeminent neoclassicist, John Flaxman. Cameron's use of colored glass was further amplified by the placement of large mirrors within the walls.[49]

The suite for Paul, although on a more intimate scale and with lower ceilings than Catherine's main apartment, is the greater achievement, a masterpiece of wall decoration, parquetry, and ceiling painting. Each room has its distinctive style, yet the transitions in color and material are carefully modulated within the entire suite. Chinoiserie predominates on the walls of the Chinese Blue Salon; but the guiding spirit is classical, drawn from a tradition already superbly interpreted during the first half of the eighteenth century in the work of British architect–designers Colen Campbell (compiler of *Vitruvius Britannicus*), Richard Boyle (Lord Burlington), and William Kent.[50] The continuation of British Palladianism in the latter part of the eighteenth century suggests even more clearly the existence of a European neoclassical style shared by Clérisseau, Robert Adam, and Cameron.[51]

It is this style – suffused with motifs from the wall paintings of Pompeii and of Roman monuments – that informs the rooms of the Grand Duke's suite at Tsarskoe Selo. Although the decorative materials were less costly than those used in Catherine's apartments, the use of stucco for bas-reliefs and other ornamentation provided a similar sense of the neoclassical ambience in the Green Dining Room (Figure 352), with its stucco reliefs in the Wedgwood manner, and the Bedroom, where the glass columns of Catherine's Bedroom were replaced by similarly thin ceramic columns (Figure 353). In Paul's suite, architectural details such as columns and pilasters delineate the interior

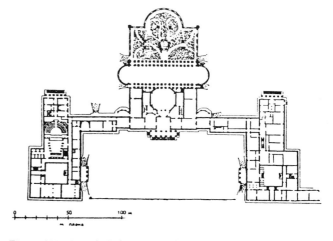

Figure 351. Tauride Palace. Petersburg. Plan by A. Shelkovnikov.

278

Figure 352. Catherine Palace, Green Dining Room. Tsarskoe Selo. Architect: Charles Cameron. (TS 2–10)

Figure 353. Catherine Palace, Grand Duke's Suite, and Bedroom. Tsarskoe Selo. Architect: Charles Cameron. (TS 2–31)

space and define the proportional relations between the walls and the dimensions of the rooms (cf. the Waiters' Room; Figure 354).

In 1780, soon after his completion of the apartments at Tsarskoe Selo, Cameron began work on the Cold Baths (or the Agate Pavilion) and the Colonnade (subsequently renamed the Cameron Gallery), both of which are adjacent to the south side of Rastrelli's palace. Nearest to the palace are the Baths, a two-story structure whose heavily rusticated lower level contained bathing facilities (including a frigidarium and tepidarium), and the upper level, in the style of a Renaissance villa with niches for statuary (Figures 355 and 356), consisted of a suite known as the Agate Pavilion.[52] Of the rooms, arranged in an intricate pattern of contrasting geometric shapes, the most luxurious are the Jasper and Agate Studies – the latter a misnomer, because the walls of both rooms are decorated with panels composed of several types of

polished jasper from the Urals.[53] They are rivaled, however, by the brilliance of the connecting Great Hall, whose walls of pink faux marbre, with Corinthian columns and bas-relief medallions on mythological themes, culminate in an elaborately coffered ceiling (Figure 357). Most of the intricate parquetry and a number of the doors in the pavilion had been designed by Velten for a mansion presented to another of Catherine's favorites, General A. D. Lanskoi. Upon the general's death in 1784, Catherine commanded that Velten's work be removed from the unfinished Lanskoi mansion, opposite the Winter Palace, and installed in the Agate Pavilion.[54] Cameron reluctantly but brilliantly complied. Indeed, the empress had granted him almost every other request for this small building, completed in 1787 at a cost in excess of 463,000 rubles.

The adjoining Cameron Gallery, connected to the Agate Pavilion by a garden terrace, is one of the hap-

Figure 354. Catherine Palace, Grand Duke's Suite and Waiters'
Room. Tsarskoe Selo. Architect: Charles Cameron. (TS 2–11)

piest conceits in eighteenth-century Russian architecture – a ground floor of massive rusticated Pudost
stone (like that of the Baths), surmounted by a delicate
peristyle of forty-four Ionic columns (Figure 358). As
an addition to the original design, Cameron made use
of the slope of the land toward the Great Pond to
create in 1786 a monumental entrance on the east
facade (Figure 359): one flight of steps (of Pudost
stone) leading to the ground level, and two in an oval
sweep leading to the upper floor. The dominant architectural elements of the east facade – the arched
entry on the ground level and the portico with four
Ionic columns – are repeated on the long side facades
(north and south) in the form of a ground arcade and
two projecting tetrastyle porticos on the upper level.
The width of the upper floor is divided into three
equal bays, the middle of which is enclosed with large
French windows providing a view of the natural park
that had been created around the Great Pond in the
1770s.[55]

The exterior gallery served for the contemplation
not only of nature, but also of classical civilization.
The collection of more than fifty bronze busts of ancient philosophers, poets, and rulers placed along the
colonnade provides a guide to the assimilation of
classical culture during the reign of Catherine, an ideological background for the development of neoclassical architecture in Russia.[56] After the completion of
the gallery in 1787, a final antique touch was provided
by the addition at the southwest corner of a rusticated
pente douce (1792–4), whose gradual incline allowed
the aged empress easier access to the park.

Indeed, Cameron had been active in the development of the grounds at Tsarskoe Selo, where in 1782,
he undertook the construction of a Chinese village
originally designed by Vasilii Neëlov, possibly with
the participation of Rinaldi.[57] As early as 1777, Rinaldi
had designed a Chinese Theater for the formal New
Garden, situated before the main courtyard of the
palace and subsequently included in the Alexander

Figure 355. Cold Baths and Agate Pavilion. Tsarskoe Selo. East facade. (TS 5–35)

Park. The theater was completed 2 years later by Ilia Neëlov, who together with his father Vasilii also constructed a large Chinese "Cross Bridge" (1776–9) over a canal in the New Garden. Cameron, too, created a number of exceptionally picturesque "Chinese" bridges, with cast-iron components, over the New Garden canals (see Plate 65).[58]

Concurrently with his work at Tsarskoe Selo, Cameron was engaged in the development of the nearby estate of Pavlovsk, recently acquired by Grand Duke Paul. The first results of Cameron's work at Pavlovsk appeared in the park, which is the most beautiful in Russia.[59] Its design is clearly indebted to English landscape gardening, developed as an integral part of neoclassical estate architecture by, among others, William Kent (at Stowe), William Chambers (Kew), Lancelot "Capability" Brown, Humphry Repton, and the German poet C. C. Hirschfeld, author of the influential *Teorie de l'art des jardins*, fragments of which were published in Russian in the 1780s.[60] Within the park vistas at Pavlovsk, Cameron created a number of pavilions, of which the first, and enduring, masterpiece is the rotunda entitled the Temple of Friendship (1780–2; see Plate 66). The monument was intended by Paul and Maria as a sign of affection to Catherine (whence its name, ultimately ironic), and allegories of friendship are portrayed in plaster medallions on the upper part of the wall.[61] The channeled columns and entablature represent the earliest proper use in Russia of the Greek Doric order (Figure 360), which would reappear at the turn of the nineteenth century

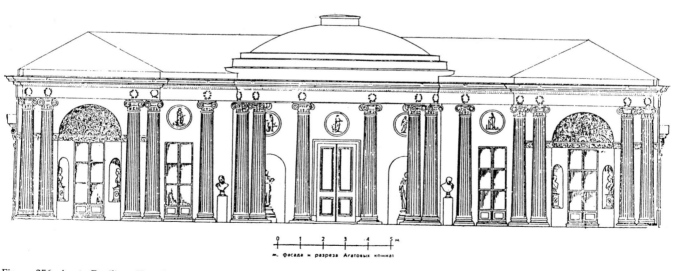

Figure 356. Agate Pavilion. Tsarskoe Selo. South elevation.

Figure 357. Agate Pavilion. Tsarskoe Selo. Plan and section, with Great Hall.

Figure 358. Cameron Gallery. Tsarskoe Selo. 1780–6. Architect: Charles Cameron. Northeast view. (TS 5–34)

imperial patronage Cameron lost little of his creative energy, and is thought to have designed the grand palace begun in 1799 for Kirill Razumovskii at the estate of Baturin (east of Chernigov). Razumovskii, who had acquired Baturin in 1750 as the last Hetman of the Ukraine, wished toward the end of his life to transform it into a center for his vast holdings and commissioned an appropriately imperial structure. The general plan for the palace and surrounding park bears a resemblance to Pavlovsk, but the palace design, with its row of major Ionic columns attached to the main facade, is far removed from his earlier Palladian model (Figure 363). After Razumovskii's death in 1803, work came to a halt on the Baturin ensemble, which rapidly fell into decline.[65]

Vincenzo Brenna

Both Cameron and Brenna (1747–1818?) owed much in their mastery of design to a thorough study of the monuments of ancient Rome, and in particular the wall paintings at the Baths (Thermae) of Titus, with elaborate decorative arabesques and an element of grotesquerie.[66] In 1776, an album of Brenna's drawings from the Thermae was published – the first of several volumes to contain his work – and the following year received a commission from Count Stanislaw Potocki to recreate the villa of Pliny the Younger (at Laurentum).[67] Following a thorough study of the monument, Brenna went to Poland in 1780, where he gained fame primarily as an interior designer of palaces and country mansions. In 1783, during a meeting between Grand Duke Paul and King Stanislaw Poniatowski of Poland, Potocki recommended Brenna to the grand duke, who hired him for work at Pavlovsk beginning in 1784.

Brenna's design of the state rooms at Pavlovsk (on the main, or first, floor) occurred within a plan that had already been defined by Cameron: a central part consisting of the Grand Vestibule (with stairs leading from the Egyptian Vestibule below); the Italian Hall, beneath the rotunda; and the Grecian hall, overlooking the park (Figure 364). Brenna decorated these rooms, intended for major state receptions and banquets, with the splendor of Roman classicism and placed special emphasis on martial regalia as a tribute to major victories over the Turks by Peter Rumiantsev and, during the Second Russo–Turkish War of 1787–92, by Alexander Suvorov. Of these rooms, Brenna's most impressive achievement was the Grecian Hall, a rectangular space with an interior court formed by sixteen Corinthian columns of green faux marble. Like

Figure 362. Pavlovsk Palace. Egyptian Vestibule. Ceiling painting by Carlo Scotti. (PV 1–1)

Cameron, Brenna made extensive use of the classical orders in his formulation of interior space.[68]

The Grecian Hall, which overlooked the expanse of the park, provided the culmination of the central space, and it also gave access on either side to enfilades containing the suite of rooms for Paul (the north enfilade) and for Maria Fedorovna (the south enfilade). Both enfilades were designed on principles of parallel development: Paul's suite, for example, began with the Hall of War; that of Maria Fedorovna began with the Hall of Peace. Each enfilade had a libary and dressing room. In some cases, the decor reinforced the apellation of the room (as in the Halls of War and Peace); in others, the name derived from the dominant decorative feature, as with the Tapestry Study (Figure 365) in Paul's suite. The most lavish decorative effects were applied to the suite of Maria Fedorovna, above all to the State Bedchamber in the French baroque style.[69]

285

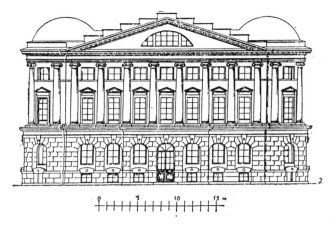

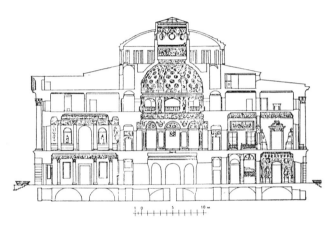

Figure 363. Razumovskii Palace at Baturin. Near Chernigov. Architect: Charles Cameron. Elevation by V. Taleporovskii.

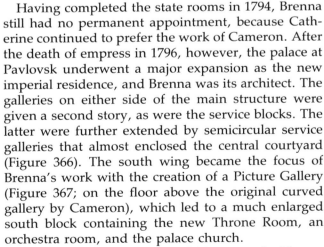

Figure 364. Pavlovsk Palace. Interior of central structure. Architects: Charles Cameron, 1782–6; Vincenzo Brenna, 1787–1800. Section by A. Kharlamova.

Figure 365. Pavlovsk Palace. Tapestry Study. Designed by Vincenzo Brenna. (PV 1–24)

Having completed the state rooms in 1794, Brenna still had no permanent appointment, because Catherine continued to prefer the work of Cameron. After the death of empress in 1796, however, the palace at Pavlovsk underwent a major expansion as the new imperial residence, and Brenna was its architect. The galleries on either side of the main structure were given a second story, as were the service blocks. The latter were further extended by semicircular service galleries that almost enclosed the central courtyard (Figure 366). The south wing became the focus of Brenna's work with the creation of a Picture Gallery (Figure 367; on the floor above the original curved gallery by Cameron), which led to a much enlarged south block containing the new Throne Room, an orchestra room, and the palace church.

Of these rooms, the most ambitious was the Throne Room (Figure 368). Originally intended as the main

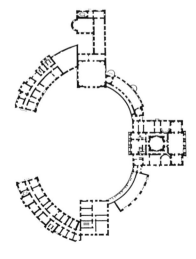

Figure 366. Pavlovsk Palace. Plan, with wing additions by Vincenzo Brenna.

dining hall, the room is afflicted with a low ceiling entirely out of proportion to the large floor space (400 square meters). With his flair for theatricality, Brenna resolved the problem by commissioning for the ceiling an enormous trompe l'oeil architectural fantasy, with a colonnade and coffered rotunda opening to a painted sky. Pietro Gonzago, a master at this type of work, submitted sketches, but the assassination of Paul in 1801 prevented the realization of the project. With considerable daring, however, the postwar restorers of the palace have implemented Gonzago's ceiling design.[70]

Although Brenna's work at Pavlovsk was largely complete by 1799,[71] the palace continued to provide work for the most distinguished of Russia's neoclassicists. In 1800, Giacomo Quarenghi designed a number of new rooms in the personal living quarters located in the south wing extended by Brenna. Quarenghi's work continued after the assassination of Paul, when Maria Fedorovna – reluctant to remain in Petersburg – made Pavlovsk her primary residence.

A fire in 1803 destroyed much of the central structure, and Andrei Voronikhin (see Chapter 12) was commissioned by Maria Fedorovna to recreate the interior as closely as possible to the original design. In so doing, Voronikhin showed sensitivity to his predecessors' work as well as his own supreme talents in the neoclassical style. And in the 1820s, Carlo Rossi, who had served his apprenticeship with Brenna at Pavlovsk, returned to the palace in 1822 to design a large library in the north wing above the Gonzago Gallery, an open terrace whose wall was painted with trompe l'oeil architectural compositions by Gonzago.

Brenna's major work at the end of the century was his construction in Petersburg of the Mikhailovskii Castle, commissioned by Paul at the end of 1796 as an impregnable residence to supplant the Winter Palace. Paul was haunted by the assassination of his father, Peter III (an act that not only led to a profound distrust of his mother, Catherine, but also gave rise to an obsessive concern about his own legitimacy), and he was determined to create an environment that

Figure 367. Pavlovsk Palace. Picture Gallery. Designed by Vincenzo Brenna. (PV 2–4)

Figure 368. Pavlovsk Palace. Throne Room. Designed by Vincenzo Brenna. Ceiling painting after a design by Pietro Gonzago. (PV 2–10)

would preserve his physical safety. The design of the Mikhailovskii Castle was originally entrusted to the brilliant – if ill-fated – Russian architect Vasilii Bazhenov (see Chapter 11). It has been argued that Bazhenov, who had entered the grand duke's service at Gatchina in 1792,[72] was in fact responsible for the basic design of the complex structure, and Brenna implemented it with certain modifications. Others have maintained that the original conception of the palace was Paul's (he had been tutored in architecture), and that Brenna, not Bazhenov, gave final shape to the plan.[73] Whatever the truth concerning the original authorship of the project, it became Brenna's own by March 1797, when Paul appointed him architect in charge of building the castle.

The site chosen for the castle had been occupied by Rastrelli's wooden Summer Palace (constructed in 1741–5; see Figure 297), which had fallen into disrepair and was razed at the beginning of Paul's reign. The castle, like the Summer Palace, was thus bounded on three sides by canals, and a moat was created for the fourth. The final plan of the castle – a square with an octagonal courtyard – produced an extraordinary variety of room configurations: oval, triangular, circular, in addition to various orthogonal combinations (Figure 369). Yet, the design proved less than practical for communication between the various suites of the building, each of which existed in quasiisolation within the wedges extending from the polygonal courtyard facade.[74] In addition, the urgent pace of construction required that building material and, in many cases, finished architectural elements be requisitioned from other building sites – notably the monumental marble facade of the entrance (Figure 370) from material intended for Rinaldi's Cathedral of St. Isaac of Dalmatia.

The Mikhailovskii Castle is thus something of a pastiche, with each facade presenting a different aspect. The one facing the Summer Garden across the Moika Canal (Figure 371) has a more domestic ap-

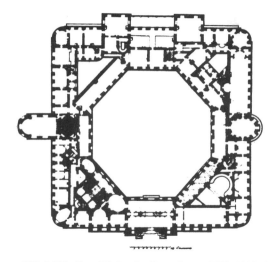

Figure 369. Mikhailovskii Castle. Petersburg. 1797–1800. Architect: Vincenzo Brenna. Plan by Carlo Rossi.

pearance, with its suites of windows and a decorative cornice. The side facades are simpler in detail, although the extension from the west facade to accommodate the palace church is richly decorated. The gilded spire of the church, as well as the bichromatic combination of a deep orange facade and stucco or stone ornamentation, represents a return to characteristics of the Petrine baroque. Even the complex geometry of the castle plan reminds of fortification design in the early eighteenth century. Yet its Italianate facades belong to a highly decorative form of neoclassicism peculiar not only to Brenna, but also Bazhenov and Rinaldi, as exemplified by the rusticated marble entrance (south), with flanking obelisks and a pediment frieze portraying "History inscribing on its tablets the Glory of Russia."

On the background of this entrance stands the most explicit Petrine reference – Carlo Rastrelli's equestrian monument to Peter the Great, modeled during the emperor's life but cast only in 1745–7. After several proposals for its location, Paul commanded that it be placed on a simple pedestal before the castle.[75] The beginning of the avenue leading to the statue and the entrance is marked by two symmetrical pavilions built in 1798–1800 to house the corps de garde. Whether designed by Bazhenov or Brenna, the pavilions display a combination of classical elements (tableaux on subjects from classical mythology and a loggia of Ionic columns above a rusticated ground floor) with baroque structural complexity: convex facades on the north and south and slight extensions on the diagonals – in the manner of the St. Andrews cross (Figures 372 and 373).

The sole entrance to the Mikhailovskii Castle led through a columned passage in the form of a Renaissance hall. From the octagonal court, access to the major parts of the castle was obtained through four main staircases, including the Grand Staircase clad in Siberian marble of various colors (Figure 374), which ascended to the emperor's state rooms and the Resurrection Hall on the south part of the castle. In the west part of the castle, another staircase led to the church, above whose iconostasis is a coffered dome with a representation of the Trinity by Carlo Scotti (Figure 375). The state rooms of Maria Fedorovna extended to the north of the church and included her Small Throne Room, with its elaborate plaster decoration, and the Raphael Gallery, with tapestries based on Raphael's frescoes in the Vatican. The gallery also contained three ceiling paintings by Jakob Mettenleiter, who frequently worked with Brenna at the imperial palaces. The largest of these allegorical paintings, "The Temple of Minerva," contained portraits of Brenna and the artist himself as the representatives of architecture and painting.[76]

The total cost of the Mikhailovskii Palace amounted to more than 6.1 million rubles. By comparison, a *Saint Sebastian* by Rubens was purchased for the palace church at the cost of 1,500 rubles; and on December 4, 1800, each of the some 4,000 construction workers was given an award of 1 ruble for the timely completion of the project.[77] Brenna, like Rastrelli and Bazhenov before him, was rewarded by promotion to the equivalent rank of major general. In December, a grand procession from the Winter Palace celebrated the dedication of the castle, yet the urgency with which it was constructed created unexpected problems, particularly in the damp winter climate. A contemporary noted that the interior plaster had not dried, and as a result, the grand state rooms – open on that occasion to the public – were suffused with a gloomy mist despite the presence of thousands of candles.[78] When the imperial family moved to the castle on February 1, 1801, penetrating dampness and cold continued to grip the building, which, as Paul had ordered, was surrounded with water barriers and strictly guarded. Unfortunately, the family lived in the castle for only 40 days: On March 11, Paul was assassinated in his own bedroom with the complicity of his personal guard and the highest of state officials.[79]

The Mikhailovskii Castle was eventually given to the Engineering School, which opened there in 1820. During the 1820s, Carlo Rossi, who had worked as Brenna's assistant on the project, redesigned much of the area surrounding the castle and increased its

Figure 370. Mikhailovskii Castle. Petersburg. Entrance facade. (P 17–6)

accessibility by filling in two of the canals. Brenna had left Russia in 1802 (taking Rossi with him on an architectural tour of Europe), and he initially enjoyed a secure retirement in France; but the vicissitudes of the Napoleonic wars reduced him to poverty, and he died in obscurity, around 1818, in Dresden.

Giacomo Quarenghi

The life and work of Giacomo Quarenghi (1744–1817), the other great Palladian in Russian architecture, is intertwined with that of both Brenna and Cameron.

Soon after his arrival in Rome (from Bergamo) in 1762, Quarenghi began studies with the painter Anton Raphael Mengs, but the latter's departure for Madrid soon thereafter propelled Quarenghi to a series of other teachers, beginning with Stefano Pozzi in whose studio he met Brenna. During this period, Quarenghi, like Brenna and Cameron, became an expert draftsman intimately familiar with the Roman ruins. His architectural education, however, proceeded fitfully with masters such as Niccolo Giansimoni, and only his discovery of Palladio's *Four Books* convinced him of the possibilities of a renewed inter-

Figure 371. Mikhailovskii Castle. Petersburg. Moika facade. (P 56–72)

pretation of classical architecture.[80] Tours of Italy – particularly the Veneto – in 1772 and 1775 further enriched his sense of the classical heritage. During the 1770s, he was actively sought out by wealthy English visitors to Rome as a guide to the city and an expert Palladian whose opinion was solicited for projects on country estates in England and Scotland.[81] His one major project in Italy was the rebuilding of the interior of the Church of St. Scolastica for the Benedictine monastery at Subiaco. Quarenghi's design (1770–6; rebuilt after World War II) shows an elegant mastery of the classical order system.[82] Having little work in Italy, Quarenghi accepted a generous contract to work in Russia and arrived, with his family, in Petersburg at the end of 1779.

During his long, prolific career in Russia, Quarenghi created the most austere form of Petersburg's Roman classicism, as exemplified by his first major project for Catherine, the English Palace at Peterhof (1780–94). The palace (destroyed during World War II) was situated in the English Park, located to the southwest of the main Peterhof park and landscaped

in 1779 as a consummate example of the "natural" style by the gardener James Meader. Both the setting and the style of the palace represented a departure from the formal garden and the baroque design of Rastrelli's palace at Peterhof.[83] In its grand simplicity, the palace reminds of the north front of Kedleston, designed by James Paine in 1759, rather than the more elaborate south front by Robert Adam. (Kedleston was among the monuments included in *Vitruvius Britannicus*, although Quarenghi would have been more familiar with the houses of Palladio.) The main facade of the English Palace, overlooking a pond, was defined by a portico with eight Corinthian columns at the summit of a broad flight of steps. The original plan called for three statues over the low pediment – a Palladian motif that Quarenghi would implement elsewhere.[84] In contrast to the severity of the exterior, the interior was decorated in the high Palladian manner appropriate to a palace intended for Catherine and her favorite Aleksei Zubov; yet Quarenghi's relative economy in the use of materials held the cost of the project (slightly over 300,000 rubles) to half that

291

Figure 372. Mikhailovskii Castle. Petersburg. Corps de garde Pavilion. 1798–1800. Architect: Vasilii Bazhenov or Vincenzo Brenna. (P 66–30)

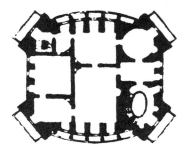

Figure 373. Mikhailovskii Castle. Petersburg. Corps de garde Pavilion. Plan.

spent by Cameron on the Agate Pavilion at Tsarskoe Selo.[85]

Quarenghi's success in Russia was immediate, and he undertook numerous imperial commissions, ranging from churches to hospitals, all marked by the classical system of orders. In 1783, he received the commission for a new building to house the Academy of Sciences, a project that had long been considered without final resolution.[86] The location of the building – next to the Kunstkammer and within the early baroque environment of Vasilevskii Island, reveals the simple and noble harmony of Quarenghi's neoclassicism (see Plate 59). The two-story building, with a granite base and a string course separating the floors, centers on an octastyle Ionic portico with an unadorned low pediment. The portico in effect frames seven window bays (also undecorated) and establishes a symmetrical progression: three windows on

either side of the portico, and five within each of the projecting facades that mark the ends of the building (Figure 376). The segmentation of the facade on both vertical and horizontal lines is complemented by a low roof and pediment (15°, but deeply set for a rich shadow relief).

Indeed, the most distinctive feature of Quarenghi's style is his Palladian-inspired portico. Throughout his career in Russia, beginning with the English Palace at Peterhof and concluding with the construction of the Smolnyi Institute for the Education of Young Noblewomen (1806–8; see Fig. 379), he used the portico as a means of organizing a large, simply detailed structural mass. His porticos typically consisted of eight columns in the Ionic order and a pediment marked with dentils. In a flawless understanding not only of the spatial relation between the height of the columns, their intercolumniation, and the angle of the pediment incline, but also of the relation of the portico to the proportions of the rest of the structure, Quarenghi achieved a clarity that epitomized the mature classical style in Russian architecture.[87]

In 1783, Quarenghi also began the Bourse, or Stock Exchange, on the eastern tip of Vasilevskii Island; and although the basic structure was completed by 1787, work came to a halt the same year (as with much other imperial construction) because of the renewal of hostilities between Russia, Turkey, and Sweden. The project ultimately led to a major disappointment at the end of Quarenghi's career: In 1805, Alexander I approved a comprehensive plan for the tip ("Strelka") of the island, Quarenghi's uncompleted building was razed, and the construction of the Bourse entrusted to the young French architect Thomas de Thomon, whose design – with peristyle – is Petersburg's most radical exercise in column and mass (see Chapter 12).[88]

But such reverses were a rarity in Quarenghi's career. During the same period, he completed a number of major state buildings, including the State Bank on Sadovaia Street (1783–9). This three-story Palladian building, with a Corinthian hexastyle portico above the main entrance on the ground floor, was connected by an open gallery on either side to an immense structure in the shape of a horseshoe (used for the bank vaults) that culminated in end facades on the street line (Figure 377).[89] Although the bank had its specific requirements that stimulated this ingenious plan, Quarenghi would henceforth give new meaning to the concept of the wing in Russian architecture. A similar design appears in his building for the Sheremetev Pilgrims' Refuge in Moscow (see Chapter 11).

Even more significant for the development of Rus-

Figure 374. Mikhailovskii Castle. Petersburg. Grand Staircase. Designed by Vincenzo Brenna. (P 106–3)

Figure 375. Mikhailovskii Castle. Petersburg. Court church. Ceiling
painting by Carlo Scotti. (P 106–14)

Figure 376. Academy of Sciences. Petersburg. Architect: Giacomo
Quarenghi. 1783–9. (P 8–9)

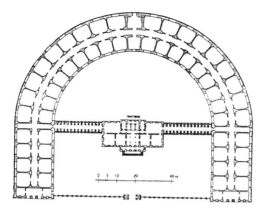

Figure 377. State Bank. Petersburg. 1783–9. Architect: Giacomo Quarenghi. Plan, elevation.

sian neoclassicism was his articulation of the facades of the service building: massive rustication and, above the ground floor, large thermal windows (semicircular with two vertical mullions) – so called because of their derivation from the Baths of Diocletian, and also much used by Palladio.[90] The genius of neoclassicism lay in its adapatability to diverse needs, and Quarenghi established the precedent for a creative union of prosaic function (barracks, warehouses, trading arcades) and monumental style, not only in Petersburg and Moscow, but throughout the Russian Empire.[91]

Although his commercial structures reveal the all-encompassing aesthetic of Russian neoclassicism, Quarenghi was no less concerned with function in imperial structures such as the Hermitage Theater (1783–7; Figure 378). Linked to Velten's Old Hermitage by a covered passage over the Winter Canal, the building accommodated a chamber theater designed as a modified amphitheater (the curve of the seating area is noticeable in the semicircular projection attached to Velten's passageway).[92] In its decorative work, the Neva facade is a notable exception to Quarenghi's usual austerity, with window pediments and decorative niches containing statues and busts of the Greek poets. The lightly rusticated ground floor provides a base for the Corinthian loggia of the upper two levels, with the harmonious effect of the whole derived from the spacing of columns and windows.

The collaboration between Quarenghi and Velten continued into the Old Hermitage, when Catherine commissioned Quarenghi in 1783 to build a gallery, or "loggia," attached to the north side of Velten's Hermitage. The structure was intended to house reproductions of the interior decorations by Raphael at the Vatican Palace. (The decorative panels – tempera on linen – were executed by Christopher Unterberger in 1778, while Quarenghi was still in Italy.[93]) The first floor of the Raphael Loggia also housed the Voltaire Library. Within the Winter Palace itself, Quarenghi undertook a major reconstruction of the state rooms extending from the Jordan Staircase along the Neva facade: a square Antechamber; the Grand Gallery, 62 meters long, with attached Corinthian faux marbre columns; and the Concert Hall, of the same dimensions as the Antechamber (see Figure 312). These interiors were destroyed in the 1837 fire, but their restoration by Vasilii Stasov preserved Quarenghi's general design and, in the case of the Concert Hall, much of its detail.[94]

So great was Quarenghi's success in the 1780s that he received many offers from grandees of the period to rebuild their mansions – in some cases only recently completed. Whatever the size, all of these urban residences displayed Quarenghi's subtle balance among the facade elements, and most were marked with a pediment over the main entrance. It should be noted that they all ultimately became institutional buildings, and continue to function as such – again demonstrating the principle of universality in late eighteenth-century neoclassicism.[95]

Quarenghi considered his masterpiece to be the building for the Smolnyi Institute for the Education of Young Women of Noble Birth, founded by Catherine in 1764 and originally housed in Rastrelli's Resurrection Convent. The plan for the institute (1806–8) combined elements from preceding projects, such as the Catherine Institute and the Liteinyi hospital, with a dentilated pediment reminiscent of the Academy of Sciences. Yet the Smolnyi Institute is both larger and more complex. The eight Ionic columns of the portico are matched with fourteen pilasters of the same order along the facade of the central building (Figure 379), and the wings extending from the main

Figure 378. Hermitage Theater. Petersburg. 1783–7. Architect: Giacomo Quarenghi. (P 16–10)

structure are marked by an attached portico of six Ionic columns. The south (right) wing contains the two-story Ceremonial Hall, whose white brilliance, with Corinthian columns of artificial marble, is among Quarenghi's best interiors.[96]

The plan of the Smolnyi Institute, with its wings, reminds that much of Quarenghi's work involves a central structure with flanking symmetrical forms – a concept that received its most extensive development in the design of the neoclassical estate house. Starov was the first to develop the idea, in works such as the Tauride Palace, and it was widely applied in Moscow and the surrounding provinces. In this respect, Quarenghi's work not only contributed to the creation of a physical environment for the Russian nobility, but also defined their privileged status in terms of classical antiquity. The Manege of the Horse Guards Regiment (1804–7; Figure 380), with its simple form but elegant Tuscan portico, suggests a classical temple, built for a military unit drawn from the nobility.[97]

In a more direct sense, his use of the central structure with flanking wings reached unprecedented dimensions in the design of manor houses, particularly on large estates located in newly consolidated areas in the south of the empire. At Lialichi, the estate of Count P. V. Zavodskii in the former Chernigov (now Briansk) Province, Quarenghi during the 1780s created a Palladian structure with a raised hexastyle Corinthian portico and a central domed rotunda. One-story wings were connected to the main structure by curved galleries, in the manner of Cameron's design at Pavlovsk. On the interior, the space beneath the

dome contained an Italian Hall – also reminiscent of the Palladian manner at Pavlovsk – around which two floors of rooms were disposed (Figure 381). The decoration included intricate stucco moldings as well as coffered ceilings (in the Great Hall) and arabesque ornmanent.[98] For all of their variety, the extent to which these estate houses share significant features of design not only reflects the number of commissions received by Quarenghi, but also suggests the establishment of a standard.[99]

Quarenghi's villa designs appeared even in Petersburg, such as his expansion, in 1783–4, of the suburban house, or dacha, of A. A. Bezborodko. Located on the right bank of the Neva opposite the Smolnyi complex, the mansion was originally built in 1773–7 by Vasilii Bazhenov, who had created a pseudo-Gothic castle not unlike his work of the same period for the imperial estate of Tsaritsyno near Moscow. Quarenghi redesigned the main facade with a dentilated pediment and provided end wings attached to the curved galleries (Figure 382). He also created a landscape park with pavilions, including a classical "ruin" that prefigures the onset of the romantic sensibility in Russian culture.[100]

It has recently been argued that Quarenghi was also the guiding spirit behind the design of the palace for the Tsarevich Paul to the north of Petersburg, on Stone Island.[101] If so, the Kamennoostrovskii (Stone Island) Palace was one of the earliest of Quarenghi's assignments in Russia, undertaken shortly after his arrival at the end of 1779. The initial work, interrupted by a flood in 1777, apparently belonged to Velten, who remained the supervising architect until the com-

Figure 379. Smolnyi Institute. Petersburg. 1806–8. Architect: Giacomo Quarenghi. Main portico. (P 24)

296

Figure 380. Manege of the Horse Guards Regiment. Petersburg.
1804–7. Architect: Giacomo Quarenghi. (P 60–16)

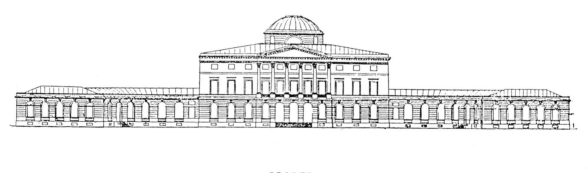

ПЛАН 1-го ЭТАЖА

Figure 381. Zavodskii estate house. Lialichi (Chernigov Province).
1780s. Architect: Giacomo Quarenghi. Section, plan.

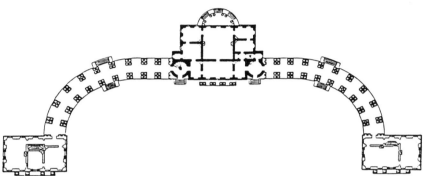

Figure 382. Bezborodko dacha. Petersburg. 1783–4. Architect: Giacomo Quarenghi. Plan, elevation.

pletion of the main structure in 1781. The palace is marked by Tuscan Doric porticoes on both the north and south facades (overlooking the Small Nevka River; Figure 383). Elsewhere, the flat roof is surmounted by a balustrade – a typical resolution for Quarenghi's palaces. The interior has been altered, but the central two-story Great Hall and gallery has preserved much of its decorative plaster work, particularly the medallions on mythological themes. Notable among the items of interior decoration were four canvas panels on classical themes painted by Hubert Robert in 1784–5.[102] By the end of the decade, Paul and Maria Fedorovna had moved to Pavlovsk, and the abandoned palace was converted by Brenna for use by the deposed Polish king Stanislaw Poniatowski.

More urban in setting was the Iusupov Palace on the Fontanka, built in the mideighteenth century and reconstructed in the 1790s in the style of a villa with landscape park. Quarenghi converted the long horizontal facade of the original building with an Ionic portico on both the park and courtyard facades. On the latter, he placed Ionic loggias connecting the cen-

tral portico with the side wings, whose pediments echo those of the central structure (Figure 384). The courtyard was enclosed in a windowless semicircular structure containing service buildings and leading to an arched entryway. On either side of the entrance extended two-story wings placed in a tangential line along the recently completed granite embankment of the Fontanka.[103] This plan maintains the sense of balance and symmetry characteristic of Quarenghi's work, despite the the fact that the facade of the palace and the Fontanka embankment are not parallel.

Among the most ingenious of Quarenghi's palace reconstructions in Petersburg was the conversion of part of the former Vorontsov Palace for religious use. The Emperor Paul had commissioned two churches, Orthodox and Roman Catholic, to be constructed at the palace as a sign of his dream of a rapprochement between the two creeds – with himself, as Grandmaster of the Maltese Order, playing a major role in the process. The Orthodox church was placed within the palace itself, but in constructing the Catholic Maltese Chapel (1798–1800), Quarenghi razed the back part of the palace quadrangle (see Figure 308)

Figure 383. Kamennoostrovskii Palace. Stone Island, Petersburg. 1776–85. Architects: Giacomo Quarenghi(?) and Georg Friedrich Velten. South facade. (L 72–50)

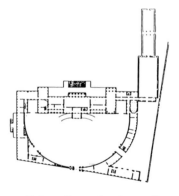

Figure 384. Iusupov Palace. Fontanka Quay, Petersburg. 1790s. Architect: Giacomo Quarenghi. Plan, elevation.

and erected a basilica connected by volutes to the flanking wings of Rastrelli's structure. The design of the small entrance was calculated for monumental effect: a pair of major Corinthian columns, attached to the facade and linked by festoons on either side of the portal, which was framed by a pediment and columns in the Doric order (Figure 385). The dentilated pediment over the facade contained one of Quarenghi's favored ornamental motifs, a round wreath

with flowing ribbons, in the middle of which was the Maltese Cross. The interior, with its decorated barrel vault ceiling, showed both richness of detail and clarity of line in the use of parallel rows of yellow faux marbre (artificial marble) Corinthian columns to mark the nave. Quarenghi attached white pilasters behind the columns and at two-thirds height to support the gallery without visual distraction from the grand effect of the colonnade.[104]

Notwithstanding the range of Quarenghi's work, he remained above all an architect of imperial palaces. His career in Russia began with the English Palace at Peterhof, and during the same period, he was also involved in the construction of pavilions in the Catherine Park at Tsarskoe Selo. The most notable among them was the Concert Hall (1782–6), described by Quarenghi as "a pavilion with a large hall for music, two studies, and an open temple dedicated to the goddess Ceres, as well as some ruins in the ancient manner close by."[105] Of the two main facades of the pavilion, the one overlooking a pond has a Tuscan portico with pediment (Figure 386), and the opposite side forms a rotunda, also in Tuscan Doric, that served as the temple to Ceres. Festoons and bucrania decorate the frieze, and the walls display bas-reliefs on themes associated with Ceres by the Russian sculptor M. I. Kozlovskii. The interior contained decorative work in plaster and faux marbre, as well as intricate wall paintings in the Roman style. The floor of the main hall included a Roman mosaic from the early third century on the theme "The Rape of Europa."[106]

The apogee of Quarenghi's work for his imperial patrons occurred in his design for one of the last great palaces on the imperial estates to the south of Petersburg: the Alexander Palace at Tsarskoe Selo. Commissioned by Catherine for her grandson Alexander and begun in 1792, the palace is a distinctive interpretation that both incorporates and transcends the Palladian and Roman styles. The residence was situated to the east of the main entrance to the Catherine Palace, yet Quarenghi's building was screened from Rastrelli's much larger structure both by a formal park (the New Garden) and by the landscaped Alexander Park. As at the English Palace, Quarenghi placed the main facade overlooking a pond (Figure 387); yet the basic plan was originally intended for Petersburg, and it retained many of the characteristics of Quarenghi's urban work, including perpendicular wings forming a courtyard for the main entrance (Figure 388).[107] The courtyard was to have been enclosed by a colonnade along the street line, but at Tsarskoe Selo, Quarenghi extended the wings and moved the double Corinthian colonnade back toward the structure, where its white

Figure 385. Maltese Chapel (Catholic) at former Vorontsov Palace. Petersburg. 1798–1800. Architect: Giacomo Quarenghi. Elevation by Quarenghi. Courtesy of the State Hermitage.

Figure 386. Concert Hall. Tsarskoe Selo. 1782–6. Architect: Giacomo Quarenghi. (TS 5–24)

Figure 387. Alexander Palace. Tsarskoe Selo. 1792–6. Architect: Giacomo Quarenghi. (TS 4–17)

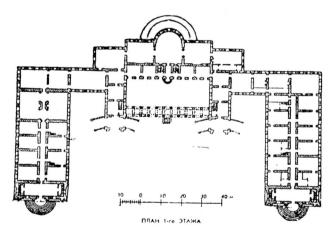

Figure 388. Alexander Palace. Tsarskoe Selo. Plan.

columns in the major order create an enclosed entrance court.

Although habitable in 1796, the Alexander Palace was not stuccoed until 1800, at which point the architectural detail was delineated in white against a yellow background, and the brilliant play of light and shadow, of space and form stood fully revealed. The design of the exterior walls follows the precedent established by Starov at the Tauride Palace in its simplicity of articulation – no window surrounds and only a drip line separating the first and second floors. Yet the detail at the various culminating points of the structure – the end facades of the wings, the colonnade – is altogether richer (Figure 389). The dentilated cornice of the structure is surmounted with a balustrade. Little of Quarenghi's interior design has been preserved at the palace, which was frequently remodeled; yet the spatial configuration was retained in the large rooms.[108]

With the passing of the reigns of Catherine and Paul, Quarenghi continued to work as imperial architect during the reign of Alexander I. At Pavlovsk, he remodeled a number of rooms on the lower floor of the south wing and of the main building (primarily the living quarters of Maria Fedorovna). But during this period, he was best known for public works such as the Smolny Institute and the Anichkov Colonnade, in which he provided a transition from the Roman

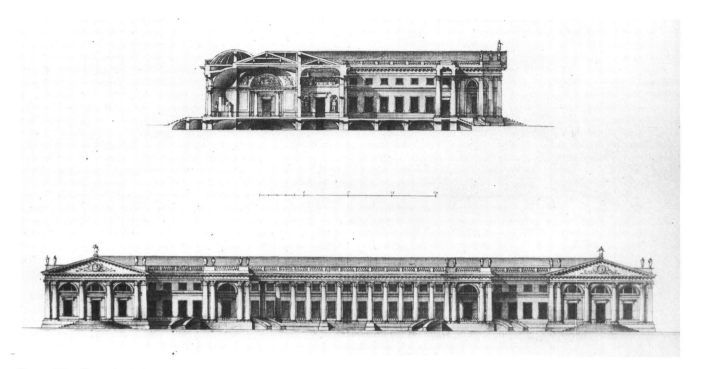

Figure 389. Alexander Palace. Tsarskoe Selo. Elevation by Quarenghi. Courtesy of the State Hermitage.

classicism of the eighteenth century to the grand ensembles of Carlo Rossi in the 1820s. Indeed, Quarenghi's career ended as the last phase of Russian neoclassicism in the post-Napoleonic period began, and he seems to proclaim the transition in his 1814 design for the Narva Gates, a triumphal arch (originally of wood) in imitation of Roman victory monuments and commemorating the Russian guards regiments who campaigned against Napoleon.[109]

After the expulsion of Napoleon's army from Russia in 1812, Alexander I initiated a competition to create a "Temple-Monument" as a memorial to the Russian sacrifice during the war. Originally intended for a site on Sparrow Hills overlooking Moscow, the project acquired a complicated history that ended with the construction of the Temple of Christ the Savior in 1837–83 on the other side of the Moscow River (see Chapter 13). The project proposals were in themselves a significant episode in Russian architecture, and Quarenghi's two proposals, submitted in 1815, were among the earliest. Both involve a grand rotunda in the manner of the Pantheon: one prefixed with a hexastyle Tuscan portico reminiscent of the Church of Sts. Peter and Paul at Courbevoie (1789) by Louis Le Masson, and the other with a higher dome and two octastyle Corinthian porticos on opposite sides.[110]

Quarenghi's ability to combine different classical orders seems to prefigure nineteenth-century eclecticism, yet the restraint and clarity of his arrangement of column and mass on the exterior (often with lavish decoration in the Roman manner on the interior) established a distinctive neoclassical aesthetic in Russia. His antecedents in Italian, English, and French architecture are many and obvious. Indeed, much of his work would not have seemed out of place in America during the same period. Yet the prolific number of his structures – if not as dramatic as those by Thomas de Thomon, Zakharov, and Rossi – established an architectural setting, an urban texture that is unmistakably of Petersburg and of Russia in its flourishing at the end of Catherine's reign.

302

CHAPTER 11

Eighteenth-Century Neoclassicism in Moscow and the Provinces

It's worth walking for an hour around the twisted, slanted streets of Moscow, and you will immediately notice that this is a city of patriarchal family existence. The houses stand apart, almost everyone of them has a wide yard, overgrown with grass.

– Vissarion Belinskii

While the architects of Petersburg developed a new classical idiom for buildings both public and private, Moscow and its surrounding provinces adapted neoclassicism in ways less concerned with the state and its high personages. Indeed, it can be argued that Moscow's culture, as well as its architecture, during the latter half of the eighteenth century represented a reaction against the *haut monde* of Petersburg. But despite the lesser scale and luxury of Moscow's architecture during this period, its buildings displayed no less a command of the tectonic and decorative principles of the neoclassicism.

Neoclassicism in Moscow and the provinces was above all an architecture of wealthy landowners and merchants: for their estate houses, for the mansions they maintained in Moscow, and for the institutions – the Noblemen's Assemblies, the charitable institutions, the churches – that represented their privileges and duties during the age of Catherine. The upheavals – social and military – of the Petrine era and of the reign of Anna Ioannovna had not been conducive to the stability needed for substantial investment in estate property. To be sure, the state had granted land and serfs to nobles by virtue of their service to the state, as well as lucrative contracts and to certain merchants and private industrialists. But apart from a few favorites of the autocrat who were allowed to retire to estates in the Russian heartland, even those of great wealth felt constrained against investment in a large estate manor – which in any event was a practice to which they were unaccustomed by their cultural traditions.[1]

The rapidity with which this changed can be at-

tributed to a series of legislative acts that on the one hand recognized the already considerable privileges accumulated to the nobility, and on the other effected a limited retreat from constant involvement in European conflicts (such as the Seven Years War) and great power politics, in which Russia had achieved major status in a remarkably short time at such enormous cost. Thus, the brief reign of Peter III witnessed not only Russia's controversial withdrawal from the Seven Years War – to the great relief of Prussia – but also the promulgation in February 1762 of the Edict on the Freedom of the Nobility. The general opinion as to the edict's significance has been stated by Richard Pipes: "Altogether, it is difficult to exaggerate the importance of the edict of 1762 for Russia's social and cultural history. With this single act the monarchy created a large, privileged, Westernised leisure class, such as Russia had never known before."[2]

To be sure, there were still restrictions on the nobility, and the apogee of that class's virtually unlimited authority over the countryside, as well as its release from its obligations to the state, did not occur until the granting of the unique Charter of the Nobility by Catherine the Great in 1785 – which led to new heights of expenditure on the great country estates of the central provinces. Yet even in the 1760s, the process was well under way, with the example of the imperial estates and palaces to provide direction in matters of design and taste. Only a few of the wealthiest or most favored grandees could afford the services of a Quarenghi or a Starov, but the genius of neoclassicism lay in its adaptability, and a number of wealthy Russians relied on the talents of serf architects and craftsmen to implement designs taken directly or indirectly from Petersburg or western sources.

Yet neoclassicism was more than a fashionable imitation of the palaces of the autocrats who had bestowed privilege upon the landed nobility (as well as certain industrialists whose wealth qualified them for entry into the nobility – an opportunity some pointedly refused to accept). Indeed, the extent of imperial largess stimulated a search for a myth, an ideology to legitimize this accession to privilege. For some of the recently created nobility, this involved an attempt to locate the origins of their new power in medieval institutions.[3] For Catherine, who summoned a special Legislative Commission in 1767, the concept of the nobility as a ruling class (ultimately subservient to the autocracy) was based on political philosophers from classical and modern times, including, paradoxically, Montesquieu, author of *Esprit des Lois*.

It is not necessary here to recount the subtleties and contradictions in the definition of noble privilege during the second half of the eighteenth century. The ready justification for the new power – cultural, social, and to an extent political – lay in a classical heritage that Russia had only recently acquired.[4] Not only did the classics, revived in the culture of Renaissance Italy and Baroque France, provide a model for the concept of noble *virtu*, but the very iconography of classical art and architecture implied a validation of privilege for the Russian elite.

Thus, the assimilation of the aesthetic principles of neoclassicism in literature and the fine arts was paralleled in architecture and the applied arts by the reproduction of scenes from Homer and Ovid – as well as from the history of classical Greece and Rome – extolling courage, sacrifice, honor, or peaceful domestic pursuits draped in the mythology of Olympus. Although it is unlikely that those who commissioned these decorative paintings and friezes for their neoclassical mansions inevitably did so with an awareness of a philosophical *moralité*, there is evidence to indicate that the message of classical art did indeed justify the sense of a privileged class in late eighteenth-century Russia.

The Neoclassical Estate Manor

The design of estate houses in the western manner begins in Moscow with the Petrine era.[5] Yet it is difficult to define with precision the evolution of this form, because the few extant examples have been so frequently remodeled.[6] By the 1760s, however, the vocabulary of neoclassicism had been introduced to Moscow and the surrounding area by architects such as Karl Blank, whose late baroque churches and other structures (see Chapter 9) – at Voronovo, for example – showed greater restraint in the application of surface ornament than did contemporary work in Petersburg. Soon thereafter, Blank was involved in the creation of Kuskovo, one of the first major neoclassical estate ensembles in the Moscow area – and the best preserved.

The village of Kuskovo, located to the north of Moscow, was acquired in 1715 by Boris Sheremetev – a close associate of Peter and commanding general at the battle of Poltava – who built there a wooden summer residence. Kuskovo's accession to magnificence began soon after the marriage of Peter Borisovich Sheremetev to Varvara Cherkasskaia in 1743; for not only did the union produce one of the greatest private fortunes in Russia, but the dowry also included a number of talented serf architects and painters who were to play the major role in implementing Sheremetev's considerable plans for the estate.[7] The enhancement of the estate grounds, located next to the Cherkasskii estate of Veshniaki, was no doubt stimulated by the proximity of Rastrelli's palace for Empress Elizabeth at Perovo – in the same area to the northeast of Moscow.

The earliest extant building at Kuskovo is the Church of the Mandylion Icon of the Savior (Figure 390), built in 1737–8 in the simplified baroque style of the period – and now missing its cornice statuary. The first building designed after the marriage of Peter Sheremetev, however, is the brick Dutch House, constructed in 1749 as a memorial to Peter the Great and to his fondness for things Dutch (among other exhibits, the house contained a collection of Delft porcelain, and the walls of some of the rooms were covered with Dutch tile). On the exterior, the pavilion is a simple, finely proportioned statement of seventeenth-century Dutch urban architecture – a theme that Karl Blank realized on a larger scale at Voronovo in the 1760s.

Architectural design at Kuskovo during this initial period was done under the supervision of Iurii Kologrivov, whose study in Italy is reflected in his design of the Italian House (1754–5), in the style of a late Renaissance villa (Figure 391). Having largely rejected their own seventeenth-century architecture, Russian builders of the post-Petrine period assiduously recreated a variety of European styles from the same period. After Kologrivov's death in 1754, construction was supervised by the serf Fedor Argunov, who in

Figure 390. Estate house and Church of the Savior at Kuskovo. Moscow. South (main) facade. (M 93–2)

1755–61 built the Grotto pavilion to a design resembling the Grotto at Tsarskoe Selo (see Figure 306). Although the statuary that first graced the roof has not survived, the niches between the rusticated paired columns contain statues of Zeus, Venus, Flora, Ceres, and Diana (Figure 392).[8] The interior is a tour de force of intricate ornamental patterns from Mediterranean shells embedded in a mixture of stucco and sand (Figure 393). The central space of the Grotto culminates in a dome, whose lunettes admit light through a green scrim, creating an aquatic ambience appropriate to the pavilion's designation.

In 1765, Karl Blank assumed the duties of architect at Kuskovo, where he remained until 1780.[9] During this time, he supervised the reconstruction of the mansion, and designed the Hermitage (1765–7), a two-story pavilion whose plasticity of form reminds of the work of Rastrelli and Chevakinskii at Tsarskoe Selo two decades earlier, as well as the transitional style of Rinaldi for his pavilions at Oranienbaum. Like Rinaldi, Blank contained his baroque design, composed of cylinders and projecting polygonal shapes, within a facade of Corinthian pilasters and a sharply delineated cornice decorated with festoons (Figure 394). The hemispherical dome is surmounted by a reproduction of the statue of the goddess Flora originally done in the 1770s by Pierre Laurent.[10] The rich visual texture of the Hermitage and its silhouette is enhanced by its location at the intersection of eight of the garden paths – each of which frames a view of the pavilion.

The main enterprise at Kuskovo during the late eighteenth century was the creation of an imposing Sheremetev summer residence. The rebuilding of the original structure had begun by the 1750s, and in 1755, the large pond in front of the house was excavated. Yet the grand design of the mansion took shape only in the late 1760s, under the supervision of Blank.[11] The final plan of the main facade and much of the interior followed designs commissioned from Charles de Wailly, whose work for Catherine has been noted in the preceding chapter. The structure rested on a limestone and brick foundation, but the walls were of wood; and whereas the texture of the plank facing is clearly visible on close inspection, the articulation of the facade conveyed the impression of masonry, with balusters beneath the windows and simply etched panels above. Framed by flanking projections with a curved pediment over Ionic columns and classical motifs carved in wood, the main portico is reached by curving ramps and culminates in a pediment with an elaborately carved Sheremetev crest.

The interior is defined by two parallel enfilades – one overlooking the pond (the "state," or formal

305

Figure 391. Italian House, Kuskovo. 1754–5. Architect: Iurii Kologrivov. (M 91–12)

Figure 393. Grotto, Kuskovo. Interior. (M 92–10)

Figure 392. Grotto, Kuskovo. 1755–61. Architect: Fedor Argunov. East facade. (M 91–11)

rooms) and the other facing the formal garden (with the living rooms on a more intimate scale). Because Kuskovo was not intended as a "major" palace, much of the interior decoration is derived either from existing Sheremetev palaces (in Petersburg) or from standard patterns – as in the design of the parquet floors. In addition, the molding is of paper-mache or plaster, whereas the larger, architectural details are of faux marbre. Despite this illusionistic use of material (suited to the theatrical nature of the house, with the rooms like stage sets distinct in character and decor), the design and its implementation represent the most accomplished example of French-inspired neoclassical decor in Moscow.

The vestibule – decorated with vases of alabaster, grisaille murals of scenes from classical mythology, scagliola pilasters, and capitals of paper-mache and plaster – opens on either side to a view of the main enfilade of drawing rooms (including the Music Room, with its Chippendale chairs, Flemish tapestries, and busts of Peter and Vavara Sheremetev by Fedot Shubin) leading to a blaze of color in the Mauve drawing room of the southwest corner. The color themes of each room – stated primarily by fabrics such as silk damask, satin, and brocatel – are coordinated not only in relation to the adjoining rooms, but also with regard to the exterior setting and the quality of the natural light through the large windows.[12] The perpendicular turn at the Mauve room leads to the State Bedroom (Figure 395), a replica of the same room in the Sheremetev palace on the Fontanka (see Chapter 9). Adjoining the State Bedroom is the suite used by the family and connected to the enfilade on the park facade. This suite contains such Russian elements as the ceramic stove with decorative motifs that combine the traditional and the neoclassical.

The other half of the main enfilade leads from the vestibule through the green Billiard Room to the Dining Room, with its portraits of Boris and Anna Sheremetev and Aleksei and Maria Cherkasskii (the parents of Peter and Varvara Sheremetev) by the serf painter Ivan Argunov. The ceiling painting of Juno by Louis Jean-François Lagrenée has remained well-preserved, but the centerpiece of the room is a large trellised niche with a marble bust of Alexander the Great (Figure 396), whose form is one of the clearest

Figure 395. Estate house, Kuskovo. 1769–75. State Bedroom. (M 141–34)

allusions to an iconographic system that pervades this and subsequent Russian mansions of the neoclassical period.

The references to heroic classicism culminate in the Ballroom, or Mirror Gallery, located at the center of the park enfilade and named for the mirrored inset French windows of the interior wall that reflect the light admitted by their counterparts overlooking the formal park. Mirrors are frequently used in the major rooms at Kuskovo to enlarge the impression of space and to enhance the lustre provided by natural light, torchères, and gilded candelabras – a technique that had been explored by Rastrelli and his predecessors in the design of the imperial palaces of Petersburg. And whereas the Kuskovo ballroom (also used for formal dinners) is smaller than Rastrelli's Great Hall at Tsarksoe Selo (see Figure 304), the monumentality of its design is no less apparent.

The decoration of the Ballroom displays the iconography of the estate culture, particularly in the ceiling painting, executed by Lagrenée and renovated in the 1880s, represents the apotheosis of Peter Shere-

Figure 394. Hermitage, Kuskovo. 1765–7. Architect: Karl Blank. East facade. (M 91–3)

Figure 396. Estate house, Kuskovo. Dining Room. (M 141–14)

metev surrounded by various muses. The borders of the ceiling are decorated with paintings of his various orders, including the crosses of St. Andrew and St. Anne. The heroic values proclaimed by classical iconography are still more evident in a series of gilded relief panels – designed by Johann Just for the ends of the ballroom – that depict the exploits of Gaius Mucius Scaevola, the mythic Roman hero of the sixth century B.C. who, having failed to assassinate the Etruscan king Porsenna, held his right hand to the fire as a sign of indifference to physical pain. The Mucius Scaevola legend acquired great resonance in Russia at the time of the Napoleonic invasion, when it can be said to have penetrated the popular consciousness as a symbol of self-sacrifice and patriotic devotion. For Peter Sheremetev and his contemporaries, the panels would have served as further expression of the standards of antiquity upheld by the elite of the Russian nobility.

Although the ballroom extends to the full height of the interior, the other rooms along the park enfilade comprise living suites, and have lower ceilings than the state rooms. The additional space above forms an entresol composed of servants' rooms with low ceilings (slightly above human height), but well illuminated by a second level of small windows extending the length of the park facade.[13] The skilfull distribution of space within the floor plan (Figure 397) and the means of circulation between the enfilades create an unusual variety of perspectives as one moves through the house – and out to the steps leading to the parterre of the formal garden.[14] From this point, the view opens directly to the imposing greenhouse (1761–3), built by Fedor Argunov and containing a refined system for year-round horticulture and the development of exotic tropical plants.[15]

Within the parterre itself are two monuments to Catherine the Great, including a column with an allegorical statue of Minerva. The empress visited Kuskovo in 1783, the year of Peter Sheremetev's election to the honorific post as head of the Moscow nobility. This placed still greater demands on his already legendary hospitality, which had made Kuskovo and its park a center for festive celebrations open to the public

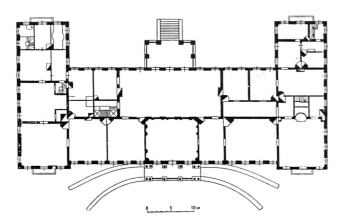

Figure 397. Estate house, Kuskovo. Plan. From Tikhomirov, *Arkhitektura moskovskikh usadeb*.

and at times involving several thousand visitors.[16] In the 1790s, however, Sheremetev's son Nikolai tired of the scale of entertainment and perhaps also of the style of Kuskovo. He had passed much of his youth in Holland and France, was familiar with recent developments in western art, and – typically for third-generation fortunes – preferred to devote himself to the pursuit of the arts, with a special interest in theater.

Having formed at Kuskovo the leading serf theatrical troupe in Russia, Nikolai Sheremetev in 1792 undertook the construction of a palace-theater at his neighboring estate of Ostankino, a former Cherkasskii village whose church, built by the serf Pavel Potekhin, so brilliantly exemplifies the late seventeenth-century ornamental style (see Figure 191).[17] Sheremetev, the owner of 210,000 serfs and vast land holdings, could well afford to build an entire estate around a theater, and the dimensions of the central structure, culminating in a rotunda, are much larger than those of the Kuskovo mansion. Several architects submitted proposals, including Giacomo Quarenghi, author of a number of major projects in Moscow (discussed later). The basic plan for the structure, its facades, and the adjoining park is attributed to Francesco Camporesi, although during the next 6 years, Sheremetev turned to Quarenghi, Karl Blank, and even Vincenzo Brenna for modifications, as well as additions to the wings.[18] The construction was supervised by Sheremetev's serf architects Aleksei Mironov, Grigorii Dikushin, and Pavel Argunov (son of the painter Ivan Argunov), who had apprenticed with Bazhenov in Petersburg.

The entire ensemble of palace and pavilions at Ostankino was created within the space of a decade. The central building (Figure 398) has an elevated portico

of six Corinthian columns and culminates in a rotunda with Palladian overtones (for all of its monumental appearance, the structure is built of wood covered with stucco). This establishes a center for a ramifying series of wings and attached pavilions that were used for living space (Figure 399). The interior is dominated by the theater, which is two stories in height and extends across much of the central block. Its floor was ingeniously designed to serve also as grand ballroom. The upper floor, or bel étage, consists of an enfilade of state rooms that open onto the portico, and a picture gallery.

On the ground floor, galleries extend from either side of the central structure to the two main pavilions: the Italian (west), with a sculpture gallery; and the Egyptian (east), containing a concert hall. The west facade of the Italian Pavilion ends in a rotunda, and the large windows of both pavilions achieve a union between the luxuriant interior and the park beyond. Indeed, the main rectangle of the park, enclosed on three sides by trees and lined with statuary, has been characterized as a "quasiinterior" space.[19] The harmony of park and palace is facilitated by the unity of the park facade (Figure 400), defined by a grand loggia of ten Ionic columns and a pediment with the carved coat of arms.

The facades of the palace and its pavilions are liberally decorated with statuary placed in niches, as well as friezes composed of abstract patterns and classical tableaux (of particular note are the bas-reliefs of sacrifice to Jupiter and Demeter by Fedor Gordeev and Gavriil Zamaraev). In 1801, Alexander I visited Ostankino as a part of his coronation ceremonies; but soon thereafter, the theater waned, no doubt in response to the illness and death, in 1803, of Zhemchugova, the leading actress of the troup and Nikolai Sheremetev's wife. After Sheremetev's own premature death in 1809, the palace remained in the family as a little-used monument to the culture fostered by the Russian nobility at its zenith.

Of the major Moscow estate houses of the late eighteenth century, the third to have survived largely intact is the palace at Arkhangelskoe. Although the building was not completed until the 1820s and much of its interior reflects the tastes of a later period, the basic design and surviving form of the palace nonetheless derive from the Catherinian era. Arkhangelskoe was acquired in 1703 by Prince Dmitrii Golitsyn, a close associate of Peter the Great. It is a telling commentary on gentry service during Peter's reign that Golitsyn did not see the estate until 27 years later –

Figure 398. Ostankino Palace. Moscow. 1792–1800. Architects: Francesco Camporesi and Pavel Argunov. South facade. (M 41–3)

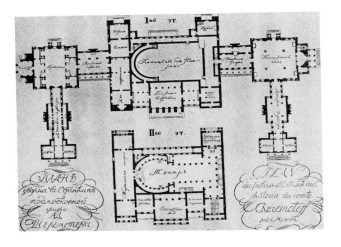

Figure 399. Ostankino Palace. Moscow. Plan of first and second floors, by I. Golosov.

and then only because he had fallen into disfavor with Empress Anne, and retreated to the estate as a form of retirement.[20] The energetic and cultured Golitsyn set about rebuilding the estate and park in the style of the baroque, but his arrest on suspicion of sedition in 1736 led to the confiscation of the estate, which remained untended until the 1770s, when Golitsyn's grandson Nikolai resumed control of the property.

There is little documentary information on Nikolai Golitsyn's rebuilding of the estate, but by 1780, the old house had been razed, and work began on the wings of a new mansion to a plan commissioned from the French architect Charles de Gerne, who never visited Russia. One of the most striking features of the palace is its park facade, set on a terraced hill. The design of the terrace, built in the 1790s, has been attributed to Giacomo Trombaro, who immigrated to Russia in 1779 and worked as a court architect in

Petersburg.[21] The palace was still far from complete at the time of Golitsyn's death in 1809.

The following year his heirs sold the estate to Nikolai Iusupov, who continued and amplified the work begun by his predecessor.[22] Only a small part of Iusupov's magnificent art collection had been evacuated or hidden when French detachments briefly occupied the palace in 1812; yet the primary damage to the palace and its park statuary occurred after the French retreat, when the Iusupov peasants rampaged through the grounds during a local uprising – an event that reveals the precarious position of a culture based on a serf economy. After the restoration of order, many prominent Moscow architects participated in the completion of the estate, but during the 1820s, supervision of the work was given to Evgraf Tiurin, who restored the palace to new heights of magnificance after a fire in 1820 destroyed much of the interior (the Iusupov art collection was, however, saved).

The Arkhangelskoe palace thus represents an amalgamation of five decades of neoclassical architecture and interior decoration. The monumental courtyard gates, built in 1817 by Stepan Melnikov and framed with paired Tuscan Doric columns (Figure 401), set the tone for the classical restraint of the palace facade, flanked by colonnades of paired Tuscan columns and marked in the center by a tetrastyle portico in the Ionic order – all to dimensions and proportions canonized by Vignola.[23] The cornice and the pediment of the portico are heavily dentilated, but the walls, with large windows appropriate to a country house reserved for the warmer season, are devoid of decoration (cf. Starov's Tauride Palace, Figure 350). The central structure culminates in a belvedere, or narrow rotunda, marked by paired Corinthian columns that frame French windows with fanlights and keystones.

The interior of the Arkhangelskoe palace is arranged along two enfilades facing the courtyard (north) and park terrace (south), respectively, and linked at either end by transverse enfilades (Figure 402).[24] The central, and in all respects dominant, interior is the Oval Hall, which extends from the park facade to form the half rotunda of the terrace. Both major enfilades lead to this brilliant two-story hall, with French windows between paired Corinthian columns and pilasters of yellow marble. The columns support a cornice with balusters beneath lunettes that on the park facade admit light for the coffered dome, at whose center a painted figure of a female nude hovers above an enormous chandelier (Figure 403). With its vistas of the park, the Oval Hall reminds that great Russian country houses usually possessed such a space – like the Ballroom at Kuskovo – whose di-

Figure 400. Ostankino Palace. Moscow. Park (north) facade. (M 97–2)

mensions and illumination effected a transition between the interior and the estate park.

The park at Arkhangelskoe contains a greater variety of terrain and landscape than either Kuskovo or Ostankino. The pavilions are situated within the groves on either side of the parterre (240 × 70 meters) and formal garden, which extends southward to the banks of the Moscow River. Of the surviving pavilions on the west side, the central part of the former Library pavilion (renamed the Tea House) is F. I. Pettondi's compact interpretation of a classical rotunda, with a rusticated stucco facade and coffered dome on Corinthian columns. In the same area is the stuccoed wooden estate theater (1817–18; designed by Osip Bove, and built by Tiurin and Melnikov), notable for its Palladian interior by the Italian theater designer Pietro Gonzago, who came to Russia in 1791 at the invitation of Iusopov.[25] On the east side of the park, near the sixteenth-century Church of the Archangel Michael (see Figure 192) is another ensemble, including the imposing arch and Corinthian columns of the

Holy Gates (so named for framing the path to the church), built in 1823–4 to a design by Tiurin.

Hardly had the palace and pavilions been completed, when Nikolai Iusupov died in 1831. His heirs showed little interest or ability in maintaining the estate until the beginning of the twentieth century, when a revival of interest in estate culture placed Arkhangelskoe at the center of attention of artists and critics such as Alexander Benois.[26] During the two decades before the 1917 revolution, the Iusupovs devoted considerable resources to maintaining the estate, and in 1910 commissioned the leading neoclassical revivalist Roman Klein to create a family mausoleum – never used for its intended purpose – whose magnificence serves as a fitting elegy to a milieu already vanished by the time of its completion (see Figure 622).

Kuskovo, Ostankino, and Arkhangelskoe illuminate the various stylistic developments of Russian neo-

311

Figure 401. Arkhangelskoe Palace. Near Moscow. Entrance Gates to main courtyard. 1817. Architect: Stepan Melnikov. (MR 15–35a)

the Demidovs were ennobled and had access to the highest levels of court and society.[27] Akinfii's son Nikita continued to be involved in the supervision of his share of the family factories, inherited in 1745; but by the time of Catherine's reign, he began to devote much of his effort to cultural pursuits, patronage of the arts and sciences, and, in 1771–3, to a grand tour of Europe with his third wife.[28] Like his two brothers, Nikita possessed numerous residences: in Moscow, the Urals, and Petersburg.

In the late 1770s, Nikita Demidov turned his attention to the estate at Petrovskoe, where he apparently commissioned Matvei Kazakov to build a large mansion with detached, flanking wings.[29] The genesis of the design of this palatial edifice, which burned in the 1930s and survives only in the magnificent ruins of its brick walls and limestone columns (see Plate 68), has been the cause of much dispute. The discovery at the beginning of this century of a cornerstone with an inscription, the date 1776, and Kazakov's name clearly marked seemed to establish the architect's identity[30]; yet the similarity of the design to the centralized structures of Vasilii Bazhenov has led to

classical estate architecture, from the early part of Catherine's reign to that of Alexander I. And by the collaborative nature of their creation, enhanced by talented serf architects and artisans, these houses and pavilions possess a generality of character that typifies the times in which they were built – quasibaroque festivity, monumental Palladianism, and the academic elegance of the late neoclassical (Empire) style.

There were, however, monuments of a single presiding genius, and perhaps the most impressive was the house built for Nikita Demidov at the estate of Petrovskoe, near the village of Alabino to the west of Moscow. At the beginning of the eighteenth century, the estate, then known as Kniazhishchevo, belonged to P. P. Shafirov, a close associate of Peter the Great and a distinguished diplomat. In the 1740s, Shafirov's heirs sold the estate to Akinfii Demidov, one of the most prominent of Russia's eighteenth-century industrialists and holder of a vast fortune in mines, metalworking, and related plants in the Urals. As a result of their great wealth and services to the state,

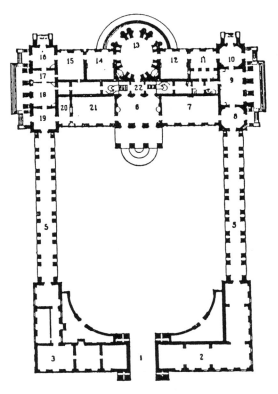

Figure 402. Arkhangelskoe Palace. Near Moscow. 1780–1831. Architects: Charles de Gerne and Evgraf Tiurin. Plan. From Tikhomirov, *Arkhitektura moskovskikh usadeb.*

Figure 403. Arkhangelskoe Palace. Near Moscow. Oval Hall. (MR 14–11)

the supposition that while Kazakov might have built the mansion, its true author was Kazakov's mentor, Bazhenov.[31]

The work of Bazhenov and Kazakov in Moscow will be examined in what follows; but whatever the extent of their mutual work at Petrovskoe (whose design was by no means beyond Kazakov's abilities as an architect), the grandeur of the structure is beyond dispute. Each of its four symmetrial facades contained a loggia of four Tuscan Doric columns of the major order, flanked by pilasters, that support the entablature and cornice. Behind each of the loggias was a large state room (Figure 404). The beveled corner projections, with an Ionic portico of two columns, represent the facades of smaller rectangular rooms, or studies, at the ends of diagonal corridors. The corridors intersected in a circular hall beneath the dome above the center of the structure (this plan was repeated on the second story). The diagonal configuration was repeated in 4 two-story wings – with rusticated facades – that defined the corners of the *cour d'honneur* (Figure 405) and were linked by a brick wall. Beyond the central ensemble lay a landscaped park.

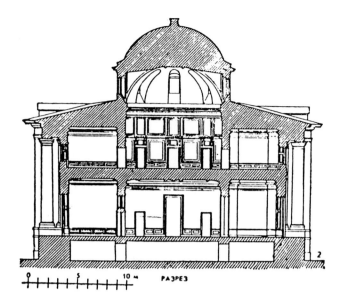

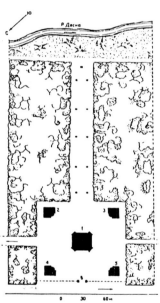

Figure 405. Demidov mansion at Petrovskoe-Alabino. Near Moscow. Section and general plan by D. P. Sukhova.

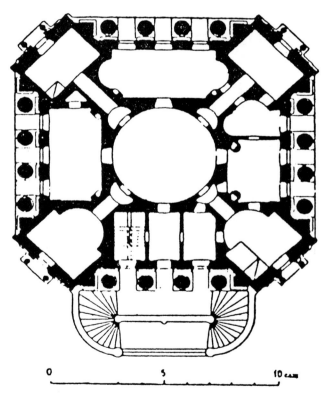

Figure 404. Demidov mansion at Petrovskoe-Alabino. Near Moscow. 1776–80s. Architect: Matvei Kazakov. Plan. From Tikhomirov, *Arkhitektura moskovskikh usadeb*.

The fortune that built the Demidov mansion at Petrovskoe was rapidly dissipated by Nikita's son Nikolai, who moved in the highest aristocratic circles and spent accordingly. Much of the Demidov industrial complex was mortgaged or sold, in addition to a number of estates; and Nikolai Demidov might well have ended in bankruptcy had he not had the very good fortune to marry Baronness Elizaveta, daughter of Alexander Stroganov, at the beginning of the nineteenth century.[32] The Stroganovs had been among the Demidovs' oldest commercial rivals, and after the marital union, they promptly restored order to the Demidov industrial enterprise, which lasted until well into the nineteenth century. Yet after Nikita's death in 1788, the grand estate at Petrovskoe fell into neglect.[33]

The Stroganovs themselves were not inactive in the Moscow area at the end of the eighteenth century; and although Alexander Stroganov chose not to build on the Demidov scale, he too commissioned a neo-classical villa for the family estate at Brattsevo, to the northwest of Moscow (now within the city limits). The Stroganovs were preoccupied with their extensive palaces and cultural activities in Petersburg; yet the design and placement of the Brattsevo villa suggest that the architect was none other than their former serf and one of the great Russian neoclassicists at the turn of the century, Andrei Voronikhin (see Chapter 12).[34] The structure is centered on the interior as well as exterior around a domed rotunda (Figure 406), whose form is reflected in half rotundas projecting from the east and west facades. The main facades – north and south – are marked by Ionic porticos on the background of a rusticated projection of the facade. Above the portico, a balustrade frames the thermal window of the upper story.

The economy of this compact, centralized design (Figure 407) integrates decorative elements into the texture of the structure itself, which is in gentle harmony with its landscaped setting – above a green sward on the slope of a hill. Within the "natural" park of this modest retreat, the single monument is as restrained and elegant as the house itself: a domed pavilion of Ionic columns surrounding a square block in imitation of a classical altar (also attributed to Voronikhin). There could be no clearer expression of the secularization of gentry culture than this noble idealized form, open to the surrounding nature, but also entirely self-sufficient and centered beneath the coffered ceiling of the dome. (The village of Brattsevo has its seventeenth-century church, which is separated from the park grounds, however, by a road and is invisible from the estate.)

Although less refined in its design and detail than the Brattsevo villa, the mansion at the Durasov estate of Liublino (northeast Moscow) can lay claim to possess one of the most idiosyncratic plans of the period, a genuine example of symbolic architecture (or *architecture parlant*). Attributed to Ivan Egotov,[35] the design consists of four wings that radiate from a round central hall and are connected by a colonnade in the Composite order (Figure 408). The genesis of the con-

Figure 406. Stroganov villa at Brattsevo. Moscow. Late eighteenth century. Architect: Andrei Voronikhin(?). (M 49–1)

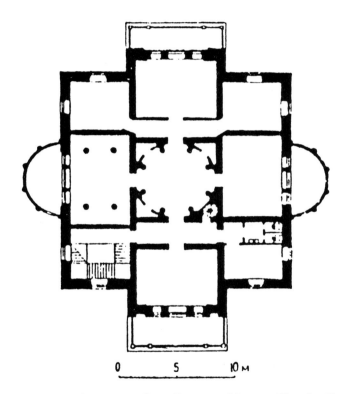

0   5   10 M

Figure 407. Stroganov villa at Brattsevo. Moscow. Plan, by G. Oranskaia.

figuration is said to have originated with N. A. Durasov's desire to memorialize his attainment of the Order of St. Anne, whose encircled cross is reproduced in the form of the house (Figure 409).

Yet the elaborate conceit of the design of the Liublino mansion serves one of the most important functions of the estate house – to provide a sheltered yet

315

Figure 408. Durasov mansion at Liublino. Moscow. 1801. Architect: Ivan Egotov. (M 38)

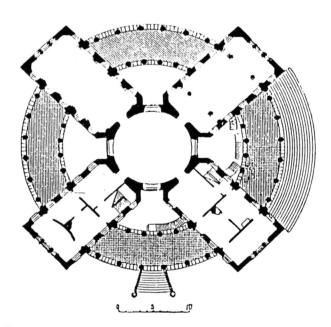

Figure 409. Durasov mansion at Liublino. Moscow. Plan, by O. Sotnikova.

immediate view of surrounding nature. On the brightly illuminated interior, the state rooms and the central hall are decorated with grisaille trompe l'oeil wall paintings of architectural motifs and friezes with such attention to detail as to be distinguished only with difficulty from the plaster medallions that also decorate the upper parts of the walls. The interior walls themselves are a combination of various shades of faux marbre typical both urban and country mansions in Moscow at the end of the eighteenth century.

So rich was central Russian estate culture at the turn of the nineteenth century, that a thorough survey of the architecture of country mansions (many no longer extant) in the area of Moscow and its surrounding provinces alone would require a separate volume. Some of the manors reveal an unexpected similarity with "Greek Revival" architecture in the American antebellum south – such as the two-story stuccoed wooden estate house at Valuevo (southwest of Moscow), built in 1810–11 (Figure 410). The Ionic portico, with veranda, and belvedere speak of influences from grander homes; yet Valuevo, owned by

Figure 410. Estate house, Valuevo. Near Moscow. 1810–11. (MR 5–76)

the archeologist Alexander Musin-Pushkin (publisher of Russia's great medieval epic, *The Igor Tale*) is itself of considerable merit for the excellent state of preservation of its architecture and the unity of its ensemble (Figure 411).[36]

In contrast to the neoclassical style of the mansion and its wings – connected to the central structure by Doric colonnades – the offices and service buildings flanking the manor have a rough, unstuccoed brick surface with rusticated pillars, whereas the corner towers of the brick wall enclosing the front of the estate are in a late variant of the Gothic revival (c. 1830s). Thus, the design of the ensemble proceeds from the refined mansion in the center to more "archaic" and eccentric forms. The English-style landscape park beyond the mansion contains a similar contrast between the neoclassical Hunting House,

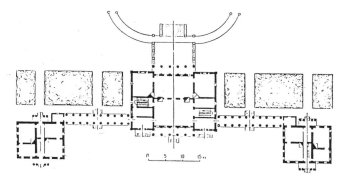

Figure 411. Valuevo. Near Moscow. Plan. From Tikhomirov, *Arkhitcktura moskovskikh usadeb.*

with light yellow walls, white trim, and Tuscan portico, which rests over the heavy rustication of a grotto.

Nikolai Lvov and the Natural Order of Neoclassicism

The triumph of the "English," or natural landscape, park on Russian country estates during the latter part of the eighteenth century represents the considerable influence of the change in tastes introduced by Catherine the Great at imperial estates such as Tsarskoe Selo (see Chapter 10). Yet the adaptation of the natural setting to the architectural design of the neoclassical manor and its auxiliary buildings quickly assumed a Russian character in the work of Nikolai Lvov and Andrei Bolotov. Although their contributions and other developments in landscape gardening can only be cursorily mentioned in this survey of architectural history, the desire to contemplate "unfettered" nature, with its immutable laws, complemented the belief in the natural logic and meaning of neoclassical forms in architecture.[37]

The origins of this intellectual, aesthetic, and cultural union of neoclassicism and natural principles are many and diverse – including in no small measure English and French literature (e.g., Horace Walpole and, above all, Rousseau).[38] For Bolotov, an autodidact and polymath who in the early 1780s worked assiduously on the park at the imperial estate of Bogoroditsk (Tula Province), the landscape park and its pavilions could be used to induce specific moods, such as melancholy, especially valued in this sentimental, preromantic era.[39]

Nikolai Lvov, too, was an inventor and autodidact, well acquainted with the literary culture of his day; but unlike the enthusiastic dilettante Bolotov, Lvov was also an architect of the highest order, whose work in both Petersburg and the provinces is eclipsed only in comparison to the extraordinary wealth of architectural talent during the latter decades of Catherine's reign. In Petersburg, Lvov was known for his design of the Neva Gates of the Peter–Paul Fortress (1786–7; see Fig. 272), and his three-story building for the Petersburg Post Office (1782–9), with a rusticated ground floor.[40]

Lvov's greatest works, however, were built in the provinces, beginning with the Cathedral of St. Joseph in Mogilev, designed in 1780 and built in 1781–98 under the supervision of the Scottish architect Adam Menelaws, who arrived in Russia in 1784. The Doric hexastyle porticos of the centralized design were unusual for the unadorned rigor of their design (comparable to Starov's work at the Trinity Cathedral in Petersburg), and took their inspiration in part from the temples at Paestum – an increasingly influential source in Russian architecture. The double-shelled central dome, however, is a reflection of Lvov's fascination with the engineering of the Pantheon.[41]

In similar style, although more complex in design, is Lvov's Cathedral of Sts. Boris and Gleb at the Monastery of the same name in Torzhok (to the north of Tver, on the main road from Moscow to Petersburg).[42] Built in 1785–96, the cathedral is one of the masterpieces of Russian neoclassicism (Figure 412). The hexastyle Tuscan portico on the west facade, repeated on the east (apsidal) end, provides a visual transition to the domical dome, which rests above a polygonal drum with a large thermal window. The cathedral thus reflects some of the basic elements of Russo–Byzantine church architecture, not only in the centralized plan, but also in the appearance on the exterior of arched bays reminiscent of the cathedrals of twelfth-century Novgorod. To be sure, the arches contain classically inspired thermal windows, yet the ability to integrate traditional features of Russian architecture into the classical system is a mark of Lvov's genius. Within the Torzhok cathedral, the massive split-corner piers are faced with Doric columns that support open arches over the arms of the cross. The arches in turn lead upward to the thermal windows and the central coffered dome, which on the interior is hemispherical. Again, the classical rigor of the design is stated with remarkable clarity – referring both

to the Pantheon and the thermae – yet the interior space is suited to the needs of the Orthodox liturgy.

These great neoclassical cathedrals, like the secular and functional Petersburg Post Office, are firmly in the manner of Lvov's idol Palladio, whom he studied with great care and whose work he saw *in situ* in Italy. His efforts bore fruit in 1798 with the first published edition in Russian translation of Palladio's *Quattro libri*, in the introduction to which he proclaimed "Long live the Palladian taste in my fatherland. French curls and English subtlety have enough imitators without us."[43] Lvov – like the other major Palladians in Russia, Quarenghi and Cameron – was interested primarily in Palladio's "rural" architecture, and above all the villas; but whereas Quarenghi and Cameron adapted principles taken from the Palladian villas to both urban and country settings, Lvov applied them almost exclusively to the landscaped environment of the estate – or the open spaces of provincial towns.[44]

Thus, in their Palladian style, Lvov's cathedrals resemble the estate houses and pavilions that he created on a number of estates, including his own, in the Torzhok area.[45] Despite the remarkable scale of his designs for the estates of grandees such as General and Senator F. I. Glebov (at Znamenskoe–Raek), Lvov's most accomplished work was at his own estate of Cherenchitsy (now Nikolskoe), where in 1784 he designed a rotundal church–mausoleum (built in 1789–1804) that is one of his most accomplished mon-

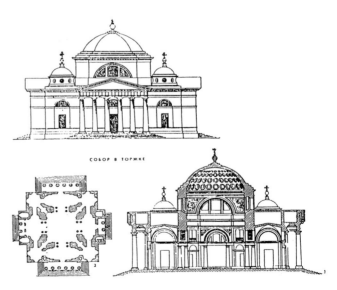

Figure 412. Cathedral of Sts. Boris and Gleb, Borisoglebsk Monastery. Torzhok. 1785–96. Architect: Nikolai Lvov. West elevation, plan, and section by N. Lvov.

uments. More eccentric is his Church of the Trinity at the estate of Prince A. A. Viazemskii at Aleksandrovskoe (on the southern outskirts of Petersburg), which uses a similar rotunda form, surrounded by sixteen Ionic columns and prefaced on the west by a pyramidal bell tower (Figure 413). Built in 1785–7, the structure has impeccable classical antecedents (the Temple of Vesta and the reproductions of the pyramids in Rome)[46]; yet it also exemplifies the secularization of Russian church design that had begun in the Naryshkin era at the end of the seventeenth century.[47]

The rapidity with which the unity summarized in Lvov's work was dissipated in Russian neoclassical estate houses is exemplified in the Alexandrine Palace on the estate of Neskuchnoe (Figure 414; now in south Moscow), whose basic form presumably dates from a rebuilding of an earlier mansion in the 1790s for Fedor Orlov – one of the four brothers favored during the early reign of Catherine – shortly before his death in 1796.[48] The building was sold to Nicholas I in 1832, at which point the court architect Evgraf Tiurin began a series of modifications, without, however, changing the basic appearance. The central portico, with its clusters of columns and arches, possesses a polished monumentality, but without the harmony of parts that distinguishes the more rigorous forms of neoclassicism.

Neoclassicism and Its Antithesis: Bazhenov in Moscow

Although neoclassicism in Moscow may have centered on house design, the city was not devoid of institutional buildings commissioned by the state. Among them, the most imposing was the Foundling Home, begun in 1764, possibly to a design by Velten, although the first stage of the vast complex was completed in 1767 under the direction of Karl Blank. The Foundling Home was intended not merely as a charitable foundation, but also an experiment in model education initiated by Ivan Betskoi. Supported by Catherine's views on the possibilities of "enlightened" education, the Home was among several institutions, primarily in Petersburg (such as the School at the Academy of Arts, and the Institute for the Education of Young Noblewomen; see Chapter 10) whose purpose was to create an ideal citizen. Yet in the example of the Foundling Home, the idealistic visions, which derived vaguely from John Locke and Rousseau, proved ill-adapted to reality, and the administration of the Home proved a major source of disappointment to Betskoi.[49]

From the perspective of architecture and planning, however, the Foundling Home had a substantial impact on the development of Moscow. Located just beyond Kitai-gorod, on the left bank of the Moscow River, the general plan of the Home called for a central administrative building, flanked on both west and east by two large quadrangular buildings (each 130 meters in length). All of the structures were to be four stories in height, with rusticated walls for the lower two floors.[50] The complex was intended to house 8,000 children; and although the east wing was not built, the middle of this century (by which time the entire complex had been converted to use for a military institute), the austere design of Karl Blank's west quadrangle accommodated several thousand children through the innovative (for the time) design of a central corridor with rooms on either side.[51] The main administrative building, which resembles Velten's Aleksandrovskii Institute in Petersburg (1764; see Chapter 10), was erected in 1771–81 with funds provided by Prokopii Demidov, brother of Nikita.[52]

The other large neoclassical structure in central Moscow served as a visual complement to the Foundling Home and was located opposite it across the Moscow River. Nikolai Legran's design for the Military Commissariat (Kriegskommissariat; 1778–80s) included a three-story central administrative building facing the river and flanked by two-story wings whose corners ended in domed round towers (Figure 415). The wings, which were intended for ammunition storage, continued at right angles to form an open quadrangle at the back of the building. This imposing military structure was begun in the aftermath of the Pugachev rebellion (which at one point seemed to threaten Moscow itself), as well as the conclusion of the First Russo–Turkish War – both in 1774.

Even as partially completed, the Foundling Home – as well as the Kriegskommissariat – challenged the medieval ambience of Moscow, and its size may have suggested the feasibility of a gargantuan, utopian plan to rebuild the Kremlin as a Russian acropolis. The author of the project, Vasilii Bazhenov (1737–99), is one of the most distinctive figures in the history of Russian architecture, and one of the most perplexing. In his work, the Muscovite flair for eccentric architecture received full expression, yet he was also capable of a richly articulated neoclassical style that took the Roman Empire as its model and inspiration.

Raised in Moscow and apprenticed as a decorator to Dmitrii Ukhtomskii in 1753–5, Bazhenov enrolled briefly at the recently founded Moscow University and then pursued his architectural studies within the Petersburg Academy of Sciences – whose arts curriculum was reorganized as the Academy of Arts in 1759. At the Academy, he studied under Savva Chevakinskii and Ivan Kokorinov.[53] In 1760, Bazhenov went to Paris on a stipend to work in the studio of royal architect Charles de Wailly, where he absorbed the latter's neoclassicism.[54] Bazhenov's success in Paris – he was recommended for the Prix de Rome, but denied on the technicality of his religion – brought him to the attention of high personages serving in the diplomatic corps, such as Ivan Chernyshev, and to Ivan Shuvalov (president of the Academy of Arts), who gave additional funds for Bazhenov's study in Rome. Honorary membership in a number of Italian academies and societies followed in 1764, and he returned to acclaim in Paris that same year. Despite his success, he was plagued by constant financial difficulties, and returned to Petersburg in May 1765.

Having been designated an academician, Bazhenov was not, however, chosen as a professor at the Academy of Arts.[55] Thus began a series of reversals that would plague his career in the following decade; yet Bazhenov also made the acquaintance of Catherine's son, the future Emperor Paul, and maintained contacts among the highly placed of the capital. Under the patronage of Grigorii Orlov, Bazhenov's appointment to the rank of capitan in the artillery apparently led to his first major commission – the Petersburg Arsenal (1767; on Liteinyi Prospekt).[56] Its style combined austere classicism with certain preclassical elements – oval windows, rounded corners – that frequently appear in Bazhenov's later work.

Denied appropriate recognition at the Academy,

Figure 413. Church of the Trinity at Aleksandrovskoe. Near Petersburg. 1785–7. Architect: Nikolai Lvov.

320

Figure 414. Alexandrine Palace at Neskuchnoe. Moscow. (M 157–13)

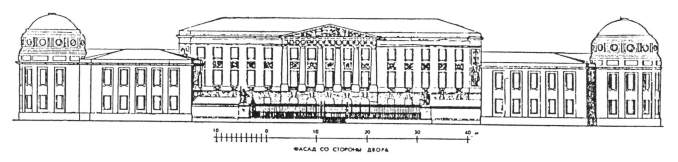

ФАСАД СО СТОРОНЫ ДВОРА

Figure 415. Kriegskommissariat. Moscow. 1778–80s. Architect: Nikolai Legran. Elevation.

Bazhenov was fortunate in being transferred in 1767 to Moscow. Few details of his early work in the city are available, but it is known that in 1768, he was commanded to inspect the great wooden royal palace at Kolomenskoe, which dated from the time of Aleksei Mikhailovich. Built of pine, with details of oak and other durable forms of wood, the structure was in a state of decay and Bazhenov recommended its demolition.[57] Nonetheless, it is likely that its rambling and picturesque form stimulated the imagination of the architect – as did the Kremlin in which he grew up. Bazhenov's work would soon manifest an idiosyncracy that parallels the development of the pseudo-Gothic elsewhere in Europe, yet incorporates characteristics of medieval Muscovite architecture in a dis-

tinctively picturesque manner. Indeed, an early example of the curious blending of the pseudo-Gothic with the brick and limestone decoration peculiar to seventeenth-century Moscow churches is the Church of the Icon of the Sign at the village of Znamenka, in Tambov Province. Although documentation is lacking – as it is for other, similar churches – it would appear that the church at Znamenka, completed only in 1789 and consecrated in 1796, was designed by Bazhenov in 1768.[58] Its fantastic decorative forms of brick and limestone (Figure 416) are imposed over a symmetrical, centralized design with pinnacles instead of cupolas. The use of ogival pediments and the pyramidal massing of the central structure gives the impression of Gothic butressing, although the basic design is sim-

321

Figure 416. Church of the Icon of the Sign at Znamenka. Tambov Province. 1768–89. Architect: Vasilii Bazhenov(?). Southwest view.

model of the Great Kremlin Palace indicate that the entire Kremlin frontage along the Moscow River was to be reconstructed as a four-story palace, with the lower two, service, floors rusticated and the upper two, intended for the court proper, designed as an enclosed colonnade of the Ionic order. Of the medieval architectural ensemble, the grandiose plan envisioned the preservation only of the main Kremlin cathedrals within this Ionic and Corinthian ambience. After the creation of the splendid model (itself costing 60,000 rubles and made, ironically, of wood from the dismantled palace at Kolomenskoe), preliminary excavations were undertaken, and a portion of the south Kremlin walls, as well as certain decrepit structures, was dismantled by the time of a solemn dedicatory ceremony in 1773. The estimated cost of the project (perhaps as much as 50 million rubles) exceeded all previous bounds, yet the apparently limitless resources of the empire removed all such practical considerations.[60]

Indeed, the Kremlin project was perceived by Mus-

ilar to that of the Church of the Dormition on Pokrovka Street in Moscow (see Figure 252).

In view of Bazhenov's appreciation of and attraction to the possibilities of revived medieval styles – which would be developed to such effect in his designs for the imperial estate at Tsaritsyno – it is remarkable that in the project to rebuild the Kremlin itself, Bazhenov should have turned resolutely to neoclassicism. The idea of rebuilding the decrepit Kremlin palaces had been broached by Betskoi in 1763, but Bazhenov's fertile imagination transformed this relatively modest project into a vaster scheme, which again was relayed by Orlov to the Empress. By 1768, Bazhenov was at work on the plans, whose dimensions were far larger than anything Rastrelli had conceived.[59]

Had the rebuilding been implemented, the Kremlin would have been transformed into a system of squares and palaces, with boulevards radiating into the city (Figure 417). Bazhenov's plans and a wooden

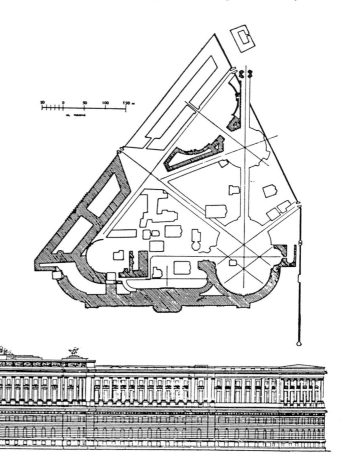

Figure 417. Plan and Moscow River elevation for the reconstruction of the Kremlin. 1768. Architect: Vasilii Bazhenov.

322

covites as redressing the imbalance in construction between the two capitals, although Catherine supported the project as a means of impressing upon foreign envoys the strength of Russia at the onset of a major war with Turkey between 1768 and 1774. (In this regard, it is worth remembering Elizabeth's determined effort to complete the new Winter Palace during the Seven Years War.) By 1773, however, the war with Turkey was all but won, and fiscal reality intruded – in no small part because of the strained financial situation brought about by the war. Two years later, in 1775, Catherine canceled the enterprise.

From the perspective of architectural and cultural preservation, Catherine's decision – whatever its motives – must be considered a major reprieve for Russian architectural history, for the plan to rebuild the Kremlin would not only have destroyed a series of major monuments (particularly the Kremlin walls and towers), but would also have violated the essential environment for the Kremlin cathedrals. Nonetheless, Bazhenov's choice of the classical orders for the renewal of the Kremlin possessed a certain logic. In the most obvious sense, the neoclassical style appealed to Catherine for both aesthetic and ideological reasons. Her intention to redesign Russian provincial towns according to an ordered plan, with major neoclassical administrative buildings dominating the center, would have received its logical culmination in the Kremlin as Acropolis. Furthermore, Bazhenov's plan can be seen as a continuation of visionary schemes, such as those of Boris Godunov, to recreate the sacred precincts of the Kremlin.

The Kremlin project also reflected a desire to reformulate the language of architecture as a means of claiming a cultural heritage from classical antiquity. Although this process had begun during the reign of Peter the Great, Bazhenov's design involved a statement more radical than even the architectural transformation wrought by Peter – who never advocated the destruction of the medieval Russian architectural heritage. For Bazhenov (and his supporters), the neoclassical Kremlin was a choice that could be justified by the appeal to the system of classical orders, but it was, nonetheless, a choice. In this sense, the Kremlin project, not to mention the pseudo-Gothic fancies of Bazhenov's later work, prefigures nineteenth-century historicism with its selective use of architectural styles, not only for decoration, but for the purposes of ideological expression.

And there was no lack of pronouncements on Bazhenov's part, commenting not only on the need for logic and order in architecture as stated in the classical monuments, but also on the transfer of the ancient imperial heritage to Russia through the use of the classical orders.[61] Of particular interest is his "Short discourse on the Kremlin construction" (1769 or 1770), which gave a detailed analysis of various monuments of antiquity, culminating in the classical architecture of Greece and Rome, which had been revived more recently in Rome and Paris.[62] Bazhenov described the purposes underlying the Expedition for the Construction of the Kremlin, founded in 1768, which became under his command not only a collective devoted to a specific project, but also an institution for the training of architects.[63] In the discourse on the Kremlin reconstruction, Bazhenov asserted that contemporary Russian architecture, epitomized in this project and the imperial largess that supported it, would overshadow the grandeur of established European cultures to the west.

Although the claims of his statement were ironically denied in 1775, Bazhenov was by no means the last architect to measure the heroic scale of Russian construction against the monumentality of western architecture. These claims were most emphatically stated in the solemn oration given by Bazhenov on the occasion of the official laying of the foundation stone, on June 1, 1773.[64] Catherine's absence from the ceremony was a sign of her waning enthusiasm for the project; yet Bazhenov's proclamations gave renewed expression to the vision of Moscow as a third Rome, a new "Tsargrad" (Constantinople). Bazhenov surveyed the architectural traditions of medieval Moscow in comparison to western architecture – including the Gothic – and noted their refinement under the guiding principles of classical architecture (Catherine herself was designated the "Russian Palladio"!). At the same time, references in the oration to Russian victories against Turkey echoed imperial designs in the direction of Constantinople. Thus, the architectural glories reflected in the Kremlin project could be interpreted – like the allegorical pavilions at Tsarskoe Selo – as a further step toward legitimizing Russia's assumption of the cultural and political legacy of the lost Byzantine empire.[65]

Bazhenov's proficiency in adapting diverse architectural idioms was spectacularly displayed in his next major project for the empress, who in 1775 had purchased from Prince S. Kantemir the estate of Chernaia Griaz ("Black Dirt") to the south of Moscow.[66] Her intention was to create a series of country residences in the area, of which the complex of palaces, pavilions, and service buildings at the renamed Tsaritsyno was to be the most extensive, rivaling the imperial estates near Petersburg. In this setting marked by ravines and a small river, Catherine chose to dispense

with the neoclassical, and in 1776, Bazhenov designed for her an ensemble in the "Moorish-Gothic" style (Figure 418). Despite the precedent of his churches and pavilions, Tsaritsyno seems unexpected from an architect so thoroughly at home in the neoclassical idiom, for Bazhenov's creation is a reinterpretation of old Muscovite elements and materials – limestone and brick – cloaked in the Gothic revival, and planned in the intricate geometrical arrangements of the mid-eighteenth-century baroque.[67]

One of the larger pavilions was subsequently known as the Opera House (1776–8), with the two-headed eagle outlined in limestone above the cornice and an panoply of limestone decorative elements – much of it classically inspired – on the brick facade.[68] In contrast to the stuccoed facades typical of Petersburg architecture (or, in rare cases, natural stone facing), Bazhenov's combination of brick and limestone detail for the imperial regalia verges on the parodistic, as though Moscow had only reluctantly accepted the notion of an imperial architectural style. Indeed, the design of exterior walls of unsurfaced brick would not again appear in a major monument until the middle of the nineteenth century – tellingly, in connection with the revival of pre-Petrine forms for a "national" style of architecture. Thus, the architect who intended to reshape the Kremlin as a neoclassical citadel also anticipated the romantic interpretation of the national style originating in the brick buildings of medieval Muscovy (see Chapter 13).

The most exquisite product of Bazhenov's fancy is also the smallest of his structures at Tsaritsyno, the Patterned, or "Figured," Gate (1776–8; Figure 419), which framed the entrance into the park. The architect himself referred to the Gothic style of the gate as

nezhnaia ("gentle," although probably a Gallicism for "precieux").[69] The sentimentalism of this term captures the pseudo-Gothic mixture of styles, intended to summon an aura of the past through a carefully contrived aesthetic vision. The limestone lower walls of the gate – which suggest equally western or Russian medieval architecture – provide a base for elaborate brick towers, whose form in miniature displays certain motifs of the Kremlin walls. Within the brick and limestone arch, a pattern of suspended limestone blocks reproduces the tracery of Gothic lancet windows. The historicist quality of the gate design prefigures the development of eclectic architecture of the nineteenth century as an exercise in historical consciousness.

The concluding phases of construction at Tsaritsyno (which experienced serious delays after 1778) revealed Bazhenov's Russo–Gothic sensibility on a considerably larger scale. Work on the palace structures for the imperial family began in 1779 and progressed with much difficulty through 1782, by which time the walls had been completed for two palaces to be used by Catherine and the tsarevich Paul, as well as a third structure for Paul's children.[70] The fate of these buildings, not extant, will be noted in what follows; their only known illustrations are contained in Bazhenov's early project sketch for Tsaritsyno (see Figure 418), which reveals an exuberantly decorated exterior.

Larger than any of these palace structures taken separately was the adjacent kitchen and service wing – known as the Klebnyi dom – begun by 1784. Designed in the form of a quadrangle with rounded corners (Figure 420), the building contained two stories with lancet windows on the first floor and composite trefoil windows on the upper story. Although less inventive

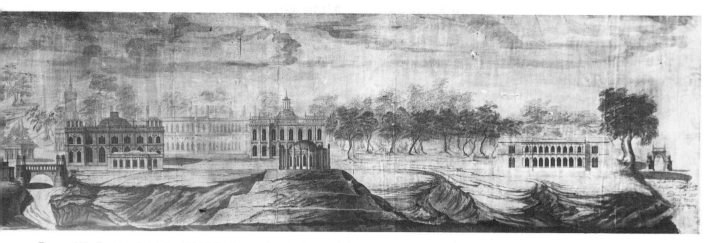

Figure 418. Project sketch by Vasilii Bazhenov for the imperial estate at Tsaritsyno. Moscow. 1776–80s. The Opera House and Patterned Gate are at the right, the main palace is in the center, and various pavilions as well as the two bridges are to the left. Courtesy of Shchusev State Historical Architectural Museum, Moscow.

in its limestone detail than the imperial pavilions, the service wing was connected to the main palace compound by a colonnade and gate that comprise one of the most bizarre forms in eighteenth-century Russian architecture. In particular, the semicircular brick arch, studded with limestone "teeth," creates a vaguely menacing air that is simultaneously undercut by the coronet motif of the flanking towers (Figure 421).

Figure 419. Patterned Gate, Tsaritsyno. 1776–8. Architect: Vasilii Bazhenov. (M 42–9)

The final flurry of construction during 1784 (in preparation for a state visit by the Empress in 1785) gave rise to other major structures, such as the Octagonal pavilion, also known as the second Cavaliers Wing.[71] The elaborate limestone figures that decorate this pavilion, as well as earlier structures of similar function, have suggested to some the cryptic symbols of Freemasonry, to which Bazhenov belonged.[72] No less inventive in its decorative motifs is the Bridge over the ravine (Figure 422; one of the last structures to be completed by Bazhenov at Tsaritsyno), with its radiant bursts of limestone emanating from the supporting arches on either end and an array of ornaments that resembles folk art in its geometric figures.

Alas, Bazhenov was the most ill-starred of Russia's great architects. For all of his attempts to receive financial guarantees at the outset of work on the estate, payments from the treasury soon manifested the familiar waning of patronage and a reluctance to meet previously stated commitments on the part of the imperial court. Despite these difficulties, Bazhenov had made extraordinary progress (his original plan called for the complex to be completed within 3 years). Yet hardly had the walls been completed for most of the structures, after 10 years of work and often inadequate means, when Catherine again halted construction after her inspection visit of 1785, commanded that the centerpiece of the ensemble – the imperial palaces – be razed, and in 1786, entrusted their rebuilding to Matvei Kazakov, Bazhenov's assistant.[73]

Kazakov in his turn conceived a monumental, if less imaginative, palace that combined the pseudo-Gothic with obvious elements of the classical order system, particularly in the columns of the projecting

Figure 420. Service Wing (*Klebnyi dom*), Tsaritsyno. 1784 (unfinished). Architect: Vasilii Bazhenov. On the left, a portion of the arcade leading to the courtyard gate. (M 43–3)

square towers (Figure 423). Kazakov already had one major "Gothic" palace to his credit – the Petrovskii Transit Palace (1775–82; see what follows), used by Catherine for her visits to Moscow. Thus, the new design was readily produced and work began on the then leveled site in 1786. The two palaces envisioned by Bazhenov were placed at either end of a rectagular core (Figure 424), whose second story rose above the entire length of the structure. The onset of a second Turkish war (1787–91), however, again led to reduced means and further delays. The walls of the two-storied palace were covered with a temporary roof in 1793; and after Catherine's death in 1796, the project was canceled. Whether they preferred Bazhenov's work or Kazakov's, subsequent visitors commented effusively on the grand nature of the abandoned site, which appealed to the sentimental, romantic tastes of the late early nineteenth century.[74]

There is a fine irony in the fact that Tsaritsyno, which included among its pavilions specially designed "ruins," should itself have become so grand and picturesque a ruin in a manner not unworthy of Piranesi. Yet the Tsaritsyno estate, created in the spirit of literary (primarily English) visions of the Gothic, was entirely removed from the English estate culture that had created over centuries a series of distinctive manor houses enhanced by landscape parks. Bazhenov intended in one massive enterprise to create an architectural fantasy doubly removed from its putative Gothic prototypes, yet related to Moscow's own past – no longer a matter to be ignored, but rather a source of increasing fascination on the part of Russians who were aware of the seductive appeal of the

past in European culture and wished to find the same in their own history.

Among the last major monuments in Moscow to be attributed to Bazhenov, the Pashkov House (1784–8; Figure 425) marks a reaffirmation of neoclassicism.[75] Built as Bazhenov's work at Tsaritsyno reached its culmination – and untimely conclusion – the stuccoed brick mansion for Life Guards Captain P. E. Pashkov represents Moscow's answer to the palaces of Petersburg. Indeed, nothing in Petersburg of the same period can surpass it, and yet this neoclassical palace is situated in an entirely different environment, isolated on Vagankov Hill overlooking the sixteenth-century Kremlin walls Bazhenov had intended to rebuild in the most grandiose of neoclasscial schemes.

Figure 421. Service arcade and gate, Tsaritsyno. 1784. Architect: Vasilii Bazhenov. (M 43–2)

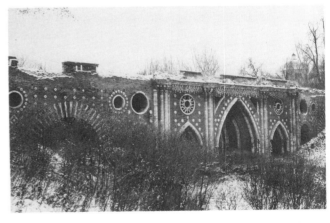

Figure 422. Bridge over the Ravine, Tsaritsyno. 1784. Architect: Vasilii Bazhenov. (M 44–5)

Figure 423. Main Palace, Tsaritsyno. 1786–93 (unfinished). Architect: Matvei Kazakov. (M 143–34)

Even the style of the Pashkov mansion is distinct from Petersburg architecture and reminds of the English baroque at the turn of the eighteenth century, exemplified by Chatsworth, country house of the Duke of Devonshire.[76] (The classicized facade detail is particularly close in both mansions.) The two wings, with Ionic porticoes, are separated from the main structure by rusticated galleries, whose length is half that of the central facade. This distance, and its relation to the height of the wings, creates a balanced system of proportions uniting the three elements. Although each of the component parts has sufficient space to be appreciated separately, one is always aware of their relation to the whole.[77]

During the late 1780s, Bazhenov completed his repertoire of classical forms with the rebuilding of the late seventeenth-century Church of the Transfiguration, subsequently named after one of its chapels dedicated to the Mother of God, Consolation of all who grieve. Located on Great Ordynka Street – in the heart of Zamoskvoreche, a merchant district across the Moscow River to the south of the Kremlin – the church

was endowed by the merchant A. I. Dolgov, who commissioned Bazhenov to rebuild the refectory and the bell tower (the main sanctuary was reconstructed by Bove in the 1830s).[78] The Ionic portico of the refectory (Figure 426), with columns of honey-colored stone, is placed within a facade marked by circular windows and rounded corners that convey a baroque quality characteristic of Bazhenov's neoclassicism. The greater achievement, however, is the round bell

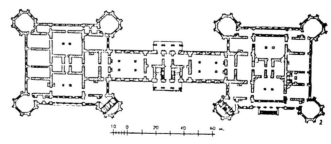

Figure 424. Main Palace, Tsaritsyno. Architect: Matvei Kazakov. Plan adapted from the Matvei Kazakov *Al'bom.*

tower – a rare example of this shape in Moscow church architecture. The campanile is composed of three ascending tiers, also with limestone columns.

Although the 1780s had brought disappointment and uncertainty to Bazhenov in the resolution of the Tsaritsyno project and his subsequent move to Gatchina, he retained connections with important patrons – most notably, the tsarevich Paul. By the end of the eighteenth century, he achieved long overdue recognition from the Academy of Arts, to which he was elected as its first vice-president in February 1799. Within a month of his appointment, Bazhenov was at work on a series of projects, including a report on much needed improvements in the organization of the academy.[79] Although the Emperor Paul personally approved of much in the report, the death of Bazhenov in August of the same year deprived the reform projects of their essential support. Nonetheless, Bazhenov's legacy as a teacher remained a major force in the development of Moscow, above all in the work of his brilliant pupil Matvei Kazakov.

Matvei Kazakov and the Creation of Neoclassical Moscow

A survey of the list of buildings by Matvei Kazakov demonstrates the remarkable adaptability of neoclassicism to virtually any monumental structure – church, hospital, government building, assembly hall, or university. His genius and prolific creativity contributed immeasureably to the formation of a distinctively neoclassical idiom in Moscow, just as Quarenghi did in Petersburg during the same period.[80] Kazakov was also fortunate in his mentors, beginning with Dmitrii Ukhtomskii, in whose school he studied in the 1750s. After Ukhtomskii's retirement in 1760, the school was directed by Peter Nikitin, who supervised the rebuilding of the ancient city of Tver after its destruction by fire in 1763. Nikitin's design is considered one of the best examples of neoclassical city planning in Russia, and Kazakov was closely involved in the many aspects of the project. And in 1768, Kazakov's work came to the attention of Bazhenov, who had undertaken the massive Kremlin project. Thus, despite his lack of travel and study abroad, Kazakov was educated by the best of Russian architects.

His first masterpiece was the Petrovskii Transit Palace, commissioned for Catherine on the northern outskirts of Moscow and built in 1775–82. Like the concurrent work of Bazhenov at Tsaritsyno, Kazakov's palace combined the fashion for the Gothic revival with motifs drawn from medieval Russian architecture – such as the use of limestone ornament on brick walls and the flared columns on the main facade (Figure 427). The pitched gables and dormers give the exterior a fragmented appearance that is, however, overcome by a great dome over the rotunda at the center of the structure, with lavish plaster decoration closely resembling Kazakov's design of a similar space in the Church of the Metropolitan Philip (1777–88; see Figure 431).[81] The Petrovskii Palace plan (Figure 428) includes flanking, turreted wings that extend from the main facade to a low semicircular sweep with two guard towers at the entrance gates. On close inspection, the peculiar design of the palace owes much to the baroque – particularly in the window surrounds beneath the dome – despite the rustic "gothick" style associated with country estate architecture.

In the same period, Kazakov's classical training produced one of the most important state buildings of Catherine's reign – the Senate in the Kremlin. After a reform in the legal system in 1763, Moscow, the second capital, was designated as the seat of two of the country's highest judicial bodies, including that concerned with the rights of the nobility. The need to provide space for the Senate led in 1776 to a project competition between Kazakov and Karl Blank. Kazakov's winning entry exploited a large but awkward lot wedged in the northeast corner of the Kremlin to create a triangular four-storied building. The plan (Figure 429) is symmetrical with two interior wings that allow more convenient passage between the sides of the equilateral triangle.

The insertion of interior wings within the Senate triangle also created three courtyards. The central of these forms a pentagon containing at its apex the dominant feature of the entire structure – the great rotunda, which provided the main assembly space for the deliberations of the Senate, or high court. Encircled on the outside with a Doric colonnade, the interior of the rotunda (Figure 430) was magnificently finished with Corinthian columns, between which are bas-reliefs by Gavriil Zamaraev on allegorical subjects by the great poet Gavriil Derzhavin and his comrade, the poet–architect Nikolai Lvov. The upper part of the rotunda, above the cornice–gallery supported by the columns, contained large plaster medallions with portraits of Russian princes and tsars in classicized form.[82]

The main Senate facade, facing west toward the Arsenal, also has at its center a dome, above an oval vestibule. The large scale of the building, and of its long facade, is moderated by its division into two rusticated ground floors and two upper stories seg-

Figure 425. Pashkov House. Moscow. 1784–8. Architect: Vasilii Bazhenov(?). (M 45–11)

mented by Doric pilasters. The Doric entrance portico is on a slighly smaller scale, thus focusing attention on the passageway to the central courtyard. The use of slightly projecting bays at the center and the ends provides a visual frame for the mass – a solution that Andreian Zakharov was to adopt, in a more heroic manner, for the building of the Admiralty in Petersburg (see Chapter 12). On a lesser scale, the Senate was also imitated for administrative buildings in many provincial Russian towns during the next half century.[83]

Kazakov's skill in integrating the rotunda form into a larger structure is evident in many of his designs, including the Demidov mansion at Petrovskoe (see the foregoing). It appears most persistently, however, in adaptations of the classical rotunda to church design, one of the earliest examples of which is his Church of the Metropolitan Philip in Moscow (1777–88; Figure 431).[84] On the east, the round structure projects a rectangular apse – thus reversing the usual formal juxtaposition of apse and cuboid main mass. On the west, the rotunda is deformed by an incongrous low refectory of the mideighteenth century and a bell tower, which were originally attached to the seventeenth-century church on this site. Even without these components, the proportions of the Kaza-

kov church are awkward, particularly in the relation between the undersized porticos and the bulk of the exterior. On the interior, the plaster ornament is lavishly applied in the best Kazakov manner (Figure 432). In the central area beneath the rotunda dome, large Ionic columns form a semicircle behind which an arcade of Doric pillars supports the choir gallery (Figure 433). In the sanctuary, a smaller Corinthian rotunda defines the altar. Although this profusion of forms threatens visually to overwhelm the rather small space of the interior, the structural design represents an innovative resolution of the centralized Orthodox plan, achieved by a reference to pre-Christian Roman architecture.

The classical antecedents for this use of the rotunda were still more clearly stated in the Baryshnikov mausoleum–church (not extant) begun in 1784 on their estate of Nikolo-Pogoreloe near Dorogobuzh. The Baryshnikovs were among Kazakov's major patrons, and his design for them is on a heroic scale. The plan (Figure 434) resembles that of the Philip church, yet the squared projection from the rotunda here serves as the large portico on the west – rather than an extension for the apse – and thus conveys a greater functional logic. The attached Ionic columns of the exterior are matched by Corinthian pilasters on the

Figure 426. Church of the Transfiguration, and Mother of God Consolation of all who grieve. Moscow. Late 1780s. Architect: Vasilii Bazhenov. South view. (M 112–36)

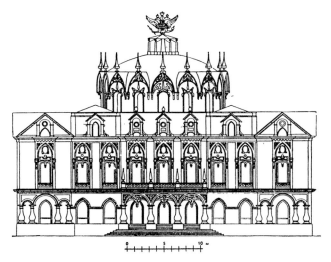

Figure 427. Petrovskii Transit Palace. Moscow. 1775–82. Architect: Matvei Kazakov. Elevation adapted from the Matvei Kazakov *Al'bom*.

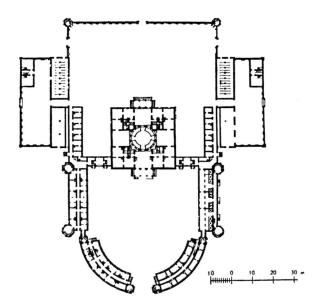

Figure 428. Petrovskii Transit Palace. Plan adapted from the Matvei Kazakov *Al'bom*.

interior (Figure 434), thus creating a greater sense of space in a building whose function did not require a choir gallery. Without a bell tower and refectory, the scale and proportions of the Baryshnikov mausoleum, as well as the dome above the rotunda, show a refinement that places it beyond the level of an architectural curiosity such as the Church of St. Philip.[85]

In addition to his imperial commissions and churches, Kazakov also built for Moscow's cultural and charitable institutions, such as the university. Although a plot facing the west wall of the Kremlin had been purchased for the central university building in 1757, not until 1786 did work begin on the main structure (construction of the wings started in 1782). The center of the four-storied building was defined by an Ionic portico of eight columns surmounted with a rotunda that marked the great Ceremonial Hall (Figure 435). The articulation of the facade resembles that of the Senate, with ground floors rusticated and the two upper stories marked by simple fenestration (Figure 436). In each case, the proportional harmony conveyed a sense of institutional order, as well as the rational basis of both the legal and educational systems.[86]

More severely deformed since the time of its initial construction is the Moscow Noblemen's Assembly, the main part of which was built in 1784–7 on the site (and incorporating the walls of) the central Moscow estate house of Prince Vasilii Dolgorukii. Greatly damaged in the 1812 fire, the structure was rebuilt by

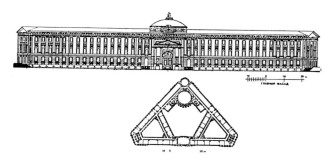

Figure 429. Senate, Moscow Kremlin. 1776–87. Architect: Matvei Kazakov. Plan and elevation adapted from the Matvei Kazakov *Al'bom*.

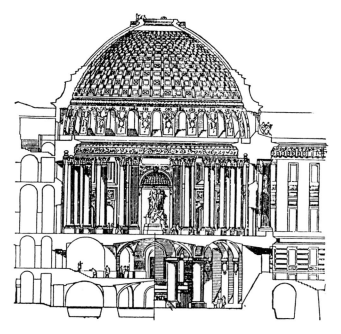

Figure 430. Senate, Moscow Kremlin. Main rotunda. Section.

Kazakov's student Aleksei Bakarev in 1814 and fundamentally altered by A. F. Meisner in 1903.[87] Thus, the present exterior of the Noblemen's Assembly – designated the House of Trade Unions – bears only a distant resemblance to the design by Kazakov. The one relatively well-preserved part is the great Hall of Columns, whose height originally arose above the rest of the structure to admit light through a row of magnificent lunettes. Now contained within the expanded building, the hall, with its Corinthian columns supporting an elaborate cornice (Figure 437), still bears testimony to the wealth of Moscow's gentry culture during the reign of Catherine.

In a better state of preservation is the Golitsyn Hospital, the last of Kazakov's major designs in Moscow (1796–1801). Located on the Kaluga Road to the south of the Moscow River, the hospital was donated by Dmitrii Golitsyn, who conceived of it as part of a complex including a spacious park on land that had belonged to his estate. The three-storied main structure, entered through a monumental hexastyle Tuscan portico, centers on a rotunda–church that is among Kazakov's most accomplished works (Figure 438).[88] The two-storied Ionic colonnade supports a coffered ceiling beneath a hemispherical dome, and an arcade with secondary Corinthian columns adds a richness of detail and plasticity of form that Kazakov had developed over the past two decades. From the exterior, the hemisphere, visually reinforced by two flanking domed bell towers, unifies the lengthy horizontal facade, which leads on either side to two-storied wings (Figure 439). The side wings impart to the hospital the ambiance of a spacious country estate house, yet they also "unfold" at a further right angle

Figure 431. Church of the Metropolitan Philip. Moscow. 1777–88. Architect: Matvei Kazakov. South view. (M 119–20)

Figure 432. Church of the Metropolitan Philip. Moscow. Interior.
(M 52–13)

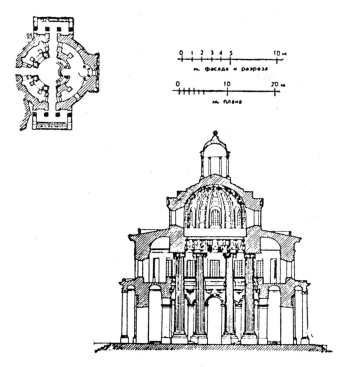

Figure 433. Church of the Metropolitan Philip. Moscow. Section, plan.

and extend parallel to the Kaluga Road. Each of these wings has its meticulously detailed entryway.

◇   ◇   ◇

For all of Matvei Kazakov's prodigious output in the forms surveyed before (and he was involved in the building of at least two other hospitals: the Pavlovskii, 1802–7; and the New Catherine, 1786–90), it could be argued that his greatest contribution to the neoclassical ambiance of Moscow lay in his design of city mansions. Over the centuries, Moscow had witnessed the evolution of a type of urban residential compound (the *gorodskaia usadba*, or "urban estate") that consisted of a main house and adjoining service buildings – all usually of wood – grouped within an enclosure. In the latter part of the eighteenth century, new mansions in the central districts of the city typically had a neoclassical facade, with portico and lower side wings, situated flush with the street. A passageway led from the street to a courtyard, which in turn gave access to the main entrance of the house. In less densely developed areas of the city, the mansion might be set back from the street, with wings or other flanking structures enclosing a courtyard in front of the main facade of the building.[89] In either configuration, the interior would frequently adhere to an arrangement of rooms along an enfilade, with state

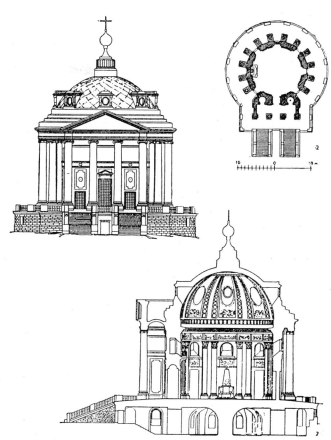

Figure 434. Baryshnikov mausoleum and estate church (not extant). Nikolo-Pogoreloe. Plan, section, and west elevation by L. I. Batalov and A. M. Kharlamov.

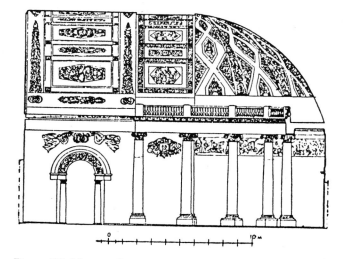

Figure 435. Moscow University. 1786–93. Architect: Matvei Kazakov. Ceremonial hall (rebuilt by Domenico Gilardi). Section by N. L. Apostolova.

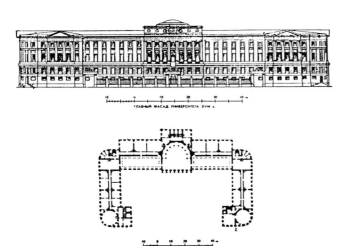

Figure 436. Moscow University. Plan and elevation adapted from the Matvei Kazakov *Al'bom*.

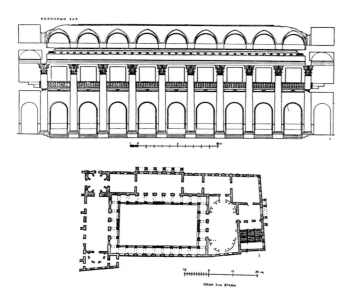

Figure 437. Noblemen's Assembly. Moscow. 1784–7. Architect: Matvei Kazakov. Hall of Columns, section by L. I. Batalov.

rooms in front and smaller living rooms – often with a mezzanine – in the back.[90]

Kazakov's most luxurious mansion was that created in 1789–91 for retired Brigadier I. I. Demidov on Gorokhov Lane. A house and park already existed on the semiurban site during the preceding generation (the 1760s and 1770s), but Kazakov's rebuilding of the earlier house resulted in a residence unprecedented in Moscow for the expense of its decorative work.[91] At the center of the facade, richly endowed with stucco ornament, is a hexastyle Corinthian portico,

raised above a rusticated ground story. The interior is dominated by a series of state rooms known as the Golden Rooms for the lavish gilt work on every carved element. The combination of gold leaf with expensive fabric wall coverings and painted ceilings suggests a setting more appropriate to the Petersburg baroque four decades earlier.

More typical of Kazakov's urban houses, however, is the three-storied mansion built in 1793–9 for the merchant M. P. Gubin, whose wealth was based on factories in the Urals. Kazakov proved particularly successful in resolving the problem of creating a monumental yet balanced structure within the confines of Moscow's often narrow central streets, which hindered a perception of the main facade. For the Gubin mansion, Kazakov created a loggia effect with a semirecessed portico, yet the Corinthian capitals and pediment project strongly over the facade without obstructing passage along the street (Figure 440).[92] Kazakov added flanking two-story extensions with an inset arch supported by paired ironic pilasters. The interior, now poorly maintained, shows a restrained, elegant form of neoclassical decoration, with the cool tones of the grisaille neo-Egyptian motifs in the main vestibule and the delicate polychrome for ceiling paintings – particularly of flower garlands – in the smaller rooms.

The more spacious territory of the house for Kazakov's merchant patron I. I. Baryshnikov on Miasnitskii Street, to the northeast of central Moscow,

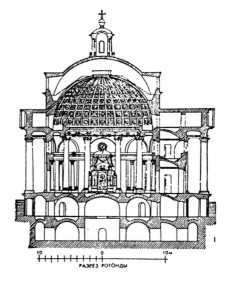

Figure 438. Golitsyn Hospital. Moscow. 1796–1801. Architect: Matvei Kazakov. Rotunda, section adapted from the Matvei Kazakov *Al'bom*.

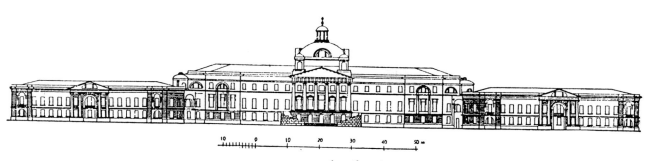

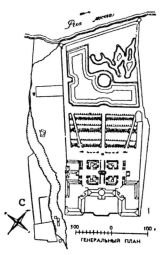

Figure 439. Golitsyn Hospital. Moscow. Elevation adapted from the Matvei Kazakov *Al'bom*.

permitted the creation of a front courtyard, framed by entrance gates and pylons, with flanking two-storied wings. As was common in Moscow, the mansion grew in stages, between 1793 and 1802, with the reconstruction and expansion of earlier structures on the site. The project's central, unifying element is its elevated portico of Corinthian columns in the major order (Figure 441). Designed in Kazakov's best Palladian manner, with columns paired at either end, the projecting portico and frieze represent a late development in eighteenth-century Moscow neoclassicism – as does the mezzanine above the main floor (all of these elements were among the last phase of rebuilding).[93] As in Kazakov's other mansions, the strong pediment replaces the dome of the rotunda that defined the central mass of his major public buildings, yet circular and oval forms figured largely in the design of the interior, particularly the great main hall, or ballroom. Situated at the end of the east wing overlooking the street, this room, almost square in configuration, contains an inscribed circle of faux marbre Corinthian columns supporting a richly molded corn-

ice that in turn frames an ethereal ceiling painting – one of the most skilfull examples of this widely used genre in the decoration of neoclassical mansions.[94]

The foregoing three houses surveyed provide a view of the variety with which Kazakov applied the neoclassical idiom in the design of grand residences for wealthy Moscow merchants who, although limited in social privilege in comparison with the nobility, were able to flaunt their wealth with the building of such residences. These examples by no means exhaust Kazakov's houses, a number of which were destroyed in 1812. Among those reconstructed and later modified beyond recognition in the twentieth century, the most prominent is the former residence of the Moscow Governor General – now the building of the Moscow City Council.[95] In all too many cases, however, Kazakov's work was irrevocably damaged during the great fire. Upon hearing the news of the fire, the invalid architect, evacuated with his family during the approach of the French, received a trauma that led to his death on October 26, 1812.[96] Yet much of his greatest work miraculously survived with little damage, including the Senate in the heart of the Kremlin.

Rodion Kazakov

In the creation of neoclassical Moscow, Matvei Kazakov was joined by younger architects such as Rodion Kazakov (no relation), who distinguished himself above all in the design of churches. The largest among them is the Church of Martin the Confessor (1782–93) in the Taganka district, a monumental exercise in column and mass (Figure 442), that despite its luxury projects a cold monochromatic impression – particularly in comparison with the polychrome of the seventeenth-century churches in the same area.[97] The appearance of this superbly constructed church might suggest that Russian Orthodoxy had indeed become the captive of the bureacratic formalism of the Holy Synod and of wealth without a popular spiritual following.

335

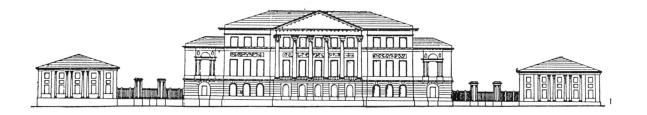

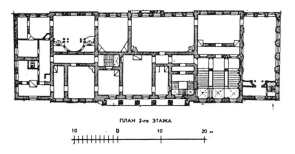

ПЛАН 2-го ЭТАЖА

Figure 440. Gubin house. Moscow. 1793–9. Architect: Matvei Kazakov. Elevation adapted from the Matvei Kazakov *Al'bom.*

Figure 441. Baryshnikov house. Moscow. 1793–1802. Architect: Matvei Kazakov. Portico, main facade. (M 121–16)

These impressions are countered by the bright form of the smaller Church of St. Varvara (1796–1804) on Varvarka Street, leading into Kitai-gorod from Red Square. Built with funds provided by I. I. Baryshnikov and another merchant, N. A. Samgin, the vertical forms of the church predominate without overpowering their surrounding (Figure 443). The white trim of the orange stucco facade intensifies the clear lines and proportions of the central cube, with dome and lantern. The attached square bell tower, buttressed on the south by a semicylinder containing a staircase, reiterates the contrast of forms, rounded and square. The rich Corinthian tetrastyle porticos on the north and south facades convey the sense of a Greek cross plan to what is essentially an elongated rectangle with apse and narthex.[98] On the south, the portico is elevated on a high base, created on the downward slope of the site, which allowed the architect to emphasize the verticality of the structure without exaggerating the dimensions of the columns and dome. The combination of sparse facade detail and a strongly projected Corinthian portico is characteristic of the Moscow neoclassicism at the turn of the century (cf. the Baryshnikov house).

Rodion Kazakov's legacy as a designer of mansions is clouded by the uncertainties of attribution. It is now generally accepted on stylistic evidence that he was the main architect for the Batashov house in the eastern region of Moscow, beyond the Iauza River.[99] Built in 1796–1805 for I. R. Batashov, a prominent industrialist and owner of ironworking plants, the mansion is comparable to the Pashkov house attributed to Bazhenov in its grand scale and richness of ornament. The centerpiece of the house (Figure 444) is a hexastyle Corinthian portico in the major order, elevated over a rusticated ground floor with mascaroni.

The main courtyard of the Batashov house is delineated along the street by two large, detached wings that anchor an iron fence with granite pillars reminiscent of the scale and design of the Summer Garden fence in Petersburg. The central gate and propylae, with crouching lions, not only frame the portico, but also comprise a monumental work in their own right.

Figure 442. Church of St. Martin the Confessor. Moscow. 1782–93. Architect: Rodion Kazakov. Southwest view. (M 113–22)

The symmetry of the main facade provides order to an ensemble composed of the mansion and its service buildings, extending into an adjacent park. Situated at the crest of one of the many small hills in the district, the Batashov house gave an especially clear view of other monuments on prominent topographical points, such as the Church of St. Martin the Confessor and the Church of St. Simeon the Stylite. The heightened rotunda and large dome of the latter were completed by 1812 (architect unknown) with funds provided by Batashov, who may have been motivated by the desire to have a distant rotunda on his horizon.[100]

◇ ◇ ◇

Whatever the uncertainties of attribution, for every late eighteenth-century mansion by Matvei or Rodion Kazakov in Moscow, there existed several for which there is no acknowledged architect. In many cases, there was indeed probably no hired architect, but rather a master builder (often a serf) who could apply typical devices of the period to the exterior and leave

the interior decoration to groups of craftsmen who specialized in these matters. With various stages of rebuilding, the residence would acquire its neoclassical order gradually. It is noteworthy, therefore, that these structures often evolved into works of considerable grace and proportional harmony.[101]

An example of this process is the A. F. Talyzin house on Vozdvizhenka Street, near the west wall of the Kremlin. An irregular quadrangle composed of several structures, some dating to the seventeenth century, the Talyzin ensemble is unified by the main house, constructed in 1787 and situated along the street line.[102] The center of the structure is marked by six pilasters whose elaborate Corinthian capitals provide a visual dominant to the even, symmetrical facade (Figure 445). The state rooms on the second floor are arranged on an enfilade overlooking the street, and the ballroom is located on the courtyard side. Despite its adaptation as an exhibition space for the Shchusev State Museum of Architecture, much of the interior decoration has been preserved, including ceil-

Figure 443. Church of St. Varvara. Moscow. 1796–1804. Architect: Rodion Kazakov. Southwest view. (M 132–27)

Figure 444. Batashov house. Moscow. 1796–1805. Architect: Rodion Kazakov. Main entrance, central facade. (M 112–23)

ing paintings and numerous high-relief plaster panels on themes drawn from classical mythology (Figure 446).[103]

Smaller, but with the same sense of proportional harmony inherent in the order system is the late eighteenth-century house of Prince Stepan Kurakin, located on New Basman Street (Figure 447). The classical allegorical ornament interspersed in the portico has, remarkably, remained with little damage. Although in 1801, Stepan Kurakin became the head of the Expedition for the Construction of the Kremlin and thus the superior of Rodion Kazakov (the chief architect), there is no evidence that the latter participated in work on the house; indeed, they seem to have heartily detested each other.[104]

Quarenghi in Moscow

As Moscow's architects developed a neoclassical idiom that combined grace and monumentality, Petersburg's great Palladian, Giacomo Quarenghi, also participated in a number of major projects, including the Catherine (Golovin) Palace, located in the district beyond the Iauza River. At the end of the 1760s, the Annenhof Palace – a reconstruction of the Golovin Palace of the Petrine era – had reached a state of disrepair that made its destruction inevitable. Catherine initiated a new palace to designs by Rinaldi, but the walls were soon razed because of faulty materials and yet another rebuilding was entrusted to Karl Blank, who completed the basic structure in 1781. Quarenghi was commissioned to endow the shell of the palace with greater monumentality, and in response, he created a massive loggia with sixteen sand-

stone columns striped in various shades of gray – virtually the only feature of the lavishly outfitted palace to have remained intact.[105] After the death of Catherine, Paul in his inimitable manner converted the palace into a barracks.

A happier fate befell Quarenghi's design for the Sheremetev Homeless Refuge, also begun by another architect, Elizvoi Nazarov, who in the late 1790s built near the Sukhareva Tower a large curved building (with end wings) to house an almshouse and hospital for the indigent. Quarenghi subsequently entered the project as a personal friend of Nikolai Sheremetev, whom he had served as a consultant during the building of the palace at Ostankino.[106] Inconsolable after the early death of Praskovia Kovaleva-Zhemchugova, his wife, in 1803, Sheremetev commissioned Quarenghi to modify the central church of the refuge into a solemn memorial to her.[107] Quarenghi was well acquainted with the peculiar challenge of the curved facade, having designed one for the State Bank in

Figure 445. Talyzin house. Moscow. 1787. Main facade. (M 151–28)

Petersburg with a double colonnade across the diameter (see Figure 377). The Sheremetev Refuge, like Kazakov's Golitsyn Hospital, had the advantage of a clearly defined functional center: the church–mausoleum. Quarenghi emphasized this point of the building with a large dome of low pitch, but the central point is the semicircular double Tuscan colonnade that extends from the center, with its long pediment, and creates an open rotunda–temple (Figure 448). The opposing contours of the colonnade and the main facade – an enclosure within an enclosure – not only emphasize the plasticity of the structure, but also provide a dramatic setting at the center (Figure 449). Quarenghi's design for the interior of the main rotunda (completed only in 1810, after the death of Sheremetev himself) displays the austere magnificence of high neoclassicism, and includes sculptural reliefs by Zamaraev and ceiling paintings by Giovanni Scotti.

Quarenghi's other monumental public structure in

Figure 446. Talyzin house. Moscow. Interior, enfilade with plaster panels. (M 116–0)

Moscow, Old Gostinnyi Dvor (trading center), is located in the commercial district of Kitai-gorod. The merchants who paid for the structure were notoriously slow in providing the funds (like their Petersburg counterparts during the construction of that city's Gostinnyi Dvor); but even in unfinished form, the structure dominated its surroundings. Quarenghi was a prolific designer of such trading centers, and the plan that he sent to Moscow in 1789 called for a large arcaded trapezoid whose sides could be completed as the need arose.[108] The actual construction of the Old Gostinnyi Dvor was implemented by local architects S. A. Karin and I. A. Selikhov under the supervision of Matvei Kazakov, who introduced various changes (the slope of the site led to differences in the size of the arcading), and by 1805, they had completed only parts of three sides of the project. Subsequent extensions and modifications in the nineteenth century disfigured Quarenghi's original plan for an open exterior arcade with an enclosed interior corridor around the courtyard perimeter.[109] Nonetheless, the extant structure (Figure 450) retains the monumentality of Quarenghi's Corinthian columns, whose measured intervals frame the two-storied arcade.

The grandest of Quarenghi's projects for Moscow was intended for A. A. Bezborodko, chancellor during the latter part of Catherine's reign and the architect's frequent patron. Bezborodko had one palace in Moscow – the Slobodskoi Palace, so named for its location in the old "German Quarter" (nemetskaia sloboda) – which Quarenghi redesigned with surpassing luxury in 1790–4; but in 1796, that residence was donated to the Emperor Paul for his Moscow coronation. Paul reciprocated by paying Bezborodko 630,000 rubles and donating land for a new palace.[110] After rejecting the possibility of purchasing a mansion from the hard-pressed Nikolai N. Demidov, Bezborodko decided in 1797 to build a new residence that would, in his words, "at the very least show posterity that in our time and in our land there was a knowledge of taste."[111]

Bezborodko had unquestionably chosen the architect with the surest sense of taste, and one not to be daunted by the scale of the project. As fate would have it, the structure was hardly beyond the foundation when Bezborodko died, in June 1798, and all work terminated. Quarenghi's project drawings have, however, survived and indicate not only the dimensions of the palace – whose enormous wings, with Corinthian loggias, contained quadrangular courtyards – but also the magnificence of the design (Figure 451). The sketches of the interior, which was to con-

Figure 447. Stepan Kurakin house on New Basman Street. Moscow. Late eighteenth century. Elevation from the Matvei Kazakov *Al'bom.* Courtesy of the Shchusev State Museum of Architecture, Moscow.

Figure 448. Sheremetev Homeless Refuge. Moscow. 1796–1810. Architects: Elizvoi Nazarov and Giacomo Quarenghi. Main portal. (M 119–24)

340

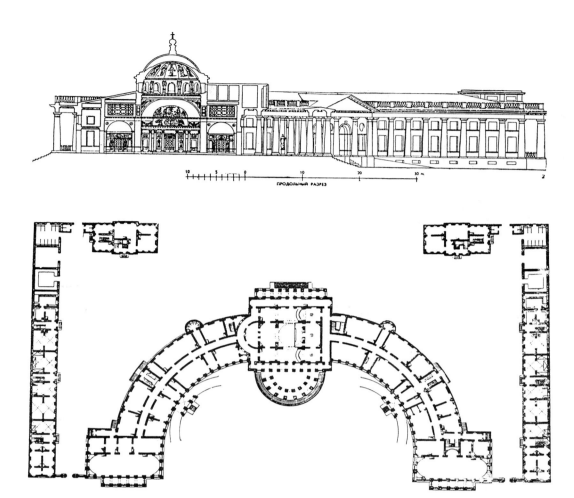

Figure 449. Sheremetev Homeless Refuge. Moscow. Elevation and plan by V. N. Taleporovskii.

tain a theater modeled on Quarenghi's Hermitage Theater in Petersburg, indicate that Bezborodko intended to create a museum ambiance for a collection of classical art – a century in advance of the realization of such a project in Moscow (see Chapter 14). Even though unrealized, the project influenced the development of Russian landscape gardening, with its extensive plans for a formal as well as a "natural" garden apparently devised by both Quarenghi and Nikolai Lvov.[112]

Neoclassicism in the Provinces

The attempt during the reign of Catherine to endow Moscow with a rational plan and an enlightened, neoclassical appearance – in some respects a notable failure – served as a model for the implementation of new town plans (over 300 by the time of Catherine's

death in 1796), not only in areas recently assimilated by the empire in the south and east, but also in medieval cities whose decrepit fortified rings were replaced by a grid pattern of streets, radial boulevards, and squares.[113] This transformation, pursued to widely varying degrees, was not simply an aesthetic decision, although Catherine was known to spend lavishly on matters of taste. Rather, it touched upon the central question, radically posed by Peter the Great with the founding of St. Petersburg, of the existence of a properly ordered state and the extension of the capital's control over the vast reaches of Russia. Thus, the reconstruction of provincial towns involved concerns ranging from the need to prevent devastating fires to zoning measures that determined property rights and social status. The process of addressing these issues evolved in several stages: the creation of the Commission for the Masonry Construction of St. Petersburg and Moscow in 1762; the summoning of

341

Figure 450. Old Gostinnyi Dvor (trading rows). Moscow. 1789–1805; midnineteenth century. Main architect: Giacomo Quarenghi. South arcade. (M 53–1)

the Legislative Commission in 1767; the implementing of a new administrative code for the provinces in 1775; and the promulgation of a "Charter for the rights of Cities" in 1785 – to name only those most directly relevant.

The first application of the new planning measures occurred with the rebuilding of the ancient city of Tver after a fire in 1763 that leveled most of the town. The Commission for the Masonry Construction of St. Petersburg and Moscow promptly issued guidelines for the resurrection of the town under the direction of Ivan Betskoi, who thereby expanded the Commission's brief to include supervision of urban planning virtually anywhere in the empire. Later in the same year, the Commission approved a town plan for Tver submitted by Peter Nikitin (assisted by Matvey Kazakov), which established a number of devices used in subsequent cases, such as the street grid and a general principle of geometric regularity. In addition, the plan experimented with the development of uniform designs for various classes of residential and commercial structure – a variant of the "model house" approach adopted in Petersburg in the first part of the eighteenth century.[114] In a vast country that wished to create an efficient administrative apparatus – and "state culture" – with only a small professional class (including architects), such methods had the obvious benefits of standardization. The models could be applied by builders with no extensive training in design, with the reasonable certainty that a functional structure of a certain size and appearance would result.

As the Commission's surveyors moved throughout the empire, each designated administrative center received its new plan. If the juxtaposition of neoclassical administrative buildings and mansions with medieval cathedrals was frequently awkward (as in Vladimir), there were other plans that to this day have retained the clarity of design and functional logic that was the Commission's ideal.[115] One such example is the city of Kaluga, which at the end of the eighteenth century was a prosperous trading and transportation center some 160 kilometers to the southwest of Moscow. Its plan, a large trapezoid, was formulated in 1778 by Peter Nikitin, who also worked on the site and oversaw much of the construction.[116] On the site of the former Kremlin and at the junction of two main roads from Moscow and Tula, he stipulated a trading center (Gostinnyi Dvor) whose focus was an arcade in a pseudo-Gothic style of brick with limestone trim, built in two stages between 1784 and 1796.[117]

Kaluga's wealth was reflected in mansions, commissioned primarily by merchants, whose scale and style imitated similar residences in Moscow. The most impressive among them – and, happily, the best preserved – is the Zolotarev house, comparable in every respect to such Moscow monuments as the Talyzin or Kolychev houses. Built in 1805–8 by an unknown architect for the merchant P. M. Zolotarev, son of a noted Kaluga silversmith and a descendent of traders in precious metals (the family name derives from "goldsmith"), the two-storied stuccoed brick structure is situated flush with the street line and is flanked by two arched entryways that lead to a courtyard and park extending to the banks of the Oka River. The center of the structure (palazzo might be a more appropriate term for this classically inspired masterpiece) is marked by a pediment and slightly recessed pilasters that create three segments, each of which contains a high-relief plaster panel on themes from the Iliad: the quarrel of the godesses, the judgment of Paris, and the Sacrifice.[118] The flanking entryways, with exquisite wrought-iron tracery, are appropriately decorated with relief figures of trumpeting glory (Figure 452), and even the service buildings enclosing the courtyard display plaster medallions drawn from classical mythology, as though masquerading as pavilions within the relatively narrow confines of the site. The entrances to the house, placed within each of the side facades, are framed by elaborate cast-iron portecocheres.

Zolotarev's profession brought him into wealthy circles in both Moscow and Petersburg, where he gained a familiarity with the latest in neoclassical architecture and design. This is most evident in the interior of the house, decorated by the Moscow firm

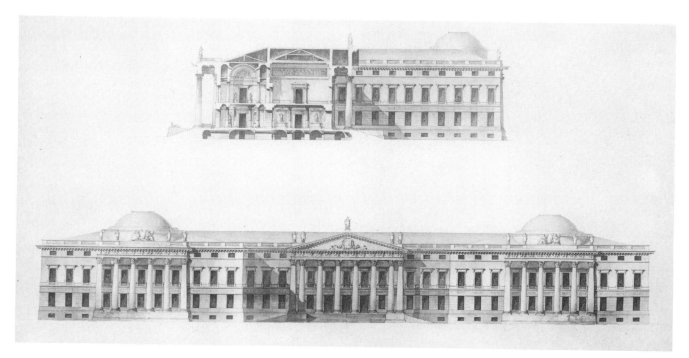

Figure 451. Bezborodko Palace. Moscow. 1797. Architect: Giacomo Quarenghi. Elevation, section by Quarenghi. Courtesy of the Shchusev State Museum of Architecture, Moscow.

Figure 452. Zolotarev house. Kaluga. East entrance. (KL 4–9a)

of S. P. Campioni. From the vestibule, done entirely in grisaille trompe l'oeil to the small "bosquet," whose walls and ceiling are covered with paintings of exotic plants and trellised ivy, the main enfilade of the house is a showpiece of the decorative arts. The largest space is the ballroom, with a wall painting in the style of Hubert Robert: classical ruins in a romantic landscape. The main part of the ceiling is painted in grisaille, with a border frieze illustrating in amphora style various scences from classical mythology. The upper part of the walls are decorated with high-relief plaster medallions on allegorical themes.[119] It is likely that Campioni's group included Italian master artisans, who produced the best examples of such work in both Moscow and Petersburg. The Zolotarev house demonstrates the degree to which wealthy merchants from the provinces had accepted the cultural iconography of neoclassicism in its most refined expression.

Although unrivaled in the quality of its design, the Zolotarev house was not an isolated example of architectural excellence in Kaluga.[120] (Even the War of 1812, so destructive for large areas of central Russia, proved a boon to Kaluga, whose strategic location made it a staging and supply point for the Russian counteroffensive against Napoleon's retreating armies – and further contributed to the town's prosperity.) The city also had its more modest townhouses, whose design derived from model projects (Figure

343

Figure 453. House built to standardized (model) design. Kaluga. Late eighteenth century. (KL 1–6a)

453). And the ensemble was completed by neoclassical churches and bell towers, resembling the work of Rodion Kazakov, as well as institutional buildings such as the Noblemen's Assembly. For certain Russian architectural critics at the beginning of the twentieth century, this creative unity in the design of provincial towns was part of a golden age in Russian culture.

◇   ◇   ◇

Few, if any, provincial centers could equal Kaluga in the number and brilliance of its stately residences; yet in some respects, the most coherent plan was developed for the medieval city of Kostroma, at the confluence of the Kostroma and Volga Rivers. The new plan, developed in 1781–4, left intact the medieval Kremlin and its Dormition Cathedral (rebuilt in 1775–8; not extant), but established immediately to the north a new center, from which radiated twelve streets (Figure 454).[121] Over the next five decades, through the 1830s, the Kostroma plan was developed with consistency and logic by a number of architects, including Stepan Vorotilov, Karl Kler, and P. I. Fursov – the most productive architect of Kostroma, where he worked for three decades after graduating from the Imperial Academy of Arts in 1817.[122]

The central square of Kostroma was bordered by a series of trading rows, which were typically named after their primary commodity: the Flour (Large and Small), Fish, Gingerbread, Butter, and Vegetable, or Tobacco (to a plan by the Petersburg architect Vasilii Stasov), in addition to the Trifle and the Red arcades. The Large Flour Rows (Figure 455) comprised an arcaded quadrangle similar in size and design to the

Red arcade, located across the central square; both were designed by Karl Kler and built with modifications by Vorotilov in 1789–93. The visual dominant of the west side of the Red arcade is a bell tower (Figure 456) constructed in 1792 by Vorotilov and adjacent to the small pentacupolar Church of the Transfiguration on the Rows, dating from the early part of the century. The result demonstrates that an architect with a sensitivity to scale and complementary form could achieve a harmony of neoclassical design with earlier Russian architectural forms. The Red arcade was enhanced during the 1820s by construction within the quadrangle of the Trifle Rows, elongated rectangular structures with simple, but visually effective, Tuscan colonnades.

In 1823–6, Fursov also built the Kostroma fire tower (Figure 457), perhaps the greatest work of the city's neoclassical renaissance and, appropriately, the one that addressed the scourge of fire that the new town plan was intended to alleviate. The main building, containing administrative offices and housing for the firefighters, resembles a classical temple, with a majestic Ionic portico. Above the pediment is a low rusticated block (an extension of the lower walls), which serves as a base for the watchtower – itself resembling a small temple, with a rusticated shaft and volutes supporting the observation platform. The detail and proportions of the complex structure are in all respects a marvel of calculation. On either side of the central block, one-story arcaded stables and a carriage shed extend symetrically; their horizontal lines provide a contrast to the tower in a concluding merger

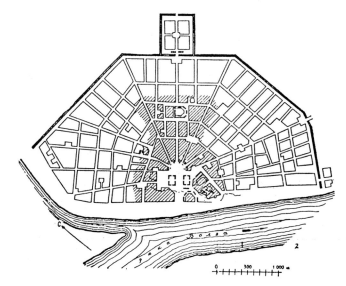

Figure 454. Town plan of Kostroma. 1781–4.

Figure 455. Large Flour Trading Rows. Kostroma. 1789–93. Architects: Karl Kler and Stepan Vorotilov. (KO 1–10)

Figure 456. Red Arcade bell tower. Kostroma. 1792. Architect: Stepan Vorotilov. In foreground: Trifle Trading Rows. 1820s. Architect: P. I. Fursov. On left: Church of the Transfiguration on the Trading Rows. Early eighteenth century. (KO 1–16)

preliminary plan for rebuilding Kazan and entrusted its implementation to Vasilii Kaftyrev (another of Dmitrii Ukhtomskii's students), who arrived in the city in 1767 and submitted a final version the following year.[123]

Over the next 15 years, Kaftyrev developed a plan – viable to this day – that imposed geometrical order on a complex topographical environment. Unfortunately, many of the neoclassical buildings that made Kazan one of Russia's most imposing cities (despite a population of only 25,000 at the beginning of the century) were destroyed or heavily damaged in the fires of 1815 and 1842, including the Gostinnyi Dvor, built by F. E. Emelianov in 1798 with a grand portico of eighteen Ionic columns.[124] Although restored after 1815, the building was substantially modifed following the 1842 fire by the removal of the portico, thus depriving the main street leading from the Kremlin of an important visual mark.

At the other end of the same street is Kazan's surviving neoclassical masterpiece, the main building of Kazan University. Founded in 1804, Kazan University was one of the most important Russian scientific in-

Figure 457. Fire tower. Kostroma. 1823–6. Architect: P. I. Fursov. (KO 1–13)

of form and function. Fursov complemented the fire tower with the building in 1823–5 of the Hauptwacht, located in the adjacent wedge formed by the central radial streets. Also of stuccoed brick with white trim, the main facade is decorated with classical elements, from the Tuscan Doric portico to the window surrounds and the stuccoed military regalia that signifies the building's purpose.

The extent and scale of the neoclassical rebuilding of the provinces is epitomized by the city of Kazan, which had become the major transportation and trading center on the Volga before the railroads realigned economic power along the river during the latter half of the nineteenth century. Fire remained a scourge of the city, which was largely destroyed in 1742, 1749, 1765, 1797, 1815, and 1842. In addition, the city suffered heavily in 1774 during a seige by the rebel forces of Emelian Pugachev. After the 1765 fire, Aleksei Kvasov, the main architect of the Commission for the Construction of Petersburg and Moscow, prepared a

Figure 458. Kazan University, main building. 1822–5. Architect: P. G. Piatnitskii. (KZ 3–13)

stitutions in Russian during the nineteenth century. Its central building, constructed in 1822–5 by P. G. Piatnitskii (a student of Andrei Voronikhin), reflects that significance with an enormous facade, 160 meters in length, broken by three Ionic porticos: hexastyle on each end and dodecastyle in the middle (Figure 458). The clarity of the design and the proportional relations of the columns, the facade, and the attic above the central portico preclude monotony. In the 1830s, the main structure was complemented by additional buildings designed by M. P. Korinfskii, also a student of Voronikhin.[125] There is a fine irony that the construction of this ensemble to a rigorous, rectilinear design should have been supported and overseen by university rector Nikolai Lobachevskii, the creator of non-Euclidean geometry.

The spread of neoclassical architecture throughout Russia during the late eighteenth century might seem a mechanical and superficial process, whose order bore little relation to underlying physical and social

reality. Not only the system of classical orders, but the decorative motifs that drew so profusely on classical themes might seem a pretentious affectation. As the French diplomat Count Segur sardonically noted: "As soon as the Russian nobility entered the path of enlightenment, they began to imitate the Patricians of Rome. . . . At that time one could meet more than one Lucullus in Moscow."[126]

There is, however, evidence direct and indirect to suggest that classical culture in its many ramifications was consciously and widely assimilated among the still small educated population in Russia. Indeed, having promulgated a secular cultural revolution throughout the eighteenth century, Russia's ruling elite – while professing loyalty to the Orthodox Church – could turn to a system of secular values inherent in classical mythology and history, values that elevated service to the state and the maintenance of social stability through a code of honor. That certain of these values might prove contradictory soon became evident to those unable to tolerate autocracy and serfdom. But during the two decades of warfare in

Europe following the French Revolution, Russian feats of arms and military involvement on several fronts would have suggested parallels with the exploits of classical heroes. (Great Britain and revolutionary France had pursued the analogy thoroughly in their own art and architecture.)

In this regard, it is no coincidence that martial valor played so large a role in the secular neoclassical iconography that replaced the wonder-working icons and religious imagery of the militant Orthodox Church – fervent supporter of the expansion of medieval Muscovy. Many of the architectural monuments discussed before display a pervasive homage to *virtus* and valor; yet in none of them is it more clearly stated than in the Moscow Military Hospital by Ivan Egotov. Built in 1798–1802 as an expansion of a hospital founded by Peter the Great at Lefortovo, the large structure was centered on a loggia (Figure 459), with doubled Cornithian columns, that suggests the influence of Egotov's mentor Matvei Kazakov.[127] The high-relief plaster work includes military regalia in the pediment and the panels "Healing" and "Blessing" on either side of the loggia, as well as statues (not extant) to Hippocrates and a classical warrior in niches on either side of the entrance.

Egotov had created a worthy example of public architecture, functional, low in cost, and a major addition to the scientific establishment of Moscow. As an object of civic pride, the pathos of its neoclassical imagery, containing references to noble sacrifice and healing, exemplifies society's idealization of the heroism of military service. By the middle of the nine-

Figure 459. Moscow Military Hospital. 1798–1802. Architect: Ivan Egotov. Photograph c. 1900. From Iurii Shamurin, *Ocherki klassicheskoi Moskvy*.

teenth century, the expression "state architecture" (or "barracks architecture") had become a pejorative term for the imperial neoclassical style. Before that time, however, heroic neoclassicism would achieve its final and most eloquent expression in the reign of Alexander I.

CHAPTER 12

The Early Nineteenth Century: Alexandrine Neoclassicism

Why should we fear to be compared with [the Romans] in magnificence?

– Carlo Rossi

The goal of a new, "civilized" architectural environment, so assiduously pursued by Russia's eighteenth-century autocrats, reached its apogee during the reign of Catherine's grandson Alexander I, from 1801 to 1825. With renewed energy and resources, and with new interpretations of the neoclassical style, Alexander's architects either extended or initiated the majority of Petersburg's neoclassical ensembles, thus creating not only a hierarchy of primary and secondary architectural space in the imperial city, but also an interrelation between its various ensembles. In certain respects, this process continued uninterruptedly even after the dissolution in 1796 of Catherine's primary planning agency, the Commission for the Masonry Construction of St. Petersburg and Moscow.

During the reign of Alexander, however, Petersburg's population more than doubled (from 200,000 to 440,000); and with the intensified expansion of the capital after the final victory over Napoleon, the emperor reestablished a central planning bureau, known as the Committee for Construction Projects and Hydraulic Works.[1] In the words of an observer of the time:

[Alexander] wanted to make Petersburg more beautiful than any of the European capitals he had visited. For this purpose he decided to set up a special architectural committee under the chairmanship of [General Augustin de] Béthencourt. Neither the legalilty of private ownership, nor the structural durability of public or private buildings was the business of this committee: it was to be concerned only with examining designs for new facades, to accept, reject, or alter them, and also to engage in the planning of streets and squares, projects for canals, bridges, and the better construction of the outlying parts of the city – devoted, in a word, solely to the city's external beauty.[2]

No building, private or public, was to escape the scrutiny of this most thorough of Petersburg's planning commissions.

In the implementation of his design, Alexander was fortunate to have at his command a group of architects whose vision matched his own: Andrei Voronikhin, Thomas de Thomon, Adrian Zakharov, Vasilii Stasov, and Carlo Rossi – the most prolific creator of monumental space in Petersburg. The sense of measure that pervades their work can be traced in part to Starov and Quarenghi, but the rhetorical style and the bold geometric emphasis of Petersburg architecture at the beginning of the nineteenth century also owes a debt to the French neoclassicism of such architects as Claude-Nicolas Ledoux and Etienne-Louis Boullée. For four decades during the reigns of Alexander and Nicholas I, neoclassicism brilliantly represented imperial Russian might; yet it eventually yielded to a surfeit of detail, to new construction technologies that encouraged a different approach to architectonics, and to different ideological expectations for architecture.

Andrei Voronikhin

The new phase in the building of neoclassical Petersburg originated during the brief reign of Paul I (1796–1801). Despite the tragic and often ludicrous events of the 5 years preceding his assassination by the palace guard, Paul's reign witnessed the victorious campaign of Alexander Suvorov over the armies of revolutionary France, and new Russian initiatives in the Mediterranean – not unconnected with Paul's involvement in the Maltese Order. Indeed, the idea of a rapprochement between Orthodoxy and Roman Catholicism may well have influenced the design of the most imposing of Petersburg's cathedrals, commissioned in 1800 and dedicated to the Icon of the Kazan Mother of God.

Its architect, Andrei Voronikhin (1759–1814), was not well known in Petersburg, having built no structure remotely comparable to the cathedral. Although born a serf on one of the Stroganov estates in the Urals, his circumstances were fortunate, for the Stroganovs were not only one of the most richest families in Russia, but also knowledgeable patrons of the arts. Having recognized Voronikhin's talent, they brought him to Moscow in 1777, where he studied for 2 years with Bazhenov and Matvei Kazakov. In 1779, Voronikhin was drawn into the Stroganov circle in Petersburg, and granted his freedom in 1786. Voronikhin accompanied Count Alexander Stroganov's son Pavel on his travels throughout Russia in 1781–5 and, between 1786 and 1790, in Europe – Switzerland, Germany, and France.

Before returning to Russia in 1790, Voronikhin had private architectural training in Paris, although the details of his work there are unknown. But what remains of his first major project – the remodeling in 1793 of Rastrelli's Stroganov Palace – shows a thorough understanding of neoclassical architectural form and interior decoration.[3] By the end of the eighteenth century, he had clearly impressed his noble patrons, as well as the Academy of Arts, which named him an academician in painting in 1799. After a period of decline, vigorously criticized by Vasilii Bazhenov, the Academy had experienced a revival under the leadership of Voronikhin's patron, Alexander Stroganov, who was its president in 1800–11.[4] Voronikhin received the official designation as architect for his design, in 1800, of the Colonnade that frames the Grand Cascade at Peterhof. During the same period, he was also engaged in redesigning many of the interiors at the Pavlovsk palace. Although neither of these projects is insignificant, they gave no hint of the magnitude of Voronikhin's work in the capital itself.

As early as the 1780s, there had been plans to rebuild Mikhail Zemtsov's modest Church of the Nativity of the Virgin on Nevskii Prospekt, the repository of the miraculous Icon of the Kazan Mother of God, which had been brought to the city by Peter the Great, and was considered the palladium of the Romanovs. Quarenghi subsequently submitted a proposal for the church's reconstruction, but it has not survived. In 1799, Paul reopened the competition for a new cathedral, to be dedicated to the icon of the Kazan Mother of God.[5] The design of the grand temple was to suggest the emperor's desire to effect a reconciliation with Roman Catholicism and, implicitly, to establish his capital as a new Rome – yet another version of the Russian obsession with heavenly cities. (The scuplted frieze on the apse of the completed Cathedral of the Kazan Mother of God portrays the Entry of Christ into Jerusalem, thus establishing a link with the Cathedral of the Intercession on the Moat in Moscow – an earlier monument to Russian messianism.) As a bastion of united Christianity, Petersburg would have a cathedral to rival St. Peter's in Rome.

Charles Cameron and Thomas de Thomon were among those competing for the project, and though Paul had approved Cameron's design in October 1800, he reversed himself a month later and appointed a commission, headed by Stroganov, to direct the construction. The commission promptly chose Voronikhin as the architect. Although Voronikhin's qualifications were strenuously questioned at first, the wisdom of this decision and Stroganov's faith in "his" architect were substantiated during the course of work, not simply in the organization of so large a construction project, but in the magnificent eloquence of the design itself. Voronikhin's cathedral (Figure 460) is redolent of monumental classicism as interpreted in Saint Peter's and, more to the point, Jacques Germain Soufflot's Sainte Geneviève in Paris (the Panthéon, 1755–92).[6] In Russia, Voronikhin's sole predecessor in a Roman classical exercise of this magnitude was Bazhenov, whose designs for the Great Kremlin Palace and, possibly, the Pashkov mansion may well have influenced Voronikhin.[7]

The body of the Kazan Cathedral is in the form of a Latin cross, with Corinthian porticoes on the north, south, and west, and a semicircular apse, with attic frieze, on the east (Figure 461).[8] The structure is surmounted by a large attic. Over the crossing is an elongated dome, above a drum whose pilasters echo the rows of columns below. In an earlier variant of the plan, the dome and the drum were considerably larger, and the drum was surrounded by a colonnade – a detail reminiscent of the Panthéon. In its present form, slender over so massive a structure, the dome produces a curiously light effect.

The placement of the cathedral in relation to Nevskii Prospekt – with various palaces, but not particularly imposing at the beginning of the century – demanded an ingenious solution. Because the cathedral's main, east–west axis parallels the Prospekt, the

Figure 460. Cathedral of the Kazan Mother of God. Petersburg. 1801–11. Architect: Andrei Voronikhin. North view. (P 78–25)

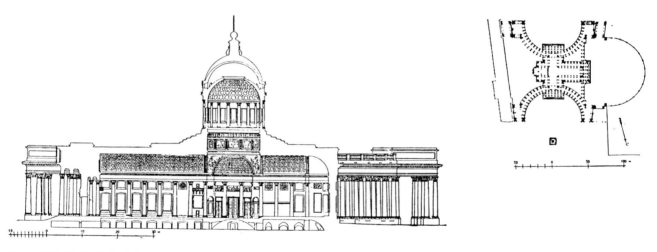

Figure 461. Cathedral of the Kazan Mother of God. Petersburg. Longitudinal section and original plan (with two colonnades).

architect had to create a monumental resolution for the cathedral's north facade, facing the street, than for its actual main entrance on the west.[9] His "deception" is a vast curving colonnade, anchored at the east and west ends by a portico of square pylons, culminating in an attic frieze (Figure 462). With its sharply defined entablature and balustrade, the Cor-

inthian colonnade sweeps from both ends toward the north portico and dome, which are barely strong enough to focus the energy released along this grand arc. In the original plan, there was to be a second colonnade on the south side, but because of cost overruns, it remained unbuilt.[10]

The general impression projected by the Kazan Ca-

350

Figure 462. Cathedral of the Kazan Mother of God. Petersburg. Colonnade. East end block. (P 44–4)

thedral is of grand austerity, yet Voronikhin devoted considerable effort to its exterior decoration. The brick walls of the structure are surfaced with Pudost stone, a limestone tufa obtained near Gatchina that is tractable when quarried, but hardens on exposure to air, thus providing an ideal substance for detailed sculpting.[11] Voronikhin exploited these properties in designing friezes on biblical subjects for the east and west end blocks and the apse, as well as sculpted panels for the three porticoes. The exterior columns and capitals, arranged in ranks of four, are also of Pudost stone, and various details are rendered in granite (three different types), limestone, and marble. Heretofore, only Rinaldi's Marble Palace had made such lavish use of stone. In addition, bronze was extensively used for statuary – such as statues by S. S. Pimenov of the "national" saints Vladimir and Alexander Nevskii, placed on either side of the north portal. The great doors of the north portal were covered with bronze panels, which Voronikhin based on Lorenzo Ghiberti's designs for the doors of the Baptistery in Florence.[12]

The interior centers around the cupolar space are defined by massive pylons, above which the pendentives with Evangelists support a drum with a grisaille frieze of scenes from the life of Christ. There could be no clearer indication of the triumph of the neoclassical iconographic system than this frieze (Figure 463), which transposes central episodes of the Christian faith to the idiom of pre-Christian classical art – Christ as classical hero. Indeed, by the time of its completion, the cathedral had already acquired the aura of a national military shrine: captured French

trophies were placed there in 1812; and the interment within the cathedral in July 1813 of the body of Field Marshal Mikhail Kutuzov, commander-in-chief of the Russian armies against Napoleon, enhanced the cathedral's role as a sanctum of patriotic and military ideals.

By the same token, the Cathedral of the Kazan Mother of God was intended as a monument specifically to the divine protection extended to the Romanov dynasty, and it would appear that no cost was spared to endow the interior with a magnificent finish, even to gilding the bronze capitals of the interior colonnade.[13] From the coffered, double-shelled cupola to the fifty-six paired Corinthian columns of polished red granite, 10.7 meters in height, that line the central nave and arms of the cruciform structure, the cathedral proclaims the immutable power of state and religion. Yet the cathedral was built by a freed serf, whose unerring sense of form and taste established a mastery over the costly materials (this in contrast to St. Isaac's Cathedral, whose lavish display of the decorative arts overwhelms the structure; see Chapter 13). Even the barrel vaults seem weightless with their network of hexagonal coffering and inset rosettes. The painting of the interior, supervised by the Academy of Arts, included works on canvas as well as on plaster. Among the prominent artists involved with the two iconostases – painted in an academic, classical style – were Vasilii Borovikovskii and Andrei I. Ivanov, a professor at the academy and father of one of the most famous of nineteenth-century Russian artists, Alexander Ivanov.[14]

The Kazan Cathedral and colonnade form one of the earliest examples of coherent spatial planning in Petersburg (with the exception of monastic institutions such as the convent at Smolnyi). During the eighteenth century, large palace ensembles had been erected along the Neva River and the canals, but the design of the areas surrounding such monuments as the Winter Palace had been deferred. By the time of the cathedral's completion, in 1811, the development of the capital's parks and squares was well under way, with new projects by Andreian Zakharov and others. But although the Voronikhin design for the Kazan Cathedral site was not fully realized, nor was it allotted the open square on the south that he had intended, its integration of architectural form and public space performs the complex task of anchoring the city's main thoroughfare at its center.

Voronikhin's other large structure in the capital, the Mining Institute, was completed the same year as the Kazan Cathedral, but in a very different form of neoclassicism. In 1806, he had been commissioned to

Figure 463. Cathedral of the Kazan Mother of God. Petersburg. Interior, dome. (P 64–34)

building. At either end, he placed allegorical statues representing the struggle between the gods and earth: "The Abduction of Persephone" and "Heracles Crushing Antaeus" by Vasilii Demut-Malinovskii and Stepan Pimenov. As with the Kazan Cathedral, Voronikhin emphasized the role of monumental sculpture and its iconography as a part of the comprehensive project design. In 1819–21 (several years after Voronikhin's untimely death), Alexander Postnikov designed the central hall of the institute, flanked by Ionic columns and used to display the main part of the institute's mineral collection. For the same space, Giovanni Scotti in 1822 produced ceiling paintings depicting imperial patronage of mining in the sculpted technique of grisaille.[16]

Thomas de Thomon

The Mining Institute marks the western end of the great ensemble of neoclassical and baroque monuments extending along the Neva River quay on Vasilevskii Island. At the opposite end, on the island's eastern point (*strelka*) stands another ensemble illustrative of early Alexandrine neoclassicism in its Greek form – the Bourse, or Stock Exchange (1805–10). Its architect, the French émigré Jean Thomas de Thomon, received his education in Paris, where he appears to have studied with Claude-Nicolas Ledoux (his early sketches indicate that architect's influence). He settled in Petersburg in 1790 and remained there until his death, in 1813.[17] The Bourse, the most important of his works to have survived, had been begun in 1783 to plans by Quarenghi. But at the beginning of Alexander's reign, Quarenghi's building (halted in 1787 because of the onset of the second Russo–Turkish

unify and expand the five buildings of the Mining Institute, located on the right bank of the Neva, on Vasilevskii Island (Figure 464).[15] Established by Catherine in 1773, the Mining Institute rapidly became one of the most important Russian technological centers, particularly with the exploitation of the mineral resources of the Ural Mountains. To provide a focal point for the institute, Voronikhin devised for the main entrance a portico of twelve Greek Doric columns (channeled and without base) and the proper entablature with pediment (Figure 465). The columns are echoed by channeled pilasters on the interior of the portico.

The apparent simplicity is worthy of Quarenghi, but Voronikhin worked on a larger scale. Whereas Quarenghi used Tuscan Doric porticoes, usually of eight columns, to mark the center of long, undecorated facades, Voronikhin extended the dodecastyle portico almost the length of the institute's central

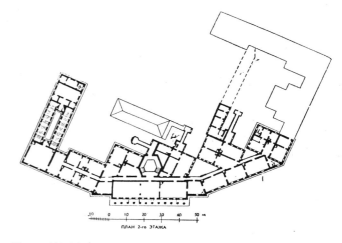

Figure 464. Mining Institute. Petersburg. 1806–11. Architect: Andrei Voronikhin. Plan.

Figure 465. Mining Institute. Petersburg. Portico. (P 20–11)

War) was razed and Thomon received the commission to design a new structure. The reason for this drastic change seems to have been Thomon's ability to grasp the sense of ensemble in the new comprehensive plan for the tip of Vasilevskii Island by Andreian Zakharov. Whereas Quarenghi's Bourse was oriented toward the Winter Palace and thus subordinate to the left bank of the Neva, Thomon shifted the main axis to the northeast, to the tip of the island itself (see Plate 69), and created a more severe "Greek" structure than that designed by Quarenghi.[18] To emphasize the visual role of the Bourse, the central element in the expanse of water between the Fortress and the left bank of Neva, Thomon placed two rostral columns (Figure 466) on either side, with allegorical figures at their base personifying Russia's major rivers. In addition to their monumental decorative function, the columns, which have spiral staircases on the interior, were to serve as beacons.

Thomon's Bourse (Figure 467) displays his familiarity with the temples at Paestum, which had exerted a major influence of the development of neoclassicism in Europe at the end of the eighteenth century – particularly a refinement of a noble "archaic" style.[19] Yet, as Hugh Honour has stated, the Bourse is "a free essay in temple architecture, not a piece of historical revivalism."[20] The massive stylobate of red granite supports a peristyle of forty-four Tuscan Doric columns with pronounced entasis and a large echinus (Figure 468). The peristyle encloses the rusticated stuccoed brick walls, at each end of which, above the entablature, stands allegorical statuary of Pudost stone representing maritime commerce ("Neptune with Two Rivers" and "Navigation with Mercury and two Rivers").

On the interior, the stock exchange was designed with a spacious trading hall, whose ceiling consisted of a single coffered barrel vault.[21] Each end of the

Figure 466. Bourse (Stock Exchange). Petersburg. General view, with rostral columns. (P 90–3)

main hall leads into a vestibule of the same width and also barrel-vaulted, but on an axis perpendicular to the central space (Figure 469). Three stories of offices extend the length of the building on either side of the central halls. Natural light for the interior is admitted by a rectangular skylight and by large semicircular fan windows on either end, whose form is repeated on the inner wall between the vestibule and main hall. (Thomon's project sketches show considerable sen-

sitivity to the effect of natural light on interior form.)

Within this precise rectangular structure, the semicircle is a recurrent motif, in the fan windows that extend along the upper walls of the side facades as well as in the relieving arches above the keystone pediments of the large first-floor windows, which are framed by the columns and their pilasters. Thus, every element of the exterior is calculated with attention to geometric proportions as well as to the contrasting vectors of curve and straight line. The extraordinary success of Thomon's design indicates that the vitality of imperial Russian architecture during the early nineteenth century lay not only in the variety generated within the aesthetic system of neoclassicism, but also in its ability to renew itself through the work of young architects whose brilliance was recognized and supported by the court bureaucracy. Alexander in effect provided Thomas de Thomon with the opportunity to realize what Claude-Nicholas Ledoux had only proposed – monumental civic structures in a heroic, archaic classical manner. The architect did not, however, live to see the official opening of the Bourse in 1816, 3 years after his death.

Thomas de Thomon's other extant major work in Petersburg is the Laval house. The eighteenth-century residence on the site had belonged to the Stroganovs,

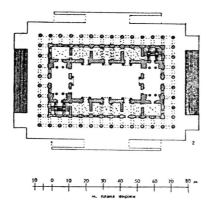

Figure 467. Bourse (Stock Exchange). Petersburg. Plan.

and in the 1790s, Voronikhin remodeled it for them.[22] In 1800, however, the house was acquired by Countess A. G. Laval, who in 1806 commissioned Thomon to rebuild and enlarge the structure. Having removed Voronikhin's tetrastyle portico at the main entrance, Thomon slightly advanced the main facade, whose nine windows establish a proportional system for all three floors (Figure 470). The ground floor is articulated in a manner similar to the walls of the Bourse: rusticated stucco with arched windows and keystone. A larger keystone pediment marks the main door, beside which are two granite lions, perhaps designed by Thomon himself. The upper floors are segmented by an Ionic colonnade extending the width of the original house. For the extensions, Ionic porticos frame a three-part window on the bel etage. Above the pediments are stucco relief panels depicting Apollo and the Muses.

On the interior, much of Thomon's original work is preserved, although portions of the house were remodeled as early as 1818. The entrance hall, framed by massive Doric columns, leads up to a rotunda with attached red granite Ionic columns and a coffered dome with inset rosettes. The state rooms by Thomon display materials and decorative motifs characteristic of the period – faux marbre, elaborate plaster work, wall paintings in a variety of styles, and grisaille friezes on themes of Roman nobility and devotion to duty.[23] The rich elegance of the neoclassical interior served as a setting for one of the most influential literary salons in Petersburg, presided over by Countess Laval. Its visitors included Alexander Griboedov, Adam Mickiewicz, Mikhail Lermontov, Ivan Krylov, and Vasilii Zhukovskii. At one such evening in 1828, Aleksander Pushkin gave a first reading of his tragedy *Boris Godunov*.

Indeed, the house witnessed a tragedy of its own that would have befitted the classical friezes portrayed on its walls: Sergei Trubetskoi, who had married the daughter of Countess Laval, was a leader of the Decembrists, whose abortive coup attempt against Nicholas I in December 1825 signaled the further de-

Figure 468. Bourse (Stock Exchange). Petersburg. 1805–10. Architect: Thomas de Thomon. (P 82–21)

355

cline of the political power of the Russian nobility as well as the widening gulf between educated social opinion and the autocracy.[24] Although there was no evidence implicating Countess Laval, the noble conspirators frequently gathered there at the invitation of Trubetskoi; and Ekaterina Trubetskaia was the first of the Decembrists' wives to voluntarily follow her husband into Siberian exile. These events once again raise the question of the larger significance of neoclassical iconography: decorative fashion or a reflection of individual values and a social code of personal honor. The Laval mansion was one of the last neoclassical town houses in Petersburg, as the increasing density of urban construction led to the design of wealthy residences within large apartment-style edifices.

Andreian Zakharov

By the time Thomas de Thomon had completed the Bourse, in 1810, work was well under way on a much larger project across the Neva: the third version of the Admiralty. As noted in Chapter 8, the docks and administrative building of the Admiralty were first built by Peter the Great and then rebuilt, in the 1730s, by Ivan Korobov (see Figure 293). The final rebuilding of the structure occurred only after Alexander's advisers had debated the wisdom of leaving this utilitarian structure, with its functioning shipworks, in the center of the capital – facing, in fact, the southwest facade of the Winter Palace. Indeed, following a fire in 1783, there had been plans to move the Admiralty to the fleet base at Kronstadt, but the proposal was not implemented. By 1806, plans submitted by Andreian Zakharov for a reconstruction of the large, decrepit complex had been approved; and although he died in 1811, long before the completion of construction in 1823, no significant changes were made in his design.[25]

Born in 1761 to the family of a minor Admiralty official, Zakharov attended the Academy of Arts; and after graduation, in 1782, he studied in Paris for 4 years under the direction of Jean François Thérèse Chalgrin, creator of the Arc de Triomphe. During this period, Zakharov traveled extensively in Italy. Although appointed in 1787 to the faculty of the Petersburg Academy of Arts – where he became a

Figure 469. Bourse (Stock Exchange). Petersburg. Model of interior.

Figure 470. Laval house. Petersburg. 1806–10. Architect: Thomas de Thomon. (P 18–1)

professor of architecture – Zakharov devoted more of his attention to the practice of architecture, and in 1805, became the chief Admiralty architect. In addition to a number of buildings for the admiralty in the Petersburg area (including a hospital and barracks), Zakharov designed in 1806–9 two warehouse complexes that again suggest the archaic simplicity of designs by Boullee and Ledoux.[26] His plan for the point of Vasilevskii Island provided a setting for the work of Thomon and subsequent architects, and although few of his projects were built, the Admiralty design alone suffices to ensure his reputation in the history of European neoclassicism.

In reconstructing Korobov's partially destroyed Admiralty, Zakharov expanded its length from 300 to 375 meters, in addition to which were two perpen-

dicular wings almost half that long extending to the river. From the perspective of the Neva River, the complex consisted of two pi-shaped buildings, one within the other (Figure 471), which were originally separated by a narrow canal. The inner building served the Admiralty dockyard, which it enclosed on three sides, and the outer contained administrative offices. On the other side was a large square – now a park – along the main facade. Its center is marked by a tower and spire (Figure 472), which envelop Korobov's original tower, and contains an arch, flanked by statues of nymphs supporting the globe (sculptor: Feodosii Shchedrin).[27] The attic frieze portrays Neptune handing Peter the Great the trident, symbol of power over the seas (Figure 473). Above the corners of the attic are statues of Alexander the Great, Ajax,

357

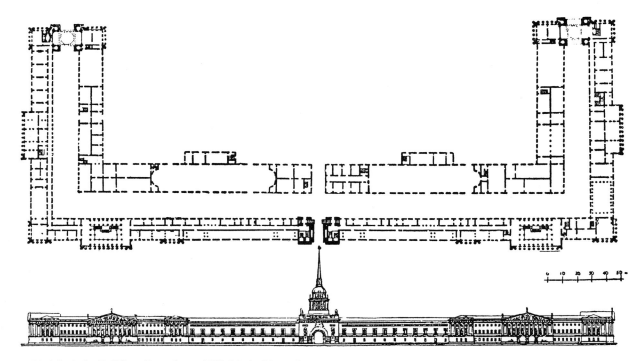

Figure 471. Admiralty Building. Petersburg. 1810–23. Architect: Andreian Zakharov. Plan and elevation of park facade.

Achilles, and Pyrrhus. The base of the spire rests on an Ionic peristyle, whose cornice supports twenty-eight allegorical and mythological statues representing the seasons, the elements, and the winds (see Plate 70). Not since the twelfth-century Cathedral of St. Dmitrii in Vladimir had architecture and sculpture combined so richly to proclaim temporal power and divine protection.

Zakharov also understood the virtues of simplicity: On either side of the tower, a rusticated ground floor defines the base of the facade, above which are two rows of simply articulated windows. (Later, a third row of windows replaced the stucco frieze that had originally run along the upper part of the facade.) At each end of the facade is a segment marked by a dodecastyle Doric portico with a pediment containing a sculpted frieze (see Plate 71). This "unit" is bounded by projections with six Doric columns. Each of the perpendicular wings has a similar Doric portico of twelve columns, with flanking hexastyle projections; and each culminates at the Neva in an end block, with a large rusticated arch flanked by Doric columns (Figure 474).

The Admiralty end blocks have been called "essays in solid geometry,"[28] perhaps the most radical attempt to achieve the monumental purity of volume idealized at the end of the eighteenth century. Zakharov had

solved the problem of horizontal repetition by using classical orders at key points on simple geometric forms, whose surface provided a setting for Zakharov's large rusticated arches and high-relief sculpture. The use of portico, pavilion, and spire, the restrained window detail, and the heroic sculpture on pediments and at the base of the spire produce, miraculously, a sense of both richness and simplicity.

Carlo Rossi

With the completion of the Bourse, the Admiralty, and the Kazan Cathedral, Petersburg had acquired architectural foci around which its landscape could be organized.[29] The Bourse defined the tip of Vasilevskii Island, and the Admiralty dominated not only the left bank of the Neva, but also the three major arteries radiating from its tower and spire into the interior of the city. The final development of a coherent design linking and complementing the city's monuments occurred under the direction of Carlo Rossi, the last of Alexander's "immortals," an architect and urban planner of genius. He created or redesigned no fewer than thirteen squares and twelve streets in the central part of Petersburg, and as an architect, he is responsible for four major ensembles, each of which forms an essential link in his grand design.[30]

Rossi was born to an Italian ballerina who had settled in Pavlovsk – an ideal environment for Rossi's architectural education. Brenna recognized his talent and supervised his apprenticeship during the building and interior decoration of the imperial palace at Pavlovsk. By 1796, Rossi was named Brenna's assistant, and participated not only in the completion of the Pavlovsk palace, but also in Brenna's work on the palace at Gatchina, and at the Mikhailovskii Castle. In 1802, Brenna and Rossi left for a 3-year sojourn in Europe (Florence, Rome, Paris). It is clear from Rossi's writings as well as his designs that the architecture of Rome produced an especially deep effect on him.

In a note attached to his unrealized, gargantuan plan for a new Admiralty quay, conceived shortly after his return from Italy, he wrote: "Why should we fear to be compared with them [the Romans] in magnificence? By this word one should not mean a surfeit of decoration, but grandeur of form, nobility of proportions, and indestructibility."[31]

From 1806 to 1814, Rossi worked primarily in Moscow and in the provincial city of Tver. Among the more curious of his early projects was a design for an immense bell tower in a flamboyant Gothic revival style for the Nilov monastic hermitage on Lake Seliger (between Moscow and Petersburg). Rossi also experimented with Russian wooden architecture in the design of an ensemble of houses in the "peasant" style

Figure 472. Admiralty. Petersburg. Park facade. (P 22–11)

Figure 473. Admiralty. Petersburg. Tower, with frieze and statuary. (P 77–24)

of the Elagin Palace is Corinthian, and the hexastyle portico of its main facade (Figure 475), with attic, bears a resemblance to that of Cameron's palace at Pavlovsk. This facade, which overlooks the park and interior of the island, is framed by two additional porticos of paired columns with pediments, thus giving a decorative emphasis to Rossi's use of classical orders. The opposite facade, which overlooks the expanse of the Middle Nevka River (Figure 476), is also given a monumental treatment, particularly in the design of the three-story half rotunda that extends from the center of the facade and is flanked on either end by Corinthian porticos. Although the proportions are awkward, the decorative detail and the ornamental vases show an elegant richness that will characterize Rossi's subsequent imperial work.

The interior staterooms of the Elagin Palace are arranged in a series of enfilades leading from a central vestibule and large oval hall (Figure 477). Their decoration expands upon the work that Rossi had done as an assistant at Pavlovsk, and later at Tver, with wall paintings and the use of architectural elements (usually of faux marbre) reflecting the design and structural arrangement of the individual rooms.[36] On this and later projects, Rossi had gathered a collective of artists and artisans who implemented his designs superbly; among them were the sculptors Vasilii Demut-Malinovskii and Stepan Pimenov, and the painters Giovanni Battista Scotti, Pietro Scotti, Antonio Vighi, and Barnabas Medici.

For the Elagin Palace, Rossi designed an ensemble of service buildings and park pavilions in the same heroic – which in the case of the kitchen and service building, with its Doric portico and niches for statuary, represents an extreme in the disjunction of neoclassical style and function (Figure 478).[37] Among the park structures, the Pavilion at the Granite Pier is among Rossi's best, although it has not been well maintained (the channeling of the Greek Doric columns has been effaced on the lower segment). On the pier side, the pavilion projects an open rotunda, half of which is inscribed in the square structure. The opposite facade has a Doric portico, and the sides of the small structure provide a background for cast-iron sacrificial urns. The stucco frieze (festoons and classical masks) beneath the entablature is characteristic of Rossi's exterior decorative work – richly articulated yet carefully isolated to allow for an unhindered perception of both detail and context.

◇   ◇   ◇

Rossi's work on the architectural replanning of the imperial ensembles in central Petersburg opens with

for the village of Glazovo at Pavlovsk.[32] Upon returning to Petersburg in 1814, he rapidly assumed authority in the formulation of Alexander's general plan for the city. An examination of Rossi's projects would require a separate volume, for he worked not only as an architect, but also as the interior designer of numerous palaces, including the grand Gallery of 1812 in the Winter Palace (1826).[33] Furthermore, in 1816, Rossi was commissioned to rebuild yet again the Anichkov Palace, which had just been presented by Alexander I to the future Nicholas I as a wedding present. Rossi's work, completed in 1820, included not only the palace, but also service buildings and two symmetrical pavilions in the neoclassical style with statuary on the theme of ''Russian heroes'' by Stepan Pimenov.[34]

Rossi's first major comprehensive project in Petersburg was the palace ensemble and park designed in 1818 on Elagin Island (adjacent to Stone Island) for Maria Fedorovna, mother of Alexander I.[35] The order

the Mikhailovskii Palace, built in 1819–25 for Mikhail Pavlovich, brother of Alexander I, on unused park land near Brenna's Mikhailovskii Castle. In building the palace, Rossi also designed a large surrounding area, which included the Mikhailovskii Park, with its pavilions, as well as square in front of the palace (now known as Pushkin Square) and a street connecting the square with Nevskii Prospekt. Rossi either built or specified the style for the buildings leading to the Prospekt, thus creating a setting to display the palace.[38]

The facade of the Mikhailovskii Palace defines Rossi's Roman style: opulent and in the Corinthian order (see Plate 72). Between the columns attached to and extending the length of the facade is a frieze of classical figures, designed by Rossi and executed by Demut-Malinovskii and Pimenov. This central part of the palace is flanked by two slightly projecting wings with large Venetian windows (Figure 479), the relative simplicity of which frames the richer texture of the center. The courtyard was completed by one-story service quadrangles (since enlarged) on either side.

The facade is Rossi's first to resolve the problem of articulating an extensive horizontal space. Interestingly, the park facade (Figure 480) conveys a sense of greater monumentality by replacing the central portico with a loggia of twelve Corinthian columns, flanked by porticos and pediments. As on the front wall, a figured frieze on Roman themes extends the length of the park facade.

The Mikhailovskii Palace interior – Rossi's most imposing – centers on a vestibule–atrium that extends to a ferrovitreous ceiling and contains a grand staircase (Figures 481 and 482). The upper level of the atrium is defined by a peristyle of Corinthian columns that support an entablature, above which are trompe l'oeil depictions of atlantes in grisaille. Both of the main floors of the palace contain enfilades of rooms along the front facade, but the second level contained the most magnificent state rooms. Apart from their ceilings, however, little has remained of the decoration of the rooms after their conversion to museum use in 1890 by Vasilii Svinin.[39]

The major exceptions are the vestibule and the large

Figure 474. Admiralty. Petersburg. East end block. (P 79–7)

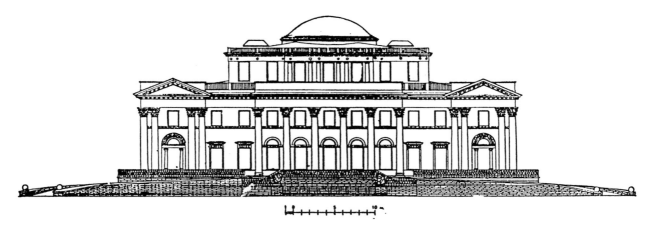

Figure 475. Elagin Palace. Petersburg. 1818–24. Architect: Carlo Rossi. Elevation of the main facade.

Figure 476. Elagin Palace. Petersburg. View across the Middle Nevka River. (P 50–9)

sitting room (also known as the White Column Hall), which overlooks the park and is Rossi's most elaborate combination of architecture and the decorative arts. The space is divided into three parts by the placement of Corinthian faux marbre columns that frame the painted and gilded decoration of the polished walls and the ceiling. As elsewhere in the palace, the decor combines friezes and panels in plaster and grisaille on heroic Roman themes, with arabesques and polychrome figured motifs that reflect the style of Raphael. Rossi's use of artificial materials and his scrupulosity in budgetary matters held the cost of the spacious palace to some 7 million rubles – less than half the cost of the Mikhailovskii Castle.[40] The Mikhailovskii Park behind the palace has only one pa-

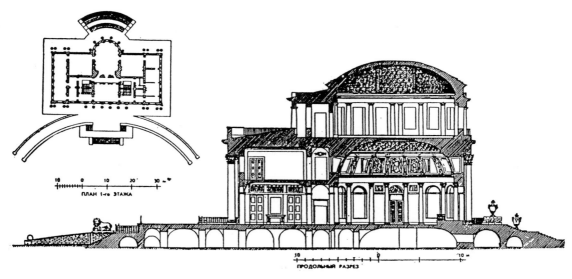

Figure 477. Elagin Palace. Petersburg. Plan and section.

362

Figure 478. Elagin Palace. Petersburg. Kitchen and service building. Architect: Carlo Rossi. (P 51–1a)

Figure 479. Mikhailovskii Palace. Petersburg. 1819–25. Architect: Carlo Rossi. Main facade. (P 101–29)

vilion, built by Rossi in 1825, but it is one of his best, consisting of two square chambers linked by a Doric colonnade that expands into the park as a half rotunda. The delicate facade overlooking the Moika Canal is effectively counterposed to a granite landing stage designed by Rossi.

Concurrently with the construction of the Mikhailovskii Palace, Rossi undertook a far greater project, in terms of both size and conceptual daring. The area between the south facade of the Winter Palace and the Moika Canal had been partially developed, but no comprehensive plan for the space had yet been implemented. Rossi's task – which began in 1819 and was completed in 1829 – consisted of two parts: to construct an administrative complex for the General Staff and the Ministries of Finance and Foreign affairs; and, in so doing, to create an imposing public square

in front of the Winter Palace. His solution called for the ministerial complex, subsequently known as the General Staff Building, to take the form of a large arc facing the palace (Figure 483). The interior configuration of the complex consists of a system of courtyards and light wells formed by perpendicular extensions that link the main facade with adjacent structures on the Moika Canal and Nevskii Prospekt.

The center of the main facade is dominated by a triumphal arch, surmounted by a chariot of victory. Despite the monumental size of the statuary – winged victory in a chariot pulled by six horses restrained by two warriors – the weight was kept under 20 tons by molding the figures of copper plate over an iron skeleton.[41] In the design of the arch, Rossi not only centered the enormous facade, but linked it to the surrounding area, particularly by the passageway

Figure 480. Mikhailovskii Palace. Petersburg. Park facade. (P 31–8)

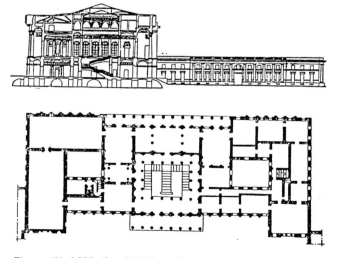

Figure 481. Mikhailovskii Palace. Petersburg. Plan and section.

Figure 482. Mikhailovskii Palace. Petersburg. Main vestibule. (P 83–21)

through the triumphal arch (known as Small Million Street), leading from Palace Square to Nevskii Prospekt. The passageway is composed of a series of three arches, the first two of which are located on an axis with the central gates to the Winter Palace, and the last follows the turn of the passage toward the Prospekt. The light that enters between the arches enhances the perception of depth and illuminates the decorative detail of this unique procession of framed space toward the city's main square (Figure 484).

The Palace Square facade of the General Staff building – devoid of decoration except for a cornice frieze, a balustrade, and columns flanking the arch – forms the perfect complement to the baroque panoply of Rastrelli's Winter Palace. The color scheme for this and for most of Rossi's other monuments was to be light gray with white trim, but later generations have preferred more assertive tones: yellow with white trim, and the metallic sculpture of military regalia painted black. Yet more important than the color is

the contour of the main facade, which not only imposes order over a vast urban terrain, but also channels movement within that space. The dramatic nature of that space in relation to massed humanity (military parades or demonstrations) has played a major role in the course of modern history.[42]

◇   ◇   ◇

Rossi's concept of ensemble was applied even more rigorously in the design for a new theater ensemble facing Nevskii Prospekt near the Anichkov park. Rossi worked on variant designs for the space over a period of a decade (1816–27) before beginning construction of the central element, the Alexandrine Theater. Facing a square formed by the Anichkov park and the Public Library (which Rossi would expand during the same period), the theater established the style for flanking buildings leading to yet another square on a diagonal approach to the Fontanka Canal (Figure 485). The front of the theater is marked by a loggia of Corinthian columns of the major order, culminating in a sculpture of Apollo in a quadriga (Figure 486). The side facades are rendered with an equal concern for the monumental, particularly in the porticos of eight Corinthian columns whose proportional relations to the rest of the structure visually reduce the large mass of the theater. The most striking feature of the exterior decoration is the frieze with festoons framing tragic theatrical masks.

The interior of the Alexandrine Theater, arranged in five tiers and with a capacity of approximately 1,400, contained a system of stairways that allowed access to specific areas and increased the space available for the audience (including the tsar's loge) and for the stage – one of the largest in Europe at the time of its completion.[43] The interior decoration made extensive use of cast-iron components, and the design of the balconies obstructed as few as possible of the sight lines – both characteristic of Rossi's concern with functionalism and economy in his monumental buildings. In addition, the extensive use of iron in struc-

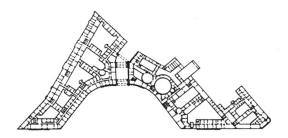

Figure 483. Building of the General Staff. Petersburg. 1819–29. Architect: Carlo Rossi. Plan.

Figure 484. Building of the General Staff. Petersburg. View from Palace Square, with the dome of the General Staff library. (P 79–15)

tural and decorative work reduced the danger of fire – a threat that would be all too dramatically realized at the Winter Palace in 1837 (see Chapter 13). Although the theater and surrounding complex of buildings are of stuccoed brick, the advancing role of structural engineering in Russian architecture is evident in the design of the upper structure of the theater, with a truss-frame system of metal supports above the ceiling (Figure 487). This system was designed by Rossi in consultation with Mathew Clark, chief engineer at the Aleksandrovskii Iron Foundry, which produced the metal components used in Rossi's work.[44]

The rear facade of the Alexandrine Theater is no less monumental than the front, and is more effectively framed – the narrow corridor of Theater Street (see Plate 73), formed by two long facades with a rusticated ground floor and paired Doric columns (formerly the Ministry of Education and the Theater Directorate), opens onto Chernyshev Square on the

Fontanka. Dramatic perspective, so frequently a part of the Petersburg cityscape, achieves on Theater Street a hypnotic effect, drawing the viewer toward the theater. In the opposite direction, Rossi designed the buildings fronting Chernyshev Square; and while the square was not completed to his original specifications for a large monument, the building facades themselves – with Doric columns over a rusticated base – create another ensemble that serves as a gateway to three streets that radiate from it: one leading to the Apraksin trading center, the second to Sadovaia Street, and the third to the theater.[45] In addition, the Chernyshev Bridge provides access from the square to the opposite bank of the Fontanka. Here, as at the Building of the General Staff, Rossi's plan called for the stuccoed surfaces to be painted gray with white trim, and the metal statuary to be toned bronze. And here as well, this subtle shading was discarded in favor of brighter tones as early as the latter half of the century.

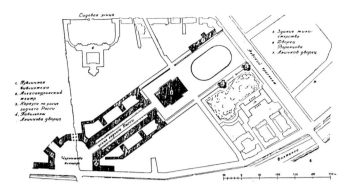

Figure 485. Alexandrine Theater ensemble. Petersburg. Architect: Carlo Rossi. Site plan.

Apart from the small pavilions of the Anichkov park, the only component of the theater ensemble to have retained something like the original colors is the new building of the Public Library (1828–34), created by Rossi as part of an expansion of the library building (on Sadovaia Street), built in 1796–1801 by Egor Sokolov.[46] Following Sokolov, Rossi took the Ionic order for a loggia of eighteen columns elevated above a rusticated ground floor and extending across the central facade. The iconographic references to the functions of the library include a statue of Minerva (wisdom) above the central attic; an intercolumnar frieze on knowledge; and statues of classical poets and philosophers, also placed among the columns. As in other aspects of neoclassicism, Rossi's use of allegorical statuary represents the culmination of a belief in the civilizing mission and message of architecture.

Rossi's last ensemble, the buildings for the Senate and Holy Synod (1829–34), was designed to complete the system of city squares extending from Palace Square, past the Admiralty Square, and into the area of Falconet's statue to Peter the Great (see Figure 337). In the area near the southwest corner of Zakharov's masterpiece, Auguste Montferrand built in 1817–20 a large residence for Prince Lobanov-Rostovskii (Figure 488), triangular in plan and with Corinthian porticos and loggias.[47] The unusual plan of the Lobanov-Rostovskii house is the result of a site formed by the intersection of Voznesenskii Prospekt – one of the three boulevards radiating from the Admiralty – with the boundaries of St. Isaac's Square, where Montferrand had in 1818 successfully proposed a plan for the reconstruction of the cathedral of St. Isaac (see Chapter 13). Thus, much construction was already under way

when work began on the Senate complex.[48] In rebuilding the Senate, Rossi created a monumental facade for the Neva (Figure 489), and then curved the building into the area of Senate Square, where the extended facade of the Senate and Synod buildings (Figure 490) formed a southern boundary to the network of urban space that began with Palace Square. The structure also defined a new perpendicular axis to the interior of the city, between Quarenghi's Horse Guards Manege and the Cathedral of St. Isaac.

Although the general plan created by Rossi for this final grand public space in the imperial ensemble was realized, he himself was not in good health after 1832 and did not supervise the construction of the two buildings – nor did he do the detail drawings that were such an important aspect of his other major projects. This perhaps explains a certain clutter and clumsiness, particularly in the use of statuary on the long facade of the two buildings of the Senate and Synod, which in their general design display Rossi's characteristic tectonic clarity: paired porticoes framing the two structures, with a loggia and stepped attic in the center of each – all in the Corinthian order.

The arch that joins the two structures and provides a tunnel perspective of Galernyi Street (Figure 491) illustrates the contradictions of the final structure: a clearly defined base and a surfeit of statuary. The crowded figures in the attic frieze appear to be engaged in an useemly tussle for space, and the presiding angels – painted black instead of bronze – resemble nothing so much as vultures, particularly when seen in profile. Indeed, the very nature of the Synod building, the center of the bureaucratic administration of a stultified official church, seems evident in the heavy-handed confusion of the facade decoration. Nonetheless, the scale and structural rhythm of the design for the Senate and Synod provide an appropriate setting for one of the city's most important public spaces.

By 1832, Rossi had been relieved (in part for reasons of health) of his role as a guiding force in the city's planning and imperial construction. Having done so much to create the architectural symbols of imperial grandeur, he had little patience with bureaucratic pomposity, and was reprimanded on at least two occasions in 1831 – once by Nicholas I – for his "crude and offensive expressions."[49] Although he showed no ambitions for high rank, he was one of the most highly paid architects in Petersburg. Yet he was scrupulous about the 60 million rubles entrusted to his projects – and died, in 1849, in poverty. The minors among his ten children (by two marriages) were eventually granted state pensions. His legacy is at once

Figure 486. Alexandrine Theater. Petersburg. 1828–32. Architect: Carlo Rossi. (P 43–9)

the culmination of neoclassicism and its extreme, a moment poised at the point of decline and reaction against an attempt to impose architectural unity on a changing urban environment.

Vasilii Stasov

Rossi's contemporary, Vasilii Stasov (1769–1848), complemented the great ensembles with monuments for both elevated and prosaic puposes.[50] The early stage of his career in Petersburg was involved with the construction of living space, even then an expensive commodity in the central city. His rebuilding of two eighteenth-century structures on Nevskii Prospekt as a single apartment house (the Kotomin building, 1812–15) is a significant early example of the application of the classical system of orders to an urban block for mixed use – commercial and residential.[51] Doric loggias at either end unite the two lower floors, and the bel etage displays an alternating series of windows with pediments in the style of the Renaissance. The horizontal profile of the building is marked by a string course and a projecting cornice. Other apartment buildings of the period, including those attributed to Stasov, follow much the same pattern.[52]

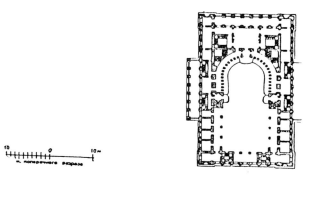

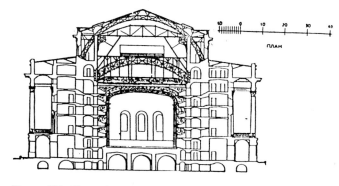

Figure 487. Alexandrine Theater. Petersburg. Plan and section, by Rossi.

367

Figure 488. Lobanov-Rostovskii house. Petersburg. 1817–20. Architect: Auguste Ricard Montferrand. (P 35–3a)

Figure 489. Building of the Senate and Holy Synod. Petersburg. 1829–34. Architect: Carlo Rossi. (P 28–6)

Larger than even the grandest of Moscow's urban mansions, the Petersburg residential block by its very form led to a diffusion of the classical tectonic system and its later replacement by the eclectic decoration of facades (see Chapter 13). During the first half of the nineteenth century, residential areas in Petersburg were still relatively undifferentiated by class, and a perimeter housing block could contain on its various levels the most diverse segments of the population – a phenomenon noted in detail by many Russian writers (particularly Nikolai Gogol and Fedor Dostoevskii). Even palatial structures such as the Lobanov-Rostovskii mansion contained residential space rented by laborers, clerks, and petty merchantry, as well as cafes and taverns of varying quality.[53] Indeed, the housing block ultimately influenced the design of palaces.

Stasov was also involved in the design of another, more specialized form of housing: barracks for Petersburg's elite military units, an architectural genre that proliferated so rapidly during the late neoclassical period that the style became associated with military regimentation. Stasov's Barracks of the Pavlovskii Regiment (1817–19) is the grandest of these structures, both in terms of size and ornament.[54] Far larger than a normal city block in size, the regimental building has various facades marked with massive Doric porticos, whose hypertrophied attic decoration undoubtedly served as a source for Soviet pseudoclassicism during the Stalin era.

In comparison with the barracks, Stasov demonstrated greater ingenuity in his designs for horses. The Court Stables, originally built in 1720–3 by Nicholas Friedrich Göbel on the Moika Canal, were reconstructed in 1817–23 by Stasov, who preserved the foundation and much of the walls of the complex plan (Figure 492).[55] The Doric loggias of the end blocks support recessed thermal windows that rise above the cornice binding most of the structure. Every detail of the exterior clarifies and enriches the form of the building, which centers on a large cuboid church with dome and Ionic loggia (Figure 493). The iconography of the stucco panels (by Demut-Malinovskii) on either side of the loggia is evocative of burden: on the right, the Entry of Christ into Jerusalem, and on the left, the Christ Bearing the Cross.[56]

Stasov's most notable accomplishments in Petersburg were two large churches that combined the cross-inscribed, pentacupolar form with neoclassical articulation. In 1827–9, he redesigned the Cathedral of the Transfiguration of the Savior, after a fire that seriously damaged the previous church, built in the early eighteenth century by Zemtsov and Pietro Trezzini for the Preobrazhenskii Guards Regiment.[57] The structure, which retains the eighteenth-century walls, is centered on a large portico with four Ionic columns (Figure 494). Its pediment is perfectly in balance with both the lower and upper parts of the structure –

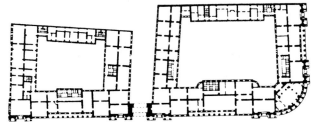

Figure 490. Building of the Senate and Holy Synod. Petersburg. Plan.

Figure 491. Building of the Senate and Holy Synod. Petersburg. Central arch. (P 60–14)

including a widely spaced pentacupolar design with ribbed hemispherical domes. Stucco panels on biblical scenes in the classical manner decorate the upper wall surface of the exterior. As with Stasov's other churches, the interior is of clean line and relatively austere decoration. The iron fence surrounding the church is composed of battle trophies, such as cannon, taken during the Russo–Turkish war of 1828.

The considerably larger Cathedral of the Trinity (1828–35) is to this day one of the most prominent landmarks of the southern part of the old city. Also supported by an elite regiment, the Izmailovskii, the church was originally built in wood with an unusual (for a Russian church) cruciform plan (Figure 495).[58] Stasov reproduced the plan with mighty hexastyle Corinthian porticos extending the width of each arm of the cross. The upper walls of the entire structure are banded by a stucco frieze with festoons comparable to those of Rossi's Alexandrine theater, but the white walls are otherwise as clear as those of early medieval churches, with only a single large arched window on each surface (Figure 496). The dark blue

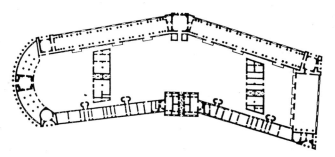

Figure 492. Court Stables. Petersburg. 1817–23. Architect: Vasilii Stasov. Plan.

metal domes are arranged at the points of the compass, as dictated by the plan of the church.

The most impressive feature of the Izmailovskii Trinity Cathedral is the central dome, whose size (over 26 meters in diameter) and detail resemble those of Starov's Trinity Cathedral as well as the Kazan Cathedral; yet no other pentacupolar church in Petersburg – including the Resurrection Cathedral at Smolnyi Convent and St Isaac's (then under construc-

Figure 493. Court Stables and Church. Petersburg. (P 110–6)

tion) – achieves the same pyramidal effect through the spacing and size of the subsidiary domes. The colonnade of Corinthian columns attached to the drum beneath the dome creates a large rotunda, clearly seen in its high elevation above the central crossing. The flanking cupolas are decorated with cornices and balustrades with iron urns. On the interior, the cruciform design is accented by paired columns at the main points of the plan.

During his prolific career, Stasov was responsible for the rebuilding or completion of churches by other architects, most notably the interior of Rastrelli's Cathedral of the Resurrection (1832–5; see Figure 446); and less successfully, the ruins of the ancient Church of the Tithe in Kiev. He also played a major role in the rapid reconstruction of the Winter Palace after the fire of 1837, rebuilding Rastrelli's grand Jordan Staircase as well as a number of major halls by other architects such as Quarenghi and Rossi (the 1812 Gallery) – with sensitivity toward the designs of his predecessors.[59] His rebuilding in 1838 of the Nevskii Enfilade, containing the main state rooms of the palace, also involved some of the most advanced engineering work of that period in Europe, as the

damaged wooden beams of the ceilings and roof were replaced by metal components designed by Mathew Clark. The iron strut-frame spans with elliptical beams over the largest halls (up to 21 meters) were particularly ingenious, and they still function.[60]

Stasov's grasp of proportion in classical architecture was brilliantly applied in little-known structures in Novgorod Province at the Arakcheev estate of Gruzino, where he built a lighthouse (1815) and bell tower (1822; destroyed in World War II), both of which were composed of open rotundas above a rusticated square tower base.[61] The design of the bell tower was particularly bold, with diverse geometric shapes – rectangular and circular – in a harmonious form of great height. Even prosaic neighborhood markets acquired under his design a striking form derived from simple elements precisely arranged – as in his Tuscan colonnade for the triangular Iamskoi (Coachman's) Market, built in Petersburg in 1817–19.[62]

Beyond the pleiade of master architects that defined Alexandrine neoclassicism in Petersburg, there ex-

370

isted lesser architects whose work forms an indispensable complement to the monuments of Rossi, Stasov, Zakharov, Thomon, Voronikhin, and Quarenghi.[63] Among the most active of them was Luigi Rusca, a native of Lugano, who like his contemporary Quarenghi used a portico and pediment on an otherwise sparsely decorated facade. In addition to a number of large houses (such as the one built on the Catherine Canal for the Jesuit Order in 1801) and the superb main facade for the barracks of the Cavalry Guards Regiment (1800–3),[64] Rusca participated in the remodeling of the Winter Palace at the beginning of the nineteenth century. His best work includes the Church of the Mother of God Consolation to All Who Grieve (1817–18), a square design with a hexastyle Ionic portico and pediments on the backdrop of a large attic that emphasizes the blocklike, cuboid quality of the structure. The most interesting feature of the design is a circular colonnade that encompasses most of the interior space and in effect creates a rotunda, marked on the exterior by a low drum and dome.[65]

Rusca's use of small forms to provide a major accent defines the other of his masterpieces, the Feather Lane Portico, built in 1802–6 as a monumental en-

trance to the Feather Lane trading rows parallel to the west facade of Gostinnyi Dvor. The trading rows building itself (1797–8; architect unidentified) was situated in the space between Vallin de la Mothe's monumental commercial edifice and Quarenghi's recently completed Silver Rows (for jewelry). The unprepossessing appearance of the Feather Rows in an architecturally distinguished context led to Rusca's commission to create a solemn Doric hexastyle por-

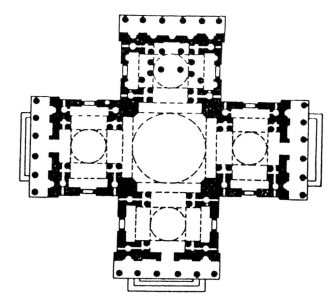

Figure 495. Cathedral of the Trinity. Petersburg. 1828–35. Architect: Vasilii Stasov. Plan.

Figure 494. Cathedral of the Transfiguration of the Savior. Petersburg. 1827–9. Architect: Vasilii Stasov. West facade. (P 42–3a)

Figure 496. Cathedral of the Trinity. Petersburg. Southeast view. (P 65–19)

371

tico, with a large attic, facing Nevskii Prospekt (Figure 497). The wisdom of Rusca's design was enhanced by Carlo Rossi, whose street connecting the Mikhailovskii Palace square with Nevskii Prospekt opens onto a view of the Feather Lane Portico.[66]

On the Point of Vasilevskii Island, Giovanni Lucchini performed a similar service by amplifying Thomon's Bourse with flanking Customs Warehouses (1826–32; their location and dimensions had been defined by Zakharov in his 1804 master plan). Their complex plan not only outlines the island's tip, but also creates an interior semicircular plaza beyond the west facade of the Bourse. Their design reflects the characteristic neoclassical blending of function and the order system – in this case, major Tuscan Doric loggias framed by end blocks with large arched windows. Beyond the north warehouse, Lucchini constructed the Customs House (1829–32), whose elevated Ionic portico with statuary above the pediments suggests the style of Quarenghi (Figure 498). The central interior court of the building is dramatically illuminated by a large drum and cupola.[67]

Figure 497. Feather Lane Portico. Petersburg. 1802–6. Architect: Luigi Rusca. (P 64–88)

The work of these and other architects completed the neoclassical ensemble of Petersburg, even as the style yielded during the 1830s to aesthetic and ideological imperatives antithetical to the forms and the universalism of neoclassical architecture. At the beginning of the twentieth century, however, the aestheticism of Petersburg's late neoclassical period would experience a triumphant, if brief, return when a nostalgia for the cultural and social values of a heroic, precapitalist era asserted itself in the work and critical writings of a group of neoclassical revivalists (see Chapter 14).

The Rebuilding of Moscow: Osip Bove

In Moscow, the final phase of neoclassicism was greatly determined – and stimulated – by the need to rebuild the city, most of which lay in ruin. The catastrophic fire that began with the entry of French troops into the city in the fall of 1812 destroyed the majority of the buildings produced during a half century of neoclassical planning and development, since the reign of Catherine the Great. In general terms, some 6,500 of 9,000 buildings in Moscow were severely damaged or destroyed – including houses and small shops, but also some of the greatest of the neoclassical monuments, such as the Pashkov House.[68] (The city's brick medieval churches seem to have fared better, although many were also in need of extensive repair.) The effort to rebuild the city began almost immediately after the retreat of the French, and the establishment the following year (1813) of the Commission for Construction in Moscow provided planning oversight with a rigor obtained from decades of large-scale projects in imperial Russia.[69]

The general plan, submitted by William Hastie in 1814 and approved by the authorities in Petersburg, envisioned a costly system of new main streets and squares and the extensive redrawing of the city's historic districts.[70] Practicality dictated a more limited approach that incorporated basic outlines of the city as it existed before the fire, and a revised plan, approved in 1817, determined much of the subsequent appearance of Moscow. Although the commission appointed a number of architects responsible for the development of individual districts, the de facto chief architect for the reconstruction was Osip Bove, a native of Petersburg but trained in Moscow.[71]

The design aspect of the reconstruction occurred on two levels: one for major buildings of state and society, and another for the majority of private houses. Designs for the street facades of private residences were to be submitted to Bove's office for approval, in accordance with yet another set of neoclassical model plans (in three volumes), compiled in 1809–12 for public and private use throughout the empire.[72] The standardization reflected a persistent impulse among Russian adminstrators since the time of Peter the Great; yet, in addition to its perceived aesthetic virtues, it also facilitated the speed and economy of recovery while preserving an acceptable level of standards. One indication of the cost of the rebuilding for individuals is the smaller size of both houses and lots in post–1812 Moscow. The use of a mezzanine instead of a full second story became common, and houses tended to be flush with the street

Figure 498. Customs House. Petersburg. Architect: Giovanni Luchini. (P 76–3)

line, without a front courtyard. Furthermore, many stuccoed houses with masonry detail were in fact built of logs on a masonry base and covered with lathing to support the stucco (Figure 499).[73]

One of the first tasks was the restoration of Red Square, and specifically the area of Trading Rows, where much of the city's commerce was conducted. In designing a neoclassical colonnade facing the east wall of the Kremlin, Bove created an impression of order when in fact there was very little in the dark network of shops and stalls extending into Kitaigorod. The domed central block of the rows was placed directly across from the dome of Kazakov's Senate Building, thus creating a visual axis for the newly cleared Red Square.[74]

Bove also supervised the formation of one of Moscow's great public spaces, Theater Square, intended as a setting for the revived Petrovskii Theater (subsequently known as the Bolshoi), which had burned in 1805 and not been rebuilt.[75] The new theater (1821–4) was designed by the Petersburg architect Andrei Mikhailov and by Bove, with a grand Ionic portico surmounted by a statue of Apollo in a quadriga (Figure 500; cf. Rossi's design for the Alexandrine Theater

in Petersburg). Its neoclassical form has not survived: A fire in 1853 destroyed the entire interior of the theater, and when rebuilt by Albert Kavos in the 1850s, the main facade was substantially modified by the addition of Renaissance elements characteristic of the era of eclecticism (Figure 501).[76] The buildings flanking Theater Square were planned as uniform, subordinate structures, two-storied with a ground-floor arcade. The plan was not realized as intended, with the partial exception of the building now housing the Malyi (small) Theater.

On the other side of the Kremlin, along its west wall, Bove in 1821–3 created the Kremlin (later Alexander) Park over what had been the Neglinnaia River bed (since rerouted underground). The long expanse of the park centered on the architect's design of a grotto, with Greek Doric columns, at the foot of the Middle Arsenal Tower (Figure 502). The same area witnessed one of the great engineering feats of the period with the construction of Manege in a period of 6 months in 1817. Intended for riding exercises and cavalry reviews, the building required a large unobstructed space (45 meters in width, without interior supports). The design, with its roof of trussed

Figure 499. House on Little Molchanovka Street. Moscow. C. 1820. The sign proclaims that the poet Mikhail Lermontov lived here between 1830–2. (M 47–12)

last, heroic phase of neoclassicism.[79] Archival photographs of the interior (unlike many Empire houses, this one still functioned as a residence at the beginning of this century) reveal the persistence of both the arch and monumentality (Figure 506) – and the strategies the inhabitants used to create livable, intimate space within such an interior. In particular, double columns supporting an architrave were frequently used to form an alcove, which provided a means of draping and enclosing space within the main sitting rooms and bedrooms. Even smaller Empire houses adopted this device in the design of state rooms, whose size could be adjusted as conditions required.

Many of the most imposing of these houses were located on the Boulevard Ring, a series of linked, tree-lined avenues (including Novinskii Boulevard), formed on the territory of the former Belyi Gorod wall, which had been leveled in the 1770s. Little of the 1775 proposal for a ring boulevard was implemented, however, until the fire of 1812 provided the opportunity for a thorough replanning of the central city. During the same period, yet another system of avenues, the Garden Ring, was formed on the site of the previous earthen rampart (Zemliannoi val).[80] Throughout much of the nineteenth century, the area between the two concentric rings was still largely composed of

wooden beams, was formulated by General of Engineers Augustin de Béthencourt, and subsequently reinforced in 1823–4, at which time Bove was commissioned to provide the architectural detailing: attached Tuscan Doric columns (frequently used to endow prosaic buildings with a heroic cast) and a cornice frieze containing military heraldic devices (Figure 503). The work was finished in 1825.[77]

On a more intimate scale, Bove distinguished himself in the rebuilding of the N. S. Gagarin house on Novinskii Boulevard (1817; one of the few Moscow monuments to be destroyed in World War II, during an air attack in July 1941).[78] Although relatively modest in size, the house displays the balance and above all the richness of decorative detail that epitomizes the late neoclassical, or "Empire," style in Moscow. (The latter term was borrowed from French usage, and in architecture, it generally refers to late neoclassicism in Moscow and the provinces.) Its plan called for flanking wings at street level and connected to the central block by a curved gallery (Figure 504). The main entrance, flanked by a complex portico of Doric columns, resembled a victory arch, with winged figures of glory above a large recessed fan window (Figure 505).

The arch is a persistent motif in Bove's work after 1812, and it is not implausible to see its use as a symbol of Moscow's victorious resurgence, celebrated in the

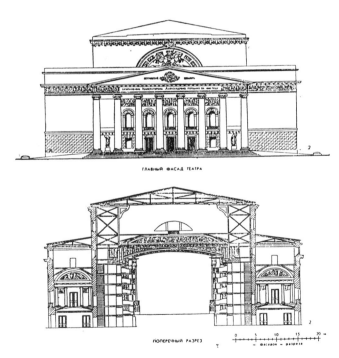

Figure 500. Bolshoi Theater. Moscow. 1821–4. Architects: Andrei Mikhailov and Osip (Giuseppi) Bove. Front elevation and transverse section, by O. Bove.

Figure 501. Bolshoi Theater. Moscow. As rebuilt by Albert Kavos in the 1850s. (M 147–19)

houses laid out on the *dvor* principle – a spacious enclosed lot with a courtyard in front or in back and service buildings placed around the perimeter.[81]

Toward the end of a career that involved so many facets of Moscow's planning and reconstruction, Bove began what is arguably his most accomplished structure: the rotunda for the sanctuary of the Church of the Mother of God, Consolation of All Who Sorrow, added in 1830s to the vestibule that had been built by Bazhenov in the 1780s (see Figure 426). The structure is an elaborate play of circular forms: A drum supporting a hemispherical dome is circumscribed within the larger diameter of the rotunda on the first floor, which contains the apse. The north and south portals are framed by simple Ionic porticos, with limestone columns juxtaposed against the stuccoed facade (Figure 507). The facade is punctuated by an arcade of fan windows, beneath which the main windows are framed by Doric limestone pilasters. Although they are not deeply recessed, the arches represent an elegant variant on a motif central to both his architecture and interior design.[82]

Bove's design of the church serves as a frame for an array of decorative work characteristic of Moscow neoclassicism in its final phase. The intricate mullions of the fan windows resemble the much larger window design within the central arch of the Gargarin house; but the more remarkable feature of the exterior ornament is the carved and molded friezes beneath the cornice of the rotunda, on the portico, and particularly in the arches, with heads of cherubim alternating with acanthus leaves. The gilt patterns in bold relief on the door panels complement the sense of rigorous order combined with imaginative detail. On the interior, the same qualities pervade one of the culminating examples of a spatial configuration that had been introduced by Kazakov over 50 years earlier in the Church of the Metropolitan Philip. An Ionic colonnade supports the drum and defines the inner circle, well illuminated by the large windows of the drum and dome. The interior is distinguished by its design and craftsmanship, notable even in the floor, composed of patterned iron panels. In this, it epitomizes the union of opposites in late neoclassical aestheticism:

Figure 502. Alexander Park Grotto. Moscow Kremlin. 1821–3. Architect: Osip Bove. In the background: Middle Arsenal Tower (1493–5) and the Arsenal (early eighteenth century). (M 158–11)

Figure 503. Manege. Moscow. 1817; 1823–5. Architects: Augustin de Béthencourt and Osip Bove. (M 55–11)

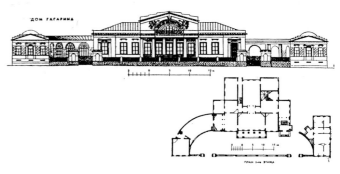

Figure 504. N. S. Gagarin house. Moscow. 1817 (destroyed in 1941). Architect: Osip Bove. Plan and elevation by A. M. Kharlamova.

Figure 505. N. S. Gagarin house (not extant). Moscow. Main portico. Photograph from a private archive.

an austere elegance combined with rich ornamentation.

Domenico Gilardi

The principles established by Bove in rebuilding Moscow were extended by other neoclassicists, such as Domenico Gilardi, member of an Italian–Swiss clan of architects, artists, and artisans who had worked in Moscow since 1787.[83] In that year, his father, Giovanni, arrived in Moscow and in the ensuing three decades established a solid reputation as an architect, most notably for the building of the Aleksandrovskii Institute (1809–11), whose facade, with a large Corinthian portico, displayed the "estate-house" design typical of medical and educational institutions in neoclassical Moscow. Indeed, the form closely resembles that of the adjacent Mariinskii Hospital for the Indi-

376

Figure 506. N. S. Gagarin house (not extant). Moscow. State bedroom. Photograph (early 1900s) from a private archive.

gent, whose construction Giovanni Gilardi had supervised (possibly to a plan by Andrei Mikhailov).[84]

Domenico Gilardi arrived in Moscow in 1796, at the age of 11. Three years later, he was sent to Petersburg, where he apprenticed with a series of Italian painters and subsequently returned to Italy for further study (at the Milan Academy), in the course of which he switched his attention to the study of architecture. He returned to Moscow in 1811 to work with his father, was evacuated to Kazan during the Napoleonic invasion, and the following year resumed an active career in the rebuilding of Moscow.

His first major work was the reconstruction, in 1817–19, of the ruined main building of Moscow University, originally designed by Matvei Kazakov. Gilardi wisely followed the general configuration of Kazakov's structure, yet introduced significant changes. The central portico (Figure 508), elevated on a limestone base, was enlarged and its columns were reerected in the Greek Doric order (Kazakov had used Ionic) with bold channeling in the manner of Voronikhin's portico for the Mining Institute (see Figure 465). The frieze behind the columns – portraying the nine muses – was executed by the sculptor Gavriil Zamaraev, who had worked with Kazakov on the interior decoration of the main hall of the Kremlin Senate. To accentuate the portico, Gilardi eliminated most of the decoration (such as Kazakov's pilasters) from the remainder of the facade, with the exception of mascaroni on the keystones above the windows of the rusticated first floor and other minor ornamentation between the upper windows.

Behind the portico of the university building, Gilardi increased the size of the dome over the main Ceremonial Hall.[85] This allowed a greater pitch of the interior dome (in fact, a half dome), for which he designed Moscow's crowning masterpiece of trompe l'oeil painting in a monumental sculpted style. The curved space is delineated by ribs, within which is an elaborate pattern of rhomboids with inset figures – all in grisaille. Friezes at the base of the dome, also in grisaille, allegorically depict the arts and sciences, as well as classical philosophers and Apollo with the muses. The idyllic scenes contrasted with the rigid and obscurantist educational policy in effect during the latter half of Alexander's reign, when classical iconography assumed an increasingly ambivalent content.

Figure 507. Church of the Mother of God, Consolation of All who Sorrow. Moscow. Rotunda (with sanctuary). 1830s. Architect: Osip Bove. (M 112–35)

Other extant civic structures by Gilardi include the more elaborately decorated Catherine Institute (1818, with portico added in 1826–7); and the Guardians (Orphanage) Council of the Foundling Home, designed in 1821 and built in 1823–6.[86] Its original plan called for a large central structure, with Ionic portico and a dome over the central hall (Figure 509). On either side were detached wings connected to the main building by a masonry fence with massive inscribed arches. This design was much altered in 1846, when Dmitrii Bykovskii expanded the institution by building in the space between the wings and the center (Figure 510).[87] Nonetheless, the extant structure and its surviving interior are considered among the best examples of late neoclassicism in Moscow, with the large arches, elaborate plaster molding, and grisaille wall paintings in arabesque as well as figured motifs. Although the decorative devices seem at times hypertrophied, the proportions are true in a Piranesian manner. It can also be assumed that the interior forms and decoration – like that of the exterior – were intended to impress upon those who entered the solemn and noble attributes of public duty – in this case, the maintenance and education of orphans.

In addition to his public buildings, Domenico Gilardi gained great renown with his house designs, which in fact bore a considerable resemblance to the former, especially the Guardians' Council. Indeed, his first major commission for a private residence was the mansion of Lieutenant-General P. M. Lunin, whose brother was director of the council.[88] The monumental symmetry of its neoclassical facades – especially the Corinthian loggia of the main structure (Figure 511) – conceals a complex plan arising out of the remaining walls of a series of eighteenth-century structures grouped around a typical Moscow *dvor*, now reconfigured by the new design of the Boulevard Ring. From the street, the house appears to be two separate houses: the smaller, with an elevated Ionic portico (intended as one of the service wings, completed around 1818); and the main house, not completed until 1823, at which point the Lunin's heirs sold the estate to the Commercial (later State) Bank.[89]

The ready transformation from residence to financial institution is a telling comment on the nature of Moscow neoclassicism. The similarities between the design of hospitals, social institutions, and imposing private residences such as the Lunin house indicate that the definition of architectural form by function was antithetical to neoclassicism, which subsumed usefulness and beauty within a supposedly immutable aesthetic system. The architecture of Petersburg also furnishes examples of this suprafunctional aes-

Figure 508. Moscow University. Central part of Old Building. 1817–19. Architect: Domenico Gilardi. (55–8)

thetics, but Moscow, with its greater space, allowed the complexities of an individual plan to be more readily perceived – and compared with other structures.

Gilardi's most accomplished work of this period is the mansion commissioned by Prince Sergei Gagarin (brother of Nikolai, owner of the house by Bove on Novinskii Boulevard) and built in 1822–3 on Povarskii Street.[90] The main facade dispenses with the portico as such, but replaces it with a variation consisting of three window arches of identical height beneath a pediment (Figure 512). The recessed windows are framed by Doric columns supporting architraves – a solution that reminds of Bove's use of the arch and the fondness of both architects for inset columnar structures in the manner of an aedicule.

On the interior, many details of the design resemble both the Lunin house and the Guardians' Council: the large framing arches, often with inset columns supporting an architrave; the use of a dome on high pendentives to illuminate the central space of the structure; the grisaille ceiling and cornice paintings in the manner of a sculpted classical frieze; and the allegorical sculpture, which in the main vestibulte is devoted to the muses of theater and music, two of the owner's main interests.[91] The harmony of the plan (Figure 513) creates a unity between interior and exterior (in contrast to the divorce between the two in the Lunin house). Indeed, the development of the Gagarin House around a central core with a progression of unfolding space (Figure 514) – rather than the rigidly arranged enfilade – anticipates innovations in housing design much later in the century.

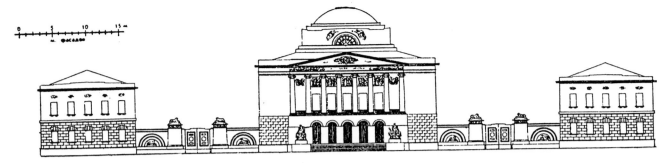

Figure 509. Building of the Guardians' Council. Moscow. 1821; 1823–6. Domenico Gilardi. Elevation.

Figure 510. Building of the Guardians' Council. Moscow. With additions by Dmitrii Bykovskii in 1846. (M157–14)

During the 1820s and the beginning of the next decade, Gilardi also worked extensively on a number of suburban or country estates in the Moscow area. As the closest among them to central Moscow, the estate house for the merchants V. N. and P. N. Usachev (1829–31) has features typical to both city and country mansions. The urban quality is stated in the elevated Ionic portico and the three-storied main structure (Figure 515), whereas the rural ambiance is enhanced by a *pente douce* leading into a park whose pavilions represent some the last specimens of that small form of neoclassical architecture.[92] The extant decoration of the interior (the house is now an institute of sports medicine) includes a number of brightly colored wall and ceiling paintings, whose themes are primarily floral, with festoons and trompe l'oeil bowers.

A more extensive exercise in estate architecture took place to the east of Moscow at the village of Vlakhernskoe, owned by Prince S. M. Golitsyn. The estate of Kuzminki, as it was known, had evolved through several stages in the eighteenth and early nineteenth centuries, with the participation of some of the leading architects of the period (Rodion Kazakov, Egotov, Bazhenov, Voronikhin). Gilardi had himself worked there in the 1810s with his father, and he returned there over the following decade to expand the estate ensemble on a grand scale.[93] The manor house, built by Kazakov and Egotov at the end of the eighteenth century (destroyed by fire in 1915), remained largely untouched, with modifications only to flanking structures and the main entrance. In 1830,

Figure 512. S. S. Gagarin house. Moscow. 1822–3. Architect: Domenico Gilardi. (M 184–17)

Figure 511. P. M. Lunin house. Moscow. 1817–22. Architect: Domenico Gilardi. (M 184–7)

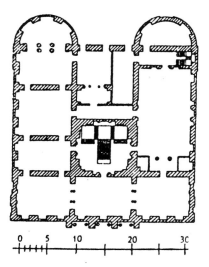

Figure 513. S. S. Gagarin house. Moscow. Plan, by M. V. Pershin.

381

Figure 514. S. S. Gagarin house. Moscow. Great hall and rotunda. (M 124–5)

Gilardi began the final phase of the park, which he focused on a view across the estate pond to a Doric colonnade called the propylaea, visible through a clearing in the surrounding grove.

Gilardi had, however, created a far greater monument, also across the lake, but on an axis perpendicular to the line from the mansion to the propylaea. An enclosed compound for the estate horse farm (*konnyi dvor*) had existed on this site, and its foundations became the base of Gilardi's design not only of a new stables, but also a complex of three structures, linked by a wall with inscribed arches that served to mask the more prosaic structures of the farm. The centerpiece of this design was a music pavilion consisting of a large, solid masonry arch (Figure 516) enclosing eight paired Tuscan columns (four from the front) with entablature and a sculpted group – a design re-

sembling that used in the main vestibule of the Sergei Gagarin house then under construction in Moscow.

The majestic columns of the Music Pavilion are not allotted even an illusionistic role of tectonic support (as in a portico or loggia), but are framed – enshrined – as supports for a work of art: in this case, the statuary, the entablature, and the columns themselves. (The effect was enhanced in front of the arch by statuary groups, replaced in 1845 by enlarged iron replicas of the statues of horse and master by Peter Klodt for the Anichkov Bridge in Petersburg.) Although the surrounding stables have not remained intact and the arch has been much neglected, it is one of the most striking examples of the reinterpretation of neoclassicism in the architecture of Moscow. Rather than adhere to a typical treatment of classical forms (such as the triumphal arch), Gilardi deconstructs the various elements and reassembles them in a way that focuses on the peculiar nature of each: the colonnade, the entablature, rustication that reaches the level of the cornice, and a hypertrophied decorative element on either side of the arch. It is little wonder that the Music Pavilion was a major source of inspiration for neoclassicists such as Vladimir Shchuko at the beginning of the twentieth century.[94]

The last and largest of Gilardi's public buildings in Moscow, the Trade School of the Foundling Home (one of the first industrial trade schools in Russia), is also his least successful. The considerable size of the project, begun in 1827, resulted in a dissipation of the formal elements (such as the attic statuary) that had achieved a heroic effect in his other public buildings.[95] Indeed, the decline of Russian neoclassicism was accompanied by its inability to define a tectonic system for major buildings that were not a part of the culture of the neoclassical era (e.g., a trade school). Yet the

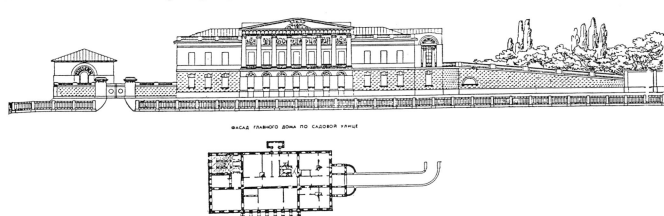

Figure 515. Usachev estate house. Moscow. 1829–31. Architect: Domenico Gilardi. Plan and elevation by D. Gilardi.

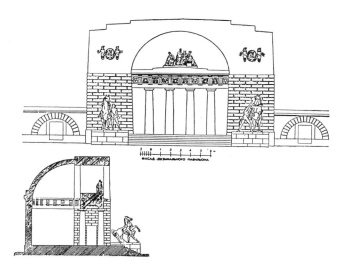

Figure 516. Music pavilion at Kuzminki. Near Moscow. Architect: Domenico Gilardi. Elevation and section by A. M. Kharlamova.

structure functioned, and still does – as the Bauman Technical Institute. In view of the extent of the Trade School, which was completed only in 1832, Gilardi requested the assistance of Afanasii Grigorev, with whom he had worked on a number of the prior projects, and who was to join Bove and Gilardi as the architects most responsible for the final flourishing of Moscow neoclassicism.

Afanasii Grigorev

Like Voronikhin, Grigorev was born a serf (in distant Tambov Province); and although his owner, a certain N. V. Kretov, did not possess the wealth and influence of the Stroganovs, he recognized talent. The young Afanasii Grigorev was sent to Moscow, where he apprenticed with the family of Giovanni Gilardi, and in 1804, at the age of 22, he received his freedom.[96] Following the precedent of the Gilardis', Grigorev in 1808 entered the service of the Foundling Home, one of the major sources of public works projects in Moscow during the first third of the nineteenth century. After the retreat of the French army, Grigorev plunged into the architectural reconstruction of the city and soon distinguished himself as a designer of houses. Although some of his most important work in this area has been destroyed, the surviving houses attributed to him comprise the best examples of the more intimate residential scale of Moscow after the fire. They were less grand than those built by Bove and Gilardi, yet they were also less likely to be sold for debts, as was the case with the Lunin and Gagarin mansions, whose owners could not afford to maintain

their recently completed mansions in the reduced circumstances of the nobility after the Napoleonic wars.

Among the extant houses attributed to Grigorev, the most complex in design is that built in 1814–15 for retired Guards officer A. P. Khrushchev. Constructed of logs, with the upper walls stuccoed and detailed to resemble masonry, the one-story house with mezzanine was built on the vaulted limestone basement level of the prewar structure.[97] Its corner location on Prechistenka Street offered the opportunity, exploited by Grigorev, of creating two "main" facades, each with an Ionic portico (Figure 517). Neither in fact frames the entrance, which is situated to the side of the Khrushchev Lane portico. This facade is therefore assigned priority, indicated by four pairs of Ionic columns beneath a richly sculpted pediment, and by the curved terrace that serves both as a base for the facade as well as a transition to Prechistenka Street. The second portico, facing Prechistenka, functions as a support for the mezzanine balcony, thus allowing the inhabitants an elevated, unobstructed view of the busy street below.[98]

The plan of the Khrushchev house (Figure 518) contains a compact enfilade of rooms facing Prechistenka, and, at a right angle, a ballroom extending for most of the front of the house. The state rooms display much the same approach found in the larger mansions: ceilings with painted arabesques and trompe l'oeil motifs, inset columns supporting architraves, and elaborate plaster molding. Of particular interest is the barrel-vaulted ceiling of the large hall. The form of this house is typical of other, less distinguished residences of the period, in which comfort and financial exigencies began to determine new forms of spatial arrangements in housing design. Despite its decorative detail, the modest scale of the Khrushchev house exemplifies the reduced means available for the maintenance of homes in "postfire" Moscow.[99] Yet the open configuration of the city allowed even a relatively small private dwelling to exist as a detached structure on a lot with subsidiary structures (in contrast to the density of Petersburg); and it is in Moscow that the term *osobniak* (a separate, detached home) gains currency as a variation on the urban "estate house" (*gorodskaia usad'ba*) that had seen so many permutations since the medieval period.

A few steps along Prechistenka, and on the opposite side of the street, is another of the urban villas attributed to Grigorev. Built between 1817 and 1822 for the poet and translator Avraam V. Lopukhin and his brother David, the house is even smaller than that of Khrushchev, yet it exhibits no less a perfection of scale and harmony of decorative elements (Figure

Figure 517. A. P. Khrushchev house. Moscow. 1814–15. Architect: Afanasii Grigorev. (M 149–15)

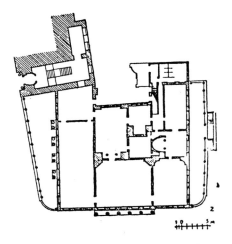

Figure 518. A. P. Khrushchev house. Moscow. Plan.

519).[100] The Lopukhin house, too, is a log structure on a limestone base, with a stuccoed facade imitating masonry motifs: large keystones over the side windows (otherwise absolutely simple and precisely proportioned in the manner of Grigorev's master Giacomo Quarenghi); rustication between the windows (as at the Khrushchev house); ornamental medallions on either side of the facade; and in the center, an Ionic portico that frames classical tableaux (attributed to Gavriil Zamaraev) consisting of portraits of a Roman family. The site plan conformed to a pattern

common after the fire, with the main house facing the street, a separate residential wing behind on one boundary of the lot, and a service building on the other boundary. The entrance to the main house is from the side courtyard.

The interior of the Lopukhin house follows a typical plan of two axes arranged perpendicularly (Figure 520): one containing the vestibule and long ballroom, and the other an enfilade of state rooms. (The everyday living quarters were in a third enfilade, parallel to and in back of the staterooms, with an entresole above.) This is likely the best preserved early nineteenth-century house in Moscow, not in terms of its furnishings, which have long since disappeared, but for the quality and extent of its painted decoration, and particularly its ceilings, which have been maintained in the major rooms.[101] The intricate detail of the *plafond* designs combines the subtle shadings of grisaille with rich polychrome medallions.

The modulations of color and mood proceed from one room to the next, from the grisaille trompe l'oeil coffering on the vaulted ceiling of the oval vestibule, to the arabesques of the ballroom ceiling (also in grisaille) that frame medallions with polychrome vases. The curved ceiling of the small living room provides a setting for the aedicule motif (two Ionic columns supporting an architrave), and the flat ceiling of the large living room displays an elaborate trompe l'oeil, whose the false relief is edged with painted shadows

384

appearing as though cast by the light of the central chandelier. The interior corners of the room are curved by white ceramic stoves, extending from floor to ceiling, and this provides a frame for a quatrefoil element consisting of the head of Mercury surrounded by four white ceramic plates with centered paintings of butterflies, as though in museum display. The most startling effect occurs in the state bedroom, with an alcove defined by Corinthian columns supporting an architrave, and a vaulted ceiling decorated in floral festoons and arabesques. The pattern reveals a grotesque smiling mask on each of the four pendentives, with a mouth formed by the festoons.

In addition to his collaboration on most of Gilardi's major projects, such as the Guardians' Council, Grigorev also constructed in 1826–8 the remarkable neoclassical Church of the Trinity at the village of Ershovo (near Zvenigorod). Although the church was destroyed during the Battle of Moscow in 1941, the preserved drawings and photographs reveal Grigorev's fusion of medieval and neoclassical elements. The traditional cuboid cross-inscribed plan, with an apse, is cloaked in the classical detail of porticos, pediments, and cornices; yet the variant plans reveal a gradual heightening of the structure, until a final, implemented version, which consisted of a rotundal bell tower over the central cube.[102] Grigorev had thus re-turned to the structural combination of bell tower and church that had been devised by Muscovite architects in the Naryshkin style at the end of the seventeenth century.[103]

Grigorev is frequently identified as the author of the Church of the Large Ascension in Moscow, although this is now under question. The church was first begun in 1798 next to a late seventeenth-century "small" Church of the Ascension on the estate of Grigorii Potemkin. The new church, whose original architect has not been determined (Kazakov?), was not finished before the fire of 1812, which severely damaged it. A rebuilding began in 1827, with modifications by Fedor Shestakov in an austere form of neoclassicism (Figure 521), with a large central cube, and a vestibule and apse of the same height (a planned bell tower was never built). The simple, volumetric emphasis of the design reminds of the early traditions of medieval Russian architecture. It is now believed that Bove added the Ionic porticos to the north and south facades.[104] After Shestakov's death in 1835, Grigorev may have been involved in the continuation of work on the church, completed only in 1848.[105] Despite the uncertainty of some attributions in the list of Grigorev's work, his must be considered one of the culminating interpretations of Moscow neoclassicism.

Figure 519. Lopukhin house. Moscow. 1817–22. Architect: Afanasii Grigorev. (M 157–24)

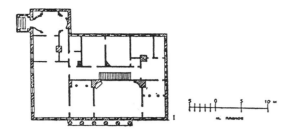

Figure 520. Lopukhin house. Moscow. Plan.

Stasov, Menelaws, and Tiurin in Moscow

Although Moscow's rebuilding was primarily the work of local architects (in some cases trained in Petersburg), the practice of implementing plans by Petersburg architects continued – as in Andrei Mikhailov's role in the reconstruction of the Bolshoi Theater. The most prominent of architects from the northern capital to work in Moscow was Vasilii Stasov, who was born and raised in Moscow. Although of impoverished noble background, Stasov had access to an excellent education, which, combined with his native genius, allowed him to advance rapidly in both social and professional terms. Before 1812, his time was divided between Moscow, Petersburg, and Europe (primarily Italy); but after the loss of their home in the 1812 fire, Stasov moved his family to Petersburg and made an architectural career whose highlights were discussed earlier.[106]

Stasov's role in the reconstruction of Moscow began in 1816 with plans for a restored imperial palace in the Kremlin (later rebuilt by Konstantin Ton). His monumental achievement, however, derived from a rather prosaic source: a series of designs for provision warehouses – primarily for Petersburg – drawn up between 1816 and 1821. When the need arose to build new space for army provisions storage in Moscow at the end of the 1820s, Stasov's final warehouse variant of 1821 served as a basis.[107] The actual construction of the Provision Warehouses in 1829–31 was implemented by Fedor Shestakov. As has been noted, Stasov combined the functional requirements of such buildings with a variant of late neoclassicism that emphasized the archaic purity of the Doric order, imposed on a sharply defined structural mass with little ornament.

The Moscow warehouse (Figure 522) consists of three large two-story buildings with battered, or tapered, walls and tapering main portals in a manner considered "Egyptian" (similar to the Guard stables at Tsarskoe Selo). The portals are surmounted by pediments and a recessed window arch, but there are no columns; only the entablature specifies the Doric order. The hipped roofs, with ventilation dormers, serve to accent both the mass of the ensemble and

Figure 521. Church of the Large Ascension. Moscow. 1798–1848. Architects: Fedor Shestakov, Osip Bove(?) and Afanasii Grigorev(?). Southeast view. (M 156–28)

Figure 522. Provision Warehouses. Moscow. 1821; 1829–31. Architects: Vasilii Stasov and Fedor Shestakov. (M 103–12)

the proportional relations among the three components. Eminently functional, the Provision Warehouses achieve an ideal combination of the aesthetic and useful.

A busier approach to neoclassical detail is displayed in the work of Adam Menelaws – whose career is also associated primarily with Petersburg, particularly his romantic–eclectic designs for the imperial estates (see Chapter 13). In Moscow, however, the two mansions attributed to him – both for the Razumovskii brothers – adhere faithfully to neoclassicism. The earlier of the two, for Count Aleksei K. Razumovskii on Gorokhovoe Field, was originally constructed in 1799–1803 in the manner of a suburban estate. The large wooden central structure (Figure 523), with stuccoed facades in imitation of masonry and a rusticated ground floor, had flanking wings attached by curved galleries – a feature similar to the plan of the Gagarin house by Bove. The most notable feature of the design is the main entrance, consisting of a recessed arch and coffered vaulting. The center of the arch is divided by two Ionic columns supporting an architrave that serves to frame the entrance and the statues flanking it (Flora and Hercules). The stairs flow around the central columns, and on either side of the arch, elevated porticoes with paired Ionic columns protect the lower steps of the divided staircase. In 1833, the house was acquired by the Foundling Home, which commissioned Grigorev to build ancillary structures for the institution's use in 1842.[108]

The second mansion attributed to Menelaws was commissioned by Lev. K. Razumovskii, who had ac-

quired a large lot fronting Tverskaia Street in the center of the city (a Moscow urban estate, with a sizeable park in the back).[109] In 1811, a projecting left wing was added to the house, balanced by a wing on the right during the rebuilding of the house in 1814–17. The central portico (Figure 524), with unadorned pediment and eight Greek Doric columns elevated over a ground-floor arcade, reminds of the strength of Gilardi's portico for the Moscow University building. In 1831, the house was rented by the English Club (a social organization for the Moscow nobility), which gave its name to the building and remained there until 1917. The interior decor has in places been preserved, particularly in the vestibule (Cornithian columns, molded cornices, trompe l'oeil motifs, and a ceiling painting of Mars and Venus).[110]

The transition from neoclassicism is exemplified in the work of the Moscow architect Evgraf Tiurin, whose career begins with his participation in the reconstruction of the Kremlin Palace in 1817–19.[111] During this period, he was engaged in the expansion of the palace and estate pavilions at Arkhangelskoe, as well as the rebuilding of the estate house – known as the Alexandrine Palace – at Neskuchnoe (see both in Chapter 11). In the central part of Moscow, Tiurin designed two important monuments, the first of which was the "new building" of Moscow University. Tiurin's design was, in fact, a rebuilding of an existing structure, the former mansion of A. I. Pashkov, cousin of the owner of the grand Pashkov House two blocks away.[112] Over the next 3 years, Tiurin adapted the interior for the university's use, and placed an

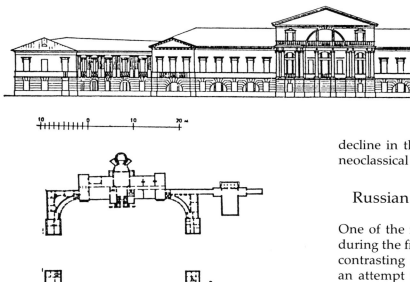

Figure 523. A. K. Razumovskii house. Moscow. 1799–1803. Architect: Adam Menelaws. Modified in late 1830s–early 1840s by Afanasii Grigorev. Elevation of original facade (reconstructed by A. K. Andreev).

Ionic portico at the center of the three-story main building. He also modified the large north wing (formerly the Pashkov manege, and after 1805, a public theater) to contain the library and the university Church of St. Tatiana. The church is the most interesting of Tiurin's designs, a "streamlined" horizontal facade with high attic ending in a curved Doric loggia, overlooking the street, that contains the apse.

A very different interpretation of neoclassicism is conveyed in Tiurin's rebuilding of the Cathedral of the Epiphany in Elokhovo, to the northeast of central Moscow (now the cathedral of the Patriarch of the Russian Orthodox Church).[113] The main structure, rebuilt between 1837 and 1845, is his attempt to combine the neoclassical system with earlier forms of Orthodox architecture, evident in the pyramidal massing of five cupolas. Where Stasov succeeded in clearly articulating, in both form and detail, the relation between the central and the subsidiary domes of his Petersburg regimental cathedrals, Tiurin surrendered this bold neoclassical harmony to conflicting impulses: a simplification of the classical orders on one hand, and on the other, a surfeit of preclassical, baroque elements in the treatment of the entablature and the window surrounds. This loss of clarity, even in comparison with his Church of St. Tatiana, is already a sign of a decline in the understanding and application of the neoclassical aesthetic.

Russian Neoclassicism: Decline and Fall

One of the most popular literary exercises in Russia during the first half of the nineteenth century was the contrasting description of Petersburg and Moscow, an attempt to define a "physiognomy," a character of the two cities in a way that would define what the Russians had themselves become in the century since the end of Peter's reign. These essays of the 1830s and 1840s appeared at a watershed in the country's development – social, political, cultural. It was an age of the stultifying aftermath of the Decembrist tragedy, and yet rich with possibilities for progress. Whatever the political position of the observer, it was clear that an age of apparent stability had passed, and with it the architectural verities of neoclassicism. Hence, the sensitivity to architectural nuance in the descriptions of the two capitals, whose differing environments each registered the changing of one order for another.

Among the most affecting commentaries on late neoclassical Moscow came from the influential social and literary critic Vissarion Belinskii. In his essay "Petersburg and Moscow," he wrote:

Although a genuine Petersburger is never amazed or enthused by anything, he would not be able to contain an exclamation when, having walked around the boulevards that encircle Moscow – its best ornament, which Petersburg might well envy – when going down and uphill, he would see on all sides an amphitheater of roofs mixed with the greenery of gardens....

Many streets in Moscow...consist primarily of the "lords'" (a Moscow word!) houses. Here you see more comfort, than huge size or elegance. In everything and on everything is the stamp of family life: a comfortable home, spacious, but nonetheless for one family group; a wide yard, and on summer evenings numerous domestic servants around the gates. Everywhere there is separation and privacy [osobnost'], everyone lives in his own home and firmly fences himself off from his neighbor.[114]

The glory of Moscow neoclassicism was indeed its houses, large and small, for merchants as well as nobility. Many are not attributed as to architect (in numerous cases, possibly a trained serf), and yet they display with remarkable frequency a command of the classical order system. This proficiency can be explained in part by the standardized plans emanating from Petersburg, but equally important is the implied and pervasive sense of stable aesthetic and cultural values – based, as Belinskii observes, on the family, whose virtues were so insistently idealized in numerous classical friezes and wall paintings. To be sure, Moscow also had its examples of imposing public architecture, and even a rare planned ensemble. Yet with far fewer bureaucratic and court institutions than Petersburg, it experienced correspondingly less state patronage in architecture. Thus, even though the 1812 fire obliterated much of Moscow's architectural heritage, the rebuilt city retained many familiar landmarks (particularly churches) that not only linked it with the medieval past, but also provided a context that diluted the force of the neoclassical ideal.

In Petersburg, with seemingly boundless support, but without the mediating elements of livable scale and hospitable landscape, Alexandrine neoclassicism achieved a magnificent formal triumph during the first quarter of the century. The great architects of the period understood how to concentrate the forces provided by the classical order system at strategic points in their designs, with economy of ornament and an absolute sense of proportion based both on precise calculation and the individual eye. Yet this genius and the seemingly immutable laws could not be perpetuated in an age that questioned, in Europe as well as Russia, the cultural assumptions and values that underlay neoclassicism (rationalism and the existence of a universal, natural order applicable to society as to the arts).

The beginning of the reign of Nicholas I – accompanied by a tragic attempt, in December 1825 – placed in sharp relief the contradictions that would destroy neoclassicism as an aesthetic system and as an expression of state authority. The appeal of eclecticism will be examined in the following chapter, but neoclassicism itself was undercut by a growing perception of the divergence between the myth of neoclassical heroism – whose iconography was drawn from carefully cultivated and instructive legends of personal honor – and the reality of Russian life in the major cities as well as the provinces. A system of design devoid of content (functional and ideological) became associated with the dead hand of reaction, whose ultimate symbol was General Aleksei Arakcheev.

It was for Arakcheev's estate in Novgorod Province

that Stasov designed some of his (and Russia's) best neoclassical monuments; yet it was also Arakcheev the martinet who devised the military communes that epitomized the reactionary direction of the latter part of Alexander's reign. Although intended as a rational, and even benign, enterprise to allow Russian troops to live with their families in self-supporting agricultural communities, the fanaticism of military regulation in the communes caused a number of revolts, punished with the usual cruelty. It is telling that the buildings for such communes were designed in the stripped classical style related to the standardized designs used elsewhere in the empire – here carried to an ultimate, sinister extreme. For certain intellectual critics of neoclassicism, Arakcheev and "barracks architecture" became synonymous with the style that had lost the glory given it by Zakharov and his peers.[115]

In fact, state institutions and private property owners often used a standardized form of neoclassicism to meet more economically the needs of a growing urban environment during the 1830s,[116] yet this attempt to exploit neoclassicism with little attention to the proportional, formal relations led to a routinization. It is ironic that in the late 1830s and 1840s, the persistent complaints against the monotony of neoclassicism – a style linked in Russia with the precapitalist era – should prefigure similar diatribes against the monotony and sterility of nineteenth-century industrial cities in the work of writers such as Charles Dickens (cf. *Hard Times*).[117]

Perhaps the most significant critique of neoclassical architecture is contained in Nikolai Gogol's long essay "On the Architecture of the Present Time," which appeared in a collection of his work entitled *Arabesques* (1835). Although rambling and highly impressionistic, Gogol's opinions merit attention, not only because he had achieved a position as one of Russia's most important writers, but, more specifically, because his commentary provides a register of opinions, unequivocally stated, at a dividing point in the history of Russian architecture:

To all city edifices they have begun to impart a smooth, simple form. They try to make houses as similar to one another as possible, yet they are more similar to sheds or barracks than to happy residences for people. The completely smooth form gains not the least vitality from small regular windows, which resemble squinting eyes in relation to the entire building. And this is the architecture we were recently so proud of as the perfection of taste, and we built entire towns in this spirit. . . . That is why the new towns have no appearance: they are so regular, so smooth, so

Figure 524. L. K. Razumovskii house. Moscow. Central portico. Photograph c. 1900. From Iurii Shamurin, *Ocherki klassicheskoi Moskvy*.

monotonous, that having gone down one street you already feel bored and refuse to look at another. It's a row of walls and nothing else.[118]

This then was the ultimate Russian interpretation of the noble quest for what has been called "geometric purism," the apotheosis of volume and form in the works of Zakharov and Thomon.[119] From revolutionary France to young Russia, geometry becomes synonymous not with ideal, universal laws but with the abstractions of an empire, ruled by decree from an abstract city. The young Carlo Rossi had proclaimed that Petersburg need not fear comparison with Rome in the grandeur of its architecture; and shortly thereafter, Stasov, in a text accompanying his 1811 project for a neoclassical memorial to the battle of Poltava (Peter's epic victory) stated that architecture – noble and neoclassical – must contribute to the "arousal of present and future generations to similar deeds."[120]

Yet there was little consensus as to what those deeds should be, particularly after 1825. Were they to be found in the liberal, antiautocratic ideals of Alexander Herzen and Nikolai Ogarev, both products of neoclassical Moscow? Certainly they were not shared by the elite surrounding the autocracy, which demonstrated little interest in maintaining neoclassicism in the face of new nationalist doctrines of absolute authority. As will be seen in the following chapter, statism, populism, and technological innovation disposed of neoclassicism in favor of a fundamentally altered language of architecture.

PART IV

The Formation of
Modern Russian Architecture

CHAPTER 13

Nineteenth-Century Historicism and Eclecticism

> . . . you really can't define our current architecture. It's a sort of disorderly mess, entirely, by the way, appropriate to the disorder of the present moment.
>
> – Fedor Dostoevskii, *Diary of a Writer*, 1873.

Relations between European architecture and literary culture have existed since the Renaissance; and in the eighteenth century, the age of reason and the fashion for Gothic novels had their effect on the development of neoclassicism and the pseudo-Gothic, respectively. Yet Russian architecture of the postclassical nineteenth century exceeds the earlier styles in its link to literary, ideological programs. Indeed, writers such as Nikolai Gogol, an amateur of architecture, and Fedor Dostoevskii, a trained engineer, assumed the burden of architectural criticism in the middle third of the nineteenth century. At the base of this literary interpretation of architecture lay an attempt to define the direction of Russian society in an era of change, particularly in the cities, where architects were engaged in a process of transforming the urban environment in an array of eclectic styles.[1]

Although most architects may have considered style a matter of taste, there were those who placed a specific cultural and social meaning upon the use of style in architecture. Almost every facet of Russian culture, architecture included, could ultimately be related to a struggle between competing political ideologies, each of which justified its position by referring to the "people." Those who commented on the significance of new currents in architecture included apologists for the existing regime; but in the broader sense, socioaesthetic commentary fell to the Russian intelligentsia, those literati and political thinkers disposed to critical, antiauthoritarian thought.[2]

The many reasons (including ideological) for the decline of neoclassicism have been alluded to in the preceding chapter. Classical models continued to be revered, particularly in educational curricula, yet the competing claims for new tectonic and decorative forms argued for a greater response to function and physical setting, both of which stimulated an eclectic approach based on an appeal to the national character and its cultural heritage. An article published in 1840 in the pioneering *Khudozhestvennaia gazeta* (*Arts Gazette*) proclaimed that "Every climate, every people, every age has its special style, which corresponds to particular needs or satisfies special goals."[3]

Paradoxically, the postclassical age almost by definition lacked a style of its own. Although the basic function of architecture remained to provide shelter in so inhospitable a climate, its form became linked to history – and to literary interpretations of history. Gogol provides the significant example in his essay, published in 1835, on contemporary architecture, in which he writes of the fragmentation of social and aesthetic consciousness in the new age: "Our age is so petty, its desires are so dispersed, our knowledge is so encyclopedic, that we cannot concentrate our thoughts on one subject; and against our will we split all our creations into trifles and charming toys. We have the marvelous gift of making everything insignificant."[4]

Having said that, Gogol offers an extreme architectural vision that is nothing if not dispersed, encyclopedic – and perhaps trivialized. In opposition to the universal measure of neoclassicism, he appeals for a visually stimulating urban architecture composed of all styles: "A city should consist of varied masses, if you will, in order to provide pleasure to the eye. Let there be gathered in it more diverse tastes. Let there rise on one and the same street something sombre and Gothic; something eastern, burdened under the luxury of ornament; something Egyptian, colossal; and something Greek, suffused with slender proportions." And so on, for several lines, enumerating additional styles.[5]

Gogol proposes the creation of an ersatz architectural tradition (disconcertingly close to modern theme parks) for a nation that still had the vaguest sense of its own architectural history. Even function is supplanted by the desire to create an aesthetic cityscape that would enlighten as well as delight its citizens. As for the person capable of designing this new environment:

The architect–creator should have a deep knowledge of all forms of architecture. He least of all should neglect the taste of those peoples to whom we usually show disdain in artistic matters. [Would not the Russians themselves fall into this category?] He must be all-embracing, must study and assimilate all their innumerable variations. But most important, he should learn everything as an idea, and not in its petty surface form and parts. But in order to master the idea, he must be a genius and a poet.[6]

Gogol's romantic concept of the creative architect lay far from Russian – or any other – reality, but his predilection for Gothic architecture was shared by a number of Russian critics and architects, including Alexander Briullov, the one contemporary architect whose work Gogol praised.[7] Although a highly imaginative and idiosyncratic form of pseudo-Gothic architecture had flourished in Russia during the reign of Catherine, the postclassical Gothic revival not only was more widely applied, but also appeared specifically as an antidote to neoclassicism. Indeed, the new Gothic can be considered the first, if short-lived, stylistic development after neoclassicism to lay claim to both aesthetic and historical significance.

The Gothic Revival

As in the late eighteenth century, the new Gothic wave was frequently used to create a picturesque environment on country estates. Nicholas I adopted the style as his own, and was generous in commissioning ensembles in the style from architects such as Adam Menelaws, who designed several pavilions for the Alexander Park at Tsarskoe Selo: the "Chapelle" pavilion (1825–8), a tower with Gothic motifs and "ruined" walls attached; the Arsenal pavilion, completed in 1834 by the same architect, on the base of Rastrelli's "Mon Bijou"; and the Farm (1818–22) – to name only a few.[8] The same architect also designed pseudo-Gothic residences and other buildings for Nicholas I

in the Alexandria Park (named in honor of Nicholas' wife) at Peterhof. The most famous of these is the Cottage (1826–9), which became the epitome of taste, and stimulated the fashion for Gothic design.[9] The most impressive example of the Gothic revival at the Alexandria Park was the Capella (much damaged during the war), designed in 1829 by the great Prussian architect Karl-Friedrich Schinkel and built by Menelaws in 1831–2.[10]

Equally famed for his use of the Gothic revival was Alexander Briullov, praised in Gogol's essay of the early 1830s as an encouraging sign of the improvement of taste in architecture. One of Briullov's most admired monuments in the Gothic style was the church (not extant) designed for the Shuvalov estate at Pargolovo. Intended as a burial monument to P. A. Shuvalov by his widow, the chapel, built in 1831–40, had a slender spire in the west decorated with pinnacles and crockets in a delicate picturesque style.[11] Perhaps the most pervasive influence of the Gothic revival was in the area of interior design; and here, too, Briullov played a central role, particularly in his design of the suite of rooms for Empress Alexandra Fedorovna, wife of Nicholas, in the rebuilt Winter Palace (1838). Although most of the rooms in the lavishly decorated suite were in an Italinate or "Pompeian" style, the ceiling of the Boudoir consisted of intricate fan vaults in imitation of the late Gothic.[12]

The design of picturesque pseudo-Gothic ensembles was by no means limited to imperial estates. The most coherent design in the Gothic manner was created by Mikhail Bykovskii on the estate of Marfino, near Moscow.[13] Also of interest are early attempts to combine – in a sense equate – the pseudo-Gothic with the ornamentalism of Russia's late medieval architecture, as exemplified in Ivan Mironovskii's design for the Synodal Typography in Moscow's Kitai-gorod (1811–15; Figure 525). The Gothic Revival culminated in Russia with yet another extensive complex of buildings commissioned by Nicholas for Peterhof and designed during the 1840s and 1850s by Nikolai Benois.[14] The adaptability of the Gothic Revival to public structures ensured its use for many decades to come, but its role as a dominant style in the postclassical era soon declined: It, too, was seen as inappropriate for the functional approach demanded by modern architecture.[15]

Utopian Visions and Retrospective Dreams

Function, however, proved a difficult concept to define in a period of technological and social change.

394

Figure 525. Synodal Printing Office, main (east) entrance. Moscow. 1811–15. Architect: Ivan Mironovskii. (M 160–28)

Whereas literati suggested that the public should be served with something visually more stimulating than the now monotonous neoclassicism, architects themselves took a more limited approach. They criticized late neoclassicism for excessive use of the column and for the divorce of the symmetrical facade from the needs of the interior plan, but they by no means dispensed with facade decoration, which by the middle of the century was applied in an unprecedented profusion – from imperial palaces by Shtakenshneider to apartment houses for the well-to-do.[16] On the most direct level, the new display of ornament was related to wealth, fashion, and the status projected by the property owner. In a broader sense, repetitive facade ornament can be seen as a reflection of a new era of industrial standardization – and of the bureaucracy whose minions filled Petersburg's ever greater numbers of multistoried houses.

It must be noted, however, that the majority of apartment houses designed during the middle third

395

of the nineteenth century in Petersburg and immortalized in the novels of Dostoevskii represent, paradoxically, an extension of the neoclassical style that had been previously applied to large urban blocks by architects such as Vasilii Stasov and Paul Jacot (Figure 526).[17] Reduced to the barest ornamental details in a vaguely classical manner, these buildings retained the often irrational planning features – again noted in the novels of Dostoevskii – that ensued from the joining of neoclassical tectonics and planning to large-scale structures built for speculative purposes.[18] In this transitional period, therefore, when the conditions of an evolving urban order were so obviously unsatisfactory, utopian visions of a new living environment seized the imagination of certain prominent writers.[19]

Gogol himself wrote enthusiastically of new materials and new cities created of metal and glass:

In our century there are such inventions and such new elements wholly belonging to it, from which one can fashion buildings never before erected anywhere. Take, for example, those suspended ornaments that began to appear not long ago. For the time being, suspended architecture appears only in loges, balconies, and small bridges. But if entire floors were to be suspended, if bold arches were to be spanned, if entire masses were to be placed on open iron supports rather than heavy columns [here follow several phrases devoted to tower architecture cloaked in iron ornaments] – what lightness, what aesthetic airiness [*vozdushnost'*] our buildings would then acquire![20]

Although these lines might be assigned to the realm of "aerial castles," Gogol's vision suggested by no means improbable goals for architecture; and his fondness of buildings of a pronounced vertical silhouette – whether Gothic or futuristic – would be amply realized in American architecture a few decades later. In Russia, his tower architecture was tentatively considered by professional architects only at the beginning of the twentieth century, but aerial cities and suspended architecture were to become a characteristic of Soviet avant-garde design workshops during the brief flourishing of architectural innovation in the 1920s (see Chapter 15). To be sure, Gogol, like many of his contemporaries as well as Soviet utopians of the 1920s, wished to summon a new age without addressing the economic realities underlying architecture and urban planning. But it is precisely the Russian ability to formulate such suprapractical – if not immaterial – possibilities that contributed to the western interest in modern Russian concepts of design and urban space.

The radicalization of ideological positions and the onset of political struggle in the 1860s led to new concepts of a highly structured living environment derived from French utopian social theories. The most famous and appealing of these schemes was provided in Nikolai Chernyshevskii's novel *What is to be Done?* (1863), with its dream depiction of "new people" leading a harmonious existence in phalansteries, or communes. These latter were based in part on the work of Charles Fourier (1772–1837) and his disciples, whose doctrine of Fouriérisme envisioned an ideal communal existence of sexual and material freedom and equality. Chernyshevskii's elaboration of this vision in his immensely popular novel represents a peculiar combination of ideal communities with the implicit regimentation of the Arakcheev colonies (Chernyshevskii's supporters would, of course, have rejected the comparison).

The communal living space, comfortably equipped and capable of accommodating some 3,000 inhabitants, was surrounded by green zones that represented his answer to the constricted, dehumanizing urban environment epitomized by Petersburg.[21] In keeping with his primarily agrarian view of communalism, industry is allotted little role in this vision. Indeed, the phalansteries, separated from each other by a few miles, represented an early form of "deurbanization" that would be resurrected by certain Soviet planners in the 1920s. Chernyshevskii's vision was dependent on technology, even to the point of domed "palaces" of aluminum and glass inspired by Paxton's Crystal Palace; but in contrast to idealistic futurist utopias, Chernyshevskii was primarily interested in the social nexus of his new harmony, and relegated architecture to a subordinate, functional position in relation to society and the fine arts.[22] None of these Russian utopian schemes led to specific planning for a more humane built environment in the nineteenth century. Although the English garden city movement, and its offshoots elsewhere, stimulated interest among certain Russian architects and planners at the beginning of the twentieth century, they lacked the material support to implement even these pragmatic plans.[23]

Apart from utopias, the competing claims for a new aesthetic basis for architecure implied widely disparate views of the spiritual, expressive capabilities of architectural form. At times, this quest bordered on the verge of mysticism, as epitomized in Alexander Vitberg's design in 1817 for a memorial Church of Christ the Savior, dedicated to the Russian sacrifice in the Napoleonic invasion and projected for a site on Sparrow Hills overlooking the city across the Moscow River. Vitberg was primarily an artist with a strong interest in the symbolic meaning of architecture, and his mystical piety accords well with the last

Figure 526. Apartment house of the Dutch Reformed Church. Petersburg. 1834–9. Architect: Paul Jacot. (P 84–3)

years of Alexander's reign. Yet he produced very little during his complicated, tragic life, which included exile to Viatka on a false criminal charge. In exile, however, he gained the support of one of the most influential Russian thinkers of the nineteenth century, Alexander Herzen, who took it upon himself to explain and praise Vitberg's project in his book *My Past and Thoughts*.

As drawn by Vitberg, the temple is characterized by exaggerated classical forms, articulated in an excessively detailed manner that obscures any possibility of geometric grandeur (Figure 527). In Vitberg's description, as conveyed to Herzen, the structure proceeded symbolically in three parts: from the base, or crypt (cut into the hill and representing the body in the grave), to a cruciform main structure (representing the soul and composed of gigantic Corinthian porticos attached to a square), and finally to a cylinder supporting a dome symbolic of the divine spirit.[24] Vitberg had limited experience as an architect, and his project was ridden with contradictions arising from his use of an established tectonic system to express a vision that might have called at the very least for an essay in Gothic Revival; but Vitberg rejected the Gothic possibility without grasping a language appropriate to his transcendent vision.[25] (That feat would be accomplished – again conceptually – after the 1917 revolution in Tatlin's Monument to the Third International; see Chapter 15.)

Although work on Vitberg's project stopped at the foundation level, Nicholas I reopened the idea of a memorial complex soon after his accession to power. By 1828, it had become clear that such a large structure could not be supported on the site – chosen for its symbolic significance – so close to the steep incline of Sparrow Hills, and a renewed competition led in 1832 to the approval of a project submitted by Konstantin Ton that had the imprimatur of the tsar himself as a style expressive of the national spirit. The "Russo–Byzantine" style, as it came to be known, had germinated in Ton's work throughout the 1820s, beginning, paradoxically, with his 6 years of study in Italy and France (1819–26) after graduating from the Academy of Arts in 1815.[26] Ton returned to Petersburg in 1827, where he embarked upon an active practice and continued to work at the Academy. The influence of medieval Russian architecture first appeared in Ton's work in a competition project, submitted in 1830, for the Church of St. Catherine in the Kolomna district of Petersburg.[27] The success of this design, as well as the assiduous support of A. N. Olenin, president of the Academy of Art, brought Ton to the attention of

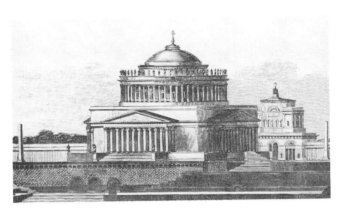

Figure 527. Project for the memorial Church of Christ the Savior. 1817. Architect: Alexander Vitberg. Courtesy of the Shchusev State Museum of Architecture, Moscow.

Nicholas, at whose behest he entered the competition for the Church of Christ the Savior.

Although a scientific interest in the development of old Russian church architecture was still in its beginning stages, Ton fluently assimilated its structural features and devised what would be seen as a faithful reflection of the medieval spirit in his articulation of the facades and the cupolar structures of his cruciform or cross-inscribed churches.[28] In fact, these designs – and above all that of the Church of Christ the Savior (Figure 528) – consisted of a pastiche of external elements, medieval and even neoclassical, applied in a manner that bore little relation to the plasticity of structure or to the internal logic of the building. Thus, as Borisova has noted, Ton's church exteriors acquired a "narrative" quality typical of eclecticism.[29] By the same process, they were also ideally suited for their ideological function as an expression of the concept, promulgated during the reign of Nicholas, of "official nationality," whose triad of "Orthodoxy, nationality, and autocracy" represented an attempt to face the challenge of western modernity by accepting certain technical advances, while resisting antiautocratic western political and social ideas by reinventing the Russian past and its ethos.[30] Because they gave specific visual content to this doctrine, Ton's church designs were in 1838 published in a large album, which in 1841 was designated by Nicholas as the proper guide for new Orthodox church construction in the empire.[31]

For all its transparent subordination to ideological purposes, the Ton's design for the Church (*khram*, or "temple") of Christ the Savior effectively established a landmark in central Moscow. Located up the Moscow River on Prechistenka Quay within sight of the Kremlin, the church was higher than the bell tower of Ivan the Great (102 meters); yet its position on lower ground and the horizontality of the basic structure (with vertical accents) conveyed a very different silhouette from the massing of spires and towers within the Kremlin and its immediate vicinity, although one historian has compared the church to another monument to the victory of the Russian people over their enemies – the Cathedral of the Intercession on the Moat (i.e., St. Basil's, also generally referred to as a *khram*).[32]

Indeed, despite the segmentation of Ton's church into bays in imitation of the vertical outlines of early medieval churches, its form emphasized the impression of a horizontal, earthbound mass. It is immediately evident that despite their smaller size, the earlier monuments possessed a much clearer sense of vertical development by virtue of a more refined system of proportions in the massing of structural components. The plan of the church was essentially cruciform, with massive corner piers whose outlines were reflected on the exterior by domed corner bays. In the

Figure 528. Church of Christ the Savior. Moscow. 1832; 1839–83; consecrated in 1889; razed in 1931. Architect: Konstantin Ton. West view, c. 1890.

abstract, the plan (Figure 529) closely ressembles that of the large Cathedral of the Don Mother of God at Donskoi Monastery (see Figure 235); yet here, too, the earlier monument has a stronger sense of compact form and vertical development. Ton dissipated the vertical impact of his structure through the low pitch of the gilded main cupola, one of the "Byzantine" components of the design; and in so doing, he tempered the great size of the structure in relation to the surrounding area. Whether the ponderous outlines of the church existed in harmony with its urban setting is a debatable issue – and a moot one, because the church, which was a marvel of engineering, with foundation trenches to a depth of 40 meters, was barbarously destroyed in 1931–2.[33]

Concurrently with work on the Church of Christ the Savior, Nicholas initiated the rebuilding of the Great Kremlin Palace, which had been severely damaged in the 1812 occupation and subsequently repaired by Stasov, Ivan Mironovskii, and others. During the 1820s, at least three major plans were submitted for its reconstruction and expansion.[34] Only in 1838 was Ton appointed to supervise the project, which provided an imposing facade for the Kremlin above the Moscow River (Figure 530) and created a stylistically appropriate link with the Terem Palace, the Faceted Chambers, and the Annunciation Cathedral within the interior of the Kremlin. The stylization was most closely related to the ornate window surrounds of the seventeenth-century Terem Palace.[35]

In complement to the Kremlin Palace, Ton was commissioned to build the adjacent Armory, an historical museum containing imperial and medieval Russian treasures. (The name derives from the Armory Chamber – *Oruzheinaia palata* – devoted to the crafting of

weapons, and one of several medieval "chambers" in the Kremlin that produced valuable objects for the grand prince, or tsar.[36]) The style of the museum is a hybrid of gothic and romanesque features on the interior. The main facade (Figure 531), leading to the Borovitskii Tower and Gates, also displays elements that could be defined as Renaissance, romanesque, and neoclassical.[37] The double-arched windows of the two-story halls of the upper museum are framed by attached limestone columns in a manner common to late neoclassicism in Russia; but the shafts of the columns are decorated with the foliate motifs and strapwork of late seventeenth-century Russian architectural ornamentation. This limited, yet highly visible, concession to a historical Russian style within an essentially western tectonic system is indicative of the cautious way in which even Ton understood and incorporated traditional Russian motifs. Indeed, his approach differed little from that of Ivan Mironovskii's design for the Synodal Printing Office (see Figure 525).

Ton's legacy as a master builder has survived in his secular imperial structures, but the destruction of his churches, erected in Moscow, Petersburg, Sevastopol, Tomsk, and other Russian cities, ensued as part of an antireligious campaign cloaked by an unjust identification of the architect with the repressive policies of the imperial autocracy.[38] Although Nicholas and certain of his ministers exploited Ton's work for their own purposes, and although he worked, as did many other architects, for the court, his churches possessed qualities of design and construction that made them valuable artifacts of midnineteenth century Russian culture. One can criticize his church designs for their ponderous inability to recapture the logic and the spirit of styles they were intended to reinterpret. Yet his work had the advantages and disadvantages of its historical position during the reign of a tsar more interested in engineering than in architecture – relegated to a picturesque, historicist approach for ideological purposes.

Imperial Eclecticism: Montferrand

The making of the Church of Christ the Savior was in many ways paralleled by the other major ecclesiastical building of Nicholas's reign – equally epochal in its construction. The Cathedral of St. Isaac of Dalmatia also had its several design stages.[39] The first masonry version (located near the site that Falconet would use for his monument to Peter the Great) was built in 1717–27 to a design by Mattarnovy, but poor foundation work led to its disuse by the middle of

Figure 529. Church of Christ the Savior. Moscow. Plan.

Figure 530. Great Kremlin Palace. Moscow. 1838–50s. Main architect: Konstantin Ton. (M 63–1)

the eighteenth century. After a number of false starts, the rebuilding of the church began in 1762 to a plan by Rinaldi, but foundation problems continued to plague the project, and Paul entrusted it to Brenna, who completed the church in 1802 to a lesser plan. The Siberian marble intended for its interior and exterior was redirected to Paul's Mikhailovskii Castle.

Dissatisfied with the hastily completed cathedral, Alexander I initiated a new competition at the beginning of his reign; and in 1818, the project was awarded to the young French architect and veteran of Napoleon's army, Auguste Ricard de Montferrand. In 1814, Montferrand, without prospects for advancement after the defeat of Napoleon, sent an album of project sketches to Alexander, who invited him to Russia. Even this sudden rise to prominence in a distant country could not have prepared for the architect's unexpected victory in the cathedral competition, which is comparable to Voronikhin's commission for the Kazan Cathedral and involved an equally protracted defense of the architect's abilities. With the beginning of structural work, Montferrand dismantled parts of

Rinaldi's cathedral (situated to the east of Senate Square), but incorporated substantial segments of its walls in his own structure – particularly for the central transverse aisle.[40]

The plan of St. Isaac's cathedral (Figure 532) can be classified as "inscribed cross," but with a longitudinal extension in the manner of a basilica. This basic fusion of different traditions and elements continues throughout the design, which began as a straightforward exercise in neoclassicism similar to the churches of Stasov.[41] The culmination of the structure was a large drum in the form of a rotunda and a dome surmounted by a lantern. At each corner of the central cube, the design called for smaller cupolas over drums that also served as the church bell towers. Montferrand's opponents successfully reopened consideration of the project in 1822, and only after an energetic counteroffensive by the architect was his new variant of the project approved in April 1825.[42]

As the plan was modified over the ensuing decade, the corner towers became much smaller and were relegated exclusively to use as bell cotes (they admit

400

no light into the interior). At the same time, new points of emphasis, such as the bronze statues of angels with a torchère at the corners of the extended length of the structure emphasized its horizontal mass (Figure 533). The gilded ribbed dome, resting above a rotunda with monolithic Corinthian columns of red granite and a balustrade, was at the time of its construction one of the largest in Europe (almost 25.8 meters in outer diameter and 2,226 metric tons in weight) and technically the most advanced in its triple-shelled iron form and truss system (see Figure 532).[43] The tension between the great height of the cupola and the horizontal emphasis of the structure can be seen as a defect of a structure designed at a period in which the harmony of classical tectonics was no longer clearly understood – or valued. Montfer-

Figure 531. Armory. Moscow Kremlin. 1844–51. Main architect: Konstantin Ton. (M 173–10)

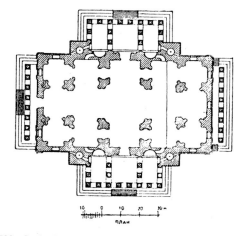

Figure 532. Cathedral of St. Isaac of Dalmatia. Petersburg. 1818–58. Architect: Auguste Ricard Montferrand. Plan, longitudinal section.

rand had, of course, received an impeccable classical training as an architecture student in France, yet the constant revisions of the plan and the project's many oversight committees led to a diffusion of purpose and the creation of autonomous segments within the design.

This is particularly noticeable in the major role alloted to sculpture in the design. Not even Voronikhin's Kazan Cathedral was decorated so profusely, or to such specific ideological intent (the west pediment, for example, contains the sculpted group "St. Isaac blessing the Emperor Theodosius and his wife Flaccilla," with its message of the union of sacred and secular authority blessed by God). The exterior bronze sculpture – most of which was entrusted to Ivan Vitali, a student of Paolo Triscorni – included statues for niches set within the marble-clad facades; figures of the apostles above the pediments, with the four Evangelists situated at the peak of each pediment; and angels at the corners and above the rotundal balustrade.[44] Sculpted reliefs provide a narrative focus and weight to the pediments, which rest on monolithic red granite columns quarried near Vyborg and each weighing some 114 metric tons.

Although the porticos and pediments, with their gargantuan dimensions, serve as a visual transition to the dome and as a centering element to the building, the general design fails to link its dispersed segments – particularly the corner bell towers. Like the Church of Christ the Savior in Moscow, the scale of St. Isaac's Cathedral, with its eclectic mixture of Renaissance, baroque, and neoclassical elements imposed upon a cross-inscribed plan, eluded a single controlling presence – this in vivid contrast to Voronikhin's Kazan Cathedral.

The interior of St. Isaac's Cathedral reveals a similar clash of material and technical brillance with spatial clarity and harmony. To enumerate the size and cost of the precious metals and semiprecious stones (lapis lazuli, porphyry, marble, malachite) used to encrust the massive piers, the iconostasis, and the vaulting would exceed normal comprehension – as, indeed, does a view of the interior *in situ*. The Russian love of color and narrative on church interiors, denied by the relative austerity of neoclassicism, here returns with a force amplified by technical means unknown to the medieval church. The malachite surfaces of the iconostasis columns and the pervasive use of gilt for architectural details are two of the more obvious examples.[45] The interior walls were richly decorated with paintings,[46] as well as mosaic panels (particularly in the iconstasis) by Russian masters who mastered the technique after four years of study in the mid–

401

Figure 533. Cathedral of St. Isaac of Dalmatia. South view. (P 77–32)

1840s at the Barberi studio in Rome. This resurrection of a long-lost art would have significant ramifications for the development of Russian architecture and monumental art at the end of the century.[47] Finally, and most unusually for a Russian Orthodox church, Montferrand installed a large stained-glass image of the resurrected Christ (crafted in Munich) for the main altar window.[48]

The completion of the Cathedral of St. Isaac established a new visual dominant in the Petersburg cityscape: Its dome was visible from points throughout the city and its great mass defined not only the south side of Senate Square, but also the north side of the new St. Isaac's Square. In this respect, Montferrand, whose cathedral differed fundamentally from the neoclassicism of Carlo Rossi, completed the latter's system of squares for the central city.

Similarly, Montferrand also provided the final accent to Palace Square with his design the Alexander Column (1830–4; see Figure 484), considered the world's tallest victory column (47.5 meters).[49] For the final variant of the monument, Montferrand designed a red granite monolith (from the same quarry near Vyborg) that echoed the array of columns in the surrounding buildings by Rastrelli and Rossi without visually conflicting with either of the monumental facades. The column is surmounted by a large bronze statue of an angel holding a cross (by Boris Orlovskii), and its base is covered with bronze bas-reliefs designed by Giovanni Scotti on the theme of Alexander's victory over the Napoleon. Yet it is not the sculpture, but the architectural appropriateness of the monument in relation to its environment that so distinguishes Montferrand's design.

The Neo-Renaissance Style

Even as the Alexander Column took its place, the final design of Palace Square was underway. After an unsuccessful competition in 1827 for the Building of the Guards Staff (Ton, Rossi, Stasov, Alexander Briullov, and Montferrand all submitted proposals), the renewed project was given to Briullov in 1837.[50] His design pays homage to the classical ambience established by Rossi, yet the main facade, with its attached Ionic columns, has more to do with the seventeenth-century French baroque than with Russian neoclassicism. The heavy cornice, the diffusion of the center (the main accents are the two-story portals on either end), and the ornamentation of the lower floors all demonstrate the mixture of styles characteristic of early eclecticism. To be sure, Briullov, whose Gothic Revival designs have been noted earlier, was one of the best proponents of the new eclecticism with a Renaissance cast. This is demonstrated in his reconstruction of the service building for the Marble Palace (1844–7; Figure 534), which involved the adding of a third story and providing the stuccoed brick facades with a mixture of Renaissance and classicizing detail.[51]

The concluding element in the Hermitage ensemble along Palace Quay is also one of the most distinguished examples of the new eclecticism. Located between the Old Hermitage and the Guards Staff building, the New Hermitage (1839–51; Figure 535) was commissioned by Nicholas as an extension to the exhibit space of the Hermitage complex – indeed, it was the first building in Russia designed specifically as a public museum for a major art collection.[52] Its architect, Leo von Klenze, was reknowned for his design of the Grecian-style Glyptothek, or museum of sculpture, in Munich (1816–34); but he was also worked in the Renaissance style, which he adopted for the New Hermitage. Within this framework, he placed classical elements that reflected the building's purpose, such as statues in facade niches of notable artists of ancient Greece and Renaissance Italy (by Johann Halbig). The main (south) facade also con-

Figure 534. Service building of the Marble Palace. Petersburg. 1844–7. Architect: Alexander Briullov. (P 41–1)

tained terra-cotta and bronze reliefs produced by the galvanostatic method, earlier applied at St. Isaac's Cathedral. The windows of the upper story are divided by granite herms, and the museum culminates in a cornice decorated with iron ornament and two pavilions above the projecting wings on each end. The most striking feature of the main facade is the portico, with ten massive gray granite atlantes, sculpted by Alexander Terebenev and 150 "peasant" assistants.[53]

The interior is organized around a stairway of majestic design and proportions, faced with yellow faux marbre and flanked on the upper level by gray granite Corinthian columns. The lower floor, composed of four enfilades forming a quadrangle, is devoted primarily to statuary and the plastic arts, and its larger halls have elaborately vaulted or coffered ceilings in both Renaissance and antique styles. On the upper level, the staircase leads to the Gallery of the History of Ancient Painting, composed of nine quadrilaterals with domed vaults containing relief medallions of prominent artists (including Klenze himself) on the pendentives (Figure 536). The walls contain scenes depicting the development of painting among the ancients, around which are painted arabesques in the manner of Raphael. The construction of the New Hermitage necessitated the demolition of Quarenghi's Raphael Loggia; but all of the decorative work of the Loggia gallery was preserved and reassembled on the same site along the east facade (overlooking the Winter Canal) in the new building. The other rooms of the upper floor are richly decorated in polychrome and gilt, including intricately carved grotesques in lavish array for the central exhibition halls with skylights.

Figure 535. New Hermitage. Petersburg. 1839–52. Architect: Leo von Klenze. (P 36–2)

Although the neo-Renaissance monuments could not rival the baroque and neoclassical ensembles of Petersburg, they complemented both major styles, and continued urban planning in an era that lacked a dominant architectural aesthetic. A notable example of this extension was the building of the Nicholas Railway Station (1843–51; Figure 537), terminus of the first Russian long-distance rail line, connecting Moscow and Petersburg. Nicholas was an avid proponent of railway development (a reflection of his interest in engineering and technology), and the station, located on Nevskii Prospekt at the intersection with the old Novgorod road, was allotted a major place in the urban fabric, facing a newly designed square (Znamenskii, after the Church of the Icon of the Sign built by Fedor Demertsov at the beginning of the nineteenth century; not extant).

The design of the station, by Konstantin Ton, fol-

lowed the Renaissance manner, yet symbolically reflected architectural elements of both cities. The ground floor is arcaded, with double-arched window bays similar to those used by Ton for the Great Kremlin Palace. Although intended as an emblem of medieval Muscovy, the double-arched bay was in fact imported by Fioravanti for the west porch of the Dormition Cathedral and subsequently widely used by Russian architects in the form of a decorative pendant.[54] The upper level of the station proclaims its allegiance to Petersburg, with attached columns and a baroque cornice in the style of Rastrelli, as well as a campanile resembling that for the city hall on Nevskii Prospekt (1799–1804; architect: Giacomo Ferrari). Ton constructed a companion station for the Moscow terminus – similar in scale, but in mediocre imitation of Petersburg classicism. The station sheds, as well as all other buildings along the Moscow–Petersburg

Plate 49. Church of the Deposition of the Robe on Don Street. Moscow. 1702. Southeast view.

Plate 50. Church of St. John the Warrior. Moscow. 1709–17. Southwest view.

Plate 51. Church of the Archangel Gabriel (Menshikov Tower). Moscow. 1701–7. Southwest view.

Plate 52. Gate Church of the Tikhvin Mother of God, Donskoi Monastery. Moscow. 1713–14. South view.

Plate 53. Cathedral of Sts. Peter and Paul, Peter-Paul Fortress. St. Petersburg. 1712–32. Architect: Domenico Trezzini. Southwest view.

Plate 54. Cathedral of Sts. Peter and Paul, Peter-Paul Fortress. Iconostasis by Ivan Zarudnyi.

Plate 55. Church of the Annunciation, Alexander Nevskii Monastery. Petersburg. 1717–22. Architects: Domenico Trezzini and Theodor Schwertfeger. Northwest view.

Plate 56. The Academy of Sciences (left). 1783–9. Architect: Giacomo Quarenghi. The Kunstkammer (right).
1718–34. Architect: Georg Johann Mattarnovy. Vasilevskii Island Quay, Neva River. Petersburg.

Plate 57. The Great Palace and Samson Fountain. Peterhof.
North facade.

Plate 58. Catherine Palace. Tsarskoe Selo. 1748–56. Architect: Bartolomeo Francesco Rastrelli. Park facade.

Plate 59. Winter Palace. Petersburg. 1754–64. Architect: Bartolomeo Francesco Ras[...] Square facade.

Plate 60. Church of St. Andrew. Kiev. 1747–67. Architect: Bartolomeo Francesco Rastrelli, with the assistance of Ivan Michurin. Southwest view.

Plate 61. Cathedral of the Resurrection, Smolnyi Convent. Petersburg. 1748–64. Architect: Bartolomeo Francesco Rastrelli. West facade.

Plate 62. Cathedral of St. Nicholas. Petersburg. 1753–62. Architect: Savva Chevakinskii. West facade.

Plate 63. Cathedral of St. Nicholas, bell tower. 1756–8. Architect: Savva Chevakinskii. East silhouette.

Plate 64. Trinity–St. Sergius Monastery. Bell tower: 1741–70. Architect: Dmitrii Ukhtomskii. Southeast view.

line, were designed by Rudolf Zheliazevich.[55]

The social and economic changes underway in Russia, even before the reign of Alexander II and the liberation of the serfs, provided a major impetus for the construction of functional urban buildings. Perhaps the most visible product of this transformation, apart from railway stations, was the shopping arcade, or "passage." Zheliazevich, for example, adopted the neo-Renaissance style for the famous Passage on Nevskii Prospekt (1846–8).[56] The pioneer for such structures in Russia, however, was Mikhail Bykovskii, who in 1835 had designed a "bazar" modeled on the Palais Royale, or the Passage du Grand Cerf (1824–6) in Paris. In 1840–1, he implemented this design for a passage commissioned by the entrepreneur Mikhail Golitsyn in the fashionable shopping district of Kuznetskii Bridge. Known as the Golitsyn Passage, the two-story structure with twenty-four shops and walkways covered by a skylight, combined neoclassical

Figure 537. Nicholas Station. Petersburg. 1843–51. Architect: Konstantin Ton. (P 85–2)

with Renaissance details, and amazed contemporaries with its innovation and convenience.[57]

The growth of the urban population that stimulated a new tempo of construction in commerce and housing also stimulated the building of new theaters, for which the premier architect was Albert Kavos, who had worked with Rossi on the construction of the Alexandrine Theater. In 1855, he rebuilt the Bolshoi Theater in Moscow (see Figure 501) after a fire in 1853 that gutted the structure. In Petersburg, he constructed in 1848 a large wooden building that contained both a circus ring and a theater stage – an intriguing but awkward arrangement. After it burned in 1859, he designed a luxuriously decorated opera house that opened in 1860 and was subsequently named the Mariinskii (after Maria, wife of Alexander II). This theater, with its extensive wooden construction, was remodeled in 1883–6 by Viktor Shreter, who added a surfeit of ornament to the more restrained, neo-Renaissance facades by Kavos that is still visible in the upper part of the structure (Figure 538).[58]

Shtakenshneider

Although the postneoclassical era witnessed the displacement of the imperial design in architecture by an eclecticism directed by other economic and social forces, the reign of Nicholas also initiated the last major phase of palace construction in Petersburg. The architect who directed this undertaking, Andrei Shtakenshneider, lacked the genius of the great imperial architects of the preceding century, but he skil-

Figure 536. New Hermitage. Petersburg. Gallery of Ancient Painting. Architect: Leo von Klenze. (P 91–18)

Figure 538. Mariinskii Theater. Petersburg. 1859–60. Architect: Albert Kavos. Rebuilt 1883–6 by Viktor Shreter. (P 84–11)

fully exploited the possibilities of eclecticism to produce a blend of the neo-Renaissance and neo-baroque. He was educated at the Academy of Arts and entered his career under the direction of Montferrand. In the 1830s, he, like Rossi before him, received commissions for designs in the "Russian" style, the most delightful of which was the stylized peasant log house at Peterhof – the so-called Nikolskii house (1833–5; not extant).[59]

Other exercises in the Russian style included a large project to rebuild the palace at Kolomenskoe; but after a year's travel in Europe in 1837 (at the expense of the court), Shtakenshneider returned to a period of intensive construction for his royal patrons in Petersburg. His first project was the Mariinskii Palace (1839–44; Figure 539) built for the grand duchess Maria Nikolaevich on the opposite side of St. Isaac's Square from the cathedral. It is a conservative design, relying heavily on the precedent of neoclassicism (as did the the cathedral), with its Corinthian columns and pilasters. Yet there are fundamental differences with neoclassicism.[60] Although the center of the building is clearly defined, it lacks the emphasis an earlier architect would have created by means of a pediment (instead of an attic) and by highlighting tectonic elements in white on a pastel background. The reaction against the bichromatic system of facade decoration is typical of the eclectic period in Petersburg, partic-

ularly in its imitation of the masonry monuments of Renaissance Italy. Indeed, for the facade, Shtakenshneider used a local reddish-brown sandstone, considered easier to maintain than stucco over brick. Other Renaissance motifs appear in the ornamental details, and the general design is perhaps most indebted to the seventeenth-century French baroque. The interior design follows the eclectic practice of decorating each main room in a different style.

For his next major commission – the rebuilding of a palace for Prince K. E. Beloselskii-Belozerskii on Nevskii Prospekt (1846–8), Shtakenshneider turned to Rastrelli for his inspiration.[61] Although considerably smaller than the imperial palaces, the monumental detail of the two-storied facade imposes its order on the surrounding space at the Anichkov Bridge. Like the Stroganov Palace, on which it is so obviously modeled, the building faces two main public spaces: Nevskii and a major canal – in this instance, the Fontanka. The plasticity of Rastrelli's cornice and pediment designs is replaced with a softer, curved pediment over the mezzanine at the center of each facade, but Shtakenshneider's elan appeared fully in his choice of a deep-red facade as a background for the neo-baroque detail.

Shtakenshneider returned to imperial palace construction in Petersburg in the early 1850s: first, the construction of the Nikolaevskii Palace (1853–61) for

406

Figure 539. Mariinskii Palace. Petersburg. 1839–44. Architect: Andrei Shtakenshneider. (P 119–15)

grand duke Nikolai Nikolaevich. The large three-storied structure is one of his most austere designs, and exemplifies the horizontality and diffusion of tectonic emphasis in eclecticism, especially in its neo-Renaissance form. Cornices separate each floor and emphasize the second, or bel etage, which contains a series of small balconies.[62]

The New Mikhailovskii Palace is an altogether more exuberant piece of work, combining different stylistic elements. Built in 1857–61 on Palace Quay for grand duke Mikhail Nikolaevich, the structure (Figure 540) is horizontally segmented by string courses into three floors in a manner similar to that of the Nikolaevskii Palace, under construction at the same time. The latter was built on an exposed location that permitted perception in three dimensions; but although the New Mikhailovskii Palace lacked this visual depth, the architect compensated by designing a central projection with attached Corinthian columns, caryatids, and a plethora of cornices and pediments. The statuary was sculpted in terra-cotta by David Jensen, one of Shtakenshneider's closest collaborators.[63] The interior was decorated in the typical fashion for eclectic clutter. The second-floor state rooms, each in a different style, are particularly lavish, including the grand Salon in a neo-rococo style.

While the construction of the Nikolaevskii and New Mikhailovskii Palaces was underway, Shtakenshnei-der indulged his eclecticism in a redesign of many of the Hermitage interiors. The most spectacular result was the Pavilion Hall of the north pavilion of the Small Hermitage (1850–8), which overlooked the Neva River on one side and a terrace garden (converted by Shtakenshneider into a conservatory) on the other. The hall is a masterpiece of space and light, with white marble Corinthian columns, walls of white faux marbre, and gilt decoration intensifying the effect of the light from the windows on the north and south facades. Indeed, the perimeter of the hall is defined by two-storied arcades, including a double arcade that supports a passageway over the hall (Figure 541) and connects arcaded galleries on the upper floor at each end. Within the south portion of the hall, whose floor contains a mosaic copy of a floor from the baths at Ocriculum, the east wall contains a semirotunda niche framed by columns of gray–green marble, and the west opens to a marble staircase leading to the galleries.[64] Shtakenshneider's mixture of Renaissance, neoclassical, and Roman elements here attains a unified aesthetic environment that astounds the millions of visitors that pass through the space.

During the same period (1851–9), Shtakenshneider undertook an extensive remodeling of the adjacent Old Hermitage for use by the royal heir (after the opening of the New Hermitage, a large part of the art collection was reinstalled, thus freeing the old building for other uses). Among the accomplishments of this work was the Sovet Staircase, so named because of its use by the state council, or *sovet*. The centerpiece of Shtakenshneider's design, however, was the two-storied Great Hall (now the Hall of Leonardo da Vinci), which overlooks the Neva River from the bel etage and was part of two parallel enfilades – one for state rooms and the other for living quarters.[65] The dimensions of the room are enhanced by walls of white faux marbre, edged with strips of light green and pink marble. The attached Corinthian columns and pilasters that segment the room are of veined gray Italian marble on high bases of dark-red porphyry. Gilt is liberally applied to the architectural details, including the molded coffers of the ceiling, whose cross beams are supported by herms. The august state functions of the room – before its reconversion to museum use – are signified by relief medallions (sculpted by Jensen) of six Russian generals, including Suvorov, Kutuzov, and Potemkin.

If the major part of Shtakenshneider's work occurred as a result of his imperial commissions within Petersburg, his most interesting designs were created on a more modest scale in the 1840s and 1850s for the suburban estate of Peterhof. In style, most of these pavilions represent variations on Italian villas, and they were situated overlooking the ponds in Peterhof's system of natural parks. All of these pavilions were destroyed or severely damaged during World War II, and only the Belvedere (1851–6) – a variation on a Greek temple, with polychrome walls and a peristyle on the second floor – has been restored to an approximation of its original form.[66]

As in the preceding century, transformations in the

Figure 540. New Mikhailovskii Palace. Petersburg. 1857–61. Architect: Andrei Shtakenshneider. (P 34–8a)

style of palace architecture were reflected in the design of private mansions during the middle third of the nineteenth century. Among the many eclectic examples, two adjacent houses by Montferrand serve as landmarks in the early stages of this development. In 1836, he designed a house for the industrialist Pavel Demidov on Morskaia Street, a block from St. Isaac's Square. From the base of gray granite and the massively rusticated stucco walls to the caryatids (or terms) supporting the central balcony, the ponderous neo-baroque facade of the Demidov house signaled the increasingly common alliance between flamboyant architecture and wealthy patrons.[67]

A more innovative design is Montferrand's reconstruction, in 1835–40, of the adjacent house, also owned by Demidov and acquired by Princess V. F. Gagarina in the 1870s.[68] Instead of the typical Petersburg town house with facade flush to the street, Montferrand designed an urban villa, with a narrow setback structure of two stories and a terrace over the carriage entrance to the courtyard. The front of the house continues as a high one-story arcaded facade, whose center is marked by attached columns and an attic frieze – also reflecting the cultural pretentions of Demidov. By the middle of the century, the neo-baroque style had triumphed, if briefly, as an expression of wealth and fashion, leading to such extremes as the mansion for Princess Z. I. Iusupova on Liteinyi Prospekt (1852–8; Figure 542), designed by Harald Bosse and Ludwig Bonstedt. The interior was decorated with the characteristic spume of stucco and gilt.[69]

In contrast to these Petersburg effusions was Nikolai Nikitin's use of the Russian vernacular style in his design of the Pogodin *Izba*, or "hut," (1850s) for the suburban Moscow estate of the historian and writer Mikhail Pogodin. Pogodin was an ardent supporter of "official nationality," as well as a collector of historical relics, and the choice of style demonstrated the romantic concept that architecture could revive a sense of the national identity and link traditional Russian culture to a new cultural environment.[70] Nikitin, who would later serve as first secretary of the Moscow Architectural Society, created a stylized interpretation of a square log cottage, decorated with carved bargeboards and window surrounds (Figure 543). The Russian vernacular style had been used earlier by Rossi and Shtakenshneider as a stylistic caprice in the suburbs of Petersburg; but in Moscow, Pogodin's reputation as a distinguished specialist of Russian history and a professor at Moscow University endowed the structure with a cultural significance out of proportion to its modest size.

Figure 541. Small Hermitage, Pavilion Hall. Petersburg. 1850–8. Architect: Andrei Shtakenshneider. (P 37–1)

Although the monarchist Pogodin was roundly condemned by "progressive" forces, he, too, subscribed to the idealized notion of the Russian folk, expressed in its culture and artifacts. Indeed, the study of history merged with a study of medieval Russian architecture, which after decades of neglect seemed to bear vivid witness to the nation's past at a time of momentous changes.[71]

After the Reforms: Architecture and the New Urbanism

The era of reforms that began with the liberation of the serfs in 1861 gave new impetus to a process of reconstruction in Russia's largest cities. With the expanded role of private capital and the need to build for an increasingly populous and economically complex urban setting, the state bureacracy and the imperial court lost their preeminence as the source of major architectural commissions.[72] Although this transformation did not begin with the reign of Alex-

ander II, his social policies of the 1860s and the Great Reforms provided the underpinnings for an enlarged economically rational use of architectural resources as well as for the development of professional organizations – from training institutes to architectural societies – to define and regulate the practice of architecture in a period of unprecedented growth.[73]

The new professionalization of architecture accompanied an increased demand for architects competent to construct a variety of buildings (primarily for commercial exploitation in cities) for a diverse clientele in a cost-effective, reliable way that also, when necessary, met certain aesthetic expectations. In this respect, Russian architects followed a path familiar to their counterparts in Britain, France, and Germany.[74] Expanded opportunity, however, failed to foster the climate of excellence associated with earlier imperial architecture, in part because of a more "democratic" environment in which the buildings commissioned were very different from those built with lavish subsidies by the court. Here, again, Russia reflected the broader stylistic confusion in European architecture during the nineteenth century.[75]

Indeed, the more advanced economic powers of western and central Europe provided a model for architectural innovation in Russia. Many Russian architects continued to tour and study abroad after formal studies in their homeland. And Russian architectural schools, like their counterparts in the west, underwent reforms intended to improve the technical aspects of architectural training (cf. Eugene Viollet-le-Duc's 1863 program for curricular reform at the Ecole des Beaux-Arts in Paris). Architectural education at schools such as the Academy of Arts and the Institute of Civil Engineering in Petersburg and the Moscow School of Painting, Sculpture, and Architecture owed much to comparable institutions in Berlin and Paris.[76]

With rising, if fitful, investment, Russian architecture made impressive progress in meeting new social and economic needs, with results that are very much in evidence today. Among the innovative structures were shopping arcades (or *passages*), large enclosed markets, educational institutions, banks and other financial institutions, hospitals, public theaters, exhibit halls, hotels, and city administrative buildings (the result of a limited extension of local governmental authority in the later part of the century). The intensive construction of railway stations during the 1840s and 1850s continued in Moscow and Petersburg throughout the following decades as new lines opened and some of the early stations were demolished to make way for grander structures. The

Figure 542. Zinaida Iusupova house. Petersburg. 1852–8. Architects: Harold Bosse and Ludwig Bonshtedt. (P 66–16)

Figure 543. Pogodin izba. Moscow. 1850s. Architect: Nikolai Nikitin. (M 74–4)

which had less usable land than Moscow. According to the census of 1881, 19 percent of Petersburg's houses had one story, 42 percent two stories, 21 percent three stories, and 18 percent four stories.[79] The rows of apartment blocks dating from the 1860s to the beginning of the century give an impression of stylistic chaos, mitigated by a more or less uniform building height.

The more prosperous the area, the more saturated with decoration the building facades. Every major architectural style was imitated or paraphrased on the facades of commercial and housing structures in Petersburg during the later part of the nineteenth century: neo-Renaissance, neo-baroque, neo-Greek, Louis XVI, Russian Revival, and Moorish. Mixed or unrecognizable styles, however, may have predominated. The primary building materials of brick and stucco could be adapted readily to florid architectural ornamentation, as new imperial residences and houses for the nouveau riche began to resemble one another.

A notable example of the former is the Palace of Grand Prince Vladimir Alexandrovich (Figure 544), constructed in 1867–72 by Alexander Rezanov along with Andrei Huhn, Ieronim Kitner, and Viktor Shreter, all of whom were to play major roles in late nineteenth-century architecture. The exterior of the palace is in the style of the early Florentine Renaissance, but the grand rooms ranged from Louis XVI to Gothic to Moorish and at least four other period styles, with wall paintings by Vasilii Vereshchagin.[80] Not only does the palace resemble the luxurious private dwellings along the quay where it is situated, but

increasing needs of industry – notably, the metal-working factories – encouraged the development of engineering techniques for the design of large enclosed interiors.[77] Similar techniques were applied to railway platform sheds. In addition to cast-iron columns, long in use, more flexible iron beams and girders became essential in building large truss-supported roofs over unobstructed work space.

During the post-Reform decades, when the population of both Moscow and Petersburg grew rapidly, the greatest need was for housing. Petersburg, with not quite 500,000 inhabitants in 1858, increased to 667,000 in 1869; 861,000 in 1881; and 954,000 in 1890.[78] The rate of growth rose even more rapidly thereafter. The increase in the number and size of apartment buildings was particualry impressive in Petersburg,

Figure 544. Palace of Grand Prince Vladimir Aleksandrovich. Petersburg. 1867–72. Main architect: Alexander Rezanov. (P 34–8)

Figure 545. Porokhovshchikov house. Moscow. 1872. Architect: Andrei Huhn. (M 150–34)

it was also built with much the same attention to cost and materials: the rustication was stucco and many details were cast in portland cement.[81] As the proliferation of eclectic buildings increased, so did architectural criticism by both amateurs and professionals, in lay as well as professional publications. Much of the architectural commentary of the period questions the subordination of style to financial considerations.[82]

In Moscow, the effects of architectural fashion during the post-Reform era were less pronounced. Although Moscow grew as rapidly as Petersburg – between the early 1860s and 1897, the population of the city proper more than doubled, from approximately 400,000 to almost 980,000 – and its economic growth continued during these decades,[83] the effects were less noticeable there. Moscow covered a greater area and had both fewer government institutions and a smaller population (Petersburg in 1881 had 861,000 inhabitants; Moscow in 1882 had 753,000). As a result, Moscow's architects did not confront the intensely commercial demands made on those in Petersburg, who designed blocks of speculative buildings, densely constructed and saturated with facade ornamentation.

To be sure, eclecticism and historicism also pervaded Moscow; but historicist designs there focused on medieval, pre-Petrine architectural monuments in the city, from the Kremlin and Red Square to the churches in every neighborhood. The ready adaptation of the idioms of medieval Muscovy to the city's architecture during the 1870s and 1880s – stimulated by the historical displays at the 1872 Polytechnic Exhibition and the 1880 All-Russian Arts and Industry Exhibition (both held in Moscow) – frequently led to the saturated application of decorative motifs from the sixteenth and seventeenth centuries.

Among the examples of the wooden vernacular style in Moscow during the 1870s, Andrei Huhn's house for the Moscow merchant Alexander Porokhovshchikov (1872) is notable for recreating the decorative and structural elements of traditional wooden architecture, albeit with inside plumbing (Figure 545).[84] The style here, as in the Pogodin Hut (see Figure 543), had an underlying logic. Porokhovshchikov was a leading member of the Slavic Committee, formed to support the liberation of the Balkan

411

Slavs from Turkish rule and, coincidentally, to extend Russian influence into the area under the guise of Pan-Slavism.[85] As a major contributor to the nationalist cause, Porokhovshchikov presumably chose the traditional Russian style as a programmatic statement. Yet Huhn was working concurrently with Rezanov in Petersburg on the Palace of Vladimir Alexandrovich, defined by a very different assortment of borrowed styles.

The cultural implications of the revival of pre-Petrine architectural styles during the 1870s and 1880s gave the architecture of Moscow more aesthetic coherence and direction than that of Petersburg, where the bureaucracy distrusted the Pan-Slav movement and where few examples existed of either vernacular or pre-Petrine Russian architecture. In addition, with more land available, architects in Moscow designed structures with a depth and plasticity suggestive of medieval architecture. These qualities, combined with the cultural mission reflected in the Russian revival, helped to shape Moscow's major buildings during the final decades of the century.

Among them, the Historical Museum (1874–83) is the most imposing (Figure 546). Both the collection and the impetus to house it derived from the Polytechnical Exhibition of 1872, many of whose display pavilions were located near the eventual site of the museum.[86] The museum was to express Russian historical consciousness on a site in the shadow of the Kremlin walls – an intention clearly conveyed in the announcement of the project.[87] The winner of the competition to design the Historical Museum was Vladimir Shervud (sherwood; of English descent), a graduate, in 1857, of the Moscow School of Painting and Sculpture. During his early years as an art student, he became acquainted with a group of Moscow intellectuals and artists identified with the Slavophile movement, among them Iurii Samarin, Mikhail Pogodin, Nikolai Gogol, and Ivan Shevyrev. Shervud's account of his meetings with this group reveals that he, too, came to advocate a renewed Russian sense of identity derived from traditional sources and reinterpreted in the arts.[88]

His design is a two-dimensional gloss on sixteenth- and seventeenth-century decorative motifs. Because the museum was located on an elongated site at the northwest entrance to Red Square, with relatively narrow passages on both sides, it has one main facade facing Red Square and another facing Okhotnyi Riad at the exit from Red Square. In Shervud's design, each facade is a balanced surface, with projecting porches and towers and medieval decorative elements in bold relief. The same pedagogic spirit pervades the interior

halls, designed and decorated by a collective of artists (including Viktor Vasnetsov) and historians, who chose decorative motifs from the various ages of Russian history and even prehistory.[89] The structural work and interior plan were supervised by the engineer Anatolii Semenov, who had served as secretary of the Moscow Architectural Society in 1871–2.

Under pressure to create an emblem of national identity, Shervud had incorporated as many historical references as possible. The result, fragmented and busy with detail, contrasts with the Kremlin towers, austerely monumental, and Saint Basil's, which has a complex centralized plan. Even by the standards of Shervud's contemporaries, the symmetrical adaptation of Russian motifs is cautious when compared to the work of Ivan Ropet (Petrov) and Viktor Hartman, whose buildings and published designs did much to propagate the revived Russian style during the latter part of the century (Figure 547). Many of their most interesting designs were large temporary wooden structures for fairs and exhibitions, such as the People's Theater by Hartman at the 1872 exhibition. The architects' drawings reveal the freedom with which they incorporated traditional Russian decorative elements into asymmetrical plans resembling those of pre-Petrine architecture.[90] Yet for all the rigidity of Shervud's interpretation of architecture as national identity, the Historical Museum succeeds as an imposing counterweight to the other monuments on Red Square.

The Brick Style and Rational Architecture

The Historical Museum also demonstrated a renewed appreciation for the aesthetic properties of unsurfaced brick. Earlier exposed-brick structures of the nineteenth century in Petersburg and Moscow were usually utilitarian (e.g., Peter Tamanskii's Kronwerk for the Peter–Paul Fortress). With the major exception of pseudo-Gothic structures by Bazhenov and Kazakov, brick buildings of any importance in Moscow were stuccoed, as they had been since the beginning of the eighteenth century in Petersburg. Before the time of Peter the Great, however, Moscow's brick churches and secular structures were often painted or whitewashed, but the texture of the brick remained visible.

After the completion of the Historical Museum, a number of unstuccoed brick buildings arose in Moscow, such as Mikhail Chichagov's design for the Korsh Theater (1884–5). Chichagov made sensible use of Russian decorative and structural elements (such

Figure 546. Historical Museum. Moscow. 1874–83. Architect: Vladimir Shervud. South facade. (M 104–2)

413

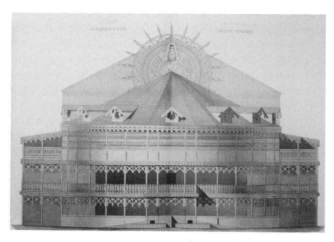

Figure 547. People's Theater for 1872 Polytechnic Exhibition. Moscow. Architect: Viktor Hartmann. *Motivy russkoi arkhitektury, 1875.* Courtesy of the Library of Congress.

as the pointed decorative gable, or *kokoshnik*), but also exploited the plasticity of brick to emphasize the depth of his building and its mildly asymmetrical distribution of shapes (Figure 548). To be sure, there were buildings in the Russian revival style whose decorative motifs were applied on a smooth facade of stuccoed brick. The design work for the Polytechnic Museum (1873–7) – another institution whose origins were linked to the 1872 exhibition – like that for the Historical Musuem, was divided between the architect of the facade, Ippolit Monighetti, and the structural engineer, Nikolai Shokhin (Figure 549).[91]

Although the use of red brick in Moscow was initially justified by its association with medieval structures, the material also appeared in more rational and less ornamental ways. By the turn of the century, Moscow architects such as Lev Kekushev and Fedor Shekhtel would use the unobstructed brick surface as a primary aesthetic medium of the style moderne. In the 1870s, however, Petersburg had the strongest advocates of a "brick style" that related structure to aesthetics. Although most of the city's nonindustrial structures maintained the local tradition of applying stucco over brick, the very lack of medieval monuments freed architects to use brick without the colorful pseudo-historical ornament used in Moscow.

One of the leading proponents of the use of brick was Viktor Shreter, who advocated brick without stucco as a durable, rational, and economical material.[92] In addition, Shreter demonstrated by using different colors of brick in decorative patterns that it need not be monotonous. In propagating the brick style, Shreter was joined by Ieronim Kitner, who used the term "rational" to connote qualities opposed to the

eclectic decoration of stuccoed buildings.[93] Although for Kitner and Shreter the meaning of the "rational" cannot be equated with the rationalism of the 1920s (in the work of Nikolai Ladovskii and others), the proponents of the brick style in the late 1870s appreciated the relation between the functional and aesthetic qualities of such materials as brick, iron, and glass.[94]

The disparate views of rationalism are particularly evident in the career of Nikolai Sultanov, who was a dedicated student of medieval Russian architecture and felt that it best represented the national genius. Like many Russian intellectuals of his time, he related his professional practice to broader social and cultural questions. In a speech delivered in 1882 at the opening of a new building for the Construction School (now the Institute of Civil Engineering), Sultanov called for spiritual values transcending the material, and praised the "Russian style" (with its practical reliance on brick) as a means to a national and rational architecture: "The new national movement does not contradict our banner – that of the rational movement – but actually coincides with it."[95] Despite the dichotomy between historicism and functionalism, there could be little doubt by the end of the nineteenth century that the building of large commercial and industrial structures – whatever the style of facade – required a reliance on technology and on the collaboration between the architects and engineers produced in ever greater numbers by professional schools.[96]

Architecture for Commerce

In this respect, as in many others, the rebuilding of the Upper Trading Rows was a turning point in Russian architectural history, not only because it represented the apogee of the expression of the Russian Revival style, but also because it demanded advanced functional technology on a scale unprecedented in Russian civil architecture. The site, facing the Kremlin, had been occupied by a neoclassical trading arcade constructed by Osip Bove after the 1812 fire; but by the 1860s, it had fallen into disrepair.[97] Not until November 1888 did the Society of City Trading Rows, a private company formed to rebuild the complex, announce a design competition; the winning proposal was by Alexander Pomerantsev, an academician at the Academy of Arts in Petersburg.

Pomerantsev derived his plan from the galleria, or *passage*, which had been used elsewhere in Europe (particularly in Milan) as well as in Russia for fashionable retail trade throughout the nineteenth century.[98] But nothing equalled the size of the new Upper Trading Rows, with its 1,000 to 1,200 shops for retail and wholesale trade (Figure 550). Although the design of this many units with proper access, illumination, and ventilation required a commitment to new technological methods, the location of the Trading Rows demanded a structure whose style would reflect that of the historic monuments on Red Square.[99]

Like Shervud, Pomerantsev organized the facade decoration in a balanced scheme, here dominated at the main entrance by two symmetrical towers in the style of the Kremlin walls. The Historical Museum had the compositional advantage of a relatively narrow main facade, in contrast to that of the Trading Rows, which extends for 242 meters. Pomerantsev delineated the space with a sharply molded string course between the floors to emphasize horizontality and to separate the layers of window surrounds and arches. On the main facade, each level is a different type of stone: red Finnish granite, Tarussa marble, and limestone – all capped with a massive cornice.[100]

Considerable ingenuity was required, however, to reconcile the historicist facade with the commercial function of the interior – which, it should be noted, readily dispensed with the Russian style in favor of Italian Renaissance detail for the three parallel arcades that extend the length of the complex (Figure 551). Each arcade has three levels, with rows of shops on the first and second and offices on the third. Walkways of reinforced concrete (possibly the first use of this technique in Russia) span each gallery on the second and third levels; in addition, the arcades are connected at each end and in the middle. Illumination

Figure 549. Polytechnic Museum. Moscow. 1873–7. Architects: Ippolit Monighetti and Nikolai Sultanov. (M 166–24)

is provided by arched skylights (Figure 552) whose design ranks among the remarkable achievements of civil engineering in Russia during the nineteenth century.[101]

The genius behind this union of the aesthetic and the functional was Vladimir Shukhov (1853–1939), one of the most versatile of Russia's civil engineers. After graduating from Moscow's Technical School in 1876, Shukhov spent several months in the United States. Although little is known about his itinerary, it no doubt gave him the opportunity to study examples of American construction technology.[102] In 1878, he moved to Moscow, where he specialized in designing metal constructions; and by the time of the Trading Rows competition, he had acquired a reputation for technical expertise in fields as diverse as bridge construction, petroleum engineering, and the design of large metal-frame arched roofs. His later fame rests primarily on his metal "webbed" towers, including the water tower for the 1896 Nizhnii Novgorod Exhibition and a 160-meter radio tower in the Shabolovka district of Moscow. At the 1896 exhibition, he also built two large pavilions that represent not only a daring use of metal-frame construction – and possibly the first use of a metal-membrane roof – but also structures of remarkable aesthetic appeal (Figures 553 and 554).

That the enormous structure of the Upper Trading Rows functioned, if imperfectly, is a tribute both to Shukhov's design and to the technical proficiency of Russian architecture toward the end of the century. Yet despite these impressive resources, the Upper Trading Rows, with its encrustation of historical motifs, revealed a disjunction between the national style and the rational, functional demands of modern ur-

Figure 548. Korsh Theater. Moscow. 1884–5. Architect: Mikhail Chichagov. (M 133–33)

Figure 550. Upper Trading Rows. Moscow. 1889–93. Architect:
Aleksandr Pomerantsev. (M 166–30)

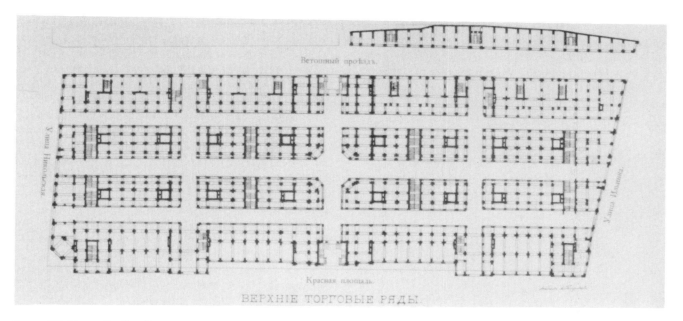

Figure 551. Upper Trading Rows. Moscow. Plan.

416

ban architecture. As a result of the divergence of style and function, only the upper galleries benefited fully from Shukhov's design in glass and iron; the lower level of shops (more desirable in commercial terms) lacked proper light and ventilation.

The shortcomings of the Upper Trading Rows did not, however, discourage another major commercial project in the pseudo-Russian style: the Middle Trading Rows (1890–1), next to the Upper Rows on land that slopes down from Red Square to the Moscow River (Figure 555). The architect was Roman Klein, who had placed second in the competition for the Upper Rows and became one of the most productive architects in Moscow at the turn of the century. After studying for 2 years at the Moscow School of Painting, Sculpture, and Architecture, he worked as a drafts-

Figure 554. Elliptical pavilion, 1896 Nizhnii Novgorod Exhibition. Engineer: Vladimir Shukhov. Architect: V. A. Nossov. Interior. *Vidy rabot proizvedenykh stroitelnoi firmy Bari na vserossiiskoi vystavke 1896 v N. Novgorode.*

Figure 552. Upper Trading Rows, central passage. Moscow. (M 160–6)

Figure 553. Round Pavilion, Construction and Engineering Section, 1896 Nizhnii Novgorod Exhibition. Engineer: Vladimir Shukhov. Architect: V. A. Nossov. *Vidy rabot proizvedenykh stroitelnoi firmy Bari na vserossiiskoi vystavke 1896 v N. Novgorode.*

man for Shervud on the Historical Museum and then proceeded to Petersburg, where he studied at the Academy of Arts between 1877–82. On graduating, he traveled to Italy and France, where he worked for a time in the studio of Charles Garnier, creator of the building for the Paris Opera. When he returned to Russia in the mid–1880s, he eventually resettled in Moscow, the center of his activity for the next three decades.[103] The Middle Trading Rows follow the decorative patterns of the other buildings on Red Square, but with less ornamental saturation. The large wall surface, however, admits little natural light into the structure, which has no skylight design comparable to the Upper Trading Rows.[104]

In the same central area of the city, the Moscow

417

Figure 555. Middle Trading Rows. Moscow. 1890–1. Architect: Roman Klein. (M 166–33)

city government undertook what was to be the city's last major exercise in the Russian style, the city hall, or *duma*. The project had long been under discussion – since the early 1870s, when Alexander Rezanov and Andrei Huhn, then completing work on the Palace of Vladimir Alexandrovich in Petersburg, presented the first design proposal, for a fanciful recreation of the pseudo-Russian style in the manner of Hartman and Ropet.[105] The revival of plans for the Duma building in 1886 initiated a series of design competitions that demonstrated the difficulty of reconciling pressures for a "Russian" style with architects' concepts of structure and purpose. Dmitrii Chichagov (the brother of Mikhail Chichagov, who designed the Korsh Theater in the national style) was one of three architects asked to submit facade designs, but the influential Archaeological Society declared them incompatible with a genuine Russian style.[106] A new proposal by Chichagov, acceptable to the society, did not please the Duma. After subsequent competitions,

Chichagov was finally authorized to begin construction in 1890.

Such interference in the design process may explain why Chichagov applied Russian decorative elements mechanically on the large Duma building (Figure 556), in contrast to his brother Mikhail's skillful distribution of such elements on the smaller Korsh Theater. Medieval decoration lies heavily along the flat, symmetrical surface of the Duma in a scheme more rigid than that of the neighboring Russian revival structures by Shervud and Pomerantsev. Although the buildings seem related, the Duma is not effectively part of Red Square: Its red brick main facade looks toward the great portico of the Bolshoi Theater, thus further violating the stylistic unity of one of Moscow's few remaining neoclassical ensembles. Inside, the Duma demonstrates the technical proficiency of the architects working in the Russian style; yet the style was used most successfully in the 1890s when applied to smaller structures, such as the mansions designed by Boris Freudenberg for Peter Shchukin (Figure 557).

The Russian Style in Petersburg

The impact of the Russian Revival style was comparatively muted in Petersburg, where other, eclectic, styles dominated. In the design of certain large apartment buildings, the Russian Revival coexisted with a more eclectic approach (Figure 558). Yet the ideology and aesthetics of the national style found expression in one major Petersburg architectural project of the end of the century: the Church of the Resurrection of the Savior on the Blood (1883–1907), built on the site where Alexander II was assassinated by terrorists of the People's Will political movement. After an extensive review of the first designs submitted, all, as frequently happened in such competitions, were judged insufficiently Russian. In the subsequent competition, Alfred Parland received first prize for a design based on the sixteenth-century Cathedral of the Intercession on Red Square, to which, in fact, it bears only superficial resemblance.[107]

Although the Resurrection Church is incongruous within the Petersburg ensemble, it is both striking and appropriate as a monument to a tsar who had toler-ated Pan-Slavism and had involved Russia in a war with Turkey in the Balkans (during his reign, many Russians awaited the imminent fall of Constantinople to Russia as part of the Orthodox patrimony). No other structure of the period reveals so clearly the link between architecture, Orthodoxy, and political purpose. For this major ecclesiastical project of the late nineteenth century Parland – a designer of many churches – drew not on the neo-Byzantine (the usual official preference), but on the "populist" style of the Russian Revival.[108] Although both styles enjoyed official favor, the Church of the Resurrection is distinct from the Russian Orthodox cathedrals constructed in the Byzantine manner, not only in Russia proper, but in other parts of the empire, such as Warsaw, and even beyond (in Sofia, Bulgaria).

Considerable technological ingenuity was required to ensure the stability of the massive structure, built on the edge of the Catherine Canal. Neither the engineering nor the architecture of the church, however, was as challenging as the mosaic panels on both the interior and exterior of the building (see Plate 74). These increased the time of construction to more than 20 years from the first groundwork in 1886. The exterior mosaic panels, designed by a group of artists

Figure 556. Moscow City Duma. 1890–2. Architect: Dmitrii Chichagov. (M 133–36a)

Figure 557. Shchukin house. Moscow. 1894. Project sketch by Boris Freudenberg. *Zodchii, 1893.*

including Viktor Vasnetsov, were made by the firm of A. A. Frolov and placed within a facade of pressed yellow brick.[109]

Abramtsevo

The ponderous uses of tradition exemplified by the Upper Trading Rows and the Church of the Resurrection were countered by a new aesthetic revival that began in the arts and crafts movement centered at Abramtsevo, the estate of Savva Mamontov. Through his patronage, there arose a congenial environment for artistic experimentation after purchasing the estate in 1870 from a daughter of Sergei Aksakov, a prominent Slavophile whose hospitality had made Abramtsevo a haven for noted writers and intellectuals.[110] The purchase occurred the year following the death of Mamontov's father, whose considerable fortune he inherited and enlarged as one of Russia's most energetic railway developers. Mamontov's "colony" thus provides a quintessential example of the productive relation between entrepreneur and artist in late nineteenth-century Russia. Although Abramtsevo would be rivaled by another center of the arts and crafts revival at Talashkino (Smolensk Province), on the estate of Princess Maria Tenisheva, Mamon-

tov's group was unique in its breadth of artistic interests and its influence on architecture and design.

In the early 1870s, both Viktor Hartman and Ivan Ropet worked at the estate. Hartman, shortly before his death in 1873, built a studio at Abramtsevo, with richly carved wooden decorations typical of the crafts revival. Ropet's "Teremok" bathhouse nearby, more interesting structurally than Hartman's work, adapts a log structure to asymmetrical shapes united under a steep trapezoidal roof that serves as a backdrop for the window and porch gables (Figure 559). In its fanciful manner, the Teremok is a foretaste of the free-style, sculpted architecture at the turn of the century; and in this, it prefigures the design of the church at

Figure 558. Petersburg Credit Society building (left). C. 1875. Architects: Viktor Shreter and E. Kruger. N. P. Basin apartment house (right). 1878–81. Architects: Nikolai Basin and Nikolai Nikonov. (M 157–0)

Figure 559. *Teremok* bathhouse. Abramtsevo. (MR 8–8)

420

Abramtsevo, which unified the colony's creative diversity.

The communal effort in building the Abramtsevo church, dedicated to the Icon of the Savior "not created by hand" (*nerukotvornyi*), has become legendary in Russian art history – the realization of a artistic synthesis by a group dedicated to preserving art in the spiritual life of the people.[111] The design of the church (see Plate 75) derived not from the Byzantine or seventeenth-century Muscovite styles prevalent in Russian church architecture of the time, but from the less grandiose traditions of medieval Novgorod and Pskov. Because the church was small and essentially an "amateur" production, unconstrained by committees or academic rules, it had none of the saturated archaeological detail expected of the Russian style. Early sketches for the project by Vasilii Polenov were based on the modest Church of the Transfiguration of the Savior on the Nereditsa (1198; see Figure 37) near Novgorod. The artists at Abramtsevo also studied churches near Rostov, which influenced Vasnetsov's subsequent modifications of the design, built in 1880–1.[112] In recurring to this more intimate style – long appreciated by art historians, but little noticed by architects – the Abramtsevo group reclaimed a part of Russian architecture that emphasized structural clarity and the relation between material and form.

There are few "quotations" in this building: The exaggerated contours, the large curved segmented window on the south wall, and the carved limestone details do not reproduce with archaeological precision the small churches of Novgorod or Pskov – which in any event had been rebuilt extensively over the centuries. Yet the deeper structural similarity is recognizable, presented without the decorative detail that cluttered most examples of the Russian revival style (Figure 560). The decoration of the interior and the design of the furnishings involved not only Polenov and Vasnetsov, but also the painters Ilia Repin and Apollonarii Vasnetsov (Viktor's brother), the sculptor Mark Antokolskii, and Savva Mamontov's wife, Elizaveta Mamontova, offspring of the Sapozhnikov silk-manufacturing dynasty. Mamontova participated actively in the Abramtsevo crafts circle, whose cause she promoted tirelessly along with Elena Polenova, Vasilii's sister.

Each of the craft workshops contributed to the decoration of the church. The furniture and woodworking shop, established by Elena Polenova in 1882, provided the interior furnishings in an arts and crafts style continued in Vasnetsov's designs at the turn of the century. The church was also decorated with ceramic tiles: inside, on the traditional Russian stove, and outside, in ornamental strips around the cupola drum and burial chapel. In 1889, Polenova organized the ceramics workshop into a full-fledged enterprise, drawing on the talent of Mikhail Vrubel, whose ceramic designs are preserved in tile stoves in the estate house at Abramtsevo. The artists' group at Abramtsevo continued to work on the church and its design: Ten years after the church was completed, Vasnetsov added a chapel on the north facade, where in 1892, Mamontov's invalid son Andrei was buried. In 1918, Savva Mamontov was buried in the same chapel.

Abramtsevo's role as a precursor of a cultural revival at the turn of the century is further illustrated by the interrelation between the arts that characterized many of the community's activities – not simply the crafts, the visual arts, and architecture, but also drama, music, and set design. Participants in the estate's "amateur" productions included Fedor Chaliapin and Konstantin Stanislavskii-Alekseev (another product of the Moscow merchant elite). One of

Figure 560. Church of the Icon of the Savior. Abramtsevo. South view. (ZG 6–23)

421

the most notable cultural events at Abramtsevo occurred in 1886, when Rimskii-Korsakov's opera *The Snow Maiden* was produced. The sets, designed by Vasnetsov, prefigure the neo-Russian element in style moderne architecture 15 years later.

The architectural collaboration at Abramtsevo was not the last occasion when a painter there designed an architectural landmark. In 1896, Konstantin Korovin, who had painted stage settings for Mamontov's opera productions, designed the Pavilion of the Far North (Figure 561) at the All-Russian Arts and Industry Exhibition in Nizhnii Novgorod. Though more modest than the large pavilions by Shukhov and Pomerantsev for the same exhibition, Korovin's innovative design exemplified his understanding of structure derived from traditional (in this case, wooden) forms. The pavilion has no trace of the ornate "folk" decoration associated with Russian wooden architecture in the nineteenth century; instead, Korovin used his materials to create a simply defined sculpted mass expressive of structural logic.

Korovin, like Vasnetsov at Abramtsevo, used no technologically advanced materials or construction methods. The approach of both artists to architectural form suggested rather an aesthetic means of transcending the clash between technology and historicism.[113] Precisely at this juncture, ahead of the new styles in both painting and architecture, the Abramtsevo artists – Polenov, Viktor Vasnetsov, Korovin, and others – introduced their painterly conception of mass and space into architectonic form.

The Search for a Unifying Idea

In the final decade of the nineteenth century, the implications of the Abramtsevo experiment were still far removed from the world of professional architecture, which paid homage to a variety of styles and schools such as the Beaux Arts, the Italian Renaissance, and the Gothic Revival. The Beaux Arts approach was represented in Petersburg by institutional buildings such as the Stieglitz Museum, attached to the School of Technical Design, endowed by Baron A. L. Stieglitz and constructed by Georg Krakau and Robert Gedike in 1879–81. The museum, begun in 1885, was designed by Maximilian Mesmakher to house the Stieglitz collection of Renaissance art and to further the education of the students at the school. Due to the elaborate work of the interior, representing various forms of sixteenth-century Italian decorative art, construction was not completed until 1895.[114] Another Beaux Arts monument is the Mutual Credit So-

Figure 561. Pavilion of the Far North. 1896 Nizhnii Novgorod Exhibition. Architect: Konstantin Korovin. *Vidy Vserossiiskoi khudozhestvennoi promyshlennoi vystavki 1896 g. v Nizhnem Novgorode.* Courtesy of the Slavic and Baltic Division, New York Public Library.

Figure 562. Mutual Credit Society Building. Petersburg. 1888–90. Architect: Pavel Siuzor. (P 101–17)

ciety Building (Figure 562), constructed in 1888–90 by Pavel Siuzor, one of the most prolific of Petersburg architects.[115] His palatial financial institution is accented in the center by a two-story arched window and statuary. Most of Siuzor's work involved the design of large apartment complexes, of which the most imposing, built in 1898–1900 for Ratkov–Rozhnov, seems to have taken its courtyard entrance arch from Rossi's Arch of the General Staff – an example of adaptive use of heroic forms from an earlier era for commercial purposes at the turn of the century.

In Moscow, the Beaux Arts style was represented by Boris Freudenberg's building for the Sandunov Baths (1894–5; Figure 563), also containing apartments and commercial space. Here, too, the entrance arch of this ebullient structure provides a focal point, more clearly defined and integrated than the corresponding motif in Siuzor's work. Rising to the cornice line, the arch establishes the basic motif, reflected in the second-story windows and repeated in their mullions. The depiction above the arch of nymphs on horseback emerging from the waves and blowing triton shells typifies the riot of high-relief sculpture characteristic of architecture for Moscow's free-spending merchant milieu. And the Moorish style of the interior court and baths carries the fantasy still further.

Variations on the Renaissance style often revealed considerable wit, as in Konstantin Bykovskii's building for the Moscow University Zoological Museum (completed in 1902), with sculpted animal and floral forms interspersed among the capitals and entablature of the classical system of orders. Among the several Moscow mansions in the Beaux Arts and Gothic Revival styles, the extravagance of the 1890s is especially obvious in the house that V. A. Mazyrin built in 1894–5 for Varvara Morozova, a leading figure in Moscow's progressive cultural and intellectual circles. Trees now obscure the extent of the structure (Figure 564), but the twisted columns at the entrance and the shell-encrusted facade identify its source as Portuguese Renaissance, probably copied from the Palácio de Pena at Sintra.[116] The interior is a series of grand spaces for entertaining – a theater, a ballroom, a banquet hall, and a central atrium in the Roman style – whose frenetic eclecticism exemplifies both the cultural pretensions of the entrepreneurial elite and their urge to engage in a conspicuous display of wealth.

In view of the construction activity in major Russian cities in the 1890s, members of the architectural profession might well have felt both a sense of accomplishment and some doubt about the future of a practice based on variations of Russian revival or French and Italian Renaissance styles. These mixed feelings surfaced in discussions of the relationship between a distinctly national style and rationalism in architecture during the first and second Congresses of Russian Architects (1892, 1895), arranged by the Petersburg and Moscow architectural societies.[117]

At the second congress, Konstantin Bykovskii, president of the Moscow Architectural Society and designer of the State Bank in Moscow, as well as the Zoological Museum, made an address that attempted to reconcile the national past with modernity. He commented not only on the activities of the society, founded by his father, Mikhail Bykovskii, in 1867, but also confronted yet again the issues of purpose and direction in Russian architecture:

The romanticism that embraced Europe in the first half of our century counterposed to classicism a fascination with the Middle Ages. . . .

Instead of imitating of classical styles, architects attempted to reproduce other styles previously rejected. The material suitable for architectural reworking is overwhelmingly varied, creating an especially difficult position for the architecture of our time. It is essential to orient oneself in all this material, to find a guiding thread that will finally bring us out of empty eclecticism. We must work to assimilate the material from the past so firmly that we can deal with it independently and say in architecture a new original word.[118]

In Bykovskii's statement are traces of ideas from many sources, including John Ruskin and Viollet-le-Duc. But Bykovskii gives a curiously Russian twist to

Figure 563. Sandunov Baths. Moscow. 1894–5. Architect: Boris Freudenberg. (M 147–37)

Figure 564. A. A. Morozov house. Moscow. 1894–8. Architect: V. A. Mazyrin. (M 162–12)

familiar pronouncements about the need to revive and recreate architecture when he speaks tautologically of "a new original word" in architecture. Dostoevskii frequently expresses the notion that a culture can say a "new word"; Bykovskii's echo of this idea provides further evidence of a literary approach to defining the function of architecture in the culture as a whole.

The inability of Russian architecture to achieve its expressive potential, according to Bykovskii, is related to the lack of cohesion in Russian society:

They are right who lament the lack of originality in contemporary Russian architecture; but they are wrong in considering none of the complexity of this phenomenon and in paying no attention to the role of social developments, of architects, and of contemporary life, in which one senses the lack of a unifying idea.[119]

The notion that architecture in an increasingly diverse technological and economic setting might need something other than a "unifying idea" eluded Bykovskii and most other architectural critics of the period. Indeed, beneath the search for an ideological imperative lay a sense of architecture's inability to address pressing social needs within the prevailing system. Even as that system inexorably declined, new architectural movements followed rapidly in an attempt to redesign the urban environment through a synthesis of the decorative arts and architecture.

CHAPTER 14

Modernism During the Early Twentieth Century

No one who holds art dear can oppose this movement [modernism], whose force is not in the subjective views of individuals but in a deep and solid bond with our culture, our technology, the best democratic aspirations of our century, and the nascent demands of the truly beautiful.

– Vladimir Apyshkov, 1905

The entire epoch of bourgeois and democratic modernism has given Petersburg *nothing*. Only the restoration of previous architectural canons can increase the beauty of our city.

– Georgii Lukomskii, 1913

The appearance of the "New style" – or *style moderne* – in Russia's major cities at the turn of the century has many obvious influences, but no clear point of origin.[1] There were no programmatic statements like Otto Wagner's *Moderne Architektur* or harbingers like Joseph Olbrich's Secession House in Vienna. At the turn of the century, however, there were signs of an awareness of new developments in western and central Europe that would stimulate a major aesthetic and technological redirection of Russian architecture.[2] The greater attention given to building technology at the turn of the century did not imply that aesthetic issues had been neglected in favor of pragmatism. The frequent references in architectural journals to John Ruskin, William Morris, the English Arts and Crafts Movement, and the work of artists associated with the Abramtsevo community demonstrated that aestheticism in both design and architecture enjoyed great vigor in an era of commercial development.[3]

The essential precondition for the new style was the continued expansion, not only of the population of large cities such as Moscow and Petersburg, but also the rise of a class of private patrons whose wealth derived from capitalist, entrepreneurial activity. Although Russian merchants had played a significant role in the construction of medieval parish churches, and although individual property owners had since the eighteenth century built early forms of the apartment building, the few decades before World War I witnessed an unprecedented period of private initiative and investment in the construction of Russian cities. The results were correspondingly varied in both style and taste as architects strove to accommodate the deluge of work involved in the creation of an urban infrastructure under social and economic conditions that were still far from modern.[4]

In view of the diversity of its sources and forms, and of the demands placed upon it, the style moderne proved to be fundamentally eclectic – not in the nineteenth-century sense of the patterned facade or the historicist stylization, but in the inventive combination of structure, material, and decorative motif. Russian architectural practice at this time was remarkably adaptable and receptive to the striking visual effect, and the work of every notable proponent of the new style demonstrated an ability to interpret it in widely divergent ways. This was particularly evident in Moscow, where an expanding economy and a number of gifted architects gave the style moderne its most distinctive expression.

Figure 565. Hotel Metropole. Moscow. 1899–1905. Architect: William Walcot. (M 147–18)

The Beginnings of the Style Moderne in Moscow

The extent of the change entailed in the new style first appeared on a large scale in Moscow's Hotel Metropole, the planning for which began at the end of the nineteenth century. Commissioned by the Petersburg Insurance Society to provide Moscow with a hotel that would meet international standards of design and luxury, the Metropole had a complicated construction history. Even the winning design of William Walcot was modified – in certain respects, almost beyond recognition – before work began in 1899.[5] During the 5 years of construction, other architects were involved in the project, most notably Lev Kekushev, who supervised the construction and added a number of elements of his own.

There are many aspects of the Metropole that classify it as a landmark of the style moderne; although it has elements of horizontal and vertical emphasis, and a large arched panel at the center of the main

facade, the facade itself contains virtually no reference to the order system (Figure 565). The new style developed a concept of tectonics in which structural mass could be shaped without reference to illusionistic supporting elements. Texture and material acquired the dominant expressive role, exemplified at the Metropole by the progression from an arcade with stone facing on the ground floor to the upper floors in plaster over brick, with inset windows lacking any decorative frame. The central two stories are contained within two horizontal strips formed by wrought-iron balconies; vertical accents – both functional and decorative – are provided by glass bays in the center and at the corners of the main facade. The patterned brick surface of the uppermost floor completes the contrast of texture and material, in which the decorative arts and structural form are combined.

This new relation between structure and material at the Metropole enabled the architect to use the facade as a ground upon which other art forms could be displayed, such as the plaster frieze by Nikolai

426

Andreev on the theme "The Four Seasons" (along the fourth floor), and seven ceramic panels designed by Alexander Golovin above the fifth story. Most prominently, the great arch at the center of the main facade contains the ceramic panel "The Princess of Dreams" (from the play *La Princess lointaine* by Edmond Rostand), designed by Mikhail Vrubel. It is significant that both Vrubel and Golovin had been active in the Abramtsevo community, whose commitment to the arts and crafts revival and to an integrated concept of structure and decoration are so largely displayed at the Metropole. A new aestheticism asserted its presence in a reinforced-concrete building, financed by an insurance company, and demanding the most advanced technical resources. As the first major example of the new style in Moscow, the Metropole also revealed a tension between structure and decoration characteristic of the early phase of the moderne.

Concurrently with the construction of the Hotel Metropole, Viktor Vasnetsov, architect of the Abramtsevo church, implemented similar principles on a far larger scale in his design for the expansion of the Tretiakov Art Gallery, devoted to the public display of Russian art in Moscow. Vasnetsov did not, in fact, build the entire gallery. Although the precise dates are unclear, he was commissioned around 1900 to create a new main entrance and facade for the gallery, which had been available to the public since 1892, when the merchant Pavel Tretiakov donated his collection to the city of Moscow.[6] The building that housed the collection formed part of an earlier complex of structures, including the Tretiakov home, whose space was initially expanded in 1873 to accommodate a private art collection. In providing a focal point for the assortment of structures around a central yard, Vasnetsov created an entrance structure for the long building that held most of the paintings. Work on the facade decoration can be firmly dated to 1903 and was probably completed in 1905.[7]

Vasnetsov's design of the entrance consisted of a brick facade, lightly stuccoed and painted, that provided a clear spatial outline as well as a base for the Russian folk-style decorative bands along the upper part of the facade. The strips include a ceramic frieze resembling fin de siècle symbolist painting, a large inscription (announcing the Tretiakov donation) on a white background in a medieval Russian stylization, and a decorative brick border. The superb quality of architectural ceramic work in Moscow, much of which was provided by the expanded Abramtsevo ceramic workshop (now relocated to Moscow), did much to encourage the use of traditional decorative elements within a new architectural aesthetic.[8] The adaptation

of Russian motifs at the entrance to the Tretiakov Gallery differs from that of the "pseudo-Russian" style, with its facades encumbered with a literal reproduction of decorative motifs. For Vasnetsov, a solitary window with decorative surround fulfills the function of a museum display, are carefully considered reference to an artistic system of the past.

The New Apartment House

The most decisive impact of the style moderne in the transformation of Moscow occurred in the construction of housing, with an emphasis on the decorative arts and a rational arrangement of interior space. Indeed, in Moscow, the large apartment building is a product of new standards of efficiency, comfort, and technological progress, suited to accommodate the growth of a middle class living in the central area of Moscow – whose limits were expanding with the tram network.[9] This trend is represented in N. M. Proskurin's two large apartment blocks on Sretenskii Boulevard, built in 1899–1902 for the Rossiia Insurance Company (Figure 566). Like many apartments of the 1890s, the building contains elements from the Italian Renaissance, combined with Gothic pinnacles on the corner tower in imitation of the Kremlin Spasskii Tower. Yet the scale and quality of the apartment complex were unprecedented in Moscow.[10] The substantial investment required for a building and services on this scale was generally available only from insurance companies (as with the Hotel Metropole), and the Rossiia firm had undertaken another apartment complex the preceding year (1898) on Lubianka Square.

A more flamboyant use of the plasticity of material occurred in the work of Lev Kekushev, whose apartment house for Isakov on Prechistenka Street (1906) combined the style moderne with neobaroque sculpted figures typical of art nouveau. But apart from the curved mullions of the windows and the undulating metal cornice, the main expressive element of the design centered on Kekushev's molding of the brick facade, which emphasizes the tensile properties of the material that had been so praised as the ideal medium for rational architecture three decades earlier.[11]

Structural fantasy and the Jugendstil influence reign in Georgii Makaev's apartment house of 1905 on Vvedenskii (now Podsosenskii) Lane. At the corner tower, with its floral plasticity and three-storied tulips, the two main facades intersect (Figure 567). Although architects in the nineteenth century fre-

Figure 566. Apartment house of the Rossiia Insurance Company.
Moscow. 1899–1902. Architect: N. M. Proskurin. *Zodchii,* 1905.

quently exploited a corner location with a projecting
tower, none resembled Makaev's flamboyant design,
which is reinforced by the asymmetrical decoration
on each of the facades. The windows of the building
are for the most part plain rectangles cut into a wall
of roughcast, whose undecorated background highlights the plaster strips on the facade, the window
surrounds on the first floor, and the projecting bays.
The contrasts in material, from the various stuccos
and reinforced concrete cornice to the iron work of
the balconies, emphasize the architect's deliberate
play between structure and texture (in Russian,
faktura).

In the midst of these stylistic effusions, there were
apartment complexes whose design reflected the need
to provide more economical living space, such as L.
Shishkovskii's eight-story apartment house for F. I.
Afremov (1904). Located on Sadovyi-Spasskii Street,
the building resulted from the boom in construction
along the Garden Ring, a circular thoroughfare com-

posed of tree-lined segments. The extension of a tram
network in 1904 brought such districts within convenient reach of the center, whereas the larger sites
available in areas around the Ring permitted new configurations in apartment blocks. The Afremov building had perpendicular wings extending from the back
facade, thus increasing the amount of space while
providing additional light and ventilation. The union
of function and aesthetics was epitomized by Fedor
Shekhtel's design of an apartment building (1904) on
Miasnitskaia Street for the Stroganov School of Technical Design. Combining the tectonic functionalism
of brick walls with delicate polychrome ceramic
panels for its window bays, the structure rests on a
ground floor of reinforced concrete, which made technically feasible the large squares of plate glass for shop
windows on the street level.[12] Shekhtel also devised
an open ground plan that solved the problem of claus-
trophobic courtyard space typical of Russian perimeter apartment plans.

428

Figure 567. Apartment house, Podsosenskii Lane. Moscow. 1905. Architect: Georgii Makaev. (M 154–21)

Although apartment construction in Moscow greatly accelerated during the first decade of the twentieth century, almost all projects with any claim to architectural distinction remained beyond the reach of the vast majority of the city's population. Advances in building technology, along with a concern for functionalism, comfort, and hygiene, sustained the new style, yet these functional and aesthetic innovations could not adequately address the larger social concerns of the city. The economic system that supported the speculative construction of apartment complexes remained untouched by social reform, despite the rise of housing cooperatives and privately subsidized apartment buildings designed by architects such as T. Ia. Bardt and Karl Nirnzee. Indeed, unscrupulous owners could gain more profit per square meter in overcrowded, substandard buildings for transients and the *Lumpenproletariat* than did the builders of apartments for the more prosperous.[13]

Thus, apartments in style moderne buildings were designed primarily for a developing urban population – middle class or upper – with the means to demand and pay for comfort and convenience in a modern building. The larger of these apartments typically had three or four main rooms overlooking the street, and the bedrooms and service areas (kitchen, storage, bathroom) were relegated to the building's interior.[14] This configuration required two staircases, one at the front entrance and one at the back, service, entrance. The pomposity of the deluxe apartment house in Moscow reached its apogee in V. E. Dubovskii's medieval "castle" for A. T. Filatova on the Arbat (1913–14; Figure 568). Although a considerable improvement over nineteenth-century apartment designs, such buildings were exceptions to the general housing situation. Upon their expropriation after the revolution, when the housing crisis became still more severe, the spacious floor plans were converted into communal apartments, with one family per room.

The Neo-Russian Style

Whatever the stylistic emphasis, all of the apartment houses surveyed before show a resemblance to some continental source such as Paris or Vienna. Yet the possibilities of using traditional motifs in a modern context, demonstrated by Vasnetsov in his design for the Tretiakov Gallery, also appeared in the construction of apartment buildings that attempted to cloak modern design by returning to a preindustrial crafts aesthetic. The prominence of the crafts revival and the use of often stagy folk motifs demonstrate a confluence of purpose among artists, set designers, and architects at the turn of the century. The Vasnetsov brothers (Viktor and Apollonarii) as well as Golovin, Korovin, Vrubel, Maliutin, Shekhtel, Polenov, and others had each explored the connection between architecture and decorative art.[15] The close relation between material and structure in the medieval or folk traditions of pre-Petrine Russian architecture received a renewed aesthetic interpretation in the "neo-Russian" variant of the style moderne, which strove for an aesthetic transformation of the urban milieu rather than the ideological message of the earlier Russian Revival style.

No one in Moscow proclaimed these possibilities more brightly than the artist Sergei Maliutin in his design for the apartment house of N. P. Pertsov at Prechistenka Quay (1905–7). Maliutin had worked at the arts and crafts community at Talashkino, the estate of Princess Maria Tenisheva, who also served as patroness of the community.[16] In 1901, he designed the *teremok* at Talashkino, a log structure decorated

Figure 568. Filatova apartment house. Moscow. 1913–14. Architect:
V. E. Dubovskii. (M 151–2)

with fanciful interpretations of Russian folk art and
resembling the Russian pavilion designed by Konstantin Korovin and Alexander Golovin for the 1900
Paris Exposition. Examples of Maliutin's craftwork
were also displayed at this pavilion.

In the Pertsov building, Maliutin used ceramic
panels and other ornamentation based on exaggerated, abstract representations of folk art (see Plate
101). The staginess of Maliutin's sketch for the building – reproduced in the 1907 issue of the *Annual of
the Society of Architect-Artists* – masked the basic structure with a panoply of steeply pitched roofs, towers,

elaborately decorated balconies and window surrounds, and large ceramic panels as well as unusual
door and window openings. Maliutin intended to reproduce the asymmetry of the medieval *teremok*, a
word that includes the concepts of "tower" and
"chambers." The ideal proved beyond reach, however, and Maliutin's original design was considerably
modified by Nikolai Zhukov, the architect who constructed the building (Figure 569).

By no means all contemporary observers were convinced of the value of this aesthetic stagecraft. The
critic and art historian Igor Grabar, pleased by the

Figure 569. Pertsov apartment house. Moscow. 1905–7. Architects: Sergei Maliutin and Nikolai Zhukov. *Ezhegodnik Obshchestva arkhitektorov-khudozhnikov,* 1907.

success of the Russian pavilion in Paris, acknowledged the aesthetic pleasures of genuine folk art; yet the excessive indulgence in these motifs leads to a new form of cliché – and to furniture that is, in his words, "hellishly uncomfortable." In contemporary life, he notes, "one wants in everyday surroundings a measure of comfort, of calm, one wants to eat and rest in peace, without having to face endless lines and colors crawling at you from the wall in front, like the glass of a kalaidescope."[17]

Russian decoration was used in a different but equally exuberant manner in an apartment house

built c. 1909 by P. K. Michini on Chistoprudnyi Boulevard for the Church of the Trinity "on the Mire"). Located a few blocks from the large apartment complex by Proskurin, the building was designed by the artist Sergei Vashkov, known for his church furnishings offered through the firm of P. I. Olovianishnikov and Sons.[18] Vashkov applied to the exterior of the building a low-relief pattern of flora and fauna derived from the limestone carvings of twelfth-century Vladimir churches, such as the St. Dmitrii Cathedral. Although it lacked the color of the Pertsov apartments, Vashkov's building demonstrated the curious

431

uses of medieval ornament in modern secular architecture.

The neo-Russian style was very much a part of secular aestheticism at the beginning of the century; yet the style's affinity with Russian medieval architecture also facilitated new interpretations of church architecture. (The Abramtsevo church played a seminal role in this development.) The Orthodox hierarchy continued to support the historicist designs of the nineteenth century; but within influential semiofficial circles, the need to revive church architecture was seriously discussed.[19] Yet, most of the innovative church designs of the early twentieth century were commissioned by individuals or private groups (such as Old Believers) for whom the bureaucracy of the Holy Synod had little meaning. Indeed, it is appropriate that the spirit of enterprise underlying the style moderne should have appeared in the design of churches often commissioned by the same groups that contributed greatly to Russia's economic development.[20] The release of Old Believer communities from legal restrictions after 1905 stimulated a surge of church construction in Moscow and, to a lesser extent, in Petersburg. Forbidden for centuries to build places of worship (except briefly during the reign of Catherine the Great), the Old Believer communities frequently adapted simple medieval forms antedating the great Schism of the seventeenth century – in other words, they turned to the churches of Novgorod and Pskov that had inspired the Abramtsevo artists.

Ilia Bondarenko, one of the most prolific of the new church architects, designed at least three Old Believer churches in Moscow, of which the most adventuresome was the Church of the Resurrection of Christ on Tokmakov Lane (1907–8; Figure 570), built for the Maritime Community (*Pomorskoe soglasie*). The basic form derives from wooden architecture of the far north, but Bondarenko's interpretation is highly idiosyncratic, with the pitched roof of its bell cote on truncated pillars over the narthex. Two angels are portrayed carrying an icon on the gable beneath the tower roof, in mosaic or ceramic tiles set into the background of pressed brick of the main facade. By applying modern techniques such as reinforced concrete for the vaulting, Bondarenko created an unobstructed interior space capable of accommodating 500 people, in addition to the narthex with separate coat rooms for men and women. A lower floor, or half basement, had five meeting rooms and service space for maintenance and heating.[21]

Ironically, the most creative modern interpretation of Russian church architecture came from an architect who would later design the Lenin Mausoleum and other symbols of Soviet power. Aleksei Shchusev, educated at the Academy of Arts, assumed a prominent position in the Petersburg Society of Architects before moving his practice to Moscow after 1905. At a meeting of the Petersburg Society in 1905, he delivered a talk entitled "Thoughts on Creative Freedom in Religious Architecture" that roundly condemned the tasteless brilliance of official Orthodox church design.[22] Shchusev's announced response was to create a place of worship whose interior and exterior would, in the words of the *Zodchii* article, exemplify that "endearing, naive, and at the same time diverse sense of artistry of the Orthodox church."

Shchusev embarked on the construction of other churches, including the Trinity Cathedral at the Pochaev Monastery (1905–12; located in the western Ukraine), based on the style of early twelfth-century Novgorod monastery cathedrals. The whitewashed brick walls of the building provided a backdrop for mosaic panels and wall paintings, designed by Shchusev and Nikolai Roerich, over the portals on the south, west, and north facades.[23] Shchusev was also responsible for the reconstruction of the twelfth-century Church of St. Basil at Ovruch (see Figure 19); when it was completed in 1910, the architect was named Academician of Architecture at the Academy of Arts.[24]

In Moscow, Shchusev undertook one major church project: the Church of the Intercession (1908–12) at the Martha-Mary Cloister, a religious and charitable foundation supported by Grand Duchess Elizaveta Fedorovna. Like the Trinity Cathedral at Pochaev – and many of his other churches – the Church of the Intercession shows an affinity with the style of twelfth-century monastery churches in Novgorod (Figure 571). Yet the unstuccoed walls of uniform brick, the pointed gables, and the exaggerated proportions of both the apse and the refectory have no direct antecedents in Novgorod churches, nor does the ornamental limestone carving (in the Vladimir style) placed haphazardly on the walls of the north porch.[25] The Church of the Intercession combines elements from several medieval traditions, and only the simplified, or "naive," outlines of the structure suggest the debt to Novgorod and Pskov.

Among the most dramatic examples of the modern free-style approach to Russian church architecture were those designs that incorporated the tent tower, or *shatior*. Modern technology made it possible to erect such towers over the central crossing of the church without the need for the massive brick walls typical of sixteenth-century tent churches (see Chapter 6). The new *shatior* created a picturesque silhouette and at the same time suggested a rejection of official Or-

Figure 570. Church of the Resurrection of Christ on Tokmakov Lane. Moscow. 1907–8. Architect: Ilia Bondarenko. Southwest view. *Ezhegodnik Obshchestva arkhitektorov-khudozhnikov*, 1908.

thodox architecture – as in Shekhtel's 1910 design for an Old Believer church at Balakovo (on the Volga River between Samara and Saratov).[26] In some cases, the design of Orthodox parish churches also used the tent tower, as in the Church of the Resurrection at Sokolniki (1909–13), by P. A. Tolstykh (Figure 572). The style moderne's emphasis on the plasticity of structure is evident in Tolstykh's treatment of the bays and apse, and in his use of color – white and green over stuccoed brick, with the white outlining the main components of the building. A brilliant array of cupolas surrounds the central tower.[27]

The Private Dwelling

The transformation of architectural design wrought by the style moderne achieved its most brilliant expression in the design of private houses, created largely for the Russian nouveau riche, despite glimmerings of a broader, populist impulse toward de-

tached suburban houses in a few large cities. Moscow provided an especially congenial environment for monuments to the mercantile spirit, evident in the late nineteenth-century mansions for the numerous Morozovs (see Chapter 13), as well as Russian revival mansions by Vasnetsov, Erikhson, and Pozdeev. By the turn of the century, the construction of houses for the more adventuresome of Moscow's entrepreneurial elite turned to contemporary design, including the sinuous ironwork of art nouveau, as well as blocklike structures of glass and brick. The two houses that William Walcot built for the Moscow Construction Company, a pioneering development firm, are among the best examples of the severely modern, functionalist aesthetic in Russia (Figure 573).[28]

The most prolific designer of houses among Moscow's modernists was Lev Kekushev (1863–1919), who received his professional training at Petersburg's Institute of Civil Engineering between 1883–8, and subsequently moved to Moscow. Kekushev was an accomplished eclectic, with a inexhaustible repertoire of styles, which included early work in the Beaux Arts manner. In the late 1890s, his houses ranged from I. I. Nekrasov's half-timbered dacha with steep gables (described as an "American house" in a 1903 issue of *Zodchii*) to neo-Renaissance designs.[29] By the end of

Figure 571. Church of the Intercession, Mary-Martha Cloister. Moscow. 1908–12. Architect: Aleksei Shchusev. (M 123–10)

433

Figure 572. Church of the Resurrection in Sokolniki. Moscow. 1909–13. Architect: P. A. Tolstykh. East view. (M 57–1)

the century, he turned to the modern style in his house for E. List (1898–9), with its counterpointing of brick and stone in a rectangular, asymmetrical structure.[30] A similar approach to the plasticity of material appeared in his own house (1901), which resembles an American or English model in its corner tower and steeply pitched roof. Toward the end of the decade, Kekushev experimented with contoured elements in his Mindovskii house on Povarskii Street (1903; Figure 574). The house is a compilation of decorative motifs, with a Secession-style attic over the main entrance. The large windows are divided by mullions in flowing, sinuous patterns that provide textural contrast to the contours of the masonry.

The definitive examples in modern domestic architecture were produced by Fedor Shekhtel, whose

work at the beginning of the century carried the design of the private house beyond a concern for new amenities and construction techniques to a comprehensive aesthetic approach worthy of such contemporaries as Joseph Maria Olbrich, Josef Hoffman, and Charles Rennie Mackintosh. Having studied at the Moscow School of Painting, Sculpture, and Architecture in the late 1870s, Shekhtel achieved his first success as a graphic designer and creator of stage sets during the 1880s.[31] Indeed, his enduring fascination with the theater can be seen as a major impulse behind the theatricality of his later architectural work. Shekhtel's apprenticeship occurred in the firm of Alexander Kaminskii, an architect whose heavily decorated, eclectic style was popular among Moscow's merchant elite during the latter half of the nineteenth

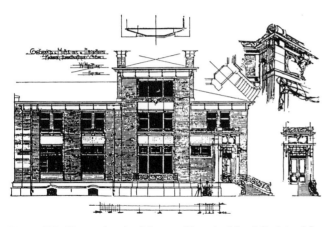

Figure 573. House for the Moscow Homebuilders' Society. Moscow. 1903. Architect: William Walcot. *Ezhegodnik Obshchestva arkhitektorov-khudozhnikov*, 1906.

century. During the 1890s, Shektel adopted a similarly flamboyant, eclectic approach in suburban mansions for various members of the Morozov family, but in his large urban homes, he used a more coherent neo-Gothic style to explore the dynamic relation between the structure of interior space and its projection in the design of the exterior. His most prominent examples in the latter category include houses for Zinaida Morozova (1893) and K. V. Kuznetsova (1896).[32]

From this use of gothic stylization as a path to structural innovation, Shekhtel moved to a radically modern idiom in his house for Stepan Pavlovich Riabushinskii in central Moscow. Begun in 1900 and finished by 1903, the Riabushinskii house displays a stylistic affinity with houses designed by Olbrich at the Matildenhöhe community, yet it also incorporates the emphasis on decorative arts pioneered at Abramtsevo. Shekhtel based his design on the play of contrasting elements, angular and sinuous, precise in line and complex in decorative form. The planes of yellow glazed brick provide a backdrop for an array of ornamental effects: large windows with bentwood details; wrought-iron railings in a fish-scale pattern; and, along the top of the walls, a mosaic frieze depicting irises on a background of clouds and azure sky. The frieze is the most arresting feature of the exterior, not only for its colors and the oneiric forms of the irises, but for the way it encompasses the structure of the house.

Shekhtel's design of the flat roof (similar to houses by Walcot and Kekushev during this period) projects beyond the walls in a precise, orthogonal line (Figure 575). As a counterpoint to precision, the sculpted forms of the porches on the side and front of the house suggest the entrance to a grotto. This submerged,

aquatic ambiance continues in the interior with the use of a pale color scheme dominated by green and blue, and with the repetition of aquatic motifs such as the fish-scale pattern in wrought iron and the frothy pattern within the large stained-glass window of the central stairway.[33]

It is in the design of the stairway that Shekhtel approached the limits of the free-form possibilities of the style moderne. This central space, extending the height of the house, serves as a core around which the rooms are grouped. The rooms themselves are modest in scale, designed for family life rather than public display (Figure 576). Yet the stairway is one of the most theatrical moments in Russian modernism, a frozen wave cascading from the upper story to the bottom landing. Its lapidary form is cast in "artificial marble," an aggregate consisting of concrete mixed with marble and granite chips that give it a striated, deep-gray color. At the foot of the stairs, the wave surges to create a column capped with a lamp of stained glass and bronze in the form of an aquatic medusa (see Plate 76). The tentacles of the lamp are complemented at the top of the stairway by a red polished-stone column and capital with sculpted lizards.

One can assume that this theatrical, "decadent" display reflected the desire to affirm a new cultural identity on the part of Stepan Riabushinskii; yet it must be remembered that Riabushinskiis adhered to a conservative Old Believer sect of Russian Orthodoxy, as did a number of Moscow's prominent merchants. Not until after 1905 were the various Old Believer sects given official permission to construct places of worship, and Shekhtel acknowledged the private nature of this religious schism by designing a house chapel, with its separate staircase, at the back of the structure above the second story. Here, in contrast to the main part of the interior, the colors are boldly stated: red and gold for the dome and pendentives over a dark, patterned wall. These are the colors of medieval Russian icons, which Riabushinskii collected, and they are applied in a setting sensitive to religious values as well as aesthetically innovative.

It is a mark of Shekhtel's diversity that he should have built another mansion in 1901 that bears little resemblance to the Riabushinskii house. Designed for Alexandra Derozhinskaia, wife of a wealthy Moscow industrialist, this house rejects elaborate decoration in favor of a monumental definition of mass and space in an international modern style (Figure 577). Craftsmanship is not ignored: the front of the house is guarded by an iron railing with the rotated triangle motif; and the pale-green brickwork of the facade is

Figure 574. Mindovskii house. Moscow. 1903–4. Architect: Lev Kekushev. *Ezhegodnik Moskovskogo arkhitekturnogo obshchestva*, 1910–11.

integrated with the window transoms and the massive concrete cornice. Shekhtel combines these structural elements and volumes at a central point with a minimum of decoration. The main window, extending to the cornice line of the two-storied structure, not only indicates the proportional for the house, but by its projection from the facade also serves as a form of triumphal arch. This central dominant culminates in two concrete cylinders, clenched by ferro concrete over a window strip that suggests the brutalism of the "machine age."[34]

The influence of British and American domestic architecture is more evident in Moscow's outlying areas, where a number of new houses were constructed on a scale and in styles that suggest comparison with large suburban mansions in America. The most striking in terms of the modernity of its design and the seeming anomaly of its very existence in Russia was the dacha built around 1909 for V. A. Nosikov by V. A. Simov and Leonid Vesnin (Figure 578). The dacha was built in the northwest Moscow

suburb of Ivankovo, and in its broad space it combines elements from Norman Shaw, Charles Voysey, and the American Shingle Style as developed in the 1870s and 1880s by Henry Hobson Richardson, the most favored American architect in Russia at the beginning of the century.[35]

Despite the contradictions in the country's economic system and distribution of wealth, the creation of a new generation of entrepreneurs led to a favorable environment for the building of large private mansions and opened possibilities for access to single-family dwellings in new areas around Moscow that were to be linked by the construction of a ring railroad.[36] The Moscow Ring Railroad was overly ambitious for its time and did not succeed financially, in part because of the lack of a sizeable middle-income population who might have afforded houses in a suburban development. Because of this attenuated growth, detached dwellings of a modern design, whether in the central city or on its outskirts, remained primarily the perogative of the well-to-do;

436

Figure 575. Stepan Riabushinskii house. Moscow. 1900–2. Architect: Fedor Shekhtel. (M 170–13)

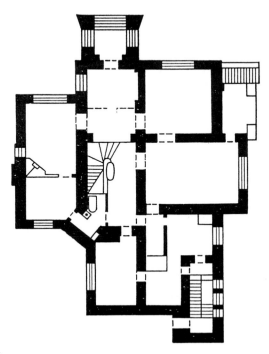

Figure 576. Stepan Riabushinskii house. Plan.

and thus the development and design of detached, private houses remained peripheral in the remaking of a modern social order in Russia.

Public and Commercial Buildings

As a style created by private patronage, the moderne served to express the cultural ethos of an entrepreneurial elite. One of the major public monuments endowed by this elite was the building of the Moscow Art Theater, designed by Shekhtel and largely supported by the Maecenas Savva Morozov, who ensured the company's financial stability in 1899. Its subsequent success with the plays of Chekhov enabled the company to commission a new theater space, but the budget was severely restricted.[37] Although the project envisioned a complete reworking of the facade of the structure, which had been built and rebuilt since the early nineteenth century, only parts of Shekhtel's design were realized, including the suspended iron lanterns, the ground-floor windows, and the company's seagull logo. The most dramatic element is the right entrance, framed with Abramtsevo tile and a sculpted frieze entitled "The Wave," by Anna Golubkina.[38]

The essential part of Shekhtel's work at the Moscow Art Theater is the innovative design of the interior, with a seating capacity of 1,300. Its stencilled decoration suggests the style of Charles Rennie Mackintosh, as does the wainscotting and woodwork of the lobbies. The contours of the small foyer areas and tearoom are carried into the auditorium, where the decorative scheme draws attention to the stage. The polished oak of the balconies and wainscotting conveys a sense of richness of material without ostentation, and the off-white walls provide both a contrast to the wood as well as a base for the modernistic pattern of lines extending from the ceiling to the proscenium. All aspects of the interior design were supervised by Shekhtel.

The renovation of the Moscow Art Theater was completed in 1902, at which time Shekhtel was engaged in another major project, the rebuilding of the Iaroslavl Railway Station, main terminus for a network of railways leading from Moscow through Iaroslavl to Arkhangelsk. The redesign of the Iaroslavl Station took place concurrently with Viktor Vasnetsov's work at the Tretiakov Gallery; and like his mentor Vasnetsov, Shekhtel reinterpreted Russian decorative elements in a modern idiom related to the "neo-Russian" style. The direct precedent for Shekhtel's use of the style was the series of Russian wooden

437

Figure 577. Derozhinskaia house. Moscow. 1901. Architect: Fedor Shekhtel. Photograph c. 1902.

pavilions that he constructed for the 1901 Glasgow Exposition, with their traditional vernacular elements recreated in a manner that emphasized color and the plasticity of form.[39]

The same characteristics are obvious in the entrance facade of the station (Figure 579), with towers on each corner modeled on the brick fortresses and monastery walls of Moscow and Iaroslavl. As at the Hotel Metropole, the arts and crafts movement originating in Abramtsevo provided the means for incorporating applied arts into the new architecture. Ceramic tiles form a green and brown frieze along the main facade of gray pressed brick, which merges into the exuberant main entrance. At this central point, related to the Glasgow pavilions, the decorative effects of ceramic, stucco, and iron are combined with attention to texture and symbolism, as in the wild strawberries of the northern forests in ceramic tile on turrets flanking the entrance.

In commercial architecture at the end of the century, Shekhtel used the multistoried arch, with spandrel beams and plate glass, as a defining tectonic element in two commercial structures: the headquarters for the Kuznetsov porcelain firm (1898) and the Arshinov store in Kitai-gorod (1899), with its facade of glazed green brick. Shekhtel's use of glazed brick – in the Riabushinskii and Derozhinskaia houses as well as a number of commercial buildings – exemplifies the fusion of aestheticism and durability, resistent to the elements and to pollution. On a considerably larger scale, Shekhtel's 1901 building for the Moscow Insurance Society on Old Square (behind the Kitai-gorod wall) represents a shift from the Renaissance detail and arched facades of the preceding buildings to an orthogonal, grid framework of brick and reinforced concrete.[40] Although the Insurance Society building (Figure 580) – more commonly known as "Boiars' Court," after the hotel situated in the build-

Figure 578. Nosikov dacha. Near Moscow. C. 1909. Architects: V. A. Simov, Leonid Vesnin. *Ezhegodnik Moskovskogo arkhitekturnogo obshchestva*, 1910–11.

ing – retains a number of stucco decorative devices familiar from earlier buildings, the rationalism of its design signaled the beginning of the modern era in Moscow's financial district.

The clearest expression of the new rationalist approach in Shekhtel's work occurred in three commercial buildings of the first decade of the century. Two were built for the Riabushinskiis: the Riabushinskii Brothers Bank (1903), in the center of Moscow's financial district (one block from the Upper Trading Rows); and the office and printing works of their newspaper, *Utro Rossii* (1907; Figure 581).[41] The main facades of both consisted of a plate-glass grid with a surface of high-quality pressed brick and virtually no ornament, although the corners are rounded and articulated.

The culmination of Shekhtel's efforts in the creation

Figure 579. Iaroslavl Railway Station. Moscow. 1902. Architect: Fedor Shekhtel. *Zodchii*, 1905.

Figure 580. Moscow Insurance Society Building (Boiars' Court).
1901. Architect: Fedor Shekhtel. (M 185–10)

of a modern business environment was the building
for the Moscow Merchants' Society, located on New
Square two blocks above Shekhtel's much larger
Boiars' Court building. Like his other commercial
structures, the Moscow Merchants' building (1909;
Figure 582) did not involve advanced construction
technology by western (especially American) standards: load-bearing brick walls and iron columns for
interior support, with a reinforced concrete and plate-
glass grid for the front and north side facades. With
little ornamentation, these elements were combined
with a sense of proportion and material contrast.[42]

Although a pioneer in the development of commercial architecture, Shekhtel was by no means the
only Moscow architect to excel in this respect. One
of the purest examples of the style moderne was Adolf
Erikhson's office building for the publishing magnate
Ivan Sytin, who published not only the newspaper
Russkoe slovo (*The Russian Word*), but also popular mass
editions of both Russian and foreign literature. Sytin
required a structure with commercial and production

areas, and Erikhson's design of the Sytin Printing
House (1905–7) extensively used ferroconcrete for
unobstructed work space, illuminated by large windows. The frame of the main facade is sheathed in
glazed brick, with modern details (including a female
mask) under the cornice and at the corners of the
building.[43] Whereas the decorative details resemble
Viennese design, the grid pattern is typical of Moscow
commercial architecture in the new style.

In the retail trade, the largest development was
Roman Klein's department store for the British firm
of Muir and Mirrielees (1906–8). As in the Hotel Metropole, the primary goal lay in creating a setting that
would provide convenience to the customer and at
the same time rationalize the operation of retail mer-
chandizing from small shops in trading to one universal store. With Klein's design of a reinforced
concrete frame to support the structure, the Muir and
Mirrielees store was probably the first in Moscow to
use a system of suspended exterior walls, whose
strips of plate glass provided natural illumination for

the interior (Figure 583). Klein chose to emphasize the lines of the facade grid, but he stopped at creating a frame in the Louis Sullivan manner, and instead endowed the building with a Gothic decorative overlay that is particularly noticeable along the roof line and on the corner tower. In addition to pinnacles, lancet windows, and crockets, a large rose window dominates one corner of the south facade; yet these elements do not alter in any substantial way a perception of the building's grid. Even the ornament was based upon the innovative use of materials such as zinc (with an overlay of copper to simulate bronze) and marble aggregrate.[44]

Redefining Modernism in Commercial Architecture

The adoption of functional, grid-based designs for commercial architecture led toward the end of the 1900s to the use of classical details in the architecture of Moscow's business district, whose new office buildings were of an unprecedented scale in either Moscow or Petersburg. In his building for the Northern Insurance Company (1909–11; codesigned by the Petersburg architect Marian Peretiatkovich, assisted by Viacheslav Oltarzhevskii), Rerberg defined the structure with a grid of reinforced concrete and plate glass. Classical elements, such as festoons and masks, appear sparsely on the facade, with the exception of a tower on Ilinka Street and two corner rotundas on the side facing the Kitai-gorod wall (Figure 584). These domed structures punctuate the labyrinthine plan of the complex, consisting of four connected buildings; and the architect's use of classical detail at such strategic points places the vertical columns of the grid in a stripped classical tectonic system.

The most thorough application of the grid appeared in Ivan Kuznetsov's Business Court (Delovoi dvor, 1912–13), a hotel and office complex located on New Square. The initiator of the project was Nikolai Vtorov, once of the most enterprising of Moscow's capitalists and, in the words of a contemporary observer, "the first to break the age-old traditions in favor of a rational and intelligent organization of commercial business."[45] Vtorov located his project just beyond the Kitai-gorod wall (a block from "Boiars' Court," by Shekhtel) and stipulated an advanced construction design. The plan included an elongated hotel in three attached segments and a trapezoidal office building for wholesale trade – each five to six stories in height. Kuznetsov complied with the functional requirements in his ferroconcrete structure, but he also provided a

Figure 581. *Utro Rossii* Building. Moscow. 1907. Architect: Fedor Shekhtel. (M 133–80)

Figure 582. Moscow Merchants' Society Building. 1909. Architect: Fedor Shekhtel. *Ezhegodnik Moskovskogo arkhitekturnogo obshchestva, 1910–11.*

Figure 583. Muir and Mirrielees department store. Moscow. 1906–
8. Architect: Roman Klein. *Ezhegodnik Moskovskogo arkhitekturnogo
obshchestva*, 1909.

neoclassical "cover" to mitigate the rigorous application of the grid design on the exterior and to provide
an imposing frame for the main entrances (Figure
585).

There was, however, one architect who used the
new materials to monumental effect without recourse
to decorative elements. Alexander Kuznetsov graduated from the Institute of Civil Engineering in 1896,
completed a supplementary course at the Berlin Polytechnikum, and in 1899 began work as an assistant
to Shekhtel.[46] The author of projects as diverse as a
modern mansion in suburban Moscow and large textile mills, Kuznetsov was commissioned to design a
building to house the Stroganov School workshops
(1914), in which the structural components were of
reinforced concrete. The structure's glazed walls and

clear lines remind of the functional aesthetic of the
Werkbund, yet Kuznetsov provided a stripped neoclassical rotunda in his design of the entrance, situated within a right angle connecting the two main
wings (Figure 586).[47]

The New Classicism in Moscow

The compromise between neoclassical detailing and
modern functionalism occurred in virtually every major type of building in Moscow. Although the city
lacked the massed neoclassical facades of Petersburg,
architects were able to create classically inspired structures at dominant points in the cityscape, such as
Roman Klein's Museum of Fine Arts (1897–1912), Il-

arion Ivanov-Schitz's building for the Shaniavskii People's University (1910–13), and Sergei Solovev's school for the Higher Women's Courses (1910–12). Even the "Iar" Restaurant (c. 1909; substantially rebuilt after the revolution), a pleasure palace designed by Adolf Erikhson near the fashionable suburban district of Petrovskii Park, displayed the fashion for classical Empire-style decorative elements combined with details derived from the Vienna Secession (Figure 587). The easy merger of the two reminds that the

Secession had a strong classical current in the work of Otto Wagner.

Ilarion Ivanov-Schitz was a particularly successful proponent of modern stripped classicism with a Secessionist cast, as in his design for the Merchants' Club on Dmitrovka Street (1907–8; subsequently the Komsomol Theater). This bastion of merchant status displayed a recessed Ionic portico flanked by square towers and Roman decorative motifs (Figure 588). The spirit of modernity is even more evident in the interior with streamlined, abstract decorative shapes that resemble Viennese motifs of the 1910s, but also anticipate Deco design during the 1920s.

The most versatile and productive adherent of the new classicism in Moscow was Roman Klein, whose contributions to the Russian Revival style, as well as to the moderne, have been noted before.[48] Of the approximately sixty buildings completed by Klein in Moscow, the majority follow some variant of classicism – a reflection of his trip to Italy in 1882, a year after his graduation from the classically based curriculum of the Academy of Arts. The most prominent of these buildings was the Museum of Fine Arts, established by Professor Ivan Tsvetaev for the study of classical and renaissance art under the auspices of Moscow University. In 1897, Klein won the design competition sponsored by the Academy of Arts, and he devoted much of the next 15 years to a project that had more than its share of frustrations.[49]

Completed in 1912, the Museum of Fine Arts signaled Moscow's accession to a cultural position befitting its status as an international metropolis. The impressive finish of the museum's interior as well as the granite- and marble-clad exterior (Figure 589) suggest comparisons with museums and public buildings erected in Europe and America during the same period. The main staircase is one of the most imposing creations of the new classicism and shows the influence of Klenze's design for the New Hermitage. Yet the contrast between Klein's classicism and Vasnetsov's vibrant design for the Tretiakov Gallery – both styles emblematic of the original collections within – exemplifies the stylistic polarities in Russian architecture at the beginning of the century.

The use of the neoclassical revival as a reflection of new wealth in Moscow also appears in a number of mansions, such as that built for Gavriil Gavriilovich Tarasov in 1909–12 by Ivan Zholtovskii, one of the most accomplished proponents of the new classicism in Moscow.[50] The Tarasov brothers, whose wealth derived from the wholesale trade of manufactured goods in the south of Russia, were legendary eccentrics, yet the second generation rapidly moved into

Figure 584. Northern Insurance Company Building. Moscow. 1909–11. Architects: Ivan Rerberg, Marian Peretiatkovich, and Viacheslav Oltarzhevskii. (M 59–32)

Figure 585. Delovoi Dvor. Moscow. 1912–13. Architect: Ivan Kuznetsov. Main entrance. (M 185–8)

the world of artistic culture in both the theater and in architecture. It would be difficult to imagine a more assertive statement of high culture than Zholtovskii's design of the Tarasov mansion (Figure 590), which was modeled on Palladio's Palazzo Thiena in Vicenza[51] and whose heavily rusticated granite facade contained chiseled Latin inscriptions – including one beginning with the Romanized name "Gavrielus Tarasov." A similar display in a different manner was created by the firm of Adamovich and Maiat, who adapted Moscow's own Empire style for a mansion commissioned by the manufacturer and financier Nikolai Vtorov.[52] In choosing a design derived from Moscow's neoclassical mansions of the early nineteenth century (particularly the work of Gilardi and Bove), the architects created a hypertrophied, mannered stylization.

Moscow's final exercise in classical monumentality before the revolution was the design for the Kiev Railway Station, across the Moscow River via Klein's newly rebuilt Borodino Bridge (1912–13). Work on the station began in 1914; by 1917, the basic structure was complete, although the final details were not finished until 1920. The architect, Ivan Rerberg, graduated from Petersburg's Institute of Military Engineering in 1896 and had served as an assistant to Klein in the

construction of the Museum of Fine Arts. In the design of the main terminal building, he adapted the Moscow Empire model, with attached Ionic columns on the main facade and end blocks containing arched entrances and surmounted with domed rotundas. A clock tower on the right corner provides the visual dominant to the entire ensemble. The great platform shed represents the epitome of functionalism in its curved ferrovitreous vault (47 meters in width, 30 in height, and 231 in length), projected and built by the same Shukhov who had created a revolution in the integration of architecture and engineering in Russia.[53]

Petersburg Moderne

In contrast to Moscow, the Petersburg environment consisted of contiguous buildings arranged within a city plan that followed the straightedge wherever its deltaic terrain permitted. The city's height restrictions also encouraged perspectival uniformity. In this setting, the plasticity of structure in the style moderne frequently assumed a two-dimensional form dependent on the texture of materials and the shaping of the facade of a building. As for architectural patron-

444

age, Petersburg's socioeconomic structure created a financial elite composed less of self-made entrepreneurial dynasties from the Russian heartland, than of financiers and entrepreneurs who seem to have had little desire for the declarations of cultural identity that marked the Morozovs, Riabushinskiis, and others in Moscow's merchant circles.

There are exceptions to this dichotomy, but they too illustrate characteristic differences between the new style in Moscow and in Petersburg. The rustic, expressive shapes of the Scandinavian (particularly Finnish) moderne appeared in the designs of private houses on Petersburg's Kamennyi Ostrov (Stone Island), whereas Moscow's suburban mansions displayed an orientation toward English and American domestic architecture. By the end of the first decade of this century, those who commissioned large houses in the Petersburg suburbs showed a preference for the neoclassical revival in the Empire style or the Italian villa.

The more visible uses of the new style first occurred in the decoration of apartment facades at the turn of the century.[54] Of the several hundred building projects undertaken in the city between 1898 and 1915, only a small fraction applied the new style in anything other than a fragmentary, decorative manner – if at all.[55] There were, nonetheless, architects whose work defined a distinctive and comprehensive variant of the new style in Russia known as the "Northern moderne." Fedor Lidval was the most productive among them, and his career ranged from the early moderne to the more austere neoclassical revival. Not only do Lidval's buildings – primarily apartment houses and banks – epitomize the multifaceted stylistic developments of that era, they also represent the alliance between large projects and capitalist financial resources.

Lidval received his professional training at the Academy of Arts from 1890 to 1896, with final study in the workshop of Leontii Benois, whose conserva-

Figure 586. Stroganov School workshops. Moscow. 1914. Architect: Alexander Kuznetsov. (M 193–36)

Figure 587. Iar Restaurant. Moscow. C. 1909. Architect: Adolf Erikson. *Ezhegodnik Moskovskogo arkhitekturnogo obshchestva*, 1910–11.

tive adherence to the Renaissance style for his own buildings in no way hampered the imagination of his students.[56] Indeed, the first of Lidval's major projects – an apartment house listed under the name of his wife, I. B. Lidval – is one of the clearest expressions of the new style. Begun in 1899, the building displays the integration of structural and decorative elements within a plan that departs from the unbroken facade typical of the city's housing. The building is located at the head of Kamennoostrovskii Prospekt on the Petersburg Side (across the Neva River north of the city center), which became a showcase for middle-class and luxury apartment housing.[57] When the entire project was completed in 1904, it formed a pi-shaped plan with two facades on Kamennoostrovskii Prospekt and a landscaped courtyard in the center (Figure 591). With this design, much imitated, Lidval avoided the cramped inner courtyard of Petersburg's apartment blocks, and created a parklike setting that also endowed the building with a sense of depth.[58]

The facade of the Lidval apartment complex exploited a variety of materials to create a sense of texture and plasticity unusual in Petersburg architecture before 1900. The rusticated treatment of irregular

Figure 588. Merchants' Club. Moscow. 1907–8. Architect: Ilarion Ivanov-Schitz. *Ezhegodnik Moskovskogo arkhitekturnogo obshchestva*, 1909.

446

stone blocks on the ground floor of the building yields to a broad swath of rough-cast walls for the upper floors and vertical ornamental strips between the windows (Figure 592). The outlines of those windows facing the street frequently deviate from the rectangular, and complement the molded plasticity of the building. On the interior, the main stairwells display crafted materials ranging from stained glass and wrought iron to ceramic floor tiles.

The use of contrasting materials and textures on facades became a characteristic feature of Livdal's other style moderne projects, such as the Meltser building (1904–5), which served as the Petersburg headquarters of the Kodak Camera Company. An even bolder and more "archaic" handling of surface materials appears in an apartment house by Ippolit Pretro on Bolshoi Prospekt – also on the "Petersburg

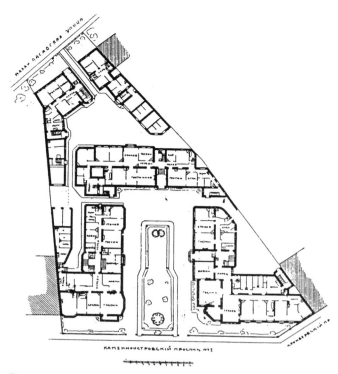

Figure 591. Lidval apartment house. Plan. *Ezhegodnik Obshchestva arkhitektorov-khudozhnikov,* 1906.

Figure 589. Museum of Fine Arts. Moscow. 1897–1912. Architect: Roman Klein. (M 73–21)

Figure 590. Tarasov house. Moscow. 1909–12. Architect: Ivan Zholtovskii. (M 103–3)

Side." Built for N. T. Putilova, a member of the family that owned the gigantic Putilov metalworking factory in Petersburg, this massive structure (Figure 593; 1906–7) resembles contemporary Finnish architecture by the firm of Eliel Saarinen, Herman Gesellius, and Armas Lindgren (cf. the Pohjola Insurance Company in Helsinki).[59] Pretro applied large, rough-hewn blocks for his ground floor and for the triangular frames of the building's main cavelike points of entry.

Such devices function as an elaborate conceit that masks modern urban housing behind forms reflecting a romantic, nationalist reaction to the industrial age with primitive modes of expression in the arts. This tactile impression, with irregular fenestration, is increased by the use of rough-cast – another distinctive feature of the "northern moderne." (In Moscow, by contrast, brick remained the preferred material for wall surfaces, with such refinements as glazed brick and ceramic panels in the work of Shekhtel.) Occupying an entire block, the Putilova building had the advantage of a three-dimensional profile.

Amid the prolific designs of modern apartment buildings in Petersburg, the work of Aleksei Bubyr goes beyond that of Pretro in the originality of its approach to structure as a sculpted, textured block.

447

Figure 592. Lidval apartment house. Central courtyard facade. (P 70–26)

A 1902 graduate of the Institute of Civil Engineering, Bubyr often collaborated with the architect Nikolai Vasilev, who also designed a number of large housing projects in Petersburg.[60] Yet he himself developed the rationalist side of the style moderne, with equal attention to aesthetics and engineering – in particular the use of reinforced concrete. The apartment house that he built in 1910–12 on the Fontanka Quay (No. 159) is striking not only for its lack of ornamentation, but also for its molded outline (Figure 594). In constructing the facade, Bubyr resorted to the familiar device of unfinished granite on the lower surface, but only to the level of the first-floor window ledge. For the most part, the walls are covered with gray roughcast; yet the facade is framed by a top floor and corner bays of smooth, light stucco. Bubyr designed multistoried window bays that intensify the vertical lines of the facade, and at the same time provide more light for the main rooms of each apartment. The upper stories culminate in a complex line beginning as a mansard roof with low, narrow dormers (in effect, a

seventh story), and rising at the corners to high gables and a series of pyramidal forms covered by ceramic roofing tiles.

An altogether different form is the 1911 apartment house by Karl Baldi on Bolshoi Dvorianskii Street (No. 21), which is one of the few examples to integrate modern materials into the aesthetic resolution of the facade. Its horizontal outline is broken by three semicircular bays – on either end and in the middle – that rise above a rusticated ground floor with large shop windows (Figures 595 and 596). The wrought-iron balcony work contains both neoclassical and art nouveau patterns. Within this saturated facade are five smaller window bays united into a single shaft of glass and metal extending from the third to the fifth floors. Although hardly revolutionary, the design is unusual by Petersburg standards in the functional union between material and design. There is little ornamentation on the metal casing of the shafts, and the

Figure 593. Putilova apartment house. Petersburg. 1906–7. Architect: Ippolit Pretro. (P 89–5)

Figure 594. Apartment house, No. 159 Fontanka Quay. Petersburg.
1910–11. Architect: Aleksei Bubyr. (P 84–26)

windows in the masonry part of the facade are also
largely devoid of decoration; but it is the glass bays
that create an interior space whose access to natural
light set a new standard in Russian architecture at the
beginning of the century.[61]

In Petersburg as in Moscow, the speculative apartment buildings in the style moderne and in the classicized variant that superceded the new style met only
a fraction of the city's housing needs. There were,
however, limited attempts to design new developments that would address the need for workers' housing. The most notable among them is the Harbor
Workers Village (Gavanskii rabochii gorodok), built
by Nikolai Dmitriev at the western end of Vasilevskii
Island.[62] Dmitriev had expended considerable effort
in a comparative study of approaches to the urban
crisis in housing (particularly for workers and their
families) throughout Europe, and his housing project,
launched in 1904 with considerable philanthropic
support, was intended as a model for further progress
in this area. Architecturally, the five buildings of the

complex (Figure 597) were solidly designed, with the
modest eclectic decoration fitting easily into the structure. That the project had less than a major impact
on housing need in Petersburg was hardly the fault
of the architect and planner, but rather of much larger
problems in the prevailing economic and social
system.[63]

Modernism and the Private House in Petersburg

As Petersburg moved fitfully toward accommodating
the housing needs of its citizens through apartment
construction, the development of new areas in the
north of the city (especially along Kamennoostrovskii
Prospekt) provided space for that rarest of forms in
Petersburg architecture – the detached mansion. Of
the Petersburg houses that displayed the new decorative aesthetic, many were attached structures built
in the nineteenth century and redesigned at the be-

449

Figure 595. Apartment house, No. 21 Bolshaia Dvorianskaia Street.
Petersburg. 1911. Architect: Karl Baldi. (P 84–13)

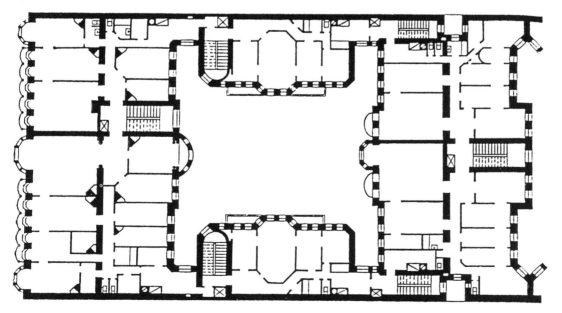

Figure 596. Apartment house, No. 21 Bolshaia Dvorianskaia Street.
Plan.

450

Figure 597. Harbor Workers' Village. Petersburg. 1904–8. Architect: Nikolai Dmitriev. (P 89–36)

ginning of the twentieth, as exemplified by the E. I. Nabokova house on Morskaia Street, rebuilt in 1901–2 by Mikhail Geisler.

The grandest of the new mansions was that built for the prima ballerina Matilda Kshesinskaia by Alexander Gogen (von Hohen), who also worked for the imperial family. The house (Figure 598) derives much from Viennese architecture as defined by Otto Wagner and the Secession; Kshesinskaia maintained close relations with the imperial court (she had been Nicholas' mistress before his marriage and accession to the throne), and her position in the theater world provided additional incentive for entertainment on a lavish scale. Gogen thus combined a family dwelling with a grand social space in the main rooms on the first floor – all decorated in an eclectic manner.

On the exterior Gogen's interpretation of the new style emerges in a coherent, if austere, design. From the rough-stone surface of the base, the walls ascend in a progressive refinement of material: a rusticated granite facing reaches midway to the first floor, before yielding to the precise surface of pale-yellow pressed brick for the upper part of the walls. Upon this durable facade, Gogen applies decorative work that, by Moscow standards, is muted in color and dominated by heavily articulated iron work. On the street facade, a dark ceramic tile frieze, decorated with attached iron

garlands and segmented by large wrought-iron consoles, extends beneath the flat, projecting cornice. No section of the mansion is without some form of ornamental iron work in the linear patterns of the Secession, from the cupola railing above the corner of the central structure to the curved glass and metal bay of the conservatory attached to the main hall.[64]

A more radical exercise in modernism was the house designed by Vladimir Apyshkov for the financier S. N. Chaev (1906–7). Apyshkov gave a discerning critique of the style moderne in his 1905 book *The Rational in the Latest Architecture*, which summarized new aesthetic developments throughout Europe, as well as in Russia.[65] Thus, the complex plan of the Chaev house, with its circular modules (Figure 599), can be viewed as an abstract statement of the possibilities of the new style (Figure 600). The composition of the house around a central module, open to a skylight, would be in itself sufficient to qualify the Chaev house as a radical experiment; but Apyshkov's uses of the design are still more ingenious: the second-floor gallery was in fact built as a picture gallery, from which one could observe the central space as well as the conservatory cylinder, which faced the courtyard and contained the main staircase.[66] In keeping with the owner's desire for adequate natural lighting throughout the house, the floor of the servants'

451

Figure 598. Kshesinskaia house. Petersburg. 1904–6. Architect: Alexander Gogen. (P 57–19)

dining area – placed directly above the circular picture gallery – was constructed of translucent glass plates. The conservatory consisted of an illuminated tropical garden, with a special ventilation system that prevented the moisture-laden atmosphere from penetrating the rest of the house. Although three of the main rooms of the house were decorated in period styles to match the Chaev's furniture, the other rooms "followed the principle of simplicity – smooth ceilings with simple cornices that do not gather dust; smooth stuccoed walls."[67] On the exterior, the flat angularity of the roof and its parapet was originally adorned by a streamlined statue of a female nude, poised between two granite pillars above the arched window of the central bay. The crowning irony in Apyshkov's relation to modernism would occur six years later with his retrospective, neoclassical design for a second Chaev mansion in the suburb of Stone Island in north Petersburg.

Stone Island was, in fact, the one area in Petersburg in which the style moderne achieved something approaching a coherent expression of a new aesthetic unity in architecture and the decorative arts. This was due in large part to the parklike setting of the island, which had served as a resort and dacha community throughout the nineteenth century, and had only be-

gun to acquire the trappings of a wealthy suburban development at the turn of the century.[68] The E. K. Gausvald dacha (1898), designed by Vasilii Schöne and Vladimir Chagin, was one of the earliest examples of the new style in Russia. This charming oddity has several characteristics of art nouveau, and suggests a familiarity with the work of Victor Horta or Hector Guimard.

Schöne's next project on Stone Island – his own house – took some two years in the design stage and involved an extensive complex of surrounding buildings. The house itself, built during 1902–4, is related to the British vernacular revival – particularly the work of Charles Voysey and H. M. Baillie Scott whose reknown in Russia has been noted earlier.[69] Schöne drew upon features associated with vernacular traditions in European architecture, such as the pitched roof and white rendered walls (Figure 601). Even more obvious are the connections between Schöne's work and that of Central European modernists from the Vienna Secession, such as Joseph Olbrich, whose work was well known in Petersburg and Moscow.[70]

The vernacular revival in Petersburg found its most dramatic expression in the house that Roman Meltser built for himself in the center of Stone Island (1901–4; Figure 602).[71] The design is related to the northern

452

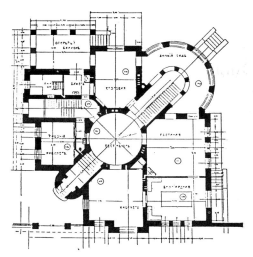

Домъ особнякъ С. Н. Чаева, Спб. Лицейская, 7.
I. этажъ.

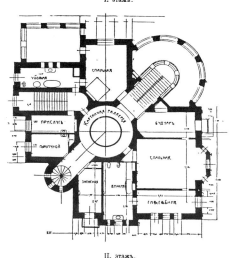

II. этажъ.

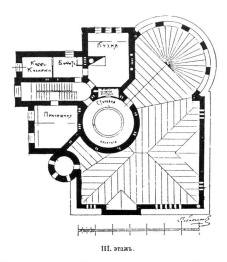

III. этажъ.

Figure 599. Chaev house. Plan. Petersburg. 1906–7. Architect: Vladimir Apyshkov, *Zodchii*, 1908.

Figure 600. Chaev house. Petersburg. *Zodchii*, 1908.

traditions of Russia and of Finland, whose arts and crafts revival was well known in Petersburg. Meltser's contrast between fieldstone for the lower walls on two sides of the house (the other sides are of red brick) and a log structure for the upper walls reminds of contemporary Finnish architecture – particularly the studio of Saarinen, Lindgren, and Gesellius at Hvitträsk, completed in 1902. Other elements of the Meltser house, such as the large carved sunburst over the main entrance, bear comparison with the stylized folk designs of Sergei Maliutin for the Tenisheva estate at Talashkino.[72] In addition to the contrast of materials for the walls (rounded log walls over a brick base), the visual impact of the house derives from its great height, which ascends through a series of steeply pitched roofs to a battered brick chimney towering over the very center of the structure. Although the floor plan is a relatively simple arrangement, the chimney and adjacent spiral staircase form a core that represents a variant of the centralized structure of the style moderne.

New Commercial Architecture in Petersburg

In the design of public buildings for banking and commerce, the modern style evolved rapidly toward a stripped classicism. The harbingers of the new style in commercial architecture include Karl Shmidt's building for the firm of Carl Fabergé (1899; Figure 603), near Nevskii Prospekt. The Fabergé building displayed trappings of pseudo-Gothic architecture on the facade, combined with extensive use of plate-glass

Figure 601. Project sketch for Schöne house, Stone Island. Petersburg. 1902–4. Architect: Vasilii Schöne. *Ezhegodnik Obshchestva arkhitektorov-khudozhnikov*, 1906.

Figure 602. Meltser house, Stone Island. Petersburg. 1901–4. Architect: Roman Meltser. *Ezhegodnik Obshchestva arkhitektorov-khudozhnikov*, 1906.

454

windows. The design for Fabergé emphasizes the texture of hewn stone, from the polished red granite columns and facing of the first-floor arcade to the opposition of rough-cut and smooth blocks of gray granite on the upper floors. It is on the basis of the facade that the Fabergé building has been designated "proto-moderne."[73]

Along Nevskii Prospekt itself, there were structures that proclaimed modernity, among which the most flamboyant is the Eliseev building and food emporium, built by Gavriil Baranovskii in 1902–4, and subsequently enlarged in 1906 (Figure 604). On the ground level, the main structure contains a richly decorated high-ceilinged hall for the display of Petersburg's most luxurious selection of wine and comestibles. The next level contained a large theater, a reflection of Eliseev's passion for that art form; and on the slightly recessed attic level of the rectangular structure, Baranovskii included office space.[74] With extensive use of metal decorative elements above the entrance and as a frame for the two-storied stained-glass arched window, the Eliseev building establishes a landmark along the north side of Nevskii Prospekt.

A more noticeable "marker" from the same period is the headquarters of the Singer Sewing Machine Company (1902–4; Figure 605), at the corner of Nevskii Prospekt and the Catherine Canal. Its architect, Pavel Siuzor, graduated from the Academy of Arts in 1866, and thus spans virtually the entire period of this study, from eclecticism to the style moderne and the neoclassical revival. As the dean of Petersburg's architects at the beginning of the century, Siuzor had established a career remarkable not only for prodigious output, but also for its success in adapting to stylistic and technical innovations.[75]

Among the technical advances in the Singer Building is the application of something approaching a skeletal structural system, although not the steel frame of the type widely used in America. The exterior facades are supported with a ferroconcrete and brick frame, whereas the interior floors (also reinforced concrete) rest on iron columns (Figure 606). By surfacing the arcade of the first two floors with rusticated blocks of polished red granite, and using a lighter, gray granite for the upper stories, Siuzor created a visual base for the structure, which rises in granite-surfaced piers and glass window shafts that extend from the third to the sixth floors in a secondary arcade pattern. The plate-glass windows, divided by two mullions, reach from floor to ceiling; and within the glass shafts, the base of each of the floors is marked by a spandrel and a bronze balcony rail with art nouveau tracery. The culminating architectural motif of

Figure 603. Fabergé Building. Petersburg. 1899. Architect: Karl Schmidt. (P 100–18)

Figure 604. Eliseev Building. Petersburg. 1902–4. Architect: Gavriil Baranovskii. (P 78–35)

the building is the elongated ferrovitreous cupola at whose summit two female figures, draped in bronze folds, support a globe with the Singer logo. The glass-enclosed cupola and globe could be illuminated for advertising purposes; and because they were not considered a usable part of the structure, the Singer Company managed to exceed the height restrictions on Nevskii Prospekt.

Despite its eclectic combination of Beaux Arts and art nouveau decorative elements within the functional grid design, the Singer Building represented a major step in the development of modern commercial architecture in Petersburg. No doubt the standards of the American clients played a substantial role in the inclusion of various innovative features, as well as the efficiency of the design, in which Siuzor was assisted by Petersburg architects such as Evgenii Baumgarten and Marian Peretiatkovich. As the main architect, Siuzor presided over a project that more than any other in his time symbolized the possibilities of Russia's integration into the capitalist economic system of Europe and America.[76]

Toward the end of the first decade, the style moderne as a decorative system for commercial architecture yielded to a more rectilinear design. In some instances, this led to the use of classicizing elements within a modern tectonic system, exemplified by the Building of the Guards Economic Society. Built in 1908–9 by a team of architects that included Ernest Virrikh, Stepan Krichinskii, and Nikolai Vasilev, the building (Figure 607) served as a department store that catered to the upper strata of elite Petersburg Guards regiments, and was at the time of its completion the city's most modern facility for retail trade. Like Roman Klein's building for Muir and Mirrielees, the Guards building was essentially a ferroconcrete structure, with extensive use of plate glass and surfaced with natural stone. Although the classical motifs are particularly evident in the rotunda above the corner of the building, the facade is shaped by the alternation of structural elements and a ferrovitreous membrane. The interior of the Guards Economic Society provides evidence of Virrikh's reputation as a specialist in the use of ferroconcrete (Figure 608). The

455

Figure 605. Singer Building. Petersburg. 1902–4. Architect: Pavel Siuzor. (P–42)

main hall, rising the full height of the building, is surrounded by three gallery levels.[77] The reinforced concrete arches over the hall are decorated with coffers and rosettes; yet the classical details do not distract from the central space and its arched roof of glass in an iron frame.

Modern rationalism was capable of a more "romantic" interpretation, as in the Passage on Liteinyi Prospekt.[78] Designed in 1911 by Nikolai Vasilev, the project represents an evolution of the style moderne architecture after the more decorative features of the style had disappeared. The Passage (1912–13) has no superficial decorative elements of any provenance. In this extended facade – plate glass within a two-story masonry grid – Vasilev introduced an element characteristic of the moderne in Petersburg, and in Finland. The ferroconcrete piers that separate the window bays are surfaced with rusticated gray granite that reminds of the new style's emphasis on the texture of material, and of Saarinen's use of red granite

for the Helsinki railway station. Within the profiled arches is a highly abstracted grid design on the second floor above each main entrance. The grid is of bronzed iron, as are the window transoms.

It would appear that the inspiration for the reduced, "stripped" classicism in Petersburg architecture after 1910 derives from the monumental design by Peter Behrens for the new German Embassy in Petersburg (1911–12). Behrens received less attention in the Russian press than his Viennese contemporaries, whose designs would have been more amenable for commercial architecture in Russia; yet this leading representative of the *Werkbund* was undoubtedly known to Petersburg architects through German architectural journals.[79] His contribution to this key site in central Petersburg is all the more remarkable for the difficult trapezoidal site on which the embassy is situated. Behrens' solution was to create in effect two independent, yet joined, structures, surfaced in roughhewn red granite. The main part, facing St. Isaac's

456

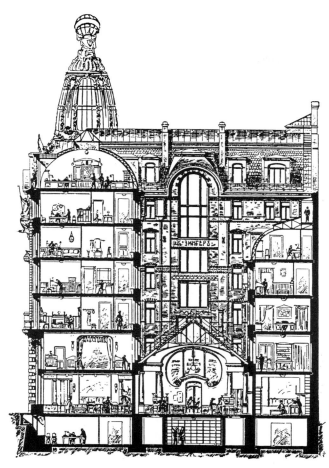

Figure 606. Singer Building. Section. *Ezhegodnik Obshchestva arkhitektorov-khudozhnikov*, 1906.

classicism for apartment and commercial architecture. In 1911–12, he constructed a building on Nevskii Prospekt for the trading firm of F. Mertens (furriers), whose clarity of design illustrates the merging of modern architecture with classical details (Figure 610). The advances in construction technology and design that had been introduced as part of the "new style" could hardly be abandoned by architects building in a commercial environment, whatever their use of architectural ornament. For architects such as Vasilev and Lialevich, and Kuznetsov in Moscow, the opposition between the moderne and *neoklassitsizm* was largely irrelevant. In 1910, for example, Lialevich and Marian Peretiatkovich designed an expressionistic, free-form project for the Sytnyi Market (Figure 611), and Iakov Gevirts adapted ancient forms from Middle East architecture for a strikingly modern synagogue and Jewish cemetery on the southern outskirts of Petersburg.[81]

Square and containing the embassy's state and reception rooms, is defined on the exterior by a horizontal frame of pilasters, attic, and base (Figure 609). By eliminating the acute corner angle, Behrens attached a second rectangular structure – extending along the side street and containing consular offices and staff quarters – at an angle to the main facade. This arrangement joined the two parts, and yet left each a discrete unit. In contemporary criticism on the building, its integrity of design and unity were associated with an absence of architectural ornamentation.[80]

Whatever the impact of Behrens' monument on Petersburg architecture, the stylistic gamut of Vasilev's work – from the florid style moderne to stripped classicism in commercial architecture – is repeated in the careers of many of his contemporaries, such as Lidval, Apyshkov, Ohl, and Marian Lialevich. Lialevich, who studied with Leontii Benois and graduated from the Academy of Arts in 1901, became a proponent of neo-

Figure 607. Guards' Economic Society. Petersburg. 1908–9. Architects: Ernest Virrikh, Stepan Krichinskii, and Nikolai Vasilev. (P 101–20)

457

Figure 608. Guards' Economic Society. Interior. *Zodchii*, 1910.

Neoclassical Revival

There were, however, architects and critics for whom the neoclassical revival in architecture formed not simply an aesthetic movement, but an essential part of a cultural and ideological platform to revive a sense of national direction during the instability of the prewar decade. Neoclassicism, criticized during the reign of Nicholas I and neglected thereafter, suddenly reappeared as an expression of nobility and imperial grandeur, in opposition to the questionable, bourgeois values of the style moderne.[82] The development of the neoclassical revival is illuminated by the work of the architect and designer Ivan Fomin. In 1894, he entered the Imperial Academy of Arts, but interrupted his studies in 1896 following a political protest, after which he left for a year in France and returned to Moscow as an architectural assistant. His mentors at the turn of the century included modernists such as Fedor Shekhtel and Lev Kekushev, and Fomin himself made a significant contribution to the new style with his interior designs and project sketches for houses.[83]

The seminal influence on Fomin was the aesthete and critic Alexander Benois, who in 1902 published an article entitled "Picturesque Petersburg" in *Mir iskusstva*. Benois defended the capital's classical architectural heritage and proclaimed that one must "save [Petersburg] from destruction, stop the barbarous deformation, and preserve its beauty from the encroachments of crude boors who treat the city with such incredible carelessness."[84] The implications of Benois's statement were immediately clear to his contemporaries: Petersburg was being destroyed by entrepreneurs whose new buildings violated the spirit of the imperial architectural ensemble.[85] To those who criticized his attack on modern architecture, Benois responded with another critical essay, "The Beauty of Petersburg," in *Mir iskusstva*: "The quest for profit and the reconstruction of buildings is entirely natural,

Figure 609. German embassy. Petersburg. 1911–12. Architect: Peter Behrens. (P 78–9)

Figure 610. Mertens Building. Petersburg. 1911–12. Architect: Marian Lialevich. (P 101–27)

458

Figure 611. Project sketch for Sytnyi Market. Architects: Marian Lialevich and Marian Peretiatkovich. *Ezhegodnik Obshchestva arkhitektorov-khudozhnikov*, 1910.

but it is unforgivable when buildings are disfigured in the process. . . . Unfortunately our architects . . . prefer pathetic parodies in the deutsche Renaissance, in French Rococo, in the gothic (the Fabergé building), or more recently – oh horrors! – the absurdly interpreted style moderne."[86] In 1904, Fomin published his own panegyric, also in *Mir iskusstva*, to the neoclassical architecture of early nineteenth-century Moscow, contrasted to the sterility of urban architecture: "By some strange stylistic act of a trivialized species of people and their talentless artists, multi-storied buildings are already replacing these amazing structures from the epoch of Catherine II and Alexander I. There remain so few of them. All the more valuable are they."[87]

In 1905–9, Fomin studied at the Academy of Arts in the architectural studio of Leontii Benois, where he not only produced neoclassical project sketches of exceptional brilliance, but also engaged in scholarly and archival work for a major exhibition of eighteenth-century Russian art and architecture. Although

originally scheduled for 1908 at the Academy of Arts, the Historical Exhibition of Architecture did not open until 1911, at which point it celebrated the critical reappraisal of neoclassicism that had been brought about so largely by Fomin, whose work now included a number of neoclassical revival houses.[88] Indeed, throughout Stone Island, the construction of magnificent, impeccably detailed mansions in the revival style attested to its nostalgic appeal for entrepreneurs such as Chaev and Mertens.[89]

Nevertheless, it was large-scale developments that the neoclassical revival had to justify itself as an alternative to the moderne in shaping the urban environment. An early example of modernized classicism can be found in the work of Fedor Lidval (1870–1945), who built two banks in the latter style between 1907–9: the Second Mutual Credit Society and the Azov-Don Bank (Figure 612).[90] Both exploit the texture and color of granite, as well as the sculptural qualities of natural stone in the decoration of the facade. And both made extensive use of iron structural compo-

Figure 612. Azov-Don Bank. Petersburg. Architect: Fedor Lidval. *Ezhegodnik Obshchestva arkhitektorov-khudozhnikov,* 1909.

nents on the interior to support the transaction halls and adjoining office space. Lidval had established that essential connection between neoclassicism and modern, "bourgeois" architecture by melding a functional commercial structure and an aesthetic system derived from monumental architecture of Petersburg.

Another neoclassicist, Marian Peretiatkovich, turned to the Italian Renaissance, which he had studied as a pupil of Leontii Benois at the Academy and seen during his diploma trip to Italy in 1906.[91] His design for the Vavelberg Building, which contained the Petersburg Trade Bank, combined features of the Florentine quattrocento, such as the resticated stone work of Michelozzo's Palazzo Medici, with the double arcade of the Palace of Doges in Venice (Figure 613). On a narrower facade, Peretiatkovich repeated the style of the Renaissance palazzo in his design for the Russian Bank of Trade and Industry (1912–14), which incorporated elements of sixteenth-century Italian palaces. A more severe form of late imperial neoclassicism characterizes Lidval's Hotel Astoria on St. Isaac's Square (1911–12; Figure 614), a six-story building with a few highly visible decorative elements, such as the classical urns and channeled pilasters along the austere granite facade. Lidval also created a number of prominent apartment buildings with a sensitive yet sparse application of classical and Renaissance detail.

The most ambitious attempt to apply classical elements to city planning occurred on Golodai Island, an undeveloped area to the north of Vasilevskii Island in the northwest part of the city. In view of the Russian interest in English concepts of town planning, it

is revealing that in 1911, an English investment firm initiated a project, called "New Petersburg," for a community occupying much of the western part of the island (about 1 square kilometer).[92] The general design for the project was entrusted to Fomin, who intended to create a monumental housing development for the city's middle class (Figure 615). Yet very little of the New Petersburg project ever materialized. In 1912, he constructed one of the five-story apartment blocks, whose "Roman" facades followed the curve of the semicircular entrance park. For Georgii Lukomskii, the leading proponent of the neoclassical revival, the New Petersburg project gave hope for the creation of a "part of the city with a truly European appearance and a strict unity of classical architectural ensembles, situated on the shores of an open sea."[93] Financial reasons and the onset of the First World War, halted construction after the initial stages of the project.

Despite the failure of "New Petersburg," Kamennoostrovskii Prospekt flourished as it had since the beginning of the century, when the tram line appeared and Lidval completed his first major apartment complex in the style moderne. Foremost in this

Figure 613. Vavelberg building. Petersburg. 1910–12. Architect: Marian Peretiatkovich. (P 84–19)

development was Vladimir Shchuko, who graduated from the Academy of Arts in 1904 and, like Fomin, was awarded a diploma trip to Italy. The early careers of the two architects contain significant parallels: the effect of Italian architecture on their work and their appreciation for the varieties of Russian neoclassicism, so brilliantly reinterpreted in Shchuko's pavilions for the 1911 Rome and Turin exhibitions.[94]

Shchuko's first apartment house on Kamennoos-

Figure 614. Hotel Astoria. Petersburg. 1911–12. Architect: Fedor Lidval. (P 108–21)

Figure 615. Sketch for New Petersburg (housing development on Golodai Island). Architect: Ivan Fomin. *Ezhegodnik Obshchestva arkhitektorov-khudozhnikov*, 1913.

461

trovskii Prospekt, No. 63 (1908–10), was constructed for Konstantin Markov, a military engineer and real estate developer who had done the initial structural design. The building, whose fifth story is situated above the profiled cornice, represents a variation on the Italian Renaissance style, with loggias, ionic pilasters, and carved ornamental panels (Figure 616). His subsequent, and adjacent, apartment house for Markov (No. 65; 1910–11) adopted a more forceful display in its massive articulation of the classical order. The attached composite columns rise four floors, from the top of the ground floor to the attic floor, which is itself designed in the form of a colossal broken cornice. The shafts of projecting window bays are wedged between the columns that define the main part of the facade in a slender balance between practicality and pomposity.[95]

At the Fourth Congress of Russian Architects, held in Petersburg in January 1911, Lukomskii gave the most forceful advocacy of the neoclassical revival as the proper style of the times. Having dismissed the style moderne as a rootless invention of "a little decade-long epoch of individualism," the critic noted the return to principles in architecture: "Having endured an epoch of agitated searching for a new form, new beauty and ornamentation, and having been convinced of the impossibility of bright achievements without correspondingly new constructive devices and materials, architecture – like art – became ashamed of its irrationality, and is again joyously repeating and taking as its base the old national forms, while waiting for the decisive discoveries of an iron architecture that has not yet found its superb form."[96]

Yet the very cult of individualism that both Fomin and Lukomskii had criticized in their commentary on the demise of the style moderne now flourished within the varieties of the neoclassical revival – whether in Petersburg or in Moscow. Whatever the ideological implications in the transition from the style moderne to the classical model, the economic,

Figure 616. Markov apartment house, No. 63 Kamennoostrovskii Prospekt. Petersburg. 1908–10. Architect: Vladimir Shchuko. In middle distance, Markov apartment house, No. 65 Kamennoostrovskii Prospekt. (L 73–36)

Figure 617. Rozenshtein apartment house, No. 35 Kamennoostrovskii Prospekt. Petersburg. 1913–15. Architect: Andrei Belogrud. (L–49)

entrepreneurial basis of apartment construction remained the same – as is evident in the two idiosyncratic Italianate apartment houses that Andrei Belogrud built between 1912 and 1915 for the developer Konstantin Rozenshtein, at the intersection of Kamennoostrovskii and Bolshoi Prospekt on the Petersburg Side (Figure 617). Designers of neoclassical buildings, no less than those of the moderne, used stylistic identity as an advertisement for the amenities that justified the cost of living at a fashionable address. In praising the return to classical monumentality for modern urban housing, Lukomskii was imposing an architectural ideal from the precapitalist era within an environment created by and for private financial interests.[97] Yet the inability to achieve a coherent modern urban environment could not be resolved by an appeal to nostalgia.

On the eve of World War I, proponents of a new, rational era in architecture dismissed both the moderne and the neoclassical revival, while Lukomskii

and Lialevich wrote of their a belief in the coming of a new era, but remained advocates of classical tectonics.[98] For Lukomskii, architecture's mission was to restrain the future and its attendant chaos in favor of aesthetic principles representative of moral strength. There could be no clearer statement of this position than the introduction to his 1913 article "New Petersburg." Taking a monarchist position in the year of the Romanov tercentenary, the critic insisted that great architecture must derive from the power of the state and Church: "Therefore, all efforts to present a 'New Petersburg' only on the basis of proposed conditions in economy and hygiene can lead to nothing other than pale, gray facades. For just this reason, the entire epoch of bourgeois and democratic modernism has given Petersburg *nothing*. Only the restoration of previous architectural canons can increase the beauty of our city.... A completely ideal [solution] is unthinkable. We do not have the conditions to create it. It is necessary to limit ourselves to retrospectivism."[99]

Indeed, retrospective sentiments in Russian architecture displayed a resurgence during the half decade before World War I. The neo-Russian style, which had formed part of the modern aesthetic movement at the beginning of the century, turned toward a more insistent, "escapist" form of architectural fantasy, as demonstrated in Shchusev's winning design for the Kazan Railway Station (1913–26) – an elaborate seventeenth-century stylization (Figure 618) based on fortress towers in Moscow and Kazan, and located opposite Shekhtel's style moderne masterpiece, the Iaroslavl Station.[100] In Moscow, Ivan Kuznetsov adopted the *teremok* design for the Savvinskoe Pod-

Figure 618. Kazan Railway Station. Moscow. 1913–26. Architect: Aleksei Shchusev. Elevation.

vore office building and hostel (1907), with a ceramic facade in ethereal polychrome.

Retrospectivism also included church construction that encompassed archaeological-historical designs by architects such as Vasilii Kosiakov and Stepan Krichinskii. Vladimir Pokrovskii based his church designs on Muscovite architecture of the sixteenth and seventeenth centuries. Pokrovskii was the architect of commercial projects in the neomedieval style Nizhnii Novgorod, Petersburg, and Moscow (the Loan Bank; 1913–15). Yet his fame rested primarily on churches distinguished by their large size and centralized tower designs in the manner of sixteenth-century Muscovite architecture. In addition, he designed the Cathedral of St. Theodore (1909–11) at Tsarskoe Selo. Modeled on the Annunciation Cathedral of the Kremlin, this church served as the center of a medieval "village," the Fedorovskii Gorodok, designed in collaboration with Stepan Krichinskii for the emperor.[101]

Such was the versatility of Russian architectural practice that in the midst of the retrospective movement, buildings of startling modernity were also constructed. A. M. Ginzburg, for example, published vaguely neoclassical designs for resort spas; yet his House of Public Meetings (1912) in Ekaterinoslav (now Dnepropetrovsk) is one of the most modernistic creations of this century, with its masterful use of ferroconcrete in both the asymmetrical plasticty of the structure and the futuristic shape of its window openings (Figure 619). Little is known of Ginzburg after the revolution (he is not to be confused with the noted Constructivist theoretician Moisei Ginzburg), but his idiosyncratic visionary projects are comparable to those of Antonio Sant'Elia and Tony Garnier.[102]

As architects pursued their modernist or retrospective visions, the antidemocratic sentiments of much architectural criticism before the war revealed a lack of faith in the viability of the bourgeoisie as a source of governance – social, political, or cultural. The ultimate ramifications of this line of thought appeared in Lukomskii's book *Sovremennyi Petrograd* (Contemporary Petrograd), published a few months before the first, so-called "bourgeois," revolution in February 1917: "It is more and more evident that contemporary Petrograd is losing its national, noble character; is becoming more trivial, European. Only a common, amicable effort in matters of construction, only an artistic dictatorship in the distribution of building sites and the attraction of the best resources will save the capital and give it an even more powerful and beautiful appearance than it had during its best days in the epoch of Alexander I."[103] The nostalgic

Figure 619. Public theater and club. Ekaterinoslav. 1912. Architect: A. M. Ginzburg. *Moskovskii arkhitekturnyi mir*, 1913.

reference to Petersburg during the golden age of Alexander I, a century earlier, represented an attempt to revive the glorious myth of the imperial capital and of Russia itself. A stunning reversal: After almost a century of criticism directed against neoclassicism as an alien, monotonous style bureaucratically imposed to the exclusion of vibrant national traditions, neoclassical architecture was proclaimed by Lukomskii and other critics as the purest expression of Russian culture.

In its final phase, the neoclassical revival produced exquisitely refined buildings, even as the old order moved inexorably toward collapse. It is appropriate that two of the most accomplished of these buildings should have been shrines to the dead. In 1911–13 Fomin designed his neoclassical masterpiece, the Stone Island palace (modestly called a *dacha*) for the prominent diplomat A. A. Polovtsov. The site is perhaps the most desirable on the island: situated across the expanse of the Middle Nevka River from Rossi's Elagin Palace. The original plan for the project was conceived in 1909 by Karl Shmidt; but after the death of the senior Polovtsov, the family decided to continue the project as a memorial and hired Fomin to produce a grander design, based upon motifs of the Russian empire style.[104] The courtyard facade (Figure 620), including both wings and the central structure, is masked by an ionic colonnade, and a portico of double columns frames the central enfilade.

The attention to detail and the scale of the design – more appropriate to a museum than a dwelling – continues on the interior of the Polovtsov dacha, leading through a circular vestibule to the Gobelin Hall (so named for the five tapestries it contained from the family collection). Everything about this two-storied hall proclaims the heroic sensibility, from the coffered ceiling to the large gilded white doors in the Empire style.[105] The distant echoes of Pompeii, whose exca-

Figure 620. Polovtsov dacha, Stone Island. Petersburg. 1911–13.
Architect: Ivan Fomin. (L–45)

Figure 621. Abamalek-Lazarev house. Petersburg. 1913–15. Architect: Ivan Fomin. (L–46)

Figure 622. Iusupov mausoleum, Arkhangelskoe. Near Moscow. 1911–16. Architect: Roman Klein. (MR 13–8)

vations were again the subject of much attention in *Zodchii*, are reinforced by wall paintings of classical ruins (in the style of Paestum) on the lunettes – a homage to a dead civilization. Beyond this central space, the double doors open onto the White-columned Hall, whose columns of white scagliola support a ceiling of three vaults, of which the main one was preserved from the dacha of Baron Ludwig Stieglitz (into whose family and fortune Polovtsov married) that originally stood on the site in the early nineteenth century.[106] The Polovtsov dacha is perhaps the greatest of Russian houses at the beginning of this century – and one of the last.

Fomin applied the style in a very different setting for the town house of Prince S. S. Abamalek-Lazarev on the Moika Quay (1913–15). The structure included three buildings from the eighteenth century, but Fomin's main task was to rebuild a four-story structure on the Moika, with a facade that adapted and in subtle ways exaggerated classicizing details such as Corinthian pilasters and medallions with a plaster relief of dancing figures (Figure 621). On the interior, Fomin used classical features similar to those of the Polovtsov house, but with even greater ingenuity in view of the spatial constraints. The state rooms were finished in a luxurious recreation of the nineteenth-century neoclassical ambience: coffered ceilings, false marble columns, intricate parquetry, plaster relief medallions, and wall and ceiling paintings.[107]

The ultimate use of neoclassicism as architecture *in memoriam* occurred at Arkhangelskoe, near Moscow, where Roman Klein constructed in 1909–16 a mausoleum for the Iusupov family in the Palladian style, with a domed chapel and curved, double colonnade extending from either side (Figure 622).[108] The design and materials (including gray granite and marble for the structure) are of the highest quality, as is the interior decorative work, created by Ivan Nivinskii, who had also supervised the wall painting for Klein at the Museum of Fine Arts.

From the perspective of the innovators of the 1920s, Russian architecture of the early twentieth century – whether moderne or neoclassical – had achieved little in meeting the requirements of the modern age. Within the relatively short time and limited economic resources available to it, Russian capitalism had provided architects with a means to approach the problems of the modern urban environment, but not to solve them.[109] Architecture, however, exists within a specific social context; and had the late imperial social and economic order encouraged a more rational use of resources, architects undoubtedly would have shown a greater sense of purpose in meeting social needs such as urban housing. Yet the diversity and "bourgeois" individualism associated with prerevolutionary architecture offers compelling evidence of a culture able to thrive and to create without centralized direction or a "unifying idea."

CHAPTER 15

Revolution and Reaction in Soviet Architecture

"October 1917 marked the beginning of the Russian Revolution and the opening of a new page in the history of human society. It is to this social revolution, rather than to the technological revolution, that the basic elements of Russian architecture are tied."[1] In 1930, when this passage appeared in El Lissitzky's essay *Russia: Architecture for a World Revolution,* little remained of the foment that had motivated the radical experiment in Russian architecture in the 1920s. With an irony no doubt unintended, Lissitzky had stated a truth that would acquire a new dimension in the Stalinist era, as the Communist Party erected its monuments with little concern for the technological revolution and the experimental, at times utopian, quests of the preceding decade. But for the approximately 15 years of its existence, the great post-Revolutionary experiment in its many manifestations endeavored to alter conceptions of architectural space, to create an environment that would inculcate new social values, and at the same time to utilize the most advanced structural and technological principles.

The assumption that a revolution in architecure (along with the other arts) would inevitably accompany a political revolution was soon put to the test by social and economic realities. Russia's rapidly developing industrial base was a shambles after a war, a revolution, and a civil war; technological resources were extremely limited in what was still a predominantly rural nation; and Moscow's population – poorly housed before the war – increased dramatically as the city became in 1918 the administrative center of a thoroughly administered state. One of that state's

earliest edicts, in August 1918, repealed the right to private ownership of urban real estate.

To be sure, the pre-Revolutionary building boom had established a viable foundation, in both architectural theory and practice, for urban development on a large scale. Furthermore, the Russian architectural profession was relatively intact after the emigration that decimated other areas of Russian culture after the revolution. And the most prominent art and architectural schools in Moscow and Petrograd were capable of providing a base for the development of new cadres, despite sometimes sweeping changes in the composition of the faculty. Nonetheless, the task of resuscitating these institutions, of allocating resources for new construction, and of devising a plan for coordinating further development could only have been Herculean.

Even as the country plunged into civil war, groups of architects in Moscow and Petrograd designed workers' settlements that represent an extension of the "garden city" movement that had already tentatively appeared in Russia during the decade before the First World War.[2] More monumental designs drew upon massive, archaic forms of neoclassicism (reminiscent of the heroic architectural visions of the French Revolution), such as projects by Ivan Fomin and Andrei Belogrud for a Palace of Workers in Petrograd.[3] Indeed, with the collapse of commercial architecture, many designs of the first years of Soviet power consisted of classically inspired monuments to revolutions and revolutionary thinkers, European as well as Russian. To prominent examples to be implemented were the Freedom Obelisk (1918–19; not extant) by Dmitrii Osipov and the sculptor Nikolai Andreev; and the monument on Mars Field in Petrograd to those who perished in the revolution (1919) by Lev Rudnev and Ivan Fomin.[4]

Other projects were built of wood – cheap, still readily available, and technologically undemanding. In 1920, Ivan Fomin used wood, with gypsum details, for rostral columns and a triumphal entrance to newly converted rest homes for workers on Stone Island, earlier the site of elegant suburban mansions (see Chapter 14).[5] The most impressive such exercise, with a combination of both modernist and traditional designs, was the 1923 All-Russian Agricultural and Cottage Industry Exhibition, situated to the north of central Moscow. From Ivan Zholtovskii's monumental double arched entrance to the futuristic open frame tower of the *Izvestiia* pavilion (Boris Gladkov, Vera Mukhina, Alexandra Ekster), the variety of wooden pavilion designs served as a symbol of a society reemerging toward prosperity and development in the countryside. The most ingenious union of function, modern design, and rational use of limited materials was Konstantin Melnikov's pavilion for the "Makhorka" tobacco factory, with its well-illuminated interior and a series of ascending levels leading to the final room, from which the visitors descended via a spiral staircase.[6] For more prosaic purposes, the old Russian technique of building from standardized, precut wooden components was refined for workers' housing in provincial industrial towns.[7]

Paradoxically, the poverty and social chaos of the early revolutionary years propelled architects and artists toward radical ideas on design, many of which were related to an already thriving modernist movement in the visual arts. For example, Lissitzky's concepts of space and form, along with those of Kazimir Malevich and Vladimir Tatlin, played a major part in the development of an architecture expressed in "stereometric forms," purified of the decorative elements of the eclectic past. The experiments of Lissitzky, Vasilii Kandinskii, and Malevich in painting and of Tatlin and Alexander Rodchenko in sculpture had created the possibility of a new architectural movement, defined by Lissitzky as a synthesis with painting and sculpture.[8]

A New Rationalism

Within the diversity of architectural schools and alliances in the immediate post-Revolutionary period, one Moscow institution served as the preeminent gathering ground for architects and artists dedicated to innovation in the arts and to an exploration of the social ramifications of the new aesthetic movement. Named VKhUTEMAS (the Russian acronym for Higher Artistic and Technical Workshops), the organization was formed from the merger, in 1918, of two pre-Revolutionary art schools: the Stroganov School and the Moscow School of Painting, Sculpture, and Architecture (see Chapter 14).[9] Orginally known as the Free Workshops, the new entity acquired its name after a reorganization in 1920.[10] In 1925, it was reorganized yet again, subsequently to be called the Higher Artistic and Technical Institute (VKhUTEIN). VKhUTEMAS-VKhUTEIN was by no means the only Moscow institution concerned with the teaching and practice of architecture in the 1920s, but it was unique in the scope of its concerns (which included the visual and the applied arts) as well as in the variety of programs and viewpoints that existed there before its closing, in 1930.

Theoretical direction for VKhUTEMAS was provided by the Institute of Artistic Culture (INKhUK, also founded in 1920), which attempted to establish a science "examining analytically and synthetically the basic elements both for the separate arts and for art as a whole."[11] Its first program-curriculum, developed by Kandinskii, was found too abstract by many at INKhUK, and Kandinskii soon left for Germany and the Bauhaus. But the concern with abstract, theoretical principles did not abate with Kandinskii's departure. Indeed, the issue of theory versus construction became a major source of factional dispute in Russian modernism.

In the early 1920s, a group of faculty members at the Higher Workshops established the Working Group at INKhUK, and began to exhibit architectural sketches, both in Russia and in Germany (for example, in Berlin in 1922). In 1923, the nucleus of the group – which included Nikolai Ladovskii, Vladimir Krinskii, Nikolai Dokuchaev, and for a time Lissitzky – formed the Association of New Architects (ASNOVA), an organization devoted to the "establishment of general principles in architecture and its liberation from atrophied forms."[12] Its members called themselves Rationalists, a term signifying the study of basic geometric principles, their development in space, and the psychological bases of perception of architectural forms.

The pedagogical and theoretical programs developed by Ladovskii and his colleagues were closely related to the work of Lissitzky and Malevich, whose abstract architectonic models (Lissitzky's "Prouns," and Malevich's *planity* or *arkhitektony;* Figure 623) rep-

Plate 65. Alexander Park. Tsarskoe Selo. 1782–8. Chinese Bridge designed by Charles Cameron (1782–8).

Plate 66. Temple of Friendship. Pavlovsk. 1782. Architect: Charles Cameron.

Plate 67. Imperial Palace. Pavlovsk. 1780–96. Architect: Charles Cameron. Park facade.

Plate 68. Ruins of Demidov mansion at Petrovskoe-Alabino. Near Moscow. 1776–85. Architect: Matvei Kazakov(?).

Plate 69. Bourse (Stock Exchange), Vasilevskii Island. Petersburg. 1805–10. Architect: Thomas de Thomon.

Plate 71. Admiralty. Petersburg. Pediment detail.

Plate 70. Admiralty. Petersburg. 1806–23. Architect: Andreian Zakharov. Park facade.

Plate 72. Mikhailovskii Palace. Petersburg. 1819–23. Architect: Carlo Rossi.

Plate 73. Alexandrine Theater. Petersburg. 1828–32. Architect: Carlo Rossi. View from Theater Street.

Plate 74. Church of the Resurrection of the Savior on the Blood. Petersburg. 1883–1907. Architect: Alfred Parland. South view.

Plate 75. Church of the Icon of the Savior. Abramtsevo. 1881–2. Architect: Viktor Vasnetsov. Northwest view.

Plate 76. S. P. Riabushinskii house. Moscow. 1900–2. Architect: Fedor Shekhtel. Main stairway.

Plate 77. Central Union of Consumer Cooperatives (Tsentrosoiuz) Building. 1929–36. Architect: Le Corbusier, assisted by Pierre Jeanneret and Nikolai Kolli.

Plate 78. Rusakov Club. Moscow. 1927–9. Architect: Konstantin Melnikov.

Plate 79. Church of the Transfiguration of the Savior, from the village of Kozliatevo. Now at the Museum of Wooden Architecture, Suzdal. Southwest view.

Plate 80. Church of the Transfiguration of the Savior at Kizhi. 1714. West view.

resented the ultimate refinement in "pure" spatial forms. For Malevich, architectonic forms were a logical extension of his "Suprematism."[13] Even as art (and sculpture) continued to exert a profound influence on the development of modern architectural design – in Russia as elsewhere – so architecture came to be seen as the dominant, unifying element in a synthesis of art forms. (Cf. the work of Walter Gropius and Bruno Taut during the same period.)

Both Malevich and Lissitzky were actively involved in another organization propagating the ideas of a new architecture. Known as the Affirmers of New Art (UNOVIS, in the Russian acronym), the group originated in Vitebsk under the direction of Malevich; and 3 years after its founding, in 1919, most of the members moved with Malevich to the Petrograd Institute of Artistic Culture, where they combined forces with the artist Tatlin and Nikolai Punin. There were branches of the Affirmers in several Russian cities, Moscow included, and doubtless the staff at INKhUK was familiar with the objectives of UNOVIS, which sought "the optimal harmony of the simplest geometric forms." The Unovis curriculum began with "the study of color, and of the principles of contemporary movements in art, beginning with Cézanne and concluding with Suprematism; then a transition to the study of the properties of various materials; and only afterwards, concentrated work on specific projects."[14]

The pedagogical program developed by Ladovskii, Dokuchaev, and others was not accepted without protest by many architects (including Alexander Vesnin), who considered the ASNOVA approach pseudoscientific and excessively abstract. As early as 1922, Ivan Zholtovskii, commissioned to assess the Ladovskii group, found many of their views untenable, but suggested that they be allowed to function as a studio, "in view of their sincerity and passion."[15] Such was the tolerance of the 1920s. For much of that decade, Ladovskii, Dokuchaev, and other members of AS-NOVA focused largely on aesthetic principles of architectural shapes that were designed to produce the ideal physical and psychological environment.

In terms of actual construction, the ASNOVA group produced little: Dokuchaev, in his article, "Contemporary Russian Architecture and Western Parallels" (1927), complained of bias in the award of projects by juries hostile to ASNOVA, and spoke of a "blockade"[16]; but by the end of the 1920s, ASNOVA architects participated actively in architectural competitions. In 1928, Ladovskii and his closest followers seceded from the association to found the Association of Architects-Urbanists, with a concentration on ur-

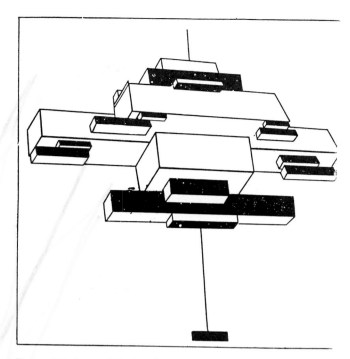

Figure 623. *Future "Planits" [habitats] for Earthlings*. Artist: Kazimir Malevich. Suprematist architecture of pure forms.

ban planning; and in 1932, ASNOVA was absorbed, along with other architectural groups, into the Union of Soviet Architects.[17] It would be a mistake to consider the Association excessively concerned with abstruse theoretical problems at the expense of architectural practice, for many of the designs from its studios were far-sighted and might have been quite practical had the Soviet Union possessed the necessary technology and materials. As early as 1922, Krinskii and the Ladovskii studio designed a skyscraper (projected for Moscow's Lubianka Square) in a style that prefigures Howe and Lescaze's Philadelphia Saving Fund building (1932), one of the first International Modern skyscrapers.

Constructivism

Most of the projects realized during the 1920s belong to a group of architects known as the Constructivists (or Functionalists). For all of the polemical fury generated by debates between the Rationalists and Constructivists, their origins and goals had much in common. Like the Rationalists, the Constructivists drew inspiration from modernism in painting and sculpture – particularly the latter. In 1920, the year of genesis for so much in Russian modernism, the brothers Naum Gabo and Anton Pevsner released their

469

"Realistic Manifesto," with its praise of kinetic rhythms and negation of outmoded concepts of volume; yet they reaffirmed the integrity of art and disputed the credo of the faction within INKhUK that called upon artists and designers to turn to utilitarian, "productionist" (and political) goals.[18]

Indeed, the importance of "pure" artistic experiments in spatial constructions to the evolution of the principles of Constructivism is demonstrated in the work of Alexander Rodchenko, who in 1921 stated that "construction is the contemporary demand for organization and the utilitarian application of materials."[19] The most dramatic expression of form as a function of material revealed in space was Vladimir Tatlin's utopian project for a monument to the Third International (1919–20; Figure 624), intended to be 400 meters in height, with a spiral steel frame containing a rotating series of geometric forms: at the base, a cube (for a legislature), requiring a year to complete its revolution; in the middle, a pyramid (for executive offices of the international Communist movement), rotating once a month; and at the top, a cylinder (for

offices of mass communication), rotating once a day.[20] Although putatively designed to be erected, the monument was dismissed as technologically infeasible when the large model constructed by Tatlin was brought to Moscow for exhibition and discussion. Even as a model, the design contributed greatly to a sense of dynamic development in society and the arts, and was to be followed by other utopian architectural projects that at times seemed to deny the very properties of material.[21] Yet the designs of Tatlin, Lissitzky, and other architects and students at the VKhUTEIN workshops gave notice of a new movement that glorified the rigorous logic of undecorated form as an extension of material, and that intended to participate fully in the shaping of Soviet society.

In the early 1920s, the evolution of Constructivist ideas at INKhUK passed through a number of polemical phases (the term *konstruktivizm* was still broadly interpreted and had not yet acquired the "functionalist" architectural emphasis of the mid–1920s). The pure-art faction, influenced by Kandinskii, was opposed by the "productionists" – associated with the Left Front of the Arts – who anticipated an age of engineers supervising the mass production of useful, nonartistic objects.[22] A reaction to both sides, particularly the former, led in 1921 to the formation of a group of artists-constructivists: Alexander Vesnin, architect; Aleksei Gan, art critic and propagandist[23]; Rodchenko, sculptor and photographer; Vladimir and Georgii Sternberg, poster designers; and Varvara Stepanova, set designer.

As at the beginning of the century, Russian artists and architects of the modern movement experienced considerable success in Europe, particularly among the intelligentsia, who were often favorably disposed toward the social experiment underway in the Soviet Union and saw the Russian avant-garde – particularly the Constructivists – as a fitting manifestation of an unshackled society. Lissitzky, who spent much of the 1920s in Germany, but maintained contacts in the Soviet Union, served admirably as a propagandist for the movement. During that decade, many Russian artists active at VKhUTEMAS and INKhUK visited the west (Kandinsky, Malevich, Gabo, Pevsner), and a number of western architects visited, and in many cases worked in, the Soviet Union (Bruno Taut, Ernst May, Erich Mendelsohn, Le Corbusier).[24] Exhibitions of modernist Soviet art were held in various German cities, in the Netherlands, in Paris, Venice, and New York; and western architectural journals such as *L'esprit nouveau* and *De Stijl* wrote of Constructivism and of the latest developments in Russian architecture. The Soviets reciprocated: Ties between INKhUK and

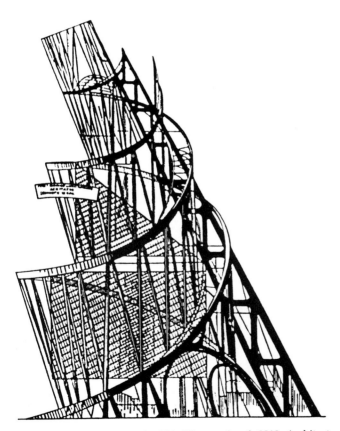

Figure 624. Monument to the Third International. 1919. Architect: Vladimir Tatlin. Sketch.

the Bauhaus were close, and at exhibits in Moscow during the middle and late 1920s, Russian architects could see the work of their counterparts in Germany (Mendelsohn, Max Berg, Walter Gropius, Mies van der Rohe), the Netherlands (Gerrit Rietveld, J. J. P. Oud), and France (Le Corbusier).[25]

Until 1925, the Constructivists had little more to show in actual construction than their more theoretically minded colleagues, the Rationalists. The exigencies of social and economic reconstruction drastically limited the resources available, particularly for structures requiring a relatively intensive use of modern technology. In fact, the most advanced of Constructivist works in the early 1920s were wooden set designs by Alexander Vesnin, Varvara Stepanova, and Liubov Popova.[26] (Konstantin Melnikov's Makhorka Pavilion of 1923 cannot be properly called "Constructivist," although its form shows similarities with the Constructivist design.)

Yet by 1924, Constructivist architects, whatever their tangible achievements, had acquired vigorous leadership in the persons of Alexander Vesnin and Moisei Ginzburg, the latter of who proved to be an articulate and combative spokesman in polemics with Asnova. In 1924, Ginzburg's book *Style and Epoch* appeared in print, which established the theoretical and historical base for a new architecture in a new age, devoid above all of the eclecticism and aestheticism of capitalist architecture at the turn of the century.[27] The following year, the Constructivists founded the Union of Contemporary Architects (OSA); and in 1926, the Union began publishing the journal *Contemporary Architecture*, edited by Ginzburg and Vesnin.

The crux of the debate between the Rationalists, or formalists, and the Constructivists lay in the relative importance assigned to aesthetic theory as opposed to a functionalism derived from technology and materials. In 1923, the poet Vladimir Maiakovskii exhorted the Constructivists: "Beware of becoming just another aesthetic school!"; although this statement could be dismissed as another bit of the "infantile leftist" sloganeering so characteristic of the early 1920s (in 1920, the Constructivists had declared "uncompromising war on art"), Constructivist ideologues maintained that the work of the architect must not be separated from the utilitarian demands of technology. Ginzburg accused the Rationalists of ignoring this principle. Asnova countered by finding the constructivists guilty of "technological fetishism." Constructivists responded with the terms "naive," "abstract," and "formalist."[28] Yet both groups shared a concern for the relation between architecture and social planning; and both insisted on a clearly defined structural

mass, based on simple, uncluttered geometric forms.

This geometric laconism is uncompromisingly applied in the Constructivist buildings erected in Moscow in the late 1920s and early 1930s. A comparison of Shekhtel's building for the Moscow Mercantile Society (see Figure 582) – one of the most advanced prerevolutionary designs – with Grigorii Barkhin's *Izvestiia* Building (1927; Figure 625) reveals that the facades of both are defined by an orthogonal grid, both make extensive use of glass within the grid, both create an unobstructed off-center glass shaft (a stairwell, on the left), and both have a large service entrance at the left corner. But the visual effects are strikingly different, and it is a difference that says much about the Constructivist aesthetic. Shekhtel modulated the effect of the grid with glazed-brick facing applied to the piers, and by a judicious use of the curve: over the service entrance, in the niches of the top story, and in the brick facing that covers the piers. Barkhin, by contrast, adopts a resolutely angular approach: There is no rounding – or "compromise" – of the points of intersection between vertical and horizontal,

Figure 625. *Izvestiia* Building. Moscow. 1927. Architect: Grigorii Barkhin. (M 133–27)

no concession to an aesthetic mediation of material and structure. Both the horizontal and vertical lines are further stressed by a series of simple balconies, placed asymmetrically on the facade; and when the curve is used, it is used fully, as a circle in the four windows of the top story. The circle and square dominate here as clearly as they do in Constructivist set designs by Stepanova.[29]

Barkhin's geometrical display is limited to the street facade of the *Izvestiia* Building, but the juxtaposition of square and circle is developed in depth by Ilia Golosov in his Zuev Workers' Club (1927–9). Graduating from the Moscow School of Painting, Sculpture, and Architecture in 1912, Golosov began his career before the revolution with designs in a predictable Neoclassical revival style. In the early 1920s, he taught with Melnikov at VKhUTEMAS, and, like Melnikov, built or projected a number of wooden exhibition pavilions. At the same time, he produced rather eclectic, "romantic" sketches for competitions on a grand scale such as the Moscow Palace of Labor project (1922–3), with the arched roof of its central auditorium suggesting the shape of a dynamo.[30] By 1925, Golosov's acceptance of Constructivist principles became markedly evident in a number of large office building designs, streamlined and reduced to a balance of rectilinear elements. In the few projects that were realized (primarily apartment buildings), the divergence between the crisp lines of his drawings and the realities of Soviet construction methods is all too evident.[31]

The Zuev Club, however, was built with atypical concern for the integrity of the design, despite its complex contours (Figure 626). Many such clubs were built in the late 1920s and 1930s, and in the most pragmatic sense, they were intended to provide a meeting and recreational space for both workers and professionals (whose alternative might have been the tavern). On the level of ideology, the workers' clubs provided an opportunity for the integration of architecture and social politics in the creation of communal structures, and they firmly announced the leading role of the Communist Party in the creation of a new society. It is not surprising, therefore, that the club concept (or "palace of labor") stimulated some of the most interesting designs of the period.[32]

The Zuev Club has been shabbily maintained, like most Constructivist buildings. But the vigor of Golosov's concept has not diminished. The large corner cylinder, containing a stairwell enclosed in glass, is clenched with a rectangular extension of one of the upper floors. The resulting contrast of shapes epitomizes Constructivist architecture, both in its display

Figure 626. Zuev Club. Moscow. 1927–9. Architect: Ilia Golosov. (M 46)

of unadorned steel, glass, and concrete, and in its massing of sharply defined volumes. A new industrial aesthetic created a building that resembles a machine, symbolizing the machine age. Yet the bold modeling of its forms recalls the work of architects such as Bazhenov, whose neoclassical designs display a similar volumetric approach. (An example in Moscow is Bazhenov's Iushkov mansion, 1973, which also turns on a corner cylinder – and by fitting coincidence served as the main location of VKhUTEMAS.)

More significant, however, are the similarities between Constructivist buildings – and the Zuev Club in particular – and the plasticity of early medieval Russian architecture. The most obvious examples in support of this comparison are the monastery cathedrals constructed in Novgorod at the beginning of twelfth century (Iurev Monastery, Antoniev Monastery; see Figures 28 and 30). The clearly outlined mass of the exterior, reflecting the interior division and support of the structure, exemplifies the fusion of function and tectonics that appears in much constructivist architecture. The corner cylinder at the Antoniev Monastery cathedral served the same function as its Zuev Club counterpart: to provide access to the upper levels of the main structure.

Yet the parallel between the medieval and modern should not be limited to isolated functional or structural similarities. Rather, it can be argued that the style so sympathetically received by the international modern movement in architecture was deeply rooted a perception of structure deriving from the oldest traditions of Russo-Byzantine architecture – the ability to interpret form without ornament. If the development of modern Russian painting is indebted to the rediscovery of the forms and painterly values of medieval icon painting (as is widely acknowledged), then modern Russian architecture also bears within itself an equivalent understanding of the essential elements of structure – themselves capable of symbolic interpretation – that were logically and economically expressed in the high medieval period.

The organization of interior space at the Zuev Club also devolves upon the staircase cylinder, whose wall of glass not only illuminates with a brilliance unusual in Moscow architecture, but also highlights the radial construction of the reinforced-concrete beams beneath the upper landing (Figure 627). The dynamism of this machinelike space, which served to concentrate motion within the building, is both function and lyric in its relation to the urban landscape beyond the walls. Golosov, like Shekhtel, Konstantin Melnikov, and Le Corbusier, was particularly attuned to the properties of the glass membrane in defining the relation between interior and exterior space; but he went beyond them in his use of glazed components to endow the structure with the sense of a living organism whose interior workings – people moving from one level to another within the building – were exposed to view.[33] By 1933, however, Golosov, like many of his contemporaries, had abandoned this idealistic view of an open structure in favor of a massive, opaque neoclassicism.[34]

The Aesthetics of Functionalism: Moisei Ginzburg; Le Corbusier

Not all buildings of the Constructivist movement explored tectonic relations as inventively as did Golosov, and, in general, the buildings of the period avoided dramatic juxtapositions of form in favor of

Figure 627. Zuev Club. Glass cylinder. Interior. (S 7–32)

more severe lines that delinated structure in its most basic outlines. The main proponent of this functionalism, Moisei Ginzburg, noted that "the method of functional thought by no means negates the extremely important task of architectural design. It merely establishes the laws for this design and forces the architect to locate [design] in functionally justified elements."[35] In this and other statements of 1926–7, Ginzburg attempted to defend his Constructivist, functional approach to architecture from those who considered it indifferent to the question of aesthetics, and at the same time to insist on the logical unity of form and function.

Despite technological and material limitations, there are Moscow structures that bear out his claim. One of the earliest, Boris Velikovskii's building for the State Trade Agency (Gostorg, 1925–7), was never completed to the architect's specifications. Its recessed central structure, with flanking blocks that extend to the street line, was originally intended to serve as a base for an office tower (fourteen stories in all).[36] As it exists (Figure 628), the six-floor structure is probably the period's most severely functional design, with its ferroconcrete skeleton set within horizontal strips of glass, interrupted only by vertical slabs of concrete on the flanking projections. Despite its unkempt appearance, the proportions of the structural frame and the fenestration, as well as the variations in depth along Gostorg's street facade attest to a sensitivity to proportion that is noteworthy in comparison with the lack of such qualities in recent functionalist design in Soviet architecture.

Perhaps the most accomplished example of the functional aesthetic is Ginzburg's own creation, the apartment house for the People's Commissariat of Finance (Narkomfin, 1928–30), designed in collaboration with Ignatii Milinis. Ginzburg had just completed his architectural training at the Milan Academy of Arts when the First World War broke out; and after returning to Russia, he continued his studies at the eminent Riga Polytechnikum (then evacuated to Moscow).[37] In addition to his theoretical works establishing the principles of Constructivism in architecture, Ginzburg contributed greatly in the 1920s to the development of new concepts of housing, with particular emphasis on the social aspects of modern communal housing. Although in the debate over the feasibility of "deurbanization" as opposed to greater urban concentration Ginzburg had stated his support for decentralization, his housing designs could achieve a massive scale – as in his 1925 project for a textile workers' apartment building (unbuilt).[38]

Figure 628. State Trade Agency (Gostorg) Building. Moscow. 1925–7. Architect: Boris Velikovskii. (M 45)

474

The smaller scale of the Narkomfin building (intended for 200 residents) contributed only marginally to a solution for resolving the urban housing crisis, but it illustrates admirably Ginzburg's statements on the necessary interdependence of aesthetics and functional design, "from the interior to the exterior." Built to contain apartments, as well as dormitory rooms arranged in a communal living system, the interior was meticulously designed, like that of many Constructivist buildings.[39] The main structure, adjoined at one end by a large block for communal services, rested on pilotis (now enclosed); and the structure culminated in an open-frame solarium. The front, or east, facade of the building is defined by the sweeping horizontal lines of window strips and, on the lower floors, of connecting balconies.

The horizontality of the Narkomfin east facade, which follows the design of the straight interior corridors (facing the morning sun and suitable for calisthenics) along the length of the building, exists in counterpoint to the split-level design of the apartments themselves, which are marvels of spatial ingenuity. The complexity of this arrangement is delineated with greater clarity on the west facade: the floors are grouped in strips of two, and each end of the facade is marked by a stairwell shaft (Figure 629). The effect is austere, yet impressive in rhythm and balance. Larger communal apartment buildings of the period were necessarily less refined in detail; yet a few examples, such as Ivan Nikolaev's massive eight-story dormitory (1,000 rooms, each 6 meters square, for 2,000 students) built in 1929–30 on Donskoi Lane in south Moscow, were strikingly futuristic in the streamlined contours of their machine-age design.[40]

Ginzburg's implementation of his concept of functionalism for the Narkomfin project not only created a remarkable example of Russian modernist architecture, but also demonstrated how closely such works were related to contemporary architecture in the rest of Europe. Without losing its individuality, the building seems to echo Gropius and De Stijl, and within a few years of its completion, Alvar Aalto was to continue this experiment in communal living space with his Paimio Tuberculosis Sanatorium (1933), a building with formal similarities to the Narkomfin apartment building. The closest affinity, however, is with Le Corbusier's notion of the Unité d'Habitation. Le Corbusier and Ginzburg were personally acquainted, and in 1927, the French architect was included on the board of *Contemporary Architecture*, edited by Ginzburg and Alexander Vesnin. The following year, Le Corbusier made the first of his three visits to the Soviet Union (the last in 1930).

Figure 629. Apartment house for the People's Commissariat of Finance (Narkomfin). Moscow. 1928–30. Architects: Moisei Ginzburg and Ivan Milinis. West facade. (M 56–5)

Le Corbusier's active collaboration in Russian architecture involved enormous conceptual projects that remained unrealized, such as his plan for the reconstruction of Moscow, one of whose variants would have required leveling much of the existing city (but not major architectural monuments).[41] In addition, for the Palace of Soviets competition in 1931, he submitted a boldly modernistic proposal that was rejected. His enduring legacy, however, was the design for the headquarters for the Central Union of Consumers' Cooperatives (Tsentrosoiuz, 1929–36). Assisted by his cousin Pierre Jeanneret, and the Soviet architect Nikolai Kolli, Le Corbusier succeeded in completing the building on the intended scale, but without many of its planned technical refinements, such as an advanced system of circulating cooled or heated air through the double-glazed facade (see Plate 77). Only eight stories tall, the building is an impressive mass composed of three elongated blocks. The center block is set back from Kirov Street, and the other two flank it in a perpendicular arrangement extending to the street line. Two of the blocks are sheathed in a glass-curtain wall, framed in red tufa; and the central block rests on pilotis – now enclosed, although a restoration is supposed to return the ground floor to a semblance of its original appearance.[42] The rear of the building contains subsidiary structures, including a meeting hall and club space. The main components of the interior are connected by spiral ramps.

The Tsentrosoiuz building was one of the last modernist works to be completed in Moscow. Yet the Constructivist–functionalist movement continued to thrive into the 1930s, as demonstrated by Panteleimon Golosov's *Pravda* Building (1931–5), which included a nine-story office block fronted by the lower printing plant, with its streamlined, horizontal window lines.[43] The versatile Aleksei Shchusev, Russia's most gifted designer of churches before the Revolution and subsequently the author of the Lenin Mausolem, also contributed to the late flourishing of the Constructivist style in his office building for Commissariat of Agriculture (1929–33; Figure 630).[44] Its surface of masonry panels and glass, suspended from a ferroconcrete skeleton, is articulated in a masterful play of curved and orthogonal lines.

During this period, even such neoclassicists as Ivan Fomin combined Constructivist concepts with stripped classicism in his design for the Dinamo Society housing and office complex (1928–9), near Liubianka, or Dzerzhinskii, Square. The facade of the seven-story administrative sector was divided with paired attached columns extending for six stories, and the flat surface of the seventh served as an entablature, marked with large circular windows in a manner reminiscent of Barkhin's *Izvestiia* Building.[45] Indeed, the concept of this design derives ultimately from Behrens' building for the German Embassy in Petersburg (see Figure 609), whose expression of monumental power anticipates the ways of totalitarian architecture in the Soviet Union. The second component of the Dinamo complex was a narrow fourteen-story apartment building in an angular style more closely associated with Constructivism.

Figure 630. Building for the Commissariat of Agriculture. Moscow. 1929–33. Architect: Aleksei Shchusev. (M 166–18)

During the Constructivist era, however, the latent force of reaction in Soviet architecture could be seen in the work of unreconstructed traditionalists such as Ivan Zholtovskii, who adopted a neo-Renaissance style for the State Bank office building (1927–9).[46] Another of the prerevolutionary Neoclassicists, Ivan Rerberg, also firmly rejected modernism in his design for the Central Telegraph Building (1926–7), whose strategic location at the foot of Tverskaia Street failed to inspire the architect to anything more than a capricious, ungainly form of stripped classicism.[47]

The Vesnin Brothers

Among the many architects whose work adhered to the principles of Constructivism, perhaps the most stalwart and productive proponents of the movement were the Vesnin brothers: Leonid, Viktor, and Alexander, all of whom completed their education in Petersburg before the First World War.[48] Leonid and

Viktor embarked on flourishing careers, one of whose landmarks was the design by Viktor Vesnin and A. Miliukov for the Roll office and cinema complex (1913) in a modernized classical style.[49] Alexander, the most artistically gifted of the three, worked in Tatlin's studio between 1912 and 1914, and also revealed a brilliant talent as stage designer. It was in this capacity, during the material restrictions of the early postrevolutionary years, that the Vesnins – Alexander in particular – began to explore the methods of dynamic construction in space, with the obvious influence of Tatlin. The most remarkable product of this phase was Alexander Vesnin's set design in 1922 for Alexander Tairov's production of ''The Man who was Thursday'' at the Moscow Chamber (Kamernyi) Theater.[50] With its intersecting planes and ramps, the set not only emphasized the dynamic of the actors' motion, but also bridged the gap between the abstract constructions of artists such as Lissitskii, Malevich, and Pevsner and the design of functional buildings.

The Vesnins' progression from dynamic, avant-garde set constructions to the much larger scale of major architectural projects was soon evident in their design of 1923 for the Palace of Labor competition (Figure 631). Although their submission was awarded only third prize, it served as a programmatic statement in the development of a Constructivist aesthetic, combining both monumentality and severe functionalism in the massing of simple geometric shapes in a complex balance.[51] The center of the plan was the oval meeting hall in the form of an amphitheater, 75 × 67 meters in size. The array of radio masts and docking ports for airships around the top were functionally justified, despite their futuristic appearance in the context of an exhausted country reestablishing a modicum of civilized existence.

In 1925, Alexander and Viktor Vesnin, together with Moisei Ginzburg, founded the Constructivist organization OSA (the preceding year, Alexander had designed the book jacket for *Style and Epoch*).[52] With the quickening tempo of construction during the late 1920s, all three brothers were actively engaged in projects extending from the Caucasus to the colossal hydroelectric dam across the Dnieper River, the DneproGES, designed by Viktor Vesnin in collaboration with Nikolai Kolli and others. The Vesnins' design of the Mostorg department store in central Moscow (1927–9; Figure 632) represents an attempt to provide modern retail space during the brief flourishing of commerce toward the end of the NEP period. Located on an awkward trapezoidal lot in the Krasnaia Presnia working-class district, the store, with its double-glazed facade framed by a ferroconcrete structure, appeared strikingly modern when first constructed in its context of nineteenth-century brick buildings. It has since suffered by the addition of another story and by a lack of proper maintenance.[53]

Like other major architects of the late 1920s, the Vesnins were much concerned with the creation of institutions for social communication. One of the most modernistic of such designs – and one of the last Constructivist buildings in Moscow – was the club for the Society of Tsarist Political Prisoners, begun in 1931. In addition to meeting rooms and a theater hall, the extensive complex was to contain a museum. In 1934, however, the society was disbanded (an ominous prelude to the great Stalinist purges, which would create an altogether new society of political prisoners), and the larger plans for a museum were eliminated. Even in this truncated and deformed version (Figure 633), the harmony of the pure, undecorated volumetric forms is evident – and reflects, if coincidentally, some of the oldest formal traditions in Russian architecture.[54]

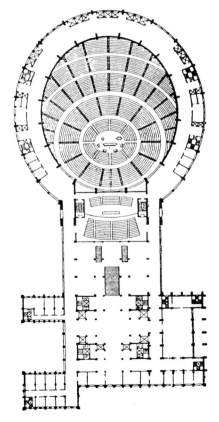

Figure 631. Project for the Palace of Labor in Moscow. 1923. Architects: Alexander, Leonid, and Viktor Vesnin. Plan, sketch from M. A. Il'in, *Vesniny*.

477

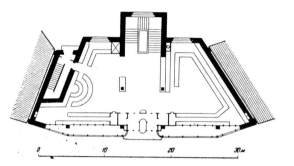

Figure 632. Mostorg Department Store. Moscow. 1927–9. Architects: Vesnin brothers.

The culminating project in the Vesnins' Constructivist oeuvre was an extension of the concept of the workers' club, conceived as a large complex of three buildings to serve the social needs of the Proletarian District, a factory and workers' district in southeast Moscow. The site overlooked the Moscow River and was adjacent to the Simonov Monastery, part of whose walls were razed in the course of constructing the project. Yet the largest part of the ensemble, a theater with a circular hall designed to seat 4,000, was never built, nor was the projected sports building. The central element, however, was the club building itself (Figure 634), built between 1931 and 1937. This period was marred by the death of Leonid, in 1933, and by the increasing need to defend their Constructivist designs.

Nonetheless, they persevered to a remarkable degree, bending to the system, but without rejecting the work that stood at the center of the Constructivist movement. In their writings, it is clear that Viktor and Alexander Vesnin considered the Proletarian Region club one of their most significant works, not only for its union of functions – a 1,000-seat theater, ballroom, meeting halls, exhibition space – but also for the way in which form followed function and space flowed

effortlessly from one component to another.[55] The way in which the design combined an acute aesthetic sensibility with function was particularly important at a time when Constructivism was under attack ostensibly for its inability to recognize the people's aesthetic needs. In the club building, the Vesnins' fluency was reflected on the exterior in such details as the contours of the large rounded bay window over the entrance to the auditorium, and a semicircular conservatory extending from the river facade. The club also included a small astronomy observatory, whose design added to the variety of the building's upper structure.

Indeed, the encouragement of popular astronomy served one of the regime's key goals of combatting religion and inculcating the ideology of atheism through a scientific explanation of the forces of the cosmos. The most notable institution in Moscow promoting a wider knowledge of astronomy was, predictably, the new city planetarium (1927–9), in the Krasnaia Presnia region. Its architects, Mikhail Barshch and Mikhail Siniavskii, were among the Constructivists, and succeeded in using the more futur-

Figure 633. Club for the Society of Tsarist Political Prisoners. Moscow. 1931–4. Architects: Vesnin brothers. (M 155–9)

Figure 634. Palace of Culture for the Proletarian District. Moscow. 1932–7. Architects: Vesnin brothers.

478

istic possibilities of functional design to symbolize the new age of science in the service of a socialist society. The thin parabolic ferroconcrete roof, resembling a beehive, reveals a typical Constructivist emphasis on the plasticity of materials applied with modern technology.[56] (Constructivist designs varied between the resolutely angular and the use of the curve on a massive, structure-forming scale.) On the interior of the ferroconcrete shell, a hemispherical ceiling screen was suspended over a circular 500-seat auditorium located on the second floor of the structure (Figure 635). That floor was supported by ferroconcrete beams radiating from a massive central column on the ground level – a technique analogous to Golosov's design of the upper landing within the cylinder of the Zuev Club (see Figure 627), and also curiously reminiscent of single-column designs supporting the ceilings of refectory halls in medieval Novgorod and Moscow.

Constructivism Beyond Moscow

For all of the variety displayed by Moscow's Constructivist architects, and with all of the resources dedicated to rebuilding the city to reflect a new social order, Moscow by no means possessed a monopoly on modernist architecture. Leningrad, Nizhnii Novgorod (or Gorkii), Sverdlovsk, Kazan, and Kharkov, among others, saw the implementation of major projects that illustrated the extent to which ideas developed at INKhUK and applied by the Constructivists had been assimilated into general architectural practice. The export of new ideas to other Soviet cities was stimulated by the overproduction of architects in the educational center of Leningrad, whose economy was still unequipped to absorb them in the 1920s.[57]

In Leningrad, which under the direction of Sergei Kirov had begun to recover from its precipitous economic and political decline after the revolution, Constructivist architecture was particularly noticeable in the design of administrative and cultural centers for the city's largest outer districts, where workers' housing was under construction. (The historic central districts of the city remained largely intact, by virtue of a comprehensive preservation policy and the limited resources of an abandoned capital.) One of the earliest examples was the Moscow–Narva District House of Culture (1925–7; later renamed the Gorkii Palace of Culture), by Alexander Gegello and David Krichevskii. Essentially, a symmetrical structure designed around a wedge-shaped amphitheater of 1,900 seats, the compact building demonstrated the beginnings of a functional monumentality dictated by actual circum-

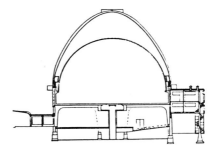

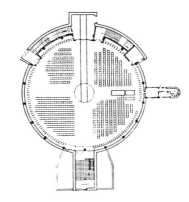

Figure 635. Planetarium. Moscow. 1927–9. Architects: Mikhail Barshch and Mikhail Siniavskii. Section. From Bylinkin et al., *Istoriia sovetskoi arkhitektury*.

stances – ignored in the earlier Workers' Palace and Palace of Labor competitions.[58]

The construction of a number of model projects occurred in the same district, including workers' housing by Gegello and others on Tractor Street (1925–7); a department store and "factory-kitchen" (to eliminate the need for cooking at home) built in 1929–30 in a streamlined early Bauhaus style by Armen Barutchev and others; and the Tenth Anniversary of October School (1925–7) designed by Alexander Nikolskii on Strike Prospekt.[59] The centerpiece of the district (subsequently renamed Kirov) was the House of Soviets (1930–4; Figure 636), designed by Noi Trotskii. Its long four-story office block, defined by horizontal window strips, ends on one side in a perpendicular wing with a rounded facade, and on the other in a severely angular ten-story tower with corner balconies.[60]

A similarly austere, unadorned style emphasizing the basic geometry of forms was adopted by Igor Ivanovich Fomin and V. Daugul for the Moscow District House of Soviets (1931–5; on Moscow Prospekt). Yet the facade, composed of segmented windows of identical size, signifies the repetition of an incipient bureacratic style rather than the streamlined dynamic of earlier Constructivist work.[61] During the same period, 1931–5, Igor Fomin and Evgenii Levinson designed an apartment complex for use by the Leningrad Soviet in the fashionable prerevolutionary Petrograd District, on the bank of the Karpovka River near Kamennoostrovskii Prospekt (subsequently renamed after Kirov). With an open passageway supported by granite columns in the center of the curved facade (Figure 637), the design echoes the work of Ginzburg and, especially, of Le Corbusier. A stylobate of gray granite provides a base for the rest of the structure, whose facade is coated in artistic concrete with a scored surface.[62] The careful attention to such details of architectural and decorative design are unusual for this period and indicate the privileged status of the city bureaucrats for whom the structure was built. With their balconies and wide windows overlooking the wooded river bank, some of the building's seventy-six apartments reached a size of six rooms (on two levels) – this at a time when desirable prerevolutionary apartments of similar size were being subdivided for the use of one family to a room.

The monumentality of the projects described before suggests an increasing social differentiation within the Soviet Union, as well as the power and prevalence of the bureaucracy. Each of these developments supported an architectural reaction described in the following sections. But during the transitional period of the first Five-Year Plan (1928–32), the functionalist aesthetic still influenced the determination of form, as is exemplified in the enormous Moscow apartment complex known as the Government House (Figure 638) on Serafimovich Street, designed by Boris Iofan with the assistance of Dmitrii Iofan. Like many of the

leading Soviet architects, Boris Iofan had traveled extensively in Italy and become devoted to Italian architecture in all its variety.[63] Returning to the Soviet Union in 1924, Iofan designed workers' housing in Moscow and the provinces until 1927, when he began work on the Government House, which was far larger than other experimental housing projects such as Ginzburg's Narkomfin building, under construction at the same time.

Located diagonally from the Kremlin across the Moscow River and intended for use by the upper echelons of the party and government (the Central Committee of the party and the Council of People's Commissars), the complex was in fact a small city, three hectars in size and containing some 500 apartments, as well as a library, a gymnasium, a club, and an array of services and shops for the elite.[64] Iofan accommodated these many functions within an ensemble of several buildings, constructed of a ferroconcrete skeleton with brick infill. Despite the uniformity of the fenestration and the lack of ornament, the project possessed its own "skyline," with setback roof structures; and the arrangement of three interior courtyards between the buildings (connected by enclosed passages raised on pilotis) provided further variety to the design. The side facing the Moscow River on the Bersenevka Quay was symmetrically planned, with apartment towers flanking the facade of the club (later converted to a variety theater) and all linked by a large stripped colonnade symbolizing the structure's relation to the neoclassical architecture of central Moscow to the north across the river.

The south side of the ensemble is, however, the more interesting by virtue of Iofan's design of the attached Udarnik (Shockworker) Cinema, whose silhouette provides a transition from the surrounding area to the massive grouping of apartment buildings (see Figure 638). Its form echoes the "dynamo" shape of the final variant of Ilia Golosov's proposal for the 1923 Palace of Labor competition, with a series of stepped arches forming the roof over the 1,600-seat auditorium.[65] Despite its Constructivist aspects, the Government House already shows a turning toward classicizing elements, such as the general symmetry of its design and the use of colonnades. By the time of its completion in 1931 (work on the interior actually continued several more years because of an inability to install demanding technical features), Iofan had irrevocably embarked on the path of a conservative, classicist monumentality at the service of a totalitarian state.

As will be seen in more detail, Iofan was by no means alone in his turn from functionalism to Stalinist

Figure 636. Moscow–Narva (Kirov) House of Soviets. Leningrad. 1930–4. Architect: Noi Trotskii. (P 90–23)

480

Figure 637. Apartment house of the Leningrad Soviet. 1931–5. Architects: Igor Fomin and Evgenii Levinson. (P 71–16)

monumentalism. Sergei Chernyshev, for example, moved from the archival austerity of the Marxism–Leninism Institute (1927), with unadorned pilaster strips segmenting a facade of plain rectangular windows, to the massive Ionic portico of the Moscow Highway Institute (late 1940s) – an expression of his lifelong interest in Moscow neoclasscism.[66]

One of the clearest examples of the amalgamation of functionalism and incipient monumentality occurred with the construction of the main library of the Soviet Union, the Lenin Library. The competition for the project, in 1928, produced a number of avant-garde proposals, but the project was awarded to a more conservative, eclectic design by Vladimir Shchuko and Vladimir Gelfreikh. The jury's decision was yet another premonition of the stylistic and cultural reaction in Soviet architecture, because Shchuko had been one of the most accomplished proponents of the monumental neoclassical revival in Petersburg before the First World War (see Chapter 14).[67]

To be sure, the classicizing elements, such as the colonnade and portico (Figure 639), were very much in the modernized, stripped manner[68]; and the statuary above the cornice of the main structure was an elaboration that evolved over the extended period of construction, which embodied the transition from modernism to conservative forms. The library was not completed until 1940, and the outfitting of the main reading rooms continued well after the war. The statuary, the frieze above the main portico, and the bronze reliefs of noted thinkers between the pylons of the facade signaled a return to a traditional (Renaissance and classical) synthesis of monumental art forms as a means of expressing – or manipulating – ideological content in architecture.

Konstantin Melnikov

Within the divide created by the opposition between Constructivism and incipient monumentalilty, there were a few Russian architects who stood apart from

Figure 638. Government House. Moscow. 1927–31. Architects: Boris and Dmitrii Iofan. (M 69–5)

any particular faction. The greatest of these was Konstantin Melnikov. Although not a Constructivist, he was closely acquainted with the group, and like most of them had received a thorough grounding in classical architecture before developing his distinctive version of a modern architectural aesthetic. Although some of his earliest masterpieces were wooden pavilions, no longer extant, his design for the Soviet Pavilion at the Paris Exhibition of Decorative Arts (1925) presented to the west one of its first views of the achievements of Russian modernism. With great ingenuity, Melnikov's dynamic, angular arrangment of forms connecting the entrance with the exhibit rooms concealed the compact floor space of the structure.[69]

While in Paris, Melnikov was invited to design a parking garage with 1,000 spaces for the city. Nothing came of his exuberant designs, intended to be constructed over the Seine.[70] Upon his return to Moscow, however, his first major commission was the design in 1926 of a large garage on Bakhmetev Street for newly acquired British Leyland buses. Designed as a parallelogram, the bus garage included angled entrance and exit facades with six monumental portals – in front, each framed in chaneled concrete under a single pediment, and in back (Figure 640), each portal

constructed as an independent brick unit separated by strips of glass panes and culminating in circular windows (certain of these details have since been lost). The following year Melnikov received another industrial commission, for a truck garage on Novoriazanskaia Street. The design is both vigorous and functional, with the main garage contained in a semicircular structure and the administrative block in the middle. The end facades of the semicircle are articulated with vertical vitreous strips and circular windows set within an angled portal facade.[71]

A similarly bold, expressionistic shaping of structure appeared in his Rusakov Club (1927–9; see Plate 78), for the Union of Municipal Workers. It is the most dramatic of the workers' clubs, with its three cantilevered wedges plunging toward a point at the rear of the building (Figure 641). The effect of the three massive projections, separated by glass shafts in the front, is not only visually striking, but functional as well, in providing a slope for the seats of the theater within. The building has been called "expressionist," and it indeed proclaims itself more loudly than most other structures of the period – Melnikov's included.[72] His Kauchuk and "Burevestnik" factory clubs (both 1927–9), by contrast, show a greater resemblance to the work of the Constructivists such as Ilia Golosov, particularly in its contrast of curved and orthogonal shapes and its use of the cylinder.[73]

The cylinder is the essential element of the most private of Melnikov's buildings, the house that he built for himself in 1927–9. Situated on a small wooded lot on one of the side streets of Moscow's Arbat region, the Melnikov house consists of two interlocking vertical cylinders, whose entrance is defined by a rectangular glass facade between two pylons (Figure 642). The taller cylinder, to the rear, is perforated by numerous hexagonal windows that distribute natural light throughout the artist's studio and bedroom, while framing the exterior landscape in isolated segments of color and texture. The Melnikov dwelling belongs to that category architects' houses – from Frank Lloyd Wright's Robie House to the Alvar Aalto's Villa Mairea – that represent a distillation of the architect's thought, a credo. The Melnikov house does not resemble any of them; indeed, its contours form a sharp contrast to the angularity of modern house designs by Wright or Gerrit Rietveld or Le Courbusier.[74] Like the Riabushinskii house, it consists of contrasting principles, notably the open double-glazed front set within a tower that reminds of a fortress, protected from the large blocks of flats that surround it. This rounded sufficiency suggests that the house's true affinity lies not with twentieth-century architecture, but the late eighteenth-century design for a spherical house by another visionary, Claude-Nicolas Ledoux, creator of secular temples.

There is a purified, altarlike quality about the interior of the Melnikov house, in its shape and in the way the light enters through a multitude of narrow windows – both reminiscent of the apsidal space of

Figure 639. Lenin State Library. Moscow. 1928–40. Architects: Vladimir Shchuko and Vladimir Gelfreikh. (M 107–0)

Figure 640. Bakhmetev Street bus garage. Moscow. 1926. Architect: Konstantin Melnikov. (M 177–8)

large fourteenth-century Novgorod churches, as well as the tower churches at Kolomenskoe. The individuality so uncompromisingly stated in the Melnikov house ensured the architect's banishment from active professional life during the following decades, during which he was left to draw sketches for projects whose grandiosity suggests comparison with Boullée or Ledoux. Yet his house has survived and is entering an uncertain period of restoration.[75]

As Melnikov became increasingly isolated in the 1930s, his fantastic designs for such major competitions as the Palace of Soviets (in 1932) and the skyscraper Commissariat of Heavy Industry (Narkomtiazhprom, in 1934) seem to be declarations of freedom from the mundane constraints of practicality and feasibility.[76] Even his two designs that were implemented – parking garages for Intourist (1934–6) and Gosplan (1936) – were dynamically sculpted facades symbolizing motion, with little relation to the function of the structure itself.[77] Melnikov was tireless in exploring new concepts relating architecture to human psychology (his design of an experimental sleep environment, for the 1929 Green City project) and to kinetics – his projected monument to Christopher Columbus, also 1929, which resumed a theme broached by Tatlin a decade earlier in his Monument to the Third International.[78]

Figure 641. Rusakov Club. Moscow. 1927–9. Architect: Konstantin Mclnikov. (M 177–11)

In addition to Melnikov, there were other isolated geniuses who continued to explore visionary architecture on paper. Iakov Chernikhov of Leningrad worked primarily in the realm of architectural theory, beginning with Suprematism and moving from Constructivism to an idiosyncratic, romantic expressionism.[79] In addition to his theoretical treatises, he created in the 1930s volumes of "architectural fictions" and fantasy drawings (in the cycles "Picturesque Architecture" and "Palace Architecture") of remarkable inventiveness, ranging from archaic, geological forms to visions of a future environment. If, as Emil Kaufmann has stated in reference to Piranesi, "any period of extraordinary excitement will easily become a heyday for architectural fantasies,"[80] then the work of Chernikhov expresses exquisitely the transition from the early period of revolutionary enthusiasm to an era of frenzied industrialization culminating in Stalinist megalomania.

The 1930s: Architecture and the Totalitarian State

During the early 5-year plans, the obvious metaphorical connections between "construction" and the creation of a new society were exploited to the full as a part of the cultural revolution promulgated by Stalin and his party apparatus. Not only was the new to be built, but the old had to be destroyed. The clearest example of this socioarchitectural dialectic was the demolition of Konstantin Ton's massive Church of Christ the Redeemer (see Chapter 13), and the international competition for a new building on the site, the Palace of Soviets. The dimensions announced at the first stage of the competition in 1931 approach the realm of fantasy: a main hall for 15,000, and a conference hall for 6,000, in addition to numerous smaller meeting spaces and offices.[81] Of the 160 projects submitted from several countries in addition to the Soviet Union, 16 were awarded prizes, but none met the guidelines established by the construction committee, whose commentary on the process provides a view of the move toward classical models that would become a basis for "socialist realism" in architecture.

At the same time, the Palace of Soviets was to exploit modern technology on a gargantuan scale in ways that became clearer during the fourth phase of competition, in 1932–3. By the middle of 1933, the project had been awarded to a team consisting of Boris Iofan, Shchuko, and Gelfreikh, who over the next 6 years developed the artistic and technical aspects of the structure to their final, hypertrophied forms: halls with a seating capacity of 21,000 and 6,000, set within

Figure 642. Melnikov house. Moscow. 1927–9. Architect: Konstantin Melnikov. Rear cylinder. (M 155–19)

a sprawling rectangular base with endless columniation. From this stylobate, a tiered columnar structure formed of massive pylons was to rise to a height of 315 meters, above which was to be a 100-meter statue of Lenin (Figure 643).[82] Despite the stupendous megalomania of the project, Iofan and his collaborators were committed to its implementation. A trip to the United States in 1935 gave an encouraging view of the technical possibilities, and by 1937, work had begun on the enormous foundation pit, excavated to limestone bedrock at a depth of 20 meters below the level of the adjacent Moscow River. By 1940, the steel frame began to rise above ground level from the concentric circles of the ferroconcrete foundation; but the outbreak of war halted construction and the steel was extracted for military uses, including "hedgehogs" for the defense of Moscow in the fall of 1941. Various attempts to resurrect – and diminish – the project proved futile, and in 1958–60, the foundation pit was

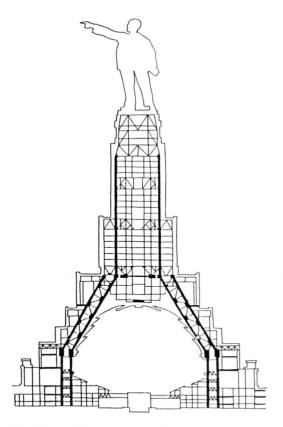

Figure 643. Palace of Soviets project. Moscow. 1930s. Architects: Boris Iofan, Vladimir Shchuko, and Vladimir Gelfreikh. Section.

converted into the basin for a gargantuan outdoor heated swimming pool (130 meters in diameter) designed by Dmitrii Chechulin.[83] Yet despite the failure of the Palace of Soviets project, the process of its development provided the technological experience and a number of the design motifs for the postwar Stalinist skyscrapers.

Even the more practical scale of urban construction in the 1930s achieved startling results. For not only was architecture commanded to glorify the achievements of the new industrial power, but the very cityscape of the country's two major urban centers was visibly transformed. The earlier disputes between the "urbanists" and "deurbanists" was resolved in favor of regulated but intensive urban development, as set forth in a speech by Stalin's satrap Lazar Kaganovich at the Central Committee plenum in June 1931.[84] As a result, both Moscow and Leningrad developed new comprehensive city plans that were to serve as a setting for the new monumental architecture.

By the time the Moscow plan, by Vladimir Semenov and Sergei Chernyshev, was formally adopted in 1935, measures were underway to implement a major

reconstruction of the Soviet capital.[85] The Okhotnyi Riad market area between the Bolshoi Theater and the Kremlin was cleared, and the former Tverskaia Street – renamed in honor of Maxim Gorky in 1932 – was widened and endowed in 1936–40 with rows of buildings designed primarily by Arkadii Mordvinov in an eclectic style that defines the early phase of Stalinist architecture.[86] Other major projects included the construction of Peace Prospekt as the main thoroughfare in the north of the city – with the concomitant razing of Sukharev Tower (see Chapter 7); the design of the Gorky Park of Culture and Rest (1934–6, to a design by Alexander Vlasov; and the construction of the first phases of the Moscow subway.[87]

In Leningrad, the 1935 city plan, devised by Lev Ilin and modified in the late 1930s by Nikolai Baranov, involved a shift from the historical central districts to a new grand avenue – Moscow Prospekt – leading to the south and to a proposed administrative complex centered on the House of Soviets (Figure 644).[88] This building, and the plaza surrounding it, formed perhaps the most grandiose project of the 1930s (if one considers the Moscow Palace of Soviets to have been, in effect, utopian). Ultimately, the project was reduced in scale, and the outbreak of war curtailed construction still further; but the House of Soviets (1936–41), designed by an architectural collective headed by Noi Trotskii, was completed in the purest form of totalitarian monumentality: 220 meters long and 150 meters in depth, including a semicircular projection from the east facade containing a 3,000-seat auditorium. The central facade is marked by twenty attached columns, above which is a massive frieze depicting scenes from the construction and defense of the socialist homeland. The design on the one hand attempts to draw upon the legacy of classical architecture and city planning in Petersburg with its great open squares and correspondingly capacious architectural facades, and on the other proposes to supercede that legacy by sheer exaggeration of scale.[89]

The creation of such monumentally eclectic projects reflected not simply a shift in favor of traditionalists in the process of architectural competitions, but an insistence on the reeducation of the intelligentsia in the ways of subordination to a monomania that equated the state, the party, the people – and Stalin. In the architectural profession, the Stalinist "general line" was imposed skillfully and methodically – as it had been in the other arts. Various factional disputes continued through the early 1930s, while the party tightened its control as a "mediator." In this atmo-

Figure 644. House of Soviets. Leningrad. 1936–41. Architects: Noi Trotskii et al. *Arkhitektura Leningrada*, 1937.

sphere, architects of the dwindling avant-garde succumbed to disunity, and incorrigible individuals such as Melnikov became targets for the self-righteous invective of hackdom.[90] The first phase of this process concluded in 1932, when architectural groups such as OSA (Constructivists), ASNOVA (Rationalists), VOPRA (the organization of "proletarian architects"), and the Moscow and Leningrad Architectural societies were abolished. In the same year, the Union of Soviet Architects was established as the profession's sole legitimate organization.

As the public campaign against "formalism" intensified, ideological control solidified within the union. One particular target was Ivan Leonidov (an associate of Ginzburg's), who built very little, but whose designs, ranging from the visionary to the functional, made his name a term of abuse for the reactionaries.[91] At architectural conferences in 1934 and 1935, both formalism and retrospectivism were condemned, thus creating the curious situation in which architects as diverse as Ivan Fomin and Melnikov found themselves in open disfavor.

There were, however, indications that retrospectivism would play a major role in the new monumentalism. In 1934, Zholtovskii constructed a seven-story apartment building (at 16 Marx Prospekt; Figure 645) in a pompous neoclassical revival style strongly related to Shchuko's work in Petersburg before the First World War (see Figure 616). Its gargantuan attached columns reached five stories, and culminated in mammoth composite capitals.[92] During the same period, even these hypertrophied forms were exceeded in the design by Pavel Abrosimov and Ivan Fomin for the

Building of the Ukrainian Government in Kiev (1934–8).[93] In 1935, the Vesnin brothers attempted a mild reply to the growing retrospectivist tendency by stating that "the canonization of an old form, however excellent, is a brake on the development of content."[94]

But retrospectivism was not to be denied. The new concept of "socialist realism" had to be given content, which by the Stalinist dialectic was to be derived not from an innovative – if occasionally dreary – functionalism (now labeled formalism), but from conservative neoclassical and neo-Muscovite styles (the epitome of formalism in a modern context).[95] Among the formulators of the style were architects such as Zholtovskii, who had never abandoned the prerevolutionary Renaissance, classicist origins of his career; and Shchusev, who collaborated with Zholtovskii in the design of a pompous, porticoed design for the Palace of Soviets and subsequently applied an eclectic medley of classicizing elements to his design of the capital's new showcase hotel, the "Moskva" (1930–5; Figure 646), on the site of the former Okhotnyi Riad.[96] The project was intended to demonstrate that Soviet architects, craftsmen, and technology could be used to produce a hotel equaling the highest international standards. Therefore, much attention was given to the furnishings and decorative details of the main halls and the deluxe suites – a precedent that would be expanded to lavish extent after the war.

Facing the side facade of the Hotel Moskva was a more austere product of the new monumentalism, the building for the central Soviet administrative apparatus: the Council of Labor and Defense, subsequently the Council of People's Commissariats, and

487

Figure 645. Apartment house, 16 Marx Prospekt. Moscow. 1934.
Architect: Ivan Zholtovskii. (M 55–5a)

still later Gosplan (the main state planning agency). Its architect, Arkadii Langman, had already completed the Dinamo Stadium in the north of Moscow (1927, with L. Cherikover), as well as a building for the Commissariat of Interior Affairs (1932–3) near Fomin's Dinamo Society (also connected with the state police).[97] The council building (1932–6) is of relatively low height – ten stories – in relation to the length of its facade, and this horizontality is massively confirmed by the unadorned cornice that caps the building and from which rises a low attic. The vertical pylons that segment the facade convey the (intimidating) impression of a barred surface, and for both its supporters and detractors, the building has represented the epitome of the centralized and seemingly omnipotent administrative culture.

A more exuberant and appealing interpretation of 1930s' monumentalism appeared in the work of An-

drei Burov, who had studied at VKhUTEMAS in the Vesnin workshop and during the 1920s enjoyed a varied, productive career that included a number of pavilions, the interior of Soviet ocean liners, and sets for Sergei Eisenstein's film *The Old and the New*.[98] In the early 1930s, he served Stalin's industrialization campaign by participating in the design of the Cheliabinsk Tractor Plant, for which purpose he was sent to Detroit to observe the work of Albert Kahn's firm, responsible for the overall design and construction of this and many other major industrial plants in the Soviet Union from April 1929 to May 1932.[99] During the 1920s, Burov also created designs (unrealized) for theaters and workers' clubs in the best Constructivist manner.

With the shift of stylistic and ideological emphasis in the 1930s, Burov responded by producing on the one hand exquisitely mannered classical designs, such as the red facade with white ceramic and gold trim for the extension to the headquarters of the Union of Architects in Moscow (1939–40),[100] and on the other apartment buildings that avoided neo-Renaissance pomposity by using prefabricated concrete components and panels formed in extravagant botanical designs (for example, the apartment house he built in 1935 with the assistance of Boris Blokhin at Leningrad Prospekt No. 25 in Moscow).[101] Burov's career reflects, paradoxically, the high level of culture offered to young architects favored by fortune during the 1930s. In 1935, he was able, for example, to complete graduate work at the Academy of Architecture, which had been founded to define the aesthetic content of Socialist Realism, with its basic premise of the "critical assimilation of the heritage." the architecture of the totalitarian state was, in imitation of its imperial predecessors, to adapt academic styles to a new ideological and technical environment.[102]

Even as the functional, streamlined architecture of industrial production – in Marxist terms, the base – took shape with the help of western engineers and specialists in the Urals and on the Volga (particularly in Stalingrad), the blossoming of surface decoration on the buildings of the new administrative and cul-

tural "superstructure" reflected a dimunition of functionalism in favor of a blatant display of power. This development cannot be attributed solely to the will of Stalin or of his closest advisers, although they undoubtedly approved of it.[103] Rather, it represented both a reaction against "standardized," monotonous architecture associated with Constructivism (whose projects were often subverted by the poor quality of finish and technology), and a preference by the "people" – or the rapidly evolving party elite – for an architecture of decoration and monumentality representative of the achievements of the new society.

Just as eighteenth-century autocrats had erected triumphal arches and extravagant palaces in celebration of the state, its victories, and their supreme role in both, so the new order expected its achievements to be celebrated – in the name of the masses that it mobilized – with an appropriately grandiloquent style. The elaboration of multistoried monoliths in Moscow symbolized the hierarchy of technoadministrative cadres and enclosed them from the masses, whose spartan conditions were masked in the 1930s by grand "parks of culture," by the construction of the Moscow subway, and by the stagey, ornamented building facades that arose along the large boulevards

Figure 646. Hotel Moskva. Moscow. 1930–5. Final architect: Aleksei Shchusev. (M 171–37)

and squares of reconstructed Moscow. Russian modernism had no place in this architectural order, and its demise was completed at the First All-Union Congress of Architects in June 1937 as former modernists accepted the party's direction or remained silent.[104]

The hyperbole of Soviet architecture in the late 1930s has many manifestations, but an extreme example of the attempt to equate architecture with the symbols of state power occurred in the design of Moscow's Central Theater of the Red Army (1934–40), designed by Karo Alabian and Vasilii Simbirtsev (products of the "proletarian" architectural movement – VOPRA – in the late 1920s).[105] The relatively small 1,200-seat auditorium was placed in a much larger pentagon with triangular extensions at each point, thus creating a plan in imitation of the (red) star of the army. Even the columns of the peristyle, which echoed the shape of the two-story base, conformed to the star shape. Above the base rose a central structure of similar configuration with a loggia and a modernized "tempietto" on the top.

This eclectic amalgamation of motifs was repeated throughout the Soviet republics, as elements of local cultures in the Caucasus and Central Asia found their way not only onto buildings in Baku and Erevan, but even into the architecture of Moscow, capital of an indestructible multinational state. (The influence of Moscow's All-Union Agricultural Exhibit, reconstructed in 1939 with a number of national pavilions, was a catalyst in the architectural expression of imperium.[106]) Indeed, the fusion of eastern and western motifs is one of the rare distinctive features of Stalinist architecture in the 1930s – in contrast to motifs adapted from neoclassicism or American skyscraper design. As an expression of the Soviet Union's unique place between the vast potential of the east and the technological might of the west, architecture in all of its variety was projected as evidence for the Soviet's claim to have created a new culture, symbolized abroad by Boris Iofan's sleek Deco design for the Soviet pavilion at the 1937 Paris World's Fair.[107] Even the Moscow Canal, whose 128 kilometers linked Moscow's northwest reservoir at Khimki with the upper Volga River, was endowed with monumental classical structures at major locks. When completed in 1937, this most significant of Soviet hydraulic projects in the 1930s gave notice that the will of Stalin, like that of Peter I, had tamed nature itself. Yet beneath this ubiquitous monumentality – by turns bombastic and superbly detailed – lay another realm of "architecture": that of the GULAG archipelago, whose population increased to unimaginable numbers in the late 1930s and whose form, like that of workers' slums, rarely figures in architectural history.

Postwar Reconstruction

The unprecedented destruction visited upon the Soviet Union by the Second World War (approximately thirty percent of the national wealth) ushered in a final era of monumental construction projects, as cities such as Stalingrad, Smolensk, Minsk, Kharkov, and Kiev were rebuilt from the ground up. Yet the surge of hope brought about by victory and the limited easement of totalitarian thought control during the war proved ephemeral. By 1948, modest attempts at cultural liberalization had been crushed – most notably in literature and music – and architecture reached even greater heights of bombast, epitomized in the late 1940s and early 1950s by the rise of "Stalinist gothic" buildings. Cities from Warsaw to Tashkent exhibited details of the style; but the center remained Moscow, where eight tower buildings were to display a pastiche of decorative motifs adapted from early twentieth-century Manhattan neo-Gothic skyscrapers such as the Woolworth Building, as well as classicizing elements from the unbuilt Palace of Soviets, and crowned with motifs from sixteenth- and seventeenth-century Muscovite architecture.

Ultimately, only seven of the towers were built (the eighth was intended for a site to the southeast of Red Square now occupied by the Hotel Rossiia).[108] Their placement defined certain key points in the topography of the city – a role emphasized by their large spires, redolent both of medieval bell towers and of the spires of Petersburg. The role of a vertical dominant in organizing a low, seemingly chaotic array of surrounding structures had long been a feature of Russian architecture; and although not all of these "tall buildings" (vysotnye zdaniia) were originally designed with the spires, they obtained them in the final designs as a recognition of their symbolic and visual role in a city that would retain a largely horizontal, "communal" profile.

To the southeast of the city center, Dmitrii Chechulin, assisted by a team of architects and engineers, erected in 1948–52 a twenty-four-story apartment building with ramifying wings on the Kotelnicheskaia Quay at the confluence of the Iauza and Moscow rivers. On the north of the Boulevard Ring, Aleksei Dushkin designed an office and apartment building at Lermontov Square (1953); and in the same area, Leonid Poliakov built the Hotel Leningrad (1949–53) near the Leningrad Station. The west portion of the

Boulevard Ring was marked by an apartment building by Mikhail Posokhin and A. Mdoiants at Insurrection Square (1950–4); and at the southwest portion of the Ring stands the Ministry of Foreign Affairs and Foreign Trade on Smolensk Square, by Vladimir Gelfreikh and Mikhail Minkus (1948–53; Figure 647). Further to the southwest, beyond the Moscow River, is perhaps the most grotesque of the seven: the Hotel ukraina, by Arkadii Mordvinov (1950–6).

But of the most imposing of all was the new central building of Moscow State University on Lenin (formerly Sparrow) Hills. Where Vitberg had thought to create a pantheon to Russian heroes in the 1812 war (see Chapter 13), Lev Rudnev, Pavel Abrosimov, and Alexander Khriakov built in 1949–53 a tower with spire overlooking all Moscow (Figure 648). The main architect, Rudnev, had played an important role in defining Soviet monumentalism with buildings such as the M. V. Frunze Military Academy (1932–7; in collaboration with V. O. Munts), whose rectangular

Figure 648. Moscow State University. 1949–53. Architects: Lev Rudnev, Pavel Abrosimov, and Aleksandr Khriakov. (M 127–18)

mass was defined in early "totalitarian style" by an unyielding grid of square windows above a long sylobate.[109] The new university building represents a later, flamboyant stage of totalitarian architecture, and was designed as a self-contained and tightly regulated community, a melding of utopian notions of communism with the unparalleled elitism of the late Stalinist period.[110] Although it too suggests elements of early Manhattan skyscraper design, its vast and sprawling semetry is unique. Wasteful of interior space and bombastic, the Moscow University tower – like its lesser spired counterparts – does exactly what it was intended to do: dominate the city.

The decision in late Stalinist architecture to revert to models of the imperial period and of American capitalism might seem ironic, but Stalin and his associates had a greater sympathy for the monumentality of prerevolutionary culture than for the innovative, rationalist, cosmopolitan thought of the 1920s, loud in its debates and obviously a hotbed of deviationism. Monumental architecture in a historicist form allowed for a "narrative" style that could express "the main ideas of the epoch" – reminiscent of the call for a unifying sociocultural idea in architecture at the beginning of the century (see Chapter 14).[111] Even more significant than the revival of the neoclassical revival

Figure 647. Ministry of Foreign Affairs and Foreign Trade. Moscow. 1948–53. Architects: Vladimir Gelfreikh and Mikhail Minkus. (M 57–3)

was the reversion to neo-Muscovite forms following the Second World War. Apart from nationalistic overtones, this move provided a link with the architecture of potentates such as Ivan the Terrible, whose role in Russian history was glorified during the Stalinist era (cf. Eisenstein's cinematic interpretation of Ivan).

Both autocrats built for grandiose and symbolic effect; yet the votive tower churches had only limited uses as churches, and the Stalin-era towers were vastly regressive in their wasted space and elaborate decoration – isolated points of opulence in a country wracked by destruction and deprivation. This lack of functional and economic rationalism (what other country emerging from the ashes of the war permitted itself this luxury?) exemplifies the principle elucidated by the Czech semiotician Jan Mukařovský, of substitution for vanished functions.[112] The usual considerations of design, material, and use of a structure were displaced by symbolic functions, denoting, in the case of Stalinist Russia, the power of the state, the glory of Muscovite culture, the central position of Moscow in the Communist world, and, by implication, the omnipotence of Stalin himself – the "Great Architect of Communism."

The Post-Stalinist Era and the Return of Functionalism

In the period following Stalin's death, in March 1953, a sober reassessment of priorities – particularly the housing crisis in Moscow and other cities – led to a functionalism that had been among the goals of Soviet design and planning during the 1920s. Teams of engineers and architects began to produce standardized plans that could be widely applied with relatively simple technology, while the pursuit of a historical framework for architectural style was largely discarded – as indicated by the abolition of the Academy of Architecture in the early Khrushchev era.[113] The acceleration of standardized construction achieved an impressive volume, first with five-story apartment buildings that appeared throughout the country, and subsequently with mass-produced buildings as high as twenty stories – in rare cases even higher.[114]

The industrialization of building and the curbing of decorative pomposity produced, however, a different set of problems. Apart from the general monotony of design, even the creative project must be adapted to the processes of standardized, "industrial" construction, based on prefabricated modules or precast concrete forms assembled on site. The seams and cracks that result from such methods of assembly give many contemporary buildings a shoddy appearance. Whatever the project – housing, administrative or commercial, education, entertainment – Soviet architects were faced with a narrow range of options limited by mass construction methods and meagre financial resources. Indeed, it could be claimed that architecture had been supplanted by engineering in the routinized production of buildings issuing from design bureaus.

Even showcase projects with considerable support have shared in the general monotony. The most prolific practitioner of postwar Soviet modernism was Mikhail Posokhin, who had collaborated in the design of the Stalinist apartment tower on Insurrection Square, but then shifted into the new functionalism, interpreted in Moscow on a monumental scale appropriate to the confidence of the Sputnik era. His design for the Kremlin Palace of Congresses (1959–61, in collaboration with A. Mndoiants and others) had the appearance of a modern concert hall of huge proportions, whose marble-clad rectangular outline was marked by narrow pylons – also faced with white marble – and multistoried shafts of plate glass.[115] The main virtue of its style was the relatively unobtrusive effect of so large a structure on the historic Kremlin ensemble, part of which had already been destroyed in the 1930s. In its primary function as the site of Communist Party meetings, the Palace of Congresses officially opened on the first day of the Twenty-Second Party Congress, which was to witness the culmination of Nikita Khrushchev's de-Stalinization campaign. Indeed, the contrast between late Stalinist architecture and the neutral modern style of the Khrushchev "palace" could not have been greater, nor more expressive of the pragmatic values of a technocratic state.

Posokhin subsequently adapted the international modern style, with its glass and aluminum facades, to industrialized methods of construction in the creation of such ensembles as Kalinin Prospekt (1964–9; also known as the New Arbat), extending westward from the Kremlin and Arbat Square. Its identical towers and shopping complexes provided the capital with the facade of cosmopolitan prosperity (and its leaders with a direct highway to their dachas), but the complex wreaked incalculable and lasting damage on the original Arbat district.[116] To the right of the bridge that takes Kalinin Prospekt over the Moscow River, Posokhin and Mndoiants interpreted modernism in more dramatic fashion in their "open-book" design for the building of the Council of Mutual Economic Assistance (1964–9), the institution through which Moscow controlled its economic relations with the countries of the Warsaw Pact.[117] In a similar repetitive

Figure 649. Troparevo housing area. Moscow. 1970s. Architects: A. Samsonov and A. Bergelson. (M 57–8)

style, a team headed by Dmitrii Chechulin (and assisted with Komsomol labor) built the gargantuan Hotel Rossiia near Red Square in 1964–9, with accommodations for 6,000 guests in single or double rooms.[118] The hotel was built on a site that had been intended for one of the postwar Stalinist towers. Although Chechulin's design also destroyed an historic, viable district of several blocks in Kitai-gorod, the new era at least allowed the preservation of ancient landmarks (mostly churches) that now surround the hotel in artificial juxtaposition.

In view of Posokhin's leading role in remaking the capital during the Brezhnev era, it is not surprising that he was entrusted with devising a new general plan for Moscow, which was accepted by the Central Committee and Council of Ministers in 1971. The city's boundary was extended to the limits of the new ring expressway (and even some areas beyond), within which were eight large zones.[119] The outer zones contained numerous developing "microregions," designed within a system of new transportation arteries. These areas were marked above all by vast "housing massifs" with thousands of apartments (Figure 649). Some had considerable pretensions to design and variety of configuration, such as Iasenevo (late 1970s; Ia. Belopolskii, A. Rochegov et al.); Chertanovo North, built to house 22,000 (late 1970s–early 1980s; Posokhin, L. Diubek et al.); Troparevo (1970s; A. Samsonov, A. Bergelson et al.); and Strogino, home for 150,000 (late 1970s–early 1980s).[120]

Even the radical ideals of the "house-commune" of the 1920s returned in at least one project: the House of New Living (*dom novogo byta*; 1969; N. Osterman,

A. Petrushkova et al.), with 812 apartments designed primarily for young marrieds who were not yet prepared for the rigors of household life and could make use of the project's centralized services. However, many of the technological marvels remained on the drawing board, and the project proved hardly more successful than its predecessors; it was soon converted to a graduate student dormitory for Moscow State University and other institutions.[121] Yet for all of the variations, these endlessly serried slabs of apartment buildings represent the fulfillment of a vision propounded at its rationalist, surreal extreme by the German architect Ludwig Hilberseimer as early as the mid–1920s.[122]

Not all Russian architecture of the modern period descended to nondescript conformity. Construction technology appeared spectacularly in the futuristic Ostankino Television Tower (1967; N. Nikitin, L. Batalov et al.), a reinforced concrete monolith of impressive design and engineering (Figure 650).[123] The ferroconcrete shaft reaches a height of 385 meters (on a foundation of only 4 meters), above which a steel frame superstructure for antennas rises another 150 meters. Technological ingenuity is also displayed in the design of contemporary sports arenas – which, like television, served the regime's propaganda interests. Vast stadium complexes began to take shape even in the late Stalinist period, such as Leningrad's Kirov Stadium on Krestovskii Island (1950; A. Nikolskii et al.) and culminating with the Luzhniki stadium complex in south Moscow (1955–6; A. Vlasov et al.). The emphasis on the culture of sports, which reached a crescendo in the preparations for the 1980 Olympics,

493

Figure 650. Ostankino television tower. Moscow. 1967. Architects: N. Nikitin, L. Batalov, et al. In foreground, Monument to the Conquest of Space. 1964. Sculptor: A. P. Faidysh-Kradievskii. Architect: Mikhail Barshch. (M 145–24)

Figure 651. "Friendship" Sporting Hall. Moscow. 1978–9. Architects: Iurii Bolshakov et al. (M 52)

produced some of the most interesting forms in contemporary Russian architecture, such as the multipurpose "Friendship" Sporting Hall at Luzhniki (1978–9; Figure 651), designed by Iurii Bolshakov and others with a main arena holding up to 4,000 spectators. Even more dramatic in its high technology and streamlined, sweeping lines is the Velotrek bicycle racing stadium in the west Moscow suburb of Krylatskoe (1978–9; Natalia Voronina et al.), with a bifurcated roof composed of rolled steel membranes 4-millimeters thick stretched between a pair of tilted elliptical arches on each side, supported by a truss frame system (Figure 652). The velodrome's soaring contours symbolize the speed for which the elegantly functional structure and its high, banked track of polished Siberian larch were designed.[124]

Whatever the engineering achievements of projects with highly specialized technical requirements, most architectural design has remained subordinate to mass construction techniques. There are, however, projects that ingeniously exploit these limitations, such as the Children's Music Theater near Moscow State University (1979; Figure 653). Its architects, Alexander Velikanov and V. Krasilnikov, have written: "Architects are forced to use methods and construction materials worked out by construction and architectural practice, and this places its mark on the architecture of a building, especially under conditions of industrialized construction."[125] Wishing to create a monolithic structure of simple geometric contrasts but unable to use the techniques of poured, textured concrete that characterize western "brutalism," the architects sheathed the facade in textured stone and concrete panels, decorated with fanciful sculpture from children's fables to provide relief within the horizontal mass of the building.[126] The seams that mark prefabricated architecture are here integrated into the rough surface, thus adapting standardized components to a boldly sculpted design. Similar in approach but greatly overbearing in manner is the design for the Blokhin Oncology Center (1972–9; Igor Vinogradskii et al.), whose twenty-two story central tower (Figure 654) – impressive and functional though it is – would seem to offer no hope to those treated within.

Even as new methods are developed to integrate prefabricated components into a design aesthetic, there are also signs of a return to the texture of the brick surface, despite its more costly, labor-intensive demands. The brick facade has been skillfully applied in a number of recent apartment developments in Moscow and Leningrad; but the most successful example is the new extension to the Taganka Drama Theater in Moscow (1974–81; A. Anisimov et al.), with its austere intersecting planes of red brick creating a vivid play of light and shadow on the surface (Figure 655).[127]

During the 1980s, there has been a tentative return to monumentality in certain large projects, such as the Building of the Council of Ministers of the Russian Republic (now known as the "White House," the center of the Russian government), whose design by Dmitrii Chechulin is a variation of the architect's 1934 project for Aeroflot headquarters in Moscow – thus reviving early Soviet monumentalism in the most di-

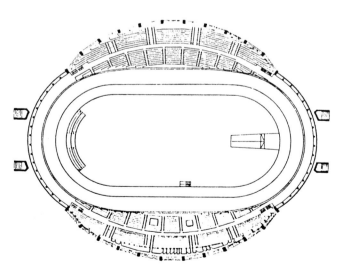

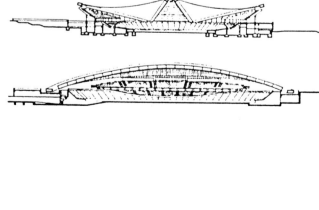

Figure 652. Velotrek bicycle racing stadium. Moscow. 1979–80. Architects: Natalia Voronina et al. *Arkhitektura SSSR*, 1986.

Figure 653. Children's Music Theater. Moscow. 1979. Architects: Alexander Velikanov and V. Krasilnikov. (M 53)

rect sense.[128] Even the multistoried arches that led into the courtyards of Stalinist apartment complexes have reappeared in an attempt to deal with the monotony of the endlessly repeated facade. Perhaps the most striking, if rather shoddy, example is the Leningrad housing development by V. Sokolov and P. Kurochkin on October Prospekt, Vasilevskii Island (Figure 656; designed in 1979–83 and built in 1983–6).

In the same area of Vasilevskii Island, the Hotel "Pribaltiskaia" (1976–8) was constructed to very high standards by a Swedish firm, primarily to accommodate foreign tourists. The architect of record, Nikolai Baranov, created a design on a typical Soviet scale reminiscent of the work of Posokhin in Moscow; but when Soviet planners wish to build a structure intended to impress visitors from the west, they often hire a western firm: Moscow's Hotel Cosmos (French), the second international terminal at Sheremetevo Airport (German), and the International Trade Center on the Moscow River, built by a major New York firm, although listed as a Posokhin design in Soviet sources.[129]

The large scale that has been equated with efficiency in postwar Russian architecture has concomitantly led to the neglect of often essential details of design and urban planning. Deprived of a sense of direct participation in the design process or of work on a human scale, architects have countered by protesting their plight and by participating vigorously in international design competitions focusing on concepts rather than on the material limitations that so restrict their own environment. This reaction is epitomized by the "paper architecture" movement of the 1980s, whose drawings occasionally suggest the utopian, unrealized projects of early Soviet architecture, but whose superb draftsmanship more often creates a form of meta-architecture, a commentary – satirical or surrealistic – on architecture.[130]

The results of this architecture of fantasy and protest give every indication that the creative spirit is very much present, yet architecture must continue to provide shelter in the most material sense. The Gorbachev era and the subsequent fragmentation of the monolithic Soviet state have seen the rise of hopes for a general social and cultural revival based on moral values and respect for the individual; but this transformation has also brought to the surface a broad array of problems – long ignored and ranging from the ecological to the ethnic – that appears virtually insurmountable. Under such conditions, the construction industry will itself contract, leading perhaps to a revival of the architecture on a human scale within

Figure 654. Blokhin Oncology Center. Moscow. 1972–9. Architect:
Igor Vinogradskii. (M 155–29)

Figure 655. Taganka Drama Theater. Moscow. 1974–81. Architects:
A. Anisimov and Iu. Gnedovskii. (M 109–11)

Figure 656. Apartment complex, Vasilevskii Island. Leningrad. 1983–6. Architects: V. Sokolov and P. Kurochkin. (L 80–7)

a society in desperate need of housing and other services. For the present, however, architectural values are most tangibly represented in the popular movement for historic preservation, which has provided the initiative needed to impede the shocking neglect and destruction of Russia's architectural heritage in this century.[131] With as yet no clear direction into the future, the vital ideas of architecture remain in the past, whose surviving monuments – of Moscow, of St. Petersburg (again so named), of Constructivism and medieval churches – bear mute witness to the turbulent history and indomitable spirit of the Russian people.

Appendices

Russian Wooden Architecture

Medieval Russian chronicles contain intriguing references to complex churches of wood, such as the first church of Saint Sophia in Novgorod (989?), an oak structure with thirteen "tops" (presumably some form of cupola).[1] From extensive archaeological and historical data, it is evident that wood was used for almost every type of structure in Russia until well into the eighteenth century. By virtue of their settlement within a vast forested zone, Russians were fully aware of the strengths of wood, which they exploited to remarkable effect for churches, dwellings, and fortifications. Fire and decay, however, have long since destroyed the work of early medieval Russian carpenters. Little has been preserved from before the eighteenth century, and attributions of log churches to the fifteenth and sixteenth centuries are extremely rare, as well as questionable. Indeed, the earliest dating is c. 1391, for the small Church of the Resurrection of Lazarus from the Murom Monastery on the shores of Lake Onega (Figure 657).[2] Despite the lack of verifiable evidence, commentary on the characteristics of early Russian wooden architecture has often proceeded on the assumption that such traditional forms were inherently conservative and can be inferred from surviving log buildings of a later period.[3]

The oldest examples of Russian wooden architecture are churches, which were used more carefully than houses, and which could last as long as three to four centuries – provided rotting logs were promptly replaced (a common procedure) and the roof properly maintained. Whatever the problems of chronology and evolution, it has been possible to establish a typology of such structures.[4] The simplest type of

wooden church, such as the Church of the Deposition of the Robe from Borodavo (possibly as early as 1486; Figure 658) or the Church of the Dormition from the village of Nikulino (1599; Figure 659), resembles the basic unit of the peasant house, with its pitched roof and rectangular "cell" (*klet*).[5] The plan is linear, along an east–west axis, with one unit for the service and another, the *trapeza*, as a form of vestibule. Such churches often have two additional units: an apse, containing the altar, on the east; and a bell tower attached to the vestibule (Figures 660 and 661).

The more elaborate churches of this type, like the larger peasant houses, were decorated with carved end boards that protected the ends of the roof beams, and with carved galleries on raised porches. The variations on this form are many, and include churches with a roof of two planes above the higher central structure to better protect the walls from moisture, as in the Church of St. Nicholas at Tukholia (seventeenth century; Figure 662).[6] Still more complex variants possessed multiple gables with extensive carving, such as the Church of St. Nicholas at Miakishevo (latter half of seventeenth century; Figure 663).[7] Other churches of this plan had very high pitched roofs, which shedded snow more rapidly (Figures 664 and 665).

Although the steeply pitched roof gave the larger cell churches an imposing silhouette, the vertical line is much more emphatic in the "tent" – or *shatior* – type of wooden church, so named for the shape of its central tower. The linear arrangement is here replaced with a centralized plan, whose cuboid core is surmounted by an octahedron supporting an eight-

Figure 657. Church of the Resurrection of Lazarus, from Murom Monastery, Lake Onega. Now at Kizhi. Late fourteenth century(?). Northeast view. (KZ 1–18)

Figure 658. Church of the Deposition of the Robe, from Borodavo. Now at St. Kirill-Belozersk Monastery. 1485. Southeast view. (KI 2–29)

Figure 659. Church of the Dormition, from Nikulino. Now at Vitoslavlitsy Museum, Novgorod. 1599. Southeast view. (N 9–3)

Figure 660. Church of the Dormition, from Fomiskoe. Now at Ipatievskii Monastery, Kostroma. 1721. South view. (KO 2–20)

Figure 661. Archangel Michael Chapel, from Lelikozero. Now at Kizhi. Late eighteenth century(?). Southwest view. (KZ 4–22)

Figure 662. Church of St. Nicholas, from Tukholia. Now at Novgorod. Seventeenth century. Northwest view. (N 22)

Figure 663. Church of St. Nicholas, from Miakishevo. Now at Novgorod. Late seventeenth century. South view. (N 9–9)

Figure 664. Church of the Transfiguration, from Spas-Vezhi. Now
at Ipatievskii Monastery, Kostroma. 1628. Southeast view. (KO 1–
24)

Figure 665. Church of St. Nicholas, from Glotovo. Now at Suzdal.
1766. Southwest view. (SZ 9)

sided tower, as in the Church of the Dormition at Kuritsko (1595; Figure 666).[8] There were more complex variations that developed a cruciform plan with flanking domes, illustrated in the Church of the Nativity of the Virgin at Peredki, a monastic structure first mentioned in 1539 (Figure 667).[9] The Peredki church is notable for its gallery on three sides, raised above the highest snow drifts on a beautifully designed system of projecting logs (*pomochi*). Although the bulk of the church (approximately 30 meters in height) is austerely monumental, details such as the gallery remind how closely aesthetics and function were combined in log churches.

The disfavor directed toward the *shatior* by the church hierarchy in the midseventeenth century (see Chapter 7) resulted in a waning of that design. Yet the Russian love of verticality in church design, which indicated the presence of man and his devotion to God in the vast northern forests, found expression in a third type of log church, the tiered, or *iarusnyi*, structure, in which a pyramidal silhouette ascends in a series of diminishing octahedrons over the main part of the building. In some cases, the tower is set within a linear plan, as superbly illustrated in the Church of St. Nicholas at Vysokii Ostrov (1757; Figure 668). When seen from the east (Figure 669), the design suggests the form of a pagoda. In this church, as in those surveyed before, the two basic methods of joining the pine logs were the notch (*oblo s ostatkom*) for round logs, and the mortise and tenon (*lapa*) for both round and square logs when greater precision of detail and stability were required – such as the apsidal structure of the St. Nicholas Church. In its purest form, the tiered design consisted of a cruciform plan with octahedrons rising from the core of the structure, as in the Church of Transfiguration at Kozliatevo (1756; see Plate 79), consisting of mortised, square logs. The vertical design of this church is accented by decorative barrel-shaped gables over the arms of the cruciform plan and repeated in smaller variants above the octahedrons.

Whatever the form, the methods of construction demanded great skill and knowledge of the properties of wood. The logs were cut in late fall after the final ring of the tree – usually pine, with some fir – had hardened, and they were left on the ground until the beginning of building season, in late spring. The logs were then taken to the construction site, where master carpenters trimmed, notched, and, if necessary, planed them.[10] The most common tools were the ax (of which there were various types adapted to specific functions) and the adze, as well as wedged spikes for splitting logs and a primitive type of spokeshave, or

drawing knife, for making concave incisions along a log. (Russian log structures almost never used clay caulking, but relied instead on the tight fit of one log above another, with materials such as moss or hemp for insulation in dwellings.[11]) There was little use for saws, which would have opened the grain of the wood to moisture, as opposed to the proper stroke of the ax, which closed the grain. Nails were also traditionally dispensed with, even in the roof, whose planks – usually double-layered – were designed with a groove fit and wedged at the top into a ridge beam.

Whether notched or mortised, the logs just beneath the roof were usually extended in length, so as to support an overhang for protection against moisture runoff. This flare (*poval*) is one of the most graceful, if unobtrusive, details of Russian wooden architecture, and is completely functional. The tips of the roof planks often displayed carved tips, which in sunlight cast a bold pattern of shadows against the texture of the log walls. If the church culminated in a *shatior*, the base of the tower would be surrounded by an overhang at a much lower angle (*politsa*). Such towers were usually planked, but in some instances, they were covered with carved shingles, as were the cupolas. These shingles (*lemekhi* or *cheshui* – "fish scales"), among the most ingenious features of Russian wooden architecture, were curved and wedged to follow the contours of the cupola frame. Typically, the shingles were carved from moist aspen, which ages from a golden hue to silver, and forms a brilliant contrast to the logs of the structure.

The supreme example of these time-honored methods of construction – and of the genius of Russian wooden architecture – is the tiered Church of the Transfiguration of the Savior on Kizhi Island (the northwest part of Lake Onega), built in 1714 ostensibly in honor of Peter the Great's victories over the Swedes, although a Transfiguration Church had existed at Kizhi since at least the early seventeenth century.[12] As with the Cathedral of the Intercession on Red Square in Moscow, the impression produced by the main Kizhi church is one of overwhelming profusion and complexity; yet the design is the very essence of logic – tectonic and aesthetic (Figure 670). Located on open space in the southwest part of the island, the church formed the center of a *pogost*, a term which by the eighteenth century had come to mean an enclosed cemetery with a parish or district church. Its high pyramidal silhouette (37 meters) signified from a great distance consecrated ground, and the design of the structure reinforces at every point that symbolic purpose.

The core is an octahedron in three tiers, buttressed

Figure 666. Church of the Dormition, from Kuritsko. Now at Novgorod. 1595. Southeast view. (N 9–8)

Figure 667. Church of the Nativity of the Virgin, from Peredki.
Now at Novgorod. 1539(?). Southeast view. (P 15–11)

Figure 668. Church of St. Nicholas, from Vysokii Ostrov. Now at
Novgorod. 1757. Southeast view. (N 9–5)

512

Figure 669. Church of St. Nicholas, from Vysokii Ostrov. Now at
Novgorod. East view. (N 9–4)

Figure 670. Church of the Transfiguration of the Savior. Kizhi. 1714.
Northeast view. (PV 2–33)

on the lowest – and largest – tier by rectangular extensions at the four compass points. These extensions are also stepped, and thus each of the four provides two additional *bochka* gables surmounted by a cupola. The eight cupolas of these extensions merge with eight above the main octahedron, and four more surmount the next octahedron. The final octagonal tier supports the culminating, largest cupola, and the twenty-second cupola rests over an unobtrusive apse extending from the east. The harmony created in this intricated pattern of cupolas and structure is capable of extended analysis, so varied are the impressions that it produces (Figure 671).[13] The natural properties of materials are fully exploited for aesthetic effect in the contrast between the dark walls of aged pine logs and the brilliant silver of the cupolas, covered with a total of some 30,000 curved aspen shinges with stepped points (see Plate 80). This elaborate superstructure provided an efficient system of ventilation to preserve the structure from rot; yet as was typical of tall wooden churches, the superstructure was not visible from the interior, which was capped at a low level by a painted ceiling, or "sky" (*nebo*), over the central part of the church. Apart from the religious imagery of the iconostasis, the interior walls were unpainted – also typical of Russian log churches.[14]

The Church of the Transfiguration was used only during the brief northern summer. It was not uncommon in Russian settlements (Suzdal, for example) to have paired churches, for summer and winter. At the Kizhi pogost, the adjoining "winter" Church of the Intercession, built in 1764, provides an admirable visual complement to the ensemble (Figure 672). Whereas the Transfiguration soars, the Intercession accentuates the horizontal, with an extended vestibule that could be used for community meetings (another feature of many northern wooden churches). Also in contrast to the Transfiguration, the Intercession Church has a prominent altar apse with a large barrel gable and cupola – a further accent on the horizontal axis of the structure. The upper part of the Intercession Church represents one of the formal variations that does not fall into the three categories defined heretofore. Although there is some evidence to suggest that the church originally had a tent tower, the crown of eight cupolas surrounding the main cupolas at the top of the octahedron is a dramatic and satisfying resolution that enhances, rather than competes with, the form of the Transfiguration Church. The final element of the pogost ensemble was a freestanding bell tower with a tent roof between and in front of the two churches (late eighteenth century, rebuilt in 1874). The pogost was enclosed by a low

Figure 671. Church of the Transfiguration of the Savior. Kizhi. West view. (KZ 5–5)

wall of horizontal logs on a base of fieldstone, reinforced with perpendicular extensions and two square towers on the north side, all protected by plank roofing. Access is provided through a stout wooden gate in front of the Church of the Intercession.[15]

The extraordinary variety and beauty of Russian log churches should not obscure the main purpose of wooden architecture, which was to provide housing. Although log houses were often humble affairs and even in the best cases would not have rivaled the distinctive form of the church, they too could demonstrate artistry of design as well as economy of function.[16] The center of the peasant log house – whatever its size – was the large masonry stove (Figure 673) used not only for cooking, but also for heating the main living space during the long winters. The stove could be ventilated in two ways that define the two basic types of peasant house: the "white" and the "black." In the former, the smoke was released through a brick chimney, and in the latter, the smoke

Figure 672. Church of the Intercession. Kizhi. North view. (KZ 4–0)

Figure 673. Iakovlev house, from the village of Kleshcheila. Now at Kizhi. 1880–1900(?). Main room, second floor. (KZ 2–2)

516

drifted up toward the ceiling and a wooden duct that collected the smoke and expelled it. This "black" variant was the more common, even for large houses; and due to the ingenuity of the design, the smoke did not foul the entire room, but only an area under the roof that could be scraped down.

In the central part of Russia, the house typically formed the main component of a *dvor*, or yard enclosed by a solid fence and containing various sheds for animals and farm implements.[17] In the more severe climate of the far north, these units were combined into a single, self-sufficient structure with three basic configurations: a long rectangular structure (*brus*) with the living quarters on one side and the storage sheds and livestock on the other, larger side (Figure 674); a rectangular structure with the barn attached to the side and extending back at a right angle (*glagol*); and, the most complex, a two-story structure with the living quarters in front and the barn in back under a greatly extended roof (*koshel*; Figure 675).

Traditionally, log houses, whether large or small, were decorated with elaborate window surrounds and end boards (*prichelina*), which were either carved or, in more elaborate designs, sawn. In the eighteenth and nineteenth centuries, patterns derived from folk motifs became particularly elaborate[18]; yet during the same period, carpenters began to adapt urban architectural motifs such as baroque window surrounds (Figure 676) that they might have observed during seasonal work in the cities, or at the country dachas of city residents. Within the cities themselves, wooden houses remained the majority well into the nineteenth century (even longer in the provinces); but with the spread of saw mills, the log walls of these houses were frequently covered in plank siding, which provided opportunities for still more elaborate designs (Figure 677).[19] Vernacular architecture from central Russian cities such as Riazan to the Siberian cities of Tobol'sk and Tomsk thus served as a showcase for artisanal skills that reflected the owner's wealth and link with Russian peasant traditions.

Indeed, during the nineteenth century, the peasant's log house became a symbol of Russian national identity, as exemplified in the "Hut" built on the Moscow estate of the eminent history professor Mikhail Pogodin and, in the 1870s, in the log house built by the pan-Slavist Porokhovshchikov (see Chapter 13). The fashion for this display of traditional wooden forms was accompanied not only by an increasing

Figure 674. Iakovlev house. Now at Kizhi Side and rear view, with ramp to barn. (KZ 2–7)

517

Figure 675. Sergin house, from the village on Munozero. Now at Kizhi. 1880s. With barn extending from the rear. (KZ 2–21)

scholarly interest in the study of Russian wooden architecture, but also by the postulation of log structures as the source of the major forms indigenous to Russian architecture. The leading proponent of this idea was Ivan Zabelin, a meticulous scholar who deduced from his research that the basic elements of native Russian architecture were present in and ultimately derived from wood.[20] Zabelin was followed by other students of traditional Russian church and vernacular architecture, such as V. V. Suslov, who placed a high value on wooden forms.[21]

These concepts of wooden derivation could be reasonably defended, if not proven; yet the scholarly dispute (albeit with nationalist overtones) moved into a virulent phase during the Stalinist period, particularly with its exclusive emphasis on the nativist origins of such monuments as the "tent" votive churches of sixteenth and seventeenth-century Mus-

covy.[22] Although the ideological conformity of that period has passed, there are still those who would attribute a major role to wooden forms in the evolution of Russian architecture – an argument that is likely to continue without firm proof. Paradoxically, such claims risk excluding Russian architecture from serious, exhaustive study as a part of the culture of masonry architecture in western civilization. Logic suggests that the great Russian monuments in brick and stone must have developed as a process related to similar developments elsewhere, primarily in Byzantium and the west. To argue that Russian architecture is ultimately idiosyncratic – rather than capable of idiosyncratic variations at certain moments – is to deny Russia's place in the continuum of art history and in the comity of nations with which it obviously shares so much.

Rather, the remarkable and distinctive achieve-

Figure 676. Ekimovaia house, from Ryshevo. Now at Novgorod. Second half of nineteenth century. With "baroque" window decoration. (P 15–12)

ments of Russian master carpenters can be seen both as a highly developed, specific response to a demanding physical and geographical environment, and as an expression of values that can also be traced in Russian masonry architecture: the striving for verticality in church architecture, with its symbolic references to the relation between God and man; the fondness for elaborate ornamentation; and a plasticity of structural form. It is clear that the rigors of the far northern climate produced a shelter environment that excluded or reduced light – even in the precious and limited time when the sun was visible. The windows were small, and interior lamps – where they existed – were dim. All the more necessary and comprehensible then was the urge to create vivid, towering forms of churches that would catch and reflect the light, whether on a blinding winter day or a long summer evening. Such forms, created from the materials available in the northern forests, reaffirmed the survival and the innate longings of the soul. The fact that wooden architecture occasionally displayed a shared aesthetic with masonry forms—particularly in medieval churches – suggests not an overarching theory of derivation, but rather parallel developments and mutual inspiration.

Figure 677. Wooden house. Riazan. Late nineteenth century. (RZ 4–13)

520

APPENDIX II

Illustrated Architectural Elements

The following illustrations identify selected Russian and European architectural terms and three common types of cruciform church plans.

Eleventh Century, Kievan Rus

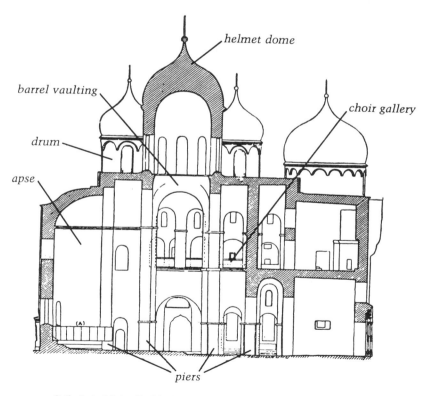

Cathedral of Saint Sophia. Novgorod. 1045–52. Section.

Fourteenth Century, Novgorod

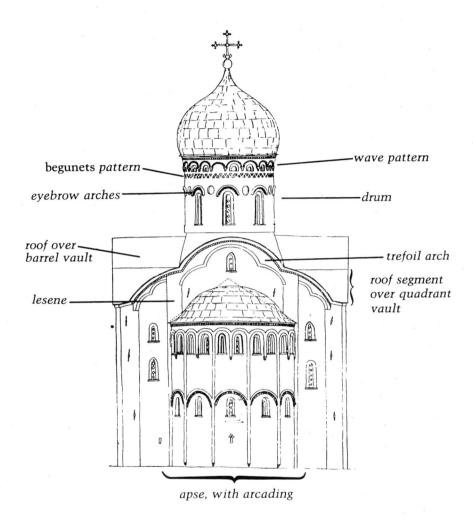

begunets *pattern* ———

wave pattern

eyebrow arches ———

——— *drum*

roof over—
barrel vault

——— *trefoil arch*

roof segment
over quadrant
vault

lesene ———

apse, with arcading

Church of Saint Theodore Stratilites on the Brook. Novgorod. 1361.

Fifteenth Century, Moscow

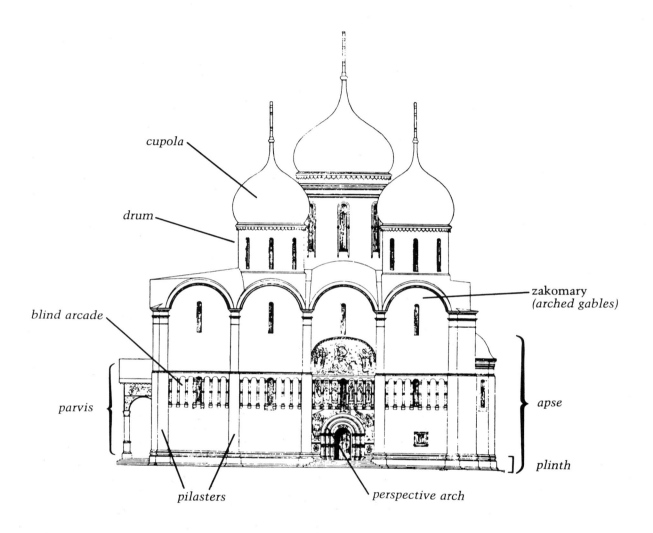

cupola

drum

blind arcade

parvis

pilasters

zakomary (arched gables)

apse

plinth

perspective arch

Cathedral of the Dormition. The Kremlin, Moscow. 1475–9.
South elevation.

Sixteenth Century, Moscow

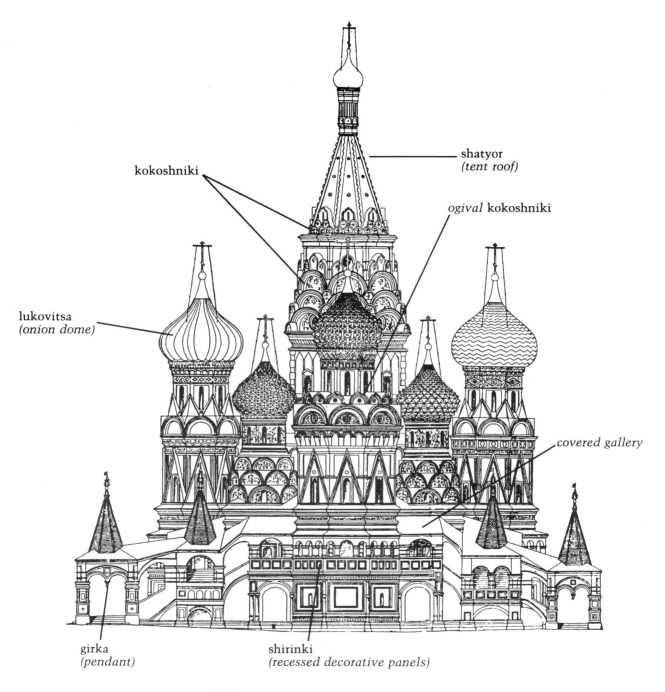

kokoshniki

shatyor
(tent roof)

ogival kokoshniki

lukovitsa
(onion dome)

covered gallery

girka
(pendant)

shirinki
(recessed decorative panels)

Cathedral of the Intercession (Saint Basil's). Moscow 1555–61.

Wooden Church

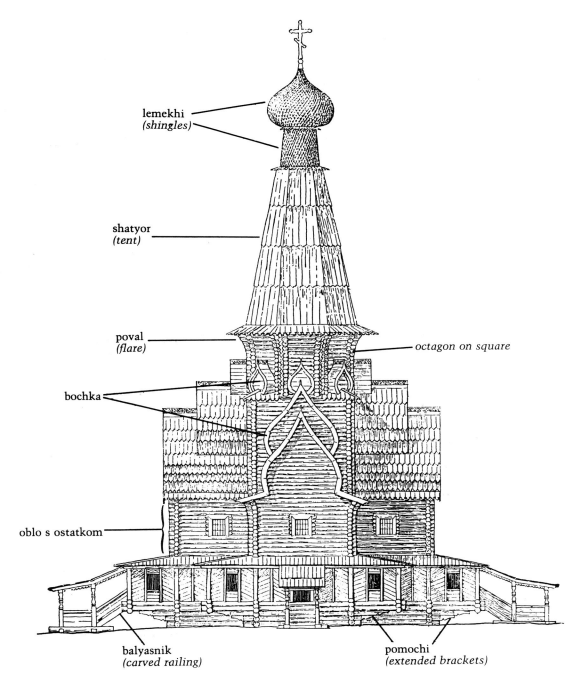

lemekhi
(shingles)

shatyor
(tent)

poval
(flare)

octagon on square

bochka

oblo s ostatkom

balyasnik
(carved railing)

pomochi
(extended brackets)

Church of the Presentation. Osinovo (Arkhangelsk region). 1684.

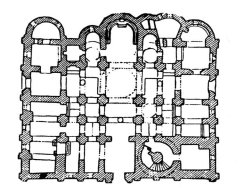

Cross-domed plan.
Cathedral of Saint Sophia.
Novgorod.

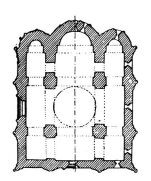

Inscribed cross (quincunx).
Cathedral of Saint Dmitri.
Vladimir.

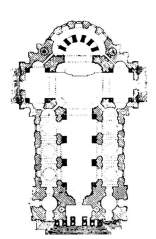

Latin cross.
Cathedral of the Trinity,
Alexander Nevsky Monastery.
Leningrad.

Notes

Introduction

1. "Ob arkhitekture nyneshnego vremeni," in N. V. Gogol', *Sobranie sochinenii v shesti tomakh* (Moscow, 1959), vol. 6, p. 59.
2. The beginnings of Russian architectural historiography are chronicled in T. A. Slavina, *Issledovateli russkogo zodchestva* (Leningrad, 1983). See also E. I. Kirichenko, *Russkaia arkhitektura 1830–1910-kh godov* (Moscow, 1978), pp. 57–8.
3. A. Benua, *Zhizn' khudozhnika: Vospominaniia* (New York, 1955), p. 70.
4. See Erwin Panofsky, *Gothic Architecture and Scholasticism* (New York, 1957).
5. E. A. Borisova, *Russkaia arkhitektura vtoroi poloviny XIX veka* (Moscow, 1979), p. 92.
6. On the overwhelming contrast between sacred and secular architecture in the early medieval period, see, for example, N. N. Voronin, *Zodchestvo Severo-Vostochnoi Rusi XII–XV vekov* (Moscow, 1961), vol. 1. pp. 49–50. One explicit medieval statement on the uses of magnificent architecture – above all the church – as an element of power and authority was issued by John, exarch of Bulgaria, in the treatise *Shestodnev*. Further commentary is contained in D. S. Likhachev, "Printsip ansamblia v drevnerusskoi estetike," in A. L. Mongait, ed., *Kul'tura drevnei Rusi* (Moscow, 1966), pp. 118–20.
7. See William C. Brumfield, "Anti-Modernism and the Neoclassical Revival in Russian Architecture, 1906–1916," *Journal of the Society of Archtiectural Historians,* 48 (1989): 371–86.

Chapter 1

1. An English translation can be found in S. H. Cross, *The Russian Primary Chronicle* (Cambridge, 1930). For a brief, lucid summary of the controversy concerning the rise of the Kievan state, see N. V. Riasanovsky, *A History of Russia* (New York, 1963), pp. 25–30. A more detailed examination is set forth in works such as G. Vernadsky, *Kievan Russia,* and B. D. Grekov, *Kievskaia Rus'* (Moscow, 1953) – also available in English. The latter vigorously challenges the "Normanist" theory, in which the Vikings are assigned a major role in the political and cultural development of the eastern Slavs.
2. For a detailed reexamination of the circumstances surrounding the official acceptance of Orthodox Christianity in 988, see Andrzej Poppe, "The Political Background to the Baptism of Rus': Byzantine–Russian Relations between 986–89," *Dumbarton Oaks Papers,* 30 (1976), pp. 197–244; reprinted in Andrzej Poppe, *The Rise of Christian Russia* (London, 1982).
3. There were, undoubtedly, a large number of buildings in Kiev – and other settlements of ancient Rus – before the advent of Byzantine influence; but by all evidence, they were rudimentary in form and intended for the basic needs of housing, trade, and defense. For a description of the remains of a small pagan temple in Kiev, see P. P. Tolonchko and Ia. E. Borovskii, "Iazichnitske kapishche v 'gorodi' Volodimira," in L. L. Vashchenko, ed., *Arkheologiia Kieva* (Kiev, 1979), pp. 3–10.
4. In his account of the spread of Christian architecture throughout the Roman Empire in the fourth and fifth centuries, Richard Krautheimer writes: "Yet wherever evidence is available, it leads to the conclusion that the architects in charge of the new buildings had come from abroad, frequently in the suite of the court. On the other hand, masons, as a rule, were home-bred." *Early Christian and Byzantine Architecture* (New York, 1979), p. 71. Something of the same process may have occurred in Kiev in the tenth century, although masons, too, were probably imported at the earliest stages. Located on the periphery of the Byzan-

tine cultural sphere, Kiev soon developed its own style, but continued to benefit from successive waves of Greek masters and artists. The most thorough study of the relation between Middle Byzantine architecture and that of Kievan Rus is A. I. Komech, *Drevnerusskoe zodchestvo kontsa X – nachala XII v.: Vizantiiskoe nasledie i stanovlenie samostoiatel'noi traditsii* (Moscow, 1987). More generally on Byzantine culture and the art of the Orthodox Church, see V. V. Bychkov, *Vizantiiskaia estetika* (Moscow, 1977); Gervase Matheu, *Byzantine Aesthetics* (New York, 1964); Jarosláv Pelikan, *The Spirit of Eastern Christendom (600–1700)* (Chicago, 1974); and Timothy Ware, *The Orthodox Church* (Harmondsworth, 1969).

5. An exhaustive account of the historical and archaeological evidence concerning the Church of the Tithe is contained in Mikhail Karger, *Drevnii Kiev* (Moscow–Leningrad, 1962), 2: 9–59. For the composition of the walls and an inventory of decorative fragments, see pp. 49–59. More recent commentary is provided in P. A. Rappoport, *Russkaia arkhitektura X–XIII vv.*, vol. E1–47 in the series *Arkheologiia SSSR: Svod arkheologicheskikh istochnikov* (Leningrad, 1982), pp. 7–8; Iu. S. Aseev, *Arkhitektura drevnego Kieva* (Kiev, 1982), pp. 28–35; and Komech, *Drevnerusskoe zodchestvo*, pp. 168–77.

6. The development of the cross-domed church is discussed in Krautheimer, *Byzantine Architecture*, pp. 299–315. Whereas the term *cross-domed* is appropriate for large churches such as St. Sophia in Kiev and Novgorod, and the destroyed Church of St. Irene in Kiev (1037) – each with five or more aisles – some medievalists have advocated a specific term to designate the more modest, compact plan typical of much Middle Byzantine and early Russian architecture. Called variously the inscribed cross, cross-in-square, or quincunx, this plan is defined as containing nine units – a central bay with drum and cupola, four barrel-vaulted extensions representing the arms of the cross, and four corner bays (sometimes with cupolas) – and epitomized in the Nea Ekklesia in Constantinople (consecrated in 881), although an earlier derivation is considered possible. See ibid., pp. 359–63. The use of these terms has, however, led to confusion in the description of Kievan monuments: Krautheimer characterizes not only St. Sophia in Kiev, but also the Cathedral of the Transfiguration in Chernigov as "cross-domed" (pp. 309–10), but later states that the quincunx is "almost universally accepted all over the sphere of Byzantine and dependent architecture, from the tenth century to the fall of Constantinople, and surviving in Russia and the Balkans far beyond" (p. 360). In addition, he considers untenable the hypothesis that derives the quincunx from the cross-dome type (pp. 360–1). Soviet scholarship uses both the general term *krestovokupolnyi* (cross-domed) and "inscribed cross." Komech simplifies matters by calling all churches of Kievan Rus from the eleventh to the thirteenth centuries four-piered, that is, inscribed-cross structures that, whatever their ultimate complexity, derive from a central bay whose drum and cupola rest on four free-standing piers. See Komech, *Drevnerusskoe zodchestvo*, p. 263.

7. There has been much controversy surrounding the dates of construction of St. Sophia: The Novgorod chronicle gives 1017 as the date of the cathedral's founding, whereas the Kievan chronicle indicates 1037. For a summary of the various positions, see Karger, *Drevnii Kiev*, pp. 98–104. Karger, incidentally, accepts 1037 for the beginning of construction, which, in his opinion, was completed in the 1040s. Andrzej Poppe also argues in favor of 1037, with a completion date in the 1050s. See Andrzej Poppe, "The Building of the Church of St. Sophia in Kiev," *Journal of Medieval History*, 7 (1981), 15–66; reprinted in Andrzej Poppe, *The Rise of Christian Russia*. Other supporters of the later date include Komech, *Drevnerusskoe zodchestvo*, pp. 178–81; and Iu. S. Aseev, "K voprosu o vremeni osnovaniia Kievskogo Sofiiskogo sobora," *Sovetskaia arkheologiia*, 1980, no. 3: 135–40.

8. For a discussion of the mystical concept of Sophia, or the Divine Wisdom, and its reflection in the art and architecture of the Orthodox Church, see Donald M. Fiene, "What is the Appearance of the Divine Sophia?," *Slavic Review*, 48 (1989): 449–76.

9. Speculation on the origins and significance of the multidomed churches of medieval Rus is presented in G. Ia. Mokeev, "Mnogoglavye khramy Drevnei Rusi," *Arkhitekturnoe nasledstvo*, 26 (1978): 41–52. Mokeev's interpretation of the numerological significance of the domes is challenged in I. L. Buseva-Davydova and A. L. Batalov, "O metodologii izucheniia simvoliki arkhitektury," in A. A. Voronov, ed., *Istoriia arkhitektury: Ob"ekt, predmet i metof issledovaniia* (Moscow, 1988), pp. 92–9.

10. The complex structure of the St. Sophia cathedral, with its strong vertical emphasis, has been analyzed by K. N. Afanasev in terms of an elaborate system of proportional relations. See *Postroenie arkhitekturnoi formy drevnerusskimi zodchimi* (Moscow, 1961), pp. 58–60. Komech has argued for a more pragmatic and less precise method of construction, in which the building's proportions were determined by the need to create an extensive choir gallery for the grand prince's family and retinue. See his "Rol' kniazheskogo zakaza v postroenii Sofiiskogo sobora v Kieve," in V. N. Lazarev, ed., *Drevnerusskoe iskusstvo: Khudozhestvennaia kul'tura domongol'skoi Rusi* (Moscow, 1971), pp. 50–64; and "Postroenie vertikal'noi kompozitsii Sofiiskogo sobora v Kieva," in *Sovetskaia arkheologiia*, 3 (1968): 232–8. The literature on the Cathedral of St. Sophia is copious, but little is available in English. Among the fundamental works are N. I. Kresal'nii, *Sofiiskii zapovidnik u Kievi* (Kiev, 1960) and M. K. Karger, *Drevnii Kiev*, vol. 2, pp. 98–206. The latter contains extensive bibliographic references.

11. The frescoes and mosaics of St. Sophia have been meticulously studied by V. N. Lazarev, whose book *Mozaiki Sofii Kievskoi* (Moscow, 1960) remains the fundamental work on the subject. For a broader survey of Russian mosaics and frescoes, see his *Drevnerusskie mozaiki i freski: XI–XV vv.* (Moscow, 1973).

12. A detailed analysis of the Cathedral of the Transfiguration in Chernigov and its relation to Byzantine architec-

ture is presented in A. I. Komech, "Spaso-Probrazhenskii sobor v Chernigove," in G. V. Popov, ed., *Drevnerusskoe iskusstvo: Zarubezhnye sviazi* (Moscow, 1975), pp. 9–26; and *Drevnerusskoe zodchestvo*, pp. 134–68. Additional descriptions of this and other monuments in Chernigov are contained in G. N. Logvin, *Chernigov, Novgorod-Severskii, Glukhov, Putivl* (Moscow, 1965); Iu. S. Aseev, entries on Kievan architecture in *Istoriia ukrains'koho mystetstva* (Kiev, 1969), vol. 1, pp. 153–223; P. A. Rappoport, *Russkaia arkhitektura X–XIII vv.*, passim; and Volodymyr I. Mezentsev, "The Masonry Churches of Medieval Chernihiv," *Harvard Ukrainian Studies*, vol. XI, nos. 3–4, pp. 365–83.

13. The progress of the construction of the Cathedral of the Transfiguration is noted in Rappoport, *Russkaia arkhitektura X–XIII vv.*, p. 40; and Mezentsev, "Masonry Churches," 367–8.

14. For a survey of the history of the Kiev Cave Monastery – or Lavra (the highest rank of Orthodox monastery) – see S. K. Kilesso, *Kievo-Pecherskaia lavra* (Moscow, 1975).

15. An analysis of the complex construction history of the Cathedral of the Dormition is presented by M. V. Kholostenko, "Uspenskii sobor pecherskogo monastiria," in the collection *Starodavnii Kyiv* (Kiev, 1975), pp. 107–70; and "Novi doslidzhennia Ioanno-Predtechenskoi tserkvi ta rekonstruktsiia Uspenskoho soboru Kievo-Pecherskoi lavri," in *Arkheologichni doslidzennia staro-davnoho Kyiva* (Kiev, 1976), pp. 131–65. See also Karger, *Drevnii Kiev*, 2: 345–69; Iu. S. Aseev, *Arkhitektura drenego Kieva*, pp. 78–90; Rappoport, *Russkaia arkhitektura X–XIII vv.*, pp. 23–5; and Komech, *Drevnerusskoe zodchestvo*, pp. 268–74. Results of recent archeological work and a rebuttal of the hypothesis that the cathedral was originally pentacupolar are presented in Iu. S. Aseev and V. A. Kharlamov, "Ob arkhitekture Uspenskogo sobora Pecherskogo Monastyria v Kieve (issledovanniia 1982 g.)," *Arkhitekturnoe nasledstvo*, 34 (1986): 209–14.

16. For commentary on the Dormition Cathedral as a major monument in defining this stylistic identity, see Aseev, *Arkhitektura drevnego Kieva*, pp. 78–9; and Komech, *Drevnerusskoe zodchestvo*, p. 273.

17. For a reconstruction and analysis of the original plan of the Cathedral of the Archangel Michael at Vydubetskii Monastery, see Karger, *Drevnii Kiev*, 2: 345–69. Further discussion of the monument is contained in Aseev, pp. 104–6; Rappoport, *Russkaia arkhitektura X–XIII vv.*, pp. 26–7; and Komech, *Drevnerusskoe zodchestvo*, pp. 264–8.

18. On the development of local traits of representation and color in the mosaics of the Archangel Michael Cathedral, see V. N. Lazarev, *Mikhailovskie mozaiki* (Moscow, 1966), p. 87.

19. A hypothetical reconstruction and plan of the Church of Archangel Michael the Golden-Domed is contained in Aseev, *Arkhitektura drevnego Kieva*, p. 92; see also pp. 99–102. Both Aseev and Komech (*Drevnerusskoe zodchestvo*, pp. 275–80) emphasize the development of the *zakomary* as regular feature of the definition of the roofline – both a decorative element and a reflection of the vaulting on the interior. For an archaeological summary of masonry construction on the site of the St. Dmitrii (later Michael the Golden-Domed) Monastery, see Rappoport, *Russkaia arkhitektura X–XIII vv.*, pp. 16–17.

20. G. K. Vagner, *Belokamennaia rez'ba drevnego Suzdalia* (Moscow, 1975), pp. 15, 79.

21. Despite the preservation of the narthex of the Church of the Savior at Berestovo, there has been some difference of opinion as to the original appearance of the structure. Karger's views are presented in *Drevnii Kiev*, vol. 2, pp. 374–91. Aseev's hypothetical reconstruction is illustrated *Arkhitektura drevnego Kieva*, p. 105, with further discussion on pp. 110–12. There is general agreement that the main bay of the south, west, and north facades had an enclosed porch whose vault followed a trefoil contour. The possibility that the roofline might also have adopted the trefoil shape (a form that appeared later in the architecture of Novgorod – and possibly in Kiev itself) rather than the newly established horizontal row of *zakomary* cannot be proven, as Komech notes in *Drevnerusskoe zodchestvo*, pp. 292–7. Although the foundation of the Savior Monastery is dated to 1072, there is no documentary reference to the construction of the church itself, which is first mentioned under the year 1138 in the chronicle. See Rappoport, *Russkaia arkhitektura X–XIII vv.*, pp. 22–3.

22. For a description of the masonry technique at the Berestovo church, see Karger, *Drevnii Kiev*, vol. 2, pp. 390–1; and Kilesso, *Kievo-Pecherskaia lavra*, p. 55. A comparison of the masonry construction of this and other Kievan churches with that found in contemporary South Slavic monuments is provided in N. I. Brunov, "K voprosu o nekotorykh sviaziakh russkoi arkhitekture s zodchestvom iuzhnykh slavian," *Arkhitekturnoe nasledstvo*, 2 (1952): 3–42. Kilesso also presents illustrations of surviving fragments of the church's twelfth-century frescoes (Figures 38, 39, 42).

23. The urban development of Kiev during the twelfth century is examined in I. S. Krasovskii, "Nekotorye osobennosti gradostroitel'prnoi struktury Kieva serediny XII v.," *Arkhitekturnoe nasledstvo*, 25 (1976): 12–18.

24. The first specific reference to the Church of St. Cyril is under the year 1171, by which time it was being used as a burial place for the Olgovichi. See Rappoport, *Russkaia arkhitektura X–XIII vv.*, pp. 20–1, with references to the church in both the Laurentian and Hypatian redactions of the Kievan chronicle.

25. The 1880s restoration of St. Cyril's was carried out under the direction of the distinguished archaeologist A. V. Prakhov, who was clearly dedicated to the work, implemented it as carefully as possible under the conditions of the time, and published a detailed description of his work in 1883. Among those who participated in the restoration was Mikhail Vrubel – now acknowledged as the most original of Russian painters of the late nineteenth century – who repainted certain areas that had lost almost all of their original work. For an account (with photographs) of the latest restoration process, see I. P. Dorofienko and P. Ia. Red'ko, "Raskrytie fresok XII v. v Kirkllovskoi tserkvi Kieva," in O. I. Podobedova, ed., *Drevne russkoe iskussto:*

Monumental'naia zhivopis' XI–XVII vv. (Moscow, 1980), pp. 45–51. The newly cleaned scenes from the life of St. Cyril of Alexandria are described by N. V. Blinderova, "Zhitie Kirilla a Afanasiia Aleksandriiskikh v rospisiakh Kirillovskoi tserkvi," in the same volume, pp. 52–60. For a description of the church and a listing of its frescoes, see Aseev, *Arkhitektura drevnego Kieva*, pp. 119–25; and Karger, *Drevnii Kiev*, vol. 2, pp. 442–53.

26. The challenge to the earlier dating of the Cathedral of Sts. Boris and Gleb has been advanced in Karger, *Drevnii Kiev*, 2: 480; and by Aseev in *Istoriia ukrains'koho mystetstva*, I: 199–200. On the basis of stylistic features, Aseev and others now place the cathedral's construction at some point in the 1170s, but that is only an educated guess. For a defense of the earlier dating, see, among others, N. V. Kholostenko, "Issledovaniia Borisoglebskogo sobora v Chernigove," *Sovetskaia arkheologiia*, 1967, no. 2: 188–210. The archeological investigations of the site are summarized in Rappoport, *Russkaia arkhitektura X–XIII vv.*, pp. 41–3.

27. The postwar reconstruction of the Cathedral of Sts. Boris and Gleb, directed by N. Kholostenko, has elicited criticism, partly because of the placement of the capitals (their diameter does not correspond to that of the attached columns on which they rest), and partly because of the stucco, whose thick, smooth surface does not reproduce what is considered to have been the original appearance – of a thin layer, scored to resemble ashlar. See Aseev, *Istoriia ukrains'hoho mystetstva*, I: 199; and Logvin, *Chernigov.* Kholostenko's views on the capitals are presented in "Neizvestnye pamiatniki monumental'noi skul'ptury drevnei Rusi: Relefy Borisoglebskogo sobora v Chernigove," *Iskusstvo*, 1953, no. 3: 84–91. The possible connections with Romanesque architecture have been frequently stated by Aseev, both in reference to this church and to the late twelfth-century churches of Rus in general. See, for example, Aseev, *Arkhitektura Kyivs'koi Rusi* (Kiev, 1969), p. 133, in reference to the capitals of the Cathedral of Sts. Boris and Gleb; and pp. 136–8, which note Romanesque traits in the Cathedral of the Dormition at Eletskii Monastery (see what follows) and suggest that the Romanesque influence was more widespread in Chernigov than in Kiev. See also Aseev, *Arkhitektura drevnego Kieva*, p. 128.

28. A description of the structure of the Dormition Cathedral and a summary of possible construction dates are contained in Rappoport, *Russkaia arkhitektura X–XIII vv.*, pp. 45–6. For a formal analysis of the proportional system of the cathedral, see I. Sh. Shevelov, "Proportsii i kompozitsiia Uspenskoi Eletskoi tserkvi v Chernigove," *Arkhitekturnoe nasledstvo*, 19 (1972): 32–42.

29. See archaeological description in Rappoport, pp. 46–7. For a photograph of the original masonry wall, covered with stucco and scored to resemble stone work, see Aseev, *Arkhitektura Kyivs'koi Rusi*, p. 143.

30. Two other churches in Chernigov have been precisely dated to the late twelfth century: the Church of the Archangel Michael (1174) and the Church of the Annunciation (1186), both built by Sviatoslav Vsevolodovich, who had become the grand prince in Kiev. Unfortunately, neither of the churches has survived, with the exception of intriguing fragments such as mosaics from the floor of the Church of the Annunciation. See Rappoport, *Russkaia arkhitektura X–XIII vv.*, pp. 43–4; and Aseev, *Arkhitektura Kyivs'koi Rusi*, pp. 144–5.

31. For a detailed description of Schusev's reconstruction of the Church of St. Basil in Ovruch, see K. N. Afanas'ev, *A. V. Shchusev* (Moscow, 1978), pp. 18–21. Shchusev as assisted on site by the future Constructivist architect Leonid Vesnin (see Chapters 14 and 15).

32. A description of the archaeological data is provided in Rappoport, *Russkaia arkhitektura X–XIII vv.*, pp. 29–30. The date of the Ovruch church was refined by Aseev, who found a grafitto with the date 1192 on a fragment of the stuccoed interior. See Aseev, *Arkhitektura drevnego Kieva*, p. 138. For Aseev's variant reconstruction of the church, see *Arkhitektura Kyivs'koi Rusi*, p. 164.

33. Aseev has advanced the argument that the foundations of a church first discovered in 1878 and reexcavated in 1947 on Voznesenskii Slope in Kiev are in fact those of the Church of St. Basil. See *Arkhitektura drevnego Kieva*, p. 141, with Aseev's reconstruction, p. 139. A description of the site is contained in Karger, *Drevnii Kiev*, vol. 2, pp. 237–49; and the findings are summarized in Rappoport, *Russkaia arkhitektura X–XIII vv.*, pp. 17–18. Rappoport does not commit to a precise identification, but on the basis of the foundation, places the church on Voznesenskii slope within a series of other churches typified by St. Basil's in Ovruch, St. Paraskeva in Chernigov, and an excavated, unnamed church in Smolensk. As the center of the Rostislavich dynasty, Smolensk is thought to have exerted considerable influence on church architecture in the central part of Rus during the late twelfth century. See N. N. Voronin and P. A. Rappoport, *Zodchestvo Smolenska, XII–XIII vv.* (Moscow, 1979), pp. 363–5. It is interesting to note that another Church of St. Basil, built at the beginning of the 1180s by Riurik's predecessor, Sviatoslav Vsevolodovich, not only has been precisely identified, but survived (under the name of the Church of the Three Saints) until its destruction in 1935–6. See Karger, *Drevnii Kiev*, vol. 2, pp. 454–62; and Rappoport, *Russkaia arkhitektura X–XIII vv.*, pp. 10–11.

34. The restoration of the Church of St. Paraskeva was done under the supervision of P. D. Baranovskii, with the participation of G. M. Shtender. See Rappoport, *Russkaia arkhitektura X–XIII vv.*, pp. 44–5.

35. Ibid., p. 44. Further analysis is contained in Aseev, *Arkhitektura Kyivs'koi Rusi*, pp. 170–4; and *Arkhitektura drevnego Kiev*, pp. 137–8, which casts doubt on the theory that the architect of the St. Paraskeva Church might have been the Kievan builder Petr Miloneg.

36. See Riasanovsky, *A History of Russia*, pp. 44–6.

37. For a description of the renovation of Kiev's monuments in the seventeenth and eighteenth centuries, see Karger, passim. There have been modest attempts at regaining the original appearance of Kiev's early monuments: In particular, the stucco has been removed from portions of the exterior of eleventh- and twelfth-century church walls. One such project has involved the Cathedral of Archangel Michael at Vydubetskii Monastery, but because of topographical changes, only a portion of the structure can be restored.

Chapter 2

1. For this and subsequent references in English from the Novgorod chronicle, see entries under the appropriate year in *The Chronicle of Novgorod*, Robert Mitchell and Nevill Forbes, transl. (London, 1914). A useful chronological synopsis of the history of medieval Novgorod (from the chronicles) is contained in M. N. Tikhomirov, ed., *Novgorod: k 1100-letiiu goroda* (Moscow, 1964), pp. 297–313.

2. Although the architecture of Novgorod churches naturally derived from the Byzantine tradition, via Kiev, the city's extensive trading contacts in the Baltic suggest the possibility of the assimilation of other, western, architectural motifs. A formal (stylistic) comparison of the medieval churches of Novgorod and Pskov with contemporary monuments in western Europe, including France and Italy, is provided in P. N. Maksimov, "Zarubezhnye sviazi v arkhitekture Novgoroda i Pskova XI–nachala XVI vekov," *Arkhitekturnoe nasledstvo*, 12 (1960): 23–44.

3. Summaries of the archaeological data uncovered in Novgorod are presented in A. V. Artsikhovskii, "Novgorod Velikii po arkheologicheskim dannym," pp. 38–47; and S. N. Orlov, "K topografii Novgoroda X–XVI vv.," in M. N. Tikhomirov, ed., *Novgorod: k 1100-letiiu goroda*, pp. 264–85. For a more general survey, see A. L. Mongait, *Archeology in the U.S.S.R.* (Baltimore, 1961). Novgorod continues to be one of the most productive sites for the archaeological study of life in medieval Russia, and the material presented in the foregoing works has been greatly supplemented by recent discoveries concerning both the topography of the ancient city and its culture. For an appreciation of the latter topic, see D. S. Likhachev, *Novgorod Velikii: Ocherk istorii kul'tury Novgoroda X–XVII vv.* (Moscow, 1959).

4. There were, in fact, churches from the late twelfth and the thirteenth centuries that made extensive use of bricks in the construction of walls, but these buildings are attributed – for that reason – to masons from other cities (e.g., the Church of St. Paraskeva Piatnitsa, 1207, and the Church of Sts. Peter and Paul on Sinichia Hill, 1185–92; see what follows). For an account of the variations in construction material, see Mikhail Karger, *Novgorod: Architectural Monuments 11th–17th centuries* (Leningrad, 1975), pp. 6, 13.

5. It is gratifying to note that recent Soviet restorations have occasionally removed the whitewashed stucco that over the years had been applied to the exteriors of churches. Not only does the natural wall surface reveal the ingenuity with which Novgorod's masons constructed and decorated their churches, but also the original rough texture creates a striking visual effect, particularly when illuminated by soft light. Given that all significant modifications in the history

of ancient monuments are architecturally of interest, establishing the appropriate period of restoration is a complex issue. Many of the churches of Novgorod and Pskov were so frequently rebuilt or altered that it is often impossible to recreate the original appearance of a structure.

6. Medieval chronicle references to the construction history of the St. Sophia Cathedral are summarized in P. A. Rappoport, *Russkaia arkhitektura X–XIII vv.*, vol. E1–47 in the series *Arkheologiia SSSR: Svod arkheologicheskikh istochnikov* (Leningrad, 1982), p. 65. According to the Third Novgorod chronicle, St. Sophia was consecrated in 1052, shortly before the death of Prince Vladimir, whose body was interred in the cathedral. See also V. G. Briusova, "Stranitsa iz istorii Sofiiskogo sobora Novgoroda," in A. L. Mongait, ed., *Kul'tura drevnei Rusi* (Moscow, 1966), pp. 42–6.

7. For a discussion of Kiev's role in the construction of St. Sophia in Novgorod, see A. I. Komech, *Drevnerusskoe zodchestvo kontsa X–nachala XII v.: Vizantiiskoe nasledie i stanovlenie samostoiatel'noi traditsii* (Moscow, 1987), pp. 236–7.

8. Rappoport, *Russkaia arkhitektura X–XIII vv.*, p. 65.

9. Opinions concerning the dates of construction of the exterior galleries of the Novgorod cathedral have varied, but it is now commonly assumed that their evolution occurred simultaneously with building of the main structure. See ibid., p. 66. The development of the plan of St. Sophia, with an emphasis on the chapels within the galleries, is analyzed in Komech, "Rol' pridelov v formirovanii obshchei kompozitsii Sofiiskogo sobora v Novgorode," in G. K. Vagner and D. S. Likhachev, eds., *Srednevekovaia Rus'* (Moscow, 1976), pp. 147–51.

10. Most of the interior of St. Sophia is covered with paintings of much later provenance – primarily the nineteenth century. For a summary and illustration of the earliest fragments, see, V. N. Lazarev, *Drevnerusskie mozaiki i freski: XI–XV vv.* (Moscow, 1973), pp. 174–8; "O rospisi Sofii Novgorodskoi," in V. N. Lazarev, ed., *Drevnerusskoe iskusstvo: Khudozhestvennaia kul'prtura Novgoroda* (Moscow, 1968), pp. 7–62; and *Vizantiiskoe i drevnerusskoe iskusstvo* (Moscow, 1978), pp. 116–74.

11. See Komech, *Drevnerusskoe zodchestvo*, pp. 251–3.

12. At certain points in the history of medieval Rus, a crude form of succession operated, whereby the principality of Novgorod was entrusted to the Kievan grand prince's eldest son, who transferred it to his eldest, etc.

13. For a summary of the archaeological data from the site of the Church of the Annunciation, see Rappoport, *Russkaia arkhitektura X–XIII vv.*, p. 74. There had been no significant masonry construction in Novgorod since the completion of St. Sophia 50 years earlier, and Komech argues that the architects for the church could only have been provided by Vladimir Monomakh. *Drevnerusskoe zodchestvo kontsa X–nachala XII v.*, p. 299.

14. A detailed description of the Church of St. Nicholas and its partial restoration is contained in G. M. Shtender, "Arkhitektura domongol'skogo perioda," in Tikhomirov, *Novgorod: k 1100-letiiu goroda*, pp. 186–9. See also Rappoport, *Russkaia arkhitektura X–XIII vv.*, pp. 70–1. According

to Shtender, the structure would originally have had a greater height than it does at present due to an accretion of soil around the base of the church to a depth of almost 2.5 meters. The same observation could be made of other twelfth-century churches in Novgorod, particularly those in low-lying areas prone to flooding. For an analysis of the great proportional height of this church (only 1.5 meters less than the Novgorod St. Sophia), see Komech, *Drevnerusskoe zodchestvo kontsa X–nachala XII v.*, pp. 304–5. Noting that the choir gallery of St. Nicholas is placed at the same height as that in St. Sophia, Komech states that the church would have combined structural elements of the Novgorod cathedral (Mstislav's desire to create a rival structure) with the general plan first applied at the Church of the Annunciation and imported from the south.

15. See Komech, *Drevnerusskoe zodchestvo kontsa X–nachala XII v.*, p. 309.

16. See Shtender, "Arkhitektura domongol'skogo perioda," p. 190; and Rappoport, *Russkaia arkhitektura X–XIII vv.*, pp. 67–8. Komech provides a detailed explanation of the church's innovations in form (noted by Shtender) and their possible origins in *Drevnerusskoe zodchestvo kontsa X–nachala XII v.*, pp. 309–14.

17. The chronicle references and archaeological data are contained in Rappoport, *Russkaia arkhitektura X–XIII vv.*, p. 73. The Third Novgorod chronicle notes that Prince Vsevolod was present at the consecration of the church in 1140 – an obvious error, because Vsevolod had died in 1137 (the year following his expulsion from Novgorod). It is now assumed that the consecration occurred in 1130 – transformed by scribal error into the later date.

18. The central aisle of St. George is approximately the same width and length as that of the Novgorod St. Sophia, and the side aisles of St. George are in fact larger than those of the Cathedral of St. Sophia. The latter, however, has two aisles on each side, giving a larger total space even without the addition of the attached galleries. See Komech, *Drevnerusskoe zodchestvo*, pp. 306, 308.

19. See V. N. Lazarev, *Novgorodian Icon-Painting* (Moscow, 1976), pp. 7–11.

20. The Church of John the Baptist in Petriatin Court (or Opoki, in the Trading Side) was built by Vsevolod in 1127–30 and presented to the corporation of merchants specializing in the lucrative wax trade. Subsequently, it served as a center for the resolution of commercial disputes. The original church, of traditional form and modest scale, was replaced in 1184; but little remains even of that structure, which was razed and rebuilt in 1453 by Archbishop Evfimii, a staunch opponent of Muscovite expansionism who wished to reproduce a church reminiscent of Novgorod's twelfth-century glory. The present structure is, therefore, a considerable stylistic anachronism. See Rappoport, *Russkaia arkhitektura X–XIII vv.*, pp. 68–9.

21. For evidence linking Vsevolod to the construction of Cathedral of the Transfiguration of the Savior, see G. F. Alferova, "Sobor Spaso-Mirozhskogo monastyria," *Arkhitekturnoe nasledstvo*, 1958, no. 10: 5, 24; Lazarev, *Drevnerus-*

skie mozaiki i freski: XI–XV vv., p. 187; and Rappoport, *Russkaia arkhitektura X–XIII vv.*, p. 81.

22. Evidence in support of a later group of princes (in the 1140s) as the primary donors is based on monastery records from the sixteenth century and is presented in M. N. Soboleva, "Stenopis' Spaso-Preobrazhenskogo sobora Mirozhskogo monastiria v Pskove," in V. N. Lazarev, ed., *Drevnerusskoe iskusstvo: Khudozhestvennaia kul'tura Pskova* (Moscow, 1968), pp. 39–42. Soboleva argues that the church was built between 1148 and 1154 (p. 43), and was painted only in 1157–8, after the death of Nifont and under the patronage of Iurii Dolgorukii's son Andrei Bogoliubskii. Lazarev finds the later date unconvincing, *Drevnerusskie mozaiki i freski: XI–XV vv.*, p. 187.

23. On the Byzantine prototypes, see Alferova, "Sobor Spaso-Mirozhskogo monastyria," pp. 3–22; and Iu. P. Spegal'skii, *Pskov: Khudozhestvennye pamiatniki* (Leningrad, 1972), pp. 20–2.

24. For a detailed analysis and schematic identification of the frescoes, see Soboleva, "Stenopis' Spaso-Preobrazhenskogo sobora," pp. 7–50, with a comparison between Byzantine work and the Pskov frescoes on pp. 38–9. See also Lazarev, *Drevnerusskie mozaiki i freski: XI–XV vv.*, Plates 187–206.

25. For a detailed account of Pokryshkin's restoration work and the postwar restoration of 1956–8 supervised by Grigorii Shtender, see G. M. Shtender, "Vosstanovlenie Nereditsy," in *Novgorodskii istoricheskii sbornik* (Novgorod, 1962), pp. 169–205; and "Arkhitektura domongol'skogo perioda," in Tikhomirov, *Novgorod: k 1100-letiiu goroda*, pp. 194–201 (a 1946 photograph of the ruins is reproduced on p. 193).

26. Archaeological evidence seems to indicate that the *zakomary* were also edged with brick in the dogtooth pattern – a detail omitted in the postwar reconstruction. For a description of structural details, see Rappoport, *Russkaia arkhitektura X–XIII vv.*, pp. 74–5.

27. Three churches with their original frescoes largely intact were destroyed on the eastern edge of Novgorod during the Second World War: the Church of the Savior on the Nereditsa, the Church of the Savior at Kovalevo (whose exterior has now been restored; see Chapter 4), and the Church of the Dormition at Volotovo. There are prewar photographs of the interior of the Church of the Transfiguration, some of which are included in Lazarev, *Drevnerusskie mozaiki i freski: XI–XV vv.*, Plates 242–76.

28. For a description of archaeological work at the Church of the Annunciation, see Shtender, "Arkhitektura domongol'skogo perioda," pp. 191–2; Rappoport, *Russkaia arkhitektura X–XIII vv.*, p. 72. An analysis of the frescoes in the light of recent restorations is presented in G. S. Batkhel', "Novye dannye o freskakh tserkvi Blagoveshcheniia na Miachine bliz Novgoroda," in V. N. Lazarev, ed., *Drevnerusskoe iskusstvo: Khudozhestvennaia kul'tura domongol'skoi Rusi* (Moscow, 1972), pp. 245–54; and Lazarev, *Drevnerusskie mozaiki i freski: XI–XV vv.*, Plates 230–8.

29. Shtender, "Arkhitektura domongol'skogo perioda," pp. 192–3.

30. The most detailed analysis of the reconstruction of the Church of St. Paraskeva is ibid., pp. 201–14. On the existence of foreign "companies" in medieval Novgorod, see E. A. Rybina, *Inozemnye dvory v Novgorode XII–XVII vv.* (Moscow, 1986).

31. A discussion of the Paraskeva church in relation to the architecture of Smolensk is contained in N. N. Voronin and P. A. Rappoport, *Zodchestvo Smolenska XII–XIII vv.* (Leningrad, 1979), pp. 348–53.

32. For a recent survey of the early medieval architecture of Smolensk, see P. A. Rappoport, *Zodchestvo drevnei Rusi* (Leningrad, 1986), pp. 120–8, with a model of the latest reconstruction of the Archangel Michael church by S. S. Pod"iapol'skii on p. 123. A more detailed analysis of the church is presented in Pod"iapol'skii's chapter in Voronin and Rappoport, *Zodchestvo Smolenska*, pp. 163–95. The remains of the cathedral at the Trinity Monastery are analyzed in ibid., pp. 196–220.

33. Shtender, "Arkhitektura domongol'skogo perioda," p. 211.

34. Rappoport, *Russkaia arkhitektura X–XIII vv.*, p. 75. For a more detailed analysis of the Peryn church, see R. Katsnel'son, "Drevniaia tserkov' v Perynskom skity bliz Novgoroda," *Arkhitekturnoe nasledstvo*, 2 (1952): 69–85.

35. For a critical appraisal of Alexander's policy – supported by the Orthodox Church – of accommodation with the Mongols, see John Fennell, *The Crisis of Medieval Russia 1200–1304* (London–New York, 1985), pp. 107–13, 116–18.

Chapter 3

1. From the *Primary Chronicle* (under A.M. 6532). For the English translation, see S. H. Cross, *The Russian Primary Chronicle* (Cambridge, 1930).

2. For a description of evidence relating to the existence of the first Church of the Savior in Vladimir, see N. N. Voronin, *Zodchestvo Severo-Vostochnoi Rusi XII–XV vekov* (Moscow, 1961), vol. 1, pp. 39–44; and P. A. Rappoport *Russkaia arkhitektura X–XIII vv.*, vol. E1–47 in the series *Arkheologiia SSSR: Svod arkheologicheskikh istochnikov* (Leningrad, 1982), p. 56.

3. For archaeological data on the Church of St. George, see ibid., pp. 55–6; also Voronin, *Zodchestvo Severo-Vostochnoi Rusi*, vol. 1, pp. 91–100.

4. For a description of the original and present forms of the Church of Sts. Boris and Gleb, see ibid, pp. 67–76; and Rappoport, *Russkaia arkhitektura X–XIII vv.*, p. 60.

5. The Cathedral of the Transfiguration of the Savior at Pereslavl'-Zalesskii is the subject of a detailed analysis in A. Chiniakov, "Arkhitekturnyi pamiatnik vremeni Iuriia Dolgorukogo," *Arkhitekturnoe nasledstvo*, 2 (1952): 43–66. See also Voronin, *Zodchestvo Severo-Vostochnoi Rusi*, vol. 1, pp. 77–90; and I. P. Purishchev, *Pereslavl'-Zalesskii* (Moscow, 1970), pp. 9–11.

6. Archaeological details of the structure are analyzed in Rappoport, *Russkaia arkhitektura X–XIII vv.*, pp. 62–3.

7. A summary of Andrei Bogoliubskii's rule and his re-

lations with Kiev is contained in John Fennell, *The Crisis of Medieval Russia 1200–1304* (London–New York, 1985), pp. 2–6. The account of the battle in the Novgorod chronicle is entered under [A.M.] 6677 and 6678. For an English version, see *The Chronicle of Novgorod*, Robert Michell and Nevill Forbes, transl., pp. 26–7.

8. A thorough description of the surviving fragments of the original carvings appears in G. K. Vagner, *Skul'ptura drevnei Rusi XII v.: Vladimir-Bogoliubovo* (Moscow, 1969), pp. 95–124.

9. The connection with Barbarossa was made by Vasilii N. Tatishchev (1686–1750) in *Istoriia Rossiiskaia s samykh drevneishikh vremen* (Petersburg, 1774), vol. 3, p. 127. Tatishchev was among earliest Russian historians in the modern sense, but his medieval manuscript source for this claim is not extant. Nonetheless, the idea receives support in Vagner, *Skul'ptura drevnei Rusi*, pp. 84–5.

10. For extant fragments of the arcade frescoes, see Lazarev, *Drevnerusskie mozaiki i freski: XI–XV vv.*, Plates 152–3.

11. Voronin, *Zodchestvo Severo-Vostochnoi Rusi*, vol. 1, pp. 128–48; and Rappoport, p. 56. For a discussion of the protective role bestowed upon gate churches in medieval Rus, see V. P. Vygolov, *Arkhitektura Moskovskoi Rusi serediny XV veka* (Moscow, 1988), pp. 156–8. A survey of medieval Russian fortification design is presented in V. V. Kostochkin, *Krepostnoe Zodchestvo drevnei Rusi* (Moscow, 1969).

12. One of the churches was dedicated to the Apostle Andrew, who was popularly believed to have been the first Christian emissary to the lands of Rus. For source references, see Rappoport, *Russkaia arkhitektura X–XIII vv.*, p. 57.

13. N. N. Voronin supervised archaeological excavations at the site in 1934–8, and his book contains the most extensive published description: Voronin, *Zodchestvo Severo-Vostochnoi Rusi*, vol. 1, pp. 201–61. For a discussion of the iconographic meaning of extant fragments of the limestone carving and a comparison with Romanesque work, see Vagner, *Skul'ptura drevnei Rusi*, pp. 66–95. Both books contain the authors' sketches of the reconstructed compound, as well as photographs of surviving fragments.

14. The account in the Kievan chronicle is contained in V. Lebedev and V. Panov, eds., *Drevnerusskie letopisi* (Moscow–Leningrad, 1936), pp. 223–6 (under A.M. 6683).

15. *Drevnerusskie letopisi*, p. 223.

16. For a discussion of the relation between the institution of the feast day of the Intercession of the Virgin (in 1165–6) and the iconography of the church on the Nerl, see Voronin, *Zodchestvo Severo-Vostochnoi Rusi*, vol. 1, p. 122; and Vagner, *Skul'ptura drevnei Rusi*, pp. 140–2. In addition, the church was built in memory of Andrei's son Iziaslav, who died in 1165. On this basis, Rappoport (*Russkaia arkhitektura X–XIII vv.*, p. 58) assigns a date of 1166 to the church, rather than the commonly accepted 1165.

17. For a reconstruction of the original form, see Nikolai Voronin, *Vladimir, Bogolyubovo, Suzdal, Yurev-Polskoi* (Moscow, 1971), p. 145; and Rappoport, *Russkaia arkhitektura X–XIII vv.*, pp. 58–9.

18. For a discussion of the original appearance of the cupola, see A. Vlasiuk, "Pervonachal'naia forma kupola tserkvi Pokrova na Nerli," *Arkhitekturnoe nasledstvo*, 2 (1952): 67–8.

19. An elaborate mathematical analysis of the proportional relations in the structure of the Church of the Intercession is contained in A. V. Ikonnikov and G. P. Stepanov, *Osnovy arkhitketurnoi kompozitsii* (Moscow, 1971), pp. 93–4. The formula underlying the balance of asymmetrical spaces in the church is based on a modification of the golden section and can be expressed by the relation 1:1.118. Although this discovery does not shed any further light on the provenance of the design, the foregoing relation can be derived from the difference between the traditional Russian measures *mernaia sazhen* (179.4 cm.) and *sazhen bez cheti* (197.2 cm) and thus would not have involved an improbably complicated series of geometric calculations. For an analysis of the measurements that led to this observation, see I. Sh. Shevelov, *Geometricheskaia garmoniia* (Kostroma, 1963). For a more detailed analysis of systems of measurement for construction purposes in medieval Rus, see I. A. Bondarenko, "K voprosu ob ispol'zovanii mer dliny v drevnerusskom zodchestve," *Arkhitekturnoe nasledstvo*, 36 (1988): 54–63. Even with these systems of calculation, the usual approach to the design of a masonry church was by reference to a prototype or earlier model. See T. N. Viatchanina, "O znachenii obraztsa v drevnerusskoi arkhitekture," *Arkhitekturnoe nasledstvo*, 32 (1984): 26–31.

20. A detailed analysis of the iconographic system of the Church of the Intercession is presented in Vagner, *Skul'ptura drevnei Rusi*, pp. 125–49.

21. Vagner proposes that three groups of masters worked on the carvings at the Church of the Intercession. Among them would have been a remnant of the foreigners referred to in the chronicles as working on his earlier projects. In addition, stylistic comparisons suggest the presence of masters ("two or three") from Galich, in the extreme western part of Rus. Vagner argues for an assimilation of Romanesque features at the Church of the Intercession, rather than a firm influence: ibid., pp. 186–91. A more general discussion of the presence of Romanesque elements in medieval Russian architecture, with particular reference to perspective portals, is contained in V. N. Lazarev, *Iskusstvo srednevekovoi Rusi i Zapad* (Moscow, 1970), p. 12. For an analysis of substantive differences in the structural and symbolic roles of perspective portals in western European and medieval Russian churches, see T. P. Kudriavtseva, "K voprosu o 'romanskikh' vliianiiakh vo Vladimiro-Suzdal'skom zodchestve," *Arkhitekturnoe nasledstvo*, 23 (1975): 30–6. Other possible conduits for Romanesque motifs into the culture of Vladimir include church vessels, such as twelfth-century reliquaries from the Rhine region that were transported to Vladimir. See V. P. Darkevich, "Romanskaia tserkovnaia utvar' iz Severo-Vostochnoi Rusi," in A. L. Mongait, ed., *Kul'tura drevnei Rusi* (Moscow, 1966), pp. 61–70.

22. A discussion of the iconographic significance of the image of David is contained in Vagner, *Skul'ptura drevnei Rusi*, pp. 130–4.

23. It has been noted that the Feast of the Intercession of the Virgin – October 1 – occurs at a time of the year, after the harvest, when marriages were traditionally made. The Christian holiday may have superseded an ancient ceremony devoted to a pagan goddess. See ibid., p. 140.

24. A number of the carved consoles at the Church of Intercession has been replaced over the centuries – some as recently as the past few decades. The original work and the probable replacements are identified in ibid., pp. 147–8.

25. For a succinct definition of the place of the *Physiologus* within medieval Russian literature, see. D. S. Mirsky, *A History of Russian Literature* (New York, 1960), p. 9. A standard encyclopedic reference to the work is in N. G. L. Hammond and H. H. Scullard, eds., *Oxford Classical Dictionary*, 2nd ed. (London, 1973), p. 832. The *Physiologus* is mentioned frequently by historians of medieval Russian art, including Vagner, *Skul'ptura drevnei Rusi*, p. 144 and passim.

26. Ibid., p. 200.

27. *Drevnerusskie letopisi*, p. 225. It is possible that the Kievan scribe wished to emphasize the pervasive cultural influence of Kiev, but it is also reasonable to assume that Kievan architecture would have continued to play a role in church design throughout Rus in the twelfth century.

28. N. N. Voronin, *Zodchestvo Severo-Vostochnoi Rusi*, vol. 1, pp. 354–75; and Rappoport, *Russkaia arkhitektura X–XIII vv.*, pp. 51–2.

29. Some of the decorative stonework on the north and south walls was transferred from the original cathedral. See Vagner, *Skul'ptura drevnei Rusi*, pp. 97, 207, 214. As in Andrei's time, the new arcade frieze probably contained frescoes of a row of saints. See Rappoport, *Russkaia arkhitektura X–XIII vv.*, p. 52. Almost nothing has been preserved of the interior frescoes commissioned by Vsevolod. See Lazarev, *Drevnerusskie mozaiki i freski: XI–XV vv.*, Plates 154–5.

30. If one considered the new aisles an integral part of the central structure, rather than an attachment to it (as in the Kiev and Novgorod Sophia cathedrals), then the Vladimir cathedral could be considered the largest in medieval Rus. For a comparison, to scale, of the plans of extant or uncovered churches through the thirteenth century, see Rappoport, *Russkaia arkhitektura X–XIII vv.*, pp. 118–31.

31. See ibid., pp. 54–5; and Voronin, *Zodchestvo Severo-Vostochnoi Rusi*, vol. 1, pp. 378–95. Fragments of the stone carving of the monastery church are illustrated in Vagner, *Skul'ptura drevnei Rusi*, pp. 220–9. On the basis on the carved archivolts of the west portal, Vagner states that the romanesque motifs of Bogoliubskii's time had been replaced by south Slavic motifs from Serbia. Cf. p. 229.

32. A description of the church structure is given in Voronin, *Zodchestvo Severo-Vostochnoi Rusi*, vol. 1, pp. 396–437.

33. For a survey of possible sources, see Vagner, *Skul'ptura drevnei Rusi*, pp. 390–415. The central importance of Ar-

menia in the development of medieval sculptural ornament was most vigorously proposed by Jurij Strzygowski, in *Die Baukunst der Armenier und Europa* (Vienna, 1918). In English, Strzygowski's theories were restated and elaborated upon in David R. Buxton, *Russian Medieval Architecture, with an Account of the Transcaucasian Styles and their Influence in the West* (Cambridge, 1934). Vagner's predictably critical comments on Strzygowski and his influence on such noted Russian art historians as A. I. Nekrasov (sent to the GULAG during the terror of the late 1930s) is contained in fn. 67, p. 428. Nekrasov's concepts of Russian art history, which are now current in the work of a number of leading Soviet medievalists, were often presented in a manner that challenged established academic interpretations on such sensitive issues as the origins and evolution of Russian art. He was sceptical of an emphasis on importance of wooden architecture to the development of major architectural forms in Russia, he consistently applied Marxist criticism to a discussion of the relation between art and society (leading to the charge of vulgar sociologism), and he was a comparativist in approach to stylistic questions (hence the link with Strzygowski). Among the published books of A. I. Nekrasov are: *Ocherki dekorativnogo iskusstva Drevnei Rusi* (Moscow, 1924); *Vizantiiskoe i russkoe iskusstvo* (Moscow, 1924); *Vozniknovenie moskovskogo iskusstva* (Moscow, 1929); *Ocherki po istorii drevnerusskogo zodchestva XI–XVII vekov* (Moscow, 1936); and *Drevnerusskoe izobrazitel'noe iskusstvo* (Moscow, 1937).

34. "On the Aesthetic Attitude in Romanesque Art," in Meyer Schapiro, *Romanesque Art: Selected Papers* (New York, 1977), p. 16. Indeed, the similarities between the western romanesque and the Suzdalian churches, whose basic form derived from Byzantium, are closer than Schapiro knew. Earlier in the same paper (p. 10), he defined different attitudes toward decoration in the two Christianities: the western being more receptive to diverse decorative motifs – even secular in origin – than the eastern, which officially venerated the image. Yet the twelfth-century churches of Vladimir show the same ability to incorporate both sacred and secular images, some perhaps of pagan derivation.

35. Sketches of the prerenovation appearance of the St. Dmitrii church are reproduced in Vagner, *Skul'ptura drevnei Rusi*, pp. 234, 236. It has been proposed that the galleries were not part of the original plan, but were constructed in the 1220s; however, current research indicates that they were built with the main structure. See Rappoport, *Russkaia arkhitektura X–XIII vv.*, p. 54.

36. It has also been suggested that in addition to the *Physiologos*, a source for the fanciful creatures and images of the natural world in Suzdalian church sculpture might have been the "Golubinaia kniga" (*glubinaia kniga* – "profound book"), an equivalent "encyclopedia" of knowledge interpreted in the Christian context in early medieval Rus. See I. Tolstoi and N. Kondakov, *Russkie drevnosti v pamiatnikakh iskusstva*, vol. 6, *Pamiatniki Vladimira, Novgoroda i Pskova* (St. Petersburg, 1899), p. 36. Vagner gives qualified support to this view (see *Skul'ptura drevnei Rusi*, pp. 196, 364).

37. Vagner argued that the seated prince in the central

zakomary was in fact Solomon and proceeded on that assumption to create an elaborate symbolic network (ibid., pp. 250, 254, and passim). Subsequently, restorers uncovered a clear inscription with the name David (as at the Church of the Intercession on the Nerl). This does not, however, eliminate Solomon from the facade sculpture or from the larger semantic context of the ruler and God's creation. On the cathedral facades, Solomon appears in three sites: on the left zakomara of the west facade, enthroned in the archivolt of the south portal, and on the north facade. A reappraisal of the David/Solomon motif is contained in Vagner, "Ob otkrytii reznykh nadpisei sredi fasadnoi skul'ptury Dmitrievskogo sobora vo Vladimire," *Sovetskaia arkheologiia*, 1976, no. 1: 270–2. An earlier interpretation of the seated figure as Solomon appeared in Tolstoi and Kondakov, pp. 30–1.

38. Vagner (*Skul'ptura drevnei Rusi*, p. 260) notes that the St. Dmitrii version of the apotheosis of Alexander differs from the usual regalia portrayed elsewhere in medieval Europe, but conforms to the details given in later variants of the Alexander romance. See also ibid., p. 455, n. 475. An illustration of a twelfth-century Byzantine relief of the Apotheosis of Alexander, on the facade of the Cathedral of St. Mark in Venice, is contained in under the heading "Alessandro," in *Enciclopedia Italiana*, vol. 2 (Milan–Rome, 1929), p. 337. For reference information on the Alexander romance, see "Pseudo-Callisthenes," *Oxford Classical Dictionary*, 2nd ed., p. 894.

39. Of the five sons – Konstantin, Georgii, Iaroslav, Vladimir, and Sviatoslav – Vagner suggests that the one on Vsevolod's knee would be the youngest (Sviatoslav), born during the construction of the cathedral (p. 258). In Voronin's opinion, the more likely choice is Vladimir, whose baptismal name was Dmitrii (as was Vsevolod's). See Voronin, *Zodchestvo Severo-Vostochnoi Rusi*, vol. 1, p. 436.

40. A summary of analyses of the frieze and its nineteenth-century replacement statuary (including the half-figure saints) is provided in Vagner, *Skul'ptura drevnei Rusi*, pp. 245–8.

41. On the drum, only an image of Christ, two evangelists, and three saints with scrolls are considered twelfth-century work. As Vagner notes, the drum – particularly the lower part – was damaged during the 1830s restoration, and most of the medallions were replaced (ibid., pp. 242, 258).

42. For a description and illustrations of the extant frescoes at the Cathedral of St. Dmitrii, see Lazarev, *Drevnerusskie mozaiki i freski: XI–XV vv.*, pp. 36–8, and Plates 157–71; and the large-format album (with extensive scholarly documentation) by V. Plugin, *Freski Dmitrievskogo sobora* (Leningrad, 1974).

43. Lazarev, *Drevnerusskie mozaiki i freski: XI–XV vv.*, p. 35.

44. See Rappoport, *Russkaia arkhitektura X–XIII vv.*, p. 55; Voronin, *Zodchestvo Severo-Vostochnoi Rusi*, vol. 1, pp. 438–45.

45. For archaeological data on Konstantin's churches in Rostov and Iaroslavl, see ibid., vol. 2, pp. 55–66; and Rappoport, *Russkaia arkhitektura X–XIII vv.*, pp. 61–2. Bogoliubskii's Dormition Cathedral in Rostov collapsed in 1204; the new cathedral was not consecrated until 1231.

46. See Rappoport, *Russkaia arkhitektura X–XIII vv.*, pp. 59–60; and Voronin, *Zodchestvo Severo-Vostochnoi Rusi*, vol. 2, pp. 19–42. There is some confusion in thirteenth-century sources as to the early history of the cathedral. Vagner supports the debatable hypothesis that at the beginning of the twelfth century, Vladimir Monomachus constructed a church (whose foundations have been discovered slightly to the north of the present church), but that it quickly fell into ruin and was rebuilt by Iurii Dolgorukii in 1148, whose church was subsequently replaced by Iurii Vsevolodovich. See Vagner, *Belokamennaia rez'ba drevnego Suzdalia* (Moscow, 1975), pp. 14–25.

47. Vagner's reconstruction of a three-domed structure with a carved ornamental pattern covering the central bay is reproduced in ibid., p. 32.

48. For an exegesis of the scenes, with copious illustrations, see ibid., pp. 97–142.

49. There is still disagreement as to the original height and form of the roofline of the St. George Cathedral. See Rappoport, *Russkaia arkhitektura X–XIII vv.*, p. 64.

50. A detailed description of the structure is contained in Voronin, *Zodchestvo Severo-Vostochnoi Rusi*, vol. 2, pp. 68–107. The north facade is analyzed, with a hypothetical reconstruction of the missing elements in G. K. Vagner, "K voprosu o rekonstruktsii severnogo facada Georgievskogo sobora v Iur'eve-Pol'skom," *Arkhitekturnoe nasledstvo*, 14 (1962): 27–34.

51. The carving and its reconstruction at the Cathedral of St. George is the subject of the first of Georgii Vagner's three books on the stone churches of Suzdalia: *Skul'ptura Vladimiro-Suzdalskoi Rusi* (Moscow, 1964). Vagner's exhaustive analysis is admirably summarized and illustrated in Nikolai Voronin, *Vladimir, Bogolyubovo, Suzdal, Yurev-Polskoi* (in English), pp. 294–308.

52. Neither of the Nizhnii Novgorod churches is extant. For a description of the archaeological remains, see Voronin, *Zodchestvo Severo-Vostochnoi Rusi*, vol. 2, pp. 43–54; and Rappoport, *Russkaia arkhitektura X–XIII vv.*, p. 61.

53. Novgorod chronicle, under A.M. 6732. See Michell and Forbes, *The Chronicle of Novgorod*, pp. 63–6.

54. V. Lebedev and V. Panov, eds. *Drevnerusskie letopisi*, pp. 270–1. The Mongols ignited wood placed against the walls of the Dormition Cathedral, but the structure remained intact.

55. "O nichtozhestve literatury russkoi" (On the Insignificance of Russian Literature), Aleksandr Pushkin, *Polnoe sobranie sochinenii v desiati tomakh* (Moscow, 1964), vol. 7, p. 307.

Chapter 4

1. A detailed discussion of new developments in building materials as illustrated by the Church of St. Nicholas at Lipno is presented by L. M. Shuliak, "Arkhitektura kontsa XIII–XV v.," in M. N. Tikhomirov, ed., *Novgorod: k 1100-letiiu goroda* (Moscow, 1964), pp. 217–19. Photographs before and after the restoration of the church are reproduced in Tikhomirov, pp. 217, 221. For an authoritative theoretical analysis and summation of the results of 30 years of restoration work on the churches of Novgorod (with critical commentary on the details of a number of the restored churches discussed below), see G. M. Shtender, "Restavratsiia pamiatnikov novgorodskogo zodchestva," in D. S. Likhachev, ed., *Vosstanovlenie pamiatnikov kul'tury (Problemy restavratsii)* (Moscow, 1981), pp. 43–72. An early detailed analysis of the structure is provided by P. Maksimov, "Tserkov' Nikoly na Lipne bliz Novgoroda," *Arkhitekturnoe nasledstvo*, 2 (1952): 86–104.

2. An archaeological description of two early fourteenth-century churches – the Archangel Michael at the Marketplace (1300) and the Annunciation at Gorodishche (1342) – is contained in Shuliak, "Arkhitektura kontsa XIII–XV v.," pp. 220, 222–3.

3. See Lazarev, *Drevnerusskie mozaiki i freski: XI–XV vv.*, pp. 64–6; and a selection of prewar photographs of the frescoes, Plates 367–78. Lazarev suggests (p. 65) that the painters could have been from the monastic community of Mount Athos, where both the Russian and the Serbian Church had major presence. A more detailed analysis by the same author is contained in "Kovalevskaia rospis' i problema iuzhnoslavianskikh sviazei v russkoi zhivopisi XIV veka," in V. N. Lazarev, ed., *Russkaia srednevekovaia zhivopis'* (Moscow, 1970), pp. 238–74. A description of the reconstruction of fragments of the Kovalevo frescoes, smashed to bits in the Second World War, is presented with reference to their architectural setting in A. P. Grekov, "Iz opyta rabot po spaseniiu rospisi tserkvi Spasa na Kovaleve v Novgorode," in O. I. Podobedova, ed., *Drevnerusskoe iskusstvo: Monumental'naia zhivopis' XI–XVII vv.* (Moscow, 1980), pp. 176–95. For a summary in English of the Grekovs' heroic efforts, see Henrik Birnbaum, "Ancient Russian Art – Its Destruction and Restoration," *Essays in Early Slavic Civilization* (Munich, 1981), p. 302. A recent analysis of the Kovalevo frescoes and other examples of frescoes from fourteenth- and fifteenth-century Novgorod churches is presented in L. I. Lifshits, *Monumental'naia zhivopis' Novgoroda XIV–XV vekov* (Moscow, 1987). Profusely illustrated, the volume contains an appendix with schematic guides to the location and identification of each fresco fragment in these churches.

4. Commissioned by the Novgorod archbishop Moses for a small monastery, the Volotovo church was of modest proportions and distinguished only by its frescoes, which were apparently painted by an unknown Novgorod master. See Lazarev, *Drevnerusskie mozaiki i freski*, pp. 60–4. During the Second World War, the Volotovo church shared the fate of the other churches in Novgorod's eastern suburbs (Nereditsa, Lipno, Kovalevo). Its partial restoration has lagged behind that of the other reconstructed monuments, although its frescoes were photographed and painted before the war. They are the subject of an album based on prewar photographs by L. A. Matsulevich and colored sketches of the frescoes: Mikhail V. Alpatov, *Freski tserkvi Uspeniia na*

Volotovom pole (Moscow, 1977). See also Lifshits, *Monumental'naia zhivopis'*, pp. 495–9.

5.   See Shuliak, "Arkhitektura kontsa XIII–XV v.," p. 238, fn. 143; also Iu. N. Dmitriev, "O formakh pokrytiia v novgorodskom zodchestve XIV–XVI vekov, *Drevnerusskoe iskusstvo XV–nachala XVI veka* (Moscow, 1963), pp. 198–9.

6.   An examination of construction techniques utilized in one of the most prolific periods of Novgorodian architecture – the second half of the fourteenth century and the beginning of the fifteenth – is contained in Shuliak, "Arkhitektura kontsa XIII–XV v.," pp. 228–32.

7.   Ibid., p. 234.

8.   Lazarev, *Drevnerusskie mozaiki i freski*, pp. 58–9, with illustrations of the St. Theodore frescoes in plates 326–34. For a descriptive analysis of the extant fragments, see V. M. Kovaleva, "Zhivopis' tserkvi Fedora Stratilata v Novgorode po materialam otkrytii 1974–1976 gg.," in O. I. Podobedova, ed., *Drevnerusskoe iskusstvo: Monumental'naia zhivopis' XI–XVII vv.* (Moscow, 1980), pp. 161–75. See also Lifshits, *Monumental'naia zhivopis'*, pp. 508–11.

9.   For a history of the construction of the Church of the Transfiguration on Elijah Street (with commentary on its predecessor churches), see Gerol'd I. Vzdornov, *Freski Feofana Greka v tserkvi Spasa Preobrazheniia v Novgorode* (Moscow, 1976), pp. 9–17.

10.   On the west facade, the Church of the Transfiguration had an enclosed extension and bell tower, which were razed (perhaps in the late eighteenth century) and replaced. The later variants have since been removed, and the west facade now shows the arch of the original extension. See Brumfield, *Gold in Azure*, p. 59.

11.   Information on the life of Theophanes is provided in Viktor Lazarev, *Feofan Grek i ego shkola* (Moscow, 1961), pp. 9–11, 111–13. We are fortunate in having an account of Theophanes by a contemporary, Epiphanius the Wise, a monk at the Savior-Andronicus Monastery in Moscow. Epiphanius met Theophanes after the latter had moved to Moscow (by the early 1390s), and in a letter written around 1415 to Cyril of Tver presented his extensive, psychologically astute impressions of the painter. See *Izbornik* (Moscow, 1969), pp. 398–401.

12.   The most thorough study of the Transfiguration frescoes (with comprehensive photographic documentation) is Vzdornov, *Freski Feofana Greka*. For a detailed schematic guide, see Lifshits, *Monumental'naia zhivopis'*, pp. 500–3.

13.   For example, Lazarev, *Drevnerusskie mozaiki i freski*, p. 56. Lazarev deals more substantively with the Hesychast theme in *Feofan Grek i ego shkola*, pp. 18–29.

14.   For comments on the monastic, eschatological emphasis in the Transfiguration frescoes, see Vzdornov, *Freski Feofana Greka*, pp. 153–61. A survey of the literature concerning the relation of Hesychasm to the work of Theophanes is presented in ibid., pp. 236–58. One of the leading authorities on the theme is M. V. Alpatov, author of "Iskusstvo Feofana Greka i uchenie isikhastov," *Vizantiiskii vremennik*, 33 (1972): 190–202. The same theme is discussed in his text to the album *Feofan Grek* (Moscow, 1979), pp. 9–20, passim.

15.   Following the Second World War, the severely damaged Church of Sts. Peter and Paul in Slavno was restored by analogy with churches of similar plan and period. See Shuliak, "Arkhitektura kontsa XIII–XV v.," pp. 235–6.

16.   Shuliak, who refers to the church as the Nativity of the Virgin in Molotkovo, notes that the western part of the church, as well as the vaults, the roof, and much of the apsidal structure were rebuilt in the seventeenth century (ibid., p. 236).

17.   For commentary and illustrations of the frescoes on the interior of the Church of the Nativity of Christ in the Cemetery, see Lazarev, *Drevnerusskie mozaiki i freski*, p. 66, and Plates 380–2. For a note on the structure, see Shuliak, "Arkhitektura kontsa XIII–XV v.," p. 236. See also Lifshits, *Monumental'naia zhivopis'*, pp. 511–13.

18.   Shuliak notes that the trefoil roof and vaulting, traces of which were found in a recent restoration, were replaced in the sixteenth century (ibid., p. 238). Like most such churches, the west facade had an enclosed extension, subsequently rebuilt.

19.   See ibid, pp. 238–9.

20.   For a list of later modifications to the Church of St. John, see ibid., pp. 239–40.

21.   The position of the Church of the Twelve Apostles at a turning point in Novgorod architecture is briefly discussed in ibid., pp. 243–4.

22.   For a description of changes in the production of brick, see ibid., p. 242.

23.   The Novgorod chronicle account of archbishop Evfimii's construction projects within the citadel (or *detinets*) is contained in *Novgorodskaia pervaia letopis' starshego i mladshego izvodov* (Moscow–Leningrad, 1950), pp. 416–23. The reference to "Germans" appears on p. 416. For an analysis of the reception hall of the Faceted Chambers and its relation to late Gothic brick structures in the Baltic area (such as the castle at Marienburg), see V. P. Vygolov, *Arkhitektura Moskovskoi Rusi serediny XV veka* (Moscow, 1988), pp. 126–8.

24.   The Church of St. Dmitrii and its ornamentation are analyzed in P. N. Maksimov, "Tserkov' Dmitriia Solunskogo v Novgorode," *Arkhitekturnoe nasledstvo*, 14 (1962): 35–46. Maksimov argues that the decorative brick patterns illustrated in this church influenced the development of ornamental limestone carving in early Moscow churches (see pp. 43–5). Similar decorative and structural devices were applied in the building of new churches, such as St. Simeon at the Zverin Monastery (1467). Some 7 meters in length and width, the church is typical of the "miniaturization" of Novgorod churches during the middle of the fifteenth century, with details such as pilaster strips characteristic of much larger structures. The colorful interior frescoes, including much work dating to the fifteenth century, have been well preserved. See Lifshits, *Monumental' naia zhivopis'*, pp. 517–20.

25.   For a summary of the revival of Novgorodian architecture and a replanning of the city at the beginning of the sixteenth century, see L. E. Krasnorech'ev, "Arkhitektura

XVI v.," in M. N. Tikhomirov, ed., *Novgorod: k 1100-letiiu goroda*, pp. 244–53.

26. A detailed analysis of the construction history of the Church of Women Bearing Myrrh is provided in T. V. Gladenko, "Tserkov' Zhen Mironosits," M. N. Tikhomirov, ed., *Novgorod: k 1100-letiiu goroda*, pp. 254–8. Archaeological data on the roof are contained on pp. 256–7. A still more traditional form appeared in the Church of St. Clement, built in 1520 by the Muscovite merchant Vasilii Tarakanov on the site of an earlier church dating from 1386 (collapsed in 1516). See Brumfield, *Gold in Azure*, p. 68. The structure and decoration, which reproduce the features of fourteenth-century architecture, have been expertly restored in a project supervised by T. V. Gladenko. See Gladenko, "Tserkov' Klimenta," in M. N. Tikhomirov, ed., *Novgorod: k 1100-letiiu goroda*, pp. 261–3.

27. A detailed description of the structure of the Church of St. Prokopii appears in Gladenko, "Tserkov' Prokopiia," M. N. Tikhomirov, ed., *Novgorod: k 1100-letiiu goroda*, pp. 258–61.

28. See Krasnorech'ev, "Arkhitektura XVI v.," pp. 245–6.

29. Ibid., p. 247.

30. This innovative ensemble, whose covered, connecting gallery would be imitated to much effect in the Novgorod area is under restoration. See ibid., pp. 250–1.

31. John Fennell, *The Crisis of Medieval Russia 1200–1304* (London–New York, 1983), pp. 133–5.

32. Iu. P. Spegal'skii, *Pskov: Khudozhestvennye pamiatniki* (Leningrad, 1972), p. 25. See also V. D. Beletskii, "Arkheologicheskie dannye k datirovke krepostnykh sten Dovmontova goroda v Pskove," *Arkheologicheskie sbornik Gosudarstvennogo Ermitazha*, 12 (1970): pp. 68–73. For the subsequent development of the center of Pskov, see G. Ia. Mokeev, "Stolichnyi tsentr Pskova kontsa XV v.," *Arkhitekturnoe nasledstvo*, 24 (1976): 60–71.

33. Archaeological data on the Trinity Cathedral, originally constructed in the twelfth century (probably 1190s), are presented in P. A. Rappoport, *Russkaia arkhitektura X–XIII vv.*, vol. E1–47, *Arkheologiia SSSR: Svod arkheologicheskikh istochnikov* (Leningrad, 1982), p. 79. Although completely rebuilt in the fourteenth century, the Trinity Cathedral is thought to have retained many of the features of the twelfth-century design. A detailed discussion of the cathedral in relation to the architecture of twelfth-century Smolensk is contained in N. N. Voronin, P. A. Rappoport, *Zodchestvo Smolenska, XII–XIII vv.*, pp. 365–71. See also Spegal'skii, *Pskov*, pp. 33–5.

34. Spegal'skii notes that both the cement ground and the limestone whitewash contained impurities that added a polychromatic element (light yellow or pink tones) to the exterior wall surface (ibid., pp. 36–7).

35. For a detailed recreation of the original appearance of the Church of St. Basil, see ibid., pp. 127–30. Shortly before his death, Spegal'skii published an article stating that the church was built not in the fifteenth century, but in the middle of the sixteenth: "Tserkov' Vasiliia na Gorke v Pskove," *Sovetskaia arkheologiia*, 1970, no. 2: 252. Nonetheless, the date 1413, documented in medieval sources, remains accepted in contemporary scholarship – including Spegal'skii's own posthumously published book on Pskov.

36. Spegal'skii, *Pskov*, pp. 43, 56. Further discussion of the evolution of the multiplanar roof in Pskov is contained in P. N. Maksimov, "Zarubezhnye sviazi v arkhitekture Novgoroda i Pskova XI–nachala XVI vekov," *Arkhitekturnoe nasledstvo*, 12 (1960): 42.

37. The complex construction history of the Church of Sts. Kozma and Demian is set forth in Spegal'skii, *Pskov*, pp. 205–8.

38. The Church of the Epiphany was severely damaged by fire at the beginning of the Second World War. For a reconstruction of its original form – and a sharp criticism of its postwar restoration – see ibid., pp. 212–14.

39. A detailed analysis of the belfry at the Cave Monastery and a comparison with other Pskov belfries is contained in Mikhail Kraskovskii's pioneering survey "Pskovskie zvonnitsy," *Zodchii*, 1906, no. 28: 292–3. The architectural development of the monastery is examined in G. Rabinovich, "Arkhitekturnyi ansambl' Pskovo-Pecherskogo monastyria," *Arkhitekturnoe nasledstvo*, 6 (1956): 57–86.

40. Commentary on St. Nicholas church and its postwar restoration appears in Spegal'skii, *Pskov*, pp. 130–4.

41. For a discussion of the "Third Rome" proclamation and its relation to other church-sponsored writings glorifying Moscow's role as a defender of Orthodoxy, see Robert O. Crummey, *The Formation of Muscovy 1304–1613* (London–New York, 1987), pp. 136–7. The political implications of the Filofei document for the image of the Muscovite ruler is discussed in Michael Cherniavsky, *Tsar and People: Studies in Russian Myths* (New Haven, 1961), pp. 38–42. See also V. Malinin, *Starets Eleasarova monastyria Filofei i ego poslaniia* (Kiev, 1901); Dimitri Strémooukhoff, "Moscow the Third Rome: Sources of the Doctrine," *Speculum* (January 1953): 84–101; and N[ikolay] Andreyev, "Filofey and his epistle to Ivan Vasilyevich," *Slavonic and East European Review*, 38 (1959): 1–3. A sceptical interpretation of the "Third Rome" doctrine, within the context of Byzantine influence on Muscovy, is presented in John Meyendorff, "Was There Ever a 'Third Rome'? Remarks on the Byzantine Legacy in Russia," in John Yiannias, ed., *The Byzantine Tradition after the Fall of Constantinople* (Charlottesville, 1991), pp. 45–60.

Chapter 5

1. There are a number of works that attempt to reconstruct the early history of Moscow. One of the classic studies is I. E. Zabelin, *Istoriia goroda Moskvy* (Moscow, 1902). An authoritative Soviet study is L. V. Cherepnin, *Obrazovanie Russkogo tsentralizovannogo gosudarstva v XIV–XV vekhakh* (Moscow, 1960). A political history in English is J. L. I. Fennell, *The Emergence of Moscow 1304–1359* (Berkeley, 1968). A survey of archaeological and historical data relating to the city's earliest stages of development is contained in A. I. Komech and V. I. Pluzhnikov, eds., *Pamiatniki arkhitektury*

Moskvy: Kreml', Kitai-gorod, Tsentral'nye ploshchadi (Moscow, 1983), pp. 21–7.

2. For a discussion of Daniil's reign, with references to the sparse evidence from medieval chronicles, see Fennell, *The Emergence of Moscow*, pp. 47–51.

3. For a survey of this protracted, debilitating struggle, see ibid., pp. 60–110.

4. Ibid., pp. 111–21.

5. For a survey of archaeological data on the earliest stone churches in the Kremlin (which is first referred to by that name in 1331), see Komech and Pluzhnikov, *Kreml'*, pp. 28–9, 262–4. In addition to the Dormition Cathedral, the early attested monuments include the Church of John Climacus (1329), the Church of the Savior in the Woods (1330s; rebuilt at the end of the eighteenth century and destroyed in 1932), and the Cathedral of the Archangel Michael (1333–40). On the basis of excavations under the auspices of the State Museum of the Moscow Kremlin, claims have been made by V. I. Fedorov and N. S. Sheliapina for the existence of an earlier stone church, dedicated to St. Dmitrii and constructed toward the end of the thirteenth century. A summary of their work is contained in *Arkheologicheskie otkrytiia 1968 goda* (Moscow, 1969), pp. 81–3. See also N. S. Sheliapina, "K istorii izucheniia Uspenskogo sobora moskovskogo Kremlia," *Sovetskaia arkheologiia*, 1972, no. 1: 200–14. The claims for the existence of the Dmitrii church are tentatively accepted in Komech and Pluzhnikov, *Kreml'*, p. 262, but are rejected as "mythical" in V. P. Vygolov, *Arkhitektura Moskovskoi Rusi serediny XV veka* (Moscow, 1988), p. 60. A survey of archaeological and restoration projects in the Kremlin is presented in O. A. Shvidkovskii et al., eds., *Sokhranenie arkhitekturnykh pamiatnikov moskovskogo Kremlia* (Moscow, 1977).

6. N. N. Voronin compares the Dormition Cathedral with earlier monuments of Suzdalia in *Zodchestvo Severo-Vostochnoi Rusi XII–XV vekov*, vol. 2, p. 152.

7. For commentary on the relation between the Orthodox Church and Ivan Kalita, see Fennell, *The Emergence of Moscow*, pp. 191–2; and Crummey, *The Formation of Muscovy*, p. 40. See also John Meyendorff, *Byzantium and the Rise of Russia* (Cambridge, 1981).

8. On Dmitrii Donskoi's reconstruction of the Kremlin walls, see Komech and Pluzhnikov, *Kreml'*, pp. 30–1 (with map indicating monasteries and century of founding on p. 32), 263.

9. From the vita of Sergius by Epiphanius the Wise. An English translation is contained in Serge Zenkovsky, ed., *Medieval Russia's Epics, Chronicles, and Tales* (New York, 1963), pp. 208–36, with particular reference to p. 230. For a discussion of the cultural significance of the Orthodox Church in the Russian revival at the end of the fourteenth century, see D. S. Likhachev, *Kul'tura Rusi vremeni Andreia Rubleva i Epifaniia Premudrogo (konets XIV–nachalo XV v.)* (Moscow–Leningrad, 1962).

10. On the Church of St. Nicholas at Kamenskoe, see Voronin, *Zodchestvo Severo-Vostochnoi Rusi*, vol. 2, pp. 321–4; M. A. Ilin, "Redkii pamiatnik drevnerusskoi arkhitektury (Khram sela Kamenskogo)," *Istorii SSSR*, 1969, no. 3: 150–5; and B. L. Al'tshuller, "Novye issledovaniia Nikol'skoi tserkvi sela Kamenskogo," *Arkhitekturnoe nasledstvo*, 20 (1972): 17–25. The Moscow area also contains substantial fragments of a still earlier church, similar in design to St. Nicholas at Kamenskoe. Located on the outskirts of Kolomna (a major trading center to the south of Moscow), the Church of John the Baptist at Gorodishche has been tentatively dated to the 1360s; and although much rebuilt, its lower walls – of rough limestone – have been preserved and suggest a plan similar to that of the Kamenskoe church. See Voronin, *Zodchestvo Severo-Vostochnoi Rusi*, vol. 2, pp. 204–5; and M. V. Fekhner, *Kolomna* (Moscow, 1966), pp. 63–4.

11. T. V. Nikolaeva, *Drevnii Zvenigorod* (Moscow, 1978), p. 9.

12. The Dormition Cathedral is presumed to have been completed in 1400 and the Nativity Cathedral somewhat later. See Voronin, *Zodchestvo Severo-Vostochnoi Rusi*, vol. 2, pp. 290–8; and 299–306. It is now believed that Andrei Rublev painted a number of the original frescoes of the Dormition Cathedral, including two figures (Sts. Flor and Lavr) that have survived on the east (altar) piers. See Lazarev, *Drevnerusskie mozaiki i freski: XI–XV vv.* (Moscow, 1973), pp. 71–2, and Plates 393–4.

13. In comparison with the resolution of exterior segmentation and interior structure in pre-Mongol limestone churches, the disjunction between the two in early fifteenth-century churches can be seen as evidence of a lack of aesthetic perception. Yet the later designs have been defended as a new means of defining a balance of structure and form that created a sense of monumentality and vertical emphasis within the still limited means of Muscovy's princes. See P. N. Maksimov, "O kompozitsionnom masterstve moskovskikh zodchikh nachala XV v.," *Arkhitekturnoe nasledstvo*, 21 (1973): 44–7. N. F. Gulianitskii pursues the matter further by noting that the independent segmentation of the facade represents a movement toward an order system: "It is characteristic that the first elements of the order system in the form of pilasters with a base and capital can be traced in early Muscovite churches, when there began to appear a divergence from the tectonic system of Vladimir-Suzdal church architecture and toward the formation of a new structure of segmentation." See "O svoeobrazii i preemstvenykh sviaziakh ordernogo iazyka v russkoi arkhitekture," *Arkhitekturnoe nasledstvo*, 23 (1975): 15.

14. A convincing analysis of fourteenth-century Serbian – and, more generally, Byzantine – elements in the ornamental carving of the early cathedrals at Zvenigorod and Zagorsk is presented in M. A. Il'in, "Dekorativnye reznye poiasa rannemoskovskogo kamennogo zodchestva," in G. V. Popov, ed., *Drevnerusskoe iskusstvo: Zarubezhnye sviazi* (Moscow, 1975), pp. 223–39.

15. A detailed history of the Holy Trinity lavra is presented in a number of works by V. I. Baldin, including *Arkhitekturnyi ansambl Troitse-Sergievoi lavry* (Moscow, 1976); and his chapter "Arkhitektura," in N. N. Voronin and V. V. Kos-

tochkin, eds., *Troitse-Sergieva lavra: Khudozhestvennye pamiatniki* (Moscow, 1968), pp. 15–71.

16. Baldin, "Arkhitektura," pp. 17–18.

17. N. I. Brunov considered the presence of capitals above the pilaster strips at the Trinity Cathedral to be an early Russian attempt to assimilate the order system through an evolution of typically Russian forms. See Brunov et al., *Istoriia russkoi arkhitektury* (Moscow, 1956), p. 85.

18. Iu. A. Lebedeva, "Andrei Rublev i zhivopis' XV veka," in Voronin and Kostochkin, *Troitse-Sergieva lavra*, pp. 77–8.

19. The painting of Rublev's Trinity icon has not been dated with any precision and could possibly have occurred for the second log church over the grave of Sergius. It is more probable, however, that such a monumental icon would have been painted for the stone church just as its structure was completed and ready for consecration (around 1423). See ibid., p. 78. A survey of the extant rows of icons dating from 1427–9 in the iconostasis, with indications as to probable authorship, is contained in ibid., pp. 79–92.

20. For a discussion of the origins and early form of the Russian iconostasis, see L. V. Betin, "Ob arkhitekturnoi kompozitsii drevnerusskikh vysokikh ikonostasov," in V. D. Lazarev, ed., *Drevnerusskoe iskusstvo. Khudozhestvennaia kul'tura Moskvy i prilezhashchikh k nei kniazhestv. XIV–XVI vv.* (Moscow, 1970), pp. 41–56; and idem, "Istoricheskie osnovy drevnerusskogo vysokogo ikonostasa," ibid., pp. 57–72. In his comments on the development of the icon screen, M. A. Il'in notes the hypothetical nature of the task, because no surviving inconstasis (as opposed to the icons themselves) predates the seventeenth century: "Nekotorye predpolozheniia ob arkhitekture russkikh ikonostasov na rubezhe XIV–XV vv.," in A. L. Mongait, ed., *Kul'tura drevnei Rusi* (Moscow, 1966), pp. 79–88. The relation between the iconostasis and interior space, with specific reference to the Trinity Cathedral, is analyzed in N. F. Gulianitskii, "O vnutrennem prostranstve v kompozitsii rannemoskovskikh khramov," *Arkhitketurnoe nasledstvo*, 33 (1985): 211–17. See also V. I. Baldin, "Arkhitektura Troitskogo sobora Troitse-Sergievoi lavry," *Arkhitekturnoe nasledstvo*, 6 (1956): 21–56, esp. p. 31.

21. See M. A. Il'in and T. V. Moiseeva, *Moskva i Podmoskov'e* (Moscow, 1979), p. 470. N. I. Brunov was among the first to advance the hypothesis concerning the evolution of the tower church from the corbeled arches of the inscribed-cross form. See, for example, "K voprosu o nekotorykh sviaziakh russkoi arkhitektury s zodchestvom iuzhnykh slavian," *Arkhitekturnoe nasledstvo*, 2 (1952): 3–42. This view was challenged (with specific reference to the Andronikov Monastery cathedral) in M. A. Il'in's monograph on sixteenth-century tower churches: *Russkoe shatrovoe zodchestvo. Pamiatniki serediny XVI veka* (Moscow, 1980), pp. 20–2. The question of sixteenth-century tower churches is addressed in Chapter 6.

22. For a reference to Rublev's work at Andronikov Monastery, see Lebedeva, "Andrei Rublev i zhivopis'," pp. 77–8.

23. V. P. Vygolov cites documentary evidence suggesting that around 1462, the Trinity Tower was rebuilt at least partly in brick: *Arkhitektura Moskovskoi Rusi serediny XV veka* (Moscow, 1988), p. 135. Vygolov argues that builders experienced in the use of brick could have been imported initially from Novgorod, where the material was extensively used in the fourteenth and fifteenth centuries (pp. 222–3).

24. See M. A. Il'in, "Pskovskie zodchie v Moskve v kontse XV veka," in V. N. Lazarev, ed., *Drevnerusskoe iskusstvo: Khudozhestvennaia kul'tura Pskova* (Moscow, 1968), pp. 192–3, with reference to remnants of Gothic decorative motifs in the decoration of the apse of the Church of the Holy Ghost (see what follows). A more extensive analysis of the work of the Pskov builders is presented by G. I. Vzdornov, "Postroiki pskovskoi arteli zodchikh v Moskve (Po letopisnoi stat'e 1476 goda)," in V. N. Lazarev, ed., *Drevnerusskoe iskusstvo: Khudozhestvennaia kul'tura Pskova* (Moscow, 1968), pp. 174–88.

25. For an account of the "riddle" of the belfry – which was concealed in an eighteenth-century rebuilding of the roof – and the access to it, see ibid., pp. 180–1. A description of the restoration of the church to its earlier form is contained in V. I. Baldin and Iu. N. Gerasimov, "Dukhovskaia tserkov' Troitse-Sergieva monastyria," *Arkhitekturnoe nasledstvo*, 19 (1972): 53–65.

26. Vzdornov states that the ornamental motifs themselves were typical to the Moscow region: "Postroiki pskovskoi arteli," pp. 178–9. As for the facade of the Holy Spirit church, the material used was a type of plinthos rather than the larger Moscow brick or the "super" Italian brick introduced in the 1470s. Vzdornov proposes that the smaller brick was closer in size and weight to the rough limestone slabs used in Pskov (ibid., p. 176).

27. See ibid., pp. 182–4. It should be noted that P. N. Maksimov disputes the role of the Pskov masters for the Kremlin churches because of the considerable differences in the manner of the churches' construction. See "K voprosu ob avtorstve Blagoveshchenskogo sobora i Rizpolozhenskoi tserkvi v Moskovskom Kremle," *Arkhitekturnoe nasledstvo*, 16 (1967): 13–18. Both Il'in and Vzdornov, however, accept the Pskov authorship in their respective articles on the Deposition and Annunciation churches.

28. The similarity to the Andronikov Monastery cathedral is noted in Il'in, "Pskovskie zodchie v Moskve v kontse XV veka," pp. 194–5.

29. The present icon stand in the Annunciation Cathedral is a much later version, although several of the original icons themselves have been preserved. There is some question as to the original design of the stand: Was it placed between the east piers, as in Zvenigorod, or did it conceal the piers, as in the Trinity Monastery Cathedral (see n. 19)? For a survey of the history of the construction and painting of the Annunciation Cathedral, see Komech and Pluzhnikov, *Kreml'*, pp. 318–20. See also N. A. Maiasova, "K istorii ikonostasa Blagoveshchenskogo sobora Moskovskogo Kremlia," in A. L. Mongait, ed., *Kul'tura drevnei Rusi* (Moscow, 1966), pp. 152–7. A general photograph of the iconostasis

(of considerable size in relation to the cramped central space) is reproduced in Alpatov, *Feofan Grek* (Moscow, 1979), p. 142.

30. For a reconstruction by N. D. Vinogradov of the appearance of the Annunciation Cathedral as rebuilt in the 1480s, see Brunov, *Istoriia russkoi arkhitektury*, p. 95. Although accepting the basic features of the reconstruction, Vzdornov notes certain corrections pertaining to the terrace attached to the side facades (p. 186). Il'in notes that the walls of the cathedral were of the newly developed brick – not the plinthos used in the Church of the Holy Ghost: "Pskovskie zodchie v Moskve v kontse XV veka," p. 195.

31. Although there are no references to the construction of the Church of St. Anne, the probable time is outlined in Komech and Pluzhnikov, eds., *Kreml'*, p. 447.

32. For a catalog of modifications to the original structure of the Nativity Cathedral, see G. V. Makarevich et al., eds., *Pamiatniki arkhitektury Moskvy: Belyi Gorod* (Moscow, 1989), pp. 212–14.

33. A detailed study of this neglected period in Russian architectural history is presented in Vygolov, *Arkhitektura Moskovskoi Rusi serediny XV veka* (Moscow, 1988). For a list of the major projects, beginning with construction commissioned in the Kremlin by Metropolitan Jonah in 1450 and 1451, see pp. 211–12.

34. For an analysis of the 1471 rebuilding of the Cathedral of St. George in Iurev-Pol'skoi, see ibid., pp. 74–92. It is not entirely clear whether Ermolin, in his various commissions from Ivan III, actually served as an architect. For a survey of his career, based on the famous "Ermolin Chronicle," see A. M. Viktorov, "V. Ermolin," in Iu. S. Iaralov, ed., *Zodchie Moskvy XV–XIX vv* (Moscow, 1981), pp. 34–41.

35. Vygolov, *Arkhitektura Moskovskoi Rusi*, p. 182.

36. The role of Philip in the 1472 rebuilding of the Dormition Cathedral is examined in ibid., pp. 182–8, with a comparative discussion of the various, sometimes competing, chronicle accounts of this major event (pp. 179–81). The submerged animosity between Ivan III and Philip probably originated from Ivan's need to limit the growing area of land under church control, and Philip was deeply suspicious of the Italian retinue that accompanied Sophia Paleologue to her new residence in Moscow. See S. M. Zemtsov and V. L. Glazychev, *Aristotel' F'oravanti* (Moscow, 1985), pp. 83–4.

37. A collation of chronicle accounts of the collapse is presented in Vygolov, *Arkhitektura Moskovskoi Rusi*, pp. 190–2. In addition to the usual technical reasons, it has been suggested, on the basis of a complaint by Vasilii Ermolin (who withdrew from the project in 1472), that the great haste with which Philip drove the builders led to carelessness in construction. See P. N. Maksimov, "K voprosu ob avtorstve Blagoveshchenskogo sobora i Rizpolozhenskoi tserkvi v Moskovskom Kremle," *Arkhitekturnoe nasledstvo*, 16 (1967): 16. The great size of the cathedral in comparison with previous Muscovite churches is analyzed in B. A. Ognev, "Nekotorye problemy rannemoskovskogo zodchestva," *Arkhitekturnoe nasledstvo*, 12 (1960): 48–9.

38. Zemtsov and Glazychev, *F'oravanti*, pp. 69–70.

39. A colorful account of the meeting between Tolbuzin and Fioravanti (based on a flattering description by Tolbuzin) is provided in V. Snegirev, *Aristotel' Fioravanti i perestroika moskovskogo kremlia* (Moscow, 1935). A more judicious view of Tolbuzin's encomium and of his motives for writing it is provided in Zemtsov and Glazychev, *F'oravanti*, pp. 80, 82. For an informed Italian account of Fioravanti's encounter with the Russians and his work in Moscow, see Piero Cazzola, "I 'Mastri frjazy' a Mosca sullo scorcio del quindicesimo secolo (dalle Cronache russe e da documenti di Archivi italiani)," *Arte Lombarda*, 44/45 (1976): 158–66.

40. Fioravanti's years in Milan (1458–64) are chronicled in Zemtsov and Glazychev, *F'oravanti*, pp. 44–54. For an Italian chronology, see Sandra Tugnoli Pattaro, "Le opere bolognesi de Aristotele Fioravanti architetto e ingegnere del secolo quindicesimo," *Arte Lombarda*, 44/45 (1976): 35–70.

41. For a description of the wall construction (a brick inner wall between the limestone facades), see S. M. Zemtsov, "Arkhitektory Moskvy vtoroi poloviny XV i pervoi poloviny XVI veka," in Iu. S. Iaralov, ed., *Zodchie Moskvy XV–XIX vv* (Moscow, 1981), p. 53. See also Zemtsov and Glazychev, *F'oravanti*, p. 88.

42. See analytical scheme of the cathedral section by I. Fedorov, ibid., p. 104.

43. See ibid., p. 157. The plan is also reproduced in Nikolaus Pevsner, *An Outline of European Architecture* (Harmondsworth, 1963), p. 186.

44. It is possible that a choir gallery might originally have been intended as a link with the palace of the grand prince (to the west of the cathedral) had the location of the Church of the Deposition not interfered. During the pre-Mongol period of strong princely authority, it had been the Russian custom (derived from Byzantium) to link the ruler's residence with a cathedral; yet the importance of the Dormition Cathedral as a symbol of state perhaps transcended even the specific needs of the grand prince, who in any event transformed the Annunciation Cathedral into his court church. For a discussion of the effect of the iconostasis and the initial possibility of a choir gallery on Fioravanti's design, see Zemtsov and Glazychev, *F'oravanti*, pp. 89–93.

45. In the midseventeenth century, the poorly maintained frescoes were stripped from the walls, which were repainted in 1642–3 along the schematic outlines of the original work. In the 1890s, and again in the 1920s, fragments of the original frescoes were uncovered in chapels located in the apsidal structure. A survey of the history of the cathedral's painting, and of modifications to both painting and structure, is contained in Komech and Pluzhnikov, *Kreml'*, pp. 315–17. A more detailed description of the cathedral and its chapels is presented by Z. P. Cheliubeeva in M. V. Alpatov, ed., *Uspenskii sobor moskovskogo kremlia* (Moscow, 1971), pp. 27–35. For a description of the earliest extant frescoes (probably the work of Dionisii or his school around 1479–81), see Lazarev, *Drevnerusskie mozaiki i freski: XI–XV vv.* (Moscow, 1973), pp. 75–6, and Plates 427–9.

46. Cheliubeeva, *Uspenskii sobor*, p. 28. The original method of gilding copper plates involved the use of mercury under intense heat – a highly toxic process. At the same time, the deep red–gold color of the Dormition Cathedral domes has become an essential part of the Kremlin ensemble. The most recent restoration, in the late 1970s, resolved the dilemma by retaining the extant copper sheets, with repairs where necessary. For a description of the restoration process, see Shvidkovskii, ed., *Sokhranenie arkhitekturnykh pamiatnikov moskovskogo Kremlia*, pp. 28–9.

47. See Vygolov, *Arkhitektura Moskovskoi Rusi*, pp. 133–5.

48. The Kremlin walls and towers are described in detail, with plans, in Komech and Pluzhnikov, eds., *Kreml'*, pp. 300–14.

49. The Savior Tower is of exceptional interest not only for the great clock by Halloway (replaced in 1707 by a Dutch carillon, again replaced in the eighteenth and nineteenth centuries), but also for large painted limestone reliefs of mounted figures of St. George (parts of which are preserved) and St. Dmitrii of Salonika – guardian saints of the Moscow princes. Although the sculptor of the statues, dating from 1464 and 1466, respectively, is unknown, the chronicles state that they were done under the supervision of Vasilii Ermolin. See Vygolov, *Arkhitektura Moskovskoi Rusi*, pp. 135–69.

50. See A. S. Ramelli, "Il Cremlino di Mosca, esempio di architettura militare," in *Arte Lombarda*, 44/45 (1976): 130–8. Marco Friazin (called Marco Ruffo by Nikolai Karamzin and later historians of Russian antiquity) arrived in Moscow no later than 1484 and is last mentioned in 1491. See S. M. Zemtsov, "Arkhitektory Moskvy," pp. 59–61.

51. For a biographical sketch of Anton Friazin, who may have arrived in Moscow with an Italian delegation as early as 1469, see Zemtsov, "Arkhitektory Moskvy," pp. 44–6. The Beklemishev Tower was among those blown up by the retreating French in 1812, but it was carefully reconstructed in 1817–19 by Osip Bove.

52. Pietro Antonio Solari (c. 1450–93) was the son of the sculptor Guiniforte Solari. Like Fioravanti, he had worked for the Sforzas in Milan and had participated in the building of the Ospedale Maggiore. See Zemtsov, "Arkhitektory Moskvy," pp. 61–8; and Cazzola, "I 'Mastri frjazy' a Mosca," pp. 166–7. A more detailed account is presented in Solari's work is presented in P. Cazzola, "P. A. Solari, architetto lombardo in Russia," *Arte Lombarda*, 14 (1969): 45–52.

53. The construction history and subsequent modifications to the Granovitaia palata are surveyed in Komech and Pluzhnikov, eds., *Kreml'*, pp. 330–1.

54. Indeed, Andrei's energy incurred the ill will of Ivan III – his older brother – with whom he had long feuded until a truce in 1481. At that time, construction began on a substantial kremlin at Ulgich, with the princely chambers and the masonry Cathedral of the Transfiguration of the Savior (destroyed and rebuilt in the seventeenth century). In 1491, Ivan suddenly imprisoned Andrei in Pereslavl-Zalesskii, where he soon died. See B. M. Kirikov, *Uglich* (Leningrad, 1984), pp. 25–6; and S. E. Novikov, *Uglich: Pamiatniki arkhitektury i iskusstva* (Moscow, 1988), pp. 13–14. Kirikov, pp. 28–30, gives a comparative analysis of the chambers with the secular architecture of fifteenth-century Novgorod.

55. A. Vlasiuk examines the Crimean interlude in Aleviz's journey and its relation to his Moscow work in "O rabote zodchego Aleviza Novogo v Bakhchisarae i v Moskovskom Kremle," *Arkhitekturnoe nasledstvo*, 10 (1958): 101–10.

56. A judicious appraisal of the theories concerning the Italian identity of Aleviz Novyi, with particular emphasis on the person of Alvise Lamberti de Montagnana, is presented by S. S. Pod"iapol'skii, "Venetsianskie istoki arkhitektury moskovskogo Arkhangel'skogo sobora," in G. V. Popov, ed., *Drevnerusskoe iskusstvo: Zarubezhnye sviazi* (Moscow, 1975), pp. 274–9. See also Giuliana Mazzi, "Indagini archivistiche per Alvise Lamberti da Montagnana," in *Arte Lombarda*, 44/45 (1976): 96–101. A biographical sketch is contained in S. M. Zemtsov, "Arkhitektory Moskvy," pp. 70–6.

Aleviz Staryi (the "Elder"), who came to Moscow from Milan in 1494, has been tentatively identified as the engineer Aloisio da Caresano. See Virginio Bussi, "Nota su Aloisio Caresano, architetto vercellese della seconda metà del XV secolo, morto forse in Russia nella prima metà del XVI secolo," in *Arte Lombarda*, 44/45 (1976): 237–8; also S. M. Zemtsov, "Arkhitektory Moskvy," pp. 68–9. In addition to the northwest Kremlin wall, he built a new Kremlin palace in 1499–1508 (see Komech and Pluzhnikov, eds., *Kreml'*, p. 326; also pp. 266, 281).

57. A detailed study of the Italianate decorative elements of the Archangel Cathedral is presented in A. Vlasiuk, "Novye issledovaniia arkhitektury Arkhangel'skogo sobora v Moskovskom kremle," *Arkhitekturnoe nasledstvo*, 2 (1952): 105–32. See also E. S. Sizov, "Novye materialy po Arkhangel'skomu soboru moskovskogo kremlia. Kogda byl postroen Arkhangel'skii sobor?," *Arkhitekturnoe nasledstvo*, 15 (1963): 176–7.

58. Pod"iapol'skii has pressed cogent claim for the northern Italian origins of Aleviz's delineation of the central aisle and crossing of the Archangel Cathedral, as well as the articulation of the facades. See "Venetsianskie istoki arkhitektury moskovskogo Arkhangel'skogo sobora," pp. 251–62. Pod"iapol'skii notes (ibid., p. 255) that there is no precedent for the six-piered, cross-inscribed church in Muscovite architecture, whose churches followed a four-piered, single-cupola pattern (the Dormition Cathedral is sui generis). In the ancient cities of Suzdalia, there were, of course, churches that followed the more complex six-piered plan with a narthex, and it is possible the Aleviz toured some of them. Even so, the architect would have recognized a plan quite familiar from his own Venetian culture.

59. See A. V. Vorob'ev and V. A. Smyslova, "O galeree arkhangel'skogo sobora," *Arkhitekturnoe nasledstvo*, 15 (1963): 178–81.

60. The practice of painting a brick wall a more vivid shade of red (known in Russian as *pod kirpich*, or "in the manner

of brick") became very widespread in the sixteenth and seventeenth centuries. The Italianate structures such as the Rusticated Chambers and the Archangel Cathedral established the practice of counterpointing painted brick walls with limestone decoration. There are Soviet specialists who argue that the polychromatic facades of such Kremlin monuments, including the bell tower of Ivan the Great, should replace the more recent white stucco. See M. P. Kudriavtsev, "Problema tsveta pri restavratsii pamiatnikov arkhitektury," in *Metodika i praktika sokhraneniia pamiatnikov arkhitektury* (Moscow, 1974), pp. 77–8. On the other side are those who insist that the polychromatic St. Basil's and the massive red Kremlin walls demand the counterbalance of the central white mass of the Kremlin ensemble. See Iu. Raninskii, "Ansambl i gorod," *Arkhitektura i stroitel'stvo Moskvy*, 1976, no. 3: 34. To complicate matters, the Kremlin walls themselves have frequently been painted white until the twentieth century.

61. John Summerson, *The Classical Language of Architecture* (London, 1980), p. 25.

62. An examination of the parallels between the developing architecture of Muscovy and a sense of classicism in architectural form is provided in N. F. Gulianitskii, "Traditsii klassiki i cherty renessansa v arkhitekture Moskvy XV–XVII vv.," *Arkhitekturnoe nasledstvo*, 26 (1978): 13–30. See also, by the same author, "O svoeobrazii i preemstvenykh sviaziakh ordernogo iazyka v russkoi arkhitekture," *Arkhitekturnoe nasledstvo*, 23 (1975): 14–17. A broader treatment of these themes, particularly the possibility of a "pre-Renaissance" in medieval Russian culture is presented in a number of works by the eminent cultural historian Dmitrii Likhachev. See, for example, *Chelovek v literature drevnei Rusi* (Moscow, 1970), with its emphasis on the development of "democratic" or humanistic principles in literary culture in the medieval period (through the seventeenth century). If Likhachev's arguments occasionally seem strained, this can be attributed to the often attentuated nature of humanistic culture in Russia.

63. A survey of influence of the Archangel Cathedral on sixteenth-century Russian architecture is presented by T. N. Viatchanina, "Arkhangel'skii sobor moskovskogo kremlia kak obrazets v russkom zodchestve XVI v.," *Arkhitekturnoe nasledstvo*, 34 (1986): 215–23. Viatchanina dismisses the view that the influence was limited and superficial, and argues that as the century progressed, Russian architects moved from a limited borrowing of decorative motifs to a deeper understanding and adaptation of the tectonic system of the cathedral. See p. 223. Lazarev had maintained that the influence was decorative, rather than tectonic: *Iskusstvo srednevekovoi Rusi i Zapad (XI–XV vv.)* (Moscow, 1970), p. 50.

64. For a thorough analysis of the Ascension Cathedral and a discussion of both the architectural and symbolic relation of its form to the Cathedral of the Archangel, see A. L. Batalov, "Sobor Voznesenskogo monastyria v moskovskom kremle," *Pamiatniki kul'tury. Novye otkrytiia. 1983*, X (1985): 468–82. The attribution of the cathedral to Aleviz Novyi is accepted in Komech and Pluzhnikov, *Kreml',*

p. 273. In addition to his great cathedral, Aleviz is thought to have built, or reconstructed, other churches in the Kremlin, including the Resurrection of Lazarus, 1514 (also known as the Nativity of the Virgin in the Antechamber; see ibid., p. 329); the Nativity of John the Baptist in the Grove (ibid., pp. 268–9); and possibly John Climacus, 1518, which was placed within the bell tower of Ivan the Great. Aleviz is also known, or thought, to have built a number of churches elsewhere in the city, including the Church of the Metropolitan Peter at the Upper Petrovskii Monastery (see Chapter 6). For a tentative list, see A. L. Batalov, "Osobennosti 'Ital'ianizmov' v moskovskom kamennom zodchestve rubezha XVI–XVII vv.," *Arkhitekturnoe nasledstvo*, 34 (1986): 238–9. See also S. M. Zemtsov, "Arkhitektory Moskvy," pp. 71, 76.

65. The bell tower was built on the site of the Church of John Climacus "under the bells" (perhaps similar to the Church of the Holy Ghost at the Trinity–St. Sergius Monastery), originally built in 1392 and subsequently rebuilt within the lower level of the Bell Tower of Ivan the Great – presumably in 1518 by Aleviz Novyi. See Komech and Pluzhnikov, *Kreml'*, p. 323; also S. M. Zemtsov, "Arkhitektory Moskvy," pp. 76–7.

66. Komech and Pluzhnikov, *Kreml'*, p. 319.

67. For commentary on the Byzantine and Tatar models in Muscovy's developing concept of autocracy – as reflected in the changing title of the ruler – see Michael Cherniavsky, "Khan or Basileus: An Aspect of Russian Medieval Political Theory," in Michael Cherniavsky, ed., *The Structure of Russian History* (New York, 1970), pp. 65–79.

Chapter 6

1. As has been noted in Chapter 3, Suzdal's thirteenth-century limestone Nativity Cathedral, whose vaulting and upper walls collapsed in 1445, was rebuilt on the order of Vasilii III in 1528 with a brick upper tier and a pentacupolar roof in the style of large Muscovite churches, thus also uniting the pre- and post-Mongol building traditions in central Russia.

2. M. A. Il'in, *Russkoe shatrovoe zodchestvo. Pamiatniki serediny XVI veka*, p. 23.

3. An analysis of the structure of the Cathedral of the Intercession at Aleksandrova Sloboda and a comparison with other churches of the same period is presented in G. N. Bocharov and V. P. Vygolov, *Aleksandrovskaia Sloboda* (Moscow, 1970), pp. 9–11. In the eighteenth century, the dedication of the cathedral was changed to the Holy Trinity – located in what had become the Dormition Convent.

4. The Italian legacy was still more apparent in the Cathedral of the Transfiguration of the Savior at the Iaroslavl Transfiguration Monastery, commissioned by Basil and built in 1505–16 on the site of a thirteenth-century cathedral damaged by fire in 1501. The monastery had been strong in its support of the Moscow princes since the acquisition of the Iaroslavl principality by Ivan III in 1463, and its political importance stimulated the endowment of the new cathedral – as noted in T. N. Viatchanina, "Arkhangel'skii sobor moskovskogo kremlia kak obrazets v russkom zodchestve XVI v.," *Arkhitekturnoe nasledstvo*, 34 (1986): 216–17. Although disfigured by later modifications, the cathedral's Italianate details are visible: the rudimentary cornice entablature; the level row of zakomary, each with an oculus; and preserved fragments of carved limestone scallop patterns. Yet the basic design of the cathedral resembles the traditional Russian form of the Intercession Convent in Suzdal; its borrowed elements are essentially decorative. See E. M. Karavaeva, "Sobor Spasskogo monastyria v Iaroslavle," *Arkhitekturnoe nasledstvo*, 15 (1963): 40.

Other examples of the cuboid structure include the Dormition Cathedral at Dmitrov (35 kilometers to the north of Moscow), commissioned by Iurii Ivanovich – prince of Dmitrov and younger brother of Vasilii III – built at some point between 1509 and 1533, and subsequently much modified. The still visible core structure displays a simple entablature and oculi arranged in a trefoil around a central round window in each zakomara (as in the Archangel Cathedral). Although designed with only three bays on each facade (the typical cuboid form), the Dormition Cathedral is pentacupolar and sufficiently large to symbolize the political pretensions of its builder, who in the difficult period before the birth of Basil's son actively promoted his own cause as heir to the throne in Moscow. See Viatchanina, "Arkhangel'skii sobor," pp. 218–19.

5. The Trinity Monastery in Pereslavl-Zalesskii was founded in 1508 by the monk Daniil, who became a spiritual adviser and confessor of Vasilii III and was thus aware of the concern over Basil's lack of a heir. Upon the birth of Ivan, Daniil performed the baptismal rites. For information on the foundation of the new Trinity Cathedral by Basil as a response to these events, see Ivan Purishev, *Pereslavl'-Zalesskii* (Moscow, 1970), pp. 15–16. Purishev, along with other historians such as N. N. Voronin, gives the year of Ivan's birth as 1530, but Il'in gives the accepted date as late August 1529: *Russkoe shatrovoe zodchestvo*, p. 23.

6. Purishev, *Pereslavl'-Zalesskii*, p. 23.

7. Similar in design is the Church of St. Nikita (1560–4) at the Nikitskii Monastery on the outskirts of Pereslavl-Zalesskii. Commissioned by Ivan IV on the site of an earlier church endowed by his father, Vasilii III, the Church of St. Nikita had a pentacupolar roof and two chapels attached on the east corners. It has long been under restoration and is now in catastrophic condition. See Purishev, pp. 17–18. A description of the monastery is contained in L. I. Denisov, *Pravoslavnye monastyri rossiiskoi imperii* (Moscow, 1908), pp. 95–7.

8. A summary of archaeological data on the pre-Mongol versions of the Dormition Cathedral in Rostov is provided in P. A. Rappoport, *Russkaia arkhitektura X–XIII vv.*, pp. 61–2. Although the vaulting of the thirteenth-century structure had collapsed at the beginning of the fifteenth century, it was repaired and continued to stand until the complete rebuilding around the turn of the sixteenth century. Ar-

guments in favor of a relatively early dating (the late fifteenth century) are presented in V. S. Banige, *Kreml' Rostova Velikogo: XVI–XVII veka* (Moscow, 1976), pp. 62, 66.

9. Ibid., p. 62.

10. A description of the monastery and a history of the eponymous Icon of the Smolensk Mother of God are contained in *Moskva zlatoglavaia*, p. 131. There has been some question as to the date of construction of the cathedral, but 1524–5 is now generally accepted. See Iu. M. Ovsiannikov, *Novodevichii monastyr'* (Moscow, 1968); Ovsiannikov notes its resemblance not only to the Dormition Cathedral, but also to the cathedral at the Intercession Convent in Suzdal, with which it is closely related historically as well as architecturally. See also L. S. Retkovskaia, *Novodevichii monastyr'* (Moscow, 1956).

11. For the dimensions and other structural details of the Trinity–Sergius Dormition Cathedral, see V. I. Baldin, "Arkhitektura," in Voronin and Kostochkin, eds., *Troitse-Sergieva lavra: Khudozhestvennye pamiatniki* (Moscow, 1968), pp. 30–1.

12. O. A. Belobrova, "Zhivopis' XVI–XVII vekov," in Voronin and Kostochkin, *Troitse-Sergieva lavra*, pp. 102–3.

13. See G. I. Vzdornov, *Vologda* (Leningrad, 1978), pp. 12, 20–2; and G. N. Bocharov and V. P. Vygolov, *Vologda. Kirillov. Ferapontovo. Belozersk* (Moscow, 1979), pp. 26–8. Like the Dormition Cathedral at the Trinity–Sergius Monastery, the Cathedral of St. Sophia was not consecrated until after the death of Ivan the Terrible – 1588 in the case of the Vologda cathedral. According to the colorful explanation in a folk poem, a piece of the cathedral vaulting fell on Ivan the Terrible as he inspected the work, and in his anger, he wished to destroy the structure. Dissuaded, he commanded that it not be consecrated, and promptly abandoned Vologda. A fragment of the poem is reproduced in Vzdornov, *Vologda*, p. 21. The most evocative portrait of Vologda on the eve of the cataclysmic changes of this century is Georgii Lukomskii, *Vologda i ee starina* (St. Petersburg, 1914).

14. A survey of sixteenth-century fortress construction is contained in N. I. Brunov et al., *Istoriia russkoi arkhitektury* (Moscow, 1956), pp. 118–27. Medieval Russian fortification designs are compared in V. V. Kostochkin, *Krepostnoe zodchestvo drevnei Rusi* (Moscow, 1969), pp. 7–27.

15. See D. J. B. Shaw, "Southern Frontiers of Muscovy, 1550–1700," in J. H. Bater and R. A. French, eds., *Studies in Russian Historical Geography* (London, 1983), vol. 1, pp. 117–42.

16. The great fortress at Kolomna, whose brick and limestone walls were pilfered for construction material from the latter part of the eighteenth century to the 1930s, has been the subject of detailed study. See T. Sergeeva-Kozina, "Kolomenskii kreml'," *Arkhitekturnoe nasledstvo*, 2 (1952): 133–63; M. V. Fekhner, *Kolomna* (Moscow, 1966), pp. 13–22; and N. N. Godlevskii, "Planirovka kremlia Kolomny v XVI–XVII vv.," *Arkhitekturnoe nasledstvo*, 16 (1967): 19–28.

17. The evolution of the Tula fortress in the sixteenth and seventeenth centuries is described in N. N. Godlevskii, "Planirovka i zastroika Tul'skogo kremlia v XVI–XVII vv.,"

Arkhitekturnoe nasledstvo, 18 (1969): 25–9. For the expansion of sixteenth-century fortifications in Pskov, see Iu. P. Spegal'skii, *Pskov: Khudozhestvennye pamiatniki*, pp. 74–5.

18. For an authoritative historical survey of the development of the Kitai-gorod district, see Komech and Pluzhnikov, eds., *Tsentral'nye ploshchadi*, pp. 349–86. The origins of the name are obscure and often confused with the Russian word for China (*Kitai*), although the district was never a "Chinatown"; but one current linguistic explanation links the term to a wattle and earthen fortification (also "kitai," perhaps related to the plant *kita*) formed when a moat was dug around the district in 1534. At that time, what had been known as the Velikii Posad, or Great Settlement, assumed the name that it has to this day. See ibid., p. 362. See also A. N. Kirpichnikov, "Kreposti bastionnogo tipa v srednevekovoi Rossii," in *Pamiatniki kul'tury. Novye otkrytiia. Ezhegodnik. 1978* (Leningrad, 1979), pp. 471–99.

19. Komech and Pluzhnikov, eds., *Tsentral'nye ploshchadi*, p. 363–4.

20. The most authoritative study of Petrok's biography and work – with copious references to the *Polnyi svod russkikh letopisei* – is S. S. Pod"iapol'skii, "Arkhitektor Petrok Malyi," in V. P. Vygolov et al., eds., *Pamiatniki russkoi arkhitektury i monumental'nogo iskusstva: Stil', atributsii, datirovki* (Moscow, 1983), pp. 34–50. Much of the available information on Petrok comes from a deposition taken upon the arrest of one Petr Friazin, who was apprehended in 1539 at the western border while attempting to flee from the unsettled court situation in the early years (or regency) of Ivan IV. One must, of course, assume the identity of Petrok and Petr Friazin (see ibid., p. 44). Although Petrok had converted to Orthodoxy, married a Russian, and established firm roots in the adopted country, attempts to escape were frequent among foreign specialists thrown into the unfamiliar and often suddenly threatening environment of Moscow court politics. As Pod"iapol'skii points out (pp. 44–5), failed escape was not always punished in the case of foreigners with particularly valued skills.

21. The "structural" view of the evolution of the tower church was presented by N. I. Brunov not in Russian, but in M. Alpatov and N. Brunov, "Nachrichten aus Moskau," *Byzantinische Zeitschrift*, 24 (1924): 485–92. Il'in criticizes this approach as excessively broad in *Russkoe shatrovoe zodchestvo*, p. 20. A similar statement of the technical approach, emphasizing the structural details unique to masonry, was presented in G. Gol'ts, "Arkhitektura b. tserkvi Vozneseniia v sele Kolomenskom," in *Russkaia arkhitektura* (Moscow, 1940), pp. 55–6. A more recent proponent of this view is Iu. P. Spegal'skii, who, in an article published posthumously, made a comparative analysis of the evolution of masonry vaulting systems within Russian church architecture, leading to the Church of the Ascension. See Spegal'skii, "K voprosu o vzaimovliianii dereviannogo i kamennogo zodchestva v Drevnei Rusi," *Arkhitekturnoe nasledstvo*, 19 (1972): 66–75.

22. See Makarevich et al., eds., *Pamiatniki arkhitektury Moskvy:*, pp. 181–2, with a reconstruction of the original form by B. P. Dedushkino, p. 169. Exterior trompe l'oeil decoration and other modifications introduced in the late seventeenth and early eighteenth centuries had previously led to the assumption that the Church of the Metropolitan Peter dated from the later period, particularly because its form is reproduced in a number of late seventeenth-century churches. See B. P. Dedushkino, "K istorii ansamblia moskovskogo Vysoko-Petrovskogo monastyria," in *Drevnerusskoe iskusstvo XVII v.* (Moscow, 1964), pp. 253–71.

23. Voronin dates the Savior-Evfimii tower to the first decade of the sixteenth century and links the dedication of its small church (John the Baptist) to the birth of Ivan IV, in *Vladimir, Bogolyubovo, Suzdal, Yurev-Polskoi* (Moscow, 1971), pp. 244–5. Il'in challenges this view of the dedication, which he construes as a votive church related to Basil's earlier marriage to Solomoniia Saburova. See *Russkoe shatrovoe zodchestvo*, pp. 23–4.

24. For a survey of the ensemble at Kolomenskoe, see M. A. Gra and B. B. Zhiromskii, *Kolomenskoe* (Moscow, 1971).

25. The leading proponent of wooden derivation theory was Ivan Zabelin, who first published his essay "Cherty samobytnosti v drevnerusskom zodchestve," in *Drevniaia i Novaia Rossiia*, 1878, no. 3: 185–203; and 1878, no. 4: 282–303. It subsequently appeared as a separate volume under the same title (Moscow, 1900). Zabelin's case rested on formal similarities, as did that of Nikolai Sultanov, but for entirely different purposes. Sultanov related the tent form to masonry churches in the Caucasus with a pyramidal roof over the central drum. See "Russkie shatrovye tserkvi i ikh sootnoshenie k gruzino-armianskim piramidal'nym polkytiiam," *Trudy V Arkheologicheskogo s'esda v Tiflise v 1881 g.* (Moscow, 1887), p. 230 and passim. The chronicle discoveries by M. N. Tikhomirov were first published as "Maloizvestnye letopisnye pamiatniki XVI v," *Istoricheskie zapiski*, 1941, no. 10: 88; and "Letopisnye pamiatniki b Sinodal'nogo patriarshego sobraniia," *Istoricheskie zapiski*, 1942, no. 13: p. 268.

26. During the 1920s, A. I. Nekrasov began to attack the Zabelin position with a series of works supporting the idea of a western, Romanesque provenance for the tent roof. The Speyer Cathedral (eleventh and twelfth centuries) is one among many such examples included in Kenneth John Conant, *Carolingian and Romanesque Architecture* (Baltimore, 1959). Nekrasov's view culminated in 1936 with his sharply polemical criticism of the wooden-derivation theory as "reactionary" (i.e., nationalistic), and a remnant of "monarchist ideology." See *Ocherki po istorii drevnerusskogo zodchestva XI–XVII vekov* (Moscow, 1936), p. 244. Such views were not appreciated in the late 1930s. Apart from formal comparisons with western structures, there is no direct evidence for Nekrasov's position, presented within the pseudo-Marxist framework that the Soviets call "vulgar sociologism." It has, however, been revived by V. V. Filatov in his work on the Cathedral of the Intercession on Red Square, "Vnutrennii dekor Pokrovskogo stolpa," in G. V. Popov, ed., *Drevnerusskoe iskuustvo. Zarubezhnye sviazi* (Moscow, 1975), p. 357.

A critical summary of the various positions in the debate, including relevant chronicle references, was first presented in M. A. Il'in, *Kamennaia letopis' moskovskoi Rusi: svetskie osnovy kamennogo zodchestva XV–XVII vv.* (Moscow, 1966), pp. 33–40; and subsequently elaborated in *Russkoe shatrovoe zodchestvo*.

27. The question of the derivation of the *shatior* is not likely to be resolved solely by a typological, formal approach. The ontological and semiological aspects of the question (the reasons for its appearance on the estate of the Moscow grand prince in 1530) are addressed by Il'in in *Russkoe shatrovoe zodchestvo*, pp. 40–1; and idem., "K izucheniiu tserkvi Vozneseniia v Kolomenskom," in O. I. Podobedova, ed., *Drevnerusskoe iskusstvo. Problemy i atributsii* (Moscow, 1977), pp. 355–6.

28. Among other supporting evidence, V. A. Bulkin notes that the Ascension Church at Kolomenskoe was completed shortly before Petrok began work on the Church of the Resurrection in the Moscow Kremlin. See "O tserkvi Vozneseniia v Kolomenskom," in *Kul'tura srednevekovoi Rusi* (Leningrad, 1974), pp. 113–16.

29. A reconstruction of the original form of the Church of the Resurrection (subsequently renamed the Church of the Nativity of Christ; demolished by the French in 1812), as well as further material in support of Petrok's authorship of the Kolomenskoe church is presented in Pod"iapol'skii, "Arkhitektor Petrok Malyi," pp. 46–9. In his *Kamennaia letopis' moskovskoi Rusi*, published in 1962, M. A. Il'in stated that the unknown architect of the Church of the Ascension was "undoubtedly a Russian master" (p. 45). Yet Il'in, too, eventually accepted stylistic evidence in favor of an Italian architect (most logically Petrok). See M. A. Il'in and T. V. Moiseeva, *Moskva i Podmoskov'e* (Moscow, 1979), p. 480, which includes recent evidence such as the uncovering by restorers in 1977 of the date 1533 on one of the capitals – unlikely to have been written by a Russian, because the date was in Arabic numerals and corresponded to the western calendar rather than the Muscovite, which counted from Anno Mundi.

30. This pattern is particularly effective in the contrast between the brick structure and the limestone pattern of the *shatior* – a contrast obscured, however, by the application in the late 1970s of whitewash over the entire exterior. Although there is historical evidence to support the use of whitewash and although it creates an imposing monolith from a distance, it has been argued that the brick surface should have been left uncovered, in P. Zinov'ev, "Spornyi eksperiment," *Stroitel'stvo i arkhitektura Moskvy*, 1979, no. 7: 32. See also William C. Brumfield, "St. Basil's and Other Curiosities," *Harvard Magazine*, 1982, no. 6: 42–8. References to the Italian use of the rhomboid pattern are contained in Il'in, *Russkoe shatrovoe zodchestvo*, pp. 35–6.

31. On the use of the order system at Kolomenskoe and its parallels with examples of Italian Renaissance architec-

ture, see Pod"iapol'skii, "Arkhitektor Petrok Malyi," pp. 47–8. For a discussion of the Church of the Ascension as a Russian parallel to the architectonic perfection of classical Greek architecture, see N. F. Gulianitskii, "Traditsii klassiki i cherty renessansa v arkhitekture Moskvy XV–XVII vv.," *Arkhitekturnoe nasledstvo*, 26 (1978): 19–22. Gulianitskii suggests that the system of orders appears not only in specific details, but in the proportional system of the structure. See also Gulianitskii, "O svoeobrazii i preemstvennykh sviaziakh ordernogo iazyka v russkoi arkhitekture," *Arkhitekturnoe nasledstvo*, 23 (1975): 17.

32. Il'in has commented extensively on the process of secularization (*obmirshchenie*) in sixteenth-century Russian culture as a major influence on artistic form. See, for example, *Russkoe shatrovoe zodchestvo*, p. 19; and *Kamennaia letopis' moskovskoi Rusi*.

33. In reference to the structure as beacon and watchtower, it should be noted that in the sixteenth and seventeenth centuries, the tent tower form, whether for church or fortress, was referred to in certain chronicle manuscripts as *kostrovoi*, a term related to *kostior*, one of whose meanings corresponds precisely to the English word "fagot": a bundle or pyramid of firewood "as used for fuel . . . or as a means of burning heretics alive" (*Webster's New Third International Dictionary*). The concept of piling wood seems to have been transformed into the image of a fortification tower, as indicated in *Tolkovyi slovar' zhivogo velikorusskogo iazyka Vladimira Dalia*, 3rd ed., vol. 2 (Petersburg–Moscow, 1905), p. 447. See also Il'in, *Kamennaia letopis' moskovskoi Rusi*, p. 38.

34. It was long thought, on the basis of a faulty understanding of manuscript evidence, that the Church of the Decapitation of John the Baptist dated from 1529. A. I. Nekrasov demonstrated the untenability of the date and, on the basis of an analysis of the altar dedications of the church, suggested a date of 1547. See *Ocherki po istorii drevnerusskogo zodchestva XI–XVII vekov*, p. 256 and passim. His analysis was extended, with corrections on the altar dedications, by Gra and Zhiromskii, and by Il'in. Il'in argues that the church would have been completed before 1554, the birth year of Ivan's second son, Ivan, named after the Byzantine theologian John Chrysostom. See *Russkoe shatrovoe zodchestvo*, pp. 56–7.

35. Commentary and a diagram of the structural function of the drum are contained in G. A. Shteiman, "Osobennosti konstruktsii russkikh kamennykh sooruzhenii XVI–XVII vv.," *Arkhitekturnoe nasledstvo*, 20 (1972): 42–3.

36. See Il'in, *Kamennaia letopis' moskovskoi Rusi*, p. 48; Gra and Zhiromskii, p. 114; and Il'in, *Russkoe shatrovoe zodchestvo*, p. 57. Il'in explains the omission of a chapel dedicated to St. Anastasiia, the eponym for Ivan's first wife, by the personal, familial nature of the church (related, that is, to the dynasty of the tsar and his ancestors).

37. See Pod"iapol'skii, "Arkhitektor Petrok Malyi," pp. 49–50.

38. In his later work, however, Il'in went so far as to state

– without documentary evidence – that "an Italian master worked side by side with a Russian architect" at the Diakovo church. His argument is based on the presence of a modified order system in the design of the facades, yet this system is so abstract and simplified as to call into question his assertion. See *Russkoe shatrovoe zodchestvo*, p. 61.

39. For a concise discussion of Filarete's work in relation to his quattrocento contemporaries, see Nikolaus Pevsner, *An Outline of European Architecture* (Harmondsworth, 1963), pp. 185–7. The resemblance between the Diakovo monument and the various examples of Renaissance centralized churches, particularly as projected in the *Tratatto*, has been noted by, among others, A. I. Nekrasov, *Ocherki po istorii drevnerusskogo zodchestva*, pp. 259–61; V. A. Bulkin, "Ital'ianizmy v drevnerusskom zodchestve kontsa XV–XVI vekov," *Vestnik Leningradskogo gosudarstvennogo universitetal*, 20 (1973): 59–66; and Frank Kämpfer, "La concezione teologica ed architecttonica della cattedrale 'Vasilii Blazhennyi' a Mosca," *Arte Lombarda*, 44/45 (1976): 191–8. See also Pod"iapol'skii, "Arkhitektor Petrok Malyi," p. 49, n. 48. For an analysis of the iconography of centralized Italian church designs of the Quattrocento, with emphasis on Filarete's treatise, see Iu. E. Revzina, "Nekotorye ikonograficheskie istochniki tsentricheskikh khramov XV v. v Italii," in A. L. Batalov, ed., *Ikonografiia arkhitektury* (Moscow, 1991), pp. 69–101. There is no comparison with Russian centralized churches of the following century in this article, whose content reveals the gulf between the philosophical interpretations of the centralized form in the Quattrocento, and the very different, political uses of the form in Muscovy.

40. Brunov suggests not only that the Italians brought plans and architectural commentary with them for use in Moscow, but that their use also spread to Russian masters familiar with the Italians' work. This practice was evidently interrupted by the general cultural decline in Muscovy in the latter part of the sixteenth century, when builders again reverted to the use of rough schematic drawings – if that. Only during the second half of the following century did the practice of detailed architectural plans reappear. See N. I. Brunov, *Khram Vasiliia Blazhennogo v Moskve: Pokrovskii Sobor* (Moscow, 1988), p. 44; and A. Tits, *Zagadki drevnerusskogo chertezha* (Moscow, 1978).

41. See, for example, documents cited in V. L. Snegirev, *Pamiatnik arkhitektury khram Vasiliia Blazhennogo* (Moscow, 1953), pp. 36–7.

42. There has been considerable question as to the identity – indeed, the names – of the architects. Not until the end of the nineteenth century were manuscripts revealed that mentioned a certain Barma (designated in the Piskarev Compilation as the leader of construction, but with no further information), and Postnik, the latter from Pskov and presumed identical to Postnik Iakovlev, known from other sources. Other theories, based on the resemblance "Barma" and "Postnik" to a sobriquet rather than a first name, suggest that Postnik's actual name was Ivan, or that Bram and Postnik were in fact the same person. For a survey of the relevant documents, see V. L. Snegirev, *Pamiatnik arkhitektury khram Vasiliia Blazhennogo*, pp. 32–41. N. Sobolev, the leading specialist on the archaeology of the Cathedral of the Intercession, states that on the basis of an exhaustive comparison of construction methods of the Diakovo church and the Intercession Cathedral, there is good reason to assume the architects of the two monuments to be identical. See "Proekt rekonstruktsii pamiatnika arkhitektury-khrama Vasiliia Blazhennogo v Moskve," *Arkhitektura SSSR*, 1977, no. 2: 48.

No extant Russian document contains a reference to Ivan the Terrible's blinding of the architect to prevent the construction of an even greater structure. This legend, which has appeared in relation to renowned architectural monuments in the west, gained currency in seventeenth-century accounts of Russia by western travelers such as Adam Olearius. See Snegirev, *Pamiatnik arkhitektury*, p. 30.

43. Brunov provides an elaborate interpretation of the cathedral as an intermediary between the Kremlin and the Posad. See *Khram Vasiliia Blazhennogo*, pp. 40–1, 49–56.

44. For an excellent selection of engravings depicting the Kitai-gorod and its relation to the Kremlin, see Komech and Pluzhnikov, eds., *Tsentral'nye ploshchadi*, pp. 82–110, esp. pp. 82–9, containing a reproduction of the panorama of the city in the midseventeenth travel account by A. Mayerberg, *Iter in Moschoviam*.

45. It has been suggested that the sudden appearance of symmetrical plans for large churches consisting of separate units with their own entrances was related to the great church council of 1551, whose record, or Stoglav, codified many aspects of the life of the church. Among them was the stipulation that chapels (*pridely*) of a church should, insofar as possible, exist as discrete components. See I. Malyshev, "Zhemchuzhina russkogo zodchestva: Restavratsiia khrama Vasiliia Blazhennogo," *Stroitel'stvo i arkhitektura Moskvy*, 1980, no. 7: 24–6.

46. A detailed reconstruction of the cathedral plan as it evolved over three centuries is presented in Sobolev, "Proekt rekonstruktsii," pp. 42–8.

47. As a result of the shift of the main tower, the small chapels on the west lose the interior corner of their cube and are reduced to a size capable of containing only a handful of worshipers. Brunov offers a similar analysis – with differences in detail – of the multiaxial nature of the north and south views in *Khram Vasiliia Blazhennogo*, p. 55.

48. Documentary material on the construction of the cathedral is collated, with references to the chronicles, in Il'in, *Russkoe shatrovoe zodchestvo*, pp. 64–6.

49. As indicated in the seventeenth-century manuscript cited in Snegirev, *Pamiatnik arkhitektury*, p. 33–4. See also Il'in, *Russkoe shatrovoe zodchestvo*, pp. 64–5.

50. Ibid., pp. 68–9, with references to A. Klibanov, *Reformatsionnye dvizheniia v Rossii* (Moscow, 1960). Further comments on the symbolic significance of the dedication to the Trinity are contained in Brunov, *Khram Vasiliia Blazhennogo*, pp. 193–7.

51. Il'in, *Russkoe shatrovoe zodchestvo*, p. 64. It is not clear which was the added church (if one accepts the reliability of the account), yet one recent work identifies the ninth as the west church, the Entry of Christ into Jerusalem. See Il'in and Moiseeva, *Moskva i Podmoskov'e*, p. 434.

52. On the relation of wooden church architecture to the Cathedral of the Intercession, see Brunov, *Khram Vasiliia Blazhennogo*, pp. 58–9, 61.

53. The Brunelleschi design is discussed and illustrated in Pevsner, pp. 181–2. On the comparisons with Leonardo da Vinci, Bramante, and Filarete, see Brunov, *Khram Vasiliia Blazhennogo*, pp. 60–1.

54. Despite errors in detail, Michael Cherniavskii provides a lucid statement of the Intercession Cathedral as an immensely powerful symbol of the new Muscovite identity after the taking of Kazan. See his chapter "Russia," in O. Ranum, ed., *National Consciousness, History, and Political Culture in Early-Modern Europe* (Baltimore, 1975), pp. 127, 130. The rise of a Muscovite sense of destiny as an Orthodox state is examined in various contemporary documents by Brunov, Khram Vasiliia Blazhennogo, pp. 209–15. Of special interest is the Muscovite assertion – included in epistles attributed to Ivan himself – that western Christianity had fallen into captivity and should be returned to the true faith (pp. 212–13).

55. For a hypothetical reconstruction of the 1561 appearance of the cathedral, see Sobolev, "Proekt rekonstruktsii," p. 48.

56. The eight small cupolas were removed as a fragile hazard during a renovation of the cathedral in 1781–4; ibid., p. 44. The original placement of the small cupolas is indicated in Sobolev's reconstructions of the facades.

57. Much of this material was uncovered in a restoration conducted under the supervision of N. P. Sychev in 1957–61. For an analysis of the interior decorative patterns and their relation to western Gothic architecture, see Filatov, "Vnutrennii dekor Pokrovskogo stolpa," 354–61. Concerning the interior inscription, see Sobolev, "Proekt rekonstruktsii," p. 43.

58. See Filatov, "Vnutrennii dekor," pp. 355–6.

59. Ibid., pp. 358–60.

60. The most lucid exposition of the Jerusalem idea in sixteenth- and seventeenth-century Russian architecture is A. L. Batalov and T. N. Viatchanina, "Ob ideinom znachenii i interpretatsii ierusalimskogo obraztsa v russkoi arkhitekture XVI–XVII vv," *Arkhitekturnoe nasledstvo*, 36 (1988): 22–42. It should be noted that there were earlier sixteenth-century examples of the Palm Sunday ritual procession in Russia (Novgorod, for example), but its institution in Moscow is unquestionably linked with the symbolism of the victory over Kazan. Il'in was one of the first to explicate the significance of this ritual in relation to the Intercession Cathedral. See *Kamennaia letopis' moskovskoi Rusi*, pp. 50–2; and his later comments in *Russkoe shatrovoe zodchestvo*, pp. 70–1. For more extensive commentary on the Jerusalem motif in sixteenth-century Russian culture and in the Intercession Cathedral, see Brunov, pp. 219–30; also see Frank Kämpfer, "La concezione teologica," pp. 191–8.

61. Batalov and Viatchanina, "Ob ideinom znachenii," pp. 30–1. The Palm Sunday ritual procession to the Intercession Cathedral continued until 1636. Batalov and Viatchanina note that when the ritual was revived, in 1656, the reverse, and more logical movement, into the Kremlin from the Red Square was instituted (see p. 31, n. 41).

62. On Olearius, see Komech and Pluzhnikov, eds., *Tsentral'nye ploshchadi*, p. 77. Other references to the cathedral as "Jerusalem" are contained in Batalov and Viatchanina, "Ob ideinom znachenii," p. 30.

63. Il'in, *Russkoe shatrovoe zodchestvo*, p. 67.

64. Referring to the connection of the Intercession Cathedral with the culture of Pskov, Il'in has observed that the names of two of the main component churches – the Trinity and the Entry of Christ into Jerusalem – are identical to those of the major shrines in Pskov: the Trinity Cathedral and the Church of the Entry of into Jerusalem, the latter of which served in 1471 as the center of a church convocation to celebrate the union of Novgorod to Moscow. (See Il'in, *Kamennaia letopis' moskovskoi Rusi*, p. 51.) This event reinforces the concept of the Intercession Cathedral as a symbol of Moscow's bringing together of the Russian lands. On the significance of the image of the Pskov Saint Nicholas Velikoretsk as part of a multivalent interpretation of the component churches of the Intercession Cathedral, see S. L. Batalov, "K interpretatsii arkhitektury sobora Pokrova na Rvu," in A. L. Batalov, ed., *Ikonografiia arkhitektury* (Moscow, 1990), pp. 18–23.

65. A summary of the life of Vasilii the Blessed is contained in *Entsiklopedicheskii slovar'* (Petersburg, 1900), s.v. "Vasilii Blazhennyi." Vasilii died on August 2, and it is noteworthy that both Tsar Ivan and the Metropolitan Macarius participated in the funeral ritual, which must have occurred only a few weeks before the major battles at Kazan. Ivan's demonstrative reverence before Vasilii reflects not only his own piety (later grotesquely deformed), but also a shrewd knowledge of the religious spirit of his subjects.

66. On the Chapel of Vasilii the Blessed as an early example of the Godunov style, see A. L. Batalov, "Chetyre pamiatnika arkhitektury Moskve kontsa XVI v.," *Arkhitekturnoe nasledstvo*, 32 (1984): 47–53.

67. The connection between the appearance of the onion dome in late sixteenth-century Russian church architecture and the most revered of Russian cathedral reliquaries (known as "Large Zions"), depicting the onion-domed canopy that existed over the Holy Sepulchre between the mideleventh and midtwelfth centuries is set forth by A. M. Lidov, "Ierusalimskii kuvuklii. O proiskhozhdenii lukovichnykh glav," in Batalov, ed., *Ikonografiia arkhitektury*, pp. 57–68. (This article also surveys earlier theories of the origins of the onion dome.) Lidov's argument focuses particularly on the reliquary, or Large Zion, used on the most solemn occasions in the Kremlin Dormition Cathedral. For an illustration of this vessel, see E. I. Smirnova et al., *Go-*

sudarstvennaia oruzheinaia palata moskovskogo kremlia (Moscow, 1969), Plates 14 and 15, with a description in the appendix, n.p.

68. For a survey of the successive modifications to the cathedral, see Sobolev, "Proekt rekonstruktsii," pp. 42–8; and Komech and Pluzhnikov, eds., *Tsentral'nye ploshchadi*, pp. 401–2. There is no precise evidence as to when the painted ornamentation first appeared, but the earliest reference to painting occurs in connection with a major renovation in 1682. See Snegirov, *Pamiatnik arkhitektury*, pp. 85–6. The "Sigismund plan" of the city, drawn for the Polish king Sigismund III in 1610, shows the cathedral and the surrounding chapels before their amalgamation in the 1670s. See Komech and Pluzhnikov, *Tsentral'nye ploshchadi*, p. 65. The relation between the evolving form of the cathedral and its various popular designations is discussed in I. L. Buseva-Davydova, "Ob izmenenii oblika i nazvanii sobora Pokrova na Rvu," in *Arkhitekturnoe nasledie Moskvy* (Moscow, 1988), pp. 40–51.

69. The Annunciation Cathedral in Kazan was built by Pskov masons under the direction of Postnik Iakovlev – apparently the same Pskov builder involved in the design of the Cathedral of the Intercession on the Moat – and Ivan Shiriai. Despite the frequent modifications to the Cathedral (leading to its deformation in the nineteenth century), the link with Pskov is clearly stated not only in the decorative brick bands on the apse and on the cupola drums, but in the general resemblance of the structure to its namesake in the Kremlin – also presumed to have been built by masters from Pskov. A description and hypothetical reconstruction of the original form of the Kazan Annunciation Cathedral are contained in V. P. Ostroumov, *Kazan'* (Kazan, 1978), pp. 34–7. See also M. Fekhner, *Velikie Bulgary. Kazan'. Sviiazhsk* (Moscow, 1978), p. 80. The influence of Pskov architecture on the intensive church building campaign within the newly conquered khanate is still more evident in the Dormition Cathedral (1556–60) of the Dormition Monastery at the Sviiazhsk fort, a center of Orthodox missionary activity among the Tatar population. See ibid., pp. 235–6.

70. On the connection between the exterior detail of the Archangel Cathedral and the Annuciation chapels, see Viatchanina, "Arkhangel'skii sobor moskovskogo kremlia," pp. 219–20.

71. For a survey of some of the extensive literature on the latter part of Ivan the Terrible's reign, see Crummey, *The Formation of Muscovy*, pp. 158–76.

72. Bocharov and Vygolov, *Aleksandrovskaia Sloboda*, p. 8.

73. For foreign accounts of the origins of the churches, constructed with money taken from Novgorod, see ibid., p. 26.

74. The complex form of the Trinity Church, with its many additions, is analyzed in ibid., pp. 26–9; as is the much modified Dormition Church, pp. 34–9. Both churches, and particularly the latter, display decorative motifs of Italian origin, although Bocharov and Vygolov's as-

sertion that Aleviz's Archangel Michael Cathedral served as a prototype has been challenged by A. L. Batalov, who argues that the Italian motifs were not directly borrowed in these two churches, but rather refracted through the example of the earlier Intercession Cathedral at Aleksandrova Sloboda. See "Osobennosti 'Ital'ianizmov' v moskovskom kamennom zodchestve," pp. 239–41.

75. The dates and stages of rebuilding of the Church of the Crucifixion are discussed in Bocharov and Vygolov, *Aleksandrovskaia Sloboda*, pp. 22–3.

76. See Il'in, *Russkoe shatrovoe zodchestvo*, p. 25. The earlier view that the structure was originally built as a bell tower later in the sixteenth century, then converted to the Church of St. George in the seventeenth, is presented in Gra and Zheromskii, pp. 112–13.

77. For a revision, based on structural and stylistic features, of the date of the refectory Dormition Church, see Il'in, *Russkoe shatrovoe zodchestvo*, pp. 29–30.

78. On the crown estate at Ostrov (given by Peter the Great to Aleksandr Menshikov at the beginning of the eighteenth century and subsequently donated by Catherine II to Aleksei Orlov in 1765), see E. N. Pod"iapol'skaia, *Pamiatniki arkhitektury moskovskoi oblasti*, vol. 1, pp. 310–11.

79. See Il'in, *Russkoe shatrovoe zodchestvo*, pp. 75–7.

80. Purishev, pp. 19, 21.

81. For a survey of other late sixteenth-century tower churches – the Church of the Resurrection at Gorodno, the Cathedral of Sts. Boris and Gleb at Staritsa, and the Church of Sts. Kozma and Demian in Murom – see Il'in, *Russkoe shatrovoe zodchestvo*. An unusual variant is the now much disfigured Cathedral of the Transfiguration at the Solovetsk Monastery, a large cuboid structure built in 1558–66, with a tent tower over the central crossing. See Il'in, pp. 100–5; and S. A. Sharov, "O zavershenii Spaso-Preobrazhenskogo sobora Solovetskogo monastyria," *Arkhitekturnoe nasledstvo*, 34 (1986): 224–9.

82. On the construction of the Sviiazhsk fort, see Fekhner, *Velikie Bulgary. Kazan'. Sviiazhsk*, pp. 217–21. The development of prefabricated log structures in the sixteenth century is analyzed in V. V. Kostochkin, "Iz istorii russkogo sbornogo stroitel'stva XVI v.," *Arkhitekturnoe nasledstvo*, 18 (1969): 125–34.

83. On the walls of Pskov in the sixteenth century, see Spegal'skii, *Pskov*, pp. 74–5. For an account of the 1581 siege of Pskov and the role of religious imagery in its defense, see Brumfield, *Gold in Azure*, pp. 80–3.

84. An architectural survey of the Pskov Cave Monastery is contained in T. N. Mikhel'son, "Pechory," in L. I. Maliakov, ed., *Dostoprimechatel'nosti Pskovskoi oblasti* (Leningrad, 1987), pp. 288–300.

85. The most authoritative recent study of Godunov's reign in R. G. Skrynnikov, *Boris Godunov* (Moscow, 1978).

86. Later designated the "small," to distinguish it from the monastery's large cathedral with the same dedication built at the end of the seventeenth century. A comparative analysis of the Basil the Blessed Chapel and the Donskoi

Monastery Small Cathedral is presented in Batalov, "Chetyre pamiatnika arkhitektury Moskvy kontsa XVI v.," pp. 47–9.

87. On the victory over Kasy-Girei and its relation to the foundation of the monastery, see Iu. I. Arenkova and G. I. Mekhova, *Donskoi monastyr'* (Moscow, 1970), pp. 4–6.

88. For further commentary on the parallels drawn between the Snipe Field victory, the Don icon, and the founding of the Donskoi Monastery, see N. F. Gulianitskii, "Osvoboditel'nye idei Rusi v obrazakh pamiatnikov arkhitektury XVI–pervoi poloviny XVII vv.," *Arkhitekturnoe nasledstvo*, 32 (1984): 32–5. Guliantiskii also notes that in 1618, the last serious Polish raid on Moscow during the "Time of Troubles" was repulsed at Donskoi Monastery – an event that confirmed the cathedral's importance as a model for further votive churches in the early seventeenth century.

89. An analysis of the structural system of the Donskoi cathedral is presented in Arenkova and Mekhova, pp. 7–8. More generally on the evolution of churches without interior piers, see G. A. Shteiman, "Besstolpnye pokrytiia v arkhitekture XVI–XVII vekov," *Arkhitekturnoe nasledstvo*, 14 (1962): 47–62; and by the same author, "Konstruktivnye priemy resheniia vertikal'nykh sooruzhenii v kamennom zodchestve XVI–XVII vekov," *Arkhitekturnoe nasledstov*, 15 (1963): 79–87.

90. The Donskoi cathedral and the Trinity Church are further linked by their machicolation beneath the corbelled arches within the vault – an unusual device in the construction of such churches, although machicolation was not infrequent on the exterior of major structures in central Moscow (cf. the Intercession Cathedral on the Moat). A detailed structural analysis of the two churches, with attention to the vaulting techniques, is presented in Batalov, "Chetyre pamiatnika arkhitektury Moskvy kontsa XVI v.," pp. 50, 52.

91. On the political events surrounding the reconstruction of the Ascension Cathedral (not extant), which was intended as the place of burial for Irina Godunova as wife of Tsar Fedor, see Batalov, "Sobor Voznesenskogo monastyria v moskovskom kremle," pp. 477–80.

92. The stylistic and symbolic links between the Archangel Michael Cathedral and the Godunov churches, with reference to the Trinity Church at Khoroshevo, are analyzed in Batalov, "Sobor Voznesenskogo monastyria v moskovskom kremle," pp. 478–80; and "Osobennosti 'Ital'ianizmov' v moskovskom kamennom zodchestve rubezha XVI-XVII vv.," pp. 244–5. See also Viatchanina, "Arkhangel'skii sobor moskovskogo kremlia," pp. 220–1.

93. On the Viaziomy estate, see Pod"iapol'skaia, *Pamiatniki*, vol. 2, pp. 76–80.

94. The stylistic transfer between the Archangel Cathedral and the Viaziomy Church of the Trinity is analyzed in Viatchanina, "Arkhangel'skii sobor moskovskogo kremlia," p. 222. See also Batalov, "Sobor Voznesenskogo monastyria," p. 478; and "Osobennosti 'Ital'ianizmov'," p. 245.

95. The roof of the Trinity Church was rebuilt at the end

of the seventeenth century with a level cornice, but it has since been restored to the earlier configuration. See L. Soboleva, "Issledovatel'skie i restavratsionnye raboty po tserkvi preobrazheniia v usad'be Viazëmy," in *Teoriia i praktika restavratsionnykh rabot* (Moscow, 1972), pp. 84–98.

96. Among the first specialists to appreciate the Viaziomy belfry was Mikhail Krasovskii, in his *Ocherk istorii moskovskogo perioda drevnerusskogo tserkovnogo zodchestva* (Moscow, 1911), p. 226. On the basis of its Italinate motifs, Krasovskii considered the Viaziomy ensemble to have been built by an Italian (ibid., p. 257).

97. On the church at Besedy, much modified in the nineteenth century, see Pod"iapol'skaia, *Pamiatniki*, vol. 1, p. 301.

98. A schematic analysis of the system of churches along the river network of the Moscow area is provided in M. P. Kudriavtsev, "Sistemy prirechnykh ansamblei Moskvy XVII v.," *Arkhitekturnoe nasledstvo*, 34 (1986): 17–25, with reference to the churches at Besedy and Ostrov, the latter anchoring the southern end of the system (pp. 17–18).

99. An analysis of the Godunov compound at Borisov Gorodok is presented in P. A. Rappoport, "Zodchii Borisa Godunova," in A. L. Mongait, ed., *Kul'tura drevnei Rusi* (Moscow, 1966), pp. 215–21.

100. On the attribution of the Godunov churches to Kon, see Arenkova and Mekhova, pp. 12–15. This attribution is rejected, however, in the most extensive biography of Kon, by V. V. Kostochkin, *Gosudarev master Fedor Kon'* (Moscow, 1964), p. 6.

101. See Rappoport, "Zodchii Borisa Godunova," pp. 218–20.

102. See Brunov et al., *Istoriia russkoi arkhitektury*, pp. 165–6.

103. Ibid., pp. 163–4.

104. See Komech and Pluzhnikov, eds., *Tsentral'nye ploshchadi*, pp. 60–1. On the matter of greater regularity in urban construction, the first useful "plans" of Moscow, or schematic drawings with some topographic accuracy, appeared during Godunov's reign. Ibid., p. 50.

105. On the expansion of Moscow's defensive system, see ibid., pp. 47, 60.

106. An authoritative interpreter of Godunov's design for the Kremlin is Il'in, whose research on the topic is summarized in *Kamennaia letopis' moskovskoi Rusi*, pp. 56–8.

107. The Jerusalem prototype for the Kremlin Holy of Holies is discussed in Batalov and Viatchanina, "Ob ideinom znachenii i interpretatsii ierusalimskogo obraztsa," pp. 22–8. On the form of the Anastasis and its rotunda, see Krautheimer, *Early Christian and Byzantine Architecture*, pp. 77–8.

108. A survey of historical material on this complex and difficult period can be found in the relevant sections of histories of Russia by Riasanovsky and Crummey. For a more detailed account by the leading Soviet specialist, see Ruslan G. Skrynnikov, *The Time of Troubles: Russia in Crisis, 1604–1618*, Hugh Graham, transl. (Gulf Breeze, Florida, 1988).

Chapter 7

1. On the commemorative function of the Intercession Church at Rubtsovo, see Gulianitskii, "Osvoboditel'nye idei Rusi v obrazakh pamiatnikov arkhitektury XVI-pervoi poloviny XVII vv.," *Arkhitekturnoe nasledstvo*, 32 (1984): 34–5.

2. The Kazan Cathedral is discussed and illustrated in ibid., pp. 39–40.

3. For a summary of the results of Pozharskii's campaign of church construction, see ibid., p. 39. On Pozharskii's assiduous efforts to revive architecture and the crafts on his many estates, see Iu. M. Eskin, "Dmitrii Pozharskii," *Voprosy istorii*, 1976, no. 8: 118.

4. A detailed historical analysis of the Intercession Church is presented in N. F. Gulianitskii, "Tserkov' Pokrova v Medvedkove i russkoe zodchestvo XVI-XVII vv.," *Arkhitekturnoe nasledstvo*, 28 (1980): 52–64.

5. The Medvedkovo church also bears a telling similarity to the Godunov Church of Sts. Boris and Gleb (see what preceded), which would have been personally known to Pozharskii according to Gulianitskii, "Tserkov' Pokrova," pp. 58–9.

6. Elevations of the Nizhnii Novgorod churches are reproduced in Gulianitskii, "Osvoboditel'nye idei," pp. 36–7.

7. On the Monastery of the Metropolitan Aleksii and a structural analysis of the Dormition Church, see Kirikov, *Uglich*, pp. 65–8.

8. The movement toward the decorative and purely symbolic use of elements exemplified by tower churches with multiple "tents" is defined in Gulianitskii, "Tserkov' Pokrova," p. 55. On the possible local symbolic references in the triad of towers, see Gulianitskii, "Osvoboditel'nye idei," pp. 45–6. The structural system of the churches with multiple towers at Uglich and Riazan is analyzed in Shteiman, "Besstolpnye pokrytiia v arkhitekture XVI–XVII vekov," pp. 60–2.

9. Ibid., p. 42. On the Solovetsk Transfiguration Monastery, see Denisov, *Pravoslavnye monastyri*, pp. 10–19.

10. Gulianitskii, "Osvoboditel'nye idei," p. 42.

11. See V. I. Baldin, "Monastyr' v pervoi polovine XVII veka," in Voronin and Kostochkin, eds., *Troitse-Sergieva lavra*, p. 41. Gulianitskii notes the topographic importance of the church as a visual dominant for the newly created cannoneers' quarter established for the monastery guard after the lifting of the siege in 1610 ("Osvoboditel'nye idei," p. 43).

12. See Il'in and Moiseeva, *Moskva i Podmoskov'e*, pp. 463–4.

13. Ibid., pp. 453–4.

14. The Riazan Holy Spirit is unusual not only for its combination of two towers, but also as one of the few buildings of the period to have a named architect, Vasilii Zubov. G. K. Vagner, *Starye russkie goroda* (Moscow, 1980), pp. 387–8.

15. Iaroslavl was among the earliest cities to recover from the Time of Troubles, and one of the early signs of that recovery in architecture is the pentacupolar Church of St. Nicholas Nadein (1620–2; subsequently much modified), which possesses a sense of traditional, monumental form last seen in Russian church design during the 1560s. The St. Nicholas Church is also of interest as an example of the increasing role assumed in large architectural projects by merchant donors. Nadei Sveteshnikov, whose first name was attached to the church dedication, had supported the cause of national liberation (like many prominent Iaroslavl merchants) during the Time of Troubles, and he subsequently achieved enormous wealth as the tsar's purchasing agent. For a reconstruction and analysis of the St. Nicholas Church, as well as a biographical profile of its donor, see B. V. Gnedovskii and E. D. Dobrovol'skaia, *Iaroslavl'. Tutaev* (Moscow, 1981), pp. 54–68.

16. A brief note on Anikei and Nifantii Skripin, and on their considerable power within both church and state, is contained in ibid., pp. 88–9.

17. Illustrated commentary on the frescoes of the Elijah church is presented in ibid., pp. 93–116; and V. G. Briusova, *Freski Iaroslavlia* (Moscow, 1969), pp. 71–88. The donation of the frescoes by Iulita Skripina reminds that the northeast chapel was dedicated to Sts. Gurii, Samon, and Aviv, patrons of conjugal happiness. The frescoes in the enclosed gallery and Chapel of the Deposition of the Robe date primarily from 1715–16. An analysis of the synthetic, architectonic qualities of the frescoes is contained in M. A. Nekrasova, "Novoe v sinteze zhivopisi i arkhitektury XVII veka (rospis' tserkvi Il'i Proroka v Iaroslavle)," in V. N. Lazarev, ed., *Drevnerusskoe iskusstvo: XVII vek* (Moscow, 1964), pp. 89–109.

18. A survey of the Nikitnikov family in the seventeenth century is contained in E. S. Ovchinnikova, *Tserkov' Troitsy v Nikitnikakh* (Moscow, 1970), pp. 5–12. For a broader study, see Paul Bushkovitch, *The Merchants of Moscow, 1580–1650* (Cambridge, 1980).

19. Komech and Pluzhnikov, eds., *Tsentral'nye ploshchadi*, pp. 453–4.

20. Ibid., p. 16.

21. On the Terem Palace, see Brunov, *Istoriia russkoi arkhitektury*, pp. 193–6; and Komech and Pluzhnikov, eds., *Tsentral'nye ploshchadi*, pp. 333–4.

22. The Piscator Bible has been proposed as a source for the iconography and composition of the Trinity frescoes. See Ovchinnikova, *Tserkov' Troitsy*, pp. 128–9.

23. On the identity of the fresco artists, see ibid., pp. 132–3. Simon Ushakov subsequently painted many of the icons for the church iconostasis.

24. For a typology of Russian church architecture during this period, see M. P. Kudriavtsev and G. Ia. Mokeev, "O tipichnom russkom khrame XVII v.," *Arkhitekturnoe nasledstvo*, 29 (1981): 70–9. Numerous examples of the "ship" form in Moscow churches are illustrated in *Moskva zlatoglavaia*.

25. The reinforcing elements and vaulting systems of typ-

ical seventeenth-century churches are described in Shteiman, "Osobennosti konstruktsii russkikh kamennykh sooruzhenii XVI–XVII vv.," pp. 47–9.

26. On the professional, craft boundaries of Moscow districts and their integration into the city as a whole, see T. P. Kudriavtseva, "Struktura i kompozitsionnye osobennosti slobody russkogo goroda XVI–XVII vv.," *Arkhitekturnoe nasledstvo*, 32 (1984): 13–25. More generally on the organic nature of development within late medieval Russian towns, see A. S. Shchenkov, "Struktura russkikh gorodov XVI–XVII vv. i ikh esteticheskoe vospriiatie," *Arkhitekturnoe nasledstvo*, 32 (1984): 3–12. Western reactions to the environment of seventeenth-century Russian cities is surveyed in James Cracraft, *The Petrine Revolution in Russian Architecture* (Chicago, 1988), passim.

27. Il'in and Moiseeva, *Moskva i Podmoskov'e*, p. 456.

28. Closely related in design to the Dormition on Potters' Lane is the Church of St. George on Pskov Hill, built in 1657 and named after a quarter in Kitai-gorod settled by merchants from Pskov. Built on the site of a church of 1462 dedicated to St. George, the church was also known as the Intercession, and has had numerous local designations. In a borrowing from the Pskov custom of converting church basements into storehouses, the lower part of the church – situated on a steep bank – was divided into vaulted chambers for storage. See Komech and Pluzhnikov, eds., *Tsentral'nye ploshchadi*, pp. 456–7.

29. On the restoration, see G. V. Alferova, "Issledovanie i restavratsiia palat Averkiia Kirillova," *Iz istorii restavratsii pamiatnikov kul'tury* (Moscow, 1974), pp. 136–50.

30. On the St. Nicholas Church, see Il'in and Moiseeva, *Moskva i Podmoskov'e*, p. 467.

31. A history of the Ostankino church is contained in L. A. Lepskaia, M. Z. Sarkisova et al., *Ostankinskii dvorets-muzei: Tvorchestvo krepostnykh* (Leningrad, 1982), pp. 7–9.

32. A description of the Archangel Church structure, as well as information on the frequent changes of ownership at Arkhangelskoe, is presented in Pod"iapol'skaia, ed., *Pamiatniki arkhitektury moskovskoi oblasti*, vol. 1, p. 278.

33. An analysis of the complex structure of the Taininskoe church is contained in Pod"iapol'skaia, ed., *Pamiatniki arkhitektury moskovskoi oblasti*, vol. 2, p. 42. A similar resolution of the west front appears in a church of the monastic complex at Viazhishche near Novgorod (see what follows).

34. The Church of the Resurrection and the Kadashi district comprised the life work of the Soviet scholar Gali Alferova, whose exhaustive study culminated in the monograph *Pamiatnik russkogo zodchestva v Kadashakh* (Moscow, 1974). In addition to an architectural and restoration analysis, the volume provides the general cultural and historical setting within which the church was built. Alferova notes with some bitterness that her plans to convert the abandoned church to a museum were thwarted by local (party?) interests after its preliminatry reconstruction. See p. 99.

A more recent detailed study, with drawings, of the Kadashi settlement and its significance in the composition of Moscow at the turn of the eighteenth century is presented in T. N. Kudriavtseva, "Kadashevskaia sloboda v Moskve i ee razvitie v kontse XVII–XVIII vvv. (gradostroitel'nyi analiz," *Arkhitekturnoe nasledstvo*, 27 (1979): 38–48. Kudriavtseva's work on the *slobody*, or guild and commercial districts, as coherent visual ensembles related to the landscape dominants of central Moscow was later expanded in her article "Struktura i kompozitsionnye osobennosti slobody russkogo goroda XVI–XVII vv."

35. Il'in and Moiseeva, *Moskva i Podmoskov'e*, p. 448. Turchaninov was a close ally of Patriarch Nikon and much involved in his monumental construction projects (see what follows).

36. As Alferova points out in *Pamiatnik russkogo zodchestva v Kadashakh*, the limestone carving has seriously deteriorated because of industrial pollution and the replacement stone is not as durable as the original.

37. A thorough structural typology of the Iaroslavl masonry churches (particularly the large "cold" churches intended for use in the warmer months) is developed in S. S. Popadiuk, "Arkhitekturnye formy 'kholodnykh' khramov 'iaroslavskoi shkoly," in V. P. Vygolov et al., eds., *Pamiatniki russkoi arkhitektury i monumental'nogo iskusstva: Stil', atributsii, datirovki* (Moscow, 1983), pp. 64–91.

38. A description of the Korovniki ensemble is contained in Gnedovskii and Dobrovol'skaia, *Iaroslavl'*, pp. 116–29.

39. Measurements and other data on this "stretching" of the four-piered structure are presented in Popadiuk, "Arkhitekturnye formy," pp. 65–6. It must be emphasized that the shift of the piers away from the center did not occur at the expense of the east and west bays, whose walls were also shifted; hence, the increased length of the structure without the addition of two piers.

40. Concerning the interior structure of the second church at Korovniki, see Gnedovskii and Dobrovol'skaia, *Iaroslavl'*, p. 129.

41. The innovations introduced at the Tutaev Cathedral and their variation at Tolchkovo are analyzed in Popadiuk, "Arkhitekturnye formy," pp. 84–8. See also Iu. Ia. Gerchuk and M. I. Domshlak, *Khudozhestvennye pamiatniki verkhnei Volgi* (Moscow, 1976), pp. 127–30.

42. The north chapel of the Church of John the Baptist is dedicated to the Kazan saints Gurii and Varsanofii. Unfortunately, the pentacupolar structure of the chapels has long been obscured by an interminable "restoration." In addition, the Tolchkovo church is surrounded by a large industrial plant that in places directly abuts upon the church site.

43. The frescoes and their relation to the structure of the Tolchkovo church are surveyed in Gnedovskii and Dobrovol'skaia, *Iaroslavl'*, pp. 191–208. More detailed commentary and illustration are provided in Briusova, *Freski Iaroslavlia*, pp. 90–107.

44. A summary of the contemporary account of the construction of the St. Theodore Church is presented in Gnedovskii and Dobrovol'skaia, *Iaroslavl'*, p. 185. The attached gallery was not added until 1736.

45. On the St. Theodore frescoes, which include an un-usually large number of "realistic" battle scenes portraying the victories of the Russian Orthodox over their enemies, see ibid., p. 186–8.

46. On the Nazarev brothers, of whom Akindin played a major role in holding the allegiance of Iaroslavl to Moscow during the Time of Troubles, see ibid., pp. 69, 71. The com-plex plan of the Church of the Nativity is reproduced on p. 66.

47. For the text of the inscription as it pertains to the Nazarevs, see ibid., pp. 78–9. The Nazarevs were intrepid traders whose network extended not only down the Volga to Astrakhan, but well into Siberia and even into Central Asia, where it is entirely possible that they would have seen examples of the brilliant use of tile and ceramic inscriptions on the Islamic monuments of Bukhara. By this period, how-ever, the production of ornmental tiles in Muscovy was developing from other sources to the west, whose types and uses of ceramic decoration were distinct from those of Central Asia.

48. The gate chapel of the Nativity Church was dedicated to Sts. Gurii, Samon, and Aviv – as at the Elijah Church (see before, n. 17). The reference here is undoubtedly to the donor Gurii Nazarev.

49. On the Nativity Church frescoes, see Briusova, *Freski Iaroslavlia*, pp. 126–31; and Gnedovskii and Dobrovol'skaia, *Iaroslavl'*, pp. 85–7. Briusova dates the frescoes to 1700 (?), but both sources attribute the work to the painter Dmitrii Semenov.

50. Popadiuk, "Arkhitekturnye formy," pp. 89–90, gives a detailed analysis of the profiled ceramic entablature, as well as the larger relation between structure and facade decoration at the Epiphany Church.

51. On the varieties of ceramic decoration at the Epi-phany Church, see Gnedovskii and Dobrovol'skaia, *Iaros-lavl'*, pp. 170–1.

52. The frescoes are briefly described and illustrated in Briusova, *Freski Iaroslavlia*, pp. 122–5. See also Gnedovskii and Dobrovol'skaia, *Iaroslavl'*, pp. 152–6, 171, 174.

53. Subsequent modifications in the middle of the eight-eenth century deformed the original design of the Resur-rection Church – particularly the roof, which had followed the contours of the zakomary, and the gallery, whose dec-orative open arcade was enclosed. As in Iaroslavl, the Church of the Resurrection in Kostroma was constructed largely with funds provided by a local merchant – K. G. Isakov. See V. N. Ivanov, *Kostroma* (Moscow, 1978), p. 139. Some of the interior frescoes have been preserved, although not to the extent of the major Iaroslavl monuments. See ibid., pp. 102–6, 140.

54. Among the best examples of parish architecture in Kaluga is the Church of the Intercession on the Moat built in 1687 near the moat that had formerly surrounded Ka-luga's log fortress. The whitewashed church combines an array of odd pediments and kokoshniki with isolated fea-tures of the classical system of orders – such as the denti-lation within the architrave strip above the windows – that

illustrate the idiosyncratic, decorative uses of western ar-chitectural elements, which in any event had passed through many filters before reaching the builders of pro-vincial Russian towns. On the Church of the Intercession, see M. V. Fekhner, *Kaluga. Borovsk* (Moscow, 1972), p. 78. The present bell tower (eighteenth century) rests on the lower walls of the original tower, which may have had a tent roof.

Numerous studies have been devoted to the monuments of the major medieval Russian towns. Among the more recent are: S. I. Maslenitsyn, *Murom* (Moscow, 1971), with superb illustrations of seventeenth-century churches and monasteries; P. A. Tel'tevskii, *Velikii Ustiug* (Moscow, 1977); and G. Vzdornov, *Vologda* (Leningrad, 1978).

55. Nikon's association with the Monastery of the Trans-figuration would prove ironic when the Solovki community became in the most literal sense one of the last bastions of resistance to the liturgical changes promulgated by Nikon and imposed with main force by the state.

56. Nikon in fact precipitated the crisis by renouncing the patriarch's throne in an unsuccessful attempt to obtain the tsar's submission. A survey of the ecclesiastical position of Nikon within the social and political setting of the time is presented in M. A. Il'in, *Kamennaia letopis' moskovskoi Rusi*, pp. 93–105. The most detailed account of the relations be-tween patriach and tsar is N. Kapterev, *Patriarkh Nikon i Tsar' Aleksei Mikhailovich*, 2 vols. (Sergiev Posad, 1909–12).

57. For a wide-ranging analysis of the Russian Church schism and its implications, see Michael Cherniavsky, "The Old Believers and the New Religion," *Slavic Review*, XXV, no. 1 (March 1966): 1–39. See also James H. Billington, *The Icon and the Axe* (New York, 1966), pp. 127–44.

58. The function of ornamentalism in late seventeenth-century church architecture as a reflection of a secularizing tendency in Muscovite society is analyzed in Il'in, *Kamennaia letopis' moskovskoi Rusi*, pp. 207–25.

59. The architectural and symbolic aspects of the con-struction of the Iversk Monastery at Valdai are discussed in M. A. Il'in, *Kamennaia letopis' moskovskoi Rusi*, pp. 106–148. See also G. V. Alferova, "K voprosu o stroitel'noi deia-tel'nosti patriarkha Nikona," *Arkhitekturnoe nasledstvo*, 18 (1969): 30–44. A brief account of the monastery's early his-tory is presented in Denisov, *Pravoslavnye monastyri*, pp. 582–3, with bibliographical references to more detailed accounts of the monastery.

60. In 1552, Nikon went to Solovki to transfer from the Transfiguration Monastery to Moscow the relics of Phillip, who had been canonized after an assiduous campaign by Nikon that further demonstrates his intentions to insist on the inviolability of the church. In 1681, the Church of the Apostle Phillip was rededicated to the Twelve Apostles. See Komech and Pluzhnikov, eds., *Tsentral'nye ploshchadi*, pp. 340–1.

61. The various pronouncements against the *shatior* are reproduced and discussed in S. Zabello, V. Ivanov, and P. Maksimov, *Russkoe dereviannoe zodchestvo* (Moscow, 1942), p. 9; Il'in, *Kamennaia letopis' moskovskoi Rusi*, p. 96; M. Preo-

brazhenskii, *Pamiatniki drevnerusskogo zodchestva v predelakh Kaluzhskoi gubernii* (St. Petersburg, 1891), p. 59, with reference Nikon's prescription of "round" instead of pointed (i.e., onion?) domes for chapels at the Church of the Dormition in Veshniaki (1644–5; near Moscow) – which itself was built with a *shatior*. See also I. E. Zabelin, *Russkoe iskusstvo: Cherty samobytnosti v drevnerusskom zodchestve* (Moscow, 1900), p. 29; V., "Kak stroilis' khramy," in the architectural periodical *Nedelia stroitleia*, 1891, nos. 46–7, 438, with a warning in 1675 by Metropolitan Joseph against the use of the *shatior* for a church in Voronezh (suggesting that the form continued to tempt church builders); and S. P. Zavarikhin, *Russkaia arkhitekturnaia kritika* (Leningrad, 1989), p. 39. I. L. Buseva-Davydov and A. L. Batalov argue against a reductive symbolism in interpreting Nikon's fondness for the pentacupolar form, seen not as an expression of canonical symbolism but a preference for traditional forms. See "O metodologii izucheniia simvoliki arkhitektury," in A. A. Voronova, ed., *Istroiia arkhitektury: Ob"ekt, predmet i metod issledovaniia* (Moscow, 1988), pp. 95–96.

62. This motive for opposing the *shatior*, with its commemoration of secular events, is mentioned in Gulianitskii, "Tserkov' Pokrova," p. 56; and N. A. Evsina, *Arkhitekturnaia teoriia v Rossii XVIII v.* (Moscow, 1975), p. 12.

63. The most detailed account of the monastery at New Jerusalem is by Archimandrite Leonid [Kavelin], *Istoricheskoe opisanie stavropigial'nogo Voskresenskogo, Novyi Ierusalim imenuemogo monastyria* (Moscow, 1876). Il' in gives a detailed analysis of Nikon's design and construction at the monastery in *Kamennaia letopis' moskovskoi Rusi*, pp. 176–204. See also Alferova, "K voprosu o stroitel'noi deiatel'nosti patriarkha Nikona."

64. Il'in, *Kamennaia letopis' moskovskoi Rusi*, pp. 199–200. Nikon pilfered sufficiently to do serious damage to the Boris and Gleb Cathedral, which was finally dismantled in 1804. Concerning its original form, see Il'in, *Russkoe shatrovoe zodchestvo*, pp. 85–96.

65. There have been ingenious attempts to explain the presence of the *shatior* over the Eleon chapel, including the possibility that a chapel did not "count" in Nikon's prohibition. See ibid., pp. 194–5.

66. Amico's account, dating from 1596, was republished in 1620 in Florence as *Trattato delle piante et imagini de Sacri Edifizi di terra Santa* (subsequently translated into English). The first to draw attention to the similarity in plan between the Amico illustrations and New Jerusalem cathedral was N. Ivanovskii, "Proskinitarii Arseniia Sukhanova," in *Pravoslavnyi Palestenskii sbornik*, v. VII, no. 3 (21) (St. Petersburg, 1889): 130–4. Further discussion and a comparison of the plans of the two monuments are contained in Il'in, *Kamennaia letopis' moskovskoi Rusi*, pp. 188–94. (The Amico volume also contained a drawing of the chapel on Mount Eleon, also recreated at New Jerusalem.) The other possible sources for the Resurrection Cathedral were a model brought to Moscow in 1649 by Patriach Paisy of Jerusalem, and accounts by Russian pilgrims. See ibid., pp. 183–8.

67. On the continuity of Nikon's project with earlier expressions of Jerusalem in Muscovite architecture, see A. L. Batalov and T. N. Viatchanina, "Ob ideinom znachenii i interpretatsii ierusalimskogo obraztsa," pp. 36–9.

68. As noted in ibid., p. 37, in relation to Nikon.

69. Il'in notes that the great impact of the Resurrection Cathedral on late seventeenth-century church architecture – particularly in its ceramic work – actually affected the renewed decoration of its prototpye, the Cathedral of the Intercession on Red Square. See *Kamennaia letopis' moskovskoi Rusi*, pp. 201–2. For a summary of the scholarly literature concerning the broad influence of the cathedral, in both structural and decorative terms, see Batalov and Viatchanina, pp. 38–41. The innovative role of Belorussian craftsmen at work on the project and its ceramic detailing (with elements of the system of orders) is discussed in L. A. J. Hughes, "Belorussian craftsmen in late seventeenth-century Russia and their influence on Muscovite architecture," *The Journal of Byelorussian Studies*, 3 (1976): 332–3.

70. The construction history of the monastery and surrounding structures is summarized in *Pamiatniki arkhitektury moskovskoi oblasti*, vol. 1, pp. 187–92.

71. On the concept of ideal cities in Renaissance Europe, see Georg Münter, *Idealstädte: Ihre Geschichte vom 15.–17. Jahrhundert* (Berlin, 1957).

72. A recent study of the Rostov Kremlin is V. S. Banige, *Kreml' Rostova Velikogo: XVI–XVII veka* (Moscow, 1976), with copious illustrations.

73. G. K. Vagner, *Starye russkie goroda*, p. 385.

74. The Resurrection frescoes have in fact been attributed to various masters from Iaroslavl and Kostroma. Excellent illustrations are reproduced in Banige, Figures 41–55. See also Briusova, *Freski Iaroslavlia*, pp. 44–61.

75. Banige, *Kreml' Rostova Velikogo*, p. 102.

76. The frescoes are reproduced in ibid., Figures 71–84; see also Briusova, pp. 62–5. Vagner notes that the style embodies the contradictory impulses in late seventeenth-century Russian painting, with relatively realistic figure detail combined with an archaic, "Gothicized" rendering of Mary in the style of the trecento. See *Starye russkie goroda*, p. 386. Complementing the Savior Church, but beyond the southwest portion of the walls, stands the Church of St. Gregory the Theologian, built in 1670 as the first refectory church at the Court of the Metropolitan.

77. Banige, *Kreml' Rostova Velikogo*, p. 82.

78. An authoritative history of Tobolsk and its architecture is V. V. Kirillov, *Tobol'sk* (Moscow, 1984). More generally on the building of new towns in Muscovy during this period, see G. V. Alferova, "K voprosu o stroitel'stve gorodov v Moskovskom gosudarstve v XVI–XVII vv.," *Arkhitekturnoe nasledstvo*, 28 (1980):20–8.

79. Kirillov examines the energetic activity of the Siberian Office in supporting construction in "Sibirskii prikaz i ego rol' v organizovannom stroitel'stve gorodov na novykh zemliakh," *Arkhitekturnoe nasledstvo*, 28 (1980): 13–19. See also T. S. Proskuriakova, "Planirovochnye kompozitsii gorodov-krepostei Sibiri (vtoroi poloviny XVII–60-e gg. XVIII v.)," *Arkhitekturnoe nasledstvo*, 25 (1976): 57–71; and S. V. Kopylova, *Kamennoe stroitel'stvo v Sibiri konets XVII–XVIII v.* (Novosibirsk, 1979).

80. V. V. Kirillov, "Metody proektirovaniia Semena Remezova," *Arkhitekturnoe nasledstvo*, 22 (1974): 53–62. Kirillov notes two conflicting impulses in the early Petrine development of masonry architecture Tobolsk: one emphasizing the imposing, commemorative aspect, with an array of towers; and the other emphasizing efficiency and regularity of construction ("Ansambl' Tobol'skogo kremlia," in T. V. Alekseeva, ed., *Russkoe iskusstvo pervoi chetverti XVIII veka: Materialy i issledovaniia* [Moscow, 1974], p. 66). The same duality of impulse can be detected throughout much of the history of Russian (and Soviet) architecture.

81. The Kazan walls subsequently suffered damage from artillery fire during the siege of the city in 1774 by the forces of the rebel and pretender to the throne Emelian Pugachev. See V. P. Ostroumov, *Kazan'*, p. 34.

82. See Ostroumov, pp. 44–7, with reference to the presence of local, Tatar elements in the design. See also M. Fekhner, *Velikie Bulgary. Kazan'. Sviiazhsk*, p. 73.

83. On the Savior–St. Evfimii Monastery, see Denisov, *Pravoslavnye monastyri*, pp. 98–102.

84. V. Ivanov, *Kostroma*, p. 62; and Denisov, *Pravoslavnye monastyri*, pp. 319–21. The Romanovs had been exiled to Kostroma by Boris Godunov, who made rich donations to the monastery and considered his ancestry to be derived from the monastery's fourteenth-century founder, the converted Tatar prince Chet (see Ivanov, p. 53).

85. There are numerous accounts of these dramatic events, usually from the perspective of Peter the Great. For a recent, authoritative account of Sophia's life and reign, see Lindsey Hughes, *Sophia, Regent of Russia, 1657–1704* (New Haven, 1990).

86. On the development of the refectory church in Russia (such a combination is apparently unknown in Greece, Bulgaria, or Serbia), see V. P. Vygolov, *Arkhitektura Moskovskoi Rusi seredin y XV veka* (Moscow, 1988), pp. 122–4. Early examples of refectory churches mentioned in Chapter 6 include the Conception of St. Anne (1551) at the Intercession Convent in Suzdal.

87. On the history of the development of refectory structures at the Trinity–St. Sergius Monastery, see ibid., pp. 113–22.

88. At the opposite, north end of the monastery enclosure stands another palace structure with trompe l'oeil rustication: the tsar's Chambers (*chertogi*), simple in its elongated rectangular design, but with elaborate window surrounds that reveal the transition between medieval and modern (western) architectural details at the end of the century. On the tsar's Chambers, see V. I. Baldin, "Arkhitektura," in Voronin and Kostochkin, eds., *Troitse-Sergieva Lavra*, p. 50. The evolution in window surrounds is analyzed in V. I. Pluzhnikov, "Rasprostranenie zapadnogo dekora v petrovskom zodchestve," G. V. Popov, ed.,

Drevnerusskoe iskusstvo: Zarubezhnye sviazi (Moscow, 1975), pp. 362–70. The most richly ornamented structure at the monastery is the small chapel built in the 1680s over a holy spring at the southwest corner of the Dormition Cathedral, with ornament derived from elements of intricately carved wooden iconostases (particularly the grapevine motif).

89. Baldin, "Arkhitektura," pp. 53–4.

90. See Denisov, *Pravoslavnye monastyri*, pp. 414–17.

91. The cathedral actually contains two churches, the lower of which (used in the winter) is dedicated to St. Athanasius of Athos and the upper to the Icon of the Mother of God of the Sign. This bifurcation accounts for the distinctive apsidal structure on two levels. Komech and Pluzhnikov, eds., *Tsentral'nye ploshchadi*, pp. 450–2.

92. Denisov, *Pravoslavnye monastyri*, pp. 393–9.

93. The development of the Izmailovo estate and the scholarly literature thereupon are surveyed in A. P. Vergunov and V. A. Gorokhov, *Russkie sady i parki* (Moscow, 1988), pp. 159–67. A more detailed discussion of the architecture is contained in A. Chiniakov, "Arkhitekturnye pamiatniki Izmailova," *Arkhitekturnoe nasledstvo*, 2 (1952): 193–220.

94. An architectural survey of the Simonov Monastery is contained in R. Katsnel'son, "Ansambl' Simonova monastyria v Moskve," *Arkhitekturnoe nasledstvo*, 6 (1956): 87–106. On the Polish connection, which is plausible in view of the greater Russian receptivity to Polish and Belorussian cultural influence in the latter part of the seventeenth century, see M. Ilyin, *Moscow* (Moscow, 1968), p. 92. On the connection with northern Europe (Holland and the Baltic), see Komech and Pluzhnikov, eds., *Tsentral'nye ploshchadi*, p. 121; and Boris Vipper, "Russkaia arkhitektura XVII veka i ee istoricheskoe mesto," in the same author's collection of essays, compiled by N. A. Evsina, *Arkhitektura russkogo barokko* (Moscow, 1978), pp. 20–2. Il'in, too, acknowledged the Dutch influence in general on the formation of a Moscow baroque decorative style; see "K voprosu o prirode arkhitekturnogo ubranstva moskovskogo barokko," in V. N. Lazarev, ed., *Drevnerusskoe iskusstvo: XVII vek*, pp. 232–5. Information on the importation of western architectural treatises by Dutch merchants and diplomats in the seventeenth century is summarized in Lindsey A. J. Hughes, "Western European Graphic Material as a Source for Moscow Baroque Architecture," *Slavonic and East European Review*, 55 (1977): 437, 441–2.

95. The history and architecture of the Novodevichii Convent are examined in Iu. M. Ovsiannikov, *Novodevichii monastyr'* (Moscow, 1968). See also Denisov, pp. 498–503. The name of the convent honors the bringing of the new Icon of the Smolensk Mother of God Hodegetria to Moscow after the taking of Smolensk by Basil III.

96. On Golitsyn's extensive involvement in architectural matters, see Batalov and Viatchanina, pp. 39–40 (with regard to propagating the decorative devices of the New Jerusalem cathedral); and Hughes, "Western European Graphic Material," pp. 439–40, on his acquisition of western architectural manuals and their possible influence on the design of his estate churches and at the Novodevichii Convent.

97. Modifications to the refectory church in the nineteenth century eliminated its original decorative pentacupolar form (the middle cupola remains) and contoured roof line; but the facades of the central cube are extant, and show a complex entablature with attached columns framing the bays and window surrounds. For reproductions of early eighteenth-century drawings with the Dormition Church portrayed (distantly) in its original pentacupolar form, see Komech and Pluzhnikov, eds., *Tsentral'nye ploshchadi*, pp. 93–9.

98. The terrace of the Intercession Church continues to the adjacent Chambers of the Tsarevna Mariia Alekseevna (Mariinskie palaty), one of two sisters of Peter I who retired to Novodevichii Convent (a practice to ensure dynastic stability). Both tsarevnas had their chambers, built in the 1680s, in the manner of stone *palaty* of wealthy Muscovites. The roster of women of high birth sequestered in the convent increased in 1689, when Peter I placed Sophia under house arrest there after the quelling of her attempted coup, supported by the *streltsy*. In 1727, Peter I's first wife, Evdokiia Lopukhina, who had taken monastic vows at the Suzdal Intercession Convent in 1698, was transferred on order of Peter II to Novodevichii Convent, where she occupied the chambers of the Tsarevna Ekaterina – now known as the Lopukhin Chambers.

99. The Upper Petrovskii Monastery is also site of the small Church of the Metropolitan Peter (see Figure 136), long considered a seminal example of Moscow baroque tower churches. The monastery's long dormitory was built in the 1690s with support provided by Kirill Naryshkin (father of Peter I's mother), who in his final years took monastic vows. An architectural survey of the monastery is contained in G. V. Makarevich, ed., *Pamiatniki arkhitektury Moskvy: Belyi gorod*, pp. 180–8. A more detailed analysis (but with certain questionable attributions) is provided in B. P. Dedushkino, "K istorii ansambli moskovskogo Vysoko-Petrovskogo monastyria," in V. N. Lazarev, ed., *Drevnerusskoe iskusstvo: XVII vek*, pp. 253–71.

100. The history of the St. Nicholas Monastery is briefly summarized in Denisov, *Pravoslavnye monastyri*, pp. 574–5. An exhaustive analysis of the use of architectural ceramics in seventeenth-century Novgorod, with particular emphasis on the refectory Church of St. John the Theologian at Viazhishchi, is contained in V. P. Vygolov, "Monumental 'no-dekorativnaia keramika Novgoroda kontsa XVII veka. Izraztsy Viazhitskogo monastyria," in V. N. Lazarev, ed., *Drevnerusskoe iskusstvo: Khudozhestvennaia kul'tura Novgoroda* (Moscow, 1968), pp. 237–66.

101. For biographic information and sources references on the metropolitan and archimandrite, see ibid., pp. 240–5.

102. Ibid., p. 265,

103. On Metropolitan Evfimii, see ibid., pp. 245–6, with source references.

104. N. Soshina, "Krutitskii teremok v Moskve," *Arkhi-

tekturnoe nasledstvo*, 6 (1956): 136–7.

105. The political ramifications of the construction of the new cathedral are discussed in Arenkova and Mekhova, *Donskoi monastyr'*, pp. 17–19.

106. An excellent example of this design in the Church of St. Catherine, Chernigov (1715). See Brumfield, *Gold in Azure*, p. 31.

107. On the other hand, it has been noted that the design of the new Donskoi cathedral differs fundamentally with the proposed Ukrainian prototypes, and is to the contrary a structural whole rather than an agglomeration of towers around a central crossing. See Arenkova and Mekhova, *Donskoi monastyr'*, p. 21.

108. On the monastery's maneuvering between the two factions – Sophia and Golitsyn on one hand, and Peter and his Naryshkin relatives on the other – see ibid., p. 19.

109. The term "Moscow baroque" gained currency from the F. F. Gornostaev's chapter on late seventeenth-century architecture entitled "Barokko Moskvy," in Igor Grabar, ed., *Istoriia russkogo iskusstva*, vol. 2 (Moscow, 1910), pp. 417–67. For a survey of the positions on the use of the term, see Lindsey A. J. Hughes, "Moscow Baroque – A Controversial Style," *Transactions of the Association of Russian–American Scholars in the U.S.A.*, 15 (1982): 69–93 (illustrated). See also Cracraft, *The Petrine Revolution* (Chicago, 1988), pp. 85–93. An earlier use of the related term "Russian baroque" appeared in Nikolai Sultanov's *Istoriia arkhitektury* (St. Petersburg, 1896), which adopted a comparative approach to western and Russian architecture. See T. A. Slavina, *Issledovateli russkogo zodchestva* (Leningrad, 1983), p. 111.

110. The clearest critique of this manifest deficiency is Boris Vipper, "Russkaia arkhitektura XVII veka i ee istoricheskoe mesto," *Arkhitektura russkogo barokko*, pp. 25–8; and "Arkhitektura russkogo barokko," ibid,. p. 33.

111. See Hughes, "Western European Graphic Material."

112. On the similarity of the wooden tiered churches, see V. P. Vygolov, "O razvitii iarusnykh form v zodchestve kontsa XVII veka," in V. N. Lazarev, ed., *Drevnerusskoe iskusstvo: XVII vek* (Moscow, 1964), p. 248. Vygolov's article focuses, however, on early masonry examples of the tiered church. Further commentary on the origins of the tiered structure is presented in I. L. Buseva-Davydova, "Ob istokakh kompozitsionnogo tipa 'vosmerik na chetverike' v russkoi arkhitekture kontsa XVII v.," *Arkhitekturnoe nasledstvo*, 33 (1985): 220–6.

113. The late fifteenth-century Church of the Holy Spirit at the Trinity–St. Sergius Monastery had been a rare attempt to place a belfry above the central church structure; and although its design has been considered a prototype for both sixteenth- and seventeenth-century tower churches, the similarity is distant from the narrower, highly decorated forms of the Naryshkin style.

114. A prototypical example was the Church of the Resurrection by the Cattle Yard, built in 1683 on the estate of Lev Naryshkin at the outskirts of Riazan. The church consisted of a cube supporting an octagonal structure, above whose dome was an octagonal lantern or belfry – hardly a clear statement of ascending tiers. An archival photograph of the Riazan church is reproduced in Vygolov, ''O razvitii iarusnykh form,'' p. 245. The article enumerates the earliest examples of the tiered form.

115. For an analysis of the innovative role of the Church of Josaphat, see ibid., p. 246. See also Chiniakov, ''Arkhitekturnye pamiatniki Izmailova''; and Komech and Pluzhnikov, eds., *Tsentral'nye ploshchadi*, pp. 122–3, with excellent archival photographs.

116. On the Ziuzino estate, see *Pamiatniki usadebnogo iskusstva, I: Moskovskii uezd* (Moscow, 1928), p. 31. It is worth noting that they began the church almost immediately after acquiring the estate, as a sign of their wealth and ownership.

117. In 1866, a refectory and bell tower were added to the church over the site of the seventeenth-century manor. See M. A. Il'in, *Podmoskov'e* (Moscow, 1974), pp. 13–15; and Pod''iapol'skaia, *Pamiatniki arkhitektury moskovskoi oblasti*, vol. 2, p. 155.

118. In 1799, the property was acquired by Nikolai Sheremetev, thus accounting for its present name ''Sheremetev Court.'' See G. V. Makarevich, ed., *Belyi gorod*, pp. 76–7.

119. N. F. Gulianitskii argues that the tectonic quality of the Church of the Intercession at Fili approaches the ''canonical.'' See ''Traditsii klassiki i cherty renessansa v arkhitekture Moskvy XV-XVII vv.,'' *Arkhitekturnoe nasledstvo*, 26 (1978): 22. For a further analysis of the adaptation of the order system (as defined by Vignola) in Russian church architecture of the late eighteenth century, see O. I. Braitseva, ''Novoe i traditsionnoe v khramovom zodchestve Moskvy kontsa XVII v.,'' *Arkhitekturnoe nasledstvo*, 26 (1978): 31–40.

120. The biographical information on Bukhvostov is drawn from the two major monographs on the architect: M. A. Il'in, *Zodchii Iakov Bukhvostov* (Moscow, 1959); and P. A. Tel'tevskii, *Zodchii Bukhvostov* (Moscow, 1960). Both works also describe the system of construction contracting in the late seventeenth century.

121. On the building of the Riazan cathedral, see Il'in, *Bukhvostov*, pp. 51–60; and Tel'tevskii, *Bukhvostov*, pp. 31–58. See also G. K. Vagner, *Riazan'*, pp. 30–3.

122. Vagner places the decorative motifs of the carved limestone elements into four categories: geometric, natural plant, arabesque plant, and floral. Ibid., p. 32.

123. Il'in claims the existence of an eighteenth-century document, not extant, that identified Bukhvostov as the architecture of the Troitse-Lykovo church. See *Zodchii Iakov Bukhvostov*, pp. 111–32.

124. One scholar has compared the Church of the Trinity at Troitse-Lykovo to a bride arrayed in a Russian wedding dress, admiring her reflection in the waters of the Moscow. See V. Podkliuchnikov, *Tri pamiatnika XVII stoletiia* (Moscow, 1945), p. 20. For the placement of this church within the string of sixteenth- and seventeenth-century monuments along the course of the Moscow River, see M. P. Kudriavtsev, ''Sistemy prirechnykh ansamblei Moskvy XVII

v.,'' *Arkhitekturnoe nasledstvo*, 34 (1986): 17–25.

125. The connection between the exterior decoration to the iconstasis is explored in Gornostaev, ''Barokko Moskvy,'' pp. 430, 454. Of considerable interest is the appearance of quite similar decorative devices in another ''peripheral'' culture, Mexico, at precisely the same time. The twisted columns and grapevine motif (symbolic of the Eucharist) also appear in the late Solomonic phase of the Mexican baroque, as illustrated in the retablos ''Seven Sorrows of the Virgin,'' done in 1690. See *Mexico: Splendor of 30 Centuries* (New York, 1990), pp. 339–42.

126. On the founding and subsequent history of the Dubrovitsy church, see G. I. Vzdornov, ''Zametki o pamiatnikakh russkoi arkhitektury kontsa XVII–nachala XVIII v.,'' in T. V. Alekseeva, ed., *Russkoe iskusstvo XVIII veka* (Moscow, 1973), pp. 20–5; and Pod''iapol'skaia, *Pamiatniki arkhitektury moskovskoi oblasti*, vol. 2, p. 126. More specific material on the origins of the interior work is presented in T. A. Gatova, ''Iz istorii dekorativnoi skul'ptury Moskvy nachala XVIII v.,'' in T. V. Alekseeva, ed., *Russkoe iskusstvo XVIII veka* (Moscow, 1973), pp. 40–1.

127. The Perovo church has been little studied, but the similarities with the Dubrovitsy church are noted in Vipper, *Arkhitektura russkogo barokko*, pp. 36–7. See also A. I. Nekrasov, *Barokko v Rossii* (Moscow, 1926), p. 19.

128. Appropriately, exceptions can be found in the decoration of provincial Russian churches – more difficult to control – where folk craftsmen were able to provide interiors with brightly colored religious statuary.

129. See Gatova, ''Iz istorii dekorativnoi skul'ptury Moskvy nachala XVIII v.,'' pp. 31–44.

130. A history of the Dormition Church, with archival photographs, is contained in G. V. Makarevich, ed., *Belyi gorod*, pp. 272–3, 279. The development of Pokrovka Street and the role of the church in defining that urban ensemble are analysed in O. I. Braitseva, ''Ob ansamble ul. Pokrovki kontsa XVII v. v Belom gorode Moskvy,'' *Arkhitekturnoe nasledstvo*, 28 (1980): 47–51. For an analysis of the complex order system of the Dormition Church, see Braitseva, ''Novoe i traditsionnoe,'' pp. 33–8.

131. A history of the Stroganov community at Solvychegodsk and its architectural patronage is presented in G. Bocharov and V. Vygolov, *Sol'vychegodsk. Velikii Ustiug. Tot'ma* (Moscow, 1983), with reference to the Presentation Cathedral on pp. 74–9. An authoritative monograph on the ''Stroganov style'' is O. I. Braitseva, *Stroganovskie postroiki rubezha XVII–XVIII vv.* (Moscow, 1977).

132. On the Stroganov church in Kazan, see S. Agafonov, *Gor'kii. Balakhna. Makar'ev* (Moscow, 1987), pp. 186–95 (with illustrations).

133. M. Fekhner, *Velikie Bulgary. Kazan'. Sviiazhsk*, pp. 98–9.

134. On the Pogankin Palaty, see Iu. P. Spegal'skii, *Pskov*, pp. 178–80.

135. The history of the Old English Court is summarized in Komech and Pluzhnikov, eds., *Tsentral'nye ploshchadi*, pp. 448–9.

136. O. P. Shchenkova analyzes the evolution of Kitai-gorod as a commercial center during the seventeenth century in "Kitai-gorod v strukture tsentra Moskvy XVII v," *Arkhitekturnoe nasledstvo*, 29 (1981): 56–62. Attempts to regulate city construction during the same period are examined in T. S. Proskuriakova, "O reguliarnosti v russkom gradostroitel'stve XVII-XVIII vv.," *Arkhitekturnoe nasledstvo*, 28 (1980): 37–46.

137. The increasing construction of masonry residences in the pre-Petrine period is examined in A. A. Tits, *Russkoe kamennoe zhiloe zodchestvo XVII v.* (Moscow, 1966). The same author has traced the increasing use of architectural "plans" during this period, both in the planning of entire lots and individual structures. He notes, however, that these sketches were of use primarily to the client rather than the builders, who continued to work in the traditional ways of measurement by sight and construction according to prototype (*po obraztsu*). See "Chertezh v russkoi stroitel'noi praktike XVII veka," in V. N. Lazarev, ed., *Drevnerusskoe iskusstvo: XVII vek* (Moscow, 1964), pp. 215–31.

138. The various layers of the mansion are examined in G. V. Alferova's detailed account of the restoration of the structure between 1954 and 1964, "Issledovanie i restavratsiia palat Averkiia Kirillova," *Iz istorii restavratsii pamiatnikov kul'tury* (Moscow, 1974), pp. 136–50.

139. Komech and Pluzhnikov, eds., *Tsentral'nye ploshchadi*, p. 126.

140. A formal analysis of the varieties of early eighteenth-century church architecture (based on a comprehensive sampling) is presented in V. I. Pluzhnikov, "Sootnoshenie ob"emnykh form v russkom kul'tovom zodchestve nachala XVIII veka," in T. V. Alekseeva, ed., *Russkoe iskusstvo pervoi chetverti XVIII veka* (Moscow, 1974), pp. 81–108.

141. A design similar to St. John the Warrior appeared in the small Cathedral of the Savior at the Zaikonospasskii Monastery. Located in Kitai-gorod on a constricted lot (formerly part of the St. Nicholas Monastery), the cathedral was begun in 1661 with the construction of the lower church (Moscow churches typically had a "warm" church beneath a more visible upper church with a different dedication). Between 1701 and 1709, this structure received a vestibule and the tower of the upper church. This small monastery was also the site of one of the most influential early centers of western education in Muscovy – the Slavonic–Greek–Latin Academy, founded in the 1660s by the humanist and poet Simeon Polotskii. In 1685–7, a "Collegium" was built for the school and much enlarged by Peter in the 1720s. See Komech and Pluzhnikov, eds., *Tsentral'nye ploshchadi*, pp. 417–18. For a historical description of the Zaikonospasskii Monastery, see Denisov, pp. 401–4.

142. On the construction of the Menshikov Tower, see G. V. Makarevich, ed., *Belyi gorod*, pp. 245–9. Although Zarudnyi's authorship of the church has been questioned, Vzdornov reaffirms his role as architect on the basis of documentary evidence. See "Zametki o pamiatnikakh russkoi arkhitektury kontsa XVII–nachala XVIII v.," pp. 25–30. The Italian–Swiss provenance of the interior sculpture is investigated in Gatova, "Iz istorii dekorativnoi skul'ptury Moskvy nachala XVIII v.," pp. 31–8.

143. After the building of Petersburg began in earnest, Menshikov resettled there in 1710, and the interior work on his Moscow church proceeded slowly. A lightning strike in 1723 not only toppled the wooden spire, but, during the ensuing fire, destroyed the supports for an English chiming clock and fifty bells, all of which plunged below, taking with them much of the vaulting and interior decoration. Although two attached chapels continued to function, the main structure was not rebuilt until 1773–9, at which time the uppermost octagonal tier was replaced with an elongated decorative cupola and the facades were stuccoed. The facade ornamentation, however, dates from the beginning of the eighteenth century – as does most of the structure. See Makarevich, ed., *Belyi gorod*, pp. 246–7.

144. An analysis of the construction history of the Lefortovo palace is R. P. Podol'skii, "Petrovskii dvorets na Iauze," *Arkhitekturnoe nasledstvo*, 1 (1951): 14–55. For contemporary examples of domestic architecture in Moscow in the early baroque period, see A. Petrov, "Palaty fel'dmarshala B. P. Sheremeteva i F. M. Apraksina v Moskve," *Arkhitekturnoe nasledstvo*, 6 (1956): 138–46.

145. Komech and Pluzhnikov, eds., *Tsentral'nye ploshchadi*, pp. 343–4. For a more detailed analysis of the Arsenal construction, see Iu. I. Arenkova, "Arsenal v Kremle. Istoriia stroitel'stva," in T. V. Alekseeva, ed., *Russkoe iskusstvo barokko: Materialy i issledovaniia* (Moscow, 1977), pp. 43–54.

Chapter 8

1. Books beyond counting have been published on Peter the Great and aspects of his reign. A recent survey of the topic and of the diplomatic moves surrounding his conduct of the Great Northern War is contained in Paul Dukes, *The Making of Russian Absolutism 1613–1801* (London–New York, 1982), pp. 59–101. For a selection of commentary on Peter from the classics of Russian historiography, see Marc Raeff, *Peter the Great: Reformer or Revolutionary* (Lexington, Mass., 1963). Also in English translation is Vasili Klyuchevsky, *Peter the Great* (New York, 1958). A recent authoritative Russian interpretation is E. Anisimov, *Vremia petrovskikh reform* (Leningrad, 1989).

2. The standard Soviet history of Petersburg's early years is M. P. Viatkin, ed., *Ocherki istorii Leningrada*, vol. 1, *Period feodalizma (1703–1861 gg.)* (Moscow–Leningrad, 1955). The most authoritative account of the planning and construction of Petersburg in its first decades is contained in S. P. Luppov, *Istoriia stroitel'stvo Peterburga v pervoi chetverti XVIII veka* (Moscow, 1957). A recent detailed study in English is James Cracraft, *The Petrine Revolution in Russian Architecture* (Chicago, 1988).

3. A. V. Bunin has argued that despite the frenetic construction of Petersburg's early history, a rational plan for its development was present from the beginning. See *Istoriia gradostroitel'nogo iskusstva* (Moscow, 1979), p. 410.

4. Luppov, pp. 78–81.

5. The Office of City Affairs (renamed the Office of Construction in 1723) is examined in E. Beletskaia et al., "*Obraztsovye" proekty v zhiloi zastroike russkikh gorodov XVIII–XIX vv.* (Moscow, 1961), pp. 14–15, passim. Attempts to legislate construction codes during the Petrine period are examined in T. M. Sytina, "Russkoe arkhitekturnoe zakonodatel'stvo pervoi cherverti XVIII v," *Arkhitekturnoe naslsedstvo*, 18 (1969): 67–73.

6. Timber and grain were particularly vital to the functioning of Petersburg, and both depended on uncertain access through waterways to the interior of the country. For Menshikov's involvement in these logistic matters as governor of St. Petersburg, see N. I. Pavlenko, *Aleksandr Danilovich Menshikov* (Moscow, 1983), pp. 77–9.

7. Luppov, p. 50.

8. For an analysis of Peter's voyage to Europe as it affected his artistic tastes, see V. F. Levinson-Lessing, "Pervoe puteshestvie Petra I za granitsu," in G. N. Komelova, ed., *Kul'tura i iskusstvo petrovskogo vremeni* (Leningrad, 1977), pp. 5–36. The considerable evidence of Peter's direct involvement in the design of Petersburg is presented in M. V. Iogansen, "Ob avtore general'nogo plana Peterburga petrovskogo vremeni," in T. V. Alekseeva, ed., *Ot Srednevekov'ia k Novomu vremeni* (Moscow, 1984), pp. 50–72, esp. pp. 66–7.

9. On Trezzini's designs for model (*obraztsovye*) houses, see N. Krasheninnikova, V. Shilkov, "Proekty obraztsovykh zagorodnykh domov D. Trezini i zastroika beregov Fontanki," *Arkhitekturnoe nasledstvo*, 7 (1955): 5–12. Peter's commission of standardized designs from Trezzini (and, in 1717, from Le Blond) has been studied as part of a long Russian tradition of rapid, standardized construction. See E. Beletskaia et al., "*Obraztsovye" proekty v zhiloi zastroike russkikh gorodov XVIII–XIX vv.* (Moscow, 1961); and S. S. Ozhegov, *Tipovoe i povtornoe stroitel'stvo v Rossii v XVIII–XIX vekakh* (Moscow, 1984), pp. 16–23, with reproductions of Trezzini's model houses designed in 1714.

10. For a comprehensive history of the development of Vasilevskii Island (particularly its point, or *strelka*), see M. S. Bunin, *Strelka Vasilevskogo ostrova* (Moscow–Leningrad, 1957). Trezzini's involvement in the development of Vasilevskii Island is analyzed in M. V. Iogansen, "Raboty D. Trezini po planirovke i zastroike Strelki Vasil'evskogo ostrova," in T. V. Alekseeva, ed., *Russkoe iskusstvo XVIII v.* (Moscow, 1973), pp. 45–55.

11. A contemporary account of the construction chaos is reproduced in S. L. Ptashitskii, "Peterburg v 1720 godu. Zapiski poliaka-ochevidtsa," *Russkaia starina*, 25 (1879): 267–73. See also excerpts from F. C. Weber, *The Present State of Russia* (London, 1723), quoted or paraphrased in Cracraft, pp. 198–210. Charming sketches of the rustic appearance of Petersburg between 1718 and 1722 by Fedor Vasil'ev are contained in E. I. Gavrilova, " 'Sankt Piterburkh' 1718–1722 goda v naturnykh risunkakh Fedora Vasil'eva," in T. V.

Alekseeva, ed., *Russkoe iskusstvo pervoi chetverti XVIII veka* (Moscow, 1974), pp. 119–40. A broader, more stately view of the city appears in a remarkable panorama executed by the engraver Aleksei Zubov for Peter in 1716. An analysis of the panorama, which conveys perhaps our most accurate view of early Petrine architecture in Petersburg is contained in G. N. Komelova, " 'Panorama Peterburga' – graviura raboty A. F. Zubova," in G. N. Komelova, ed., *Kul'tura i iskusstvo petrovskogo vremeni* (Leningrad, 1977), pp. 111–43. Superb reproductions of this and other early views of the city are contained in Iu. M. Denisov et al., *Gorod glazami khudozhnikov: Peterburg–Petrograd–Leningrad v proizvedeniiakh zhivopisi i grafiki* (Leningrad, 1978). See also A. N. Voronikhina, *Peterburg i ego okrestnosti v chertezhakh i risunkakh arkhitektorov pervoi treti XVIII veka* (Leningrad, 1972).

12. For Le Blond's response to the initial work at Petersburg, see M. V. Iogansen, "Ob avtore general'nogo plana Peterburga petrovskogo vremeni," pp. 61–2. A detailed analysis of Le Blond's contributions to the development of architecture in Petersburg is provided in N. V. Kaliazina, "Arkhitektor Leblon v Rossii (1716–1719)," in Alekseeva, *Ot Srednevekov'ia k novomu vremeni*, pp. 94–123. See also I. A. Egorov, *The Architectural Planning of Saint Petersburg: Its development in the 18th and 19th Centuries* (Athens, Ohio, 1969), pp. 11–26; and T. F. Savarenskaia et al., *Istoriia gradostroitle'nogo iskusstva. Pozdnii feodalizm i kapitalizm* (Moscow, 1989), pp. 107–9.

13. Iogansen, "Ob avtore general'nogo plana Peterburga petrovskogo vremeni," p. 64. In defense of Le Blond's plan, see Kaliazina, "Arkhitektor Leblon," pp. 114–15.

14. Iogansen suggests that the system of three radial prospects was a "paraphrase on a purely Russian scale" of the design at Versailles. "Ob avtore general'nogo plana Peterburga petrovskogo vremeni," p. 67. She also notes, however, that it is difficult to distinguish the prospects among the various streets radiating from the Admiralty on early maps (ibid.). Apparently the earliest extant map with the three prospects clearly indicated is a plan for the protection of the city against flooding, drawn up in 1727 by the governor-general, Count Buchard Christoph Münnich. See Luppov, p. 53, with a reproduction on p. 55.

15. Igor' Grabar', *Istoriia russkogo iskusstva*, vol. 3 (Moscow, 1912), p. 10.

16. In recent years, the evolution of architectural thought in Russia at the turn of the eighteenth century and in the following decades has been the subject of much study. In her monograph on early modern Russian architectural theory, N. A. Evsina demonstrates that Peter and this agents did not simply invite foreign architects to Russia, but made a comprehensive effort to assimiliate, to create a new architectural language (in every sense). See *Arkhitekturnaia teoriia v Rossii XVIII v.* (Moscow, 1975), and particularly Chapter 2. See also N. A. Evsina, "Iz istorii arkhitekturnykh vzgliadov i teorii nachala XVIII veka," in Alekseeva, *Russkoe iskusstvo pervoi chetverti XVIII veka*, pp. 9–26. As Evsina indicates (pp. 36–8), this assimilation involved the rapid translation of classic architectural treatises, of which the first to

be published was that of Vignola, appearing in Russian editions in 1709, 1712, and 1722. Vitruvius also existed in an early Russian translation, which although unpublished was widely disseminated. See V. Shilkov, "Russkii perevod Vitruviia nachala XVIII veka," *Arkhitekturnoe nasledstvo*, 7 (1955): 89–92; and A. Tits, "Neizvestnyi russkii traktat po arkhitekture," in Alekseeva, *Russkoe iskusstvo XVIII v.* (1968), pp. 17–31. More specifically on the language of architecture, see E. P. Zenkevich and G. S. Lebedeva, "Evoliutsiia poniatiia 'teoriia' i 'praktika' v russkoi arkhitektunoi mysli XVIII veka," *Arkhitekturnoe nasledstvo*, 36 (1988): 94–105. Peter the Great's own numerous directives on matters of design and construction had a considerable effect on the development of a critical consciousness toward architectural style in Russia. See S. P. Zavarikhin, *Russkaia arkhitekturnaia kritika seredina XIII–nachalo XX vv.* (Leningrad, 1989), pp. 42, 44.

The role of foreigners in the formation of Russian cadres is examined in E. A. Borisova, " 'Arkhitekturnye ucheniki' petrovskogo vremeni i ikh obuchenie v komandakh zodchikh-inostrantsev v Peterburge," in Alekseeva, *Russkoe iskusstvo pervoi chetverti XVIII veka*, pp. 9–26.

17. A detailed study of Trezzini's life, with archival references and a comprehensive chronological listing of his work but with a text bordering on the chaotic, is Iu. M. Ovsiannikov, *Dominiko Trezini* (Leningrad, 1987). Trezzini is also the subject of two monographs by Irina Lisaevich, *Pervyi arkhitektor Peterburga* (Leningrad, 1971); and *Domeniko Trezini* (Leningrad, 1986).

18. For an early eighteenth-century view of Kronshlot, situated in shallows off the southeast point of Kotlin Island, see N. D. Kremshevskaia, "Kronshtadt," in A. N. Petrov et al., *Pamiatniki arkhitektury prigorodov Leningrada* (Leningrad, 1983), p. 542, with map and further description on pp. 540–1.

19. Ovsiannikov, *Trezini*, p. 36.

20. Peter's knowledge of fortifications is examined in regard to his plan, implemented by Trezzini, for the fortress of Shlisselburg (formerly the Swedish fort Noteburg, or, in Russian, Oreshek) on the upper reaches of the Neva in M. V. Iogansen and A. N. Kirpichnikov, " 'Petrovskii Shlissel'burg' (po novootkrytym arkhivnym materialam)," in Alekseeva, *Russkoe iskusstvo pervoi chetverti XVIII veka*, pp. 27–52. For a survey of the historical development of this key fortress, see Iu. M Gogolitsyn et al., *Pamiatniki arkhitektury Leningradskoi Oblasti* (Leningrad, 1987), pp. 88–99.

21. Clockwise from the upper bastion on the Neva River, nthe bastions were named (with the beginning dates of their masonry construction): Peter I (1717), Naryshkin (later Catherine; 1725), Trubetskoi (1708), Zotov (1707), Golovkin (later Anna; 1707), and Menshikov (later Peter II; 1706). The bastions were long under construction: the first (Menshikov) bastion was not completed until 1729, and the others were continued after Trezzini's death by Ch. A. Minnich. In the 1770s and 1780s, the walls and bastions on the Neva side were faced with granite. See A. N. Petrov et al., *Pamiatniki arkhitektury Leningrada* (Leningrad, 1972), p. 29.

22. The original Peter Gate statuary was transferred to the rebuilt gates, but by 1722, Peter wished to have it recreated in a more durable medium to accompany the two-headed imperial eagle cast in lead by F. Wassoult. The sculptor Bartolomeo Carlo Rastrelli was the original choice for this work, but Peter rejected his bid as too expensive. Although Saint Peter and four flanking allegorical statues have not been preserved, the existing sculpture, completed after Peter's death, is now attributed to Nicolas Pineau. See Petrov, *Pamiatniki arkhitektury Leningrada*, pp. 31, 33; and Ovsiannikov, p. 39.

23. For a description of the Peter's Dutch carillon, which cost the very considerable sum of 45,000 rubles, see Edward V. Williams, *The Bells of Russia: History and Technology* (Princeton, 1985), pp. 82–4; 291, n. 15.

24. A list of the Russian painters who decorated the interior of the cathedral is included in Petrov, *Pamiatniki arkhitektury Leningrada*, p. 29.

25. Ibid., and Ovsiannikov, *Trezini*, pp. 101–2, for brief accounts – with unresolved questions – on the making of the iconostasis.

26. For commentary on the relation between Prokopovich (1681–1736) and Peter, see James Cracraft, "Feofan Prokopovich," in J. G. Garrard, ed., *The Eighteenth Century in Russia* (Oxford, 1973), pp. 75–105.

27. The original appearance of the church is discussed in E. Timofeeva, "Pervonachal'nyi oblik Petropavlovskogo sobora," *Arkhitekturnoe nasledstvo*, 7 (1955): 93–108.

28. See A. I. Kudriavtsev and G. N. Shkoda, *Aleksandro-Nevskaia Lavra: Arkhitekturnyi ansambl' i pamiatniki Nekropolei* (Leningrad, 1986), p. 6.

29. The coffin of Alexander Nevskii was taken from the Nativity Monastery in Vladimir in August 1723, and remained at the Schlisselburg fortress until August 1724, when it was solemnly transferred to the monastery Church of the Annunciation and of Alexander Nevskii to celebrate the third anniversary of the Treaty of Nystadt.

30. The model of Schwertfeger's cathedral is reproduced in ibid., p. 14. The same work gives a detailed survey of the monastery's complicated construction history and frequent changes of architects.

31. Leibniz was greatly impressed by Peter the Great, both as a person and as one who could, it seemed, implement rational premises in government on a far greater scale than possible elsewhere in Europe. Yet western thinkers who approved of Peter's vast intentions (Leibniz was by no means alone) ignored the brutal and frequently irrational manner with which these ideas were applied. (A contrary view of Peter the Great and his western admirers is trenchantly expressed in Princess Dashkov's memoirs, republished in Russian as Ekaterina Dashkova, *Zapiski: 1743–1810* [Leningrad, 1985], pp. 126–8.) Leibniz's letters and other writings concerning Peter are collected in *Sbornik pisem i memrialov Leibnitsa, otnosiashchikhsia k Rossii i Petru I* (St. Petersburg, 1873). Briefly on the Colleges, see Dukes, *The Making of Russian Absolutism*, pp. 75–6.

32. See B. R. Vipper, *Arkhitektura russkogo barokko* (Moscow, 1978), p. 44. (This edition of Vipper's collected writings on the Russian baroque includes not only his original notes, but also a thorough, updated annotation by N. A. Evsina.) In 1714, Trezzini had developed a similar concept for a temporary, timber-framed (Fachwerk) Senate office building, located at Trinity Square on the northern, Petersburgh Side of the city. See M. V. Iogansen, "Zdanie 'mazankovykh kollegii' na Troitskoi ploshchadi Peterburga," in Alekseeva, *Ot Srednevekov'ia k novomu vremeni*, pp. 73–86.

33. The design and construction of the Twelve Colleges are described in Petrov, *Pamiatniki arkhitektury Leningrada*, p. 94; and Ovsiannikov, *Trezini*, pp. 126–9.

34. For site plans of the tip of Vasilevskii Island, with the outlines of the cathedral, see Iogansen, "Raboty D. Trezini po planirovke i zastroike Strelki Vasil'evskogo ostrova," Plates 22, 26, 27. A section sketch of the Tessin design for the cathedral is contained in A. N. Voronikhina et al., *Arkhitekturnaia grafika Rossii: Pervaia polovina XVIII veka* (Leningrad, 1981), p. 138.

35. Additional information on Swedish builders in Petersburg is provided in L. N. Semenova, "Uchastie shvedskikh masterovykh v stroitel'stve Peterburga (pervaia chetvert' XVIII v.)," in *Istoricheskie sviazi Skandinavii i Rossii. IX–XX vv.* (Leningrad, 1970).

36. *Pamiatniki arkhitektury Leningrada*, p. 221.

37. The architects involved in constructing the Kunstkammer were Nicolaus-Friedrich Härbel (a Swiss architect who worked in Petersburg from 1719 until his death in 1724), Gaetano Chiaveri, and Mikhail Zemtsov, who finished the building. Zemtsov will be discussed in what follows. An analysis of Chiaveri's work in Petersburg is contained in V. F. Shilkov, "Dve raboty arkhitektora Kiaveri v Rossii," *Arkhitekturnoe nasledstvo*, 9 (1959): 61–4. The upper part of the Kunstkammer tower was destroyed by fire in 1747 and not rebuilt in Savva Chevakinskii's restoration of the structure in 1754–8. It remained in this state until a postwar reconstruction in 1947 (the two-hundredth anniversary of the fire). See *Pamiatniki arkhitektury Leningrada*, p. 95.

38. For the link between Schlüter and the design of the Kunstkammer, see Grabar', *Istoriia russkogo iskusstva*, vol. 3, p. 78; and, more generally on Schlüter's work in Russia, V. S. Voinov, "Andreas Shliuter – arkhitektor Petra (K voprosu o formirovanii stilia 'Petrovskoe barokko')," *Sovetskoe iskusstvoznanie*, 1976, no. 1: 367–77.

39. The construction of the first two masonry Winter Palaces (there had been an earlier one of wood) is described, with a selection of early engravings, in Iu. M. Denisov, "Ischeznuvshie dvortsy," in V. I. Piliavskii and V. F. Levinson-Lessing, *Ermitazh: Istoriia i arkhitektura zdaniia* (Leningrad, 1974), pp. 23–6. See also Ovsiannikov, pp. 141–7, and Plates 33–6. Ovsiannikov recounts (p. 147) the discovery by G. Mikhailov and V. Galochkin in 1985 of some 20

meters of the original Mattarnovy wall incorporated into Giacomo Quarenghi's Hermitage Theater (see Chapter 10). For a reproduction of Mattarnovy's palace plan and elevation in the Hermitage State Museum archives, see Voronikhina, *Arkhitekturnaia grafika Rossii*, pp. 59–60.

40. The design of the Summer Garden, laid out in the Dutch style, is described in T. B. Dubiago, *Letnii sad* (Moscow–Leningrad, 1951). The Summer Garden marble statuary, primarily late seventeenth- and early eighteenth-century Italian work purchased by Peter, served as yet another means of propagating a cultural revolution in the Russian context. See O. Ia. Neverov, "Pamiatniki antichnogo iskusstva v Rossii petrovskogo vremeni," in Komelova, *Kul'tura i iskusstvo petrovskogo vremeni*, pp. 46–53. An account of the shock created by the statues is presented in Ovsiannikov, pp. 68–70. On the cultural function of the Petrine gardens, see A. P. Vergunov and V. A. Gorokhov, *Russkie sady i parki* (Moscow, 1988), pp. 39–70.

41. N. V. Kaliazina provides a documented survey of interior paintings in Petrine palaces in "Monumental'no-dekorativnaia zhivopis' v dvortsovom inter'ere pervoi chetverti XVIII veka (k probleme razvitiia stilia barokko v Rossii)," in T. V. Alekseeva, ed., *Russkoe iskusstvo barokko* (Moscow, 1977), pp. 55–69, esp. pp. 64–5, n. 2.

42. For a detailed study of the Menshikov Palace, see N. V. Kaliazina et al., *Dvorets Menshikova* (Moscow, 1986). An engraving of the palace in 1716 by A. I. Rostovtsev, and reconstructions by G. Mikhailov and V. Galochkin of its appearance in two successive stages are contained in Ovsiannikov, Plates 22–4.

43. The ceiling paintings are analyzed in Kaliazina, "Monumental'no-dekorativnaia zhivopis'," pp. 58–9. A similarly informed analysis of the plaster work is contained in N. V. Kaliazina, "Lepnoi dekor v zhilom inter'ere Peterburga pervoi chetverti XVIII veka," in Alekseeva, *Russkoe iskusstvo pervoi chetverti XVIII veka*, pp. 111–12.

44. See A. Tits, "Neizvestnyi russkii traktat po arkhitekture," p. 29, with reference to use of the composite order in Menshikov's 1707 rebuilding of the Lefortovo Palace in Moscow.

45. See Petrov, *Pamiatniki arkhitektury prigorodov Leningrada*, pp. 550–1, with Ottomar Elliger's 1727 engraving and a photograph of the current, much altered state of the palace. Braunstein also built a palace for the tsar on Kotlin Island, which had in 1712 been considered by Peter as a major settlement for the new capital, and not simply a naval citadel. See Luppov, pp. 26–8.

46. See A. Petrov, "Palaty Kikina," *Arkhitekturnoe nasledstvo*, 4 (1953): 141–7; and Petrov, *Pamiatniki arkhitektury Leningrada*, p. 221. Adapted for use by the Horse Guards in the 1730s, the building was modified by Bartolomeo Rastrelli. Extensive shell damage during World War II allowed a restoration to its original appearance.

47. For a reproduction of Braunstein's 1716 site plan of Peterhof, see Voronikhina, *Arkhitekturnaia grafika Rossii*, p. 28. Ibid., pp. 117–18, for Peter's own guiding sketches

of Peterhof, which are discussed in V. Shilkov, "Chetyre risunka Petra I po planirovke Petergofa," *Arkhitekturnoe nasledstvo*, 4 (1953): 35–40. There are many studies of and guides to Peterhof, including the detailed and authoritative A. G. Raskin, N. I. Arkipov, "Petrodvorets," in Petrov, *Pamiatniki arkhitektury prigorodov Leningrada*, pp. 322–479. The most comprehensive photographic survey, with commentary on individual rooms within the palaces, is Abram Raskin, *Petrodvorets (Petergof)* (Leningrad, 1979); also available in English.

48. Le Blond's French antecedents are traced in Kaliazina, "Arkhitektor Leblon v Rossii," pp. 102; 116, n. 3; with particular reference to his supplement in the 1710 (second) edition of A. C. D'Aviler's popular *Cours d'Architecture...*, first published in 1691. An exhaustive analysis of the development of interior space in Russian palaces and mansions is presented, with diagrams, in L. V. Tydman, "Razvitie vnutrennego prostranstva domov-dvortsov 1700–1760-kh godov," in *Ot Srednevekov'ia k novomu vremeni*, pp. 180–210.

49. For a survey of construction during the first decade of the main palace, see *Pamiatniki arkhitektury prigorodov Leningrada*, pp. 344–6. Engravings of the palace as it existed in 1717 and in 1724, after the extension by Michetti, are reproduced in I. M. Gurevich et al., *Bol'shoi petergofskii dvorets* (Leningrad, 1979), pp. 13–15.

50. See Kaliazina, "Monumental'no-dekorativnaia zhivopis'," pp. 59–61, with an inventory of Pillement's other work, pp. 64–5. Photographs of the State Hall are contained in Raskin, pp. 291–301. On the postwar restoration of "Mon plaisir," see A. Gessen and M. Tikhomirova. "Raboty po restavratsii dvortsa Monplesir v Petrodvortse," in *Teoriia i praktika restavratsionnykh rabot* (Moscow, 1972), pp. 99–108.

51. On the Petrine canals, which failed to realize their promise, see R. A. French, "Canals in Pre-Revolutionary Russia," in J. H. Bater and R. A. French, eds., *Studies in Russian Historical Geography*, vol. 2 (London, 1983). The extensive system of waterways, including the 24-kilometer Ropshinskii Canal, that fed the parks at Petrodvorets is described in *Pamiatniki arkhitektury prigorodov Leningrada*, pp. 440–3. One of the most intricate aquatic ensembles, the "Chessboard Hill" Cascade (also known as the Dragon Cascade) leading to the two Roman Fountains, is examined in V. F. Shilkov, "Kaskad 'Shakhmatnaia gora' i 'Rimskie' fontany v Petrodvortse," *Arkhitekturnoe nasledstvo*, 9 (1959): 176–80.

52. The Hermitage was extensively redecorated by Rastrelli in 1756–7, but the basic design remains untouched. See *Pamiatniki arkhitektury prigorodov Leningrada*, pp. 426–7.

53. In 1743–4, before Rastrelli began his work at Tsarskoe Selo, Mikhail Zemtsov had devised a plan for extending the palace with galleries and end pavilions. His model gives an idea of the original Braunstein structure. See A. N. Petrov, *Gorod Pushkin. Dvortsy i parki* (Leningrad, 1977), pp. 12–13.

54. *Pamiatniki arkhitektury prigorodov Leningrada*, p. 480. Although Oranienbaum, renamed Lomonosov in 1948, was in the battle zone from the fall of 1941 to January 1944, it remained in Russian hands as a bridgehead on the south shore of the Gulf of Finland. The palace, therefore, emerged relatively intact, but its interior had already been much changed in the late eighteenth and nineteenth centuries. See also G. I. Solosina, *Gorod Lomonosov (Oranienbaum)* (Moscow, 1954); and the profusely illustrated A. G. Raskin, *Gorod Lomonosov: Dvortsovo-parkovye ansambli XVIII veka* (Leningrad, 1979). Menshikov also commissioned other, smaller residences closer to the imperial estates. See T. Dubiago, "Usad'by petrovskogo vremeni v okrestnostiakh Peterburga," *Arkhitekturnoe nasledstvo*, 4 (1953): 125–41.

55. On Makhaev's drawings (including Oranienbaum) and the two collections of engravings made from them, see G. N. Komelova, *Vidy Peterburga i ego okrestnostei serediny XVIII veka* (Leningrad, 1968); and Komelova, "K istorii sozdaniia gravirovannykh vidov Peterburga i ego okrestnostei M. I. Makhaevym." *Trudy Gosudarstvennogo Ermitazha*, 11 (1970): 36–56.

56. For the wooden residence at Strelna, see Petrov, *Pamiatniki arkhitektury prigorodov Leningrada*, pp. 596–9.

57. Le Blond's sketches of the original designs of the Strelna palace and one pavilion are reproduced in Voronikhina, *Arkhitekturnaia grafika Rossii*, pp. 55–6. Plans of the palace and grounds are provided in *Pamiatniki arkhitektury prigorodov Leningrada*, pp. 580–94.

58. On the Catherinental Palace, see V. Raam, *Arkhitekturnye pamiatniki Estonii* (Leningrad, 1974), pp. 96–7; M. Lumiste, *Kadriorgskii dvorets* (Tallin, 1976); and Vipper, p. 52, with photographs of the White Hall, pp. 173–4. For a broader survey of Michetti's Russian work, see G. G. Grimm, "Proekty arkhitektora N. Miketti dlia Peterburga i ego okrestnostei v sobranii Gosudarstvennogo Ermitazha," *Soobshcheniia Gosudarstvennogo Ermitazha*, 13 (1958): 21–4.

59. This and other biographical details are provided in M. V. Iogansen's monograph on the architect, *Mikhail Zemtsov* (Leningrad, 1975).

60. Sketches of the Summer Garden and Zemtsov's work therein are reproduced in Iogansen, *Mikhail Zemtsov*, pp. 32–4, 36, 38, 52; see also Voronikhina, *Arkhitekturnaia grafika Rossii*, pp. 43–50, with some differences in identification.

61. For a concise discussion of the events surrounding the accession of Anna Ioannovna, and of her place among eighteenth-century Russian autocrats, see Dukes, *The Making of Russian Absolutism*, pp. 104–10, passim.

62. A survey of Korobov's work is contained in V. Piliavskii, "Ivan Kuz'mich Korobov," *Arkhitekturnoe nasledstvo*, 4 (1953): 41–62; and P. Podol'skii, "Ivan Korobov," *Sovetskaia arkhitektura*, 3 (1952): 105–16.

63. See E. Moskalenko, "Shpil' Admiralteistva i ego konstruktsiia," *Arkhitekturnoe nasledstvo*, 4 (1953): 177–8.

Chapter 9

1. Because of seasonal fluctuations in the work force of Petersburg, and for lack of comprehensive statistical data, there is little agreement on the early population of the city until 1750, when a census of adults provides the basis for an estimated total population of 95,000. See G. I. Kochin, "Naselenie Peterburga do 60-kh godov XVIII v.," in *Ocherki istorii Leningrada*, vol. 1, pp. 102–3.

2.   An analysis of common housing design in Petersburg is contained in A. N. Petrov, "Peterburgskii zhiloi dom 30–40-kh godov XVIII stoletiia," *Ezhegodnik Instituta istorii iskusstv 1960. Zhivopis' i arkhitektura* (Moscow, 1961), pp. 132–57.

3.   As architect of the Ministry (college) of the Admiralty, Korobov would have been a likely choice to design the Church of St. Panteleimon, dedicated to naval victories. For brief comments on the history of the building, see *Pamiatniki arkhitektury Leningrada*, p. 267.

4.   Iogansen, *Mikhail Zemtsov*, pp. 104–6. Iogansen notes that due to the unpopularity of Anne's reign, the fires were rumored to be the work of arsonists (p. 105). This is an accusation that would be repeated after subsequent great fires in Petersburg during times of social and political unrest (as, for example, in 1863).

5.   On the work of the commission, see V. Shilkov, "Proekty planirovki Peterburga 1737–1740 godov," *Arkhitekturnoe nasledstvo*, 4 (1953): 7–13; and A. I. Gegello and V. F. Shilkov, "Arkhitektura i planirovka Peterburga do 60-kh godov XVIII v," in *Ocherki istorii Leningrada*, vol. 1, pp. 138–41. A reproduction of the 1737 Petersburg map, published by the Academy of Sciences in 1741, is contained in ibid., pp. 144–5. As the military topographer Johann von Sichheim provided the maps for the newly defined five parts of the city, Eropkin would plot his recommendations for construction. See Iogansen, *Mikhail Zemtsov*, pp. 107–9. A broader view of the planning and development of Petersburg in the 1730–40s is provided in N. F. Gulianitskii, "Gradostroitel'nye osobennosti Peterburga i cherty russkoi arkhitektury serediny XVIII v.," *Arkhitekturnoe nasledstvo*, 27 (1979): 12–21.

6.   Ibid., pp. 109–18.

7.   The treatise was first published as "Dolzhnost' Arkhitekturnoi Ekspeditsii. Traktat-kodeks 1737–1740," with an introduction by D. Arkin, in *Arkhitekturnyi arkhiv*, 1 (1946): 7–100. For a detailed analysis of its contents, see Evsina, *Arkhitekturnaia teoriia v Rossii XVIII v.*, pp. 78–93.

8.   Iogansen, *Zemtsov*, pp. 43–4. A more detailed survey of architectural education in the mideighteenth century is provided in E. A. Borisova, "Arkhitekturnoe obrazovanie v Kantseliarii ot stroenii vo vtoroi chetverti XVIII veka," in *Ezhegodnik Instituta istorii iskusstv 1960. Zhivopis' i arkhitektura* (Moscow, 1961), pp. 97–109.

9.   Arkin, *Arkhitekturnyi arkhiv*, p. 9.

10.   See Iogansen, *Zemtsov*, pp. 119–20, for other repercussions of the repression among architects associated with Eropkin.

11.   There have been numerous surveys of Rastrelli's work, among which one of the most perceptive is B. R. Vipper, *Arkhitektura russkogo barokko*, pp. 65–94. Subsequent studies include D. Arkin, *Rastrelli* (Moscow, 1954), and Iu. M. Denisov and A. N. Petrov, *Zodchii Rastrelli: Materialy k izucheniiu*

tvorchestva (Leningrad, 1963), which includes a comprehensive listing of known Rastrelli graphic material in Russian, Polish, Swedish, and Austrian collections. A recent monograph is Iu. Ovsiannikov, *Franchesko Bartolomeo Rastrelli* (Leningrad, 1982). Certain Soviet scholars have attempted to standardize the Rastrellis' names as Bartolomeo Carlo and Francesco Bartolomeo. See, for example, Iu. M. Ovsiannikov, "Novye materialy o zhizni i tvorchestve F.-B. Rastrelli, *Sovetskoe iskusstvoznanie '79*, Moscow, 1980, no. 1; and T. V. Alekseeva, "Franchesko-Bartolomeo Rastrelli i russkaia kul'tura," in T. V. Alekseeva, ed., *Ot Srednevekov'ia k novomu vremeni* (Moscow, 1984), p. 140, n. 1. The present volume will continue, however, to present the order of their names as used by Boris Vipper and standard western biographical sources.

12.   Vipper, *Arkhitektura russkogo barokko*, p. 67.

13.   For Antiokh Kantemir's amusing reference to Rastrelli's skill as a decorator of buildings, see ibid., p. 67.

14.   P. N. Petrov, an early student of Rastrelli's work, suggested that he returned to Europe twice, in the early 1720s and again in 1725 (cf. "Materialy dlia biografii grafa Rastrelli," *Zodchii*, 1876, 5: 55). Vipper (p. 67) accepts only the latter date as plausible. Hamilton is sceptical of any suggestion that he returned to Paris, but argues that his work shows a familiarity with the baroque of Austria and Northern Italy – a knowledge that he might have gained either by travel or by the study of published editions of the set designs and architectural engravings of Ferdinando and Giuseppe Balli Bibiena. See George Heard Hamilton, *The Art and Architecture of Russia* (Baltimore, 1975), pp. 196, 305, nn. 12, 13.

15.   For questions raised by ambiguous court documents concerning the Rastrellis' respective roles in projects of the early 1730s, see Ovsiannikov, *Rastrelli*, pp. 29–31. Bartolomeo Francesco Rastrelli's detailed summary of his work, compiled in 1764, lists the major projects as his own.

16.   A thorough study of the Annenhof palaces is provided in O. S. Evangulova, *Dvortsovo-parkovye ansambli Moskvy pervoi poloviny XVIII veka* (Moscow, 1969). For reproductions of project drawings, see Denisov and Petrov, *Zodchii Rastrelli*, Plates 1–38.

17.   Denisov and Petrov, *Zodchii Rastrelli*, Plates 57–71.

18.   For a history of the construction of the Third Winter Palace, with plans and elevation sketches, see Denisov, "Ischeznuvshie dvortsy," pp. 26–35. A more detailed catalogue of project drawings is contained in Denisov and Petrov, Plates 128–61. On the history of the Makhaev drawings, see G. N. Komelova, "K istorii sozdaniia gravirovannykh vidov Peterburga i ego okrestnostei M. I. Makhaevym," *Trudy Gosudarstvennogo Ermitazha*, 11 (1970): 36–56. Makhaev's drawings of the Winter Palace are described and reproduced in Komelova, *Vidy Peterburga*, pp. 14–24.

19.   Rastrelli's 1764 inventory (*relatsiia*) of work completed was first published in Z. Batowski, *Architekt Rastrelli o swych pracach* (Lwow, 1939), and republished in Russian in "Materialy o zhizni i tvorchestve Franchesko Bartolomeo Ras-

563

trelli," in *Soobscheniia kabineta teorii i istorii arkhitektury SSSR,* 1 (1940), 17–38; with an introductory article by D. Arkin. The foregoing passage is quoted on p. 31.

20. Denisov, "Ischeznuvshie dvortsy," pp. 29. With the rebuilding of the palace in the 1750s, the Amber Study was reinstalled in the Catherine Palace at Tsarskoe Selo, where it remained until its disappearance, or destruction, during World War II. Although the room is being recreated at the Catherine Palace with the help of prewar photographs, the mystery of its disappearance continues to engage German writers. See Karl-Heinz Janssen, "Grossfahndung nach dem Bernsteinzimmer," *Die Zeit,* 47 (November 24, 1984): 12–14.

21. A description of Rastrelli's work for Biron is provided in Boris Vipper's chapter "Rastrelli v Pribaltike" in his *Arkhitektura russkogo barokko,* pp. 86–94. For a more detailed study, see the same author's *Baroque Art in Latvia* (Riga, 1939). Vipper notes (p. 88) that the designs for Ruhental and Mitau (held at the Albertine in Vienna) were ready in 1734, when Biron had already become the de facto ruler of Courland.

22. Ovsiannikov offers a colorful account of the expense of the Mitau palace in *Rastrelli,* pp. 49–52.

23. The text of the petition is reproduced in Ovsiannikov, *Rastrelli,* pp. 66–67 (archival reference: TsGADA, f. 17, ed. khr. 298, 11. 7–8). Vipper seems to have been unaware of this document and the circumstances surrounding it. In *Arkhitektura russkogo barokko,* p. 71, he states that the indispensable Rastrelli suffered no loss of rank or pay during the transition between rulers. In 1744, the architect's father, who had completed some of his best statuary at the end of Anne's reign, died at the age of 74.

24. Ovsiannikov, *Rastrelli,* p. 72.

25. On the construction of the Third Summer Palace, see Denisov and Petrov, *Zodchii Rastrelli,* p. 9, and Figures 75–127. Details from the Makhaev engraving and a plan of the palace are presented in Ovsiannikov, *Rastrelli,* Plates 21–5.

26. Vipper, *Arkhitektura russkogo barokko,* p. 72.

27. Arguments in support of Zemtsov's authorship of the Anichkov Palace and a reproduction of the main facade elevation by his assistant Grigorii Dmitriev (who died in 1746) are contained in Iogansen, *Mikhail Zemtsov,* pp. 129–30. For a chronicle of modifications to the palace, see *Pamiatniki arkhitektury Leningrada,* p. 155–6.

28. For an analysis of the evolution of Rastrelli's use of the enfilade, see Vipper, *Arkhitektura russkogo barokko,* p. 77.

29. A survey of work on the interior of the Peterhof palace is contained in N. I. Arkhipov and A. G. Raskin, *Petrodvorets* (Leningrad–Moscow, 1961), pp. 47–51. Detailed photographic documentation and a description of individual rooms are also found in Raskin, *Petrodvorets (Petergof)* (Leningrad, 1979), pp. 57–81, with a list of rooms by Rastrelli, pp. 337–8. See also the chapter on Petrodvorets by Raskin and Arkhipov in *Pamiatniki arkhitektury prigorodov Leningrada,* pp. 344–71.

30. Biographical information on the work of Tarsia and Valeriani in Russia is contained in notes compiled by Jacob von Stählin, a Swabian poet who was invited to join the Russian Academy of Sciences (founded in 1724). Soon after his arrival, in 1735, Stählin was appointed professor of elocution at the Academy, where he chronicled the lives of artists in Russia until 1783. His notes on painting were first published in Russian in "(Ia. Shtelin) Zapiski o zhivopisi i zhivopistsakh v Rossii," Alekseeva, ed., *Russkoe iskusstvo barokko* (Moscow, 1977), pp. 180–211; with the accompanying article by K. V. Malinovskii, "Iakob fon Shtelin i ego zapiski po istorii russkoi zhivopisi XVIII veka," ibid., pp. 173–9.

31. Catherine the Great, *Zapiski Imperatritsy Ekateriny Vtoroi* (St. Petersburg, 1907), pp. 120–1. Rastrelli himself complained about the need to spend an inordinate amount of time supervising work at Tsarskoe Selo for lack of qualified supervisors and master masons. See Ovsiannikov, *Rastrelli,* p. 116. The most lavish and sensitive study of the imperial estate at Tsarskoe Selo is Aleksandr Benois, *Tsarskoe selo v Tsarstvovanie Elizavety Petrovny* (St. Petersburg, 1910). Project drawings for Rastrelli's work at Tsarskoe Selo are contained in Denisov and Petrov, Plates 444–75.

32. Arkin, *Rastrelli,* p. 105.

33. William Coxe, *Travels into Poland, Russia, Sweden, and Denmark* (London, 1785), 1: 477.

34. Sir Nathaniel Wraxall, *A Tour through Some of the Norethern Parts of Europe, Particuarly Copenhagen, Stockholm, and Petersbourgh* (London, 1775).

35. For a description of the interior as designed by Rastrelli, see A. N. Petrov, *Gorod Pushkin. Dvortsy i parki,* pp. 48–63. A more detailed presentation is contained in the same author's earlier work, *Pushkin. Dvortsy i parki* (Leningrad, 1969).

36. Vipper, *Arkhitektura russkogo barokko,* p. 80.

37. See V. I. Loktev, "B. Rastrelli i problemy barokko v arkhitekture," in A. V. Livatov et al., eds., *Barokko v slavianskikh kul'turakh* (Moscow, 1982), pp. 299–315, with particular reference to pp. 305–6. Loktev's comments are made in response to Grabar's criticism (in *Istoriia russkogo iskusstva,* vol. 3) of the Rastrelli palaces as insufficiently refined to be considered true rococo.

38. Quoted in Ovsiannikov, *Rastrelli,* p. 124. The building of the Hermitage is recounted in *Pamiatniki arkhitektury prigorodov Leningrada,* p. 62.

39. Much has been written on the statuary of the Old Park at Tsarskoe Selo. See, for example, Petrov, *Gorod Pushkin,* pp. 91–6.

40. For an archival photograph of the interior of the central room of the Hermitage, see *Pamiatniki arkhitektury prigorodov Leningrada,* p. 63. In the preceding book, published in 1983, Petrov states (p. 62) that the restoration of the Hermitage is nearing completion. As of 1990, his optimistic assertion is, regrettably, far from the case.

41. A description of Mon Bijou and of its reconstruction by Menelaws, who specialized in the pseudo-Gothic style, is contained in Petrov, *Gorod Pushkin,* pp. 175–7. See also Ovsiannikov, *Rastrelli,* pp. 125–6. An original wooden model of the pavilion was apparently still preserved at the turn of this century.

42. It should be noted that Rastrelli's suburban work also included the small Srednerogatskii Palace on the road to Tsarskoe Selo and, on the road to Peterhof, the Sivers Dacha – a brick villa, far more substantial than the usual dacha structure. On the latter, see Iu. Denisov, "Usad'ba XVIII veka na Petergofskoi doroge," *Arkhitekturnoe nasledstvo*, 4 (1953): 148–54.

43. Rumors of large sums of English money used to subsidize construction of the Vorontsov mansion (in exchange for Russian support of English interests in the confrontation with France) are repeated in Ovsiannikov, *Rastrelli*, p. 124.

44. The Vorontsov Palace is discussed in Denisov and Petrov, p. 11, with project sketches included under catalog nos. 334–7. Further information is contained in *Pamiatniki arkhitektury Leningrada*, pp. 201–3. The palace has been converted to use as a Suvorov cadet school.

45. For further commentary on the integral relation between the two main facades of the Stroganov Palace, see V. I. Pluzhnikov's survey of the development of the baroque facade in Russian secular and church architecture: "Organizatsiia fasada v arkhitekture russkogo barokko," in Alekseeva, ed., *Russkoe iskusstvo barokko*, p. 96.

46. The symbolic and aesthetic significance of Rastrelli's use of the lion motif – also frequent at the Catherine Palace – is discussed in T. V. Alekseeva, "Franchesko-Bartolomeo Rastrelli i russkaia kul'tura," in *Ot Srednevekov'ia k novomu vremeni*, pp. 135–6.

47. Quoted in Ovsiannikov, *Rastrelli*, p. 139.

48. The most authoritative recent history of the design and construction of the Winter Palace is Iu. M. Denisov, "Zimnii dvorets Rastrelli," in Piliavskii and Levinson-Lessing, eds., *Ermitazh: Istoriia i arkhitektura zdaniia* (Leningrad, 1974), pp. 39–64.

49. On Rastrelli's temporary palace for Elizabeth, see Denisov, "Ischeznuvshie dvortsy," pp. 32–7.

50. Peter III's remarks are quoted in Denisov, "Zimnii dvorets Rastrelli," p. 47.

51. S. B. Alekseeva provides an analysis of the various sculptural elements of the Winter Palace, in terms not only of the plasticity of the facade, but also of their domination of the extensive space around the palace. See her "Arkhitektura i dekorativnaia plastika Zimnego dvortsa," in T. V. Alekseeva, ed., *Russkoe iskusstvo barokko* (Moscow, 1977), pp. 128–58. Earlier variants of the plan had a weaker segmentation of an even greater number of windows on the facades. See Denisov, "Zimnii dvorets Rastrelli," pp. 42–3.

In his survey of the design of the facade in the Russian baroque, V. I. Pluzhnikov states: "The facades of the baroque, perhaps to a greater degree than those of any other architectural style, are distinguished by their theatricality, imposing a dynamic on stable elements of the structure and creating a rhythmic complexity unrequired in a functional sense, and sometimes in opposition to it" ("Organizatsiia fasada v arkhitekture russkogo barokko," p. 88). Russian architecture had witnessed earlier examples of the dichotomy between the resolution of the facade and the structure (particularly in the seventeenth century), but not until the imperial era had the demands of architectural rhetoric been imposed on so large a mass, intended to project authority, wealth, and the control of a vast space.

It has been argued that Rastrelli, particularly at the Winter Palace, created an unusual variation on the rococo. On the interior, Rastrelli applied the system of classical orders – an approach considered by Igor Grabar to reveal a defect in his understanding of the rococo, but one that allowed a greater monumentalilty in the style. And on the exterior, Rastrelli's use of scale transformed rococo motifs from their largely decorative, interior function (in French design) to components of a genuine architectural style. See V. I. Loktev, "B. Rastrelli i problemy Barokko v arkhitekture," in A. V. Lipatov et al., eds., *Barokko v slavianskikh kul'turakh* (Moscow, 1982), pp. 299–315.

52. On the original color, see Denisov, "Zimnii dvorets Rastrelli," p. 46; with archival reference, p. 269, n. 19.

53. Rastrelli's extant project sketches for the Winter Palace are provided in Denisov and Petrov, *Zodchii Rastrelli*, catalog items 172–297.

54. The circumstances surrounding the Winter Palace fire are described in V. M. Glinka, "Pozhar 1837 goda," Piliavskii and Levinson-Lessing, eds., *Ermitazh: Istoriia i arkhitektura zdaniia* (Leningrad, 1974), pp. 107–18. On the rebuilding of the palace, V. I. Piliavskii, "Vosstanovlenie Zimnego dvortsa posle pozhara 1837 goda," ibid., 119–72. See also Richard M. Haywood, "The Winter Palace in St. Petersburg: Destruction by Fire and Reconstruction, December 1837–March 1839," in *Jarbücher für Geschichte Osteuropas*, 27 (1979): 161–80.

55. The building has not been without its critics. The prominent historian of Russian art, Igor Grabar, described it as "incontestably a genuine palace, stern and serious architecture," but also wrote that the building does not inspire, that its weakness is inherent in the very conception, in the "incredible extension of this gigantic rectangle, whose lines are interrupted only by feeble projections in the facade." Grabar', *Istoriia russkogo iskusstva*, vol. 3, p. 223.

56. Boris Vipper noted that for all of the power and the variety of the Winter Palace, there is a certain "ambiguity" in Rastrelli's design that derives from the contradictions between the waning baroque style and the rise of a neo-classical architectural aesthetic. Vipper, *Arkhitektura russkogo barokko*, p. 83. Loktev, however, argues that in the Winter Palace, Rastrelli brings the rococo of the interior to the exterior as a compositional system, thus recreating the rococo as a full-fledged architectural (as opposed to decorative) style. See "B. Rastrelli," pp. 308–12.

57. Rastrelli had originally designed a large square (subsequently Palace Square) that would have contained his father's equestrian statue of Peter the Great, but this project was not realized. For an analysis of the relation between Rastrelli's architectural designs and their urban context, see S. B. Alekseeva, "Arkhitektura i dekorativnaia plastika Zimnego dvortsa"; and N. F. Gulianitskii, "O maloissledovannoi storone tvorcheskogo metoda V. V. Rastrelli-gradostroitelia," *Arkhitekturnoe nasledstvo*, 21 (1973): 24–43.

58. For an account of this, and other difficulties encountered by Michurin, see Ovsiannikov, *Rastrelli*, pp. 82–4.

59. A summary of the various renovations of the church, with bibliographical references, is contained in *Pamiatniki gradostroitel'stva i arkhitektury Ukrainskoi SSR*, vol. 1, Iu. S. Aseev, ed. (Kiev, 1983), pp. 16–17.

60. For an analysis of the adaptation of the traditional pentacupolar design in Russian baroque church architecture, see T. P. Fedotova, "K probleme piatiglaviia v arkhitekture barokko pervoi poloviny XVIII v.," in Alekseeva, *Russkoe iskusstvo barokko: Materialy i issledovaniia*, pp. 70–87. In view of the Italian origins of so many of Russia's architects, it is logical to assume, as Fedotova does, that seventeenth-century Italian churches (especially the work of Borromini) were influential in the Russian integration of baroque decoration with the concept of the central dome and surrounding towers. It must also be remembered that centralized church designs were very much a part of the Roman baroque, as is demonstrated in Rudolf Wittkower, *Architectural Principles in the Age of Humanism* (New York, 1971).

61. The iconostasis of the St. Nicholas Cathedral is described and illustrated in *Pamiatniki arkhitektury Leningrada*, pp. 269–70. A survey of Chevakinskii's work is presented in A. N. Petrov, "S. I. Chevakinskii i peterburgskaia arkhitektura serediny XVIII veka," in Grabar, *Russkaia arkhitektura pervoi poloviny XVIII v.*, pp. 363–72.

62. See *Pamiatniki arkhitektury Leningrada*, p. 203. The Sheremetev palace, located on the Fontanka and now known as "Fontannyi dom," was associated with two of Russia's greatest poets: Alexander Pushkin and Anna Akhmatova, who lived there both before and after World War II.

63. Ibid., p. 205.

64. A comprehensive survey and listing of Ukhtomskii's work is provided in A. A. Kiparisova and R. G. Koroleva, *Arkhitektor Dmitrii Vasil'evich Ukhtomskii. 1719–1774. Katalog* (Moscow, 1973). Ukhtomskii was also a successful pedagogue, whose school, formally established in 1749, trained a number of capable architects – and some of Russia's greatest in the latter part of the eighteenth century. See ibid., pp. 24–6; and A. I. Mikhailov, *Arkhitektor D. V. Ukhtomskii i ego shkola* (Moscow, 1954).

65. Kiparisova, *Arkhitektor Ukhtomskii*, pp. 19–20, with sketches and photograph of the Red Gates, pp. 67–71.

66. An analysis of the construction history and evolving design of the Trinity–St. Sergius bell tower is provided in A. Mikhailov, "K istorii proektirovaniia i stroitel'stva kolokol'ni Troitse-Sergievoi lavry," *Arkhitekturnoe nasledstvo*, 1 (1951): 67–77; and G. I. Vzdornov, "Stroitel'stvo kolokol'ni Troitse-Segievoi lavry (v svete novykh dannykh)," *Arkhitekturnoe nasledstvo*, 14 (1962): 125–34.

67. The place of the Ukhtomskii bell tower in the evolution of an order system is discussed in N. F. Gulianitskii, "O svoeobrazii i preemstvenykh sviaziakh ordernogo iazyka v russkoi arkhitekture," *Arkhitekturnoe nasledstvo*, 23 (1975): 21. Gulianitskii notes that the obligatory use of project drawings for large projects by the mideighteenth century

facilitated the introduction of classical orders. Yet Mikhailov points out that Ukhtomskii's use of elements of the classical orders was far from codified. See *Arkhitektor D. V. Ukhtomskii*, p. 154.

68. The relation between sixteenth- and seventeenth-century Russian architecture (particularly the "tent" form) and Rastrelli's work at New Jerusalem is concisely discussed in Alekseeva, "Franchesko-Bartolomeo Rastrelli i russkaia kul'tura," p. 134, with excellent accompanying illustrations.

69. On the church at Voronovo, see M. A. Il'in, *Podmoskov'e* (Moscow, 1974), pp. 107, 111; and E. N. Pod"iapol'skaia, *Pamiatniki arkhitektury moskovskoi oblasti*, vol. 2, p. 121.

70. A selection of Pietro Antonio Trezzini's project sketches, including the Church of the Transfiguration, is reproduced in Voronikhina, *Arkhitekturnaia grafika Rossii*, pp. 138–41. G. I. Vzdornov provides a survey of Trezzini's work in "Arkhitektor P'etro Antonio Trezini i ego postroiki," Alekseeva, ed., *Russkoe iskusstvo XVIII v.* (Moscow, 1968), pp. 139–56. Although Lisaevich and Ovsiannikov suggest in their monographs on Domenico Trezzini that Pietro was his son, Vzdornov disputes this claim (p. 140) and notes that Pietro arrived in Russia only in 1726. The accepted date of his departure from Russia is 1751 (cf. ibid., p. 151).

Chapter 10

1. Apart from the personal tastes and ideology of the autocrat, the role of increased economic growth and the consequent demand for utilitarian structures in an acceptable architectural style throughout the empire served as a stimulus in the transition to neoclassical architecture. See A. F. Krasheninnikov, "Nekotorye osobennosti perelomnogo perioda mezhdu barokko i klassitsizmom v russkoi arkhitekture," in Alekseeva, ed., *Russkoe iskusstvo XVIII v.: Materialy i issledovaniia* (Moscow, 1973), pp. 97–102. Particularly apt is Krasheninnikov's analysis of a stylistic cycle alternating between the pragmatic and the highly decorative (pp. 101–2). Thus, the late baroque actually bears a greater resemblance to late seventeenth-century ornamental architecture than to its predecessor, the Petrine baroque, which, like neoclassicism, tended toward a more functional resolution of architectural tasks in a manner that could be easily reproduced. In this respect, the impulse to produce designs for model houses and other structures returns with full force in the neoclassical period.

2. Rastrelli's project sketches for Gostinnyi Dvor are listed and illustrated in Denisov and Petrov, *Zodchii Rastrelli*, items 351–8.

3. A history of Rastrelli's plans for Gostinnyi dvor and their revision by Vallin de la Mothe is provided in V. Nechaev, "Rastrelli i Delamot. Iz istorii postroiki Gostinnogo dvora," in *Starina i iskusstva: Sbornik statei* (Leningrad, 1928), pp. 3–21. The successive restorations of Gostinnyi Dvor are chronicled in *Pamiatniki arkhitektury Leningrada*, pp. 153–5.

4. For a narrative of Rastrelli's final work in Courland, see Ovsiannikov, *Rastrelli*, pp. 175–83. Rastrelli's final years were spent in a peripatetic existence between Mitau, Berlin, Italy, and Petersburg. After a brief trip to Italy in 1769, he returned to Petersburg in 1770 and petitioned for election to the Academy of Arts. In 1771, he was granted honorary status in the academy, but his proposal that the academy or imperial court acquire and publish his annotated collection of project sketches was unsuccessful. (The sketches and Rastrelli's description passed in the eighteenth century from Russia to Poland, where they were finally sold, in 1932, to the National Library in Warsaw.) Shortly after his election to the academy, Rastrelli died, at the age of 71. The circumstances remain an enigma: Neither the precise date nor the place of burial is known. The imperial government did, however, provide a pension to his descendents.

5. "Pis'ma Imperatritsy Ekateriny II k Grimmu," *Sbornik Imperatorskogo Russkogo istoricheskogo obshchestva*, 23: (Petersburg, 1885), p. 157.

6. See, for example, John Summerson's illuminating comments on the assimilation of Roman temple architecture in Claude Perrault's design of the east front of the Louvre (1667–70) in *The Classical Language of Architecture*, pp. 69–70.

7. Hugh Honour, *Neo-Classicism*, 2nd ed. (Baltimore, 1975), p. 18. For a Russian survey of the style and its origins, see N. N. Kovalenskaia, *Russkii klassitsizm* (Moscow, 1964).

8. There are a number of studies of the Academy of Arts and the building that houses it. A general history is V. G. Lisovskii, *Akademiia khudozhestv* (Leningrad, 1972), reissued in expanded form as *Akademiia khudozhestv: Istoriko-iskusstvovedcheskii ocherk* (Leningrad, 1982). An account of the prolonged effort to establish the Academy of Arts as an institution separate both from the Academy of Sciences and Moscow University, see E. I. Gavrilova, "Lomonosov i osnovanie Akademii khudozhestv," Alekseeva, ed., *Russkoe iskusstvo XVIII v.: Materialy i issledovaniia* (Moscow, 1973), pp. 66–75. A design for an earlier variant of the institution, intended for Moscow, was submitted by the French architect Jacques-François Blondel the younger in 1757. With its mansard roof, the Blondel's project closely followed the style of early French classicism; and although the design was unsuited to the climate and building traditions of Moscow, it serves as a harbinger of the stylistic changes to follow. See N. A. Evsina, "Proekty uchebnykh zdanii v Rossii XVIII veka," in Alekseeva, ed., *Russkoe iskusstvo XVIII veka* (Moscow, 1968), pp. 117–19. On the planning of the building in Petersburg, see A. Krasheninnikov, "Novye dannye po istorii zdaniia Akademii khudozhestv," *Arkhitekturnoe nasledstvo*, 7 (1955): 125–39.

9. For information on architectural volumes received in Russia during the mideighteenth century, see N. A. Evsina, *Arkhitekturnaia teoriia v Rossii vtoroi poloviny XVIII-nachala XIX veka* (Moscow, 1985), pp. 102–4.

10. Ibid., 128–9.

11. Ibid., 68–70, for a summary of Golitsyn's essay, which remains unpublished.

12. A survey of the construction history of the academy is contained in Lisovskii, *Akademiia khudozhestv*, pp. 24–7. Neither Kokorinov, who died in 1772, nor Vallin de la Mothe, who left Russia in 1775, saw the completion of the basic structure.

13. On the Razumovskii Palace (now the central building of the Herzen Pedagogical Institute), see *Pamiatniki arkhitektury Leningrada*, pp. 203–5.

14. The Iusupov palace underwent a major extension and rebuilding in the 1830s (architect: Andrei Mikhailov), but the original structure is extant. Ibid., pp. 207–9. It was in this palace that Grigorii Rasputin was assassinated in December 1916 by a group of monarchist conspirators led by Felix Iusupov.

15. See A. F. Krasheninnikov, "Lesnye sklady na ostrove Novaia Gollandiia v Peterburge," *Arkhitekturnoe nasledstvo*, 19 (1972): 96–101.

16. The most authoritative study of Velten's career is provided in two works by Militsa Korshunova: *Arkhitektor Iurii Fel'ten: Katalog vystavki* (Leningrad, 1982); and the more extensive monograph, *Iurii Fel'ten* (Leningrad, 1988). His education is examined in E. N. Suslova, "Uchenicheskie gody Iu. M. Fel'tena," *Arkhitekturnoe nasledstvo*, 9 (1959): 69–72.

17. A number of scholarly works has been devoted to the Commission on the Construction of Petersburg and Moscow. A brief bibliography is provided in Evsina, pp. 189–90, n. 4. For a general survey of the work of the commission, whose brief extended far beyond Petersburg and Moscow, see Savarenskaia et al., *Istoriia gradostroitel'nogo iskusstva*, pp. 139–53. Also see Ozhegov, *Tipovoe i povtornoe stroitel'stvo v Rossii v XVIII–XIX vekakh*, p. 50 and passim. After the establishment of the commission, the Construction Office (*kantselariia*; see Chapter 8) devoted itself entirely to building for the imperial court. On the planning of Petersburg during Catherine's reign, see B. Vasil'ev, "K istorii planirovki Peterburga vo vtoroi polovine XVIII veka," *Arkhitekturnoe nasledstvo*, 4 (1953): 14–29.

18. On Velten's designs for the Palace Quay, see Korshunova, *Iurii Fel'ten*, pp. 39–44. More generally on the embankments of Petersburg, see V. I. Kochedamov, *Naberezhnye Nevy* (Leningrad, 1954). The initial supervisor of construction of the granite embankment has been identified as Ignazio Ludovico Rossi, born in Moscow in 1705 and involved as a master craftsman in a number of major construction projects in Petersburg. See K. V. Malinovskii, "V granit odelasia Neva: Ob avtorstve pervoi kamennoi naberezhnoi Peterburga," *Stroitel'stvo i arkhitektura Leningrada*, 1981, no. 11: 32–35.

19. One view of the complicated and often obscure history and attribution of the Summer Garden fence is presented in Korshunova, *Iurii Fel'ten*, pp. 40–4. Korshunova suggests (p. 44) that the basic design of the fence was derived from the work of Daniel Marot, as published in *Oeuvre de Sr. Marot architecte de Guilliame III Roi de la Grande Bretagne* (Amsterdam, 1712). The large central gate was replaced in 1870 by a chapel – not extant – commemorating the deliverance of Alexander II from an assassination attempt by Dmitrii Karakozov near this site in 1866.

20. The details of this feud and of the long and difficult process of modeling and casting the Falconet's statue (completed in 1777) go beyond the bounds of architectural history. It is the subject of an exhaustive monograph by Avraam Kaganovich, *"Mednyi vsadnik": Istoriia sozdaniia monumenta* (Leningrad, 1975), with frequent references to Velten's involvement in the project.

21. In addition to Velten's palace, the Chesme victory stimulated a variety of artistic commissions by Catherine. The battle was depicted in a number of large canvasses by Richard Payton and Jacob Phillipe Hackaert, which Velten integrated into his design of the Throne and Chesme Halls at Peterhof. See Korshunova, *Iurii Fel'ten*, pp. 68–70; and A. G. Cross, "Richard Paton and the Battle of Chesme," *Study Group on the Eighteenth Century Newsletter*, 14 (1986): 31–7.

22. Korshunova draws analogies between the Chesme palace and possible English prototypes, including the work of John Thorpe during the late seventeenth century (Thorpe's authorship of these palaces is now in doubt), as well as mideighteenth-century work by Roger Morris and Robert Mylne (Inveraray Castle) and Henry Flitcroft. The castle at Longford, Wiltshire (sixteenth century, with later alterations; misattributed to Thorpe), had a triangular plan and appeared in vol. 5 of *Vitruvius Britanicus* (1771). See Korshunova, *Fel'ten*, pp. 72–3.

23. The stylistic variety of Velten's churches reminds that architecture during the reign of Catherine was by no means limited to neoclassicism, however central its position in late eighteenth-century Russian culture. Velten used the flamboyant pseudo-Gothic in the design of the Chesme church, and he devised a more restrained Gothic variant for a small church – also dedicated to John the Baptist – on the boulevard to Stone Island (Kamennyi Ostrov) in the northern suburbs of Petersburg. His other churches, however, display a form of neoclassicism typically defined by a central ionic portico, such as the Armenian Church on Nevskii Prospekt (1771–1780), and the Lutheran churches of St. Catherine on Bolshoi Prospekt, Vasilevskii Island (1768–71) and St. Anne (1775–9), whose apsidal structure is expanded to a half rotunda with an ionic colonnade and balustrade. The definitive attribution of Velten's churches is contained in N. V. Murashova, "Avtorstvo ustanovleno," *Stroitel'stvo i arkhitektura Leningrada*, 1978, no. 2: 42–5. The building of the Armenian Church, endowed by the fabulously wealthy merchant Ivan Lazarev (Lazarian), is described in Korshunova, *Fel'ten*, pp. 96–8.

24. The "ruined" appearance of the Ruin was increased during World War II, when the trees planted on the slope of the attached brick wall were uprooted. The structure, however, remains largely intact. See Petrov, *Gorod Pushkin: Dvortsy i Parki* (Leningrad, 1977), pp. 118–19; and *Pamiatniki arkhitektury prigorodov Leningrada*, p. 92.

25. For commentary on the Column House, see Robert Rosenblum, *Transformations in Late Eighteenth Century Art* (Princeton, 1967), pp. 115–16.

26. D. O. Shvidkovskii gives a convincing interpretation of the architectural text of park pavilions in "Prosvetitel'skaia kontseptsiia sredy v russkikh dvortsovo-parkovykh ansambliakh vtoroi poloviny XVIII veka," in I. E. Danilova, ed., *Vek prosveshcheniia: Rossiia i Frantsiia* (Moscow, 1989), pp. 185–99.

27. The Catherine Park, like the palace, was named in honor of Peter the Great's wife Catherine I. For a concise survey of the Neëlovs' work, see E. A. Borisova, "Arkhitektory Neelovy," *Arkhitekturnoe nasledstvo*, 4 (1953): 73–90.

28. See *Pamiatniki arkhitektury prigorodov Leningrada*, pp. 116–17.

29. On the building of the Lycee, see ibid., p. 132.

30. Korshunova, *Fel'ten*, p. 91.

31. Piliavskii and Levinson-Lessing, *Ermitazh*, pp. 201–2.

32. A brief sketch of Rinaldi's life is provided in D. A. Kiuchariants, *Antonio Rinal'di* (Leningrad, 1976), pp. 7–14. See also G. G. Grimm's section on Rinaldi in Grabar', *Istoriia russkogo iskusstva*, 6 (1915): 68–76.

33. A study of Rinaldi's work at Oranienbaum can be found in L. Nevostrueva, "Ansambl' Rinal'di v gorode Lomonosove," *Arkhitekturnoe nasledstvo*, 7 (1955): 109–24. See also Raskin, *Gorod Lomonosov: Dvortsovo-parkovye ansambli XVIII veka* (Leningrad, 1979); and the detailed description by A. Petrov and E. Petrova in *Pamiatniki arkhitektury prigorodov Leningrada*, pp. 500–38. The rich complexity of his ceiling designs is noted in G. G. Grimm, *Arkhitektura perekrytii russkogo klassitsizma* (Leningrad, 1939), pp. 4–5, with further references to his work at Gatchina, pp. 25–7.

34. The track at the Oranienbaum Sledding Hill fell into disrepair after the reign of Catherine, and was dismantled in 1801 (the colonnade flanking the track was removed in 1858–61). Despite the "frivolous" nature of the structure, it demonstrated a harmony of form and function, as well as a skillful adaptation of the traditional Russian construction of wooden sledding hills. See Raskin, *Gorod Lomonosov*, pp. 40–2.

35. On the interior decoration of the Sledding Hill, see *Pamiatniki arkhitektury prigorodov Leningrada*, pp. 534–8.

36. Both the interior and exterior of the Gatchina palace were severely damaged during World War II. A restoration is currently underway, but much of Rinaldi's original work has been lost. See *Pamiatniki arkhitektury prigorodov Leningrada*, pp. 266–75, with color reproductions of a superb series of watercolors of the interior painted by E. Gau and L. Premazzi in the 1870s. For a more detailed, annotated study of the palace and its grounds, see V. Makarov and A. Petrov, *Gatchina* (Leningrad, 1974). A brief analysis of the types of Pudost stone, which appeared in a number of major structures at the end of the eighteenth century, is contained in ibid., p. 77, n. 2.

37. Ibid., pp. 44–5. In 1771, Rinaldi had designed a more elaborate monument to the Chesme victory in the rostral column at Tsarskoe Selo (completed in 1776). Situated in the middle of the Large Pond, the column is a dominant in the landscape of the lower Catherine Park, and reminds

that Rinaldi, like Velten, was involved in the enhancement of the parks at Tsarskoe Selo during the 1770s. His great obelisk of 1771 commemorating Petr Rumiantsev's victory over the Turkish army at Kagul (Moldavia) in July 1770 is referred to in at least two poems by Alexander Pushkin: "Vospominaniia v Tsarskom Sele" (both the 1814 and 1829 versions) and "Elegiia" (1819). Rinaldi also designed a triumphal arch for the Orlov Gates (also known as the Gatchina Gates, over the road from the Catherine Park to Gatchina), erected between 1777 and 1782 to honor Grigorii Orlov's role in restoring order to Moscow in 1771 after an outbreak of plague. Each of these monuments adheres to the classical style, and each exploits the variety of colors and textures of marble. The obelisk contains three types of marble, whereas the Orlov Gates are composed of pink marble from Karelia for the attached columns and panels on a background of gray marble that surfaces the brick structure.

38. Details of the financial transactions involved in Catherine's purchase of Grigorii Orlov's property are contained in Makarov and Petrov, *Gatchina*, pp. 76–7.

39. A description of the types of marble used on the surface of the palace is contained in A. A. Kedrinskii et al., *Vosstanovlenie pamiatnikov arkhitektury Leningrada* (Leningrad, 1983), pp. 136–7. The authors note that the marble surface has suffered from a combination of climatic rigors (particularly cold and moisture) and industrial pollution, and has required substantial restoration. On the relation between decoration and structure in the design of the palace, see D. A. Kiuchariants, "Sintez iskusstv v arkhitekture Mramornogo dvortsa v Leningrade," *Arkhitekturnoe nasledstvo*, 16 (1967): 71–80.

40. During his remodeling of the Marble Palace, Briullov enlarged the palace service building – on the adjacent lot upriver – to dimensions that rivaled those of the palace itself. His eclectic combination of Renaissance and Greek styles in the stuccoed building complements Rinaldi's masterpiece and illuminates the continuing interpretation of classically inspired architectural motifs over the period of a century (see Chapter 13).

41. On Starov, see N. N. Belekhov and A. N. Petrov, *Ivan Starov: Materialy k izucheniiu tvorchestva* (Moscow, 1950).

42. For a discussion of the estate at Bogoroditsk and the development of the park by the noted Russian specialist in rural economy and landscape design, Andrei Bolotov, see Vergunov and Gorokhov, *Russkie sady*, pp. 362–9.

43. Starov's involvement in the development of plans for provincial cities is examined in V. F. Shilkov, "Raboty A. V. Kvasova i I. E. Starova po planirovke russkikh gorodov," *Arkhitekturnoe nasledstvo*, 4 (1953): 30–4.

44. This final stage in the design of the Trinity Cathedral is analyzed by A. I. Kudriavtsev and G. N. Shkoda, *Aleksandro-Nevskaia Lavra*, pp. 25–30.

45. Gould, one of the major figures in the development of the imperial parks during the reign of Catherine, had his own house on the grounds of the Tauride Palace. Designed by Fedor Volkov, architect of a number of Petersburg's monumental army barracks in the neoclassical style, the Gould house is itself a model of estate architecture.

46. Toward the end of the nineteenth century, a large section of the park surrounding the Tauride Palace was sold for speculative development; and in 1906–7, the palace acquired new fame – and further modifications – as the site of Russia's short-lived *duma*, or legislative body. From the exterior, however, the Tauride Palace remains the supreme example of the noble simplicity of Russian neoclassical domestic architecture. For a survey of the construction and design of the Tauride Palace, as well as its subsequent modifications, see *Pamiatniki arkhitektury Leningrada*, pp. 211–17.

47. Cameron's biographical deception is examined in Tamara Talbot Rice, "Charles Cameron, Architect to the Imperial Russian Court," *Charles Cameron* (London, 1967), pp. 8–10. See also Dmitrij Shividovsky [i.e., Shvidkovskii], "The Empress and the Architect," *Country Life* (Nov. 16, 1989), pp. 90–2; and John Robinson, "A Dazzling Adventurer: Charles Cameron – the Lost Early Years," *Apollo* (January 1992), pp. 58–78. A basic Soviet monograph on Cameron is V. N. Taleporovskii, *Charl'z Kameron* (Moscow, 1939). Cameron's volume on the Roman baths was reproduced, with commentary by V. P. Zubov, as *Termy rimlian* (Moscow, 1939).

48. Letter of June 22, 1781, in "Pis'ma Imperatritsy Ekateriny II k Grimmu," *Sbornik Imperatorskogo Russkogo istoricheskogo obshchestva*, vol. 23 (text in French). An analysis of Clérisseau's influence on the development of neoclassicism in Russia is contained in Thomas McCormick, *Charles-Louis Clérisseau and the Genesis of Neoclassicism* (Cambridge, M.I.T. Press: 1990).

49. Detailed illustrations of these interiors – particularly Catherine's Bedroom – in their prewar state are contained in Grimm, *Arkhitektura perekrytii*, pp. 59–68, with an analysis of Cameron's approach to ceiling design, p. 7.

50. The early phase of the new Palladian movement in Britain is surveyed in Peter Kidson et al., *A History of English Architecture* (Harmondsworth, 1969), pp. 222–31. Kent's interior designs, which prefigure much in late eighteenth-century Russian decoration, are examined in Margaret Jourdain, *The Work of William Kent* (London, 1941).

51. The role of Clérisseau has been acknowledged, but there are also numerous similarities between Cameron's work at Tsarskoe Selo and interiors by Robert Adam – particularly his Etruscan Room (late 1770s) at Osterly Park and the interiors at Syon House (1762–9). The spirit of Adam is still more pervasive in Cameron's work at Pavlovsk.

52. D. O. Shvidkovskii notes that in designing the Cold Baths and Agate Pavilion, Cameron was particularly influenced by his study of the baths of Hadrian's villa at Tivoli, more intimate in scale than the larger public baths of Rome. See "K voprosu rekonstruktsii ansamblia Tsarskogo sela Ch. Kameronom," *Arkhitekturnoe nasledstvo*, 33 (1985): 63. Proceeding clockwise from the left of the oval rotunda entrance to the Agate Pavilion, the rooms are the Small Study, the Oval Study, the Jasper Study, the Great Hall, the Agate Study, the Staircase (to the baths), and the Library. Detailed illustrations of the interior, with emphasis on ceiling designs, are presented in Grimm, *Arkhitektura perekrytii*, pp. 69–78.

53. For an analysis of the decorative stonework, and an explanation for the confusion in the use of the term "agate," see M. G. Voronov and G. D. Khodasevich, *Arkhitekturnyi ansambl' Kamerona v Pushkine* (Leningrad, 1982), pp. 47–51.

54. Ibid., pp. 54–5.

55. For a survey of the development of the "natural park" to the south of the formal Catherine Park at Tsarskoe Selo, see Vergunov and Gorokhov, *Russkie sady i parki*, pp. 225–7, 232. In the landscaping of the park, Vasilii Neëlov, who was sent by Catherine to England to observe methods of gardening in 1771, had the assistance of John Bush (Johann Busch), one of the many gardeners that she hired from England. Neëlov's sojourn in England is included in A. G. Cross, *"By the Banks of the Thames": Russians in Eighteenth-Century Britain* (Newtonville, Mass., 1980). The role of Neëlov and his two sons, Ilia and Pavel, in the design of the pavilions at the Catherine Park (both old and new) has been noted before – as have the contributions of Velten and Rinaldi. See also G. P. Balog, V. V. Demus et al., *Muzei i parki Pushkina* (Leningrad, 1969), pp. 20–3; Petrov, *Gorod Pushkin*, pp. 114–18; and *Pamiatniki arkhitektury prigorodov Leningrada*, p. 72. On the topic of the spread of English landscape gardening in Russia, see A. G. Cross, "Catherine the Great and Whately's *Observations on Modern Gardening*," *Study Group on Eighteenth-Century Russia Newsletter*, 18 (1990): 21–9.

56. A detailed survey of the bronze busts, including one by Fedot Shubin of the great Russian polymath Lomonosov, is contained in Voronov and Khodasevich, *Arkhitekturnyi ansambl' Kamerona*, pp. 20–37.

57. Like the fashion for the pseudo-Gothic, the use of a Chinese decorative style for many of the pavilions at Tsarskoe Selo was likely inspired by the example of English park pavilions. See *Pamiatniki arkhitektury prigorodov Leningrada*, pp. 112–17; and Petrov, *Gorod Pushkin*, pp. 148–58. Petrov notes the work of William Chambers and William and John Halfpenny as possible sources of influence (p. 148). After years of disrepair and ruin following World War II, the Chinese Village is now being reconstructed.

58. Perhaps the most idiosyncratic design by Cameron in the area of Tsarskoe Selo was the project for a cathedral for the new town of Sofiia, established by Catherine in 1780 as a suburban "development" near the imperial palace, but also another component in the grand allegorical system expressive of her claims toward the Ottoman Empire and, ultimately, Constantinople. Cameron's design included features from the Hagia Sophia, particularly in the form of the drum beneath the main dome. The project, however, proved impossibly grandiose, and its modification – perhaps by Starov – is one of the early examples of the high neoclassical style in Russian church architecture (1782–8). In plan, the church is symmetrical, a cross inscribed within

a square, with a Tuscan Doric portico on each facade. The town of Sofiia soon withered for lack of interest, and after Catherine's death, most of the existing structures – except the cathedral – were dismantled for reuse in Tsarskoe Selo. On the Sofiia cathedral, see *Pamiatniki arkhitektury prigorodov Leningrada*, p. 156. A concise account of the origins and planning of Sofiia is presented in D. O. Shvidkovskii, "K voprosu rekonstruktsii ansamblia Tsarskogo sela Ch. Kameronom," pp. 65–8.

59. There has been much debate as to the identity of the designer of the Pavlovsk park. Isobel Rae makes a case for Capability Brown as the main source of the Pavlovsk park in *Charles Cameron: Architect to the Court of Russia* (London, 1971), p. 70. That claim has been disputed, however, and credit for the original design is usually given to Cameron himself.

60. Hirschfeld's writings on gardens appeared in the journal *Ekonomicheskii magazin*, edited by Andrei Bolotov, himself a leading figure in the development of the Russian landscape garden in the final decades of the century. Much has been written on the rise of the eighteenth-century landscape garden in Europe and its relation to literature, painting, and the history of ideas. Among recent works are John Dixon Hunt, *The Figure in the Landscape: Poetry Painting and Gardening During the Eighteenth Century* (London, 1976); and Edward Malins, *English Landscaping and Literature, 1660–1840* (London, 1966). On specific English gardeners, see Edward Hyams, *Capability Brown and Humphry Repton* (London, 1971). The most sensitive Russian treatment of the theme is D. S. Likhachev, *Poeziia sadov* (Leningrad, 1982), with particular reference to Romanticism in the landscaping of gardens, pp. 193–287.

For a survey of Cameron's work at the Pavlovsk Park, see Vergunov and Gorokhov, pp. 243–8; and *Pamiatniki arkhitektury prigorodov Leningrada*, p. 212 and passim.

61. *Pamiatniki arkhitektury prigorodov Leningrada*, pp. 236–8.

62. On Palladio in Russia, see V. N. Grashchenko, "Nasledie Palladio v arkhitekture russkogo klassitsizma," *Sovetskoe iskusstvoznanie*, 1981, no. 2: 201–34. See also Hamilton, p. 307, n. 24.

63. For excellent details of Cameron's interior designs at Pavlovsk, with particular attention to ceilings and moldings, see Grimm, *Arkhitektura perekrytii*, pp. 7, 79–87.

64. After the fire of 1803, Cameron's work was restored by Voronikhin, and the Scotti's ceiling (1786) was repainted by his son Giovanni. See *Pamiatniki arkhitektury prigorodov Leningrada*, pp. 184, 188; also V. V. Antonov, *Zhivopistsy-dekoratory Skotti v Rossii*, in T. V. Alekseeva, ed., *Russkoe iskusstvo vtoroi poloviny XVIII-pervoi poloviny XIX v.* (Moscow, 1979), pp. 69–107.

65. For a concise description of the ensemble at Baturin, see Vergunov and Gorokhov, p. 283; and F. F. Gornostaev, *Stroitel'stvo grafov Razumovskikh na Chernigovshchine* (Moscow, 1911). Although Cameron is most frequently mentioned as its architect, attribution of the Baturin palace has long been the subject of debate, and some historians now argue that Adam Menelaws (or Menelas) was the actual architect. See D. O. Shvidkovskii, "K polemike 1910-kh gg. ob atributsii dvortsa Razumovskikh v Baturine," in A. L. Batalov and I. A. Bondarenko, eds., *Restavratsiia i arkhitekturnaia arkheologiia* (Moscow, 1991), pp. 234–9; and Dmitrij Shividkovsky [sic], "Architect to Three Emperors: Adam Menelas in Russia," *Apollo* (January 1992): 37–41. On the current state of the palace, see N. L. Zharikov, ed., *Pamiatniki gradostroitel'stva i arkhitektury Ukrainskoi SSR* (Kiev, 1983–6), vol. IV, pp. 291–2. Cameron continued to work in Russia until his death in 1812, following which his wife returned to Britain with his architectural archive.

66. On Brenna's work with the thermae, see V. K. Shuiskii, *Vinchentso Brenna* (Leningrad, 1986), pp. 8–12. Much of the Roman work studied by Cameron and Brenna subsequently proved to be from the lower vaults of the Golden House of Nero, on which the baths were constructed. It should also be noted that Raphael had drawn on much of the same material over two centuries earlier for his work at the Vatican (the Loggia) and his design for the Villa Madama in Rome (1517; uncompleted). In both projects, but particularly the latter, Raphael and his assistants revived the extraordinarily inventive Roman grotesques in wall decoration. There is some basis for the claims that Brenna reinterpreted this aspect of Raphael's work in the designs at Pavlovsk (the boudoir of Maria Fedorovna, for example; see Shuiskii, *Brenna*, p. 35); yet Brenna and Cameron were themselves well acquainted with the original Roman material.

67. Ibid., pp. 12–15. A reproduction (p. 14) of a Brenna drawing of the Thermae wall paintings shows a trompe l'oeil of narrow columns supporting interior canopies – similar to Cameron's designs at Tsarskoe Selo.

68. Brenna's pride in the Grecian Room and its architectonic features are conveyed in a letter of 1789 to his former patron Count Potocki, quoted in ibid., p. 27.

69. Many of the bedroom furnishings were, in fact, from the French royal workshops. The design and furnishings of each room are described in Valeria Belanina, *Pavlovsk* (Moscow, 1987).

70. *Pamiatniki arkhitektury prigorodov Leningrada*, p. 210. For other Gonzago ceiling sketches at Pavlovsk, see Grimm, *Arkhitektura perekrytii*, pp. 143–6. His work as park designer as well as painter at Pavlovsk is examined in A. Efros, "Gonzago v Pavlovske," in A. Efros, *Mastera raznykh epokh* (Moscow, 1979).

71. As Brenna's work at Pavlovsk lessened in the early 1790s, he was engaged to expand and remodel much of Rinaldi's work at the Gatchina palace, which had been repurchased by Catherine from the Orlov family in 1783 and presented to the grand duke. As at Pavlovsk, Brenna added a second story to the curved wings on either side of the central structure, and also expanded the service blocks at the end of the wings. A number of his new Gatchina interiors showed a quasibaroque manner that maintained the spirit of Rinaldi's original designs. A description of Brenna's work at Gatchina – park pavilions as well as palace interiors – is contained in V. K. Shuiskii, *Brenna*, pp. 84–119. See also Makarov and Petrov, p. 13 and passim. His interior designs are illustrated in the prewar Grimm, *Arkhitektura perekrytii*, pp. 8, 108–30.

72. On Bazhenov's stay at Gatchina, see L. K. Abramov, "Novye materialy of rabotakh V. I. Bazhenova v Gatchine," *Arkhitekturnoe nasledsto*, 1 (1951): 78–85.

73. The early stages of the published debate concerning the authorship of the Mikhailovskii Castle are summarized in V. L. Snegirev, *Zodchii Bazhenov* (Moscow, 1962), pp. 191–8. Snegirev argues, of course, in favor of Bazhenov as the original architect. On the other side, the most recent proponent of Brenna's decisive role is Shuiskii, who questions Bazhenov's authorship of a 1792 drawing – with Bazhenov's signed comments (illegible), but executed by Lavrentii Miller – for a project resembling the Mikhailovskii Castle (*Brenna*, pp. 193–4, n. 79). Bazhenov's removal from the Mikhailovskii Castle project is attributed by Shuiskii, without specific evidence, to critical remarks that Bazhenov might have directed toward Paul's original sketch for the castle (reproduced on p. 122). Others have suggested that it was a matter of Bazhenov's ill health.

74. The official historian of the palace, August Kotzebue, noted that it was necessary to ascend and descend numerous staircases in order to reach a destination within the palace (for the quote see ibid., p. 148). This author can attest to the accuracy of Kotzebue's observation.

75. For a survey of the many proposals for Rastrelli's equestrian statue, see ibid., pp. 135–8.

76. The postwar restoration of the Raphael Gallery, the Small Throne Room, and the palace church, as well as other interior spaces, is described in Kedrinskii et al., pp. 145–58. Shuiskii provides an inventory of the major rooms of the palace, pp. 148–61.

77. Ibid., pp. 129, 139–40.

78. Kotzebue is, again, the source of much of this information. Ibid., 147–8.

79. For commentary on this event and a summary of historians' assessment of Paul, see Dukes, *The Making of Russian Absolutism*, pp. 180–1.

80. Quarenghi's formative study in Italy is surveyed in V. N. Taleporovskii, *Kvarengi: materialy k izucheniiu tvorchestva* (Leningrad–Moscow, 1954), pp. 4–5; and M. F. Korshunova, *Dzhakomo Kvarengi* (Leningrad, 1977), pp. 10–15. See also V. I. Piliavskii, *D. Kvarengi: Arkhitektor. Khudozhnik* (Leningrad, 1981).

81. Korshunova, *Kvarengi*, pp. 18–20.

82. Ibid., pp. 15–17, with illustration.

83. James Meader arrived in Petersburg from London (where he was hired by the Russian ambassador Aleksei Musin-Pushkin) in May 1779. His park at Peterhof is described in E. N. Glezer, *Arkhitekturnyi ansambl' Angliiskogo parka* (Leningrad, 1979), pp. 10–16; and Korshunova, *Kvarengi*, pp. 28–31. Quarenghi praised Meader's work in his own volume, *Edifices construits à Saint Petersbourg d'aprés les plans du Chevalier de Quarenghi et sous sa direction* (Petersburg, 1810), vol. 1, p. 11.

84. For project sketches and a construction history of the English Palace, see Glezer, *Arkhitekturnyi ansambl'*, pp. 36–47. Catherine also commissioned Quarenghi to design two summer houses near the English Palace: one for Paul and the other for her grandsons Alexander and Constantine. After her death, these uncompleted pavilions were dismantled.

85. Quarenghi's interior decoration, characterized by elaborate plaster work serving as a frame for painted ornamentation, is illustrated in Grimm, *Arkhitektura perekrytii*, pp. 6–7, 28–45. For an inventory of the rooms, see Glezer, *Arkhitekturnyi ansambl'*, pp. 49–90. Following the death of Catherine, Paul turned the recently completed and unused palace into a barracks, with attendant damage to the interior. Despite a restoration by Quarenghi in 1805, the palace still had no "tenant," and was used only sporadically. Figures on its cast are presented in ibid., p. 124. Taleporovskii notes (*Kvarengi*, p. 48) that Quarenghi's economy of design was primarily an aesthetic decision that also allowed greater flexibility in financial matters.

86. Earlier proposals for the Academy of Sciences are discussed in E. A. Borisova, "O rannikh proektakh zdanii Akademii nauk," T. V. Alekseeva, ed., *Russkoe iskusstvo XVIII v.: Materialy i issledovaniia* (Moscow, 1973), pp. 56–65.

87. For a comparative analysis of the proportional relations in the facades of major buildings by Quarenghi, see Taleporovskii, *Kvarengi*, pp. 66–70. On the low, "stretched" incline of his pediments, see p. 47. A more general comment on the Palladian element in his work is presented in M. A. Il'in, "O palladianstve v tvorchestve D. Kvarengi i N. L'vova," in T. V. Alekseeva, ed., *Russkoe iskusstvo XVIII veka* (Moscow, 1973), pp. 103–8.

88. A detailed analysis of Quarenghi's design for the Bourse, with extensive graphic material, is contained in M. V. Iogansen, "Raboty Kvarengi na Strelke Vasil'evskogo ostrova v Peterburge," in T. V. Alekseeva, ed., *Russkoe iskusstvo vtoroi poloviny XVIII–pervoi poloviny XIX v.* (Moscow, 1979), pp. 7–17. Project drawings are reproduced in Taleporovskii, *Kvarengi*, Plates 96–8. See also Korshunova, *Kvarengi*, pp. 42–5.

89. *Pamiatniki arkhitektury Leningrada*, pp. 255.

90. For commentary on Quarenghi's frequent use of the thermal – or in Russian, "Italian" – window, see Taleporovskii, *Kvarengi*, pp. 71–2.

91. Indeed, Quarenghi, together with Starov, was influential in extending the neoclassical canon throughout the empire in the design not only of country mansions, but also commercial structures such as the Gostinnyi Dvor in Moscow (see Chapter 11) and the Trading Rows for the Siberian city of Irkutsk. A brief survey of Quarenghi's commercial designs for the provinces, from Irkutsk to Kursk, is contained in Korshunova, *Kvarengi*, pp. 82–4.

In Petersburg, Quarenghi increased the available space for commerce with the construction of a number of trading centers. Each represents a variation on the arcaded shopping structure, introduced by Rastrelli and Vallin de la Mothe for the Gostinnyi Dvor on Nevskii Prospekt. For the jewelers Quarenghi designed the Silver Rows (1784–7; also on Nevskii Prospekt), with a rusticated arcade on the street level and a Tuscan Doric enclosed arcade for the two upper stories. His Small Gostinnyi Dvor (1790s) has Venetian windows above a rusticated open arcade; and the largest of his markets, the New Bourse Gostinny Dvor on Vasilevskii Island (c. 1800), was rusticated on both levels. (The latter was adapted for office use by Leningrad University and has a third floor added in 1936 by Vladimir Piliavskii. See *Pamiatniki arkhitektury Leningrada*, p. 99.) The most curious in terms of plan is the triangular Round Market on the Moika (1790s; attributed to Quarenghi). The most elegant in terms of design is the Anichkov Trading Rows (1803–5; an enclosed colonnade owned by the Office of the Imperial Household and located on the Fontanka at the Anichkov Palace), yet he was criticized for combining Ionic columns with a Doric entablature. Quarenghi sarcastically noted this criticism of the Trading Rows in his letters to Antonio Canova. See Korshunova, *Kvarengi*, pp. 116–18. On the design of the building, see Taleporovskii, *Kvarengi*, pp. 31–2.

92. For the evolution of the Hermitage Theater design (built in three stages) and a description of the interior, see Piliavskii and Levinson-Lessing, *Ermitazh*, pp. 213–22 (with project sketches). Quarenghi's description is contained in *Edifices construits*, vol. 1, p. 32.

93. Parts of the Raphael Loggia were modified by the construction of the New Hermitage, beginning in 1839. See Korshunova, *Kvarengi*, pp. 50–3; and Piliavskii and Levinson-Lessing, *Ermitazh*, pp. 203–7.

94. Ibid., pp. 83–4. For project sketches, see Taleporovskii, *Kvarengi*, Plates 54–9. During the 1780s, Quarenghi also constructed what was in effect a separate building integrated within the Winter Palace and connecting it to the Small Hermitage. The main floor of this structure contained two more state rooms by Quarenghi, including the Apollo Hall at the entrance to the Hermitage art collection. On the same axis, but in the opposite direction, was the Marble Hall, richly sheathed in polychrome Russian marble, with attached Corinthian columns. So imposing were its dimensions (some 800 square meters) and decor that Catherine designated it the new Throne Hall and dedicated in 1795 to St. George, whose name it finally assumed. Again, Quarenghi's work was destroyed in 1837, and only its proportions were retained in Stasov's reconstruction. On the original construction of the Marble and Apollo Halls, see Piliavskii and Levinson-Lessing, *Ermitazh*, pp. 78–84. For a history of the complicated reconstruction of the Marble Hall, in white Carrara marble, between 1838 and 1843, see pp. 161–5.

95. In 1782–3, Quarenghi added an octastyle Ionic portico to the former Boris Kurakin mansion on the English Quay in a remodeling to accommodate the Collegium, or Ministry, of Foreign Affairs. See A. F. Krashennikov, "Zdanie byvshei Inostrannoi kollegii v Leningrade," *Arkhitekturnoe nasledstvo*, 20 (1972): 64–9. In the early 1780s, Quarenghi converted two houses near the main Post Office into a palace for A. A. Bezborodko, whose many duties for Catherine

included supervision of the postal service, which after his death acquired the building for official use. In 1784–8, Quarenghi built a mansion with pediment and balcony, but no portico, for the merchant F. Groten on Palace Quay (later known as the Saltykov House, and later still the English Embassy). The large house that he constructed in 1788 opposite the Admiralty for I. Fitinhof, president of the Collegium of Medicine, was converted in 1804 into the Building of Province Offices. For descriptions of these mansions in *Pamiatniki arkhitektury Leningrada*, see the Bezborodko Palace, p. 217; the Ministry of Foreign Affairs, p. 253; the Saltykov house, p. 115; the Fitinhof mansion, p. 69.

A variation on these urban houses is evident in his Main Pharmacy (1789–96), with flanking Corinthian pilasters at the center of one facade and attached columns for the other. The existing building for the Main Pharmacy (and Medical collegium) deviates in certain respects from Quarenghi's specifications. See Taleporovskii, *Kvarengi*, p. 29, and Plates 146, 147. Even the last of his buildings in Petersburg, the Anglican Church, has its portico of attached Corinthian columns and three statues over the pediment (1814; on the English Quay).

On a considerably larger scale, Quarenghi placed a portico of three-quarter Corinthian columns over a rusticated entrance arcade for the Catherine Institute near the Anichkov Bridge (1804–7; located on the site of Mikhail Zemtsov's "Italian" Palace), thus providing a visual center to an extended facade along the narrow Fontanka quay. Quarenghi's designs of pediment and portico vary in their proportions as well as the significance that they impart to a building. At the Charity Hospital on Liteinyi Prospekt (1803–5), his Ionic octastyle portico protects a curving entrance drive, and with its two flanking service wings, the plan of the hospital suggests a country manor; yet the lack of dentilation or any other ornament suggests the building's severe and prosaic function. The Charity Hospital, later named the Mariinskii, was founded to commemorate the centenary of St. Petersburg. See G. Popov, *Mariinskaia bol'nitsa dlia bednykh* (St. Petersburg, 1905). Korshunova, *Kvarengi*, pp. 118–19, discusses this and other medical institutions by Quarenghi. Its plan and elevation are contained in Taleporovskii, *Kvarengi*, Plate 180.

96. Korshunova, *Kvarengi*, pp. 120–4. For project drawings and plans, see Taleporovskii, Plates 184, 186, 187. It was in the Ceremonial Hall that Lenin proclaimed the establishment of Soviet power in November 1917.

97. *Pamiatniki arkhitektury Leningrada*, p. 77. An analysis of the classical resolution of the Manege facade proportions is presented in Taleporovskii, *Kvarengi*, pp. 71–73, with splendid project drawings, Plates 157–60. See also the comparative analysis of the Petersburg Manege with the one designed by Quarenghi for Munich, ibid., p. 31, Plates 161–2.

98. Documentary material on the construction of Lialichi is contained in F. F. Gornostaev, *Dvortsy i tserkvi iuga* (Moscow, 1914); also Taleporovskii, *Kvarengi*, pp. 25–6, and Plates 120–30, illustrating the palace and its interior decoration as it still existed in 1911. War damage has left only a few outbuildings and the church extant. Piliavskii also attributes to Quarenghi the design of the Stol'noe manor, built in the 1780s and similar to Lialichi (*D. Kvarengi*, pp. 153–4).

In contrast, Quarenghi's design of a large villa for Pavel Stroganov on the estate of Khoten (Kharkov Province) is suggestive of his urban designs in Petersburg. Instead of a centralized plan with rotunda, horizontal lines predominate in this two-story building marked in the center by a hexastyle portico with pediment statuary. See Taleporovskii, *Kvarengi*, p. 27, with project drawings, Plates 131–3; and Vergunov and Gorokhov, *Russkie sady*, pp. 284–5. See also the elgaic commentary on the neglect of Khoten in G. K. Lukomskii, *Starinnye usad' by Khar'kovskoi gubernii* (Petrograd, 1917).

99. For comments on the typology of Quarenghi estate houses, see Taleporovskii, *Kvarengi*, pp. 50–1.

100. *Pamiatniki arkhitektury Leningrada*, p. 241; Korshunova, pp. 61–3. In addition to his Petersburg houses, Bezborodko commissioned Quarenghi to build in Moscow yet another mansion, the scale of which would have dwarfed most of the architect's previous work (see Chapter 11).

101. For the attribution to Quarenghi, see V. A. Vitiazeva, *Nevskie Ostrova* (Leningrad, 1986), pp. 26–7. The Kamennoostrovskii Palace was long attributed to Bazhenov, and subsequently to Velten, who seems to have supervised its construction. See also *Pamiatniki arkhitektury Leningrada*, p. 211; and Korshunova, *Iurii Fel'ten*, pp. 94–5.

102. Vitiazeva, *Nevskie Ostrova*, pp. 28–30.

103. The palace on the Fontanka should not be confused with the Iusupov Palace on the Moika, by Vallin de la Mothe (see the preceding). In 1810, the Fontanka palace became the premises of the newly established Institute of Transportation Engineers. *Pamiatniki arkhitektury Leningrada*, p. 219; Taleporovskii, *Kvarengi*, pp. 17–18; Korshunova, *Kvarengi*, pp. 68–9, with a plan of the palace grounds, p. 71.

104. Quarenghi's son Giulio commented on the classical antecedents for the placement of the interior columns in the Maltese Chapel. See *Fabbriche e disegni di Giacomo Quarenghi architetto de S. M. L'Imperatore di Russia cavaliere di Malta e di S. Wolodimiro illustrate dal cavaliere Giulio suo figlio* (Mantova, 1844), p. 35; quoted in Taleporovskii, pp. 29–30. See also *Disegni di Giacomo Quarenghi: Catalogo della Mostra* (Venice, 1967); and Korshunova, *Kvarengi*, pp. 111–14. Taleporovskii also notes the inventiveness with which Quarenghi used faux marbre in colors and patterns that bore no relation to an imitation of natural marble (p. 91). The current use of the palace as a military cadet school prevents a proper viewing of this magnificent structure.

105. From a letter of 1785 to Luigi Marchesi, quoted in Taleporovskii, p. 10. See also *Pamiatniki arkhitektury prigorodov Leningrada*, p. 80.

106. For details of the ceiling decoration in both the main hall and the study, see Grimm, *Arkhitektura perekrytii*, pp. 46–50. On the design of the floor, Korshunova, *Kvarengi*, pp. 74, 76. Catherine called the Concert Hall a "temple of friendship," and for the intimate musical gatherings refreshments were prepared in the nearby kitchen pavilion, or Kitchen Ruin, designed by Quarenghi in 1785–6 in romantic imitation of a ruined Italian rotunda, with shattered columns, fragments of classical bas reliefs (by Carlo Albani), and brick walls partially stripped of stucco. Project sketches as well as prewar photographs of both the Concert Hall and the Kitchen Ruins are contained in Taleporovskii, *Kvarengi*, Plates 22–32.

In the same area of the Catherine park, and during the same period, Quarenghi erected a Turkish "kiosk" pavilion (not extant), reflecting, as did other park structures at Tsarskoe Selo, Catherine's interests in the Ottoman Empire. On a more personal level, she commissioned Quarenghi to build a mausoleum to contain the body of one of her favorites, A. D. Lanskoi, who died from a hunting accident at Tsarskoe Selo in 1784. The domed cruciform structure, with a rusticated, windowless ground floor and thermal windows on the facade of each of the four arms, seems both Roman and Byzantine. See *Pamiatniki arkhitektury prigorodov Leningrada*, p. 156.

107. For a survey of the variant plans of the Alexander Palace, see Taleporovskii, *Kvarengi*, pp. 24–5. The resemblance of the plan to Starov's design for the Tauride Palace is noted in Petrov, *Gorod Pushkin*, p. 160.

108. An example of the classical economy of his design at the Alexander Palace is the adaptation of the exterior bays with thermal windows (as on the end facades) for use on the interior as a semicircular open arch placed over faux marbre columns and pilasters at the passage from one state room to another. For project drawings of the interior and prerevolutionary photographs with the original configuration of the state rooms, see Taleporovskii, *Kvarengi*, Plates 114–17. The building houses a naval institute and as of this writing is not open for viewing.

109. After prolonged discussion, a more durable replica of the gates was begun in 1827 under the supervision of Vasilii Stasov, who designed a brick structure sheathed in copper. An exhaustive analysis of the construction of the Narva Triumphal Gates and of their iconographic significance is contained in A. G. Raskin, *Triumfal'nye arki Leningrada* (Leningrad, 1977), pp. 98–136. Quarenghi's project drawings are reproduced in Taleporovskii, *Kvarengi*, Plates 191–4. For his design of the arch, Quarenghi was awarded the Order of St. Vladimir and given hereditary rights as a Russian nobleman. Soon after his death in Petersburg in March 1817, his widow and son Giulio returned to Bergamo with their archive of Quarenghi's work.

110. See ibid., Plates 195–8.

Chapter 11

1. The lack of a firm association between the hereditary Russian nobility and a specific estate before the eighteenth century has been frequently noted. See, for example, Paul Dukes, *Catherine the Great and the Russian Nobility* (Cambridge, 1967), p. 18.

2. Richard Pipes, *Karamzin's Memoir on Ancient and Modern Russia: A Translation and Analysis* (New York, 1966), p. 15. Pipes' introductory essay provides a lucid summary of the stages in the accrual of privilege by the eighteenth-century Russian nobility; see pp. 6–20. For a complementary, but more reserved interpretation of the edict's significance, see Paul Dukes, *The Making of Russian Absolutism*, pp. 135–8. The relevant documents are reproduced in Paul Dukes, *Russian under Catherine the Great: Volume One: Select Documents on Government and Society* (Newtonville, Mass., 1978). A recent monograph of the subject is Robert Jones, *The Emancipation of the Russian Nobility* (Princeton, 1973).

3. See Pipes, *Karamzin's Memoir*, p. 15.

4. A specific example of the appeal to classical precedent in the definition of noble privileges was Prince N. Davydov's suggestion (at the discussions of the 1767 Legislative Commission) for the ranking of various groups of nobility as had been suggested by Plato and Aristotle and implemented in Rome. See Dukes, *Catherine the Great and the Russian Nobility*, pp. 152–3.

5. Among the earliest Moscow manors in the western manner was Glinki, built in the 1730s by James Bruce, of Scottish descent and one of Peter's most important advisors on matters of military technology. Although simple in design and modest in size, the Glinki mansion represents a rare surviving example of the major evolution between the functional estate houses of the pre-Petrine period and the new concepts of the country manor as an expression of culture and the art of building. On the Glinki manor house, see N. Ia. Tikhomirov, *Arkhitektura podmoskovnykh usadeb* (Moscow, 1955), pp. 48–50. The same work also contains a survey of other Moscow estate houses from the first half of the eighteenth century. The evolution of the manor house during this period, and its contrast with the preceding era, is analyzed in S. Toropov, *Podmoskovnye usad'by* (Moscow, 1947), pp. 5–9.

In Moscow proper, one of the first suburban mansions of the new style was commissioned by Peter I on the former estate of another of his associates, Fedor Golovin. First built by Golovin in 1702 on the banks of the Iauza River near Lefortovo, the house was complemented by other Petrine structures intended to create an environment in the "European manner." In the 1730s, the same area, east of the central part of Moscow, provided the site for Bartolomeo Francesco Rastrelli's palace complex at Annenhof, followed in 1747 by the suburban wooden palace that he built in his usual baroque style for Empress Elizabeth at Perovo (whose earlier "Moscow baroque" Church of the Icon of the Sign was noted in the preceding chapter). The Golovin estate and park are described, along with other early Moscow ensembles, in Vergunov and Gorokhov, *Russkie sady i parki*, pp. 167–70.

6. The house at the Vorontsov estate at Voronovo illustrates the process: first built in the middle of the eighteenth century by Ivan Vorontsov (who was permitted by Elizabeth to retire at an early age from state service), the mansion was enlarged by Artemii Ivanovich Vorontsov at the end of the century to a plan by Nikolai Lvov, with three stories in the grand Palladian style. Over the same period, the estate also acquired a number of other monuments, particularly those designed by Karl Blank in the 1760s, such as the Church of the Savior and the stylized Dutch House with a tiered pediment decorated in the manner of the late seventeenth century.

In 1800, the Voronovo estate was acquired by Fedor Rostopchin, governor-general of Moscow and a lover of English landscape parks, who brought the surroundings to their apogee. In 1812, however, the mansion's location near the invasion route led Rostopchin to set it afire as Kutuzov's army abandoned the area. The remnants of the severely damaged central structure were soon rebuilt on a smaller scale, which was again enlarged at the end of the nineteenth century by the Sheremetevs, who added a mansard roof. In 1949, the mansion was expanded still further as a "rest home," without, however, distorting the basic design of the Sheremetev variant – itself considerably different in appearance from the Lvov design. For a detailed history of the Voronovo estate, see S. N. Palentreer, *Usad'ba Voronovo* (Moscow, 1960). See also M. A. Il'in, *Podmoskov'e* (Moscow, 1974), pp. 107–12.

A similar series of transformations occurred with many other eighteenth-century country mansions, such as the one at Volkonskii estate of Sukhanovo (to the south of Moscow). Built by an unknown architect at the end of the eighteenth century, the house was frequently rebuilt during the nineteenth century, and burned to the ground following the 1917 revolution. It was rebuilt in the neoclassical style in 1945–6 as a rest home (used by the Writers Union). Sukhanovo is most famous, however, for its slightly later pseudo-Gothic service buildings and the Volkonskii mausoleum, a rotunda constructed in 1813 by Afanasii Grigorev or Domenico Gilardi. The basic monograph on Sukhanovo is D. Arkin, *Sukhanovo* (Moscow, 1958). A more concise survey is provided in Pod''iapol'skaia, ed., *Pamiatniki arkhitektury moskovskoi oblasti*, vol. 1, pp. 313–16. It should be noted that the rebuilding during the immediate postwar period of mansions at Sukhanovo, Voronovo, and other former estates represents a telling comment on the elitism of the final phase of Stalinist rule.

7. An architectural survey of the Kuskovo ensemble is provided by L. V. Tydman in I. M. Glozman, ed., *Kuskovo. Ostankino. Arkhangel'skoe* (Moscow, 1976), pp. 15–74. See also Vergunov and Gorokhov, pp. 178–85. A lavishly illustrated text in English is Olga Baranova, *Kuskovo* (Leningrad, 1983).

8. For a reproduction of a 1770s engraving of the Kuskovo Grotto, based on a drawing supervised by Mikhail Makhaev, see ibid., Plate 75. The history of eighteenth-century albums of views of the estate is presented in the introduction to Baranova (no pagination).

9. Pierre Laurent also compiled an album of engravings (based largely on drawings by Makhaev) of the estate that provides the best documentary source for the eighteenth-century appearance of Kuskovo. Later in the century, his state of Flora was replaced by one of Ganymede. See Vergunov and Gorokhov, *Russkie sady*, p. 183.

10. On the legacy of Karl Blank at Kuskovo, see L. V. Tydman, "Rabota arkhitektora K. I. Blanka v Kuskove (Zakazchik i arkhitektor v XVIII v.)," in T. V. Alekseeva, ed., *Russkoe iskusstov barokko* (Moscow, 1977), pp. 216–25.

11. Peter Sheremetev involved himself in all aspects of the design of the house and kept copious records, which document the involvement of serf architects and artisans in the project until its completion in 1775.

12. The use of color and light as organizing principles within the enfilades of state rooms is analyzed in Vergunov and Gorokhov, *Russkie sady*, p. 179.

13. Tydman gives a perceptive analysis of the relation of the entresol rooms, with their contrasting simplicity, to the rooms of the enfilade below. See *Kuskovo. Ostankino. Arkhangel'skoe*, pp. 46–7.

14. The example of Kuskovo in the evolving design of large state rooms in the Russian country house is examined in R. M. Baiburova, "Zal i gostinaia usadebnogo doma russkogo klassitsizma," in V. P. Vygolov et al., eds., *Pamiatniki russkoi arkhitektury i monumental'nogo iskusstva* (Moscow, 1983), pp. 113–14.

15. On the formal garden, as well as the larger park at Kuskovo, see Vladimir Zgura, "Kuskovskii reguliarnyi sad," *Sredi kollektsionerov*, 1924, nos. 5–6: 4–19.

16. Vergunov and Gorokhov, *Russkie sady*, p. 182.

17. A recent history of the Ostankino estate and its architecture is L. A. Lepskaia, M. Z. Sarkisova et al., *Ostankinskii dvorets-muzei: Tvorchestvo krepostnykh* (Leningrad, 1982). See also I. G. Semenova, "Ostankino," in I. M. Glozman, ed., *Kuskovo. Ostankino. Arkhangel'skoe*, pp. 75–124; and N. A. Elizarova, *Ostankino* (Moscow, 1966). There were several, related considerations behind the move from Kuskovo to Ostankino, in particular Sheremetev's decision to marry the troupe's lead actress and his former serf Praskovia Kovaleva (stage name Zhemchugova). Three years after their marriage in 1800, Zhemchugova died of consumption. See Iurii Shamurin, *Podmoskovnyia* (Moscow, 1912), p. 52.

18. Semenova, "Ostankino," pp. 78–9.

19. On the relation between the formal garden and the palace, see Vergunov and Gorokhov, *Russkie sady*, pp. 187–92.

20. An architectural survey of the palace and grounds at Arkhangelskoe is contained in V. L. Rapoport and N. T. Unaniants, "Arkhangel'skoe," in I. M. Glozman, ed., *Kuskovo. Ostankino. Arkhangel'skoe*, pp. 125–200. See also V. Poznanskii, *Arkhangel'skoe* (Moscow, 1966). On the later phases of construction, see Tikhomirov, *Arkhitektura podmoskovnykh usadeb*, pp. 160–88, with illustrations.

21. Rapoport and Unaniants, "Arkhangel'skoe," p. 132.

22. Iusupov's contribution to the Arkhangelskoe ensem-

ble is discussed in Shamurin, *Podmoskovnyia* (Moscow, 1912), p. 41.

23. Rapoport and Unaniants, "Arkhangel'skoe," p. 141.

24. The major state rooms of the Arkhangelskoe palace were designed primarily for the display of Iusupov's art collection, which included antique statuary in the Hall of Antiquities, located at the center of the west enfilade and flanked by two corner salons containing work by, and in the style of, Hubert Robert, a French painter much sought after during the late eighteenth century for his idealized landscapes with classical ruins (cf. the Kamennoostrovskii Palace in Petersburg). Among other gallery-rooms, the most notable is the Venetian, or Tiepolo, Hall (north enfilade, to the right of the central vestibule), containing the artist's vast canvases "The Meeting of Antony and Cleopatra" and "The Feast of Cleopatra." The family living quarters, situated in the east enfilade, were on a much more modest and intimate scale.

25. Tikhomirov, *Arkhitektura podmoskovnykh usabeb*, pp. 180–1, 187.

26. The Arkhangelskoe estate was featured in some of the most prestigious of early twentieth-century cultural publications. See, for example, B. Veniaminov, "Arkhangel'skoe," in Sergei Diagilev's *Mir iskusstva*, 1904, no. 2: 31–40 (with 35 photographs).

27. The Demidov dynasty is the suject of a monograph by Hugh D. Hudson, Jr., *The Rise of the Demidov Family and the Russian Iron Industry in the Eighteenth Century* (Newton-ville, Mass. 1986).

28. On Nikita Akinfievich Demidov, see ibid., pp. 80–96. His lavish style of life and his expenditures during the tour of Europe are noted on pp. 93–6.

29. The estate of Petrovskoe (given the dual name of the nearby village of Alabino to avoid confusion with other estates of the same name in the Moscow area) has been the subject of much investigation. Among the more informative works are Sergei Toropov, "Petrovskoe-Demidovykh," *Sredi kollektsionerov*, 1924, nos. 7–8: 20–5; Tikhomirov, *Arkhitektura podmoskovnykh*, pp. 108–12; A. I. Vlasiuk, A. I. Kaplun, and A. A. Kirparisova, *Kazakov* (Moscow, 1955), pp. 88–97; M. A. Il'in, *Podmoskov'e*, pp. 113–15; and Pod''iapol'skaia, ed., *Pamiatniki arkhitektury moskovskoi oblasti*, vol. 2, pp. 61–4.

30. Toropov, "Petrovskoe-Demidovykh," p. 20.

31. The complex geometry of the plan argues in favor of Bazhenov's participation, yet this is only supposition, as is so much else in the career of that architect. The argument for Bazhenov is advanced by I. E. Grabar' "V poiskakh neizvestnykh postroek V. I. Bazhenova," in *Neizvestnye i predpolagaemye postroiki V. I. Bazhenova* (Moscow, 1951), pp. 123–5. The entrance pavilions to the Mikhailovskii Castle in Petersburg (see Chapter 10) bear a considerable resemblance to the form of the Demidov mansion at Petrovskoe, but they were built later and have been attributed to Brenna as well as Bazhenov. The plan of the mansion also bears a close resemblance to Ivan Starov's design

of a mansion for the Demidovs at Taitsy (1774–80s), near Petersburg. See Il'in, *Podmoskov'e*, p. 114.

32. See Hudson, *The Rise of the Demidov Family,* p. 113.

33. Following Nikolai's death in Florence in 1828, the next Demidov generation reached new heights of financial profligacy, and in 1852 the estate was sold to the Princes Meshcherskii, who in the ensuing decades stripped the mansion of most of its interior work. Toropov indignantly notes the Meshcherskiis' meretricious vandalism in "Petrovskoe-Demidovykh," p. 25.

34. On Brattsevo, see Toropov, *Podmoskovnye usad'by*, pp. 27–8; and M. A. Il'in and T. V. Moiseeva, *Moskva i Podmoskov'e*, p. 457.

35. Undeservedly little has been written on the Liublino estate. See Tikhomirov, *Arkhitektura podmoskovnykh*, p. 193.

36. On the Valuevo estate and park, see ibid., pp. 132–3; and Pod''iapol'skaia, ed., *Pamiatniki arkhitektury moskovskoi oblasti*, vol. 1, pp. 302–4.

37. The most thoughtful Russian examination of the intellectual bases of the landscape garden in the neoclassical era is Dmitrii Likhachev, *Poeziia sadov* (Leningrad, 1982), pp. 189–300. Likhachev, too, has written on the deliberate and complementary contrast between nature and neoclassical architecture (pp. 286–7). See also M. A. Anikst and V. S. Turchin, *. . . v okrestnostiakh Moskvy*, with reproductions and extensive excerpts from eighteenth-century manuals on gardening and the design of parks. A survey of the work of Bolotov and Lvov in garden design is contained in Vergunov and Gorokhov, *Russkie sady*, pp. 110–16.

38. In *Poeziia sadov*, Likhachev frequently refers to contemporary literary culture in both Russia and the West. On the views of pre-Romantics such as Nikolai Karamzin toward the "enhancement" of nature (in opposition to Rousseau's complete faith in untouched nature), see E. P. Shchukina, " 'Natural'nyi sad' russkoi usad'by v kontse XVIIIv," in T. V. Alekseeva, ed., *Russkoe iskusstvo XVIII v.: Materialy i issledovaniia* (Moscow, 1973), pp. 109–10. Further commentary on the literary aspects of the natural garden is contained in Priscilla Roosevelt, "Tatiana's Garden: Noble Sensibilities and Estate Park Design in the Romantic Era," *Slavic Review*, 49 (1990): 335–49.

39. For commentary (not altogether complimentary) on Bolotov's work at Bogoroditsk, see V. Makarov, "Andrei Bolotov i sadovoe iskusstvo v Rossii XVIII veka," *Sredi kollektsionerov*, 1924, nos. 5–6: 27–32. More generally on Bolotov's opinion on the salutary effects of landscape design, see E. P. Shchukina, " 'Natural'nyi sad' russkoi usad'by v kontse XVIIIv," pp. 109–17.

40. Lvov's building for the post office continues in its original function to this day. An authoritative biography, with particular emphasis on his literary work and his connections with contemporary Russian artists (such as Borovikovskii) and poets (such as Gavriil Derzhavin), is A. N. Glumov, *N. A. L'vov* (Moscow, 1980). For closer attention to Lvov's work as an architect, see M. V. Budylina, O. I. Braitseva, and A. M. Kharlamova, *Arkhitektor N. A. L'vov*

(Moscow, 1961); and N. I. Nikulina, *Nikolai L'vov* (Leningrad, 1971).

41. See ibid., pp. 26–31. On classical prototypes in the work of Lvov, with specific reference to the Pantheon, see M. B. Mikhailova, "Tipy sooruzhenii antichnosti v arkhitekture russkogo klassitsizma," *Arkhitekturnoe nasledstvo*, 26 (1978): 4–5. The double-shelled dome in Lvov's other work is discussed in the "Afterword" by A. M. Kharlamova to Glumov, *N. A. L'vov*, pp. 192–3.

42. On the Monastery of Sts. Boris and Gleb, see Denisov, *Pravoslavnye monastyri*, pp. 837–9. Briefly on the Torzhok cathedral, see Nikulina, p. 88. More detail on the architecture of Torzhok is provided in L. V. Andreev, "Istoricheskoe iadro Torzhka i ego glavnye arkhitekturnye ansambli," *Arkhitekturnoe nasledstvo*, 29 (1981): 18–26.

43. Although plates were prepared for volumes three and four, only the first volume of Lvov's translation, from the edition *Il quattro libri del l'architecture di Andrea Palladio* (Venice, 1616), was published, as *Chetyre knigi Palladievoi arkhitektury* (Petersburg, 1798). See Evsina, *Arkhitekturnaia teoriia v Rossii vtoroi poloviny XVIII–nachala XIX veka*, pp. 44–5.

44. On the predominant influence of Palladio's villas in Russian architecture (particularly the work of Lvov and Quarenghi), see M. A. Il'in, "O palladianstve v tvorchestve D. Kvarengi i N. L'vova," in T. V. Alekseeva, ed., *Russkoe iskusstvo XVIII veka* (Moscow, 1973), pp. 104–5. See also V. N. Grashchenko, "Nasledie Palladio v arkhitekture russkogo klassitsizma," in *Sovetskoe iskusstvoznanie*, 1981, no. 2: 201–34.

45. Lvov also rebuilt the mansion at Voronovo, largely destroyed in 1812. For a survey of Lvov's estate architecture, see Glumov, *L'vov*, pp. 116–20, with an illustrated supplement at the end.

46. A comparison of the Trinity Church with its Roman antecedents is given in Mikhailova, "Tipy sooruzhenii antichnosti," pp. 3–4. A more detailed analysis of the church, its prototypes, and its attribution to Lvov is presented in Nikulina, pp. 74–82. See also Petrov et al., *Pamiatniki arkhitektury Leningrada*, p. 279. The church is commonly referred to as "Kulich and Paskha" for its resemblance to the shape of the traditional Easter round cake and the pyramid mold of soft cheese.

47. For Lvov, and for many of his contemporaries, buildings of all designations – temple, house, or pavilion – could be subsumed within a unified aesthetic and tectonic system based on the principles of the classical orders, whether defined by Vitruvius or Palladio. Equally important for Lvov, however, was architecture in an open, picturesque setting closely related to the qualities valued in the idealized landscapes of painters such as Hubert Robert. Lvov's extensive work in park design and his estate pavilions indicate not only a superb understanding of architectural form and interior design, but also an appreciation of the building as noble ruin.

48. A detailed reexamination of the provenance and dates of the Alexandrine Palace is contained in G. M. An-

tsiferova, "Dvorets v Neskuchnom," in Vygolov, ed., *Pamiatniki russkoi arkhitektury*, pp. 92–111.

49. For a summary of Betskoi's pedagogical activities, see B. Krasnobaev, *Ocherki istorii russkoi kul'tury XVIII veka* (Moscow, 1972), pp. 71–80; on the Foundling Home, pp. 73–4. Commentary on the design in relation to contemporary French culture is contained in N. A. Luk'ianov, "Moskovskii Vospitatel'nyi dom i problemy russkogo klassitsizma," in N. T. Eneeva, ed., *Pamiatnik v kontekste kul'tury* (Moscow, 1991), pp. 53–62. Betskoi published a large edition on the home, with engravings: *Uchrezhdenie Imperatorskogo Vospitatel'nogo doma* (St. Petersburg, 1767).

50. A reproduction of the 1767 engraving of the projected form is contained in Brunov, *Istoriia russkoi arkhitektury*, p. 353.

51. On the design and innovations of the west wing, see N. A. Evsina, "Proekty uchebnykh zdanii v Rossii XVIII veka," in T. V. Alekseeva, ed., *Russkoe iskusstvo XVIII veka*, p. 123.

52. The construction history of the Foundling Home is summarized in G. V. Makarevich, ed., *Pamiatniki arkhitektury Moskvy: Belyi gorod*, pp. 335–8. For an account of Prokopii Demidov's support for the home and his attitudes toward Betskoi's attempt to create a new educated class in Russia, see Hudson, *The Rise of the Demidov Family*, pp. 101–6.

53. The following biographical details are taken primarily from V. L. Snegirev's monograph, *Zodchii Bazhenov* (Moscow, 1962).

54. On Bazhenov's study with de Wailly, see ibid., pp. 35–7. Snegirev also notes that Bazhenov worked in an unofficial capacity with Sufflot; ibid., p. 37.

55. Bazhenov had reason to expect the appointment, but was denied for reasons of internal politics, perhaps related to the irritable president of the Academy, Ivan Betskoi. See ibid., pp. 56–8.

56. As in so many subsequent cases, there is no documentary confirmation for the attribution of the Petersburg Arsenal to Bazhenov. See A. I. Mikhailov, *Bazhenov* (Moscow, 1957), p. 42; and Snegirev, *Bazhenov*, p. 58. During the nineteenth century, the Arsenal was converted to use as the district court – an institution whose unpopularity led to the burning of the building during the disturbances at the beginning of 1917. Orlov continued to use his influence on Bazhenov's behalf, although the architectural commissions only rarely resulted in actual construction. Among the unrealized projects was a grandiose design for the Institute for the Education of Young Noblewomen at the Smolnyi Convent, with elements of the baroque that suggest Rastrelli's work and with a geometrically complex floor plan. For a reproduction of the plan for the institute, see, ibid., p. 59.

57. Ibid., p. 61.

58. The attribution to Bazhenov was advanced in a number of publications by N. A. Kozhin, who placed the church and other Russian examples of the pseudo-Gothic within the tradition of seventeenth-century Russian architecture. See, for example, his "K genezisu russkoi lozhnoi gotiki," *Akademiia arkhitektury*, 1 (1934): 114–21. On the tenuous nature of the attribution of the Znamenka and other pseudo-Gothic churches to Bazhenov, see A. I. Mikhailov, *Bazhenov* (Moscow, 1951), pp. 166, 168; and Snegirev, *Bazhenov*, pp. 30–1, 61, 115.

59. On the planning for the reconstruction of the Kremlin, see Mikhailov, *Bazhenov*, pp. 49–110.

60. For the financial calculations, see Snegirev, *Bazhenov*, p. 77.

61. Among the documents related to Bazhenov's Kremlin project is the "Opinion of the Architect Bazhenov concerning the Kremlin" (1768), published in N. Morenets, "Novye materialy o V. I. Bazhenove," *Arkhitekturnoe nasledstvo*, 1 (1951): 94–104. Other sources for Bazehnov's pronouncements are noted in Snegirev, *Bazhenov*, pp. 64, 67.

62. In the discourse, Bazhenov insisted that the architectural brilliance of the western cultures was related to the respect they accorded to architecture and the arts – a significant statement for the development of a modern professional conciousness among Russian architects. Bazhenov's text included a survey of architectural duties and principles – derived primarily from Vitruvius, but similar to Eropkin's views set forth at the end of the 1730s (see Chapter 9). On the "Short Discourse on the Kremlin Construction," see ibid., pp. 67–71. The document was written by Bazhenov's assistant Fedor Karzhavin, with emendations by Bazhenov, who one can assume was the actual author of the document.

63. The most brilliant product of this system – complementing the more rigid curriculum of the Academy in Petersburg – was Matvei Kazakov, chosen by Bazhenov as his primary assistant. On the educational aspect of the Kremlin project, see Mikhailov, *Bazhenov*, pp. 79–81, 306–13; and Snegirev, *Bazhenov*, pp. 100–4. The training of architects in Moscow during this period is also discussed in M. V. Budylina, "Arkhitekturnoe obrazovanie v Kamennom prikaze (1775–1782)," *Arkhitekturnoe nasledstvo*, 15 (1963): 111–20.

64. Although the text of the Kremlin speech (reproduced in Snegirev, *Bazhenov*, pp. 220–3) was long attributed to the distinguished Russian poet Alexander Sumarokov, a close acquaintance of the architect and a participant in the ceremony, it would appear that Bazhenov was the primary author. Ibid., p. 83.

65. Even as the Kremlin project came to a halt, Catherine commissioned Bazhenov in 1775 to create on Moscow's Khodinka Field a large triumphal setting for the celebration of the successful conclusion of the Turkish war. The large open space was contoured in imitation of the Crimea (with a pond and miniature ships) and filled with pavilions and theaters whose eclectic styles represented the exotic varieties of architecture in the Ottoman Empire. Ibid., p. 110. At the same time, most of the structures – whether wood or masonry – were finished in brick red with white trim, in the manner of medieval Muscovite architecture (as portrayed in the drawings of his assistant Matvei Kazakov).

66. A summary of the history of the estate and Catherine's purchase is presented in Mikhailov, *Bazhenov*, p. 112; and Snegirev, *Bazhenov*, pp. 114–15.

67. A selection of Bazhenov's plans at Tsaritsyno is presented in Mikhailov, *Bazhenov*, pp. 119–22. The first of the structures to be completed, the "Patterned" Bridge (1776–8), established the decorative system of patterned brickwork with limestone decoration in a merger of "gothick" with the medieval Muscovite masonry construction. Many of the early pavilions are not extant, but the walls of the small Private – or Semicircular – Palace still stand, with their exuberant limestone decoration culminating in a radiant burst around the monogram of Catherine. On the Private Palace, see ibid, pp. 124–5; with plan, p. 126. Like many of Bazhenov's pavilions at Tsaritsyno, the domed roof of the palace was originally covered with bright yellow ceramic tiles, associated in Catherine's mind with medieval architecture. The poor quality of the material, however, justified Bazhenov's reluctance to apply this technique, and the tiles were subsequently replaced by Matvei Kazakov with iron roofs. See Mikhailov, *Bazhenov*, pp. 151–2.

68. Although Bazhenov's plan for the "Opera House" has not been discovered, see ibid., pp. 125–7, for a discussion of the probable original design.

69. Bazhenov's characterization of the gate is quoted in ibid., p. 127. The architect used the same term in reference to the Gothic style of other structures at Tsaritsyno.

70. On Bazhenov's imperial palaces at Tsaritsyno, see ibid., pp. 130–9.

71. Ibid., pp. 149–50.

72. A sympathetic account of Bazhenov's involvement in Freemasonry is contained in Snegirev, *Bazhenov*, pp. 105–8. On possible masonic symbolism in the decorative motifs, see Mikhailov, *Bazhenov*, pp. 140, 147, passim. See also O. A. Medvedkova, "Tsaritsynskaia psevdogotika V. I. Bazhenova: opyt interpretatsii," in A. L. Batalov, ed., *Ikonografiia arkhitektury* (Moscow, 1990), pp. 153–73.

73. A more detailed study would be required to assay whether Catherine's decision was indeed related to her suspicion of the possibility of an incipient opposition circle among Moscow's grandees (perhaps connected to Freemasonry), or whether the style and elaborate designs – both of the exterior facades and interior plans – seemed to her oppressive in comparison with the stately grandeur of her suburban Petersburg palaces. The evidence in either case is largely speculative. For descriptions of Catherine's visit and its aftermath, see Snegirev, *Bazhenov*, pp. 130–1; and Mikhailov, *Bazhenov*, p. 156. It has been suggested, with little evidence, that Bazehnov's masonic affiliation was shared by the tsarevich Paul (cf. Snegirev, *Bazhenov*, p. 131), who did indeed give Bazhenov refuge and work at Gatchina after the Tsaritsyno debacle.

74. For a selection of Russian commentary on the ruins, as well as a survey of their subsequent fate, see ibid., pp. 133–4. On the cultural impact of the ruins in early nineteenth-century Russian literature, see S. V. Sergeev, "Pamiatnik v khudozhestvennom kontekste: vospriiatie usad'by Ekateriny II v Tsairtsyno v russkoi kul'ture pervoi treti XIX v.," in A. A. Voronov et al., eds., *Problemy istorii arkhitektury* (Moscow, 1990), part II, pp. 48–53. Russian restorers have attempted to complete one of the larger structures (the *khlebnyi dom*), but the project has been plagued with various delays.

75.   On the genesis of the mansion, see V. Eingorn, *K stopiatidesiatiletiiu sushchestvovaniia zdaniia Vsesoiuznoi biblioteki imeni V. I. Lenina* (Moscow, 1936); Mikhailov, *Bazhenov*, pp. 202–30; and N. L Krasheninnikova and P. A. Tel'tevskii, *Staroe zdanie Gosudarstvennoi Biblioteki SSSR imeni V. I. Lenina (dom Pashkova)* (Moscow, 1957). The Pashkov family archives burned during the fire of 1812, and there is no evidence confirming Bazhenov as the architect. The case is made largely on the basis of stylistic affinities between the Pashkov house and Bazhenov's project for the Great Kremlin Palace. See Snegirev, pp. 162–7; and Z. B. Krylova, "Novoe podtverzhdenie avtorstva V. I. Bazhenova v sozdanii byvsh. doma Pashkova (nyne Gos. Biblioteka im. Lenina)," *Arkhitektura SSSR*, 1955, no. 10: 47. For a summary of the history of the mansion (which in 1861 was converted into the Rumiantsev Museum, later the repository of rare books and manuscripts at the State Lenin Library), see G. V. Makarevich, ed., *Belyi gorod*, pp. 55–7.

76.   The Pashkov mansion has also been compared to eighteenth-century French architecture. See Iu. P. Kivokurtsev, "Skhodstvo arkhitektury doma b. Pashkova (Leninskoi biblioteki) s frantsuzskoi arkhitekturoi XVIII stoletiia," *Akademiia arkhitektury*, 1937, no. 2: 46–50.

77.   Less imposing, but possibly more influential, is the mansion attributed to Bazhenov and constructed in 1793–5 for Lieutenant General Ivan Iushkov. Located on a corner lot at the intersection of Miasnitskii Street with a small side street, it consists of a rotundal corner tower connecting two perpendicular facades. In this case, the major Ionic columns rest on a rusticated base, whose dimensions are echoed in the cornice. The upper floors are recessed. The complex geometry of the interior plan, which contains a magnificent oval colonnade at the head of the main staircase and several rooms with rounded configurations, is related to Bazhenov's work at Tsaritsyno. See Snegirev, *Bazhenov*, pp. 155–8; and Makarevich, ed., *Belyi gorod*, pp. 251–3, with plans. After its acquisition by the Moscow Arts Society in 1844, the Iushkov house served as the location of the School of Painting, Sculpture, and Architecture – and after 1917 of the art schools Vkhutemas and Vkhutein.

Other houses attributed to Bazhenov but now disfigured or not extant are discussed in N. Krasheninnikova, "K voprosu ob atributsii byvshego doma Dolgova na 1-y Meshchanskoi ulitse," *Arkhitekturnoe nasledstvo*, 1 (1951): 86–93; and "Sobstvennye doma V. I. Bazhenova v Moskve," *Arkhitekturnoe nasledstvo*, 1 (1951): 105–7. See also A. A. Kiparisova, "Neopublikovannye proekty Moskovskikh zodchikh kontsa XVIII in nachala XIX vekov," *Arkhitekturnoe nasledstvo*, 1 (1951): 108–34.

78.   Snegirev, *Bazhenov*, p. 162.

79.   On Bazhenov's activities at the academy in 1799, see ibid., pp. 201–5.

80.   A concise survey of Kazakov's work is provided in M. A. Il'in, *Kazakov* (Moscow, 1955). A more detailed study is A. I. Vlasiuk, A. I. Kaplun, and A. A. Kiparisova, *Kazakov* (Moscow, 1957).

81.   The Petrovskii Palace is currently occupied by administrative offices for the Russian space program and is therefore off limits to architectural historians. Photographs of the building and the interior of the rotunda are contained in M. Il'in, *Moskva: Pamiatniki arkhitektury XVIII-pervoi treti XIX veka* (Moscow, 1975), pp. 209–12.

82.   The medallions were copied from marble originals by Fedot Shubin for the Chesme Palace near Petersburg. See Komech and Pluzhnikov, eds., *Tsentral'nye ploshchadi*, pp. 344–5.

83.   Il'in, *Kazakov*, p. 19.

84.   The Church of the Metropolitan Philip was projected as the centerpiece of an unbuilt legation in Moscow for the Metropolitan Platon. See Il'in and Moiseeva, *Moskva i Podmoskov'e*, pp. 460–1.

85.   The Baryshnikov mausoleum served as a prototype for Kazakov's design of the Church of the Ascension on Gorokhovoe Field (1790–3) in Moscow. Kazakov's most complex adaptation of the rotunda to church architecture appeared on a smaller scale in the Church of Sts. Kozma and Demian on Pokrovka Street (1791–3), composed of three rotundas attached to a central rotunda: on the apse and at the northwest and southwest. The circular form of the Kozma and Demian church was repeated in the attached bell tower, with a dome that echoed that of the main structure. The interior of the church was completed only in 1803. See Makarevich, ed., *Belyi gorod*, pp. 297–8.

86.   Kazakov's design for the university did not survive in its original form: During the 1812 fire, it was severely damaged, and a rebuilding by Domenico Gilardi, while preserving certain of the dimensions of the original, is a landmark of late Moscow neoclassicism (see Chapter 12). The original elevation of the Kazakov university building is reproduced in ibid., pp. 22–3; with further information on the history and plan of the building, pp. 99–101. See also E. Beletskaia, "Vosstanovlenie zdanii Moskovskogo universiteta posle pozhara 1812 goda," *Arkhitekturnoe nasledstvo*, 1 (1951): 175–90.

87.   On the Noblemen's Assembly, see Makarevich, ed., *Belyi gorod*, pp. 143–6; and A. Kiparisova, "Neopublikovannye proekty moskovskikh zodchikh kontsa XVIII i nachala XIX vekov," *Arkhitekturnoe nasledstvo*, 1 (1951): 108–18. The central hall was the site of some of the most notorious show trials of the 1930s.

88.   The rotunda–church–mausoleum of the Golitsyn Hospital contained an elaborate sculpted burial monument to Dmitrii Golitsyn. See Il'in and Moiseeva, *Moskva i Podmoskov'e*, pp. 468–9.

89.   For a comparative analysis of the alternative plans for urban houses and their relation to the evolution of the street network in Moscow in the latter half of the eighteenth century, see Komech and Pluzhnikov, eds., *Tsentral'nye ploshchadi*, pp. 142–6.

90. This pattern shows numerous parallels with suburban estate houses such as that at Kuskovo. A discussion of the spatial arrangments in Moscow's neoclassical homes is contained in L. V. Tydman, "Ob"emno-prostranstvennaia kompozitsiia domov-dvortsov XVIII v.," in V. P. Vygolov, ed., *Pamiatniki russkoi arkhitektury i monumental'nogo iskusstva* (Moscow, 1985), pp. 127–47; and Evgenii Nikolaev, *Klassicheskaia Moskva* (Moscow, 1975), pp. 184–210. A more general analysis is presented in R. M. Baiburova, "Russkii usadebnyi inter'er epokhi klassitsizma. Planirovochnye kompozitsii," in V. P. Vygolov, ed., *Pamiatniki russkoi arkhitektury i monumental'nogo iskusstva* (Moscow, 1908), pp. 140–61. For a well-illustrated survey of the furnishings of the interiors, see I. A. Bartenev and V. N. Batazhkova, *Russkii inter'er XVIII-XIX v* (Leningrad, 1977).

91. On the I. I. Demidov mansion, see Il'in and Moiseev, *Moskva i Podmoskov'e*, pp. 471–2. In 1858, the house was sold to the Boundary Office, and subsequently retained its relation to mapmaking as a Soviet geodetic institute. Detailed information on the construction of the house is presented in Nikolaev, *Klassichskaia Moskva*, pp. 114–16.

92. A plan and analysis of the Gubin mansion are contained in Makarevich, ed., *Belyi gorod*, pp. 189–91. See also Nikolaev, *Klassichskaia Moskva*, pp. 112–13; and Baiburova, "Russkii usadebnyi inter'er," pp. 152, 155. Elevations and plans of Kazakov's houses, as collected in albums produced by the architect's workshop, are reproduced in E. A. Beletskaia, *Arkhitekturnye al'bomy M. F. Kazakova* (Moscow, 1956). Also included in this, one of the last projects of Kazakov's life, are contemporary houses by other architects. Many were destroyed in 1812 or subsequently rebuilt; thus, the albums, kept in the archives of the Shchusev Museum of Architecture in Moscow, are a valuable source of visual documentation for neoclassical Moscow of the late eighteenth century. For a selection of photographs, including the major houses by Kazakov, see M. A. Il'in, *Moskva. Pamiatniki arkhitektury XVIII–pervoi treti XIX veka* (Moscow, 1975).

93. For a detailed plan of the Baryshnikov mansion, see A. I. Komech and V. I. Pluzhnikov, eds., *Pamiatniki arkhitektury Moskvy: Zemlianoi gorod* (Moscow, 1989), pp. 242–4. The various stages of construction are analyzed in Nikolaev, *Klassichskaia Moskva*, pp. 102–7.

94. Much of the interior decoration of the Baryshnikov mansion has been preserved, although in a cluttered state. Like many former Moscow and Petersburg palatial residences, the house is crudely used by the institutions that pay to maintain it (in this case, a sanitation institute).

95. Kazakov rebuilt the house of the governor-general twice. The first version, originally designed by an unknown architect, was included in Kazakov's album instead of his own later version of 1791. A reproduction of the earlier version is contained in Makarevich, ed., *Belyi gorod*, p. 129. For a description of the later version, substantially rebuilt with the addition of two stories by Dmitrii Chechulin in 1947, see ibid., pp. 147–8.

96. Il'in, *Kazakov*, p. 49.

97. For a sympathetic critical analysis of the St. Martin church, see T. V. Alekseeva, "Iz istorii chastnogo stroitel'stva v Moskve kontsa XVIII veka. Doma A. B. Kurakina," in T. V. Alekseeva, *Issledovaniia i nakhodki* (Moscow, 1976), p. 135.

98. A plan of the Varvara Church is contained in Komech and Pluzhnikov, eds., *Tsentral'nye ploshchadi*, p. 459.

99. Detailed plans of the Batashov ensemble are contained in Komech and Pluzhnikov, eds., *Zemlianoi gorod*, pp. 310–14. Precisely because of the richness of the design in comparison with the more restrained, dry character of Rodion Kazakov's work, one specialist has questioned the attribution of the house to that architect. See Alekseeva, "Iz istorii chastnogo stroitel'stva v Moskve kontsa XVIII veka. Doma A. B. Kurakina," p. 136.

100. For a perceptive analysis of the location of the Batashov house as an example of this characteristic feature of Moscow's "organic" architectural growth – producing a system of sight lines merging architecture and topograpy – see Nikolaev, *Klassichskaia Moskva*, pp. 13–21. The texture of urban Moscow as organized around neoclassical monuments in the late eighteenth century is also examined in N. F. Gulianitskii, "O kompozitsii zdanii v ansamblevoi zastroike Moskvy perioda klassitsizma," *Arkhitekturnoe nasledstvo*, 24 (1976): 20–7. On the St. Simeon Church, see Komech and Pluzhnikov, eds., *Zemlianoi gorod*, pp. 314–15.

The scale, if not the variety, of the Batashov house was rivaled by the mansion constructed in 1799–1801 for Alexander Kurakin on Old Basman Street. Although the house (converted for use as the Alexander Commercial Institute in the latter part of the nineteenth century) is not extant, photographs and original site plans show an ensemble – including a large semicircular service building – as complex as that of the Batashov house. The main facade, which fronted along the street, contained a grand Corinthian portico and attached, symmetrical wings. The A. B. Kurakin house on Old Basman Street (not to be confused with the residence of his brother Stepan on New Basman Street) is the subject of Alekseeva's article, "Iz istorii chastnogo stroitel'stva v Moskve kontsa XVIII veka. Doma A. B. Kurakina," pp. 125–48, with documentation demonstrating Rodion Kazakov's authorship.

An approximation of the design of the portico is evident in a smaller estate house built by Rodion Kazakov at the turn of the nineteenth century on a Stroganov estate across the Iauza River (above the Savior–Andronikov Monastery). Flanked by symmetrical attached wings, the Corinthian portico in the major order projects from a spacious facade, carefully balanced in its proportions and with little surface decoration.

101. One example relatively well preserved is the Lobkova-Golitsyn house, built in 1782–1800, but composed of an agglomeration of parts extending along a small lane off Tverskaia Street in the central city. They are unified only by the articulation of the facade with pilaster strips and small loggia of attached columns over the carriage entrance to the courtyard. On the interior, the state rooms are aligned

along an enfilade, unifying two different states of construction. Typical features of late neoclassical interior design include oval or semicircular alcoves, such as the sitting room, within larger orthogonal spaces; faux marbre for columns and wall surfaces; and high-relief plaster tableaux on panels. On the A. I. Lobkova house, acquired by A. B. Golitsyn in 1820, see Makarevich. ed., *Belyi gorod*, pp. 154–6, with plans.

102. Plans and a construction history of the Talyzin house are presented in Makarevich, ed., *Belyi gorod*, pp. 79–81.

103. More compact in form but similar in design to the Talyzin house is the Kolychev house (end of the eighteenth century) on Bolshaia Nikitskaia (Herzen) Street. Perfectly balanced on both its vertical and horizontal lines, the main structure, with six main Corinthian pilasters, is flanked by attached wings containing entrances to the interior courtyard. Detailed plans and a selection of interior photographs of the Kolychev house (adapted for use by the School of Synodal Church Singers and now part of the Moscow Conservatory) are contained in Makarevich, ed., *Belyi gorod*, pp. 109–11. For a survey of the ensemble of neoclassical houses on Bolshaia Nikitskaia Street, see Nikolaev, *Klassicheskaia Moskva*, pp. 39–84.

104. On the hypercritical attitude of Stepan Kurakin toward Rodion Kazakov, see Alekseeva, "Iz istorii chastnogo stroitel'stva v Moskve kontsa XVIII veka. Doma A. B. Kurakina," pp. 137–8. The large house of Stepan Kurakin's brother Alexander (designed by Rodion Kazakov; discussed above) was located on the neighboring Old Basman Street.

105. The Catherine Palace was the major component in an extensive redevelopment in the late eighteenth century of the Iauza district and the former "Nemetskaia sloboda." See N. F. Gulianitskii, "Moskva Iauzskaia," *Arkhitekturnoe nasledstvo*, 34 (1986): 34–43. A general survey of Quarenghi's work in Moscow is presented by A. F. Krasheninnikov, "Dzhakomo Kvarengi," in Iu. S. Iaralov, ed., *Zodchie Moskvy XV–XIX vv*, pp. 189–94.

106. Quarenghi had earlier (c. 1790) participated in a competition to design a palace for Sheremetev in Kitai-gorod that would have housed the prince's rich collection of art. His extensive drawings for the building suggest a temple of the arts, with the majestic portico and use of statuary in architecture. The palace remained unbuilt, however, as Sheremetev shifted his attention to Ostankino. See Korshunova, *Kvarengi*, pp. 101–2.

107. See Krasheninnikov, "Dzhakomo Kvarengi," p. 192; and Il'in and Moiseeva, *Moskva i Podmoskov'e*, pp. 454–5.

108. Had the projected Sheremetev Palace been constructed, Quarenghi would have single handedly refashioned the core of the city's oldest trading district in the neoclassical manner. Plans and a survey of the construction history of the Old Gostinnyi Dvor are presented in Komech and Pluzhnikov, eds., *Tsentral'nye ploshchadi*, pp. 433–4. See also Krasheninnikov, "Dzhakomo Kvarengi," pp. 192–3. The intensive development of commercial architecture in Kitai-gorod in the late eighteenth century is discussed in O. P. Shchenkova, "Kitai-gorod – torgovyi tsentr Moskvy

v kontse XVIII–pervoi polovine XIX v.," *Arkhitekturnoe nasledstvo*, 33 (1985): 31–9; with particular reference to the rebuilding of the Old Gostinnyi Dvor, pp. 34–5. For a more general analysis of the transformation of Kitai-gorod during the same period, see idem., "Arkhitektura Kitai-goroda Moskvy perioda klasitsizma," *Arkhitekturnoe nasledstvo*, 36 (1988): 175–86.

109. Quarenghi's project drawings with the original arcaded form are reproduced in Taleporovskii, *Kvarengi*, Plates 103, 104.

110. The palaces of A. A. Bezborodko in Moscow are discussed in Taleporovskii, *Kvarengi*, pp. 27–8, with extensive project drawings; Korshunova, pp. 105–7; and Krasheninnikov, "Dzhakomo Kvarengi," p. 193.

111. Bezborodko's statement is contained in a letter of November 23, 1797, to Count S. R. Vorontsov; quoted, with source reference, in Taleporovskii, *Kvarengi*, p. 27.

112. The apparent collaboration between Quarenghi and Lvov – both ardent Palladians and both aware of the relation between the natural park and the proper setting of the neoclassical mansion – is discussed in Korshunova, *Kvarengi*, pp. 105–8.

113. A survey of new approaches to city planning in Russia during the latter half of the eighteenth century is contained in T. F. Savarenskaia, D. O. Shvidkovskii, and F. A. Petrov, *Istoriia gradostroitel'nogo iskusstva. Pozdnii feodalizm i kapitalizm* (Moscow, 1989), pp. 137–60. A concise treatment in English is Robert E. Jones, "Urban Planning and the Development of Provincial Towns in Russia During the Reign of Catherine II," in J. G. Garrard, ed., *The Eighteenth Century in Russia* (Oxford, 1973), pp. 321–44. A more extensive, if traditional analysis is provided in V. A. Shkvarnikov, *Ocherk istorii planirovki i zastroiki russkikh gorodov* (Moscow, 1954). According to Savarenskaia (p. 163), 300 new town plans were drawn up by the Commission, and over 100 by successor agencies. A total of 416 was included in the 1839 Book of Plans and Drawings, appended to the Compendium of Laws (PSZ).

114. For an analysis and illustrations of the Tver model forms and their subsequent influence, see S. S. Ozhegov, *Tipovoe i povtornoe stroitel'stvo v Rossii v XVIII–XIX vekakh* (Moscow, 1984), pp. 52–8.

115. The implementation of the new plans did not invariably run counter to traditional city plans. On their interrelation in the late eighteenth century, see N. F. Gulianitskii, "Cherty preemstvennosti v kompozitsii tsentrov russkikh pereplanirovannykh v XVIII v. gorodov," *Arkhitekturnoe nasledstvo*, 29 (1981): 3–17; and idem., "Russkii reguliarnyi gorod na traditsionnoi osnove," *Arkhitekturnoe nasledstvo*, 33 (1985): 3–13.

116. On the Nikitin plan for Kaluga, see Savarenskaia et al., *Istoriia gradostroitel'nogo iskusstva*, pp. 148–51.

117. The development of the Kaluga trading center is outlined in Margarita Fekhner, *Kaluga* (Moscow, 1972), pp. 117–21. The Gostinnyi Dvor building has been occasionally been attributed to Bazhenov, not on the basis of firm evidence, but on a general stylistic resemblance to his pseudo-Gothic designs. For a survey of centralized trading rows as an organizing element in the new town plans (including those for Kaluga and Kostroma), see A. A. Maksimov, "Torgovye tsentry v planirovkakh russkikh gorodov vtoroi poloviny XVIII-nachala XIX v.," V. P. Vygolov, ed., *Pamiatniki russkoi arkhitektury i monumental'nogo iskusstva* (Moscow, 1980), pp. 126–39.

118. A detailed description of the Zolatarev house (also known as the Kologrivova house, after its last private owner at the beginning of this century) is contained in Fekhner, *Kaluga*, pp. 88–96.

119. The adjoining, smaller state rooms, such as the large salon and the bedroom, are similarly decorated with faux marbre columns, elaborate trompe l'oeil ceiling paintings, and a series of plaster medallions narrating the progress of love – from Cupid's arrow to Cupid enchained to a statue of Minerva (symbolizing marriage) in the state bedroom.

120. A survey of Kaluga's early nineteenth-century town houses is presented in Fekhner, *Kaluga*.

121. On the plan of Kostroma, see Savarenskaia et al., *Istoriia gradostroitel'nogo iskusstva*, p. 147.

122. An architectural survey of neoclassical Kostroma is contained in Vladimir Ivanov, *Kostroma* (Moscow, 1978), pp. 144–64. A sensitive evocation of the old town at the time of the Romanov Tercentenary in 1913 is provided in Georgii K. Lukomskii, *Kostroma* (St. Petersburg, 1913). The town's connection with the founder of the Romanov dynasty, Mikhail (noted in Chapter 7), influenced the building of memorial structures only beginning with the nineteenth century.

123. On the replanning of Kazan, see V. P. Ostroumov, *Kazan'* (Kazan, 1978), pp. 73–81; and M. Fekhner, *Velikie Bulgary. Kazan'. Sviiazhsk* (Moscow, 1978), pp. 109–117, 120.

124. Ostroumov, *Kazan'*, p. 87.

125. For a survey of the construction of the neoclassical ensemble of the University of Kazan, see ibid., pp. 111–16; and Fekhner, *Kazan'*, pp. 133–47.

126. Quoted in Korshunova, *Kvarengi*, p. 100.

127. On the Military Hospital, see Il'in and Moiseeva, *Moskva i Podmoskov'e*, p. 473. Egotov's work in Moscow, including the hospital, is surveyed in M. S. Nikol'skaia, "I. V. Egotov," Iu. S. Iaralov, ed., *Zodchie Moskvy XV–XIX vv*, pp. 178–85.

Chapter 12

1. For a survey of planning initiatives in Petersburg in the first quarter of the nineteenth century, see Savarenskaia et al., *Istoriia gradostroitel'nogo iskusstva*, pp. 175–85. Much archival material on the topic is presented in N. Leiboshits and V. Piliavskii, "Materialy k istorii planirovki Peterburga v pervoi polovine XIX veka," *Arkhitekturnoe nasledstvo*, 7 (1955): 39–66.

2. Quoted in Grabar, *Istoriia russkogo iskusstva*, vol. 6, p. 466.

3. A recent monography on Voronikhin is V. G. Lisov-

skii, *Andrei Voronikhin* (Leningrad, 1971). See also G. G. Grimm, *Arkhitektor Voronikhin* (Leningrad, 1963). For illustrations of Voronikhin's interior work at the Stroganov Palace – with particular emphasis on the astonishing perspectival work in the design of the palace's Mineral Study – see Grimm, *Arkhitektura perekrytii*, pp. 88–107, 156–60.

Voronikhin's other work for the Stroganovs in Petersburg is not extant; the dacha that he decorated for them on Black River in 1797 was destroyed in this century. On the Stroganov dacha, portrayed by Swedish landscape painter Benjamin Paterssen, see G. Komelova et al., *Peterburg v proizvedeniiakh Patersena* (Moscow, 1978), p. 18. (A more detailed study of Paterssen's work, a major pictorial source for Petersburg at the turn of the nineteenth century, is presented in B. L. Vasil'ev, "Peterburg kontsa XVIII–nachala XIX vekov v izobrazhenii V. Patersena," *Arkhitekturnoe nasledstvo*, 9 [1959]: 28–44.) Voronikhin himself sketched the dacha in 1799, for which he was awarded the title "Academician of Perspective Painting" by the Academy of Arts. It is now thought that the architect of the dacha was F. I. Demertsov.

4. Stroganov's tenure at the Academy of Arts is reviewed in V. G. Lisovskii, *Akademiia khudozhestv*, pp. 52–62.

5. A history of the genesis and construction of the Kazan Cathedral is contained in Ia. I. Shurygin, *Kazanskii sobor* (Leningrad, 1987), pp. 3–85.

6. For a discussion of the Kazan Cathedral within the context of European neoclassicism, see M. B. Mikhailova, "K voprosu o meste ansamblia Kazanskogo sobora v evropeiskoi arkhitekture," *Arkhitekturnoe nasledstvo*, 24 (1976): 41–50. Mikhailova, who sees only the most general and questionable stylistic resemblance between the Kazan Cathedral and St. Peter's, draws a comparison with the Church of San Francesco di Paola in Naples, built in 1817–28 by Pietro Bianchi. Although later than the Voronikhin structure, both manifest similarities in the neoclassical approach to monumental public space.

7. For a discussion of the possibility of a link between Bazhenov's work and Voronikhin's design for the Kazan Cathedral, see Lisovskii, *Voronikhin*, pp. 87–105. Lisovskii considers the evidence insufficient to establish a case of direct influence. It must be noted, however, that Voronikhin had studied with Bazhenov, and that both Russians had a first-hand acquaintance with the work of distinguished French neoclassicists such as de Wailly and Chalgrin.

8. For a structural description, see A. N. Petrov et al., *Pamiatniki arkhitektury Leningrada* (Leningrad, 1972), pp. 143–4.

9. A brief, innovative perception of the painterly qualities of Voronikhin's cathedral design – each perspective in two dimensions – is presented in O. A. Medvedkova, "Tvorchestvo Voronikhina i romanticheskie tendentsii v nachale XIX v." in A. A. Voronov et al., eds., *Problemy istorii arkhitektury* (Moscow, 1990), Part II, pp. 84–6.

10. The strength of the two colonnades would have obscured the "main" structure, if not altogether reduce it to insignificance. The unrealized plans for the south colonnade are recounted in Shurygin, *Kazanskii sobor*, p. 27. Although encroaching apartment construction and lack of landscaping gave the south facade a somewhat abandoned appearance, the southeast view is nonetheless the clearest perception of the church structure proper.

11. The postwar restoration of the exterior, including the cleaning of the Pudost stone surface, is described in A. A. Kedrinskii et al., *Vosstanovlenie pamiatnikov arkhitektury Leningrada* (Leningrad, 1983), pp. 192–4.

12. On the statuary and the iconographic system of the Kazan Cathedral sculpture, see I. M. Shmidt, "Arkhitekturno-skul'pturnyi kompleks Kazanskogo sobora i ego znachenie," in T. V. Alekseeva, ed., *Russkoe iskusstvo vtoroi poloviny XVIII–pervoi poloviny XIX v.* (Moscow, 1979), pp. 18–37. See also Shurygin, *Kazanskii sobor*, pp. 42–65.

13. The bronze capitals were originally gilded, but the gold was improperly fixed, and in the ensuing chemical reaction, the capitals acquired a dark coloration. See Shurygin, *Kazanskii sobor*, p. 36.

14. On the work of the younger Ivanov, who labored over vast canvases with socioreligious themes, see George Hamilton, *The Art and Architecture of Russia* (Harmondsworth, 1983), pp. 365–8. A detailed survey of the interior painting is presented in Shurygin, *Kazanskii sobor*, pp. 65–86.

15. Petrov et al., *Pamiatniki arkhitektury Leningrada*, p. 361.

16. For an analysis of the painting and its painstaking restoration after severe damage in World War II, see Kedrinskii et al., *Vosstanovlenie pamiatnikov*, pp. 195–201.

17. Thomas de Thomon's work is surveyed in G. D. Oschepkov, *Arkhitektor Tomon. Materialy k izucheniiu tvorchestva* (Moscow, 1950). His early architectural sketches and sketches of Italy are preserved at the Hermitage State Museum. See A. V. Khamano, "Al'bomy 'Souvenir d'Italie' Toma de Tomona," *Panorama iskusstv*, 7 (1984): 295–307.

18. A comparison of Quarenghi's and Thomas de Thomon's plans is presented in Koshunova, *Kvarengi*, pp. 42–3; and G. D. Oshchepkov et al., *Zdanie tsentral'nogo voenno-morskogo muzeiia (b. Birzha) v Leningrade* (Leningrad, 1957), pp. 6, 9. See also M. S. Bunin, *Strelka Vasilevskogo ostrova* (Moscow–Leningrad, 1957).

19. For commentary on the Paestum phenomenon in European neoclassicism, see Joselita Raspi Serra, ed., *Paestum and the Doric Revival 1750–1830* (Florence, 1986).

20. Hugh Honour, *Neo-classicism* (Harmondsworth, 1968), p. 109.

21. A compendium of elevations and precise detail drawings of the Bourse is contained in Oshchepkov et al., *Zdanie*.

22. A summary of the prior ownership of the Laval house is presented in Petrov et al., *Pamiatniki arkhitektury Leningrada*, p. 73. Voronikhin's working sketches for the Stroganovs have been preserved, and, therefore, much can be reconstructed of his version of the structure. See Kedrinskii et al., *Vosstanovlenie pamiatnikov*, p. 202.

23. On the interior and its restoration after severe damage in World War II, see Kedrinskii et al., *Vosstanovlenie pamiatnikov*, pp. 202–9.

24. On the irreconcilable split between enlightened thought and autocracy, see Nicholas Riasanovsky, *A Parting of Ways: Government and the Educated Public in Russia 1801–1855* (Oxford, 1976).

25. A survey of Zakharov's work is presented in V. I. Piliavskii and N. Ia. Leiboshits, *Zodchii Zakharov* (Leningrad, 1963). See also N. Leiboshits, "Novye materialy ob A. D. Zakharove," *Arkhitekturnoe nasledstvo*, 4 (1953): 95–103; and V. K. Shuiskii, *Andreian Zakharov* (Leningrad, 1989).

26. On Zakharov's warehouse projects for the Petersburg port and for the Provisions Island (on the left bank of the Neva, opposite the Mining Institute), see N. I. Brunov, *Istoriia russkoi arkhitektury* (Moscow, 1956), pp. 444, 447.

27. E. Moskalenko, "Shpil' Admiralteistva i ego konstruktsiia," *Arkhitekturnoe nasledstvo*, 4 (1953): 177–88.

28. Honour, *Neo-classicism*, p. 130. Honour relates this simplicity of design to the late eighteenth-century philosophical search, embodied by Goethe's Altar of Good Fortune, for deep symbolism in simple universal forms. The ideological basis of an architecture of "geometric purism" or "geometric idealism," derived from natural laws of the universe (and especially prevalent in the work of Ledoux), is discussed in Rosenblum, *Transformations in Late Eighteenth Century Art* (Princeton, 1967), pp. 120–7. See also Emil Kaufmann, *Three Revolutionary Architects – Boullée, Ledoux and Lequeu, Transactions of the American Philosophical Society*, vol. 42 (1952); and idem, *Architecture in the Age of Reason* (Harvard University Press, Cambridge, Mass., 1955), pp. 160–80, with brief reference to French stylistic currents in Russia, p. 179.

29. An illuminating analysis of Petersburg's system of open space and architectural ensemble is S. B. Alekseeva, "Rol' monumental'no-dekorativnoi skul'ptury v formifovanii ansamblia tsentral'nykh ploshchadei Peterburga pervoi poloviny XIX v," in T. V. Alekseeva, ed., *Russkoe iskusstvo vtoroi poloviny XVIII–pervoi poloviny XIX v.* (Moscow, 1979), pp. 38–68.

30. A general monograph on Rossi's life and work is M. Z. Taranovskaia, *Karl Rossi* (Leningrad, 1978).

31. On the Admiralty Quay project, see V. Kochedamov, "Proekt naberezhnoi u Admiralteistva Zodchego K. I. Rossi," *Arkhitekturnoe nasledstvo*, 4 (1953): 111–14. For Rossi's description, see ibid., p. 113.

32. Rossi's designs for Nilova Pustyn' are briefly discussed by Taranovskaia (*Karl Rossi*, pp. 33–4), who states that they demonstrate the "unique forms of Russian national architecture" in the manner of Bazhenov and Kazakov (p. 33). In fact, the bell tower shows a much clearer influence of the western Gothic revival than, although Rossi also seems to have pursued the attempt, explored by Bazhenov and Kazakov, to conflate western and Russian medieval architecture. For a description of the vernacular designs for Glazovo, see idem., pp. 52–4.

33. A comprehensive catalogue of Rossi's architectural

drawings, as well as designs of decorative objects, is N. I. Nikulina, ed., *Karl Ivanovich Rossi. Katalog* (Leningrad, 1975). On Rossi's design of the 1812 Gallery in the Winter Palace, see V. I. Piliavskii, ed., *Ermitazh. Istoriia i arkhitektura zdanii* (Leningrad, 1974), pp. 85–7; and V. M. Glinka, Iu. M. Denisov, M. V. Iogansen et al., *Ermitazh. Istoriia stroitel'stva i arkhitektury zdanii* (Leningrad, 1989), pp. 162–5.

34. On the Anichkov Palace, see Taranovskaia, *Karl Rossi,* pp. 64–9.

35. The land and an earlier residence (which Rossi completely rebuilt) had belonged to one of Catherine's grandees, I. P. Elagin. A history of the palace and park, and its relation to the design of the earlier Stone Island Palace (see Chapter 10) is given in V. A. Vitiazeva, *Nevskie ostrova* (Leningrad, 1986), pp. 43–50. See also Taranovskaia, *Karl Rossi,* pp. 76–92.

36. The interior of the palace was destroyed by artillery and fire during World War II. On the painstaking restoration of the interior, see Kedrinskii et al., *Vosstanovlenie pamiatnikov,* pp. 210–21.

37. Heroic designs of palace service buildings in Russia were not new to Rossi, as similar structures at Tsaritsyno (uncompleted) and the Marble Palace demonstrate. The entire complex of palace, service buildings, and park pavilions on Elagin Island is surveyed in Petrov et al., *Pamiatniki arkhitektury Leningrada,* p. 186–95.

38. Rossi's general plan for the area around the Mikhailovskii Palace is described in Taranovskaia, *Karl Rossi,* pp. 101–12, 123–4.

39. The remodeling of the palace interior by Vasilii Svinin, and his reconstruction of the entire east service quandrangle for museum purposes (now the Ethnographic Museum), is criticized in ibid., 125–6. See also Petrov et al., *Pamiatniki arkhitektury Leningrada,* p. 175. The palace itself, in expanded form, is now the State Russian Museum.

40. Taranovskaia, *Karl Rossi,* p. 122. Above the enfilade of state rooms on the park facade Rossi created an entresol – probably used for service purposes and now part of the storage facilities at the Russian Museum.

41. On the design and construction of the chariot group, see Taranovskaia, *Karl Rossi,* pp. 135–6, 142.

42. Blair A. Ruble discusses the function of the plazas in central Petersburg as an element enriching public space and the life of the city in "From Palace Square to Moscow Square: St. Petersburg's Century-Long Retreat from Public Space," in William C. Brumfield, ed., *Reshaping Russian Architecture* (New York and Cambridge, 1990), pp. 10–12, 16–21.

43. The design of the interior is described in detail in Taranovskaia, *Karl Rossi,* pp. 181–9.

44. On the metal construction technique, see A. L. Punin, *Arkhitektura Peterburga serediny XIX veka* (Leningrad, 1990), pp. 96–7. By sad irony, the brilliant design of the metal ceiling structure at the theater became a pretext for a personal vendetta against Rossi within the Committee for Construction and Hydraulic Projects. See Taranovskaia, *Karl Rossi,* pp. 193–6. Mathew Clark, who collaborated in the construction of a number of major Petersburg monuments (particularly the metal statuary), arrived in Russia as an apprentice from Scotland in 1785 and embarked on a long career leading to the directorship of the Aleksandrovskii plant, the country's most advanced metalworking factory in the first part of the nineteenth century. See A. G. Raskin, *Triumfal'nye arki Leningrada,* p. 123.

45. The planning of the ensemble surrounding the theater is surveyed in Taranovskaia, *Karl Rossi,* 170–4.

46. The various stages in the rebuilding of the library complex are surveyed in Petrov et al., *Pamiatniki arkhitektury Leningrada,* pp. 181, 185.

47. At the entrance of the Lobanov-Rostovskii house are two statues of lions designed by Paolo Triscorni and immortalized in Pushkin's great poem on Petersburg, *The Bronze Horseman.* See A. L. Rotach and O. A. Chekanova, *Monferran* (Leningrad, 1979), pp. 30–2; and Petrov et al., *Pamiatniki arkhitektury Leningrada,* p. 85.

48. The Senate had occupied a house facing the Neva and owned first by Alexander Menshikov and subsequently by A. P. Bestuzhev-Riumin. The transfer of the Senate to the baroque building in 1763 was followed in the 1780s by a remodeling (perhaps by Ivan Starov) in the neoclassical style. The construction history of the Senate is surveyed in Taranovskaia, *Karl Rossi,* pp. 151–6; and Petrov et al., *Pamiatniki arkhitektury Leningrada,* p. 75.

49. Taranovskaia, *Karl Rossi,* p. 197.

50. The standard monograph on Stasov's work is V. I. Piliavskii, *Stasov – Arkhitektor* (Leningrad, 1963).

51. On the Kotomin building – later modified by the removal of a Doric portico of attached columns in the center of the building – see Petrov et al., *Pamiatniki arkhitektury Leningrada,* pp. 135, 139. The building is renowned in Russian literary history as the site of the cafe Wolff and Beranger, a favorite haunt of Alexander Pushkin.

52. For other apartment projects attributed to Stasov, see ibid., pp. 133, 141.

53. On the development of the Petersburg apartment block – stimulated in the late eighteenth century by the authorities' wish to control the expensive territorial expansion of the city – see E. I. Kirichenko, "Zhilaia zastroika Peterburga epokhi klassitsizma i ee vliianie na razvitie arkhitektury," *Arkhitekturnoe nasledstvo,* 16 (1967): 81–95. Kirichenko proposes that the increased density of construction in Petersburg brought about by the new apartment blocks influenced the design of monumental ensembles, particularly by Rossi, in the first third of the nineteenth century. See also idem, "Dokhodnye zhilye doma Moskvy i Peterburga (1770–1830-e gg.)," *Arkhitekturnoe nasledstvo,* 14 (1962): 135–58.

54. Petrov et al., *Pamiatniki arkhitektury Leningrada,* pp. 116–17. Other elite barracks of the period by Fedor Volkov, Luigi Rusca, and others are surveyed in ibid., pp. 353–7, 363.

55. Ibid., p. 363. The church of the Court Stables is another of the city's many landmarks associated with Alexander Pushkin – tragically in this case, for it was here that a funeral service was covertly arranged on February 1, 1837, after the poet's death from wounds incurred in a pistol duel.

56. In addition, Stasov did the original, archaic design of the main guard stables at Tsarskoe Selo (1822–4), although the design was modified by the actual builder, Smaragd Shustov, the architect of the Imperial Stables Office. See Petrov et al., *Pamiatniki arkhitektury prigorodov Leningrada*, p. 138. Stasov's mastery of monumental detail was also demonstrated at Tsarskoe Selo in his design (1826) of the Greek Doric pylons for the gates to the Cold Baths adjacent to the Catherine Palace.

57. Petrov et al., *Pamiatniki arkhitektury Leningrada*, p. 399.

58. Ibid.

59. For a survey of Stasov's massive undertaking in the restoration of the Winter Palace, see V. M. Glinka et al., *Ermitazh*, pp. 206–32.

60. On the system devised by Clark for the iron strut framework above the ceiling of the state rooms, see ibid., pp. 198–200; and Punin, *Arkhitektura Peterburga serediny XIX veka*, pp. 97–9. Among Stasov's other metal designs was a monumental arch over the entrance of the Moscow Road into Petersburg. Although the project had been proposed in the decade after the Napoleonic wars as another memorial to the Russian triumph, Quarenghi's Narva Gates (completed by Stasov) remained the victory arch to the 1812–14 conflict. Following the Russian successes in wars against Persia (1826–8) and Turkey, the idea of an arch over the Moscow road was revived. Stasov's proposal for twelve Greek Doric channeled columns – six across, with a spacing in the middle the width of "two carriages" – was approved in 1838. After detailed preparations and casting of the iron columns (over 15 meters high), construction was completed in 1834. A history of the design of the Moscow Gates is presented in Raskin, *Triumfal'nye arki Leningrada*, pp. 182–208.

61. See Brunov, *Istoriia*, pp. 484–5.

62. Petrov et al., *Pamiatniki arkhitektury Leningrada*, p. 367. In addition to the Iamskoi Market, Stasov designed other utilitarian structures in Petersburg, including a warehouse near the barracks of the Izmailovskii Regiment.

63. Perhaps the most productive of the lesser classicists was Andrei Mikhailov, who designed the Church of St. Catherine on Vasilevskii Island, 1811–23; the Garden Wing of the Academy of Arts, 1819–21, with a perfect Greek Doric portico; and numerous other monuments. Among other neoclassical architects (the list is not comprehensive) are Domenico Adamini, builder of a large apartment house (1823–7) on the Moika Canal near Mars Field; Avraam Melnikov (Church of St. Nicholas, 1820–6); Vincenzo Beretti (Guard House on Haymarket Square, 1818–20); David Visconti (Catholic Church of St. Stanislas, 1823–5); and Ludovic Charlemagne, whose Golovin dacha (1823–4) is a noble example of the neoclassical style in wood. The most impressive wooden monument in the "Empire" style is the Stone Island Theater, built in 1827 by Smaragd Shustov and rebuilt, with modifications in 1844 by Albert Kavos.

64. On the complex plan of the Cavalry Guards barracks, see ibid., 355.

65. Ibid., p. 397.

66. Ibid., p. 153.

67. Ibid., p. 101. The Customs House is now the re-nowned Pushkin House of the Institute of Russian Literature.

68. Of the many accounts of the aftermath of the 1812 fire, a standard Soviet reference is *Istoriia Moskvy*, vol. 3, *Period razlozheniia krepostnogo stroia* (Moscow, 1954), pp. 110–35.

69. An analysis of the damage and the rebuilding of Moscow is presented in M. Budylina, "Planirovka i zastroika Moskvy posle pozhara 1812 goda," *Arkhitekturnoe nasledstvo*, 1 (1951): 135–74. A recent survey of the replanning of the city is Savarenskaia et al., *Istoriia gradostroitel'nogo iskusstva*, pp. 199–204. In English, see Albert Schmidt, "The Restoration of Moscow after 1812," *Slavic Review* 40 (1981): 37–48.

70. On Hastie in Russia, see Albert Schmidt, "William Hastie, Scottish Planner of Russian Cities," *Proceedings of the American Philosophical Society*, 114 (1970): 226–43.

71. Bove's work is surveyed in Z. K. Pokrovskaia, *Arkhitektor O. I. Bove (1784–1834)* (Moscow, 1964).

72. It is generally accepted that the volumes of model plans were authored by Rusca, Hastie, and Stasov (and possibly Zakharov). See E. A. Beletskaia et al., "*Obraztsovye*" *proekty v zhiloi zastroike russkikh gorodov XVIII–XIX vv* (Moscow, 1961). Ozhegov, however, notes the lack of precise evidence in the attribution (see *Tipovoe i povtornoe stroitel'stvo*, p. 162). Ozhegov's analysis and reproduction of a number of the facade designs – as well as comparative illustrations of their use in Moscow – are presented in ibid., pp. 81–92. See also L. E. Chernozubova, "Obraztsovye proekty planirovki zhilykh kvartalov i ploshchadei nachala XIX v.," *Arkhitekturnoe nasledstvo*, 15 (1963): 188–92.

73. A detailed analysis of structure and interior plans of early nineteenth-century Moscow houses is contained in R. M. Baiburova, "Russkii usadebnyi inter'er," in V. P. Vygolov et al., ed., *Pamiatniki russkoi arkhitektury i monumental'nogo iskusstva* (Moscow, 1980), pp. 154–61; and in the same volume, L. V. Tydman, "Prostranstvo inter'era v moskovskikh osobniakakh pervoi poloviny XIX v.," pp. 162–81. On wooden residences, see A. Okh and M. Fekhner, "Novye issledovaniia po dereviannym zhilym domam nachala XIX veka v Moskve," *Arkhitekturnoe nasledstvo*, 5 (1955): 115–40. A selection of facade elevations of typical modest homes (for both nobility and merchantry) is contained in Brunov, *Istoriia*, p. 492. The new regulations for building wooden houses (promulgated for reasons of fire safety as well as aesthetics) are included in an analysis of the reconstruction of Moscow by L. E. Chernozubova, "Iz istorii zastroiki Moskvy v pervoi polovine XIX v.," *Arkhitekturnoe nasledstvo*, 9 (1959): 15–27.

74. On Bove's rebuilding of the Upper Trading Rows, see Komech and Pluzhnikov, eds., *Tsentral'nye ploshchadi*, pp. 154–5. A half century later, Bove's Upper Trading Rows had reached such a state of decrepitude that necessitated their replacement, in what proved to be one of the building projects of the century (discussed in Chapter 13).

75. On Theater Square as part of a system of planned spaces (including the Alexander Garden) around the Kremlin, see N. F. Gulianitskii, "O kompozitsii zdanii v ansamblevoi zastroike Moskvy perioda klassitsizma," *Arkhitekturnoe nasledstvo*, 24 (1976): 31–3.

76. The vicissitudes of the building of the Bolshoi (Petrovskii) Theater, originally constructed in 1776–80 and named after its location on Petrovka Street, are chronicled in Komech and Pluzhnikov, eds., *Tsentral'nye ploshchadi*, pp. 483–4; and Brunov, *Istoriia*, p. 496.

77. The building of the Manege is chronicled in M. Budylina, "Istoriia postroiki Manezha v Moskve," *Arkhitekturnoe nasledstvo*, 2 (1952): 236–49. See also Komech and Pluzhnikov, eds., *Tsentral'nye ploshchadi*, p. 480. In reference to military triumph, Bove designed a triumphal arch (1827–34) over the Tver highway at the main entrance to Moscow from Petersburg. (Although dismantled in the 1930s, the arch was reerected in 1969 on Kutuzov Prospekt, not far from a memorial complex to the Battle of Borodino in the western part of the city.) Among his other notable public buildings is the First City Hospital (1828–33), located on the Kaluga Road adjacent to Kazakov's Golitsyn Hospital, which it resembles in its general plan.

78. On the N. S. Gagarin house, see Brunov, *Istoriia*, pp. 497–8; and Komech and Pluzhnikov, eds., *Zemlianoi gorod*, p. 27.

79. Gulianitskii discusses the frequent use of the arch in Bove's work in "O kompozitsii zdanii v ansamblevoi zastroike Moskvy," pp. 34–5.

80. A brief survey of the development of the ring avenues is provided in Savarenskaia et al., *Istoriia gradostroitel'nogo iskusstva*, pp. 200–1. See also Schmidt, "The Restoration of Moscow."

81. A comparison of urban residental plans in early nineteenth-century Moscow is contained in Komech and Pluzhnikov, eds., *Tsentral'nye ploshchadi*, pp. 142, 145.

82. Gulianitskii, "O kompozitsii zdanii v ansamblevoi zastroike Moskvy," pp. 35–6.

83. The standard monograph on Domenico Gilardi is E. A. Beletskaia and Z. K. Pokrovskaia, *D. I. Zhiliardi* (Moscow, 1980). See pp. 8–10 for the family background of Gilardi (the correct western spelling of the name; the Russian transliteration is Zhiliardi, but elements of the two are mistakenly combined in some recent western publications).

84. Ibid., pp. 9–10. Mikhail Dostoevskii, father of Fedor, served in the Mariinskii Hospital, which is where the great writer was born.

85. On the reconstruction of the main building of Moscow University, see E. A. Beletskaia, "Vosstanovlenie zdaniia Moskovskogo universiteta posle pozhara 1812 goda," *Arkhitekturnoe nasledstvo*, 1 (1951): 175–90. An analysis and drawings of the dome construction at the university is presented in Beletskaia and Pokrovskaia, *D. I. Zhiliardi*, pp. 30–8.

86. With the retirement of Giovanni Gilardi in 1818 from service as architect to the Foundling Home, his son Domenico assumed the post, and soon thereafter began work in the reconstruction of another charitable institution: the Widows' Home – a former military hospital whose remaining walls were incorporated into an expanded building for the widows of those who had served in the military. The long facade was anchored by a portico of eight Tuscan columns.

87. On the building of the Guardians' Council (*Opekunskii sovet*), see ibid., pp. 60–71; and Makarevich, ed., *Belyi gorod*, p. 345.

88. Beletskaia and Pokrovskaia, *D. I. Zhiliardi*, p. 51.

89. E. V. Karaulov provides a thorough description of the Lunin house in "Dom Luninykh v Moskve," *Arkhitekturnoe nasledstvo*, 20 (1972): 75–84. An analysis of the plans of the constituent parts of the house is also presented in Makarevich, ed., *Belyi gorod*, pp. 113–17.

90. On the S. S. Gagarin house, see Komech and Pluzhnikov, eds., *Zemlianoi gorod*, p. 150; and Beletskaia and Pokrovskaia, *D. I. Zhiliardi*, pp. 72–84.

91. Gagarin subsequently became director of the imperial theaters (1829–33), but by that time, he had already sold his Moscow home to the Moscow office of the Auction and Breeding Stables to cover substantial debts (ibid., p. 161).

92. The original plan of the Usachev estate park is reproduced in ibid., pp. 122–3. Most of the park pavilions have been destroyed in the Soviet period.

93. On the early stages of the design of the Kuzminki estate, see ibid., p. 86.

94. The monumentalism of Gilardi's work at Kuzminiki appeared on other estates, such as the horse farm of Count A. G. Orlov at Khrenovoe (1820s; Voronezh Province), whose domed manege displays the Doric order. Although documentary evidence is lacking, the main building of the Khrenovoe horse farm (which still functions in the original building) has been attributed to Gilardi on the basis of stylistic analysis. See ibid., pp. 97–8, 102.

Gilardi also used the rotunda for a mausoleum at Otrada, the estate of Count Vladimir G. Orlov at Semenovskoe (in Moscow Province). Designed in 1832, the year of Gilardi's departure from Russia, the mausoleum was completed by his cousin Alexander Gilardi (who also finished certain of the projects at Kuzminki). Although it lacks some of the original detail, the basic structure is extant: a drum and dome supported by a circle of paired Ionic columns, which are in turn contained within the outer circle of the rotunda. A Doric portico frames the entrance to the mausoleum, whose exterior walls are of unstuccoed brick. The plan is similar to that of Bove's Church of the Mother of God (the rotundal form was suggested as a model for Orthodox churches in the 1820s). The earlier variants of the project (first intended as a museum to the exploits of the Orlov brothers) are reproduced in Beletskaia and Pokrovskaia, *D. I. Zhiliardi*, pp. 132–3, 135. Semenovskoe is a rare grand estate in the Moscow region that has been largely preserved. See Pod'iapol'skaia, ed., *Pamiatniki arkhitektury moskovskoi oblasti*, vol. 2, pp. 279–84.

Most of Domenico Gilardi's estate work in the 1830s demonstrates an ornamental, fragmented manner, exemplified in the pavilions at the Usachev estate, the Octagon at the Zakrevskii dacha in Moscow, and rotunda–mausoleum at the Stakhovich estate of Palno-Mikhailovko, near the town of Elets (in the area of the central Russian spa of Lipetsk). A survey of these and other memorial estate structures attributed to Gilardi is presented in pp. 137–46. See also N. Krasheninnikova, "Iz neopublikovannykh rabot I. i D. Zhiliardi," *Arkhitekturnoe nasledstvo*, 1 (1951): 191–201.

95. The building site of the Trade School was occupied by the ruined walls of the Sloboda Palace in Lefortovo, which had burned in 1812. The project is the analyzed in Beletskaia and Pokrovskaia, *D. I. Zhiliardi*, pp. 99–117.

96. A recent study of Grigorev's life and work is presented in E. A. Beletskaia's introductory biographical sketch "A. G. Grigor'ev. Ocherk zhizni i tvorchestva," in V. I. Baldin, ed., *Arkhitektor Afanasii Grigor'evich Grigor'ev. 1782–1868* (Moscow, 1976).

97. It was not uncommon in eighteenth-century Moscow to built wooden houses over a stone basement, and just as common to rebuilt them in a similar manner. The former owner of the Khrushchev lot was Prince Bariatinskii. On the Khrushchev house (also known as the Seleznev house, after its later owners), see Komech and Pluzhnikov, eds., *Zemlianoi gorod*, pp. 62–4.

98. The compositional ingenuity of Grigorev's corner design – both as architecture and as an element of urban planning – is noted in Gulianitskii, "O kompozitsii zdanii v ansamblevoi zastroike Moskvy," pp. 37–8.

99. For a comparison of post–1812 house designs in Moscow with those of the late eighteenth century, see E. I. Kirichenko, "Ob osobennostiakh zhiloi zastroiki poslepozharnoi Moskvy," *Arkhitekturnoe nasledstvo*, 32 (1984): 60–1.

100. On the Lopukhin (later Stanitskii) house, see Beletskaia, "A. G. Grigor'ev," pp. 15–16; and Komech and Pluzhnikov, eds., *Zemlianoi gorod*, pp. 61–2.

101. In 1920, the house was converted to a museum dedicated to Lev Tolstoi. Although there is no evidence that the great writer ever set foot in the house, the conversion had the advantage of preserving the structure and its wall paintings, with access to the public.

102. On the Trinity Church at Ershovo, see Beletskaia, "A. G. Grigor'ev," pp. 17–18, with reproductions of the variant plans, pp. 81–5.

103. Grigorev also left project drawings, dating from 1829–1830 for a gargantuan pentacupolar church thought to have been his proposal for the competition to design a temple–monument commemorating the Russian sacrifice during the Napoleonic wars. For commentary and sketches of Grigorev's large church project, see ibid., pp. 19–20, 88–9. In addition, Grigorev is considered the architect of the Church of the Resurrection and ancillary structures at Vagankov Cemetery (1822), the Church of the Trinity at Piatnitskii Cemetery (1830–5), and the Church of the Trinity in Vishniaki (1824–6) – all in a late neoclassical style with bell towers on the west. Documentation concerning the cemetery churches is presented in Baldin, ed., *Arkhitektor Afanasii Grigor'evich Grigor'ev*, pp. 41, 53. On the Trinity Church in Vishniaki, located on Piatnitskii Street, see E. A. Beletskaia, "A. Grigor'ev," in Iu. S. Iaralov, ed., *Zodchie Moskvy XV–XIX vv.* (Moscow, 1981), p. 223; and A. V. Ikonnikov, *Kamennaia letopis' Moskvy* (Moscow, 1978), p. 258.

104. A history of the construction of the Ascension Church, with reference to Bove, is contained in Komech and Pluzhnikov, eds., *Zemlianoi gorod*, pp. 139–40.

105. On the case for Grigorev's participation, see Beletskaia, "A. G. Grigor'ev," pp. 21, 91. It is frequently noted that the great poet Alexander Pushkin was married in the Ascension Church, in February 1831; but at that time, only the vestibule was completed. See E. A. Beletskaia, "Zdes' venchalsia Pushkin," *Stroitel'stvo i arkhitektura Moskvy*, 1976, no. 12: 22–4.

106. Stasov's early Moscow biography is recounted in S. P. Iakovlev, "V. Stasov," in Iaralov, ed., *Zodchie Moskvy XV–XIX vv.*, pp. 230–5.

107. On the Provision Warehouses, see Iakovlev, "V. Stasov," pp. 238–40; and Iu. Rusakov, "Predvaritel'nyi variant proekta Proviantskikh skladov," *Arkhitekturnoe nasledstvo*, 4 (1953): 108–10. Iakovlev, along with many earlier sources, gives the construction dates as 1830–5. An earlier date of 1829–31 is now given in Komech and Pluzhnikov, eds., *Zemlianoi gorod*, p. 82.

108. The complex construction history of the A. K. Razumovskii house is detailed in E. A. Beletskaia, "Iz istorii stroitel'stva doma Razumovskogo," *Arkhitekturnoe nasledstvo*, 9 (1959): 189–96. See also idem, "A. G. Grigor'ev," pp. 21–2.

109. The previous owner, A. M. Kheraskov (brother of the eighteenth-century neoclassical poet Mikhail Kheraskov), had constructed in the 1780s a masonry house that was subsequently rebuilt at the beginning of the nineteenth century – presumably by Menelaws, although the attribution is very much open to question. On the L. K. Razumovskii house (since 1922, the Museum of the Revolution), see Iu. Ferdman, "Rekonstruktsiia Tsentral'nogo muzeia Revoliutsii SSSR," *Stroitel'stvo i arkhitektura Moskvy*, 1986, no. 7: 10–12. The attribution of the building to Menelaws has been persistently questioned; and on the basis of stylistic similarities between the channeled Doric columns of the portico and the portico of the rebuilt Moscow University, some have suggested that the design might belong to Domenico Gilardi. See Komech and Pluzhnikov, eds., *Zemlianoi gorod*, p. 185. The building – particularly the wings – was extensively remodeled throughout the late nineteenth and early twentieth centuries, although after the war, the exterior was restored to an approximation of its appearance in the 1820s.

110. It would be pleasant to think that the building was preserved by its confraternity of nobles; but in fact the house, located on a prime lot, was deformed at the turn of the century by commercial usage (like so many surviving but poorly maintained Moscow mansions during that period). Iurii Shamurin's sensitive study of Moscow neoclassicism, *Ocherki klassicheskoi Moskvy* (Moscow, 1914), contains a number of photographs of such monuments in all of their noble decrepitude.

111. Tiurin's career is briefly surveyed in A. V. Solov'ev, "E. Tiurin," Iaralov, ed., *Zodchie Moskvy XV–XIX vv.*, pp. 186–8.

112. Located adjacent to the university on Mokhovaia Street, the A. I. Pashkov mansion was acquired in 1833 by the university for additional space. On the conversion of the Pashkov estate to the university building, see Makarevich, ed., *Belyi gorod*, pp. 102–4.

113. There is surprisingly little information on the construction history of the Epiphany Cathedral. For example, the entry in *Moskva zlatoglavaia* (p. 102) is quite brief as well as misleading on the later construction of the church. The bell tower and vestibule contain eighteenth-century work, including fragments from the initial structure built in 1722–31; but the bell tower itself appears to have been redone by Tiurin.

114. V. G. Belinskii, *Polnoe sobranie sochinenii*, vol. 8 (Moscow, 1955), p. 391. Belinskii's essay originally appeared in a collection entitled *The Physiology of Petersburg*, edited by Nikolai Nekrasov and published in 1845. Similar essays were written by Alexander Hertzen and Apollon Grigorev, both brilliant observers of Moscow's traditional landscape in the first half of the nineteenth century. See Robert Whittaker, " 'My Literary and Moral Wanderings': Apollon Grigor'ev and the Changing Cultural Topography of Moscow," *Slavic Review* 42 (1983): 390–407.

115. Perhaps the most vehement condemnation of neoclassicism as "barracks architecture" came from the pen of the poet Aleksei K. Tolstoi (1817–75), who in his long, semi-autobiographical poem "Portrait" (1874) reminisces of his noble upbringing and of the yellow estate houses with their obligatory portico. For Tolstoi's narrator, neoclassicism may have had its origins in the revolutionary spirit of Napoleonic France, but in Russia, the uniformity of neoclassical elements and the grandomania of geometric city plans are associated with Arakcheev – and even the Mongols! See A. K. Tolstoi, *Sobranie sochinenii v chetyrekh tomakh*, vol. 1 (Moscow, 1963), pp. 543–4. A concise analysis of this change of mood toward neoclassical architecture is presented in A. L. Punin, "Pochemu soshel so stseny klassitsizm?" *Stroitel'stvo i arkhitektura Leningrada*, 1978, no. 7: 39–43.

116. For examples, see Punin, *Arkhitektura Peterburga serediny XIX veka*, pp. 18–19; and E. I. Kirichenko, "Dokhodnye zhilye doma Moskvy i Peterburga (1770–1830-e gg.)," *Arkhitekturnoe nasledstvo*, 14 (1962): 135–58.

117. Examples of contemporary commentary on the monotony of Petersburg's neoclassical urban environment are provided in Punin, *Arkhitektura Peterburga serediny XIX veka*, pp. 20–1.

118. "Ob arkhitekture nyneshnego vremeni," in N. V. Gogol', *Sobranie sochinenii v shesti tomakh*, vol. 6 (Moscow, 1959), p. 46.

119. On geometric purism in neoclassical architecture, see Rosenblum, *Transformations in Late Eighteenth Century Art*, p. 127. Of the radical concepts of certain French neoclassicists, such as Ledoux, Kaufmann has written: "Out of the turmoil of the Revolution emerged the calmest and purest geometrical forms." See *Architecture in the Age of Reason*, p. 164. These forms were by no means readily accepted in France, however, and in the work of Boullée, they tended to ignore function as well as "the triviality of romanticizing architecture" (ibid., p. 162).

120. Quoted in Piliavskii, *Stasov – Arkhitektor*, p. 53.

Chapter 13

1. The relation between architecture and the larger context of literary criticism and scientific positivism in Russia during the nineteenth century is explored in E. I. Kirichenko, "Problema natsional'nogo stilia v arkhitekture Rossii 70-kh gg. XIX v.," *Arkhitekturnoe nasledstvo*, 25 (1976): 135–7; and idem, "Problemy stilia i zhanra v russkoi arkhitekture vtoroi chetverti XIX v.," *Arkhitektura SSSR*, 1983, nos. 3–4: 112–15. For a broader analysis of the literary aspects of the relation, see E. A. Borisova, "Nekotorye osobennosti vospriiatiia gorodskoi sredy i russkaia literatura vtoroi poloviny XIX v.," in G. Iu. Sternin, ed., *Tipologiia russkogo realizma vtoroi poloviny XIX veka* (Moscow, 1979), pp. 252–85.

2. On the origins of the Russian intelligentsia, see Martin Malia, "What is the Intelligentsia," in Richard Pipes, ed., *The Russian Intelligentsia* (New York, 1961), pp. 1–18.

3. *Khudozhestvennaia gazeta*, 1840, no. 3: 17. Although unsigned, the article may have been written by Nestor Kukolnik, an editor of the paper who frequently commented on architecture. See A. L. Punin, *Arkhitektura Peterburga serediny XIX veka* (Leningrad, 1990), p. 17.

4. N. V. Gogol', "Ob arkhitekture nyneshnego vremeni," in *Sobranie sochinenii v shesti tomakh*, vol. 6 (Moscow, 1959), pp. 51.

5. Ibid., p. 57. Gogol was, however, fascinated by the classical architecture of Rome (both ancient and Renaissance), as revealed in his "Rome," published in 1842.

6. Gogol', "Ob arkhitekture nyneshnego vremeni," p. 57.

7. At the end of his essay, Gogol placed a brief, but highly laudatory note on the work of Briullov. See ibid., p. 61.

8. On Menelaws' work at Tsarskoe Selo, see A. N. Petrov et al., *Pamiatniki arkhitektury prigorodov Leningrada* (Leningrad, 1983), pp. 120–6. Although there is not yet a definitive monograph on Menelaws, a survey of his work is presented by A. K. Andreev, "Adam Menelas," in *Problemy sinteza iskusstv i arkhitektury* 7 (1977): 38–59. See also Dmitrij Shividkovsky, "Architect to Three Emperors: Adam Menelas in Russia," *Apollo* (January 1992), pp. 37–41.

9. On the Alexandria Park, which was devised by Menelaws, and the Cottage at Peterhof, see Petrov et al., *Pamiatniki arkhitektury prigorodov Leningrada*, pp. 444–53. A recent monograph, profusely illustrated, is V. M. Tenikhina and V. V. Znamenov, *Kottedzh* (Leningrad, 1990). Punin comments on the role of the Cottage in establishing new interior fashions in *Arkhitektura Peterburga serediny XIX veka*, pp. 70–1.

10. The Gothic Capella is described and illustrated in Petrov et al., *Pamiatniki arkhitektury prigorodov Leningrada*, pp. 450–1. Although Schinkel (1781–1841) is known primarily for his Grecian style, he was an early adherent of the Gothic revival.

11. On the chapel at Pargolovo and the considerable impression that it had on contemporaries, see Punin, *Arkhitektura Peterburga serediny XIX veka*, pp. 32, 34–6. Briullov's career is surveyed in G. A. Ol', *Aleksandr Briullov* (Leningrad, 1983).

12. On the Boudoir of Alexandra Fedorovna, see V. M. Glinka et al., *Ermitazh*, pp. 242–3. The room was especially praised for its "architectonic" purity in A. P. Bashutskii's laudatory account of the rebuilt Winter Palace, *Vozobnovlenie Zimnego dvortsa v Sankt-Peterburge* (Petersburg, 1839) – a document that itself played an important part in disseminating public knowledge of new stylistic fashions in architecture and interior design. See p. 118. A broader survey of changing fashions in interior design is presented in I. A. Bartenev and V. N. Batazhkov, *Russkii inter'er XIX veka* (Leningrad, 1984).

13. Marfino was owned by V. G. Orlov. After his death (1831), the property was inherited by his daughter Sofia Panina, who was married to Nikita Panin, one of the main conspirators in the assassination of the emperor Paul and consequently exiled to his estates in Smolensk Province. During the 1820s, Bykovskii received several commissions from Panin, who assiduously cultivated his estate holdings. Subsequently, Sofia Panina commissioned Bykovskii to redesign the Marfino park and buildings as a Gothic landscape. Spires and crenellation abound throughout the Marfino ensemble, beginning with an Italianate bridge situated between two ponds, and leading to the main house, decorated in the Gothic style, but symmetrically planned in the neoclassical manner. Work on the estate terminated after her death in 1846. A detailed history of Bykovskii's work at Marfino is provided in E. I. Kirichenko, *Mikhail Bykovskii* (Moscow, 1988), pp. 143–67. See ibid., p. 247.

14. The most flamboyant example of the Peterhof Gothic Revival was the Manége, centerpiece of the large ensemble of the Court Stables (1848–55). On the exterior, the building displays lancet windows, pinnacles, and other decorative devices of the style, yet the interior of the manége impresses still more with its timber hammerbeam roof. A telling juxtaposition is provided by Benois' design for the New Peterhof Railway Station (1854–7). Both stable and station use the Gothic style, not only because of Nicholas's fondness for it, but also because of its suitability for extended, high-roofed structures whose structural weight is carried by the exterior walls. But the magnificently crafted wooden roof of the stables is replaced in the station and its platform shed by the innovative technology of an iron-beamed trussed roof – impervious to engine sparks and symbolic of the new machine age. The Gothic Stables are described in Petrov et al., *Pamiatniki arkhitektury prigorodov Leningrada*, pp. 474–6. Nikolai Benois, founder of a dynasty of distinguished architects, designers, and artists, is the subject of an excellent monograph by M. I. Barteneva, *Nikolai Benua* (Leningrad, 1985). On the New Peterhof Station and its engineering, see Punin, *Arkhitektura Peterburga serediny XIX veka*, p. 202; and Petrov et al., *Pamiatniki arkhitektury prigorodov Leningrada*, pp. 476–7.

15. See Punin, *Arkhitektura Peterburga serediny XIX veka*, p. 39, for a sampling of opinion in the 1850s on the impracticibility of the pseudo-Gothic.

16. An example of one architect's denial of the general validity of neoclassical architecture, in favor of a more varied stylistic approach, is contained in Bykovskii's lecture "On the Unreliability of the Opinion that Greek or Greco-Roman architecture can be universal and that beauty in Architecture is Based on the Five Known Orders." The lecture was delivered in May 1834, at the Moscow Court Architectural School, and subsequently published as "Rech' o neosnovatel'nosti mneniia, chto arkhitketura grecheskaia, ili greko-rimskaia, mozhet byt' vseobshcheiu i chto krasota arkhitektury osnovyvaetsia na piati izvestnykh chinopolozheniiakh, govorenaia na torzhestvennom akte Moskovskogo dvortsovogo arkhitekturnogo uchilishcha Mikhailom Bykovskim maiia 8 dnia 1834 goda," (Moscow, 1834). The speech is discussed in Punin, *Arkhitektura Peterburga serediny XIX veka*, pp. 27–8. See also Kirichenko, *Mikhail Bykovskii*, pp. 39–44. The publication of this lecture (an unusual occasion for a Russian architect) is testimony to the general, if not universal, accord given the subversion of neoclassicism.

17. On the work of Jacot, see E. I. Kirichenko, "Materialy o tvorchestve arkhitektora P. P. Zhako," *Arkhitekturnoe nasledstvo*, 18 (1969): 83–99. A more general analysis of the impact of late neoclassical apartment blocks on the further development of the Petersburg milieu is presented in idem, "Zhilaia zastroika Peterburga epokhi klassitsizma i ee vliianie na razvitie arkhitektury," *Arkhitekturnoe nasledstvo*, 16 (1967): 81–95. See also Punin, *Arkhitektura Peterburga serediny XIX veka*, pp. 257–65.

18. The residual effects of neoclassicism in the design of midnineteenth-century Petersburg apartments are discussed in E. A. Borisova, "Nekotorye osobennosti vospriiatiia gorodskoi sredy," pp. 279–81, with references to the portrayal of this milieu in the work of Dostoevskii.

19. The details of the utopia varied according to the political views of the author, but they were predicated on technological advances that would allow control over the the environment through the use of materials such as iron and glass on an unprecedented scale. The writer Vladimir Odoevskii (1804–69) took the longest view, in his uncompleted novella *4338 A.D.*, fragments of which were published in 1835 and 1840. Like many fantastists, Odoevskii envisioned air travel and new forms of energy, from natural sources such as the sun as well as from electricity. Odoevskii's vision of the future Petersburg encompassed rationally planned megaregions, marked with large towers that served as a link with forms of air transportation such as "galvanostats" or "aerostats." Little attention is given to the economic basis of the new society; indeed, both England and America are briefly lampooned for their unrestrained mercantile spirit. See V. F. Odoevskii, *Povesti i rasskazy* (Moscow, 1959), pp. 422, 448. In her commentary on Odoevskii's utopian vision and its architectural setting, Kirichenko emphasizes his opposition to the soulless frenzy of western capitalism. See E. I. Kirichenko, *Arkhitekturnye teorii XIX veka v Rossii* (Moscow, 1986), pp. 81–7. Although Odoevskii worked on the utopian fanatasy until the end of his life, it was never completed. A comprehensive version of the extant fragments was published in the 1920s, during a period of renewed interest in utopian built environments (see Chapter 15). For a publication history of the novella, see Odoevskii, *Povesti*, pp. 490–1. For the text, see ibid., pp. 416–48. Odoevskii explains the date of his title (2,500 years after 1838) as 1 year before a catastrophic collision – predicted by "certain astronomers" – between Earth and the comet Viela. Ibid., p. 416.

A more "realistic" utopian vision is presented in Vladimir Sollogub's satirical tale *Tarantas*, whose title derives from the ramshackle vehicle in which the two protagonists travel through a landscape of mismanagement, from Moscow to Kazan. Perhaps the greatest of this work's virtues are the drawings by Grigorii Gagarin, who captured not only the revived interest in Russian vernacular architecture, but also the laughable charade of late neoclassical facades in provincial Russian architecture. *Tarantas*, published in 1845, has been reissued in a facsimile edition (Moscow, 1985), with extensive commentary on Gagarin's work. For examples of Gagarin's flattering view of ornamented Russian vernacular architecture in wood, see ibid., p. 224.

Sollogub's dim view of Russian reality concludes with a "dream" of Moscow in the future, in which the dishonesty, slovenliness, and poverty that characterize contemporary Russia are replaced by a clean, well-regulated city propelling prosperity throughout the land. The new architecture, brightly portrayed in Gagarin's drawing of the transformed Moscow, combines styles representative of many cultures and historical epochs in a manner similar to Gogol's visionary urban environment. The transformed mercantile district of Zamoskvoreche contains a plethora of monumental styles, including the pseudo-Gothic, Moorish, Venetian, Byzantine, and other combinations of eastern and western forms. Yet the Kremlin maintains its dominant position as the city on the hill, and it appears that Sollogub's intention is to meld the miracles of technology with a new society in which the split between the educated elite and the people would be healed through a return to "authentic," traditional Russian culture.

It was Gagargin, personally acquainted with prominent architects such as Konstantin Ton, who endowed Sollogub's vague and charitable vision of Russian brotherhood and urban harmony with eclectic forms. The Orthodox Church retains an important role in Sollogub's fantasy, and among Gagarin's structures is a large domed church reminiscent of Ton's Church of Christ the Redeemer (discussed later in this chapter), then under construction in Moscow. See ibid., p. 271. Further commentary on Gagarin's architectural fantasy is provided by A. Kantor, "Grigorii Gagarin – illustrator 'Tarantas'," in the volume of commentary accompanying the 1985 reprint, p. 46. Sollogub was virtually the only Slavophile supporter to make specific comments on architecture, its style, and its societal functions. See Kirichenko, *Arkhitekturnye teorii*, pp. 92–7. A survey of midnineteenth-century utopian programs for an urban environment in Russia is presented in T. V. Savarenskaia et al., *Istoriia gradostroitel'nogo iskusstva* (Moscow, 1989), pp. 211–16.

20. Gogol', "Ob arkhitekture nyneshnego vremeni," pp. 60–1.

21. For a visualization of Chernyshevskii's phalanstery as presented in *What is to be Done?*, see I. G. Ivanova's drawing in Savarenskaia et al., *Istoriia gradostroitel'nogo iskusstva*, p. 215.

22. A discussion of Chernyshevskii's materialistic aesthetics and its deprecatory view of architecture is contained in Kirichenko, *Arkhitekturnye teorii*, pp. 175–81. Chernyshevskii's moral authority and his considerable role in the formation of progressive social opinion in Russia endowed his aesthetic and critical views with the weight of holy writ. Whatever the interpretation of his attitude toward architecture, Kirichenko considers his aesthetic program to have been enormously influential in the development of functionalism in architectural thought during the second half of the century. See ibid., p. 181.

23. For a survey of these efforts, see William C. Brumfield, *The Origins of Modernism in Russian Architecture* (Berkeley, 1991), pp. 193–5, 295.

24. Vitberg's commentary, as contained in his "Notes" (*Zapiski*), was compiled by his fellow exile in Viatka, Herzen. They have since been published in A. G. Gertsen, *Polnoe sobranie sochinenii*, vol. 1 (Moscow, 1954), with Vitberg's description of the temple on pp. 381–90. Herzen's references to the project in *Byloe i dumy* are contained in ibid., vol. 8 (Moscow, 1956), pp. 281–3. Herzen, it must be noted, was writing as the official version of the memorial, submitted by Konstantin Ton and approved by Nicholas, was under construction. His sympathy for a fellow exile and his antipathy to Nicholas obviously influenced his approval of Vitberg's project, which, however, remained primarily a verbally expressed idea rather than a tectonic form – one of the earliest examples of Russian architecture's subordination to literary programs in the nineteenth century. Extensive commentary on Vitberg's project is presented in Kirichenko, *Arkhitekturnye teorii*, pp. 104–10.

25. As quoted in A. G. Gertsen, vol. 1, p. 390.

26. An account of this period of study is contained in the standard monograph on Ton, T. A. Slavina, *Konstantin Ton* (Leningrad, 1989), pp. 21–31. One of Ton's earliest mature projects was an Orthodox church in the form of an early Christian basilica (1820).

27. For a recounting of the genesis of the St. Catherine Church at Kolomna (Ton also designed a St. Catherine in Tsarskoe Selo), see ibid., pp. 33–8. Of particular interest is Slavina's comparison (pp. 106–7) of the interior design of the Kolomna church with the interior design of the Cathedral of the Intercession on the Moat in Moscow.

28. Ton's church designs reflect the serious study of medieval Russian architecture that had been encouraged by Olenin at the Academy. Ibid., pp. 104–5.

29. See E. A. Borisova, *Russkaia arkhitektura vtoroi poloviny XIX veka* (Moscow, 1979), p. 105.

30. On the doctrine of official nationality, formulated in 1833 by the minister of education Sergei Uvarov, see Nicholas Riasanovsky, *Nicholas I and Official Nationality in Rus-*

sia, *1825–1855* (Berkeley, 1967), pp. 73–183. Nicholas's shrewd exploitation of the doctrine as a means of claiming a place for autocracy within the romantic shift away from the eighteenth-century rationalist concept of "citizen" toward the idea of the "people" is noted in Kirichenko, *Arkhitekturnye teorii,* pp. 98–101.

31. The album was published at official court suggestion but at Ton's own expense. See Slavina, *Konstantin Ton,* p. 86. On the ideological significance of the publication of Ton's church designs, see Kirichenko, *Arkhitekturnye teorii,* p. 99; and Punin, *Arkhitektura Peterburga serediny XIX veka,* pp. 51–2.

32. E. I. Kirichenko, "Arkhitekturnye ansambli Moskvy 1830–1860-kh gg.," *Arkhitekturnoe nasledstvo,* 24 (1976): 8.

33. On the engineering work for the church, see Slavina, *Konstantin Ton,* pp. 115–17.

34. Ibid., pp. 157–61.

35. For the design of the interior of the Great Kremlin Palace, Ton was joined by the court architect Friedrich Richter, who boldly combined neoclassical, baroque, gothic, and medieval Russian motifs. As an "archaic," historical device, Ton freely used elaborate barrel and groin vaults for the main halls, of which the grandest is the two-storied Hall of St. George, in honor of recipients of the highest Russian military honor. On the interior of the palace, see ibid., pp. 166–82. See also Komech and Pluzhnikov, eds., *Tsentral'nye ploshchadi,* p. 339.

36. A survey of the history and collection of the Armory is contained in E. I. Smirnova et al., *Gosudarstvennaia oruzheinaia palata moskovskogo kremlia* (Moscow, 1969).

37. The stylistic variety of the Armory is analyzed in Slavina, *Konstantin Ton,* 182–4.

38. Slavina, who resolutely defends the architect's reputation in *Konstantin Ton,* chronicles the criticisms directed against his work, beginning with contemporaries such as Herzen.

39. The construction history of the Cathedral of St. Isaac is surveyed in G. P. Butikov and G. A. Khvostova, *Isaakievskii sobor* (Leningrad, 1979). An analysis of the cathedral in the context of Montferran's work is presented in Rotach and Chekanova, *Monferran* (Leningrad, 1979).

40. The plans of the two structures – by Rinaldi and Montferrand – are compared in ibid., pp. 28–9, 33.

41. A sketch of the 1818 design is reproduced in Butikov and Khvostova, *Isaakievskii sobor,* p. 15. Cf. the final, 1825 design, p. 21.

42. A detailed account of the critique of Montferrand's project is contained in Rotach and Chekanova, *Monferran,* pp. 36–61.

43. On the construction of the cupola, begun in 1838, see ibid., pp. 79–84; and Butikov and Khvostova, *Isaakievskii sobor,* pp. 39–40. Statistics for the building are provided in ibid., pp. 166–7.

44. For a description of the exterior statuary, see ibid., pp. 74–87; and Rotach and Chekanova, *Monferran,* pp. 87–97.

45. A description of the decoration of the cathedral interior is contained in Butikov and Khvostova, *Isaakievskii sobor,* pp. 89–128. Detailed illustrations are presented in George Butikov, *St Isaac's Cathedral* (Leningrad, 1974).

46. The paintings, which vary greatly in quality, are especially loud, as dictated by the general ambiance. In defense of the artists, who were led by Vasilii Shebuev, Rector of the Academy of Arts, it must be noted that the emperor interfered throughout the process of the painting and often stipulated the style or models (usually Renaissance) to be followed. In addition, the Holy Synod also contributed its detailed recommendations and prohibitions. Despite the surfeit of ornament beneath it, the Karl Briullov's painting of the Mother of God surrounded by a host of saints on the hemispherical inner dome remains the center of attention. Briullov began the project in 1842 in a state of exaltation characteristic of the Romantic era; but the rigors of working over such a large area in the uncompleted building ruined his health (he died in Italy in 1852), and Peter Basin finished the details to Briullov's sketches. The main vaults were primarily the work of Fedor Bruni. See Butikov and Khvostova, *Isaakievskii sobor,* pp. 103–18. For a study of the work of Briullov, Bruni, Shebuev, and Basin (among others) in relation to the romanticism and historicism of the period 1820–50, see Magdalina Rakova, *Russkaia istoricheskaia zhivopis' serediny deviatnadtsatogo veka* (Moscow, 1979).

47. For a description of the cathedral's mosaic work, see Butikov and Khvostova, *Isaakievskii sobor,* pp. 118–23.

48. The suggestion for the stained-glass altar panel originated with Leo von Klenze, architect of the New Hermitage, who had been invited by Nicholas in 1841 to submit a plan for the decoration of the cathedral interior. Although Montferrand repulsed this further challenge to his supervision of the design (the cathedral committee rejected Klenze's plan), the use of stained glass – an art then being resurrected in Germany – was unanimously approved. See ibid., pp. 89–90, 123–8.

49. A history of the making of the Alexander Column is contained in Rotach and Chekanova, *Monferran,* pp. 121–40.

50. Petrov et al., *Pamiatniki arkhitektury Leningrada,* p. 69.

51. Ibid., p. 115. The transitional nature of the Guards building and the Marble Palace service building in the movement from classicism to eclecticism is noted in Punin, *Arkhitektura Peterburga serediny XIX veka,* pp. 75–7.

52. On the genesis of the New Hermitage project, see V. M. Glinka et al., *Ermitazh,* pp. 404–7. Klenze produced the plans in his Munich workshop, and made yearly visits to inspect the progress of work, but the actual construction was overseen by Stasov.

53. Ibid., p. 412.

54. A history and stylistic analysis of the Nicholas Station is contained in Slavina, *Konstantin Ton,* pp. 94–100.

55. Punin provides a history of the construction of railway stations in Petersburg during the midnineteenth century, including the Nicholas, the Warsaw, and the Baltic – all in the neo-Renaissance style – in *Arkhitektura Peterburga serediny XIX veka,* pp. 190–203.

56. The work of Zheliazevich, who specialized in technically innovative, functional buildings related to commerce and transportation, is surveyed in ibid., pp. 133–5; 181–3. For a study of the development of shopping galleries in Moscow (and Petersburg) during the nineteenth century, see William C. Brumfield, "Dai bassifondi all'edificio superiore dei Torgovye Rjady: il design delle gallerie commerciali di Mosca," *Ricerche de Storia dell'arte*, 39 (1989): 7–16.

57. The passage also had the support of the governor-general of Moscow, Dmitrii Golitsyn, who supported a number of initiatives (often rejected by local merchants) to improve the planning of central Moscow. See Kirichenko, *Mikhail Bykovskii*, pp. 103–6. Kirichenko notes that the Golitsyn Passage was the subject of a laudatory booklet, published in 1842 – another early example of the growing public commentary on architecture in Russia.

58. On Kavos's work as a builder of theaters, see Punin, *Arkhitektura Peterburga serediny XIX veka*, pp. 176–9.

59. A recent monograph on Shtakenshneider is T. A. Petrova, *Andrei Shtakenshneider* (Leningrad, 1978). On the Nikolskii house (*domik*), see ibid., pp. 18–20; and Punin, *Arkhitektura Peterburga serediny XIX veka*, pp. 60–2.

60. The contrast between neoclassical and Renaissance elements in the design of the Mariinskii Palace is further discussed in Petrova, *Shtakenshneider*, p. 30.

61. On the construction history of the palace, and its acquisition by grand duke Sergei Aleksandrovich in 1884, see ibid., pp. 41–55.

62. Punin comments on the neo-Renaissance diffusion of the classical system of orders at the Nikolaevskii Palace in *Arkhitektura Peterburga serediny XIX veka*, pp. 205–6. See also Petrov et al., *Pamiatniki arkhitektury Leningrada*, p. 287.

63. On the New Mikhailovskii Palace and Jensen's work in terra-cotta, see Petrova, *Shtakenshneider*, pp. 161–2.

64. The decoration of the Pavilion Hall is described in ibid., pp. 116–19; and V. M. Glinka et al., *Ermitazh*, pp. 332–40. Shtakenshneider also remodeled many of the Winter Palace suites (some of which remain) in the 1840s and 1850s. See ibid., pp. 288–300.

65. Petrova, *Shtakenshneider*, pp. 125–7; and Glinka et al., *Ermitazh*, pp. 378, 380.

66. Shtakenshneider's work at Peterhof and other suburban estates is surveyed in Petrova, *Shtakenshneider*, pp. 55–98. See also Petrov et al., *Pamiatniki arkhitektury prigorodov Leningrada*, pp. 446, 456–66.

67. Punin notes that the Demidov house contained both Italian Renaissance and baroque elements. See *Arkhitektura Peterburga serediny XIX veka*, p. 72. The house and its interior are described in Petrova, *Shtakenshneider*, pp. 151–6. In 1911, the house was acquired by the Italian embassy, which dismantled the malachite wall surfaces of the famed Malachite Room (situated in the center of the bel etage) upon the embassy's evacuation following the revolution.

68. On the Gagarina house (as it is now known), see Punin, *Arkhitektura Peterburga serediny XIX veka*, p. 72; and Petrov et al., *Pamiatniki arkhitektury Leningrada*, p. 319.

69. Ibid., p. 325. A more restrained interpretation of the baroque was Bosse's mansion for E. M. Buturlina (1857–60), a three-storied structure closely modeled on the early work of Rastrelli. A survey of Bosse's work is presented in V. Andreeva, "G. E. Bosse – arkhitektor–novator," *Arkhitektura SSSR*, 1988, no. 1: 88–95.

70. Pogodin himself was born a serf, whose family was freed by their owner in 1806. On Pogodin's role in Russian intellectual life in the middle third of the century, see Riasanovsky, *Nicholas I*, pp. 53–8.

71. The development of the study of Russian architecture is the subject of a substantial monograph by T. A. Slavina, *Issledovateli russkogo zodchestva: Russkaia istoriko-arkhitekturnaia nauka XVIII–nachala XX veka* (Leningrad, 1983). The work of Vladimir Suslov, one of the major architect–restorers, is discussed in A. V. Suslova and T. A. Slavina, *Vladimir Suslov* (Leningrad, 1978). Kirichenko argues that at this watershed in Russian history (the 1850s), the romantic first phase of eclecticism began to yield to a more careful use of historical motifs (historicism). See "Romantizm i istorizm v russkoi arkhitekture XIX veka (K voprosu o dvukh fazakh razvitiia eklektiki)," *Arkhitekturnoe nasledstvo*, 36 (1988): 130–55. Punin disputes this distinction, and places the boundary between early and late eclecticism – both of which emphasized historical motifs – in the 1860s. See *Arkhitektura Peterburga serediny XIX veka*, pp. 5–6.

72. Elena Borisova's *Russkaia arkhitektura vtoroi poloviny XIX veka* (Moscow, 1979) frequently refers to the relation between capitalist development and architectural practice, especially in Chapters 3 ("Obraz goroda vtoroi poloviny XIX v.") and 4 ("Razvitie novykh tipov sooruzhenii i ego vliianie na arkhihtekturno-khudozhestvennyi protsess").

73. The development of a sense of professional cohesion in architecture led to the formation of two major architectural associations: the Moscow Architectural Society, chartered in 1867, and the Petersburg Society of Architects (1870). The founder and first president of the Moscow group was Mikhail Bykovskii (1801–85), a noted architect whose work during four decades ranged from church and palace architecture to commercial structures. He was also the father of Konstantin Bykovskii, president of the Moscow society in 1894–1903 and one of its most active spokesmen. For a detailed study of the elder Bykovskii's work, see Kirichenko, *Mikhail Bykovskii*.

The first president of the Petersburg society was Alexander Rezanov, a prominent architect and, from 1871, rector of the Imperial Academy of Arts. Among the most significant achievements of the Petersburg society was the initiation of the journal *Zodchii* (*Architect*) at the beginning of 1872. For 45 years, until the end of 1917, this authoritative publication served not only as a record of the architectural profession throughout Russia, but also provided a conduit for technical information and ideas developed in Russia, as well as in Europe and the United States. For detailed information on the foundation of the societies and various architectural journals, see Iu. S. Iaralov, ed., *100 let obschestvennykh arkhitekturnykh organizatsii v SSSR, 1867–1967* (Moscow, 1967). See also V. Shreter, "K istorii S-

Petersburgskogo Obshchestva Arkhitektorov," in *Zodchii*, 1894, no. 5: 35–7; and L. N. Benois and M. F. Geisler, "25-letie osnovaniia S-Peterburgskogo Obshchestva Arkhitektorov," *Zodchii*, 1895, no. 11: 82–90.

74. See Joan Bassin, *Architectural Competitions in Nineteenth-Century England* (Ann Arbor, 1984), pp. 4–12, for a discussion of the professionalization of English architecture during the nineteenth century. Despite great differences in economic and social structures, the similarities in the development of a professional identity among architects in the two countries are striking, and derive in both cases from new possibilities offered by rapid economic and industrial growth.

75. Robert Macleod notes this stylistic confusion – at times creative – in nineteenth-century British architecture in *Style and Society: Architectural Ideology in Britain 1835–1914* (London, 1971). His own interpretation of the effects of professionalism and a market economy on architecture in Britain amplifies that of Bassin (see pp. 123–6). See also Bassin, pp. 6–7, for reference to the patronage of "corporate groups" in the expansion of architectural opportunity.

An extensive discussion of the interrelation between social change and architectural development in Russia during the latter half of the century is contained in Borisova, *Russkaia arkhitektura*, pp. 168–72. For a study of the impact of industrial development on the urban setting, see James H. Bater, "The Industrialization of Moscow and St. Petersburg" in James Bater and R. A. French, eds., *Studies in Russian Historical Geography*, vol. 2 (London, 1983), pp. 279–303.

76. The connections with German schools were the most closely developed. Two of the most prominent architects teaching at the Academy of Arts in Petersburg were both educated in Germany: Ludwig Bonstedt (1822–85) at the Bauakademie and the Berlin Academy of Arts; and Harold Bosse (1812–94) in Darmstadt. Although born in Petersburg, Bonstedt left Russia for Germany in 1863, after 5 years as professor at the Petersburg Academy of Arts. In 1872, he won first prize in the competition for the design of the Reichstag, but his design was not built. More information on Bonstedt is contained in the biographical sketch by V. S. Shreter in *Zodchii*, 1872, no. 5: 112–14; and in the obituary, also by Shreter, published in *Zodchii*, 1886, no. 1: 1–3. For a brief account of Bosse's work by one of his contemporaries, see *Zodchii*, 1894, no. 12: 91. A more detailed survey is presented in V. Andreev, "G. E. Bosse – arkhitektor–novator," *Arkhitektura SSSR*, 1988, no. 1: 88–95.

77. A Soviet study of nineteenth-century industrial architecture is A. L. Punin's *Arkhitkturnye pamiatniki Peterburga: vtoraia polovina XIX veka* (Leningrad, 1981), particularly the chapter "Metallicheskie konstruktsii mostov i promyshlennykh zdanii" (pp. 77–92), and the preceding chapter, pp. 63–76. The impact of Joseph Paxton's Crystal Palace is noted on p. 75. See also N. A. Smurova, "Inzhenernye sooruzheniia i ikh vliianie na razvitie russkoi khudozhestvennoi kultury" (with particular emphasis on the work of Vladimir Shukhov) in Iu. S. Lebedev, ed., *Kon-

struktsii i arkhitekturnaia forma v russkom zodchestve XIX–achala XX vv.* (Moscow, 1977), pp. 60–93; and Iu. P. Volchok, "Stanovlenie novykh tektonicheskikh sistem v promyshlennoi arkhitekture," ibid., pp. 94–126.

78. See B. M. Kochakov, ed., *Ocherki Istorii Leningrada*, vol. 2, *Period Kapitalizma* (Moscow–Leningrad, 1957), p. 173, for precise data and sources.

79. From the entry "Sankt-Peterburg" in *Entsiklopedicheskii Slovar'* (St. Petersburg, 1900), LVI, 319.

80. A contemporary report on the palace, including a thorough cost analysis, is contained in "Dom E. I. V. Velikogo Kniazia Vladimira Aleksandrovicha," *Zodchii*, no. 3, pp. 41–2; nos. 4–5, pp. 63–4; and nos. 7–8, pp. 89–90. *Zodchii* also included detailed drawings and plans of the structure (which the editors call a "house") in the volumes for 1875 and 1878.

81. Punin, *Arkhitketurnye pamiatniki*, p. 166. Some of the city's wealthiest citizens recreated the opulence of imperial palaces. The Ratkov-Rozhnov house, a few steps up Palace Quay from the Palace of Vladimir Aleksandrovich, is one such imitation. The project began in 1875 when the architect Karl Rackhau was hired to rebuild an early eighteenth-century structure on the site. By the completion of construction in 1877, the building had become the property of V. A. Ratkov-Rozhnov, the mayor of Petersburg, who owned seventeen buildings in the city, many of them as eclectic as the house on Palace Quay, with its classical and baroque elements combined with "Egyptian" caryatids. The major rooms of the Ratkov-Rozhnov house, like those in the Palace of Vladimir Alexandrovich, were designed in a variety of period styles. Ibid., p. 169. A biography of Karl Rachau (1830–80) and illustrations of several of his buildings are contained in "K. K. Rackhau," *Zodchii*, 1882, no. 1: 12–13.

82. On the proliferation of Russian architectural criticism during this period, see William C. Brumfield, *The Origins of Modernism in Russian Architecture* (Berkeley, 1991), pp. 4, 6, 8. No one attacked the saturated facade, "without a single breathing space," more sarcastically than the prominent cultural critic Vladimir Stasov:

[Eclecticism] is architecture copied from old models, from books and albums, from photographs and drawings, the architecture of clever people who get smart in class and then with great indifference turn out goods by the yard and by the pound. . . . If it suits you, here are five yards of Greek "classicism"; if not, here are three and a quarter of Italian "Renaissance." Don't like that? Well then, here, if you please, is a little piece of the highest sort of "rococo Louis XV," and if that's not it, here is a nice bit of "Romanesque," six ounces of "Gothic," or a whole gross of "Russian."

This passage appeared in the introduction to "Nasha arkhitektura," the third section in Stasov's four-part survey of the arts in Russian during the reign of Alexander II, "Dvadtsat' piat' let russkogo iskusstva," first published during 1882 and 1883 in the journal *Vestnik Evropy*. Quoted from V. V. Stasov, *Izbrannye sochineniia*, (Moscow, 1952), II, 499. In the same article, Stasov writes approvingly of attempts to create a Russian national style in architecture, even though such attempts were a part of the electicism that he criticized.

83. Population figures are taken from Akademiia Nauk SSSR, Institut Istorii, *Istoriia Moskvy*, vol. 4, *Period promyshlennogo kapitalizma* (Moscow, 1954), p. 227. The same volume also has extensive information on the economic growth of Moscow during the latter part of the nineteenth century.

84. For a contemporary description of the Porokhovshchikov house, see D. Liushin, "Dereviannyi dom g-na Porokhovshchikova," *Zodchii*, 1872, no. 2: 16. This volume also contains a plan and architectural drawings of the structure.

85. Further information on the involvement of Moscow's merchants in the cause of Pan-Slavism (with specific reference to Porokhovshchikov) can be found in Thomas Owen, *Capitalism and Politics in Russia: A Social History of the Moscow Merchants, 1855–1905* (New York, 1981), pp. 89–93.

86. Presented as part of the bicentennial observance of Peter the Great's birth, the exhibition is recognized as a landmark in Russian cultural history, with ramifications extending both to the arts and to technology. Its sponsor, the Society of Lovers of the Natural Sciences, Anthropology, and Ethnography, arranged for the display of some 12,000 exhibits at sites throughout Moscow, and it is a measure of the organizers' sense of purpose that many of these items were eventually to form the basis of collections at Moscow's Polytechnical and Historical museums. The Moscow Architectural Society sponsored the architectural section, including historical displays of models of major monuments and architectural documents from both Petersburg and Moscow. In addition to this tribute to national architectural traditions, the Exhibitions also featured new construction technology. See Borisova, *Russkaia arkhitektura*, pp. 155–7; also E. I. Kirichenko, *Moskva na rubezhe dvukh stoletii* (Moscow, 1977), p. 26. For a detailed contemporary account, see V. Kuroedov, "Obzor arkhitekturnoi chasti politekhnicheskoi vystavki v Moskve," *Zodchii*, 1872, no. 7: 105–12; and no. 8: 139–42.

87. One account, in the newspaper *Golos* (*Voice*) in 1875, noted: "The museum will tell us loudly, clearly, and justly who we were, who we are, what our worth is as a people, and consequently what place belongs to us in the family of nations of the civilized world. Here is the political meaning of the museum." The same account stated that the winning design had been inspired by the monuments on Red Square (the Kremlin towers, and the Cathedral of the Intercession), as well as various sixteenth- and seventeenth-century monuments in Muscovy. "Moskovskie zametki," *Golos*, 1875, no. 235: 1 (quoted in Borisova, *Russkaia arkhitektura*, p. 294).

For a detailed analysis of the competition process for the design of the Historical Museum, see E. I. Kirichenko, "Arkhitektor V. O. Shervud i ego teoreticheskie vozzreniia," *Arkhitekturnoe nasledstvo*, no. 22 (1974): 3–7; also, Kirichenko, *Moskva na rubezhe*, pp. 36–9; and by the same author, "The Historical Museum: A Moscow design competition 1875–83," in Catherine Cooke, ed., *Uses of Tradition in Russian and Soviet Architecture* (London, 1987), pp. 24–6. In their programmatic statement *The Sense and Meaning of the [Historical] Museum* (1873), A. S. Uvarov and I. E. Zabelin noted:

"The path that neglects history has never led to good. . . . A people wishing to achieve greatness must know its history, under the pain of ceasing to be a great people. . . . Museums are one of the most powerful means for the achievement of a people's self awareness – the highest goal of history." Quoted in E. I. Kirichenko, "Arkhitektor V. O. Shervud i ego teoreticheskikh vozzreniia," p. 4.

88. For excerpts from Shervud's notebooks, see V. Voropaev, " 'Menia ochen' zanimal Gogol '. . .': Iz 'Zapisok' V. O. Shervuda," *Literaturnaia gazeta* (April 9, 1986): 6. The notebooks are kept in the Manuscript Division of the Lenin Library in Moscow. In her article on Shervud, E. I. Kirichenko gives a detailed analysis of his wish to establish a scientific basis for a Russian architectural style, exemplified by the design of the Historical Museum. Yet his attempt to rise above historically based decorative detail in the formation of a national style proved a difficult, if not impossible, task. In a letter of May 1874 to the historian Ivan Zabelin, Shervud complained that his preliminary designs for the museum produced only "nice architectural houses for a wealthy client or, even more, for provincial city halls." "Arkhitektor V. O. Shervud i ego teoreticheskie vozzreniia," pp. 3–7.

89. An analysis of the iconography of the museum interior is presented in E. I. Kirichenko, "Istorism myshleniia i tip muzeinogo zdaniia v russkoi arkhitekture serediny i vtoroi poloviny XIX v.," in G. Iu. Sternin, ed., *Vzaimosviaz' iskusstv v khudozhestvennom razvitii Rossii vtoroi poloviny XIX v.* (Moscow, 1982), pp. 135–42.

90. An informative survey of Ropet's work and his view of the role of historical interpretation in architecture is provided in E. I. Kirichenko, "Arkhitektor I. P. Ropet," *Arkhitekturnoe nasledstvo*, 20 (1972): 85–93. Despite Ropet's attempt to incorporate stylistic features of Russian vernacular architecture into his work, Kirichenko notes that his use of the "Russian style" was not the antithesis to eclecticism, but rather another eclectic manifestation (p. 87). Reproductions of the designs of both Hartman and Ropet were included in a series of illustrated volumes entitled *Motivy russkoi arkhitektury* (Petersburg, n.d. [apparently 1890s]). See particularly vol. 2, for the year 1875.

91. Information on the competition for the Polytechnic Museum project and the changes introduced into the final plan is contained in Kirichenko, *Moskva na rubezhe*, p. 48. Nikolai Shokhin (1819–95), who graduated from the architectural school attached to the Kremlin Court Office, had extensive experience in the restoration of medieval Russian monuments in the Kremlin and elsewhere in Moscow, yet his original design for the museum was Italianate. Monighetti's contribution was to redesign the facades in the Russian style.

92. Shreter's views and work were illustrated in two of his articles: V. Shreter, "Dom V. F. Shtrausa v S-Peterburge," *Zodchii*, 1874, no. 12: 145–7, with illustrations; and idem, "Obyvatel'skii dom i fabrika shelkovykh izdelii A. I. Nissena," *Zodchii*, 1873, no. 2: 139. His career is the subject of a comprehensive, annotated monograph by T. I. Nikolaeva, *Viktor Shreter* (Leningrad, 1991).

594

93. I. S. Kitner, "Kirpichnaia arkhitektura," *Zodchii*, 1872, no. 6: 84. For a survey of Ieronim Kitner's leading role in the architectural profession in Petersburg, as well as that of his sons Maksim and Richard, see Iu. I. Kitner, "Dinastiia arkhitektorov," *Stroitelstvo i arkhitektura Leningrada*, 1978, no. 4: 42–5.

94. The mentor of the rationalists was Apollinarii Krasovskii, a leader in Russian architectural education during the nineteenth century. Krasovskii's textbook *Civil Architecture*, first published in 1851 and reissued in a second edition in 1886, served generations of Russian civil engineers and architects, many of whom studied under him during his 37-year tenure at Petersburg's Construction School. (In 1882, the school became the Institute of Civil Engineers as part of an upgrading that Krasovskii had long supported.) In the book, he wrote:

> Architecture should not tend exclusively toward either the useful or the beautiful; its basic rule is the transformation of the one into the other. . . . Tectonics or construction is the main source of architectural forms. The role of art in the composition consists only in conveying artistic finish to the crude forms of tectonics. . . . The property of a material and the best possible means of applying it determine the means of construction, and construction itself determines the external form of both parts and buildings.

A. Krasovskii, *Grazhdanskaia arkhitektura* (St. Petersburg, 1886), pp. 5, 12. For further work on Krasovskii, see A. L. Punin, "Idei ratsionalizma v russkoi arkhitekture vtoroi poloviny XIX veka," in *Arkhitektura SSSR*, 1962, no. 11: 55–8. An assessment of Krasovskii's work by his contemporaries is contained in his obituary in *Zodchii*, 1875, no. 9: 102–3.

95. N. V. Sultanov, "Odna iz zadach stroitel'nogo uchilishche," *Zodchii*, 1882, no. 5: 71. For those who interpreted rationalism more strictly, Sultanov's speech was an apostasy, announced at an institute established to provide the highest technological training. When the speech was published in *Zodchii* in May 1882, S. Zosimovskii, a civil engineer, quickly responded, writing in the following number of *Zodchii* that artistic concerns are "an abnormal phenomenon for civil engineers," and irrelevant to technology. See "Po povodu rechi grazhdanskogo inzhenera Sultanova 'Odna iz zadach stroitel'nogo uchilishche,'" *Zodchii*, 1882, no. 6: 85.

96. On the development of professional training in both engineering and architecture, see Brumfield, *Origins of Modernism*, pp. 19–20.

97. See E. I. Kirichenko, *Moskva na rubezhe*, pp. 41–2, with references to the design competition for the Upper Trading Rows.

98. A brief sketch of the architectural evolution of the *passage* in Petersburg is presented in Punin, pp. 97–100; see also *Konstruktsii i arkhitekturnaia forma*, pp. 143–57. For the larger context of ferrovitreous galleries and halls in Britain and France, see Bassin, pp. 65–6.

99. Borisova, *Russkaia arkhitektura*, p. 306. Detailed photographs of the old trading rows, as well as the construction of the new building for the Upper Trading Rows appeared in the album *Torgovye riady na Krasnoi ploshchadi v Moskve* (Kiev, 1893).

100. I. P. Mashkov, ed., *Putevoditel' po Moskve* (Moscow, 1913), pp. 259–62. A description and detailed plan of the Upper Trading Rows are also contained in Komech and Pluzhnikov, eds., *Pamiatniki arkhitektury Moskvy: Kreml', Kitai-gorod, Tsentral'nye ploshchadi*, pp. 404–5.

101. Each of the skylights weighs some 50,000 puds (819 metric tons) and has over 20,000 panes of glass. The components were made by Otto Krel, the director of the Petersburg Metal Factory and builder of a number of metal-framed public markets in Petersburg, and were assembled under the supervision of the engineer Ivan Rylskii.

102. Shukhov's trip to the United States is described in G. M. Kovelman's biographical study *Tvorchestvo pochetnogo akademika inzhenera Vladimira Grigorevicha Shukhova* (Moscow, 1961), pp. 16–19. The growing Russian interest in American architecture and construction technology is exemplified by Sergei Kuleshov's travel account, "Eskizy amerikanskoi arkhitektury i tekhniki," which appeared in several issues of *Zodchii* in 1877. For more on this account of American cities by a Russian architect, see William C. Brumfield, "Russian Perceptions of American Architecture, 1870–1917," in *Reshaping Russian Architecture* (New York: Cambridge University Press, 1990), pp. 47–51. Shukhov's work at the 1896 Nizhnii Novgorod exhibition is illustrated in *Vidy rabot proizvedennykh stroitel'noi firmy Bari na vserossiiskoi vystavke 1896 v N. Novgorode* (Moscow, 1896). See also Nina Smurova, "Arkhitketurno-stroitel'nye dostizheniia Vserossiiskoi vystavki 1896 g. i ee rol' v razvitii otechestvennoi arkhitektury," in *Problemy istorii sovetskoi arkhitektury* (Moscow, 1976), vol. 2, pp. 14–19.

103. Smirnova surveys Klein's life and work in the chapter "R. Klein," in S. M. Zemtsov, ed., *Zodchie Moskvy* (Moscow, 1981), pp. 288–300.

104. In 1909, the society of merchants that owned the Middle Trading Rows petitioned, unsuccessfully, to enlarge the windows. In 1914, a second petition to rebuild in the French Renaissance style was granted, but not implemented. Klein himself was responsible for the merchants' dissatisfaction with the original style; his own design for the Muir and Mirrielees firm (1906–8), discussed in Chapter 14, demonstrated the superiority of plate glass for modern commercial trade.

105. Rezanov's article "Proekt zdanii gorodskoi dumy v Moskve," *Zodchii*, 1876, nos. 8–9: 93–4, gives a summary of the initiatives leading to his original design for the Duma. Although not chosen in the final competition, Rezanov's project showed considerably more originality in the facade design than did Chichagov's final proposal. Rezanov's drawing of the main facade appeared in *Zodchii* (1876): Plate 36 (Plate 18 shows the ground plan), and a revised version of the facade – codesigned with Andrei Huhn – was published in *Zodchii* (1888): Plate 58.

106. E. I. Kirichenko, *Moskva na rubezhe*, p. 47.

107. The 1882 volume of *Zodchii* contains excellent illustrations of the competition designs: four prizes and one honorable mention by architects including Kitner and

Huhn, Leontii Benois, Shreter, and Bogomolov. None of these designs shows any resemblance to the Russian style eventually chosen.

108. Parland's detailed, self-justificatory account of the design and construction of the Church of the Resurrection appeared in *Zodchii*, 1907, no. 35: 374–8, with illustrations. The church was also the subject of a lavishly produced brochure, with plans and architectural drawings: *Kratkii otchet o postroike Khrama Voskreseniia Khristova sooruzhennogo na meste smertel'nogo poraneniia v Boze pochivshiego Imperatora Aleksandra II* (Petersburg, 1907).

109. Vasnetsov designed four mosaic scenes of the Crucifixion for the pediments of the church's west entrance porches. His work for the church represents a revival of interest in medieval art forms that would ramify both in his own work as a painter, designer, and architect and in that of other artists, such as Mikhail Vrubel and Ivan Nesterov. A report on the mosaic work of A. A. Frolov (including the Church of the Resurrection) appeared in *Nedelia stroitelia* (the weekly supplement to *Zodchii*) (1900): 180–2. Frolov also did extensive designs for secular structures, including mosaic panels for the Upper Trading Rows. A partial listing of these projects is contained in the obituary "A. A. Frolov," *Stroitel'*, 1897, nos. 13–14: 539–40.

110. For a commentary on Mamontov's transformation of Abramtsevo, see G. Iu. Sternin, "Abramtsevo: ot 'usad'by' k 'dache,'" in the same author's *Russkaia khudozhestvennaia kul'tura vtoroi poloviny XIX–nachala XX veka* (Moscow, 1984), pp. 187–8. See also E. R. Arenzon, "Ot Kireeva do Abramtseva. K biografii Savvy Ivanovicha Mamontova," *Panorama iskusstv*, 6 (1986): 359–82.

111. In her memoirs of Abramtsevo, Natalia Polenova (the daughter of the painter Vasilii Polenov) notes that the church was built to embody not only aesthetic but also spiritual ideals. Her account is presented in *Abramtsevo: vospominaniia* (Moscow, 1922), pp. 30–43. See also Borisova, *Russkaia arkhitektura*, pp. 256–7.

112. Reproductions of project sketches by Polenov and Vasnetsov appear in Polenova, *Abramtsevo*, pp. 33, 35, 36. The original sketches for the building were largely the work of Polenov, one of the earliest members of the Abramtsevo circle. Viktor Vasnetsov, a painter of subjects from the Russian past, refashioned the sketches into an architectural project. It should be noted that in the nineteenth century, the Church of the Savior on the Nereditsa looked quite different (particularly in the roof line) from its present appearance, based on a reconstruction at the turn of the century. It is this earlier form of the church that shows in Polenov's drawing. For a detailed account of the design of the Abramtsevo church, see N. V. Masalina, "Tserkov' v Abramtseve," in E. A. Borisova, ed., *Iz istorii russkogo iskusstva vtoroi poloviny XIX–nachala XX veka* (Moscow, 1978), pp. 47–58.

113. Elena Borisova comments on the creative involvement of the Abramtsevo painters in architecture: "The main thing, perhaps, is that precisely in architectural creativity artists could satisfy that tendency to the plastic, that professional architects felt somewhat later, for which painters had

still not found a place on their canvases." *Russkaia arkhitektura*, p. 264.

114. On the history of the Stieglitz Museum, see T. E. Tyzhnenko, "Muzei nachinaetsia s facada," *Leningradskaia panorama*, 1983, no. 5: 31–4; and Petrov, ed., *Pamiatniki arkhitektury Leningrada*, p. 381.

115. Siuzor's career is surveyed in V. G. Isachenko, "V shirokom diapazone," *Leningradskaia panorama*, 1985, no. 10: 28–31. He also designed the Russian headquarters of the Singer Sewing Machine Company on Nevskii Prospekt (see Chapter 14).

116. The A. A. Morozov mansion (the deed was held by Morozova's estranged husband Abram Abramovich) was widely publicized as one of Moscow's marvels at the beginning of the century. Its plan is reproduced in Makarevich et al., *Belyi gorod*, pp. 82–3.

117. For a survey of the architectural congress debates, see Brumfield, *Origins of Modernism*, pp. 40–5.

118. Konstantin Bykovskii, "Zadachi arkhitektury XIX veka" (The Tasks of Architecture in the Nineteenth Century), in *Trudy II s'ezda russkikh arkhitektorov* (Moscow, 1899), p. 18.

119. Ibid.

Chapter 14

1. On the appearance of the terms "new style" and "style moderne" as applied to Russian architecture, see Brumfield, *The Origins of Modernism in Russian Architecture* (Berkeley, 1991), pp. 47–8.

2. The speeches delivered at the Third Congress of Russian Architects, held in Petersburg in 1900, made no substantial reference to architectural innovation, yet the speakers had finally abandoned the debate over the relevance of medieval Russian architecture for the creation of a "national" style. Indeed, this was the first major conference in which engineering topics clearly predominated over the aesthetic. The proceedings of the 1900 congress of architects were published as *Trudy III s"ezda russkikh zodchikh* (Petersburg, 1905).

3. The propagation of modernism in Russian architecture at the turn of the century involved reports in professional journals of new directions in western architecture and design, as well as commentary and publicity concerning the appearance of the "new style" in Russia. For a survey of the critical debates and exhibits of modern design in Moscow and Petersburg, see Brumfield, *The Origins of Modernism*, pp. 47–62. A recent survey of the Viennese presence in Moscow's style moderne is M. V. Nashchokina, "Venskie motivy v arkhitekture Moskvy nachala XX veka," in A. A. Voronov, ed., *Voprosy istorii arkhitektury* (Moscow, 1990), pp. 94–109.

4. A general discussion of Russian social and economic development during the two decades before the revolution is Teodor Shanin, *The Roots of Otherness: Russia's Turn of the Century*, 2 vols. (New Haven, 1986). See also Edith Clowes et al., eds., *Between Tsar and People: Educated Society and the*

Quest for Public Identity in Late Imperial Russia (Princeton, 1991). The most perceptive general formulation of Russia's late industrial boom remains Alexander Gerschenkron, *Europe in the Russian Mirror: Four Lectures in Economic History* (New York: Cambridge University Press, 1969).

5. Walcot's original design is reproduced in Brumfield, *The Origins of Modernism*, p. 67. The construction history of the Metropole is surveyed in V. M. Chekmarev, "Obnovlenie gostinitsy 'Metropol,' " *Arkhitektura i stroitel'stvo Moskvy*, 1987, no. 6: 22–5; and by the same author, "Mir khudozhestvennykh obrazov gostinitsy 'Metropol,' " in A. S. Loginova, ed., *Muzei 10*, pp. 35–47.

6. The most authoritative history of the Tretiakov Gallery is D. Ia. Bezrukova, *Tretiakov i istoriia sozdaniia ego galerei* (Moscow, 1970).

7. Vasnetsov's work on the facade in 1903 is mentioned in the journal *Zodchii*, 1903, no. 36: 427, and photographs of the completed building appeared in architectural publications by 1906.

8. On the Abramtsevo workshop's role in the development of architectural ceramics in Moscow, see E. R. Arenzon, " 'Abramtsevo' v Moskve: K istorii khudozhestvenno-keramicheskogo predpriiatiia S. I. Mamontova," in *Muzei 10*, pp. 95–102. For photographs of the museum, see Brumfield, *The Origins of Modernism*, Plate 10.

9. Despite a desperate housing shortage for the lower classes, large parts of the city were still underbuilt; therefore, the construction of large apartment complexes were usually designed to attract a sufficiently properous clientele. On the design of apartments at the beginning of the twentieth century, see E. I. Kirichenko, "O nekotorykh osobennostiakh evoliutsii gorodskikh mnogokvartirnykh domov vtoroi poloviny XIX–nachala XX vekov (Ot otdel'nogo doma k kompleksy," *Arkhitekturnoe nasledstvo*, 15 (1963): 153–70; and "Prostranstvennaia organizatsiia zhilykh kompleksov Moskvy i Peterburga v nachale XX v.," *Arkhitekturnoe nasledstvo*, 19 (1972): 118–36.

10. Indeed, the primitive services offered by Moscow at the time made it essential that such a large project provide its own source of water, heat, and electricity. The Proskurin design is analyzed in detail in Elena Vokhovitskaia and Aleksei Tarkhanov, "Dom 'Rossiia,' " *Dekorativnoe iskusstvo*, 1986, no. 7: 34–8.

11. For a survey of apartment construction by Kekushev and other Moscow architects, see Brumfield, *Origins of Modernism*, pp. 71–7.

12. The inclusion of such amenities was not common in Moscow; retail commercial outlets were generally located in galleries and trading rows at the center. The growing commercial use of the ground floor of apartment buildings at the turn of the century in Moscow is closely related to developments in construction technology. See M. A. Kozlovskaia, "Konstruktivnye struktury i arkhitekturnye formy grazhdanskikh zdanii," in Iu. S. Lebedev, ed., *Konstruktsii i arkhitekturnaia forma v russkom zodchestve XIX nachala XX vv.* (Moscow, 1977), p. 129. A comprehensive analysis of Shekhtel's work is presented in Brumfield, *Origins of Modernism*, pp. 120–73.

13. A clear admission of the limited possibilities available to the architectural profession in addressing the housing question in Russian cities can be found in a lecture by S. Ia. Timokhovich at the Second Congress of Russian Architects, published in *Trudy II s"ezda russkikh zodchikh v Moskve* (Moscow, 1899), pp. 179–85. Entitled "Proekt blagoustroennikh kvartir v gigienicheskom i sanitarnom otnosheniiakh," the lecture assessed the need for "well organized apartments from a hygienic and sanitary point of view" in four categories of housing: (1) luxury apartments; (2) "midlevel" (*srednei ruki*) apartment houses; (3) cheap apartments and furnished rooms; and (4) attics, basements, and flophouses. For practical reasons, only the second category offered possibilities for real and immediate improvement in design; regardless of humanitarian considerations, the lower categories were dismissed as beyond the control of architects. In Soviet scholarship, the disparity between housing levels in Moscow at the beginning of the century has been examined by P. and B. Gol'denberg, in *Planirovka zhilogo kvartala Moskvy* (Moscow, 1935), pp. 126–78. See also E. I. Kirichenko, "O nekotorykh osobennostiakh evoliutsii gorodskikh mnogokvartirnykh domov vtoroi poloviny XIX-nachala XX vv.," *Arkhitekturnoe nasledstvo*, 15 (1963): 158–61. Attempts to provide cheap housing subsidized by the bequest of the merchant. G. G. Solodovnikov catered almost entirely to a growing "white-collar" service population. See Brumfield, *Origins of Modernism*, p. 77; and Robert Thurston, *Liberal City, Conservative State: Moscow and Russia's Urban Crisis, 1906–1914* (Oxford, 1987), pp. 143–4.

14. Vladimir Kirillov provides a detailed analysis of the typical arrangement of apartment space in the fashionable buildings of the period in *Arkhitektura russkogo moderna* (Moscow, 1979), pp. 90–3. A more general survey can be found in Gol'denberg, *Planirovka*, pp. 136–9; and Kirichenko, "O nekotorykh osobennostiakh," pp. 167–9.

15. See William Brumfield, "The Decorative Arts in Russian Architecture: 1900–1907," *The Journal of Decorative and Propaganda Arts*, no. 5 (1987): 12–27.

16. A recent monograph on the Talashkino community, including Maliutin, is L. S. Zhuravleva, *Talashkino* (Moscow, 1989). See also Sergei Diagilev, "Neskol'ko slov o S. V. Maliutine," *Mir iskusstva*, 1903, no. 4: 157–60. In Diagilev's view, Maliutin, together with the Finnish painter and designer Gallen-Kalela, had established in the north of Europe the basis for a "second rinascimento" that would eventually lead to a "new aesthetic, a new Florence." Ibid., pp. 159–60.

17. It is revealing that Grabar's solution for a revival of furniture design in Russia stems not from modernized folk art, but from a revival of Russia's Empire furniture designs of the turn of the nineteenth century – thus anticipating the revival of neoclassicism in both architecture and interior design later in the decade. "Neskol'ko myslei o sovremennom prikladnom iskusstve v Rossii," *Mir iskusstva*, 1902, no. 3: 51–6.

Maliutin's defenders have argued that because the theatrical facade in the neo-Russian variant of the new style endowed the apartment dwelling with aesthetic significance, the disjunction between the exterior and interior of the prosaic apartments themselves was justified. It even affirmed the importance of the theater in countering, by the "magic" of mythic symbol and theatrical design, the modern urban tendency toward conformity and alienation. The Pertsov building was the main subject of a laudatory, illustrated essay (unsigned) on the neo-Russian style: "Mastera russkogo stilia," *Moskovskii arkhitekturnyi mir*, no. 2 (1912): 43–9. A defense of theatricality in the design of apartment houses appeared in P. Sokolov, "Krasota arkhitekturnykh form," *Zodchii*, 1912, no. 49: 490. For an theoretical discussion of the neo-Russian variant of the style moderne and its theatrical quality, see Borisova, "Neorusskii stil' v russkoi arkhitekture predrevoliutsionnykh let," in E. A. Borisova et al., eds., *Iz istorii russkogo iskusstva vtoroi poloviny XIX–nachala XX veka* (Moscow, 1978), pp. 59–71.

18. Illustrations of Vashkov's work for the Olovianishnikov firm appeared frequently in the architectural annuals, which also contained elaborately designed advertisements for the same firm. For example, see *Ezhegodnik Moskovskogo arkhitekturnogo obshchestva*, no. 1 (1909): 19. Photographs of the apartment house appeared in the same issue. V. P. Vygolov refers to Vashkov's work at the Trinity Church apartments in his chapter "Inter'er," in *Russkaia khudozhestvennaia kul'tura kontsa XIX–nachala XX veka (1908–1917)* (Moscow, 1980), vol. 4, pp. 369, 371.

19. For an analysis of critical discussions concerning a revival of church architecture, see William C. Brumfield, "The 'New Style' and the Revival of Orthodox Church Architecture, 1900–1914," in William Brumfield and Milos Velimirovic, eds., *Christianity and the Arts in Russia* (New York: Cambridge University Press, 1991), pp. 105–7, 112–13. A succinct survey of the church between reform and reaction during this period is provided in Gregory L. Freeze, " 'Going to the Intelligentsia': The Church and Its Urban Mission in Post-Reform Russia," in Clowes et al., eds., *Between Tsar and People*, pp. 215–32.

20. For a discussion of the Old Believer role in Russian economic and social history, see Alexander Gerschenkron, *Europe in the Russian Mirror*. See n. 4.

21. An elaborately carved iconostasis in the church contained a number of valuable icons. In this church for *bespopovtsy*, who had no priest or altar, the church ritual occurred in front of the iconostasis, and the space behind it was used as a council room for the community elders. The simplicity of the interior, illuminated by large tinted windows, resembled that of a Protestant meeting house. Contemporary accounts note the considerable effort applied to furnishing this church – now vandalized almost beyond repair – in antiqued bronze, silk, carved stained oak, and wrought iron. Information on the construction of the Tokmakov Lane church was published in "Khram Staroobriadtsev Pomorskogo soglasiia v Moskve," *Zodchii*, 1908, no. 48: 440; and I. P. Mashkov, *Putevoditel' po Moskve* (Moscow, 1913), pp. 205–6. Mashkov places the cost of the church at 150,000 rubles.

22. According to Shchusev, the decline stemmed from the interference in the design process by clergy, donors, and official institutions, and from the inability of architects themselves to devise anything more than a crude, uninformed imitation of historical prototypes. Aleksei Shchusev, "Mysli o svobode tvorchestva v religioznoi arkhitekture," *Zodchii*, 1905, no. 11: 132. Shchusev went considerably beyond church architecture to the role of tradition in architecture. In his view, the new emphasis on rationality in construction must not deny traditional nonfunctional elements that are significant in the perception of structure. For an analysis of this principle in the neo-Russian variant of the style moderne, with particular reference to Shchusev's churches, see Borisova, "Neorusskii stil'," pp. 61, 65–6. For a more detailed description of Shchusev's churches, see K. N. Afanas'ev, *A. V. Shchusev* (Moscow, 1978), pp. 15–36.

23. At the time of its completion, the cathedral was accorded the rare distinction of a special illustrated supplement – thirteen splendidly reproduced photographs – in the 1912–13 *Annual of the Moscow Architectural Society: Ezhegodnik Moskovskogo Arkhitekturnogo Obshchestva*, no. 3 (1912–13): 135–47. A recent description of the Pochaev cathedral is contained in N. L. Zharikov, ed., *Pamiatniki gradostroitel'stva i arkhitektura Ukrainskoi SSR* (Kiev, 1983–6), vol. 4, pp. 78–80. Nikolai Roerich's collaboration with Shchusev in the decoration of the Trinity Cathedral (as well as other churches by Shchusev and Vladimir Pokrovskii) is discussed in L. V. Korotkina, "Rabota N. K. Rerikha s arkhitektorami A. V. Shchusevym i V. A. Pokrovskim," in *Muzei 10*, 156–61.

24. Zharikov, *Pamiatniki*, vol. 2, pp. 153–4.

25. On the Mary-Martha church, see Mashkov, *Putevoditel' po Moskve*, p. 194; also *Moskva Zlatoglavaia*, p. 65.

26. A description and project sketch of the Balakovo church appeared in *Zodchii*, 1911, no. 51: 541, and Plate 60.

27. The structural logic and dynamic symbolism of the medieval church, particularly in its tower form, also attracted the brothers Leonid, Viktor, and Alexander Vesnin, who subsequently became three of the most prominent architects of Soviet Constructivism. During the decade before the revolution, they designed a number of churches, including at least four in Nizhnii Novgorod Province and one in Moscow Province. They used structural elements from the medieval churches in an analytical, aestheticized manner that spoke to the architects' interests in new forms and tectonic principles. For a list of churches by the Vesnin brothers, see K. I. Murashkov, ed., *Vesniny: Katalog-putevoditel' po fondam muzeia* (Moscow, 1981), pp. 79–83.

28. A critical appraisal of the Walcot houses appeared in the article "Sovremennaia Moskva" (Contemporary Moscow), *Zodchii*, 1904, no. 17: 201. A survey of Walcot's education and career in Russia is contained in Sergei Romaniuk, "Vil'iam Val'kot (1874–1943)," *Stroitel'stvo i arkhitektura Moskvy*, 1986, no. 6: 24–7.

29. For a discussion of American influence on Russian domestic architecture, see William C. Brumfield, "Russian Perceptions of American Architecture, 1870–1917," in *Reshaping Russian Architecture: Western Technology, Utopian*

Dreams (New York: Cambridge University Press, 1990), pp. 43–66. Also in 1906, the leading Russian architectural journal *Zodchii* published designs of duplexes and single-family suburban homes by K. G. Skolimovskii.

30.   Kekushev's report on the house was published in "Dom O. A. Lista v Moskve," *Zodchii*, 1901, no. 4: 48. The cost of construction was listed at 100,000 rubles. On other Kekushev houses, see Brumfield, *Origins of Modernism*, pp. 85–91.

31.   A survey of Shekhtel's set designs is presented in E. I. Kirichenko, "Teatral'nye raboty F. O. Shekhtelia 1880-kh godov v muzeiakh Moskvy," in Loginova, ed., *Muzei 10*, pp. 162–73.

32.   For examples of Shekhtel's early work, see Brumfield, *Origins of Modernism*, pp. 121–3.

33.   For links between the aquatic motif and Rimskii-Korsakov's opera *Sadko*, see ibid., p. 310, fn. 23.

34.   The Derozhinskaia house and its international modern interior (paralleled by the work of Hoffman, Olbrich, and Mackintosh) are examined in Brumfield, *Origins of Modernism*, pp. 144–51.

35.   See ibid., pp. 91–2.

36.   Plans for the Moscow Ring Railway and the designs of some of its stations were presented in "Sooruzhenie Moskovskoi zheleznoi dorogi," *Zodchii*, 1909, no. 10: 105–9.

37.   Shekhtel, whose friendship with Chekhov and his family originated in the late 1870s, refused to accept a fee for his own work at the theater.

38.   For more detailed commentary on the theater, see Brumfield, *Origins of Modernism*, pp. 151–3.

39.   On Shekhtel's Glasgow pavilions, see ibid., pp. 141–4; and Catherine Cooke, "Shekhtel in Kelvingrove and Mackintosh on the Petrovka," *Scottish Slavonic Review*, 10 (1988): 177–205.

40.   E. I. Kirichenko notes the relation between the commanding presence of the Kitai-gorod wall (not extant) and the long horizontal lines of Shekhtel's Moscow Insurance building in *Moskva na rubezhe stoletii* (Moscow, 1978), pp. 63–4.

41.   The *Utro Rossii* (*Morning of Russia*) building is of particular interest as a reflection of the social idealism of the Riabushinskii family. The newspaper, under the guidance of Pavel P. Riabushinskii, served the political goals of a group of the merchant elite who wished to create a constitutional, economically liberal political party to further the interests of capitalist development in Russia. That movement failed, and the newspaper was frequently the target of tsarist censorship. The Riabushinskii attempt to forge a new political coalition representing the interests of a Russian bourgeoisie is set forth in James West, "The Riabushinskii Circle: Russian Industrialists in Search of a Bourgeoisie, 1909–1914," *Jahrbücher für Geschichte Osteuropas* 32 (1984): 358–77. See also V. S. Diakin, *Samoderzhavie burzhuaziia i dvorianstvo v 1907–1911 gg.* (Leningrad, 1978), pp. 185–91.

42.   In this union of form and function, Shekhtel expressed the spirit of a new economic order in Russia. See William C. Brumfield, "Building for the Bourgeoisie: The Quest for a Modern Style in Russian Architecture," in Clowes et al., eds., *Between Tsar and People*, pp. 308–24.

43.   For a history of the Sytin Printing Works and the subsequent fate of the building, see R. E. Krupnova and V. A. Rezvin, *Ulitsa Gor'kogo, 18* (Moscow, 1984), pp. 14–17. During the 1930s, the brick facing was removed from the first floor and replaced with rusticated stucco. During the same period, the original interior underwent a complete modification.

44.   A description of innovative elements in Klein's structural design of the Muir and Mirrielees store is presented in M. A. Kozlovskaia, "Konstruktivnye struktury i arkhitekturnye formy grazhdanskikh zdanii," in Lebedev, ed., *Konstruktsii i arkhitekturnaia forma*, pp. 155–6. On Klein's eclectic treatment of the exterior, see Kirichenko, *Moskva na rubezhe stoletii*, p. 102.

45.   Pavel Buryshkin, *Moskva kupecheskaia* (New York, 1954), p. 198. A discussion of the structure of the Delovoi dvor project is contained in Kozlovskaia, "Konstruktivnye struktury," pp. 139–42.

46.   M. P. Makotinskii, "A. V. Kuznetsov," in M. I. Astaf'eva-Dlugach et al., *Zodchie Moskvy XX veka*, pp. 104–5.

47.   The building for the Stroganov Workshops illustrated a program that Alexander Kuznetsov had propounded at the Fifth (and final) Congress of Russian Architects, held in Moscow in 1913. Whereas the congress proceedings illustrated as never before the dimensions of the split between engineering and architecture, Kuznetsov's own presentation argued the opposite. Because of the increased freedom provided by ferroconcrete in the design of buildings, Kuznetsov proposed that the properties and uses of this material should be intensively studied in architectural schools. Due to the outbreak of war, however, the proceedings of the Fifth Congress were never published, and Kuznetsov's lecture appeared as a two-part article "Arkhitektura zhelezobetona," *Zodchii*, 1915, no. 19: 191–8; and no. 20: 203–9. For a critical assessment of the Fifth Congress and the noticeable split between the architecture and engineering sections, see *Russkaia khudozhestvennaia kul'tura kontsa XIX–nachala XX veka (1908–1917)*, pp. 332–3.

48.   L. M. Smirnov surveys Klein's work in Iu. S. Iaralov and S. M. Zemtsov, eds., *Zodchie Moskvy* (Moscow, 1981), pp. 288–300.

49.   The uncompleted building was damaged by fire in December 1904; and between 1906 and 1908, the continuation of work was threatened by a financial depression that effected the largess of Ivan Nechaev-Maltsev, one of the leading manufacturers of glassware in Russia and the major private donor to the museum. The museum was originally named after Alexander III, although the government provided only 200,000 rubles toward its construction, in comparison with over 2 million from Nechaev-Maltsev. Although many of Moscow's greatest cultural institutions derived their support from the local merchant elite, Tsvetaev was largely rebuffed in his efforts to raise money in Moscow. Nechaev-Maltsev was a resident of Petersburg. Now named in honor of Alexander Pushkin, the museum is the subject of an exhaustive, two-volume study based on Klein's correspondence with Tsvetaev: I. E. Danilova, ed., *Gosudarstvennyi muzei izobrazitel'nykh iskusstv im. A. S. Pushkina: Istoriia sozdaniia muzeia v perepiske professora I. V. Tsvetaeva s arkhitektorom R. I. Kleinom i drugikh dokumentakh (1898–1912)* (Moscow, 1977).

50. A survey of Zholtovskii's prerevolutionary work is presented in "I. V. Zholtovskii," M. I. Astaf'eva-Dlugach and Iu. P. Volshok, eds., *Zodchie Moskvy: XX vek*, pp. 48–60.

51. Pavel A. Buryshkin, *Moskva kupecheskaia*, p. 201.

52. A brief survey of the Vtorov clan is presented in ibid., pp. 197–200. In 1934, the house was converted to the residence of the American ambassador ("Spaso House"). See Brumfield, *Origins of Modernism*, pp. 274, 277.

53. Specifications of the Kiev (formerly Briansk) Railway Station are presented in G. M. Shchebro, "I. Rerberg," in Astaf'eva-Dlugach and Volshok, eds., *Zodchie Moskvy: XX vek*, pp. 65–6.

54. For early examples of style moderne apartment buildings in Petersburg and their critical reception, see Brumfield, *Origins of Modernism*, pp. 174–5.

55. For an exhaustive listing of buildings related to the new style between 1897–1915 (grouped by region in Leningrad), see B. M. Kirikov, "Peterburgskii modern," *Panorama iskusstv*, no. 10 (1978): 99–148; with an informative introductory essay by Kirikov. Obviously, most of the several hundred buildings in the 27-page list are of no distinction; but the list is a useful guide to the architectural development of the city, even though a number of major structures of the period are excluded because they are not classified as part of the "Petersburg moderne."

56. The career of Leontii Benois, whose work was frequently featured in *Zodchii*, is summarized in V. G. Lisovskii and L. A. Iudina, "Zamechatel'nyi zodchii i pedagog," *Stroitel'stvo i arkhitektura Leningrada*, 1979, no. 2: 35–8. In addition to Lidval, the students of Benois included Aleksei Shchusev, Nikolai Vasilev, Marian Lialevich, Vasilii Shchuko, Marian Peretiatkovich, Andrei Belogrud, Ivan Fomin, Vasilii Pokrovskii, Oskar Munts, and many other architects.

57. For an analysis of the factors impinging upon the development of the outlying areas of Petersburg, see James H. Bater, *St. Petersburg: Industrialization and Change* (Montreal, 1976), pp. 317, 323–33. See also B. M. Kochakov, ed., *Ocherki istorii Leningrada, Vol. 3, Period imperializma i burzhuazno-demokraticheskikh revoliutsii* (Moscow–Leningrad, 1956), pp. 906–8, 914–15, 920.

58. A detailed plan, with several photographs of the Lidval apartment complex, appeared in *Ezhegodnik Obshchestva Arkhitektorov-Khudozhnikov*, 1 (1906): 58–63. Lidval's career is surveyed by V. G. Lisovskii in "Master Peterburgskogo moderna," *Stroitel'stvo i arkhitektura Leningrada*, 1980, no. 1: 34–8. The most extensive appreciation of his work was provided by his protegé Andrei Ohl (Ol'), architect and author of the monograph *F. Lidval* (St. Petersburg, 1914).

59. Although none of these architects worked in Petersburg, the proximity of Helsinki and the appearance of major articles on Finland in the Russian architectural press suggest the possibility of a shared approach to materials and design. In April 1903, for example, the prominent critic and supporter of the moderne Pavel Makarov published an article in *Zodchii* on the work of Saarinen, Gesellius, and Lindgren (in addition to other Finnish designers), with photographs of the 1901 building for the Pohjola Insurance Company. The use of heavily rusticated stone facing for this structure became a trademark of the Finnish national style in Helsinki (cf. Gesellius' building for the National Museum), and a number of Petersburg architects similarly used the texture of natural stone (usually granite) as a distinctive feature of the "northern moderne."

60. For a discussion of Bubyr's engineering achievements, see V. G. Isachenko, "Pobornik novogo stilia: Stranitsy tvorcheskoi biografii A. F. Bubyria," *Stroitel'stvo i arkhitektura Leningrada*, 1978, no. 3: 44–7. On Vasilev, see Brumfield, *Origins of Modernism*, pp. 187–91. V. G. Lisovskii summarizes Vasilev's large apartment projects in "Master shkoly natsional'nogo romantizma," *Stroitel'stvo i arkhitektura Leningrada*, 1975, no. 4: 44. A list of buildings designed by each architect is contained in V. G. Isachenko et al., eds., *Arkhitektory-stroiteli Peterburga-Petrograda nachala XX veka* (Leningrad, 1982).

61. M. A. Kozlovskaia provides an analysis, with plans, of the technical structure of the apartment house by Baldi in Lebedev, ed., *Konstruktsii i arkhitekturnaia forma*, pp. 133–5.

62. Dmitriev's career is surveyed in V. G. Isachenko, "Trud otdannyi narodu," *Leningradskaia panorama*, 1982, no. 3: 30–3.

63. On the housing crisis as viewed by Petersburg architects at the beginning of the century, see Brumfield, *Origins of Modernism*, pp. 194–6. A detailed description of the Workers Village is contained in a review of the completed project presented to the Petersburg Society of Architects on December 10, 1906, and published shortly thereafter in *Zodchii*, 1906, no. 52: 523–4. The project, its virtues, and its inability to solve the larger housing needs were extensively discussed in *Zodchii* throughout 1907 (references given in Brumfield, *Origins of Modernism*). On the development of the theory and practice of planned communities for workers in Russia (usually unrealized), see A. I. Vlasiuk, "K istorii proektirovaniia i stroitel'stva zhilishch dlia rabochikh v kontse XIX v. v Rossii," *Arkhitekturnoe nasledstvo*, 15 (1963): 171–5; idem, "Rabochie gorodki Peterburga vtoroi poloviny XIX–nachala XX v.," *Arkhitekturnoe nasledstvo*, 16 (1967): 121–7; and E. I. Kirichenko, "O nekotorykh osobennostiakh evoliutsii gorodskikh mnogokvartirnykh domov vtoroi poloviny XIX–nachala XX vv.," *Arkhitekturnoe nasledstvo*, 15 (1963): 161–6.

64. A favorable critique of the Kshesinskaia mansion is provided in B. M. Kirikov, "Obrazets stilia modern. Novye materialy ob inter'erakh pamiatnika arkhitektury," *Stroitel'stvo i arkhitektura Leningrada*, 1976, no. 6: 38–41. Among

the accounts of the mansion as Bolshevik headquarters in the spring of 1917, two in English include Edmund Wilson, *To the Finland Station* (New York, 1940), pp. 473–4; and Adam Ulam, *The Bolsheviks* (New York, 1965), p. 323, fn. 9. See also description in A. N. Petrov et al., *Pamiatniki arkhitektury Leningrada* (Leningrad, 1971), pp. 335, 337; and "V stenakh shtaba bol'shevikov," *Leningradskaia panorama*, 1987, no. 11: 4–6. Kshesinskaia's own indulgent description of the house appears in her memoirs: Mathilde Kshessinska, *Dancing in Petersburg*, Arnold Haskell, trans. (New York, 1961), p. 104. The vicissitudes of both owner and house in 1917 are described in the same book, pp. 163, 167–71.

65. See Brumfield, *Origins of Modernism*, pp. 58–9.

66. One of the most unusual features of the house was the design of the third floor, which occupied only about a third as much space as the other floors, and contained a large kitchen and laundry. Whereas mansions of this period usually placed such service facilities in a wing adjacent to the main living and dining areas, or in the basement (as in the Kshesinskaia house), Chaev stipulated that they occupy the uppermost floor in order to "eliminate any possibility that odors associated with such spaces should penetrate the reception or living rooms." From a description of the Chaev mansion in *Zodchii*, 1908, no. 48: 440–1.

67. Ibid., p. 441.

68. A survey of the development of Petersburg's islands north of the Neva River is provided by V. A. Vitiazeva, *Nevskie ostrova* (Leningrad, 1986). A more detailed description specifically of Stone Island appears in the same author's *Kamennyi Ostrov* (Leningrad, 1991).

69. See n. 34.

70. The influence of Baillie Scott, in particular, on the design of Olbrich's own house at Matildenhöhe is suggested by Ian Latham, *Joseph Maria Olbrich* (New York, 1980), p. 58. The Keller house is described and illustrated on pp. 86–9.

71. A graduate of the Academy of Arts in 1884, Meltser was active in various aspects of interior design as well as architecture, and his enterprises ranged from commissions for the Imperial Court to the production of affordable furnishings for the middle class. In each case, Meltser drew upon the resources of the large factory founded by his father Friedrich Meltser and specializing in interior furnishings. A list of Meltser's work in Petersburg (including participation in the redecorating of the Winter Palace) is contained in V. G. Isachenko et al., eds., *Arkhitektory-stroiteli Peterburga-Petrograda nachala XX veka* (Leningrad, 1982), pp. 94–5. For additional information on the Meltser factory, see "Iubilei R. F. Mel'tsera," *Zodchii*, 1903, no. 45: 555–6.

72. On the design of the Meltser house (interior as well as exterior) and its similarities to the work of Maliutin at Talashkino, see Brumfield, *Origins of Modernism*, pp. 80, 208–9.

73. The term "gothicized premoderne" is used in I. G. Tokareva, "V poiskakh 'novogo stilia,'" *Leningradskaia panorama*, 1987, no. 8: 33. M. A. Kozlovskaia gives a concise analysis of the structure of the Fabergé building in Lebedev, ed., *Konstruktsii i arkhitekturnaia forma*, p. 132.

74. Baranovskii's design for the Eliseev building did not place a premium on tectonic logic. The exaggerated monumentality of the front facade is composed of a three-story arch contained between two massive corner piers that do not in fact bear the weight of the structure; nor does the facade convey an accurate impression of the structural frame of the interior. Kozlovskaia analyzes the relation between structure and facade in op. cit., pp. 149–50.

75. The important role of Siuzor's apartment houses in the Leningrad ensemble is discussed in V. G. Isachenko, "V shirokom diapazone," *Leningradskaia panorama*, 1985, no. 10: 28–31.

76. For a survey of comments on American skyscrapers in the Russian architectural press, see William C. Brumfield, "Russian Perceptions of American Architecture, 1870–1917," in *Reshaping Russian Architecture*, pp. 53, 60–2. A detailed description of the Singer Building in Petersburg, with photographs and a listing of the technical consultants, appeared in *Zodchii*, 1906, no. 39: 390–1, Plates 41–3.

77. The Building of the Guards Economic Society was described and illustrated in *Zodchii*, 1910, no. 478: 471–3, Plates 48–50. The cost of the structure was listed as 1.2 million rubles.

78. *Pamiatniki arkhitektury Leningrada*, pp. 385–7. Vasilev wrote a description of the Passage in *Zodchii* (1913): no. 10 119, Plate 5.

79. The design of Behrens' house at Matildenhöhe was featured in Pavel Makarov's report on the 1901 Darmstadt exhibition, *Zodchii*, 1902, no. 33: 372–3.

80. Early responses to the German Embassy building include an unsigned article in *Moskovskii arkhitekturnyi mir* (1913): 103–7; and Marian Lialevich, "Dom germanskogo posol'stva," *Peterburgskaia gazeta*, 1913, no. 19. A critique of the embassy – with favorable commentary on Behrens's rough-hewn interpretation of neoclassicism, but with no mention of his name – appeared in an article signed with the initial "G.," "Dom germanskogo posol'stva," *Arkhitekturno-khudozhestvennyi ezhenedel'nik*, 1914, no. 2: 5–7. After the beginning of the war, another article in the same journal showed a predictable nationalist reaction against the embassy building and its symbolic projection of German might, in Martell, "Razgadannyi rebus," *Arkhitekturno-khudozhestvennyi ezhenedel'nik*, 1914, no. 26: 253–5. For a more detailed analysis of reaction to the embassy design, see Brumfield, *Origins of Modernism*, pp. 227–8.

81. On the Sytnyi Market, see Borisova and Kazhdan, *Russkaia arkhitektura*, pp. 113, 130–1. Unfortunately, the synagogue designed by Gevirts has been neglected in the critical literature, although his other work is listed in Isachenko, *Arkhitektory-Stroiteli*, pp. 38–9. See Brumfield, *Origins of Modernism*, pp. 232–5.

82. The primary forum for neoclassical aestheticism in the arts was the elegantly produced journal *Apollon*, founded in 1909 by the poet Sergei Makovskii. Although literary in its orientation, *Apollon* published frequent commentary on architecture, and certain issues contained lavishly illustrated surveys of neoclassical architecture –

particularly in Petersburg, which, appropriately, served as the center of the movement. The relation between style and ideology in the movement are analyzed in William C. Brumfield, "Anti-Modernism and the Neoclassical Revival in Russian Architecture, 1906–1916," *Journal of the Society of Arhcitectural Historians*, 48 (1989): 371–86.

83. This aspect of Fomin's early career is examined in V. G. Lisovskii, *I. A. Fomin* (Leningrad, 1979), pp. 10–11. Fomin's designs for houses in both the modern and neoclassical styles appeared in *Ezhegodnik Obshchestva Arkhitektorov-Khudozhnikov*, no. 1 (1906): 116–19. His work in subsequent issues of the architectural annual was devoted to variations on the classical theme.

84. Alexander Benois, "Zhivopisnyi Peterburg," *Mir iskusstva*, 1902, no. 1: 1–5.

85. The response to Benois on the part of architectural critics who supported the style moderne was predictably negative. See Brumfield, *The Origins of Modernism*, p. 51.

86. Alexander Benois, "Krasota Peterburga," *Mir iskusstva*, 1902, no. 8: 138–42.

87. Ivan Fomin, "Moskovskii klassitsizm," *Mir iskusstva*, 1904, no. 7: 187.

88. On Fomin's early houses (including a number of estate mansions), see Lisovskii, 53–68.

89. For a survey of neoclassical revival mansions in Petersburg, see Brumfield, *The Origins of Modernism*, pp. 270–3.

90. Lidval's work in both the style moderne and the neoclassical revival is summarized in V. G. Lisovskii, "Master Peterburgskogo moderna," *Stroitel'stvo i arkhitektura Leningrada*, 1980, no. 1: 34–8.

91. A survey of the career of Peretiatkovich is contained in the obituary by G. Kosmachevskii, *Zodchii*, 1916, no. 23: 219–20; and in B. M. Kirikov, "Mar'ian Mar'ianovich Peretiatkovich," *Stroitel'stvo i arkhitektura Leningrada*, 1973, no. 1: 30–1. For an analysis of Renaissance elements and theories in the Russian neoclassical revival, see G. I. Revzin, "Renessansnye motivy v arkhitekture neoklassitsizma nachala XX veka," A. L. Batalov, ed., *Ikonografiia arkhitektury* (Moscow, 1990), pp. 187–211.

92. The information on the New Petersburg project is contained in a technical report by the noted Petersburg civil engineer Alexander Montag, "Izmenenie plana ostrova Golodaia," *Zodchii*, 1915, no. 49: 510; and from Georgii Lukomskii, "O postroike Novogo Peterburga," *Zodchii*, 1912, no. 52: 519–21.

93. In "O postroike Novogo Peterburga," pp. 520–1. On Lukomskii's work as a standard bearer of the neoclassical revival, see Brumfield, "Anti-Modernism and the Neoclassical Revival."

94. A number of Shchuko's sketches appeared in *Ezhegodnik Obshchestva arkhitektorov-khudozhnikov*, no. 2 (1907): 142–5, as well as in other issues of this annual. Although Shchuko's Italian exhibition pavilions did not have a strong impact on his domestic work, they were among the most finely conceived of his neoclassical revival projects. The standard monograph on Shchuko is Tatiana Slavina, *Vladimir Shchuko*, Leningrad, 1978.

95. Despite his praise for the loggias and the subtlety in detail of Shchuko's first building, Lukomskii was even more impressed by the hypertrophied forms of the second, which proved that the classical system of orders could be applied on a scale commensurate with the demands of a modern city. See Lukomskii, "Novyi Peterburg (Mysli o sovremennom stroitel'stve)," *Apollon*, 1913, no. 2: 25.

96. Lukomskii, "Arkhitekturnye vkusy sovremennosti," *Trudy IV S"ezda russkikh zodchikh* (Petersburg, 1911), p. 28. A similar attack against "excessive" individualism appeared in Lukomskii's "Novyi Peterburg," p. 9.

97. Indeed, Lukomskii did so quite consciously, as is evident in the comments on Fomin from his 1913 survey of contemporary neoclassical architecture in *Apollon*: "Fomin's art does not at all correspond to the contemporary economic spirit of calculation and triviality, of contemporary cheapness and bad workmanship; and this, of course, makes it difficult for him to work on the construction of apartment houses." "Novyi Peterburg," p. 22.

98. The ideological pronouncements of architectural critics during the 1910s (usually directed, implicitly or explicitly) against the bourgeoisie or the current order) are examined in Brumfield, *The Origins of Modernism*, pp. 289–95.

99. "Novyi Peterburg," p. 10.

100. Shchusev's winning proposal for the Kazan Railway Station was the subject of detailed reports in *Arkhitekturno-khudozhestvennyi ezhenedel'nik*, 1914, no. 4: 46–8; 1915, no. 19: 217–19. Shekhtel himself had submitted a similar historicist proposal for the station in 1911, and turned to a skillful blending of medieval elements in a number of projects in Nizhnii Novgorod. See Brumfield, *The Origins of Modernism*, pp. 167–9. Ever the master of styles, Shekhtel also created in the neoclassical mode, for his own (third) house in house and for the Chekhov Museum in Taganrog. See ibid., 165–6.

101. For an analysis of Pokrovskii's work in the context of the retrospective stylization in church architecture, see Brumfield, "The 'New Style' and the Revival of Orthodox Church Architecture, 1900–1914," in Brumfield and Velimirovic, eds., *Christianity and the Arts in Russia*, pp. 119–20.

102. For a brief discussion of A. M. Ginzburg's work, see Borisova and Kazhdan, *Russkaia arkhitektura*, p. 138, with illustrations on p. 141. Although Ginzburg has received little attention in Soviet publications, numerous photographs and sketches of his work appeared in *Moskovskii arkhitekturnyi mir*, 2 (1913): 92–7; 3 (1914): 111–16; and 4 (1915): 78.

103. *Sovremennyi Petrograd* (Petrograd, n.d.), p. 30. Subtitled "A Sketch of the history of the appearance and development of neoclassical construction," the volume represents a compendium of Lukomskii's major writings on the neoclassical revival – including the 1913 and 1914 issues of *Apollon* – with an expanded preface, in which the preceding quotation appears. It is further ironic that Lukomskii's solution for controlled urban design would become,

in basic terms, the accepted practice in the Soviet period. Even the neoclassical revival proved easily transferable to the heroic enthusiasm of the early period of Soviet power, when architects such as Fomin, Belogrud, and Shchuko produced numerous designs for public buildings in the so-called "Red Doric" or "proletarian classical" manner. Two remarkable examples of the Red Doric style are project sketches, dating from 1919, by Fomin and Belogrud for a palace of workers, reproduced in A. M. Zhuravlev, A. V. Ikonnikov, and A. G. Rochegov, *Arkhitektura sovetskoi Rossii* (Moscow, 1987), pp, 56, 59.

104. Schmidt's work on the original design and his subsequent replacement by Fomin are noted in I. G. Tokareva, "V poiskakh 'novogo stilia,'" *Leningradskaia panorama*, 1987, no. 8: 35.

105. See Brumfield, *Origins of Modernism*, pp. 266–8. The extensive interior decoration of the Polovtsov dacha, which involved the work of Roman Meltser and the painter Ivan Bogdaninskii, was not completed until 1916, at which point the house had less than a year to serve as a monument to a statesman instrumental in Russia's expansionist policy in the Far East and in the construction of the Chinese–Eastern Railway through Manchuria. The importance of the Polovtsov mansion as the summa of the neoclassical revival is indicated by its extensive photographic coverage in the major journals. Lukomskii's "Novyi Peterburg" (in *Apollon*) included four photographs of the house; fourteen more, including many views of the interior, appeared in *Ezhegodnik Obshchestva arkhitektorov-khudozhnikov*, no. 11 (1916): 95–109; and *Zodchii* published a lyrical view in the illustrated supplement to its 1916 volume.

106. Vitiazeva, *Nevskie Ostrova*, p. 118.

107. A detailed analysis of the Abamalek-Lazarev mansion is contained in Lisovskii, *I. A. Fomin*, pp. 53–60. Several photographs appeared in *Ezhegodnik Obshchestva arkhitektorov-khudozhnikov*, no. 11 (1916): 110–16.

108. Klein's sketches for the Iusupov mausoleum appeared in *Ezhegodnik Moskovskogo arkhitekturnogo obshchestva*, no. 1 (1909): 35–7. His assistant in the project was Grigorii Barkhin, later a leading Constructivist architect.

109. More damning than the inability to address immediate issues was the lack of a coherent theoretical system that would have guided architecture to a union of technology and design. It is on this point that the leading theoretician of Russian Constructivist architecture, Moisei Ginzburg, dismissed prerevolutionary modernism. See Brumfield, *Origins of Modernism*, pp. 294–6; and Moisei Ginzburg, *Style and Epoch* (1924), Anatole Senkevitch, trans. and ed. (Cambridge, Mass.: M.I.T. Press, 1982), p. 42.

Chapter 15

1. From El Lissitsky's essay, originally published in Austria in 1930 as *Russland, Die Rekonstruktion der Architektur in der Sowjetunion*, and republished, with supplementary material, in 1965 in Germany as *Russland: Architektur für eine Weltrevolution*. The English translation, by Eric Dluhosch, draws its title from the German edition. See *Russia: Architecture for a World Revolution* (Cambridge, Mass.: M.I.T. Press, 1970), p. 27.

2. A survey of new plans for workers' communities is contained in V. E. Khazanova, *Sovetskaia arkhitektura pervykh let oktiabria* (Moscow, 1970), pp. 51–71. More generally on early planned communities in Russia, see S. Frederick Starr, "The Revival and Schism of Urban Planning in Twentieth-Century Russia," in Michael Hamm, ed., *The City in Russian History* (Lexington, Ky., 1976), pp. 222–42; and Brumfield, *Origins of Modernism*, pp. 295, 321, n. 95.

3. For reproductions of the Fomin and Belogrud submissions, see A. M. Zhuravlev, A. V. Ikonnikov, and A. G. Rochegov, *Arkhitektura sovetskoi Rossii* (Moscow, 1987), pp. 56, 59. The Belogrud design was modeled on the Castel Sant'Angelo in Rome, with additional components in the Florentine style. For a detailed, annotated analysis of the projects for this competition, see Khazanova, *Sovetskaia arkhitektura pervykh let oktiabria*, pp. 125–7.

4. A survey of revolutionary monuments (including the early variants of Shchusev's Lenin Mausoleum) is contained in ibid., pp. 151–67.

5. On Fomin's Rostral columns, see Zhuravlev et al., *Arkhitektura sovetskoi Rossii*, pp. 66–7. His contribution to the design of the workers' rest zone on Stone Island is described in V. A. Vitiazeva, *Kamennyi ostrov* (Leningrad, 1991), pp. 222–4.

6. The 1923 Agricultural Exhibition is examined in Khazanova, *Sovetskaia arkhitektura pervykh let oktiabria*, pp. 167–73. On Melnikov's Makhorka pavilion, see S. Frederick Starr, *Konstantin Melnikov: Solo Architect in a Mass Society* (Princeton, 1978), pp. 59–63; and S. Kazakov, "Promyshlennaia arkhitektura Konstantina Melnikova," *Arkhitektura SSSR*, 1990, no. 4: 82 (with detailed drawings).

7. See N. P. Bylinkin, V. N. Kalmykova, A. V. Riabushin, and G. V. Sergeeva, *Istoriia sovetskoi arkhitektury (1917–1954 gg.)* (Moscow, 1985), p. 48.

8. Lissitsky, *Russia: Architecture*, pp. 28–34. An English survey of these developments is contained in Camilla Gray, *The Russian Experiment in Art. 1863–1922* (New York, 1986), pp. 240–1 and passim.

9. For a summary of the organizational history of VKhUTEMAS, see Khazanova, *Sovetskaia arkhitektura pervykh let oktiabria*, pp. 200–1. See also Christina Lodder, *Russian Constructivism* (New Haven, 1983), pp. 113–14.

10. The revolutionary ambiance of the Free Workshops is conveyed in Elena Ovsiannikova, "Svobodnye ili gosudarstvennye," *Dekorativnoe iskusstvo SSSR*, 1988, no. 10: 23–7.

11. Khazanova, *Sovetskaia arkhitektura pervykh let oktiabria*, p. 204.

12. See V. E. Khazanova, *Iz istorii sovetskoi arkhitektury 1926–1932 gg.* (Moscow, 1970), pp. 39–41. On Ladovskii, see S. O. Khan-Magomedov, "N. Ladovskii," in M. I. Astaf'-

eva-Dlugach et al., *Zodchie Moskvy: XX vek* (Moscow, 1988), pp. 135–44. A biographical sketch and excerpts from the writings of Dokuchaev are contained in M. G. Barkhin, ed., *Mastera sovetskoi arkhitektury ob arkhitekture* (Moscow, 1975), vol. 2, pp. 186–210. On Krinskii, see ibid., pp. 105–27.

13. See Kazimir Malevich, *The Nonobjective World*, Howard Dearstyne, trans. (Chicago, 1959), pp. 27–102, with illustrations. See also Khazanova, *Sovetskaia arkhitektura pervykh let oktiabria*, pp. 24–6; and A. Shumov, "Ot ploskosti k prostranstvu," *Arkhitektura SSSR*, 1990, no. 4: 54–60.

14. Ibid., pp. 18, 203. The UNOVIS program was closely related to Ladovskii's method at ASNOVA. See ibid., p. 38, n. 25.

15. Ibid.

16. Dokuchaev, "Sovremennaia russkaia arkhitektura i zapadnye paralleli," *Sovetskoe iskusstvo*, 1927, no. 1: 5–12; no. 2: 5–15. This article summarizes Dokuchaev's interpretation of Rationalism in the context of contemporary architecture. See also Khazanova, *Iz istorii sovetskoi arkhitektury 1926–1932 gg.*, pp. 45–50.

17. For material on the Union of Architects-Urbanists (ARU), see ibid., pp. 123–46. The innovative views of Nikolai Miliutin on city planning and the linear city are developed in his book *Problema stroitel'stva sotsialisticheskikh gorodov: Osnovnye voprosy ratsional'noi planirovki i stroitel'stva naselennykh mest SSSR* (Moscow, 1930); translated into English by Arthur Sprague as *Sotsgorod: The Problem of Building Socialist Cities*, with notes and introduction by George Collins and William Alex (Cambridge, Mass.: M.I.T. Press, 1974). See also Lissitsky, pp. 50–66. Soviet surveys of urban planning between 1918 and 1932 include Khazanova, *Sovetskaia arkhitektura pervykh let oktiabria*, pp. 43–100; K. N. Afanasev and V. E. Khazanova, *Iz istorii sovetskoi arkhitektury 1917–1925 gg.* (Moscow, 1963), pp. 7–128, includes documents and plans; and the chapter by Selim Khan-Magomedov on city planning in Iu. S. Iaralov, ed., *Arkhitektura sovetskoi Rossii* (Moscow, 1975). A definitive monograph on approaches to urban planning from the late 1920s through the 1930s is Khazanova, *Sovetskaia arkhitektura pervoi piatiletki* (Moscow, 1980). A compilation of documents of the period is K. N. Afanas'ev and V. E. Khazanova, *Iz istorii sovetskoi arkhitektury 1928–1932 gg. Dokumenty i materialy. K problemam goroda, sotsialisticheskogo rasseleniia, byta* (Moscow, 1973). In English, see Maurice Parkins, *City Planning in Soviet Russia* (Chicago, 1953), and Anatole Kopp, *Town and Revolution: Soviet Architecture and City Planning* (New York, 1970).

18. The *Realistic Manifesto* and the Pevsner brothers' relation to the Moscow avant-garde are examined in Lodder, *Russian Constructivism*, pp. 34–42. See also Steven A. Nash, "Sculptures of Purity and Possibility," and Christina Lodder, "Gabo in Russia and Germany," in Steven A. Nash and Jörn Merkert, eds., *Naum Gabo: Sixty Years of Constructivism* (Munich, 1985), pp. 23–6 and 51–4, respectively.

19. For a summary of Rodchenko's role in the formulation of the Constructivist view of geometric form as a func-

tion of economy of material, see Lodder, *Russian Constructivism*, pp. 22–9. See also Alexander Lavrentjev, "Alexander Rodchenko's Architectural Language," in Alessandra Latour, ed., *Alexander Rodchenko 1891–1956* (New York, 1987), n.p.; and David Elliott, ed., *Rodchenko and the Arts of Revolutionary Russia* (New York, 1979).

20. Tatlin's monument is one of the most frequently analyzed works in the history of avant-garde architecture. The development of Tatlin's concept and the form of the model are described in Lodder, *Russian Constructivism*, pp. 55–66. A contemporary interpretation of the monument was provided in Nikolai Punin, *Pamiatnik III Internatsionala* (Petrograd, 1920).

21. These subsequent visionary projects were by no means lightly regarded. See Milka Bliznakov, "The Realization of Utopia: Western Technology and Soviet Avant-Garde Architecture," in William Brumfield, ed., *Reshaping Russian Architecture* (New York, 1991), pp. 145–75.

22. A concise history of the Constructivists and their Union of Contemporary Architects (OSA) is contained in Afanas'ev and Khazanova, *Iz istorii sovetskoi arkhitektury 1926–1932 gg.*, pp. 65–8, with statements pertaining to the movement on pp. 69–105. Extensive studies on the movement in English include Anatole Kopp, *Constructivist Architecture in the USSR* (New York, 1985); and Selim O. Khan-Magomedov, *Pioneers of Soviet Architecture* (New York, 1987). The impact of the Constructivist movement in architectural design is surveyed in Lodder, *Russian Constructivism*, pp. 118–80. The bibliographies contained in the foregoing works can be supplemented by Anatole Senkevitch, Jr., *Soviet Architecture, 1917–1962: A Bibliographic Guide to Source Material* (Charlottesville, Va., 1974).

23. Aleksei Gan's programmatic statement *Konstruktivism* (Tver, 1922) adopted an extremely antiaesthetic approach that would be pursued by the major architectural theoretician of the movement, Moisei Ginzburg. Gan's work is examined in Khazanova, *Sovetskaia arkhitektura pervykh let oktiabria*, pp. 20–2. For a description in English of his views, see Lodder, *Russian Constructivism*, pp. 98–9; and John Bowlt, ed., *Russian Art of the Avant-Garde: Theory and Criticism* (New York, 1976), pp. 217–25.

24. For a study of western modernist architects who worked in the Soviet Union, see Anatole Kopp, "Foreign Architects in the Soviet Union During the First Two Five-Year Plans," in Brumfield, ed., *Reshaping Russian Architecture*, pp. 176–214.

25. I. Kokkinaki surveys the links between Soviet and western architects of this period, with emphasis on De Stijl, in "K voprosu o vzaimosviaziakh sovetskikh i zarubezhnykh arkhitektorov v 1920–1930-e gody," in I. M. Shmidt et al., eds., *Voprosy sovetskogo izobrazitel'nogo iskusstva i arkhitektury* (Moscow, 1976), pp. 350–82.

26. Popova's development of architectonic forms in painting and her substantial contributions to Constructivism are noted in Magdalena Dabrowski, *Liubov Popova* (New York, 1991), pp. 20–5.

27. *Stil' i epokha* (Moscow, 1924). In English: *Style and Epoch*, Anatole Senkevitch, trans. (Cambridge, Mass.: M.I.T. Press, 1982). On the Constructivist approach (primarily Ginzburg's) to design, see Catherine Cooke, " 'Form is a Function X': The Development of the Constructivist Architects Design Method," in Catherine Cooke, ed., *Russian Avant-Garde Art and Architecture* (London, 1983), pp. 34–49.

28. See relevant documents in Afanas'ev and Khazanova, *Iz istorii sovetskoi arkhitektury 1926–1932 gg.*, pp. 43–4, 50–3, 70–2.

29. A brief survey of Barkhin's work is presented in K. N. Afanas'ev, "G. B. Barkhin," M. I. Astaf'eva-Dlugach et al., *Zodchie Moskvy: XX vek*, pp. 117–21. Afanas'ev provides a geometric analysis of the *Izvestiia* Building facade in "Grigorii Borisovich Barkhin," *Arkhitektura SSSR*, 1981, no. 11: 60–3. For a concise review in English of Barkhin's work, see Oleg A. Shvidkovsky, ed., *Building in the USSR, 1917–1932* (London, 1971), pp. 78–86.

30. The standard monograph, richly illustrated, on Golosov's life and work is S. O. Khan-Magomedov, *Il'ia Golosov* (Moscow, 1988). In English, see Shvidkovsky, ed., *Building in the USSR*, pp. 106–14.

31. See, for example, the plan and photographs of a Golosov housing development in Ivanovo-Voznesensk, ibid., pp. 150–1.

32. The principles of workers' clubs are discussed in Lissitsky, *Russia*, pp. 43–5; and Khan-Magomedov, "Formirovanie novykh tipov obshchestvennykh zdanii," in Iaralov, ed., *Arkhitektura sovetskoi Rossii*, pp. 69–76. A more detailed study, with documents, is K. N. Afanas'ev, ed., *Iz istorii sovetskoi arkhitektury 1926–1932 gg. Dokumenty i materialy. Rabochie kluby i dvortsy kul'tury* (Moscow, 1984).

33. See ibid., pp. 163–4, for an analysis of Golosov's frequent use of the glass cylinder within a rectangular design.

34. For Golosov's varying commentary (from the early 1920s and the 1930s) on the opposition of Constructivism and classical architectural principles, see ibid., pp. 184–6.

35. Moisei Ginzburg, "Funktsional'nyi metod i forma," in *Sovremennaia arkhitektura*, 1926, no. 4: 89–92. Included in Afanas'ev and Khazanova, *Iz istorii sovetskoi arkhitektury 1926–1932 gg.*, pp. 72–93.

36. Bylinkin et al., *Istoriia sovetskoi arkhitektury*, pp. 54–5. A. V. Ikonnikov, *Arkhitektura Moskvy. XX vek* (Moscow, 1984), p. 54.

37. The standard monograph on Ginzburg's work is Selim O. Khan-Magomedov, *M. Ia. Ginzburg* (Moscow, 1972). A biographical sketch and a selection of writings is presented in Barkhin, ed., *Mastera sovetskoi arkhitektury ob arkhitekture*, vol. 2, pp. 266–320. For a survey in English, see the introduction by Anatole Senkevitch to Ginzburg, *Style and Epoch*.

38. For an analysis of Ginzburg's work within the context of housing and urban planning debates, see Khazanova, *Sovetskaia arkhitektura pervoi piatiletki*, pp. 72–4, 164–5, passim. On the relation between housing, social policy, and the new urban environment as explored by Ginzburg and the Constructivists, see Hugh D. Hudson, Jr., "The Social Condenser of Our Epoch: The Association of Contemporary Architects and the Creation of a New Way of Life in Revolutionary Russia," *Jahrbücher für Osteuropas*, 34 (1986): 557–78.

39. For plans of the various Narkomfin apartment configurations and photographs of the building in its original form, see Bylinkin et al., *Istoriia sovetskoi arkhitektury*, pp. 46–7. A discussion of the building from the perspective of theories of communal housing is presented in Khazanova, *Sovetskaia arkhitektura pervoi piatiletki*, pp. 168–71.

40. On the Nikolaev dormitory (with plans), see Bylinkin et al., *Istoriia sovetskoi arkhitektury*, pp. 42–3, 45; and Zhuravlev et al., *Arkhitektura sovetskoi Rossii*, pp. 87–8. A biographical sketch of Nikolaev is contained in Astaf'eva-Dlugach et al., *Zodchie Moskvy: XX vek*, pp. 278–85.

41. The most thorough study of Le Corbusier's work in Russia, is Jean-Louis Cohen, *Le Corbusier and the Mystique of the USSR* (Princeton, 1991). For a Russian analysis of Corbusier's plan for Moscow, see Khazanova, *Sovetskaia arkhitektura pervoi piatiletki*, pp. 260–4.

42. On the restoration of the Tsentrosoiuz building, see A. V. Ikonnikov, *Kamenia letopis' Moskvy*, p. 197.

43. A brief biographical sketch of Panteleimon Golosov is contained in Astaf'eva-Dlugach et al., *Zodchie Moskvy: XX vek*, pp. 155–9.

44. The Narkomzem (agriculture) building was originally known as the Koopinsoiuz. Its design, implemented in collaboration with D. D. Bulgakov, I. A. Frantsuz, and G. K. Iakovlev, is given cursory treatment in the standard biography of Shchusev by K. N. Afanas'ev, *A. V. Shchusev*, pp. 90–1. See also Ikonnikov, *Arkhitektura Moskvy*, p. 56.

45. Fomin's work in Soviet Moscow is surveyed in Astaf'eva-Dlugach et al., *Zodchie Moskvy: XX vek*, pp. 72–9. On the Dinamo building, see also Zhuravlev et al., *Arkhitektura sovetskoi Rossii*, pp. 102–3. An emphasis on his Soviet classicism is presented in M. Il'in, *Ivan Aleksandrovich Fomin* (Moscow, 1946), pp. 27–47.

46. Zholtovskii had spent 3 years in his beloved Italy (1923–6) before returning to work in Moscow. For a survey of his Soviet work, see Astaf'eva-Dlugach et al., *Zodchie Moskvy: XX vek*, pp. 48–60. On the State Bank building, see also Zhuravlev et al., *Arkhitektura sovetskoi Rossii*, p. 101.

47. The Telegraph Building project was much sought after, and the competition stimulated a number of innovative designs – which made Rerberg's victory all the more revealing as to the ultimate direction of Soviet architecture. On Rerberg's Soviet work, see Astaf'eva-Dlugach et al., *Zodchie Moskvy: XX vek*, pp. 61–71.

48. Leonid Vesnin graduated from the Petersburg Academy of Arts in 1909, and Alexander and Viktor graduated from the Institute of Civil Engineering in 1912. Among the many Soviet studies of the Vesnins are M. A. Il'in's pioneering *Vesniny* (Moscow, 1960); A. G. Chiniakov, *Brat'ia Vesniny* (Moscow, 1970); and S. O. Khan-Magomedov, *Alek-*

sandr Vesnin (Moscow, 1983). Much valuable information is also contained in the following catalogues of their work published by the Shchusev Museum of Architecture: A. I. Manina, *Arkhitektory brat'ia Vesniny* (Moscow, 1983); and K. I. Murashov, ed., *Vesniny: Katalog-putevoditel' po fondam muzeiia* (Moscow, 1981; no illustrations). A concise survey of their work is provided in Astaf'eva-Dlugach et al., *Zodchie Moskvy: XX vek*, pp. 122–34. A romanticized, "local" biography is Larisa L. Poliakova, *Zodchie brat'ia Vesniny* (Iaroslavl, 1989). In English, see Selim Khan-Magomedov, *Aleksandr Vesnin and Russian Constructivism* (New York, 1986); and Shvidkovskii, *Building in the USSR*, pp. 42–56.

49. For examples of the diversity of the work of Viktor and Leonid Vesnin before the revolution, see Brumfield, *The Origins of Modernism in Russian Architecture*.

50. The set design for this play by G. K. Chesterton is one of Alexander Vesnin's most frequently illustrated works. See, for example, Gray, *The Russian Experiment in Art*, p. 267; and Khan-Magomedov, *Aleksandr Vesnin and Russian Constructivism*. On the relation between avant-garde Soviet set design and architecture, with emphasis on the Vesnins, see Christina Lodder, "Constructivist Theater as a Laboratory for an Architectural Aesthetic," *Architectural Association Quarterly*, 1979, no. 2: 24–35.

51. The Vesnins' Palace of Labor project has also been frequently discussed as one of the seminal works of Constructivist architecture. Khazanova analyzes the project in the context of the competition, in *Sovetskaia arkhitektura pervykh let oktiabria*, pp. 136–45. The jury awarded first place to Noi Trotskii's cavernous butressed hall in a medieval Italian style reminiscent of the work of Belogrud.

52. See Manina, *Arkhitektory brat'ia Vesniny*, p. 42.

53. A survey of retail store construction in Moscow of this period is provided in Ikonnikov, *Arkhitektura Moskvy*, pp. 67–8. See also Blair A. Ruble, "Moscow's Revolutionary Architecture and Its Aftermath: A critical Guide," in Brumfield, ed., *Reshaping Russian Architecture*, pp. 124–5.

54. The building subsequently became the Cinema Actors' Theater.

55. The Vesnins frequently referred to the Proletarian Region Workers club in justification of their concept of Constructivism, even after Soviet architecture had taken a sharply reactionary course. For example, in their article "Novoe po forme i soderzhaniiu," *Arkhitekturnaia gazeta*, (December 31, 1936), Alexander and Viktor emphasize the relation between interior and exterior. Quoted in Barkhin, ed., *Mastera sovetskoi arkhitektury ob arkhitekture*, vol. 2, pp. 65–6. The club subsequently became the property of the adjacent Likhachev Auto Factory.

56. The planetarium structure is analyzed in Bylinkin et al., *Istoriia sovetskoi arkhitektury*, pp. 64–5. See also Ikonnikov, *Arkhitektura Moskvy*, p. 66, who notes that the original ramp for the entrance has been defaced in a remodeling.

57. G. Gorvits provides an account of large project designs in Kharkov (capital of the Ukrainian S.S.R. until 1934) by architects from Leningrad – which had a surfeit of architects as a result of the shift of major construction to Moscow. In its years as the Ukrainian capital, Kharkov was the site of some of the most ambitious architectural complexes of modern functionalism. See "Iz istorii tvorcheskikh sviazei arkhitektorov Leningrada i pervoi stolitsy Ukrainy," in Shmidt, ed., *Voprosy*, pp. 311–49. For a survey of developments in other Soviet cities, see Iaralov, *Arkhitektura sovetskoi Rossii*, pp. 5–31.

58. On the Moscow–Narva District House of Culture, see Petrov et al., *Pamiatniki arkhitektury Leningrada*, pp. 455–6; and Zhuravlev et al., *Arkhitektura sovetskoi Rossii*, pp. 104–5. A biographical sketch of Gegello and a selection of his writings is contained in Barkhin, ed., *Mastera sovetskoi arkhitektury ob arkhitekture*, vol. 2, pp. 245–65.

59. These three buildings are analyzed in Petrov et al., *Pamiatniki arkhitektury Leningrada*, pp. 453–5, 457–8.

60. On the Moscow–Narva (later Kirov) House of Soviets, see ibid., p. 459; and Zhuravlev et al., *Arkhitektura sovetskoi Rossii*, p. 97.

61. On the Moscow District House of Soviets, see ibid., pp. 98–9.

62. A description of the apartment complex is provided in Petrov et al., *Pamiatniki arkhitektury Leningrada*, pp. 475, 479. See also Zhuravlev et al., *Arkhitektura sovetskoi Rossii*, pp. 145–7, with plan.

63. In fact, Boris Iofan received his architectural training in Rome, at the Regio Instituto Superiore de bell arti, and subsequently studied engineering in that city. His older brother Dmitrii had graduated from the Academy of Arts in Petersburg. For a biographical sketch of Boris Iofan and excerpts from his writings, see Barkhin, ed., *Mastera sovetskoi arkhitektury ob arkhitekture*, vol. 2, pp. 211–44. The standard monograph is Isaak Eigel', *Boris Iofan* (Moscow, 1978).

64. See ibid., pp. 39–42. As a microcosm of the upper reaches of Soviet society, the building served as the setting of Iurii Trifonov's novel *Dom na naberezhnoi* (Moscow, 1976), translated into English as *House on the Embankment* (New York, 1983).

65. The innovation aspects of the Udarnik Cinema, including a sectioned roof that could be opened to the sky, are discussed in Eigel', *Boris Iofan*, pp. 53–4. Although designed in the era of silent film, the excellent acoustics and advanced design of the trapezoidal auditorium made it admirably equipped as the first Soviet sound cinema.

66. A survey of Chernyshev's work as an architect and city planner is contained in Astaf'eva-Dlugach et al., *Zodchie Moskvy: XX vek*, pp. 145–54.

67. Shchuko's work in Moscow (including the Lenin Library) is summarized in Astaf'eva-Dlugach et al., *Zodchie Moskvy: XX vek*, pp. 109–16. The design of the Lenin Library is discussed in Bylinkin et al., *Istoriia sovetskoi arkhitektury*, pp. 67, 70–1, with plan.

68. The similarities between the Lenin Library exterior – particularly the squared columns – and the contemporary architecture of Fascist Italy are notable. Soviet reaction to Fascist architecture was ambivalent: On overt ideological grounds, it was condemned. Yet the appeal of the Italian architectural tradition, so admired by many Soviet architects, and the obvious – if unadmitted – parallels in the adaptation of monumental architecture to political, statist goals led to an unconcealed interest in Fascist architecture (to which it might be added that Italian Fascism appeared a less virulent phenomenon than German National Socialism, which developed its own form of monumental classicism). The Thirteenth International Congress of Architects, held in Rome in 1935 and attended by prominent Soviet architects such as Viktor Vesnin, provided a pretext for Soviet commentary on the architecture of Fascist Italy. See, for example, Vesnin's article "O sovremennoi ital'ianskoi arkhitekture," in the volume devoted to Soviet impressions of the Italian excursion: *Arkhitekturnye zapiski. Rim–Pompei–Florentsiia–Venetsiia–Vichentsa–Parizh. Iz materialov sovetskoi delegatsii na XIII Mezhdunarodnom arkhitekturnom kongresse* (Moscow, 1937), pp. 141–54; and L. I. Rempel', "K kharakteristike arkhitektury fashistkoi Italii," *Akademiia arkhitektury*, 2 (1935): 50–61. Later Soviet exercises in classicist architecture would abandon the modernized form in favor of adaptations of the varieties of Russian neoclassicism – including the early twentieth-century neoclassical revival.

69. On Melnikov's Paris pavilion, see Starr, *Melnikov*, pp. 87–99. A recent Soviet monograph on the architect is S. O. Khan-Magomedov, *Konstantin Mel'nikov* (Moscow, 1991).

70. Melnikov's designs for the Paris garage are illustrated and discussed in Starr, *Melnikov*, pp. 103–5; and in Kazakov, "Promyshlennaia arkhitektura Konstantina Melnikova," pp. 82–3, 85.

71. Plans and archival photographs of the Moscow garages are presented in ibid., pp. 84–7; and Starr, *Melnikov*, pp. 108–12. The Rodchenko photograph on p. 109 is of the interior of the truck garage, not the Leyland garage (as indicated in caption 97). See also Astaf'eva-Dlugach et al., *Zodchie Moskvy: XX vek*, pp. 193–4.

72. A discussion of the link between the Rusakov Club and expressionism (à la Erich Mendelsohn) is contained in Starr, *Melnikov*, pp. 135–7.

73. A laudatory contemporary account of Melnikov's clubs in Nikolai V. Lukhmanov, *Arkhitektura kluba* (Moscow, 1930). Lukhmanov notes that these clubs were not completed to Melnikov's original specifications.

74. There have been many formal comparisons with the Melnikov house, including the structure that so appealed to Le Courbusier – the American grain elevator. See, for example, Starr, *Melnikov*, pp. 63, 119. An early example of Soviet praise of the American grain elevator (with photographs) appeared in the editorial commentary "Estetika sovremennosti," *Arkhitektura*, 1923, nos. 1–2: 3–6.

75. For a detailed spatial analysis of the house, with comments on the decay of parts of the structure, see V. Rezvin, "Dom arkhitektora K. S. Mel'nikova," *Arkhitektura SSSR*, 1984, no. 4: 84–5. More recently, see Peter Lizon, "International Call for Saving Melnikov House in Moscow," *Architecture* (September 1989): 28.

76. For sketches of these project designs, see Starr, *Melnikov*, pp. 158–61, 193–9. The Heavy Industry project was to be built on the site of GUM (formerly the Upper Trading Rows) facing Red Square.

77. Sketches of the garages, which were modified during construction, are included in *Konstantin Stepanovich Mel'nikov*, Plates 132–5. See also Astaf'eva-Dlugach et al., *Zodchie Moskvy: XX vek*, p. 198.

78. Melnikov's concept of kinetic architecture is discussed in Astaf'eva-Dlugach et al., *Zodchie Moskvy: XX vek*, p. 197. On the "Sleep Sonata" project, see Starr, *Melnikov*, pp. 177–9.

79. Chernikhov was the author of six books related to the principles of architectural form, including *Osnovy sovremennoi arkhitektury* (Leningrad, 1930); *Konstruktsiia arkhitekturnyikh i mashinykh form* (Leningrad, 1931); and *Arkhitekturnye fantazii* (Leningrad, 1933). A survey and analysis of Chernikhov's work is contained in Andrei Chernikhov, " 'Artist show us your world . . .': Iakov Chernikhov 1889–1951," in Cooke, ed., *Russian Avant-Garde Art and Architecture*, pp. 64–72; and Catherine Cooke, "Chernikhov. The Construction of architectural and machine forms," ibid., pp. 73–80. See also Zhuravlev et al., *Arkhitektura sovetskoi Rossii*, pp. 122–3.

80. Kaufmann, *Architecture in the Age of Reason*, p. 105.

81. A summary of the Palace of Soviets competition is presented in Bylinkin et al., *Istoriia sovetskoi arkhitektury*, pp. 70–4; Ikonnikov, *Arkhitektura Moskvy*, pp. 79–80, 94–7; and Antonia Cunliffe, "The Competition for the Place of Soviets in Moscow, 1931–33," *Architectural Association Quarterly*, 1979, no. 2: 36–48. Commentary on the first phase of competition and reproductions of a large sample of entries – including the three main winners, by Boris Iofan, the American architect George O. Hamilton, and Zholtovskii – are presented in N. Zapletin, "Dvorets Sovetov SSSR (po materialam konkursa)," *Sovetskaia arkhitektura*, 1932, nos. 2–3: 10–116.

82. For a detailed analysis of the Iofan design in its variant forms, see Eigel', *Boris Iofan*, pp. 80–117.

83. Ikonnikov, *Arkhitektura Moskvy*, p. 97.

84. Nikolai Miliutin reported on this shift of policy and presented a face-saving adaptation of his own theories to it in "Vazhneishie zadachi sovremennogo etapa sovetskoi arkhitektury," *Sovetskaia arkhitektura*, 1932, nos. 2–3: 3–9.

85. An analysis of the 1935 plan by Semenov (known as a prerevolutionary disciple of the English Garden City theorist Ebenezer Howard), as well as competing proposals in 1931–3, is presented in V. N. Belousov and O. V. Smirnova, *V. N. Semenov* (Moscow, 1980), pp. 80–102. For discussions leading to the plan, see also Khazanova, *Sovetskaia arkhitektura pervoi piatiletki*, pp. 273–303. Semenov's views, which included an attack on Constructivism in the name of resurrecting the art in architecture, were presented in a series of articles in *Stroitel'stvo Moskvy* in 1932–3, and recapitulated in the chapter "Arkhitekturnaia rekonstruktsiia Moskvy," in *Voprosy arkhitektury* (Moscow, 1935), pp. 119–58.

86. The work of Mordvinov, a consummate party hack, is surveyed in Astaf'eva-Dlugach et al., *Zodchie Moskvy: XX vek*, pp. 244–50. His apartment houses on Gorkii Street were built at an accelerated pace that included the extensive use of prefabricated components.

87. A survey of Moscow's major reconstruction projects during the late 1930s is contained in Bylinkin et al., *Istoriia sovetskoi arkhitektury*, pp. 83–7.

88. For a discussion of the 1935 Leningrad plan and the design of Moscow (Moskovskii, and after the war, Stalin) Prospekt, see Blair A. Ruble, "From Palace Square to Moscow Square: St. Petersburg's Century-long Retreat from Public Space," in Brumfield, ed., *Reshaping Russian Architecture,* pp. 29–30.

89. A description of the House of Soviets is contained in Petrov et al., *Pamiatniki arkhitektury Leningrada*, p. 469. Articles on the structure appeared regularly in *Arkhitektura Leningrada* between 1937 and 1940, including Trotskii's own "Dom sovetov v Leningrade," *Arkhitektura Leningrada*, 1937, no. 2: 8–19. See also Ruble, "From Palace Square to Moscow Square," pp. 31–6. Trotskii's work is examined in a monograph by T. E. Suzdaleva, *N. A. Trotskii* (Leningrad, 1991).

90. The attack on Melnikov, within the context of architectural "debates" in the mid–1930s is recounted in Starr, *Melnikov*, pp. 214–27.

91. The most thorough study of Ivan Leonidov's work is Andrei Gozak and Andrei Leonidov, *Ivan Leonidov: The Complete Works* (New York, 1988).

92. On the Zholtovskii building and the controversy that it provoked upon completion in 1934, see Astaf'eva-Dlugach et al., *Zodchie Moskvy: XX vek,* pp. 57–8.

93. The work of Abrosimov, a disciple of Shchuko, is surveyed in Barkhin, ed., *Mastera sovetskoi arkhitektury ob arkhitekture*, vol. 2, pp. 447–9.

94. "Forma i soderzhanie," in *Arkhitekturnaia gazeta* (April 8, 1935). Quoted in M. A. Il'in, *Vesniny*, p. 111.

95. The fundamental, ideological shift in approaches to architecture during the Stalinist era is the subject of an excellent and provocative study by Vladimir Papernyi, *Kul'tura Dva* (Ann Arbor, 1985).

96. On the Hotel Moskva, which was begun as a clumsy "Constructivist" design by L. Savel'ev and S. Stapran, see Afanas'ev, *Shchusev*, pp. 108–11. To the frequent criticism of the hotel's busy eclecticism, Shchusev agreed with the justification that the project he was given and the architects he worked with were poorly prepared.

97. Langman's work in Moscow is surveyed in Astaf'eva-Dlugach et al., *Zodchie Moskvy: XX vek*, pp. 182–9. In reference to his work for the Commissariat for Internal Affairs, it should be noted that Shchusev in 1939–40 designed and partially implemented an expansion for the headquarters of the dreaded security police on Liubianka (or Dzerzhinskii) Square. See Afanas'ev, *Shchusev*, pp. 171–3, where the project is referred to in the typical Soviet euphemism as an "administrative building."

98. A summary of Burov's career and excerpts from his writings are contained in Barkhin, ed., *Mastera sovetskoi arkhitektury ob arkhitekture*, vol. 2, pp. 456–91. The standard monograph is O. I. Rzhekhina, R. N. Blashkevich, and R. G. Burova, *A. K. Burov* (Moscow, 1984).

99. On the role played by the Albert Kahn firm in Soviet industrial construction – with ramifications that extended far beyond the end of their contract (because of currency restrictions) in 1932 – see Bliznakov, "The Realization of Utopia," in Brumfield, ed., *Reshaping Russian Architecture,* pp. 154–7; and Kopp, "Foreign Architects in the Soviet Union During the First Two Five-Year Plans," ibid., pp. 201–4. The Soviet architect of record for the Cheliabinsk plant was A. Fisenko, a leading specialist in factory design. For a survey of early Soviet industrial architecture and an analysis of significant examples from the 1930s (such as the Likhachev Auto Plant in Moscow), see Bylinkin et al., *Istoriia sovetskoi arkhitektury*, pp. 31–6; 105–9.

100. Burov's design for the facade of the House of Architects was taken from a fresco by Piero della Francesco in the Church of San Francesco in Arezzo. See Rzhekhina et al., *Burov*, p. 64.

101. Burov's innovative work combining ornament and factory-produced structural components is discussed in ibid., pp. 74–86. See also Ikonnikov, *Arkhitektura Moskvy*, pp. 93–4; and Bylinkin et al., *Istoriia sovetskoi arkhitektury*, pp. 120–3.

102. On the ideology of the principle of "critical assimilation" in Socialist Realist architecture, see Cunliffe, "The Competition for the Place of Soviets," pp. 41–2. The basic forum of the academy's mission was the journal *Akademiia arkhitektury*, published 1934–7. A corollary of the emphasis on "critical assimilation" was the raising of the cultural level of the architectural elite, to which end Burov and his contemporaries at the academy were sent on an extended trip to Europe. This exposed them, in time-honored Russian fashion, to the masterpieces of western culture, yet also enabled them to meet distinguished contemporary architects such as Le Corbusier, with whom Burov maintained a long correspondence dating from his meeting with the Swiss architect in Moscow in 1928. See Barkhin, ed., *Mastera sovetskoi arkhitektury ob arkhitekture*, vol. 2, pp. 458.

103. For a concise discussion of the Stalinist administrative apparatus and the development of Soviet architecture, see S. Frederick Starr, "The Social Character of Stalinist Architecture," *Architectural Association Quarterly*, 1979, no. 2: 49–55. The topic is addressed in its many ramifications in Papernyi's *Kul'tura Dva*.

104. On the 1937 congress, see Starr, *Melnikov*, pp. 220–7.

105. A summary of Alabian's career and a brief selection of his writings is contained in Barkhin, ed., *Mastera sovetskoi arkhitektury ob arkhitekture*, vol. 2, pp. 406–22. On the design of the Red Army theater, see Astaf'eva-Dlugach et al., *Zodchie Moskvy: XX vek*, pp. 254–5; and Ikonnikov, *Arkhitektura Moskvy*, pp. 102–3.

106. A survey of the 1939 version of the exhibit (subsequently the Exhibition of Economic Achievements, or VDNKh) is contained in Bylinkin et al., *Istoriia sovetskoi ar-*

khitektury, pp. 158–60. Commentary on individual pavilions within the ideological context of Soviet culture is contained in Papernyi, *Kul'tura dva*.

107. The pedestal of the 1937 Paris pavilion was crowned by Vera Mukhina's statue of the worker and collective farm woman. See Bylinkin et al., *Istoriia sovetskoi arkhitektury*, pp. 160–1.

108. A lavish survey of the Stalin-era towers is presented in V. K. Oltarzhevskii, *Stroitel'stvo vysotnykh zdanii v Moskve* (Moscow, 1953). Oltarzhevskii, who had worked with Rerberg before the revolution in the design of one of Moscow's first "towers" (the Northern Insurance Company), went to the United States for study purposes in the 1920s and became one of the leading Soviets experts in western skyscraper construction. He ran afoul of the Stalinist purge machinery in the 1930s; but after returning from penal exile, he was elevated in the late 1940s to the position of Doctor of Architecture in obvious recognition of his now desirable expertise in tall buildings. Briefer surveys of the Moscow towers include Ikonnikov, *Arkhitektura Moskvy*, pp. 112–19; and Zhuravlev et al., *Arkhitektura sovetskoi Rossii*, pp. 185–90.

109. For a brief survey of Rudnev's career, see Astaf'eva-Dlugach et al., *Zodchie Moskvy: XX vek*, pp. 167–74; and V. Ass (Rudnev's assistant), "Lev Rudnev," *Arkhitektura SSSR*, 1985, no. 1: 101–7. A similar grid was adopted by Gegello, N. Trotskii, and Andrei Ol' in their design of the Leningrad NKVD (state police) headquarters (1931–2) – another example of talented and well-educated architects in service to the totalitarian state. See Petrov et al., *Pamiatniki arkhitektury Leningrada*, p. 475.

110. In the original published design, the Moscow University tower was surmounted by a gargantuan, idealized statue of a Soviet scholar. Although Stalin had suggested that the Palace of Soviets serve as a pedestal for the 100-meter statue of Lenin, it was probably he who insisted, shrewdly, that this particular statue be replaced by a spire – thus unifying Moscow with a series of needle-pointed "tall buildings." Reproductions of the earlier design are found in Papernyi, *Kul'tura Dva*, p. 336.

111. The most insistent statement on the role of monumental historicism in late Stalinist architecture came from critics such as Mikhail Tsapenko and Ivan Matsa, formerly head of VOPRA and a leading figure in the Academy of Architecture. See, for example, Matsa, "Sovetskaia arkhitektura – novyi etap v razvitii mirovoi arkhitektury," *Arkhitektura SSSR*, 17–18 (1947): 11–14; and Tsapenko, *O realisticheskikh osnovakh sovetskoi arkhitektury* (Moscow, 1952). A concise summary of their work and its repressive atmosphere is presented in Zhuravlev et al., *Arkhitektura sovetskoi Rossii*, pp. 180–1.

112. See "On the Problem of Functions in Architecture," in *Structure, Sign, and Function: Selected Essays by Jan Mukařovský*, John Burbank and Peter Steiner, trans. and eds. (New Haven, 1978), pp. 236–50, with specific reference to p. 245.

113. One clear statement of the shift from historicist ornamentation was Lev Rudnev's article "O formalizme i klassike," *Arkhitektura SSSR*, 1954, no. 11: 30–2.

114. The early stages of Soviet industrialized apartment construction, between 1955 and 1960, are surveyed in Zhuravlev et al., *Arkhitektura sovetskoi Rossii*, pp. 215–29. In English, see William C. Brumfield, "Architecture and Urban Planning," in James Cracraft, ed., *The Soviet Union Today: An Interpretive Guide* (Chicago, 1988), pp. 164–74.

115. The Kremlin Palace of Congresses is described in Ikonnikov, *Arkhitektura Moskvy*, pp. 136–8.

116. The negative impact of such renewal projects on the urban fabric are addressed in the round-table discussion "Problemy kompleksnoi rekonstruktsii v tsentre Moskvy," *Stroitel'stvo i arkhitektura Moskvy*, 1982, no. 6: 5–7. One discussant speaks of the danger of creating "dead zones" by moving residents out of the center city, which becomes a purely administrative center.

117. Plans and descriptions of the Kalinin Prospket ensemble and the CMEA (or SEV) building are contained in Ikonnikov, *Arkhitektura Moskvy*, pp. 146–53.

118. On the building of the Hotel Rossiia, see ibid., pp. 155–6.

119. Summaries of the 1971 Moscow plan are provided in ibid., pp. 163–8; and N. P. Bylinkin and A. V. Riabushin, eds., *Sovremennaia sovetskaia arkhitektura. 1955–1980 gg.* (Moscow, 1985), pp. 11–16. The latter volume also surveys developments in city planning elsewhere in the Soviet Union during the same period. See ibid., pp. 18–44.

120. Chertanovo North, an "experimental complex" with advanced design features and cost overruns, is described in M. V. Posokhin and D. K. Diubek, *Eksperimental'nyi zhiloi raion Chertanovo-Severnoe*, in the architectural series of *Znanie*, 1976, no. 10. In English, see Brumfield, "Architecture and Urban Planning," pp. 170–1. A survey of the design and construction of Soviet apartment complexes during the 1960s and 1970s is contained in Bylinkin and Riabushin, eds., *Sovremennaia sovetskaia arkhitektura*, pp. 77–108; and Ikonnikov, *Arkhitektura Moskvy*, pp. 157–63, 171–83.

121. On the House of New Living, see ibid., p. 163; and Bylinkin and Riabushin, eds., *Sovremennaia sovetskaia arkhitektura*, pp. 107–8. This author can attest that 10 years after its construction, the building had reached a state of extreme dilapidation.

122. See Richard Pommer et al., *In the Shadow of Mies: Ludwig Hilberseimer* (Chicago, 1988), with copious illustrations that reveal the similarities.

123. The Ostankino tower, part of a television studio complex (1964–9; L. Batalov et al.) near the former Ostankino estate, is described in Ikonnikov, *Arkhitektura Moskvy*, pp. 153–4; and Bylinkin and Riabushin, eds., *Sovremennaia sovetskaia arkhitektura*, pp. 149–52, with comparative silhouettes of other notable modern towers.

124. The Luzhniki complex, with its Lenin Stadium and other facilities, is described in Ikonnikov, *Arkhitektura Moskvy*, pp. 134–6. Other stadiums, including the Friendship Sports Hall, are included in ibid., pp. 204–9; and Bylinkin and Riabushin, eds., *Sovremennaia sovetskaia arkhitektura*, pp. 156–62. The splendid Krylatskoe Velodrome is analyzed by V. Khanzhi (one of the project engineers), "Velotrek v Krylatskom," *Arkhitektura SSSR*, 1986, no. 3: 26–31. The steel membrame roof was applied in other Moscow Olympic stadiums, and reminds of Shukhov's pioneering use of this technique in his 1896 Nizhnii Novgorod pavilions (see Chapter 14).

125. V. Krasil'nikov and A. Velikanov, *Moskovskii gosudarstvennyi Detskii muzykal'nyi teatr* (Moscow, 1979), n.p.

126. In 1980, poured concrete composed almost half of the concrete used in the Soviet Union; and although much of this can be accounted for in foundations, dams, and industrial structures, poured concrete (or "monolithic" concrete, as the Russians call it) is being used with increasing sophistication and with some awareness of its aesthetic properties – as demonstrated in the Ostankino television tower. See V. P. Belov, *Monolitnyi zhelezobeton,* in the architectural series of *Znanie,* 1977, no. 10.

127. A description and plan of the Taganka extension, sensitively integrated into the site of the old (and still preserved) theater, are contained in Ikonnikov, *Arkhitektura Moskvy,* pp. 200–2. Examples of theater architecture, usually awkward or ostentatious, are presented in Zhuravlev et al., *Arkhitektura sovetskoi Rossii,* pp. 314–20.

128. For a comparison of the two projects, see Papernyi, *Kul'tura "dva,"* p. 335. See also Ikonnikov, *Arkhitektura Moskvy,* p. 194.

129. See ibid., p. 216.

130. On the paper architecture phenomenon, see Catherine Cooke's recent article "A Picnic by the Roadside or Work in Hand for the Future," *Architectural Association Files,* 18 (1989): 15–24; and D. K. Bernshtein, "O fenomene 'bumazhnoi arkhitektury' 1980-kh godov," in I. A. Azizian, ed., *Teoriia arkhitektury,* pp. 111–35.

131. On the movement for architectural preservation, see William C. Brumfield, "St. Basil's and Other Curiosities," *Harvard Magazine,* 1982, no. 6: 42–8; and idem., "Russia's Glorious Churches," *Historic Preservation* (February 1985): 42–6.

Appendix I

1. *Polnoe sobranie russkikh letopisei,* vol. 3, p. 208. An excellent survey of early chronicle references to log construction is presented in M. I. Mil'chik and Iu. S. Ushakov, *Dereviannaia arkhitektura russkogo severa* (Leningrad, 1981), pp. 5–6.

2. On the Lazarus Church, see A. V. Opolovnikov, "Lazarevskaia tserkov' Muromskogo monastyria," *Arkhitekturnoe nasledstvo,* 18 (1969): 106–11. In English, see Alexander Frolov, *Petrozavodsk and Kizhi* (Moscow, 1983), p. 104. The church is dated to the late sixteenth century in V. P. Orfinskii, *Logika krasoty* (Petrozavodsk, 1978), pp. 59–60.

3. The argument for chronological stability was propounded by one of the earliest historians of Russian wooden architecture, Ivan Zabelin, in *Domashnii byt russkikh tsarei v XVI i XVII stoletiiakh* (Moscow, 1872), vol. 1, p. 27. A revisionist view in favor of substantial changes in Russian wooden architecture is presented in Iu. P. Spegal'skii, *Zhilishche Severo-Zapadnoi Rusi IX–XIII vekov* (Leningrad, 1972).

The difficulties presented by the lack of remains are discussed in S. Agafonov, "Nekotorye ischeznuvshie tipy drevnerusskikh dereviannykh postroek," *Arkhitekturnoe nasledstvo,* 2 (1951): 173–86.

4. The basic categories of the Russian wooden church were elucidated, with superb photographs by the artist Ivan Bilibin and others, by F. Gornostaev in Igor Grabar', *Istoriia russkogo iskusstva,* vol. 1 (Moscow, 1909). Surveys in English include Alexander Opolovnikov and Yelena Opolovnikova, *The Wooden Architecture of Russia,* edited by David Buxton (New York, 1989); and David Buxton, *The Wooden Churches of Eastern Europe: An Introductory Survey* (Cambridge, 1981).

5. The Borodavo church, on display at the St. Cyril Belozersk Monastery, is dated in Bocharov and Vygolov, *Vologda. Kirillov. Ferapontovo. Belozersk,* p. 161. The Nikulino church, now at the Vitoslavlitsy open-air museum near Novgorod, is described in L. A. Filippova, *"Vitoslavlitsy" – muzei dereviannogo zodchestva* (Leningrad, 1979), pp. 37–8. A more detailed study of the Novgorod churches is L. E. Krasnorech'ev and L. Ia. Tyntareva, *"Kak mera i krasota skazhut"* (Leningrad, 1971).

6. The St. Nicholas Church at Tukholia, previous variants of which are attested as early as 1478, is described in Filippova, *"Vitoslavlitsy,"* pp. 45–8.

7. The Miakishevo church, whose dates are uncertain, is described in ibid., pp. 53–6.

8. On the Kuritsko church, see ibid., pp. 49–52. The construction of wooden "tent" towers and their relation to the rest of the structure are analyzed in S. Agafonov, "K voprosu ob otkrytykh vnutr' shatrakh v russkom dereviannom zodchestve," *Arkhitekturnoe nasledstvo,* 2 (1951): 187–92.

9. The Peredki church is the oldest surviving example of wooden architecture from the Novgorod region. Ibid., pp. 30–6. The complex restoration of the church is described in Krasnorech'ev and Tyntareva, *Kak mera,* p. 38.

10. The division of labor and contractual arrangements between the peasants who supplied the wood and the master carpenters who built the church are described in Mil'chik and Ushakov, *Dereviannaia arkhitektura,* pp. 36–46.

11. These tools are illustrated in ibid., pp. 40–1, 44–5.

12. The literature on the Kizhi Transfiguration Church and its immediate ensemble is extensive, including sections in such general works as A. V. Opolovnikov, *Russkii Sever* (Moscow, 1977), pp. 202–38; and in English, Frolov, *Petrozavodsk and Kizhi,* pp. 83–101.

13. See, for example, L. M. Lisenko, "Garmonicheskie postroeniia v arkhitekture tserkvei Kizhskogo pogosta," *Arkhitekturnoe nasledstvo,* 18 (1969): 125–34.

14. The interior and the iconostasis are described in Frolov, *Petrozavodsk and Kizhi,* pp. 92–3.

15. On the bell tower, ibid., pp. 98–9. By the middle of this century, nothing remained of the wall apart from the foundation stones. For commentary on the restoration of the wall, based on a similar structures at Vodlozero and Pochozero, see ibid., pp. 99–101.

16. The construction of large log houses, drawn from late seventeenth-century documents, is described in Mil'chik and Ushakov, *Dereviannaia arkhitektura*, pp. 13–35. The design of houses, sheds, and other structures in the far north in more recent times is detailed in Iurii S. Ushakov, *Dereviannoe zodchestvo russkogo Severa (narodnye traditsii i sovremennye problemy)* (Leningrad, 1974); and in A. V. Opolovnikov, *Russkoe dereviannoe zodchestvo* (Moscow, 1983). See also a lyrical appreciation of traditional log houses in A. Opolovnikov and G. Ostrovskii, *Rus' dereviannaia: Obrazy russkogo dereviannogo zodchesetva* (Moscow, 1981), pp. 16–38.

17. An analysis of country housing configurations is presented in A. A. Shennikov, ''Krest''ianskie usad'by XVI–XVII vv. (Verkhnee Povolzh'e, severo-zapadnye i severnaia chasti Evropeiskoi Rossii),'' *Arkhitekturnoe nasledstvo*, 15 (1963): 88–101.

18. Sawn gingerbread decorative motifs are the subject of an excellent monograph by A. I. Skvortsov, *Russkaia narodnaia propil'naia rez'ba* (Leningrad, 1984), which devotes special attention to a typology of window surrounds.

19. Siberian cities such as Tomsk were rich in such wooden ornament, as illustrated in E. I. Dreizin, *Dereviannaia arkhitektura Tomska* (Moscow, 1975).

20. Zabelin's most famous statement on the nativist theory was a lecture first delivered in 1871 and subsequently reworked in book form for three editions, the last of which was *Russkoe iskusstvo. Cherty samobytnosti v russkom zodchestve* (Moscow, 1900). Zabelin's place in the historiography of Russian architecture is recounted in T. A. Slavina, *Issledovateli russkogo zodchestva* (Leningrad, 1983), pp. 82–96.

21. Indeed, the major work of Suslov's career was a comprehensive study of Russian wooden architecture, which remained unpublished. See ibid., pp. 105–9, passim; and A. V. Suslova and T. A. Slavina, *Vladimir Suslov* (Leningrad, 1978).

22. For commentary on the dispute over wooden portotypes, particularly as it focused on the Church of the Ascension at Kolomenskoe, see Chapter 6, with accompanying annotation.

Bibliography

Abramov, L. K. "Novye materialy o rabotakh V. I. Bazhenova v Gatchine," *Arkhitekturnoe nasledstvo,* 1 (1951): 78–85.

Afanas'ev, K. N. *Postroenie arkhitekturnoi formy drevnerusskimi zodchimi.* Moscow, 1961.

———— *A. V. Shchusev.* Moscow, 1978.

———— "Grigorii Borisovich Barkhin," *Arkhitektura SSSR,* no. 11 (1981) 60–3.

Afanasev, K. N., and V. E. Khazanova. *Iz istorii sovetskoi arkhitektury 1917–1925 gg.* Moscow, 1963.

———— *Iz istorii sovetskoi arkhitektury 1928–1932 gg. Dokumenty i materialy. K problemam goroda, sotsialisticheskogo rasseleniia, byta.* Moscow, 1973.

———— *Iz istorii sovetskoi arkhitektury 1928–1932 gg. Dokumenty i materialy. Rabochie kluby i dvortsy kul'tury.* Moscow, 1984.

Agafonov, S. "Nekotorye ischeznuvshie tipy drevenerusskikh dereviannykh postroek," *Arkhitekturnoe nasledstvo,* 2 (1951): 173–86.

———— "K voprosu ob otkrytykh vnutr' shatrakh v russkom dereviannom zodchestve," *Arkhitekturnoe nasledstvo,* 2 (1951): 187–92.

———— *Gor'kii. Balakhna. Makar'ev.* Moscow, 1987.

Akademiia Nauk SSSR, Institut Istorii, *Istoriia Moskvy, Vol. 4, Period promyshlennogo kapitalizma.* Moscow, 1954.

Alekseev, A. D., and G. Iu. Sternin, eds. *Russkaia khudozhestvennaia kul'tura kontsa XIX-nachala XX veka (1895–1907),* vol. 2. Moscow, 1969.

———— *Russkaia khudozhestvennaia kul'tura kontsa XIX-nachala XX veka (1908–1917),* vol. 4. Moscow, 1980.

Alekseeva, S. B. "Arkhitektura i dekorativnaia plastika Zimnego dvortsa." In *Russkoe iskusstvo barokko: Materialy i issledovaniia,* edited by T. V. Alekseeva, pp. 128–58. Moscow, 1977.

———— "Rol' monumental'no-dekorativnoi skul'ptury v formirovanii ansamblia tsentral'nykh poloshchadei Peterburga pervoi poloviny XIX v." In *Russkoe iskusstvo vtoroi poloviny XVIII–pervoi poloviny XIX v.,* edited by T. V. Alekseeva, pp. 38–68. Moscow, 1979.

Alekseeva, Tat'iana V. *Issledovaniia i nakhodki.* Moscow, 1976.

———— "Franchesko-Bartolomeo Rastrelli i russkaia kul'tura." In *Ot Srednevekov'ia k novomu vremeni,* edited by T. V. Alekseeva, pp. 131–40. Moscow, 1984.

————, ed. *Russkoe iskusstvo XVIII v.: Materialy i issledovaniia.* Moscow, 1968.

———— *Russkoe iskusstvo XVIII v.: Materialy i issledovaniia.* Moscow, 1973.

———— *Russkoe iskusstvo pervoi chetverti XVIII veka: Materialy i issledovaniia.* Moscow, 1974.

———— *Russkoe iskusstvo barokko: Materialy i issledovaniia.* Moscow, 1977.

———— *Russkoe iskusstvo vtoroi poloviny XVIII–pervoi poloviny XIX v.: Materialy i issledovaniia.* Moscow, 1979.

———— *Ot Srednevekov'ia k Novomu vremeni.* Moscow, 1984.

Alferova, G. V. "Sobor Spaso-Mirozhskogo monastyria," *Arkhitekturnoe nasledstvo,* 10 (1958): 3–32.

———— "K voprosu o stroitel'noi deiatel'nosti patriarkha Nikona," *Arkhitekturnoe nasledstvo,* 18 (1969): 30–44.

———— "Issledovanie i restavratsii palat Averkiia Kirillova." In *Iz istorii restavratsii pamiatnikov kul'tury.* Moscow, 1974.

———— "K voprosu o stroitel'stve gorodov v Moskovskom gosudarstve v XVI–XVII vv.," *Arkhitekturnoe nasledstvo,* 28 (1980): 20–8.

Alpatov, M. *Arkhitektura russkogo klassitsizma nachala XIX veka.* Moscow, 1961.

Alpatov, Mikhail V. *Andrei Rublev.* Moscow, 1972.

———— "Iskusstvo Feofana Greka i uchenie isikhastov," *Vizantiiskii vremennik,* 33 (1972): 190–202.

———— *Freski tserkvi Uspeniia na Volotovom pole.* Moscow, 1977.

———— *Feofan Grek.* Moscow, 1979.

Alpatov, M. V., ed. *Uspenskii sobor moskovskogo kremlia.* Moscow, 1971.

Al'tshuller, B. L. "Novye issledovaniia Nikol'skoi tserkvi sela Kamenskogo," *Arkhitekturnoe nasledstvo,* 20 (1972): 17–25.

Andreev, A. K. "Adam Menelas." In *Problemy sinteza iskusstv i arkhitektury,* 7 (1977): 38–59.

Andreev, L. V. "Istoricheskoe iadro Torzhka i ego glavnye arkhitekturnye ansambli," *Arkhitekturnoe nasledstvo,* 29 (1981): 18–26.

Andreev, V. "G. E. Bosse – arkhitektor–novator," *Arkhitektura SSSR,* 1988, no. 1: 88–95.

Andreyev, N. [ikolay] "Filofey and his epistle to Ivan Vasilyevich," *Slavonic and East European Review,* 38 (1959): 1–31.

Anikst, M. A., and V. S. Turchin. . . . *v okrestnostiakh Moskvy.* Moscow, 1979.

Anisimov, Evgenii. *Vremia petrovskikh reform.* Leningrad, 1989.

Antonov, V. *Zhivopistsy-dekoratory Skotti v Rossii.* In *Russkoe iskusstvo vtoroi poloviny XVIII–pervoi poloviny XIX v.,* pp. 69–107. Moscow, 1979.

Antsiferova, G. M. "Dvorets v Neskuchnom." In *Pamiatniki russkoi arkhitektury i monumental'nogo iskusstva: Stil', atributsii, datirovki,* edited by V. P. Vygolov et al., pp. 92–111. Moscow, 1983.

Antsyferov, N. P. *Dusha Peterburga.* Petersburg, 1922.

Arenkova, Iuliia I. "Arsenal v Kremle. Istoriia stroitel'stva." In *Russkoe iskusstvo barokko: Materialy i issledovaniia,* edited by T. V. Alekseeva, pp. 43–54. Moscow, 1977.

Arenkova, Iuliia I., and Galina I. Mekhova. *Donskoi monastyr'.* Moscow, 1970.

Arenzon, E. R. "Ot Kireeva do Abramtseva. K biografii Savvy Ivanovicha Mamontova," *Panorama iskusstv,* 6 (1986): 359–82.

——— " 'Abramtsevo' v Moskve: K istorii khudozhestvenno-keramicheskogo predpriiatiia S. I. Mamontova." In *Muzei 10,* pp. 95–102. Moscow, 1989.

Arkhipov, N. I., and A. G. Raskin. *Petrodvorets.* Leningrad–Moscow, 1961.

——— *Bartolomeo Karlo Rastrelli.* Leningrad–Moscow, 1964.

Arkin, D., ed. "Dolzhnost' Arkhitekturnoi Ekspeditsii. Traktat-kodeks 1737–1740," *Arkhitekturnyi arkhiv,* 1 (1946): 7–100.

——— *Rastrelli.* Moscow, 1954.

——— *Sukhanovo.* Moscow, 1958.

Artsikhovskii, A. V. "Novgorod Velikii po arkheologicheskim dannym." In *Novgorod: k 1100-letiiu goroda,* edited by M. N. Tikhomirov, pp. 38–47. Moscow, 1964.

——— "K voprosu o vremeni osnovaniia Kievskogo Sofiiskogo sobora," *Sovetskaia arkheologiia,* 1980, no. 3: pp. 135–40.

Aseev, Iu. S. *Arkhitektura Kyivs'koi Rusi.* Kiev, 1969

——— *Arkhitektura drevnego Kieva.* Kiev, 1982.

Aseev, Iu. S., and V. A. Kharlamov. "Ob arkhitekture Uspenskogo sobora Pecherskogo Monastyria v Kieve (issledovanniia 1982 g.)," *Arkhitekturnoe nasledstvo,* 34 (1986): 209–14.

Ass, V. "Lev Rudnev," *Arkhitektura SSSR,* 1985, no. 1: 101–7.

Astaf'eva-Dlugach, M. I., Iu. P. Volchok, and A. M. Zhuravlev. *Zodchie Moskvy XX v.* Moscow, 1988.

Azizian, I. A., ed. *Teoriia arkhitektury. Sbornik nauchnykh trudov.* Moscow, 1988.

Azizian, I. A., G. I. Lebedeva, and E. L. Beliaeva, eds. *Arkhitektura i kul'tura,* 2 parts. Moscow, 1990.

Baiburova, R. M. "Russkii usadebnyi inter'er epokhi Klassitsizma. Planirovochnye kompozitsii." In *Pamiatniki russkoi arkhitektury i monumental'nogo iskusstva,* edited by V. P. Vygolov A. P. Vlasiuk, and V. I. Pluzhnikov, pp. 140–61. Moscow, 1980.

——— "Zal i gostinaia usadebnogo doma russkogo klassitsizma." In *Pamiatniki russkoi arkhitektury i monumental'nogo iskusstva,* edited by V. P. Vygolov A. P. Vlasiuk, and V. I. Pluzhniko, pp. 113–14. Moscow, 1983.

——— "Gorodskoi usadebnyi dom russkogo klassitsizma i frantsuzskii klassitsisticheskii otel." In *Pamiatniki russkoi arkhitektury i monumental'nogo iskusstva,* edited by V. P. Vygolov, A. P. Vlasiuk, and V. I. Pluzhnikov, pp. 116–26. Moscow, 1985.

Baldin, V. I. "Arkhitektura Troitskogo sobora Troitse-Sergievoi lavry," *Arkhitekturnoe nasledstvo,* 6 (1956): 21–56.

——— *Arkhitekturnyi ansambl Troitse-Sergievoi lavry.* Moscow, 1976.

Baldin, V. I., and Iu. N. Gerasimov. "Dukhovskaia tserkov' Troitse-Sergieva monastyria," *Arkhitekturnoe nasledstvo,* 19 (1972): 53–65.

Balog, G. P., E. S. Gladkova, L. V. Emina, and V. V. Lemus. *Muzei i parki Pushkina.* Leningrad, 1969.

Banige, Vladimir S. *Kreml' Rostova Velikogo: XVI–XVII veka.* Moscow, 1976.

Baranova, Olga. *Kuskovo: 18th-Century Russian Estate and the Museum of Ceramics.* Leningrad, 1983.

Barkhin, M. G. *Arkhitektura i gorod. Problemy razvitiia sovetskoto zodchestva.* Moscow, 1979.

———, ed. *Mastera sovetskoi arkhitektury ob arkhitekture,* 2 vols. Moscow, 1975.

Bartenev, I. A., and V. N. Batazhkova. *Russkii inter'er XVIII-XIX v.* Leningrad, 1977.

——— *Russkii inter'er XIX veka.* Leningrad, 1984.

Barteneva, M. I. *Nikolai Benua.* Leningrad, 1985.

Bashutskii, A. P. *Vozobnovlenie Zimnego dvortsa v Sankt-Peterburge.* Petersburg, 1839.

Bassin, Joan. *Architectural Competitions in Nineteenth-Century England.* Ann Arbor, 1984.

Batalov, A. L. "Chetyre pamiatnika arkhitektury Moskve kontsa XVI v.," *Arkhitekturnoe nasledstvo,* 32 (1984): 47–53.

——— "Sobor Voznesenskogo monastyria v moskovskom kremle," *Pamiatniki kul'tury. Novye otkrytiia. 1983,* X (1985): 468–82.

——— "Osobennosti 'Ital'ianizmov' v moskovskom kamennom zodchestve rubezha XVI-XVII vv.," *Arkhitekturnoe nasledstvo,* 34 (1986): 238–45.

———— "K interpretatsii arkhitektury sobora Pokrova na Rvu (O granitsakh ikonograficheskogo metoda)." In *Ikonografiia arkhitektury. Sbornik nauchnykh trudov,* edited by A. L. Batalov, pp. 15–37. Moscow, 1990.

————, ed. *Ikonografiia arkhitektury. Sbornik nauchnykh trudov.* Moscow, 1990.

Batalov, A. L., and I. A. Bondarenko, eds. *Restavratsiia i arkhitekturnaia arkheologiia. Novye materialy i issledovaniia.* Moscow, 1991.

Batalov, A. L., and T. N. Viatchanina. "Ob ideinom znachenii i interpretatsii ierusalimskogo obraztsa v russkoi arkhitekture XVI-XVII vv," *Arkhitekturnoe nasledstvo,* 36 (1988): 22–42.

Bater, James H. "The Industrialization of Moscow and St. Petersburg." In *Studies in Russian Historical Geography,* edited by James H. Bater and R. A. French, vol. 2, pp. 279–303. London, 1983.

Bater, James H., and R. A. French, eds. *Studies in Russian Historical Geography.* 2 vols. London, 1983.

Batkhel', G. S. "Novye dannye o freskakh tserkvi Blagoveshcheniia na Miachine bliz Novgoroda." In *Drevnerusskoe iskusstvo: Khudozhestvennaia kul'tura Domongol'skoi Rusi,* edited by V. N. Lazarev, pp. 245–54. Moscow, 1972.

Bekker, A. "Novye normy dlia zhiloi zastroiki Moskvy," *Stroitel'stvo i arkhitektura Moskvy,* 1980, no. 1: 17–18.

Belanina, Valeria. *Pavlovsk.* Moscow, 1987.

Belekhov, N. N., and A. N. Petrov. *Ivan Starov: Materialy k izucheniiu tvorchestva.* Moscow, 1950.

Beletskaia, E. A. "Vosstanovlenie zdanii Moskovskogo universiteta posle pozhara 1812 goda." *Arkhitekturnoe nasledstvo,* 1 (1951): 175–90.

———— *Arkhitekturnye al'bomy M. F. Kazakova.* Moscow, 1956.

———— "Iz istorii stroitel'stva doma Razumovskogo," *Arkhitekturnoe nasledstvo,* 9 (1959): 189–96.

Beletskaia, E., N. Krasheninnikova, L. Chernozubova, and I. Ern. *"Obraztsovye" proekty v zhiloi zastroike russkikh gorodov XVIII-XIX vv.* Moscow, 1961.

Beletskaia, E. A., and Z. K. Pokrovskaia, *D. I. Zhiliardi.* Moscow, 1980.

Beletskii, V. D. "Arkheologicheskie dannye k datirovke krepostnykh sten Dovmontova goroda v Pskove," *Arkheologicheskie sbornik Gosudarstvennogo Ermitazha,* 12 (1970): 68–80.

Belousov, V. N., and O. V. Smirnova. *V. N. Semenov.* Moscow, 1980.

Benois, Alexander. "Zhivopisnyi Peterburg," *Mir iskusstva,* no. 1 (1902): 1–5.

———— "Krasota Peterburga," *Mir iskusstva,* 1902, no. 8: 138–42.

———— *Tsarskoe selo v Tsarstvovanie Elizavety Petrovny.* St. Petersburg, 1910.

Benois, L. N., and M. F. Geisler. "25-letie osnovaniia S-Peterburgskogo Obshchestva Arkhitektorov," *Zodchii,* 1985, no. 11: 82–90.

Bernshtein, D. K. "O fenomene 'bumazhnoi arkhitketury' 1980-kh godov." In *Teoriia arkhitektury,* edited by I. A. Azizian, pp. 111–35. Moscow, 1988.

Betin, L. V. "Istoricheskie osnovy drevnerusskogo vysokogo ikonostasa." In *Drevnerusskoe iskusstvo. Khudozhestvennaia kul'tura Moskvy i prilezhashchikh k nei kniazhestv. XIV–XVI vv.,* edited by V. N. Lazarev, pp. 57–72. Moscow, 1970.

———— "Ob arkhitekturnoi kompozitsii drevnerusskikh vysokikh ikonostasov." In *Drevnerusskoe iskusstvo. Khudozhestvennaia kul'tura Moskvy i prilezhashchikh k nei kniazhestv. XIV–XVI vv.,* edited by V. N. Lazarev, pp. 41–56. Moscow, 1970.

Bezrukova, D. Ia. *Tretiakov i istoriia sozdaniia ego galerei.* Moscow, 1970.

Billington, James H. *The Icon and the Axe.* New York, 1966.

Birnbaum, Henrik. *Essays in Early Slavic Civilization.* Munich, 1981.

Bliznakov, Milka. "The Realization of Utopia: Western Technology and Soviet Avant-Garde Architecture." In *Reshaping Russian Architecture,* edited by William Brumfield, pp. 145–75. New York: Cambridge University Press, 1991.

Bocharov, Genrikh N., and Vsevolod P. Vygolov. *Aleksandrovskaia Sloboda.* Moscow, 1970.

———— *Vologda. Kirillov. Ferapontovo. Belozersk.* Moscow, 1979.

———— *Sol'vychegodsk. Velikii Ustiug. Tot'ma.* Moscow, 1983.

Bogdanov, Andrei I. *Istoricheskoe, geograficheskoe i topograficheskoe opisanie Sankt-Peterburga ot nachala zavedeniia s 1703 po 1751.* Completed in 1750; published with foreword by Vasilii Rubanov. Petersburg, 1779.

Bondarenko, I. A. "K voprosu ob ispol'zovanii mer dliny v drevnerusskom zodchestve," *Arkhitekturnoe nasledstvo,* 36 (1988): 54–63.

Borisova, E. A. "Arkhitektory Neelovy," *Arkhitekturnoe nasledstvo,* 4 (1953): 73–90.

———— "Arkhitekturnoe obrazovanie v Kantseliarii ot stroenii vo vtoroi chetverti XVIII veka." In *Ezhegodnik Instituta istorii iskusstv 1960. Zhivopis' i arkhitektura,* pp. 97–109. Moscow, 1961.

———— "O rannikh proektakh zdanii Akademii nauk." In *Russkoe iskusstvo XVIII v.: Materialy i issledovaniia,* edited by T. V. Alekseeva, pp. 56–65. Moscow, 1973.

———— " 'Arkhitekturnye ucheniki' petrovskogo vremeni i ikh obuchenie v komandakh zodchikh-inostrantsev v Peterburge." In *Russkoe iskusstvo pervoi chetverti XVIII veka,* edited by T. V. Alekseeva, pp. 9–26. Moscow, 1974.

———— "Neorusskii stil' v russkoi arkhitekture predrevoliutsionnykh let." In *Iz istorii russkogo iskusstva vtoroi poloviny XIX–nachala XX veka,* edited by E. A. Borisova, G.G. Pospelov, and G. Iu. Sternin pp. 59–71. Moscow, 1978.

———— "Nekotorye osobennosti vospriiatiia gorodskoi sredy i russkaia literatura vtoroi poloviny XIX v." In *Tipologiia russkogo realizma vtoroi poloviny XIX veka,* edited by G. Iu. Sternin, pp. 252–85. Moscow, 1979.

———— *Russkaia arkhitektura vtoroi poloviny XIX veka.* Moscow, 1979.

Borisova, E. A., and T. P. Kazhdan. *Russkaia arkhitektura kontsa XIX–nachala XX veka.* Moscow, 1971.

Borisova, E. A., G. G. Pospelova, and G. Iu. Sternin, eds.

Iz istorii russkogo iskusstva vtoroi poloviny XIX–nachala XX veka. Moscow, 1978.

Borisova, V. G. "Stranitsa iz istorii Sofiiskogo sobora Novgoroda." In *Kul'tura drevnei Rusi,* edited by A. L. Mongait, pp. 42–6. Moscow, 1966.

Bowlt, John, ed. *Russian Art of the Avant-Garde: Theory and Criticism.* New York, 1976.

Bozherianov, I. N. *Nevskii Prospekt: 1703–1903.* St. Petersburg, 1903.

Braitseva, O. I. "Novye konstruktivnye priemy v russkoi arkhitekture kontsa XVII–nachala XVIII veka," *Arkhitekturnoe nasledstvo,* 12 (1960): 133–52.

—— "Nekotorye osobennosti ordernykh kompozitsii v russkoi arkhitekture rubezha XVII–XVIII vv.," *Arkhitekturnoe nasledstvo,* 18 (1969): 45–60.

—— "Nadvratnaia tserkov' Troitse-Sergieva monastyria," *Arkhitekturnoe nasledstvo,* 19 (1972): 83–92.

—— "Novoe v kompozitsii vkhodov russkikh khramov kontsa XVII v.," *Arkhitekturnoe nasledstvo,* 23 (1975): 37–51.

—— *Stroganovskie postroiki rubezha XVII–XVIII vv.* Moscow, 1977.

—— "Novoe i traditsionnoe v khramovom zodchestve Moskvy kontsa XVII v.," *Arkhitekturnoe nasledstvo,* 26 (1978): 31–40.

—— "Ob ansamble ul. Pokrovki kontsa XVII v. v Belom gorode Moskvy," *Arkhitekturnoe nasledstvo,* 28 (1980): 47–51.

—— "Ulitsy Maroseika i Pokorvka v Moskve nachala XIX v.," *Arkhitekturnoe nasledstvo,* 29 (1981): 63–9.

Briusov, V. G. *Freski Iaroslavlia.* Moscow, 1969.

Brown, Peter. *Society and the Holy in Late Antiquity.* Berkeley, 1982.

Bruk, Ia. V., and L. I. Iovleva. *Gosudarstvennaia Tret'iakovskaia galereia: Ocherki istorii (1856–1917).* Leningrad, 1981.

Brumfield, William Craft. "St. Basil's and Other Curiosities," *Harvard Magazine,* 1982, no. 6: 42–8.

—— *Gold in Azure: One Thousand Years of Russian Architecture.* Boston, 1983.

—— "Russia's Glorious Churches," *Historic Preservation* (February 1985): 42–6.

—— "The Decorative Arts in Russian Architecture: 1900–1907," *The Journal of Decorative and Propaganda Arts,* no. 5 (1987): 12–27.

—— "Architecture and Urban Planning." In *The Soviet Union Today: An Interpretive Guide,* edited by James Cracraft, pp. 164–74. Chicago, 1988.

—— "Anti-Modernism and the Neoclassical Revival in Russian Architecture, 1906–1916," *Journal of the Society of Architectural Historians,* 48 (1989): 371–86.

—— "Dai bassifondi all'edificio superiore dei Torgovye Rjady: il design delle gallerie commerciali di Mosca," *Ricerche de Storia dell'arte,* 39 (1989): 7–16.

—— "Russian Perceptions of American Architecture, 1870–1917." In *Reshaping Russian Architecture,* edited by William C. Brumfield, pp. 43–66. New York: Cambridge University Press, 1990.

—— "Building for the Bourgeoisie: The Quest for a Modern Style in Russian Architecture." In *Between Tsar and People,* edited by Edith Clowes, Samuel Kassow, and James West, pp. 308–24. Princeton, 1991.

—— "The 'New Style' and the Revival of Orthodox Church Architecture, 1900–1914." In *Christianity and the Arts in Russia,* edited by William Brumfield and Milos Velimirovic, pp. 105–23. New York: Cambridge University Press, 1991.

—— *The Origins of Modernism in Russian Architecture.* Berkeley, 1991.

——, ed. *Reshaping Russian Architecture: Western Technology, Utopian Dreams.* New York: Cambridge University Press, 1990.

Brumfield, William and Milos Velimirovic, eds. *Christianity and the Arts in Russia.* New York Cambridge University Press, 1991.

Brunov, N. I. "K voprosu o nekotorykh sviaziakh russkoi arkhitektury s zodchestvom iuzhnykh slavian," *Arkhitekturnoe nasledstvo,* 2 (1952): 3–42.

—— *Khram Vasiliia Blazhennogo v Moskve: Pokrovskii Sobor.* Moscow, 1988.

Brunov, N. I., A.I. Vlasiuk, and A. G. Chiniakov. *Istoriia russkoi arkhitektury.* Moscow, 1956.

Budylina, M. "Planirovka i zastroika Moskvy posle pozhara 1812 goda." *Arkhitekturnoe nasledstvo,* 1 (1951): 135–74.

—— "Istoriia postroiki Manezha v Moskve." *Arkhitekturnoe nasledstvo,* 2 (1952): 236–49.

—— *Istoriia russkoi arkhitektury.* Moscow, 1956.

—— "Arkhitekturnoe obrazovanie v Kamennom prikaze (1775–1782)," *Arkhitekturnoe nasledstvo,* 15 (1963): 111–20.

Bulkin, V. A. "Ital'ianizmy v drevnerusskom zodchestve kontsa XV–XVI vekov," *Vestnik Leningradskogo gosudarstvennogo universitetal,* 20 (1973): 59–66.

—— "O tserkvi Vozneseniia v Kolomenskom." In *Kul'tura srednevekovoi Rusi,* pp. 113–16. Leningrad, 1974.

Bunin, A. V. *Istoriia gradostroitel'nogo iskusstva.* Moscow, 1979.

Bunin, M. S. *Strelka Vasilevskogo ostrova.* Moscow–Leningrad, 1957.

Buryshkin, Pavel. *Moskva kupecheskaia.* New York, 1954.

Buseva-Davydova, I. L. "Ob istokakh kompozitsionnogo tipa 'vosmerik n chetverike' v russkoi arkhitekture kontsa XVII v.," *Arkhitekturnoe nasledstvo,* 33 (1985): 220–6.

—— "Zapadnye vliianiia v russkoi arkhitekture XVII v." In *Problemy istorii arkhitektury,* edited by A. A. Voronov, N. A. Smolina, A. Ia. Flier, and Iu. E. Revzina, part 2, pp. 161–2. Moscow, 1990.

Buseva-Davydova, I. L., and A. L. Batalov. "O metodologii izucheniia simvoliki arkhitektury." In *Istoriia arkhitektury. Ob'ekt, premet i metod issledovaniia,* edited by A. A. Voronov, pp. 92–9. Moscow, 1988.

Bussi, Virginio. "Nota su Aloisio Caresano, architetto vercellese della seconda metà del XV secolo, morto forse in Russia nella prima metà del XVI secolo," *Arte Lombarda,* 44/45 (1976): 237–8.

Butikov, Georgii P. *Isaakievskii sobor.* Leningrad, 1974.

615

Butikov, G. P., and G. A. Khvostova. *Isaakievskii sobor*. Leningrad, 1979.

Buxton, David R. *Russian Medieval Architecture, with an Account of the Transcaucasian Styles and their Influence in the West*. Cambridge, 1934.

———— *The Wooden Churches of Eastern Europe: An Introductory Survey*. Cambridge, 1981.

Bychkov, V. V. *Vizantiiskaia estetika*. Moscow, 1977.

Bylinkin, N. P., and A. V. Riabushin, eds. *Sovremennaia sovetskaia arkhitektura. 1955–1980 gg*. Moscow, 1985.

Bylinkin, N. P., V. N. Kalmykova, A. V. Riabushin, and G. V. Sergeeva. *Istoriia sovetskoi arkhitektury (1917–1954 gg.)*. Moscow, 1985.

Catherine the Great. *Zapiski Imperatritsy Ekateriny Vtoroi*. St. Petersburg, 1907.

Cazzola, Piero. "Artisti italiani a Mosca," *Le vie del mondo*, 9 (1967): 1042–56.

———— "I 'Mastri frjazy' a Mosca sullo scorcio del quindicesimo secolo (dalle Cronache russe e da documenti di Archivi italiani)," *Arte Lombarda*, 44/45 (1976): 157–72.

Chekmarev, V. M. "Obnovlenie gostinitsy 'Metropol,' " *Arkhitektura i stroitel'stvo Moskvy*, 1987, no. 6: 22–5.

———— "Mir khudozhestvennykh obrazov gostinitsy 'Metropol.' " In *Muzei 10*, edited by A. S. Loginova, pp. 35–47. Moscow, 1989.

Cherepnin, L. V. *Obrazovanie Russkogo tsentralizovannogo gosudarstva v XIV–XV vekakh*. Moscow, 1960.

Cherniavsky, Michael. *Tsar and People: Studies in Russian Myths*. New Haven, 1961.

———— "The Old Believers and the New Religion." *Slavic Review*, XXV, no. 1 (March 1966): 1–39.

————, ed. *The Structure of Russian History*. New York, 1970.

Chernikhov, Andrei. " 'Artist show us your world . . .': Iakov Chernikhov 1889–1951." In *Russian Avant-Garde Art and Architecture*, edited by Catherine Cooke, pp. 64–72. London, 1983.

Chernikhov, Iakov. *Osnovy sovremennoi arkhitektury*. Leningrad, 1930.

———— *Konstruktsiia arkhitekturnyikh i mashinykh form*. Leningrad, 1931.

———— *Arkhitekturnye fantazii*. Leningrad, 1933.

Chernozubova, L. E. "Obraztsovye proekty planirovki zhilykh kvartalov i ploshchadei nachala XIX v.," *Arkhitekturnoe nasledstvo*, 15 (1963): 188–92.

Chernyshev, M. B. In *Kul'tura drevnei Rusi*, edited by A. L. Mongait, pp. 289–93. Moscow, 1966.

Chiniakov, A. "Arkhitekturnye pamiatniki Izmailova," *Arkhitekturnoe nasledstvo*, 2 (1952): 193–220.

———— "Arkhitekturnyi pamiatnik vremeni Iuriia Dolgorukogo," *Arkhitekturnoe nasledstvo*, 2 (1952): 43–66.

———— "O nekotorykh osobennostiakh drevnerusskogo gradostroitel'stva," *Arkhitekturnoe nasledstvo*, 12 (1960): 3–22.

———— *Brat'ia Vesniny*. Moscow, 1970.

Clowes, Edith, Samuel Kassow, and James West, eds. *Between Tsar and People: Educated Society and the Quest for Public Identity in Late Imperial Russia*. Princeton, 1991.

Cohen, Jean-Louis. *Le Corbusier and the Mystique of the USSR*. Princeton, 1991.

Conant, Kenneth John. *Carolingian and Romanesque Architecture*. Baltimore, 1959.

Cooke, Catherine. " 'Form Is a Function X': The Development of the Constructivist Architects Design Method." In *Russian Avant-Garde Art and Architecture*, edited by Catherine Cooke, pp. 34–49. London, 1983.

———— "Shekhtel in Kelvingrove and Mackintosh on the Petrovka," *Scottish Slavonic Review*, 10 (1988): 177–205.

———— "A Picnic by the Roadside, or Work in Hand for the Future?" *Architectural Association Files*, 18 (1989): 15–24.

————, ed. *Russian Avant-Garde Art and Architecture*. London, 1983.

Coxe, William. *Travels into Poland, Russia, Sweden, and Denmark*. London, 1785.

Cracraft, James. "Feofan Prokopovich." In *The Eighteenth Century in Russia*, edited by J. G. Garrard, pp. 75–105. Oxford, 1973.

———— *The Petrine Revolution in Russian Architecture*. Chicago, 1988.

————, ed. *The Soviet Union Today: An Interpretive Guide*. Chicago, 1988.

Cross, A. G. *Russia Under Western Eyes*. London, 1971.

———— "By the Banks of the Thames": Russians in Eighteenth-Century Britain. Newtonville, Mass., 1980.

———— "Richard Paton and the Battle of Chesme," *Study Group on the Eighteenth Century Newsletter*, 14 (1986): 31–7.

———— "Catherine the Great and Whately's *Observations on Modern Gardening*," *Study Group on Eighteenth-Century Russia Newsletter*, 18 (1990): 21–29.

Cross, Samuel Hazard. *The Russian Primary Chronicle*. Cambridge, 1930.

Crummey, Robert O. *The Formation of Muscovy 1304–1613*. London–New York, 1987.

Cunliffe, Antonia. "The Competition for the Place of Soviets in Moscow, 1931–33," *Architectural Association Quarterly*, 1979, no. 2: 36–48.

Dabrowski, Magdalena. *Liubov Popova*. New York, 1991.

Dashkova, Ekaterina. *Zapiski: 1743–1810*. Leningrad, 1985.

Danilova, I. E., ed. *Gosudarstvennyi muzei izobrazitel'nykh iskusstv im. A. S. Pushkina: Istoriia sozdaniia muzeia v perepiske professora I. V. Tsvetaeva s arkhitektorom R. I. Kleinom i drugikh dokumentakh (1898–1912)*, 2 vols. Moscow, 1977.

———— *Vek prosveshcheniia: Rossiia i Frantsiia*. Moscow, 1989.

Darkevich, V. P. "Romanskaia tserkvonaia utvar' iz Severovostochnoi Rusi." In *Kul'tura drevnei Rusi*, edited by A. L. Mongait, pp. 61–70. Moscow, 1966.

Dedushkino, B. P. "K istorii ansamblia moskovskogo Vysoko-Petrovskogo monastyria." In *Drevnerusskoe iskusstvo XVII v.*, pp. 253–71. Moscow, 1964.

Denisov, Iu[rii M.]. "Usad'ba XVIII veka na Petergofskoi doroge," *Arkhitekturnoe nasledstvo*, 4 (1953): 148–54.

———— "Ischeznuvshie dvortsy." In *Ermitazh: Istoriia i arkhitektura zdaniia*, edited by V. I. Piliavskii and V. F. Levinson-Lessing, pp. 19–38. Leningrad, 1974.

Denisov, Iu. M., and A. N. Petrov. *Zodchii Rastrelli: Materialy k izucheniiu tvorchestva*. Leningrad, 1963.

Denisov, Iu. M., A. G. Gordin, N. M. Kozyreva, L. K.

Koshkareva, and T. M. Sokolina. *Gorod glazami khudozhnikov: Peterburg–Petrograd–Leningrad v proizvedeniiakh zhivopisi i grafiki.* Leningrad, 1978.

Denisov, Leonid I. *Pravoslavnye monastyri rossiiskoi imperii.* Moscow, 1908.

Diagilev, Sergei. "Neskol'ko slov o S. V. Maliutine," *Mir iskusstva*, 1903, no. 4: 157–60.

Diakin, Valentin. *Samoderzhavie burzhuaziia i dvorianstvo v 1907–1911 gg.* Leningrad, 1978.

Dmitriev, Iu. N. "O formakh pokrytiia v novgorodskom zodchestve XIV–XVI vekov." In *Drevnerusskoe iskusstvo XV–nachala XVI veka*, edited by V. N. Lazarev, pp. 196–207. Moscow, 1963.

Dmitriev, Lev, and Dmitrii Likhachev, eds. *Pamiatniki literatury drevnei rusi konets XV–pervaia polovina XVI veka.* Moscow, 1984.

Dokuchaev, Nikolai. "Sovremennaia russkaia arkhitektura i zapadnye paralleli," *Sovetskoe iskusstvo*, 1927, no. 1: 5–12; no. 2: 5–15.

Dorofienko, I. P., and P. Ia. Red'ko, "Raskrytie fresok XII v. v Kirillovskoi tserkvi Kieva." In *Drevnerusskoe iskussto: Monumental'naia zhivopis' XI–XVII vv.*, edited by O. I. Podobedova, pp. 45–51. Moscow, 1980.

Dreizin, E. I. *Dereviannaia arkhitektura Tomska.* Moscow, 1975.

Dubiago, T. B. *Letnii sad.* Moscow–Leningrad, 1951.

———— "Usad'by petrovskogo vremeni v okrestnostiakh Peterburga," *Arkhitekturnoe nasledstvo*, 4 (1953): 125–41.

———— *Russkie reguliarnye sady i parki.* Leningrad, 1963.

Dukes, Paul. *Catherine the Great and the Russian Nobility.* Cambridge, 1967.

———— *Russian under Catherine the Great: Volume One: Select Documents on Government and Society.* Newtonville, Mass., 1978.

———— *The Making of Russian Absolutism 1613–1801.* London–New York, 1982.

Efros, A. *Mastera raznykh epokh. Izbrannye istoriko-khudozhestvennye i kriticheskie stat'i.* Moscow, 1979.

Egorov, I. A. *The Architectural Planning of Saint Petersburg: Its development in the 18th and 19th Centuries*, translated by Eric Dluhosch. Athens, Ohio, 1969.

Eigel', Isaak. *Boris Iofan.* Moscow, 1978.

Eingorn, V. *K stopiatidesiatiletiiu sushchestvovaniia zdaniia Vsesoiuznoe biblioteki imeni V. I. Lenina.* Moscow, 1936.

Elizarova, N. A. *Ostankino.* Moscow, 1966.

Elliott, David, ed. *Rodchenko and the Arts of Revolutionary Russia.* New York, 1979.

Eneeva, N. T., ed. *Pamiatnik v kontekste kul'tury.* Moscow, 1991.

Eskin, Iu. M. "Dmitrii Pozharskii," *Voprosy istorii*, 1976, no. 8: 107–19.

Evangulova, O. S. *Dvortsovo-parkovye ansambli Moskvy pervoi poloviny XVIII veka.* Moscow, 1969.

———— "K probleme stilia v iskusstve petrovskogo vremeni," *Vestnik Moskovskogo universiteta*, 3 (1974): 67–84.

Evsina, N. A. "Proekty uchebnykh zdanii v Rossii XVIII veka." In *Russkoe iskusstvo XVIII veka*, edited by T. V. Alekseeva, pp. 110–38. Moscow, 1968.

———— "Iz istorii arkhitekturnykh vzgliadov i teorii nachala XVIII veka." In *Russkoe iskusstvo pervoi chetverti XVIII veka*, edited by T. V. Alekseeva, pp. 9–26. Moscow, 1974.

———— *Arkhitekturnaia teroiia v Rossii XVIII v.* Moscow, 1975.

———— *Arkhitekturnaia teoriia v Rossii vtoroi poloviny XVIII–nachala XIX veka.* Moscow, 1985.

Fedotova, T. P. "K probleme piatiglaviia v arkhitekture barokko pervoi poloviny XVIII v." In *Russkoe iskusstvo barokko: Materialy i issledovaniia*, edited by T. V. Alekseeva, pp. 70–87. Moscow, 1977.

Fekhner, Margarita V. *Kolomna.* Moscow, 1966.

———— *Kaluga. Borovsk: Khudozhestvennye pamiatniki XVI–XX vekov.* Moscow, 1972.

———— *Velikie Bulgary. Kazan'. Sviiazhsk.* Moscow, 1978.

———— "K istorii stroitel'stva Mariinskoi bol'nitsy dlia bednykh v Moskve," *Arkhitekturnoe nasledstvo*, 31 (1983): 12–16.

Fennell, John. *The Emergence of Moscow 1304–1359.* Berkeley, 1968.

———— *The Crisis of Medieval Russia 1200–1304.* London–New York, 1985.

Fiene, Donald M. "What Is the Appearance of the Divine Sophia?," *Slavic Review*, 48 (1989), 449–76.

Filatov, V. V. "Vnutrennii dekor Pokrovskogo stolpa." In *Drevnerusskoe iskusstvo. Zarubezhnye sviazi*, edited by G. V. Popov, p. 354–61. Moscow, 1975.

Fletcher, Giles. *Of the Russe Commonwealth*, edited by Richard Pipes and John Fine. Cambridge, Mass.: Harvard University Press, 1966.

Freeze, Gregory. " 'Going to the Intelligentsia': The Church and its Urban Mission in Post-Reform Russia." In *Between Tsar and People*, edited by Edith Clowes, pp. 215–32. Princeton, 1991.

French, R. A. "Canals in Pre-Revolutionary Russia." In *Studies in Russian Historical Geography*, edited by J. H. Bater and R. A. French, vol. 2. London, 1983.

Gan, Aleksei. *Konstruktivism.* Tver, 1922.

Garrard, J. G., ed. *The Eighteenth Century in Russia.* Oxford, 1973.

Gatova, T. A. "Iz istorii dekorativnoi skul'ptury Moskvy nachala XVIII v." In *Russkoe iskusstvo XVIII veka*, edited by T. V. Alekseeva, pp. 31–44. Moscow, 1973.

Gavrilov, S. A. "Tserkov' Vozneseniia v Kolomenskom. Issledovaniia 1972–1990 gg." In *Restavratsiia i arkhitekturnaia arkheologiia. Novye materialy i issledovaniia*, edited by A. L. Batalov and I. A. Bondarenko, pp. 58–78. Moscow, 1991.

Gavrilova, E. I. "Lomonosov i osnovanie Akademii khudozhestv." In *Russkoe iskusstvo XVIII v.: Materialy i issledovaniia*, edited by T. V. Alekseeva, pp. 66–75. Moscow, 1973.

———— " 'Sankt Piterburkh' 1718–1722 goda v naturnykh risunkakh Fedora Vasil'eva." In *Russkoe iskusstvo pervoi chetverti XVIII veka: Materialy i issledovaniia*, edited by T. V. Alekseeva, pp. 119–40. Moscow, 1974.

Gerschenkron, Alexander. *Europe in the Russian Mirror: Four Lectures in Economic History.* London: Cambridge University Press, 1969.

Gertsen [Herzen], Aleksandr G. *Polnoe sobranie sochinenii*, vol. 8. Moscow, 1956.

Gessen, A., and M. Tikhomirova. "Raboty po restavratsii dvortsa Monplesir v Petrodvortse." In *Teoriia i praktika restavratsionnykh rabot*, pp. 99–108. Moscow, 1972.

Ginzburg, Moisei. *Stil' i epokha*. Moscow, 1924.

―――― *Style and Epoch*, translated and edited by Anatole Senkevitch. Cambridge, Mass., M.I.T. Press, 1982.

Glezer, Elena N. *Arkhitekturnyi ansambl' Angliiskogo parka*. Leningrad, 1979.

Glinka, V. M., Iu. M. Denisov, and M. V. Iogansen. *Ermitazh. Istoriia stroitel'stva i arkhitektury zdanii*. Leningrad, 1989.

Glozman, Iosif M., ed. *Kuskovo, Ostankino. Arkhangel'skoe*. Moscow, 1976.

Glumov, Aleksandr N. *N. A. L'vov*. Moscow, 1980.

Gnedovskii, B. V., and E. D. Dobrovol'skaia. *Iaroslavl'. Tutaev*. Moscow, 1981.

Godlevskii, N. N. "Planirovka kremlia Kolomny v XVI–XVII vv.," *Arkhitekturnoe nasledstvo*, 16 (1967): 19–28.

―――― "Planirovka i zastroika Tul'skogo kremlia v XVI–XVII vv.," *Arkhitekturnoe nasledstvo*, 18 (1969): 25–9.

Gogol', Nikolai V. *Sobranie sochinenii v shesti tomakh*. Moscow, 1959.

Gogolitsyn, Iu. M., and T. M. Gogolitsyna. *Pamiatniki arkhitektury Leningradskoi Oblasti*. Leningrad, 1987.

Gol'denberg, P., and B. Gol'denberg. *Planirovka zhilogo kvartala Moskvy*. Moscow, 1935.

Gol'ts, G. "Arkhitektura b. tserkvi Vozneseniia v sele Kolomenskom." In *Russkaia arkhitektura*, pp. 55–6. Moscow, 1940.

Gornostaev, F. F. *Dvortsy i tserkvi iuga*. Moscow, 1914.

Gozak, Andrei, and Andrei Leonidov. *Ivan Leonidov: The Complete Works*. New York, 1988.

Gra, M. A., and B. B. Zhiromskii. *Kolomenskoe*. Moscow, 1971.

Grabar, Igor' E. "Neskol'ko myslei o sovremennom prikladnom iskusstve v Rossii," *Mir iskusstva*, no. 3 (1902): 51–6.

―――― "V poiskakh neizvestnykh postroek V. I. Bazhenova." In *Neizvestnye i predpolagaemye postroiki V. I. Bazhenova*, pp. 123–5. Moscow, 1951.

Grabar', Igor' E., ed. *Istoriia russkogo iskusstva*, 6 vols. Moscow, 1910–15.

―――― *Russkaia arkhitektura pervoi poloviny XVIII v. Issledovaniia i materialy*. Moscow, 1954.

Grabar', I. E., and V. N. Lazarev. *Istoriia russkogo iskusstva*, 13 vols. Moscow, 1953–64.

Grashchenko, V. N. "Nasledie Palladio v arkhitekture russkogo klassitsizma." *Sovetskoe iskusstvoznanie*, 1981, no. 2.

Gray, Camilla. *The Russian Experiment in Art. 1863–1922*. New York, 1986.

Grekov, Alexander P. "Iz opyta rabot po spaseniiu rospisi tserkvi Spasa na Kovaleve v Novgorode." In *Drevnerusskoe iskusstvo: Monumental'naia zhivopis' XI–XVII vv.*, edited by O. I. Podobedova, pp. 176–95. Moscow, 1980.

Grimm, G. G. *Arkhitektura perekrytii russkogo klassitsizma*. Leningrad, 1939.

―――― "Proekty arkhitektora N. Miketti dlia Peterburga i ego okrestnostei v sobranii Gosudarstvennogo Ermitazha," *Soobshcheniia Gosudarstvennogo Ermitazha*, 13 (1958): 21–4.

―――― *Arkhitektor Voronikhin*. Leningrad, 1963.

Grekov, Boris D. *Kievskaia Rus'*. Moscow, 1953.

Gulianitskii, N. F. "O maloissledovannoi storone tvorcheskogo metoda V. V. Rastrelli-gradostroitelia," *Arkhitekturnoe nasledstvo*, 21 (1973): 24–43.

―――― "O svoeobrazii i preemstvennykh sviaziakh ordernogo iazyka v russkoi arkhitekture," *Arkhitekturnoe nasledstvo*, 23 (1975): 14–29.

―――― "O kompozitsii zdanii v ansamblevoi zastroike Moskvy perioda klassitsizma," *Arkhitekturnoe nasledstvo*, 24 (1976): 20–7.

―――― "Traditsii klassiki i cherty renessansa v arkhitekture Moskvy XV-XVII vv.," *Arkhitekturnoe nasledstvo*, 26 (1978): 13–30.

―――― "Gradostroitel'nye osobennosti Peterburga i cherty russkoi arkhitektury serediny XVIII v.," *Arkhitekturnoe nasledstvo*, 27 (1979): 12–21.

―――― "Tserkov' Pokrova v Medvedkove i russkoe zodchestvo XVI-XVII vv.," *Arkhitekturnoe nasledstvo*, 28 (1980): 52–64.

―――― "Cherty preemstvennosti v kompozitsii tsentrov russkikh gorodov, pereplanirovannykh v XVIII v.," *Arkhitekturnoe nasledstvo*, 29 (1981): 3–17.

―――― "Sintez professii i metod zodchego v russkoi arkhitekture kontsa XVIII v.," *Arkhitekturnoe nasledstvo*, 30 (1982): 24–31.

―――― "Osvoboditel'nye idei Rusi v obrazakh pamiatnikov arkhitektury XVI–pervoi poloviny XVII vv," *Arkhitekturnoe nasledstvo*, 32 (1984): 32–46.

―――― "O vnutrennem prostranstve v kompozitsii rannemoskovskikh khramov," *Arkhitekturnoe nasledstvo*, 33 (1985): 211–19.

―――― "Russkii reguliarnyi gorod na traditsionnoi osnove," *Arkhitekturnoe nasledstvo*, 33 (1985): 3–13.

―――― "Moskva Iauzskaia," *Arkhitekturnoe nasledstvo*, 34 (1986): 34–43.

Gurevich, I. M., V. V. Znamenov, and E. G. Miasoedova. *Bol'shoi petergofskii dvorets*. Leningrad, 1979.

Hamilton, George Heard. *The Art and Architecture of Russia*, 2nd, revised edition. Baltimore, 1975.

Hammond, N. G. L., and H. H. Scullard, eds., *Oxford Classical Dictionary*, 2nd edition. London, 1973.

Hamm, Michael, ed. *The City in Russian History*. Lexington, Ky., 1976.

Haywood, Richard M. "The Winter Palace in St. Petersburg: Destruction by Fire and Reconstruction, December 1837–March 1839," *Jahrbücher für Geschichte Osteuropas*, 27 (1979): 161–80.

Hirschfeld, C. C. L. *Theorie der Garten-Kunst*. 3 vols. Leipzig, 1779–80.

Honour, Hugh. *Neo-classicism*. Harmondsworth, 1968.

Hudson, Hugh D., Jr. *The Rise of the Demidov Family and the*

Russian Iron Industry in the Eighteenth Century. Newton-ville, Mass., 1986.

———— " 'The Social Condenser of Our Epoch': The Association of Contemporary Architects and the Creation of a New Way of Life in Revolutionary Russia," *Jahrbücher für Osteuropas,* 34 (1986): 557–78.

Hughes, L. A. J. "Belorussian craftsmen in late seventeenth-century Russia and their influence on Muscovite architecture," *The Journal of Byelorussian Studies,* 3 (1976): 332–3.

———— "Western European Graphic Material as a Source for Moscow Baroque Architecture," *Slavonic and East European Review,* 55 (1977): 433–43.

———— "Moscow Baroque – A Controversial Style," *Transactions of the Association of Russian–American Scholars in the U.S.A.,* 15 (1982): 69–93.

———— *Sophia, Regent of Russia, 1657–1704.* New Haven, 1990.

Hunt, John Dixon. *The Figure in the Landscape: Poetry Painting and Gardening during the Eighteenth Century.* London, 1976.

Hyams, Edward. *Capability Brown and Humphry Repton.* London, 1971.

Iaralov, Iu. S., ed. *100 let obshchestvennykh arkhitekturnykh organizatsii v SSSR, 1867–1967.* Moscow, 1967.

———— *Zodchie Moskvy XV–XIX vv.* Moscow, 1981.

Ikonnikov, Andrei V. *Kamennaia letopis' Moskvy.* Moscow, 1978.

———— *Arkhitektura Moskvy. XX vek.* Moscow, 1984.

Ikonnikov, A. V., and G. P. Stepanov, *Osnovy arkhitekturnoi kompozitsii.* Moscow, 1971.

Il'in, Mikhail A. *Ivan Aleksandrovich Fomin.* Moscow, 1946.

———— *Zodchii Iakov Bukhvostov.* Moscow, 1959.

———— *Vesniny.* Moscow, 1960.

———— "K voprosu o prirode arkhitekturnogo ubranstva 'moskovskogo barokko.' " In *Drevnerusskoe iskusstvo: XVII vek,* edited by V. N. Lazarev, pp. 232–5. Moscow, 1964.

———— *Kamennaia letopis' moskovskoi Rusi: svetskie osnovy kamennogo zodchestva XV–XVII vv.* Moscow, 1966.

———— "Nekotorye predpolozheniia ob arkhitekture russkikh ikonostasov na rubezhe XIV-XV vv." In *Kul'tura drevnei Rusi,* edited by A. L. Mongait, pp. 79–88. Moscow, 1966.

———— "Pskovskie zodchie v Moskve v kontse XV veka." In *Drevnerusskoe iskusstvo: Khudozhestvennaia kul'tura Pskova,* edited by V. N. Lazarev, pp. 189–96. Moscow, 1968.

———— "Redkii pamiatnik drevnerusskoi arkhitektury (Khram sela Kamenskogo)," *Istoriia SSSR,* 1969, no. 3: 150–5.

———— "O palladianstve v tvorchestve D. Kvarengi i N. L'vova." In *Russkoe iskusstvo XVIII veka,* edited by T. V. Alekseeva, pp. 103–8. Moscow, 1973.

———— *Podmoskov'e.* Moscow, 1974.

———— "Dekorativnye reznye poiasa rannemoskovskogo kamennogo zodchestva." In *Drevnerusskoe iskusstvo: Zarubezhnye sviazi,* edited by G. V. Popov, pp. 223–39. Moscow, 1975.

———— *Moskva. Pamiatniki arkhitektury XVIII–pervoi treti XIX veka.* Moscow, 1975.

———— "K izucheniiu tserkvi Vozneseniia v Kolomenskom." In *Drevnerusskoe iskusstvo: Problemy i atributsii,* edited by O. I. Podobedova, pp. 355–67. Moscow, 1977.

———— *Russkoe shatrovoe zodchestvo. Pamiatniki serediny XVI veka.* Moscow, 1980.

Il'in, M. A., and T. V. Moiseeva, *Moskva i Podmoskov'e.* Moscow, 1979.

Iogansen, Marina V. "Raboty D. Trezini po planirovke i zastroike Strelki Vasil'evskogo ostrova." In *Russkoe iskusstvo XVIII v.: Materialy i issledovaniia,* edited by T. V. Alekseeva, pp. 45–55. Moscow, 1973.

———— *Mikhail Zemtsov.* Leningrad, 1975.

———— "Raboty Kvarengi na Strelke Vasil'evskogo ostrova v Peterburge." In *Russkoe iskusstvo vtoroi poloviny XVIII-pervoi poloviny XIX v.,* edited by T. V. Alekseeva, pp. 7–17. Moscow, 1979.

———— "Ob avtore general'nogo plana Peterburga petrovskogo vremeni." In *Ot Srednevekov'ia k Novomu vremeni,* edited by T. V. Alekseeva, pp. 50–72. Moscow, 1984.

———— "Zdanie 'mazankovykh kollegii' na Troitskoi ploshchadi Peterburga." In *Ot Srednevekov'ia k novomu vremeni,* edited by T. V. Alekseeva, pp. 73–86. Moscow, 1984.

Iogansen, M. V., and A. N. Kirpichnikov. " 'Petrovskii Shlissel'burg' (po novootkrytym arkhivnym materialam)." In *Russkoe iskusstvo pervoi chetverti XVIII veka,* edited by T. V. Alekseeva, pp. 27–52. Moscow, 1974.

Isachenko, V. G. "Pobornik novogo stilia: Stranitsy tvorcheskoi biografii A. F. Bubyria," *Stroitel'stvo i arkhitektura Leningrada,* 1978, no. 3: 44–7.

———— "Trud otdannyi narodu," *Leningradskaia panorama,* 1982, no. 3: 30–3.

———— "V shirokom diapazone," *Leningradskaia panorama,* 1985, no. 10: 28–31.

Isachenko, V. G., B. M. Kirikov, and S. G. Fedorov, eds. *Arkhitektory-stroiteli Peterburga-Petrograda nachala XX veka.* Leningrad, 1982.

Ivanov, V. N. *Kostroma.* Moscow, 1978.

Ivanovskii, N. "Proskinitarii Arseniia Sukhanova." In *Pravoslavnyi Palestenskii sbornik,* VII, no. 3 (21), pp. 130–4. St. Petersburg, 1889.

Iz istorii restavratsii pamiatnikov kul'tury. Moscow, 1974.

Jones, Robert E. *The Emancipation of the Russian Nobility.* Princeton, 1973.

———— "Urban Planning and the Development of Provincial Towns in Russia During the Reign of Catherine II." In *The Eighteenth Century in Russia,* edited by J. G. Garrard, pp. 321–44. Oxford, 1973.

Jourdain, Margaret. *The Work of William Kent.* London, 1941.

Kaganovich, Avraam. *Mednyi vsadnik: Istoriia sozdaniia monumenta.* Leningrad, 1975.

Kaliazina, Ninel' V. "O dvortse admirala F. M Apraksina v Peterburge," *Trudy Gorsudarstvennogo Ermitazha,* 11 (1970): 131–40.

———— "Lepnoi dekor v zhilom inter'ere Peterburga pervoi chetverti XVIII veka." In *Russkoe iskusstvo pervoi chetverti*

XVIII veka, edited by T. V. Alekseeva, pp. 109–18. Moscow, 1974.

——— "Monumental'no-dekorativnaia zhivopis' v dvortsovom inter'ere pervoi chetverti XVIII veka (k probleme razvitiia stilia barokko v Rossii)." In *Russkoe iskusstvo barokko: Materialy i issledovaniia*, edited by R. V. Alekseeva, pp. 55–69. Moscow, 1977.

——— "Arkhitektor Leblon v Rossii (1716–1719)." In *Ot Srednevekov'ia k novomu vremeni*, edited by N. V. Alekseeva, pp. 94–123. Moscow, 1984.

Kaliazina, N. V., L. P. Dorofeeva, and G. V. Mikhailov. *Dvorets Menshikova*. Moscow, 1986.

Kämpfer, Frank. "La concezione teologica ed architecttonica della cattedrale 'Vasilii Blazennyi' a Mosca," *Arte Lombarda*, 44/45 (1976): 191–8.

Kapterev, N. *Patriarkh Nikon i Tsar' Aleksei Mikhailovich*, 2 vols. Sergiev Posad, 1909–12.

Karaulov, E. V. "Dom Luninykh v Moskve," *Arkhitekturnoe nasledstvo*, 20 (1972): 75–84.

Karavaeva, E. M. "Sobor Spasskogo monastyria v Iaroslavle (issledovanie i restavratsiia)," *Arkhitekturnoe nasledstvo*, 15 (1963): 36–50.

Karger, Mikhail. *Drevnii Kiev*. Moscow–Leningrad, 1962.

——— *Novgorod: Architectural Monuments 11th–17th Centuries*. Leningrad, 1975.

Katsnel'son, R. "Drevniaia tserkov' v Perynskom skity bliz Novgoroda," *Arkhitekturnoe nasledstvo*, 2 (1952): 69–85.

——— "Ansambl' Simonova monastyria v Moskve," *Arkhitekturnoe nasledstvo*, 6 (1956): 87–106.

Kaufmann, Emil. *Architecture in the Age of Reason*. Cambridge, Mass.: Harvard University Press, 1955.

Kavelin, Leonid. *Istoricheskoe opisanie stavropigial'nogo Voskresenskogo, Novyi Ierusalim imenuemogo monastyria*. Moscow, 1876.

Kazakov, S. "Promyshlennaia arkhitektura Konstantina Melnikova," *Arkhitektura SSSR*, 1990, no. 4: 81–7.

Kedrinskii, A. A., M. G. Kolotov, B. N. Ometov, and A. G. Raskin. *Vosstanovlenie pamiatnikov arkhitektury Leningrada*. Leningrad, 1983.

Khait, V. "Samyi teatral'nyi teatr," *Stroitel'stvo i arkhitektura Moskvy*, 1982, no. 10: 12–14.

Khan-Magomedov, Selim O. *M. Ia. Ginzburg*. Moscow, 1972.

——— *Aleksandr Vesnin*. Moscow, 1983.

——— *Aleksandr Vesnin and Russian Constructivism*. New York, 1986.

——— *Pioneers of Soviet Architecture*. New York, 1987.

——— *Il'ia Golosov*. Moscow, 1988.

——— *Konstantin Mel'nikov*. Moscow, 1991.

Khanzhin, V. "Velotrek v Krylatskom," *Arkhitektura SSSR*, 1986, no. 3: 26–31.

Kharlamova, A. M. *Nikolai L'vov*. Moscow, 1961.

Khazanova, Vigdariia E. *Iz istorii sovetskoi arkhitektury 1926–1932 gg*. Moscow, 1970.

——— *Sovetskaia arkhitektura pervykh let oktiabria*. Moscow, 1970.

——— *Sovetskaia arkhitektura pervoi piatiletki*. Moscow, 1980.

Kholostenko, M. V. "Neizvestnye pamiatniki monumental'noi skul'ptury drevnei Rusi: Relefy Borisoglebskogo sobora v Chernigove," *Iskusstvo*, no. 3 (1953): 84–91.

——— "Issledovaniia Borisoglebskogo sobora v Chernigove," *Sovetskaia arkheologiia*, no. 2 (1967): 188–210.

——— "Uspenskii sobor pecherskogo monastiria." In *Starodavnii Kyiv*, pp. 107–70. Kiev, 1975.

——— "Novi doslidzhennia Ioanno-Predtechenskoi tserkvi ta rekonstruktsiia Uspenskoho soboru Kievo-Pecherskoi lavri." In *Arkheologichni doslidzennia staro-davnoho Kyiva*, pp. 131–65. Kiev, 1976.

Kidson, Peter, Peter Murray, and Paul Thompson. *A History of English Architecture*. Harmondsworth, 1969.

Kilesso, S. K. *Kievo-Pecherskaia lavra*. Moscow, 1975.

Kiparisova, A. A. "Neopublikovannye proekty moskovskikh zodchikh kontsa XVIII i nachala XIX vekov," *Arkhitekturnoe nasledstvo*, 1 (1951): 108–34.

——— "Stanovlenie nekotorykh tipov sooruzhenii moskovskogo klassitsizma v tvorchestve D. V. Ukhtomskogo," *Arkhitekturnoe nasledstvo*, 29 (1981): 33–40.

Kiparisova, A. A., and R. G. Koroleva. *Arkhitektor Dmitrii Vasil'evich Ukhtomskii. 1719–1774. Katalog*. Moscow, 1973.

Kirichenko, Evgeniia I. "Dokhodnye zhilye doma Moskvy i Peterburga (1770–1830-e gg.)," *Arkhitekturnoe nasledstvo*, 14 (1962): 135–58.

——— "O nekotorykh osobennostiakh evoliutsii gorodskikh mnogokvartirnykh domov vtoroi poloviny XIX–nachala XX vekov (Ot otdel'nogo doma k kompleksy)," *Arkhitekturnoe nasledstvo*, 15 (1963): 153–70.

——— "Zhilaia zastroika Peterburga epokhi klassitsizma i ee vliianie na razvitie arkhitektury," *Arkhitekturnoe nasledstvo*, 16 (1967): 81–95.

——— "Materialy o tvorchestve arkhitektora P. P. Zhako," *Arkhitekturnoe nasledstvo*, 18 (1969): 83–99.

——— "Arkhitektor I. P. Ropet," *Arkhitekturnoe nasledstvo*, 20 (1972): 85–93.

"Prostranstvennaia organizatsiia zhilykh kompleksov Moskvy i Peterburga v nachale XX v.," *Arkhitekturnoe nasledstvo*, 19 (1972): 118–36.

——— *Fedor Shekhtel*. Moscow, 1973.

——— "Arkhitektor V. O. Shervud i ego teoreticheskie vozzreniia," *Arkhitekturnoe nasledstvo*, 22 (1974): 3–7.

——— "Arkhitekturnye ansambli Moskvy 1830–1860-kh gg.," *Arkhitekturnoe nasledstvo*, 24 (1976): 3–19.

——— "Problema natsional'nogo stilia v arkhitekture Rossii 70-kh gg. XIX v.," *Arkhitekturnoe nasledstvo*, 25 (1976): 131–53.

——— *Moskva na rubezhe dvukh stoletii*. Moscow, 1977.

——— "Istorizm myshleniia i tip muzeinogo zdaniia v russkoi arkhitekture serediny i vtoroi poloviny XIX v." In *Vzaimosviaz' iskusstv v khudozhestvennom razvitii Rossii vtoroi poloviny XIX v.*, edited by G. Iu. Sternin, pp. 135–42. Moscow, 1982.

——— "Problemy stilia i zhanra v russkoi arkhitekture vtoroi chetverti XIX v.," *Arkhitektura SSSR*, 1983, nos. 3–4: 112–15.

——— "Ob osobennostiakh zhiloi zastroiki poslepozharnoi Moskvy," *Arkhitekturnoe nasledstvo*, 32 (1984): 54–62.

——— *Arkhitekturnye teorii XIX veka v Rossii*. Moscow, 1986.

———— "The Historical Museum: A Moscow Design Competition 1875–83." In *Uses of Tradition in Russian and Soviet Architecture,* edited by Catherine Cooke, pp. 24–6. London, 1987.

———— *Mikhail Bykovskii.* Moscow, 1988.

———— "Romantizm i istorizm v russkoi arkhitekture XIX veka (K voprosu o dvukh fazakh razvitiia cklektiki)," *Arkhitekturnoe nasledstvo,* 36 (1988): 130–55.

Kirikov, Boris M. "Mar'ian Mar'ianovich Peretiatkovich," *Stroitel'stvo i arkhitektura Leningrada,* 1973, no. 1: 30–1.

———— "Obrazets stilia modern. Novye materialy ob inter'erakh pamiatnika arkhitektury," *Stroitel'stvo i arkhitektura Leningrada,* 1976, no. 6: 38–41.

———— *Uglich.* Leningrad, 1984.

———— "Peterburgskii modern," *Panorama iskusstv,* 10 (1987): 99–148.

Kirillov, V. V. "Ansambl' Tobol'skogo kremlia (Opyt sozdaniia obshchegorodskogo publichnogo tsentra rannepetrovskogo vremeni)." In *Russkoe iskusstvo pervoi chetverti XVIII veka: Materialy i issledovaniia,* edited by T. V. Alekseeva, pp. 53–67. Moscow, 1974.

———— "Metody proektirovaniia Semena Remezova," *Arkhitekturnoe nasledstvo,* 22 (1974): 53–62.

———— *Arkhitektura russkogo moderna.* Moscow, 1979.

———— "Sibirskii prikaz i ego rol' v organizovannom stroitel'stve gorodov na novykh zemliakh," *Arkhitekturnoe nasledstvo,* 28 (1980): 13–19.

———— *Tobol'sk.* Moscow, 1984.

Kirpichnikov, A. N. "Kreposti bastionnogo tipa v srednevekovoi Rossii." In *Pamiatniki kul'tury. Novye otkrytiia. Ezhegodnik. 1978,* pp. 471–99. Leningrad, 1979.

Kitner, Iu. I. "Dinastiia arkhitektorov," *Stroitel'stvo i arkhitektura Leningrada,* 1978, no. 4: 42–45.

Kiuchariants, D. A. "Sintez iskusstv v arkhitekture Mramornogo dvortsa v Leningrade," *Arkhitekturnoe nasledstvo,* 16 (1967): 71–80.

———— *Antonio Rinal'di.* Leningrad, 1976.

Kivokurtsev, Iu. P. "Skhodstvo arkhitektury doma b. Pashkova (Leninskoi biblioteki) s frantsuzskoi arkhitekturoi XVIII stoletiia," *Akademiia arkhitektury,* 1937, no. 2: 46–50.

Klibanov, A. *Reformatsionnye dvizheniia v Rossii.* Moscow, 1960.

Klyuchevsky, Vasili. *Peter the Great,* translated by Liliana Archibald. New York, 1958.

Kochakov, B. M., ed. *Ocherki Istorii Leningrada, Vol. 2, Period Kapitalizma.* Moscow–Leningrad, 1957.

Kochedamov, V. I. "Proekt naberezhnoi u Admiralteistva Zodchego K. I. Rossi," *Arkhitekturnoe nasledstvo,* 4 (1953): 111–14.

———— *Naberezhnye Nevy.* Leningrad, 1954.

———— *Pervye russkie goroda Sibiri.* Moscow, 1978.

Kokkinaki, I. "K voprosu o vzaimosviaziakh sovetskikh i zarubezhnykh arkhitektorov v 1920–1930-e gody." In *Voprosy sovetskogo izobrazitel'nogo iskusstva i arkhitektury,* edited by I. M. Shmidt, pp. 350–82. Moscow, 1976.

Kolmakov, N. A. "Dom i familiia Stroganovykh," *Russkaia starina,* 53 (1887): 575–602.

Komech, A. I. "Postroenie vertikal'noi kompositsii Sofiiskogo sobora v Kieva," *Sovetskaia arkheologiia,* 3 (1968), 232–8.

———— "Rol' kniazheskogo zakaza v postroenii Sofiiskogo sobora v Kieve." In *Drevnerusskoe iskusstvo: Khudozhestvennaia kul'tura domongol'skoi Rusi,* edited by V. N. Lazarev, pp. 50–64. Moscow, 1971.

———— "Spaso-Probrazhenskii sobor v Chernigove." In *Drevnerusskoe iskusstvo: Zarubezhnye sviazi,* edited by G. V. Popov, pp. 9–26. Moscow, 1975.

———— "Rol' pridelov v formirovanii obshchei kompozitsii Sofiiskogo sobora v Novgorode." In *Srednevekovaia Rus',* edited by G. K. Vagner and D. S. Likhachev, pp. 147–55. Moscow, 1976.

———— *Drevnerusskoe zodchestvo kontsa X–nachala XII v.: Vizantiiskoe nasledie i stanovlenie samostoiatel'noi traditsii.* Moscow, 1987.

Komech, A. I., and V. I. Pluzhnikov, eds. *Pamiatniki arkhitektury Moskvy: Kreml', Kitai-gorod, Tsentral'nye ploshchadi.* Moscow, 1983.

Komelova, G. N. *Vidy Peterburga i ego okrestnostei serediny XVIII veka.* Leningrad, 1968.

———— "K istorii sozdaniia gravirovannykh vidov Peterburga i ego okrestnostei M. I. Makhaevym." *Trudy Gosudarstvennogo Ermitazha,* 11 (1970): 36–56.

———— ed. *Kul'tura i iskusstvo petrovskogo vremeni: Publikatsii i issledovaniia.* Leningrad, 1977.

Komelova, G. N., G. Printseva, and I. Kotel'nikova. *Peterburg v proizvedeniiakh Patersena.* Moscow, 1978.

Kopp, Anatole. *Town and Revolution: Soviet Architecture and City Planning.* New York, 1970.

———— *Constructivist Architecture in the USSR.* New York, 1985.

———— "Foreign Architects in the Soviet Union During the First Two Five-Year Plans." In *Reshaping Russian Architecture: Western Technology, Utopian Dreams,* edited by William C. Brumfield, pp. 176–214. New York: Cambridge University Press, 1991.

Kopylova, S. V. *Kamennoe stroitel'stvo v Sibiri konets XVII–XVIII v.* Novosibirsk, 1979.

Korshunova, Militsa F. *Dzhakomo Kvarengi.* Leningrad, 1977.

———— *Arkhitektor Iurii Fel'ten: Katalog vystavki.* Leningrad, 1982.

———— *Iurii Fel'ten.* Leningrad, 1988.

Kostochkin, V. V. *Gosudarev master Fedor Kon'.* Moscow, 1964.

———— "Iz istorii russkogo sbornogo stroitel'stva XVI v.," *Arkhitekturnoe nasledstvo,* 18 (1969): 125–34.

———— *Krepostnoe zodchestvo drevnei Rusi.* Moscow, 1969.

———— "K voprosu o traditsiiakh i novatorstve v russkom zodchestve XVI–XVII vv.," *Arkhitekturnoe nasledstvo,* 27 (1979): 29–37.

Kovalenskaia, N. N. *Russkii klassitsizm.* Moscow, 1964.

Kovaleva, V. M. "Zhivopis' tserkvi Fedora Stratilata v Novgorode po materialam otkrytii 1974–1976 gg." In *Drevnerusskoe iskusstvo: Monumental'naia zhivopis' XI–XVII vv.,* edited by O. I. Podobedova, pp. 161–75. Moscow, 1980.

Kovelman, G. M. *Tvorchestvo pochetnogo akademika inzhenera Vladimira Grigorevicha Shukhova.* Moscow, 1961.

Kozhin, N. A. "K genezisu russkoi lozhnoi gotiki," *Akademiia arkhitektury*, 1 (1934): 114–21.

Krasheninnikov, A. F. "Novye dannye po istorii zdaniia Akademii khudozhestv, *Arkhitekturnoe nasledstvo*, 7 (1955): 125–39.

——— "Lesnye sklady na ostrove Novaia Gollandiia v Peterburge," *Arkhitekturnoe nasledstvo*, 19 (1972): 96–101.

——— "Zdanie byvshei Inostrannoi kollegii v Leningrade," *Arkhitekturnoe nasledstvo*, 20 (1972): 64–9.

——— "Nekotorye osobennosti perelomnogo perioda mezhdu barokko i klassitsizmom v russkoi arkhitekture." In *Russkoe iskusstvo XVIII v.: Materialy i issledovaniia*, edited by T. V. Alekseeva, pp. 97–102. Moscow, 1973.

——— "Sobstvennye doma V. I. Bazhenova v Moskve." *Arkhitekturnoe nasledstvo*, 1 (1951): 105–7.

Krasheninnikova, N. "Iz neopublikovannykh rabot I. D. Zhiliardi," *Arkhitekturnoe nasledstvo*, 1 (1951): 191–201.

——— "K voprosu ob atributsii byvshego doma Dolgova na 1-y Meshchanskoi ulitse." *Arkhitekturnoe nasledstvo*, 1 (1951): 86–93.

Krasheninnikova, N., and V. Shilkov. "Proekty obraztsovykh zagorodnykh domov D. Trezini i zastroika beregov Fontanki," *Arkhitekturnoe nasledstvo*, 7 (1955): 5–12.

Krasnobaev, Boris I. *Ocherki istorii russkoi kul'tury XVIII veka*. Moscow, 1972.

——— *Russkaia kul'tura vtoroi poloviny XVII–nachala XIX v.*. Moscow, 1983.

Krasnorech'ev, L. E., and T. V. Gladenko. "Arkhitektura XVI v." In *Novgorod: k 1100-letiiu goroda*, edited by M. N. Tikhomirov, pp. 244–63. Moscow, 1964.

Krasovskii, A. *Grazhdanskaia arkhitektura*. St. Petersburg, 1886.

Krasovskii, I. S. "Nekotorye osobennosti gradostroitel'noi struktury Kieva serediny XII v.," *Arkhitekturnoe nasledstvo*, 25 (1976): 12–18.

Krasovskii, Mikhail. "Pskovskie zvonnitsy," *Zodchii*, 1906, no. 28: 240, 249, 281, 288.

——— *Ocherk istorii moskovskogo perioda drevnerusskogo tserkovnogo zodchestva*. Moscow, 1911.

Krautheimer, Richard. *Early Christian and Byzantine Architecture*. New York, 1979.

Kresal'nii, N. I. *Sofiiskii zapovidnik u Kievi*. Kiev, 1960.

Krupnova, R. E., and V. A. Rezvin, *Ulitsa Gor'kogo, 18*. Moscow, 1984.

Krylova, Z. B. "Novoe podtverzhdenie avtorstva V. I. Bazhenova v sozdanii byvsh. doma Pashkova (nyne Gos. Biblioteka imeni Lenina," *Arkhitektura SSSR*, 1955, no. 10: 47.

Kudriavtsev, Alexander I., and Galina N. Shkoda. *Aleksandro-Nevskaia Lavra: Arkhitekturnyi ansambl' i pamiatniki Nekropolei*. Leningrad, 1986.

Kudriavtsev, M. P. "Problema tsveta pri restavratsii pamiatnikov arkhitektury." In *Metodika i praktika sokhraneniia pamiatnikov arkhitektury*, pp. 77–78. Moscow, 1974.

——— "Opyt privedeniia kompozitsii Moskvy kontsa XVII v. K idealizirovannoi skheme," *Arkhitekturnoe nasledstvo*, 30 (1982): 13–23.

——— "Sistemy prirechnykh ansamblei Moskvy XVII v.," *Arkhitekturnoe nasledstvo*, 34 (1986): 17–25.

Kudriavtsev, M. P., and T. N. Kudriavtseva. "Landshaft v kompozitsii drevnerusskogo goroda," *Arkhitekturnoe nasledstvo*, 28 (1980): 3–12.

Kudriavtsev, M. P., and G. Ia. Mokeev. "O tipichnom russkom khrame XVII v.," *Arkhitekturnoe nasledstvo*, 29 (1981): 70–9.

Kudriavtseva, T. N. "Kadashevskaia sloboda v Moskve i ee razvitie v knotse XVII–XVIII vvv. (gradostroitel'nyi analiz," *Arkhitekturnoe nasledstvo*, 27 (1979): 38–48.

——— "Struktura i kompozitsionnye osobennosti slobody russkogo goroda XVI–XVII vv.," *Arkhitekturnoe nasledstvo*, 32 (1984): 13–25.

Kudriavtseva, T. P. "K voprosu o 'romanskikh' vliianiiakh vo Vladimiro-Suzdal'skom zodchestve," *Arkhitekturnoe nasledstvo*, 23 (1975): 30–36.

Latham, Ian. *Joseph Maria Olbrich*. New York, 1980.

Latour, Alessandra, ed. *Alexander Rodchenko 1891–1956*. New York, 1987.

Lavrentjev, Alexander. "Alexander Rodchenko's Architectural Language" In *Alexander Rodchenko 1891–1956*, edited by Alessandra Latour, n.p. New York, 1987.

Lazarev, Viktor N. *Mozaiki Sofii Kievskoi*. Moscow, 1960.

——— *Feofan Grek i ego shkola*. Moscow, 1961.

——— *Mikhailovskie mozaiki*. Moscow, 1966.

——— "O rospisi Sofii Novgorodskoi." In *Drevnerusskoe iskusstvo: Khudozhestvennaia kul'ture Novgoroda*, edited by V. N. Lazarev, pp. 7–62. Moscow, 1968.

——— "Kovalevskaia rospis' i problema iuzhnoslavianskikh sviazei v russkoi zhivopisi XIV veka." In *Russkaia srednevekovaia zhivopis'*, edited by V. N. Lazarev, pp. 238–74. Moscow, 1970.

——— *Drevnerusskie mozaiki i freski: XI–XV vv*. Moscow, 1973.

——— *Novgorodian Icon-Painting*. Moscow, 1976.

——— *Vizantiiskoe i drevnerusskoe iskusstvo*. Moscow, 1978.

———, ed. *Drevnerusskoe iskusstvo: XV–nachala XVI vekov*. Moscow, 1963.

——— *Drevnerusskoe iskusstvo: XVII vek*. Moscow, 1964.

——— *Drevnerusskoe iskusstvo: Khudozhestvennaia kul'tura Novgoroda*. Moscow, 1968.

——— *Drevnerusskoe iskusstvo: Khudozhestvennaia kul'tura Pskova*. Moscow, 1968.

——— *Drevnerusskoe iskusstvo. Khudozhestvennaia kul'tura Moskvy i prilezhashchikh k nei kniazhestv. XIV–XVI vv*. Moscow, 1970.

——— *Russkaia srednevekovaia zhivopis'*. Moscow, 1970.

——— *Drevnerusskoe iskusstvo: Khudozhestvennaia kul'tura domongol'skoi Rusi*. Moscow, 1971.

Lebedev, Iu. S., ed. *Konstruktsii i arkhitekturnaia forma v russkom zodchestve XIX–nachala XX vv*. Moscow, 1977.

Lebedev, V., and V. Panov, eds. *Drevnerusskie letopisi*. Moscow–Leningrad, 1936.

Lebedeva, Iu. A. "Andrei Rublev i zhivopis' XV veka." In *Troitse-Sergieva lavra: Khudozhestvennye pamiatniki*, edited by N. N. Voronin and V. V. Kostochkin, pp. 77–93. Moscow, 1968.

Leiboshits, N. "Novye materialy ob A. D. Zakharove." *Arkhitekturnoe nasledstvo*, 4 (1953): 104–7.

622

Leiboshits, N., and V. Piliavskii. "Materialy k istorii planirovki Peterburga v pervoi polovine XIX veka," *Arkhitekturnoe nasledstvo*, 7 (1955): 39–66.

Lepskaia, L. A., and M. Z. Sarkisova. *Ostankinskii dvorets-muzei: Tvorchestvo krepostnykh.* Leningrad, 1982.

Levinson-Lessing, V. F. "Pervoe puteshestvie Petra I za granitsu." In *Kul'tura i iskusstvo petrovskogo vremeni: Publikatsii i issldeovaniia*, edited by G. N. Komelova, pp. 5–36. Leningrad, 1977.

Lidov, A. M. "Ierusalimskii kuvuklii. O proiskhozhdenii lukovichnykh glav." In *Ikonografiia arkhitektury*, edited by A. L. Batalov, pp. 57–68. Moscow, 1990.

Lifshits, L. I. *Monumental'naia zhivopis' Novgoroda XIV–XV vekov.* Moscow, 1987.

Likhachev, Dmitrii S. *Novgorod Velikii: Ocherk istorii kul'tury Novgoroda X–XVII vv.* Moscow, 1959.

——— *Kul'tura Rusi vremeni Andreia Rubleva i Epifaniia Premudrogo (konets XIV–nachalo XV v.).* Moscow–Leningrad, 1962.

——— "Printsip ansamblia v drevnerusskoi estetike." In *Kul'tura drevnei Rusi*, edited by A. L. Mongait, pp. 118–20. Moscow, 1966.

——— *Chelovek v literature drevnei Rusi.* Moscow, 1970.

——— *Poeziia sadov.* Leningrad, 1982.

———, ed. *Vosstanovlenie pamiatnikov kul'tury (Problemy restavratsii).* Moscow, 1981.

Lipatov, A. V., A. I. Rogov, and L. A. Sofronova, eds. *Barokko v slavianskikh kul'turakh.* Moscow, 1982.

Lisaevich, Irina. *Pervyi arkhitektor Peterburga.* Leningrad, 1971.

Lisenko, L. M. "Garmonicheskie postroeniia v arkhitekture tserkvei Kizhskogo pogosta," *Arkhitekturnoe nasledstvo*, 18 (1969): 125–34.

——— *Domeniko Trezini.* Leningrad, 1986.

Lisovskii, V. G. *Andrei Voronikhin.* Leningrad, 1971.

——— *Akademiia khudozhestv.* Leningrad, 1972.

——— "Master shkoly natsional'nogo romantizma," *Stroitel'stvo i arkhitektura Leningrada*, 1975, no. 4: 42–4.

——— *I. A. Fomin.* Leningrad, 1979.

——— "Master Peterburgskogo moderna," *Stroitel'stvo i arkhitektura Leningrada*, 1980, no. 1: 34–8.

——— *Akademiia khudozhestv: Istoriko-iskusstvovedcheskii ocherk.* Leningrad, 1982.

Lisovskii, V. G., and L. A. Iudina. "Zamechatel'nyi zodchii i pedagog," *Stroitel'stvo i arkhitektura Leningrada*, 1979, no. 2: 35–8.

Lissitzky, El. *Russia: Architecture for a World Revolution*, trans. by Eric Dluhosch. Cambridge, Mass., M.I.T. Press, 1970.

Lodder, Christina. "Constructivist Theater as a Laboratory for an Architectural Aesthetic," *Architectural Association Quarterly*, 1979, no. 2: 24–35.

——— *Russian Constructivism.* New Haven, 1983.

Logvin, G. N. *Chernigov, Novgorod-Severskii, Glukhov, Putivl.* Moscow, 1965.

Loktev, V. I. "B. Rastrelli i problemy Barokko v arkhitekture." In *Barokko v slavianskikh kul'turakh*, edited by A. V. Lipatov, A. I. Rogov, and L. A. Sofronova, pp. 299–315. Moscow, 1982.

Lukhmanov, Nikolai V. *Arkhitektura kluba.* Moscow, 1930.

Luk'ianov, N. A. "Moskovskii Vospitatel'nyi dom i problemy russkogo klassitsizma." In *Pamiatnik v kontekste kul'tury*, edited by N. T. Eneeva, pp. 53–62. Moscow, 1991.

Lukomskii, Georgii. "O postroike Novogo Peterburga," *Zodchii*, 1912, no. 52: 519–21.

——— "Novyi Peterburg (Mysli o sovremennom stroitel'stve)," *Apollon*, no. 2 (1913): 25.

——— *Vologda i ee starina.* St. Petersburg, 1914.

——— *Starinnye usad'by Khar'kovskoi gubernii.* Petrograd, 1917.

Lumiste, M. *Kadriorgskii dvorets.* Tallin, 1976.

Luppov, S. P. *Istoriia stroitel'stvo Peterburga v pervoi chetverti XVIII veka.* Moscow, 1957.

McCormick, Thomas. *Charles-Louis Clérisseau and the Genesis of Neoclassicism.* Cambridge, 1990.

Macleod, Robert. *Style and Society: Architectural Ideology in Britain 1835–1914.* London, 1971.

Maiasova, N. A. "K istorii ikonostasa Blagoveshchenskogo sobora Moskovskogo Kremlia." In *Kul'tura drevnei Rusi*, edited by A. L. Mongait, pp. 152–7. Moscow, 1966.

Maikov, P. M. *Ivan Ivanovich Betskoi.* Petersburg, 1904.

Makarevich, G. V., ed. *Pamiatniki arkhitektury Moskvy: Belyi Gorod.* Moscow, 1989.

Makarov, V. "Andrei Bolotov i sadovoe iskusstvo v Rossii XVIII veka," *Sredi kollektsionerov*, 1924, nos. 5–6: 27–32.

Makarov, V., and A. Petrov. *Gatchina.* Leningrad, 1974.

Maksimov, A. A. "Torgovye tsentry v planirovkakh russkikh gorodov vtoroi poloviny XVIII-nachala XIX v." In *Pamiatniki russkoi arkhitektury i monumental'nogo iskusstva*, edited by V. P. Vygolov, pp. 126–39. Moscow, 1980.

Maksimov, P. N. "Tserkov' Nikoly na Lipne bliz Novgoroda," *Arkhitekturnoe nasledstvo*, 2 (1952): 86–104.

——— "Zarubezhnye sviazi v arkhitekture Novgoroda i Pskova XI-nachala XVI vekov," *Arkhitekturnoe nasledstvo*, 12 (1960): 23–44.

——— "Tserkov' Dmitriia Solunskogo v Novgorode," *Arkhitekturnoe nasledstvo*, 14 (1962): 35–46.

——— "K voprosu ob avtorstve Blagoveshchenskogo sobora i Rizpolozhenskoi tserkvi v Moskovskom Kremle," *Arkhitekturnoe nasledstvo*, 16 (1967): 13–18.

——— "O kompozitsionnom masterstve moskobskikh zodchikh nachala XV v.," *Arkhitekturnoe nasledstvo*, 21 (1973): 44–7.

Malia, Martin. "What is the Intelligentsia." In *The Russian Intelligentsia*, edited by Richard Pipes, pp. 1–18. New York, 1961.

Maliakov, L. I., ed. *Dostoprimechatel'nosti Pskovskoi oblasti.* Leningrad, 1987.

Malinovskii, K. V. "Zapiski Iakoba Shtelina o russkoi arkhitekture XVIII veka." In *Problemy sinteza iskusstva i arkhitektury.* Leningrad, 1977.

——— "V granit odelsai Neva: Ob avtorstve pervoi kamennoi naberezhnoi Peterburga," *Stroitel'stvo i arkhitektura Leningrada*, 1981, no. 11: 32–35.

Malins, Edward. *English Landscaping and Literature, 1660–1840.* London, 1966.

Malyshev, I. Zhemchuzhina russkogo zodchestva: Restavratsiia khrama Vasiliia Blazhennogo," *Stroitel'stvo i arkhitektura Moskvy*, 1980, no. 7: 24–6.

Manina, A. I. *Arkhitektory brat'ia Vesniny*. Moscow, 1983.

Mashkov, I. P. *Putevoditel' po Moskve*. Moscow, 1913.

Masalina, N. V. "Tserkov' v Abramtseve." In *Iz istorii russkogo iskusstva vtoroi poloviny XIX–nachala XX veka*, edited
by E. A. Borisova, pp. 47–58. Moscow, 1978.

Maslenitsyn, Stanislav I. *Murom*. Moscow, 1971.

Matheu, Gervase. *Byzantine Aesthetics*. New York, 1964.

Mazzi, Giuliana. "Indagini archivistiche per Alvise Lamberti da Montagnana," *Arte Lombarda*, 44/45 (1976): 96–
101.

Medvedkova, O. A. "Tsaritsynskaia psevdogotika V. I.
Bazhenova: opyt interpretatsii." In *Ikonografiia arkhitektury*, edited by A. L. Batalov, pp. 153–73. Moscow, 1990.

——— "Tvorchestvo Voronikhina i romanticheskie tendentsii v nachale XIX v." In *Problemy istorii arkhitektury*,
edited by A. A. Voronov, Part II, pp. 84–6. Moscow, 1990.

Meyendorff, John. *Byzantium and the Rise of Russia*. Cambridge, 1981.

Mezentsev, Volodymyr I. "The Masonry Churches of Medieval Chernihiv," *Harvard Ukrainian Studies*, XI, nos. 3–
4 (1987): 365–83.

Mikhailov, A. I. *Bazhenov*. Moscow, 1951.

——— "K istorii proektirovaniia i stroitel'stva kolokol'ni
Troitse-Sergievoi lavry," *Arkhitekturnoe nasledstvo*, 1
(1951): 67–77.

——— "Tvorchestvo Rastrelli i traditsii russkoi arkhitektury," *Arkhitekturnoe nasledstvo*, 1 (1951): 62–6.

——— *Arkhitektor D. V. Ukhtomskii i ego shkola*. Moscow,
1954.

Mikhailova, M. B. "K voprosu o meste ansamblia Kazanskogo sobora v evropeiskoi arkhitekture," *Arkhitekturnoe
nasledstvo*, 24 (1976): 41–50.

——— "Tipy sooruzhenii antichnosti v arkhitekture russkogo klassitsizma," *Arkhitekturnoe nasledstvo*, 26 (1978):
4–5.

——— "Printsip zavisimosti ot obraztsa pri vozvedenii
monumental'nykh zdanii klassitsizma," *Arkhitekturnoe
nasledstvo*, 31 (1983): 3–11.

Mil'chik, M. I., and Iu. S. Ushakov. *Dereviannaia arkhitektura
russkogo severa*. Leningrad, 1981.

Miliutin, Nikolai. *Problema stroitel'stva sotsialisticheskikh gorodov: Osnovnye voprosy ratsional'noi planirovki i stroitel'stva
naselennykh mest SSSR*. Moscow, 1930.

——— "Vazhneishie zadachi sovremennogo etapa sovetskoi arkhitektury," *Sovetskaia arkhitektura*, 1932, nos. 2–3:
3–9.

——— *Sotsgorod: The Problem of Building Socialist Cities*, trans.
by Arthur Sprague, with notes and introduction by
George Collins and William Alex. Cambridge, Mass.:
M.I.T. Press, 1974.

Mirsky, D. S. *A History of Russian Literature*. New York, 1960.

Mokeev, G. Ia. "Stolichnyi tsentr Pskova kontsa XV v.,"
Arkhitekturnoe nasledstvo, 24 (1976): 60–71.

——— "Mnogoglavye khramy Drevnei Rusi," *Arkhitekturnoe nasledstvo*, 26 (1978): 41–52.

———, "Sistemnye elementy planirovki drevnei Moskvy,"
Arkhitekturnoe nasledstvo, 30 (1982): 5–12.

Mongait, A. L. *Archeology in the U.S.S.R.* Baltimore, 1961.

———, ed. *Kul'tura drevnei Rusi*. Moscow, 1966.

Morenets, N. "Novye materialy o V. I. Bazhenove," *Arkhitekturnoe nasledstvo*, 1 (1951): 94–104.

Moskalenko, E. "Shpil' Admiralteistva i ego konstruktsiia,"
Arkhitekturnoe nasledstvo, 4 (1953): 177–88.

*Moskva zlatoglavaia: Pamiatniki religioznogo zodchestva Moskvy
v proshlom i nastoiashchem*. Moscow–Paris, 1979.

Mukařovský, Jan. "On the Problem of Functions in Architecture." In *Structure, Sign, and Function: Selected Essays
by Jan Mukarovsky*, translated and edited by John Burbank
and Peter Steiner, pp. 236–50. New Haven, 1978.

Münter, Georg. *Idealstädte: Ihre Geschichte vom 15.–17. Jahrhundert*. Berlin, 1957.

Murashkov, K. I., ed. *Vesniny: Katalog-putevoditel' po fondam
muzeia*. Moscow, 1981.

Murashova, N. V. "Avtorstvo ustanovleno," *Stroitel'stvo i
arkhitektura Leningrada*, 1978, no. 2: 42–5.

Nash, Steven A., and Jörn Merkert, eds. *Naum Gabo: Sixty
Years of Constructivism*. Munich, 1985.

Nashchokina, M. V. "Venskie motivy v arkhitekture
Moskvy nachala XX veka." In *Voprosy istorii arkhitektury*,
edited by A. A. Voronov, pp. 94–109. Moscow, 1990.

Nechaev, V. "Rastrelli i Delamot. Iz istorii postroiki Gostinnogo dvora." In *Starina i iskusstvo: Sbornik statei*, pp. 3–
21. Leningrad, 1928.

Nekrasov, A. I. *Vizantiiskoe i russkoe iskusstvo*. Moscow, 1924.

——— *Barokko v Rossii*. Moscow, 1926.

——— *Vozniknovenie moskovskogo iskusstva*. Moscow, 1929.

——— *Ocherki po istorii drevnerusskogo zodchestva XI–XVII
vekov*. Moscow, 1936.

Nekrasova, M. A. "Novoe v sinetze zhivopisi i arkhitektury
XVII veka (rospis' tserkvi Il'i Proroka v Iaroslavle)." In
Drevnerusskoe iskusstvo: XVII vek, edited by V. N. Lazarev,
pp. 89–109. Moscow, 1964.

Neverov, O. Ia. "Pamiatniki antichnogo iskusstva v Rossii
petrovskogo vremeni." In *Kul'tura i iskusstvo petrovskogo
vremeni: Publikatsii i issledovaniia*, edited by G. N. Komelova, pp. 37–53. Leningrad, 1977.

Nevostrueva, L. "Ansambl' Rinal'di v gorode Lomonosove," *Arkhitekturnoe nasledstvo*, 7 (1955): 109–24.

Nikolaev, Evgenii. *Klassicheskaia Moskva*. Moscow, 1975.

Nikolaeva, T. I. *Viktor Shreter*. Leningrad, 1991.

Nikolaeva, T. V. "Nekotorye problemy rannemoskovskogo
zodchestva," *Arkhitekturnoe nasledstvo*, 12 (1960): 45–62.

——— *Drevnii Zvenigorod*. Moscow, 1978.

Nikulina, N. I. *Nikolai L'vov*. Leningrad, 1971.

Nikulina, N. I., and N. G. Efimova. *Karl Ivanovich Rossi.
1775–1849. Katalog*. Leningrad, 1975.

Nosov, Nikolai, E., ed. *Istoricheskie sviazi Skandinavii i Rossii.
IX–XX vv.* Leningrad, 1970.

Novikov, S. E. *Uglich: Pamiatniki arkhitektury i iskusstva*. Moscow, 1988.

Odoevskii, V. F. *Povesti i rasskazy*. Moscow, 1959.

Ognev, V. A. "O pozakomarnykh pokrytiiakh," *Arkhitekturnoe nasledstvo*, 10 (1958): 43–58.

Okh, A., and M. Fekhner. "Novye issledovaniia po dereviannym zhilym domam nachala XIX veka v Moskve." *Arkhitekturnoe nasledstvo*, 5 (1955): 115–40.

Ol', Andrei. *F. Lidval.* S. Petersburg, 1914.

Ol', G. A. *Aleksandr Briullov.* Leningrad, 1983.

Oltarzhevskii, Viacheslav K. *Stroitel'stvo vysotnykh zdanii v Moskve.* Moscow, 1953.

Opolovnikov, A. V. "Lazarevskaia tserkov' Muromskogo monastyria," *Arkhitekturnoe nasledstvo*, 18 (1969): 106–11.

——— *Russkie Sever.* Moscow, 1977.

——— *Russkoe dereviannoe zodchestvo.* Moscow, 1983.

Opolovnikov, A., and G. Ostrovskii. *Rus' dereviannaia: Obrazy russkogo dereviannogo zodchestva.* Moscow, 1981.

Opolovnikov, Alexander, and Yelena Opolovnikova. *The Wooden Architecture of Russia*, edited by David Buxton. New York, 1989.

Orlov, S. N. "K topografii Novgoroda X–XVI vv." In *Novgorod: k 1100-letiiu goroda*, edited by M. N. Tikhomirov, pp. 264–85. Moscow, 1964.

Oshchepkov, G. D. *Arkhitektor Tomon. Materialy k izucheniiu tvorchestva.* Moscow, 1950.

——— *Zdanie tsentral'nogo voenno-morskogo muzeia (b. Birzha) v Leningrade.* Leningrad, 1957.

Ostroumov, V. P. *Kazan': Ocherki po istorii goroda i ego arkhitektury.* Kazan, 1978.

Ovchinnikova, Ekaterina S. *Tserkov' Troitsy v Nikitnikakh.* Moscow, 1970.

Ovsiannikov, Iurii M. *Novodevichii monastyr'.* Moscow, 1968.

——— "Novye materialy o zhizni i tvorchestve F.-B. Rastrelli, *Sovetskoe iskusstvoznanie '79*, no. 1 (Moscow, 1980): 340–51.

——— *Franchesko Bartolomeo Rastrelli.* Leningrad, 1982.

——— *Dominiko Trezzini.* Leningrad, 1987.

Ovsiannikova, Elena. "Svobodnye ili gosudarstvennye," *Dekorativnoe iskusstvo SSSR*, 1988, no. 10: 23–7.

Owen, Thomas. *Capitalism and Politics in Russia: A Social History of the Moscow Merchants, 1855–1905.* New York, 1981.

Ozhegov, S. S. *Tipovoe i povtornoe stroitel'stvo v Rossii v XVIII–XIX vekakh.* Moscow, 1984.

Palentreer, S. N. *Usad'ba Voronovo.* Moscow, 1960.

Papernyi, Vladimir. *Kul'tura Dva.* Ann Arbor, 1985.

Parkins, Maurice. *City Planning in Soviet Russia.* Chicago, 1953.

Pattaro, Sandra Tugnoli. "Le opere bolognesi de Aristotele Fioravanti architetto e ingegnere del secolo quindicesimo," *Arte Lombarda*, 44/45 (1976): 35–70.

Pavlenko, N. I. *Aleksandr Danilovich Menshikov.* Moscow, 1983.

Pelikan, Jaroslav. *The Spirit of Eastern Christendom (600–1700).* Chicago, 1974.

Petrov, A[natolii] N. "Palaty Kikina," *Arkhitekturnoe nasledstvo*, 4 (1953): 141–7.

——— "S. I. Chevakinskii i peterburgskaia arkhitektura serediny XVIII veka." In *Russkaia arkhitektura pervoi poloviny XVIII v.*, edited by I. E. Grabar, pp. 363–70. Moscow, 1954.

——— "Palaty fel'dmarshala B. P. Sheremeteva i F. M.

Apraksina v Moskve," *Arkhitekturnoe nasledstvo*, 6 (1956): 138–46.

——— "Peterburgskii zhiloi dom 30–40-kh godov XVIII stoletiia." In *Ezhegodnik Instituta istorii iskusstv 1960. Zhivopis' i arkhitektura*, pp. 132–57. Moscow, 1961.

——— *Pushkin. Dvortsy i parki.* Leningrad, 1969.

——— *Gorod Pushkin. Dvortsy i parki.* Leningrad, 1977.

Petrov, A. N., E. A. Borisova, A. P. Naumenko, and A. V. Povelikhina. *Pamiatniki arkhitektury Leningrada.* Leningrad, 1972.

Petrov, A. N., E. N. Petrova, A. G. Raskin, N. I. Arkhipov, A. F. Krasheninnikov, and N. D. Kremshevskaia. *Pamiatniki arkhitektury prigorodov Leningrada.* Leningrad, 1983.

Petrova, T. A. *Andrei Shtakenshneider.* Leningrad, 1978.

Pevsner, Nikolaus. *An Outline of European Architecture.* Harmondsworth, 1963.

Piliavskii, V. "Ivan Kuz'mich Korobov," *Arkhitekturnoe nasledstvo*, 4 (1953): 41–62.

——— *Stasov – Arkhitektor.* Leningrad, 1963.

——— *Zodchii Vasilii Petrovich Stasov (1769–1848).* Leningrad, 1970.

——— "Proekty triumfal'nykh sooruzhenii D. Kvarengi v Rossii," *Arkhitekturnoe nasledstvo*, 28 (1980): 71–9.

——— *D. Kvarengi: Arkhitektor. Khudozhnik.* Leningrad, 1981.

Piliavskii V. I., and N. Ia. Leiboshits. *Zodchii Zakharov.* Leningrad, 1963.

Piliavskii V. I., and N. Ia. Gorshkova. *Russkaia arkhitektura XI–nachala XX v. (Ukazatel' izbrannoi literatury na russkom iazyke za 1811–1975 gg.).* Leningrad, 1978.

Piliavskii V. I., and V. F. Levinson-Lessing, eds. *Ermitazh: Istoriia i arkhitektura zdaniia.* Leningrad, 1974.

Piliavskii, V. I., A. A. Tits, and Iu. S. Ushakov. *Istoriia russkoi arkhitektury.* Leningrad, 1984.

Pipes, Richard, ed. *The Russian Intelligentsia.* New York, 1961.

——— *Karamzin's Memoir on Ancient and Modern Russia: A Translation and Analysis.* New York, 1966.

Plugin, V. *Freski Dmitrievskogo sobora.* Leningrad, 1974.

Pluzhnikov, V. I. "Sootnoshenie ob"emnykh form v russkom kul'tovom zodchestve nachala XVIII veka." In *Russkoe iskusstvo pervoi chetverti XVIII veka*, edited by T. V. Alekseeva, pp. 81–108. Moscow, 1974.

——— "Rasprostranenie zapadnogo dekora v petrovskom zodchestve." In *Drevnerusskoe iskusstvo: Zarubezhnye sviazi*, edited by G. V. Popov, pp. 362–70. Moscow, 1975.

——— "Organizatsiia fasada v arkhitekture russkogo barokko." In *Russkoe iskusstvo barokko: Materialy i issledovaniia*, edited by T. V. Alekseeva, pp. 88–127. Moscow, 1977.

Pod"iapol'skaia, E. N. *Pamiatniki arkhitektury moskovskoi oblasti*, 2 vols. Moscow, 1975.

Pod"iapol'skii, S. S. "Venetsianskie istoki arkhitektury moskovskogo Arkhangel'skogo sobora." In *Drevne-russkoe iskusstvo: Zarubezhnye sviazi*, edited by G. V. Popov, pp. 252–79. Moscow, 1975.

——— "Arkhitektor Petrok Malyi." In *Pamiatniki russkoi arkhitektury i monumental'nogo iskusstva: Stil', atributsii, da-*

tirovki, edited by V. P. Vygolov, pp. 34–50. Moscow, 1983.

——— "Novshestva v tekhnike moskovskogo kamennogo stroitel'stva kontsa XV–nachala XVI v." In *Problemy istorii arkhitektury*, edited by A. A. Voronov, N. A. Smolina, A. Ia. Flier, and Iu. E. Revzina, part 2, pp. 141–5. Moscow, 1990.

——— "Ital'ianskie stroitel'nye mastera v Rossii v kontse XV–nachala XVI veka po dannym pis'mennykh istochnikov (opyt sostavleniia slovaria)." In *Restavratsiia i arkhitekturnaia arkheologiia. Novye materialy i issledovaniia*, edited by A. L. Batalov and I. A. Bondarenko, pp. 218–33. Moscow, 1991.

Podkliuchnikov, V. *Tri pamiatnika XVII stoletiia: Tserkov' v Filiakh, Tserkov' v Uborakh, Tserkov' v Troitskom-Lykove*. Moscow, 1945.

Podobedova, Olga I., ed. *Drevnerusskoe iskusstvo: Problemy i atributsii*. Moscow, 1977.

——— *Drevnerusskoe iskusstvo: Monumental'naia zhivopis' XI–XVII vv*. Moscow, 1980.

Podol'skii, P. "Petrovskii dvorets na Iauze," *Arkhitekturnoe nasledstvo*, 1 (1951): 14–55.

——— "Ivan Korobov." *Sovetskaia arkhitektura*, 3 (1952): 105–16.

Pokrovskaia, Zinaida K. *Arkhitektor O. I. Bove (1784–1834)*. Moscow, 1964.

Polenova, Natalia. *Abramtsevo: vospominaniia*. Moscow, 1922.

Polnyi svod russkikh letopisei.

Popadiuk, S. S. "Arkhitekturnye formy 'kholodnykh' khramov 'iaroslavskoi shkoly." In *Pamiatniki russkoi arkhitektury i monumental'nogo iskusstva: Stil', atributsii, datirovki*, edited by V. P. Vygolov et al., pp. 64–91. Moscow, 1983.

Popov, G. *Mariinskaia bol'nitsa dlia bednykh*. St. Petersburg, 1905.

Popov, G. V., ed. *Drevnerusskoe iskusstvo: Zarubezhnye sviazi*. Moscow, 1975.

Poppe, Andrzej. "The Political Background to the Baptism of Rus': Byzantine-Russian Relations between 986–89," *Dumbarton Oaks Papers*, 30 (1976): 197–244.

——— "The Building of the Church of St. Sophia in Kiev," *Journal of Medieval History*, 7 (1981): 15–66.

——— *The Rise of Christian Russia*. London, 1982.

Posokhin, M. V., and D. K. Diubek. *Eksperimental'nyi zhiloi raion Chertanovo-Severnoe*, Znanie (architectural series), 1976, no. 10.

Preobrazhenskii, M. *Pamiatniki drevnerusskogo zodchestva v predelakh Kaluzhskoi gubernii*. St. Petersburg, 1891.

Proskuriakova, T. S. "Planirovochnye kompozitsii gorodov-krepostei Sibiri (vtoroi poloviny XVII–60-e gg. XVIII v.)," *Arkhitekturnoe nasledstvo*, 25 (1976): 57–71.

——— "O reguliarnosti v russkom gradostroitel'stve XVII–XVIII vv.," *Arkhitekturnoe nasledstvo*, 28 (1980): 37–46.

Ptashitskii, S. L. "Peterburg v 1720 godu. Zapiski poliaka-ochevidtsa," *Russkaia starina*, 25 (1879): 267–73.

Punin, A. L. "Idei ratsionalizma v russkoi arkhitekture vtoroi poloviny XIX veka," in *Arkhitektura SSSR*, 1962, no. 11: 55–8.

——— "Pochemu soshel so stseny klassitsizm?," *Stroitel'stvo i arkhitektura Leningrada*, 1978, no. 7: 39–43.

——— *Arkhitketurnye pamiatniki Peterburga: vtoraia polovina XIX veka*. Leningrad, 1981.

——— *Arkhitektura Peterburga serediny XIX veka*. Leningrad, 1990.

Purishev, Ivan P. *Pereslavl'-Zalesskii*. Moscow, 1970.

Quarenghi, Giacomo. *Edifices construits à Saint Petersbourg d'après les plans du Chevalier de Quarenghi et sous sa direction*. Petersburg, 1810.

Raam, Villem. *Arkhitekturnye pamiatniki Estonii*. Leningrad, 1974.

Rabba, Joel. *The Moscow Kremlin: Mirror of the Newborn Muscovite State*. Tel Aviv, 1975.

Rabinovich, G. "Arkhitekturnyi ansambl' Pskovo-Pecherskogo monastyria," *Arkhitekturnoe nasledstvo*, 6 (1956): 57–86.

Rae, Isobel. *Charles Cameron: Architect to the Court of Russia*. London, 1971.

Raeff, Marc. *Peter the Great: Reformer or Revolutionary*. Lexington, Mass., 1963.

Rakova, Magdalina. *Russkaia istoricheskaia zhivopis' serediny deviatnadtsatogo veka*. Moscow, 1979.

Ramelli, A. S. "Il Cremlino di Mosca, esempio di architettura militare," *Arte Lombarda*, 44/45 (1976): 130–8.

Raninskii, Iu. "Ansambl i gorod," *Arkhitektura i stroitel'stvo Moskvy*, 1976, no. 3: 34.

Ranum, O., ed. *National Consciousness, History, and Political Culture in Early-Modern Europe*. Baltimore, 1975.

Rappaport, Alexander. G. "Ob intellektual'nom suverenitete arkhitektury." In *Arkhitektura i kul'tura*, edited by I. A. Azizian, G. I. Lebedeva, and E. L. Beliaeva, Part 1, pp. 43–7. Moscow, 1990.

Rappoport, Pavel A. "Zodchii Borisa Godunova." In *Kul'tura drevnei Rusi*, edited by A. L. Mongait, pp. 215–21. Moscow, 1966.

——— *Russkaia arkhitektura X–XIII vv.*, Arkheologiia SSSR: Svod arkheologicheskikh istochnikov, Vol. E1–47. Leningrad, 1982.

——— *Zodchestvo drevnei Rusi*. Leningrad, 1986.

Raskin, Abram. *Gorod Lomonosov: Dvortsovo-parkovye ansambli XVIII veka*. Leningrad, 1979.

——— *Petrodvorets (Petergof)*. Leningrad, 1979.

Rempel', L. I. "K kharakteristike arkhitektury fashistkoi Italii," *Akademiia arkhitektury*, 2 (1935): 50–61.

Retkovskaia, L. S. *Novodevichii monastyr'*. Moscow, 1956.

Revsin, G. I. "Renessansnye motivy v arkhitekture neoklassitsizma nachala XX veka." In *Ikonografiia arkhitektury*, edited by A. L. Batalov, pp. 187–211. Moscow, 1990.

——— "Sad moderna i neoklassitsizm." In *Voprosy istorii arkhitektury*, edited by A. A. Voronov, pp. 126–38. Moscow, 1990.

Revzina, Iu. E. "Nekotorye ikonograficheskie istochniki tsentricheskikh khramov XV veka v Italii." In *Ikonografiia arkhitektury*, edited by A. L. Batalov, pp. 69–101. Moscow, 1990.

Rezvin, V. "Dom arkhitektora K. S. Mel'nikova," *Arkhitektura SSSR*, 1984, no. 4: 84–5.

Riasanovsky, Nicholas V. *A History of Russia*. New York, 1963.

—— *Nicholas I and Official Nationality in Russia, 1825–1855*. Berkeley, 1967.

—— *A Parting of Ways: Government and the Educated Public in Russia 1801–1855*. Oxford, 1976.

Rice, Tamara Talbot. "Charles Cameron, Architect to the Imperial Russian Court." In *Charles Cameron*, pp. 8–10. London, 1967.

Robinson, John Martin. "A Dazzling Adventurer: Charles Cameron – the Lost Early Years," *Apollo* (January 1992), pp. 31–5.

Romaniuk, Sergei. "Vil'iam Val'kot (1874–1943)," *Stroitel'stvo i arkhitektura Moskvy*, 1986, no. 6: 24–7.

Roosevelt, Priscilla R. "Tatiana's Garden: Noble Sensibilities and Estate Park Design in the Romantic Era," *Slavic Review*, 49 (1990): 335–49.

Rosenblum, R. *Transformations in Late Eighteenth Century Art*. Princeton, 1967.

Rotach, A. L., and O. A. Chekanova. *Monferran*. Leningrad, 1979.

Ruble, Blair A. "From Palace Square to Moscow Square: St. Petersburg's Century-Long Retreat from Public Space." In *Reshaping Russian Architecture: Western Technology, Utopian Dreams*, edited by William C. Brumfield, pp. 10–42. New York: Cambridge University Press, 1991.

—— "Moscow's Revolutionary Architecture and its Aftermath: A Critical Guide." In *Reshaping Russian Architecture: Western Technology, Utopian Dreams*, edited by William C. Brumfield, pp. 111–44. New York: Cambridge University Press, 1991.

Rudnev, Lev. "O formalizme i klassike," *Arkhitektura SSSR*, no. 11 (1954): 30–2.

Rybina, E. A. *Inozemnye dvory v Novgorode XII–XVII vv.* Moscow, 1986.

Rzhekhina, O. I, R. N. Blashkevich, and R. G. Burova, *A. K. Burov*. Moscow, 1984.

Samoilova, N. "Arkhitektor Viktor Aleksandrovich Vesnin," *Arkhitektura SSSR*, 1982, no. 4: 32–40.

Savarenskaia, T. F., D. O. Shvidkovskii, and F. A. Petrov. *Istoriia gradostroitel'nogo iskusstva. Pozdnii feodalizm i kapitalizm*. Moscow, 1989.

Schmidt, Albert. "William Hastie, Scottish Planner of Russian Cities," *Proceedings of the American Philosophical Society*, 114 (1970): 226–43.

—— "The Restoration of Moscow after 1812," *Slavic Review* 40 (1981): 37–48.

—— *The Architecture and Planning of Classical Moscow: A Cultural History*. Philadelphia, 1989.

Sedov, Aleksei P. *Iaropolets*. Moscow, 1980.

Semenova, L. N. "Uchastie shvedskikh masterovykh v stroitel'stve Peterburga (pervaia chetvert' XVIII v.)." In *Istoricheskie sviazi Skandinavii i Rossii. IX–XX vv.*, edited by N. E. Nosov, pp. 269–81. Leningrad, 1970.

Senkevitch, Anatole. *Soviet Architecture 1917–1962: A Bibliographical Guide to Source Material*. Charlottesville, Va., 1974.

Sergeev, S. V. "Pamiatnik v khudozhestvennom kontekste: vospriiatie usad'by Ekateriny II v Tsaritsyno v russkoi kul'ture pervoi treti XIX v." In *Problemy istorii arkhitektury*, edited by A. A. Voronov, Part II, pp. 48–53. Moscow, 1990.

Sergeeva-Kozina, T. "Kolomenskii kreml'," *Arkhitekturnoe nasledstvo*, 2 (1952): 133–63.

Serra, Joselita Raspi, ed. *Paestum and the Doric Revival 1750–1830*. Florence, 1986.

Shamurin, Iurii. *Podmoskovnyia*. Moscow, 1912.

Shanin, Teodor. *The Roots of Otherness: Russia's Turn of the Century*, 2 vols. New Haven, 1986.

Sharov, S. A. "O zavershenii Spaso-Preobrazhenskogo sobora Solovetskogo monastyria," *Arkhitekturnoe nasledstvo*, 34 (1986): 224–9.

Shaw, D. J. B. "Southern Frontiers of Muscovy, 1550–1700." In *Studies in Russian Historical Geography*, edited by J. H. Bater and R. A. French, Vol. 1, pp. 117–42. London, 1983.

Shchenkov, A. S. "Struktura russkikh gorodov XVI–XVII vv. i ikh esteticheskoe vospriiatie," *Arkhitekturnoe nasledstvo*, 32 (1984): 3–12.

Shchenkova, O. P. "Kitai-gorod v strukture tsentra Moskvy XVII v," *Arkhitekturnoe nasledstvo*, 29 (1981): 56–62.

—— "Kitai-gorod – torgovyi tsentr Moskvy v kontse XVIII–pervoi polovine XIX v.," *Arkhitekturnoe nasledstvo*, 33 (1985): 31–9.

—— "Arkhitektura Kitai-goroda Moskvy perioda klasitsizma," *Arkhitekturnoe nasledstvo*, 36 (1988): 175–86.

Shchukina, E. P. "Metodika vosstanovleniie sadov i parkov XVIII–XIX vv." In *Teoriia i praktika restavratsionnykh rabot*, pp. 30–8. Moscow, 1972.

—— " 'Natural'nyi sad' russkoi usad'by v knotse XVIIIv." In *Russkoe iskusstvo XVIII v.: Materialy i issledovaniia*, edited by T. V. Alekseeva, pp. 109–17. Moscow, 1973.

Sheliapina, N. S. "K istorii izucheniia Uspenskogo sobora moskovskogo Kremlia," *Sovetskaia arkheologiia*, 1972, no. 1: 200–14.

Shennikov, A. A. "Krest"ianskie usad'by XVI–XVII vv. (Verknee Povolzh'e, severo-zapadnye i severnaia chasti Evropeiskoi Rossii)," *Arkhitekturnoe nasledstvo*, 15 (1963): 88–101.

Shevelov, I. Sh. *Geometricheskaia garmoniia*. Kostroma, 1963.

—— "Proportsii i kompozitsiia Uspenskoi Eletskoi tserkvi v Chernigove," *Arkhitekturnoe nasledstvo*, 19 (1972): 32–42.

Shilkov, V. F. "Chetyre risunka Petra I po planirovke Petergofa," *Arkhitekturnoe nasledstvo*, 4 (1953): 35–40.

—— "Proekty planirovki Peterburga 1737–1740 godov," *Arkhitekturnoe nasledstvo*, 4 (1953): 7–13.

—— "Raboty A. V. Kvasova i I. E. Starova po planirovke russkikh gorodov," *Arkhitekturnoe nasledstvo*, 4 (1953): 30–4.

—— "Arkhitektory-inostrantsy pri Petre I." In *Russkaia arkhitektura pervoi poloviny XVIII v.*, edited by I. E. Grabar, pp. 118–67. Moscow, 1954.

—— "Russkii perevod Vitruviia nachala XVIII veka," *Arkhitekturnoe nasledstvo*, 7 (1955): 89–92.

—— "Dve raboty arkhitektora Kiaveri v Rossii," *Arkhitekturnoe nasledstvo*, 9 (1959): 61–4.

—— "Kaskad 'Shakhmatnaia gora' i 'Rimskie' fontany v

Petrodvortse," *Arkhitekturnoe nasledstvo,* 9 (1959): 176–80.

Shil'nikovskaia, V. P. *Velikii Ustiug.* Moscow, 1973.

Shkvarnikov, V. A. *Ocherk istorii planirovki i zastroiki russkikh gorodov.* Moscow, 1954.

Shmidt, I. M. "Arkhitekturno-skul'pturnyi kompleks Kazanskogo sobora i ego znachenie." In *Russkoe iskusstvo vtoroi poloviny XVIII–pervoi poloviny XIX v.,* edited by T. V. Alekseeva, pp. 18–37. Moscow, 1979.

———, ed. *Voprosy sovetskogo izobrazitel'nogo iskusstva i arkhitektury.* Moscow, 1976.

Shreter, Viktor. "K istorii S-Peterburgskogo Obshchestva Arkhitektorov," *Zodchii,* 1984, no. 5: 35–7.

Shteiman, G. A. "Besstolpnye pokrytiia v arkhitekture XVI–XVII vekov," *Arkhitekturnoe nasledstvo,* 14 (1962): 47–62.

——— "Konstruktivnye priemy resheniia vertikal'nykh sooruzhenii v kamennom zodchestve XVI–XVII vekov," *Arkhitekturnoe nasledstvo,* 15 (1963): 79–87.

——— "Osobennosti konstruktsi russkikh kamennykh sooruzhenii XVI–XVII vv.," *Arkhitekturnoe nasledstvo,* 20 (1972): 39–49.

Shtender, Grigorii M. "Vosstanovlenie Nereditsy." In *Novgorodskii istoricheskii sbornik,* pp. 169–205. Novgorod, 1962.

——— "Arkhitektura domongol'skogo perioda." In *Novgorod: k 1100-letiiu goroda,* edited by M. N. Tikhomirov, pp. 186–9. Moscow, 1964.

——— "Restavratsiia pamiatnikov novgorodskogo zodchestva." In *Vosstanovlenie pamiatnikov kul'tury (Problemy restavratsii),* edited by D. S. Likhachev, pp. 43–72. Moscow, 1981.

Shuiskii, V. K. *Vinchentso Brenna.* Leningrad, 1986.

——— *Andreian Zakharov.* Leningrad, 1989.

Shuliak, L. M. "Arkhitektura kontsa XIII–XV v." In *Novgorod: k 1100-letiiu goroda,* edited by M. N. Tikhomirov, pp. 214–44. Moscow, 1964.

Shurygin, Ia. I. *Kazanskii sobor.* Leningrad, 1987.

Shvidkovskii, Dmitrii O. "K voprosu rekonstruktsii ansamblia Tsarskogo sela Ch. Kameronom," *Arkhitekturnoe nasledstvo,* 33 (1985): 62–8.

——— "The Empress and the Architect," *Country Life* (November 16, 1989): 90–2.

——— "Prosvetitel'skaia kontseptsiia sredy v russkikh dvortsovo-parkovykh ansambliakh vtoroi poloviny XVIII veka." In *Vek prosveshcheniia: Rossiia i Frantsiia,* edited by I. E. Danilova, pp. 185–99. Moscow, 1989.

——— "K ikonografii sadovo-parkovykh ansamblei russkogo Prosveshcheniia." In *Ikonografiia arkhitektury,* edited by A. L. Batalov, pp. 174–86. Moscow, 1990.

——— "K polemike 1910-kh gg. ob atributsii dvortsa Razumovskikh v Baturine." In *Restavratsiia i arkhitekturnaia arkheologiia. Novye materialy i issledovaniia,* edited by A. L. Batalov and I. A. Bondarenko, pp. 234–9. Moscow, 1991.

——— "Architect to Three Emperors: Adam Menelas in Russia," *Apollo* (January 1992), pp. 37–41.

Shvidkovsky, Oleg A., ed. *Building in the USSR, 1917–1932.* London, 1971.

——— *Sokhranenie arkhitekturnykh pamiatnikov moskovskogo Kremlia.* Moscow, 1977.

Sizov, E. S. "Novye materialy po Arkhangel'skomu soboru moskovskogo kremlia. Kogda byl postroen Arkhangel'skii sobor?," *Arkhitekturnoe nasledstvo,* 15 (1963): 176–7.

Skrynnikov, Ruslan. *Boris Godunov.* Moscow, 1978.

——— *The Time of Troubles: Russia in Crisis, 1604–1618,* translated by Hugh Graham. Gulf Breeze, Fla. 1988.

Skvortsov, A. I. *Russkaia narodnaia propil'naia rez'ba.* Leningrad, 1984.

Slavina, T. A. *Vladimir Shchuko.* Leningrad, 1978.

——— *Issledovateli russkogo zodchestva: Russkaia istoriko-arkhitekturnaia nauka XVIII–nachala XX veka.* Leningrad, 1983.

——— *Konstantin Ton.* Leningrad, 1989.

Smirnova, E. I., A. A. Goncharova, and G. A. Markova. *Gosudarstvennaia oruzheinaia palata moskovskogo kremlia.* Moscow, 1969.

Smurova, N. A. "Arkhitekturno-stroitel'nye dostizheniia Vserossiiskoi vystavki 1896 g. i ee rol' v razvitii otechestvennoi arkhitektury." In *Problemy istorii sovetskoi arkhitektury,* vol. 2, pp. 14–19. Moscow, 1976.

——— "Inzhenernye sooruzheniia i ikh vliianie na razvitie russkoi khudozhestvennoi kultury" (with particular emphasis on the work of Vladimir Shukhov). In *Konstruktsii i arkhitekturnaia forma v russkom zodchestve XIX–nachala XX vv.,* edited by Iu. S. Lebedev, pp. 60–93. Moscow, 1977.

Snegirev, V. L. *Pamiatnik arkhitektury khram Vasiliia Blazhennogo.* Moscow, 1953.

——— *Zodchii Bazhenov.* Moscow, 1962.

Sobolev, N. "Proekt rekonstruktsii pamiatnika arkhitektury-khrama Vasiliia Blazhennogo v Moskve," *Arkhitektura SSSR,* 1977, no. 2: 42–8.

Soboleva, L. "Issledovatel'skie i restavratsionnye raboty po tserkvi preobrazheniia v usad'be Viazëmy." In *Teoriia i praktika restavratsionnykh rabot,* pp. 84–98. Moscow, 1972.

Soboleva, M. N. "Stenopis' Spaso-Preobrazhenskogo sobora Mirozhskogo monastyria v Pskove." In *Drevnerusskoe iskusstvo: Khudozhestvennaia kul'tura Pskova,* edited by V. N. Lazarev, pp. 39–42. Moscow, 1968.

Sollogub, Vladimir A. *Tarantas.* Petersburg, 1845.

Solosina, G. I. *Gorod Lomonosov (Oranienbaum).* Moscow, 1954.

Soshina, N. "Krutitskii teremok v Moskve," *Arkhitekturnoe nasledstvo,* 6 (1956): 136–7.

Spegal'skii, Iu. P. "Tserkov' Vasiliia na Gorke v Pskove," *Sovetskaia arkheologiia,* 1970, no. 2: 252–5.

——— "K voprosu o vzaimovliianii dereviannogo i kamennogo zodchestva v Drevnei Rusi," *Arkhitekturnoe nasledstvo,* 19 (1972): 66–75.

——— *Pskov: Khudozhestvennye pamiatniki.* Leningrad, 1972.

Starr, S. Frederick. "The Revival and Schism of Urban Planning in Twentieth-Century Russia." In *The City in Russian History,* edited by Michael Hamm, pp. 222–42. Lexington, Ky., 1976.

——— *Konstantin Melnikov: Solo Architect in a Mass Society.* Princeton, 1978.

——— "The Social Character of Stalinist Architecture," *Architectural Association Quarterly,* 1979, no. 2: 49–55.

Stasov, Vladimir V. *Izbrannye sochineniia.* Moscow, 1952.

Stender-Peterson, A. D. *Anthology of Old Russian Literature.* New York, 1954.

Sternin, G. Iu., ed. *Tipologiia russkogo realizma vtoroi poloviny XIX veka.* Moscow, 1979.

—— *Vzaimosviaz' iskusstv v khudozhestvennom razvitii Rossii vtoroi poloviny XIX v.* Moscow, 1982.

—— *Russkaia khudozhestvennaia kul'tura vtoroi poloviny XIX–nachala XX veka.* Moscow, 1984.

Strémooukhoff, Dimitri. "Moscow the Third Rome: Sources of the Doctrine," *Speculum* (January 1953): 84–101.

Strzygowski, Jurij. *Die Baukunst der Armenier und Europa.* Vienna, 1918.

Sultanov, Nikolai. "Russkie shatrovye tserkvi i ikh sootnoshenie k gruzino-armianskim piramidal'nym polkytiiam." In *Trudy V Arkheologicheskogo s'esda v Tiflise v 1881 g.* Moscow, 1887.

Summerson, John. *The Classical Language of Architecture.* London, 1980.

Suslova, A. V., and T. A. Slavina. *Vladimir Suslov.* Leningrad, 1978.

Suslova, E. N. "Ucheniicheskie gody Iu. M. Fel'tena," *Arkhitekturnoe nasledstvo,* 9 (1959): 69–72.

Suzdaleva, T. E. *N. A. Trotskii.* Leningrad, 1991.

Sytina, T. M. "Russkoe arkhitekturnoe zakonodatel'stvo pervoi cherverti XVIII v," *Arkhitekturnoe nasledstvo,* 18 (1969): 67–73.

Taleporovskii, V. N. *Charl'z Kameron.* Moscow, 1939.

—— *Kvarengi: materialy k izucheniiu tvorchestva.* Leningrad–Moscow, 1954.

Taranovskaia, M. Z. *Karl Rossi.* Leningrad, 1978.

Tarkhanov, Aleksei. "Dom 'Rossiia'," *Dekorativnoe iskusstvo,* 1986, no. 7: 34–8.

Tel'tevskii, Prokopii A. *Staroe zdanie gosudarstvennoi Biblioteki SSSR imeni V. I. Lenina (dom Pashkova).* Moscow, 1957.

—— *Velikii Ustiug: Arkhitektura i iskusstvo XVII–XIX vekov.* Moscow, 1977.

Tenikhina, Valentina M., and Vadim V. Znamenov. *Kottedzh.* Leningrad, 1990.

Thieme-Becker Künstler-lexikon, 36 vols. Leipzig, 1907–47.

Thurston, Robert V. *Liberal City, Conservative State: Moscow and Russia's Urban Crisis, 1906–1914.* Oxford, 1987.

Tikhomirov, M. N. "Maloizvestnye letopisnye pamiatniki XVI v." In *Istoricheskie zapiski,* 1941, no. 10: 88.

—— "Letopisnye pamiatniki b Sinodal'nogo patriarshego sobraniia." In *Istoricheskie zapiski,* 1942, no. 13: 268.

—— *Rossiia v XVI stoletii.* Moscow, 1960.

——, ed. *Novgorod: k 1100-letiiu goroda.* Moscow, 1964.

Tikhomirov, Nikolai Ia. *Arkhitektura podmoskovskikh usadeb.* Moscow, 1955.

Timofeeva, E. "Pervonachal'nyi oblik Petropavlovskogo sobora," *Arkhitekturnoe nasledstvo,* 7 (1955): 93–108.

Tits, A. A. *Russkoe kamennoe zhiloe zodchestvo XVII v.* Moscow, 1966.

—— "U istokov arkhitekturnogo chertezha." In *Kul'tura drevnei Rusi,* edited by A. L. Mongait, pp. 268–71. Moscow, 1966.

—— "Neizvestnyi russkii traktat po arkhitekture." In *Rus-skoe iskusstvo XVIII v.: Materialy i issledovaniia,* edited by T. V. Alekseeva, pp. 17–31. Moscow, 1968.

—— *Zagadki drevnerusskogo chertezha.* Moscow, 1978.

Tokareva, I. G. "V poiskakh 'novogo stilia,'" *Leningradskaia panorama,* 1987, no. 8: 33–5.

Tolochko, P. P., and Ia. E. Borovskii, "Iazichnitske kapishche v 'gorodi' Volodimira." In *Arkheologiia Kieva,* edited by L. L. Vashchenko, pp. 3–10. Kiev, 1979.

Tolstoi, I., and N. Kondakov, *Russkie drevnosti v pamiatnikakh iskusstva,* Vol. 6, *Pamiatniki Vladimira, Novgoroda i Pskova.* St. Petersburg, 1899.

Toropov, S. "Petrovskoe-Demidovykh," *Sredi kollektsionerov,* 1924, nos. 7–8: 20–5.

—— *Podmoskovnye usad'by.* Moscow, 1947. Trotskii, Noi. "Dom sovetov v Leningrade," *Arkhitektura Leningrada,* 1937, no. 2: 8–19.

Trubinov, Iu. V. "Letnii dvorets Menshikova v Peterburge," *Arkhitekturnoe nasledstvo,* 29 (1981): 41–9.

Trudy II s''ezda russkikh zodchikh v Moskve. Moscow, 1899.

Trudy III s''ezda russkikh zodchikh. Petersburg, 1905.

Tydman, L. V. "Rabota arkhitektora K. I. Blanka v Kuskove (Zakazchik i arkhitektor v XVIII v.)." In *Russkoe iskusstvo barokko,* edited by T. V. Alekseeva, pp. 216–25. Moscow, 1977.

—— "Prostranstvo inter'era v moskovskikh osobniakakh pervoi poloviny XIX v." In *Pamiatniki russkoi arkhitektury i monumental'nogo iskusstva,* edited by V. P. Vygolov, pp. 162–81. Moscow, 1980.

—— "Razvitie vnutrennego prostranstva domov-dvortsov 1700–1760-kh godov." In *Ot Srednevekov'ia k novomu vremeni,* edited by T. V. Alekseeva, pp. 180–210. Moscow, 1984.

—— "Ob''emno-prostranstvennaia kompozitsiia domov-dvortsov XVIII v." In *Pamiatniki russkoi arkhitektury i monumental'nogo iskusstva,* edited by V. P. Vygolov, pp. 127–47. Moscow, 1985.

Tyzhnenko, T. E. "Muzei nachinaetsia s facada," *Leningradskaia panorama,* 1983, no. 5: 31–4.

Ulam, Adam. *The Bolsheviks.* New York, 1965.

Ushakov, Iurii S. *Dereviannoe zopdchestvo russkogo Severa (narodnye traditsii i sovremennye problemy).* Leningrad, 1974.

Vagner, Georgii K. "K voprosu o rekonstruktsii severnogo facada Georgievskogo sobora v Iur'eve-Pol'skom," *Arkhitekturnoe nasledstvo,* 14 (1962): 27–34.

—— *Skul'ptura Vladimiro-Suzdalskoi Rusi.* Moscow, 1964.

—— *Skul'ptura drevnei Rusi XII v.: Vladimir-Bogoliubovo.* Moscow, 1969.

—— *Riazan'.* Moscow, 1971.

—— *Spaso-Andronikov monastyr'.* Moscow, 1972.

—— *Belokamennaia rez'ba drevnego Suzdalia.* Moscow, 1975.

—— "Ob otkrytii reznykh nadpisei sredi fasadnoi skul'ptury Dmitrievskogo sobora vo Vladimire," *Sovetskaia arkheologiia,* 1976, no. 1: 270–2.

—— *Starye russkie goroda: Spravochnik-putevoditel'.* Moscow, 1980.

Vagner, G. K., and D. S. Likhachev, eds. *Srednevekovaia Rus'.* Moscow, 1976.

Vashchenko, L. L., ed. *Arkheologiia Kieva.* Kiev, 1979.

Vasil'ev, B. "Arkhitektory Neelovy," *Arkhitekturnoe nasledstvo*, 4 (1953): 73–90.

—— "K istorii planirovki Peterburga vo vtoroi polovine XVIII veka," *Arkhitekturnoe nasledstvo*, 4 (1953): 14–29.

—— "Peterburg kontsa XVIII–nachala XIX vekov v izobrazhenii V. Patersena," *Arkhitekturnoe nasledstvo*, 9 (1959): 28–44.

Veniaminov, B. "Arkhangel'skoe," *Mir iskusstva*, 1904, no. 2: 31–40.

Vergunov, A. P., and V. A. Gorokhov. *Russkie sady i parki*. Moscow, 1988.

Viatchanina, T. N. "O znachenii obraztsa v drevnerusskoi arkhitekture," *Arkhitekturnoe nasledstvo*, 32 (1984): 26–31.

—— "Arkhangel'skii sobor moskovskogo kremlia kak obrazets v russkom zodchestve XVI v.," *Arkhitekturnoe nasledstvo*, 34 (1986): 215–23.

Viatkin, M. P., ed. *Ocherki istorii Leningrada, Vol. 1, Period feodalizma (1703–1861 gg.)*. Moscow–Leningrad, 1955.

Viktorov, A. M. "V. Ermolin." In *Zodchie Moskvy XV–XIX vv*, edited by Iu. S. Iaralov, pp. 34–41. Moscow, 1981.

Vipers [Vipper], B. *Baroque Art in Latvia*. Riga, 1939.

Vipper, Boris R. *Arkhitektura russkogo barokko*. Moscow, 1978.

Vitiazeva, Vera A. *Nevskie ostrova*. Leningrad, 1986.

—— *Kamennyi Ostrov*. Leningrad, 1991.

Vitiazeva, V. A., and B. M. Kirikov. *Leningrad: Putelvoditel'*. Leningrad, 1986.

Vlasiuk, A. "Novye issledovaniia arkhitektury Arkhangel'skogo sobora v Moskovskom kremle," *Arkhitekturnoe nasledstvo*, 2 (1952): 105–32.

—— "Pervonachal'naia forma kupola tserkvi Pokrova na Nerli," *Arkhitekturnoe nasledstvo*, 2 (1952): 67–8.

—— "O rabote zodchego Aleviza Novogo v Bakhchisarae i v Moskovskom Kremle," *Arkhitekturnoe nasledstvo*, 10 (1958): 101–10.

—— "K istorii proektirovaniia i stroitel'stva zhilishch dlia rabochikh v kontse XIX v. v Rossii," *Arkhitekturnoe nasledstvo*, 15 (1963): 171–5.

—— "Rabochie gorodki Peterburga vtoroi poloviny XIX–nachala XX v.," *Arkhitekturnoe nasledstvo*, 16 (1967): 121–7.

Voinov, V. S. "Andreas Shliuter – arkhitektor Petra (K voprosu o formirovanii stilia 'Petrovskoe barokko')," *Sovetskoe iskusstvoznanie*, 1976, no. 1 367–77.

Vokhovitskaia, Elena, and Aleksei Tarkhanov, "Dom 'Rossiia,'" *Dekorativnoe iskusstvo*, 1986, no. 7: 34–8.

Vorob'ev, A. V., and V. A. Smyslova. "O galeree arkhangel'skogo sobora," *Arkhitekturnoe nasledstvo*, 15 (1963): 178–81.

Voronikhina, Anna N. *Peterburg i ego okrestnosti v chertezhakh i risunkakh arkhitektorov pervoi treti XVIII veka*. Leningrad, 1972.

—— *Vidy zalov Ermitazha i zimnego dvortsa v akvareliakh i risunkakh khudozhnikov serediny XIX veka*. Moscow, 1983.

Voronikhina, A. N., N. V. Kaliazina, M. F. Korshunova, and T. A. Petrova. *Arkhitekturnaia grafika Rossii: Pervaia polovina XVIII veka*. Leningrad, 1981.

Voronikhina, A. N., and T. M. Sokolova. *Ermitazh. Zdaniia i zaly muzeia*. Leningrad, 1968.

Voronin, Nikolai N. *Zodchestvo Severo-Vostochnoi Rusi XII–XV vekov*. Vols. 1 and 2. Moscow, 1961, 1962.

—— *Vladimir, Bogolyubovo, Suzdal, Yurev-Polskoi*. Moscow, 1971.

Voronin, N. N., and V. V. Kostochkin, eds. *Troitse-Sergieva lavra: Khudozhestvennye pamiatniki*. Moscow, 1968.

Voronin, N. N., and P. A. Rappoport. *Zodchestvo Smolenska, XII–XIII vv*. Moscow, 1979.

Voronov, A. A., ed. *Istroiia arkhitektury: Ob"ekt, predmet i metod issledovaniia*. Moscow, 1988.

—— *Voprosy istorii arkhitektury*. Moscow, 1990.

Voronov, A. A., N. I. Smolina, A. Ia. Flier, and Iu. E. Revzina, eds. *Problemy istorii arkhitektury*. 2 parts. Moscow, 1990.

Voronov, M. G., and G. D. Khodasevich. *Arkhitekturnyi ansambl' Kamerona v Pushkine*. Leningrad, 1982.

Voropaev, V. " 'Menia ochen' zanimal Gogol' . . .': Iz 'Zapisok' V. O. Shervuda," *Literaturnaia gazeta* (April 9, 1986): 6.

Vygolov, Vsevolod. P. "Triumfal'nye vorota 1721 g. I. P. Zarudnogo," *Arkhitekturnoe nasledstvo*, 12 (1960): 179–82.

—— "O razvitii iarusnykh form v zodchestve kontsa XVII veka." In *Drevnerusskoe iskusstvo: XVII vek*, edited by V. N. Lazarev, pp. 236–52. Moscow, 1964.

—— "Monumental'no-dekorativnaia keramika Novgoroda kontsa XVII veka. Izraztsy Viazhitskogo monastyria." In *Drevnerusskoe iskusstvo: XVII vek*, edited by V. N. Lazarev, pp. 237–66. Moscow, 1968.

—— "Inter'er." In *Russkaia khudozhestvennaia kul'tura kontsa XIX-nachala XX veka (1908–1917)*, Vol. 4, edited by A. D. Alekseev, pp. 365–84. Moscow, 1980.

—— *Arkhitektura Moskovskoi Rusi serediny XV veka*. Moscow, 1988.

Vygolov, V. P., A. I. Vlasiuk, and V. I. Pluzhnikov, eds. *Pamiatniki russkoi arkhitektury i monumental'nogo iskusstva: Stil', atributsii, datirovki*. Moscow, 1983.

——, eds. *Pamiatniki russkoi arkhitektury i monumental'nogo iskusstva: Goroda, ansambli, zodchie*. Moscow, 1985.

Vzdornov, G[erol'd] I. "Stroitel'stvo kolokol'ni Troitse-Segievoi lavry (v svete novykh dannykh)," *Arkhitekturnoe nasledstvo*, 14 (1962): 152–34.

—— "Arkhitektor P'etro Antonio Trezini i ego postroiki." In *Russkoe iskusstvo XVIII v.: Materialy i issledovaniia*, edited by T. V. Alekseeva, pp. 139–56. Moscow, 1968.

—— "Postroiki pskovskoi arteli zodchikh v Moskve (Po letopisnoi stat'e 1476 goda)." In *Drevnerusskoe iskusstvo: Khudozhestvennaia kul'tura Pskova*, edited by V. N. Lazarev, pp. 174–88. Moscow, 1968.

—— "Zametki o pamiatnikakh russkoi arkhitektury kontsa XVII-nachala XVIII v.," In *Russkoe iskusstvo XVIII veka*, edited by T. V. Alekseeva, pp. 20–5. Moscow, 1973.

—— *Freski Feofana Greka v tserkvi Spasa Preobrazheniia v Novgorode*. Moscow, 1976.

—— *Vologda*. Leningrad, 1978.

Ware, Timothy. *The Orthodox Church*. Harmondsworth, 1969.

West, James. "The Riabushinskii Circle: Russian Industrialists in Search of a Bourgeoisie, 1909–1914," *Jahrbücher für Geschichte Osteuropas* 32 (1984): 358–77.

Williams, Edward V. *The Bells of Russia: History and Technology*. Princeton, 1985.

Wilson, Edmund. *To the Finland Station*. New York, 1940.

Wittkower, Rudolf. *Architectural Principles in the Age of Humanism*. New York, 1971.

Wraxall, Nathaniel. *A Tour through Some of the Northern Parts of Europe, Particularly Copenhagen, Stockholm, and Petersbourgh*. London, 1775.

Zabelin, Ivan E. *Russkoe iskusstvo: Cherty samobytnosti v drevnerusskom zodchestve*. Moscow, 1900.

——— *Istoriia goroda Moskvy*. Moscow, 1902.

Zabello, S., V. Ivanov, and P. Maksimov. *Russkoe dereviannoe zodchestvo*. Moscow, 1942.

Zapletin, N. "Dvorets Sovetov SSSR (po materialam konkursa)," *Sovetskaia arkhitektura*, 1932, nos. 2–3: 10–116.

Zavarikhin, S. P. *Russkaia arkhitekturnaia kritika seredina XIII–nachalo XX vv*. Leningrad, 1989.

Zemtsov, S. M. "Arkhitektory Moskvy vtoroi poloviny XV i pervoi poloviny XVI veka." In *Zodchie Moskvy XV–XIX vv*, edited by Iu. S. Iaralov. Moscow, 1981.

Zemtsov, S. M., and V. L. Glazychev, *Aristotel' F'oravanti*. Moscow, 1985.

Zenkevich, E. P., and G. S. Lebedeva. "Evoliutsiia poniatiia 'teoriia' i 'praktika' v russkoi arkhitekturnoi mysli XVIII veka," *Arkhitekturnoe nasledstvo*, 36 (1988): 94–105.

Zenkovsky, Serge, ed. *Medieval Russia's Epics, Chronicles, and Tales*. New York, 1963.

Zgura, Vladimir. "Kuskovskii reguliarnyi sad," *Sredi kollektsionerov*, 1924, nos. 5–6: 4–19.

Zharikov, N. L., ed. *Pamiatniki gradostroitel'stva i arkhitektury Ukrainskoi SSR*, 4 vols. Kiev, 1983–6.

Zhuravlev, A. M., A. V. Ikonnikov, and A. G. Rochegov. *Arkhitektura Sovetskoi Rossii*. Moscow, 1987.

Zhuravleva, L. S. *Talashkino*. Moscow, 1989.

Zinov'ev, P. "Spornyi eksperiment." In *Stroitel'stvo i arkhitektura Moskvy*, 1979, no. 7: 32.

Index

Where available, birth and death dates for architects and designers active in Russia are given in parentheses.